Child Development and Education

Teresa M. McDevitt
University of Northern Colorado

Jeanne Ellis Ormrod
University of Northern Colorado (Emerita)
University of New Hampshire

Merrill
Prentice Hall

Upper Saddle River, New Jersey
Columbus, Ohio

Library of Congress Cataloging in Publication Data

McDevitt, Teresa M.

    Child development and education / Teresa M. McDevitt, Jeanne Ellis Ormrod.

       p. cm.

    Includes bibliographical references and index.

    ISBN 0-13-761933-2

      1. Child development. 2. Adolescent psychology. 3. Educational psychology. I.

Ormrod, Jeanne Ellis. II. Title.

LB1115.M263 2002

305.231—dc21   2001031473

Vice President and Publisher: Jeffery W. Johnston
Executive Editor: Kevin M. Davis
Development Editor: Julie Peters
Production Editor: Mary Harlan
Copy Editor: Sue Snyder Kopp
Design Coordinator: Diane C. Lorenzo
Photo Coordinator: Nancy Harre Ritz
Cover Design: Alan Bumpus
Cover Photos: The Stock Market and Photodisc
Production Manager: Laura Messerly
Director of Marketing: Kevin Flanagan
Marketing Manager: Amy June
Marketing Coordinator: Barbara Koontz

This book was set in Berkeley by Carlisle Communications, Ltd. It was printed and bound by Courier Kendallville, Inc. The cover was printed by The Lehigh Press, Inc.

Photo Credits: Bill Bachmann/Photo Researchers, Inc.: p. 388; Billy E. Barnes/PhotoEdit: p. 90; Berkeley Police Department: p. 99; Robert Burke/Stone: p. 258; CNRI/Science Photo Library/Photo Researchers: p. 67 (right); Paul Conklin/PhotoEdit: pp. 136, 462; Corbis Digital Stock: pp. 413, 469; Scott Cunningham/Merrill: pp. 10, 24, 113 (left), 119, 252, 294, 415 (left), 541; Bob Daemmrich Photography, Inc.: p. 122; Deborah Davis/ PhotoEdit: p. 545; Mary Kate Denny/PhotoEdit: pp. 7, 35, 59, 77, 212, 511, 532; Laima Druskis/PH College: pp. 282, 288; Laura Dwight Photography: p. 68; John Paul Endress/Silver Burdett Ginn: p. 228; FBI: p. 67 (left); Hunter Freeman/Stone: p. 52; Tony Freeman/PhotoEdit: p. 238, 319; Jeff Greenberg/PhotoEdit: p. 176; Will Hart/PhotoEdit: pp. 124, 134, 218; Richard Hutchings/PhotoResearchers, Inc.: pp. 185 (left), 256; Catherine Karnow/ Woodfin Camp & Associates: p. 524; Richard Lord/The Image Works: p. 365; Daniel Lunghi/Merrill: p. 470; Anthony Magnacca/ Merrill: pp. 16, 170, 185 (right), 193, 279; Teresa McDevitt: p. 71; Michael Newman/PhotoEdit: pp. 17, 141, 348, 376, 559; Rosanna Olson/Stone: p. 327; Lori Adamski Peek/Stone: p. 352; PH College: pp. 69, 477; PhotoDisc, Inc.: pp. 41, 185 (center), 214, 330, 384, 406; Page Poore/PH College: p. 457; Mike Provost/Silver Burdett Ginn: p. 161; Mark Richards/PhotoEdit: p. 573; Nancy Richmond/The Image Works: p. 338; Andy Sacks/Stone: p. 335; Silver Burdett Ginn: pp. 205, 221; Superstock, Inc.: p. 191; John T. Wong/Index Stock Imagery, Inc.: p. 113 (right); Todd Yarrington/Merrill: p. 247; David Young-Wolff/PhotoEdit: pp. 156, 267, 371, 393, 415 (right), 423, 437, 501; David Young-Wolff/Stone: p. 307; Shirley Zeiberg/PH College: p. 450; and Elizabeth Zuckerman/ PhotoEdit: p. 487.

Pearson Education Ltd., *London*
Pearson Education Australia Pty. Limited, *Sydney*
Pearson Education Singapore Pte. Ltd.
Pearson Education North Asia Ltd., *Hong Kong*
Pearson Education Canada, Ltd., *Toronto*
Pearson Educación de Mexico, S.A. de C.V., *Mexico*
Pearson Education—Japan, *Tokyo*
Pearson Education Malaysia Pte. Ltd.
Pearson Education, *Upper Saddle River, New Jersey*

Merrill
Prentice Hall

10 9 8 7 6 5 4 3 2 1
ISBN: 0-13-761933-2

DEDICATION

To our children and husbands,
Connor, Alexander, and Eugene Sheehan
and
Christina, Alex, Jeffrey, and Richard Ormrod

Preface

As psychologists and teacher educators, we have been teaching child and adolescent development for many years. A primary goal in our classes has been to help students translate developmental theories into practical implications for teachers and other professionals who nurture the development of young people. The textbooks we've used in our courses have provided a solid foundation in theory and research but have offered few suggestions for working with children and adolescents in classrooms and other settings.

With this book, we bridge the gap between theory and practice. We draw from innumerable research studies conducted around the world, and from our own experiences as parents, teachers, psychologists, and researchers, to identify strategies for promoting the physical, cognitive, and social-emotional growth of children and adolescents.

Several features of this book make it different from other comprehensive textbooks about child and adolescent development. In particular, this book

- Is written specifically for educators
- Situates readers among real students and their work
- Explores core developmental issues

THE ONLY COMPREHENSIVE DEVELOPMENT
TEXT WRITTEN SPECIFICALLY FOR EDUCATORS

In selecting material for this book, we focused on concepts and principles that are important to developmental theorists and to educational practitioners. The result is a text that is uniquely useful to those who are interested in practical applications of developmental scholarship.

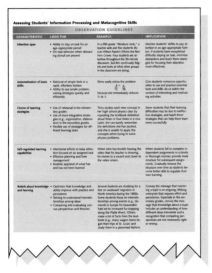

Educational Implications. Throughout every chapter, you will find extensive discussion of the relevance of this material to teachers and others who work with children. Most major topics contain sections that examine in depth the educational implications of the developmental research and theory being presented. Readers come away not only understanding current views of concepts such as children's theory construction or attachment but also seeing the relevance and application of these ideas to working with children.

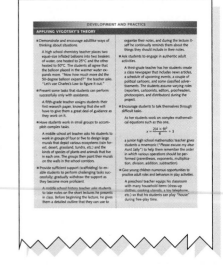

Development and Practice. In addition to consistent discussion of application throughout the text itself, we provide "Development and Practice" features that offer concrete educational strategies for facilitating student development. To help our readers move from research to practice, we include actual examples of teachers using particular strategies in classrooms.

Observation Guidelines. To work productively with children and adolescents, one must first be able to interpret their behavior. Knowledge of development provides an essential lens through which teachers must look if they are to understand children. One of the foundational goals of this text is to help teachers observe developmental nuances in their students. To this end, throughout the book we give readers "Observation Guidelines." These features offer specific characteristics to look for in students, present illustrative examples, and provide specific recommendations for teachers.

Another central focus of this text is to illustrate concepts and research with examples of real children and adolescents. Authentic case studies begin and end each chapter, and there are often separate, shorter vignettes within the bodies of chapters. In addition to these types of illustrations, the text, much more than any other similar text, also makes frequent use of real artifacts from children's journals, sketchbooks, and school assignments. It is among real children and adolescents and in the midst of the work that children and adolescents produce that developmental content becomes meaningful to teachers. More than any other text, *Child Development and Education* brings this educational context to life.

Case Studies. Each chapter begins with a case that, by being referenced throughout the chapter, is used to help illustrate and frame that chapter's content. A chapter ending case provides readers with an opportunity to apply chapter content to an instructional setting. A series of questions that accompany each of these end-of-chapter cases helps the reader in this application process.

Artifacts from Children and Adolescents. The frequent use of actual artifacts provides another forum for illustrating developmental abilities and issues. Throughout the text, actual examples of children's and adolescents' artwork, poetry, and school assignments are integrated into discussions of various concepts and applications. Not only do these artifacts offer readers authentic illustrations of chapter content, but they also help place developmental research and theory directly within an educational context.

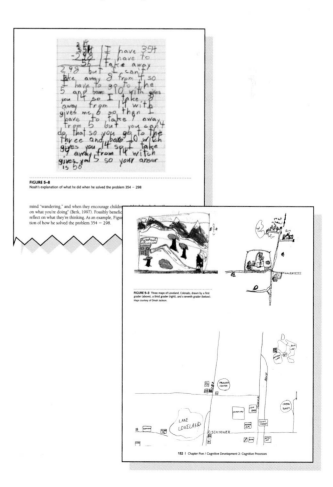

The other major goal of *Child Development and Education* is to help readers come to a broad conceptual understanding of the field of child development, to make them aware of the foundational ideas and issues that frame the field, and to provide them with a broad sense of how and when children develop various abilities. Throughout all of its chapters, the book consistently examines three core developmental issues—the relationship between biological and environmental influences on development, universality and diversity of developmental changes, and the qualitative and quantitative nature of developmental changes. Though organized topically, the book also provides an overview of developmental changes from a chronological perspective.

Basic Developmental Issues. In every chapter we examine ways in which development is the complex product of interacting forces—nature, nurture, and the children's own efforts. We also spotlight circumstances that reveal fairly universal developmental trends and areas marked with substantial diversity. Finally, we analyze developmental changes for their underlying nature: do they take the form of dramatic qualitative changes, or are they the outcome of many small, trend-like quantitative changes?

Developmental Trends. The book is organized around substantive topics of development to allow for an in-depth examination of each area of development. In the context of this topical approach, however, we also identify the unique characteristics of students during particular periods of growth. In the narrative, we frequently provide detailed chronological examples of children's abilities to give teachers a flavor of what children can do at specific ages. In almost every chapter, one or more "Developmental Trends" tables summarize typical features of four developmental periods: early childhood, middle childhood, early adolescence, and late adolescence. These tables also explain common types of individual and group differences and provide instructional implications.

Supplementary Materials

Accompanying the book are numerous supplementary materials to assist both instructors and students.

INSTRUCTOR AIDS

Videotape Package

Accompanying the textbook are seven videotapes:

Observing Children and Adolescents in School Settings. This videotape depicts a variety of teachers and students in action throughout the elementary and secondary school grades. By observing student-student and teacher-student interactions, viewers refine their abilities to interpret children's and adolescents' behaviors from a developmental perspective and can assess the value of various teaching practices.

 ABC News/Prentice Hall Video Library: Issues in Child and Adolescent Development. This videotape includes numerous segments from ABC News programs, *Good Morning America,* and *World News Tonight* on a variety of topics, such as advances in brain research, trends in language development, peer and parental influences on children, and an examination of how and why teenagers often think and act differently than children and adults.

By observing this girl's solutions to balance scale problems and listening to the explanations she offers, you get a feel for the mathematical principles she is applying and the effects that interactions with classmates have on her reasoning.

Insights into Learning. Three one-hour videotapes provide an in-depth examination of specific aspects of cognitive development:

■ *Using Balance Beams in Fourth Grade.* Fourth graders work in small groups to solve problems involving weights on a balance scale. Whole-class discussions show students offering and defending solutions. A college professor presents additional problems to probe the students' reasoning.

■ *Finding Area in Elementary Math.* Fifth graders engage in an authentic problem-solving activity in which they must calculate the area of an irregular shape using a prescribed problem-solving sequence. Small-group work and whole-class discussions are included. A college professor presents several transfer tasks to probe the students' reasoning.

■ *Designing Experiments in Seventh Grade.* Four seventh graders conduct experiments with a pendulum and discuss how various factors affect the pendulum's oscillation rate. Their teacher then conducts a lesson on separating and controlling variables. A college professor gives the students a transfer task involving separation and control of variables and reflects on the activity.

Double-Column Addition: A Teacher Uses Piaget's Theory. Second graders construct creative strategies for adding and subtracting two-digit numbers and reveal a true understanding of place value. Rather than teaching specific strategies, the teacher helps the students develop their own strategies by presenting problems, asking for possible solutions, and encouraging discussion of various approaches.

A Private Universe. This video illustrates the pervasiveness of misconceptions about two scientific phenomena—the seasons of the year and the phases of the moon—not only in high school students but also in graduates and faculty members of Harvard University. One high-achieving ninth grader's conceptions are portrayed in depth both before and after instruction. Questions that probe her reasoning following instruction reveal that she still holds onto some of her prior misconceptions.

Multimedia Guide

The Multimedia Guide helps instructors direct and enrich students' interpretation and understanding of what they learn from the videos, the compact disk, and the Companion Website.

Observation Record tables, similar to the Observation Guidelines tables in the text, help students record their observations and apply their knowledge of child and adolescent development.

Transparencies

The instructional transparencies include diagrams, artifacts, and other graphic aids similar to those found in the textbook. These transparencies are designed to help students understand, organize, and remember developmental concepts and theories presented in the text. The transparencies are also available on the Instructor's CD-ROM.

Test Bank

The test bank that accompanies the textbook contains approximately 50 test items for each chapter. Items include both knowledge-level questions (which ask students to identify or explain basic concepts and principles) and higher-level application questions (which ask students to apply what they have learned to specific situations). The test bank is available in both paper and electronic formats (Windows and Macintosh platforms).

Instructor's Manual

This manual offers numerous suggestions and resources for classroom instruction, including learning activities, supplemental lectures, case study analyses, group discussion topics, and additional media resources. Each element has been carefully crafted to provide opportunities to support, enrich, and expand upon what students read in the textbook.

Instructor's CD-ROM

This user-friendly CD-ROM provides lecture-enhancing color PowerPoint transparencies, black and white transparency masters (which can also be used as handouts), answers to end-of-chapter case study questions, in-class and out-of-class activities, and more.

STUDENT SUPPLEMENTS

Interactive Computer Simulations in Child Development

This problem-solving simulation CD-ROM allows students to participate in two "virtual" activities—manipulating variables in a pendulum experiment and assessing moral reasoning—to learn more about Piaget's theory of cognitive development and Kohlberg's theory of moral development. At the end of each simulation, students apply what they have learned to classroom situations.

Companion Website

A Companion Website (CW) provides additional support for studying and learning from the book. For each chapter, the CW includes outlines and summaries, sample multiple-choice and essay questions, links to other Websites relevant to the subject matter, and a glossary of key terms. It also includes a link to Pearson Education's Learning Network and a message board and chat room for out-of-class communication among students and the instructor. You can find this Website at www.prenhall.com/mcdevitt.

Student Study Guide

The Study Guide has several features to help readers focus their learning and studying in every chapter: (1) a brief chapter overview; (2) a description of common student beliefs and misconceptions that may interfere with effective learning; (3) focus questions that can guide an initial reading of the chapter and, during later review sessions, can provide a means of self-assessing overall comprehension of chapter content; (4) glossary of key terms introduced in the chapter; (5) application exercises that provide practice in recognizing developmental concepts and principles in children's and teachers' behaviors; and (6) sample test questions.

Acknowledgments

Although we are listed as the sole authors of this textbook, in fact many individuals have contributed in significant ways to its content and form. Our editor, Kevin Davis, was the book's catalyst, persisting for several years in his efforts to convince us to undertake such a project. We thank him for his encouragement, task focus, high standards, and wisdom. We thank him, too, for his ability to discern when he needed us to push us in particular directions and when it was better to let us follow our own instincts.

We also had the great fortune to have the support of many other talented individuals at Merrill/Prentice Hall. Julie Peters, our development editor, was a continual source of guidance, support, insight, and good humor throughout the writing process; her assistance and advice were especially helpful as we faced the innumerable little problems and challenges of such a complex endeavor. In the early stages of the project, Linda Montgomery helped us conceptualize organizational schemes, pedagogical features, and classroom artifacts. Mary Harlan masterfully guided the manuscript through the production process and was unswervingly patient when other commitments in our lives temporarily distracted us from reading page proofs, evaluating art and photos, and responding to questions. Sue Snyder Kopp worked diligently to simplify and refine our presentation, correct impurities in our language, include additional examples, and magnify our impact. Nancy Ritz sorted through hundreds of photos to identify those that could best capture key developmental principles in a visual form. Christina Kalisch and Amy Hamer handled logistical details quickly and smoothly. Marketing whizzes Kevin Flanagan, Amy June, Barbara Koontz, Suzanne Stanton, and others helped us get the word out about the book.

Stephanie Taylor and Stephanie Owens, doctoral students at the University of Northern Colorado, assisted us with smaller yet essential tasks at critical times. We appreciate their assistance with library research, photocopying, and copyright permissions. Stephanie Taylor played an additional key role as author of the Instructor's Manual and Companion Website. We are indebted, too, to Kathleen E. Fite at Southwest Texas State University for writing the Test Bank that accompanies the book.

Children, Adolescents, and Teachers. Equally important contributors to the book were the many children and teachers who provided the work samples and other artifacts that appear throughout the fourteen chapters. The work of the following students contributed immeasurably to the depth and richness of our discussions:

Davis Alcorn	Eddie Garcia	Jessica Lumbrano	Oscar Rodriguez
Jacob Alcorn	Palet Garcia	Krista Marrufo	Elizabeth Romero
Brenda Bagazuma	Veronica Garcia	Malanie Nunez	Daniela Sanchez
Ricco Branch	James Garrett, III	Dustin O'Mara	Alex Sheehan
Marsalis Bush	Mayra de la Garza	Alex Ormrod	Connor Sheehan
Eric Campos	Jared Hale	Jeff Ormrod	Alex Snow
Jenna Dargy	William Hill	Tina Ormrod	Sam Snow
Noah Davis	Brandon Jackson	Isabelle Peters	Grace Tober
Shea Davis	Rachel Johnson	Laura Prieto-Velasco	Brady Williamson
Rachel Foster	Marianne Kies	Ian Rhoades	

To ensure we included students' work from a wide variety of geographic locations and from diverse backgrounds, we contacted organizations north and south, east and west to obtain work samples that would reflect the diversity found in schools today. We want to thank these individuals for their coordination efforts: Heidi Schork and members of the Boston Youth Clean-Up Corps (BYCC), Michelle Gabor of the Salesian Boys' and Girls' Club, and Bettie Lake of the Phoenix Elementary School District. In addition, we thank the many teachers and principals who were so helpful in our efforts to identify artifacts and teaching strategies to illustrate developmental concepts; key among them were Janet Alcorn, Michael Gee, Dinah Jackson, Jesse Jensen, Erin Miguel, Michele Minichiello, Dan Moulis, Annemarie Palincsar, and Cathy Zocchi.

Reviewers and Colleagues. In addition, we received considerable encouragement, assistance, and support from our professional colleagues. Faculty and administrators at the University of Northern Colorado—especially Marlene Strathe, Steve Pulos, Bonnie Konopak, Randy Lennon, and Allen Huang—unselfishly provided information, advice, resources, and time. Developmentalists and educational psychologists at numerous institutions around the country have offered their careful and insightful reviews of one or more chapters. We are especially indebted to the following reviewers:

Karen Abrams
Keene State College

Lynley Anderman
University of Kentucky

David E. Balk
Kansas State University

Tom Batsis
Loyola Marymount University

Daniel Fasko
Morehead State University

Sherryl Browne Graves
Hunter College

Michael Green
University of North Carolina–Charlotte

Glenda Griffin
Texas A & M University

Deborah Grubb
Morehead State University

Melissa Heston
University of Northern Iowa

James E. Johnson
The Pennsylvania State University

Michael Keefer
University of Missouri–St. Louis

Judith Kieff
University of New Orleans

Nancy Knapp
University of Georgia

Mary McLellan
Northern Arizona University

Kenneth Merrell
University of Iowa

Tamera Murdock
University of Missouri–Kansas City

Bridget Murray
Indiana State University

Virginia Navarro
University of Missouri–St. Louis

Larry Nucci
University of Illinois–Chicago

Jennifer Parkhurst
Duke University

Sherrill Richarz
Washington State University

Kent Rittschof
Georgia Southern University

Linda Rogers,
Kent State University

Richard Ryan
University of Rochester

Sue Spitzer
California State University, San Bernardino

Bruce Tuckman
The Ohio State University

Kathryn Wentzel
University of Maryland–College Park

Allan Wigfield
University of Maryland–College Park

Thomas D. Yawkey
The Pennsylvania State University.

Our Families. Finally, our families have been supportive and patient over the extended period we have been preoccupied with reading, researching, writing, and editing. Our children gave of themselves in anecdotes, artwork, and diversions from our work. Our husbands picked up the slack around the house and gave us frequent emotional boosts and comic relief. Much love and many thanks to Eugene, Connor, and Alex (from Teresa) and to Richard, Tina, Alex, and Jeff (from Jeanne).

T. M. M.
J. E. O.

Brief Contents

Contents

CHAPTER 14

Growing Up in Context   539

Special Features

Child Development and Education

Krista, age 7

Myra, age 13

Making a Difference in the Lives of Children and Adolescents

CASE STUDY: TONYA

When Mary Renck Jalongo thinks back to her years as a novice teacher, one student often comes to mind:

Not only was she big for her age, she was older than anyone else in my first-grade class because she had been retained in kindergarten. Her name was Tonya and she put my patience, my professionalism, and my decision making on trial throughout my second year of teaching. Tonya would boss and bully the other children, pilfer items from their desks, or talk them into uneven "trades."

Matters worsened when I received a hostile note from a parent. It read, "This is the fourth time that Tommy's snack cake has been taken from his lunch. What are you going to do about it?"

What I did was to launch an investigation. First, I asked if anyone else was missing items from lunchboxes and discovered that many other children had been affected. Next, I tried to get someone to confess—not in the way that *my* teachers had done it, by sitting in the room until the guilty party or an informant cracked, but simply by asking the perpetrator to leave a note in my classroom mailbox. My classroom was antiquated, but it included an enclosed hallway, now equipped with coat racks and shelves that led to a restroom. Apparently, while I was preoccupied teaching my lessons, a child was stealing food. Three days later, several other children reported that they had seen Tonya "messing around people's lunchboxes." I asked her, but she denied it. At recess, I looked in her desk and found it littered with empty food wrappers. Then Tonya and I discussed it again in private and examined the evidence.

I consulted my principal about what to do. He suggested that I punish her severely; a month without recess seemed warranted, he said. I thought it might be better to call her mother, but they had no telephone and the principal assured me that, based on her failure to attend previous school functions, Tonya's mother would not come to school. Then I said I would write a note and set up a home visit. He strongly advised against that, telling me that Tonya's mother had a disease, that the house was a mess, and that she had a live-in boyfriend.

All these things were true, but I understand them differently now. Tonya's mother had lupus and was at a debilitating stage of the disease that prevented her from working, much less maintaining a spotless home. Tonya's family now consisted of mother, unofficial stepfather (also permanently disabled), and a three-year-old brother. They lived on a fixed income, and Tonya qualified for free lunches.

As a first-year teacher [at this school], I was reluctant to go against the principal's wishes, but I did draw the line at harsh punishment. When I asked Tonya *why* she took things from the other children's lunches, she simply said, "'Cause I was hungry." I asked her if she ate breakfast in the morning, and she said, "No. I have to take care of my little brother before I go to school." I asked her if having breakfast might solve the problem and she said, "Yes. My aunt would help." And so, my first big teaching problem was solved by an eight-year-old when instead of foraging for food each morning, Tonya and her brother walked down the block to her unmarried aunt's house before school and ate breakfast.

There was still the matter of repairing Tonya's damaged reputation with the other children, who had accumulated a variety of negative experiences with her and had labeled her as a thief. I stood with my arms around Tonya's shoulder in front of the class and announced that Tonya had agreed not to take things anymore, that she could be trusted, and that all was well.

Two weeks later, a child's candy bar was reported missing, and the class was quick to accuse Tonya. I took her aside and inquired about the missing candy bar. "No," she said firmly, "I didn't eat it." As I defended Tonya's innocence to her peers, I noticed how Tonya, the child who had learned to slouch to conceal her size, sat up tall and proud in her seat.

I must confess that I was wondering if Tonya might be lying when Kendra, the child who reported the stolen candy bar, said she was ill and wanted to go home. Then, with a candor only possible in a young child, Kendra said, "I have a stomachache, and you want to know why? Because I just remembered that *I* ate my candy bar on the bus this morning."

Tonya's confidence and competence flourished during the remainder of her first-grade year and throughout second grade. Then, in third grade, she had a teacher who was sarcastic and unfair. When I passed by the third-grade room, I often saw Tonya seated off by herself or washing the walls, desks, or floors as punishment for her misbehavior. She would stop at my first-grade classroom after school, and when I asked her about it, she said she just didn't like third grade and wished she could come back to first grade. Ms. M., Tonya's third-grade teacher, had the habit of choosing certain children—always the ones whose parents were influential and wealthy—for all of the classroom privileges. One day as I was passing by her classroom, the third-grade teacher said, "Alyssa, you have on such a pretty dress today, why don't you be our messenger? Be sure to show Mr. B [the principal] how nice you look!" I caught a glimpse of Tonya's face as she sat there in her secondhand clothes and felt bitter tears in my eyes.

From *Teachers' Stories: From Personal Narrative to Professional Insight* (pp. 114–117), by M. R. Jalongo, J. P. Isenberg, & G. Gerbracht, 1995, San Francisco: Jossey-Bass. Copyright © 1995 by Jossey-Bass, Inc. Adapted by permission of Jossey-Bass, Inc., a subsidiary of John Wiley & Sons, Inc.

HOW EASY IT MIGHT have been for a teacher to write Tonya off as a bully and a thief and, as the principal suggested, to punish her severely for her transgressions. Fortunately, Ms. Jalongo looked beneath the surface to find a child who was, instead, hungry and eager to please. By doing so, she identified a simple strategy—arranging for Tonya and her brother to eat breakfast with their aunt—that not only eliminated the lunch-pilfering episodes but also started Tonya on the road to establishing more positive relationships with her classmates.

Teachers play an important—in fact, a *critical*—role in the development of children and adolescents. At the very minimum, teachers provide the experiences and instruction that promote more sophisticated thinking and greater knowledge about the world. But in addition, *effective* teachers help children and adolescents develop social skills, self-confidence, and a love of learning. In some cases (perhaps in Tonya's), teachers may even provide the most caring, stable environment that students have.

In this book, we explore the course of development during childhood and adolescence, with a particular focus on the preschool, elementary, middle school, and high school years. Throughout our exploration, we continually connect what theorists and researchers have learned about human development to what educators can do to help children and adolescents become all that they are capable of becoming—not only academically, but physically, socially, and emotionally as well. We frequently illustrate such connections with examples and case studies. We also draw on our own experiences as teachers and mothers; thus, you will see references to Teresa and Jeanne, the authors, throughout the book.

Our exploration begins with an overview of the field of child and adolescent development and an examination of basic issues that the field addresses. We also survey the various perspectives that psychologists and other theorists have used to describe and explain why youngsters behave and think as they do and how their behaviors and thought processes change over time. Later, we preview characteristics that are commonly seen in various age groups. Finally, we go from theory to practice, identifying some general strategies through which teachers can make a difference in the lives of their students.

Child and Adolescent Development as a Field of Inquiry

What does it mean for children and adolescents to "develop"? When we talk about **development,** we are referring to systematic, age-related changes in the physical and psychological functioning of human beings. Sometimes we are talking about changes that almost everyone undergoes. For example, as children get older, almost all of them acquire increasingly complex

development
Systematic, age-related changes in physical and psychological functioning.

language skills. At other times, we are talking about acquisitions that differ considerably among individuals. For example, over time, some children spontaneously develop more effective ways of studying academic subject matter, but others gain little insight into how they can learn effectively unless given explicit instruction in study strategies.

In upcoming chapters, we will examine developmental changes in three general areas: physical development, cognitive development, and social-emotional development. In our discussion of **physical development,** we will investigate patterns of physical growth and maturation, the genetic bases for some human characteristics and abilities, neurological (brain) development, the acquisition of motor skills (e.g., running, using scissors), and health-promoting behaviors. Tonya, from the opening case study, was taller than her classmates. Her greater height was certainly due, at least in part, to being a year older than her peers; she may also have been genetically inclined to be tall. But environmental factors influence physical development as well; for instance, the nutritional value of children's diets affects their physical growth and energy level.

By **cognitive development,** we mean systematic changes in children's reasoning, concepts, memory, and language. For example, Tonya spent 2 years in kindergarten before moving on to first grade; perhaps she initially lacked the basic academic skills that her kindergarten teacher thought would be essential for her success in first grade. Also, you may have noticed that Tonya responded to Ms. Jalongo's questions with short, simple responses. Was her language development delayed? Probably not; as you will discover, basic language skills develop normally under a wide range of circumstances.

We will use the term **social-emotional development** to refer to changes in children's feelings, ways of coping, social relationships, and moral functioning—for instance, changes in self-esteem, social skills, and beliefs about right and wrong. Notice how Tonya became increasingly self-confident during her year in first grade, to the point where she eventually "sat up tall and proud in her seat" (Jalongo et al., 1995, p. 116). Furthermore, Tonya's stealing episodes stopped once she was getting breakfast at her aunt's house, and so it appears that she *did* have a basic respect for other children's possessions. Ms. Jalongo's efforts to repair Tonya's reputation may have helped Tonya begin to forge friendships with classmates; in the process, Ms. Jalongo may also have helped her develop more effective interpersonal skills. Peer relationships are important to all children, and Tonya's situation reminds us of the pain that children experience when rejected by classmates and other peers.

In addition to considering the normal course of children's physical, cognitive, and social-emotional development, it is important to consider the *context* within which children grow. For instance, some sort of "family" or other close, caring cluster of relationships is a critical condition for optimal development. We know that Tonya assumed responsibilities beyond her years in caring for her younger brother, that her mother was physically unable to give her much support, and that an aunt was, fortunately, able to provide the physical (and perhaps psychological) nurturance that Tonya so desperately needed. Many other factors—neighborhood, community, culture, ethnicity, income level, and so on—also contribute to the context in which children develop. For example, Tonya's financial circumstances prevented her from buying pretty dresses like those admired by her third-grade teacher, and we shudder to think about what long-term repercussions this thoughtless teacher's actions may have had on Tonya's emotional and academic growth.

As we describe the course of child and adolescent development and the factors that promote or in other ways alter it, we will base our discussions on research from the fields of psychology and, to a lesser extent, sociology and anthropology. In some cases, research findings are consistent with what we might deduce from common sense. At other times, they may be surprising, and perhaps even inconsistent with commonly held beliefs about children and adolescents. In all cases, however, developmental research gives educators a solid foundation on which to build effective teaching strategies. To cultivate our readers' appreciation for developmental research, we explore research principles early in the book (Chapter 2). In later chapters, we occasionally describe specific research studies to illustrate how researchers have reached their conclusions.

Figure 1–1 gives an overview of the book, identifying the chapters in which we will examine developmental research methods, the three domains of development (physical, cognitive, and social-emotional), and the nature of the contexts in which children and adolescents grow.

physical development
Physical and neurological growth and age-related changes in motor skills.

cognitive development
Systematic changes in reasoning, concepts, memory, and language.

social-emotional development
Systematic changes in emotional, social, and moral functioning.

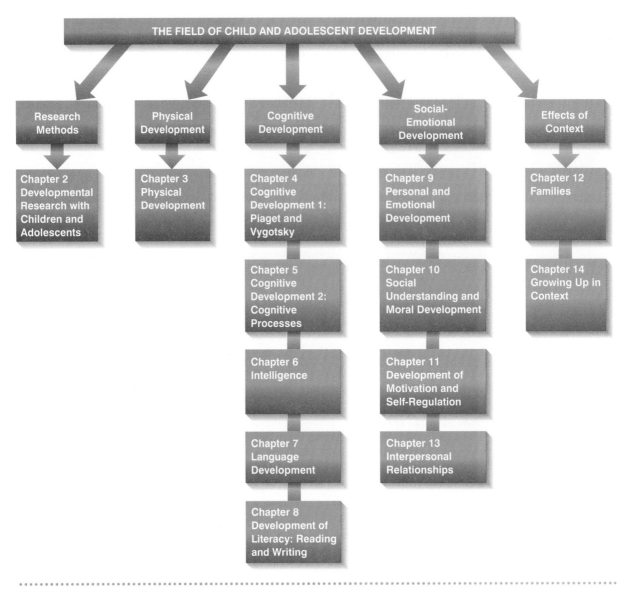

FIGURE 1–1 Overview of the book

Although it appears as if we will treat these topics as separate entities, we will frequently illustrate how, in fact, they interact with one another. For example, physical development (e.g., neurological changes) allows cognitive advancements to take place, and increases in the ability to look at situations from multiple perspectives (a cognitive ability) enable more effective social relationships. Throughout the book, we will continually consider how children develop within the contexts of schools, families, and cultural systems.

Basic Issues in the Study of Development

In their attempts to describe and explain the changes that take place during childhood and adolescence, developmental theorists have grappled with, but not yet resolved, three key issues. First, theorists disagree about the relative influences of heredity and environment on various aspects of development. Second, they speculate about the extent to which certain developmental phenomena are true for everyone, on the one hand, or unique to particular individuals, on the other. Third, when they describe how certain characteristics develop over time, some theorists portray development as occurring in discrete time periods, or *stages*, whereas others instead depict development as a series of more gradual, continuous *trends*. We now look more closely at these three issues: nature versus nurture, universality versus diversity, and qualitative versus quantitative change.

Nature and Nurture

Nature refers to inherited (genetic) influences on growth and functioning. Some inherited characteristics appear in virtually all members of the species; for instance, almost all children have natural talents for upright locomotion (walking, running, etc.), language, imitation, and the use of simple tools. Other inherited characteristics differ from one individual to another; for instance, people's stature, physical appearance, and athletic ability vary widely. Such psychological traits as temperament (e.g., the tendency to be shy vs. outgoing), aggression, and intelligence may also be partly influenced by genes (Petrill & Wilkerson, 2000; Plomin, 1989; Rowe, Almeida, & Jacobson, 1999).

Inherited characteristics and tendencies are not always evident at birth. Many emerge gradually through the process of **maturation,** genetically controlled changes that occur over the course of development. Although certain basic kinds of environmental support, such as food, are necessary for maturation to take place, a person's genetic makeup provides powerful instructions for certain changes to occur despite a wide range of environmental circumstances.

Nature's equal partner is **nurture,** the influence of factors in children's environments. Nurture includes the effects of family, peers, schools, neighborhoods, culture, the media, and the broader society in which people live. It affects children's development through multiple channels—physically through nutrition and opportunities for activity, intellectually through informal experiences and formal instruction, socially through adult role models and peer relationships, and so on.

Historically, the relative influences of nature versus nurture have been a source of considerable controversy among developmental theorists; you will find examples of such controversy in our discussions of intelligence (Chapter 6), language development (Chapter 7), temperament (Chapter 9), and aggression (Chapter 13). But increasingly, those who study development are beginning to realize that nature and nurture intermesh in ways that we can probably never tease apart. Following are several principles to keep in mind:

■ *The relative effects of heredity and environment vary for different domains of development.* Some domains seem to be heavily dictated by genetically controlled systems in the brain. For example, depth perception and the ability to distinguish among various speech sounds appear to be human birthrights activated with only a hint of experience (Flavell, 1994; Gallistel, Brown, Carey, Gelman, & Keil, 1991). Other domains, such as development in traditional school subject areas (e.g., reading, geography) and advanced accomplishments in challenging artistic and physical arenas (e.g., playing the piano, becoming a competitive basketball player), are more dependent on environmental support (Gardner, Torff, & Hatch, 1996; Olson, 1994; Watson, 1996).

Expert coaching (nurture) can enhance children's natural abilities (nature).

■ *Inherited tendencies may make children more or less responsive and susceptible to particular environmental influences.* Because of differences in their genetic makeup, some children may be easily affected by certain conditions in the environment, whereas others are less affected (Rutter, 1997). For example, children who are, by nature, timid and inhibited may be quite shy if they live in situations where they have few social contacts. If their parents and teachers encourage them to make friends, however, they may become more socially outgoing (Arcus, 1991; Kagan, 1998). In contrast, children who have more extroverted temperaments may be friendly and sociable *regardless* of the environments in which they grow up.

■ *Environment may play a greater role when conditions are extreme rather than moderate.* When youngsters have experiences typical for their culture and age group, then heredity often accounts for differences in their physical and psychological characteristics. But when they have experiences that are quite unusual—for instance, when they experience extreme deprivation—the role of environment may far outweigh the possible effects of heredity (Rowe et al., 1999). For example, as you will discover in Chapter 6, when children grow up having adequate nutrition, a loving and stable home environment, and appropriate educational experiences, heredity influences the rate at which they acquire certain intellectual abilities. But when they grow up in extremely impoverished conditions—when nutrition is inadequate and they have little physical and psychological

nature
Effects of heredity and genetically controlled maturational processes on development.

maturation
Genetically controlled changes that occur over the course of development.

nurture
Effects of environmental conditions on development.

stimulation—heredity may have little to say about their intellectual development (Plomin & Petrill, 1997; Rowe, Jacobson, & Van den Oord, 1999).

■ *Some environmental experiences play a greater role at some ages than at others.* Sometimes the members of a species need a particular kind of stimulation at a particular age to develop normally. Classic research with geese by Konrad Lorenz in the 1940s illustrates this phenomenon. Lorenz observed that newly hatched geese almost immediately began to follow their mother, and he wondered if such behavior was instinctual and therefore hereditary. To answer his question, he divided a clutch of goose eggs into two groups; one group was hatched in the mother's nest, the other in an incubator. The goslings hatched by their mother were soon following their mother around Lorenz's estate. The goslings hatched in the incubator began to follow the first moving object they saw—in this case, Dr. Lorenz—and appeared to form an emotional attachment to him. Lorenz observed that this phenomenon, called *imprinting,* occurred only when the goslings were exposed to a moving "mother" figure very early in life (see Lorenz, 1981, for an English description of this work). In more controlled laboratory studies, Hess (1958) found that ducklings would even follow a nonliving moving object (a wooden duck decoy traveling in a circle several feet in diameter). Imprinting was strongest if the ducklings were exposed to the decoy between 13 and 16 hours of age (an age span that Hess called a *critical period*), and virtually no imprinting occurred after the ducklings were 28 hours old.

Evidence has since emerged that other species may also have critical periods for certain aspects of development, such as visual perception (Blakemore, 1976; Bruer, 1999; Hubel & Wiesel, 1965). In human beings, too, some kinds of environmental stimulation have a greater effect during particular age ranges. In most cases, however, these age ranges reflect an *optimal* time, rather than the *only* time, for such stimulation. In other words, individuals may be most receptive to a certain type of stimulation at one point in their lives but can nevertheless benefit from it later as well. Furthermore, enriching experiences or explicit training at a later time can often make up for any critical experiences missed at an earlier period (Bruer, 1999). Hence, some theorists prefer to use the term **sensitive period** (rather than critical period) when talking about hereditarily determined ideal time frames for certain environmental experiences.

Sensitive periods in human development are often complex and multifaceted. In language development, for example, we find evidence for several different sensitive periods:

- Soon after birth, young infants can discriminate among the many speech sounds that human beings can utter, but by 6 months their discriminatory powers appear to be attuned primarily to those sounds produced by people in their own linguistic culture (Kuhl, Williams, & Lacerda, 1992).
- Children appear to master the grammar of a language (either their native tongue or a second language) more completely if they are exposed to it in the early years, ideally before age 4 (Johnson & Newport, 1989; Newport, 1990).
- Children can learn to pronounce a second language flawlessly only if they begin studying it before puberty; those who begin after puberty almost always have an accent (Bialystok, 1994b; Collier, 1989; Long, 1995).

Yet not all aspects of language development are characterized by a sensitive period; for instance, people can learn new words at virtually *any* time in their lives.

■ *Children make choices that affect the environments they encounter.* In addition to nature and nurture, **organismic influences**—children's own characteristics and behaviors—affect their development (the term *organism* refers to a single, living member of a particular species). Children do not sit passively waiting for their every move to be dictated by heredity or environment. Instead, they make choices, seek out information and events that they understand, modify what they do not understand and, over time, develop ideas about people and the world that they continue to accumulate and refine (Flavell, 1994; Piaget, 1985). Returning to our example of language, children ask for definitions themselves ("What *cooperate* mean, Mommy?"), seek out informants whom they think can answer their questions ("Uncle Kevin, what is this word in my computer magazine?"), and test their own informal hypotheses about concepts and their boundaries ("Daddy called that a donkey, not a horse. I wonder what the difference is"). Children may even create environments that exacerbate their genetic tendencies. For instance,

sensitive period
A period in development when certain environmental experiences have a more pronounced influence than is true at other times.

organismic influences
Characteristics and behaviors of human beings that influence later development.

a child with an irritable disposition may seek out conflicts, picking fights with peers and adults; in doing so, the child creates a more aggressive climate in which to grow.

As children get older, they are better able to seek out stimulation and create environments that suit their inherited constitutions. For example, imagine that Marissa has inherited considerable potential for developing verbal skills, such as learning vocabulary, comprehending stories, using sophisticated grammatical structures, and so on. As a baby, Marissa must rely heavily on her parents to talk to her. As a toddler, she can move around independently and ask her parents for particular kinds of stimulation ("Read book, Mommy!"). In elementary school, she might seek out particular books to read and might favor friends who will swap books with her. As a teenager, she is even more capable of defining her own environment; for instance, she may baby-sit for pocket change, take the bus to the library and bookstore, and choose books by a favorite author. Thus, we might expect that genetic tendencies become *more* powerful as children grow older—a prediction that turns out to be consistent with genetic research (Scarr & McCartney, 1983).

In many ways, then, nature and nurture are inextricably intertwined in their effects on human development. While theorists are busy debating the relative influences of nature and nurture, children manage to combine these forces skillfully and naturally. In other words, the effects of nature and nurture blend seamlessly during development (Keating, 1996b).

Universality and Diversity

Some developmental changes occur in just about everyone; such changes reflect a certain degree of **universality** in development. For instance, unless physical disabilities are present, all young children learn to sit, crawl, walk, and run, and almost invariably in that order. Other developmental changes are highly individual and idiosyncratic, reflecting **diversity.** For instance, children differ in their strength, agility, and endurance as they engage in strenuous physical activities.

Theorists differ in the extent to which they believe that developmental sequences and accomplishments are universal across all human beings, on the one hand, or unique to particular individuals, on the other. Some propose that heredity and maturation (i.e., the influence of nature) quite logically lead to universality in what develops (e.g., Gesell, 1928). They point out that, despite widely varying environments, virtually all human beings acquire basic motor skills, proficiency in language, an ability to think about the perspectives of other people, an ability to inhibit immediate impulses, and so on.

Maturation is not necessarily the only route to universality, however. The developmental psychologist Jean Piaget believed that children acquire similar ways of thinking about the world because, despite their unique interactions with objects and people, they are all apt to observe similar phenomena (e.g., objects always fall *down* rather than up, people often get angry when their possessions are snatched away). (We will look at Piaget's theory in depth in Chapter 4.)

Yet other theorists have been impressed by the diversity in cognitive and social functioning during childhood and adolescence (e.g., Baltes, Reese, & Lipsitt, 1980; Lerner, 1989). Some individual differences can be traced to the historical era in which people grew up (e.g., were their childhood experiences marked by war, economic depression, counterculture movements, societal apathy, or a computer revolution?). Differences also occur as a result of events unique to individuals and their families (e.g., did their parents divorce? did drug dealers invade their neighborhoods? did their parents win the lottery?). Finally, cultural settings are significant sources of diversity, as we will see throughout the book, and especially in Chapter 14. Children differ in the skills and competencies they acquire based on the culturally unique tools and symbols that pervade their lives (Rogoff, 1990; Wertsch & Tulviste, 1994).

Earlier, we mentioned that the relative influences of nature and nurture depend on the domain. The same point can be made about universality and diversity. Developmental pathways tend to be universal in areas that are under fairly strict maturational control, such as physical development. Diversity is more prevalent in other domains, such as cognitive, social, and moral development. Furthermore, there is always *some* diversity, even in physical development. For instance, some children are born with physical disabilities, others are seriously injured early in childhood, and still others have insufficient nutrition to develop normally. Throughout the book,

Although some developmental changes are universal, others (e.g., tastes in clothing and music) reflect the diversity in children's talents, temperaments, and interests.
Courtesy of Ricco, age 13.

universality
Characteristics and developmental progressions shared by virtually all human beings.

diversity
Characteristics and developmental progressions that differ from one individual to another.

we will find instances of developmental universality, but perhaps more often than not, we will see divergences from typical pathways.

Effective teachers are knowledgeable about the universals that characterize their students' development; they are also sensitive to the many ways in which their students are likely to be different from one another and from what is "average" for a particular age group. For example, in the opening case study, Ms. Jalongo was well aware that Tonya was in some ways different from her classmates: Tonya was taller, her bullying behavior was unusual for first graders, and her ability to cajole her classmates into uneven "trades" indicated possible sophistication in the art of persuasion. But Ms. Jalongo also suspected that Tonya, like most children, had a basic desire to make friends (a desire that is fairly universal), and so she paved the way for Tonya to repair her reputation once the stealing stopped.

One theorist has offered a simple analogy that may help you understand the roles of universality and diversity:

> Development is like a game of Scrabble. The fundamental rules of the game and the strategies for maximizing progress are essentially the same for all players. However, because everyone starts with a different set of tiles and plays a different pattern of words, each player faces unique challenges and opportunities throughout the course of the game. That is why effective educational policies and practices must be based on notions of diversity and individuality, not on norms and group averages. Although education often occurs in group settings, development always proceeds one child at a time. (Ford, 1997, p. 124)

Qualitative and Quantitative Change

Sometimes development is characterized by a rather sudden, relatively dramatic change in behavior or thinking; this is a **qualitative change.** For instance, when children learn to run, they propel their bodies forward in a way that is distinctly different from walking. When they begin to talk in two-word sentences rather than with single words, they are, for the first time, using rudimentary forms of grammar that restrict the ways in which they combine words.

Certainly not all of development involves dramatic change. More frequently, development occurs as a gradual progression, or *trend,* with many small additions to behaviors and thought processes. Such progression is **quantitative change.** For example, children grow taller gradually, over time, and with both age and experience they slowly learn more about the animal kingdom, getting along with others, and so on.

When theorists talk about qualitative change, they are talking about a systematic revamping of previously acquired knowledge and skills. Oftentimes, they use the term **stage** to refer to a period of development characterized by a particular way of behaving or thinking. In a **stage theory** of development, individuals progress through a series of stages that are qualitatively different from one another. Most stage theories are *hierarchical,* in that earlier stages provide the foundation for, and so are prerequisite to, later ones.[1]

Developmental theorists have been attracted to the idea of stages ever since the field of developmental psychology was founded (Parke, Ornstein, Rieser, & Zahn-Waxler, 1994), and you will read about several stage theories in this book. For instance, you will encounter Piaget's theory of cognitive development in Chapter 4, Erikson's theory of social-emotional development in Chapter 9, and Kohlberg's theory of moral development in Chapter 10.

Research does not entirely support the notion that children and adolescents proceed through stages one at a time in a lockstep fashion. For instance, youngsters often display characteristics of two or more stages during a single period of time, depending on the circumstances (e.g., Ceci & Roazzi, 1994; Kurtines & Gewirtz, 1991; Metz, 1995). Nor do stage progressions always ap-

As teachers work with children, they should keep in mind not only typical age trends but also the diversity in children's abilities and developmental progress.

qualitative change
Relatively dramatic developmental change that reflects considerable reorganization or modification of functioning.

quantitative change
Developmental change that involves a series of minor, trendlike modifications.

stage
A period of development characterized by a particular way of behaving or thinking.

stage theory
Theory that describes development as involving a series of qualitatively distinct changes, with these changes occurring in the same sequence for everyone.

---

[1]Note that developmentalists use the term *stage* in a somewhat narrower way than we use it in everyday speech. Parents and other adults often make comments such as "He's at the terrible twos stage" or "She's at that stage when she really worries about what her friends think." Such comments reflect the idea that children are behaving typically for their age group, but they don't necessarily imply that a *qualitative* change has taken place.

Illustrations in the Three Domains

BASIC DEVELOPMENTAL ISSUES

ISSUE	PHYSICAL DEVELOPMENT	COGNITIVE DEVELOPMENT	SOCIAL-EMOTIONAL DEVELOPMENT
Nature and Nurture	Nature masterminds the maturational unfolding of specific parts of the brain in particular sequences. Genetic factors also determine certain physical predispositions, such as a tendency toward thinness or a susceptibility to diabetes. The importance of nutrition and the effects of instruction and training on athletic skills illustrate nurture at work (Chapter 3).	Some aspects of intelligence and language seem to be genetically based. Many contemporary theorists emphasize environmental influences, such as informal learning experiences, adult modeling and mentoring, and formal schooling (Chapters 4, 5, 6, 7).	Individual differences in temperament appear to be partly controlled by heredity (nature). Environmental influences (nurture) are evident in the development of self-esteem and ethnic identity (Chapter 9).
Universality and Diversity	The emergence of key physical features (e.g., gender-specific features that develop during puberty) is universal. Diversity is evident in the ages at which children and adolescents undergo key physical developments, as well as in their general state of physical health (Chapter 3).	The components of the human information processing system (e.g., the mechanisms that support learning and memory) are universal. However, some children have more effective ways of learning and remembering information than others (Chapter 5).	The need for peer affiliation represents a universal part of development in children and adolescents. Considerable individual differences exist in prosocial behavior and aggression (Chapter 13).
Qualitative and Quantitative Change 	Some aspects of physical development (e.g., the changes associated with puberty) reflect dramatic change. Most of the time, however, physical development occurs gradually as a result of many small changes (e.g., young children grow slowly taller and then experience a rapid growth spurt in adolescence; Chapter 3).	Children's logical reasoning skills show some qualitative change; for instance, children acquire new and increasingly sophisticated ways of solving problems. Quantitative change occurs as children gradually gain knowledge in various academic disciplines (Chapters 4 and 5).	Some evidence suggests that, with appropriate social experience, children's understanding of morality undergoes qualitative change, often in conjunction with changes in logical reasoning. In a more quantitative manner, children gradually come to understand how other people's minds work and discover that others' knowledge, beliefs, and desires may be different than their own (Chapter 10).

pear to be universal across cultures (e.g., Glick, 1975; Triandis, 1995). Currently, then, few developmentalists support strict interpretations of stage theories (Parke et al., 1994).

At the same time, most theorists do not want to abandon all notions of qualitative changes in development (Flavell, 1994). At age 15, adolescents do strike most people as acting in ways that are consistently different than those of 2-year-old children. Fifteen-year-olds are not simply taller or more knowledgeable about the world; they go about their day-to-day living in what amounts to a qualitatively different style. Maturation-based developments, such as neurological increases in memory capacity and efficiency, plus an ever-expanding accumulation of knowledge and experience, probably permit and promote both gradual and occasionally dramatic changes in thinking and behaving (Case et al., 1996; Flavell, 1994).

As you read this book, you will find that the three developmental issues we've introduced here periodically resurface, both in the text and in Basic Developmental Issues tables. (The first of these tables, above, provides examples of how the issues are reflected in physical, cognitive, and social-emotional development.) Continually revisiting the issues will remind us that development is a complex process—that it is the outcome of both natural forces and environmental influences, that it displays common pathways and exceptions, and that it embodies many minor changes as well as occasional dramatic reorganizations.

Theories of Child and Adolescent Development

In the 18th and 19th centuries, the nature of *how things change* piqued the interest of many scholars, who began to investigate the histories of a variety of phenomena—animal species, geological features, culture, ideas, and so on (Dixon & Lerner, 1992). Charles Darwin's theory of natural selection and evolution provided an influential framework for looking at change in living beings, including humans. Historians in the field of child development argue over how strongly and positively their field was influenced by Darwin (Charlesworth, 1992; Dixon & Lerner, 1992). Even so, Darwin and other early theorists articulated several ideas that have provided a foundation on which many current theories of human development now rest:

- Knowledge about an individual's past can help us understand the individual's present functioning.
- Both biological capacities and environmental experiences contribute to an individual's present characteristics.
- The nature of children's development is best investigated through systematic and scientific methods of inquiry.
- The changes that children exhibit as they grow older invariably lead to improvements in their ability to function and adapt to environmental circumstances.

The last of these ideas—an assumption known as *progressive change*—has sometimes been called into question in recent decades: not all theorists believe that all developmental changes are necessarily for the best. Nevertheless, the notion of progressive change has long been a guiding principle in the field of child and adolescent development (Bronfenbrenner, Kessel, Kessen, & White, 1986).

In the first few decades of the 20th century, explicit **theories**—organized systems of principles and explanations of certain aspects of child and adolescent development—began to emerge. Over the years, such theories have directed the questions that developmental scientists ask, provided ground rules for acceptable research methods, and helped researchers make sense of their observations. In the next few pages, we survey the currently dominant theoretical perspectives of development. We then urge you to take advantage of multiple theoretical perspectives in your attempts to better understand, and thereby to work more effectively with, children and adolescents.

Dominant Theoretical Perspectives of Development

Eight theoretical approaches have dominated academic discussions about children and adolescents. We examine them briefly here and then revisit them in later chapters as they become relevant to our discussions of particular topics.

Maturational Perspectives Developmental scholars working within a **maturational perspective** emphasize the genetically guided unfolding of developmental structures, neurological organizations, and motor abilities. Historically, the best known maturational theorist was Arnold Gesell, who focused on developmental changes that occur almost automatically, without learning or instruction. From this perspective, children walk when they are physiologically ready to do so, and puberty begins when a biological clock triggers the appropriate hormones. If you recall our earlier discussion about the contributions of nature and nurture, you may be inferring (correctly) that theorists striking a maturational pose are emphasizing the nature side of the continuum. The influence of maturational theorists will be readily apparent in our discussion of physical development in Chapter 3.

Psychodynamic Perspectives Theorists taking a **psychodynamic perspective** believe that early experiences play a critical role in later characteristics and behavior. They typically focus on social and personality development and, often, abnormal development.

Sigmund Freud, the earliest psychodynamic theorist, persuasively argued that there is more to childhood than innocent play. According to Freud, young children continually find themselves embroiled in internal conflicts between impulses toward sexuality and aggression, on

theory
Organized system of principles and explanations regarding a particular phenomenon.

maturational perspective
Theoretical perspective that emphasizes genetically guided unfolding of developmental structures, neurological organizations, and motor abilities.

psychodynamic perspective
Theoretical perspective that focuses on how early experiences affect social and personality development.

the one hand, and socially sanctioned pressures to gain parental approval and be productive, on the other. Through ongoing negotiations with parents, children progress through a series of qualitatively distinct stages, eventually learning to channel their biological impulses in socially appropriate ways.

Psychodynamic perspectives often include a series of stages through which children must progress. You will find an example of a psychodynamic perspective in Erik Erikson's psychosocial theory in Chapter 9.

Cognitive-Developmental Perspectives In **cognitive-developmental perspectives**, the emphasis is on thinking processes and how they change, qualitatively, over time. In such perspectives, children typically play an active role in their own development: They seek out new and interesting experiences, try to make sense of what they see and hear, and work actively to reconcile any discrepancies between new information and what they have previously believed to be true. In the process of doing these things, children's thinking becomes more abstract and systematic.

Children develop, in part, by actively seeking out new and interesting experiences. Courtesy of Margot, age 6.

The earliest and best known cognitive-developmental theorist was Jean Piaget. With a career that spanned decades and spawned thousands of research studies around the world, Piaget touched on many aspects of children's lives, including emotional development, peer relationships, and moral reasoning. But his main focus and contributions were in cognitive development, where he investigated the nature of children's logical thinking processes about such topics as numbers, physical causality, geographical formations, and time. We will describe Piaget's work in Chapter 4. A second cognitive-developmental perspective, Lawrence Kohlberg's theory of how moral reasoning develops, is presented in Chapter 10.

Behavioral Learning Perspectives A fourth position, the **behavioral learning perspective,** stands in sharp contrast to the earlier perspectives we've described, in that developmental changes are credited almost exclusively to environmental influences (nurture). Conducting research with humans and other species (e.g., dogs, rats, pigeons), behavioral learning theorists have shown that many behaviors can be modified through appropriate environmental stimuli. For instance, they have demonstrated that children actively "work" for rewards such as food, praise, or physical contact and tend to avoid behaviors that lead to punishment.

In recent years, behavioral learning theorists have begun to realize that children don't necessarily respond mindlessly to environmental events but instead actively think about and interpret those events. They've discovered that children can learn a great deal from observing others and that, furthermore, they can anticipate the consequences of their actions and choose their behaviors accordingly. We will present the ideas of two prominent behavioral learning theorists, B. F. Skinner and Albert Bandura, in our discussion of motivation and self-regulation in Chapter 11.

Evolutionary Perspectives Reflecting the influence of Charles Darwin, **evolutionary perspectives** focus on inherited behavior patterns that enhance a child's chances for survival and reproduction. Those characteristics and behaviors that increase the chances of survival and reproduction are more likely to be genetically passed on to future generations.

Two general variants on the evolutionary theme are ethology and sociobiology. *Ethological theorists* study behavior patterns that they believe are inherited. From an ethological perspective, it makes sense that parents and infants form emotional bonds to each other ("Isn't my baby adorable?!"), that people stand alert to threat signals ("Fire!"), that they engage in courtship rituals ("Dinner at my place?"), and that they safeguard their young ("Prisons in my neighborhood? Never!"). *Sociobiologists* have similar concerns but are more interested in behaviors within a social group, including the roles that childrearing, cooperation, self-sacrifice, and other behaviors play in the long-term survival and proliferation of the group.

The evolutionary perspective reminds us to examine how children's and adolescents' behaviors may be adaptations to particular environments. For example, children do not survive their early years unless they stay out of harm's way and form social-emotional bonds with caregivers who have their best interests at heart. We will see in Chapter 9 that children form intense bonds with their caregivers and are fearful of strangers at a time when they are quite vulnerable and dependent but are beginning to explore their environment by crawling or walking.

cognitive-developmental perspective
Theoretical perspective that focuses on qualitative changes in thinking processes over time.

behavioral learning perspective
Theoretical perspective that focuses on environmental stimuli and learning processes that lead to developmental change.

evolutionary perspective
Theoretical perspective that focuses on inherited behavior patterns that enhance the survival and reproduction of the species.

Social-emotional attachments seem to be nature's way of protecting small children and inducting them into nurturant social communities.

Information Processing Perspectives **Information processing perspectives** focus on the nature of human cognitive processes—for instance, how people transform and remember the information they receive—and on how such processes change during childhood and adolescence. Early information processing theories, which emerged in the 1960s, modeled human thinking processes on the linear, this-leads-to-that ways in which computers operate. More recently, however, many theorists have acknowledged that computers and human beings probably "think" very differently (e.g., Derry, 1996; Mayer, 1996). But whether they use a computer metaphor or not, information processing theorists all attempt to describe children's and adolescents' thought processes with a fair amount of precision.

Information processing perspectives dominate much of the research in cognitive development, and so they will dominate much of our discussion of cognitive development in Chapter 5. You will also see the influence of information processing theory in our discussions of intelligence (Chapter 6), language development (Chapter 7), and literacy (Chapter 8).

Ecological and Socio-Historic Perspectives **Ecological and socio-historic perspectives** shine light on the social and cultural systems in which children and adolescents develop. Bronfenbrenner (1979) has described the *ecology,* or natural environments, of childhood, including children's immediate and extended families, neighborhoods, schools, parents' workplaces, the mass media, community services, and political systems and practices. These various social systems often interact with one another as they affect children. For example, out-of-home daycare providers assist many parents in childrearing duties, but if the out-of-home care is not responsive, safe, stimulating, and stable, then parents may become anxious about the welfare of their children and behave accordingly. You will see the influence of ecological perspectives in our discussion of "growing up in context" in Chapter 14.

Another slant on social and cultural systems comes from *socio-historic theorists,* such as Lev Vygotsky and Barbara Rogoff, who have studied children's developing capacity to use the tools and symbolic systems of their cultures and to participate fully in the traditional roles and activities of their communities. We describe Vygotsky's theory and include some of Rogoff's ideas in Chapter 4.

Life-Span Perspectives **Life-span perspectives** track developmental changes from conception to death. Some of these changes are predictable and age-related, others are more dependent on particular historic events (e.g., war, economic depression), and still others result from individual life events (e.g., divorce of parents, death of a close friend). Life-span theorists depict development as the result of dynamic interactions among maturational, contextual, historical, and cultural forces, and as a process that does not stop once people reach adulthood.

Some theorists working from perspectives we've already discussed take a life-span approach to development. For instance, Erik Erikson (a psychodynamic theorist we discuss in Chapter 9) considers social-emotional development from birth through old age. And some information processing theorists investigate how memory and cognitive processes change over the course of adulthood.

Taking an Eclectic Approach

The eight perspectives just described are summarized in Table 1–1. With so many theories, which one is right? To some extent, they all are: Each one provides unique insights into the nature of child and adolescent development that no other approach can offer. At the same time, none is completely right, in that no single theory can adequately explain all aspects of development. In a sense, any theory is like a lens that brings certain phenomena into sharp focus but leaves other phenomena blurry or unrecognizable.

Throughout the book, we introduce a variety of theoretical explanations for the phenomena we are addressing. We urge you to have an eclectic attitude about these theories, looking for the best that each has to offer. Each of the theories can help you understand some aspects of children's and adolescents' thinking and behavior, and each can give you some useful ideas about how to promote optimal development during the school years.

information processing perspective
Theoretical perspective that focuses on the precise nature of human cognitive processes.

ecological and socio-historic perspectives
Theoretical perspectives that focus on the social and cultural systems in which human beings grow and develop.

life-span perspective
Theoretical perspective that looks at developmental patterns from conception until death.

Table 1–1   Theoretical Perspectives on the Development of Children and Adolescents

THEORETICAL PERSPECTIVES	EMPHASES OF PERSPECTIVES	ILLUSTRATIONS IN CLASSROOMS
Maturational Perspectives	The development of many physical abilities depends on the genetically controlled unfolding of physiological and neurological structures.	• The pencil grip of kindergarten children depends on their level of neurological development. • During adolescence, physical changes associated with puberty are guided by maturational forces.
Psychodynamic Perspectives	Children and adolescents experience impulses related to sexuality and aggression, on the one hand, and desires for social approval and productive contributions to society, on the other. Through a series of qualitatively different stages, they learn to channel their impulses in socially acceptable ways.	• When young children cannot satisfy their immediate desires, they may lash out at others (e.g., by hitting another child). • Adolescents can release their frustrations through vigorous physical activity.
Cognitive-Developmental Perspectives	Children and adolescents-actively contribute to their own intellectual development. As they discover difficulties or contradictions in their own thinking, they formulate new ways of understanding the world. With development, intellectual operations are increasingly abstract and systematic.	• Young children better understand the nature of numbers when they can see how counting and arithmetic operations play out with concrete manipulatives. • Through interrelationships with peers, children and adolescents learn to appreciate the rights of others and can negotiate rules that ensure fairness for all.
Behavioral Learning Perspectives	Children and adolescents actively work for rewards such as food, praise, and physical contact. They learn a great deal from observing others, and as they learn which behaviors are likely to have successful outcomes, they eventually begin to regulate their own behavior.	• Many preschoolers and elementary school students eagerly seek the praise of their teachers. • Adolescents vigilantly observe and often model the ways of speaking, manner of dress, and activities of their friends.
Evolutionary Perspectives	Characteristics and behaviors that enhance an individual's chances for survival and ability to reproduce may have a genetic basis.	• Parents react quickly and strongly when they believe that some children are threatening their sons and daughters at school. • Adolescents often engage in courtship rituals at school, trying to attract the attention of the opposite sex.
Information Processing Perspectives	The ways in which children perceive, interpret, and remember information change over time. With age, children become increasingly aware of and able to control their own cognitive processes.	• Young children often experience information overload when they begin a new and complex task. • Adolescents often benefit from explicit instruction in how to study effectively.
Ecological and Socio-Historic Perspectives	The communities and cultures in which children live have a significant influence on their learning and skill development.	• Children tend to acquire the skills and attitudes that their communities value (e.g., if their parents are active readers, they are likely to read a lot themselves). • A child or adolescent often learns a great deal when working in a one-on-one mentoring relationship with an experienced adult.
Life-Span Perspectives	Developmental changes occur in individuals from conception to death. Some of these changes are predictable and age-related, others are dependent on particular historic events, and still others result from individual life events.	• Children growing up in the 21st century may have very different experiences than those that their teachers had in childhood. • Teachers' own life changes and events (e.g., marriage, relocation) affect their effectiveness in the classroom.

General Trends in Children's and Adolescents' Development

We can make our task of exploring child and adolescent development more manageable by dividing the developmental journey into shorter time periods. But how do we divide the "pie" of childhood and adolescence into meaningful "slices"? Age cutoffs are somewhat arbitrary, in that universal stages with precise timetables simply cannot be found in any domain of development. Nonetheless, preschoolers are very different from fourth graders, who in turn are very different from high school students, and so, in our upcoming discussions, we will often compare different age groups. We will typically consider four general age periods: early childhood (2–6 years), middle childhood (6–10 years), early adolescence (10–14 years), and late adolescence (14–18 years). We look briefly at each period now.

Early Childhood (2–6 Years)

Early childhood is a period of incredible creativity, fantasy, wonder, and play. Preschool-aged children see life as a forum for imagination and drama: They reinvent the world, try on new roles, and struggle to play their parts in harmony.

Language and communication skills develop rapidly during early childhood. New vocabulary, appropriate use of language in social contexts, and facility with syntax (grammar) are noticeable advancements. Language builds on daily increases in knowledge about the world and, especially, the routines of daily life.

Physical changes are apparent as well. The cautious movements of infancy give way to fluid rolling, tumbling, running, and skipping. High levels of energy and a gusto for learning radiate from movements and interactions. Young children don't walk; they run, dance, and skip. They don't talk; they chatter, sing, and moan. And they don't sit quietly on the sidelines; they handle, pour, and paste.

Socially and emotionally, preschoolers are often endearing creatures who can be trusting, giving, and affectionate. They become increasingly interested in others, are eager to spend time with playmates, and infuse their social interactions with fantasy and pretend. Yet concern for others coexists with aggressive and self-centered impulses, which occasionally interfere with effective interactions.

Middle Childhood (6–10 Years)

Whereas in early childhood interests are often transient and fleeting, middle childhood is a time of sustained attention to real-world tasks. Fantasy is not abandoned, but it plays less of a role than it did in early childhood. Instead, children become concerned with how the world works, and they show considerable interest in learning the customs, tools, and accumulated knowledge of their community and culture.

Middle childhood is a time of sustained attention to realistic tasks.

Serious commitments to peers, especially to playmates of the same age and gender, emerge. Children also begin to compare their performance to that of others: Why do I have fewer friends than Janie and Maria? Am I good enough to be picked for the baseball team? Will I ever learn to read like the other kids? When they routinely end up on the losing side in such comparisons, they are more hesitant to try new academic tasks. But diversity is common, and individual differences in academic performance become more noticeable with each passing year.

In the elementary school years, children internalize

many prohibitions they've heard repeatedly ("Don't play near the river," "Look after your little brother," "Look both ways before crossing the street"). They gain a sense of what is expected of them, and most are inclined to live up to these expectations. Rules of games and required classroom behavior become important. Sometimes children heed preestablished rules in sacred compliance, but at other times they haggle over and negotiate them.

Early Adolescence (10–14 Years)

In early adolescence, youngsters slowly lose their childlike bodies and eventually become reproductively mature. Physical developments are accompanied by equally dramatic reorganizations in learning processes, the roles assumed in families, and the nature of social relationships with peers.

The physical changes of puberty are orderly and predictable, but boys and girls alike often experience them as new, puzzling, and perhaps disconcerting events. Young adolescents sometimes look and feel awkward, and hormonal changes can lead to unpredictable mood swings. Adolescents show increasing reflectiveness about their changing selves and a heightened sensitivity to what other people think about them. Whereas they compared themselves to peers in middle childhood, they now consider how their peers might view *them*: What are they thinking of me? Why are they looking at me? How does my hair look? Am I one of the "cool" kids? Peers become a sounding board through which adolescents gain social support and seek assurance that their appearance and behaviors are acceptable.

Cognitive abilities take major strides forward in early adolescence, enabling more logical, abstract, and systematic thinking. Furthermore, the world view of young adolescents broadens well beyond family and peer group. A sense of power and idealism flickers, such that many adolescents feel entitled to challenge the existing order of things. They often become critical of social organizations, wondering why schools, inner cities, governments, and the earth's ecosystem cannot be improved overnight. They seem to sense that they are about to inherit these organizations and so want them to be better.

Diversity is present in every developmental phase, but individual differences are often most pronounced in early adolescence. Although the physical changes of puberty occur in a fairly predictable manner, the age at which they emerge can vary considerably from one individual to the next. Thus, not all "early adolescents" fall into the 10–14 age range. Some, girls especially, may begin puberty before 10. Others, boys in particular, may not begin puberty until the end of this age span.

Early and late adolescence is a time of many physical, cognitive, and emotional changes.

Late Adolescence (14–18 Years)

As teenagers continue to mature, they lose some of the gawky, uneven appearance of early adolescence and blossom into attractive young adults. Resembling young adults, late adolescents often feel entitled to make their own decisions. Common refrains often include the word *my*: "It's *my* hair, *my* body, *my* clothes, *my* room, *my* education, *my life*!"

Late adolescence can be a confusing time to make decisions. Mixed messages abound. For instance, teenagers may be encouraged to abstain from sexual activity or practice "safe sex," yet they continually encounter inviting, provocative sexual images and activities in the media. Similarly, parents and teachers urge healthy eating habits, yet junk food is everywhere—in vending machines at school, at the refreshment stand at the movie theater, and often in kitchen cabinets at home.

Fortunately, many high school students do make wise decisions: They try hard in school, explore career possibilities, gain job experience, and refrain from seriously risky behaviors. Others, however, are less judicious in their choices, experimenting with alcohol, drugs, sex, and violence and in general thinking more about here-and-now pleasures than potential long-term consequences.

Examples of Accomplishments and Areas of Diversity at Different Age Levels

DEVELOPMENTAL TRENDS

AGE	WHAT YOU MIGHT OBSERVE	DIVERSITY	IMPLICATIONS
Early Childhood (2–6) 	**Physical Development** • Increasing abilities in such motor skills as running and skipping, throwing a ball, building block towers, and using scissors • Increasing competence in basic self-care and personal hygiene **Cognitive Development** • Dramatic play with peers • Ability to draw simple figures • Some knowledge of colors, letters, and numbers • Recounting of familiar stories and events **Social-Emotional Development** • Developing understanding of gender • Emerging abilities to defer immediate gratification, share toys, and take turns • Some demonstration of sympathy for people in distress	• Children master physical milestones (e.g., skipping) at different ages. • Individual differences in fine motor and gross motor agility are substantial. • Some children enter kindergarten with few prior experiences with age-mates; others have been in group daycare since infancy. • Family and cultural backgrounds influence the kinds of skills that children have mastered by the time they begin school. • Some children have difficulty following rules, standing quietly in line, and waiting for their turn.	• Provide sensory-rich materials that encourage exploration (e.g., water table, sandbox, textured toys). • Read to children regularly to promote vocabulary and preliteracy skills. • Give children frequent opportunities to play, interact with peers, and make choices. • Hold consistent expectations for behavior so that children learn to follow rules. • Communicate regularly with parents about children's academic and social progress.
Middle Childhood (6–10) 	**Physical Development** • Ability to ride a bicycle • Successful imitation of complex physical movements • Participation in organized sports **Cognitive Development** • Development of basic skills in reading, writing, mathematics, and other academic subject areas • Ability to reason logically when aided by concrete manipulatives • Increasing awareness of how one's own abilities compare with those of classmates **Social-Emotional Development** • Desire for time with age-mates, especially friends of the same gender • Increasing responsibility in household chores • Adherence to rules in games • Understanding of basic moral rules	• Individual differences are evident in children's performance in academic areas. • Many children are unable to sit quietly for long periods. • Children differ in temperament and sociability; some are outgoing, others are more reserved and shy. • A few children may show disturbing levels of aggression toward others.	• Tailor instructional methods (e.g., cooperative groups, individualized assignments, choices in activities) and materials to meet diversity in children's talents, background knowledge, and interests. • Address deficiencies in basic skills (e.g., in reading, writing, and math) before they develop into serious developmental delays. • Provide moderately challenging new tasks that encourage children to learn new skills, perform well, and seek additional challenges. • Provide the guidance necessary to help students interact more successfully with classmates (e.g., by suggesting ways of resolving conflicts, finding a "buddy" for a newcomer to the school district).

Peer relationships remain a high priority in late adolescence, and as we will see in Chapter 13, they can be either a good or bad influence, depending on the particular peer group. Still, most adolescents continue to savor their ties with trusted adults and preserve the fundamental values—the importance of a good education, the need to be honest and fair in business dealings, and so on—that their parents and teachers have championed.

AGE	WHAT YOU MIGHT OBSERVE	DIVERSITY	IMPLICATIONS
Early Adolescence (10–14) 	**Physical Development** • Onset of puberty • Significant growth spurt **Cognitive Development** • Emerging capacity to think and reason about abstract ideas • Preliminary exposure to advanced academic content in specific subject areas **Social-Emotional Development** • Continued (and perhaps greater) interest in peer relationships • Emerging sexual interest in the opposite gender or same gender, depending on orientation • Occasional challenges to parents and teachers regarding rules and boundaries	• Young adolescents exhibit considerable variability in the age at which they begin puberty. • Academic problems often become more pronounced during adolescence; those who encounter frequent failure become less engaged in school activities. • Adolescents seek out peers whose values are compatible with their own and who will give them recognition and status. • Some young adolescents begin to engage in deviant and risky activities (e.g., unprotected sex, cigarette smoking, use of drugs and alcohol).	• Suggest and demonstrate effective study strategies as students begin to tackle challenging subject matter. • Give struggling students the extra support they need to be academically successful. • Provide a regular time and place where middle school students can seek your guidance and advice about academic or social matters (e.g., offer your classroom as a place where students can occasionally eat lunch). • Provide opportunities for students to contribute to school and classroom decision making. • Hold students accountable for their actions, and impose appropriate consequences when they break school rules.
Late Adolescence (14–18) 	**Physical Development** • Achievement of sexual maturity and adult height • For some teens, development of a regular exercise program • Development of specific eating habits (e.g., becoming a vegetarian, consuming junk food) **Cognitive Development** • In-depth study of certain academic subject areas • Consideration of career tracks and possibilities **Social-Emotional Development** • Dating • Increasing independence (e.g., driving a car, making choices about how to use free time) • Frequent questioning of existing rules and societal norms	• Some students make poor choices in the peers with whom they affiliate. • Older adolescents aspire to widely differing educational and career tracks (e.g., some aspire to college, others anticipate seeking employment immediately after high school, and still others make no plans for life after high school). • Some teens participate in extracurricular activities; those that do are more likely to stay in school until graduation. • Some teens become sexually active, and some become parents. • Teenagers' neighborhoods and communities offer differing opportunities and temptations for the after-school hours.	• Communicate caring and respect for all students. • Allow choices in academic subjects and assignments, but hold students to high standards for performance. • Provide the guidance and assistance that low-achieving students may need to be more successful. • Help students explore higher education opportunities and a variety of career paths. • Encourage involvement in extracurricular activities at school. • Arrange opportunities for students to make a difference in their communities through volunteer work and service learning projects.

Individual differences in academic achievement are substantial during the high school years. Indeed, wide variances in students' abilities are one of the biggest challenges faced by high schools today. Some low-achieving students drop out of high school altogether, perhaps as a way of shielding themselves from the stigma of academic failure. Many of the low achievers who stay in school affiliate with students who share their dim views on education.

The four periods of development just identified appear regularly in Developmental Trends tables throughout the book. These tables summarize key developmental tasks, accomplishments, and milestones at different age levels, as well as manifestations of diversity at each level. The first of these tables, which begins on page 18, gives you a flavor for children's and adolescents' accomplishments in the three domains of physical, cognitive, and social-emotional development.

From Theory to Practice

As developmental scholars have studied the hows and whys of human development, their efforts have been motivated, in large part, by a keen interest in the welfare of children. Early developmentalists actively worked with educators to improve schools for children and to establish national and regional centers that supported children and families (Beatty, 1996; White, 1992). They embraced a variety of children's causes, including support for child labor laws and improvements in elementary and secondary curricula (Cairns, 1983).

Teachers are in a unique position to be positive influences in children's lives—for instance, by creating nurturing and supportive environments to which children come each day, by presenting new challenges that encourage children to think and act in increasingly sophisticated ways, and by guiding children gently along the road toward becoming responsible contributors to adult society. In the opening case study, for example, Ms. Jalongo got at the root of Tonya's stealing episodes, paved the way for her to establish more productive relationships with her classmates, and in general created an environment in which Tonya could begin to flourish. Tonya's third-grade teacher, in contrast, passed judgment on Tonya based on superficial characteristics and never took the time to find the thinking, feeling child that lay beneath. Her thoughtless actions created a divisive environment that ultimately served none of her students.

The classroom environments that teachers establish, the instructional strategies that they implement, and the materials that they use can be effective only to the extent that such interventions take into account students' developing physical, cognitive, and social characteristics and abilities.

Developmentally appropriate practice involves awareness of, and instructional adaptations to, the age, characteristics, and developmental progress of students. It enables growing children to be active learners, recognizes that adult-type functioning is neither realistic nor valuable for children to imitate, and encourages children to work together in an ethical and democratic fashion (Kohlberg & Mayer, 1972).

In this final section of the chapter, we identify several general strategies to get you thinking like a developmentalist—in other words, strategies that promote a *developmental mind-set*. We then offer strategies for maintaining that mind-set over the long run.

Acquiring a Developmental Mind-set in the Classroom

In later chapters, we will pinpoint educational strategies that relate to specific aspects of development. Here we offer more general strategies to help you start thinking like a developmentalist:

■ *Remember that the apparent "weaknesses" of childhood and adolescence may, from a developmental standpoint, serve a purpose.* Human beings take longer to reach physical maturity than do members of any other species. For instance, although girls and boys become physiologically capable of conceiving offspring in their early teens, many continue to gain height after that time, and their brains continue to mature during the late teens and early twenties (Giedd, Blumenthal, Jeffries, Castellanos, et al., 1999; Giedd, Blumenthal, Jeffries, Rajapakse, et al., 1999; Sowell & Jernigan, 1998; Sowell, Thompson, Holmes, Jernigan, & Toga, 1999). Such a lengthy childhood allows younger members of the human race to learn all that is involved in being "human"—from survival skills to the basic patterns, beliefs, and tools of their culture (Gould, 1977; Leakey, 1994). Childhood, then, is not necessarily an "inconvenience" resulting from a body that grows too slowly for its own good. On the contrary, it probably provides the time that a growing human needs to become an effective participant in adult society.

When, as adults, we assess children's abilities in comparison to our own, the children inevitably come up short. We might describe preschoolers as being impulsive and self-centered, with only a limited ability to think about anything but their immediate circumstances. Adolescents can be rude and irresponsible and sometimes seem determined to ignore basic common sense and to trespass beyond any reasonable boundaries on their actions. From a developmental perspective, however, the "weaknesses" that children and adolescents have and the "mistakes" that they make often serve a purpose and promote development over the long run (Bjorklund & Green, 1992; Bruner, 1972). Let's examine some of the "deficits" children pos-

developmentally appropriate practice
Adapting instructional practices and materials to the age, characteristics, and developmental progress of students.

sess to see if we can recast them in a more positive light. Consider the following children, all of whom seem to have a developmental "limitation":

- Two-day-old Dominic is helpless, vulnerable, and in other ways completely incapable of attending to his own needs. His cries of hunger bring a parent running to feed and cuddle him, and in the process a strong parent-child emotional bond begins to form. Furthermore, Dominic is starting to discover that the people in his life are reliable and trustworthy.
- Five-year-old Melissa spends long hours engaged in seemingly frivolous play. Is she wasting her time? A closer look at Melissa's play reveals cognitive and social work in action—complex language, creative fantasies, cooperative turn taking with friends, and practice of adult roles.
- Eight-year-old Javier routinely overestimates what he is capable of learning and physically accomplishing. Although he may seem a bit naive, children have much to learn, and Javier's overly optimistic outlook might encourage him to persist in his attempts at new tasks despite the obstacles and setbacks he is likely to face along the way.
- Fifteen-year-old Breann believes that she is invincible to normal accidents and health hazards and so engages in many foolish, risky behaviors. Her parents and teachers are understandably concerned about her safety. But at the same time, Breann is experimenting with some of the activities and tackling some of the challenges that she is likely to encounter as an adult.

With time and experience, Dominic will become more self-sufficient, Melissa will abandon her imaginary play, Javier will be more realistic about what he can accomplish, and Breann will make more sensible choices. But in the meantime, their "less advanced" ways of behaving and thinking may ultimately help them build the foundation of knowledge and skills that will be essential as they travel the long, complex road from infancy to adulthood.

■ *Remain confident that the environment makes a difference.* Throughout the book, we will identify a myriad of ways in which environmental factors influence the course of physical, cognitive, and social-emotional development. Furthermore, even when early life circumstances have not been ideal (as was certainly the case for Tonya), thoughtful and systematic interventions during the school years can make a world of difference. A body of recent research suggests that children exhibit a certain amount of **resiliency**, in that, with nurturing environments and relationships in later years, they can often overcome harmful early experiences. Some children beat the odds, growing into healthy adults despite the high-risk environments they call home (Werner, 1989). Resiliency seems to be fostered by having a close relationship with a teacher or other caring adult who serves as a role model, friend, and source of advice and support (McLoyd, 1998b; Werner, 1995). Teachers are most likely to foster resiliency when they show affection and respect for their students, are available and willing to listen to students' views and concerns, hold high expectations for performance, and provide the encouragement and support necessary for success both in and out of the classroom (Masten & Coatsworth, 1998; McMillan & Reed, 1994; Werner, 1995).

Melanie (age 11) clearly perceives Mrs. Lorenzo's classroom to be warm and supportive.

■ *Use the universals of development to make predictions about what students probably can and cannot do at a particular age, but expect diversity at every turn.* Some developmental pathways are common to all, but exceptions are everywhere. If there are 25 children in a classroom, there will be 25 unique profiles of talents and needs. Children do not fit a single developmental mold, and teachers need to plan classroom instruction and activities in ways that respect individual differences.

All too often, new teachers rely on their own childhood memories to predict the kinds of students they are likely to have in their classrooms and the kinds of teaching methods that are likely to be effective. "What worked for us will work for others," they may assume. Yet the challenges children face today may not be the ones that either troubled or inspired children in previous generations. Consider the following trends:

- As of 1990, half of the mothers of preschool or school-age children worked outside the home (Hamburg, 1992). More and more frequently, children receive out-of-family care in daycare settings or other people's homes. Many of these out-of-home settings are

resiliency
Ability of some children and adolescents to thrive and develop despite adverse environmental conditions.

high-quality environments, but others are understaffed, unsafe, and unresponsive to children's needs. Furthermore, many children have no supervision at all during the after-school hours.

- Students and their teachers come from different backgrounds. Students of color represent 30% of the population of students in American elementary and secondary schools (Gay, 1993). At the same time, teachers of color make up less than 15% of the teaching force. Only about 8% of all K–12 teachers are African Americans, 3% are Hispanics, 1% are Asian and Pacific Islanders, and 1% are Native Americans (*Status of the American School Teacher,* 1992). In addition, the number of children living in large urban areas is increasing, whereas teachers tend to live in suburban communities, and more than 72% of teachers are female (Gay, 1993).

- The number of children of immigrant families is increasing. Today's immigrant families come from a broad array of countries, especially countries in Central and South America and southeast Asia (Board on Children and Families, 1995). By the year 2010, children of immigrants may make up 22% of the school-aged population, and most of those children will speak a language other than English (Fix & Passel, 1994). Despite the rich composition of cultures represented in American classrooms, individual teachers tend to be familiar with only one cultural perspective (Shaw, 1993).

- Almost 25% of children in the United States grow up in poverty (Hamburg, 1992). The percentage is even higher in some minority groups; for instance, 38% of Hispanic and 44% of African American children under the age of 18 live in poverty (*Statistical Abstract of the United States,* 1991). Although many children fare well despite very limited financial resources, in general children who grow up in extreme poverty are at higher risk for death, malnutrition, disease, injury, disability, father absence, and exposure to violence.

- Students with disabilities make up 11% of the students in this country (Wagner, 1995b). Increasingly, such students are educated for part or all of the school day within the general education classroom—a practice called **inclusion.**[2]

As we describe general developmental trends in this book, we will continually consider various sources of diversity. As you read the upcoming chapters, we ask you to pay particular attention to how developmental principles depend on culture and context (and in some cases disability) for their manifestation. We also urge you to think about your professional responsibility for children who come from backgrounds different from your own. Marian Wright Edelman, the president of the Children's Defense Fund, offers a poignant moral imperative to us all:

> We cannot continue as a nation to make a distinction between our children and other people's kids. Every youngster is entitled to an equal share of the American Dream. Every poor child, every black child, every white child—every child living everywhere—should have an equal shot. We need every one of them to be productive and educated and healthy. (Edelman, 1993, p. 235)

■ *Keep in mind that children and adolescents are, in many respects, very different from adults.* By knowing the characteristics and thinking abilities of students at a particular age, teachers can better tailor instruction to address students' developmental needs. The previous Developmental Trends table, like the others throughout the book, includes an "Implications" column that gives teachers suggestions for working with students at various age levels. Development and Practice features, which also appear throughout the book, provide additional ideas for teaching students at one or more age levels. The first of these features, which identifies and illustrates several general, age-appropriate teaching strategies, begins on the following page.

■ *Look for and capitalize on students' strengths.* Children can sometimes make lives difficult for teachers, as Tonya initially did in our introductory case. In such situations, educators are often tempted to throw up their hands in despair. But with extra effort, a change in tactics, and a solid

---

inclusion
Practice of educating all students, including those with severe and multiple disabilities, in neighborhood schools and general education classrooms.

[2]In the United States, federal legislation known as the *Individuals with Disabilities Education Act* (IDEA), passed in 1975 and updated several times since, mandates that children with disabilities be educated in the *least restrictive environment*—in the most typical and standard educational environment that can reasonably meet their educational needs. As a result of such legislation, more than two-thirds of students with disabilities are now educated in general education classrooms for part or all of the school day (U.S. Department of Education, 1996).

ENGAGING IN DEVELOPMENTALLY APPROPRIATE PRACTICE WITH STUDENTS AT VARIOUS AGES

Early Childhood

■ Provide reassurance to children who have difficulty separating from their families.

A daycare provider establishes a routine for the morning. After children say goodbye to their parents, they stand at the window with him, watch their parents walk to their cars, and then find an activity to join.

■ Create a classroom environment that permits children to explore their physical and cultural world.

A preschool teacher has several "stations" available to children during free-choice time, including a water table and areas for playing with blocks, doing puzzles, constructing arts and crafts, engaging in dramatic play, and listening to books on tape.

■ Introduce children to the world of literature.

A preschool teacher reads to the children at least once each day. She chooses books with entertaining stories and vivid illustrations that readily capture the children's attention, interest, and imagination.

■ Encourage self-reliance and responsibility.

A kindergarten teacher rotates daily jobs among the children. For instance, during snack time, one child hands out napkins, another pours milk into plastic cups, and a third sponges down the table after everyone has finished eating.

Middle Childhood

■ Encourage family members to become active participants in children's education.

A third-grade teacher invites children's parents and other family members to contribute in some small way to the classroom curriculum, perhaps by describing their occupations, reading a favorite book from their own childhood, demonstrating an ethnic custom, or assisting with costumes and props for the class play.

■ Ensure that all students acquire basic academic skills.

A first-grade teacher individualizes reading instruction for her students based on their current knowledge and skills. She works on mastery of letter identification and letter-sound correspondence with some, reading of simple stories with others, and selection of appropriate books with a few students who are already reading inde-

pendently. She makes sure that all children have regular opportunities to listen to stories both in small groups and on tape.

■ Give students the guidance they need to establish and maintain positive relationships with their peers.

When two second graders are quarreling on the playground, their teacher gives them several suggestions that can help them identify a reasonable compromise.

■ Encourage children to be critical learners.

When a fourth-grade teacher describes the Europeans' early explorations and settlements in the New World, he asks his students to think about what various Native American groups might have been thinking and feeling at that time.

Early Adolescence

■ Design a curriculum that is challenging and motivating and that incorporates knowledge and skills from several content areas.

A middle school teacher designs a unit on "war and conflict," integrating writing skills and knowledge of social studies. He encourages students to bring in newspaper clippings about current events and to talk and write about local political events.

■ Assign every student an advisor who looks after the student's welfare.

During homeroom with her advisees, a seventh-grade teacher personally makes sure that each student is keeping up with assignments. She also encourages students to talk with her informally about their academic and social concerns.

■ Show sensitivity to students who are undergoing the physical changes of puberty.

A junior high school physical education teacher makes sure that students have privacy when they dress and shower after physical activities.

■ Allow students to make some decisions about classroom activities and policies.

An eighth-grade language arts teacher asks students to write a review for a book of their own choosing and to select one of three possible ways of presenting their review: a written report, a poster, or an oral presentation.

(continued)

ENGAGING IN DEVELOPMENTALLY APPROPRIATE PRACTICE WITH STUDENTS AT VARIOUS AGES *(continued)*

Late Adolescence

■ Expect students to meet high standards for achievement, but give them the support and guidance they may need to meet those standards.

> An English composition teacher describes and then posts the various steps involved in writing—planning, drafting, writing, editing, and revising—and asks his students to use these steps for their essays. He then monitors his students' work and gives feedback and suggestions as necessary, making sure that students are executing each step in a way that enhances the quality of their writing.

■ Reach out to students socially and emotionally.

> A high school social studies teacher talks about the social and political movements of her own adolescence and invites her students to talk about current social practices that they find troubling.

■ Encourage students to give back to their communities.

> A high school requires all students to participate in 50 hours of volunteer work or service learning in their town.

■ Educate students about the academic requirements of jobs and colleges.

> A high school mathematics teacher frequently assigns problems commonly encountered by people in various professions.

faith in children's ability to overcome the odds, teachers can find areas of strength in *all* children and help them draw upon their own resources. As an illustration, consider how one teacher acquired a new appreciation for a student named Crystal once she made a concerted effort to look for Crystal's strong points rather than her deficiencies:

> Crystal really surprised me in the social learning center. Frankly, I always thought that Crystal was quiet and listless because you hardly hear anything from her and she seldom shows interest in anything in the class. Oh, no, you just can't believe, when doing dress-up Crystal was constantly moving, talking, and singing! When doing puppets she was constantly giving the directions! I would have never known where her strength lies if the social learning area were not available in the classroom. (Chen, Krechevsky, & Viens, 1998, p. 58)

When teachers tap into students' talents, they can use such strengths as a bridge to weaker areas. For instance, Crystal's teacher took advantage of Crystal's social skills to foster her improvement in mathematics; in particular, she asked Crystal to pose questions to classmates, tally their responses, and compare differences between groups (Chen et al., 1998).

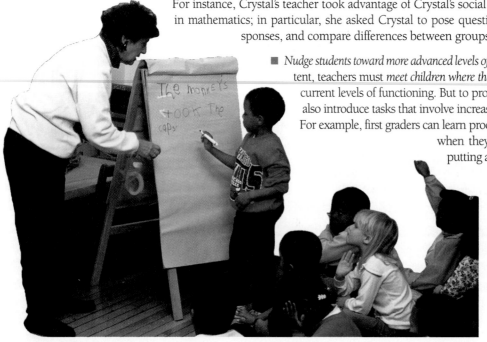

■ *Nudge students toward more advanced levels of thinking and behaving.* To some extent, teachers must *meet children where the children are*—that is, at children's current levels of functioning. But to promote development, teachers must also introduce tasks that involve increasing complexity and responsibility. For example, first graders can learn procedures that let their teacher know when they are going to the restroom (e.g., putting a clothespin on a rope next to their name). Middle school students can be shown how to use daily planners to keep track of assignments and due dates. High school students can be encouraged to edit and revise first drafts of essays according to certain specifications. Initially, students may need occasional reminders and words of praise for such behaviors, but eventually they should initiate the behaviors on their own, without any prodding or encouragement from adults.

By introducing tasks that involve increasing complexity and responsibility, teachers nudge students toward more advanced ways of thinking and behaving.

We intentionally say *nudge,* rather than *push,* children toward more advanced levels. Unreasonable expectations—expectations for behavior well beyond what children are currently capable of doing—will often lead to unnecessary failure, cause stress and frustration, and so not have the positive benefits that gentle and guided prodding is likely to have.

Maintaining the Mind-set over the Long Run

A developmental mind-set isn't something that, once acquired, necessarily lasts forever. Furthermore, researchers continue to advance the frontiers of knowledge about the nature and course of child and adolescent development. Teachers can do several things to stay on top of current findings in the field of development and keep a developmental mind-set alive:

■ *Continue to take courses in child development and teacher education.* Additional coursework is one surefire way of keeping up to date on the latest theoretical perspectives and research results on child and adolescent development and its implications for classroom practice. In general, such coursework definitely *does* enhance teaching effectiveness (Darling-Hammond, 1995).

■ *Find information and guidance through professional organizations.* Many professional organizations hold regular, often annual, meetings at which researchers and practitioners can exchange information and ideas. Such meetings allow practicing teachers to learn about the latest research findings and theoretical advances in development, discover new strategies for teaching children and adolescents in various age groups, and renew their energy and commitment to the lives of their students.

Many professional organizations also publish guidelines that can assist teachers in their choices of developmentally appropriate methods and materials. For example, the National Association for the Education of Young Children (NAEYC) offers separate recommendations for infants and toddlers, 3-year-olds, 4- and 5-year-olds, and 5- to 8-year-olds. Their recommendations for promoting cognitive development in 4- and 5-year-olds illustrate:

> *Appropriate Practice:* Children develop understanding of concepts about themselves, others, and the world around them through observation, interacting with people and real objects, and seeking solutions to concrete problems. Learnings about math, science, social studies, health, and other content areas are all integrated through meaningful activities such as those when children build with blocks; measure sand, water, or ingredients for cooking; observe changes in the environment; work with wood and tools; sort objects for a purpose; explore animals, plants, water, wheels and gears; sing and listen to music from various cultures; and draw, paint, and work with clay. Routines are followed that help children keep themselves healthy and safe.

> *Inappropriate Practice:* Instruction stresses isolated skill development through memorization and rote, such as counting, circling an item on a worksheet, memorizing facts, watching demonstrations, drilling with flashcards, or looking at maps. Children's cognitive development is seen as fragmented in content areas such as math, science, or social studies, and times are set aside to concentrate on each area. (Bredekamp, 1987, p. 56)

The National Council for Accreditation of Teacher Education (NCATE) recently published *Program Standards for Elementary Teacher Preparation* (2000). Within these standards we find some recommendations about topics appropriate for elementary school students. Although NCATE's focus is more on what teachers should do, it suggests that, among other things, students in the upper elementary grades should be able to

> examine a variety of sources (e.g., primary and secondary sources, maps, statistical data, and electronic technology-based information); acquire and manipulate data; analyze points of view; formulate well-supported oral and written arguments. (NCATE, 2000)

The National Middle School Association (NMSA) offers guidelines for meeting the developmental needs of 10- to 15-year-olds (NMSA, 1995). For instance, it suggests that every student be supported by one adult (an advisor) who supports his or her academic and personal development, perhaps within the context of a "home base" period or other group meeting time. The advisor-student relationship, when stable and caring, can help young adolescents weather the rapid developmental changes—not only physical but also cognitive and social—that they are likely to experience. NMSA also suggests that large middle schools be subdivided into "houses" or other small units in which students share several classes with the same classmates and get to know a few teachers very well. And it advocates teaching techniques that are varied, engaging, and responsive to students' cultural backgrounds, prior knowledge, and individual talents:

> Since young adolescents learn best through engagement and interaction, learning strategies feature activities that provide hands-on experiences and actively involve youngsters in learning. While direct instruction is still important, varied approaches are needed, including experiments, demonstrations, opinion pools, simulations, and independent study. (NMSA, 1995, p. 25)

The National Association of Secondary School Principals (NASSP), in partnership with the Carnegie Foundation for the Advancement of Teaching, has published a landmark book that gives some guidance to teachers and other practitioners working with high school students. *Breaking Ranks: Changing an American Institution* (1996) offers more than 80 recommendations for improving schools for adolescents. The recommendations are too numerous to include here, but they convey a consistent message that schools must become more student-centered and personalized. Illustrations of specific recommendations related to personalizing instruction include the following:

> Each student will have a Personal Plan for Progress to ensure that the high school takes individual needs into consideration and to allow students, within reasonable parameters, to design their own methods for learning in an effort to meet high standards. (NASSP, 1996, p. 11)

> Teachers will convey a sense of caring to their students so that their students feel that their teachers share a stake in their learning. (p. 21)

> Every high school student will have a Personal Adult Advocate to help him or her personalize the educational experience. (p. 29)

> High schools will create small units in which anonymity is banished. (p. 45)

Other professional organizations, especially those that focus on particular content areas (e.g., National Council of Teachers of Mathematics, National Council of Geographic Education), have identified certain accomplishments, or **standards,** that they believe students at various grade levels should achieve. For instance, published standards are now available for the fields of English, reading, mathematics, science, social studies, art, physical education, and health education. In some school districts, meeting certain standards is mandatory before students can graduate from high school.

Generally speaking, the guidelines and standards offered by professional organizations have met with broad acceptance among educators. We find them especially useful in offering innovative suggestions for making schools more responsive to students' developmental needs. However, we share a concern that others have raised that some guidelines reflect the values of particular cultures and may not always be as universally applicable as they first appear (Dahlberg, Moss, & Pence, 1999). Furthermore, some of the recommendations—for instance, those for high, common academic standards for all students—are being implemented on a trial basis, and their effects are unknown. We suspect that teachers who focus solely on these standards, without also considering students' other cognitive and social-emotional needs, will do their students a disservice.

■ *Subscribe to professional journals in child development and teaching practice.* Many professional organizations publish journals that can help teachers keep up to date with current theory, research, and applications in the field. *Child Development* (published by the Society for Research in Child Development) and *Developmental Psychology* (published by the American Psychological Association) present recent theoretical advancements and research findings. Examples of other relevant journals, many of which address implications for teachers, are *Applied Developmental Science, Journal of Applied Developmental Psychology, Young Children, Elementary School Journal, Middle School Journal, Adolescence, Journal of Early Adolescence,* and *Youth and Society.*

■ *Consult and collaborate regularly with professional colleagues.* Teachers often gain a better understanding of the strengths and needs of individual students when they meet frequently to exchange insights and ideas; in the process, they may also gain a more optimistic view of their own ability to bring about positive changes in their students' personal development and academic achievement (e.g., Weinstein, Madison, & Kuklinski, 1995). In one approach, 10 to 12 teachers, administrators, specialists and parents meet every 2 or 3 weeks to discuss and strategize about students' developmental needs (Squires, Howley, & Gahr, 1999). The following example illustrates the kinds of insights that result:

standards
General statements specifying the knowledge and skills that students should achieve and the characteristics that their accomplishments should reflect.

[W]e began to notice recurring patterns of behavior. For example, when Jordan was upset, he would usually withdraw from the group and from me for awhile. Pat pointed out that these behavior patterns are clues . . . to what the child is working on in his or her development. From . . . observations I had made, I thought that Jordan was trying to understand how to deal with conflict. Other children were trying to learn about making "friends" with other students, or dealing with issues of responsibility in homework, classwork, and on the playground. All those details that we wrote in our journals started to make more sense as they were woven into recurring patterns.

. . . I found it surprising that the children's developmental work generally had little to do with what we were studying in math, science, or social studies. . . .

We discussed this in the group, as others felt the same way. . . . If Jordan has his own developmental agenda, then, of course, other students in the class did, too. And what I was doing in the classroom, all that content, didn't match well with what they were dealing with. I felt I was trying to show a movie at the beach at noon. It would be difficult for kids to see the movie (the content of the lessons) when the sun (their developmental agendas) was so strong and bright.

. . . I found myself searching for and trying different ways to make my classroom and my teaching more attuned to students' needs. (Squires et al., 1999, p. 200)

Throughout this chapter, we have argued that children's developmental journeys are not universal; all children develop in their own, idiosyncratic fashion (Dahlberg et al., 1999). Furthermore, the outcomes of development are not predetermined at the onset; instead, children's developmental journeys depend significantly on the educational environments that parents, teachers, and other adults create. Development happens one child at a time, but it doesn't happen without "nurture." As you will discover throughout the book, teachers can do much to help students navigate their individual developmental journeys.

CASE STUDY: LATISHA

Latisha, who is 13 years old, lives in a housing project in an inner-city neighborhood in Chicago. An adult asks her to describe her life and family, her hopes and fears, and her plans for the future. She responds as follows:

My mother works at the hospital, serving food. She's worked there for 11 years, but she's been moved to different departments. I don't know what my dad does because he don't live with me. My mother's boyfriend lives with us. He's like my step father.

In my spare time I just like be at home, look at TV, or clean up, or do my homework, or play basketball, or talk on the phone. My three wishes would be to have a younger brother and sister, a car of my own, and not get killed before I'm 20 years old.

I be afraid of guns and rats. My mother she has a gun, her boyfriend has one for protection. I have shot one before and it's like a scary feeling. My uncle taught me. He took us in the country and he had targets we had to like shoot at. He showed us how to load and cock it and pull the trigger. When I pulled the trigger at first I feel happy because I learned how to shoot a gun, but afterward I didn't like it too much because I don't want to accidentally shoot nobody. I wouldn't want to shoot nobody. But it's good that I know how to shoot one just in case something happened and I have to use it.

Where I live it's a quiet neighborhood. If the gangs don't bother me or threaten me, or do anything to my family, I'm OK. If somebody say hi to me, I'll say hi to them as long as they don't threaten me . . . I got two cousins who are in gangs. One is in jail because he killed somebody. My other cousin, he stayed cool. He ain't around. He don't be over there with the gang bangers. He mostly over on the west side with his grandfather, so I don't hardly see him . . . I got friends in gangs. Some of them seven, eight years old that's too young to be in a gang . . . They be gang banging because they have no one to turn to . . . If a girl join a gang it's worser than if a boy join a gang because to be a girl you should have more sense. A boy they want to be hanging on to their friends. Their friends say gangs are cool, so they join.

The school I go to now is more funner than the school I just came from. We switch classes and we have 40 minutes for lunch. The Board of Education say that we can't wear gym shoes no more. They say it distracts other people from learning, it's because of the shoe strings and gang colors.

My teachers are good except two. My music and art teacher she's old and it seems like she shouldn't be there teaching. It seem like she should be retired and be at home, or traveling or something like that. And my history teacher, yuk! He's a stubborn old goat. He's stubborn with everybody.

When I finish school I want to be a doctor. At first I wanted to be a lawyer, but after I went to the hospital I said now I want to help people, and cure people, so I decided to be a doctor.

From " 'I Wouldn't Want to Shoot Nobody': The Out-of-School Curriculum as Described by Urban Students," by J. Williams and K. Williamson, 1992, *Action in Teacher Education, 14*(2), pp. 11–12. Adapted with permission of Association of Teacher Educators.

- In what ways do we see the contexts of family, school, neighborhood, and culture affecting Latisha's development?
- Based on your own experiences growing up, what aspects of Latisha's development would you guess are probably universal? What aspects reflect diversity?
- What clues do we have that Latisha's teachers can almost certainly have a positive impact on her long-term development and success?

SUMMARY

The Field of Child and Adolescent Development

The term *development* refers to systematic, age-related changes in the physical and psychological functioning of human beings. Developmental theorists typically focus on the nature and progression of development in three domains—physical, cognitive, and social-emotional—and look at how a variety of environmental contexts (families, neighborhoods, culture, etc.) affect its course.

Basic Developmental Issues

Three basic issues characterize the study of developmental change during childhood and adolescence: (1) nature versus nurture (the extent to which development involves a genetically controlled unfolding of characteristics and abilities vs. the extent to which environmental factors shape those characteristics and abilities), (2) universality versus diversity (the extent to which developmental progressions are common to all young people vs. the extent to which individuals are different, because of either inherited endowments or environmental conditions), and (3) qualitative versus quantitative change (the extent to which development involves major reorganizations in functioning vs. the extent to which it involves a series of minor, trend-like, modifications).

Theoretical Perspectives of Child and Adolescent Development

Developmentalists have proposed a wide variety of explanations as to how and why children and adolescents change over time. Such explanations can be categorized into eight general theoretical perspectives: maturational, psychodynamic, cognitive-developmental, behavioral learning, evolutionary, information processing, ecological and socio-historic, and life-span. These perspectives often focus on different domains of development and may place greater or lesser importance on nature versus nurture, universality versus diversity, and qualitative versus quantitative change.

General Trends in Development

Early childhood (2–6 years) is a time of imaginative play, rapid language development, significant advances in both gross motor and fine motor skills, and emerging social skills. During middle childhood (6–10 years), children begin to tackle in earnest the tasks and activities that they will need to master to participate effectively in adult society; they also develop long-term relationships with age-mates and internalize many of society's rules and prohibitions. In early adolescence (10–14 years), youngsters are somewhat preoccupied with the physical changes of puberty and are often overly sensitive to how they might appear to others; at the same time, they are beginning to think in the abstract, logical, and systematic ways that allow a critical look at society and an exploration of complex academic topics. Late adolescence (14–18 years) is, for most, a period of intensive interaction with peers and greater independence from adults; although many older adolescents make wise choices, others engage in risky and potentially dangerous behaviors.

Acquiring and Maintaining a Developmental Mind-set

Developmentally appropriate educational practice is guided by both universal developmental pathways and individual differences. Age-related physical characteristics, thinking abilities, and social skills must be important considerations in how schools, classrooms, and lessons are structured. Teachers can use several strategies to help them acquire and maintain a developmental mind-set as they work with children and adolescents. For instance, teachers can identify and capitalize on individual students' strengths. They can consider how their students' "weaknesses" may ultimately foster development over the long run. Through ongoing education, participation in professional organizations, and subscriptions to professional journals, they can keep up to date on developments in the field. And through regular collaboration with colleagues, they can maintain an optimistic outlook on their ability to have a significant positive impact on the lives of their students.

Now go to our Companion Website to assess your understanding of chapter content with Multiple-Choice Questions, apply comprehension in Essay Questions, and broaden your knowledge with links to related Developmental Psychology World Wide Web sites.

KEY CONCEPTS

development (p. 4)
physical development (p. 5)
cognitive development (p. 5)
social-emotional development (p. 5)
nature (p. 7)
maturation (p. 7)
nurture (p. 7)
sensitive period (p. 8)
organismic influences (p. 8)
universality (p. 9)
diversity (p. 9)
qualitative change (p. 10)

quantitative change (p. 10)
stage (p. 10)
stage theory (p. 10)
theory (p. 12)
maturational perspective (p. 12)
psychodynamic perspective (p. 12)
cognitive-developmental perspective (p. 13)
behavioral learning perspective (p. 13)

evolutionary perspective (p. 13)
information processing perspective (p. 14)
ecological and socio-historic perspectives (p. 14)
life-span perspective (p. 14)
developmentally appropriate practice (p. 20)
resiliency (p. 21)
inclusion (p. 22)
standards (p. 26)

Eddie, age 7

Elizabeth, age 14

Developmental Research with Children and Adolescents

CASE STUDY: MICHAEL

After grabbing a cold drink in the teacher's lounge, Barb Cohen returns to the large kindergarten classroom she shares with her coworker, Ted Delgado. It's 3:30 in the afternoon, the children are gone, and Barb savors her first chance to relax and catch her thoughts. The two teachers sit down to compare notes after a long and busy day.

"Ted, I need your ideas about Michael," Barb says. Despite being the youngest child in the class, Michael is one of the tallest. He also has a relatively sophisticated vocabulary (*chamber, cauldron, ghoul*) for a 5-year-old. But Michael's young age does seem to be a factor in other arenas. He is impulsive, rarely pays attention during group activities, can't cut with scissors, has great difficulty writing letters and numbers, and refuses to paint at the easel. But what disturbs Barb most is that he seems to be an unhappy child.

Michael is usually Barb's responsibility, but Ted has plenty of opportunity to observe him as well. This is Barb's second year as a teacher, and so she often relies on the insights that her more experienced partner has gleaned from 15 years in the classroom.

Barb digs out her teaching log and reads aloud her notes on Michael. "Jagged edges in his cutting." "Walks around just watching other children." "Doesn't make choices during free time." "Obnoxious today." "Delays in fine motor skills." "Jabbed Devon with a pencil." "Threw scissors on floor today and said, 'I hate scissors!' " "Possibly lacks self-esteem?" There are few work samples in Michael's portfolio folder, indicating that he hasn't turned in much in the way of artwork, stories, or other written products. Those that he has turned in appear to have been completed in a hurried, careless fashion.

"Not a picture of positive adjustment to kindergarten," Barb concludes.

"He does seem to be having a hard time, I agree," Ted responds. "What other ways might you look at Michael? What other observations could help you?"

"At his parent-teacher conference, his mother said that he doesn't like school," Barb recalls. "But his parents don't seem to be too concerned about his lack of progress. When I mentioned Michael's difficulty cutting in a straight line, his father laughed and said, 'I'm not much better. You should see how I cut grocery coupons out of the newspaper!"

Silently, Barb wonders if Michael's parents are causing his problems. Certainly, they don't seem to support *her* objectives for their son. She cringes as she remembers how his mother mentioned that not only did Michael dislike school, but he didn't seem to like his teachers either.

Barb refocuses on Ted's recommendation. "I like your question, Ted. What other observations could help me? Let me think about that."

The next day, during an art lesson, Barb asks the children to draw pictures of themselves. After school, she shows Ted the picture Michael drew. "Look, he's frowning in his self-portrait. He's angry. He's showing us that he doesn't feel good about himself. He has no self-esteem."

"Possibly," Ted responds thoughtfully. "But what other explanations are there for that expression? Think about it, Barb. Are there any more optimistic ways to look at Michael?"

Angered, Barb wonders why Ted won't admit that Michael is having self-esteem problems that prevent him from learning at school. Furthermore, Barb's feelings are hurt by Ted's apparent implication that Barb has a negative perception of Michael. She is, after all, spending a lot of time observing him and trying to understand and help him. Is she missing something?

BARB COHEN IS UNDERSTANDABLY concerned about Michael's progress and is wondering how she can best promote his academic, social, and personal development. Like Barb, teachers often wonder why students are having difficulties at school. To find answers, they examine students' work samples, observe students' behaviors throughout the school day, and try a variety of instructional strategies. In other words, teachers experiment. In the process, they make countless daily decisions about how to instruct, motivate, assess, discipline, inspire, and sympathize with students.

What guides teachers' decision making? Oftentimes teachers make decisions based on their existing beliefs about children and adolescents. For instance, Barb believes that self-esteem is an important factor influencing classroom performance and suspects that a lack of self-esteem may be at the root of Michael's difficulties. But her more experienced colleague is hesitant to jump to that conclusion. Like Ted Delgado, effective teachers base their decisions on ample evidence about what their students can and cannot do. To some extent, then, effective teachers do research.

As teachers conduct their informal research in the classroom, others are conducting research in a more formal and systematic fashion. These individuals are continually making new discoveries about the characteristics and thinking processes of children and adolescents at various age levels; they are also making solid advances in understanding how teachers and other practitioners can better promote the physical, cognitive, and social-emotional development of their students. Anyone who wants to work effectively with children and adolescents must keep abreast of research findings in human development and educational practice.

In this chapter, we examine the beliefs that teachers often have about the nature of children and adolescents. We then delve into basic principles and procedures of developmental and educational research. As we do so, we have two goals in mind: to help you understand and draw appropriate conclusions from the published research reports you encounter, and to help you conduct your own data collection in classroom settings.

Common Beliefs About Children and Education

All of us hold beliefs about what children are like and how adults can best work with them. For instance, by the time future teachers begin college, they already have well-established beliefs about teaching and learning, and they become increasingly comfortable with their views as they proceed through college and into the classroom (Astington & Pelletier, 1996; Kagan, 1992; Pajares, 1992). Having spent so much time in schools themselves, prospective teachers may believe that they already understand children and that anything they read in textbooks or professional journals is "just theory" that doesn't relate to the real world of classroom practice.

Our beliefs about children and schools are often so engrained that we're not even aware of them; in a sense, they've gone "underground." Even so, they often surface in our everyday behaviors (Olson & Bruner, 1996). As an example, one prevalent belief about teaching is that it is primarily a process of communicating information (perhaps about history, geology, or mathematics) in a simplified and straightforward manner to willing and attentive learners (Brookhart & Freeman, 1992; Strauss & Shilony, 1994). Such a belief often translates into relatively ineffective teaching strategies (Beatty, 1996; Clinchy, 1994). It implies that teaching is little more than "telling" and ignores students' existing understandings, reasoning abilities, interests, and needs as contributing factors to the learning process. It may also lend itself to a single-minded focus on teaching basic skills and assessing students' mastery of those skills.

College students studying to become teachers often hold relatively naive—and sometimes counterproductive—beliefs about the nature of children and teaching. Many prospective teachers

- Value the emotional needs of children but neglect the cognitive and academic variables that may influence learning (Weinstein, 1988) (recall that Barb Cohen focused on Michael's self-esteem and did not consider his cognitive ability)
- Hold unrealistic views about the classroom problems they will face and assume that they already have all the knowledge and skills they will need to teach effectively (Brookhart & Freeman, 1992; Pajares, 1992)
- Support conventional teaching practices and see little need for change in education (Edmundson, 1990; Ginsburg & Newman, 1985; Lortie, 1975)
- Believe that youngsters who are "different" in some way should adapt to the existing educational system, instead of seeing teachers as social activists who can possibly change the system to reduce discrimination (Nel, 1993)

In some instances, future teachers' beliefs about children and adolescents are at odds with what researchers find to be true. In Table 2–1, we list several faulty conceptions we have occasionally encountered in our work with students in teacher preparation programs. Sometimes our students have readily admitted these beliefs; at other times, their actions have revealed a clear commitment to them.

People's beliefs about children, development, learning, and teaching are often a product of the cultures in which they've grown up (Kruger & Tomasello, 1996). For instance, cultures vary widely in their views about the nature of physical development. Some believe that children's physical skills develop naturally and so need not be taught, whereas others deliberately teach such basic skills as sitting and walking (Mead, 1930; Super, 1981). Views about language development vary as well. Although most parents in North America and western Europe simplify their speech when they talk and interact with infants, parents in the cultures of some developing nations speak to their children in much the same way as they would speak to other adults (Kaye, 1982; Ochs, 1988; Trevarthen, 1979).

Confronting and Changing Beliefs About Children and Teaching

Teachers' beliefs about children often color what they see when they observe their students. For instance, in the following scenario, Frances Hawkins, a former preschool teacher, had been watching 5-year-old Jack from behind a one-way mirror. Jack's current teacher had just given Ms. Hawkins an earful about Jack's chronic misbehaviors in class and then temporarily left the room. At this point, Ms. Hawkins observed the following:

Jack . . . stopped by a low vase with golden leaves and took out one brown cattail already fraying at the top. . . . Then I saw Jack's attention focus on the denuded stem at the top. With care, he broke off the spare top stem. After a moment his interest seemed to shift again, not away from the brown cattail but more intently on the velvet-textured object he held protectively in his small brown hand. . . .

Jack continued to probe the looser seeds at the top very gently with the testing finger, his eyes on the finger's probing. What bit lay under his private microscope? The vast number of seeds? The way each seed was attached to the stem, the way the seeds were attached to each other, or how each looked when partially released? I couldn't know what he was thinking, perhaps all this and more.

Only after a long, delicate examination did Jack make his selection: one helicopter seed. . . . He held up the one seed and blew softly, matching his blowing to the delicacy of his miniature glider. The seed traveled, while Jack . . . watched it until it was lost somewhere in the large classroom. Content in face and posture, he gently put the still-intact marsh plant back into its vase and moved on.

The door to my observation booth opened. Startled, I turned to see [Jack's teacher] coming in. Hoping to protect the delight in the scene I had just witnessed and to forestall another unprofessional attack on Jack, I asked his age.

TABLE 2-1 Beliefs About Children and Adolescents That Are Challenged by Research

BELIEF	RESEARCH FINDINGS THAT CHALLENGE THIS BELIEF	IMPLICATION
The wounds of childhood scar people for life.	Although adverse circumstances put children at risk, serious negative outcomes are common only when negative factors persist over a long period of time. Furthermore, some children are remarkably resilient to life's stresses (Cicchetti & Garmezey, 1993; Sameroff, Seifer, Baldwin, & Baldwin, 1993; Shaw, Vondra, Hommerding, Keenan, & Dunn, 1994).	Be sensitive to the difficult circumstances facing your students, but do not assume that present hardships doom students to lasting misfortune or failure.
The best way to educate children is to mimic the home environment. If there is a mismatch between the two environments, children suffer.	Sometimes a difference between home and school is a good thing. In one study, middle school students who had few opportunities for independence and decision making at home performed better in schools that fostered and encouraged initiative and decision making (Epstein, 1983).	Keep in mind the compensatory role that schools can play in students' lives. For example, encourage independence even when students are given little independence at home.
Placing children in a literature-rich environment—one with many books and opportunities to listen to stories—virtually ensures that they will learn to read all by themselves.	Research studies certainly attest to the importance of early reading experiences and availability of good children's literature. However, children also benefit from explicit instruction in letter-sound correspondences, decoding skills, and comprehension strategies; this is especially true for children who come to school with limited experience with books and other forms of written language (Gough & Wren, 1998; Hulme & Joshi, 1998; Stanovich, 2000). Furthermore, without intervention, early difficulties in reading often persist and become more debilitating as students get older (Stanovich, 2000).	Immerse children in a literate environment, but also offer them explicit instruction in learning to decode and make sense of text. Be particularly attentive to the needs of students who struggle with reading.
The best environment for kindergarten children is an academically rigorous one. Children given early training in basic skills have a boost for life.	Some instruction in basic skills is probably beneficial for kindergartners, but too much academic pressure in kindergarten can be detrimental. Young children often thrive in learning environments that build on their natural curiosity; allow them to make choices; incorporate hands-on activities; and encourage play, small-group interaction, and personal expression (Katz, 1999a, 1999b; Shephard & Smith, 1988).	Temper your zeal in teaching basic skills to young children; give them opportunities to explore, experiment, and play.
Students who fail to make eye contact with teachers are devious and disrespectful.	Patterns of language and communication vary from one culture to another. In some cultures, it is disrespectful to look an adult in the eye or to initiate a conversation with an adult (Gilliland, 1988; Irujo, 1988; Lomawaima, 1995). Furthermore, some children with disabilities (e.g., autism) may routinely avoid eye contact.	Learn about the behavior patterns and communication styles of children whose cultural backgrounds are different from your own.

"Five."

"He is tall," I began, "and . . ."

Before I could recount his investigation, she was off: "Look at him wandering about . . . can't settle down to anything . . . does nothing . . . trouble to all." (Hawkins, 1997, p. 323)

Ms. Hawkins believed that children were naturally curious about their world and would take action to satisfy their curiosity. In contrast, Jack's teacher apparently believed that some children, Jack among them, had little inside themselves that could guide their behavior in productive directions.

Developing self-confidence in one's beliefs about children and educational practice is part of a teacher's professional growth. Equally important, however, are confronting and modifying beliefs that are inconsistent with reasonable theoretical explanations, research findings, and available data about individual students. Following are three strategies that can help you examine your own assumptions about how children develop and learn:

BELIEF	RESEARCH FINDINGS THAT CHALLENGE THIS BELIEF	IMPLICATION
Adolescence is a time of storm and stress that must simply be endured by teenagers and their parents and teachers. Adults cannot hope to exert much influence over adolescents.	Adolescence is a period of rapid physical, emotional, and social growth. Conflicts increase with parents and teachers as adolescents struggle to carve out individual identities. Yet only in about 1 in 5 families does the turmoil of adolescence lead to prolonged, extreme conflict (Montemayor, 1982). Serious conflict in adolescence is associated with juvenile delinquency, dropping out of school, and drug abuse (Brook, Brook, Gordon, Whiteman, & Cohen, 1990).	Never underestimate the emotional needs of troubled youth, but remember that juvenile delinquency and drug abuse are not the inevitable outcomes of adolescence.
Schools spend too much time teaching students' "left brains." In doing so, they're asking students to use only half of their brain power.	The left and right hemispheres of the human brain have different specializations. In right-handed people, the left hemisphere predominates in logical, analytical, and sequential thinking, and the right hemisphere predominates in spatial, simultaneous, and analogical thinking. Nevertheless, the two hemispheres are in constant communication, and studies of efforts to strengthen a particular hemisphere indicate that such "training" is relatively ineffective (Pressley & McCormick, 1995).	Diversify instructional tasks, formats, and materials for all children, but remember that most activities involve both hemispheres.
Adults are smarter than adolescents, adolescents are smarter than elementary school children, and elementary school children are smarter than preschoolers.	Thousands of research studies document convincingly that children become increasingly capable as they grow older. However, the superior learning and memory capabilities that come with age are sometimes a function of individuals' *knowledge* rather than age per se. For instance, when children know more about a topic than adults do, their ability to learn and remember new information about the topic surpasses that of adults (Chi, 1978; Rabinowitz & Glaser, 1985). Furthermore, what appear to be limitations and errors in children's thinking may actually be beneficial for development. For example, the naive and unrealistic optimism that young children have in approaching learning tasks may help them to persist in the face of frequent failure. Likewise, the more limited memory capacity of young children may help them segment the language they hear into manageable pieces, making it easier to decipher and master (Bjorklund & Green, 1992).	Keep in mind that limitations in students' thinking may sometimes serve a purpose in their long-term development.

■ *Identify metaphors that best reflect your views about the nature of children.*
Perhaps you think that children are like

Empty buckets waiting to be filled

Dry sponges that will soak up whatever moisture comes their way

Plants in a garden that need shelter from the elements

Thoughtful philosophers thinking about and questioning what they see and hear

Restless moviegoers wanting to be entertained

Stray cats who have their own, mysterious agendas

Prisoners conspiring against their wardens

Caged animals that need to be trained

We might guess that, in the earlier scenario, Ms. Hawkins thought of children, including Jack, as "thoughtful philosophers." In contrast, Jack's teacher may instead have subscribed to a "stray cat" or "caged animal" point of view.

Certainly no single metaphor is the "correct" way of thinking about children, but some metaphors lead to more productive teaching practices than others. As you read the upcoming

What are your assumptions about how children develop and learn? Your effectiveness as a teacher depends, in part, on your willingness to explore—and possibly revise—your beliefs.

chapters, we urge you to continually refine the metaphors you've identified as best reflecting your own views about children in light of the theories and research findings we present.

■ *Identify metaphors that best capture your beliefs about effective teaching practice.* How would you best describe the role of a teacher? Consider the following possibilities:

Friend	Quality control	Scientist
Parent	inspector	Gardener
Tour guide	Counselor	Drill sergeant
Cheerleader	Entertainer	Religious leader

These various metaphors yield different implications about what a teacher should do. For example, the "counselor" metaphor suggests that a teacher should focus primarily on social and emotional development and pay little heed to cognitive development. The "quality control inspector" metaphor might lead to an emphasis on simply assessing, rather than improving, children's existing abilities. Throughout the book, we describe strategies that should promote children's and adolescents' development in the physical, cognitive, and social-emotional domains. These numerous strategies indicate that a teacher's many roles cannot easily be boiled down into a single metaphor.

■ *Read current literature with an open mind but critical eye.* In our own professional growth as teachers and scholars, we have revised our beliefs about children and teaching many times over, often in response to ideas and data we've encountered in the literature. We hope that you, too, will find value in the theories and research findings you encounter throughout your professional career and that you will modify your beliefs as new ideas and data warrant.

At the same time, we urge you to look carefully at the conclusions that researchers derive from the findings they report. Research, like many human endeavors, is a worthy but fallible enterprise. In the pages that follow, we discuss the role that research plays in the study of development and then present general principles that guide appropriate implementation and interpretation of research studies.

Role of Research in the Study of Development

Research often clarifies, and may even correct, what we believe to be true about how children and adolescents develop. What is "common knowledge" to some doesn't always hold up under the careful scrutiny of researchers.

Research doesn't necessarily provide the final, definitive answer to every question about childhood and adolescence. There are often alternative theories and explanations for the patterns of data obtained, so researchers rarely know for certain when they have the "right" explanation for those data. Furthermore, researchers are probably more on target in their interpretations when they acknowledge that human development in virtually any domain—physical, cognitive, or social-emotional—is a complex and multifaceted process and that true "mastery" of a particular ability or skill is difficult to define and pin down (Flavell, 1994).

As an illustration, consider the development of *perspective taking,* the ability to determine what another person perceives, feels, and believes. Researchers have found that this ability to take other people's perspectives increases with age (Selman, 1980; Selman & Schultz, 1990), but at what point have children *mastered* it? Children of many ages can sometimes take the perspective of another. For example, 2-year-old Alex rubs his mother's head when she looks worried and asks, "Mommy, you got an ow-ee?" and 16-year-old Danielle realizes that even the "cool" kids at her high school probably feel self-conscious and insecure at times. However, these same youngsters behave differently in other settings: Alex offers his cranky older brother his "Barney friend" in a misguided gesture of sympathy, but doesn't understand that his brother is too old to take solace in stuffed toys. When Danielle walks into her first-period class, she thinks everyone will notice her new haircut—she has apparently forgotten her insight about her classmates often being *self*-conscious rather than *other*-conscious. Researchers who try to pinpoint the precise point at which young people master perspective taking are likely to be befuddled by such variability from one situation to another.

Like perspective taking, many abilities develop slowly over time, and they often appear in some contexts while remaining absent in others (Flavell, Miller, & Miller, 1993). Despite the complexity of children's development in virtually any domain, researchers remain committed to uncovering the nature of development and creating models and theories that help to explain the regularities and patterns they observe. In the sections that follow, we consider how researchers go about their work.

Key Features of Developmental Research

In the opening case study, Barb Cohen's deliberations about Michael's difficulties adjusting to kindergarten illustrate two key features of research in child and adolescent development. First, Barb forms hypotheses that might explain Michael's difficulties adjusting to kindergarten: She suspects that Michael suffers from poor self-esteem, and she speculates that his parents may be doing little to encourage his skill development. Second, she collects and interprets data: She records her observations of Michael's behavior in the classroom and keeps a portfolio of the work he has turned in. She then scrutinizes both sources of data, looking for patterns to support or disconfirm her hypotheses.

In some respects, then, Barb's efforts do constitute "research." But developmental research typically involves much more than informal observations of a child. Several features characterize research in child and adolescent development: hypothesis formation, sampling and recruitment, systematic collection and interpretation of data, ethical conduct, and public scrutiny and analysis.

Hypothesis Formation

Developmentalists rarely pull research topics out of a hat. Instead, the studies they design and conduct are guided by particular questions about the nature and course of human development and, often, by particular hypotheses and expectations about what they think they will observe. Such hypotheses are formulated out of existing theories, personal experiences, and consistent patterns in the way children and adolescents talk and behave in classrooms and other settings.

Sampling and Recruitment

To acquire knowledge about developmental phenomena, researchers need the cooperation of children, adolescents, parents, and teachers. Typically, researchers identify a particular population they want to examine and then select a smaller subgroup, or **sample,** of that population. Ideally, the people in the sample reflect the characteristics of the people in the population in question, and in roughly the same proportions. When such is not the case (and it usually *isn't*), the researchers must identify the characteristics of the sample (age, gender, income level, ethnic background, etc.) that may influence the outcome of their study.

Some youngsters and families are easier to recruit for research studies than others. As an illustration, Teresa once conducted a series of studies to investigate the development of children's beliefs about listening, asking questions such as "What do you think it means to be a good listener?" and "Whose fault is it when a listener does not understand the speaker?" She found that first graders were a snap to recruit, third graders were relatively easy but not quite as accessible, and fifth graders were harder still. (Perhaps the older children were losing her recruitment letters and parent consent forms in their backpacks, or perhaps they were more distracted with after-school activities.)

Because some people are more accessible and willing than others, developmental researchers have tended to recruit children and adolescents who come from backgrounds similar to their own. The unhappy result is that we have less information about the development of children and adolescents who come from ethnic and racial minority groups, language environments other than English-only families, and low-income communities (e.g., Coll et al., 1996; Fisher, Jackson, & Villarruel, 1998). This book refers often to research that represents the diversity present in our society's young people, but as you read, we do urge you to consider whether specific educational implications may or may not apply to the students you will teach.

Fortunately, some developmental researchers are now working vigorously to study hard-to-find populations, such as children from migrant or homeless families. These outreach efforts will eventually strengthen the conclusions we can draw about commonalities and diversity in the development of children and adolescents.

sample
The specific participants in a research study; their performance is often assumed to indicate how a larger population of individuals would perform.

Systematic Collection and Interpretation of Data

Barb Cohen has collected data about Michael in a somewhat haphazard fashion: She has made notes of whatever she's happened to see and collected whatever Michael has happened to turn in. Furthermore, her hypotheses affect her interpretations of the data. For instance, she immediately interprets Michael's frowning self-portrait as an indication of low self-esteem. But other interpretations are possible as well. The frown may have reflected an upset stomach, a dislike of drawing activities, or angry feelings toward parents or teachers. Perhaps the "frown" wasn't meant to be a frown at all. In her teaching log, Barb has noted that Michael shows "delays in fine motor skills," and the work samples in his portfolio appear to have been completed hurriedly. Perhaps an undiagnosed disability, whether in certain cognitive skills or in fine motor coordination, limits his ability to translate what he sees or imagines onto paper.

In developmental research, data collection is typically more planned and systematic. Researchers take precautions that their data collection is as objective as possible and that their own beliefs and biases don't influence their observations or measurements. They also try to consider the many ways in which their data might be interpreted, eliminating some interpretations only as the data warrant.

Ethical Conduct

A paramount concern for developmental researchers is that they conduct their research in an ethical manner, in particular that they are honest and respectful of the rights of the participants in their studies. Before conducting research, investigators submit plans to *review boards*, committees of scholars who scrutinize the plans for potential dangers to participants and deny approval to any plans that put participants at undue risk. Researchers must inform participants (and, in the case of minors, parents or guardians) of procedures that will be used, allow participants to withdraw from a study at any time, and keep individual responses anonymous and confidential. Furthermore, when describing research studies to others, researchers must represent their methods and results accurately. In general, matters of ethics must preside over knowledge building whenever a research project potentially puts children in harm's way.

Public Scrutiny and Critical Analysis

Developmental researchers conduct their research in public. When they believe they have learned something about children, they present their methods, observations, and conclusions to other scholars in the field. Their colleagues eagerly consume the results, identify limitations, spot holes in the logic, recast the results in alternative theoretical perspectives, and think about implications of the results for their own work. Experienced researchers learn to anticipate such criticisms and to eliminate as many problems as they can in their research designs.

The field of human development is strengthened by such critical analysis. At every step of the way, we must examine alternative explanations for the conclusions we favor, consider *all* available evidence, generate other plausible interpretations, and search for new tests of our hypotheses. In the process, we refine our methods, theories, and understandings of how we can best help children and adolescents.

We hope that you, too, will be able to critically analyze the developmental research studies you read and not take the researchers' conclusions at face value. But before you can do so, you must ultimately know more about data collection techniques and research designs. We turn to these two topics next.

Data Collection Techniques

Developmental researchers typically use one or more of only a handful of strategies for collecting their data. After describing these strategies, we will consider how likely data collection methods are to yield accurate and dependable results—in other words, the extent to which they have validity and reliability.

Strategies for Gathering Information

Three strategies for collecting information are self-reports (interviews and questionnaires), tests and other methods of numerical measurement, and observations of behavior. As you read our discussion of these strategies, be alert to the advantages and disadvantages that each has as a window into the minds and lives of children and adolescents.

Self-Reports   Teresa once attended a session at a professional conference with her son Connor, then 5, in tow. The featured speaker, a prominent researcher in educational psychology, introduced his topic by saying, "Today we are going to consider the history of research on children's growth and development." Connor immediately stood up straight and tall in the crowded room and announced, "I'm a kid! Let *me* tell you how children grow and develop!" Teresa, embarrassed beyond words, insisted that Connor sit down immediately, but she now wonders what he would have said.

Obviously, young people have much to tell us about their own development. When it comes to children's beliefs, intentions, hopes, and frustrations, who better to ask than the children themselves? Accordingly, some of the most informative research data come in the form of children's and adolescents' own statements about themselves—that is, in the form of **self-reports**.

Sometimes researchers pose questions in face-to-face **interviews**. For example, Jean Piaget once asked children of various ages to explain what they thought *thinking* was. Here, as an example, is a conversation with 7-year-old "Monte":[1]

Adult:	You know what it means to think?
Monte:	Yes.
Adult:	Then think of your house. What do you think with?
Monte:	The mouth.
Adult:	Can you think with the mouth shut?
Monte:	No.
Adult:	With the eyes shut?
Monte:	Yes.
Adult:	With the ears stopped up?
Monte:	Yes.
Adult:	Now shut your mouth and think of your house. Are you thinking?
Monte:	Yes.
Adult:	What did you think with?
Monte:	The mouth. (dialogue from Piaget, 1929, p. 39)

Contrast Monte's views with those of 11-year-old "Victor":

Adult:	Where is thought?
Victor:	In the head.
Adult:	If someone opened your head, would he see your thought?
Victor:	No.
Adult:	Could he touch it?
Victor:	No.
Adult:	Feel it as if it was air?
Victor:	No . . .
Adult:	What is a dream?
Victor:	It's a thought.
Adult:	What do you dream with?
Victor:	With the head.
Adult:	Are the eyes open or shut?
Victor:	Shut.
Adult:	Where is the dream whilst you are dreaming?
Victor:	In the head.
Adult:	Not in front of you?
Victor:	It's as if . . . you could see it.

---

[1] In reports of his interviews, Piaget often abbreviated or in other ways shortened the names of the children (A. Karmiloff-Smith, personal communication, October, 2000; S. Pulos, personal communication, September, 2000). Here and throughout the book we substitute his abbreviations with actual, but in most cases probably incorrect, names.

self-report
Data collection technique whereby participants are asked to describe their own characteristics and performance.

interview
Data collection technique that obtains self-report data through face-to-face conversation.

Adult:	Is there anything in front of you when you dream?
Victor:	No, nothing.
Adult:	What is inside the head?
Victor:	Thoughts.
Adult:	Is it the eyes which see something inside the head?
Victor:	No. (dialogue from Piaget, 1929, p. 54)

From these and other interviews, Piaget concluded that when children begin to conceptualize the nature of thinking (sometime around age 6), they view thoughts as concrete entities that occur in the mouth or ears. By age 11, their conceptualization has become more abstract, in that thought no longer has tangible, material qualities.

Interviews have the advantage of allowing a researcher to explore the reasoning of individual children in considerable depth. They can be very time-consuming, however, so researchers often use written **questionnaires** when they need to gather responses from a large number of participants. As an illustration, we turn to an early study by Lynd and Lynd (1929), who administered a 12-item checklist to 730 students in grades 10 through 12. The Lynds asked students to check the issues "about which you and your parents disagree." Students most often picked "the hours you get in at night" and "the number of times you go out on school nights during the week." Sound familiar? This study was replicated by Caplow, Bahr, Chadwick, Hill, and Williamson (1982), with most frequently checked items being "the hours you get in at night" and "home duties." Responses from these two surveys, administered more than five decades apart, indicate that parent-adolescent conflicts tend to center on everyday concerns, including completion of schoolwork, social life and friends, home chores, disobedience, disagreements with siblings, and personal hygiene (Montemayor, 1983).

Interviews and questionnaires certainly have their limitations. Without actually observing children and adolescents in their natural environments, researchers cannot check on the accuracy or meaning of their statements, and the information they get is limited to the particular questions that they ask. As one simple example, Teresa once asked her son Connor, then 10, if he had made his bed that morning, and he answered that he had. Later that day, as Teresa brought Connor's laundry into his bedroom, she had to tiptoe carefully to avoid the many toys and clothes strewn on the floor. Yes, he had made his bed (albeit not to military standards), but he had done little else to get his room in order. Researchers (and parents and teachers as well) get the most accurate and useful information when they ask the right questions and find a means of double-checking the veracity of what children are telling them.

Despite such difficulties, self-report techniques can give researchers vivid glimpses into the thoughts and actions of growing youths. When researchers ask children to express their views, verify children's understanding of the questions being asked, probe their understandings in a thorough yet sensitive fashion, and confirm the patterns they see with other types of data, valuable insights can result.

Tests and Other Methods of Numerical Measurement A **test** is an instrument designed to assess knowledge, abilities, or skills in a fairly consistent fashion from one individual to the next. Although tests inevitably involve observable behaviors (researchers cannot assess what they cannot see), they allow researchers and practitioners to draw inferences about learning, reasoning, and other nonobservable mental phenomena. Some tests involve paper and pencil, whereas others do not, but all typically yield one or more numbers (*scores*) that summarize performance.

Tests have long histories in schools; teachers and other school personnel often use them to determine what students do and do not know and can and cannot do. Yet tests are often used in research as well. To illustrate, in a study by Campbell and Ramey (1994), intelligence tests and other measures of cognitive development were administered at regular intervals to a sample of children from ages 3 months to 12 years. All of the children came from low-income families, and most of their mothers had not completed high school. As infants, half of the children were randomly selected to attend a daycare center in which they had activities designed to promote their cognitive, perceptual, linguistic, motor, and social development; they attended this center until they were 5 years old. The other half were assigned to a control group in which they received nutritional formula and disposable diapers as long as such items were needed, but they did not attend daycare. Test scores indicated that children who participated in the experimental daycare program made greater cognitive gains than the nonparticipants soon after

questionnaire
Data collection technique that obtains self-report data through a paper-pencil inventory.

test
Instrument designed to assess knowledge, understandings, abilities, or skills in a consistent fashion across individuals.

the program began and maintained this advantage until age 12. (A second intervention, beginning at age 5 and lasting for 3 years, was less effective.)

Some of the tests that researchers use are similar or identical to those used by practitioners. Others are designed specifically for research purposes. For instance, researchers have developed numerous instruments to assess aspects of children's motivation, self-esteem, personality, social skills, and moral development. Such instruments often have little or no usefulness to teachers but help researchers test specific hypotheses about the nature or possible causes of children's development.

Developmentalists also measure children's accomplishments and abilities in ways that we would not necessarily think of as "tests" but that nevertheless can yield numerical scores. For instance, they might record reaction times in certain decision-making tasks, ask children to find differences among similar-looking stimuli, or measure patterns of neurological activity in different parts of the brain.

Observations Researchers conduct **observations** when they carefully watch the behavior and listen to the conversations of youths, often within youngsters' natural environments. Observations can offer rich portraits of "slices" of children's lives, particularly when they take place over an extended time and are supplemented with interviews and analyses of the products (e.g., drawings, essays) that children create.

Some researchers conduct observations in a highly structured fashion, perhaps identifying and then either counting or timing certain behaviors each time they occur. For example, a researcher might select a sample of boys and girls in 10 high school history classrooms and record the number and types of questions that each student asks.

Other researchers take a less structured approach, keeping an ongoing, detailed record of significant events that take place in a particular setting, such as the playground, lunchroom, or classroom. As an illustration, a team of researchers took turns observing one 7-year-old boy, "Raymond," on a single day in 1949 (Barker & Wright, 1951). The researchers took great pains to describe Raymond's actions, the physical and social settings in which he acted, and the intentions and motives that appeared to be guiding his actions. The following is an excerpt from the description of his actions at school:

Observations of children in ordinary, familiar situations, such as a class party, can yield rich portraits of the complexity of children's lives.

10:37	He chewed on his left thumbnail and gazed off into space over the heads of the other children. Judy Marshall, who was in his direct line of vision, looked at him and whispered something. As they both raised their eyebrows, Raymond rolled his eyes upward, as if to say, "Gee, is this boring."
10:38	Then he slumped way down until his head leaned against the back of the seat and his book rested against his chest. Someone in the room whistled. Raymond looked around, as did many of the children, to locate the source of the sound. Raymond's eyes returned to his book.
10:39	He gave a large stretch, with both hands raised over his head. Suddenly he stood up and walked straight to a window at the back of the room. He carefully closed the window, peering outside with a curious, lingering look, as if he would like to stay and look a long time but knew he had better go back to his seat.
10:41	Mrs. Logan said, "You may put your readers away and get out your number workbooks." Raymond returned to his seat, bent down, and peered inside his desk. He popped up in a minute with a ballpoint pen and a pair of scissors, which he placed on top of his desk. He put his tongue between his teeth and blew hard, making a sputtery noise.
10:43	He stood up, walked very briskly to the front of the room where the teacher stood, and spoke to her in a low voice. The teacher asked aloud, "You mean you haven't any pencil?" Looking somewhat puzzled, Raymond leaned nearer and said something more to Mrs. Logan. She replied aloud, "Oh, you mean no paper." Waiting while she considered his request, he stood with his finger in his mouth and looked around the room aimlessly. Then, swinging both his arms, he ambled over to the teacher's desk where he just leaned and surveyed the children in the room. The teacher said in a calm but commanding voice, "I'll get you some paper in a minute, Raymond. Go and sit down." Raymond, looking to neither side, walked immediately to his desk and sat down. (Barker & Wright, 1951, pp. 144–145)

observation
Data collection technique whereby a researcher carefully observes and documents the behaviors of participants in a research study.

In this excerpt, Raymond appears to tolerate the demands of school with a hint of reluctance. Read the rest of the account, and you will find a boy who negotiates an impressive array of transactions with a wide range of individuals across multiple settings. The experiences of this real boy hardly fit into categories investigators might derive through an interview, survey, or test. Furthermore, even this lengthy book (a 435-page record of Raymond's single day) alters and compresses the actual activities of his day. The authors of this "specimen record" use the analogy of a pressed flower to describe their document:

> As with other field specimens, parts of the original have been altered and other parts have been lost in the process of getting and preserving it. A pressed flower in an herbarium is not the same as a flower in bloom. It is useful to botanists nonetheless. Similarly this specimen of behavior may prove useful to social scientists. (Barker & Wright, 1951, p. 1)

"Apples," courtesy of Grace, age 7.

Observations are frequently used to document characteristics and behaviors that young people display in public settings (e.g., hairstyles, dress codes, "bullying" behaviors). They are also helpful for studying actions and interactional styles that youngsters and adults may be unaware of (e.g., the frequency and types of questions that teachers direct toward boys and girls) and behaviors that violate social norms (e.g., temper tantrums, petty thefts).

Observations have their weaknesses, however. For one thing, the presence of an observer might actually change the behaviors under investigation. (Were the children distracted by the observer? Did they misbehave or, alternatively, stay on task more than usual?) Furthermore, observers' biases and expectations can influence the information they record. (Did they see what they wanted to see? Did they notice that a reprimand was given in a gentle, caring manner, or did they simply record that a criticism was given?) Finally, questions arise as to whether the behaviors observed are typical or the exception. (Was an adolescent having an especially troubling day? Are a parent's disciplinary actions consistent across different kinds of transgressions, such as refusing to eat vegetables, running recklessly into the street, failing to complete homework?)

The three data-gathering strategies we've just described are frequently used in combination, and the information collected is often more accurate and compelling as a result. Imagine, for instance, that you are a researcher interested in studying the experiences of children and adolescents who live and work on the streets. What kinds of observations would you conduct? Could you supplement your observations with other kinds of data, such as interviews with these vulnerable youngsters? Campos and her colleagues (1994) addressed such questions and decided to examine the lives of street children with a varied arsenal of data sources. They interviewed children and adolescents who worked, and in some cases also lived, on the streets of a large Brazilian city. They supplemented open-ended interviews and group discussions with structured interviews and in-depth observations of youths in specific locations throughout the city (e.g., city squares, abandoned houses, agencies that provided food or showers). The participants' self-reports indicated that those who lived on the streets fared worse than those who lived at home; for instance, 75% of the street-based youths but only 15% of the home-based youths reported engaging in illegal activities. The researchers' observations were consistent with the results of the self-reports: Compared to the home-based youths, those who lived on the street had less social support, more often engaged in substance abuse, and were sexually active at a younger age. The observational field notes of one of the researchers portrays the wrenching experience of drug dependency:

> I was in the square, the kids were sniffing thinner. L.A. was very agitated because the can had finished. L.R. said, "Look at that, just because the thinner's gone, he's in the mood, the first necklace that appears, he'll grab it." D.R. added, "It's true, when the thinner's gone they all get nervous until they get money for another can; when they buy it they . . . are calm again." (Campos et al., 1994, p. 325)

Validity in Data Collection

As they collect their data, developmental researchers must continually ask themselves how they know they are getting accurate information. In other words, they are concerned with **validity,** the extent to which a data collection technique actually assesses what it is intended to assess. Validity takes several forms, each of which is more or less important in different situa-

validity
Extent to which a data collection technique actually assesses what it is intended to assess.

tions. Data collection has *content validity* when it systematically assesses the entire range of knowledge and skills in the domain under investigation. It has *construct validity* when it accurately assesses an underlying, nonobservable trait or characteristic, such as intelligence, achievement motivation, self-esteem, or empathy.[2] It has *predictive validity* when it allows a researcher to make predictions about how children or adolescents are likely to behave or perform in other settings and in the future. The top portion of Table 2–2 presents examples of situations in which the various forms of validity are suspect.

When assessing the validity of their data collection techniques, researchers examine several types of evidence. To determine content validity, they compare their questions and tasks to the entire domain they want to assess (e.g., reading comprehension ability, mathematical problem solving, perspective taking), making sure that their instrument reflects most or all aspects of that domain in appropriate proportions. To determine construct validity, they compare their results with other indications of the characteristic in question (perhaps with teacher ratings, grade-point-averages, or results from instruments that other researchers have used). To determine predictive validity, they compare their results with relatively objective measures of participants' future performance. Researchers may draw on other sources of evidence as well, such as evidence from prior research studies about the validity of a particular approach or experts' judgments about an instrument's accuracy.

In addition to looking for evidence that their techniques measure certain things, researchers work to rule out the influence of other, irrelevant traits. For instance, do scores on a test of mathematical ability reflect children's knowledge of a particular culture (e.g., are there too many questions about American sports?)? Does a test of young children's reasoning capabilities assess their compliance and desire to please the experimenter as much as their actual reasoning skills? Only when researchers can say "no" to such questions do they have some assurance that their data collection methods are valid.

Sound developmental research also takes into account the perspectives and motives of the participants. As adults, we are predisposed to "see" children through our own "lenses." Skilled researchers recognize that young people bring their own beliefs, expectations, and agendas to their interactions with researchers. Some (adolescents especially) may give responses to shock a researcher or in some other respect undermine the research effort. For example, Jeanne's daughter Tina once came home from high school reporting that, on a lark, she and her friends had written nonsensical (and definitely inaccurate) answers on a schoolwide questionnaire. Others may tell a researcher what they think the researcher wants to hear. The following interview with 6-year-old Joey illustrates how children sometimes seek to comply with a researcher's expectations:

Researcher:	I'm interested in how children get along with their brothers and sisters. Can you tell me about any arguments you had with your brother Sam in the last few days?
Joey:	He . . . ah . . . he took my toys. We got in a fight.
Researcher:	You didn't like that, I bet. About how many times a day do you fight with Sam?
Joey:	Two.
Researcher:	Two? Twice a day? Is that all?
Joey:	Three?

Good researchers acknowledge that young research participants go into a research study with motivations, trepidations, and ways of responding that may decrease the validity of data sources. Furthermore, children and adolescents may use words and phrases that have different meanings to the adult researchers than they do to themselves. Probing in perceptive ways, searching for confirmation through a variety of sources, and reassuring children that they are not being evaluated are strategies researchers use to put children at ease and improve the validity of the data they collect.

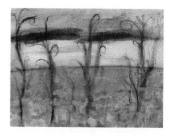

Children's complex behaviors and products tell us a great deal about how their abilities change with age. The challenge for researchers lies in evaluating such behaviors and products objectively and systematically. What criteria might a researcher use to evaluate the apple tree art on the facing page and the poppy field above? "Poppy Field" courtesy of Laura, age 10.

---

[2]The term *construct* refers to abstract concepts that theorists devise to summarize or explain certain kinds of phenomena. For instance, they developed the construct *intelligence* to explain the fact that some people learn and solve problems more quickly than others. They developed the construct *achievement motivation* to describe the consistent drive of some students to excel at academic and other pursuits.

TABLE 2–2   Questions of Validity and Reliability in Data Collection

ISSUE	QUESTION ADDRESSED	EXAMPLE OF POOR VALIDITY OR RELIABILITY
VALIDITY **Content Validity**	Does the technique yield information that reflects the entire domain being assessed?	A researcher uses a questionnaire to discover the kinds of study strategies that high school students use to prepare for tests. The instrument includes questions about what students do when they study in class but omits questions about how they study at home, as well as questions about the study environment in each situation. The strategies students use when they work unsupervised and when distractions abound (in some home situations) may be very different from those they use in situations where guidance and resources are available to them.
Construct Validity	Does the technique measure the underlying characteristic it is intended to measure?	A researcher uses preschoolers' activity level (e.g., the degree to which they move around the classroom during free play) as a measure of curiosity, neglecting the fact that activity level may also reflect other characteristics, such as hyperactivity or a desire to affiliate with energetic classmates.
Predictive Validity	Does the technique allow the researcher to make predictions?	A researcher finds that 4-year-olds' scores on a kindergarten "readiness" test have little relation to how well children perform in a kindergarten classroom.
RELIABILITY **Test-retest Reliability**	Have the effects of temporary fluctuations in participants' performance been minimized?	A researcher who is asking children about the nature of thinking finds that the children's beliefs change considerably from one day to the next, depending on how the researcher phrases the questions.
Interrater Reliability	Do two researchers classify or rate aspects of participants' performance in the same way?	As two researchers classify the behaviors they see on the playground, one "sees" aggression (Sasha intentionally slammed into Maria) while the other "sees" clumsiness (Sasha slipped and tripped into Maria).
Internal Consistency Reliability	Do different items or questions yield consistent information?	In a questionnaire designed to assess overall self-esteem, many participants respond to some questions in ways that reflect high self-esteem but respond to others in ways that reflect low self-esteem.
Alternate Forms Reliability	Do two different forms of an instrument yield similar results?	A researcher is assessing middle school students' moral reasoning by presenting one of two moral dilemmas, situations with no obvious "right" answer. The students show more advanced reasoning when given a dilemma about children their own age than when given a dilemma involving adults.

Reliability in Data Collection

Researchers must also ask whether their data collection methods are yielding consistent, dependable results—in other words, whether their methods have **reliability**. Like validity, reliability takes several forms. *Test-retest reliability* is the extent to which a test or other assessment technique yields similar results on two different occasions. *Interrater reliability* reflects the degree to which two or more observers rate or classify a particular behavior or performance in the same way. *Internal consistency reliability* is the extent to which participants respond to different questions or items in a single instrument (when all are assumed to assess the same thing) in a similar manner. *Alternate forms reliability* is at issue when a researcher uses two or more

reliability
Extent to which a data collection technique yields consistent, dependable results—results that are only minimally affected by temporary and irrelevant influences.

versions of a test or other instrument and wants to make sure that these forms yield similar scores. The bottom portion of Table 2–2 presents examples of situations in which the different forms of reliability are questionable.

In general, reliability is lower when unwanted influences (usually temporary in nature) affect the results obtained. Children and adolescents, and adults as well, inevitably perform differently on some occasions than on others, in that they may be more or less rested, well fed, cheerful, attentive, cooperative, thoughtful, honest, and articulate. Their performance is also influenced by characteristics of the researcher (e.g., gender, educational background, ethnic origin, mode of dress) and conditions within the research setting (e.g., how quiet the room is, how instructions are worded, what kinds of incentives are given for participation).

In collecting information from children and adolescents, researchers must be alert to the influence of such "nuisance" factors and then try to minimize their effects as much as possible. For instance, they often *standardize* their instructions, procedures, and time limits, making such factors as similar as possible for everyone. They make sure tests are long enough that misinterpretation or guessing on a few items doesn't seriously impact the overall scores. Before observing children or adolescents in natural settings, they identify specific criteria they will use to classify and code behaviors and train all observers to use them consistently. And ideally, they collect several different kinds of data, looking for converging patterns in the information they collect.

At first glance, reliability may seem less important than validity, but in fact reliability is *essential* for the validity of data. Researchers cannot obtain valid information about children and adolescents if their data vary considerably from one hour to the next or from one question to another. At the same time, reliability doesn't guarantee validity. For example, imagine that researchers are interested in middle school students' feelings of school pride. They decide to look at whether or not students properly dispose of the remains of their lunch (bread crust, apple cores, food wrappers, etc.) before leaving the cafeteria every day. Two observers are very consistent in the number of students they identify as either discarding their trash or leaving it on the lunch tables. Furthermore, they find that individual students are fairly consistent from one day to the next in whether they discard or abandon their trash. Although the information collected appears to be reliable, you might want to question its validity as a measure of school pride. Perhaps students who carry their lunch remains to the trash cans have simply developed that habit and do not necessarily have pride or other positive feelings toward their school. As a general principle, then, reliability is a necessary but insufficient condition for validity.

Research Designs in the Study of Children and Adolescents

Speculate with us, for a minute, about how we might examine the nature of children's *aggression,* behavior intended to harm another either physically or verbally. How might we study possible factors that lead to aggression? How might we find out whether people who are aggressive as young children tend to be more aggressive later in life? How might we determine what kinds of interventions are effective in decreasing children's aggression?

Developmental researchers often exercise considerable creativity when it comes to research design. Having posed their research questions and possibly formed one or more hypotheses, they must develop a plan for collecting the data that will answer their question. Here we describe several common designs in developmental research and illustrate them with examples of research on aggression.

Experimental and Quasi-Experimental Studies

In an **experimental study,** a researcher manipulates an aspect of the lives of children or adolescents and measures its impact on a particular characteristic or behavior that they display. Experiments typically involve an intervention, or *treatment,* of some sort. Participants are divided into two or more groups, with different groups receiving different treatments or perhaps with one group (a **control group**) receiving either no treatment or a presumably ineffective one. Following the treatment(s), the researcher looks at the groups for differences in the characteristic or behavior in question. As one simple example, a researcher might use two different methods of

experimental study
Research study in which a researcher manipulates one aspect of the environment (a treatment), controls other aspects of the environment, and assesses the treatment's effects on participants' behavior.

control group
A group of participants in a research study who do not receive the treatment under investigation; often used in an experimental study.

reducing aggressive behavior (the treatments) with two different groups of children and then measure and compare the frequency of later aggressive acts for each group.

In a true experimental design, participants are assigned to groups on a *random* basis; they have essentially no choice in the treatment (or lack thereof) that they receive. Random assignment ensures that any average differences among the groups (perhaps differences in the intelligence, motivation, or personalities of group members) are due to chance alone. Furthermore, with the exception of the particular treatment administered, the experimenter tries to make all conditions of the research experience identical or very similar for all of the groups. By doing such things, the researcher ensures that the only major difference among the groups is the experimental treatment; thus, any differences in subsequent characteristics or behaviors are almost certainly the *result* of the treatment differences.

Experiments are unique among research designs in the degree to which outside influences are controlled and therefore eliminated as possible explanations for the results obtained. For this reason, *experiments are the method of choice whenever a researcher wants to explore possible cause-effect relationships between environmental conditions (i.e., treatments) and children's characteristics and behaviors.*

However, in many situations experiments are impossible, impractical, or unethical for the issue at hand. For example, although considerable evidence indicates that parental abuse leads to more aggressive behavior in children, controlled experiments to test this idea are out of the question. A researcher would certainly not assign families to groups and then insist that parents in one group behave abusively toward their children!

When random assignment isn't a viable strategy, researchers may instead conduct a **quasi-experimental study,** one that has some elements of experimental designs but does not tightly control other possible influences on the results (Campbell & Stanley, 1963). For example, imagine that a team of researchers wants to examine the possible effects of an after-school recreation program in reducing aggressive behavior in high school students. The researchers might establish such a program at one high school and then enlist a second high school to serve as a control group. Before starting the after-school program, the researchers would collect data to ensure that students at both high schools shared certain characteristics potentially related to aggressive behavior (type of community, family income level, achievement test scores, etc.). Now imagine that, a year later, the researchers find that students at the high school with the after-school recreation program show lower rates of aggressive behavior than students in the control group. The researchers have eliminated *some* alternative explanations for the difference between the two groups; in particular, they've eliminated those characteristics that were initially similar for the two groups—and in doing so they have increased the likelihood that the differences they observed are the result of the after-school program. Because they have not, and in fact could not, make sure that the two groups were similar in *every* respect, the possibility exists that some other, unmeasured variable (perhaps motivation or some personality characteristic) accounts for the difference observed.

Some quasi-experiments involve only one group of participants. In a simple *pretest-posttest design,* the researcher measures the characteristic or behavior twice, both before and after the treatment being studied, and looks for differences in performance on the two occasions. In a *time-series design,* the researcher presents two or more treatments to the same children at different points in time and assesses changes in the children's behavior following each treatment. By using a single group of participants for all treatments, the researcher keeps such individual characteristics as intelligence and personality constant but has difficulty ruling out other events in the participants' lives that may instead be causing the changes in behavior observed.

A study by Middleton and Cartledge (1995) illustrates the use of a one-group, pretest-posttest design in investigating aggression. The researchers identified five elementary school boys who, according to their teachers, displayed high levels of physical or verbal aggression (or both). They first observed and recorded the boys' physical aggression (e.g., hitting, biting, spitting) and verbal aggression (e.g., swearing, arguing, and teasing) at school. They then trained the boys in more appropriate ways of interacting with other children (the treatment). After the training, they measured aggressive behavior once again, and four of the five boys showed a decrease in aggression. This change was probably the result of the social skills training the boys received, although it is possible that other factors in the boys' lives (perhaps something their teachers had done in the meantime, perhaps simply the fact that they had gotten a bit older) may instead have been responsible.

quasi-experimental study
Research study in which one or more experimental treatments are administered but in which random assignment to groups is not possible.

Causal-Comparative Studies

In a **causal-comparative study,** a researcher identifies two or more groups of people who are *already* different with respect to certain characteristics or prior experiences; the researcher then looks at how the groups compare on some subsequent characteristics or behaviors. For example, Mansavage (1999) compared incarcerated and nonincarcerated male adolescents between the ages of 14 and 18. She found that the two groups did *not* differ on some variables, such as incidence of "bad behaviors" or experience with punishment. The two groups did differ on hostility and humor: The incarcerated adolescents showed greater hostility and less use of humor than did the adolescents who were not incarcerated. The incarcerated adolescents were also more pessimistic than were nonincarcerated adolescents. Causal-comparative studies, like quasi-experimental studies, provide helpful glimpses into conditions of life for youngsters, but they do not allow us to draw firm conclusions about cause-effect relationships. For instance, we cannot conclude that hostility, pessimism, and a poor sense of humor caused the incarcerated students to take the paths that led to their wrongdoings and convictions. Many other explanations are possible; for instance, students who became incarcerated may have had families who offered little guidance about appropriate behavior, or perhaps their families were poor, genetically inclined to be combative, or inadequately educated.

Correlational Studies

By **correlation,** we mean the extent to which two variables are related to each other, such that one variable changes when the other variable does in a somewhat predictable fashion. The direction and strength of a correlation is often summarized by a statistic known as a **correlation coefficient,** which we describe in Figure 2–1.

In a **correlational study,** investigators do not try to change anything, as they do in an experiment. Instead, they look for naturally occurring associations among characteristics, behaviors, or other variables. As an example, in a study with 9- to 12-year-olds, Grotpeter and Crick (1996) distinguished between three groups of children: those who were *relationally aggressive* (manipulating and inflicting harm on others through such tactics as gossiping, spreading rumors, and giving peers the "silent treatment"), those who were *overtly aggressive* (hitting, shoving, or physically threatening peers), and those who were not aggressive. The researchers found differences in the nature of the friendships that the various groups maintained. For instance, compared to nonaggressive children, relationally aggressive children developed more close, intimate relationships with their friends but were often jealous; for instance, when they were playing with their friends, they would not allow other children to join their activities. Overtly aggressive children were especially aggressive toward others outside their friendship circles (often partnering with their friends in such aggression), and they were more reluctant to share secrets or disclose personal information about themselves.

Correlational studies allow us to identify associations among variables; however, they do *not* allow us to draw conclusions about cause-effect relationships between those variables. For instance, the data in Grotpeter and Crick's study of relationally and overtly aggressive children provide no definitive clues as to what factors might be leading the children to behave in particular ways toward their peers.

Often, we have found our own students encountering correlations in the developmental literature and incorrectly drawing inferences about cause and effect. For instance, a well-established finding is that, on average, children with higher self-esteem perform at higher levels in school. Logically, it might seem that self-esteem should be the cause of the higher achievement (this was certainly Barb Cohen's assumption about Michael). However, the reverse might also be true (i.e., better performance in school might lead to higher self-esteem). Or, alternatively, a third factor (perhaps teacher attention and guidance, perhaps affectionate relationships with parents) might be the cause of *both* the higher self-esteem and the higher school achievement. As a general rule, *we can never draw conclusions about causation from correlational data alone.*

Cross-Sectional Studies

In a **cross-sectional study,** a researcher compares individuals of different ages. Typically, the researcher recruits participants at two or more age levels and assesses the same characteristic or behavior for each age group. For example, in a study with first- and third-grade boys,

causal-comparative study
Research study in which relationships are identified between existing conditions in children's lives and one or more aspects of the children's behavior.

correlation
Extent to which two variables are related to each other, such that when one variable increases, the other either increases or decreases in a somewhat predictable fashion.

correlation coefficient
A statistic that indicates the nature of the relationship between two variables.

correlational study
Research study that explores relationships among variables.

cross-sectional study
Research study in which the performance of individuals at different ages is compared.

Consider the following questions:

- Do children with high self-esteem perform better in school than children with low self-esteem?
- Do two different intelligence tests given at the same time yield similar scores?
- How is children's aggressiveness related to their popularity?
- Are highly aggressive children more or less likely than less-aggressive children to feel guilty about inflicting harm?

Each of these questions asks about a relationship between two variables—whether it be the relationship between self-esteem and school performance, between two sets of intelligence test scores, between aggressiveness and popularity, or between aggressiveness and the presence of a conscience. The nature of such relationships is sometimes expressed in terms of a particular number—a statistic known as a *correlation coefficient.*

A correlation coefficient is a number between −1 and +1; most correlation coefficients are decimals (either positive or negative) somewhere between these two extremes. A correlation coefficient simultaneously tells us about the direction and strength of the relationship between the two variables.

Direction of the relationship. The sign of the coefficient (+ or −) tells us whether the relationship is positive or negative. In a *positive correlation,* as one variable increases, the other variable also increases. In a *negative correlation,* as one variable increases, the other variable decreases instead. Here are several examples:

Positive correlations
- Children with higher self-esteem achieve at higher levels at school (e.g., Marsh, 1990a).
- Children tend to get similar scores on different intelligence tests, especially when the tests have similar content (e.g., McGrew, Flanagan, Zeith, & Vanderwood, 1997).

Negative correlations
- Children who are more aggressive are less popular with their peers (e.g., Coie, Dodge, Terry, & Wright, 1991).
- Children who display low levels of aggression are more likely to have a guilty conscience about their aggressive acts than are chlildren who display higher levels of aggression (e.g., Eron, 1987).

Strength of the relationship. The size of the coefficient tells us how strong the relationship is. A number close to either +1 or −1 (e.g., +.89 or −.76) indicates a *strong correlation:* The two variables are closely related, so knowing the level of one variable allows us to predict the level of the other variable with considerable accuracy. A number close to 0 (e.g., +.15 or −.22) indicates a *weak correlation:* Knowing the level of one variable allows us to predict the level of the other variable, but we cannot predict with much accuracy. Coefficients in the middle range (e.g., those in the .40s and .50s, whether positive or negative) indicate a *moderate correlation.*

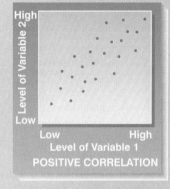

POSITIVE CORRELATION

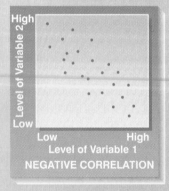

NEGATIVE CORRELATION

In the graphs above, each dot shows the degree to which a particular person shows Variables 1 and 2.

Coie and colleagues (1991) found that first graders were more likely to be targets of aggression than third graders. At both grade levels, however, boys who were more aggressive (e.g., by grabbing a toy being used by another child) were less apt to be liked by their peers.

Cross-sectional designs are frequently used to discover how children's and adolescents' thinking abilities, social skills, and other characteristics and behaviors change over time. Their major weakness is that, even though they reveal differences at different age levels, they do not necessarily indicate that age is the reason for those differences. Let's take a hypothetical example. Imagine that a researcher gives 8th-, 10th-, and 12th-grade students a questionnaire designed to measure their psychological attachment to their school (their school spirit, so to speak). The researcher finds that the students in higher grade levels respond in ways that indicate greater attachment to school. Does this mean that students become more attached to school during the high school years? Not necessarily, even if the questionnaire is a valid and reliable measure of attachment. An alternative explanation is that students with little attachment to school drop out along the way. Relatively "spiritless" students are still in school in eighth grade, but some drop out before 10th grade and others drop out before 12th grade. The age differences observed, then, are a function of which students are still in school, rather than a function of an actual increase in school attachment.

Longitudinal Studies

In a **longitudinal study,** a researcher takes one group of children or adolescents and studies them over a lengthy period of time, often for several years and sometimes even for decades.[3] An example is Eron's (1987) study of antecedents to aggression. Eron collected data about a variety of factors—family relationships, television viewing habits, attitudes about aggression, police records, and so on—potentially related to aggressive behavior. He collected data at three points in time, first when the participants in his study were in third grade, a second time 10 years later, and a third time 12 years after that. He found that aggressive behavior persisted from childhood to adulthood: Aggressive children were more likely to be aggressive adults, as manifested in such things as aggressiveness toward spouses, punitive actions toward children, and arrests for criminal behavior. Furthermore, conditions present when the participants were children (punitiveness of their own parents, tendency to watch violent television shows, apparent lack of a guilty conscience about aggressive acts) predicted their aggressiveness 10 and 22 years later.

Eron's study illustrates the two most common uses of longitudinal designs: to examine the persistence of certain characteristics, abilities, and behaviors over time; and to identify factors in children's early lives that predict their later performance. Many longitudinal studies indicate that certain aspects of early development are predictive of later tendencies and abilities. For example:

- Children's experiences in high-quality, developmentally appropriate preschools are associated with social and academic competence years later (Consortium for Longitudinal Studies, 1983; Reynolds, Mavrogenes, Bezruczko, & Hagemann, 1996; Schweinhart, Barnes, & Weikart, 1993).
- Adults tend to treat their children in the same ways their own parents treated them. For instance, they show affection and teach their children life skills similarly to how their parents did (Rossi & Rossi, 1990).

Such long-term relationships occur for a variety of reasons. Some lessons that children learn early provide the foundation for the things they learn later. In addition, genetic predispositions for temperament and talents often endure over time. Finally, some aspects of people's environments, such as financial resources and family members' behaviors, may remain relatively constant for many years.

Yet anyone who has attended a high school reunion knows that predictions about the future can be wrong. For instance, returning to our preceding example, the benefits of having attended a high-quality preschool tend to lessen over time unless students also enjoy positive school and family experiences in later years (Reynolds et al., 1996). Early progress, then, does not necessarily guarantee long-term advantages.

Conversely, children exposed to childhood stresses and adversity are not necessarily bound for a lifetime of woes. For instance, troubled children who later experience positive school experiences, receive encouragement in a harmonious family setting, and avoid deviant peer groups function better as adults and are more likely to steer clear of antisocial individuals (Rutter, Champion,

---

[3]Occasionally, a longitudinal study involves an intensive examination of children's thought processes and behaviors over a very short period of time (perhaps an hour or two). Such an approach, known as a *microgenetic design,* is most frequently used to study how children deal with, work on, and eventually master a new task.

longitudinal study
Research study in which the performance of a single group of people is tracked over a long period of time.

Quinton, Maughan, & Pickles, 1995). Similarly, girls growing up in the 1950s and 1960s who encountered such adversities as parental divorce, parental alcohol abuse, or economic hardship were more likely to have high self-esteem and good social skills if, as children, they observed their mothers coping effectively with similar problems (Moen & Erickson, 1995). In general, then, past experiences may influence later behaviors, but people continue to have new experiences and make personal choices that can either sustain them or derail them.

Naturalistic Studies

In a **naturalistic study,** a researcher examines development in natural contexts, as children and adolescents behave and interact in their families, peer groups, neighborhoods, schools, clubs, and so on. Some of these studies, known as *ethnographies,* look at the cultural norms, beliefs, social structures, and other cultural patterns of an entire group of people—perhaps a community, a classroom, or an adolescent gang. Other naturalistic studies take the form of *case studies,* wherein the researcher looks at a single child or adolescent in considerable depth over a period of time. (The latter are not to be confused with the case studies in this book, which are quite limited in scope.)

The research designs we've considered up until now typically involve considerable use of numbers (test scores, tallies of questionnaire responses, ratings of behavior, etc) and so are sometimes referred to as **quantitative research.** In contrast, many naturalistic studies rely heavily on nonnumerical aspects of people's behavior—what people do each day, how they interact with one another, what unspoken rules they follow, and so on—and may also make use of existing tools, documents, and other objects that shed light on significant aspects of the participants' world. Accordingly, most naturalistic studies fall within the domain of **qualitative research.**

Naturalistic studies vary greatly in nature, as the methods they incorporate are limited only by the researcher's imagination. However, a study by Ember and Ember (1994) can give you a flavor for the naturalistic approach. Examining records from 186 societies, the Embers found that relatively high numbers of homicides occurred in societies where parents encouraged aggression in their sons and were more hostile and less emotionally warm toward both their sons and daughters. They also drew on other researchers' descriptive accounts of particular societies. For instance, they summarized Pospisil's (1958, 1959) work with the Kapauku, who lived in the central highlands of western New Guinea. War and homicides were frequent among the Kapauku, and the Embers attributed such aggressiveness to the childhood experiences of the Kapauku:

> At about 7 years of age, a Kapauku boy begins to be under the father's control, gradually sleeping and eating only with the men and away from his mother. His father gives him a garden plot to cultivate and later a pig to raise. The father tries to train his son to be a brave warrior. His training begins when the father engages his son in mock stick fights. Gradually the fights become more serious and possibly lethal when the father and son shoot real war arrows at each other. Groups of boys play at target shooting; they also play at hitting each other over the head with sticks. Boys from neighboring villages (in the same political unit) play at war by fighting with blunt arrows and sticks. (Ember & Ember, 1994, pp. 639–640)

Although the Embers did not compare childrearing practices in North America with those of other societies, it is easy for the reader to make such a comparison. Before we conclude that we raise children more appropriately in our own societies, we should perhaps reflect on the violence and aggression we expose them to on television, in print media and movies, and in their interactions on the street.

The developmental research designs we've just described have different strengths and weaknesses. We summarize and illustrate the designs in Table 2–3.

From Research to Practice

Some developmental research studies are conducted primarily to identify effective strategies for enhancing children's and adolescents' development, and such studies clearly have relevance for practicing teachers. In contrast, other studies are conducted primarily to either overhaul or fine-tune theoretical explanations of the nature and processes of human development. Yet these studies, too, are of value to teachers, in that they advance our understanding of how and

naturalistic study
Research study in which individuals are observed in their natural environment.

quantitative research
Research study in which the data collected are predominantly numerical.

qualitative research
Research study in which the data collected are largely nonnumerical.

TABLE 2–3 Developmental Research Designs

DESIGN	ADVANTAGES AND DISADVANTAGES	EXAMPLE IN A SCHOOL SETTING
Experiment	• Well-designed experiments enable researchers to be relatively confident that a particular intervention is the cause of changes in thinking or behavior. • The tight controls required for firm conclusions about cause-effect relationships may lead to experimental conditions that do not resemble, and so may not generalize to, real-world settings.	A school district is unsure which of two textbook series is more effective for teaching scientific reasoning skills in its 10 elementary schools. It gives copies of one series to 5 schools and copies of the other series to the other 5 schools, with the schools using each series being chosen randomly. At the end of the school year, it administers a test of scientific reasoning skills to students at all 10 schools and compares the average scores of students using the two series.
Quasi-Experiment	• Quasi-experiments provide an alternative when true experiments are not possible, practical, or ethical. • Because other possible explanations for observed changes cannot be ruled out, conclusions about cause-effect relationships are speculative at best.	A middle school implements a new drug-use prevention program and compares students' knowledge and beliefs about drugs both before and after participation in the program.
Causal-Comparative Study	• Causal-comparative studies provide a second alternative when true experiments are not possible. • Observed differences among groups cannot be traced to the particular factor being investigated.	A teacher looks at the average grades for two sets of students, those who qualify for the free lunch program and those who do not. The teacher finds that the lower-income students (those eligible for free lunch) have lower grades than the higher-income students.
Correlational Study	• Correlational studies are relatively inexpensive to conduct and can yield a large body of data regarding relationships among variables. • Cause-effect relationships cannot be determined from correlations alone.	A high school teacher gives students a questionnaire that assesses their attitudes toward mathematics and then looks at the relationship between their responses to the questionnaire and the number of elective math courses in which they enroll.
Cross-Sectional Study	• Cross-sectional designs offer an efficient snapshot of how characteristics or behaviors probably change with age. • Age differences can be explained in a variety of ways, including physiological maturation, exposure to different schooling experiences, and important historical events.	The district coordinator of physical education compares 4th-, 7th-, and 10th-grade students' opinions about incorporating step aerobics activities into the school district's physical education curriculum.
Longitudinal Study	• Longitudinal studies demonstrate how individuals change as they grow older; they also allow prediction of later characteristics and behaviors from earlier characteristics and experiences. • Longitudinal studies are very expensive and time-consuming, and it is difficult to maintain a sizable sample of research participants over the duration of the study (people move, lose interest in the research, etc.).	An elementary school art teacher studies the progress students make in their painting and drawing skills from kindergarten through fifth grade.
Naturalistic Study	• Naturalistic studies capture the complexities and subtle nuances of children's environments and experiences. • Naturalistic studies are difficult and time-consuming to conduct, as they generally take a long time and involve extended, in-depth data collection.	An elementary teacher conducts a series of observations on the playground to investigate how her students respond to and interact with children who have various kinds of disabilities.

under what conditions development occurs and so suggest additional strategies for working with students.

How Research Can Help Classroom Teachers

Developmental research and the theories it advances can help teachers in several ways, all of which contribute either directly or indirectly to more effective teaching practice:

■ *Research illuminates effective and ineffective teaching practice.* Researchers routinely investigate how children and adolescents respond to different kinds of educational methods and programs. For example, researchers have examined a variety of methods aimed at helping children better understand the information they encounter in textbooks and classroom lessons (Palincsar & Brown, 1984; Paris & Jacobs, 1984; Pressley, Goodchild, Fleet, Zajchowski, & Evans, 1989). Some methods bring about dramatic improvements, but others are less effective, despite teachers' best efforts in using them.

■ *Research findings can either verify or disconfirm existing beliefs about children and adolescents.* Historically, research has contradicted many prevailing beliefs held by scientists, teachers, and parents. For example, young infants were once thought to have perceptual abilities so limited that they experienced only a "buzzing, blooming confusion" (James, 1890/1950). However, psychologists now know that some aspects of perception are quite sharp almost from birth; for instance, infants can discriminate their mothers from other women within the first few days of life (Field, Woodson, Greenberg, & Cohen, 1982; Johnson & Morton, 1991). As another example, young children were once described as being egocentric, trapped in their own ways of thinking and unable to decipher others' needs (Piaget, 1926). Today we realize that even preschool-aged children adjust their speech and other behaviors to the age and characteristics of their conversational partners (McDevitt & Ford, 1987; Shatz & Gelman, 1973). Adolescents, once believed by many to undergo an inevitable period of stress, turmoil, and rebellion (Hall, 1904), in reality more often show acceptance of parents' values and the particular practices and expectations of their culture (Mead, 1935; Sebald, 1986).

Even today, myths about children and adolescents abound. Such myths appear in the forms of newspaper articles ("Boys have higher aptitude for mathematics than girls"), assumptions of parents ("My third grader is reading at a sixth-grade level; shouldn't you at least move her up to fourth grade?"), and talk in the teachers' lounge ("Science is just too abstract for young children"). As we write this book, one myth getting widespread publicity is the idea that a child's brain develops only until about age 3, at which point it is relatively "hard-wired" and so has limited ability to change and improve. Some activists have used this idea to argue that substantial federal funds should be allocated to daycare centers and preschools, which can then provide intensive, enriching experiences for infants and young children. Although we certainly support the call for high-quality daycare and preschool environments, we find little data in the research to support the notion that children have a window of opportunity in the early years that slams shut at age 3 (e.g., see Bruer, 1999). (We look at brain development more closely in Chapter 3.)

Teachers must remember that the foundations of research that support claims about children and adolescents are uneven: Some are solid, some are shaky, some are nonexistent. Tread gingerly! Carefully scrutinizing and analyzing research enables teachers to separate the wheat from the chaff—the strong from the weak—in the claims they encounter.

■ *Research promotes new ways of thinking about children and their development.* Research results often encourage teachers to think about developmental issues they have not previously considered. For example, some teachers may not initially realize that they need to revise their assumptions about children's learning when they work with students from diverse cultures. Students from different cultures sometimes encounter obstacles in school because they communicate, behave, and learn in ways that their teachers don't understand. Unless teachers discover and think about the culturally specific communication patterns, work habits, and approaches to problem solving of their students, they may erroneously and unfairly conclude that these students are simply unable or unmotivated to achieve academic success (Gay, 1993).

As teachers-in-training visit schools to conduct observations and perhaps get their feet wet by teaching short lessons, they see many teachers—some highly effective, some less so—in action. Later, as they begin a year or semester in an internship or student teaching experience

Neurological and psychological research studies refute the popular idea that the brain develops primarily during the first 3 years of life and that opportunities for learning have their greatest impact during this period. In fact, the brain continues to develop throughout childhood and adolescence, and students of all ages can easily acquire new knowledge and skills.

and assume the role of full-time teacher, they typically emulate strategies they have seen more experienced teachers using. Yet experienced teachers, as skillful as they might be, illuminate only what teaching practice *is* at present. In contrast, advances in developmental research shine light on what teaching practice *could be* (e.g., Wong Fillmore, 1993). In other words, research points to avenues for possible educational reform.

■ *Research engenders optimism about making a difference in the lives of children and adolescents.* It is all too easy to blame students themselves (e.g., they are "dumb," "lazy," or "obnoxious") for their difficulties in learning and interacting in the classroom. Yet innumerable studies have demonstrated that, under the right conditions, the great majority of children and adolescents *do* want to be successful in their academic and social pursuits. When, by reading the research literature, teachers become aware of the complex factors that influence children—developmental levels, background experiences, individual talents and temperaments, family dynamics, cultural patterns, and so on—they discover how, and also *how much,* they can make a difference in their students' lives (Weinstein et al., 1995).

■ *Research reports provide a model of critical analysis.* Earlier in the chapter we mentioned the importance of critical analysis in evaluating research studies. Good researchers engage in critical analysis of their *own* hypotheses, data collection methods, research design, and theoretical interpretations, and they describe their line of reasoning when they publish their findings and conclusions. For instance, if researchers believe that violence on television causes children to become more aggressive, then they must explain why they hypothesize this to be true, identify appropriate methods of documenting the relationship, and determine reasonable guidelines for deciding whether their data are sufficiently compelling to support their hypothesis.

Nevertheless, researchers are only human and have difficulty evaluating their own work with a completely objective eye. So it behooves the rest of us to carefully scrutinize and critically analyze the work that they have done.

Critically Analyzing Research Studies

As you read this chapter, you may be studying the nature of research in child and adolescent development for the very first time. Nevertheless, if you ask yourself a few simple questions when you read the research literature, you can analyze research studies in much the same way experts do. Following are several questions to keep in mind:

■ *Do the data have high validity for the purpose of the research?* The data collected should provide reasonable indicators or measures of the characteristics or behaviors under investigation. No data collection method is perfect, of course. Table 2–4 revisits the three methods of data collection we've previously examined—self-reports, tests, and observations—and identifies possible distortions in each that can affect the validity of the results.

■ *Do the data have high reliability?* The data should have been influenced only minimally by temporary characteristics and other chance factors affecting participants' performance. Reliability is especially an issue with research involving young children, whose limited language skills, short attention spans, and relative inexperience with schoollike tasks and tests may lead to considerable variation in performance from one day to the next.

■ *Does the research design warrant the conclusions drawn?* Experimental studies often enable researchers to draw conclusions about cause-effect relationships, but other designs rarely do. Whenever you read a research report, ask yourself this question: *Have the researchers considered and justifiably eliminated other reasonable explanations for their results?*

■ *How substantial and compelling are the results?* Sometimes researchers find major differences between groups or dramatic effects of particular methods. For example, in a classic study by Palincsar and Brown (1984), six seventh-grade students with poor reading comprehension skills participated in twenty 30-minute sessions involving *reciprocal teaching,* a procedure whereby students learn to ask themselves and one another thought-provoking questions about what they read. Despite this relatively short intervention, the students showed remarkable improvement in their reading comprehension skills, sometimes even surpassing the performance of their classmates (Brown & Palincsar, 1987; Palincsar & Brown, 1984). The effectiveness of reciprocal teaching has

TABLE 2–4 Distortions of Information Collected from Children and Adolescents

SOURCE OF INFORMATION	POSSIBLE DISTORTION	EXAMPLE	IMPLICATION FOR TEACHERS
Self-Reports (Interviews and Questionnaires)	Memory of research participants	In a study of students' informal experiences with science at home, a second grader forgets about his family's frequent trips to the local natural history museum.	When soliciting information from students (perhaps about their life experiences or their understandings of subject matter), describe exactly what kind of information you are seeking.
	Interpretations by research participants	When asked if she has encountered any sexual harassment at her school, a teenager focuses only on unwanted physical contacts and does not share the researcher's more general definition, which also includes verbal harassment.	When asking students for their opinions and experiences, define your terms carefully.
	Defensiveness of research participants	In an anonymous survey, a middle school student prefers not to admit that she has experimented with marijuana.	Respect students' right to privacy, but recognize that students may not always be honest with you about sensitive issues.
Tests	Response style of research participants	Students rush through a test, responding quickly and not very carefully, so that they can have a longer recess.	Encourage students to work carefully and thoroughly on tests, and give them reasons and incentives for performing at their best.
	Cultural bias in test content	Some students taking a mathematics ability test have difficulty with two questions—one asking them to calculate the perimeter of a football field and another asking them to calculate the area of a baseball diamond—because they have little familiarity with these sports.	Carefully screen test content and eliminate any items that may either penalize or offend students from particular backgrounds.
	Participants' familiarity with test format	Some students in a third-grade class have never taken tests involving a matching-item format and so skip all items using this format.	Give students ample practice with the test formats you will be using.
Observations	Bias of observers	In a study of gender differences in sharing behavior, an observer expects that girls share their possessions more often than boys and so is more apt to notice such actions in girls.	Think about your own biases about students and how they may color what you "see."
	Attention limitations of observers	In a study of nonverbal communication in high school students, a researcher misses a third of the smiles, gestures, winks, and other subtle communication behaviors that the students display.	Keep in mind that you can take in only a limited amount of information in the classroom at any given period of time.
	Effects of the observer's presence	During a researcher's observations of an after-school science club, middle schoolers are unusually quiet, attentive, businesslike, and on task.	Be alert to ways that students might change their behavior when they know that you are watching.

Source: Distortions identified by Hartmann & George, 1999.

subsequently been documented in numerous other studies, and so we will revisit this technique in our discussion of literacy development in Chapter 8.

At other times, researchers report differences or effects that are probably too small to worry about. For instance, as you will discover in Chapter 6, many studies have found gender differences in verbal ability (a difference favoring females) and visual-spatial thinking (a difference favoring males). However, the differences are fairly small and are based only on group averages, so they tell us little if anything about how *individual children* are likely to perform on verbal and visual-spatial tasks. In fact, many boys have exceptional verbal ability, and many girls are excellent visual-spatial thinkers.

Keep in mind, too, that our knowledge base about children is fallible and ever-changing. The new research findings that appear each year sometimes support what we have previously thought to be true and sometimes call into question our earlier conclusions. Ideally, we must look for consistent patterns across many studies and not rely too heavily on the results of any single study.

■ *How might the researchers' biases have influenced their data collection, analyses, and interpretations?* Much as researchers strive to be objective and impartial in their work, their methods and interpretations are often influenced by their own biases and expectations. For example, researchers are more likely to publish research findings that support, rather than contradict, their beliefs and hypotheses. Unless a researcher is exceptionally open-minded, those contradictory results are likely to end up buried in the bottom drawer of a file cabinet, or perhaps even "filed" in a wastebasket or recycling bin.

Furthermore, just as many developmental studies have used predominantly White, middle-class samples (see the earlier section on "Sampling and Recruitment"), so, too, have the researchers been predominantly White, middle-class and, until recently, male. The unique perspectives of ethnic minority groups, members of alternative cultural groups, and women have been underrepresented in psychology and other disciplines (Bohan, 1995). Fortunately, cross-cultural perspectives on the development of children and adolescents are increasingly available. We will highlight many of them throughout the book as we summarize evidence on particular topics. Nonetheless, we invite you to remain vigilant to cultural gaps in the literature and the necessity of adapting instruction to the particular backgrounds of your students.

■ *Do the conclusions seem reasonable in light of your own experiences with children?* Sometimes well-meaning researchers and theorists offer advice that flies in the face of what common sense tells us is reasonable and appropriate. For example, John Watson, a trailblazing and influential psychologist in the early 20th century, warned mothers about the perils of excessive "mother love" and advised them not to "hug or kiss" their children or "let them sit in your lap" (Watson, 1928, pp. 81, 87). His ideas about parenting are questionable today, yet he touted his position with vigor to a generation of parents and nursery school teachers. Similarly, Arnold Gesell, a psychologist best known for his maturationist view of physical development (e.g., 1923, 1929), operated a nursery school in which he modeled rigorous methods of "habit training" for parents and asked them to adjust their childrearing routines to comply with regimented procedures (Beatty, 1996). Years later, some of these mothers expressed regret about following the advice of such "experts."

Furthermore, some educational practices are derived from a consideration of research in some areas but ignore findings in other areas. For example, having children who are making slower-than-average progress repeat a particular grade level makes some educational sense if we look at the problem from the standpoint of cognitive development only. If Justin repeats first grade, the assumption goes, he'll get a chance to "catch up." In fact, recent research findings have unveiled many negative social and emotional consequences associated with not allowing students to move from one grade to the next with their peers (Shephard & Smith, 1987, 1989; Watson, 1996).

■ *Are the results generalizable to the students with whom you will be working?* Fortunately, researchers typically describe the specific characteristics (e.g., age, gender, ethnicity, family income level) of the participants in their studies. If their samples are different in important ways from your own students, then you should be cautious in your use of their results. Following are some examples of questions you might ask yourself:

• A researcher finds a relationship between middle-class parents' disciplinary strategies and their children's social skills. Would a similar relationship also exist in families living in extreme economic poverty?

- A researcher finds a relationship between how openly fathers express their emotions and their children's skill in resolving conflicts with their peers. Would this relationship apply to children who do not live full-time with their fathers?
- A researcher reports results obtained for Hispanic children who are fluent in both Spanish and English. Are the results likely to apply to Hispanic children who speak only Spanish or only English?
- A researcher finds that a particular method of teaching science is highly effective with bright, highly motivated children who attend a university laboratory school. Would the same method be effective with average-ability students in a traditional public school?

Ultimately, teachers must keep their own students in mind as they consider which research findings are applicable and potentially useful in their classrooms.

The critical habits of mind we encourage you to develop about research are also relevant to your own thinking and decision making in the classroom. Good research methods and critical analysis are not just activities for professors and college students; they can also shed light on the daily dilemmas of practicing teachers. The questions researchers raise about the validity of measurement instruments are just as important in classroom teaching as they are in scholarly research. (For example, when you read the opening case study, did you wonder whether a frowning self-portrait was *really* an indication of low self-esteem?) The questions researchers raise about causal relationships between variables are of as much interest to teachers as they are to theorists. (For example, did you wonder what was at the root of Michael's adjustment difficulties in kindergarten?) In the final section of the chapter, we consider how teachers can apply common principles and practices of research in classroom settings.

Gathering Information in the Classroom

As you have seen, academic researchers work diligently to collect information about children and adolescents in a way that is sensitive, ethical, valid, and reliable. Teachers do the same. In this section, we consider two types of inquiry that classroom teachers conduct. We first look at teachers' everyday attempts to interpret, or "read," the behaviors of their students. We then describe how teachers join ranks with academic researchers by occasionally conducting systematic research in their own classrooms and schools. We conclude the chapter by offering ethical guidelines for classroom data collection.

Learning to "Read" Children and Adolescents

Teachers do their jobs more effectively when they can accurately determine what their students think, believe, know, and can do. To do so, teachers need to observe their students carefully and correctly interpret students' behaviors. In other words, they need to "read" their students (Hunt, 1981).

Teachers use many strategies to read their students (Pinnegar, 1988). They look at facial expressions and body language for signs of comprehension, insight, engagement, or boredom. They watch closely during laboratory activities, cooperative groups, and independent seatwork to see if students understand instructions and assignments. They examine students' work, listen to their discussions in class, and consider the questions they ask, all the while trying to determine not only *if* the students are learning but also *what* they are learning (Heuwinkel, 1998; Wilson, Shulman, & Richert, 1987).

Throughout the book you will find Observation Guidelines tables that can help you read children and adolescents more effectively. The first of these, which follows, suggests some general behaviors to look for. We also offer the following recommendations:

■ *Learn from experienced teachers.* Becoming a skilled "reader" of children and adolescents does not happen automatically. Beginning teachers can learn a lot by asking more experienced colleagues to provide insights about students' learning and performance. Whenever you have an opportunity to visit other teachers' classrooms, listen to what they say about their students, both as individuals and as a group. Watch how they combine what they've learned from past experience with their analyses of students' current behavior in particular activities. What do

"Reading" Students' Behaviors

OBSERVATION GUIDELINES

CHARACTERISTIC	LOOK FOR	EXAMPLE	IMPLICATION
Activity Level	• Activity level appropriate to the assigned task (might indicate motivation to do well and an understanding of the assigned task) • Hyperactivity (might indicate boredom, frustration, anxiety or, in some cases, a disability) • Listlessness (might indicate boredom, fatigue, or poor nutrition) • Requesting or volunteering for additional work (probably indicates high motivation)	Molly seems to fly off the handle whenever she encounters a problem she cannot solve easily.	Determine the probable source of students' inappropriate activity levels. Make sure assigned tasks are geared for each student's knowledge, abilities, and areas of interest. Follow up with listless students, to see if they are getting adequate meals and sleep. When a particular student is chronically hyperactive or underactive, consult with the school counselor or psychologist about possible undiagnosed disabilities.
Body Language	• Facial expressions (reflecting enjoyment, excitement, sadness, confusion, anger, or frustration) • Tenseness of limbs (might indicate intense concentration or excessive anxiety) • Slouching in seat (might indicate fatigue, boredom, or resistance to an activity) • Head on desk (might indicate intense concentration, boredom, depression, or fatigue)	Whenever his teacher engages the class in a discussion of controversial issues, Jamal participates eagerly. When she goes over the previous night's homework, however, he crosses his arms, slouches low in his seat, pulls his hat low over his eyes, and says nothing.	Use students' body language as a rough gauge of a lesson's effectiveness, and modify activities that do not appear to be engaging students' attention and interest. Speak individually and confidentially with students who often show signs of sadness or anger, and if necessary seek a school counselor's assistance.
On-Task and Off-Task Behaviors	• Ability to work well on independent assignments and in group activities (probably indicates high motivation to learn and achieve) • Frequent chattering or horseplay with classmates (might indicate low motivation to learn, lack of confidence about an assigned task, or a strong need for social interaction with peers) • Focus on irrelevant, and perhaps meaningless, activities (might indicate boredom or lack of confidence about performing a task) • Daydreaming (might indicate unwillingness or inability to complete an assigned task; might also indicate creative thinking about a task)	During a cooperative group activity, three members of a group are actively planning the group's upcoming oral presentation. Nathan, the fourth group member, doesn't participate in the discussion; instead, he fiddles with a paperclip he has found on the floor.	Identify the specific reason(s) for students' off-task behaviors, and modify lessons and assignments to be appropriate for individual students' ability levels and needs. Incorporate opportunities for social interaction throughout the school day.

(continued)

they learn from students' verbal statements? from their nonverbal actions? Are their interpretations and conclusions similar to, or different from, your own? Why might you have reached different conclusions than they have? Although the people you are observing have more experience than you do, they won't necessarily always be right!

■ *Develop your interviewing skills.* Too often, conversations between teachers and students are short, ask-a-question-and-get-an-answer exchanges. Lengthier dialogues, perhaps with an individual student or a small group of students, are far more informative. To find out what students think, believe, know, and misunderstand, teachers must not only encourage their students to talk

OBSERVATION GUIDELINES

CHARACTERISTIC	LOOK FOR	EXAMPLE	IMPLICATION
Questions and Comments	• Asking thoughtful and insightful questions about the topic at hand (indicates high task engagement and motivation) • Asking questions that have already been answered (might indicate inattentiveness or lack of understanding) • Complaining about the difficulty of an assignment (might indicate low motivation, lack of ability or confidence, or an overloaded schedule of academic and social obligations)	In a whining tone, Danusia asks, "Do we really have to include *three* arguments in our persuasive essays? I've been thinking really hard and can only come up with one!"	Read between the lines in the questions students ask and the comments they make. Consider what their questions and comments indicate about their existing knowledge, skills, motivation, and self-confidence.
Students' Work	• Careful and thorough work (indicates high motivation) • Unusual and creative ideas, artwork, or constructions (indicates high motivation and a willingness to take risks) • Numerous sloppy errors (might indicate that a student did an assignment hurriedly, has poor proofreading skills, or has a learning disability)	When Martin's social studies teacher gives several options for how students might illustrate the idea of *democracy,* Martin creates a large poster of colorful, cartoon-like characters engaging in such activities as voting, free speech, and making new laws.	When looking at and evaluating students' work, don't focus exclusively on "right" and "wrong" answers. When assessing diverse abilities (e.g., accuracy, neatness, creativity), however, do not combine them into a single "grade" for an assignment; such a grade would be meaningless and impossible to interpret.

but also follow up with probing questions and frequent reassurances that students' ideas and opinions are important and valued. Pramling (1996) urges teachers

> to become skilled at letting the children expose their ideas and also at getting the children to feel that they want to share their ideas with the teacher and the other children. Children must feel it is enjoyable to express themselves and to be thrilled by others' ideas. To achieve this means that both the teacher and the children must learn to communicate on equal terms and to share their experiences. (p. 570)

■ *Keep in mind both the advantages and limitations of paper-pencil tests.* Paper-pencil tests are often a quick and efficient way of determining what students have and have not learned. Furthermore, a well-designed test—perhaps one that probes students' reasoning and problem-solving skills—can reveal a great deal about students' thinking processes. Yet appraisals of students that rely exclusively on quiz and test scores often paint a lopsided picture of students' abilities. For instance, students who have limited reading and writing skills (perhaps because they have a learning disability, or perhaps because they have only recently begun to learn English) are likely to perform poorly. Furthermore, paper-pencil tests, by their very nature, cannot provide certain kinds of information. For instance, they tell us little if anything about students' self-confidence, motor skills, ability to work with others, or expertise at using equipment.

■ *Seize opportunities to observe children and adolescents.* Effective teachers watch students in a variety of contexts, not only in the classroom, but also in the cafeteria, on the playground, on field trips, during extracurricular activities, and with parents at parent-teacher conferences and school open houses. As you observe children and adolescents in such settings, ask yourself what they are doing, why they might be behaving this way (always consider and contrast several possible explanations!), and how they might be interpreting the events in which they participate. Shift your attention from individual students to group dynamics and then back again, as you are likely to learn different things from different levels of analysis.

■ *Continually question the validity and reliability of the information you collect.* Validity and reliability are, and *must be*, ongoing concerns not only for researchers but for teachers as well. Teachers must have some assurance that the data they gather about students and the conclusions they reach from those data are accurate and dependable.

Earlier we mentioned that virtually any method of obtaining data about children and adolescents has its weaknesses. If you look back at Table 2–4, you will find several suggestions for how teachers can minimize the influences of distortions in data collection.

■ *Always, always use multiple sources of information.* Because no single source of data ever has "perfect" validity and reliability, effective teachers use many sources of information—self-reports, tests, observations, homework, in-class creations, and anything else that might be of value—to understand and draw conclusions about their students' abilities and accomplishments.

■ *Reflect on how your beliefs and assumptions about students and their learning might influence your conclusions.* At the beginning of the chapter, we explored common beliefs about children and education. We also considered some of the metaphors that teachers might use to capture the nature of children and roles of a teacher. Such beliefs and metaphors are likely to influence how you interpret students' classroom performance and behavior. For example, if you think of a teacher as an "entertainer," you may be inclined to focus on students' enthusiasm. If you think of a teacher as a "drill sergeant," you will be more apt to look at whether students are complying with instructions and classroom rules. Try to change your focus over time—perhaps using particular metaphors as "lenses"—to learn from the various types of clues that students either intentionally or unintentionally provide. Be particularly alert to clues from students whose backgrounds are different from your own, as you are less likely to be accurate in interpreting their behavior.

As teachers gain experience, they become better able to "read" students—that is, to draw inferences about students' knowledge, beliefs, and abilities from what students do and say. Teachers must remember, however, that no single behavior is likely to be a valid and reliable reflection of what students can and cannot do.

■ *Form multiple hypotheses.* In your efforts to read children and adolescents, never be content with a single interpretation, no matter how obvious that interpretation might seem to you (remember Barb Cohen's hasty conclusion that Michael had a self-esteem problem). Always consider multiple possible explanations for the behaviors you observe and resist the temptation to settle on one of them as being "correct" until you've had a chance to eliminate other possibilities. In essence, try to behave as a researcher would: Hold your opinions in abeyance until the data are fairly compelling.

As an all-too-common example, imagine that you have begun working as a teacher in an inner-city school. Many of your students live with only one of their parents (or perhaps instead with an aunt or grandparent), and almost all of them come from low-income families. From day one, your students are unruly and difficult to control, so you spend most of your time trying to discipline them and rarely accomplish anything of an academic nature. "These students just don't care," you think to yourself. But is this really a motivation problem? What are some other possible explanations? Is the material you are trying to present too difficult for them? too easy? not relevant to their interests and needs? Have their previous classroom experiences been boring? esteem-deflating? an apparent waste of time? You must also ask yourself what *you* might do to get students engaged in learning and constructive behavior. So many questions, so many hypotheses and, obviously, so much more data to be collected!

Conducting Research as a Teacher

The research literature on children's thinking, development, and learning grows by leaps and bounds every year. Nevertheless, teachers sometimes encounter problems in the classroom that the existing research literature doesn't address. In such circumstances, they have an alternative: They can conduct their own research. When teachers conduct systematic studies of issues and problems in their own schools, with the goal of seeking more effective interventions in the lives of children, they are conducting **action research.**

Teacher research is becoming an increasingly popular endeavor among teachers, educational administrators, and other educational professionals. Such research takes numerous forms; for example, it might involve assessing the effectiveness of a new teaching technique, gathering information about students' opinions on a schoolwide issue, or conducting an in-depth case study of

action research
Systematic study of an issue or problem in one's own situation, with the goal of bringing about more productive outcomes as a result of the research.

a particular student (Cochran-Smith & Lytle, 1993; Mills, 2000). But any action research study typically involves the following four steps (Mills, 2000):

1. *Identify an area of focus.* The teacher-researcher begins with a problem and gathers some preliminary information that might shed light on the problem. Usually this involves perusing the literature for investigations of related problems and perhaps also surfing the Internet or conducting informal interviews of colleagues or students. The teacher-researcher then identifies one or more questions related to the problem and develops a research plan (data collection techniques, necessary resources, schedule, etc.) for answering those questions. At this point, any needed permissions from school administrators and review boards are obtained.

2. *Collect data.* The teacher-researcher collects data relevant to the research questions. Such data might, for example, be obtained from questionnaires, interviews, achievement tests, students' journals or portfolios, existing school records (e.g., attendance patterns, rates of referral for discipline problems), or observations. Many times, the teacher-researcher uses two or more of these sources to answer the research questions from various angles.

3. *Analyze and interpret the data.* The teacher-researcher looks for patterns in the data. Sometimes the analysis involves computing particular statistics (e.g., percentages, means, correlation coefficients); at other times, it involves an in-depth, nonnumerical inspection of the data. In either case, the teacher-researcher relates the patterns observed to the original research questions.

4. *Develop an action plan.* The final step distinguishes action research from the more traditional research studies we considered earlier: The teacher-researcher uses the information collected to *take action*—for instance, to change instructional strategies, school policies, or the classroom environment.

A good example of action research is a case study conducted by Michele Sims (1993). Initially concerned with why middle school students of average intelligence struggle to comprehend classroom material, Sims began to focus on one of her students, a quiet boy named Ricardo. She tapped a diverse array of data sources, including interviews with Ricardo, conversations with other teachers, dialogues with university faculty, her own journal reflections, and her notes of Ricardo's work. The more she learned, the better she understood who Ricardo was as an individual and how she could better foster his learning and development. She also became increasingly aware of how often she and her fellow teachers overlooked the needs of quiet students:

> We made assumptions that the quiet students weren't in as much need. My colleague phrased it well when she said, "In our minds we'd say to ourselves—'that child will be all right until we get back to him.' " But we both wanted desperately for these children to do more than just survive. (Sims, 1993, p. 288)

Action research is a powerful tool, and we urge our readers to pursue opportunities (whether in their teacher preparation programs or in later coursework or in-services) to learn more about it. Research conducted by teachers provides a forum for solving problems, broadening and deepening perspectives on real-life issues of teaching and learning, creating alliances, fostering a community spirit among teachers, drawing attention to the legitimacy of teachers' knowledge and practice, and transforming schools to promote social justice (Noffke, 1997). The Development and Practice feature on the next page offers some suggestions on steps teachers can take to get their feet wet in action research.

Ethical Guidelines for Classroom Data Collection

Whether teachers are informally "reading" their students or more formally collecting data for action research, they must behave in ways that protect students, their families, and professional colleagues. We recommend that you learn as much as possible in your teacher preparation program about your legal and ethical responsibilities in the classroom. In addition, we offer the following guidelines:

■ *Collect multiple sources of information, and be tentative in your conclusions.* Never put too much weight on any single piece of information (remember Barb Cohen's conclusion, based on a single self-portrait, that Michael had low self-esteem). Instead, collect a variety of data—writing samples, test scores, projects, informal observations of behavior, and so on—and look for general trends. Even so, be cautious in the conclusions you draw and consider multiple hy-

GETTING A FLAVOR FOR ACTION RESEARCH

■ Keep a journal of your observations and reflections in the classroom.

A high school English teacher keeps a daily log of students' comments and insights about the novels students are reading.

■ Talk with other teachers about what you are observing and hypothesizing.

A kindergarten teacher and physical education teacher discuss their mutual belief that students' intellectual development and physical development are related, and they decide to do more systematic observations to refine their hypothesis.

■ Collect information and write about students you seem unable to reach.

A middle school teacher keeps a journal of her observations of students who sit in the back of the room and appear to be mentally "tuned out." After a few weeks, she begins to form hypotheses about strategies that might capture the interest and attention of these students.

■ Conduct informal research on topics of social justice.

A high school teacher examines his school's data on enrollment in science courses, asks other teachers for possible explanations for why so few girls enroll in chemistry and physics, and offers recommendations for making these courses more "girl-friendly."

potheses to explain the patterns you see. And when sharing your perceptions of students' talents and abilities with parents, acknowledge that these are your *interpretations*, based on the data you have available, rather than irrefutable facts.

■ *Do not administer tests or research instruments that require special training*. Many instruments, especially psychological assessments and standardized achievement tests, must be administered and interpreted by individuals trained in their use. In untrained hands, they yield results that are highly suspect and, in some cases, potentially harmful.

■ *Be sensitive to students' perspectives*. Students are apt to notice any unusual attention you give them, either individually or collectively. For instance, when Michele Sims was collecting data about Ricardo, she made the following observation:

> I'm making a conscious effort to collect as much of Ricardo's work as possible. It's difficult. I think this shift in the kind of attention I'm paying to him has him somewhat rattled. I sense he has mixed feelings about this. He seems to enjoy the conversations we have, but when it comes to collecting his work, he may feel that he's being put under a microscope. Maybe he's become quite accustomed to a type of invisibility. (Sims, 1993, p. 285)

When data collection makes students feel so self-conscious that their performance is impaired, a teacher must seriously consider whether the information collected outweighs possible detrimental effects.

■ *Keep your principal informed of your research initiatives*. Principals are ultimately responsible for their teachers' actions in the classroom. Furthermore, they are knowledgeable about school district policies on classroom research.

■ *Maintain students' confidentiality at all costs*. Teachers often share results of their research with colleagues in their building or school district. Some also make their findings known to an audience beyond their own school walls; for instance, they may make presentations at regional or national conferences, post their findings on a Website, or write journal articles describing what they have learned and how such knowledge has changed their teaching practice. Yet teachers must certainly not broadcast their research findings in ways that violate students' anonymity. Protecting students' rights must be the highest priority at all times.

Knowledge about effective teaching comes from a variety of sources—not only from research and theories about development and learning, but also from teachers' own experiences as students, insights and intuitions, observations of other teachers, policy statements of school systems and governmental agencies, and personal moral codes. None of these is adequate in and of itself; all are more potent and effective when combined with other sources. Effective teachers draw from as many resources as possible when deciding how best to meet the needs of their students.

If you had to extract one theme from this chapter, we hope that you might settle on "critical analysis." When researchers and teachers apply critical analysis in their thinking, they carefully scrutinize their assumptions, wonder how they can frame their questions, brainstorm about possible methods by which they can obtain relevant information and, at every step of the way, consider numerous possible ways to accomplish their goals.

CASE STUDY: THE STUDY SKILLS CLASS

In spring semester, Deborah South is asked to teach study skills to a class of 20 low-achieving and seemingly unmotivated eighth graders. Later she describes a problem she encountered and her attempt to understand the problem through action research:

My task was to somehow take these students and miraculously make them motivated, achieving students. I was trained in a study skills program before the term started and thought that I was set to go. . . .

Within a week, I sensed we were in trouble. My twenty students often showed up with no supplies. Their behavior was atrocious. They called each other names, threw various items around the room, and walked around the classroom when they felt like it. . . .

Given this situation, I decided to do some reading about how other teachers motivate unmotivated students and to formulate some ideas about the variables that contribute to a student's success in school. Variables I investigated included adult approval, peer influence, and success in math, science, language arts, and social studies, as well as self-esteem and students' views of their academic abilities.

The majority of the data I collected was through surveys, interviews, and report card/attendance records in an effort to answer the following questions:

- How does attendance affect student performance?
- How are students influenced by their friends in completing schoolwork?
- How do adults (parents, teachers) affect the success of students?
- What levels of self-esteem do these students have?

As a result of the investigation, I learned many things. For example, for this group of students attendance does not appear to be a factor—with the exception of one student, they all come to school regularly. Not surprisingly, peer groups did affect student performance. Seventy-three percent of my students reported that their friends never encouraged doing homework or putting any effort into homework.

Another surprising result was the lack of impact of a teacher's approval on student achievement. Ninety-four percent of my students indicated that they never or seldom do their homework to receive teacher approval. Alternatively, 57 percent indicated that they often or always do their homework so that their families will be proud of them.

One of the most interesting things that arose during my study was the realization that most of my students misbehave out of frustration at their own lack of abilities. They are not being obnoxious to gain attention, but to draw attention away from the fact that they do not know how to complete the assigned work.

When I looked at report cards and compared grades over three quarters, I noticed a trend. Between the first and second quarter, student performance had increased. That is, most students were doing better than they had during the first quarter. Between the second and third quarters, however, grades dropped dramatically. I tried to determine why that drop would occur, and the only common experience shared by these twenty students was the fact that they had been moved into my class at the beginning of the third quarter. . . .

I was convinced that the "cause" of the students' unmotivated behavior was my teaching.

From "What Motivates Unmotivated Students," by D. South. In *Action Research: A Guide for the Teacher Researcher* (pp. 2–3), by G. Mills, 2000, Upper Saddle River, NJ: Merrill/Prentice Hall. Reprinted with permission of the author.

- What methods did Deborah use to collect her data? What were the potential strengths and limitations of each method?
- Deborah concluded that her own teaching led to the dramatic drop in grades from the second quarter to the third. Is her conclusion justified? Why or why not?
- Considering the information Deborah collected, what strategies might school personnel use to promote higher achievement and motivation in these students?

SUMMARY

Common Beliefs About Children and Education

By the time prospective teachers begin college, they already have well-established beliefs about children and their learning, and they become increasingly comfortable with their views as they proceed through college and into the classroom. Unfortunately, not all these beliefs are accurate portrayals of growing children and adolescents, and some may lead new teachers to use relatively ineffective—perhaps even counterproductive—teaching strategies. Research studies in child development and educational practice can help teachers revise their thinking about how children and adolescents develop and how they most effectively learn.

Basic Principles of Developmental Research

Good developmental research embodies several features: It involves hypothesis formation, appropriate sampling, systematic collection and interpretation of data, ethical conduct, and public scrutiny and critical analysis of findings and conclusions.

Data Collection Techniques

Developmental researchers use several methods for collecting data, including self-reports (interviews and questionnaires), tests and other methods of numerical measurement, and observations. Regardless of the method, the data collected should be accurate measures of the characteristics or behaviors being studied (a matter of *validity*) and should be only minimally influenced by temporary, irrelevant factors (a matter of *reliability*). Good researchers often collect two or more kinds of data relative to the same research question and look for converging patterns.

Developmental Research Designs

In their attempts to answer their research questions, developmental researchers use a variety of research designs, including experimental, quasi-experimental, causal-comparative, correlational, cross-sectional, longitudinal, and naturalistic designs. These designs differ in the extent to which they allow researchers to draw conclusions about cause-effect relationships, trace age trends over time, determine the stability of particular characteristics, identify early predictors of later performance, and observe children and adolescence in their natural environments.

Using Research in the Classroom

Developmental research helps teachers in many ways, for instance, by illuminating effective and ineffective teaching practices, promoting new ways of thinking about child and adolescent development, and engendering optimism about making a difference in students' lives. However, teachers must critically analyze the research they read to judge whether the conclusions are warranted from the data reported and whether the findings are applicable to the teachers' own situations.

Teachers often gather their own data in the classroom. Sometimes they do it very informally, such as when they "read" their students for possible clues about students' learning and thinking. At other times, they may conduct more formal research to answer specific questions they may have about their students or their teaching strategies.

Now go to our Companion Website to assess your understanding of chapter content with Multiple-Choice Questions, apply comprehension in Essay Questions, and broaden your knowledge with links to related Developmental Psychology World Wide Web sites.

KEY CONCEPTS

sample (p. 37)
self-report (p. 39)
interview (p. 39)
questionnaire (p. 40)
test (p. 40)
observation (p. 41)
validity (p. 42)
reliability (p. 44)

experimental study (p. 45)
control group (p. 45)
quasi-experimental study
  (p. 46)
causal-comparative study
  (p. 47)
correlation (p. 47)
correlation coefficient (p. 47)

correlational study (p. 47)
cross-sectional study (p. 47)
longitudinal study (p. 49)
naturalistic study (p. 50)
quantitative research (p. 50)
qualitative research (p. 50)
action research (p. 59)

Laura, age 6

Physical Development

CASE STUDY: THE SOFTBALL LEAGUE

Two brothers, Tom (age 13) and Phillip (age 15) are talking with psychologist William Pollack about the impact that organized sports have had on their lives:

"There used to be nothing to do around here," Tom told me [Dr. Pollack], referring to the small, economically depressed town where he and his brother live.

"There was like just one bowling alley, and it was closed on weekends. We had nothing to do, especially during the summer," Phillip agreed.

"Not quite a year ago," Tom explained, "three of our best friends died of an OD."

Indeed, the autumn before, three teenage boys in the same sleepy town had all drunk themselves into oblivion and then overdosed on a lethal cocktail of various barbiturates. Sure, the town had always had its problems—high unemployment, poorly funded schools, and many broken families. But this was different. Three boys, the oldest only sixteen, were gone forever.

The mood in the town was sullen the summer following the deaths, and Tom and Phillip were resolved to change things. "We went to the mayor and to the priest at our church, and we asked if we could set up a regular sports program for kids around here," Phillip explained.

"A softball league," Tom added.

"What a great idea," I told the boys.

"Yeah. At first we were just ten guys," said Tom.

"But then, like, everybody wanted to sign up—girls too," explained Phillip. "Now there are too many kids who want to play. More than a hundred. But the state government offered to help with some money and coaches."

"So it is making a difference, to have this new league?" I asked the boys.

"Hell, yeah," Phillip replied. "Now, we've got a schedule. We've got something to do."

"I'm not sure I'd be here anymore if it wasn't for the league," added Tom. "For a long time I couldn't deal with things. Now I've got a place to go." (Pollack, 1998, pp. 274)[1]

[1]From Real Boys: *Rescuing Our Sons from the Myths of Boyhood* by William Pollack, copyright © 1998 by William Pollack. Used by permission of Random House, Inc.

Art courtesy of Eric, age 12.

Perhaps the most obvious aspects of human development are the physical changes. As children get older, they grow taller, stronger, and more agile, and they become increasingly able to perform such complex physical tasks as using scissors, riding a bicycle, and playing softball. But physical development almost invariably occurs in tandem with social and emotional development, and often with cognitive advancements as well. Certainly, Tom and Phillip enjoyed the physical activities involved in playing softball—throwing and catching a ball, swinging a bat, running, and so on. As adolescents, they had muscles to move, a cardiovascular system to exercise, and energy to burn. But the benefits they gained from sports were not purely physical ones. The softball league became a way to forge friendships, develop teamwork and leadership skills, and gain ties to the larger community; the league also provided a schedule that helped the boys use their time productively. Mind, body, and spirit are not always a single, integrated entity, but neither are they separate kingdoms.

In this chapter, we explore physical development and its biological underpinnings. After examining the genetic foundations of what it means to be human and the ways in which the environment also influences physical growth, we identify several general principles of physical development. Next, we look at the physiological changes that occur in the brain over the course of childhood and adolescence, as well as at the implications these changes have for classroom practice. Later, we focus on the distinct nature of physical development during different age ranges and then look at general issues related to children's and adolescents' health and well-being. Finally, we consider how teachers can best help students with special physical needs.

Nature and Nurture in Physical Development

Genetic instructions play a major role in determining children's physical characteristics and abilities, but environmental factors can influence how such instructions are carried out. We look now at the effects of both heredity and environment in physical development and at several ways in which their influences are inextricably interwoven.

Genetic Foundations of Development

Every child comes with a set of instructions. Such instructions take the form of **genes**, which serve both as blueprints for how the body will develop and as a timetable for when various characteristics will emerge. Genes dictate the location and function of every cell in the body. They influence children's height, weight, activity level, intellectual talents, and emotional predispositions, making each child unique. But genes also give children a common human heritage, including a capacity for language, a need for social relationships, and a receptivity to learning the practices and beliefs of a culture (Bugental & Goodnow, 1998).

In essence, a gene is a small unit of chemical instructions, in the form of deoxyribonucleic acid, or **DNA**. A strand of DNA is structured like a twisted ladder—a *double helix*—with pairs of chemicals comprising each rung of the ladder (Figure 3–1). The particular configuration and sequence of the chemical pairings gives cells instructions to make specific proteins. These proteins, in turn, trigger critical chemical reactions throughout the body, giving human beings both their individuality and their resemblance to one another.

Human beings have up to 100,000 genes (Lewin, Siliciano, & Klotz, 1997). The genes are dispersed among 46 **chromosomes**, rodlike structures that reside in the center, or *nucleus*, of every cell in the body. The chromosomes are organized into 23 pairs that are easily seen under high-powered microscopes (Figure 3–2).

Conception and a Genetic Legacy Although the vast majority of human cells contain 46 chromosomes, a few have only 23 chromosomes—one from each chromosome pair. Such **germ cells**, which take the form of *sperm* in men and *ova* in women, are formed through a process in which chromosomes duplicate themselves within a cell and then pieces of gene segments exchange places within chromosome pairs. This crossing-over of genetic material is one of several ingenious mechanisms designed by nature to produce diversity in offspring.

gene
Basic unit of genetic instruction in a living cell.

DNA
Short for deoxyribonucleic acid, a double-helix shaped "ladder" of four chemicals that specifies how to build specific proteins that direct growth and developmental change.

chromosome
Rodlike structure that resides in the nucleus of every cell of the body and contains genes that guide growth and development.

germ cell
Cell that, in humans, contains 23 rather than 46 chromosomes; a male germ cell (sperm) and a female germ cell (ovum) join at conception.

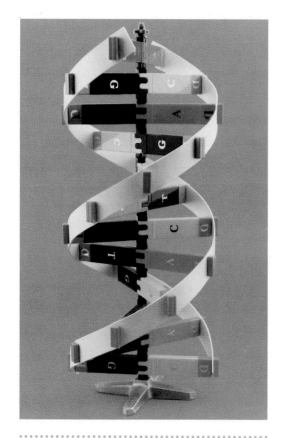

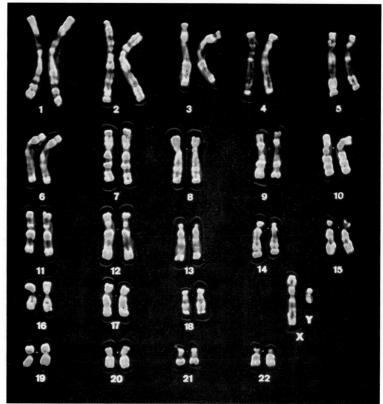

FIGURE 3–1 DNA structure. DNA molecules are structured as twisting strands of ladderlike structures.

FIGURE 3–2 Photograph of human chromosomes that have been extracted from a human cell, colored, magnified, and arranged in order of size. This set of chromosomes comes from a male, which can be deciphered by scientists from the XY structure of the 23rd pair.

Crossing-over ensures that an offspring's individual chromosomes are not identical to those of parents or potential siblings: Every time a crossover occurs, it results in a unique combination of genes. After the gene exchange, a cell containing the reconfigured chromosomes separates into two 23-chromosome germ cells. This separation occurs in a seemingly random fashion, providing a second route to individuality.

When two germ cells, one sperm and one ovum, unite in conception, the 23 chromosomes from each cell re-pair themselves, forming a **zygote** of 46 chromosomes. Under optimal circumstances, this zygote subdivides into two cells, which then also subdivide, and so on many times over, and gradually the growing cluster of cells develops into a human being. The 23rd chromosome pair determines the gender of the individual, with two *X chromosomes* (one each from the mother and father) producing a female and a combination of an X chromosome and a *Y chromosome* (from the mother and father, respectively) producing a male.

Occasionally, a zygote first splits into two separate entities, resulting in two offspring instead of one. Such **monozygotic twins** come from the same fertilized egg and so have the same genetic instructions; hence, they are often known as *identical* twins. At other times, two ova from the mother simultaneously unite with two sperm cells from the father, again resulting in two offspring. Such **dizygotic twins** (also known as *fraternal* twins) are as similar to one another as ordinary siblings: They share some genetic traits but not others.

Because monozygotic and dizygotic twins differ in the degree to which they share a common genetic heritage, researchers have studied them extensively to investigate the relative effects of heredity and environment on the development of human characteristics. In many cases, monozygotic twins are quite similar to one another in terms of how sociable they are and how they express emotion, whereas dizygotic twins are less similar (Plomin & DeFries, 1985). Even so, identical twins are *not* identical in all psychological characteristics—a sign that experience plays a significant role in shaping genetic tendencies.

zygote
Cell formed when a male sperm joins with a female ovum; it is essentially the "start" of a new human being.

monozygotic twins
Twins that began as a single zygote and so share the same genetic makeup.

dizygotic twins
Twins that began as two separate zygotes and so are as genetically similar as two siblings conceived and born at different times.

Nature and Nurture in Physical Development | **67**

Sometimes problems occur in the transmission of chromosomes from one generation to the next. For example, children with *Down syndrome* have an extra 21st chromosome, or at least an extra piece of one. Children with Down syndrome typically show delays in mental growth and are susceptible to heart defects and other health problems. Apparently, the extra 21st chromosome causes biochemical changes that redirect brain development (Carlson, 1999). In *fragile X syndrome,* part of a child's X chromosome is pinched or missing. The syndrome is associated with mild mental retardation, learning disabilities, distinctive physical features (e.g., prominent ears and a long, narrow face), and hyperactivity. For both syndromes, the severity of the disabilities varies considerably from one child to the next; for instance, some girls with fragile X syndrome have average intelligence because a normal X chromosome partially compensates for the abnormal one.

When Genes Give Conflicting Messages When the two sets of 23 chromosomes recombine into matched pairs, the corresponding genes from mom and dad also pair up. Each gene pair includes two forms of a gene—two **alleles**—for a particular physical characteristic. Sometimes the two genes in an allele pair give the same instructions ("Have brown eyes!" "Have brown eyes!"). At other times, however, they give very different instructions ("Have brown eyes!" "Have blue eyes!"). When two genes give different instructions, one gene is often more influential than its counterpart. **Dominant genes** manifest their characteristic, in a sense overriding the instructions of any **recessive gene** with which they might be paired. A recessive gene has its say only when its partner is also recessive. For example, genes for brown eyes are dominant and those for blue eyes are recessive; thus, a child with a brown-eye gene and a blue-eye gene will have brown eyes, as will a child with two brown-eye genes. Only when two blue-eye genes are paired together will a child have blue eyes.

Yet when the two genes of an allele pair "disagree," one gene doesn't always dominate completely over the other. Sometimes one gene has a stronger influence but not total domination, a phenomenon known as **codominance.** *Sickle cell anemia* is an example. In this condition, a person's red blood cells are long and curved rather than circular; these misshapen blood cells have difficulty reaching all parts of the body, leading to pain and infection. The disease develops in its full-blown form only when a person has two (recessive) alleles for it. But an individual with one recessive allele for sickle cell anemia and one dominant, "healthy" allele may experience a temporary, mild form of anemia when short of oxygen, perhaps at high altitudes or after vigorous exercise (Sullivan, 1987).

The influence of genes is sometimes even more complex. Many physiological traits and most psychological ones are dependent on multiple genes rather than on a single pair of alleles. In **polygenic inheritance,** many separate genes each exert a small influence in the expression of a trait, and they combine in their overall impact. Height is a simple example; an individual's final height as an adult is not the result of a single allele pair, but instead the outcome of several genes individually having small effects (Tanner, 1990).

Maturation and Canalization Some genes have an immediate influence on physical characteristics, but many others don't manifest themselves until later, when provoked to do so by hormonal stimulation (Tanner, 1990). Genetically controlled changes that occur over the course of development are known as **maturation.** Height is an example here as well. Children's height at birth (perhaps "length" is a more accurate descriptor for a newborn) is determined largely by prenatal conditions in the mother's uterus and is only minimally influenced by heredity at that point. By 18 months of age, however, we see a definite correlation between children's heights and the heights of their parents, presumably because genetic factors have begun to exert their influence (Tanner, 1990).

The emergence of some characteristics is tightly controlled by genetic instructions; this phenomenon is known as **canalization** (Waddington, 1957). For instance, the emergence of basic motor skills is highly canalized: Crawling, sitting, and walking appear under a wide range of circumstances. It takes extremely unusual environmental conditions for these motor skills to be stifled; they almost invariably appear without training, prompting, or encouragement. Occasionally, canalization can be influenced by specific environmental circumstances.

Positive attitudes of teachers, advocacy from parents, and federal legislation have improved educational services and opportunities for many students with genetic abnormalities and other physical disabilities.

alleles
Genes located at the same point on corresponding (paired) chromosomes and related to the same physical characteristic.

dominant gene
Gene that overrides any competing instructions in an allele pair.

recessive gene
Gene that influences growth and development only if the other gene in the allele pair is identical to it (and so also recessive).

codominance
Situation in which the two genes of an allele pair, though not identical, both have some influence on the characteristic they affect.

polygenic inheritance
Situation in which many genes combine in their influence on a particular characteristic.

maturation
Genetically controlled changes that occur over the course of development.

canalization
Tight genetic control of a particular aspect of development.

For instance, a young child exposed to heavy doses of a toxic substance (e.g., lead paint) may become canalized toward developmental delays that are not easily overridden by a more healthful and stimulating environment later on (Gottlieb, 1991, 1992).

Not all human traits are canalized, however. In fact, most of the abilities that children acquire at school—reading, writing, mathematical and scientific problem solving, musical and artistic talent, and so on—are highly susceptible to the experiences that children have both in and out of the classroom.

Environment and Its Interaction with Heredity

Genes rely on the environment to support their work. Most of the time, specific genes reside in inactive regions of the cell, and only a small subset of available genes guide the formation of proteins (Brown, 1999). You might think of genes as being like the data in a computer's memory, in that they cannot operate unless conditions are right (Brown, 1999). To make the data in a computer available for use, the computer must be turned on (adequate energy and nutrients must be available) and information must be purposefully accessed (hormones, or messenger proteins secreted by endocrine glands, must trigger the expression of genes).

Numerous environmental factors influence genetic expression, including nutrition, illness, medication, stressful events, temperature, exposure to light, and intensity of stimulation (Brown, 1999; Wilson & Foster, 1985). For example, Guatemalan children raised in the United States tend to grow taller than their parents did in Guatemala, presumably because of more abundant and diverse nutritional resources in the United States (Bogin, 1988). The environment has its effect, in part, by affecting the hormones that provoke genes into action. For example, stressful events suppress the release of certain hormones and so can indirectly suppress growth in tissues of the body and nervous system (Brown, 1999). Long-term, excessive stress can also lead to the death of neurons in the hippocampus, a component of the brain essential for memory and other cognitive functions (Lombroso & Sapolsky, 1998).

Complex psychological traits, such as personality characteristics and intellectual talents, are probably the outcomes of both polygenic inheritance and environmental experience. For instance, such aspects of temperament as cheerfulness, outgoingness, moodiness, anxiety, aggression, and risk taking seem to have genetic origins (Henderson, 1982; Rothbart & Bates, 1998; Tellegren, Lykken, Bouchard, & Wilcox, 1988). Yet these traits are clearly influenced by environmental supports, assaults, and opportunities as well (Plomin, Owen, & McGuffin, 1994). We're not born wild or shy; instead, we're born with certain tendencies that our environments may or may not cultivate.

Sandra Scarr (1992, 1993; Scarr & McCartney, 1983) has described three ways in which environmental factors may interact with genetic predispositions to nurture physical and psychological traits. A *passive gene-environment relation* occurs when parents' genes are correlated with the kind of setting in which they raise their children. For example, a father with a strong imagination and a love of art and drama may provide his son with cultural enrichment, art materials and lessons, and visits to museums and performances. An *active gene-environment relation* occurs when children have particular talents that influence the environments made

Some aspects of temperament, such as shyness, have a genetic basis but are also influenced by the environment. Although this boy is shy around his peers and has trouble separating from his mother, his parents and teacher have worked out a way to ease the transition from home to school each morning.

accessible to them. For instance, an athletic youngster may try out for the baseball team, join in on neighborhood games, request sports supplies from parents, and otherwise create occasions for sports. Finally, in an *evocative gene-environment relation,* children's own characteristics elicit specific kinds of reactions from the environment. To illustrate, a calm and compliant child may have a soothing effect on caregivers, who then respond with warmth and nurturance. A child who is quick to argue may instead provoke hostile reactions from both adults and peers.

Not only do children evoke certain kinds of environments, but they may also *seek out* environments suited to their inherited temperaments and predispositions. As an example, let's return to the opening case study. In a community with few activities to occupy children's time, Tom and Phillip took the initiative to start a softball league, whereas three of their peers instead turned to alcohol and drugs for recreation. Why did two boys identify a constructive solution to the problem while three others identified a destructive and eventually fatal one? Quite possibly, inherited differences among the boys—perhaps in sociability, emotional stability, or risk taking—nudged them toward the particular choices that they made.

Sensitive Periods: When Environment Has Its Greatest Effects In Chapter 1, we introduced the concept of *sensitive period,* an age range during which certain environmental experiences are especially important for normal development. The timing of sensitive periods is dictated by heredity, which determines *when* particular kinds of environmental stimulation come into play in the course of development.

Sensitive periods are more frequently observed in physical and perceptual development than in other developmental domains. For example, normal visual experiences in the first 2 years of life are apparently critical for the development of visual perception. Children who are born with cataracts (cloudy lenses that allow sensitivity to light but prohibit perception of shapes) are more likely to have normal vision later on if their condition is treated *before* the age of 2 (Bruer, 1999). Furthermore, some environmental influences may be highly detrimental at one phase of development yet have little or no effect at other phases. For example, children exposed to rubella (German measles) in the first 12 weeks of pregnancy are frequently born with cataracts, hearing loss, heart defects, and other abnormalities; children exposed to this disease considerably later in pregnancy remain relatively unscathed.

As you can see, then, genes do not determine appearance, behavior, or even cell functioning in any simple, predetermined fashion. They act in concert with one another; are affected by nutrition, stress, and other environmental agents; and are triggered by hormones and physiological events. Furthermore, they may be triggered at different points in development, promoting the appearance of characteristics that seem to come out of nowhere. In general, genetic influence displays considerable elasticity: It offers rough guidelines that can be either stretched or compressed, depending on the circumstances and opportunities that the environment offers.

Implications of Genetic and Environmental Influences

Genes may seem to be worlds apart from real children in classroom settings. Nevertheless, for anyone working closely with children and adolescents, the power *and* limits of genetic influence are important to understand, as they bear on the origins and course of enduring individual differences. Furthermore, a recognition that environmental factors clearly impact human development should give educators considerable optimism about the potential for significant growth in all students. With these points in mind, we offer the following recommendations for teachers:

■ *Expect and make allowances for individual differences.* Teachers who value a multitude of physical characteristics, personality types, and talents can put students at ease. Children who are tall and short, chubby and thin, coordinated and clumsy, shy and outgoing, calm and irritable *all* have a rightful place in the hearts of teachers.

■ *Remember that environmental factors influence virtually every aspect of development.* Genes have a strong effect on physiological growth and a modest effect on complex psychological characteristics. Yet viewing learning and development as being a simple outgrowth of biology can have devastating effects on children (Eisenberg, 1998). Children often live up to—perhaps more accurately, *down* to—the low expectations that others (including teachers) have for them. In Chapter 11, we will look more closely at the effects of teacher expectations.

Even if children have an inherited potential for certain talents and temperaments, their path in life is unpredictable: Environmental factors—physical conditions, social interactions, educational experiences, and so on—can affect the course of development in a myriad of ways. For instance, children who are genetically predisposed to be irritable, distractible, or aggressive *can,* with appropriate instruction and guidance, learn more adaptive and prosocial ways of responding (e.g., DeVault, Krug, & Fake, 1996; Robinson, Smith, Miller, & Brownell, 1999).

Development of a young boy at (*left to right*) ages 1, 5, 9, and 13. Notice the gradual, systematic changes: The boy grows taller, his face becomes more angular, and his trunk elongates. The boy is wearing the same T-shirt in all four photos.

■ *Encourage students to make growth-promoting choices.* Especially as they grow older, children and adolescents actively seek out experiences and environments compatible with their natural abilities, and teachers are in a key position to help them find activities and resources that allow them to use and nurture their talents. For instance, a socially outgoing student with an excessive amount of energy may frequently disrupt classroom lessons in his efforts to be sociable and active. To help him channel his energy more effectively, his teacher might encourage him to join the school drama club, a community sports program, or other groups in which he can constructively use and develop his skills.

General Principles of Physical Development

Thanks, in large part, to the influence of genetics, physical development is somewhat predictable. Researchers have identified several general principles that characterize physical growth:

■ *Different parts of the body mature at different rates.* Typical growth curves for height and weight reveal rapid increases in the first 2 years, slow but steady growth during early and middle childhood, an explosive spurt during adolescence, and then a leveling off to mature, adult levels (Hamill et al., 1979). Patterns of growth are similar for boys and girls, although girls tend to have their adolescent growth spurts about 1½ years earlier and boys, on average, end up a bit taller and heavier than girls.

Such increases are, of course, the composite result of various bodily systems getting bigger. But different parts of the body grow at different rates, and in the early years, some parts are closer than others to their eventual adult size. Heads are proportionally closer to adult size than are trunks, which are more advanced than arms and legs. In the upper limbs, the hand is closer to adult size than the forearm; the forearm is closer than the upper arm. Likewise in the lower limbs, the foot is more advanced than the calf, which is more advanced than the thigh. Figure 3–3 illustrates how relative body proportions change throughout childhood and adolescence.

Internally, things grow at different rates as well (Tanner, 1990). For instance, the lymphoid system (e.g., tonsils, adenoids, intestines, lymph nodes) grows rapidly throughout childhood (to the point where it is actually larger than adult size) and then decreases somewhat in adolescence. In contrast, the reproductive system shows fairly slow growth until adolescence, when there's a substantial burst of growth.

■ *Functioning becomes increasingly differentiated.* Every cell in the body (germ cells excepted) contains all 46 chromosomes and so has the same genetic instructions. But as cells grow, they take on specific functions, some aiding with digestion, others transporting oxygen, still others transmitting information to various points in the body, and so on. Thus, individual cells "listen" to only a subset of the many instructions they have available. This change from general to more specific functioning is known as **differentiation.**

Differentiation characterizes other aspects of physical development as well. For instance, during prenatal development, the bud of an arm becomes longer, with hands emerging slowly, then fingers. Motor skills, too, become increasingly differentiated over time: They first appear as global, unsteady actions but gradually evolve into more specific, controlled motions. For example, when trying to throw a ball, toddlers are apt to use their entire body in an intense but clumsy effort to move the ball forward. Preschoolers are more likely to move just a single arm and hand in an attempt to concentrate their efforts.

differentiation
An increase from general to more specific functioning over the course of development.

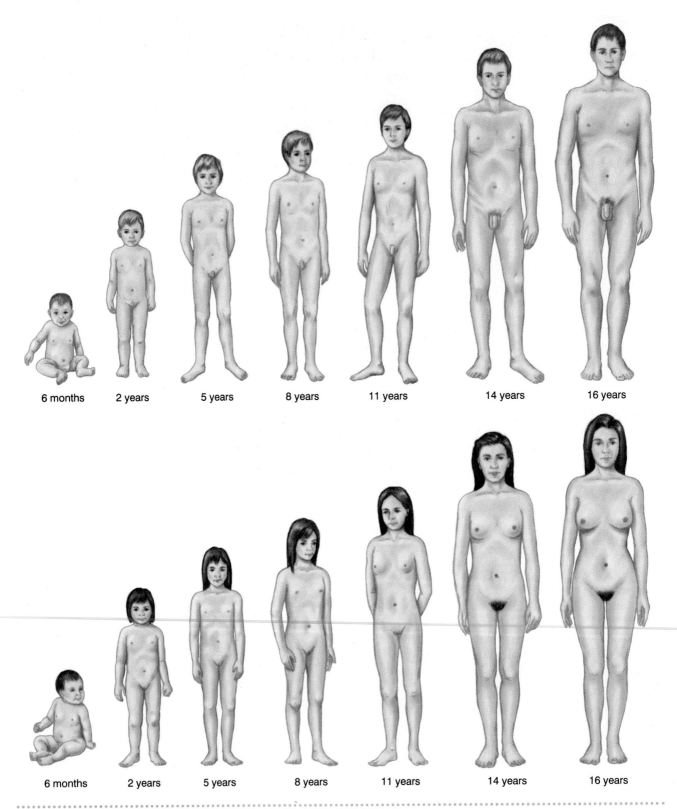

FIGURE 3–3 Physical development during childhood and adolescence. Children grow taller and heavier as they develop, and the characteristics and relative proportions of their bodies change as well.

Based on The Diagram Group (1983).

	Initial Motor Activity	Practiced Motor Activity	Mature Motor Activity
Walking			
Throwing			

FIGURE 3–4 Developmental sequences showing qualitative change in walking and overhand throwing. In walking, children tend to progress from (a) difficulty maintaining balance and using short steps with flat-footed contact, to (b) a smoother pattern, where arms are lower and there is heel-toe contact, and to (c) a relaxed gait, with reflexive arm swing. In overhand throwing, the trend is from (a) stationary feet and action mainly from the elbow, to (b) ball held behind head, arm swung forward and high over shoulder, and a definite shift forward with body weight, to (c) movement of foot on same side as throwing arm; definite rotation through hips, legs, spine, and shoulders; and a step with foot opposite the throwing arm as weight is shifted.

Based on Gallahue & Ozmun (1998).

■ *Functioning also becomes increasingly integrated.* Just as cells and body parts differentiate, so, too, must they work together. Their increasingly coordinated efforts are known as **integration** (Tanner, 1990). For instance, to see clearly, the lens of the eye must balance with the depth of the eyeball in such a way that light rays fall cleanly on the retina at the back of the eye. To throw a ball effectively, a child must carefully orchestrate the movements of the entire body—the legs and torso along with the arm and hand—to propel the ball toward a particular target.

■ *Each child follows a unique growth curve.* Children appear to have target heights that their bodies strive to attain—perhaps not as specific as 4′9″ or 6′2″, but a definite, limited target nonetheless. Growth curves are especially evident when things go temporarily awry in children's lives. Circumstances such as illness or poor nutrition may put a brief halt on height increases. But when health and adequate nutrition return, children grow rapidly. Before you know it, they're back on track—back to where we might have expected them to be given their previous rate of growth. Exceptions to this self-correcting tendency occur only when severe malnutrition is present very early in life or extends over a lengthy period of time. For instance, children who are seriously undernourished during their prenatal phase tend *not* to catch up completely, and they are at risk for later mental and behavioral deficiencies, motor difficulties, and psychiatric problems (e.g., schizophrenia; Brown et al., 1996; Chavez, Martinez, & Soberanes, 1995; Sigman, 1995).

■ *Physical development is characterized by both quantitative and qualitative changes.* Many physical changes are the outcome of a series of minor refinements. Motor skills, which may seem to the casual observer to appear overnight, are in most cases the result of numerous gradual advancements. For example, when Teresa's son Alex was 4, he wanted to snap his fingers like his older brother. Alex diligently practiced his finger snapping several times a day for 2 months yet was unable to make the desired sound. With practice, however, his movements became more fluid, and one day, much to his delight, he got it right. In Alex's eyes, the accomplishment was a quantum leap forward, but in reality it was probably the end result of repeated effort and practice.

Yet qualitative changes are seen as well. To illustrate, Figure 3–4 shows how both walking and throwing change over time. Early on, toddlers have difficulty maintaining balance and an

integration
An increasing coordination of body parts over the course of development.

General Principles of Physical Development | 73

BASIC DEVELOPMENTAL ISSUES

ISSUE	PHYSICAL GROWTH	MOTOR SKILLS	PHYSICAL HEALTH AND ACTIVITY
Nature and Nurture	Genetic instructions specify how cells divide and where they migrate during prenatal development; they also provide basic targets for mature height and weight. Yet normal progressions are contingent on healthful environmental conditions and experiences, such as adequate nutrition, activity, stimulation, affection, and protection from toxic substances.	Nature sets firm boundaries as to the motor skills a child can execute at any given age level; for instance, a 6-month old cannot run and a 10-year-old cannot clear 15 feet in the standing high jump. Organized sports programs and other opportunities for regular exercise allow children to expand, refine, and polish their developing motor skills.	Nature influences children's activity level (e.g., 3-year-olds tend to be more physically active than 17-year-olds) and susceptibility to infection and illness. Children learn habits of eating and exercise from their parents and others in their community.
Universality and Diversity	Children tend to show similar sequences in physical development (e.g., in the emergence of sexual characteristics associated with puberty) across a wide range of environments and cultures. However, the rate of development differs considerably from one child to the next, partly because of genetic diversity and partly because of diverse cultural practices related to food, exercise, and so on.	Motor skills often develop in the same, universal sequence. For example, children can, on average, pick up crumbs with their fingers at age 1, scribble with a crayon at age 2, and build a tower 10 blocks high at age 4 (Sheridan, 1975). The specific ages at which children master certain motor skills varies, due in part to genetic differences and in part to differences in environmental support (or lack of support) for practicing particular motor skills.	All children and adolescents need good nutrition, plenty of rest, and a moderate amount of physical activity to be healthy. Huge variation is present in the activity levels and eating habits of youngsters. In addition, children differ in their susceptibility to illness.
Qualitative and Quantitative Change 	Many physical advancements appear to be the result of a series of quantitative physiological changes (e.g., gradual increases in physical strength and dexterity). Qualitative changes are revealed in the different rates of change that occur in different body systems and in the characteristics that emerge at puberty.	As a general rule, children must practice motor skills for a long time before they can execute them easily and gracefully, and a series of quantitative improvements allow more complex skills to emerge. Some motor skills, such as walking and throwing a ball, also change qualitatively with maturity and practice.	Gradually and incrementally, children and adolescents gain more control over what they eat and how they spend their leisure time. Young adolescents show increased risk-taking behaviors (e.g., dangerous physical activities, experimentation with drugs and alcohol). This transition from a preoccupation with safety to a thrill-seeking mind-set reflects a qualitative change.

upright posture, take short steps, make flat-footed contact with toes turned outward, and flex their knees as their feet make contact with the ground (Gallahue & Ozmun, 1998). A few years later, they increase their stride, make heel-toe contact, swing their arms a bit, appear to lift themselves vertically as they proceed, and show increased pelvic tilt. The mature pattern of walking, achieved between ages 4 and 7, is characterized by a reflexive arm swing, a narrow base of support, a relaxed and long stride, minimal vertical lift, and a decisive heel-toe contact. Throwing a ball shows qualitative changes as well (Figure 3–4), as do such skills as jumping, galloping, and sliding (Gallahue & Ozmun, 1998).

In the Basic Development Issues table above, we summarize the ways in which physical development is both qualitative and quantitative, as well as the ways in which nature, nurture, universality, and diversity come into play.

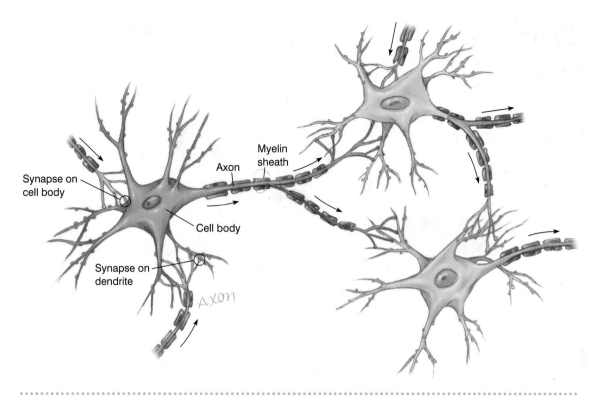

FIGURE 3–5 Neurons in the brain. The neuron on the left is receiving information from other cells. It then fires and incites other neurons to fire. Arrows show the direction of messages being sent.

Based on Carlson (1999).

The Brain and Its Development

The brain is the switchboard, command center, and computer of human functioning. It is a *switchboard* in the sense that it transmits a huge amount of information to, and receives an equal amount of information from, all parts of the body. It is a *command center* in that it regulates and coordinates the activities of various bodily systems. It is a *computer* in that it stores, organizes, and tries to make sense of the masses of data that the body collects as it interacts with its physical and social environments. Not surprisingly, then, the brain is the most complex organ in the human body.

Altogether, the brain has somewhere in the neighborhood of 180 billion cells (Teeter & Semrud-Clikeman, 1997). Many brain cells take the form of **neurons,** cells that transmit information to other cells. Neurons do their work through both architecture (Figure 3–5) and chemistry. With branchlike structures called **dendrites,** they reach out for information from other cells. With long, armlike structures called **axons,** they send information on to additional cells. The dendrites and axons of various cells come together at junctions known as **synapses.** Neurons activate one another to "fire," and in some cases *prevent* one another from firing, by sending chemical substances known as **neurotransmitters** across the synapses that join them.

Neurons in the brain are organized as communities interacting with other communities. In other words, groups of neurons grow together and communicate with other groups of neurons elsewhere in the brain and body. Most neurons have hundreds or even thousands of synapses with other neurons (Thompson, 1975), so obviously a great deal of cross-communication is possible.

Neurons are assisted by other kinds of brain cells, called **glial cells** (or *neuroglia*). These cells give neurons structural support and protect the connections among neurons. They

neuron
Cell that transmits information to other cells; also called *nerve cell*.

dendrite
Branchlike part of a neuron that receives information from other neurons.

axon
Armlike part of a neuron that sends information to other neurons.

synapse
Junction between two neurons.

neurotransmitter
Chemical substance through which one neuron sends a message to another neuron.

glial cell
Cell in the brain or other part of the nervous system that provides structural or functional support for one or more neurons; also called *neuroglia*.

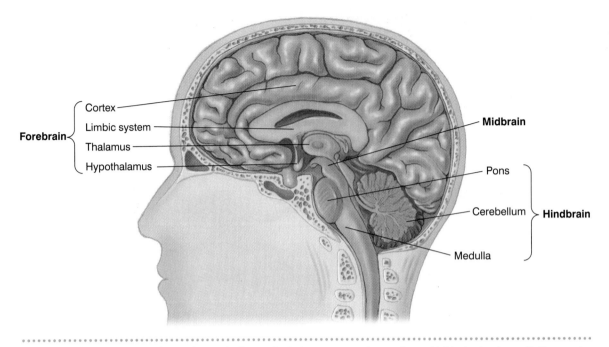

FIGURE 3–6 Structure of the human brain. The human brain is an enormously complex and intricate structure with three main parts: the hindbrain, the midbrain, and the forebrain.
Based on Carlson (1999).

also produce chemicals that neurons need to function properly, and they help to repair injured neurons and dispose of seriously damaged ones (Carlson, 1999; Teeter & Semrud-Clikeman, 1997).

Structures and Functions in the Brain

At a global level, the brain is organized into three main parts—the hindbrain, the midbrain, and the forebrain (Figure 3–6)—and each of these parts is organized further into more specialized systems with identifiable functions. The **hindbrain** controls basic physiological processes that sustain survival, including breathing, blood pressure, sleep, arousal, balance, and movement (thank your hindbrain for your slow, methodical breathing as you sleep blissfully at night). The **midbrain** connects the hindbrain to the forebrain and acts as a kind of relay station between the two; for instance, it sends messages to the forebrain about priorities for attention ("Hello! Alarm clock ringing! Hello! Alarm clock ringing!"). The **forebrain** produces complex thinking, emotional responding, and the driving forces of motivation ("6 A.M.? Ugh! I can sleep another 10 minutes if I skip breakfast").

Resting as a cap upon other parts of the brain is a portion of the forebrain known as the **cortex**. The cortex is where interpreting, reasoning, communicating, goal setting, planning, decision making, and other conscious thinking processes (collectively known as **executive functions**) take place. It also houses much of people's personalities and the habitual ways in which they respond to physical events and other human beings.

Physiologically, the cortex is highly convoluted: Bundles of nerves fold in on themselves over and over again. This physical complexity permits a huge capacity for storing information as well as for transmitting information throughout the brain. Consistent with the principle of differentiation, various parts of the cortex have specific functions, such as distinguishing among sounds, understanding spoken language, and planning speech.

The cortex is divided into two halves, or hemispheres. For the majority of people, the **left hemisphere** dominates in *analysis*, breaking up information into its constituent parts and extracting meaning from a sequence of events (Carlson, 1999; Uba & Huang, 1999). Talking, understanding speech, reading, writing, mathematical problem solving, and computer programming are all beneficiaries of left-hemisphere processing. The **right hemisphere** excels in

hindbrain
Part of the brain controlling the basic physiological processes that sustain survival.

midbrain
Part of the brain that coordinates communication between the hindbrain and forebrain.

forebrain
Part of the brain responsible for complex thinking, emotions, and motivation.

cortex
Part of the forebrain that houses conscious thinking processes (executive functions).

executive functions
Conscious thinking processes within the brain (e.g., reasoning, communicating, decision making).

left hemisphere
Left side of the cortex; largely responsible for sequential reasoning and analysis, especially in right-handed people.

right hemisphere
Right side of the cortex; largely responsible for simultaneous processing and synthesis, especially in right-handed people.

synthesis, pulling together information (especially nonlinguistic information) into a coherent whole. The right hemisphere dominates in visual activities, such as recognizing faces, detecting geometrical patterns, reading maps, and drawing. It is also the key player in appreciating musical melodies, finding humor in physical events, and recognizing various emotions in the voice and body language of others.

The intellectual specializations of the two hemispheres are assured by the physical layout of neural circuits. The left hemisphere has neurological connections to fewer regions of the brain than does the right, in keeping with its emphasis on analysis in specialized functions such as language and mathematics. The right hemisphere more liberally supports connections with a broader range of areas in the brain, permitting a wide variety of associations (Goldberg & Costa, 1981; Semrud-Clikeman & Hynd, 1991; Teeter & Semrud-Clikeman, 1997).

Researchers have been studying the specialization of the two hemispheres for many years, and their findings have been widely disseminated among scientists and the general public. But the body of evidence they have accumulated is often oversimplified or in other ways misrepresented. You may occasionally hear an educator say, "I'm trying to teach to students' right brains today" or "Billy's a left-brain kid." Such well-intentioned comments imply that various forms of thinking are confined to particular sides of the brain and that, for many students, one side is more proficient than the other. In reality, the two hemispheres are in constant communication, trading information back and forth, and so no single mental activity is exclusively the domain of one hemisphere or the other (Carlson, 1999). For example, the right hemisphere may process a complex emotion, such as the mixed feelings people often experience at high school graduation, while the left hemisphere searches for words to communicate the feelings. Each area of the cortex is informed by comparable areas in the opposite hemisphere, with understandings and behaviors often the result of the two hemispheres working together.

Having depicted typical forms of hemispheric specialization, we have news for our left-handed readers. It is common for left-handed individuals to have reversed patterns, with right hemispheres dominant in language and left hemispheres more involved in visual synthesis (Carlson, 1999). A minority of individuals appear to distribute various cognitive specializations in unique yet very successful ways across the two hemispheres (Sheehan & Smith, 1986; Witelson, 1985). For instance, people who are ambidextrous (i.e., they use both hands equally well for fine motor tasks) are more likely to have unique hemispheric specializations than people who are definitely right-handed or left-handed (Sheehan & Smith, 1986). Some evidence suggests that ambidextrous individuals are more creative than average (Gribov, 1992), although they may have greater difficulty with certain basic skills, such as discriminating left from right (Ladavas, 1988; Storfer, 1995). In addition, left-handed and ambidextrous individuals are more prone to having accidents (Daniel & Yeo, 1994).

Developmental Changes in the Brain

The brain begins as a tiny tube approximately 25 days after conception. This seemingly simple tube grows longer in places and begins to fold inward to form pockets (Rayport, 1992). Three chambers can be recognized early on, and these chambers become the forebrain, midbrain, and hindbrain. Neuron cells reproduce in the inner portion of the tube; between the 5th and 20th weeks of prenatal development, they do so at the astonishing rate of 50,000 to 100,000 new cells per second (Diamond & Hopson, 1998). Attracted by various chemical substances ("Grow toward me!") and supported by pole-like glial cells, the neurons migrate to specific locations. Once they arrive, they send out axons and dendrites in an effort to connect with one another. Those that make contact survive, and those that do not (about 50% of them) often die, reflecting nature's clever mechanisms of overproduction and selective elimination as means of maximizing its success rate (Diamond & Hopson, 1998; Huttenlocher, 1993).

Neurological development in childhood and adolescence supports more sophisticated executive functions, such as setting goals and planning future actions. Guidance from teachers helps students use these functions more effectively.

Coming from a normal, healthy prenatal environment, most newborns are well prepared for initial tasks of survival, including breathing, sucking, swallowing, crying, and forming simple associations. Yet their neurological development still has a long way to go. The development of dendrites continues after birth but now is guided by environmental stimulation and the child's own movements (Brodal, 1992; Bruer, 1999; Teeter & Semrud-Clikeman, 1997). Furthermore, glial cells grow around axons, forming a fatty sheath (*myelin*) that allows neurons to transmit their messages more quickly. This process of **myelinization** extends over a period of years, with neurons involved in basic survival skills beginning in the prenatal period and those involving motor skills and higher thinking processes coming later (Diamond & Hopson, 1998). Although the process of myelinization is most pronounced in the early years, it continues throughout childhood, adolescence, and early adulthood (Bruer, 1999).

Postnatal brain development is characterized by two additional phenomena as well (Bruer, 1999). In the first 3½ years of life, so many new synapses appear (a phenomenon known as **synaptogenesis**) that their numbers far exceed adult levels. This proliferation of synapses is followed by **synaptic pruning,** when frequently used connections strengthen and unused connections wither away. Why might brain development take this form, hungrily forming connections early on, then pruning back toward fewer connections later? In infancy and early childhood, an overconnected state prepares children for just about any kind of physical and cultural environment. It makes them neurologically adaptable, able to adjust to countless environments. But children don't live in countless environments. They live in *one* environment (admittedly a very complex one), and the synapses they keep are those most likely to serve them well in that context (Diamond & Hopson, 1998). In other words, they end up with a system that is "tried and true" for their own situation.

In middle childhood and adolescence, most neurological development occurs in the cortex, the home of the executive functions through which people control their own behavior. It appears that the building of neurological circuits supporting executive processes peaks during middle childhood (6 to 8 years) and continues to be refined into adolescence (Passler, Isaac, & Hynd, 1985). Myelinization in the frontal region of the cortex, where planning and other complex cognitive processes occur, continues well into puberty (Giedd, Blumenthal, Jeffries, Castellanos, et al., 1999; Kolb & Fantie, 1989). Yet even when the circuits are operational, they do not necessarily function at their maximum efficiency; as you will discover in Chapter 5, even high school students benefit from educational experiences that show them how to learn and think about information more effectively.

Is There a Sensitive Period in Brain Development? As we have seen, neural synapses increase dramatically in the first 3 years of life and then begin to decrease in number shortly after that. Some well-meaning individuals have interpreted this phenomenon as an indication that the first 3 years are a sensitive period (they use the stronger term *critical period*) in brain development. Accordingly, they advocate highly enriched and stimulating environments for infants, toddlers, and young preschoolers and suggest that waiting until after age 3 may be too late to promote optimal cognitive development.

Research with several species indicates that appropriate stimulation is essential for the development of *some* parts of the brain. For instance, cats, monkeys, and people who have reduced or abnormal visual stimulation when they are quite young have lifelong difficulties with visual perception, apparently as a result of irreversible neurological abnormalities (Bruer, 1999). However, the kinds of stimulation necessary for normal development in these areas of the brain are typical, everyday experiences, *not* intensive and "enriched" environments (Bruer, 1999; Greenough, Black, & Wallace, 1987). Furthermore, there is no evidence that sensitive periods exist for areas of the brain that support learning and performance in reading, mathematics, music, or other culture-specific intellectual pursuits (Bruer, 1999; Greenough et al., 1987).

Even in adulthood, the brain continues to adapt to changing circumstances (Mühlnickel, Elbert, Taub, & Flor, 1998; Nelson, 1999; Ramachandran, Rogers-Ramachandran, & Stewart, 1992; Sowell et al., 1999). Furthermore, we know from countless research studies, as well as from our own everyday observations, that human beings continue to learn new information and skills quite successfully throughout the lifespan. Teachers can reasonably assume, then, that the brain remains plastic and adaptable throughout the school years and that educational experiences at *any* age can make an important and lasting contribution to students' cognitive growth.

myelinization
The growth of a fatty sheath around neurons that allows them to transmit messages more quickly.

synaptogenesis
A universal process in brain development whereby many new synapses appear, typically in the first 3½ years of life.

synaptic pruning
A universal process in brain development whereby many synapses formed earlier wither away, especially if they have not been used frequently.

Individual Differences and Abnormal Development By and large, the general structures and connections of the brain are fairly uniform across people, and most of the variations that occur support normal cognitive functioning. In a few cases, however, brains have unusual circuits or missing or distorted structures, and such malformations often interfere with effective learning and behavior.

Some neurological disorders are not obvious at birth, or even in the first few years of life. For example, **schizophrenia,** a serious psychiatric disorder that affects one in a hundred people, often does not surface until adolescence or adulthood (Carlson, 1999). Individuals with schizophrenia display symptoms such as thought disorders (e.g., irrational ideas and disorganized thinking), hallucinations (e.g., "hearing" nonexistent voices), delusions (e.g., worrying that "everyone is out to get me"), and social withdrawal (e.g., avoiding eye contact or conversation with others). Such symptoms appear to be due, at least in part, to structural abnormalities or overactive synapses in certain parts of the brain (Carlson, 1999; Giedd, Jeffries, et al., 1999; Jacobsen, Giedd, Berquin, et al., 1997; Jacobsen, Giedd, Castellanos, et al., 1997).

What causes serious malformations in brain development? In the case of schizophrenia, genetic factors, viral infections during prenatal development, and childbirth complications may be involved (Carlson, 1999). Other neurological abnormalities may be due to drugs, alcohol, illness, or maternal stress during prenatal development; oxygen deprivation or other complications during childbirth; or inadequate nutrition or exposure to toxins (e.g., lead paint) after birth. Table 3–1 lists the possible effects of such factors.

Educational Applications of Research on Brain Development

We sometimes hear professional colleagues talk about the implications of brain research for educational practice. In fact, research in brain development is still in its infancy and does not yet give us guidance on specific ways to maximize children's neurological and cognitive growth (Bruer, 1997; Mayer, 1998; O'Boyle & Gill, 1998). However, we *can* offer a few general suggestions that the research clearly warrants:

■ *Be optimistic that high-quality educational experiences can have a significant impact throughout childhood and adolescence.* Certainly experiences in the early years are important for physical, intellectual, and social growth, but so, too, are experiences in middle childhood and adolescence. Even in late adulthood, it's not too late to learn a new language, master a new athletic skill, or work in a new medium of artistic expression. In general, windows of opportunity for learning do *not* slam shut after early childhood. Early years are learning years, but so are later ones.

■ *Don't overdo efforts to create an "enriched" environment for young children.* In their everyday experiences, young children learn a great deal about phenomena in their physical and social worlds and about the language and practices of their culture. They don't necessarily need to be taught everything they need to learn, but they *do* need to be exposed to it. In many cases, opportunities for play and informal experimentation are just as beneficial as, and sometimes even *more* beneficial than, planned and systematic instruction (Brown & Bjorklund, 1998; Bruer, 1999; Chafel, 1991).

In fact, because of neurological changes that take place in the cortex during middle childhood and adulthood, children may not even be able to benefit from certain kinds of educational experiences until the middle elementary grades at the earliest. Sustaining attention on a single topic, inhibiting socially inappropriate actions, planning ahead for the future—such capacities improve with experience but are also dependent on brain development. Accordingly, some lessons and expectations may be quite reasonable for older children yet be quite *un*reasonable for younger ones. In Chapters 4 and 5, we will look more closely at the cognitive abilities and limitations of children and adolescents of various ages and at the implications of such abilities and limitations for classroom instruction.

■ *Accommodate individual differences in neurological functioning.* Individualizing instruction is a hallmark of good teaching, and it is especially important for students who have a neurological exceptionality. For example, children who have difficulty distinguishing among the various sounds of speech may have brains with circuits that are not fully formed to permit this activity. Intensive training in speech processing seems to benefit

schizophrenia
Psychiatric condition characterized by irrational ideas and disorganized thinking.

TABLE 3–1   Examples of Risk Factors for Healthy Neurological Development

PHASE OF DEVELOPMENT	RISK FACTOR	POSSIBLE OUTCOMES
Prenatal Development	Alcohol	*Fetal alcohol syndrome:* Disruption of neuron development, growth delays, facial abnormalities, mental retardation, impulsivity, behavioral problems
	Marijuana	Premature birth, low birth weight, tremors, oversensitivity to certain kinds of stimuli
	Cocaine	Premature birth, low birth weight, small head size, lethargy, and irritability (cocaine alters the metabolism of some neurotransmitters and may influence the formation of brain structures that depend on these substances; it also reduces blood flow to the brain)
	Heroin	Premature birth, small head circumference, respiratory complications, irritability, death
	HIV infection and AIDS	Delays in motor skills, visual perception, language, and reasoning; long-term cognitive impairment; microencephaly (condition in which children have an exceptionally small head and fail to grow at normal rates)
	Maternal stress	Low birth weight, irritability, colic, restlessness
Birth	Serious birth complications (e.g., oxygen deprivation)	Cognitive, behavioral, and/or psychiatric disorders
Postnatal Development	Nutritional deficiencies	Destruction of neurons and myelin sheaths, sometimes resulting in learning and memory problems
	Exposure to lead	Cognitive and behavioral problems, epilepsy, severe motor difficulties, blindness

Sources: Chasnoff, Burns, Burns, & Schnoll, 1986; Hunt, Streissguth, Kerr, & Olson, 1995; Korkman, Autti-Raemoe, Koivulehto, & Granstroem, 1998; Kraemingk & Paquette, 1999; Mayes & Bornstein, 1997; Teeter & Semrud-Clikeman, 1997.

these children, presumably because of its effects on brain pathways (Nelson, 1999). Special educators, school psychologists, and other specialists can often provide suggestions about effective instructional strategies for working with students who have various neurological deficits.

■ *Provide extra guidance and support for students who have had early exposure to drugs and alcohol.* Children who were exposed to alcohol, cocaine, and other drugs during their prenatal development often come to school with unique needs. These students may need extra assistance in understanding abstract ideas, learning how to inhibit inappropriate responses (such as impulsively hitting bothersome classmates), and applying rules to multiple settings (e.g., "keep your hands to yourself" applies to the lunchroom and playground as well as to the classroom; Lutke, 1997). Furthermore, if students' mothers abused alcohol or drugs during pregnancy, there is a high probability that they continue to do so (O'Connor, Sigman, & Kasari, 1993). Substance-abusing parents tend to have dysfunctional relationships with their children, physically abuse and neglect their children, and use harsh and ineffective disciplinary strategies (Mayes & Bornstein, 1997). Teachers and other school personnel may be the only dependable sources of affection, nurturance, and structure that these children have.

Ultimately, teachers must remember that, with proper guidance and instruction, many children of alcohol- and drug-abusing parents can lead productive and fulfilling lives. One 17-year-old girl with fetal alcohol syndrome expressed this idea eloquently:

> There are two things I want you to know: Do not call me a victim, and do not tell me what I cannot do. Help me to find a way to do it. (Lutke, 1997, p. 188)

Physical Development Across Childhood and Adolescence

Newborn infants have a number of **reflexes**—inherited, automatic responses to certain kinds of stimulation—that enhance their chances of survival. For instance, in the *rooting reflex,* infants turn their head toward an object (perhaps a bottle, breast, or hand) that stimulates their cheek. This reflex disappears after about 3 weeks, as infants begin to turn their head and mouth voluntarily toward nourishment.

With maturation, infants acquire many physical capabilities. In the first 12 to 18 months, they learn to hold up their head, roll over, reach for objects, sit, crawl, and walk. In the second year, they walk with increasing balance and coordination, manipulate small objects, and begin to run, jump, and climb (Teresa once found 2-year-old Alex on top of the refrigerator!).

As you have seen, significant changes take place in size, bodily proportions, and neurological structures throughout childhood and adolescence, and with these changes come new, unique opportunities for physical development. We list key characteristics and acquisitions of each age group in the following Developmental Trends table and describe some in more detail in the next few pages.

Early Childhood (Ages 2–6)

Visit a local playground, and you are likely to see preschool children engaged in nonstop physical activity. Physical movement is a hallmark of early childhood, and dramatic changes occur in both gross motor and fine motor skills. **Gross motor skills** (e.g., running, hopping, tumbling, climbing, and swinging) permit locomotion around the environment. **Fine motor skills** (e.g., drawing, writing, cutting with scissors, and manipulating small objects) involve more limited, controlled, and precise movements, primarily with the hands.

During the preschool years, children typically learn such culture-specific motor skills as riding a tricycle and throwing and catching a ball. Over time, these skills become smoother and better coordinated as a result of practice, longer arms and legs, and genetically dictated increases in muscular control and strength. Optimism and persistence in motor tasks play a role as well. For instance, when Teresa's son Alex was 4, he repeatedly asked his parents to throw him a baseball as he stood poised with his bat. Not at all deterred by an abysmal batting average (about .05), Alex would frequently exclaim, "I almost got it!" His efforts paid off, as he gradually did learn to visually track the ball and coordinate his swing with the ball's path.

A lot of chatter, creative fantasy, and sheer joy accompany gross motor activity in early childhood. Children become superheroes and villains, cowgirls and horses, astronauts and aliens. During *chase play,* a young child may run after another child, pretending to be a lion or other predator (Owens, Steen, Hargrave, Flores, & Hall, 2000; Steen & Owens, 2000). Both the child doing the chasing and the one being chased work hard to keep the game going. The child wishing to be chased may yell "Chase me!," make a taunting face, and then sprint to avoid capture. The chaser joins in the game and often slows down rather than capture the other, thereby prolonging the fun. The eventual capture occurs in a friendly, if dramatic, manner, with the "victim" often squealing in excitement.

Young children also make major strides in fine motor skills. For example, most begin to scribble with a pencil or crayon when they are 18 to 24 months old, and they can draw shapes such as circles and squares when they are about 3 (Figure 3–7). By age 4 or 5, they can draw rudimentary pictures, perhaps of a "person" that consists of a circle for a head, two smaller circles and a curvy line for eyes and a mouth, and four lines sprouting from the circle that represent arms and legs (Beaty, 1998; Kellogg, 1967; McLane & McNamee, 1990). In their

FIGURE 3–7 Given access to paper and crayons or markers, most children begin scribbling when they are 18 to 24 months old. This drawing by Tina, age 2½, shows early practice in making circular shapes.

reflex
An automatic response to a particular kind of stimulation.

gross motor skills
Large movements of the body that permit locomotion around the environment.

fine motor skills
Small, precise movements of particular parts of the body, especially the hands.

Physical Development at Different Age Levels

DEVELOPMENTAL TRENDS

AGE	WHAT YOU MIGHT OBSERVE	DIVERSITY	IMPLICATIONS
Early Childhood (2–6) 	• Loss of rounded, babyish appearance, with arms and legs lengthening and taking on more mature proportions • Boundless physical energy for new gross motor skills, such as running, hopping, tumbling, climbing, and swinging • Acquisition of fine motor skills, such as functional pencil grip and use of scissors • Transition away from afternoon nap, which may initially be marked by periods of fussiness in the afternoon	• Children differ considerably in the ages at which they master various motor skills. • Boys are more physically active than girls, but girls are healthier; these differences continue throughout childhood and adolescence. • Some home environments (e.g., small apartments, homeless shelters) may limit the degree to which children can engage in vigorous physical activity; others may present hazardous environmental conditions (e.g., lead paint, toxic fumes). • Children with mental retardation have delayed motor skills.	• Provide frequent opportunities to play outside or (in inclement weather) in a gymnasium or other large indoor space. • Intersperse vigorous physical exercise with rest and quiet time. • Encourage fine motor skills through play with puzzles, blocks, doll houses, and arts and crafts. • Choose activities that accommodate diversity in children's gross and fine motor skill levels.
Middle Childhood (6–10) 	• Steady gains in height and weight • Loss and replacement of primary teeth • Refinement and consolidation of gross motor skills, and integration of such skills into structured play activities • Participation in organized sports • Increasing fluency in fine motor skills, such as handwriting and drawing	• Variations in weight and height are prominent at any single grade level. • Children begin to show specific athletic talents and interests. • Gender differences appear in children's preferences for various sports and physical activities. • Some neighborhoods do not have playgrounds or other safe play areas that foster children's gross motor skills. • Some children have delays in development of fine motor skills (e.g., their handwriting may be unusually uneven and irregular) due to neurological conditions or lack of opportunity for practice. • Some children spend much of their nonschool time in sedentary activities, such as watching television or playing video games.	• Integrate physical movement into academic activities. • Provide daily opportunities for children to engage in self-organized play activities. • Teach children the basics of various sports and physical games, and encourage them to participate in organized sports programs. • Encourage practice of fine motor skills, but don't penalize children whose fine motor precision is delayed.

writing activities, children create wavy lines or connected loops ("pseudowriting" that resembles adult cursive) at about age 4, and given sufficient experience with written language, they can often write some letters of the alphabet by age 5 (Graham & Weintraub, 1996).

Children's fine motor skills improve gradually over time with experience, practice, and normal neurological development. Some progressions involve cognitive as well as physical development; for instance, children become more competent at drawing as they are increasingly able to identify basic shapes and contours in the people and objects they want to represent on paper (Smith et al., 1998).

We see considerable individual differences in young children's fine motor skills. Some children, such as those born with certain chromosomal conditions (e.g., Down syndrome) and those exposed to alcohol during prenatal development, tend to progress more slowly than their age-mates (Barr, Streissguth, Darby, & Sampson, 1990; Bruni, 1998; Goyen, Lui, & Woods, 1998). Furthermore, some evidence indicates that some kinds of fine motor ac-

AGE	WHAT YOU MIGHT OBSERVE	DIVERSITY	IMPLICATIONS
Early Adolescence (10–14) 	• Periods of rapid growth • Beginnings of puberty; self-consciousness about bodily changes • Some risk taking behavior • Increased aggression in boys	• Onset of puberty may vary over a span of several years; puberty occurs earlier for girls than for boys. • Leisure activities may or may not include regular exercise. • Young teens differ considerably in strength and physical endurance, as well as in their specific talents for sports. Noticeable gender differences begin to appear, with boys being faster, stronger, and more confident about their physical abilities than girls. • Peer groups may or may not encourage risky behavior.	• Be a role model in terms of physical fitness and good eating habits. • Provide privacy for changing clothes and showering during physical education classes. • Explain what sexual harassment is, and do not tolerate it when it appears in the form of jokes, teasing, or physical contact. • Encourage after-school clubs and sponsored leisure activities that help teenagers spend their time constructively.
Late Adolescence (14–18)	• In girls, completion of growth spurt and attainment of mature height • In boys, ongoing increases in stature • Ravenous appetites, especially in boys • Increasing sexual activity • Greater risk taking behavior (e.g., drinking alcohol, taking illegal drugs, engaging in unprotected sexual contact, driving under the influence of drugs or alcohol), due in part to greater independence and acquisition of drivers' licenses	• Gender differences in physical abilities increase; boys are more active in organized sports programs. • Boys more actively seek sexual intimacy than girls do. • Some teens struggle with issues related to sexual orientation. • Some teens begin to rebound from earlier risky behaviors and make better decisions. • Eating disorders may appear, especially in girls. • Adolescents are less likely than younger children to get regular medical care; this is especially true for children from ethnic minority groups.	• Make sure that students know "the facts of life" about sexual intercourse and conception. • Encourage students to form goals for the future (e.g., going to college, developing athletic skills) as a way of helping them curb risky behaviors. • Develop schoolwide policies related to sexual harassment.

Sources: Eaton & Enns, 1986; Eisenberg, Martin, & Fabes, 1996; Gallahue & Ozmun, 1998; Jacklin, 1989; Linn & Hyde, 1989; Logsdon, Alleman, Straits, Belka, & Clark, 1997; National Research Council, 1993; Pellegrini & Smith, 1998; Sadker & Sadker, 1994; Sheridan, 1975; Simons-Morton, Taylor, Snider, Huang, & Fulton, 1994; Thomas & French, 1985; Wigfield, Eccles, & Pintrich, 1996.

tivities (e.g., cursive handwriting) may be easier for girls than boys (Cohen, 1997). Fortunately, explicit instruction and practice can help children improve their fine motor skills, although some individual differences in dexterity will inevitably persist (Bruni, 1998; Case-Smith, 1996).

Middle Childhood (Ages 6–10)

Children in the elementary grades typically show slow but steady gains in height and weight. Body proportions change less than in infancy or early childhood. With these slow, continuous gains come a few losses. Consider the gap-toothed smiles so common in children's elementary school pictures. One by one, children lose their 20 primary ("baby") teeth, replacing them with permanent teeth that at first appear oversized in the small mouths of 6- and 7-year-olds. Girls mature somewhat more quickly than do boys, erupting permanent teeth sooner and progressing toward skeletal maturity earlier.

ACCOMMODATING THE PHYSICAL NEEDS OF CHILDREN

■ Make sure that the classroom is free of sharp edges, peeling paint, and other environmental hazards to which young children may be particularly vulnerable.

After new carpet is installed in his classroom, a preschool teacher notices that several children complain of stomachaches and headaches. He suspects that the recently applied carpet adhesive may be to blame and, with the approval of the preschool's director, asks an outside consultant to evaluate the situation. Meanwhile, he conducts most of the day's activities outdoors or in other rooms in the building.

■ Provide frequent opportunities for children to engage in physical activity.

A preschool teacher schedules "Music and Marching" for mid-morning, "Outdoor Time" before lunch, and a nature walk to collect leaves for an art project after naptime.

■ Plan activities that will help children develop their fine motor skills.

For a unit on transportation, a first-grade teacher has students make mosaics that depict different kinds of vehicles. The students glue a variety of small objects (e.g., beads, sequins, beans, colored rice) onto line drawings of cars, trains, boats, airplanes, bicycles, and so on.

■ Design physical activities so that students with widely differing skill levels can successfully participate.

During a unit on tennis, an elementary physical education teacher has students practice the forehand stroke using tennis rackets. First she asks them to practice bouncing and then hit-ting the ball against the wall of the gymnasium. If some students master these basic skills, she asks them to see how many times in succession they can hit the ball against the wall. If any reach 5 successive hits, she tells them to vary the height of the ball from waist high to shoulder high (Logsdon, Alleman, Straits, Belka, & Clark, 1997).

■ Integrate physical activity into academic lessons.

When teaching about molecules and temperature, a fifth-grade teacher asks students to stand in a cluster in an open area of the classroom. To show the students how molecules behave when something is cold, she asks them to stay close together and move around just a little bit. To show them how molecules behave when something is hot, she asks them to spread farther apart and move more actively. (courtesy of Michele Minichiello)

■ Give children time to rest and rejuvenate.

After a kindergarten class has been playing outside, their teacher offers a snack of apple slices, crackers, and milk. Once they have cleaned up their milk cartons and napkins, the children gather around him on the floor while he reads them a storybook.

■ Respect children's growing ability to care for their own bodies.

A second-grade teacher allows children to go to the restroom whenever they need to. He teaches the children to hang a clothespin with their name on an "out rope" when they leave the room and then remove the pin when they return.

In middle childhood, children build on their emerging physical capabilities. Many gross motor skills that were once awkward are now executed in a more systematic and proficient fashion. Whereas preschoolers may run for the sheer joy of it, elementary school children put running to use in organized games and sports. They intensify their speed and coordination in running, kicking, catching, and dribbling. Stopping frequently to negotiate over rules, they accompany their physical exercise with important social lessons. Although gender differences in gross motor skills are fairly small at this age, boys begin to outperform girls on some athletic tasks, such as speed in walking long distances (National Children and Youth Fitness Study II, 1987).

Elementary-aged children improve in fine motor skills as well as gross motor ones. Their drawings, fueled by physiological maturation and cognitive advances, are more detailed and complex (Case, Okamoto, et al., 1996; Smith et al., 1998). Their handwriting becomes smaller, smoother, and more consistent (Graham & Weintraub, 1996). And they begin to tackle such fine motor activities as sewing, model building, and arts and crafts.

As children progress through middle childhood, they become increasingly aware of and sensitive about their physical appearance. Consider this fourth grader's viewpoint:

I am the ugliest girl I know. My hair is not straight enough, and it doesn't even have the dignity to be curly. My teeth are crooked from sucking my thumb and from a wet-bathing-suit-and-a-slide accident. My clothes are hand-me-downs, my skin is a greenish color that other people call "tan"

During the adolescent growth spurt, appetites increase considerably, especially for boys.

Zits by Jerry Scott and Jim Borgman. Reprinted with special permission of King Features Syndicate.

to be polite, and I don't say the right words, or say them in the right way. I'm smart enough to notice that I'm not smart enough; not so short, but not tall enough; and definitely, definitely too skinny. (Marissa Arillo, in Oldfather & West, 1999, p. 60).

Physical appearance is a major force in social interactions throughout childhood and adolescence. People respond more favorably to students that they perceive to be physically attractive, and differential treatment leads to variations in how students feel about themselves. In a variety of cultures, physical attractiveness is correlated with, and probably a causal factor in, self-esteem (Chu, 2000; Harter, 1999).

Early Adolescence (Ages 10–14)

The most obvious aspect of physical change in early adolescence is the onset of **puberty.** Ushered in by a cascade of hormones, puberty involves a series of biological changes that lead to reproductive maturity. It is marked not only by the maturation of sex-specific characteristics but also by a **growth spurt,** a rapid increase in height and weight. The hormonal increases of adolescence have other physiological repercussions as well, such as increased oil production in the face (often manifested as acne), increased activity in the sweat glands, mood swings, and emotional sensitivity (Buchanan, 1991).

Just as girls matured more quickly in middle childhood, so too do they reach puberty earlier, initiating the process sometime between ages 8 and 13 (on average, at age 10). The process begins with the onset of the growth spurt, "budding" of the breasts, and the emergence of pubic hair. Whereas such changes are typically gradual, the onset of menstruation (**menarche**) is an abrupt event. The experience can be either positive or frightening, depending on a girl's awareness and preparation ahead of time. The first menstrual period tends to occur rather late in puberty, typically sometime between 9 and 15 years. Nature apparently delays menstruation, and with it the possibility of conception, until girls are physically strong and close to their adult height and so are physiologically better able to have a successful pregnancy.

For boys, puberty gets its start somewhere between 9 and 14 years (on average, at 11½ years), when the testes enlarge and the scrotum changes in texture and color. A year or so later, the penis grows larger and pubic hair appears, and the growth spurt begins soon after. At about 13 to 14 years, boys have their first ejaculation experience (**spermarche**), often while sleeping. Boys seem to receive less information from parents about this milestone than girls do about menstruation, and little is known about boys' feelings about it. Later developments include growth of facial hair and deepening of the voice and eventually the attainment of adult height. (The course of puberty for both boys and girls is depicted in Figure 3–8.)

Notice that, for girls, the growth spurt is one of the first signs of puberty, but for boys it occurs relatively late in the sequence. The result of this discrepancy is that boys end up taller, partly because they have a longer period of steady prepubescent growth and partly because they grow a bit more during their adolescent growth spurt. With puberty, boys also gain considerably more muscle mass than girls, courtesy of the male hormone *testosterone* (Thomas & French, 1985).

puberty
Physiological changes that occur during adolescence and lead to reproductive maturation.

growth spurt
Rapid increase in height and weight during puberty.

menarche
First menstrual period in an adolescent female.

spermarche
First ejaculation in an adolescent male.

FIGURE 3–8 Maturational sequences of puberty

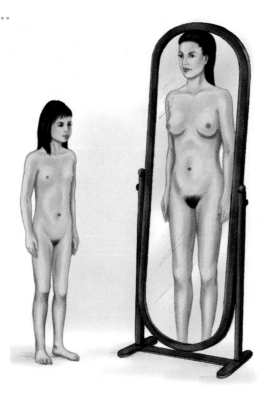

IN GIRLS

Initial elevation of breasts and beginning of growth spurt (typically between 8 and 13 years; on average, at 10 years)

Appearance of pubic hair (sometimes occurs before elevation of breasts)

Increase in size and structure of uterus, vagina, labia, and clitoris

Further development of breasts

Peak of growth spurt

Menarche, or onset of menstrual cycle (typically between 9 and 15 years)

Completion of height gain (about two years after menarche) and attainment of adult height

Completion of breast development and pubic hair growth

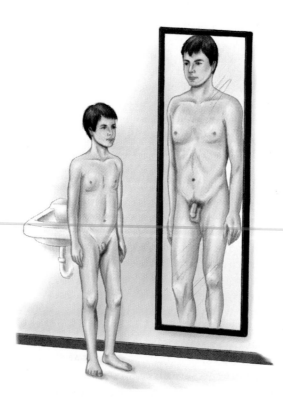

IN BOYS

Enlargement of the testes and changes in texture and color of scrotum (typically between 9 and 14 years; on average, at 11$\frac{1}{2}$ years)

Increase in penis size and appearance of pubic hair

Beginning of growth spurt (on average, at 12$\frac{1}{2}$ years)

Spermarche, or first ejaculation

Peak of growth spurt, accompanied by more rapid penis growth

Appearance of facial hair

Deepening voice, as size of larynx and length of vocal cords increase

Completion of penis growth

Completion of height gain and attainment of adult height

Completion of pubic hair growth

Accompanying the physical changes of puberty are changes in adolescents' cognitive capacities, social relationships, and feelings about themselves (Brooks-Gunn, 1989; Brooks-Gunn & Paikoff, 1992). Puberty also seems to loosen restraints on problem behaviors. For example, the onset of puberty in boys is associated with increased aggression (Olweus, Mattson, Schalling, & Low, 1998), alcohol and cigarette use (Reifman, Barnes, & Hoffman, 1999), and such behaviors as lying, shoplifting, and burglary (Cota-Robles & Neiss, 1999).

To some extent, biology affects psychology in young adolescents. The continuing development of the cortex presumably allows more complex thought, and hormonal fluctuations affect emotions. And adolescents' rapidly changing physical characteristics can be a source of either excitement or dismay. For instance, Anne Frank looked very positively on puberty, as this entry in her diary shows:

> I think what is happening to me is so wonderful, and not only what can be seen on my body, but all that is taking place inside. I never discuss myself or any of these things with anybody; that is why I have to talk to myself about them.
> Each time I have a period—and that has only been three times—I have the feeling that in spite of all the pain, unpleasantness, and nastiness, I have a sweet secret, and that is why, although it is nothing but a nuisance to me in a way, I always long for the time that I shall feel that secret within me again. (Frank, 1967, p. 146)

Yet others are not at all happy with their changing bodies. In *Reviving Ophelia,* therapist Mary Pipher (1994) describes ninth-grader Cayenne's perspective:

> She hated her looks. She thought her hair was too bright, her hips and thighs too flabby. She tried to lose weight but couldn't. She dyed her hair, but it turned a weird purple color and dried out. She felt almost every girl was prettier. She said, "Let's face it. I'm a dog." (p. 32)[2]

Curiously, psychology also affects biology, in that life experiences influence biological growth in adolescence. Family conflict seems to accelerate puberty in girls, although not in boys (Kenneth, Smith, & Palermiti, 1997). However, pubertal maturation seems to be delayed in girls who grow up in low-income families, perhaps because of less adequate nutrition (Tremblay, 1999). Also influencing physical well-being is a belief known as the **personal fable:** Young teenagers tend to think of themselves as completely unique beings within the human race (Elkind, 1981a). This belief often gives teenagers a sense of invulnerability. Because they feel immune from the normal dangers of life, they may take foolish risks, such as experimenting with drugs and alcohol and having unprotected sexual intercourse (DeRidder, 1993; Thomas, Groër, & Droppleman, 1993). (In Chapter 9, we will revisit the personal fable when we talk about the development of a sense of self in adolescence.)

Diversity in the Onset of Puberty Compared to boys, girls get a 1½-year head start on puberty. This gender difference is apparent in both the height advantage and the preoccupation with the opposite sex that many girls have in the middle school grades.

Considerable diversity exists in the timing of puberty for both girls and boys, and this diversity causes problems for some teenagers. Researchers have focused primarily on the potential vulnerabilities of *early-maturing girls* and *late-maturing boys,* whose bodies, the researchers hypothesize, are inconsistent with cultural ideals of attractiveness in the Western world. Early-maturing girls become heavier and more curvaceous earlier and so are less likely to resemble the slim and angular professional models that the popular media idealize as icons of beauty. Late-maturing boys are still "boys" when some of their peers are beginning to show signs of adultlike masculinity.

Some evidence indicates that early-maturing girls are, on average, less happy and feel less good about themselves than late-maturing girls (Susman, Nottelmann, Inoff-Germain, Dorn, & Chrousos, 1987). In addition, their more mature appearance may arouse older boys, ushering them into precocious sexual activity (Hayes & Hofferth, 1987; Stattin & Magnusson, 1990). Early-maturing girls are more likely to partake in other risky behaviors as well, including substance abuse and reckless driving (Irwin & Millstein, 1992).

As for late-maturing boys, research indicates that they get off to a slower start than other boys in several aspects of development. For instance, they tend to be less athletically inclined and less popular with peers, and they less frequently seek leadership positions at school (Gross & Duke, 1980; Jones, 1949; Simmons & Blyth, 1987). On the plus side, however, they are less likely to engage in risk-taking behaviors such as smoking, drinking, and delinquent activities (Duncan, Ritter, Dornbusch, Gross, & Carlsmith, 1985; Susman et al., 1985).

---

[2]From *Reviving Ophelia* by Mary Pipher, Ph.D., copyright © 1994 by Mary Pipher, Ph.D. Used by permission of Putnam Berkley, a division of Penguin Putnam Inc.

personal fable
Tendency for adolescents to think of themselves as unique beings that are invulnerable to normal risks and dangers.

ACCOMMODATING THE PHYSICAL NEEDS OF ADOLESCENTS

■ Accommodate the self-conscious feelings that adolescents have about their changing bodies.

A middle school boys' basketball coach gives students plenty of time to change clothes before and after practice. He also makes sure that the showers have enough curtains that each student can shower in private.

■ Keep in mind that menstruation can begin at unexpected and inopportune times.

An eighth-grade girl comes into class obviously upset, and her best friend approaches their teacher to explain that the two of them need to go to the nurse's office right away. The teacher realizes what has probably just happened and immediately gives them permission to go.

■ Make sure students understand what sexual harassment is, and do not tolerate it when it occurs.

A high school includes a sexual harassment policy in its student handbook, and homeroom teachers explain the policy very early in the school year. When a student unthinkingly violates the policy by teasing a classmate about her "big rack," his teacher takes him aside and privately explains that his comment not only constitutes sexual harassment (and so violates school policy) but also makes the girl feel unnecessarily embarrassed and uncomfortable. The boy admits that he spoke without thinking and, after class, tells the girl he's sorry.

■ Be sensitive to students' feelings about early or late maturation.

In its health curriculum, a middle school clearly describes the typical sequence of biological changes that accompany puberty. It also stresses that the timing of these changes varies widely from one person to the next and that being "normal" takes many forms.

The timing of puberty does not necessarily destine adolescents to a lifelong fate, however. For instance, the relative popularity of late-maturing girls and early-maturing boys brings only short-term gains that dissipate over time. Admired as teens, late-maturing girls and early-maturing boys may become somewhat rigid, conforming, and discontented as adults (Livson & Peshkin, 1980; Macfarlane, 1971). In contrast, early-maturing girls and late-maturing boys may develop strategies for coping with the trials and tribulations of adolescence, and these strategies may enable them to become independent, flexible, and contented adults.

Adolescents' adjustment to puberty is, to some degree, influenced by their culture, parents, and school setting (Blyth, Simmons, & Zakin, 1985; Hill, Holmbeck, Marlow, Green, & Lynch, 1985; Peterson & Taylor, 1980; Stattin & Magnusson, 1990). In some cultures, the beginning of puberty is joyously welcomed by formal celebrations, such as Bar Mitzvahs and Bat Mitzvahs for 13-year-olds of the Jewish faith and *quinceañeras* for 15-year-old girls in Mexican and Mexican American communities. School personnel can ease the transition as well, for instance, by giving some advance warning about the physiological changes that young adolescents are likely to experience and reassuring students that considerable variations in timing are all well within a "normal" range.

Late Adolescence (Ages 14–18)

At about age 15 for girls and 17 for boys, the growth spurt ends. And in the later teenage years, most adolescents reach sexual maturation. (Individual differences persist, however, especially for boys, some of whom show few signs of puberty until the high school years.) With sexual maturation comes increasing interest in sexual activity, including hugging, kissing and, for many teens, more intimate contact as well (DeLamateur & MacCorquodale, 1979). In Chapter 13, we will explore several topics related to adolescent sexuality, including dating, sexual intimacy, and sexual orientation.

Even at this point, nature continues to tinker with its handiwork. The brain in particular perseveres in refining its pathways, permitting more thoughtful control of emotions and more deliberate reflection about the possible consequences of various behaviors (Chugani, 1998; Giedd, Blumenthal, Jeffries, Rajapakse, et al., 1999). Perhaps as a result, the false sense of invulnerability tends to decline in later adolescence (Durkin, 1995; Lapsley, Jackson, Rice, & Shadid, 1988). Nevertheless, many older adolescents continue to engage in behaviors that undermine their long-term physical health—for instance, smoking cigarettes, abusing alcohol and drugs, eating too many high-salt and high-fat foods or, worse still, eating little at all—without thinking about the potential repercussions of such actions (Guthrie, Caldwell, & Hunter, 1997). We now look more closely at eating habits, alcohol and drug abuse, and other general issues related to children's and adolescents' health and physical well-being.

General Issues in Physical Well-Being

With age, children and adolescents become more aware of what "good health" is (Figure 3–9). But they also become increasingly independent decision makers and, even in late adolescence, don't always make decisions that are best for their health. In the following sections we consider several issues related to health and well-being—eating habits, physical activity, rest and sleep, and health-compromising behaviors—and identify strategies that teachers can use to promote a more healthful lifestyle for their students.

Eating Habits

As you have learned, children's nutrition affects their physical growth, brain development, and sexual maturation. Furthermore, their diet influences their energy level, concentration, and ability to perform both physical and mental tasks.

Educators often encounter children who are poorly fed, perhaps because their parents have few financial resources, are homeless, or are physically or mentally ill. Even in more fortunate circumstances, parents may rush to work in the morning and neglect to feed either themselves or their children. As an example, Teresa recalls a first grader who complained that he'd had a terrible day at school. He explained that his parents were busy professionals who never ate breakfast, and so on that particular day (as well as on many other days) he went to school with an empty stomach.

As children grow older and begin to make their own decisions about what and when to eat, the situation may deteriorate even further. For instance, in a large-scale study of American children, 24% of children ages 2 to 5 had a good diet, but only 6% of adolescents ages 13 to 18 did (Interagency Forum on Child and Family Statistics, 1999). Generally speaking, adolescents (especially boys) eat far too much "bad" stuff, such as high-fat and high-sodium foods,

FIGURE 3–9 As children grow older, they become more knowledgeable about what "good health" entails. Grace (age 11) drew this rendition of healthy and unhealthy people.

Modeled after Mayall, Bendelow, Barker, Storey, & Veltman (1996).

and far too little "good" stuff, such as fruits, vegetables, and whole grains (Robinson & Killen, 1995; Simons-Morton, Baranowski, Parcel, O'Hara, & Matteson, 1990; Subar et al., 1992).

Part of the problem is that children don't understand how eating habits relate to health. At age 5, children know that some foods (e.g., fruits, vegetables, milk) are good for them but have no idea *why* (Carey, 1985b). Even at ages 9 to 11, the vast majority of children have no idea that the body breaks food down into the essential nutrients it needs to grow and thrive (Carey, 1985b). In our own experience, such ignorance continues well into adolescence. Jeanne thinks of her son Jeff, who at 17 maintained that he could get through an entire day in perfect shape as long as he had a few donuts and several cans of cola.

Well-balanced diets are essential not only for the short run but also for children's and adolescents' long-term well-being. Excessive intake of fat, cholesterol, and sodium increases the probability of obesity and high blood pressure later in life (Nicklas, Webber, Johnson, Srinivasan, & Berenson, 1995). A good diet may be particularly important for youth of color, who often have an elevated risk for such serious medical conditions as cardiovascular disease, diabetes, and cancer (Wilson, Nicholson, & Krishnamoorthy, 1998).

Obesity Children are considered **obese** if their actual body weight exceeds their "ideal" weight (a figure that takes into account their age, gender, height, and body build) by 20% or more (Rallison, 1986). The prevalence of childhood obesity has increased over the last few decades, as has the number of children who are extremely overweight (Gortmaker, Dietz, Sobol, & Wehler, 1987). In one recent study, 22% of children between the ages of 6 and 17—more than *one fifth* of the sample—were identified as obese (Troiano, Flegal, Kuczmarski, Campbell, & Johnson, 1995).

Some obese children outgrow their baby fat, but others do not. Approximately 40% of obese 7-year-olds are obese as adults, but 70% of obese 10- to 13-year-olds become obese adults (Epstein, Wing, & Valoski, 1985). Childhood obesity is a concern in part because it may lead to serious health risks, especially in adulthood (Kedesdy & Budd, 1998). But it has social consequences as well: Other students may torment obese youngsters, calling them names and excluding them from activities.

Obesity seems to have some genetic basis, but environmental factors, such as family eating patterns, also play a role (Kedesdy & Budd, 1998). Fortunately, several interventions, including dietary counseling, combining calorie restriction with increases in physical activity, and behavioral techniques (e.g., setting specific and concrete goals, monitoring progress toward these goals, and recognizing and rewarding progress) are often effective (Kedesdy & Budd, 1998). In fact, such interventions are more successful with obese children than with obese adults, possibly because children continue to grow in height whereas adults do not, and they have a briefer history of maladaptive eating habits (cf. Epstein, 1990).

Eating Disorders Whereas some young people eat too much, others eat too little. Some develop eating disorders that seriously threaten their health. People with **anorexia nervosa** eat little if anything. In contrast, people with **bulimia** eat voraciously, especially fattening foods, and then purge their bodies by taking laxatives or forcing themselves to vomit. Individuals with eating disorders often have a distorted body image (feeling as if they are "fat" even though they appear grossly thin to others), and they may exercise compulsively in their efforts to lose additional weight (Attie, Brooks-Gunn, & Petersen, 1990; Kedesdy & Budd, 1998). In addition to jeopardizing physical health, eating disorders may slow down the bodily changes associated with puberty (Rallison, 1986).

Eating disorders are most common in adolescence and early adulthood, but they are also sometimes seen at earlier ages. Particularly when they appear before puberty, eating disorders are associated with feelings of loneliness and depression; hence, they encompass serious emotional problems as well as physical ones (Alessi, Krahn, Brehm, & Wittekindt, 1989; Attie et al., 1990). Girls are more likely to have eating disorders than boys, but 5% of anorexics are male (Stein & Reichert, 1990).

Many experts believe that society's obsession with thinness is partly to blame for anorexia nervosa and bulimia (Attie et al., 1990; Fisher & Brone, 1991; Streigel-Moore, Silberstein, & Rodin, 1986). It is fashionable for girls and women in particular to be slender; thin is "in." Psychological factors exert their force as well: Individuals may use their thinness to gain attention,

obesity
Condition in which a person weighs at least 20% more than what is optimal for good health.

anorexia nervosa
Eating disorder in which a person, in an attempt to be thin, eats little or nothing for weeks or months and seriously jeopardizes health.

bulimia
Eating disorder in which a person, in an attempt to be thin, eats a large amount of food and then purposefully purges it from the body by vomiting or taking laxatives.

stife their growing sexuality, or maintain a sense of control in the face of overbearing parents. In some cases, inherited conditions predispose people to eating disorders (Attie & Brooks-Gunn, 1989; Fisher & Brone, 1991).

Occasionally, school personnel and other adults unwittingly contribute to eating disorders. For instance, Mary Pipher (1994) describes the roots of 16-year-old Heidi's bulimia:

> Heidi said, "I've had this problem for two years, but lately it's affecting my gymnastics. I am too weak, particularly on the vault, which requires strength. It's hard to concentrate.
>
> "I blame my training for my eating disorder," Heidi continued. "Our coach has weekly weigh-ins where we count each others' ribs. If they are hard to count we're in trouble."
>
> I [Pipher] clucked in disapproval. Heidi explained that since puberty she had had trouble keeping her weight down. After meals, she was nervous that she'd eaten too much. She counted calories; she was hungry but afraid to eat. In class she pinched the fat on her side and freaked out. The first time she vomited was after a gymnastics meet. Coach took her and the other gymnasts to a steak house. Heidi ordered a double cheeseburger and onion rings. After she ate, she obsessed about the weigh-in the next day, so she decided, just this once, to get rid of her meal. She slipped into the restaurant bathroom and threw up.
>
> She blushed. "It was harder than you would think. My body resisted, but I was able to do it. It was so gross that I thought, 'I'll never do that again,' but a week later I did. At first it was weekly, then twice a week. Now it's almost every day. My dentist said that acid is eating away the enamel of my teeth."
>
> Heidi began to cry. "I feel like such a hypocrite. People look at me and see a small, healthy person. I see a person who gorges on food and is totally out of control. You wouldn't believe how much I eat. I shove food into my mouth so fast that I choke. Afterwards, my stomach feels like it will burst." (pp. 166–167)[3]

Anorexia nervosa and bulimia frequently require intensive and long-term intervention by medical and psychological specialists (Linscheid & Fleming, 1995); they are not conditions that are easily corrected simply by encouraging individuals to change their eating habits. Thus, teachers should be alert to common symptoms (increasing thinness, complaints of being "too fat," lack of energy, etc.) and should consult with a counselor or school psychologist whenever an eating disorder is suspected.

Promoting Better Eating Habits We end this section with thoughts about what educators can do to foster better nutrition and eating habits:

■ *Provide between-meal snacks for young children.* Children in preschool and the primary grades need periodic snacks as well as regular meals. Crackers, healthy cookies, fruit slices, and milk can rejuvenate active children and are particularly important for children who, for whatever reason, have come to school without eating breakfast. At the same time, however, teachers must be aware of food allergies, family food preferences, and developmental feeding abilities (e.g., possible limitations in chewing and swallowing hard substances).

■ *Regularly review the basics of good nutrition, and ask students to set goals for improving their eating habits.* Well planned school-based programs can be quite effective in changing children's and adolescents' eating habits and reducing their fat, sodium, and cholesterol intake as a result (Bush et al., 1989; Perry et al., 1989; Resnicow, Cross, & Wynder, 1991). Such programs are more likely to be successful when they ask students to set specific goals (e.g., reducing consumption of salty snacks), encourage them to chart their progress toward these goals, show them that they can stick with new eating patterns, and take cultural practices into account (Schinke, Moncher, and Singer, 1994; Wilson et al., 1998).

A logical first step in this process is to introduce students to the basic food groups and ask them to evaluate their own diets based on the recommended servings for each group. Figure 3–10 shows a third grader's analysis of her eating habits the day before.

■ *Educate students about eating disorders.* Teachers can take the glamour out of being excessively thin by educating students about eating disorders. For instance, Teresa's son Connor first learned about anorexia nervosa when his third-grade teachers talked about eating disorders as part of a unit on the human body.

---

[3]From *Reviving Ophelia* by Mary Pipher, Ph.D., copyright © 1994 by Mary Pipher, Ph.D. Used by permission of Putnam Berkley, a division of Penguin Putnam Inc.

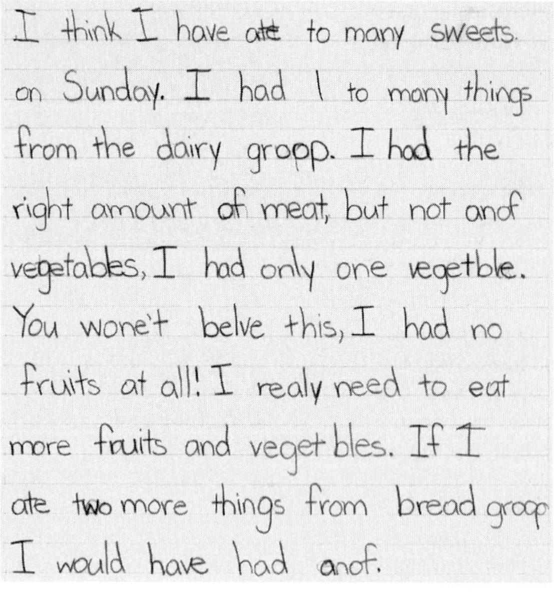

I think I have ate to many sweets. on Sunday. I had 1 to many things from the dairy groop. I had the right amount of meat, but not anof vegetables, I had only one vegetble. You wone't belve this, I had no fruits at all! I realy need to eat more fruits and veget bles. If I ate two more things from bread groop I would have had anof.

FIGURE 3–10 Charlotte (age 8) reflects on her eating habits over the weekend.

■ *Follow up when you suspect chronic nutritional problems.* Malnutrition can occur as a result of many factors. When low family income is at fault, teachers can make sure that students' families apply for free or reduced-cost lunch programs. When parental neglect or mental illness is possibly involved, teachers may need to report their suspicions to principals, counselors, psychologists, or school nurses to find the best approach to take in protecting vulnerable students.

■ *Convey respect for students' feelings.* Students who struggle with obesity or eating disorders are certainly as sensitive as their class-mates—and often even more so—when others make unflattering comments about their weight. Teachers must insist that the classroom be a "no-tease zone" regarding weight and other physical conditions.

In addition, students who are eligible for free lunches may be embarrassed about their limited financial circumstances, and simple teacher interventions can minimize the extent to which these students feel as if they stand out. For instance, a considerate staff member at one school took subsidized lunches and placed them in individual students' own lunchboxes, thus enabling students to save face when eating with peers from higher-income families (Mayall et al., 1996).

Physical Activity

Activity level increases markedly during early childhood. It then decreases during middle childhood and adolescence, sometimes by as much as 50% (Campbell, Eaton, McKeen, & Mitsutake, 1999; Rowland, 1990).

A common feature of physical activity in early and middle childhood is **rough-and-tumble play,** or good-natured "fighting." Children wrestle each other to the ground, push and shove each other, and roll around together. Perhaps in our evolutionary past, rough-and-tumble play prepared children for the fights they were likely to encounter as adolescents and adults (Humphreys & Smith, 1987). In today's world, it seems to serve other purposes, such as providing breaks from demanding intellectual tasks and establishing who is dominant in a group of children (Bjorklund & Brown, 1998; Pellegrini & Smith, 1998). Whatever the functions of rough-and-tumble play, children often find considerable pleasure in it, and when their parents and teachers insist that they stop fighting, they are likely to maintain that they are just "playing" or "messing around."

In school settings, such rough play is rarely considered acceptable, in large part because of the risk of injury. Yet children do need outlets for their seemingly boundless energy. At most schools, however, opportunities for physical activity are quite limited. Even in physical education classes, children spend much of their time listening and watching demonstrations and waiting in line for their turns to try a new skill. Elementary students spend less than 10% of physical education class time in moderate or vigorous physical activity, and middle school students spend only 17% of class time in such activity (Simons-Morton, Taylor, Snider, & Huang, 1993; Simons-Morton et al., 1994).

As children reach adolescence, exercise helps them to maintain their physical fitness and to cope more effectively with life's frustrations and stresses (Brown & Siegel, 1988). Yet school tasks become increasingly sedentary in the middle school and high school grades, and so adolescents are most likely to find opportunities for vigorous activity outside of school walls (Pate, Long, & Heath, 1994). Many adolescents do not get the exercise they need; for instance, only about half of them engage in three or more 20-minute sessions per week of moderate to vigorous exercise (Pate et al., 1994).

Throughout childhood, and especially in adolescence, boys tend to be more active than girls; for instance, they are more active on the playground and have more difficulty sitting still in class (Eaton & Enns, 1986; Sallis, 1993). During the preschool and elementary school years, gender differences in motor skills are typically quite small and are probably due more to environmental factors (such as opportunities to practice specific skills) than hereditary influences (Gallahue & Ozmun, 1998; Thomas & French, 1985). After puberty, however, boys have a significant advantage over girls in many physical activities, especially those involving height and muscular strength (Eisenberg, Martin, & Fabes, 1996; Linn & Hyde, 1989; Thomas & French, 1985).

rough-and-tumble play
Playful physical "fighting" typical in early and middle childhood.

Organized Sports In our opening case study, two enterprising teenagers were the driving force in establishing a softball league in a small, lower-income town. The league provided both a constructive use of time and an appropriate outlet for physical energy for many of the town's younger residents. As Tom and Phillip put it, "Now, we've got a schedule. We've got something to do. . . . a place to go" (Pollack, 1998, p. 274). Organized sports have other benefits as well. They provide a means through which children can maintain and enhance their physical strength, endurance, and agility. Furthermore, they promote social development by fostering communication, cooperation, and leadership skills.

But organized sports can have their downsides as well, especially when adults encourage unhealthy competition, place excessive pressure on children to perform well, and foster the development of athletically talented children at the expense of their less gifted teammates. Well-meaning parents and coaches can bolster children's confidence and athletic skills, but they can also rob children of their intrinsic enjoyment of sports (Smith & Smoll, 1997).

Generally speaking, boys are more confident than girls about their ability to play sports, and boys are almost twice as likely as girls to belong to an organized sports team (Sadker & Sadker, 1994; Wigfield et al., 1996). For boys especially, participation in sports is a prestigious activity, and talented athletes are usually quite popular with their classmates (Sadker & Sadker, 1994). Boys' top choices for physical exercise often include competitive sports, especially basketball, football, baseball, and softball (Pate et al., 1994). Girls are more likely to prefer noncompetitive activities, such as dancing, roller-skating, and walking (Pate et al., 1994).

Encouraging Physical Activity Researchers still have much to learn about how teachers and other adults can best promote healthful physical activity in children and adolescents (Taylor, Beech, & Cummings, 1998). Generally speaking, interventions with small groups tend to be more successful than programs delivered to larger audiences, and school-based interventions are more likely to be successful than those at other sites (Taylor et al., 1998). Here we offer several strategies for promoting children's and adolescents' physical activity in school settings:

■ *Be "pro-ACTIVE."* Teachers at all grade levels should incorporate opportunities for physical movement into classroom activities, allowing students to release pent-up energy and giving them a mental breather from strenuous intellectual pursuits. Regular breaks that include physical activity tend to increase students' attention to demanding cognitive tasks (Pellegrini & Bjorklund, 1997).

■ *Provide environments in which young children can safely engage in physical activity.* Open space, playground equipment, and balls and other athletic props encourage physical exercise. Equipment should be chosen carefully to allow children to experiment freely yet safely with their bodies, ideally reducing the instances in which teachers have to say "no" to particular activities (Bronson, 2000). Furthermore, the equipment should be plentiful enough that all children have access to it yet sufficiently limited that children must interact and cooperate as they use it (Frost, Shin, & Jacobs, 1998).

By the middle elementary years, children can do much of the structuring of physical activities and games themselves. Teachers should tolerate some bickering as children fuss over rules and in other ways learn to get along. Even so, they may occasionally need to intervene to minimize physical aggression and to help integrate children who do not readily join in.

■ *Make exercise an enjoyable activity.* By the time they reach high school, many young people have had several unpleasant experiences with physical exercise and, as a result, associate exercise with discomfort, failure, embarrassment, competition, boredom, injury, or regimentation (Rowland, 1990). Furthermore, the majority of adolescents do not see physical exercise as a regular part of the daily lives of their parents or other family members (Feist & Brannon, 1989).

Youngsters are more likely to engage in a physical activity if they enjoy it and find it challenging while still being within their ability level (Taylor et al., 1998). Their enjoyment can spring from a variety of sources: They may have intrinsic interest in developing particular skills (e.g., in karate), consider certain activities outlets for self-expression (e.g., as is true for dance), or appreciate the camaraderie and peer support they gain from team sports and other group activities. For example, as Jeanne works on this paragraph, she looks forward to her aerobics class later in the day, when she knows she will see a couple of her friends and be able to bounce around the gym in sync with lively music.

Regular recess and breaks for physical movement not only promote children's physical well-being but also lead to improved attention and concentration in more cognitively oriented activities.

Art courtesy of Grace, age 11.

■ *Plan physical activities with diversity in mind.* Not everyone can be a quarterback, and not everyone likes football. In fact, it's probably the minority of students who are drawn to competitive sports at all. But *all* children can find enjoyment in physical activity in some form. Offering a range of activities, from dance to volleyball, can maximize the number of students who participate. Ideally, everyone can find a niche. A child who is unusually short, for example, might look to activities that do not require a tall stature, such as soccer, cycling, or gymnastics (Rudlin, 1993). A boy who is extremely shy might be given specific jobs—perhaps setting up equipment or modeling an athletic skill at which he is especially proficient—that make him feel more comfortable in group situations. A girl in a wheelchair might go up to bat in a softball game and then have a classmate run the bases for her (an adaptive physical education instructor can give you ideas about how to modify an activity for students with disabilities).

■ *Focus on self-improvement rather than on comparison with peers.* As you will discover in Chapter 11, focusing on one's own improvement is, for most students, far more motivating than focusing on how well one's performance stacks up against that of classmates. Focusing too much on comparison with others may lead children and adolescents to believe that physical ability is largely a matter of "natural talent," when in fact most physical skills are primarily the result of considerable practice (Ames, 1984; Proctor & Dutta, 1995).

One obvious way to promote self-improvement is to teach skills in progression, from simple to complex (Gallahue & Ozmun, 1998). For example, a preschool teacher might ask children to hop on one foot as they pretend to be the "hippity hop bunny." Once they have mastered that skill, the teacher can demonstrate more complex skills, such as galloping and skipping, that involve sequenced movements on both sides of the body. Carefully sequenced lessons give children feelings of success and mastery that enhance their enjoyment of physical activities. Even in competitive sports, the emphasis should be more on how well students have "played the game"—for instance, on whether they worked well together, treated members of the opposing team with respect, and were all-around good sports—than on whether they won or lost (Gallahue & Ozmun, 1998). For instance, children have more positive attitudes about their involvement in baseball and basketball leagues when their coaches emphasize the importance of improving skills and having fun (rather than winning), give lots of positive feedback about everyone's effort and performance, and respond to mistakes with suggestions and encouragement (Smith & Smoll, 1997).

■ *Make sure that students don't overdo it.* Some students become excessively involved in sports and exercise. The soft and spongy parts of bones in growing children are susceptible to injury from repeated use, and especially from excessive weight-bearing forces (Micheli & Melhonian, 1987). Weight-training machines are almost always designed for larger bodies, exacerbating the chances for injury. Overuse injuries are also seen in distance running, distance swimming, and gymnastics (Gallahue & Ozmun, 1998). Furthermore, excessive concern about being successful in athletics can lead children and adolescents to make health-compromising choices (taking steroids, gaining or losing weight too quickly, etc.), as our earlier case of Heidi, the 16-year-old gymnast, so poignantly illustrates.

Rest and Sleep

Sleeping and resting are essential to growth and physical well-being. Sleep actually helps young people to grow, because growth hormones are released at higher rates as children snooze. In addition to promoting growth, sleep may help the brain to maintain normal functioning and promote its development (Carlson, 1999).

Time spent in sleeping decreases steadily over the course of childhood and adolescence. Newborn babies sleep 16 hours a day; in contrast, 2-year-olds sleep 12 hours, 3- to 5-year olds sleep 11 hours, 10- to 13-year-olds sleep 10 hours, and 14- to 18-year-olds sleep 8½ hours (Roffwarg, Muzio, & Dement, 1966). These figures, of course, are averages, and much variability occurs in how many hours of sleep children at any single age need and how rested they feel after sleeping a particular number of hours.

Occasional sleep problems are normal occurrences in childhood. Nightmares are common between ages 3 and 6, and children may seek reassurance from adults to battle demons of the night that seem so real. But one-fourth of all children have chronic problems sleeping (Durand, 1998). More pronounced sleep disturbances (e.g., waking repeatedly during the night) may be a symptom of serious health problems, chemical abuse, or excessive stress; for instance, repeated nightmares are common among children who have been victims of abuse or other traumatic incidents (Durand, 1998; Vignau et al., 1997). Furthermore, children with certain disabilities (e.g., cerebral palsy, severe visual impairment, autism, attention-deficit hyperactivity disorder) often have difficulty sleeping (Durand, 1998).

In our own experience, adolescents are less likely to get sufficient sleep than younger children. Although they require less sleep than they did in their earlier years, they are growing rapidly, and so their bodies need considerable time to rest. Yet their out-of-school obligations—extracurricular activities, part-time jobs, social engagements, and homework assignments—may keep them up until the wee hours of the morning. For instance, as a high school student, Jeanne's son Jeff thought nothing of working at the local grocery store until 9:00 P.M., communicating with friends on the phone or on-line for an hour after that, and then finally settling down to do his homework. Needless to say, Jeff's late hours and sleep habits were a frequent source of discussion and friction between him and his parents.

When children and adolescents don't get enough sleep, they are likely to be irritable and have difficulty with changes in routine, and any aggressive tendencies they have may worsen (Durand, 1998). In some cases, of course, they actually fall asleep in class; for instance, it's not uncommon for high school teachers (and college professors as well) to find students napping during class time—a practice hardly conducive to classroom learning!

Accommodating Students' Needs for Rest and Sleep Teachers regularly have students who do not sleep easily and soundly, including some who are truly sleep-deprived. With this in mind, we offer the following suggestions:

■ *In some cases, provide time for sleep during the school day.* It is common practice, and almost certainly *good* practice, to include an afternoon naptime in the schedule of preschoolers who attend school most or all of the day. A few older children and adolescents—for instance, those with recent brain injuries or other chronic health conditions—may need an hour or two of sleep as well, perhaps on a couch in the nurse's office (Jackson & Ormrod, 1998).

■ *Include time for rest in the daily schedule.* Young children typically give up their afternoon nap sometime between ages 2 and 5, but for quite some time after that, they need to recharge their batteries with quiet and restful activities (e.g., listening to stories or music) in the afternoon. Even older children and adolescents typically cannot "go, go, go" all day long. At any age level, students learn and perform more effectively when they take an occasional, restful break from intense physical or intellectual activity.

■ *Be alert to students who appear sleepy, irritable, or distractible.* They may be tired! Although specific advice about sleep habits is probably best left to the family physician, teachers should certainly speak with parents when they think fatigue is the source of students' difficulties in concentration, peer relationships, or classroom behavior.

■ *Give students enough time to complete out-of-school assignments, and help them plan their time so that they don't leave assigned tasks to the last minute.* At the high school level, students may have several hours of homework each night. Add to this workload adolescents' increasing involvement in extracurricular and social activities, and you have students who are seriously overcommitted timewise. Lengthy last-minute homework assignments ("For tomorrow, write a 5-page essay on the pros and cons of having labor unions") make it virtually impossible for students to plan ahead and budget their time, and when something has to be left out of the daily schedule, that "something" may very well be sleep.

Even when teachers do give adequate time for homework, many high school students (and in our own experience, many college students as well!) underestimate how long it will take them to finish assignments and don't allot time for getting a good night's sleep. Especially when an out-of-school task is lengthy and complex (a major project, a research paper, etc.), teachers should encourage regular progress by giving students deadlines for completing various parts of the task.

■ *Recognize that sleep problems can be a sign of illness or emotional stress.* Words of acknowledgement and kindness ("You look tired today, Darragh. Did you sleep all right last night?") may give students permission to share their troubles and, as a result, take the first step toward resolving them.

Health-Compromising Behaviors

Especially as they grow older and gain increasing independence from adult supervision, children and adolescents face many choices about how to spend their leisure time, and they often make their decisions without adequate knowledge about how certain behaviors are likely to affect their health and physical well-being. Here we look at health-compromising behaviors in three areas: cigarette smoking, alcohol and drug use, and sexual activity.

Cigarette Smoking An alarming number of young people smoke cigarettes. In 1998, 9% of 8th graders, 16% of 10th graders, and 22% of 12th graders were smokers (Interagency Forum on Child and Family Statistics, 1999). Boys and girls had similar patterns of smoking, but rates differed among ethnic groups. For example, 28% of White American students smoked daily, compared to 14% of Hispanic Americans and 7% of African Americans. Unfortunately, many smoking teens don't kick the habit but continue to smoke as adults.

With health risks from smoking so well publicized, it is difficult for many adults to understand adolescents' motivation to smoke. Undoubtedly "image" is a factor. Teens may smoke cigarettes as a way of looking older and showing their affiliation with certain peer groups. Advertising plays a role as well. Only three cigarette brands account for almost all of teen smoking, perhaps reflecting the youthful, fun-loving images that certain tobacco companies cultivate in the media. Use of particular brand names varies by ethnic group, reflecting differing cultural norms for different groups (Johnston, O'Malley, Bachman, & Schulenberg, 1999).

Alcohol and Drug Use Alcohol and drugs are arguably the most serious threats to physical health that adolescents face today. With their judgment impaired, teenagers often engage in reckless behaviors while under the influence of alcohol or drugs. Occasionally a single episode with a particular drug leads to permanent brain damage or even death; recall our introductory case study, in which three boys died in an attempt to get "high." Figure 3–11 lists several common sources of substance abuse in adolescence.

Given the potential hazards of alcohol and drugs, why do adolescents so frequently use them? For some, it's a matter of curiosity: Hearing about alcohol and drugs so often, not only from their peers but also from adults and the media, teens may simply want to know firsthand what all the

Alcohol depresses the central nervous system and impairs coordination, perception, speech, and decision making; for instance, heavy drinkers may talk incoherently and walk with a staggering gait. Students who drink excessively are more likely to have car accidents and commit rape. Among high school seniors, 80%–90% have tried alcohol and 25%–40% are frequent drinkers.

Inhalants are attractive to many adolescents because they cause an immediate "high" and are readily available in the form of such household substances as glue, paint thinner, aerosol paint cans, and nail polish remover. These very dangerous substances can cause brain damage and death. Approximately 1 in 5 adolescents has tried an inhalant at least once; its use is greatest among younger teenagers (e.g., eighth graders).

Marijuana delays reaction time, modifies perception, and instills a mild feeling of euphoria, but it can also heighten fears and anxieties. Students who smoke marijuana may have red eyes, dry mouths, mood changes, loss of interest in former friends and hobbies, and impaired driving. It is the most widely used mind-altering drug taken by adolescents. More than one-third of high school seniors have tried it, as have 17% of eighth graders; 6% of high school students report smoking it almost every day.

Cocaine (including *crack*, a particularly potent form) overstimulates the central nervous system and gives users a brief sense of intense euphoria; it can also cause tremors, convulsions, vomiting, respiratory problems, and heart failure. Cocaine users may be energetic, talkative, argumentative, and boastful; long-time users may appear anxious and depressed. Crack users are prone to violence and crime. One out of six high school students has tried cocaine, and 2%–5% use it regularly.

Amphetamines ("speed") are stimulants that give their users a sense of energy, alertness, confidence, and well-being. Overdoses are possible, addiction frequently occurs, and changes to the brain and heart may occur. People who use speed regularly may combat psychiatric problems, such as believing that "everyone is out to get me." In the United States, 15% of the population has tried amphetamines or another stimulant at least once.

Lysergic acid diethylamide (LSD) is a psychedelic drug that gives its users the sensation of being on an exotic journey, or "trip." It is usually swallowed as a chemical on a piece of paper or as a drop of liquid placed on the tongue. It can impair judgment, provoke anxiety, trigger underlying mental problems and, in the case of "bad trips," cause serious distress. LSD has been tried by 10% of the American population.

Methylene dioxymethamphetamine (MDMA, or "ecstasy") gives its users a sense of euphoria and exuberance, sensory enhancements and distortions, and feelings of being at peace with the world and emotionally close to others (it is sometimes called the "hug drug"). However, the sense of euphoria often leads its users to ignore bodily distress signals, such as muscle cramping and dehydration; more serious effects include convulsions, impaired heart function, and occasionally death. It is often available at dance clubs ("raves"), where its effects are intensified with music and flashing lights. MDMA use appears to be on the increase among older adolescents. In a large-scale survey conducted in 1999 (Johnston, O'Malley, & Bachman, 2000), approximately 5% of 10th and 12th graders reported having used it in the previous 12 months.

Sources: Adams, Gullotta, & Markstrom-Adams, 1994; Atwater, 1996; DanceSafe, 2000a, 2000b; Feldman & Wood, 1994; Johnston, O'Malley, & Bachman, 2000; Kulberg, 1986; Smith, 1994; J. M. Taylor, 1994.

fuss is about. But adolescence is also a time when young people seek self-definition (Who shall I be? How does it feel to be a certain kind of me?), and experimentation with new roles and behaviors (including drug use) is a typical part of that search (Durkin, 1995).

Adult behaviors, too, influence substance abuse. For instance, many adolescents who use drugs or alcohol have parents who do little to promote their children's self-confidence, desire to abide by society's rules and conventions, or ability to delay immediate pleasures to achieve long-term gains (Botvin & Scheier, 1997; Jessor & Jessor, 1977). Furthermore, drug and alcohol use is more common when people in the local community are relatively tolerant of such behavior (Poresky, Daniels, Mukerjee, & Gunnell, 1999).

Peer group norms and behaviors are yet another factor affecting substance abuse (Epstein, Botvin, Diaz, Toth, & Schinke, 1995; Segal & Stewart, 1996). To a great extent, use of alcohol and drugs is a social activity (Durkin, 1995), and teenagers may partake simply as a means of "fitting in." It's also the case, however, that teens who are inclined to violate social norms will seek out peer groups with the same inclination for trouble (Ryan, 2000). In other words, adolescents do not passively accept the practices of their peers, but instead actively search for people who have the same interests.

The majority of teenagers try alcohol or drugs at one time or another. If they find that such substances give them pleasure, satisfy their desire for thrills, alleviate their anxieties, or deaden their pain and depression, they may begin to use them regularly. Unfortunately, some young people eventually develop an **addiction** to, or biological and psychological dependence on, drugs or alcohol. They grow accustomed to using the substance and need increasing quantities to produce a desired effect; stopping use of the substance leads to intense cravings and severe physiological and psychological reactions (Hussong, Chassin, & Hicks, 1999). Teenagers who are impulsive and disruptive, perform poorly in school, find little value in an education, or have mental illness or substance abuse in their families are especially at risk for becoming dependent on alcohol and drugs (Bryant & Zimmerman, 1999; Chassin, Curran, Hussong, & Colder, 1996; Flannery, Vazsonyi, Torquati, & Fridrich, 1994; Wills, McNamara, Vaccaro, & Hirky, 1996).

Sexual Activity Teenagers get mixed messages about the appropriateness and acceptability of sexual activity in their own lives. Social and religious norms often advocate abstinence, yet television and films depict more and more scenes of explicit sexual behavior among adolescents and adults. Schools typically do little to help teens sort out these messages. Although they often include information about male and female anatomy, procreation, and birth in their health or biology curricula, they rarely offer much guidance about how to make sense of one's emerging sexuality or how to behave in romantic relationships (Pipher, 1994).

On average, adolescents are more sexually active now than they were 30 years ago. For example, for females in the United States, the median age for a first sexual experience declined from age 19 in 1971 to age 15½ in 1990 (U.S. Department of Health and Human Services, 1994). Furthermore, about half of the adolescents who are sexually active either never use contraceptives or use them only occasionally (U.S. Department of Health and Human Services, 1997). From the perspective of physical health and well-being, early sexual activity is problematic in that it can lead to a sexually transmitted disease (STD), pregnancy, or both.

Sexually transmitted diseases. STDs vary in their severity. Syphilis, gonorrhea, and chlamydia can be treated with antibiotic drugs, but teens do not always seek prompt medical help for their symptoms. Without treatment of these STDs, serious problems can occur, including infertility and sterility, heart problems, and birth defects in future offspring. No known cure is available for genital herpes, but medication can make symptoms less severe.

Undoubtedly the most life-threatening STD is acquired immune deficiency syndrome (AIDS), which weakens the immune system and allows severe infections, pneumonias, and cancers to invade the body. AIDS is caused by a virus, human immunodeficiency virus (HIV), which can be transmitted through the exchange of bodily fluids, including blood and semen, during just a single contact. The only good news about this deadly disease is that it has spurred public awareness campaigns that have led to safer sex practices, such as less intimate contact with new acquaintances and more frequent use of condoms (Catania et al., 1992; Kelly, 1995). The bad news is that safe sexual practices are not universal. As noted earlier, many adolescents believe that they are invulnerable to normal dangers, and they may falsely believe that their partner is "safe" (Fisher & Fisher, 1992; Kelly, Murphy, Sikkema, & Kalichman, 1993; Moore & Rosenthal, 1991). People with disabilities are at especially high risk for acquiring HIV and AIDS because they tend to have limited knowledge of sex and contraception, are more likely to engage in high-risk sexual behavior, and are more vulnerable to sexual abuse from others (Mason & Jaskulski, 1994).

Pregnancy. Despite popular beliefs to the contrary, teenage pregnancy rates are now lower than they were throughout much of the 20th century (Coley & Chase-Lansdale, 1998). Nevertheless, in the United States, approximately 1 teenage girl out of 10 becomes pregnant every year (Durkin, 1995; Sadker & Sadker, 1994). More than half of these pregnancies end

addiction
Physical and psychological dependence on a substance, such that increasing quantities must be taken to produce a desired effect and withdrawal produces adverse physiological and psychological effects.

in abortion or miscarriage, but many others, of course, go to full term (Chase-Lansdale & Brooks-Gunn, 1994; Henshaw, 1997). In 1997, the birthrate for American girls ages 15 to 17 was 32 per 1,000, representing a slight drop from 1991, when the rate was 39 per 1,000 (Interagency Forum on Child and Family Statistics, 1999).

Most teenage mothers live in low-income families, often with single and poorly educated parents, and believe that life offers them few if any educational or career options (Coley & Chase-Lansdale, 1998). Many also look to sex and motherhood for the love and emotional closeness that they don't find in their other relationships (Coley & Chase-Lansdale, 1998). Some cultural groups actually encourage young, single teenage girls to become pregnant. For instance, in one community in the northeastern United States, grandmothers rather than mothers typically take on childrearing duties, and they want to be as young as possible when their grandchildren are born (Stack & Burton, 1993). Thirteen-year-old Janice, who is pregnant, explains:

> I'm not having this baby for myself. The baby's grandmother wants to be a "mama" and my great-grandfather wants to see a grandchild before he goes blind from sugar. I'm just giving them something to make them happy. (Stack & Burton, 1993, p. 161)

When young mothers have not fully matured physically, and especially when they do not have access to adequate nutrition and health care, they are at greater risk for medical complications during pregnancy and delivery. Problems arise after delivery as well: On average, teenage mothers have more health problems, are less likely to complete school or keep a steady job, live in greater poverty, and have more impaired psychological functioning than their peers (Coley & Chase-Lansdale, 1998; Upchurch & McCarthy, 1990).

Addressing Health-Compromising Behaviors Schools can do a great deal to address behaviors that put their students at physical risk, and in fact they may be the *only* resource for students whose families either cannot or will not intervene. We offer a few thoughts on appropriate support:

■ *Prevent problems.* It is much easier to teach students to resist cigarettes, alcohol, and drugs than it is to treat dependence on these substances. An ounce of prevention is clearly worth a pound of cure. One important approach is to establish a "no tolerance" policy on school grounds; students are less likely to smoke, drink, or take drugs at school if they think they might be caught (Voelkl & Frone, 2000). Prevention programs within the curriculum can also make a difference. Scare tactics, instruction about the detrimental effects of tobacco or drugs, and attempts to enhance students' self-esteem are relatively *ineffective*, however. What seem to work better are programs that strive to change students' behavior, for instance by asking students to make a public commitment to stay clean and sober, teaching them how to resist peer pressure, and giving them strategies for solving social problems, curbing impulsive behaviors, and coping with anxiety (Botvin & Scheier, 1997; Forgey, Schinke, & Cole, 1997). The effects of intervention programs do diminish over time, suggesting that students' resistance to tobacco, alcohol, and drugs needs to be established *before* they face temptations and then boosted *along the way* as they confront actual peer pressure.

Ideally, prevention programs should take into consideration the cultures in which students have grown up. As an example, the Culturally Tailored Intervention is a program designed for young adolescents from predominantly African American and Hispanic American backgrounds (Forgey et al., 1997). It involves a professional storyteller who relays stories that feature African American and Hispanic heroes and heroines who face up to obstacles (e.g., poverty, discrimination, family breakup) similar to those confronting inner-city youth today. The program also includes a rap video with teen characters modeling confrontations with drug dealers, and popular peer leaders deliver part of the curriculum.

Children and adolescents are less likely to engage in health-compromising behaviors when they have constructive alternatives for their leisure time.

Approaches to preventing pregnancy and transmission of STDs among adolescents are more controversial; for instance, many parents object to schools advocating the use of condoms and other forms of "safe sex." Recent evidence suggests that having condoms available in the schools moderately increases condom use for those students who are already sexually active (and so may offer some protection against HIV infection) but does not necessarily increase rates of sexual activity (Guttmacher et al., 1997). At the present time, however, condom use is not a panacea against either infection or pregnancy. Adolescents' use of condoms is far from universal, in part because of interpersonal factors (e.g., reluctance to use a condom or to ask that a partner use one) and situational factors (e.g., impaired judgment due to alcohol or drugs; Manderson, Tye, & Rajanayagam, 1997). Programs that encourage sexual abstinence are a less controversial alternative and can be somewhat effective in the short run, although they are less so over a long period (McKay, 1993).

■ *Provide more attractive alternatives.* Children and adolescents are less likely to engage in health-compromising behaviors when they have better things to do with their time; for instance, in our opening case study, a softball league provided a more enticing and productive form of recreation than using drugs. Obviously, educators alone cannot keep their students busy and happy 24 hours a day. They can, however, advocate for after-school youth centers, community athletic leagues, and public service programs for young people. As an example, the First Choice program, which has been implemented at over 50 sites in the United States, is targeted especially at students who are at risk for dropping out of school or getting in serious trouble with the law (Collingwood, 1997). The program focuses on physical fitness, drug use prevention, and violence prevention and has several elements that appear to contribute to its success, including educational and physical activity classes, a peer fitness leadership training program, parent support training, and use of existing community resources.

■ *Ask students to keep their long-term goals continually in mind.* Students need personally relevant reasons to stay away from illegal substances and to make wise choices about sexual activity. Having long-term goals and optimism about the future can provide an impetus for resisting peer and media pressure to use drugs and alcohol or engage in unprotected premarital sex. Adolescent therapist Mary Pipher often uses the North Star as a metaphor:

> "You are in a boat that is being tossed around by the winds of the world. The voices of your parents, your teachers, your friends and the media can blow you east, then west, then back again. To stay on course you must follow your own North Star, your sense of who you truly are. Only by orienting north can you chart a course and maintain it, only by orienting north can you keep from being blown all over the sea.
>
> "True freedom has more to do with following the North Star than with going whichever way the wind blows. Sometimes it seems like freedom is blowing with the winds of the day, but that kind of freedom is really an illusion. It turns your boat in circles. Freedom is sailing toward your dreams." (Pipher, 1994, pp. 254–255)[4]

The four areas we've discussed in this section—eating habits, physical activity, rest and sleep, and health-compromising behaviors—are central to children's and adolescents' performance and success at school. In the Observation Guidelines table on the next page, we identify characteristics and behaviors that can reveal to teachers whether their students are on the right track toward physical fitness and good health. We turn now to students who have special physical needs and may require modified instructional materials or practices to help them achieve their full potential.

Special Physical Needs

Some students have long-term physical conditions that affect their classroom performance. Here we look at chronic illness, serious injuries, and physical disabilities in children and adolescents; we then identify several strategies for accommodating these conditions.

---

[4]From *Reviving Ophelia* by Mary Pipher, Ph.D., copyright © 1994 by Mary Pipher, Ph.D. Used by permission of Putnam Berkley, a division of Penguin Putnam Inc.

Assessing Students' Physical Well-Being

OBSERVATION GUIDELINES			
CHARACTERISTIC	**LOOK FOR**	**EXAMPLE**	**IMPLICATION**
Eating Habits	• Frequent consumption of junk food (candy, chips, carbonated beverages, etc.) • Unusual heaviness or thinness, especially if these characteristics become more pronounced over time • Lack of energy • Reluctance or inability to eat anything at lunchtime	Melissa is a good student, an avid runner, and a member of the student council. She is quite thin but wears baggy clothes that hide her figure, and she eats only a couple of pieces of celery for lunch. Her teacher and principal suspect an eating disorder and meet with Melissa's parents to share their suspicion.	Observe what students eat and drink during the school day. Seek free or reduced-rate breakfasts and lunches for children from low-income families. Consult with specialists and parents when students' eating habits are seriously compromising their health.
Physical Activity	• Improvements in speed, complexity, and agility of gross motor skills (e.g., running, skipping, jumping) • Proficiency in fine motor skills (e.g., tying shoes, using scissors, writing and drawing, building models, playing a musical instrument) • Restlessness and fidgeting (reflecting a need to release pent-up energy) • Bullying and other socially inappropriate behaviors during playtime • Cooperation and teamwork during organized sports activities • Overexertion (increasing the risk of injury)	During a class field day, a fifth-grade teacher organizes a soccer game with her students. Before beginning the game, she asks them to run up and down the field, individually accelerating and decelerating while kicking the ball. She then has them practice dribbling the ball while trying to evade another player. Only after such practice does she begin the game (Logsdon et al., 1997).	Incorporate regular physical activity into the daily schedule. Choose tasks and activities that students enjoy and that allow for variability in skill levels. Make sure students have mastered prerequisite skills before teaching more complex skills.
Rest and Sleep	• Listlessness and lack of energy • Inability to concentrate • Irritability and overreaction to frustration • Sleeping in class	A teacher in an all-day kindergarten notices that some of his students become cranky during the last half hour or so of school, and so he typically reserves this time for storybook reading and other quiet activities.	Provide regular opportunities for rest and rejuvenation, especially when students are quite active during much of the school day. When a student seems unusually tired day after day, talk with the student (and perhaps with the parents) about how the lack of sleep is affecting class performance and jointly seek possible solutions to the problem.
Health-Compromising Behaviors	• The smell of cigarettes on clothing • Physiological symptoms of drug use (e.g., red eyes, dilated pupils, tremors, convulsions, respiratory problems) • Distortions in speech (e.g., slurred pronunciation, fast talking, incoherence) • Poor coordination • Impaired decision making • Mood changes (e.g., anxiety, depression) • Dramatic changes in behavior (e.g., unusual energy, loss of interest in friends) • Signs of sensory distortions or hallucinations • Rapid weight gain, and a tendency to wear increasingly baggy clothes (in girls who may be pregnant)	A high school teacher notices a dramatic change in James's personality. Whereas he used to come to class ready and willing to learn, he now begins to "zone out" during class time. He slumps in his chair, either drawing pictures or staring out the window. When called on, he seems to look past the teacher and mumbles an unintelligible response. The teacher suspects drug use and so speaks with him after class to ask how he's feeling and why he seems to have lost interest in class. James denies that anything is wrong, so the teacher consults with the school counselor about the situation.	Educate students about the dangers of substance abuse and unprotected sexual activity; teach behaviors that will enable students to resist temptations, tailoring instruction to students' cultural backgrounds. Encourage participation in enjoyable and productive leisure activities that will enable students to interact with health-conscious peers. Consult with the school counselor, psychologist, or social worker when you suspect that a student is pregnant or abusing drugs or alcohol.

Chronic Illness

All children get sick now and then, but some have ongoing, long-term illnesses as a result of genetic legacies (e.g., cystic fibrosis), environmental insults (e.g., AIDS), or an interaction between the two (e.g., some forms of cancer). In the United States, two-thirds of chronically ill children and adolescents attend their neighborhood schools for part or all of the school day (Turnbull, Turnbull, Shank, & Leal, 1999). Some of them show few if any symptoms at school, but others have noticeable limitations in strength, vitality, or alertness.

Whenever teachers have students with a serious illness, they must, first and foremost, learn as much as they can about the nature and potential effects of the illness. As children get older, many of them learn how to manage their own symptoms; for instance, most children with diabetes can monitor their blood sugar levels and take appropriate follow-up action. Yet children sometimes forget to take prescribed medication, and they are not always completely reliable in assessing their status; for example, children with asthma may not realize when they are having a severe reaction (Bearison, 1998). Accordingly, teachers must monitor students' symptoms closely and seek medical assistance if conditions deteriorate.

Some students who are chronically ill feel sufficiently "different" that they are reticent about approaching and interacting with classmates (Turnbull et al., 1999). Furthermore, they may blame their physical condition (perhaps accurately, perhaps not) for any problems they have in social relationships (Kapp-Simon & Simon, 1991). As a result, they may become isolated, with few opportunities to develop interpersonal skills. We urge teachers to be attentive to chronically ill students who remain on the periphery of social interaction, as they may require some assistance in establishing and maintaining friendships. To illustrate, one program teaches adolescents with health problems such social skills as how to start conversations, how to listen empathetically, and how to resolve conflicts (Kapp-Simon & Simon, 1991).

Unfortunately, some healthy students actively avoid or reject classmates who have serious illnesses. To some extent, such reactions may result from ignorance about the nature of those illnesses. Many children, young ones especially, have naive notions about the origins of illness; for instance, preschoolers may believe that people catch colds from the sun or get cancer by being in the same room as someone with cancer (Bibace & Walsh, 1981). As children get older, their conceptions of illness gradually become more complex, they grow more attuned to their own internal body cues, and they can differentiate among types of illness (Bearison, 1998).

Educators certainly cannot leave to chance the reactions of peers to a student who has a chronic illness. Consider the experiences of Ryan White, an adolescent who contracted HIV from a blood transfusion. Many community members believed that Ryan's presence at school would jeopardize the health of other students, and so school officials initially refused to allow Ryan to attend school. After Ryan spent many months studying at home (sometimes "participating" in class through computer hook-up), a court order finally allowed him to go back to school. His homecoming was not a happy one:

> [B]eing back at school was almost as lonely as being home. Heath was still my buddy, but he wasn't in my grade. Other kids backed up against their lockers when they saw me coming, or they threw themselves against the hallway walls, shouting, "Watch out! Watch out! There he is!" Maybe some were putting me on. I think most of them were acting like that just to get to me, to make me mad mainly. I worked hard at pretending I didn't see the kids who were making fun of me.
>
> But it hurt that no one wanted to get close to me. "It's okay for him to come to school, just as long as I don't sit by him," one boy said. Some kids were so afraid they wouldn't walk in the same hall with me. I wasn't even five feet and I weighed seventy-six pounds—quite chunky for me actually. But you'd think I was some big bruiser, the way kids ran when they saw me coming. When we had to team up in class, no one wanted to be my partner. One girl complained, "If people with measles and chicken pox can't come to school, why should Ryan?" I called Mom every day at lunchtime, just to have someone to talk to. (White & Cunningham, 1991, pp. 118–119)[5]

[5]From *Ryan White: My Own Story* by Ryan White and Ann Marie Cunningham, copyright © 1991 by Jeanne White and Ann Marie Cunningham. Used by permission of Dial Books for Young Readers, an imprint of Penguin Putnam Books for Young Readers, a division of Penguin Putnam Inc.

Community residents were, of course, misinformed about the nature of HIV and AIDS, which cannot be spread through breathing, touching, or other day-to-day forms of human contact. In desperation, Ryan's family moved to a different school district, which undertook numerous initiatives to prepare the community and school for his presence. School administrators invited experts to come talk about AIDS to teachers and students, and students met individually with school staff members to air their concerns and get reassurance. Student government officers dropped by Ryan's house to say hello. When he arrived at school the first day,

> Wendy and Jill and some other student government officers met me right at the door, and helped me find all my classes. I'd kept to myself for so long, it was like being on another planet. When I walked into classrooms or the cafeteria, several kids called out at once, "Hey, Ryan! Sit with me!". . .
>
> As I left after my first day, a reporter asked me, "How do you like *this* school?"
>
> "Oh, I think I'm going to like it here," I said. He must have noticed I was beaming. I'd been welcomed with open arms. I felt like I had hundreds of friends. It seemed like everyone said to themselves, "What if you were standing in *his* shoes? How would *you* feel?" (White & Cunningham, 1991, pp. 149–150)[6]

Serious Injuries

Injuries represent a major health threat to children and adolescents. Every year, more young people die from accidental injuries than from cancer. In fact, for children and adolescents between 1 and 19 years of age, injuries are the leading cause of death (Deal, Gomby, Zippiroli, & Behrman, 2000). As children get older, their increasing independence makes them particularly susceptible to certain kinds of injuries; for example, injuries from firearms and motor vehicle accidents increase throughout the adolescent years (U.S. Department of Health and Human Services, 1997).

Although some injuries quickly heal, others have lasting effects that must be accommodated at school. For instance, each year more than one million children and adolescents sustain brain injuries as a result of playground falls, bicycle mishaps, skiing accidents, and other traumatic events (Brain Injury Association, 1999). Depending on location and severity, brain injuries can have temporary or long-term effects on both physical functioning (e.g., seizures, headaches, poor motor coordination, chronic fatigue) and psychological processes (e.g., impairments in perception, memory, concentration, language, decision making, or anger management). Thus, the assistance that teachers provide for students with brain injuries must be tailored to each student's unique needs. For one student, such assistance may mean minimizing distractions in the classroom, for another it may mean allowing extra time to complete assignments, and for still another it may mean adjusting expectations for performance, at least for the first few weeks or months (Turnbull et al., 1999).

Many childhood injuries are avoidable, of course, and schools play a key role in educating students about such preventive measures as using seat belts while riding in motor vehicles, wearing helmets while biking and skating, and installing smoke detectors at home (e.g., Klassen, MacKay, Moher, Walker, & Jones, 2000). Teachers should also be aware of students who are more vulnerable than others; for instance, children with Down syndrome are particularly susceptible to sprains and dislocations because of poor muscle tone and excessive mobility in their joints (Krebs, 1995). Unfortunately, a few injuries are intentionally inflicted by others, perhaps by abusive family members, and teachers must keep a sharp eye out for signs of abuse. (We will discuss child abuse in more depth in Chapter 12.)

Physical Disabilities

Students with physical disabilities, such as cerebral palsy, muscular dystrophy, congenital heart problems, or blindness, have the same basic needs as other students, including a good diet, regular physical activity, and adequate rest and sleep. In addition, they may need specially

---

adapted equipment (e.g., a wheelchair, a speech synthesizer, or a computer printer that prints in Braille) and a classroom layout that permits safe movement. Some students with physical disabilities, especially those with multiple handicaps, have cognitive as well as physical impairments, but many others have intellectual capabilities similar to those of their nondisabled classmates (Turnbull et al., 1999).

Because physical activity and exercise are central to promoting health, fitness, and mood, teachers must find ways to adapt physical activities for students with special needs. Basically, such adaptation involves giving as much support as necessary to enable successful performance in movement; for example, a teacher can assist students who are visually impaired by guiding their bodies into correct positions and inserting bells or other noisemakers inside playground balls (Craft, 1995). But it also means communicating expectations for success. In fact, many people with physical disabilities have gone on to become successful athletes. Consider the following examples (Winnick, 1995):

- Harry Cordellos, who was visually impaired, ran the Boston Marathon.
- Wilma Rudolph, who had birth defects and polio, became a triple Gold Medallist at the Olympics.
- Peter Gray, who had his right arm amputated, played center field for the St. Louis Browns.
- Tom Dempsey, who was born with only half a foot, set a National Football League record for the longest field goal kick.

Of course, students with disabilities are most often like students without disabilities—not superstars, but in need of physical activity nevertheless.

Accommodating Students' Special Physical Needs

Students with chronic illnesses, serious injuries, and physical disabilities are very diverse in terms of the strengths on which they can build and the weaknesses that may impede their developmental progress. Yet several general guidelines apply to *all* students with special physical needs:

■ *Keep the mind-set that every student should participate in all classroom activities to the fullest extent possible.* In recent years, students with special physical needs have increasingly participated in general education classes. Many educators have found that when they keep open minds about what their students can accomplish, and especially when they think creatively and collaboratively about how they can adapt regular classroom activities to accommodate students with special needs, almost all students can participate meaningfully in virtually all classroom activities (Logan, Alberto, Kana, & Waylor-Bowen, 1994; Salisbury, Evans, & Palombaro, 1997). To develop physically, cognitively, and socially, every child should have as "normal" and complete a school experience as possible.

■ *Seek guidance from parents or guardians and from specialized organizations.* Parents and guardians often have helpful suggestions about adjustments that would enable their children to participate more fully at school. And professional organizations—most of them easily found on the Internet—offer a wealth of ideas about adapting instruction and equipment for students with chronic physical conditions and disabilities. Two broad-based organizations are the American Alliance for Health, Physical Education, Recreation and Dance (with a subspecialty organization, Adapted Physical Activity Council) and the National Consortium for Physical Education and Recreation for Individuals with Disabilities. Other organizations focus on specific disabilities, such as the American Athletic Association for the Deaf, Wheelchair Sports USA, National Handicapped Sports, Special Olympics, United States Cerebral Palsy Athletic Association, Dwarf Athletic Association of America, and the U.S. Association for Blind Athletes.

■ *Know what to do in emergencies.* Some students have conditions that may result in occasional life-threatening situations. For example, a student with diabetes may go into insulin shock, a student with asthma may have trouble breathing, or a student with epilepsy may have a grand mal seizure. Teachers should consult with parents and school medical personnel to learn ahead of time exactly how to respond to such emergencies.

■ *Educate classmates about the disability.* As Ryan White's experiences so vividly illustrate, classmates are more likely to show kindness and respect to a student with a physical or health impairment if they understand the nature of the disability. Peers should know, for example, that AIDS cannot be spread through breathing or touching and that epileptic seizures, though frightening, are only temporary. Keep in mind, however, that a teacher should talk about a student's physical condition *only* when the student and his or her parents have given permission for the teacher to do so.

■ *Keep lines of communication open with students who are hospitalized or homebound.* Sometimes students' physical conditions keep them hospital-bound or homebound for lengthy periods of time. In such circumstances, they can often participate in classroom lessons and activities by telephone or computer hook-up. When they cannot, they may be especially appreciative of cards, letters, and photographs from classmates and teachers.

Health and physical well-being play a role not only in children's and adolescents' physical development but in their development in other domains as well. Brain development affects cognitive development, of course, and children's energy levels and endurance influence their ability to master challenging new intellectual tasks. And health and fitness indirectly affect social development, as our final case study illustrates.

CASE STUDY: LUCY

In her early teenage years, Lucy had leukemia. After a long hospitalization, plus radiation and chemotherapy treatments that resulted in temporary hair loss, Lucy's disease finally went into remission. Eventually Lucy was healthy enough to return to school, but her life at school was quite different from what it once had been. Her therapist Mary Pipher (1994) explains:

> It had been hard for her to return to school. Everyone was nice to Lucy, almost too nice, like she was a visitor from another planet, but she was left out of so many things. Her old friends had boyfriends and were involved in new activities. When she was in the hospital they would visit with flowers and magazines, but now that she was better, they didn't seem to know what to do with her.
>
> Frank [her father] said, "Lucy's personality has changed. She's quieter. She used to clown around. Now she is more serious. In some ways she seems older; she's suffered more and seen other children suffer. In some ways she's younger; she's missed a lot."
>
> Lucy had missed a great deal: ninth-grade graduation, the beginning of high school, parties, dating, sports, school activities and even puberty (the leukemia had delayed her periods and physical development). She had lots of catching up to do. She'd been so vulnerable that her parents were protective. They didn't want her to become tired, to eat junk food, to forget to take her medicines or to take any chances. Her immune system was weak and she could be in trouble with the slightest injury. Lucy, unlike most teens, didn't grimace at her parents' worries. She associated them with staying alive. (Pipher, 1994, p. 84)[7]

- Lucy's illness delayed the onset of puberty. What other effects might her illness have had on her development relative to peers? As you ponder this question, consider her cognitive and social development as well as her physical development.
- In some respects, Lucy probably developed more quickly than most students her age. What particular strengths might Lucy have had as a result of having combated a life-threatening illness?
- As a teacher, what strategies might you use to ease Lucy's return to school?

[7]From *Reviving Ophelia* by Mary Pipher, Ph.D., copyright © 1994 by Mary Pipher, Ph.D. Used by permission of Putnam Berkley, a division of Penguin Putnam Inc.

SUMMARY

Nature and Nurture in Physical Development

All students come to school with a unique set of genetic instructions that influence not only their characteristics at birth but also (through the process of *maturation*) many characteristics that emerge in childhood and adolescence. Environmental conditions have a strong say as well; for instance, nutrition and exposure to environmental toxins affect brain development. Environmental factors frequently interact with genetic predispositions as they nurture physical and psychological traits; for instance, as children grow older and more independent, they are increasingly able to seek out experiences that are compatible with their inherited talents and tendencies. And ultimately, genes require environmental support to do their work.

General Principles of Physical Development

Different systems of the body grow at different rates, with some systems "front-loading" their growth and others waiting for their turn in the spotlight. Over time, physiological functioning becomes both increasingly differentiated (e.g., different cells take on different functions) and increasingly integrated (e.g., different body parts work more closely together). Children seem to have certain targets in physical growth that their bodies aim for, even if temporarily deterred by illness or inadequate nutrition. Overall, physical development is characterized by both quantitative and qualitative change.

Development of the Brain

The human brain is a complex organ that regulates basic physiological functions (e.g., respiration and heart rate), sensations of pleasure and pain, motor skills and coordination, emotional responses, and intellectual pursuits. An intricate organizational structure, in the form of millions of interconnected circuits of neurons, supports these many functions and their interrelationships. The brain develops in a predictable and patterned manner, with support for basic survival functions (e.g., breathing, sensation, reflexes) operational first, followed by support for motor skills and, eventually, support for complex thought processes and learning. In general, human brains are remarkably similar to one another, but individual differences allow for variations in abilities and temperament and in some cases result in cognitive or psychiatric disabilities.

Physical Development in Childhood and Adolescence

Predictable changes in physical functioning occur during childhood and adolescence. Early childhood is a very busy time, packed with physical activity and the acquisition of new motor skills. Middle childhood is a time of consolidation, when growth rate slows down and children put motor skills to purposeful use. Puberty begins in early adolescence and extends over several years' time; on average, girls begin and end this sequence about 1½ years earlier than boys. Adult height and sexual maturation are attained in late adolescence.

General Issues in Physical Well-Being

Now go to our Companion Website to assess your understanding of chapter content with Multiple-Choice Questions, apply comprehension in Essay Questions, and broaden your knowledge with links to related Developmental Psychology World Wide Web sites.

Students' health depends on several factors, including their eating habits, physical activity, and rest and sleep. Some students show patterns of behavior (e.g., eating disorders, choice of sedentary activities, overcommitments that result in insufficient sleep) that may seriously jeopardize their physical well-being. In adolescence, additional health-compromising behaviors may emerge as students struggle with such temptations as cigarettes, alcohol, drugs, and sexual activity.

Special Physical Needs

Students with chronic illness, serious injuries, and physical disabilities often need modifications in instruction, equipment, or the classroom environment. Ultimately, teachers should strive to make educational experiences as "normal" as possible for these students.

KEY CONCEPTS

gene (p. 66)
DNA (p. 66)
chromosome (p. 66)
germ cell (p. 66)
zygote (p. 67)
monozygotic twins (p. 67)
dizygotic twins (p. 67)
alleles (p. 68)
dominant gene (p. 68)
recessive gene (p. 68)
codominance (p. 68)
polygenic inheritance (p. 68)
maturation (p. 68)
canalization (p. 68)
differentiation (p. 71)
integration (p. 73)

neuron (p. 75)
dendrite (p. 75)
axon (p. 75)
synapse (p. 75)
neurotransmitter (p. 75)
glial cell (p. 75)
hindbrain (p. 76)
midbrain (p. 76)
forebrain (p. 76)
cortex (p. 76)
executive functions (p. 76)
left hemisphere (p. 76)
right hemisphere (p. 76)
myelinization (p. 78)
synaptogenesis (p. 78)
synaptic pruning (p. 78)

schizophrenia (p. 79)
reflex (p. 81)
gross motor skills (p. 81)
fine motor skills (p. 81)
puberty (p. 85)
growth spurt (p. 85)
menarche (p. 85)
spermarche (p. 85)
personal fable (p. 87)
obesity (p. 90)
anorexia nervosa (p. 90)
bulimia (p. 90)
rough-and-tumble play (p. 92)
addiction (p. 98)

Symoen, age 9

Cognitive Development 1: Piaget and Vygotsky

CASE STUDY: WHALE WATCHING

Six-year-old Kerry and her mother are talking about their family's recent whale-watching expedition:

Mother:	And we went with, who'd we go with?
Kerry:	David.
Mother:	David. Who else?
Kerry:	And Nana and Papa.
Mother:	And who else? Daddy went too, didn't he?
Kerry:	Yeah.
Mother:	Yeah. Who else?
Kerry:	That's all.
Mother:	Oh, and Auntie Karen and Uncle Pete, right?
Kerry:	Yeah.
Mother:	And David's two brothers.
Kerry:	Mmhm.
Mother:	We went whale watching and um I think it turned out to be a disaster because it was rough out there and we got kind of seasick. We did see whales, but not as good as we wanted to.
Kerry:	I saw one.
Mother:	Yeah, we saw them. They're big, huh?
Kerry:	[Nods.]
Mother:	How many were there?
Kerry:	About thirteen.
Mother:	About thirteen! There were only two or three!
Kerry:	No, there wasn't, because they were runnin' back and forth like fifty times! (Hemphill & Snow, 1996, p. 182)

Courtesy of Ian, age 6.

K ERRY HAS ALMOST CERTAINLY learned something about the animal world from her whale-watching experience. By observing whales in the flesh, she has probably acquired a better understanding of the characteristics and behaviors of whales than she could gain from a verbal description, picture book illustration, or videotape. At the same time, Kerry's interpretations of what she observed may not be entirely accurate. For instance, Kerry and her mother disagree about the number of whales that the group saw, and one of them—perhaps both of them—counted incorrectly. Furthermore, Kerry can recall certain aspects of the expedition, such as the specific people who accompanied her, only with her mother's assistance.

The conversation between Kerry and her mother gives us a brief glimpse into how a young child thinks about a particular event; in other words, it illustrates cognition in action. More generally, **cognition** encompasses all the mental activities in which a person engages, including perception, categorization, understanding, inference drawing, logical reasoning, problem solving, imagination, and memory. Such processes change and evolve in many ways over the course of childhood and adolescence; for instance, Kerry's comprehension of her experiences with the animal kingdom will almost certainly improve as she grows older.

To some extent, cognitive development is a function of physiological maturation. As you discovered in Chapter 3, the brain undergoes a series of genetically controlled changes during childhood and adolescence, and such changes almost certainly allow increasingly sophisticated thinking processes over time. Yet environmental events—both informal experiences (e.g., play activities with age-mates and encounters with new, intriguing objects) and more formal, planned interventions (e.g., whale-watching trips and classroom lessons)—also play a key, in fact *essential,* role in the development of children's and adolescents' cognitive capabilities.

The nature and course of cognitive development are the focus of Chapters 4, 5, and 6. In this chapter, we consider two early theories—those of Jean Piaget and Lev Vygotsky—that have greatly enhanced our understanding of how children's thinking changes with age. In the following two chapters, we look more closely at the development of cognitive processes (Chapter 5) and the nature of intelligence (Chapter 6).

Piaget's Theory of Cognitive Development

Children of different ages often think and reason very differently about the situations they encounter and the phenomena they observe. Consider, for example, a 6-year-old and an 8-year-old in a study by Piaget (1952a). The experimenter (Exp) shows the children a box that contains about a dozen wooden beads; two of them are white and the rest are brown. The 6-year-old, whom we'll call Brian,[1] responds as follows:

Exp:	Are there more wooden beads or more brown beads?
Brian:	More brown ones, because there are two white ones.
Exp:	Are the white ones made of wood?
Brian:	Yes.
Exp:	And the brown ones?
Brian:	Yes.
Exp:	Then are there more brown ones or more wooden ones?
Brian:	More brown ones.
Exp:	What color would a necklace made of the wooden beads be?
Brian:	Brown and white. (Here [Brian] shows that he understands that all the beads are wooden.)
Exp:	And what color would a necklace made with the brown beads be?
Brian:	Brown.
Exp:	Then which would be longer, the one made with the wooden beads or the one made with the brown beads?

cognition
The various mental activities in which a person engages.

[1]Piaget identified individuals in his studies by abbreviations. We've substituted names throughout the text to allow for easier discussion.

Brian:	The one with the brown beads.
Exp:	Draw the necklaces for me.

Brian draws a series of black rings for the necklace of brown beads; he then draws a series of black rings plus two white rings for the necklace of wooden beads.

Exp:	Good. Now which will be longer, the one with the brown beads or the one with the wooden beads?
Brian:	The one with the brown beads. (dialogue from Piaget, 1952a, pp. 163–164)

The experimenter gives 8-year-old "Natalie" the same problem:

Exp:	Are there more wooden beads or more brown beads?
Natalie:	More wooden ones.
Exp:	Why?
Natalie:	Because the two white ones are made of wood as well.
Exp:	Suppose we made two necklaces, one with all the wooden beads and one with all the brown ones. Which one would be longer?
Natalie:	Well, the wooden ones and the brown ones are the same, and it would be longer with the wooden ones because there are two white ones as well. (dialogue from Piaget, 1952a, p. 176)

Brian has difficulty with a question that, to us, seems ridiculously simple. Even though all the beads are wooden and only some (albeit the majority) are brown, he concludes that there are more brown beads. Natalie, who is 2 years older, answers the question easily: Logically there *must* be more wooden beads than brown beads. Natalie exhibits **class inclusion**, the recognition that an object can belong both to a particular category and to one of its subcategories simultaneously.

In the early 1920s, Swiss biologist Jean Piaget began studying children's responses to a wide variety of problems, including the class inclusion problem just described (e.g., Piaget, 1928, 1952a, 1959, 1970; Piaget & Inhelder, 1969). He was particularly curious about the nature of knowledge and how children acquire it, borrowing from a branch of philosophy known as *genetic epistemology*. To determine where knowledge comes from and the forms that it takes at different age levels, he observed the everyday actions of infants and children and drew inferences about the logic that seemed to be influencing their behavior. He also pioneered the use of a procedure he called the **clinical method**, whereby he gave children a variety of tasks and problems (among them the "wooden beads" problem just illustrated) and asked a series of questions about each one. Piaget tailored his interviews to the particular responses that children gave, with follow-up questions varying from one child to the next, as a way of probing into the specific reasoning processes that the children were using. The results of his studies provide many unique insights about how children think and learn about the world around them.

Key Ideas in Piaget's Theory

From his observations of children in problem-solving situations, Piaget derived several concepts and principles related to the nature of cognitive development. Among the most central ones are the following:

■ *Children are active and motivated learners.* Piaget believed that children do not just passively observe and remember the things they see and hear. Instead, they are naturally curious about their world and actively seek out information to help them understand and make sense of it. They continually experiment with the objects they encounter, manipulating things and observing the effects of their actions. For example, we think back (without much nostalgia) to the days when our children were in high chairs, experimenting with (picking up, squishing, pushing, rolling, dropping, and throwing) their food as readily as they might eat it.

■ *Children organize what they learn from their experiences.* Children don't just assemble the things they learn into a collection of isolated facts. Instead, they gradually construct an overall view of how the world operates. For example, by observing that food, toys, and other objects always fall down (never up) when they are released, children begin to construct a rudimentary understanding of *gravity*. As they interact with family pets, visit zoos,

class inclusion
Recognition that something simultaneously belongs to a particular category and to one of its subcategories.

clinical method
Procedure whereby a researcher probes a child's reasoning about a task or problem, tailoring questions to what the child has previously said or done.

look at picture books, and so on, they develop an increasingly complex understanding of *animals*.

In Piaget's terminology, the things that children learn and can do are organized as **schemes**—groups of similar thoughts or actions. Initially, children's schemes are largely behavioral in nature, but over time they become increasingly mental and, eventually, abstract. To illustrate, an infant may have a scheme for putting things in her mouth, a scheme that she uses in dealing with a variety of objects, including her thumb, her toys, and her blanket. A 7-year-old may have a scheme for identifying snakes, one that includes their long, thin bodies, their lack of legs, and their slithery nature. As a 13-year-old, Jeanne's daughter Tina had her own opinion about what constitutes *fashion*—a scheme that allowed her to classify various articles of clothing on display at the mall as being either "totally awesome" or "really stupid."

Piaget proposed that children use newly acquired schemes over and over in both familiar and novel situations. In the process, they also refine the schemes and begin to use them in combination with one another. Eventually, they integrate individual schemes into larger systems of mental processes, or **operations,** and such integration allows children to think in increasingly sophisticated and logical ways. For instance, 8-year-old Natalie's reasoning about the "beads" problem shows greater integration than 6-year-old Brian's: Although both children understand that some beads are both brown and wooden, only Natalie takes both characteristics into account *simultaneously* to conclude that there must be more wooden beads than brown beads. Brian apparently can consider only one characteristic at a time; as a result, he compares the brown beads only with the *remaining* wooden beads (the white ones) and thereby concludes that there are more brown ones.

■ *Children adapt to their environment through the processes of assimilation and accommodation.* Children's developing schemes allow them to respond in ever more successful ways to their environment. Such **adaptation** occurs as a result of two complementary processes: assimilation and accommodation.

Assimilation is a process of dealing with an object or event in a way that is consistent with an existing scheme. For example, an infant may assimilate a new teddy bear into her putting-things-in-the-mouth scheme. A 7-year-old may quickly identify a new slithery object in the backyard as a snake. A 13-year-old may readily label a classmate's clothing as being either quite fashionable or "sooooo *yesterday.*"

But sometimes children cannot easily interpret a new object or event in terms of their existing schemes. In these situations, one of two forms of **accommodation** will occur: Children will either modify an existing scheme to account for the new object or event or else form an entirely new scheme to deal with it. For example, the infant may have to open her mouth wider than usual to accommodate a teddy bear's fat paw. The 13-year-old may have to revise her existing scheme of fashion according to changes in what's hot and what's not. The 7-year-old may find a long, thin, slithery thing that can't possibly be a snake because it has four legs. After some research, the child develops a new scheme—*salamander*—for this creature.

Although children's schemes change over time, the two processes through which their schemes are acquired and modified—assimilation and accommodation—remain the same throughout the course of development. Assimilation and accommodation typically work hand in hand as children develop their knowledge and understanding of the world. Children interpret each new event within the context of their existing knowledge (assimilation) but at the same time may modify their knowledge as a result of the new event (accommodation). Accommodation rarely happens without assimilation: People of any age can benefit from (accommodate to) new experiences only when they can relate those experiences to their current knowledge and beliefs.

■ *Interaction with one's physical environment is critical for cognitive development.* New experiences are essential for cognitive development to occur; without them, the modification of schemes—accommodation—cannot take place. By exploring and manipulating the world around them—by conducting many little "experiments" with various objects and substances—children learn the nature of such physical characteristics as volume and weight, discover principles related to force and gravity, acquire a better understanding of cause-effect relationships, and so on. Activities such as "fiddling" with sand and water, playing games with balls and bats, and experimenting in a science laboratory help children construct a more complete and accurate un-

scheme
In Piaget's theory, an organized group of similar actions or thoughts.

operation
In Piaget's theory, an organized and integrated system of thought processes.

adaptation
Developmental process of responding to the environment in an increasingly effective manner.

assimilation
Dealing with a new event in a way that is consistent with an existing scheme.

accommodation
Dealing with a new event by either modifying an existing scheme or forming a new one.

Children and adolescents benefit from opportunities, either informal or more structured, to explore and manipulate physical objects.

derstanding of how the physical world operates. The following anecdote from preschool teacher Frances Hawkins illustrates:

> Tommy . . . had built a tower on a base of three regular blocks on end, with a round, flat piece of Masonite on top. Then on top of this were three more blocks and Masonite, supporting in turn a third story. Each story was defined by round, flat pieces of Masonite in the structure. The tower was already taller than Tommy, and he had a piece of triangular Masonite in hand and was gently testing the tower's steadiness against his taps. Small taps and the tower would lean, settle, and become still. Again and again he varied the strength and place of the taps; watched, waited, tapped again, and finally—on purpose—did hit hard enough to topple the structure. Then the entire process of building the tower and testing it was repeated. (Hawkins, 1997, p. 200)

■ *Interaction with other people is equally critical.* As you will soon discover, young children often have difficulty seeing the world from anyone's perspective but their own. By conversing, exchanging ideas, and arguing with others, they gradually begin to realize that different individuals see things differently and that their own view of the world is not necessarily a completely accurate or logical one. Elementary school children may begin to recognize logical inconsistencies in what they say and do (e.g., recall Brian's insistence that there were more brown beads than wooden beads) when someone else points out those inconsistencies. And through discussions with classmates or adults about social and political issues, high school students slowly modify their newly emerging idealism about how the world "should" be.

■ *The process of equilibration promotes progression toward increasingly more complex forms of thought.* Piaget proposed that children are sometimes in a state of **equilibrium:** They can comfortably explain new events in terms of existing schemes. But this equilibrium doesn't continue indefinitely. As children grow, they frequently encounter situations that they cannot adequately explain in terms of their current understanding of the world. Such situations create **disequilibrium,** a sort of mental "discomfort" that spurs them to try to make sense of what they observe. By replacing, reorganizing, or better integrating their schemes (in other words, through accommodation), children eventually become able to understand and explain previously puzzling events. The movement from equilibrium to disequilibrium and back to equilibrium again is known as **equilibration.** Equilibration and children's intrinsic desire to achieve equilibrium promote the development of more complex levels of thought and knowledge.

Let's return to the case of Brian and the "beads" problem presented earlier. The experimenter asks Brian to draw two necklaces, one made with the wooden beads and one made with the brown beads. The experimenter hopes that after Brian draws a brown-and-white necklace that is longer than an all-brown necklace, he will notice that his drawings are inconsistent with his

equilibrium
State of being able to explain new events in terms of existing schemes.

disequilibrium
State of being *un*able to explain new events in terms of existing schemes.

equilibration
Movement from equilibrium to disequilibrium and back to equilibrium; a process that promotes the development of increasingly complex forms of thought and knowledge.

statement that there are more brown beads. Brian should therefore experience disequilibrium, perhaps to the point where he will reevaluate his conclusion and realize that all the brown beads *plus two white ones* must necessarily be more than the brown beads alone. In this case, however, Brian apparently is oblivious to the inconsistency, remains in equilibrium, and so has no need to revise his thinking.

■ *Children think in qualitatively different ways at different age levels.* Piaget was a *stage theorist:* He proposed that children proceed through four stages of cognitive development and that their thinking and reasoning processes are qualitatively different at each one. These qualitative changes in children's thinking are due both to neurological maturation and to the increasing integration of their knowledge and thought processes. We turn now to the nature of Piaget's stages.

Piaget's Stages of Cognitive Development

Piaget's four stages of cognitive development are as follows:

1. Sensorimotor stage (birth until about 2 years)
2. Preoperational stage (2 years until about 6 or 7 years)
3. Concrete operations stage (6 or 7 years until about 11 or 12 years)
4. Formal operations stage (11 or 12 years through adulthood)

These stages are briefly summarized in Figure 4–1.

Piaget believed that each stage builds on the accomplishments of any preceding stages, so that children must progress through the four stages in the same, invariant sequence. Furthermore, he suggested that the stages are *universal*—that they describe the cognitive development of children throughout the world.

FIGURE 4–1 Piaget's stages of cognitive development

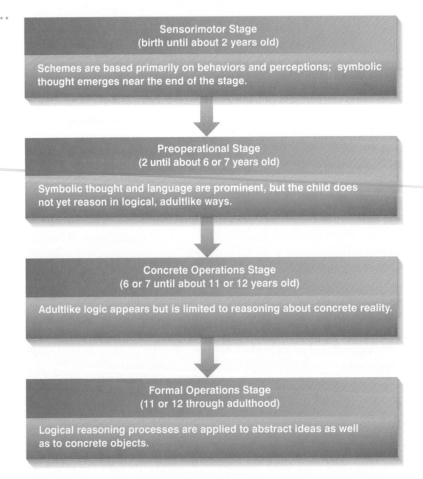

Sensorimotor Stage
(birth until about 2 years old)

Schemes are based primarily on behaviors and perceptions; symbolic thought emerges near the end of the stage.

Preoperational Stage
(2 until about 6 or 7 years old)

Symbolic thought and language are prominent, but the child does not yet reason in logical, adultlike ways.

Concrete Operations Stage
(6 or 7 until about 11 or 12 years old)

Adultlike logic appears but is limited to reasoning about concrete reality.

Formal Operations Stage
(11 or 12 through adulthood)

Logical reasoning processes are applied to abstract ideas as well as to concrete objects.

As you will discover later in the chapter, many psychologists question the notion that cognitive development is either as stagelike or as universal as Piaget believed. Nevertheless, Piaget's stages do provide insights into the nature of children's thinking at different age levels, and so we will look at them in depth. Note that the ages associated with each stage are *averages*; some children may reach a stage at a slightly younger age than average, and others may reach it at an older age. Furthermore, some children may be *transitional* from one stage to the next and so display characteristics of two adjacent stages during the same time period.

Sensorimotor Stage (Birth Until Age 2) Imagine this situation:

We show a colorful stuffed clown to 6-month-old Elena. Elena reaches for the clown in much the same way that she reaches for her teddy bear and her stacking blocks. She then drops it and squeals in delight as it falls to the floor. We pick up the clown and, as Elena watches, put it inside a box so that it is no longer visible. At this point, Elena seems to forget about her new toy and turns to play with something else.

Elena readily applies several schemes to the clown, including reaching-and-grasping, letting-go, and visually-following-a-moving-object. In the early part of the sensorimotor stage, children's schemes are based primarily on behaviors (e.g., grabbing, dropping) and perceptions (e.g., visual tracking). According to Piaget, children in this stage are not yet capable of *mental* schemes that enable them to think about objects beyond their immediate view. Elena acts as if she cannot think about a clown she cannot actually see. In other words, out of sight, out of mind.

Later in the sensorimotor stage (at about 18 months, according to Piaget), a child develops **symbolic thought,** the ability to mentally represent and think about objects and events in terms of internal, mental entities, or *symbols*. For example, Elena will eventually be able to think about a clown she has just seen without having it directly in front of her. Such symbolic thinking marks the beginning of true thought as Piaget defined it.

As infants experiment with their environments in a trial-and-error fashion, other important cognitive capabilities emerge as well. One important acquisition is **object permanence,** the realization that physical objects continue to exist even when they are removed from view. For instance, whereas 6-month-old Elena forgets about the toy clown once it is put in a box, a 12-month-old will know where the clown is and open the box to get it.

Furthermore, after repeatedly observing that certain actions lead to certain consequences, children in the sensorimotor stage acquire an understanding of cause-effect relationships. Accordingly, they begin to engage in **goal-directed behavior:** They behave in ways that they know will bring about desired results. (Whereas Elena lets go of the clown to see what will happen, an older baby or toddler might drop the clown *intentionally,* knowing in advance that it will fall to the floor and waiting eagerly to see it happen.) Older sensorimotor children also begin to combine behaviors in new and creative ways to accomplish their goals. They frequently "experiment" with such combinations in their minds first, predicting what will happen if they do such-and-such and then transforming their plans into action.

The acquisitions of the sensorimotor stage, including symbolic thought, object permanence, and goal-directed behavior, are basic building blocks on which later cognitive development depends.[2] At the same time, growing children don't entirely discard sensorimotor ways of interacting with the environment. Even as adults, we continue to use the behavioral and perceptual schemes we acquired as infants (reaching and grasping, following a moving object with our eyes, etc.), and sometimes trial-and-error experimentation is the only way to interact with a new and puzzling object.

Preoperational Stage (Age 2 Until Age 6 or 7) The ability to represent objects and events mentally (i.e., symbolic thought) gives children in the preoperational stage a greater "world view" than they had during the sensorimotor stage. They can now recall past events and envision future ones, and so they can begin to tie their experiences together into an increasingly more complex understanding of the world.

symbolic thought
Ability to represent and think about external objects and events in one's mind.

object permanence
Realization that objects continue to exist even after they are removed from view.

goal-directed behavior
Planful behavior intended to bring about an anticipated outcome.

---

[2]Piaget described the sensorimotor stage as having six substages—substages that are probably of greater interest to new parents than to teachers. If you are interested in learning about the substages of the sensorimotor stage, we refer you to Piaget (1952b), Flavell (1963), or Flavell, Miller, and Miller (1993).

Language skills virtually explode during the early part of the preoperational stage. The words in children's rapidly increasing vocabularies provide labels for newly developed mental schemes and serve as symbols that enable them to think about objects and events even when such things are not directly in sight. Furthermore, language provides the basis for a new form of social interaction: verbal communication. Children can express their thoughts and receive information from other people in a way that was not possible during the sensorimotor stage.

The advent of symbolic thought reflects itself not only in rapidly expanding language skills but also in the changing nature of children's play. Young children often engage in fantasy and make-believe, using either realistic objects or reasonable substitutes to act out the roles and behaviors of those they see around them. Piaget proposed that such pretend play enables children to practice using newly acquired symbolic schemes and familiarize themselves with the various roles they see others assume in society. The following incident involving 5-year-olds Jeff and Scott illustrates:

> In a corner of Jeff's basement, the boys make a dining area from several child-sized tables and chairs. They construct a restaurant "kitchen" with a toy sink and stove and stock it with plastic dishes and "food" items. They create menus for their restaurant, often asking a parent how to spell the words but sometimes using their knowledge of letter-sound relationships to guess how a particular word might be spelled.
>
> Jeff and Scott invite their mothers and fathers to come to the new restaurant for lunch. After seating their "customers," the boys pretend to write their meal orders on paper tablets and then scurry to the kitchen to assemble the requested lunch items. Eventually they return to serve the meals (hamburgers, French fries, and cookies—all of them plastic—plus glasses of imaginary milk), which the adults "eat" and "drink" with gusto. After the young waiters return with the final bills, the adults pay for their "meals" with nickels and leave a few pennies on the tables as tips.

With the emergence of symbolic thought, then, young children are no longer restricted to the "here and now" and so can think and act far more flexibly than they have previously. At the same time, preoperational thinking has some definite limitations, especially as we compare it to the concrete operational thinking that emerges later (see Table 4–1). For example, Piaget described young children as exhibiting **preoperational egocentrism,** the inability to view situations from another person's perspective.[3] Young children may have trouble understanding why they must share school supplies with a classmate or why they must be careful not to hurt someone else's feelings. They may play games together without ever checking to be sure that they are all playing according to the same rules. They may also exhibit **egocentric speech,** saying things without considering the perspective of the listener. They may leave out critical details as they tell a story, giving a fragmented version that a listener cannot possibly understand. As an illustration, an adult in Piaget's laboratory once told a story and asked young Giovanna to retell it:

The original:
Once upon a time, there was a lady who was called Niobe, and who had 12 sons and 12 daughters. She met a fairy who had only one son and no daughter. Then the lady laughed at the fairy because the fairy only had one boy. Then the fairy was very angry and fastened the lady to a rock. The lady cried for ten years. In the end she turned into a rock, and her tears made a stream which still runs today. (Piaget, 1959, p. 82)

Giovanna's version:
Once upon a time there was a lady who had twelve boys and twelve girls, and then a fairy [had] a boy and a girl. And then Niobe wanted to have some more sons. Then she was angry. She fastened her to a stone. He turned into a rock, and then his tears made a stream which is still running today. (p. 102)

preoperational egocentrism
Inability of a child in Piaget's preoperational stage to view situations from another person's perspective.

egocentric speech
Speaking without taking the perspective and knowledge of the listener into account.

---

[3]Bjorklund and Green (1992) have suggested that young children's egocentrism, rather than being a limitation, may actually have an adaptive function. A common finding in studies of human learning is that people can remember information more easily when they see its relevance to their own lives.

TABLE 4–1 Preoperational Versus Concrete Operational Thought

PREOPERATIONAL THOUGHT	CONCRETE OPERATIONAL THOUGHT
Preoperational egocentrism Inability to see things from someone else's perspective; thinking that one's own perspective is the only one possible. *Example:* A child tells a story without considering what prior knowledge the listener is likely to have.	**Differentiation of one's own perspective from the perspectives of others** Recognition that different people see the same things differently; realization that one's own perspective may be incorrect. *Example:* A child asks for validation of his own thoughts (e.g., "Did I get that right?").
Confusion between physical and psychological events Confusion of external, physical objects with internal thoughts; thinking that thoughts have physical reality and that objects think and feel. *Example:* A child is afraid of the "monsters" in a dark closet and worries that a doll will feel lonely if left alone at home.	**Distinction between physical and psychological events** Recognition that thoughts do not have physical reality and that physical objects don't have psychological characteristics such as "feelings." *Example:* A child realizes that imagined monsters don't exist and that dolls have no thoughts or feelings.
Lack of conservation Belief that amount changes when a substance is reshaped or re-arranged, even though nothing has been added or taken away. *Example:* A child asserts that two rows of five pennies similarly spaced have equal amounts; however, when one row is spread out so that it is longer than the other, she says that it has more pennies.	**Conservation** Recognition that amount stays the same if nothing has been added or taken away, even when the substance is reshaped or re-arranged. *Example:* A child asserts that two rows of five pennies are the same number of pennies regardless of their spacing.
Irreversibility Lack of awareness that certain processes can be undone, or reversed. *Example:* A child doesn't realize that a row of five pennies previously made longer by extra spacing can be shortened back to its original length.	**Reversibility** Ability to envision how certain processes can be reversed. *Example:* A child moves the five pennies in the longer row close together again to demonstrate that both rows have the same amount.
Reliance on perception over logic Dependence on how things appear when drawing conclusions. *Example:* A child hears a story about a girl whose uncle gives her a baby rattle as a gift. Though sad about the age-inappropriate gift, the girl in the story smiles so that she won't hurt her uncle's feelings. When looking at a picture of the smiling girl, the child concludes that the girl feels happy (Friend & Davis, 1993).	**Reliance on logic over perception** Dependence on conceptual understandings when drawing conclusions. *Example:* A child hearing the same story and seeing the picture of the smiling girl concludes that the girl *looks* happy but actually feels sad (Friend & Davis, 1993).
Centration Focus on a single physical dimension when comparing two or more objects. *Example:* When water is poured from a tall, thin glass into a short, wide glass, a child claims that there is now less water than before. He is focusing on the lesser height of the water in the second glass, without considering that the second glass is also wider than the first.	**Decentration** Consideration of two or more dimensions of objects simultaneously; recognition that one dimension may compensate for another. *Example:* A child recognizes that water poured from a tall, thin glass into a short, wide glass is still the same amount of water. He understands that the greater width of the second glass makes up for its lesser height.
Single classification Ability to classify objects in only one way at any given point in time. *Example:* A child denies that a mother can also be a doctor.	**Multiple classification** Recognition that objects may belong to several categories simultaneously (includes *class inclusion*). *Example:* A child acknowledges that a mother can also be a doctor, a jogger, and a spouse.
Transductive reasoning Reasoning that involves combining unrelated facts (e.g., inferring a cause-effect relationship simply because two events occur close together in time and space). *Example:* A child believes that clouds make the moon grow (Piaget, 1928).	**Deductive reasoning** Drawing an appropriate logical inference from two or more pieces of information. *Example:* A child deduces that if Jane is taller than Mary, and if Mary is taller than Carol, then Jane must be taller than Carol.

A   B   C

Before

B

A

C

After

FIGURE 4–2 Conservation of liquid: Do glasses A and C contain the same amount of water after the water in B is poured into C?

Notice how Giovanna never explained who "she," "her," and "he" were—things that couldn't possibly have been obvious to a listener.

In Giovanna's rendition of the story we find one reason why, from Piaget's perspective, social interaction is so important for cognitive development. Someone listening to the child's story might express confusion about who was angry and who turned into a rock. Repeated feedback from other people helps children learn that their thoughts and feelings are unique to them—that their perception of the world is not always shared by others and, in some cases, may not even reflect the true state of affairs.

Preoperational thinking is also *illogical* (at least from an adult's point of view), especially during the preschool years. As an example, recall Brian's insistence that there were more brown beads than wooden beads, an error that reflects single classification (see Table 4–1). Here is another example of the "logic" of children exhibiting preoperational thought:

We show 4-year-old Lucy the three glasses in Figure 4–2. Glasses A and B are identical in size and shape and contain an equal amount of water. We ask Lucy if the two glasses of water contain the same amount, and she replies confidently that they do. We then pour the water in Glass B into Glass C. We ask her if the two glasses of water (A and C) still have the same amount. "No," Lucy replies. She points to glass A: "That glass has more because it's taller."

Lucy's response illustrates a lack of **conservation:** She does not realize that because no water has been added or taken away, the amount of water in the two glasses must be equivalent. Young children often confuse changes in appearance with changes in amount. Piaget suggested that, in general, children in the preoperational stage depend more on perception than on logic when they reason.

As children approach the later part of the preoperational stage, perhaps at around 4 or 5 years of age, they show early signs of being logical. For example, they sometimes draw correct conclusions about conservation problems (e.g., the water glasses) or multiple classification problems (e.g., the wooden beads). They cannot yet explain *why* their conclusions are correct, however; they base their reasoning on hunches and intuition rather than on any conscious awareness of underlying logical principles. When children move into the concrete operations stage, they become increasingly able both to make logical inferences and to explain the reasoning behind their conclusions.

Concrete Operations Stage (Age 6 or 7 Years Until Age 11 or 12) At about age 6 or 7, children's thinking processes become integrated into *operations* that allow them to pull their thoughts and ideas together more effectively than they have before. As a result, concrete operational thought is more advanced than preoperational thought in a number of ways (see Table 4–1). For example, children now realize that their own thoughts and feelings are not necessarily shared by others and may reflect personal opinions rather than reality. Accordingly, they know that they can sometimes be wrong and begin to seek out external validation for their ideas, asking such questions as "What do you think?" and "Did I get that problem right?"

Children in the concrete operations stage are capable of many forms of logical thought. For instance, they show conservation: They readily understand that if nothing is added or taken away, amount stays the same despite any changes in shape or arrangement. (Hence, they would have no trouble with the water glasses problem that Lucy struggled with.) They also exhibit **multiple classification:** They can readily classify objects into two categories simultaneously. (Recall 8-year-old Natalie's ease in solving the wooden beads vs. brown beads problem.) And they demonstrate **deductive reasoning:** They can draw logical inferences from the facts they are given.

Children continue to develop their newly acquired logical thinking capabilities throughout the elementary school years. For instance, over time they become capable of dealing with increasingly more complex conservation tasks. Some forms of conservation, such as conservation of liquid and conservation of number (the latter illustrated by the "pennies" problem in Table 4–1), appear at age 6 or 7, but other forms may not appear until several years later. Consider the task involving conservation of weight depicted in Figure 4–3. Using a balance scale,

conservation
Realization that if nothing is added or taken away, amount stays the same regardless of any alterations in shape or arrangement.

multiple classification
Recognition that objects may belong to several categories simultaneously.

deductive reasoning
Drawing a logical inference about something that must be true given other information that has already been presented as true.

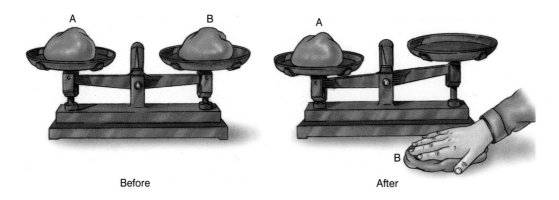

FIGURE 4–3 Conservation of weight: Balls A and B initially weigh the same. When Ball B is flattened into a pancake shape, how does its weight now compare with that of Ball A?

an adult shows a child that two balls of clay have the same weight. One ball is removed from the scale and smashed into a pancake shape. Does the pancake weigh the same as the un-smashed ball, or do the two pieces of clay weigh different amounts? Children typically do not achieve conservation of weight—that is, they do not realize that the flattened pancake weighs the same as the round ball it was previously—until sometime around age 9 to 12 (Sund, 1976).

Although children displaying concrete operational thought show many signs of logical thinking, their cognitive development is not yet complete (see Table 4–2). They have difficulty thinking about proportions and ratios, formulating and testing hypotheses, and separating and controlling variables—processes central to adult forms of mathematical and scientific reasoning. They also have trouble understanding and reasoning about abstract ideas. In mathematics, this weakness may be reflected in their confusion about such concepts as *pi* (π), *infinity,* and *negative number.* In social studies, it may limit their comprehension of such abstract notions as democracy, communism, and human rights. Finally, children who show concrete operational thought are likely to have difficulty reasoning about ideas that involve hypothetical situations or contradict reality.

A Piaget (1928) study with children of various ages illustrates. In it, the experimenter presents this problem: *Someone said, "If ever I kill myself from despair I won't choose a Friday, because Friday is a bad day and would bring me ill luck." What's silly about that?* Several children respond:

9-year-old:	People can kill themselves every day; they don't need to kill themselves on a Friday.
9-year-old:	Friday is not unlucky.
10-year-old:	Perhaps Friday will bring him good luck.
11-year-old:	He doesn't know if it will bring him ill luck. (responses from Piaget, 1928, pp. 63, 65)

The true "silliness" of the situation is, of course, that people who commit suicide don't have to worry about any subsequent bad luck. Yet many elementary school children fail to make the connection; instead, they deny that Friday is a bad day or reject the idea that people can or might kill themselves (Copeland, 1979).

Formal Operations Stage (Age 11 or 12 Through Adulthood) Consider this task:

An object suspended by a rope or string—a pendulum—swings indefinitely at a constant rate. Some pendulums swing back and forth very quickly, whereas others swing more slowly.

One or more of four variables might affect a pendulum's oscillation rate (i.e., how fast it swings): the weight of the suspended object, the force with which the object is pushed, the

When students display concrete operational thought, they can think logically about concrete objects and situations but have difficulty with more abstract forms of mathematical and scientific reasoning.

TABLE 4–2 Concrete Operational Versus Formal Operational Thought

CONCRETE OPERATIONAL THOUGHT	FORMAL OPERATIONAL THOUGHT
Dependence on concrete reality Logical reasoning only about concrete objects that are readily observed. *Example:* A child has difficulty with the concept of negative numbers, wondering how something can possibly be less than zero.	**Ability to reason about abstract, hypothetical, and contrary-to-fact ideas** Logical reasoning about things that are not tied directly to concrete, observable reality. *Example:* A child understands negative numbers and is able to use them effectively in mathematical procedures and problems.
Inability to formulate and test multiple hypotheses Identifying and testing only one hypothesis when seeking an explanation for a scientific phenomenon. *Example:* When asked what makes a pendulum swing faster or more slowly, a child states that the weight of the pendulum is the determining factor and disregards any observations she has made that contradict her hypothesis.	**Formulation and testing of multiple hypotheses** Developing and testing several hypotheses about cause-effect relationships related to a particular phenomenon. *Example:* When asked what makes a pendulum swing faster or more slowly, a child proposes that weight, length, and strength of initial push are all possible explanations and then tests the effects of each variable.
Inability to separate and control variables Confounding two or more variables when attempting to confirm or disconfirm a particular hypothesis about a cause-effect relationship. *Example:* In testing possible factors influencing the oscillation rate of a pendulum, a child adds more weight to the pendulum while at the same time also shortening the length of the pendulum.	**Separation and control of variables** Testing one variable at a time while holding all others constant, in an attempt to confirm or disconfirm a particular hypothesis about a cause-effect relationship. *Example:* In testing factors that influence a pendulum's oscillation rate, a child tests the effect of weight while keeping string length and strength of push constant and then tests the effect of length while keeping weight and push constant.
Lack of proportional reasoning Lack of understanding about the nature of proportions. *Example:* A child cannot make sense of the procedure his teacher demonstrates for converting fractions to ratios.	**Proportional reasoning** Understanding proportions and using them effectively in mathematical problem solving. *Example:* A child works easily with proportions, fractions, decimals, and ratios.
Lack of combinatorial thought Difficulty identifying all possible combinations of several objects, such that various combinations are identified in an unsystematic, random fashion. *Example:* A child asked to identify the ways in which four objects (A, B, C, D) might be combined generates four combinations (AB, CD, AD, ABCD) and then cannot think of any more.	**Combinatorial thought** Systematic identification of all possible combinations of several objects. *Example:* A child asked to identify possible combinations of four objects (A, B, C, D) generates all 15 possibilities (A, B, C, D, AB, AC, AD, BC, BD, CD, ABC, ABD, ACD, BCD, and ABCD).

height from which the object is initially released, and the length of the string that holds the object. Design an experiment that can help you determine which of these factors affect(s) a pendulum's oscillation rate.

To identify the one or more factors that influence oscillation rate, you must *separate and control variables:* You must test one factor at a time while holding all others constant. For instance, to test the hypothesis that weight makes a difference, you should try different weights while keeping constant the force with which you push each weight, the height from which you drop it, and the length of the string. Similarly, if you hypothesize that the length of the string is a critical factor, you should vary the length of the string while continuing to use the same weight and starting the pendulum in motion in the same manner. If you carefully separate and control the variables, then your observations should lead you to conclude that only *length* affects a pendulum's oscillation rate.

Piaget and his colleague Bärbel Inhelder asked children of many ages to tackle the pendulum problem. The following two examples, with children we'll call Craig and Emily, illustrate how children of different ages responded to the problem.

Craig, age 10, begins his experimentation with a long string and a 100-gram weight. He then shortens the string and changes to a 200-gram weight, which he drops from a higher point.

Exp: Did you find out anything?
Craig: The little one goes more slowly and the higher it is the faster it goes.

He puts the 50-gram weight on the same short string.

Craig: The little weight goes even faster.

He then ignores what he just observed.

Craig: To go faster, you have to pull up [shorten] the string, and the little one goes less fast because it is less heavy.
Exp: Do you still wonder what you have to do to make it go faster?
Craig: The little weight goes faster.
Exp: How can you prove it?
Craig: You have to pull up the string. (dialogue from Inhelder & Piaget, 1958, p. 71)

Emily, age 15, at first believes that each of the four factors is influential. She studies different weights with the same string length (medium) and does not notice any appreciable change.

Emily: That doesn't change the rhythm.

She then varies the string length, using the same 200-gram weight.

Emily: When the string is small, the swing is faster.

Finally, she varies the dropping point and then the strength of the push, each time using the same medium length string and the same 200-gram weight.

Emily: Nothing has changed. (dialogue from Inhelder & Piaget, 1958, pp. 75–76)

Notice how Craig changes weight and length simultaneously when he experiments, and he has difficulty separating the two variables even when he draws his conclusions (e.g., to prove that weight makes a difference, he says that "You have to pull up the string"). In contrast, Emily systematically tests each of the four variables in isolation from the other three, and she correctly concludes that only length makes a difference.

According to Piaget, several abilities essential for sophisticated scientific and mathematical reasoning emerge in formal operations (see Table 4–2). Three of these—reasoning logically about hypothetical ideas, formulating and testing hypotheses, and separating and controlling variables—together allow adolescents to use the *scientific method,* in which several possible explanations for an observed phenomenon are proposed and tested in a systematic manner. Only with formal operational thinking can people address and answer questions about cause-effect relationships in a truly scientific fashion.

Capabilities in mathematics are also likely to improve once formal operational thinking develops. Abstract problems, such as mathematical word problems, should become easier to solve. Students should become capable of understanding such concepts as *negative number* and *infinity;* for instance, they should now comprehend how temperature can be below zero and how two parallel lines will never touch even if they go on forever. And because they can now use proportions in their reasoning, they can study and understand fractions, ratios, and decimals, and they can use such proportions to solve problems.

Because adolescents capable of formal operational reasoning can deal with hypothetical and contrary-to-fact ideas, they can envision how the world might be different from, and possibly better than, the way it actually is. (Brady's cartoon in Figure 4–4 is an example.) As a result, they may exhibit some idealism

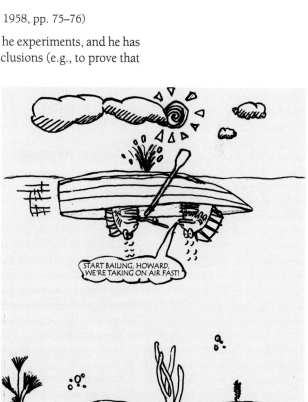

FIGURE 4–4 One characteristic of Piaget's formal operations stage is the ability to imagine alternatives to reality. At age 14, Brady Williamson drew this cartoon (partly by computer, partly by hand) of two fish rowing a boat upside-down at the water's surface.

Piaget's Theory of Cognitive Development | **121**

about social, political, religious, and ethical issues. For example, secondary school students often argue that they should be allowed to wear anything they want to school, no matter how skimpy or suggestive their fashion choices might be. They may reject their parents' political or religious affiliations and seek out alternative belief systems. Many secondary school students begin to show concern about world problems and devote some of their energy to worthy causes such as the environment, world hunger, or animal rights. Curiously, however, their devotion may sometimes be more evident in their talk than in their actions (Elkind, 1984).

As adolescents become increasingly able to reason about abstract, hypothetical, and contrary-to-fact ideas, they also become increasingly idealistic about how the world should be.

Idealistic adolescents often present recommendations for change that seem logical but aren't practical in today's world. For example, they may argue that racism would disappear overnight if people would only just begin to "love one another," or they may propose that a nation should disband its armed forces and eliminate all its weaponry as a way of moving toward world peace. Piaget suggested that adolescent idealism reflects **formal operational egocentrism,** an inability to separate one's own logical abstractions from the perspectives of others and from practical considerations. It is only through experience that adolescents eventually begin to temper their optimism with some realism about what is possible in a given time frame and with limited resources.

Current Perspectives on Piaget's Theory

Piaget's theory has inspired hundreds of research studies concerning the nature of children's cognitive development. In general, research supports Piaget's proposed *sequence* in which different abilities emerge (Flavell, 1996; Siegler & Richards, 1982). For example, the ability to reason about abstract ideas emerges only after children are already capable of reasoning about concrete objects and events, and the order in which various conservation tasks are mastered is much as Piaget proposed. Researchers have discovered, however, that Piaget was not always accurate regarding the *ages* at which various abilities appear. They have found, too, that children's logical reasoning capabilities may vary considerably from one occasion to another and are, in part, a function of previous knowledge and experiences, education, and culture. Furthermore, many researchers question the stagelike nature of cognitive development that Piaget described. We turn now to these issues; we then identify some of Piaget's enduring contributions to developmental psychology.

Capabilities of Infants A growing body of research indicates that Piaget probably underestimated the thinking capabilities of young infants. By 5 months of age, infants look surprised when objects vanish unexpectedly, supporting the idea that they have some understanding of object permanence earlier than Piaget believed (Baillargeon, 1994). Mental representation of observed events (i.e., symbolic thinking) also emerges sooner than Piaget proposed. Infants as young as 9 months can remember actions that adults perform (e.g., shaking a plastic egg, pushing a button on a box) long enough to imitate them 24 hours later (Meltzoff, 1988).

Some developmental theorists argue that infants' brains are "preprogrammed" to a certain degree—that infants are born already possessing some basic knowledge, or at least some preliminary

formal operational egocentrism
Inability of an individual in Piaget's formal operations stage to separate one's own abstract logic from the perspectives of others and from practical considerations.

intuitions, about their world (e.g., Baillargeon, 1994; Spelke, 1994). For instance, even very young infants seem to know that an object maintains its existence and shape as it moves, that one object can influence another only when the two come into contact, and that two objects cannot occupy the same space at the same time (Spelke, 1994). This idea of preprogrammed knowledge or inclinations, known as **nativism,** is particularly prevalent in theoretical views of language development; hence, we will encounter it again in Chapter 7.

The proposal that some knowledge is "built in" has been a source of considerable controversy among developmental theorists. Ultimately, we must await further research to determine the extent to which the human brain is hard-wired with what it either "knows" or is prepared to learn easily.

Capabilities of Preschoolers Preschool children are probably more competent than Piaget's description of the preoperational stage would indicate. Children as young as 3 or 4 years old are not completely egocentric; in many situations, they *can* take another person's perspective. For example, they recognize that an object looks different when viewed from different angles, and they can identify such emotions as sadness or anger in others (Lennon, Eisenberg, & Carroll, 1983; Newcombe & Huttenlocher, 1992).

Preschoolers also think more logically than Piaget suggested. They can draw logically valid deductions; for instance, they often make appropriate inferences when they listen to stories (Donaldson, 1978; Gelman & Baillargeon, 1983). Children as young as 4 sometimes show conservation; they are more likely to answer a conservation problem correctly if the transformation occurs out of sight, so that they are not misled by appearances (Donaldson, 1978; Rosser, 1994). And many supposedly preoperational children can correctly solve multiple classification problems if words are used to draw attention to the entire group; for example, many 4- and 5-year-olds realize that, in a *forest* of eight pine trees and two oak trees, there must, of course, be more trees than pine trees (Gelman & Baillargeon, 1983; Resnick, 1989; Rosser, 1994).

Why have Piaget and more recent researchers sometimes found conflicting results? Theorists have offered several explanations. One possibility is that the children in Piaget's studies sometimes misinterpreted the wordings of his problems (Reyna, 1996; Rosser, 1994). For example, when water is poured from a short, fat glass into a tall, skinny one, a child might say that the tall one has more water because she misconstrues the word *more* to mean "higher." Sometimes, too, a problem may have more pieces (e.g., more pennies in a conservation-of-number task) than a child can reasonably keep track of and remember (Gelman, 1972).

On some occasions, children may simply say what they think an adult expects them to say (Winer, Craig, & Weinbaum, 1992). For instance, when a researcher asks the same question twice (e.g., "Do the two glasses have the same amount of water?" and later, "Do they *still* have the same amount?"), children may conclude that a change *must* have occurred; otherwise, the researcher would not have repeated the question.

Capabilities of Elementary School Children Piaget may have underestimated the capabilities of elementary age children as well. Children in this age group occasionally show evidence of abstract and hypothetical thought (Carey, 1985b; Metz, 1995). As an illustration, consider this hypothetical (and therefore formal operational) situation:

All of Joan's friends are going to the museum today.
Pat is a friend of Joan.

Children as young as 9 can correctly deduce that "Pat is going to the museum today" even though the situation involves people they don't know and so has no basis in their own concrete reality (Roberge, 1970). Also, elementary school children can sometimes separate and control variables, especially when the tasks are simplified and they are given hints about the importance of controlling all variables except the one they are testing (Danner & Day, 1977; Metz, 1995; Ruffman, Perner, Olson, & Doherty, 1993).

Capabilities of Adolescents Formal operational thought processes probably emerge much more gradually than Piaget originally proposed. High school and college students often have difficulty with tasks involving such formal operational thinking abilities as separation

nativism
Theoretical perspective that some knowledge is biologically built-in and present at birth.

and control of variables, proportional reasoning, and combinatorial thought (Flieller, 1999; Kuhn, Amsel, & O'Loughlin, 1988; Pascarella & Terenzini, 1991; Siegler & Richards, 1982). Furthermore, students may demonstrate formal operational thought in one content domain while thinking more concretely in another. Evidence of formal operations typically emerges in the physical sciences earlier than in such subjects as history and geography; adolescents often have difficulty thinking about abstract and hypothetical ideas in history and geography until well into the high school years (Lovell, 1979; Tamburrini, 1982).

Effects of Prior Knowledge and Experience

Piaget believed that once children acquire a particular reasoning skill, they can apply it in virtually any context. It is becoming increasingly apparent, however, that for people of all ages, the ability to think logically in a particular situation depends on knowledge and background experiences relative to that situation. Preschoolers are less likely to exhibit the "illogic" of transductive reasoning (e.g., to say that clouds make the moon grow) when they have accurate information about cause-effect relationships (Carey, 1985a). Children as young as 4 may begin to show conservation after having experience with conservation tasks, especially if they can actively manipulate the materials of the tasks and are asked

Having a great deal of knowledge about a particular topic often allows students to engage in formal operational thought; however, the students may continue to think concretely about less familiar topics.

to discuss their reasoning with someone who already exhibits conservation (Field, 1987; Mayer, 1992; Murray, 1978). And in general, young children are more likely to think in a concrete operational rather than preoperational fashion when they are familiar with the objects they are dealing with (Ceci & Roazzi, 1994).

Formal operational thought, too, is affected by the specific knowledge and experiences that children and adolescents have acquired. Ten-year-olds can learn to solve logical problems involving hypothetical ideas if they are taught particular strategies for solving such problems (Lee, 1985). Students in the upper elementary and middle school grades are better able to separate and control variables in laboratory experiments when they have practice and guidance in doing so (Kuhn & Phelps, 1982; Ross, 1988). Junior high and high school students, and adults as well, often apply formal operational thought to topics about which they have a great deal of knowledge yet think "concrete operationally" about topics with which they are unfamiliar (Linn, Clement, Pulos, & Sullivan, 1989; Metz, 1995; Schliemann & Carraher, 1993).

As an illustration of how knowledge affects formal operational thinking, consider the fishing pond in Figure 4–5. In a study by Pulos and Linn (1981), 13-year-olds were shown a similar picture and told, "These four children go fishing every week, and one child, Herb, always catches the most fish. The other children wonder why." If you look at the picture, it is obvious that Herb is different from the three other children in several ways, including the kind of bait he uses, the length of his fishing rod, and the place where he is standing. Children who were experienced fishermen more effectively separated and controlled variables for this situation than they did for the pendulum problem described earlier, whereas the reverse was true for nonfishermen (Pulos & Linn, 1981).

One general experience that promotes more advanced reasoning is formal education: Going to school and the specific nature of one's schooling are associated with mastery of concrete operational and formal operational tasks (Artman & Cahan, 1993; Flieller, 1999). For instance, you may be happy to learn that taking college courses in a particular area (in child development, perhaps?) leads to improvements in formal reasoning skills related to that area (Lehman & Nisbett, 1990).

FIGURE 4–5 What are some possible reasons why Herb is catching more fish than the others?

Based on Pulos & Linn, 1981.

Effects of Culture Piaget proposed that his stages were universal, that they applied to children and adolescents around the globe. Yet research indicates that the course of cognitive development differs somewhat from one culture to another (Glick, 1975). For example, Mexican children whose families make pottery for a living acquire conservation skills much earlier than Piaget indicated (Price-Williams, Gordon, & Ramirez, 1969). Apparently, making pottery requires children to make frequent judgments about needed quantities of clay and water—judgments that must be fairly accurate regardless of the specific shape or form that the clay or water container takes. In other cultures, especially in those where children don't attend school, conservation appears several years later than it does in Western cultures, and formal operational reasoning may never appear at all (Cole, 1990; Fahrmeier, 1978). In such contexts, some logical reasoning skills may simply have little relevance to people's daily functioning (J. G. Miller, 1997).

Does Cognitive Development Occur in Stages? As you have seen, Piaget was not completely on target in terms of when certain abilities develop and, in some cases, whether they develop at all. He also overestimated the extent to which children generalize newly acquired reasoning skills to a broad range of tasks and contexts.

In light of all the evidence, does it still make sense to talk about discrete stages of cognitive development? A few theorists say yes. In particular, *neo-Piagetian* theorists have proposed stage theories that may more adequately account for current findings about children's logical thinking. However, most contemporary developmentalists believe that cognitive development is not as stagelike as Piaget proposed—that a child does not reason in consistently logical or illogical ways at any particular time period (Flavell, 1994). Although children exhibit certain developmental *trends* in their thinking (e.g., a trend toward increasingly abstract thought), their knowledge in particular domains will influence the sophistication of their reasoning.

A perspective known as *information processing theory* characterizes some of the general trends in cognitive processes that we are likely to see as children develop. We describe both information processing theory and neo-Piagetian theories (which draw from information processing theory as well as from Piaget's ideas) in Chapter 5.

Piaget's Enduring Contributions Despite the concerns we have raised, Piaget's theory has had a profound influence on contemporary theories of cognitive development. Piaget's lasting contributions to our understanding of children's thinking include the following:

■ *Cognitive development is, to a considerable degree, propelled by intrinsic motivation.* As you have seen, Piaget believed that children are naturally curious about their environment and so actively explore it to learn as much as they can. They are especially motivated when they encounter surprising or puzzling events (those that create disequilibrium). Many contemporary theories of cognition and cognitive development retain such notions of intrinsic motivation: Growing children *want* to learn more about the people, objects, and events around them and so naturally engage in the kinds of behaviors and activities that bring about increasingly more complex and accurate understandings over time.

■ *The nature of thinking and reasoning changes with age.* Whether we talk about discrete stages or more general trends, it is clear that *something* inside changes over time. Piaget explained these changes in terms of such concepts as *schemes* and *operations*. As you will discover in Chapter 5, contemporary theorists are more apt to speak of changes in working memory, long-term memory, cognitive strategies, metacognitive knowledge, and mental "theories" about the nature of living beings and inanimate objects.

■ *Piaget's stages provide a general idea of when new abilities are likely to emerge.* Piaget identified and documented many characteristics of children's thinking that researchers continue to study today. We list several of them in the Observation Guidelines table on the following page, where we also give suggestions for classroom practice.

Although we have, we hope, dissuaded you from taking Piaget's stages at face value, we urge you to keep them in mind when considering the kinds of tasks that children and adolescents probably can and cannot do at different ages. Some of these abilities and *in*abilities may be a function of knowledge and experience (or lack thereof) and therefore amenable to change under the right circumstances, whereas others (perhaps because of neurological factors) may be more dependent on time and maturation (Metz, 1997). It is important to remember, too, that children don't necessarily discard their earlier ways of thinking when they acquire more sophisticated ones. For instance, even when children acquire the ability to think abstractly, they may continue to think concretely, and occasionally in a "sensorimotor" fashion, about many of the situations they encounter.

■ *Piaget's clinical method reveals a great deal about children's thinking processes.* The many tasks that Piaget developed to study children's reasoning abilities—tasks dealing with conservation, classification, separation and control of variables, and so on—and the kinds of probing follow-up questions that he pioneered yield invaluable insights about the "logic" that children and adolescents use when they think about their world. Researchers and practitioners alike frequently use Piaget's tasks and method in their efforts to uncover how children and adolescents think and learn.

■ *Through their interactions with their physical and social environments, children construct their own view of the world.* Virtually all developmentalists share the view that manipulation of physical objects and interactions with other people are *essential* for cognitive development. Furthermore, the idea that children don't just "absorb" such experiences—that they actively try to interpret and make sense of them, and then integrate what they've learned into more general, personally constructed understandings—plays prominently in many contemporary views of learning and cognition. The view that people construct rather than absorb knowledge is generally known as **constructivism.** More specifically, because it focuses on constructive processes within a single person, it is sometimes called **individual constructivism.**

■ *Children benefit only from experiences that they can relate to what they already know.* In Piaget's view, accommodation typically occurs only when it is accompanied by some degree of assimilation. New knowledge, understandings, and reasoning processes (new schemes) are typically derived from previously acquired knowledge and processes (existing schemes). Contemporary developmentalists embrace this idea of *new acquisitions being based on earlier ones* almost without exception. Developmentally speaking, new knowledge, skills, and cognitive processes don't just appear out of thin air.

constructivism
Theoretical perspective proposing that learners construct a body of knowledge from their experiences, rather than absorbing knowledge at face value.

individual constructivism
Theoretical perspective that focuses on how people construct meaning from events without the assistance of others.

Assessing Students' Reasoning Skills

OBSERVATION GUIDELINES			
CHARACTERISTIC	**LOOK FOR**	**EXAMPLE**	**IMPLICATION**
Preoperational Egocentrism	• Describing events without giving listeners sufficient information to understand them • Playing group games without initially agreeing about rules • Difficulty understanding others' perspectives	Luisa doesn't understand why she must share a box of art materials with the other children at her table.	Let children know when you don't understand what they are telling you; ask them to share their ideas and opinions with one another.
Concrete Thought	• Dependence on concrete manipulatives to understand concepts and principles • Difficulty understanding abstract ideas	Tobey solves arithmetic word problems more easily when he can draw pictures of them.	Use concrete objects and examples to illustrate abstract situations.
Abstract Thought	• Ability to understand strictly verbal explanations of abstract concepts and principles • Ability to reason about hypothetical or contrary-to-fact situations	Ilsa can imagine how two parallel lines might go on forever without ever coming together.	Occasionally rely on verbal explanations (e.g., short lectures) with adolescents, but assess students' understanding frequently to make sure they understand.
Formal Operational Egocentrism	• Idealistic notions about how the world should be • Inability to adjust ideals in light of what can realistically be accomplished	Martin advocates a system of government in which all citizens contribute their earnings to a common "pool" and then withdraw money only as they need it.	Engage adolescents in discussions about challenging political and social issues.
Scientific Reasoning Skills	• Identifying multiple hypotheses for a particular phenomenon • Separation and control of variables	Serena proposes three possible explanations for a result she has obtained in her physics lab.	Have students design and conduct simple experiments; include experiments about issues related to their backgrounds and interests.
Mathematical Reasoning Skills	• Understanding and using proportions in mathematical problem solving • Identifying all possible combinations and permutations	Giorgio uses a 1:240 scale when drawing a floor plan of his school building.	Introduce abstract mathematical concepts and tasks (e.g., proportional reasoning, combinatorial thought) using simple examples (e.g., fractions such as ⅓ and ¼, all possible arrangements of 3 objects)

Educational Implications of Piaget's Theory and Post-Piagetian Research

Piaget's theory and the body of research it has inspired have numerous implications for teachers, including the following:

■ *Provide opportunities for students to experiment with physical objects and natural phenomena.* Children of all ages can learn a great deal from exploring the natural world in a hands-on fashion. At the preschool level, this might involve playing with water, sand, wooden blocks, and age-appropriate manipulative toys. During the elementary school years, it might entail such activities as throwing and catching balls, going on nature walks, working with clay and watercolor paints, or constructing Popsicle-stick structures.

Despite the increased capabilities for abstract thought in adolescence, high school students also benefit from opportunities to manipulate and experiment with concrete materials—

APPLYING PIAGET'S THEORY

■ Provide hands-on experiences with physical objects, especially when working with elementary school students. Allow and encourage students to explore and manipulate things.

A kindergarten teacher and his students work with small objects (e.g., blocks, buttons, pennies) to explore such basic elements of arithmetic as conservation of number and the idea that addition and subtraction are reversible processes.

■ Provide opportunities for students to share their ideas and perspectives with one another.

A high school history teacher has students meet in small groups to debate the pros and cons of the United States' decision to become actively involved in the Vietnam War.

■ Present puzzling phenomena.

A second-grade teacher crumples a paper towel and places it inside an otherwise empty glass. She asks students to predict what will happen to the towel when she places the glass upside-down in a bowl of water. Many students predict that the paper towel will get wet. The teacher performs the experiment; when she removes the glass from the water, the students discover that the paper towel is completely dry.

■ Relate abstract and hypothetical ideas to concrete objects and observable events.

A middle school science teacher illustrates the idea that heavy and light objects fall at the same speed by having students drop objects of various weights from a second-story window.

perhaps equipment in a science lab, cameras and film, food and cooking utensils, or wood and woodworking tools. Such opportunities allow them to discover laws of the natural world firsthand and to tie their newly emerging abstract ideas to the physical, concrete world.

■ *Explore students' reasoning with problem-solving tasks and probing questions.* By presenting a variety of Piagetian tasks involving either concrete or formal operational thinking skills—tasks involving conservation, multiple classification, separation and control of variables, proportional reasoning, and so on—and observing students' responses to such tasks, teachers can gain valuable insights into how their students think and reason. They can then tailor the classroom curriculum and instructional materials accordingly. Figure 4–6 presents an example of a Piagetian task that a teacher might use to probe students' reasoning processes about the concept of *area*.

To probe students' reasoning in novel situations, teachers need not stick to traditional Piagetian reasoning tasks. On the contrary, such strategies are applicable to a wide variety of academic domains and subject matter. For example, Liben and Downs (1989) showed young children (kindergartners, first graders, and second graders) various kinds of maps (e.g., a road map of Pennsylvania, an aerial map of Chicago, a three-dimensional relief map of a mountainous area) and asked the children to interpret what they saw. The children interpreted many of the symbols in a concrete fashion. For example, some correctly recognized some of the roads "because they are gray" but thought that the roads marked in red were actually painted red. The children also had trouble understanding the scales of the maps (a finding consistent with Piaget's belief that proportional reasoning doesn't emerge until early adolescence). For example, one child rejected the idea that a road could be a road because it was "too skinny for two cars to fit on," and another denied that mountains on a relief map were mountains because "they aren't high enough."

■ *Keep Piaget's stages in mind when interpreting children's behavior and developing lesson plans, but don't take the stages too literally.* Piaget's four stages are not always accurate descriptions of students' logical thinking capabilities. Nevertheless, teachers might think of the stages as giving some clues about the thinking and reasoning processes they are apt to see in students at various age levels (Kuhn, 1997; Metz, 1997). For example, preschool teachers should not be surprised to see young children arguing that the three pieces of a broken candy bar constitute more candy than a similar, unbroken bar (a belief that reflects lack of conservation). Elementary school teachers should recognize that their students are likely to have difficulty with proportions (e.g., fractions, decimals) and with such abstract concepts as *historical time* in history and *place value, negative number,* and *pi* in mathematics (Barton & Levstik, 1996; Byrnes, 1996; Tourniaire & Pulos, 1985). And high school teachers should expect to hear their adolescent students debating passionately about idealistic yet unrealistic notions about how society should operate.

Materials:
2 sheets of 8½" by 11" green construction paper
2 small toy (perhaps plastic) cows
24 sugar cubes or equal-size small wooden blocks

Procedure:

In Piaget's clinical method, the interviewer tailors questions to the particular things that a child has previously said and done, but such flexibility often comes only with considerable experience. Here we present a procedure that a novice interviewer might use in presenting a conservation-of-area task.

1. Lay the 2 sheets of construction paper side by side, and place a cow on each sheet. Say, *These two cows are grazing in their pastures. Do they each have the same amount of grass to eat?* The student will probably say yes. Place a cube on each sheet and say, *A farmer builds a barn in each pasture. Do the two cows still have the same amount of grass to eat, or does one cow have more than the other?* The student will probably say that the cows each have the same amount.

2. Add 3 more cubes to each sheet. On the first sheet, place the cubes next to the first cube so that they form a square. On the second sheet, scatter 3 additional cubes around the pasture. Ask, *The farmer builds three more barns in each pasture, like this. Do the cows still have the same amount of grass to eat, or does one have more?*

3. Place 8 more cubes on the first sheet, placing them next to the square so that the 12 cubes form a rectangle. Place 8 more cubes on the second sheet, scattering them around the pasture. Ask, *The farmer builds eight more barns in each pasture, like this. Do the cows still have the same amount of grass to eat, or does one have more?* After the student responds, ask, *How do you know?*

4. If the student says that both cows have the same amount, say, *The other day, someone told me that this cow has more to eat* (point to the cow on the second sheet). *What could you do or say to convince that person that the two cows have the same amount?*

Interpretation:

Students who have fully achieved conservation of area realize that the amount of grass is the same if the same number of barns are placed in each pasture, despite the different arrangements of the barns. To justify a "same" response, students might (a) explain that the same number of barns cover the same amount of grass regardless of their arrangement or (b) move the scattered barns in the second pasture into a rectangular shape similar to that of the barns in the first pasture. In Piaget's theory, conservation of area appears early in the concrete operations stage.

FIGURE 4–6 Conservation of area: An example of how a teacher might probe students' reasoning processes with Piaget's clinical method

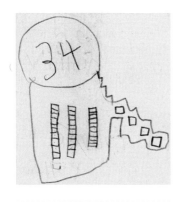

FIGURE 4–7 Noah's depiction of the number 34

Piaget's stages also provide guidance about strategies that are likely to be effective in teaching students at different grade levels. For instance, given the abstract nature of historical time, elementary school teachers planning history lessons should probably minimize the extent to which they talk about specific dates before the recent past (Barton & Levstik, 1996). Also, particularly in the elementary grades (and to a lesser degree in middle and high school), teachers should find ways to make abstract ideas more concrete for their students. As one simple example, a third-grade teacher, realizing that *place value* might be a difficult concept for third graders to comprehend, showed her students how to depict two-digit numbers with blocks, using 10-block rows for the number in the 10s column and single blocks for the number in the 1s column. We present 8-year-old Noah's drawing of "34" in Figure 4–7.

■ *Present situations and ideas that students cannot easily explain using their existing knowledge and beliefs.* Events and information that conflict with students' current understandings create disequilibrium that may motivate students to reevaluate and perhaps modify what they "know" to be true. For instance, if students believe that "light objects float and heavy objects sink" or that "wood floats and metal sinks," a teacher can present a common counterexample: a metal battleship (floating, of course) that weighs many tons.

■ *Plan group activities in which students share their beliefs and perspectives with one another.* As noted earlier, Piaget proposed that interaction with peers helps children realize that others often view the world very differently than they do and that their own ideas are not always completely logical or accurate ones. Interactions with age-mates, especially those that involve conflicts or differences of opinion, are likely to create disequilibrium and thus spur children to reevaluate their current perspectives.

Many contemporary psychologists share Piaget's belief in the importance of such **sociocognitive conflict** (e.g., Damon, 1984; Webb & Palincsar, 1996). They have offered several reasons why interactions with peers may help promote cognitive growth:

- Peers speak at a level that children can understand.
- Whereas children may accept an adult's ideas without argument, they are more willing to challenge and contest the ideas of their peers.
- When children hear competing views held by peers—individuals who presumably have knowledge and abilities similar to their own—they may be motivated to reconcile the contradictions.
(Champagne & Bunce, 1991; Damon, 1984; Hatano & Inagaki, 1991)

A study by Bell, Grossen, and Perret-Clermont (1985) illustrates the effect that sociocognitive conflict can have on young children's logical reasoning capabilities. Young children who did not yet demonstrate conservation of liquid (i.e., they stated that two differently shaped glasses contained different amounts of water) were each paired with a same-age partner and asked to play a "game" in which the two had to share equal amounts of juice. The experimenter gave the non-conserving children two glasses, one taller and thinner than the other, and asked them to pour the same amount of juice into each one. In most cases, the children poured juice to equal heights in the two glasses, which provoked disagreement from their partners. The "game" ended only after the children and their partners both agreed that they had the same amount of juice to drink. On a conservation posttest a week later, the children showed greater gains in their ability to conserve liquid than a control group who had worked with the same materials alone.

Research by Kuhn, Shaw, and Felton (1997) illustrates similar effects of peer interaction and conflict for adolescents. For five successive weeks, seventh and eighth graders met in pairs to discuss capital punishment, a topic about which many of them had strong yet varying opinions. Students were paired with different partners each week so that, over the course of the experiment, they were exposed to opinions both consistent and discrepant with their own. During the paired discussions, the students were observed asking questions that clearly challenged one another's reasoning (e.g., "What do you mean by 'justifiable'?"; "Do you think that [capital punishment] is going to stop them from doing that?"). After the fifth discussion, the researchers found that the students' reasoning about capital punishment had changed in several important ways:

- The students had a better understanding of both the pros and cons of capital punishment.
- Although few students completely reversed their positions on capital punishment, many took a less extreme stance on the issue.

sociocognitive conflict
Encountering and having to wrestle with ideas and viewpoints different from one's own.

- The students identified more reasons for believing as they did than they had before the discussions.
- The students showed greater awareness that multiple and possibly equally legitimate perspectives could exist about the issue.

When using group interaction to help students acquire more sophisticated understandings, keep in mind that students can also learn *misinformation* from one another (Good, McCaslin, & Reys, 1992). It is essential, then, that teachers closely monitor discussions and correct for any misconceptions or misinterpretations that students may pass on to their classmates.

■ *Use familiar content and tasks when asking students to reason in sophisticated ways.* Earlier we presented evidence to indicate that children and adolescents display more advanced reasoning skills when they work with topics they know well. With such evidence in mind, teachers might ask students to

- Conserve liquid within the context of a juice-sharing task (as Bell and her colleagues did).
- Separate and control variables within the context of an activity the students engage in regularly (perhaps fishing, playing sports, or riding a bicycle).
- Consider abstract ideas about subject matter that students have already studied in depth in a concrete fashion.

In Piaget's theory, cognitive development is largely an individual enterprise: By assimilating and accommodating to new experiences, children develop increasingly more advanced and integrated schemes over time. From this perspective, then, it seems that children do most of the mental "work" themselves. In contrast, another early developmental theory—that of the Russian psychologist Lev Vygotsky—places much of the responsibility for a child's development on the adults in the child's society and culture. From Vygotsky's perspective, children's interactions with adults play a critical role in fostering the development of skills and thinking capabilities essential for success in the adult world. We turn now to this very different, yet equally influential, theory of cognitive development.

Vygotsky's Theory of Cognitive Development

In the "Whale Watching" case at the beginning of the chapter, a mother helps her daughter understand and interpret what might otherwise have been a very confusing event for a 6-year-old. In particular, Mother helps Kerry recall the family members who were present, attaches labels to aspects of the experience (e.g., "disaster," "seasick"), and questions Kerry's assessment of the number of whales encountered on the trip.

Vygotsky proposed that adults promote children's cognitive development by engaging them in meaningful and challenging activities, helping them perform those activities successfully, and talking with them about their experiences. Because he emphasized the importance of society and culture for promoting cognitive growth, his theory is sometimes called the **sociocultural perspective.**

Vygotsky conducted numerous studies of children's thinking from the 1920s until his premature death from tuberculosis in 1934. Western psychologists did not fully appreciate the usefulness of his work until several decades later, when his major writings were translated into English (Vygotsky, 1962, 1978, 1987, 1997). Although Vygotsky never had the chance to develop his theory fully, his ideas are clearly evident in our views of child development and classroom practice today.

Key Ideas in Vygotsky's Theory

Vygotsky acknowledged that biological factors play a role in development: Children bring certain characteristics and dispositions to the situations they encounter, and their responses to those situations vary accordingly. Furthermore, children's behaviors, which are influenced in part by inherited traits, influence the particular experiences that they have (Vygotsky, 1997). However, Vygotsky's primary focus was on the role of nurture, and especially on the ways in

sociocultural perspective
Theoretical perspective emphasizing the importance of society and culture for promoting cognitive development.

which a child's social and cultural environments foster cognitive growth. Following are central ideas and concepts in Vygotsky's theory:

■ *Complex mental processes begin as social activities; as children develop, they gradually internalize the processes they use in social contexts and begin to use them independently.* Vygotsky proposed that many thinking processes have their roots in the social interactions (conversations, arguments, etc.) that children have with other people. Children first talk about objects and events with adults and other knowledgeable individuals; in the process, they discover how the people around them think about those objects and events.

In Vygotsky's view, dialogue with others is an essential condition for promoting cognitive development. Gradually, children incorporate into their own thinking the ways that adults and others talk about and interpret the world. The process through which social activities evolve into internal mental activities is called **internalization.**

Not all mental processes emerge through children's interactions with adults, however; some processes also develop as children interact with their peers. As an example, children frequently argue with one another about a variety of matters: how best to carry out an activity, what games to play, who did what to whom, and so on. According to Vygotsky, childhood arguments help children discover that there are often several points of view about any single situation. Eventually, children can, in essence, internalize the "arguing" process, developing the ability to look at a situation from several different angles *on their own.*

■ *Thought and language become increasingly interdependent in the first few years of life.* For us as adults, thought and language are closely interconnected. We often think in terms of the specific words that our language provides; for example, when we think about household pets, our thoughts contain words such as *cat* and *dog.* In addition, we usually express our thoughts when we converse with others; as we sometimes put it, we "speak our minds."

But Vygotsky proposed that thought and language are separate functions for infants and young toddlers. In these early years, thinking occurs independently of language, and when language appears, it is first used primarily as a means of communication rather than as a mechanism of thought. But sometime around age 2, thought and language become intertwined: Children express their thoughts when they speak, and they think at least partially in terms of words (see Figure 4–8).

When thought and language merge, we begin to see **self-talk** (also known as *private speech*), whereby children talk to themselves out loud. Recall Piaget's notion of *egocentric speech,* based on his observation that young children often say things without taking into account the listener's perspective. Vygotsky proposed that such speech is better understood as talking to *oneself* than as talking to someone else. According to Vygotsky, self-talk has a specific purpose: By talking to themselves, children learn to guide and direct their own behaviors through difficult tasks and complex maneuvers in much the same way that adults have previously guided them.

Self-talk eventually evolves into **inner speech:** Children "talk" to themselves mentally rather than aloud. They continue to direct themselves verbally through tasks and activities, but others can no longer see and hear the means by which they do it.

Taken together, self-talk and inner speech illustrate the internalization process mentioned earlier: Over time, children gradually internalize the directions that they have initially received from those around them so that they are eventually giving *themselves* directions.

Recent research has supported Vygotsky's views regarding the progression and role of self-talk and inner speech. The frequency of children's audible self-talk decreases during the preschool years, but this decrease is accompanied by an increase in whispered mumbling and silent lip movements, presumably reflecting a transition to inner speech (Bivens & Berk, 1990; Owens, 1996). Furthermore, self-talk increases when children are performing more challenging tasks—tasks at which they must work harder to complete successfully (Berk, 1994; Schimmoeller, 1998).

■ *Through both informal interactions and formal schooling, adults convey to children the ways in which their culture interprets and responds to the world.* In their interactions with children, adults share with children the *meanings* that they attach to objects, events, and, more gen-

internalization
In Vygotsky's theory, the gradual evolution of external, social activities into internal, mental activities.

self-talk
Talking to oneself as a way of guiding oneself through a task.

inner speech
"Talking" to oneself mentally rather than aloud.

erally, human experience. Such meanings are conveyed through a variety of mechanisms, including language (spoken words, writing, etc.), symbols, mathematics, art, literature, and so on. Children gradually adopt their culture's interpretations of the world by internalizing the words, concepts, symbols, and other representations that people around them use.[4] In this way, all members of a community—growing children included—can share a common perspective of "how things are and should be."

Informal conversations, such as the one between Kerry and her mother, play a major role in helping children internalize their culture. No less important in Vygotsky's eyes is formal education, where teachers systematically impart the ideas, concepts, and terminology used in various academic disciplines (Vygotsky, 1962). Although Vygotsky, like Piaget, saw value in allowing children to make some discoveries themselves, he also saw value in having adults describe the discoveries of previous generations (Karpov & Haywood, 1998).

To the extent that specific cultures pass along unique conceptual tools, ideas, and belief systems, children of different cultural backgrounds will develop somewhat different knowledge, skills, and ways of thinking. Thus, Vygotsky's theory leads us to expect greater diversity among children, at least in cognitive development, than Piaget's theory does. For example, some cultures use a wide variety of maps (road maps, maps of subway systems, shopping mall layouts) and expose children to them early and frequently, whereas other cultures rarely if ever use maps (Trawick-Smith, 2000; Whiting & Edwards, 1988). In fact, cultures differ markedly in the extent to which they represent their world and experiences on paper at all (Trawick-Smith, 2000).

■ *Children can perform more challenging tasks when assisted by more advanced and competent individuals.* Vygotsky distinguished between two kinds of abilities that children are likely to have at any particular point in their development. A child's **actual developmental level** is the upper limit of tasks that he or she can perform independently, without help from anyone else. A child's **level of potential development** is the upper limit of tasks that he or she can perform with the assistance of a more competent individual. To get a true sense of children's cognitive development, Vygotsky proposed, we should assess their capabilities both when performing alone *and* when performing with assistance.

Children can typically do more difficult things in collaboration with adults than they can do on their own. For example, children may be able to read more complex prose with the assistance of a teacher or older child than they are likely to read independently. They can play more difficult piano pieces when adults help them locate some of the notes on the keyboard or provide suggestions about what fingers to use where. And notice how a student who cannot independently solve division problems with remainders begins to learn the correct procedure through an interaction with her teacher:

Teacher:	[writes 6)̄44 on the board] 44 divided by 6. What number times 6 is close to 44?
Child:	6.
Teacher:	What's 6 times 6? [writes 6]
Child:	36.
Teacher:	36. Can you get one that's any closer? [erasing the 6]
Child:	8.
Teacher:	What's 6 times 8?
Child:	64 . . . 48.
Teacher:	48. Too big. Can you think of something . . .
Child:	6 times 7 is 42. (Pettito, 1985, p. 251)

---

[4]This process of internalizing the meanings and understandings of one's culture is sometimes called *appropriation,* a term suggested by a Russian contemporary of Vygotsky (Leont'ev, 1981).

In infancy, thought is nonverbal in nature, and language is used primarily as a means of communication.

At about 2 years of age, thought becomes verbal in nature, and language becomes a means of expressing thoughts.

With time, children begin to use *self-talk* to guide their own thoughts and behaviors.

Self-talk gradually evolves into *inner speech,* whereby children guide themselves silently (mentally) rather than aloud.

FIGURE 4–8 Vygotsky proposed that thought and language initially emerge as independent entities but eventually become intertwined.

actual developmental level
Extent to which one can successfully perform a task independently.

level of potential development
Extent to which one can successfully execute a task with the assistance of a more competent individual.

From Vygotsky's perspective, parents and teachers promote children's cognitive development in part by conveying how their culture interprets the world.

■ *Challenging tasks promote maximum cognitive growth.* The range of tasks that children cannot yet perform independently but *can* perform with the help and guidance of others is known as the **zone of proximal development (ZPD).** A child's zone of proximal development includes learning and problem-solving abilities that are just beginning to develop—abilities that are in an immature, embryonic form. Naturally, any child's ZPD will change over time; as some tasks are mastered, other, more complex ones appear on the horizon to take their place.

Vygotsky proposed that children learn very little from performing tasks they can already do independently. Instead, they develop primarily by attempting tasks they can accomplish only in collaboration with a more competent individual—that is, when they attempt tasks within their zone of proximal development. In a nutshell, it is the challenges in life—not the easy successes—that promote cognitive development.

Whereas challenging tasks are beneficial, *impossible* tasks—those that children cannot do even with considerable structure and assistance—are of no benefit whatsoever. (As a simple example, it is pointless to ask a typical kindergartner to solve for *x* in an algebraic equation.) In this way, a child's ZPD sets a limit on how quickly the child can develop cognitively.

■ *Play allows children to stretch themselves cognitively.* Recall the scenario of Jeff and Scott playing "restaurant" presented earlier in the chapter. The two boys take on several adult roles (restaurant managers, waiters, cooks) and practice a variety of adultlike behaviors: assembling the necessary materials for a restaurant, creating menus, keeping track of customers' orders, and tallying final bills. In real life, such a scenario would, of course, be impossible: Very few 5-year-old children have the cooking, reading, writing, mathematical, or organizational skills necessary to run a restaurant. Yet the element of make-believe brings the same tasks within the boys' reach (e.g., Lillard, 1993). To put this idea in Vygotsky's words:

> In play a child is always above his average age, above his daily behavior, in play it is as though he were a head taller than himself. (Vygotsky, 1978, p. 102)

In play activities, children rely on their imaginations as much as on real objects; in the process, they learn to use their thoughts to guide their behaviors. As they substitute one object for another (e.g., pretending that a cardboard box is the family car), they begin to distinguish between objects and their meanings and to respond to internal representations (e.g., the concept of *car*) as much as to external objects.

Furthermore, even when children play, their behaviors must conform to certain standards or expectations. For instance, children in preschool and the early elementary grades often act in accordance with how a "daddy," "teacher," or "waiter" would behave. In the organized group games and sports that come later, children must follow a specific set of rules. By adhering to such restrictions on their behavior, children learn to plan ahead, to think before they act, and to engage in self-restraint—skills critical for participating successfully in the adult world.

Especially within the last 20 years, many Western developmentalists have embraced and extended Vygotsky's ideas. We turn now to some modern Vygotskian perspectives about child development and educational practice.

Current Perspectives on Vygotsky's Theory

Vygotsky focused primarily on the *processes* through which children develop, rather than on the characteristics that children of particular ages are likely to exhibit. He did identify stages of development but portrayed them in only the most general terms. From our perspective, the stages are not terribly informative (we refer you to Vygotsky, 1997, pp. 214–216, if you would like to learn more about them). Largely for these reasons, Vygotsky's theory has been more difficult for researchers to test and either verify or disprove than has Piaget's theory. In fact, the most frequent criticisms of Vygotsky's ideas are his lack of precision and his inattention to details (Haenan, 1996; Hunt, 1997; Wertsch, 1984).

zone of proximal development (ZPD)
Range of tasks that one cannot yet perform independently but *can* perform with the help and guidance of others.

Despite such weaknesses, many contemporary theorists and practitioners have found Vygotsky's theory both insightful and helpful. Although they have taken Vygotsky's notions in many different directions, we can discuss much of their work within the context of several general ideas: participation in adult activities, scaffolding, apprenticeships, social construction of meaning, dynamic assessment, and the value of play.

Participation in Adult Activities Most cultures allow, and in fact often require, children to be involved in adult activities. Children's early experiences are often at the fringe of an activity—a phenomenon known as **legitimate peripheral participation** (Lave, 1991; Lave & Wenger, 1991). As the children acquire greater competence, they take an increasingly more central role in the activity until, eventually, they are full-fledged participants.

To illustrate, when our own children were preschoolers, we often let them help us bake cookies by asking them to pour the ingredients we'd measured into the mixing bowl, and we occasionally let them do some preliminary mixing as well. Similarly, when taking them to the office with us, we might have them press the appropriate buttons in the elevator, check our mailboxes, open envelopes, or deliver documents to the department secretary. In later years, we gave them increasing responsibility and independence in these arenas. For example, by the time Jeanne's son Jeff reached high school, he was baking and decorating his own cakes and cookies, and he ran errands around the community (e.g., trips to the library and post office) to help Jeanne with her book-writing efforts.

From a Vygotskian perspective, this gradual entry into adult activities increases the probability that children will engage in behaviors and thinking skills that are within their zone of proximal development. Some theorists believe that participation in everyday adult activities has an additional advantage as well. They take a **situative perspective** of cognition and cognitive development: They describe thinking as being tied to, or *situated in,* the specific tasks in which people are engaged (e.g., Light & Butterworth, 1993). They argue that children display thinking and reasoning abilities primarily within the particular contexts in which they have acquired those abilities; hence, they disagree with Piaget's view that the logical thinking abilities associated with the concrete and formal operations stages emerge independently of any single content domain. As an example, Brazilian children who work as street vendors selling gum and candy can, during their sales transactions, use mathematical operations that they seem unable to use with more traditional mathematics problems at school (Carraher, Carraher, & Schliemann, 1985). Adults' thinking can be equally context-bound; for instance, construction foremen, fishermen, and cooks more effectively use proportional reasoning when they are in their professional milieus—that is, when they are dealing with blueprints, quantities of fish, and recipes, respectively (Schliemann & Carraher, 1993). Some research findings are inconsistent with a situative perspective of cognitive abilities, however; for instance, students who learn mathematical procedures in the classroom often apply the procedures quite successfully in a wide variety of real-world contexts (Anderson, Reder, & Simon, 1997). At present, the extent to which various cognitive abilities are context-specific or context-independent is a source of considerable controversy among psychologists.

Scaffolding Theorists have given considerable thought to the kinds of assistance that can help children complete challenging tasks. The term **scaffolding** is often used here: Adults and other more competent individuals provide some form of guidance or structure that enables children to perform tasks that are in their zone of proximal development. To understand this concept, think of the scaffolding used in the construction of a new building. The *scaffold* is an external structure that provides support for the workers (e.g., a place where they can stand) until the building itself is strong enough to support them. As the building gains stability, the scaffold becomes less necessary and so is gradually removed.

In much the same way, an adult guiding a child through a new task may provide an initial scaffold to support the child's early efforts. In the teacher-student dialogue about division presented earlier, the teacher provided clues about how to proceed, such as searching for the multiple of 6 closest to, but still less than, 44. Similarly, adults provide scaffolding when they illustrate the use of particular tools or procedures, give hints about how to approach a difficult problem, or break down a complex task into smaller, easier steps (Rosenshine & Meister, 1992; Wood, Bruner, & Ross, 1976). As children become more adept at performing tasks, the scaffolding is gradually phased out, and the children are eventually performing those tasks on their own.

legitimate peripheral participation
A child's early and somewhat limited involvement in adult activities.

situative perspective
Theoretical perspective that cognitive abilities are tied to the specific contexts in which they have been acquired.

scaffolding
Support mechanism, provided by a more competent individual, that helps a child successfully perform a task within his or her zone of proximal development.

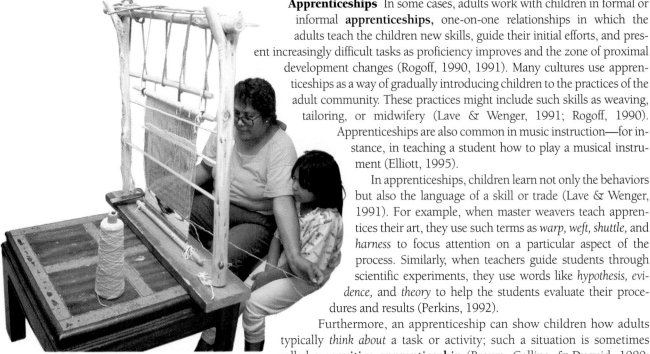

Apprenticeships In some cases, adults work with children in formal or informal **apprenticeships,** one-on-one relationships in which the adults teach the children new skills, guide their initial efforts, and present increasingly difficult tasks as proficiency improves and the zone of proximal development changes (Rogoff, 1990, 1991). Many cultures use apprenticeships as a way of gradually introducing children to the practices of the adult community. These practices might include such skills as weaving, tailoring, or midwifery (Lave & Wenger, 1991; Rogoff, 1990). Apprenticeships are also common in music instruction—for instance, in teaching a student how to play a musical instrument (Elliott, 1995).

In apprenticeships, children learn not only the behaviors but also the language of a skill or trade (Lave & Wenger, 1991). For example, when master weavers teach apprentices their art, they use such terms as *warp, weft, shuttle,* and *harness* to focus attention on a particular aspect of the process. Similarly, when teachers guide students through scientific experiments, they use words like *hypothesis, evidence,* and *theory* to help the students evaluate their procedures and results (Perkins, 1992).

In an apprenticeship, children learn both the skills and the language associated with a particular activity.

Furthermore, an apprenticeship can show children how adults typically *think about* a task or activity; such a situation is sometimes called a **cognitive apprenticeship** (Brown, Collins, & Duguid, 1989; Rogoff, 1990; Roth & Bowen, 1995). For instance, a teacher and student might work together to accomplish a challenging task or solve a difficult problem (perhaps collecting data samples in biology fieldwork, solving a mathematical brainteaser, or translating a difficult passage from German to English). In the process of talking about various aspects of the task or problem, the teacher and student together analyze the situation and develop the best approach to take, and the teacher models effective ways of thinking about and mentally processing the situation.

Although apprenticeships can differ widely from one context to another, they typically have some or all of these features (Collins, Brown, & Newman, 1989):

- *Modeling.* The adult carries out the task, simultaneously thinking aloud about the process, while the child observes and listens.
- *Coaching.* As the child performs the task, the adult gives frequent suggestions, hints, and feedback.
- *Scaffolding.* The adult provides various forms of support for the student, perhaps by simplifying the task, breaking it into smaller and more manageable components, or providing less complicated equipment.
- *Articulation.* The child explains what he or she is doing and why, allowing the adult to examine the child's knowledge, reasoning, and problem-solving strategies.
- *Reflection.* The adult asks the child to compare his or her performance with that of experts, or perhaps with an ideal model of how the task should be done.
- *Increasing complexity and diversity of tasks.* As the child gains greater proficiency, the adult presents more complex, challenging, and varied tasks to complete.
- *Exploration.* The adult encourages the child to frame questions and problems on his or her own and thereby to expand and refine acquired skills.

Social Construction of Meaning As mentioned earlier, Vygotsky proposed that, in their interactions with children, adults help children attach meaning to the objects and events around them. More recently, theorists have elaborated further on this idea. They point out that an adult such as a parent or teacher often helps a child make sense of the world through a joint discussion of a phenomenon or event they have mutually experienced (Eacott, 1999; Feuerstein, 1990; Feuerstein, Klein, & Tannenbaum, 1991; John-Steiner & Mahn, 1996). Such an interaction, sometimes called a **mediated learning experience,** encourages the child to think about the phenomenon or event in particular ways—to attach labels to it, recognize principles that underlie it, impose certain interpretations on it, and so on. For instance, in the opening case study, Kerry's mother helps Kerry better understand

apprenticeship
Situation in which a person works intensively with an expert to learn how to accomplish complex tasks.

cognitive apprenticeship
Mentorship in which a teacher and a student work together on a challenging task and the teacher suggests ways to think about the task.

mediated learning experience
Discussion between an adult and a child in which the adult helps the child make sense of an event they have mutually experienced.

the whale-watching expedition in several ways: by helping her recall the people who were present, interpreting the trip as a "disaster," describing the whales as "big," and counting the number of whales that were present. In such a conversation, the adult must, of course, consider the prior knowledge and perspectives of the child and tailor the discussion accordingly (Newson & Newson, 1975).

In addition to co-constructing meanings with adults, children often talk among themselves to derive meaning from their experiences. As we reflect back on our own childhood and adolescent years, we recall having numerous conversations with friends in joint efforts to make sense of our world, perhaps within the context of identifying the optimal food and water conditions for raising tadpoles, deciding how best to carry out an assigned school project, or figuring out why certain teenage boys were so elusive.

School is one obvious place where children and adolescents can toss around ideas about a particular issue and perhaps reach consensus about how best to interpret and understand the topic in question. As an example of how members of a classroom might work together to construct meaning, let's consider an interaction that takes place in Keisha Coleman's third-grade class (Peterson, 1992). The students are discussing how they might solve the problem $-10 + 10 = ?$. They are using a number line like this

to facilitate their discussion. Several students, including Tessa, agree that the solution is "zero" but disagree about how to use the number line to arrive at that answer. Excerpts from a discussion between Tessa and her classmate Chang (as facilitated by Ms. Coleman) follow:

Tessa:	You have to count numbers to the right. If you count numbers to the right, then you couldn't get to zero. You'd have to count to the left.
C [Ms. Coleman]:	Could you explain a little bit more about what you mean by that? I'm not quite sure I follow you. . . .
Tessa:	Because if you went that way [points to the right] then it would have to be a higher number. . . .
Chang:	I disagree with what she's trying to say. . . . Tessa says if you're counting right, then the number is—I don't really understand. She said, "If you count right, then the number has to go smaller." I don't know what she's talking about. Negative ten plus negative ten is zero. . . . What do you mean by counting to the right?
Tessa:	If you count from ten up, you can't get zero. If you count from ten left, you can get zero.
Chang:	. . . Well, negative ten is a negative number—smaller than zero.
Tessa:	I know.
Chang:	Then why do you say you can't get to zero when you're adding to negative ten, which is smaller than zero?
Tessa:	OHHHH! NOW I GET IT! This is positive. . . . You have to count right.
C:	You're saying in order to get to zero, you have to count to the right? From where, Tessa?
Tessa:	Negative 10. (Peterson, 1992, pp. 165–166)

The class continues in its efforts to pin down precisely how to use the number line to solve the problem. Eventually, Tessa offers a revised and more complete explanation. Pointing to the appropriate location on the number line, she says, "You start at negative 10. Then you add 1, 2, 3, 4, 5, 6, 7, 8, 9, 10." She moves her finger one number to the right for each number that she counts. She reaches the zero point on the number line when she counts "10" and concludes, "That equals zero."

Notice that at no time does Ms. Coleman impose her own interpretations on either the problem itself or on what Tessa and Chang have to say about the problem. Instead, she lets the two children struggle to make sense of the problem and, eventually, to agree on how best to solve it.

In recent years, many theorists have become convinced of the value of joint meaning-making discussions in helping children acquire more complex understandings of their physical, social, and academic worlds (e.g., De Corte, Greer, & Verschaffel, 1996; Hatano & Inagaki, 1993; Lampert, 1990; Sosniak & Stodolsky, 1994). This perspective, generally known as **social constructivism,** is reflected in increased advocacy for instructional practices involving student interaction—class discussions, cooperative learning activities, peer tutoring—in elementary and secondary classrooms alike.

Dynamic Assessment As noted earlier, Vygotsky believed that we can get a more complete picture of a child's cognitive development when we assess both their *actual developmental level* (the kinds of tasks they can successfully accomplish on their own) and their *level of potential development* (the kinds of tasks they can accomplish when they have the assistance of more competent individuals).

When assessing students' cognitive abilities, most school psychologists and teachers focus almost exclusively on students' *actual* developmental level: They ask students to take tests, complete assignments, and so on, without help from anyone else. To assess students' level of *potential* development, some theorists have suggested an alternative known as **dynamic assessment,** which involves (a) identifying tasks that students cannot initially do independently, (b) providing in-depth instruction and practice in behaviors and cognitive processes related to the task, and then (c) determining the extent to which each student has benefited from the instruction (Feuerstein, 1979, 1980; Kozulin & Falik, 1995; Lidz, 1997). This approach often yields more optimistic evaluations of students' cognitive capabilities than traditional measures of cognitive ability do and may be especially useful in assessing the abilities of students from diverse cultural backgrounds (Feuerstein, 1979).

Value of Play Although children's play activities may seem relatively frivolous on the surface, both Vygotsky and Piaget believed that play gives children valuable practice in adultlike behaviors. In addition, Vygotsky argued that the element of pretense in play (using a box as a car, a wooden block as a telephone, etc.) provides a means through which children begin to distinguish between objects and their meanings—a critical step in the development of thought.

Many contemporary developmentalists share Vygotsky's and Piaget's belief that play provides an arena in which youngsters can practice the skills they will need in later life. They have long been aware of the value of play for children's social development (i.e., for developing cooperation and conflict resolution skills), but increasingly they are acknowledging its importance for children's cognitive development as well. For instance, they suggest that it helps children master emerging skills, experiment with new combinations and cause-effect relationships, and (in role-playing activities) take the perspectives of people other than themselves (Chafel, 1991; Lillard, 1998; Rubin, Fein, & Vandenberg, 1983; Zervigon-Hakes, 1984). They note, too, that playful behavior is observed in many species, especially those that are relatively flexible in their behaviors (e.g., monkeys, chimpanzees, bears, dogs, cats), and so almost certainly has an adaptive purpose (Bjorklund & Green, 1992; Vandenberg, 1978).

Initially, play often takes the form of simple exploration: Infants and toddlers spend many hours manipulating toys and other objects to discover what these things can do and what effects they have. But somewhere around age 2, play takes on an element of make-believe, whereby children begin to substitute one object for another and eventually perform behaviors involving imaginary objects (e.g., "eating" imaginary food with an imaginary fork) (O'Reilly, 1995; Pederson, Rook-Green, & Elder, 1981). In the **sociodramatic play** of the preschool years, children begin to concoct elaborate scenarios in which they assume roles such as "parent," "teacher," or "doctor" (Göncü, 1993; Haight & Miller, 1993; Lyytinen, 1991). Some examples of things to look for when observing children's early play activities are presented in the Observation Guidelines table that follows.

As children reach school age, their role-playing activities gradually diminish, and other forms of play take their place. For instance, elementary school children often spend time playing cards and board games, constructing things from cardboard boxes or Legos, and engaging in team sports; many of these activities continue into adolescence as well. Although such forms of play do not mimic adult roles in as obvious a manner as "house" and "restaurant," they, too, serve a purpose. In particular, they help children and adolescents develop skills in planning, communication, cooperation, and problem solving—skills that will be important for their later success in the adult world (Bornstein, Haynes, Pascual, Painter, & Galperin, 1999; Christie & Johnsen, 1983; Sutton-Smith, 1979).

social constructivism
Theoretical perspective that focuses on people's collective efforts to impose meaning on the world.

dynamic assessment
Examining how a student's knowledge or reasoning may change as a result of learning or performing a specific task.

sociodramatic play
Play in which children take on assumed roles and act out a scenario of events.

Assessing Young Children's Play Activities

OBSERVATION GUIDELINES			
CHARACTERISTIC	**LOOK FOR**	**EXAMPLE**	**IMPLICATION**
Group Play	• Extent to which children play with one another • Extent to which children in a play group coordinate their play activities	Lamarr and Matthew are playing with trucks in the sandbox, but each boy seems to be in his own little world.	Give children opportunities to play together, and provide toys that require a cooperative effort.
Use of Symbolic Thought and Imagination	• Extent to which children use one object to stand for another • Extent to which children incorporate imaginary objects into their play	Julia tells her friend she is going to the grocery store, then opens an imaginary car door, sits on a chair inside her "car," steers an imaginary steering wheel, and says, "Beep, beep" as she blows an imaginary horn.	When equipping a play area, include objects (e.g., wooden blocks) that children can use for a variety of purposes.
Role Taking	• Extent to which children display behaviors that reflect a particular role • Extent to which children use language (e.g., tone of voice, specific words and phrases) associated with a particular person or role • Extent to which children coordinate and act out multiple roles within the context of a complex play scenario	Mark and Alisa are playing doctor. Alisa brings her teddy bear to Mark's "office" and politely says, "Good morning, Doctor. My baby has a sore throat." Mark holds a Popsicle stick against the bear's mouth and instructs the "baby" to say "aaahhh."	Provide toys and equipment associated with particular roles (e.g., toy medical kit, cooking utensils, play money).

In our discussions of Vygotsky's theory and contemporary extensions of his ideas, we have dropped numerous hints about their potential applications in the classroom. We now look more directly at educational implications.

Educational Implications of Vygotsky's Ideas

Vygotsky's work and the recent theoretical advances it has inspired yield numerous implications for classroom practice, including the following:

■ *Help students acquire the basic conceptual tools of various academic disciplines.* Through such disciplines as science, mathematics, and social studies, our culture passes along key concepts (e.g., *molecule, negative number, democracy*), symbols (e.g., H_2O, π, ∞), and visual representations (e.g., graphs, maps) that can help growing children organize and interpret the physical and social worlds in which they live. Literature, poetry, music, and fine arts help children impose meaning on the world as well—for example, by capturing the thoughts and feelings that characterize human experience.

■ *Present challenging tasks, perhaps within the context of cooperative activities.* To promote students' cognitive development, teachers should present some classroom tasks and assignments that students can perform successfully only with assistance—that is, tasks within students' zone of proximal development. To some extent, students with different zones of proximal development may need different tasks and assignments, which makes a strong case for providing as much individualized instruction as possible.

In some instances, students can accomplish challenging tasks only with the assistance of more skilled individuals, such as adults or older students. But at other times, students of equal ability can work together on difficult assignments, thereby jointly accomplishing tasks that none of them might be able to do on their own. In such situations, the students are essentially providing scaffolding for one another's efforts. Cooperative learning groups and other activities in which students work collaboratively can be highly effective in promoting both cognitive development and classroom achievement (Brown & Palincsar, 1989; Lou et al., 1996; Stevens & Slavin, 1995).

■ *Scaffold students' efforts.* When teachers provide the challenging tasks so important for cognitive development, they should also provide sufficient scaffolding to enable students to accomplish those tasks successfully. Here are some examples of how a teacher might scaffold a new and difficult task:

- Demonstrating the proper performance of the task in a way that students can easily imitate
- Dividing the task into several smaller, simpler pieces
- Providing a structure, set of steps, or guidelines for performing the task
- Asking questions that get students thinking in appropriate ways about the task
- Keeping students' attention focused on the relevant aspects of the task
- Giving frequent feedback about how students are progressing
  (Gallimore & Tharp, 1990; Good et al., 1992; Rogoff, 1990; Rosenshine & Meister, 1992; Wood et al., 1976)

As students develop increasing competence, teachers can gradually withdraw these support mechanisms and eventually allow students to perform the task independently—in other words, to stand on their own two feet.

■ *Assess students' abilities under a variety of work conditions.* Teachers need to know not only what students can and cannot do, but also under what conditions students are most likely to accomplish various tasks successfully (Calfee & Masuda, 1997). By asking students to work under varying conditions—sometimes independently, sometimes in collaboration with one or more classmates, and sometimes with teacher instruction and support—teachers get a better sense of the tasks that are in each student's zone of proximal development.

■ *Provide opportunities to engage in authentic activities.* As we've already seen, children's participation in adult activities plays a critical role in their cognitive development. Many theorists have suggested that teachers can better promote learning and cognitive development by having students engage in **authentic activities**—activities similar to those that the students may eventually encounter in the adult world—rather than in more traditional academic tasks (e.g., Hickey, 1997; Hiebert & Fisher, 1992; Lave, 1993).

Authentic activities can be identified for virtually any area of the curriculum; consider these possibilities:

Writing an editorial	Performing in a concert
Participating in a debate	Planning a family budget
Designing an electrical circuit	Conversing in a foreign language
Conducting an experiment	Making a videotape
Writing a computer program	Constructing a museum display
Creating and distributing a class newsletter	Developing a home page for the Internet

Researchers have only begun to study the effects of authentic activities on students' learning and cognitive development, but preliminary results are encouraging. For example, students may show greater improvement in writing skills when they practice by writing stories, essays, and letters to real people, rather than completing short, artificial writing exercises (Hiebert & Fisher, 1992). Likewise, students gain a more complete understanding of how to use and interpret maps when they construct their own maps than when they engage in workbook exercises involving map interpretation (Gregg & Leinhardt, 1994).

■ *Promote self-regulation by teaching children to talk themselves through difficult situations.* Through self-talk and inner speech, children begin to direct and regulate their own behaviors in much the same way that adults have previously directed them. Children who talk themselves through challenging tasks pay more attention to what they are doing and are more likely to show improvement in their performance (Berk & Spuhl, 1995).

authentic activity
Classroom activity similar to one that a student might encounter in the outside world.

Authentic activities involve tasks similar to ones that students will eventually encounter in the outside world.

Meichenbaum (1977, 1985) has successfully used five steps in teaching children how to give themselves instructions and thereby guide themselves through a new task:

1. *Cognitive modeling.* An adult model performs the desired task while verbalizing instructions that guide performance.
2. *Overt, external guidance.* The child performs the task while listening to the adult verbalize the instructions.
3. *Overt self-guidance.* The child repeats the instructions aloud (*self-talk*) while performing the task.
4. *Faded, overt self-guidance.* The child whispers the instructions while performing the task.
5. *Covert self-instruction.* The child silently thinks about the instructions (*inner speech*) while performing the task.

In this sequence of steps, depicted in Figure 4–9, the adult initially serves as a model both for the behavior itself and for the process of self-guidance. Responsibility for performing the task is soon turned over to the child; eventually, responsibility for *directing* the performance is turned over as well.

■ *Give children the chance to play.* So far, all of our suggestions—teaching concepts and symbols, presenting difficult tasks, engaging students in authentic activities, and so on—imply that facilitating children's cognitive development means giving them one or another forms of academic "work." Yet, as we have seen, informal play activities have value as well, and many theorists advocate including them in the school day, especially at the preschool level (Chafel, 1991; Hirsh-Pasek, Hyson, & Rescorla, 1990). Frost, Shin, and Jacobs (1998) have offered several suggestions for promoting preschoolers' play:

- Partition the classroom into small areas (e.g., a corner for blocks, a "housekeeping" area, an art table) that give children numerous options.
- Provide realistic toys (e.g., dolls, dress-up clothes, plastic dishes and food) that suggest certain activities and functions, as well as more versatile objects

	TASK PERFORMANCE	TASK INSTRUCTIONS
Step 1	The adult performs the task, modeling it for the child.	The adult verbalizes instructions.
Step 2	The child performs the task.	The adult verbalizes instructions.
Step 3	The child performs the task.	The child repeats the instructions aloud.
Step 4	The child performs the task.	The child whispers the instructions.
Step 5	The child performs the task.	The child thinks silently about the instructions.

FIGURE 4–9 Meichenbaum's five steps for promoting self-regulation

■ Demonstrate and encourage adultlike ways of thinking about situations.

A high school chemistry teacher places two equal-size inflated balloons into two beakers of water, one heated to 25°C and the other heated to 50°C. The students all agree that the balloon placed in the warmer water expands more. "Now *how much more* did the 50-degree balloon expand?" the teacher asks. "Let's use Charles's Law to figure it out."

■ Present some tasks that students can perform successfully only with assistance.

A fifth-grade teacher assigns students their first research paper, knowing that she will have to give them a great deal of guidance as they work on it.

■ Have students work in small groups to accomplish complex tasks.

A middle school art teacher asks his students to work in groups of four or five to design large murals that depict various ecosystems (rain forest, desert, grassland, tundra, etc.) and the kinds of species of plants and animals that live in each one. The groups then paint their murals on the walls in the school corridors.

■ Provide sufficient support (scaffolding) to enable students to perform challenging tasks successfully; gradually withdraw the support as they become more proficient.

A middle school history teacher asks students to take notes on the short lectures he presents in class. Before beginning the lecture, he gives them a detailed outline that they can use to organize their notes, and during the lecture itself he continually reminds them about the things they should include in their notes.

■ Ask students to engage in authentic adult activities.

A third-grade teacher has her students create a class newspaper that includes news articles, a schedule of upcoming events, a couple of political cartoons, and some classified advertisements. The students assume varying roles (reporters, cartoonists, editors, proofreaders, photocopiers, and distributors) during the project.

■ Encourage students to talk themselves through difficult tasks.

As her students work on complex mathematical equations such as this one,

$$x = \frac{2(4 \times 9)^2}{6} + 3$$

a junior high school mathematics teacher gives students a mnemonic ("*Please excuse my dear Aunt Sally*") to help them remember the order in which various operations should be performed (*p*arentheses, *e*xponents, *m*ultiplication, *d*ivision, *a*ddition, *s*ubtraction).

■ Give young children numerous opportunities to practice adult roles and behaviors in play activities.

A preschool teacher equips his classroom with many household items (dress-up clothes, cooking utensils, a toy telephone, etc.) so that his students can play "house" during free-play time.

(e.g., Legos, wooden blocks, cardboard boxes) that allow children to engage in fantasy and imagination.

• Provide enough toys and equipment to minimize potential conflicts, but keep them few enough in number that children must cooperate in their use.

Comparing Piaget and Vygotsky

Together, Piaget's and Vygotsky's theories give us a more complete picture of cognitive development than either one provides alone. The Developmental Trends table that follows draws on elements of both theories to describe characteristics of children and adolescents in different age ranges.

The two theories share several common themes—themes that continue to appear in more contemporary theories of cognitive development. At the same time, they have important differences that have led modern researchers to probe more deeply into the mechanisms through which children's thinking processes develop.

Common Themes

If we look beyond the very different vocabulary Piaget and Vygotsky often used to describe the phenomena they observed, we notice three themes that their theories share: challenge, readiness, and the importance of social interaction.

Challenge We see the importance of challenge most clearly in Vygotsky's concept of the *zone of proximal development:* Children benefit most from tasks that they can perform only with the assistance of more competent individuals. Challenge appears in a more disguised form in Piaget's theory, but it plays a critical role nonetheless: Children develop more sophisticated knowledge and thought processes only when they encounter phenomena they cannot adequately understand using existing schemes—in other words, phenomena that create *disequilibrium.*

Readiness In both theories, growing children may be cognitively ready for some experiences yet not be ready for others. From Piaget's perspective, children can accommodate to new objects and events only when they can also assimilate them into existing schemes; there must be some overlap between the "new" and the "old." In addition, Piaget argued that children cannot learn from an experience until they have begun the transition into a stage that allows them to deal with and conceptualize that experience appropriately (e.g., they cannot benefit from hearing abstract ideas until they have begun the transition into formal operations).

Vygotsky, too, proposed that there are limits on the tasks that children can reasonably handle at any particular time. As children acquire some capabilities, other, slightly more advanced ones emerge in an embryonic form (they fall within the child's ZPD) and can be fostered through adult assistance and guidance.

Importance of Social Interaction In Piaget's eyes, the people in a child's life present information and arguments that create disequilibrium and foster greater perspective taking. For instance, when young children disagree with one another, they gradually begin to realize that different people may have different yet equally valid viewpoints, and so they begin to shed their preoperational egocentrism.

In Vygotsky's view, social interactions provide the very foundation for thought processes: Children internalize the processes they use when they converse with others until, ultimately, they can use them independently. Furthermore, tasks within the ZPD can, by definition, be accomplished only when others assist in children's efforts.

Theoretical Differences

Following are four questions that capture key differences between Piaget's and Vygotsky's characterizations of cognitive development.

To What Extent Is Language Essential for Cognitive Development? According to Piaget, language provides verbal labels for many of the schemes that children have previously developed; it is also the primary means through which children interact with others and so can begin to incorporate multiple perspectives into their thinking. In Piaget's view, however, much of cognitive development occurs independently of language.

For Vygotsky, language is absolutely essential for cognitive development. Children's thought processes are internalized versions of social interactions that are largely verbal in nature; for instance, through self-talk and inner speech, children begin to guide their own behaviors in ways that others have previously guided them. Furthermore, in their conversations with adults, children learn the meanings that their culture ascribes to particular events and gradually begin to interpret the world in "culturally appropriate" ways.

To what extent does cognitive development depend on language? Perhaps the truth lies somewhere between Piaget's and Vygotsky's theories. Piaget probably underestimated the importance of language: Children acquire more complex understandings of phenomena and events not only through their own interactions with the world but also (as Vygotsky suggested) by learning how others *interpret* those phenomena and events. Yet Vygotsky may have overstated the case for language: Verbal exchanges may be less important for cognitive development in some cultures than in others. For instance, in a study by Rogoff, Mistry, Göncü, and Mosier (1993), adults in four cultures—middle-class communities in the United States and Turkey, a Native American community in Guatemala, and a tribal village in India—were asked to help toddlers with the difficult tasks of getting dressed and manipulating strange new toys. Adults in the United States and Turkey provided a great deal of verbal guidance as they helped the children. The Guatemalan and Indian adults conversed less with the children; instead, much of their guidance took the form of gestures and demonstrations.

Thinking and Reasoning Skills at Different Age Levels

DEVELOPMENTAL TRENDS

AGE	WHAT YOU MIGHT OBSERVE	DIVERSITY	IMPLICATIONS
Early Childhood (2–6) 	• Rapidly developing language skills • Thinking that, by adult standards, is illogical • Limited perspective-taking ability • Frequent self-talk • Sociodramatic play • Little understanding of how adults typically interpret events	• Shyness may reduce children's willingness to talk with teachers and peers and to engage in cooperative sociodramatic play. • Adultlike logic is more likely when children have accurate information about the world (e.g., about cause-effect relationships). • Adults' interpretations of some events are culturally specific.	• Provide numerous opportunities for children to interact with one another during play and other cooperative activities. • Introduce children to a variety of real-world environments and situations through field trips and picture books. • Talk with children about their experiences and possible interpretations of them.
Middle Childhood (6–10) 	• Conservation, multiple classification, and other forms of adult logic • Limited ability to reason about abstract ideas • Emergence of group games and team sports that involve coordinating multiple perspectives • Ability to participate in many adult activities (perhaps only peripherally)	• Development of logical thinking skills is affected by the importance of those skills in a child's culture. • Formal operational reasoning may occasionally appear for simple tasks and familiar contexts, especially in 9- and 10-year-olds. • Physical maturation and psychomotor skills affect success in some games and team sports.	• Use concrete manipulatives and experiences to illustrate concepts and ideas. • Supplement verbal explanations with concrete examples, pictures, and hands-on activities. • Allow time for organized play activities. • Introduce students to various adult professions, and provide opportunities to practice authentic adult tasks.
Early Adolescence (10–14) 	• Emerging ability to reason about abstract ideas • Increasing scientific reasoning abilities (e.g., separating and controlling variables, formulating and testing hypotheses) • Emerging ability to reason about mathematical proportions • Emerging idealism about political and social issues, but often without taking real-world constraints into consideration • Increasing ability to engage in adult tasks	• Students can think more abstractly when they have considerable knowledge about a topic. • Students are more likely to separate and control variables for situations with which they are familiar. • Development of formal operational reasoning skills is affected by the importance of those skills in a student's culture. • The ideals that students espouse may reflect their religious, cultural, or socioeconomic backgrounds.	• Present abstract concepts and principles central to various academic disciplines, but tie them to concrete examples. • Have students engage in scientific investigations, focusing on familiar objects and phenomena. • Assign mathematics problems that require students to use simple fractions, ratios, or decimals. • As you show students how to do a new task, also show them how you and others think about the task.
Late Adolescence (14–18) 	• Abstract thought and scientific reasoning skills more prevalent, especially for topics about which students have a substantial knowledge base • Idealistic notions tempered by more realistic considerations • Ability to perform many tasks in an adultlike manner	• Abstract thinking is more common in some content areas (e.g., mathematics, science) than in others (e.g., history, geography). • Formal operational reasoning skills are less likely to appear in cultures that don't require those skills. • Students' proficiency in particular adult tasks varies considerably from student to student and from task to task.	• Study particular disciplines in depth; introduce complex and abstract explanations and theories. • Encourage classroom discussions about social, political, and ethical issues; elicit multiple perspectives regarding these issues. • Involve students in activities that are similar or identical to the things they must eventually do as adults. • Show students how experts in a field think about the tasks they perform.

Contrasting Piaget and Vygotsky

BASIC DEVELOPMENTAL ISSUES

ISSUE	PIAGET	VYGOTSKY
Nature and Nurture	Piaget believed that biological maturation probably constrains the rate at which children acquire new thinking capabilities. However, he focused on how interactions with both the physical environment (e.g., manipulation of concrete objects) and the social environment (e.g., discussions with peers) promote cognitive development.	Vygotsky acknowledged that children's inherited traits and talents affect the ways in which they deal with the environment and hence affect the experiences that they have. But his theory primarily addresses the environmental conditions (e.g., engagement in challenging activities, guidance of more competent individuals, exposure to cultural interpretations) that influence cognitive growth.
Universality and Diversity	According to Piaget, the progression of children's reasoning capabilities is similar across cultures. Once children have mastered certain reasoning processes, they can apply those processes to a wide range of tasks. Children differ somewhat in the ages at which they acquire new abilities.	From Vygotsky's perspective, the specific cognitive abilities that children acquire depend on the cultural contexts in which the children are raised and the specific activities in which they are asked and encouraged to engage.
Qualitative and Quantitative Change 	Piaget proposed that children's logical reasoning skills progress through four, qualitatively different stages. Any particular reasoning capability continues to improve in a gradual (quantitative) fashion throughout the stage in which it first appears.	Vygotsky acknowledged that children undergo qualitative changes in their thinking but did not elaborate on the nature of these changes. Much of his theory points to gradual and presumably quantitative improvements in skills. For instance, a child may initially find a particular task impossible, later be able to execute it with adult assistance, and eventually perform it independently.

What Kinds of Experiences Promote Development? Piaget maintained that children's independent, self-motivated explorations of the physical world form the basis for many developing schemes, and children often construct these schemes with little guidance from others. In contrast, Vygotsky argued for exploratory activities that are facilitated and interpreted by more competent individuals. The distinction, then, is one of self-exploration versus guided exploration. Ideally, children almost certainly need both kinds of experiences—opportunities to manipulate and experiment with physical phenomena on their own *and* opportunities to draw upon the wisdom of prior generations (Karpov & Haywood, 1998).

What Kinds of Social Interactions Are Most Critical? Both theorists saw value in interacting with people of all ages. However, Piaget emphasized the benefits of interactions with peers (who could create conflict), whereas Vygotsky placed greater importance on interactions with adults and other more advanced individuals (who could support children in challenging tasks and help them make appropriate interpretations).

Some contemporary theorists have proposed that interactions with peers and interactions with adults play different roles in children's cognitive development (Damon, 1984; Rogoff, 1991; Webb & Palincsar, 1996). When children's development requires that they abandon old perspectives in favor of new, more complex ones, the sociocultural conflict that often occurs among age-mates (and the multiple perspective taking that emerges from it) may be optimal for bringing about such change. But when children's development instead requires that they learn new skills, the thoughtful, patient guidance of a competent adult is probably essential (e.g., Radziszewska & Rogoff, 1991).

How Influential Is Culture? In Piaget's mind, the nature of children's logical thinking skills and the progression of these skills over time are largely independent of the specific cultural context in which children are raised. In Vygotsky's view, however, culture is of paramount importance in determining the specific thinking skills that children acquire.

Vygotsky was probably more on target here. Earlier in the chapter, we presented evidence that children's reasoning skills do not necessarily appear at the same ages in different countries; in fact, some reasoning skills (especially those involving formal operational thought) may never appear at all.

In the Basic Developmental Issues table in this section, we contrast Piaget's and Vygotsky's theories in terms of our three general themes: nature and nurture, universality and diversity, and qualitative and quantitative changes. Keep in mind that neither of these theories is completely "right" or completely "wrong": Both have offered groundbreaking insights into the nature of children's thought processes and cognitive development, and both have guided the research of the theorists who followed them.

In fact, Piaget's and Vygotsky's theories complement each other to some extent, with the former helping us understand how children often reason on their own and the latter providing ideas about how adults can help them reason more effectively. The final case study describes how four young adolescents reason about a classic Piagetian task—the pendulum problem—and illustrates the scaffolding that a teacher can provide to help them reason in a more "formal operational" fashion.

FIGURE A

CASE STUDY: ADOLESCENT SCIENTISTS

Scott Sowell has just introduced the concept of *pendulum* in his seventh-grade science class. When he asks his students to identify variables that might influence the frequency with which a pendulum swings, they suggest three possibilities: the amount of weight at the bottom, the length of the pendulum, and the "angle" from which the weight is initially dropped.

Mr. Sowell divides his students into groups of four and gives each group a pendulum composed of a long string with a paperclip attached to the bottom. He also provides extra paperclips that the students can use to increase the weight at the bottom (Figure A). He gives his students the following assignment: *Design your own experiment. Think of a way to test how each one of these affects the frequency of swing. Then carry out your experiment.*

Jon, Marina, Paige, and Wensley are coming to grips with their task as Mr. Sowell approaches their table.

Marina:	We'll time the frequency as the seconds and the . . . um . . . what? (*She looks questioningly at Mr. Sowell.*)
Mr. S.:	The frequency is the number of swings within a certain time limit.

The group agrees to count the number of swings during a 15-second period. After Jon determines the current length of the string, Wensley positions the pendulum 25 degrees from vertical. When Jon says "Go" and starts a stopwatch, Wensley releases the pendulum. Marina counts the number of swings until, 15 seconds later, Jon says, "Stop." Jon records the data from the first experiment: length = 49 cm, weight = 1 paperclip, angle = 25°, frequency = 22.

The group shortens the string and adds a second paperclip onto the bottom of the first clip. They repeat their experiment and record their data: length = 36 cm, weight = 2 paperclips, angle = 45°, frequency = 25.

Wensley:	What does the weight do to it?
Marina:	We found out that the shorter it is and the heavier it is, the faster it goes.

Mr. Sowell joins the group and reviews its results from the first two tests.

Mr. S.:	What did you change between Test 1 and Test 2?
Marina:	Number of paperclips.
Mr. S.:	OK, so you changed the weight. What else did you change?
Wensley:	The length.
Marina:	And the angle.
Mr. S.:	OK, so you changed all three between the two tests. So what caused the higher frequency?
Wensley:	The length.
Marina:	No, I think it was the weight.
Jon:	I think the weight.
Paige:	The length.

| Mr. S.: | Why can't you look at your data and decide? (*The students look at him blankly.*) Take a look at the two tests. The first one had one paperclip, and the second had two. The first test had one length, and the second test had a shorter length. Why can't you come to a conclusion by looking at the two frequencies? |
| Marina: | All of the variables changed. |

Mr. Sowell nods in agreement and then moves on to another group. The four students decide to change only the weight for the next test, so they add a third paperclip to the bottom of the second. Their pendulum now looks like Figure B. They continue to perform experiments but are careful to change only one variable at a time, or so they think. In reality, each time the group adds another paperclip, the pendulum grows longer. Mr. Sowell visits the students once again.

Mr. S.:	One thing you're testing is length, right? And another thing is weight. Look at your system. Look at how you might be making a slight mistake with weight and length. (*He takes two paperclips off and then puts one back on, hanging it, as the students have done, at the bottom of the first paperclip.*)
Marina:	It's heavier *and* longer.
Mr. S.:	Can you think of a way to redesign your experiments so that you're changing only weight? How can you do things differently so that your pendulum doesn't get longer when you add paperclips?
Jon:	Hang the second paperclip from the bottom of the string instead of from the first paperclip.

When Mr. Sowell leaves, the students add another paperclip to the pendulum, making sure that the overall length of the pendulum stays the same. They perform another test and find that the pendulum's frequency is identical to what they obtained in the preceding test. Ignoring what she has just seen, Marina concludes, "So if it's heavier, the frequency is higher."

- In what ways does Mr. Sowell scaffold the students' efforts during the lab activity?
- With which one of Piaget's stages is the students' reasoning most consistent, and why?
- Use one or more of Piaget's ideas to explain why Marina persists in her belief that weight affects a pendulum's frequency, despite evidence to the contrary.
- Drawing on post-Piagetian research findings, identify a task for which the students might be better able to separate and control variables.

FIGURE B

SUMMARY

Piaget's Theory

Piaget portrayed children as active and motivated learners who, through numerous interactions with their physical and social environments, construct an increasingly more complex understanding of the world around them. Piaget proposed that cognitive development proceeds through four stages: (1) the sensorimotor stage (when cognitive functioning is based primarily on behaviors and perceptions); (2) the preoperational stage (when symbolic thought and language become prevalent, but reasoning is "illogical" by adult standards); (3) the concrete operations stage (when logical reasoning capabilities emerge but are limited to concrete objects and events); and (4) the formal operations stage (when thinking about abstract, hypothetical, and contrary-to-fact ideas becomes possible).

Developmental researchers have found that Piaget probably underestimated the capabilities of infants, preschoolers, and elementary school children yet overestimated the capabilities of adolescents. Researchers have found, too, that children's reasoning on particular tasks depends somewhat on their prior knowledge, experience, and formal schooling relative to those tasks. Most contemporary developmentalists doubt that cognitive development is as stagelike as Piaget proposed, but they acknowledge the value of his research methods and his views about motivation, the construction of knowledge, and the hierarchical nature of cognitive development.

Vygotsky's Theory

Vygotsky proposed that social activities are precursors to, and form the basis for, complex mental processes; as an example, the "arguing" process, first used in discussions with peers, is gradually internalized, such that children can eventually consider multiple perspectives when they think and reason. Vygotsky also proposed that children acquire more advanced ways of behaving and thinking by working on challenging tasks they can accomplish successfully only with the help of an adult or other more competent individual (i.e., tasks within their zone of proximal development). Adults promote cognitive development not only by assisting children with challenging tasks but also by passing along the meanings that their culture assigns to objects and events. Children can sometimes accomplish challenging tasks more successfully through self-talk and, eventually, inner speech.

Contemporary theorists have extended Vygotsky's theory in several directions. For instance, some recommend that adults introduce young children to authentic, adultlike tasks, initially providing the scaffolding necessary to accomplish those tasks successfully and gradually withdrawing the scaffolding as children become more proficient. Other theorists suggest that adults can help children better interpret their experiences through mediated learning experiences and cognitive apprenticeships.

Comparing Piaget and Vygotsky

Challenge, readiness, and social interaction are central to the theories of both Piaget and Vygotsky. However, the two perspectives differ on the role of language in cognitive development, the relative value of self-exploration versus guided exploration, the relative importance of interactions with peers versus adults, and the influence of culture.

Now go to our Companion Website to assess your understanding of chapter content with Multiple-Choice Questions, apply comprehension in Essay Questions, and broaden your knowledge with links to related Developmental Psychology World Wide Web sites.

KEY CONCEPTS

cognition (p. 110)
class inclusion (p. 111)
clinical method (p. 111)
scheme (p. 112)
operation (p. 112)
adaptation (p. 112)
assimilation (p. 112)
accommodation (p. 112)
equilibrium (p. 113)
disequilibrium (p. 113)
equilibration (p. 113)
symbolic thought (p. 115)
object permanence (p. 115)
goal-directed behavior (p. 115)
preoperational egocentrism (p. 116)
egocentric speech (p. 116)
conservation (p. 118)

multiple classification (p. 118)
deductive reasoning (p. 118)
formal operational egocentrism (p. 122)
nativism (p. 123)
constructivism (p. 126)
individual constructivism (p. 126)
sociocognitive conflict (p. 130)
sociocultural perspective (p. 131)
internalization (p. 132)
self-talk (p. 132)
inner speech (p. 132)
actual developmental level (p. 133)
level of potential development (p. 133)

zone of proximal development (ZPD) (p. 134)
legitimate peripheral participation (p. 135)
situative perspective (p. 135)
scaffolding (p. 135)
apprenticeship (p. 136)
cognitive apprenticeship (p. 136)
mediated learning experience (p. 136)
social constructivism (p. 138)
dynamic assessment (p. 138)
sociodramatic play (p. 138)
authentic activity (p. 140)

Grace, age 9

Cognitive Development 2: Cognitive Processes

CASE STUDY: HOW THE UNITED STATES BECAME A COUNTRY

Our colleague Dinah Jackson once asked students in grades 2 through 8 to write essays addressing the following question: *The land we live on has been here for a very long time, but the United States has only been a country for a little more than 200 years. How did the United States become a country?* Here are some of their responses:

Second grader:

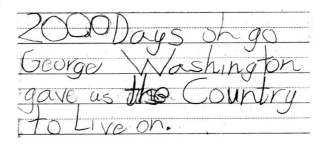

2000 Days oh go George Washington gave us ~~the~~ Country To Live on.

Third grader:

The pilgrans came over in 17 hundreds, when they came over they bilt houses. The Idiuns tihout they were mean. Then they came friends, and tot them stuff, Then winter came, and dot died, Then some had babies. So thats how we got here.

Sixth grader:

The U.S.A. became a cantry by some of the British wanting to be under a different rule than of the kings. So, they sailed to the "new world" and became a new country. The only problem was that the kings from Britin still ruled the "new world". Then they had the revolutionary war. They beat Britin, and became an independent country.

Eighth grader:

We became a country through different processes. Technology around the world finally caught up with the British. There were boats to travel with, navigating tools, and the hearts of men had a desire to expand. Many men had gone on expeditions across the sea. A very famous journey was that of Christopher Columbus. He discovered this land that we live. More and more people poured in, expecting instant wealth, freedom, and a right to share their opinions. Some immigrants were satisfied, others were displeased. Problems in other countries forced people to move on to this New World, such as potato famins and no freedom of religions. Stories that drifted through people grew about this country. Stories of golden roads and free land coaxed other families who were living in the slums. Unfortunately, there were slums in America. The people helped this country grow in industry, cultures, religions, and government. Inventions and books were now better than the Europeans. Dime-novels were invented, and the young people could read about heroes of this time. May the curiosity and eagerness of the children continue.

Responses courtesy of Dinah Jackson.

T HESE FOUR COMPOSITIONS ILLUSTRATE several changes in children's knowing and thinking as they grow older. Not surprising, of course, is an increase in knowledge: The sixth and eighth graders know considerably more—not only about the origins of their country but also about correct spelling and rules of punctuation and capitalization—than the second and third graders do. Furthermore, whereas the third grader describes the nation's history as a list of seemingly unrelated facts, the sixth and eighth graders have pulled what they have learned into an integrated whole that "hangs together." In addition, the younger children's descriptions reflect very simplistic and concrete understandings (e.g., the country was a gift from George Washington, the Pilgrims came over and built houses); in contrast, the eighth grader uses abstract concepts (e.g., technological progress, freedom of religion, overly optimistic expectations for wealth) to explain immigration to the United States.

In this chapter, we look at contemporary theories of cognition and cognitive development—theories that focus not only on changes in the nature of children's knowledge but also on changes in children's thinking and learning processes. We begin by looking at *information processing theory,* a perspective that underlies much of the current research in cognitive development. We follow up with an in-depth examination of *metacognition* and *cognitive strategies,* processes through which growing children become increasingly able to control and regulate their own thinking and learning processes. Later, we introduce *theory theory,* a perspective that describes how children construct increasingly complex, but not always accurate, understandings (theories) of their physical and mental worlds. We then build on both Piaget's theory and information processing concepts to explore *neo-Piagetian* approaches to cognitive development. Finally, we consider *exceptionalities in information processing,* including learning disabilities, attention-deficit hyperactivity disorder, and autism.

Information Processing Theory

Do children become better able to pay attention as they grow older? Do they learn and remember things more effectively as they move through the grade levels? How does the nature of their knowledge change over time? Such questions reflect the approach of **information processing theory,** a collection of theories that focus on how children receive, think about, mentally modify, and remember information, and on how such cognitive processes change over the course of development.

Information processing theory emerged in the late 1950s and early 1960s and has continued to evolve in the decades that have followed. Initially, many information processing theorists believed that human beings might think in ways similar to how computers operate, and they borrowed computer terminology to describe human thought processes. For example, they described people as *storing* (i.e., putting) information in memory and then *retrieving* it from memory (i.e., finding it) when they need it at a later time.

In recent years, however, theorists have found that people often think in distinctly *non*-computer-like ways. Much of information processing theory now has a *constructivist* flavor similar to that of Piaget's theory (Derry, 1996; Mayer, 1996). In other words, human beings construct their own unique understandings of the world; they don't simply receive and absorb knowledge from the outside world in the relatively "mindless" way that a computer does. As an example of such construction, consider once again the second grader's explanation in the opening case study:

2000 Days oh go George Washington gave us the Country to Live on.

Almost certainly, no one ever told her that Washington *gave* us the United States. Instead, she uses something she *has* been told (i.e., that Washington was a key figure in the country's early history) to concoct what is, to her, a reasonable explanation of her country's origin. Similarly, the student has probably never seen the word *ago* spelled as "oh go," yet she uses two words she *has* seen to construct a reasonable (albeit incorrect) spelling.

Key Ideas in Information Processing Theory

Information processing theorists don't always agree about the specific mechanisms involved in learning and remembering information. Nevertheless, many of them agree on several key concepts and ideas:

■ *Input from the environment provides the raw material for cognitive processing.* People receive input from the environment through the senses (sight, hearing, smell, taste, and touch) and subsequently translate that raw input into more meaningful information. The first part of this process, detecting stimuli in the environment, is **sensation;** the second part, interpreting those stimuli, is **perception.**

Because even the simplest interpretation of an environmental event takes time, many theorists believe that human memory includes a mechanism that allows people to remember raw sensory data for a very short time (perhaps 2 to 3 seconds for auditory information, and probably less than a second for visual information). We will refer to this mechanism as the **sensory register,** but theorists actually use a variety of labels (e.g., *brief sensory store, sensory buffer, iconic memory, echoic memory*) when they talk about it.

■ *In addition to a sensory register, human memory includes two other storage mechanisms: working memory and long-term memory.* **Working memory** is the component of memory where people first

information processing theory
Theoretical perspective that focuses on the specific ways in which people mentally think about ("process") the information they receive.

sensation
Physiological detection of stimuli in the environment.

perception
Cognitive interpretation of stimuli that the body has sensed.

sensory register
Component of memory that holds incoming information in an unanalyzed form for a very brief time (2–3 seconds or less).

working memory
Component of memory that enables people to actively think about and process a small amount of information.

hold new information while they mentally process it. Working memory is where most thinking, or cognitive processing, occurs; for instance, it is where people try to solve a problem or make sense of a textbook passage. **Long-term memory** is the component that allows people to keep the many things they learn from their experiences over the years, including such knowledge as when they graduated from high school and how much 2 and 2 equal, as well as such skills as how to ride a bicycle and how to use a microscope.

Working memory keeps information for only a very short time (perhaps 20 to 30 seconds unless the individual continues to think about and actively process it); hence, it is sometimes called *short-term memory*. Working memory also appears to have a limited capacity: It has only a small amount of "space" in which people can hold and think about events or ideas. As an illustration, try computing the following division problem in your head:

$$59\overline{)49,383}$$

Did you find yourself having trouble remembering some parts of the problem while you were dealing with other parts? Did you ever arrive at the correct answer of 837? Most people cannot solve a division problem with this many numbers unless they can write the problem on paper. There simply isn't "room" in working memory to hold all the numbers you need to remember to solve the problem in your head.

In contrast to working memory, long-term memory lasts an indefinitely long time. Some theorists propose that anything stored in long-term memory remains there for a lifetime, but others believe that information may slowly fade away over time, especially if its owner doesn't use it after initially storing it. Long-term memory is assumed to have an unlimited capacity: It can "hold" as much information as its owner wants to save.

To think about information previously stored in long-term memory, people must retrieve it and examine it in working memory. Thus, although people's capacity to *store* information in long-term memory may be boundless, their ability to *think about* what they've stored is limited to whatever they can hold in working memory at any one time.

■ *Attention is essential to the learning process.* Most information processing theorists believe that attention plays a key role in the interpretation of information and its storage in memory. Attention is the primary process, and perhaps the *only* process, through which information moves from the sensory register into working memory. Many theorists argue that when people *don't* pay attention to something, they essentially lose it from memory and so cannot possibly remember it later on.

■ *A variety of cognitive processes are involved in moving information from working memory to long-term memory.* Whereas attention is instrumental in moving information from the sensory register to working memory, other, more complex processes are needed if people are to remember information for longer than a minute or so. Some theorists suggest that repeating information over and over (*rehearsing* it) is sufficient for its long-term storage. Others propose that people store information effectively only when they connect it to concepts and ideas that already exist in long-term memory—for instance, when they use what they already know to *organize* or expand (i.e., *elaborate*) on the new information. The three processes just listed—rehearsal, organization, and elaboration—are examples of the *executive functions* described in Chapter 3. We will look at their development more closely later in the chapter.

■ *People control how they process information.* Some sort of cognitive "supervisor" is almost certainly necessary to ensure that a person's learning and memory processes work effectively. This mechanism, sometimes called the **central executive,** oversees the flow of information throughout the memory system. Although it is perhaps the most critical, and certainly the most "intelligent," aspect of human cognition, information processing theorists haven't yet pinned down its exact nature.

Figure 5–1 presents a model of how the mechanisms and processes just described fit together into an overall human information processing system.

■ *Cognitive development involves gradual changes in various components of the information processing system.* Information processing theorists reject Piaget's notion of discrete developmental stages. Instead, they believe that children's cognitive processes and abilities develop through

long-term memory
Component of memory that holds knowledge and skills for a relatively long time.

central executive
Component of the human information processing system that oversees the flow of information throughout the system.

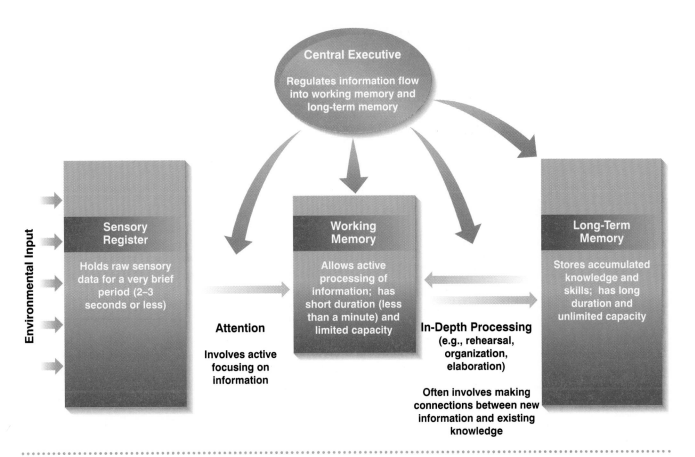

FIGURE 5–1 A model of the human information processing system

more steady and gradual *trends*. In the following sections, we look at developmental trends in sensation and perception, attention, working memory, and long-term memory.

Sensation and Perception

Many sensory capabilities are present at birth; for example, newborns can discriminate among different tastes, smells, sounds, and sound sequences (Bijeljac-Babic, Bertoncini, & Mehler, 1993; Rosenstein & Oster, 1988; Steiner, 1979). Some elements of perception (the *interpretation* of sensed stimuli) appear early as well; for instance, 1-week-old infants seem to understand that objects maintain the same shape and size even when they are rotated or moved farther away and so *look* different (Slater, Mattock, & Brown, 1990; Slater & Morison, 1985). But other sensory and perceptual capabilities, such as visual focusing, color discrimination, and the ability to locate the source of sounds, continue to develop during the first few months of life (Adams, 1987; Aslin, 1993; Hillier, Hewitt, & Morrongiello, 1992). In fact, visual perception is probably not fully developed until the preschool years, when the visual cortex of the brain reaches an adultlike form (Hickey & Peduzzi, 1987).

Experience plays a role in the development of sensation and perception. For instance, infants are more likely to show fear of heights if they have had a lot of crawling experience (Bertenthal & Campos, 1987). Furthermore, research with cats indicates the possible existence of sensitive periods in the development of visual sensation: Kittens deprived of normal sight during only the first 2 to 3 months of life have limited sensitivity to light later on (Bruer, 1999; Wiesel & Hubel, 1965).

How much can young children *remember* of what they sense and perceive? The sensory registers of 5-year-olds can apparently hold almost as much raw sensory data as those of adults (Sheingold, 1973). The significant memory differences we see between school-age children and adults, according to information processing theorists, seem to lie further along in the memory system—perhaps in attentional processes, working memory, or long-term memory.

Attention

As children grow older, their ability to pay attention changes in the following ways:

■ *Distractibility decreases; thus, sustained attention increases.* Young children's attention often moves quickly from one thing to another, and it is easily drawn to objects, events, and thoughts unrelated to whatever the children are "supposed" to be doing (Dempster & Corkill, 1999; Ruff & Lawson, 1990). Preschool and kindergarten children in free-play situations typically spend only a few minutes engaged in one activity before they move on to another (Stodolsky, 1974).

Over time, children become better able to focus their attention on a particular task and keep it there, and they are less distracted by irrelevant occurrences (Higgins & Turnure, 1984; Lane & Pearson, 1982; Ruff & Lawson, 1990). For example, in one experiment (Higgins & Turnure, 1984), children in three age groups (preschool, second grade, and sixth grade) were given age-appropriate visual discrimination tasks. Some children worked on the tasks in a quiet room, others worked in a room with a little background noise, and still others worked with a great deal of background noise. Preschool and second-grade children performed most effectively under the quiet conditions and least effectively under the very noisy conditions. But the sixth graders performed just as well in a noisy room as in a quiet room. Apparently the older children could ignore the noise, whereas the younger children could not.

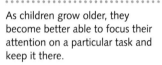

As children grow older, they become better able to focus their attention on a particular task and keep it there.

■ *Attention becomes increasingly purposeful.* During the elementary school years, children become better at identifying the information most relevant to the task at hand and paying attention accordingly (Pick & Frankel, 1974; Strutt, Anderson, & Well, 1975). As a result, their learning becomes increasingly a function of what they are *asked* to learn (Hagen & Stanovich, 1977). To illustrate, imagine that you have six cards in front of you on a table. Each card has a different background color and a picture of a different object, much like the cards in Figure 5–2. You are told to remember only the *colors* of those cards. Now the cards are flipped over, and you are asked where the green card is, where the orange card is, and so on. You are then asked to name the picture that appeared on each card. Do you think you would remember the colors of the cards (the information that you intended to learn)? Do you think you would remember the objects (information that you did *not* intend to learn)?

In a study by Maccoby and Hagen (1965), children in grades 1 through 7 were asked to perform a series of tasks similar to the one just described. The older children remembered the background colors more accurately than the younger children did. Yet the older children were no better than younger ones at remembering the objects pictured on the cards; in fact, the oldest group in the study remembered the *fewest* number of objects. Older children, then, are better at paying attention to and learning the things they *intend* to learn; they are not necessarily better at learning irrelevant information.

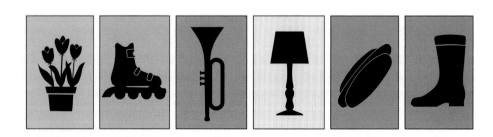

FIGURE 5–2 Imagine that you are told to remember the colors of each of these cards. After the cards are flipped over, do you think you would remember where each color appeared? Would you also remember what object appeared on each card, even though you were *not* asked to remember the objects?
Modeled after stimuli used by Maccoby & Hagen, 1965.

Working Memory

As you should recall, working memory is the component of the human information processing system where active, conscious thinking occurs. As children grow older, they become capable of thinking about a greater number of things at once and performing more complex cognitive tasks (Flavell et al., 1993; Gathercole & Hitch, 1993). This developmental trend is probably the combined result of three more specific trends related to working memory:

■ *Processing speed increases.* Children execute many cognitive processes more quickly and efficiently as they get older (Fry & Hale, 1996; Gathercole & Hitch, 1993; Siegler, 1991). For example, older children can make comparisons among similar stimuli, retrieve information from long-term memory, and solve simple problems more quickly than younger children (Cerella & Hale, 1994). Processing speed continues to increase, and thus the time to execute many mental tasks continues to *decrease*, until early adulthood (Kail, 1993).

With time and practice, some of the things that children know and can do become **automatized:** Children can perform certain mental tasks very quickly and with little or no conscious effort. Once mental activities become automatized, they take up very little "space" in working memory; as a result, children can devote more working memory capacity to other, potentially more complex tasks and problems.

As one simple example of such automatization, consider how children's reading ability improves over time. When children first begin to read, they often devote considerable mental effort to identifying the words on the page—remembering what the letter configuration FRIEND spells, sounding out an unfamiliar word such as *elementary,* and so on—and so may remember little of the content. But with increasing exposure to a variety of reading materials, word identification gradually becomes an automatized process, such that children recognize most of the words they encounter almost immediately. At this point, children can concentrate on (i.e., devote most of their working memory capacity to) what is ultimately the most important part of the reading process—understanding the ideas that an author is trying to communicate. (This is *not* to say, however, that teachers should postpone teaching reading comprehension until word recognition is automatized; we will return to this point in Chapter 8.)

Automatization increases the likelihood that a child will respond to a particular situation in a particular way. In many instances, the child will have practiced and automatized the *best* response for that situation—"best," at least, for that child's environment and culture. But different environments and cultures sometimes require very different responses, and children need to learn the most effective ways of responding within the contexts in which they are growing up. Thus, the *non*automatized cognitive processes of young children may, to some degree, be a blessing rather than a curse, in that children can practice and automatize the processes that are most likely to serve them well in their own circumstances (Bjorklund & Green, 1992).[1]

■ *Children acquire more effective cognitive processes.* Not only do children process information more quickly, but they also acquire new and better cognitive strategies as they grow older (Kail & Park, 1994). For example, when preschoolers are asked to add 3 blocks and 5 more blocks, they are likely to count all the blocks to arrive at the answer "8." In contrast, third graders given the same problem are likely to retrieve the number fact "3 + 5 = 8" from long-term memory—a strategy that involves considerably less working memory capacity. Later in the chapter, we describe some of the learning and problem-solving strategies that emerge over time.

■ *The physical capacity of working memory may increase somewhat.* Much of the apparent increase in working memory capacity is probably due to the increased speed and efficiency in children's cognitive processes, rather than to an increase in memory "space" per se (Fry & Hale,

---

[1]In Chapter 3, we considered the same idea from the standpoint of brain physiology. In the early years, many new synapses among neurons spring up (the process of *synaptogenesis*), allowing the possibility of adapting to a variety of environmental conditions. Soon after, the frequently used synapses are strengthened and the little-used synapses wither away (the process of *synaptic pruning*), resulting in a system that is especially suited for a particular environment.

automatization
Process of becoming able to respond quickly and efficiently while mentally processing or physically performing certain tasks.

1996; Gathercole & Hitch, 1993; Siegler, 1991). Theorists disagree as to whether the actual "hardware" of working memory increases and becomes more efficient with development, but some evidence suggests that it does. For instance, older children perform cognitive tasks more quickly than younger children, and adults perform them even *more* quickly, even when all groups have had extensive practice on those tasks and so presumably have automatized them (Kail, 1993).

Long-Term Memory

While working memory is an active processing center, long-term memory is more of a repository for the information and skills that people gather over the years. Some of this knowledge is almost certainly universal; for instance, children all over the globe soon learn that people typically have two legs but cats and dogs have four. Other knowledge is, of course, more dependent on children's unique experiences and on the cultural contexts in which they grow up. For example, in the four children's compositions in the opening case study, we consistently see a European American perspective of the early days of the United States: The focus is on immigration and early European colonization. Were we to ask Native American children how the United States came into being, we might get a very different perspective, perhaps one with elements of invasion, confiscation, or demolition.

As children grow older, several developmental changes in long-term memory converge to enhance their ability to understand and respond to their world:

■ *The amount of knowledge stored in long-term memory increases many times over.* This trend is an obvious one, and the four essays in the opening case study illustrate it clearly. Yet the obviousness of the trend should not negate its importance in cognitive development. Long-term memory is the repository for children's accumulating body of information and skills; thus, it provides the **knowledge base** from which children draw as they encounter, interpret, and respond to new experiences. As this knowledge base grows, then, children can interpret new experiences with increasing sophistication and respond to them with increasing effectiveness (Flavell et al., 1993).

■ *Knowledge becomes increasingly symbolic in nature.* As you should recall from Chapter 4, Piaget proposed that infants' and toddlers' schemes are predominantly sensorimotor in nature; that is, they are based on behaviors and perceptions. Near the end of the sensorimotor stage (at about 18 months, Piaget suggested), children begin to think in terms of **symbols,** mental entities (such as words) that do not necessarily reflect the perceptual and behavioral qualities of the objects or events they represent.

Piaget was probably correct in his idea that sensorimotor representations of objects and events precede symbolic representations. However, the shift from one to the other is apparently more gradual than Piaget believed. Long before children reach school age, they begin to use such symbols as words, numbers, pictures, and miniature models to represent and think about real-life objects and events (DeLoache, Miller, & Rosengren, 1997; Flavell et al., 1993). Symbolic thought is also reflected in their pretend play, such as when they use a doll as a real baby or a banana as a telephone receiver (Fein, 1979). Early symbol use is not entirely dependable, however. For example, when 3-year-old and 5-year-old children are asked to recall what happened during a recent visit to the pediatrician's office, they can do so more completely when they *act out* the visit than when they verbally describe it (Greenhoot, Ornstein, Gordon, & Baker-Ward, 1999). Furthermore, as children make the transition to more advanced forms of reasoning about Piagetian tasks, they often show such reasoning in their *gestures* before they show it in their speech (Goldin-Meadow, 1997). The following scenario illustrates:

> [A] 6-year-old child [is] attempting to justify her belief that the amount of water changed when it was poured from a tall, skinny glass into a short, wide dish. The child says, "It's different because this one's tall and that one's short," thus making it clear that she has focused on the heights of the two containers. However, in the very same utterance, the child indicates with her hand shaped like a C first the diameter of the glass and then, with a wider C, the larger diameter of the dish. The child speaks about the heights but has also noticed—not necessarily consciously—that the containers differ in width as well. (Goldin-Meadow, 1997, p. 13)

knowledge base
One's knowledge about specific topics and the world in general.

symbol
Mental entity that represents an external object or event, often without reflecting its perceptual and behavioral qualities.

Once children begin elementary school, they come face to face with a wide variety of symbols and may initially have limited success in dealing with them. For instance, elementary school teachers often use blocks and other concrete objects to represent numbers or mathematical operations, but not all kindergartners and first graders make the connection between the objects and the concepts they stand for (DeLoache et al., 1997; Uttal et al., 1998). Maps, too, are largely symbolic in nature, and as noted in the preceding chapter, children in the early grades often interpret them too literally—for instance, by thinking that a road that is red on a map is actually painted red (Liben & Downs, 1989). But as children grow older, their use of symbols to think, remember, and solve problems grows in frequency and sophistication.

■ *Children's knowledge about the world becomes increasingly integrated.* Although young children certainly know how certain aspects of their world fit together, their knowledge base consists largely of separate, isolated facts. In contrast, older children's knowledge includes many associations and interrelationships among concepts and ideas (Bjorklund, 1987; Flavell et al., 1993). This developmental change is undoubtedly one reason why older children can think more logically and draw inferences more readily: They have a more cohesive understanding of the world around them.

As an example, let's return once again to the essays in the opening case study. Notice how the third grader presents a chronological list of events without any attempt at tying them together:

> The Idiuns thout they were mean. Then they came friends, and tot them stuff. Then winter came, and alot died. Then some had babies.

In contrast, the eighth grader frequently identifies cause-effect relationships among events:

> More and more people poured in, expecting instant wealth, freedom, and a right to share their opinions. Some immigrants were satisfied, others were displeased. Problems in other countries forced peobo move on to this New World, such as potato famins and no freedom of religions. Stories that drifted through people grew about this country. Stories of golden roads and free land coaxed other families who were living in the slums.

Another example of increasing integration is seen in children's knowledge of their local communities (Forbes, Ormrod, Bernardi, Taylor, & Jackson, 1999). In Figure 5–3 we present maps that three children drew of their hometown. The first grader's "map" includes only the few features of her town (her house, her school, nearby mountains) that she knows well, and the spatial relationships among the features are inaccurate. The third grader's map shows many features of his immediate neighborhood and their proximity to one another. The seventh grader's map encompasses numerous town landmarks and their relative locations on major streets; it also makes greater use of symbols (e.g., single lines for roads, squares for buildings, and a distinctive "M" to indicate a McDonald's restaurant).

Children and adults alike sometimes organize their knowledge into what psychologists call *schemas* and *scripts*. **Schemas** (similar, but not identical, to Piaget's *schemes*) are tightly organized bodies of information about specific objects or situations; for example, you might have a schema for what a typical horse looks like (it's a certain height, and it has an elongated head, a mane, four legs, etc.) and a schema for what a typical office contains (it probably has a desk, chair, bookshelves, books, manila folders, etc.). **Scripts** encompass knowledge about the predictable sequence of events related to particular activities; for example, you probably have scripts related to how church weddings typically proceed and about what usually happens when you go to a fast-food restaurant. Schemas and scripts help children to make sense of their experiences more readily and to predict what is likely to happen in familiar contexts on future occasions.

Schemas and scripts increase in both number and complexity as children grow older (Farrar & Goodman, 1992; Flavell et al., 1993). Like Piaget's schemes, children's earliest schemas and scripts may be behavioral and perceptual in nature; for instance, toddlers can act out typical scenarios (scripts) with toys long before they have the verbal skills to describe what they are doing (Bauer & Dow, 1994). With development, these mental structures presumably loosen their ties to physical actions and perceptual qualities.

schema
Organized and internalized body of knowledge about a specific topic.

script
Schema that involves a predictable sequence of events related to a common activity.

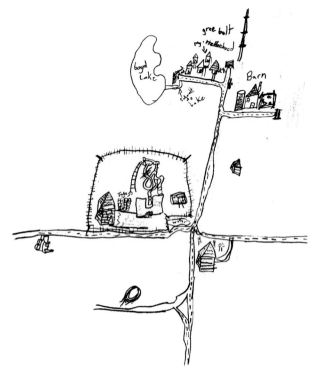

FIGURE 5–3 Three maps of Loveland, Colorado, drawn by a first grader (above), a third grader (right), and a seventh grader (below).

Maps courtesy of Dinah Jackson.

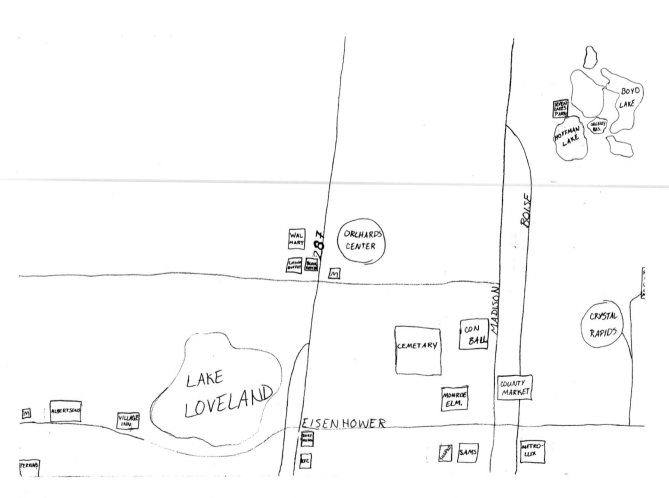

Schemas and scripts often differ somewhat from one culture to another, and such cultural differences may influence the ease with which children can understand and remember the information they encounter (Lipson, 1983; Pritchard, 1990; Reynolds, Taylor, Steffensen, Shirey, & Anderson, 1982). For example, in one study (Lipson, 1983), elementary school children read stories called "First Communion" and "Bar Mitzvah," which described coming-of-age celebrations within the Catholic and Jewish religions respectively. Children with Catholic backgrounds remembered more from "First Communion," whereas children with Jewish backgrounds remembered more from "Bar Mitzvah." In another study (Reynolds et al., 1982), eighth graders read a letter written by a young teenager, Sam, to his friend Joe. In it, Sam describes an incident in the school cafeteria earlier that day:

> I got in line behind Bubba. As usual the line was moving pretty slow and we were all getting pretty restless. For a little action Bubba turned around and said, "Hey Sam! What you doin' man? You so ugly that when the doctor delivered you he slapped your face!" Everyone laughed, but they laughed even harder when I shot back, "Oh yeah? Well, you so ugly the doctor turned around and slapped your momma!" It got even wilder when Bubba said, "Well man, at least my daddy ain't no girl scout!" We really got into it then. After a while more people got involved—4, 5, then 6. It was a riot! People helping out anyone who seemed to be getting the worst of the deal. All of a sudden Mr. Reynolds the gym teacher came over to try to quiet things down. The next thing we knew we were all in the office. The principal made us stay after school for a week; he's so straight! On top of that, he sent word home that he wanted to talk to our folks in his office Monday afternoon. Boy! Did I get it when I got home. That's the third notice I've gotten this semester. As we were leaving the principal's office, I ran into Bubba again. We decided we'd finish where we left off, but this time we would wait until we were off the school grounds. (Reynolds et al., 1982, p. 358, italics omitted)

As these children play "store," they show that they already have a well-developed script for what typically happens at the check-out counter.

Many European American students incorrectly interpreted the story as one that described physical aggression, but African American students saw it for what it really was—a story about **sounding,** a friendly exchange of insults common among male youth in some African American communities.

■ *Children's growing knowledge base facilitates more effective learning.* As a general rule, older children and adults learn new information and skills more easily than younger children. A key reason for their facility is that they have more existing knowledge (including more schemas and scripts) that they can use to help them understand and organize what they learn (Eacott, 1999; Halford, 1989; Kail, 1990). When the tables are turned—for instance, when children know more about a particular topic than adults do—then children are often the more effective learners (Chi, 1978; Rabinowitz & Glaser, 1985). For example, when Jeanne's son Alex was about 5 or 6, the two of them used to read books about lizards together. Alex always remembered more from the books than Jeanne did, because he was a self-proclaimed "lizard expert," and Jeanne knew very little about reptiles of any sort.

Educational Implications of Information Processing Theory

Our discussion of information processing theory thus far leads to several implications for classroom practice:

■ *Keep distracting stimuli to a minimum.* As you have seen, students must pay attention if they are to learn and remember information and skills related to classroom subject matter. Yet many students, young ones especially, are easily distracted by the sights and sounds around them. They can more readily concentrate on the task at hand if attractive objects remain out of view, small-group activities take place as far from one another as possible, and conversations among others in the room are relatively quiet.

Despite such precautions, students can't keep their minds on a single classroom task forever—not even highly motivated high school students. Furthermore, some students (perhaps because of a seemingly boundless supply of physical energy or perhaps because of a cognitive,

sounding
Friendly, playful exchange of insults.

APPLYING INFORMATION PROCESSING THEORY

■ Minimize distractions, especially when working with young children.

As his class begins a writing assignment, a first-grade teacher asks his students to put all objects except pencil and paper inside their desks.

■ Help students automatize essential basic skills.

Students in a fourth-grade class always have a high-interest, age-appropriate children's novel tucked in their desks. Their teacher encourages them to pull out their novels whenever they have free time (e.g., when they've finished an assignment early), partly as a way of helping them automatize their ability to recognize the printed forms of many English words.

■ Begin at a level consistent with students' existing knowledge base.

At the beginning of the school year, a ninth-grade mathematics teachers gives her students a pretest covering the mathematical concepts and operations they studied the year before. She finds that many students still have difficulty computing the perimeter and area of a rectangle. She reviews these procedures and gives students additional practice with them before beginning a unit on computing the volume of objects with rectangular sides.

■ Take students' cultural backgrounds into account when considering what they probably do and do not know.

A middle school social studies class includes students who have recently immigrated from either Mexico or the Far East. When the teacher begins a lesson on courtship and wedding traditions around the world, he asks students from various ethnic backgrounds to describe the typical dating practices and wedding ceremonies in their homelands.

■ Ask students to apply classroom material to familiar contexts.

A third-grade teacher asks her students to write word problems that shows how they might use addition in their own lives. Noah writes a problem involving himself and his sister:

> NoAH HAd 20 PENNES.
> ANd SheA HAd 15
> PENNES. HAoW MecH
> WAd that MAck.
> 35.

emotional, or behavioral disability) have a more difficult time paying attention than others. With these facts in mind, teachers should give their students regular breaks from any intensive sedentary activities that they plan (Pellegrini & Bjorklund, 1997). Some breaks are built into the daily school schedule in such forms as recess, passing periods, and lunch. Teachers may want to give students additional mental "breathers" as well—perhaps by alternating relatively sedentary cognitive activities with more physical, active ones.

■ *Remember that students can think about only a small amount of information at any one time.* Although working memory capacity increases somewhat during childhood and adolescence, students of all ages (college students included!) can mentally manipulate only a very limited amount of material in their heads at once. Thus, teachers should pace any presentation of new information slowly enough that students have time to "process" it all. Teachers should also consider writing complex problems on the chalkboard or asking students to write them on paper. And they can teach students more effective strategies for learning and solving problems (more about such strategies shortly).

■ *Give students ongoing practice in using basic information and skills.* Some information and skills are so fundamental that students should be able to retrieve and use them quickly and effortlessly. To read well, students must be able to recognize most of the words on the page without having to sound them out or look them up in the dictionary. To solve mathematical word problems, students should have such number facts as "2 + 4 = 6" and "5 × 7 = 35" on the tips of their tongues. And to write well, students should be able to form letters and words without having to stop and think about how to make an uppercase *G* or spell the word *the*.

Ultimately, students can automatize basic information and skills only through using and practicing them repeatedly (Anderson, 1983; Schneider & Shiffrin, 1977). This is definitely *not* to say that teachers should fill each school day with endless drill-and-practice exercises involving isolated facts and procedures. Teachers can promote automatization just as effectively by embedding the basics in a variety of stimulating, challenging (and perhaps authentic) activities throughout the school year.

■ *Consider not only what students say, but also what they do, when determining what they know or are ready to learn.* Earlier we described a 6-year-old who said that a tall, thin glass had more water than a short, wide dish because of the height difference between the two containers. At the same time, she showed through her gestures that the tall container had a smaller diameter than the short one. Such discrepancies in what children say and do suggest a possible readiness for developing new ideas and logical reasoning skills—for instance, a readiness for acquiring conservation of liquid (Goldin-Meadow, 1997).

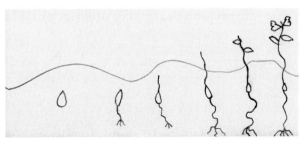

FIGURE 5–4 Noah's picture of how a seed becomes a plant

Teachers might also assess students' current knowledge by asking them to *draw* rather than describe what they have learned. For example, Figure 5–4 shows 8-year-old Noah's knowledge of how a seed becomes a plant. His picture clearly reflects his understanding that roots typically go down before a stalk grows up and that leaves gradually increase in size and number.

■ *Relate new information to students' existing knowledge base.* Numerous research studies support the idea that students learn new information more effectively when they can relate it to what they already know (e.g., Dole, Duffy, Roehler, & Pearson, 1991; McKeown & Beck, 1994). Yet students don't always make such connections on their own; for instance, they may not realize that subtraction is simply the reverse of addition or that Shakespeare's *Romeo and Juliet* has similarities to modern-day racism in the United States and to ethnic clashes in Eastern Europe. By pointing out such connections, teachers can foster not only more effective learning but also the development of a more integrated knowledge base.

The following Developmental Trends table summarizes the information processing capabilities of children and adolescents at various age levels. Up to this point, however, we have said very little about the *central executive,* the cognitive supervisor of the information processing system. Although theorists have not carefully formulated the nature of the central executive, they have learned a great deal about two of its manifestations: metacognition and cognitive strategies.

Development of Metacognition and Cognitive Strategies

As an adult with many years of formal education behind you, you have probably learned a great deal about how you think and learn. For example, you may have learned that you cannot absorb everything in a textbook the first time you read it. You may also have learned that you remember information better when you try to make sense of it based on what you already know rather than when you simply repeat it over and over again in a rote, meaningless fashion. The term **metacognition** refers both to the knowledge that people have about their own cognitive processes and to the intentional use of certain cognitive processes to improve learning and memory.

As children develop, the mental processes they use to learn information and solve problems—their **cognitive strategies**—become increasingly sophisticated and effective. Their awareness of their own thought, their beliefs about the nature of knowing and learning, and their ability to direct and regulate their own learning also change in significant ways. In the following sections we describe development in each of these areas; we then identify additional implications for instructional practice.

metacognition
Knowledge and beliefs about one's own cognitive processes, as well as efforts to regulate those cognitive processes to maximize learning and memory.

cognitive strategy
Specific mental process that people use to acquire or manipulate information.

Learning Strategies

As children get older, they develop increasingly effective methods of learning and remembering information. Toddlers and preschoolers often recognize the need to remember something but seem to have little idea of how to go about learning it, apart from looking or pointing at it (DeLoache, Cassidy, & Brown, 1985; Kail, 1990; Wellman, 1988). But as they progress through the elementary and secondary grades, children and adolescents develop several

Basic Information Processing Abilities at Different Age Levels

DEVELOPMENTAL TRENDS

AGE	WHAT YOU MIGHT OBSERVE	DIVERSITY	IMPLICATIONS
Early Childhood (2–6) 	• Short attention span • Distractibility • Emerging understanding and use of symbols • Very limited knowledge base with which to interpret new experiences	• Pronounced disabilities in information processing (e.g., ADHD, dyslexia) begin to reveal themselves in children's behavior. • Children's prior knowledge differs markedly depending on their cultural and socioeconomic backgrounds.	• Change activities often. • Keep unnecessary distractions to a minimum. • Provide a variety of experiences (field trips to the library, fire department, etc.) that enrich students' knowledge base.
Middle Childhood (6–10)	• Increasing ability to attend to important stimuli and ignore irrelevant stimuli • Increasingly symbolic nature of thought and knowledge • Gradual automatization of basic skills • Increasing exposure to environments beyond the home and family, leading to an expanding knowledge base • Knowledge of academic subject matter relatively unintegrated, especially in science and social studies	• Mild disabilities may not become evident until the middle or upper elementary grades. • Many children with learning disabilities or ADHD have short attention spans and are easily distracted. • Some children with learning disabilities have a smaller working memory capacity than their classmates.	• Intersperse sedentary activities with more physically active ones, as a way of helping children maintain attention on classroom tasks. • Give students many opportunities to practice basic knowledge and skills (e.g., number facts, word recognition), often through authentic, motivating, and challenging tasks. • Begin to explore hierarchies, cause and effect, and other interrelationships among ideas in science, history, geography, and other subject areas • Consult experts when you suspect that learning or behavior problems might reflect a cognitive disability.
Early Adolescence (10–14)	• Ability to attend to a single task for an hour or more • Basic skills in reading, writing, and mathematics (e.g., word identification, common word spellings, basic math facts) largely automatized • Growing (though not necessarily well-organized) knowledge base in various academic disciplines	• Many students with information processing difficulties have trouble paying attention for an entire class period. • Many students with sensory or physical disabilities (e.g., students who are blind or in a wheelchair) have a more limited knowledge base than their classmates, due to fewer opportunities to explore the local community.	• Provide variety in classroom tasks as a way of keeping students' attention. • Frequently point out how concepts and ideas are related to one another, both within and across academic disciplines. • Provide extra guidance and support for students with diagnosed or suspected information processing difficulties.
Late Adolescence (14–18)	• Ability to attend to a single task for lengthy periods • Extensive and somewhat integrated knowledge about some content domains	• High school students have choices in course selection, leading to differences in the extent of their knowledge base in various content domains.	• Occasionally give assignments that require students to focus on a particular task for a long period. • Consistently encourage students to think about the "hows" and "whys" of what they are learning. • Assess students' learning in ways that require them to depict relationships among ideas.

learning strategies—specific methods of learning information—that help them learn more effectively. Here we describe three learning strategies that appear during the school years: rehearsal, organization, and elaboration.

Rehearsal   What do you do if you need to remember a telephone number for a few minutes? Do you repeat it to yourself over and over as a way of keeping it in your working memory until you can dial it? This process of **rehearsal** is rare in preschoolers but increases in frequency and effectiveness throughout the elementary school years (Bjorklund & Coyle, 1995; Gathercole & Hitch, 1993; Kail, 1990).

Rehearsal takes different forms at different ages; following are some examples:

- When preschoolers are asked to remember a particular set of toys, they tend to look at, name, and handle the toys more than they would otherwise; however, such actions have little effect on their memory for the toys (Baker-Ward, Ornstein, & Holden, 1984).
- At age 6, children can be trained to repeat a list of items as a way of helping them remember those items, but even after such training they rarely use rehearsal unless specifically told to do so (Keeney, Canizzo, & Flavell, 1967).
- By age 7 or 8, children often rehearse information spontaneously, as evidenced by lip movements and whispering during a learning task. However, they tend to repeat each item they need to remember in isolation from the others (Gathercole & Hitch, 1993; Kunzinger, 1985).
- By age 9 or 10, children combine items into a single list as they rehearse (Gathercole & Hitch, 1993; Kunzinger, 1985). As an example, if they hear the list "cat . . . dog . . . horse," they will repeat "cat" after the first item, say "cat, dog" after the second, and say "cat, dog, horse" after the third. Combining the separate items during rehearsal helps children remember them more effectively.

Keep in mind, of course, that the ages we've just presented are *averages;* some children develop various forms of rehearsal sooner than others.

Organization   Take a minute to study the following 12 words; then cover them up and try to recall as many as you can.

shirt	table	hat
carrot	bed	squash
pants	potato	stool
chair	shoe	bean

In what order did you remember the words? Did you recall them in their original order, or did you rearrange them somehow? If you are like most people, then you grouped the words into three semantic categories—clothing, furniture, and vegetables—and recalled them category by category. In other words, you used **organization** to help you learn and remember the information. Research consistently shows that organized information is learned more easily and remembered more completely than unorganized information.

Even preschoolers organize information under certain circumstances. For instance, imagine that an experimenter shows you 12 identical containers, several candies, and several wooden pegs (see Figure 5–5). The experimenter places either a piece of candy or a wooden peg in each one and then closes it so that you cannot see its contents. How can you remember what each container holds? An easy yet effective strategy is to divide the containers into two groups, one with candy and one with pegs, as the experimenter fills them. Many 4-year-old children spontaneously use this strategy (DeLoache & Todd, 1988).

Yet in the preschool and early elementary years, children often have little awareness that they're organizing what they're trying to remember, and the categories they form are based on appearance, function, or common associates (e.g., table–chair, dog–cat). As children move through the late elementary, middle school, and secondary grades, however, they increasingly organize information to help them learn it, and they often do so intentionally. Furthermore, their organizational patterns become more sophisticated, reflecting semantic, and often fairly abstract, categories (e.g., furniture, animals) (Bjorklund & Jacobs, 1985; Bjorklund, Schneider, Cassel, & Ashley, 1994; DeLoache & Todd, 1988; Plumert, 1994).

learning strategy
Specific mental process used in acquiring new information.

rehearsal
Attempt to learn and remember information by repeating it over and over.

organization
Finding interrelationships among pieces of information as a way of learning them more effectively.

FIGURE 5-5

FIGURE 5–5
While you watch, an experimenter randomly places either a candy or a wooden peg into each of 12 containers and closes its lid. What simple strategy could you use to help you remember which containers hold candy?

Modeled after DeLoache & Todd, 1988.

Elaboration If we tell you that we've both spent many years living in Colorado, you will probably conclude that we either live or have lived in or near the Rocky Mountains. You might also infer that we have, perhaps, done a lot of skiing, hiking, or camping. In this situation, you are learning more than the information we actually gave you; you are also learning some information that you, yourself, supplied. This process of **elaboration**—adding additional ideas to new information based on what you already know—clearly facilitates learning and memory, sometimes quite dramatically.

Children begin to elaborate on their experiences as early as the preschool years (Fivush, Haden, & Adam, 1995). As a strategy that students *intentionally* use to help them learn, however, elaboration appears relatively late in child development (usually around puberty) and gradually increases throughout the teenage years (Flavell et al., 1993; Schneider & Pressley, 1989; Siegler, 1991). Even in high school, it is primarily students with high academic achievement who use their existing knowledge to help them learn new information. Low-achieving high school students are much less likely to use elaboration strategies as an aid to learning, and many students of all ability levels resort to rehearsal for difficult, hard-to-understand material (Pressley, 1982; Wood, Motz, & Willoughby, 1997; Wood, Willoughby, Reilley, Elliott, & DuCharme, 1994). In general, students are unlikely to engage in elaboration when they are traveling in unfamiliar waters—when they have *no* prior knowledge to which they can relate what they are studying.

Environmental and Cultural Influences on Learning Strategy Development
Environment appears to play a major role in the kinds of strategies children develop. For example, children are more likely to use effective learning strategies when teachers and other adults teach and encourage their use (Flavell et al., 1993; Ryan, Ledger, & Weed, 1987). Culture, too, makes a difference. Children in African schools have better strategies for remembering orally transmitted stories than children in American schools (Dube, 1982). Children in China and Japan rely more heavily on rehearsal than their counterparts in Western schools, perhaps because their schools place a greater emphasis on rote memorization and drill-and-practice (Ho, 1994; Purdie & Hattie, 1996). Children in typical Western schools appear to have better strategies for learning lists of words (e.g., rehearsal, organization) than unschooled children in developing nations, probably because list-learning tasks are more common in school settings (Cole & Schribner, 1977; Flavell et al., 1993).

This is not to say that schooling aids the development of *all* learning strategies, however. For instance, in a study by Kearins (1981), unschooled children in Australian aborigine

elaboration
Using prior knowledge to expand on new information and thereby learn it more effectively.

communities more effectively remembered the spatial arrangements of objects than children who attended Australian schools. The aborigine children lived in a harsh desert environment with little rainfall, and so their families moved frequently from place to place in search of new food sources. With each move, the children had to quickly learn the spatial arrangements of subtle landmarks in the local vicinity so that they could find their way home from any direction (Kearins, 1981).

Problem-Solving Strategies

As children develop, they acquire increasingly more powerful and effective ways of solving problems (e.g., Siegler, 1981, 1991). Consider the following problem: *If I have 2 apples and you give me 4 more apples, how many apples do I have altogether?* Young children can often solve such problems even if they have not yet had specific instruction in addition at school. A strategy that emerges early in development is simply to put up two fingers and then four additional fingers and count all the fingers to reach the solution of "6 apples." Somewhat later, children may begin to use a *min* strategy, whereby they start with the larger number (for the apple problem, they would start with 4) and then add on, one by one, the smaller number (e.g., counting "four apples . . . then five, six . . . six apples altogether") (Siegler & Jenkins, 1989). Still later, of course, children learn the basic addition facts (e.g., "2 + 4 = 6") that enable them to bypass the relatively inefficient counting strategies they've used earlier.

Children's problem solving sometimes involves applying certain *rules* to a particular type of problem, with more complex and effective rules evolving over time. As an example, consider the balancing task depicted in Figure 5–6. The first picture in the figure shows a wooden beam resting on a fulcrum; because the fulcrum is located at the exact middle of the beam, the beam balances, with neither side falling down. Imagine that, while holding the beam horizontal, we hang a 6-pound weight on the fourth peg to the right of the fulcrum and a 3-pound weight on the ninth peg to the left of the fulcrum. Will the beam continue to be balanced when we let go of it, or will one side fall?

Robert Siegler (1976, 1978, 1991) has found that children acquire a series of increasingly more complex rules to solve such a problem. Initially (perhaps at age 5), they consider only the amount of weight on each side of the beam; comparing 6 pounds to 3 pounds, they would predict that the right side of the beam will fall. Later (perhaps at age 9), they begin to consider distance as well as weight, recognizing that weights located farther from the fulcrum have a greater effect, but their reasoning is not precise enough to ensure correct solutions; in the balance problem in Figure 5–6, they would merely guess at how greater distance compensates

The equipment: Balance and weights

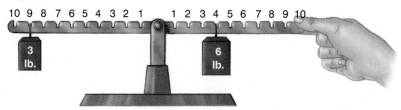

The problem:

FIGURE 5–6 A beam without weights balances on a fulcrum located at its center. After weights are hung from the beam in the manner shown here, will the beam continue to balance? If not, which side of the beam will drop?

Development of Metacognition and Cognitive Strategies | **167**

for greater weight. Eventually (perhaps in high school), they may develop a rule that reflects a multiplicative relationship between weight and distance:

For the beam to balance, the product of weight and distance on one side must equal the product of weight and distance on the other side. In cases where the two products are unequal, the side with the larger product will fall.

Applying this rule to the problem in Figure 5–6, a student would determine that the product on the left side ($3 \times 9 = 27$) is greater than the product on the right side ($6 \times 4 = 24$) and so would correctly predict that the left side will fall.

Strategy Development as "Overlapping Waves"

Information processing theorists have found that a cognitive strategy doesn't necessarily appear all at once; instead, it emerges gradually over time. For instance, children first use learning strategies (e.g., organization and elaboration) somewhat accidentally; only later do they recognize the effectiveness of these strategies and intentionally use them to remember new information (DeLoache & Todd, 1988; Flavell et al., 1993). Children also use newly acquired strategies infrequently, and often ineffectively, at the beginning. With time and practice, they become more adept at applying their strategies successfully, efficiently, and flexibly as they tackle challenging tasks (Alexander, Graham, & Harris, 1998; Flavell et al., 1993; Siegler, 1991).

Once children reach elementary school, they often have several strategies to choose from when dealing with a particular learning or problem-solving task, and so they may vary from one day to the next in their use of these strategies (Siegler & Ellis, 1996). Some strategies may be developmentally more advanced than others, yet because children initially have trouble using them effectively, they may resort to less efficient but more dependable "backup" strategies. For example, when children first learn basic number facts, they cannot always retrieve those facts quickly and easily and so may instead count on their fingers—a strategy that they *know* will yield a correct answer—when dealing with simple math problems. Eventually, however, they acquire sufficient proficiency with their new strategies that they can comfortably leave the earlier ones behind (Siegler, 1989; Siegler & Jenkins, 1989).

FIGURE 5–7 Strategic development as overlapping waves: Students gradually replace simple cognitive strategies with more advanced and effective ones. Here we see how five different strategies for dealing with the same task might change in frequency over time.

From *Children's Thinking* (3rd ed., p. 92), by R. Siegler, 1998, Upper Saddle River, NJ: Prentice Hall. Copyright 1998 by Prentice Hall. Adapted with permission of Prentice-Hall, Inc., Upper Saddle River, NJ.

From an information processing perspective, then, strategic development does *not* occur in stages, one step at a time. Instead, each strategy emerges slowly and increases in frequency and effectiveness over a lengthy period, perhaps over several months or several years. As children gain competence and confidence with more sophisticated strategies, they slowly shed their less efficient ones (Alexander et al., 1998; Flavell et al., 1993; Siegler & Jenkins, 1989). Siegler (1996b) has used the analogy of *overlapping waves,* depicted in Figure 5–7, to describe this process.

Just as there is variability in the strategies that each child uses from one occasion to the next, so, too, is there variability in the strategies that different children of the same age use for any particular situation (Siegler & Jenkins, 1989). For instance, in any high school classroom, some students may use organization and elaboration to study for a test whereas others resort to rote rehearsal. Such individual differences are due, in part, to the fact that some children and adolescents acquire competence with particular strategies sooner than others do. Other factors make a difference as well: Familiarity with the subject matter fosters more advanced strategies, as does personal interest in the task at hand (Alexander et al., 1998; Bergin, 1996; Folds, Footo, Guttentag, & Ornstein, 1990; Woody-Ramsey & Miller, 1988).

Metacognitive Awareness

metacognitive awareness
Extent to which one is able to reflect on the nature of one's own thinking processes.

In addition to acquiring new cognitive strategies, children acquire increasingly sophisticated knowledge about the nature of thinking. Such **metacognitive awareness** includes (a) awareness of the existence of thought and then, later, awareness about (b) one's own thought processes, (c) the limitations of memory, and (d) effective learning and memory strategies.

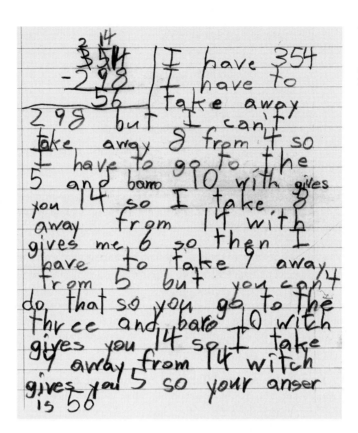

Awareness of the Existence of Thought By the time children reach the age of 3, they are aware of thinking as an entity in its own right (Flavell, Green, & Flavell, 1995). Their initial understanding of thought is quite simplistic, however. They are likely to say that a person is "thinking" only when he or she is actively engaged in a challenging task and has a thoughtful or puzzled facial expression. They also view thought and learning as relatively passive activities (e.g., the mind acquires and holds information but doesn't do much with it), rather than as the active, constructive processes that they really are (Flavell et al., 1995; Wellman, 1990).

Awareness of One's Own Thought Processes Although many preschoolers have the words *know, remember,* and *forget* in their vocabularies, they don't fully grasp the nature of knowing, remembering, and forgetting. For instance, 3-year-olds use the term *forget* simply to mean "not knowing" something, regardless of whether they knew the information at an earlier time (Lyon & Flavell, 1994). When 4- and 5-year-old children are taught a new piece of information, they may say that they've known it for quite some time (Taylor, Esbensen, & Bennett, 1994).

During the elementary and secondary school years, children and adolescents become better able to reflect on their own thought processes and so are increasingly aware of the nature of their thinking and learning (Flavell et al., 1993; Wellman & Hickling, 1994). To some extent, teachers and other adults may foster such development by talking about the mind's activities—for instance, when they speak about someone "thinking a lot" or about someone's mind "wandering," and when they encourage children to "think harder" or "keep your mind on what you're doing" (Berk, 1997). Possibly beneficial, too, is specifically *asking* children to reflect on what they're thinking. As an example, Figure 5–8 shows 8-year-old Noah's explanation of how he solved the problem 354 − 298.

Awareness of Memory Limitations Young children tend to be overly optimistic about how much they can remember. As they grow older and encounter a greater variety of learning tasks, they discover that some things are more difficult to learn than others (Bjorklund & Green, 1992; Flavell et al., 1993). They also begin to realize that their memories are not perfect—that they cannot possibly remember everything they see or hear. As an example of the latter trend, let's consider an experiment with elementary school children (Flavell, Friedrichs, & Hoyt, 1970).

Development of Metacognition and Cognitive Strategies | **169**

Children in four age groups (ranging from preschool to fourth grade) were shown strips of paper with pictures of 1 to 10 objects. The children were asked to predict how many of the objects they could remember over a short period of time. The average predictions of each age group, and the average number of objects the children actually *did* remember, were as follows:

Age Group	Predicted Number	Actual Number
Preschool	7.2	3.5
Kindergarten	8.0	3.6
Grade 2	6.0	4.4
Grade 4	6.1	5.5

Notice how all four age groups predicted that they would remember more objects than they actually could. But the older children were more realistic about the limitations of their memories than the younger ones. The kindergartners predicted they would remember eight objects, when they actually remembered fewer than four!

Children's overly optimistic assessment of their own learning and memory capabilities may actually be beneficial for their cognitive development. In particular, it may give them the confidence to try new and difficult tasks—the challenges that, from Vygotsky's perspective, promote cognitive growth—that they would probably avoid if they were more realistic about their abilities (Bjorklund & Green, 1992). Too often we have seen older children and adolescents *not* take on challenging tasks simply because they were aware of their own limitations and so had doubts that they could succeed.

Knowledge About Effective Learning and Memory Strategies   Imagine this: It is January, and you live in a cold climate. Just before you go to bed, some friends ask you to go ice skating with them right after class tomorrow. What might you do to be sure that you remember to take your ice skates to class with you?

Older children typically generate more strategies than younger children for remembering to take a pair of skates to school. Yet even kindergartners can often identify one or more effective strategies. In a classic study, Kreutzer, Leonard, & Flavell (1975) found that children in the elementary grades tend to depend on external reminders rather than on internal, mental strategies. For instance, some children said that they might write a note to themselves, and others thought that they might ask a parent to remind them. One ingenious child suggested that sleeping with his skates on would be a sure-fire way of remembering them the following morning.

As mentioned earlier, children show greater use of such internal learning and memory strategies as rehearsal, organization, and elaboration as they grow older. With experience, they also become increasingly aware of what strategies are effective in different situations (Lovett & Flavell, 1990; Short, Schatschneider, & Friebert, 1993; Wellman, 1985). For example, consider the simple idea that, when you don't learn something the first time you try, you need to study it again. This is a strategy that 8-year-olds use, but 6-year-olds do not (Masur, McIntyre, & Flavell, 1973). In a similar way, 10th graders are more aware than 8th graders of the advantages of using elaboration to learn new information (Waters, 1982). Even so, many students of all ages seem relatively uninformed about which learning strategies work most effectively in different situations (Ormrod & Jenkins, 1989; Thomas, 1993; Waters, 1982).

Self-Regulated Learning

As children and adolescents grow more aware of their own learning and memory processes, they also become more capable of directing and regulating their learning. To engage in such **self-regulated learning,** learners must have acquired capabilities such as the following (Schunk & Zimmerman, 1997; Winne, 1995a):

- Setting goals for a learning activity
- Planning an effective use of learning and study time
- Maintaining attention on the subject matter to be learned
- Identifying and using appropriate learning strategies
- Monitoring progress toward goals, evaluating the effectiveness of learning strategies, and adjusting goals or learning strategies as necessary
- Evaluating the final knowledge gained from the learning activity

Two aspects of self-regulation are planning effective use of study time and evaluating knowledge gained from a learning activity. This student planned to read one chapter during study hour and ask himself questions about it afterward.

self-regulated learning
Directing and regulating one's own cognitive processes in order to learn successfully.

As you can see, self-regulated learning is a complex, multifaceted process. In its "mature" form, it is virtually nonexistent in elementary school students. Even at the secondary level, few students can effectively regulate their own learning; those who *are* self-regulating tend to be the most academically successful (Bronson, 2000; Schunk & Zimmerman, 1997; Zimmerman & Risemberg, 1997).

Three theoretical perspectives have contributed to developmentalists' current understanding of self-regulated learning. First, of course, is information processing theorists' work regarding the nature of learning and memory. Second is social cognitive theorists' research on self-regulated behavior (more on this topic in Chapter 11). Third is Vygotsky's proposal that, through such mechanisms as self-talk and inner speech, growing children gradually transform social interactions into mental processes.

Here we look briefly at three aspects of self-regulated learning: attention control, monitoring progress toward goals, and evaluating the effectiveness of learning strategies. We then consider how the process of *co-regulation* can foster the development of self-regulation.

Attention Control   As a college student, you probably do several things to keep your attention focused on the subject matter you want to learn. Perhaps you identify a time when you know you will be alert and ready to concentrate, locate a quiet place to read, and then, as you study, try to keep your mind clear of irrelevant thoughts. Such efforts to control your own attentional processes are critical to effective self-regulated learning (Rothbart & Ahadi, 1994).

As noted earlier, many children, younger ones especially, are easily distracted by the sights and sounds around them and so have difficulty paying attention for any length of time. Yet children can learn to better control their attention through self-talk, perhaps through the five steps presented in Chapter 4 (see Figure 4–9). Through these five steps, impulsive and distractible elementary school children can effectively learn to slow themselves down and think through what they are doing (Meichenbaum & Goodman, 1971). For example, notice how one formerly impulsive student was able to talk his way through a matching task in which he needed to find two identical pictures among several very similar ones:

> I have to remember to go slowly to get it right. Look carefully at this one, now look at these carefully. Is this one different? Yes, it has an extra leaf. Good, I can eliminate this one. Now, let's look at this one. I think it's this one, but let me first check the others. Good, I'm going slow and carefully. Okay, I think it's this one. (Meichenbaum & Goodman, 1971, p. 121)

Monitoring Progress Toward Goals   When you study, what do you do to make sure you're learning the subject matter? Perhaps you think about how various ideas are either consistent or inconsistent with things you already know. Perhaps you ask yourself questions about the material and then try to answer them. Perhaps you study with friends, reviewing the material as a group and identifying possible differences of opinion about what a particular author is trying to communicate. Such activities are examples of **comprehension monitoring,** the process of checking one's understanding regularly while learning.

Children's ability to monitor their own comprehension improves throughout the school years, and so children and adolescents become increasingly aware of when they actually know something. Young children (e.g., those in the early elementary grades) often think they know or understand something before they actually do. As a result, they don't study classroom material as much as they should, and they often don't ask questions when they receive incomplete or confusing information (Markman, 1977; McDevitt, Spivey, Sheehan, Lennon, & Story, 1990). Even high school and college students sometimes have difficulty assessing their own knowledge accurately; for example, they often overestimate how well they will perform on an exam (Horgan, 1990; Ormrod & Wagner, 1987).

Evaluating the Effectiveness of Learning Strategies   Not only do children and adolescents often misjudge the degree to which they have learned something, but they may also fail to evaluate the effectiveness of the learning strategies they are using. As a result, they don't always choose the most effective learning strategies (Pressley, Levin, & Ghatala, 1984; Pressley, Ross, Levin, & Ghatala, 1984).

For example, in one study (Pressley, Ross, et al., 1984), 10- to 13-year-olds learned the definitions of new vocabulary words (e.g., *handsel* means "a small payment") using two different techniques. For some words, they used a strategy they had used in their classes many times

comprehension monitoring
Process of checking oneself to make sure one understands what one is learning.

before: Construct a sentence that contains the new vocabulary word. For other words, they were taught a new strategy: Identify a common word (*keyword*) that sounds like the vocabulary word and then construct a sentence that incorporates both the keyword and the vocabulary word's meaning. To illustrate, a keyword for *handsel* might be *hand;* thus, one could construct the sentence "She carried a *small payment* in her *hand* (Pressley, Ross, et al., 1994, p. 492). The children remembered vocabulary words' meanings much more easily using the keyword method. However, when later asked to learn additional vocabulary words, the majority of students rejected the keyword method in favor of the less effective but more familiar use-the-word-in-a-sentence method. Only when the experimenter specifically asked them to consider how they had performed previously after using each of the two methods did they spontaneously choose to use the keyword method in vocabulary learning tasks.

Co-Regulation as a Facilitator of Self-Regulation Using Vygotsky's perspective, we might reasonably suspect that self-regulated learning has its roots in, and so must be preceded by, socially regulated learning, in the following fashion: Initially, other people (e.g., parents, teachers) help children learn by setting goals for a learning activity, keeping their attention focused on the learning task, suggesting effective learning strategies, monitoring learning progress, and so on. Over time, children assume increasing responsibility for these processes; that is, they begin to set their *own* learning goals, stay on task with little prodding from others, identify potentially effective strategies, and evaluate their own learning.

Developmentally speaking, a reasonable bridge between other-regulated learning and self-regulated learning is **co-regulated learning,** in which a teacher and students share responsibility for directing the various aspects of the learning process (McCaslin & Good, 1996). For instance, the teacher and students might mutually agree on the specific goals of a learning endeavor, or the teacher might describe the criteria that indicate successful learning and then have students evaluate their own performance in light of those criteria. Initially, the teacher might provide considerable structure, or scaffolding, for the students' learning efforts; in a true Vygotskian fashion, such scaffolding is gradually removed as students become more effectively self-regulating.

Epistemological Beliefs

As people who learn new things every day, we all have ideas about what "knowledge" and "learning" are—ideas that are collectively known as **epistemological beliefs.** Included in people's epistemological beliefs are their views about

- The certainty of knowledge
- The simplicity and structure of knowledge
- The source of knowledge
- The speed of learning
- The nature of learning ability

As children and adolescents develop, many (though not all) of them change their beliefs in each of these areas; typical changes are shown in Table 5–1. For example, children in the elementary grades typically believe in the certainty of knowledge; they think that the absolute truth about any topic is somewhere "out there" waiting to be discovered (Astington & Pelletier, 1996). As they reach the high school and college years, some begin to realize that knowledge is a subjective entity and that different perspectives on a topic may be equally valid (Perry, 1968; Schommer, 1994b, 1997). Additional changes may also occur in high school; for example, students in 12th grade are more likely than 9th graders to believe that knowledge consists of complex interrelationships (rather than discrete facts), that learning happens slowly (rather than quickly), and that learning ability can improve with practice (rather than being fixed at birth) (Schommer, 1997).

Students' epistemological beliefs influence the ways in which they study and learn (Hofer & Pintrich, 1997; Purdie, Hattie, & Douglas, 1996; Schommer, 1997). For example, when students believe that knowledge is black-and-white (ideas are indisputably either right or wrong), that one either has that knowledge or doesn't, and that learning is a relatively rapid process, they give up quickly if they find themselves struggling to understand classroom material. In contrast, when students believe that knowledge is a complex body of information that is learned gradu-

co-regulated learning
Process through which a teacher and learner share responsibility for directing various aspects of the learning process.

epistemological beliefs
Beliefs regarding the nature of knowledge and knowledge acquisition.

TABLE 5-1 Developmental Changes in Epistemological Beliefs

WITH REGARD TO . . .	CHILDREN INITIALLY BELIEVE THAT . . .	AS THEY DEVELOP, THEY MAY EVENTUALLY BEGIN TO REALIZE THAT . . .
The certainty of knowledge	Knowledge about a topic is a fixed, unchanging, absolute "truth."	Knowledge about a topic (even that of experts) is a tentative, dynamic entity that continues to evolve as ongoing inquiry and research add new insights and ideas.
The simplicity and structure of knowledge	Knowledge is a collection of discrete and isolated facts.	Knowledge is a set of complex and interrelated ideas.
The source of knowledge	Knowledge comes from outside the learner; that is, it comes from a teacher or "authority" of some kind.	Knowledge is derived and constructed by learners themselves.
The speed of learning	Knowledge is acquired quickly, and in an all-or-none fashion, or else not at all. As a result, people either know something or they don't.	Knowledge is acquired gradually over time. Thus, people can have greater or lesser degrees of knowledge about a topic.
The nature of learning ability	People's ability to learn is fixed at birth (it is inherited).	People's ability to learn can improve over time with practice and the use of better strategies.

Sources: Astington & Pelletier, 1996; Hammer, 1994; Hofer & Pintrich, 1997; Hogan, 1997; Linn, Songer, & Eylon, 1996; Perry, 1968; Schommer, 1994a, 1994b, 1997.

ally with time and effort, they are likely to use a wide variety of learning strategies, and they persist until they have made sense of the ideas they are studying (Butler & Winne, 1995; Kardash & Howell, 1996; Schommer, 1994a, 1994b). Not surprisingly, then, students with more advanced epistemological beliefs achieve at higher levels in the classroom (Schommer, 1994a).

Furthermore, more advanced levels of academic achievement may, in turn, bring about more advanced views about knowledge and learning (Schommer, 1994b; Strike & Posner, 1992). The more that students get beyond the "basics" and explore the far reaches of the disciplines—whether science, mathematics, history, literature, or something else—the more they discover that learning involves acquiring an integrated and cohesive set of ideas, that even the experts don't know everything about a topic, and that truly complete and accurate "knowledge" of how the world operates may ultimately be an unattainable goal.

We speculate, however, that less sophisticated epistemological beliefs probably have some benefits for young children. Children may initially be more motivated to learn about a topic if they think there are absolute, unchanging facts (and sometimes there are!) that they can easily learn and remember. And it is often very efficient to rely on parents, teachers, and the library as authoritative sources for desired information.

Interdependence of Cognitive and Metacognitive Processes

Developmental changes in the various areas we've described—attention, memory, knowledge base, cognitive strategies, metacognitive awareness, self-regulated learning, and epistemological beliefs—are clearly interdependent. For instance, children's improving ability to pay attention and their increasing self-regulatory efforts to *control* their attention enable them to learn more from classroom activities. Their growing knowledge base, in turn, enhances their ability to use such learning strategies as organization and elaboration while reading and studying. As learning and problem-solving strategies become more effective and efficient, these strategies require less working memory capacity and so enable children to deal with more complex tasks and problems.

As adolescents' beliefs about the nature of knowledge become more sophisticated, so, too, are their learning strategies likely to change in light of those beliefs. For example, if high

Development of Metacognition and Cognitive Strategies | 173

school students conceptualize "knowledge" about a topic as a unified body of facts and inter-relations, they are more likely to use such strategies as organization and elaboration, rather than simple rehearsal, to master that topic. Furthermore, their growing comprehension-monitoring abilities give them feedback about what they are and are not learning and so may enhance their awareness of which learning strategies are effective and which are not.

Educational Implications of Metacognitive and Strategic Development

Theories and research on the development of metacognition and cognitive strategies yield several implications for instruction:

■ *Teach, model, and encourage effective learning and problem-solving strategies.* Cognitive strategies make such a difference in students' classroom achievement that teachers shouldn't leave the development of these strategies to chance. As teachers ask students to study and learn classroom subject matter, they should also give students suggestions about *how* to study and learn it. Such an approach is consistent not only with information processing theory but also with Vygotsky's proposal that adults can better promote children's cognitive development by talking about how they themselves think about challenging tasks.

A rapidly growing body of research indicates that children and adolescents *can* be taught to use more effective cognitive strategies. For instance, even 4- and 5-year-olds can be taught to organize objects into categories as a way of helping them remember the objects (Carr & Schneider, 1991; Lange & Pierce, 1992). As children encounter increasingly challenging learning tasks, organization alone is, of course, not enough. By the time they reach high school, adolescents will need to learn—and should be explicitly taught—many additional learning strategies, such as elaboration, comprehension monitoring, goal setting, note taking, and time management. Explicit instruction about how to use such strategies fosters better learning and higher classroom achievement (Hattie, Biggs, & Purdie, 1996). It is most effective when

- Strategies are taught within the context of specific academic subject matter, rather than in isolation from actual classroom tasks.
- Students learn many different strategies and the situations in which each one is appropriate.
- Students practice new strategies frequently and with a wide variety of learning and problem-solving tasks.
  (Hattie et al., 1996; Pressley, El-Dinary, Marks, Brown, & Stein, 1992)

Small-group learning activities, especially when structured in particular ways, can also promote more sophisticated cognitive strategies. One approach is to teach students to ask one another thought-provoking questions about the material they are studying. This technique, sometimes called **elaborative interrogation,** appears to promote both better recall for facts and increased integration of ideas (Kahl & Woloshyn, 1994; King, 1994; Wood et al., 1999). Following is a dialogue between two seventh graders who have been taught to use elaborative interrogation:

Jon:	How does the muscular system work, Kyle?
Kyle:	Well . . . it retracts and contracts when you move.
Jon:	Can you tell me more?
Kyle:	Um . . . well . . .
Jon:	Um, why are muscles important, Kyle?
Kyle:	They are important because if we didn't have them we couldn't move around.
Jon:	But . . . how do muscles work? Explain it more.
Kyle:	Um, muscles have tendons. Some muscles are called skeletal muscles. They are in the muscles that—like—in your arms—that have tendons that hold your muscles to your bones—to make them move and go back and forth. So you can walk and stuff.
Jon:	Good. All right! How are the skeletal muscles and the cardiac muscles the same?
Kyle:	Uhh—the cardiac and the smooth muscles?
Jon:	The cardiac and the skeletal.
Kyle:	Well, they're both a muscle. And they're both pretty strong. And they hold things. I don't really think they have much in common.
Jon:	Okay. Why don't you think they have much in common?

elaborative interrogation
Study strategy in which students develop and answer questions designed to promote elaboration of new material.

DEVELOPMENT AND PRACTICE

PROMOTING METACOGNITIVE AND STRATEGIC DEVELOPMENT

■ Encourage learning strategies appropriate for the age group.

An elementary teacher encourages his students to study their spelling words by repeating the letters of each word over and over to themselves. In contrast, a high school teacher asks her students to think about why certain historical events may have happened as they did; for example, she encourages them to speculate about the personal motives, economic circumstances, and political and social issues that may have influenced people's decision making at the time.

■ Model effective learning and problem-solving strategies and encourage students to use such strategies themselves.

A high school chemistry teacher tells her students, "Learning the symbols for all the elements is going to take some time. Some, like H for hydrogen and O for oxygen, are easy. But others, like K for potassium and Na for sodium, are more challenging. Let's take five new symbols each day and develop a strategy that can help you remember each one."

■ Identify situations in which various strategies are likely to be useful.

A fifth-grade teacher says to his class, "We've studied several features of the nine planets in our solar system—size, color, composition, distance from the sun, and duration of revolution around the sun. This sounds like a situation where a two-dimensional chart might help us organize the information."

■ Give students opportunities to practice learning with little or no help from their teacher; provide the scaffolding necessary to ensure their success.

A middle school social studies teacher distributes various magazine articles related to current events in the Middle East, making sure that each student receives an article appropriate for his or her reading level. She asks her students to read their articles over the weekend and prepare a one-paragraph summary to share with other class members. She also provides guidelines about what information students should include in their summaries.

■ Give students numerous opportunities to assess their own learning efforts and thereby to find out what they do and don't know.

A health teacher has students read a textbook chapter at home and then gives them a nongraded quiz to help them identify parts of the chapter that they may need to read again.

■ Encourage students to assess their own learning, perhaps by suggesting that they ask themselves questions both as they study and at some time later.

An elementary teacher instructs his students to study their spelling words as soon as they get home from school, then to make sure they can still remember how to spell the words after they have eaten dinner. "You might also want to ask a family member to test you on the words," he suggests.

■ Talk with students about the nature of knowledge and learning in various disciplines.

A history teacher has students read three different accounts of a particular historical event as a way of helping them discover that history is not necessarily all clear-cut facts—that there are sometimes varying perspectives on what occurred and why.

Kyle:	Because the smooth muscle is—I mean the skeletal muscle is voluntary and the cardiac muscle is involuntary. Okay, I'll ask now. What do you think would happen if we didn't have smooth muscles?
Jon:	We would have to be chewing harder. And so it would take a long time to digest food. We would have to think about digesting because the smooth muscles—like the intestines and stomach—are *involuntary*.
Kyle:	Have you really thought about it?
Jon:	Yeah.
Kyle:	Yeah, well—um—but, do you think it would *hurt* you if you didn't have smooth muscles?
Jon:	Well, yeah—because you wouldn't have muscles to push the food along—in the stomach and intestines—you'd get plugged up! Maybe you'd hafta drink liquid—just liquid stuff. Yuk. (King, Staffieri, & Adelgais, 1998, p. 141)

Elaborative interrogation is probably effective, at least in part, because it encourages students to use sophisticated learning processes (e.g., organization, elaboration) rather than rote rehearsal. Furthermore, in a Vygotskian fashion, students may eventually internalize such mutual question asking, so that they eventually ask *themselves,* and then answer, equally challenging questions as they study.

These students are asking each other thought-provoking questions about the chapter they are studying. This technique, sometimes called *elaborative interrogation,* promotes better recall for facts and increased integration of ideas.

■ *Give students frequent feedback about their learning progress.* When teachers give frequent feedback, they not only promote students' learning and classroom achievement but foster metacognitive development as well. Students who get regular and specific feedback about what they are and are not learning are likely to discover that their memories are, at best, only imperfect records of their experiences and that learning tends to be a slow, gradual process rather than a rapid, all-or-none occurrence.

Teachers can also use feedback to encourage the development of more effective learning strategies. In particular, they might ask students to study similar sets of information in two different ways—perhaps to study one using rehearsal and another using elaboration. They can then assess students' recollection of both sets of information: Presumably the more effective strategy will have promoted better learning and memory. With repeated, concrete comparisons of the effectiveness of different strategies, students will gradually discard the less effective ones for those that will serve them well as they encounter more challenging learning tasks in the years to come.

■ *Provide opportunities for students to evaluate their own learning, and help them develop mechanisms for doing so effectively.* As noted earlier, self-regulated learners monitor their progress throughout a learning task and then evaluate their ultimate success in mastering the material they have been studying. Theorists have offered several recommendations for promoting self-monitoring and self-evaluation in students:

- Teach students to ask themselves, and then answer, questions about the material they are reading and studying (Rosenshine, Meiser, & Chapman, 1996).
- Have students set specific goals for each study session and then describe their achievements relative to those objectives (Morgan, 1985).
- Provide specific criteria that students can use to judge their performance (Winne, 1995b).
- On some occasions, delay teacher feedback, so that students first have the opportunity to evaluate their own performance (Butler & Winne, 1995; Schroth, 1992).
- Encourage students to evaluate their performance realistically, and then reinforce them (e.g., with praise or extra-credit points) when their evaluations match the teacher's evaluation or some other external standard (McCaslin & Good, 1996; Schraw, Potenza, & Nebelsick-Gullet, 1993; Zuckerman, 1994).
- Have students compile **portfolios** that include samples of their work, along with a written reflection on the quality and significance of each sample (Paris & Ayres, 1994; Perry, 1998; Silver & Kenney, 1995).

portfolio
Systematic collection of a student's work over a lengthy period of time.

By engaging regularly in self-monitoring and self-evaluation of classroom assignments, students should eventually develop appropriate standards for their performance and apply those standards regularly to their accomplishments—true hallmarks of a self-regulated learner.

■ *Expect and encourage more independent learning over time.* As you have seen, self-regulated learning is a complex endeavor that involves many abilities (goal setting, attention control, flexible use of cognitive strategies, comprehension monitoring, etc.) and takes many years to master. Throughout the elementary and secondary school years, teachers must encourage and scaffold it in age-appropriate ways. For instance, they might provide examples of questions that students can use to monitor their comprehension as they read (e.g., "Explain how . . . ," "What is a new example of . . . ?"). They might provide a general organizational framework that students can follow while taking notes. They might provide guidance about how to develop a good summary (e.g., "Identify or invent a topic sentence," "Find supporting information for each main idea"). Such **metacognitive scaffolding** is most likely to be helpful when students are studying subject matter they find difficult to comprehend yet *can* comprehend if they apply appropriate metacognitive strategies (Pressley et al., 1992). In other words, metacognitive scaffolding is most beneficial when the subject matter is within students' zone of proximal development.

As students develop increasing proficiency with each self-regulating strategy, teachers can gradually withdraw the scaffolds they have previously provided. Ideally, by the time students finish high school, they should have sufficient metacognitive skills to pursue further academic education or career training programs with little or no assistance from others.

■ *Promote more sophisticated epistemological beliefs.* Teachers must communicate to students, not only in what they say but also in what they *do* (e.g., what activities they assign, how they assess students' learning), that knowledge is not a cut-and-dried set of facts and that effective learning is not simply a process of repeating those facts over and over again. For maximal learning and achievement, especially in the secondary and post-secondary school years, students must learn that

- Learning involves active construction of knowledge, rather than just a passive "reception" of it.
- Knowledge involves knowing the interrelationships among ideas as well as the ideas themselves.
- Knowledge does not always mean having clear-cut answers to difficult, complex issues.
- Understanding a body of information and ideas often requires persistence and hard work. (Hofer & Pintrich, 1997; Schommer, 1994b)

One possible way to change students' epistemological beliefs is to talk specifically about the nature of knowledge and learning—for example, to describe learning as an active, ongoing process of finding interconnections among ideas and eventually constructing one's own understanding of the world (Schommer, 1994b). But probably an even more effective approach is to provide classroom experiences that lead students to discover that knowledge is dynamic, rather than static, and to realize that successful learning sometimes occurs only through effort and persistence. For example, teachers can give their students complex problems that have no clear-cut right or wrong answers (Schommer, 1994b). They can have students read conflicting accounts and interpretations of historical events (Britt, Rouet, Georgi, & Perfetti, 1994; Leinhardt, 1994). They can ask students to compare several, possibly equally valid explanations of a particular phenomenon or event (Linn et al., 1996). And they can show students, perhaps by presenting puzzling phenomena, that their own current understandings, and sometimes even those of experts in the field, do not yet adequately explain all of human experience (Chan, Burtis, & Bereiter, 1997; Vosniadou, 1991).

Having students interact with one another may also influence their views of the nature of knowledge and learning. Heated discussions about controversial topics (e.g., pros and cons of capital punishment, interpretation of classic works of literature, or theoretical explanations of scientific phenomena) should help students gain an increased understanding that there is not always a simple "right" answer to a question or issue. Furthermore, by wrestling and struggling as a group with difficult subject matter, students may begin to understand that one's knowledge about a topic is likely to evolve and improve gradually over time. Finally, teachers must remember that group methods of inquiry are a critical feature of how the adult world tackles

metacognitive scaffolding
Supportive technique that guides students in their use of metacognitive strategies.

challenging issues and problems (Good et al., 1992; Greeno, 1997; Pogrow & Londer, 1994). By providing opportunities for students to formulate questions and problems, discuss and critique one another's explanations and analyses, and compare and evaluate potential solutions, teachers give students practice in these all-important adult strategies.

As a brief aside, we should note that, although some children have frequent opportunities to exchange ideas with adults at home (e.g., at the family dinner table), other children, including many who are at risk for academic failure and dropping out of school, rarely have opportunities to discuss academic subject matter at home. Class discussions about puzzling phenomena or controversial topics may fill a significant void in the cognitive experiences of these children (Pogrow & Londer, 1994).

Children's Construction of Theories

Growing human beings develop beliefs not only about the nature of knowledge and learning but about many other aspects of their world as well. Some psychologists have proposed that children eventually combine their beliefs into integrated belief systems, or *theories*, about particular topics (Hatano & Inagaki, 1996; Keil, 1989; Keil & Silberstein, 1996). This perspective, sometimes called **theory theory**,[2] is illustrated by the following dialogue in Keil (1989) between an experimenter (E) and child (C):

[E:] These fruits are red and shiny, and they're used to make pies and cider, and everybody calls these things apples. But some scientists went into an orchard where some of these grow and they decided to study them really carefully. They looked way deep inside them with microscopes and found out these weren't like most apples. These things had the inside parts of pears. They had all the cells of pears and everything like that, and when they looked to see where they came from they found that these came off of pear trees. And, when the seeds from this fruit were planted, pear trees grew. So what are these: apples or pears? (pp. 305–306)

C: Pears.

E: How do you know?

C: Because the seeds, when you plant the seeds a pear tree would grow, and if it were an apple, an apple tree would grow. They've got the insides of a pear and an apple wouldn't have the insides of a pear if it wasn't a pear.

E: Then how come it looks like this?

C: It's been sitting out for a long time and it turned red.

E: And it doesn't have a pear shape? . . . How did that happen?

C: (Shrug) (p. 171)[3]

This child, like many elementary school children, clearly recognizes that the essential nature of living things is determined by their internal makeup (e.g., their cells) rather than by their outward appearance. Yet children apply a very different principle to nonliving things, as another dialogue from Keil (1989) illustrates:

[E]: These things are used for holding hot liquids like coffee and tea and cocoa or milk to drink, and everybody calls these things cups. Some scientists went to the factory where some of these are made . . . to study them. They looked way deep inside with microscopes and found out these weren't like most cups. The ones made at this factory had the inside parts of bowling balls. And when they looked to see how they were made, they found out that bowling balls were ground up to make them. So what do you think these things really are: cups or bowling balls? (p. 306)

C: They're used for the same purpose as cups and they look like cups and you can drink from them and you can't bowl with them, they're definitely cups!

E: Can they still be cups if they're made out of the same stuff as bowling balls?

C: Yeah . . . and if you could melt down a glass and make it into a bowling ball without breaking it to bits, it would still be a bowling ball and not a cup. (p. 174)[3]

theory theory
Theoretical perspective proposing that children construct increasingly integrated and complex understandings of physical and mental phenomena.

---

[2]No, you're not seeing double. Although the term *theory theory* may seem rather odd, to us it suggests that many psychologists, "dry" as their academic writings might sometimes be, do indeed have a sense of humor.
[3]From Frank Keil, *Concepts, Kinds, and Cognitive Development,* 1989, The MIT Press.

In this situation, the internal makeup of cups and bowling balls is irrelevant; instead, the *function* of the object is paramount.

Children as young as 8 or 9 seem to make a basic distinction between biological entities (e.g., apples, pears) and human-made objects (e.g., cups, bowling balls). Furthermore, they seem to conceptualize the two categories in fundamentally different ways (Keil, 1987, 1989). Biological entities are defined primarily by their origins (e.g., their DNA, the parents who brought them into being). Even preschoolers will tell you that you can't change a yellow finch into a bluebird by giving it a coat of blue paint or dressing it in a "bluebird" costume (Keil, 1989). In contrast, human-made objects are defined largely by the functions they serve (e.g., holding coffee, knocking down bowling pins). Thus, if cups are melted and reshaped into bowling balls, their function changes, and so they become entirely different entities.

By the time they reach school age, most children have developed preliminary beliefs and theories about the physical world, the biological world, and, to some extent, even the mental world (Flavell et al., 1993; Wellman & Gelman, 1992). What do such theories entail? We look now at one example: children's theory of mind.

Children's Theory of Mind

As children grow older, they acquire increasingly sophisticated beliefs about the nature of the mind and the nature of thinking. John Flavell has proposed that such beliefs—their **theory of mind**—evolve over time to include five postulates (Flavell et al., 1993):

1. *The mind exists.* Children's awareness that people are thinking, feeling beings probably emerges gradually during the first 2 to 3 years of life. Although infants may not consciously know that people have thoughts and emotions, they quickly learn that human beings are different from other entities in their environment; for instance, they discover that their parents respond to their needs in ways that inanimate objects do not. Eventually, too, they learn that they can predict other people's behaviors and, in fact, can influence others by hurting, teasing, or comforting them (Flavell et al., 1993). By age 3, children refer to a variety of mental states when describing themselves and others; for instance, they use such words and phrases as *think, know,* and *feel bad* (Astington & Pelletier, 1996; Bretherton & Beeghly, 1982).

2. *The mind has connections to the physical world.* Preschoolers realize that people's mental states (e.g., their perceptions, desires, and emotions) influence their behaviors (Astington & Pelletier, 1996; Flavell et al., 1993; Wellman, 1988). For instance, a 2½-year-old is likely to predict that a child who wants a cookie may try to get one. Furthermore, preschoolers can infer people's mental states from their behaviors and other events (Flavell et al., 1993; Wellman & Woolley, 1990). For example, they reasonably conclude that a person who cannot find a lost item feels sad and will probably continue looking for it.

3. *The mind is distinct from the physical world.* By the time children are 3, they know that thoughts are not physical entities (Flavell et al., 1993; Wellman & Estes, 1986). They know, too, that they can fantasize about things—ghosts, monsters, and so on—that don't exist in reality (Wellman & Estes, 1986).

4. *The mind can represent objects and events accurately or inaccurately.* By about age 4 or 5, children realize that people's perceptions of the world do not necessarily reflect reality (Astington & Pelletier, 1996; Lillard, 1999). In one study (Wimmer & Perner, 1983), preschoolers were told a story about a boy who puts chocolate in a particular place in the kitchen; later, while he's gone, his mother moves it to a different spot. The children were asked where the boy would think the chocolate was located once he returned home. Five-year-olds understood that the boy would think it was where he had left it. In contrast, 3-year-olds mistakenly believed that the boy would know the chocolate was in its new location.

By the time they are 5, children understand not only that people sometimes have inaccurate beliefs about the world but also that people's beliefs and misbeliefs influence what they do and say (Astington & Pelletier, 1996). They know, too, that people's behaviors do not always reflect their mental states—for instance, that people who *appear* to be happy may actually feel sad (Flavell et al., 1993).

5. *The mind actively thinks about the interpretation of reality and the emotion experienced.* By the time children are 6 or 7, they can reflect on the nature of cognition—that is, they can *think*

theory of mind
Child's integrated beliefs about the existence and nature of thought.

about thinking to some degree. At this point, they understand that people interpret what they see and hear, rather than just "record" it verbatim, and so realize that people may occasionally misconstrue an event they have witnessed (Chandler & Boyes, 1982; Flavell et al., 1993). They also realize that people who have false beliefs about the world may think that their beliefs are actually correct (Astington & Pelletier, 1996).

Within this context, we find another possible explanation of the *egocentric speech* that Piaget described. As you should recall from Chapter 4, young children often tell stories without providing the details necessary for their listeners to understand. Piaget proposed that such egocentric speech reflects *preoperational egocentrism,* an inability to view a situation from another person's perspective. A theory-of-mind framework puts a different spin on this idea: Egocentric speech may reflect young children's ignorance about how the mind works; in particular, they don't yet realize that people can make sense of new information only to the extent that they have sufficient knowledge to do so (Perner, 1991).

A child's theory of mind continues to evolve throughout the elementary and secondary school years. For instance, between the ages of 5 and 10, children gain an increasing understanding that people think actively only when they are conscious, that little or no thinking occurs during deep, dreamless sleep (Flavell, Green, Flavell, & Lin, 1999). And, as noted earlier in the chapter, epistemological beliefs about the nature of learning change even during the high school years. The following Developmental Trends table summarizes what researchers have learned about the development of children's cognitive strategies, metacognitive awareness, and theory of mind.

Factors Promoting Development of a Theory of Mind   Theorists have offered several hypotheses about conditions that may promote the development of children's theories of mind. Discussions with adults about thoughts, feelings, motives, needs, and so forth almost certainly promote greater awareness about the existence of mental events as entities separate from physical reality. Parents who openly consider differing points of view during family discussions may help children realize that different points of view can legitimately exist (Astington & Pelletier, 1996). Pretend play activities, in which children assume the roles of parents, teachers, doctors, and so on, can help children to imagine what people probably think and feel in different contexts (Harris, 1989; Lillard, 1998).

Culture probably makes a difference as well. Whereas some cultures frequently explain people's behaviors in terms of people's states of mind, others are more likely to interpret behaviors in terms of situational circumstances, *without* reference to people's thoughts or feelings per se (Lillard, 1999). In the United States, children who live in urban areas often refer to people's psychological states when explaining good and bad behaviors; for example, a child might say, "He helped me to catch bugs, because he and I like to catch bugs." In contrast, children who live in rural areas are more likely to attribute people's behaviors to situational factors; for example, a child might say, "She helped me pick up my books, because if she didn't I would have missed the bus." The latter approach is evident not only in rural American cultures but also in many Asian cultures (Lillard, 1999).

How Accurate Are Children's Theories?

Up to this point, we have been discussing children's developing theories as if they are accurate (albeit incomplete) reflections of the domains they represent. But especially in the early years, children's theories develop with little or no direct instruction from other, more knowledgeable individuals. As a result, they often include naive beliefs and misconceptions[4] about how the world operates. Consider the following conversation with a 7-year-old whom we'll call Rob:

Adult:	How were the mountains made?
Rob:	Some dirt was taken from outside and it was put on the mountain and then mountains were made with it.
Adult:	Who did that?

---

[4]Theorists use a variety of terms when referring to such beliefs, including *naive beliefs, misconceptions, alternative frameworks, lay conceptions,* and *children's science* (Duit, 1991; Magnusson, Boyle, & Templin, 1994).

Cognitive Strategies and Metacognitive Awareness at Different Age Levels

DEVELOPMENTAL TRENDS

AGE	WHAT YOU MIGHT OBSERVE	DIVERSITY	IMPLICATIONS
Early Childhood (2–6) 	• General absence of intentional learning and problem-solving strategies • Belief that learning is a relatively passive activity • Overestimation of how much a person can typically remember • Growing realization that the mind does not always represent events accurately	• Children's awareness of the mind and mental events varies to the extent that the adults in their lives talk with them about thinking processes.	• Model strategies for simple memory tasks (e.g., pinning permission slips on jackets to remind children to get their parents' signatures). • Talk about thoughts and feelings as a way of helping children become more aware of their own mental life and develop a theory of mind.
Middle Childhood (6–10) 	• Use of rehearsal as the primary learning strategy • Gradual emergence of organization as a learning strategy • Emerging ability to reflect on the nature of one's own thought processes • Frequent overestimation of one's own memory capabilities • Little if any self-regulated learning	• Chinese and Japanese children rely more heavily on rehearsal than their peers in Western schools; this difference continues into adolescence. • Children with information processing difficulties are less likely to organize material as they learn it. • A few high-achieving students are capable of sustained self-regulated learning, particularly in the upper elementary grades.	• Encourage students to repeat and practice the things they need to learn. • Ask students to study information that is easy to categorize, as a way of promoting organization as a learning strategy (Best & Ornstein, 1986). • Ask students to engage in simple, self-regulated learning tasks (e.g., small-group learning tasks); give them suggestions about how to accomplish those tasks successfully.
Early Adolescence (10–14)	• Emergence of elaboration as an intentional learning strategy • Few and relatively ineffective study strategies (e.g., poor note-taking skills, little if any comprehension monitoring) • Increasing flexibility in the use of learning strategies • Emerging ability to regulate one's own learning • Belief that "knowledge" about a topic is merely a collection of discrete facts	• Students differ considerably in their use of effective learning strategies (e.g., organization, elaboration). • Some students, including many with information processing difficulties, have insufficient strategies for engaging in self-regulated learning.	• Ask questions that encourage students to elaborate on new information. • Teach and model effective strategies within the context of various subject areas. • Assign homework and other tasks that require independent learning tasks; provide sufficient structure to guide students in their efforts. • Give students frequent opportunities to assess their own learning.
Late Adolescence (14–18)	• Increase in elaboration • Growing awareness of what cognitive strategies are most effective in different situations • Increasing self-regulatory learning strategies (e.g., comprehension monitoring) • Increasing recognition that knowledge involves understanding interrelationships among ideas	• Only high-achieving students use sophisticated learning strategies (e.g., elaboration); others resort to simpler, less effective strategies (e.g., rehearsal). • Many students with information processing difficulties have insufficient reading skills to learn successfully from typical high school textbooks; furthermore, their study skills tend to be unsophisticated and relatively ineffective.	• Continue to teach and model effective learning strategies across the curriculum. • Assign more complex independent learning tasks, giving the necessary guidance to students who are not yet self-regulated learners. • Present academic disciplines as dynamic entities that continue to evolve with new discoveries, information, and ideas.

Rob:	It takes a lot of men to make mountains, there must have been at least four. They gave them the dirt and then they made themselves all alone. [*sic*]
Adult:	But if they wanted to make another mountain?
Rob:	They pull one mountain down and then they could make a prettier one. (dialogue from Piaget, 1929, p. 348)

Construction workers apparently play a major role in Rob's theory about the origins of the physical world.

Children and adolescents typically have many erroneous beliefs about the world around them; for instance, they may believe that the sun revolves around the earth, that the Great Lakes contain salt water, and that rivers can run from north to south but *not* from south to north. Sometimes such beliefs result from how things *appear* to be (Byrnes, 1996; diSessa, 1996; Duit, 1991); for example, from our perspective living here on the earth's surface, the sun looks as if it moves around the earth, rather than vice versa. Sometimes misconceptions are encouraged by common expressions in language; for instance, we often talk about the sun "rising" and "setting" (Duit, 1991; Mintzes, Trowbridge, Arnaudin, & Wandersee, 1991). Sometimes children infer incorrect cause-effect relationships between two events simply because those events often occur at the same time (Byrnes, 1996; Keil, 1991); such thinking reflects the *transductive reasoning* of which Piaget spoke. Perhaps even fairy tales and television cartoon shows play a role in promoting misconceptions (Glynn, Yeany, & Britton, 1991); as an example, after cartoon "bad guys" run off the edge of a cliff, they usually remain suspended in air until they realize that there's nothing solid holding them up. Sometimes children acquire erroneous ideas from others; in some instances, teachers or textbooks even provide such misinformation (Begg, Anas, & Farinacci, 1992; Duit, 1991).

Earlier in the chapter, we presented the principle that *children's growing knowledge base facilitates more effective learning.* This principle holds true only when that knowledge is an accurate representation of reality. When children's "knowledge" is inaccurate, it often has a counterproductive effect, in that *children's erroneous beliefs about a topic interfere with their understanding of new information related to that topic.* For example, many children in the early elementary grades believe that the earth is flat rather than round. When their teachers tell them that the earth is actually round, they may interpret that information within the context of what they already "know" and so think of the earth as being both flat *and* round—in other words, shaped like a pancake (Vosniadou, 1994).

Educational Implications of Theory Theory

Children's theories about mental events, the biological world, and the physical world have several implications for classroom practice:

■ *Remember that young children have limited ability to understand and reflect on the nature of their own and others' thoughts and feelings.* Children in the primary grades have difficulty taking other people's knowledge and thought processes into account during social interactions. And many preschoolers do not yet understand that people's perceptions of the world are sometimes inaccurate and that people's facial expressions may belie their true emotions. Such limitations must inevitably hamper young children's communication and perspective-taking skills, as you will discover in our discussions of language development and interpersonal relationships in later chapters.

■ *When introducing a new topic, determine what students already know and believe about the topic.* Teachers can more successfully address students' misconceptions when they know what those misconceptions are (Roth & Anderson, 1988; Smith, Maclin, Grosslight, & Davis, 1997; Vosniadou & Brewer, 1987). Thus, teachers should probably begin any new topic by assessing students' current beliefs about the topic, perhaps simply by asking a few informal questions that probe what students know and *misknow.*

■ *When students have misbeliefs about a topic, work actively to help them acquire more accurate understandings.* When children encounter more accurate and adultlike perspectives about the world, their existing misconceptions do not necessarily disappear. In fact, because early "knowledge" influences the interpretation of subsequent experiences, misconceptions are often quite resistant to change even in the face of blatantly contradictory information (Chambliss, 1994; Chinn & Brewer, 1993; Shuell, 1996). Thus, teachers must make a concerted effort to help students modify their early, inaccurate theories to incorporate more accurate and productive world views—in other words, to undergo **conceptual change.** Theorists and researchers have offered several strategies for promoting conceptual change in children and adolescents:

- Asking questions that challenge students' current beliefs
- Presenting phenomena that students cannot adequately explain within their existing perspectives
- Engaging students in discussions of the pros and cons of various explanations
- Pointing out, explicitly, what the differences between students' beliefs and "reality" are
- Showing how the correct explanation of an event or phenomenon is more plausible (i.e., makes more sense) than anything students themselves can offer
  (Chan et al., 1997; Chinn & Brewer, 1993; Posner, Strike, Hewson, & Gertzog, 1982; Prawat, 1989; Roth, 1990; Slusher & Anderson, 1996; Vosniadou & Brewer, 1987)

In our discussions thus far, we have drawn often from Piaget's theory and research to better understand the nature and development of children's cognitive processes; for instance, the interview with Rob about where mountains come from was conducted in Piaget's laboratory. Some contemporary theories of cognitive development rely even more heavily on Piaget's work. We turn to these *neo-Piagetian* approaches now.

Neo-Piagetian Approaches to Cognitive Development

For reasons we considered in the preceding chapter, many contemporary developmentalists have largely abandoned Piaget's early notions regarding children's cognitive development. Yet some psychologists believe that, by rejecting Piaget's theory, we may be throwing the baby out with the bath water. These psychologists have combined some of Piaget's ideas with concepts from information processing theory to construct **neo-Piagetian theories** of how children's learning and reasoning capabilities change over time (e.g., Case, 1985; Case & Okamoto, 1996; Fischer, Knight, & Van Parys, 1993).

Key Ideas in Neo-Piagetian Theories

Neo-Piagetian theorists do not always agree about the exact nature of children's thinking at different age levels or about the exact mechanisms that promote cognitive development. Nevertheless, several ideas are central to neo-Piagetian approaches:

■ *Children acquire general structures that pervade their thinking in particular content domains.* Piaget proposed that over time, children develop increasingly integrated systems of mental processes (operations) that they can apply with equal effectiveness to a wide variety of tasks and content domains. However, as noted in Chapter 4, recent research indicates that children's ability to think logically depends considerably on their specific knowledge, experiences, and instruction related to the task at hand. Thus, the sophistication of children's reasoning is far more variable from one situation to the next than Piaget predicted (Case & Edelstein, 1993; Case & Okamoto, 1996).

To address such variability, neo-Piagetians propose that children do not develop a single system of logical operations; instead, they develop more specific systems, or **structures,**[5] of concepts and thinking skills that influence thinking and reasoning capabilities within particular content domains. Accordingly, neo-Piagetian approaches are sometimes referred to as *structuralism* or *neo-structuralism* (e.g., Case & Edelstein, 1993).

■ *Cognitive development is constrained by the maturation of information processing mechanisms.* As noted earlier, children's working memory capacity increases over time; accordingly, children acquire an increasing ability to think about several things simultaneously. Neo-Piagetians

conceptual change
Revising one's knowledge and understanding of a topic in response to new information about the topic.

neo-Piagetian theory
Theoretical perspective that combines elements of both Piaget's theory and information processing theory and portrays cognitive development as involving a series of distinct stages.

structure
In neo-Piagetian theory, a specific system of concepts and thinking skills that influence thinking and reasoning in a particular content domain.

---

[5]One neo-Piagetian, Kurt Fischer, instead uses the term *skill* (e.g., Fischer & Bidell, 1991; Fischer et al., 1993).

believe that the changing capacity of working memory is, in large part, a function of neurological maturation. They further propose that children's limited working memory capacity at younger ages restricts their ability to acquire complex thinking and reasoning skills; in a sense, it places a "ceiling" on what they can accomplish at any particular age (Case & Okamoto, 1996; Fischer & Bidell, 1991; Lautrey, 1993).

■ *Formal schooling has a greater influence on cognitive development than Piaget believed.* Within the limits set by neurological maturation, formal schooling plays a critical role in children's cognitive development. For instance, Robbie Case has proposed that cognitive development results from both active attempts at learning (e.g., paying attention, thinking about how ideas are interrelated) and subconscious "associative" learning (e.g., learning gradually and unintentionally that certain stimuli are often encountered together in one's experiences). In Case's view, both forms of learning can promote the acquisition of knowledge about specific situations *and* the development of more general cognitive structures. Subsequently, specific knowledge and general structures each contribute to the development of the other in a reciprocal fashion (Case & Okamoto, 1996).

■ *Development in specific content domains can be characterized as a series of stages.* Although neo-Piagetians reject Piaget's notion that a single series of stages characterize *all* of cognitive development, they speculate that cognitive development in *specific* content domains may have a stagelike nature (e.g., Case, 1985; Case & Okamoto, 1996; Fischer & Bidell, 1991). Children's entry into a particular stage is marked by the acquisition of new abilities, which they practice and gradually master over time. Eventually, they integrate these abilities into more complex structures that mark their entry into a subsequent stage.

Recently, however, Kurt Fischer has suggested that even in a particular content domain, cognitive development is not necessarily a single series of stages through which children progress as if they were climbing rungs on a ladder. Instead, it might be better characterized as progression along "multiple strands" of skills that interconnect in a weblike fashion (Fischer et al., 1993). From this perspective, children may acquire more advanced levels of competence in a particular area through any one of several pathways. For instance, as children become increasingly proficient in reading, they may gradually develop their word decoding skills, their comprehension skills, and so on, but the relative rates at which they master each of these skills will vary from one child to the next.

To give you a better understanding of the nature of cognitive development from a neo-Piagetian perspective, we now look at a theory proposed by Robbie Case, a researcher at the University of Toronto until his untimely death in 2000.

Development of Central Conceptual Structures: Case's Theory

Case proposed that integrated networks of concepts and cognitive processes—**central conceptual structures**—form the basis for much of children's thinking, reasoning, and learning in specific content domains (Case & Okamoto, 1996; Case, Okamoto, Henderson, & McKeough, 1993). Over time, these structures undergo several major transformations, each of which marks a child's entry to the next higher stage of development.

Case speculated about the nature of children's central conceptual structures in three specific areas: social thought, spatial relationships, and number. A central conceptual structure related to *social thought* underlies children's reasoning about interpersonal relationships, their knowledge of common scripts related to human interaction, and their comprehension of short stories and other works of fiction; this structure includes children's general beliefs about human beings' mental states, intentions, and behaviors. A central conceptual structure related to *spatial relationships* underlies children's performance in such areas as drawing, construction and use of maps, replication of geometric patterns, and psychomotor activities (e.g., writing in cursive, hitting a ball with a racket); this structure enables children to align objects in space in accordance with one or more reference points (e.g., the *x*- and *y*-axes used in graphing). A central conceptual structure related to *number* underlies children's ability to reason about and manipulate mathematical quantities; this structure reflects an integrated understanding of how such mathematical concepts and operations as numbers, counting, addition, and subtraction are interrelated (Case & Okamoto, 1996).

central conceptual structure Integrated network of concepts and cognitive processes that forms the basis for much of one's thinking, reasoning, and learning in specific content domains.

From Robbie Case's neo-Piagetian perspective, children develop central conceptual structures in social thought, spatial relationships, and number (and perhaps in other areas as well). These structures affect children's reasoning and performance on a variety of relevant tasks.

Case proposed that, from ages 4 to 10, parallel changes occur in children's central conceptual structures in each of the three areas, with such changes reflecting increasing integration and multidimensional reasoning over time (Case & Okamoto, 1996). We describe the development of children's understanding of number as an example.

Development of a Central Conceptual Structure for Number   Case and his colleagues (Case & Okamoto, 1996; Case et al., 1993; Griffin, Case, & Siegler, 1994) developed a relatively precise model of the nature of children's knowledge about quantities and numbers during the preschool and elementary years. At age 4, children understand the difference between "a little" and "a lot" and recognize that addition leads to *more* objects and subtraction leads to *less;* such knowledge might take the form depicted in the top half of Figure 5–9. Furthermore, 4-year-olds can accurately count a small set of objects and conclude that the final number they reach equals the total number of objects in the set; this process is depicted in the bottom half of Figure 5–9. For example, 4-year-olds can visually compare a group of 5 objects with a group of 6 objects and tell you that the latter group contains more. They can also count accurately to either 5 or 6. Yet they *cannot* answer a question such as, "Which is more, 5 or 6?"—a question that involves knowledge of both more-versus-less and counting. It appears that they have not yet integrated their two understandings of number into a single conceptual framework.

By the time children are 6, they can easily answer simple "Which is more?" questions. Case proposed that at the age of 6, the two structures in Figure 5–9 have become integrated into the more comprehensive structure depicted in Figure 5–10. As illustrated in the figure, children's knowledge and reasoning about numbers now includes several key elements:

- Children recognize the written numerals 1, 2, 3, etc.
- They understand and can say the verbal numbers "one," "two," "three," etc.
- They have a systematic process for counting objects: They say each successive number as they touch each successive object in a group. Eventually, children count by mentally "tagging" (rather than physically touching) each object.
- They understand that movement from one number to the next is equivalent to either adding one unit to the set or subtracting one unit from it, depending on the direction of movement.
- They realize that any change in one dimension (e.g., from 3 to 4) must be accompanied by an equivalent change along other dimensions (e.g., from "three" to "four," and from ••• to ••••).
- They equate movement toward higher numbers with such concepts as "a lot," "more," and "bigger." Similarly, they equate movement toward lower numbers with such concepts as "a little," "less," and "smaller."

Neo-Piagetian Approaches to Cognitive Development | **185**

FIGURE 5–9 Hypothetical numerical structures at age 4

From "The Role of Central Conceptual Structures in the Development of Children's Thought" by R. Case, Y. Okamoto, in collaboration with S. Griffin, A. McKeough, C. Bleiker, B. Henderson, & K. M. Stephenson, 1996, *Monographs of the Society for Research in Child Development, 61*(1, Serial No. 246), p. 6. Copyright 1996 by the Society for Research in Child Development. Adapted with permission from the Society for Research in Child Development.

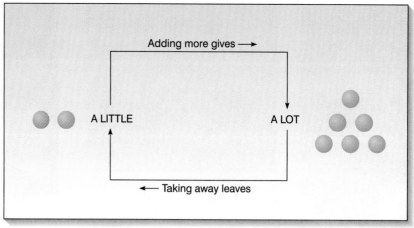

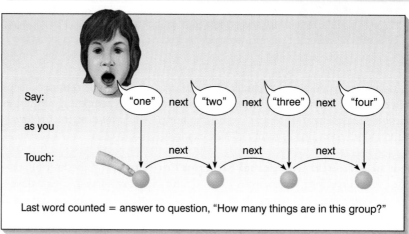

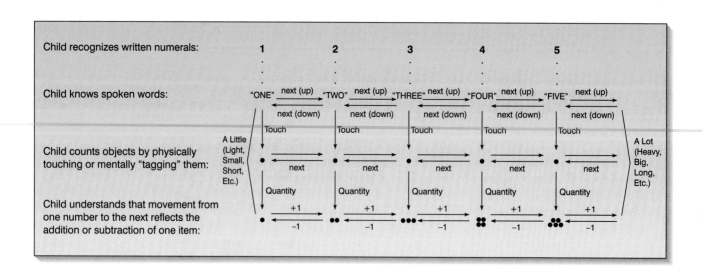

FIGURE 5–10 Hypothetical central conceptual structure at age 6

From "The Role of Central Conceptual Structures in the Development of Children's Thought" by R. Case, Y. Okamoto, in collaboration with S. Griffin, A. McKeough, C. Bleiker, B. Henderson, & K. M. Stephenson, 1996, *Monographs of the Society for Research in Child Development, 61*(1, Serial No. 246), p. 7. Copyright 1996 by the Society for Research in Child Development. Adapted with permission from the Society for Research in Child Development.

In essence, such a structure forms a mental "number line" that children can use to facilitate their understanding and execution of such processes as addition, subtraction, and comparisons of various quantities.

At age 8, Case proposed, children have sufficiently mastered this structure that they can begin using two number lines simultaneously to solve mathematical problems. For instance, they can now answer such questions as, "Which number is bigger, 32 or 28?" and "Which number is closer to 25, 21 or 18?" Such questions require them to compare digits in both the 1s column and 10s column, with each comparison taking place along a separate number line. In addition, 8-year-olds presumably have a better understanding of operations that require transformations across columns, such as "carrying 1" to the 10s column during addition or "borrowing 1" from the 10s column during subtraction.

Finally, at about age 10, children become capable of generalizing the relationships of two number lines to the entire number system. They now understand how the various columns (1s, 10s, 100s, etc.) relate to one another and can expertly move back and forth among the columns. They can also treat the answers to mathematical problems as mental entities in and of themselves and so can answer such questions as "Which number is bigger, the difference between 6 and 9 or the difference between 8 and 3?"

Case tracked the development of children's central conceptual structure for number only until age 10. He acknowledged, however, that children's understanding of numbers continues to develop well into adolescence. For instance, he pointed out that teenagers often have trouble with questions such as "What is a half of a third?" and suggested that their difficulty results from an incomplete conceptual understanding of division and the results (i.e., fractions) that it yields.

Effects of Instruction and Culture on Central Conceptual Structures Whereas Piaget downplayed the importance of education in the development of children's logical reasoning capabilities, Case believed that, within the limits of children's neurological maturation and working memory capacity, formal instruction can definitely promote the development of children's central conceptual structures (Case & Okamoto, 1996; Case et al., 1993; Griffin, Case, & Capodilupo, 1995). For instance, explicit training in such activities as counting, connecting specific number words (e.g., "three," "five") with specific quantities of objects, and making judgments about relative number (e.g., "Since this set [•••] has more than this set [••], we can say that 'three' has more than 'two' ") leads to improved performance not only in these tasks but in other quantitative tasks as well (Case & Okamoto, 1996; Griffin et al., 1995).

In several studies of children from diverse cultural backgrounds, Case found *no* significant cross-cultural differences in abilities that Case proposed are related to children's central conceptual structures for number, social thought, and spatial relations. For instance, when the drawings of Chinese and Japanese children (who receive a great deal of training in drawing skills beginning in preschool) are compared with those of Canadian and American children (who are given numerous opportunities to draw but little if any explicit instruction in how to draw), differences are found in the content and complexity of the pictures but not in the spatial relationships among the figures that the drawings contain. Similarly, Japanese and American children differ in the content of the stories they tell (reflecting cultural differences in the events they experience) but not in their storytelling skills per se (reflecting similar abilities in social thought) (Case & Okamoto, 1996). Such findings suggest that the conceptual structures Case described may develop within the context of a wide variety of educational and cultural experiences.

Educational Implications of Neo-Piagetian Theories

Neo-Piagetian theories lead to some of the same implications that we have derived from other theories. For example, like information processing theory and theory-theory approaches, neo-Piagetian approaches lead to the conclusions that teachers should relate new information to students' existing knowledge base and that they should accommodate children's limited working memory capacities. But these theories have two additional implications as well:

■ *Don't predict students' performance in one domain based on their performance in a very different domain.* From a neo-Piagetian perspective, students may develop at different rates in different content areas; for example, some students may be more advanced in social reasoning than in spatial relations, whereas the reverse may be true for other students. In the next chapter, we will see a similar idea reflected in Gardner's theory of multiple intelligences.

■ *Identify and teach concepts and skills central to students' understanding of a particular content area.* Some classroom subject matter may be information that is highly situation-specific and therefore has little relevance to students' learning in other areas. For instance, although knowing the capital city of one's home state or province is probably important, such knowledge is unlikely to impact students' overall cognitive development. But other subject matter may provide the foundation on which a great deal of subsequent learning depends; for instance, knowledge and skills related to counting, interpretation of people's motives and actions, and the ability to locate objects accurately in two-dimensional space fall into this category. If Case and his colleagues are correct, then training in such essential knowledge skills should be high on a teacher's list of instructional objectives.

Critique of Information Processing, Theory Theory, and Neo-Piagetian Approaches

The following Basic Developmental Issues table contrasts information processing theory, theory theory, and neo-Piagetian theory with respect to the three themes: nature versus nurture, universality versus diversity, and qualitative versus quantitative changes.

As you have probably realized, much work remains to be done on the nature and course of cognitive development. For instance, we do not yet have closure on the question of whether we can better characterize cognitive development in terms of stages or trends. Whereas Case has proposed that the integration of knowledge central to children's thinking in certain content domains (mathematics, social reasoning, spatial relations) occurs in a series of discrete stages, many other theorists (e.g., Keating, 1996a; Siegler, 1996a) remain unconvinced.

Nor have developmentalists completely resolved the issue of general versus domain-specific changes. General changes do seem to occur in attention, working memory capacity, learning strategies, and metacognitive awareness, and such changes probably influence children's thinking and learning across a broad range of contexts and subject areas. But to what extent do children acquire general knowledge structures (e.g., *theories* or *central conceptual structures*) that underlie much of their thinking and reasoning in particular content domains? Researchers have only recently begun to study this critical developmental question, and so a firm answer is probably many years away.

Nevertheless, contemporary theories have extended our understanding of cognitive development far beyond Piaget's and Vygotsky's early ideas. Information processing theory has made significant inroads into the question of how human beings mentally process and learn new information and how cognitive processes change over the course of childhood and adolescence. Theory theory helps us understand why children's naive beliefs (e.g., "The world is flat") may persist even in the face of contradictory evidence. The neo-Piagetian perspective has provided food for thought about the precise nature of children's knowledge in certain content areas. All three approaches have led to the conclusion that cognitive development involves more gradual changes, and the evolution of children's reasoning capabilities is more domain-specific, than Piaget suggested. And developmentalists now agree almost without exception that children's knowledge becomes increasingly integrated over time; such integration may, depending on one's theoretical perspective, take the form of *schemas, scripts, theories,* or *central conceptual structures.*

What we have learned about cognitive development helps us understand not only how children typically develop but also how some children may process information very differently from their age-mates. We turn now to exceptionalities in information processing.

Contrasting Three Theories of Cognitive Development

BASIC DEVELOPMENTAL ISSUES

ISSUE	INFORMATION PROCESSING THEORY	THEORY THEORY	NEO-PIAGETIAN THEORY
Nature and Nurture	Focus is on how environmental input is interpreted, stored, integrated, and remembered and on how formal instruction can best facilitate more effective learning and cognitive development. Information processing difficulties (learning disabilities, ADHD, autism) often have biological origins.	From interactions with their physical and social environments, children construct integrated understandings and beliefs about various physical and mental phenomena.	Both informal experiences and formal schooling promote cognitive development. However, biological maturation places an upper limit on the complexity of knowledge and skills that children can acquire at a particular age level.
Universality and Diversity	The components of the information processing system (e.g., working memory, long-term memory, central executive) are universal. However, some people use their information processing capabilities more effectively than others. People's prior knowledge and their mastery of various cognitive strategies influence the degree to which they can learn new information and skills effectively.	The specific theories that children construct are influenced by informal experiences, formal schooling, and cultural practices and beliefs.	Children develop systems of integrated concepts and thinking skills (structures) that influence much of their thinking and learning within particular content domains. In the preschool and elementary years, these structures are likely to be similar across diverse cultures; in the secondary years, they become more culture-specific.
Qualitative and Quantitative Change 	With development, children and adolescents acquire numerous cognitive strategies that are qualitatively different from one another. Each strategy evolves gradually over a lengthy period and becomes increasingly flexible, efficient, and effective. Theorists disagree about whether the physical capacity of working memory increases with age.	As children gain more information about their world, they may add to and embellish upon their theories; such changes reflect quantitative increases. Under certain conditions, however, new and compelling experiences spur children to overhaul their theories in a way that reflects qualitative change.	Structures increase in complexity in a stagelike fashion; at each successive stage, they become more complex and integrated and so are qualitatively different from preceding stages. Within each stage, children develop increasing proficiency in using newly acquired concepts and skills.

Exceptionalities in Information Processing

All human beings learn and process information in a somewhat unique, idiosyncratic manner. Because growing children have had varying experiences, their knowledge bases are somewhat different, and so the ways in which they make sense of and elaborate on new information must also be different. There are individual differences, too, in children's ability to pay attention, working memory capacity, learning and problem-solving strategies, and metacognitive awareness.

The information processing capabilities of some children are different enough as to require the use of specially adapted instructional practices and materials. Here we consider three groups of students with exceptionalities in information processing: those with learning disabilities, attention-deficit hyperactivity disorder, and autism.

Learning Disabilities

Children and adolescents with **learning disabilities** comprise the largest single category of students in need of special educational services (U.S. Department of Education, 1996). Educators have not reached complete agreement about how best to define this category.

learning disability
Significant deficit in one or more cognitive processes, to the point where special educational services are required.

Perceptual difficulty. Students may have difficulty understanding or remembering the information they receive through a particular sensory modality.

Memory difficulty. Students have less capacity to remember the information they receive, either over the short or long run; more specifically, they may have problems with either working memory or long-term memory.

Metacognitive difficulty. Students may have difficulty using effective learning strategies, monitoring their own comprehension, and in other ways regulating their own learning.

Difficulty processing oral language. Students may have trouble understanding spoken language or remembering what they have been told.

Reading difficulty. Students may have trouble recognizing printed words or comprehending what they read. An extreme form of this condition is known as *dyslexia*.

Written language difficulty. Students may have problems in handwriting, spelling, or expressing themselves coherently on paper.

Mathematical difficulty. Students may have trouble thinking about or remembering information involving numbers. For example, they may have a poor sense of time or direction or they may have difficulty learning basic number facts. An extreme form of this condition is known as *dyscalculia*.

Difficulty with social perception. Students may have trouble interpreting the social cues and signals that others give them (e.g., they may have difficulty perceiving another person's feelings or reactions to a situation) and so may respond inappropriately in social situations.

Sources: Conte, 1991; Eden, Stein, & Wood, 1995; Landau & McAninch, 1993; Lerner, 1985; Mercer, 1997; Swanson, 1993; Swanson & Cooney, 1991; Turnbull, Turnbull, Shank, & Leal, 1999; Wong, 1991.

FIGURE 5–11 Examples of information processing deficiencies in students with learning disabilities

Nevertheless, most apply the following criteria when classifying a child as having a learning disability (Mercer, Jordan, Allsopp, & Mercer, 1996; National Joint Committee on Learning Disabilities, 1994):

- *The child has significant difficulties in one or more specific cognitive processes.* For instance, the child may have difficulties in certain aspects of perception, language, memory, or metacognition. Such difficulties are typically present throughout the individual's life and are assumed to result from a specific, possibly inherited neurological dysfunction (Light & Defries, 1995; Manis, 1996). Figure 5–11 lists several forms that a student's learning disability may take.

- *The child's difficulties cannot be attributed to other disabilities, such as mental retardation, an emotional or behavioral disorder, hearing loss, or a visual impairment.* Many children with learning disabilities have average or above-average intelligence. For example, they may obtain average scores on an intelligence test, or at least on many of its subtests.

- *The child's difficulties interfere with academic achievement to such a degree that special educational services are warranted.* Students with learning disabilities invariably show poor performance in one or more specific areas of the academic curriculum; their achievement in those areas is much lower than would be expected based on their overall intelligence level. At the same time, they may exhibit achievement consistent with their intelligence in other subjects.

Several lines of research converge to indicate that learning disabilities often have a biological basis. Some children with learning abilities have slight abnormalities in parts of the brain involved in language processing (Manis, 1996). Some are apparently prone to "interference" from signals in the brain that are irrelevant to the task at hand (Dempster & Corkill, 1999). Furthermore, learning disabilities often run in families (Light & Defries, 1995; Oliver, Cole, & Hollingsworth, 1991).

Children identified as having a learning disability are a particularly heterogeneous group: They are far more different than they are similar (Bassett et al., 1996; Chalfant, 1989; National

Joint Committee on Learning Disabilities, 1994). Yet teachers are likely to see several characteristics in many of them. Students with learning disabilities may take a "passive" approach to learning rather than actively involving themselves in a learning task; for instance, they may stare at a textbook without thinking about the meaning of the words printed on the page. They are less likely to be aware of and use effective learning and problem-solving strategies. Some of them appear to have less working memory capacity than their age-mates, and so they have difficulty engaging in several cognitive processes simultaneously (Brownell, Mellard, & Deshler, 1993; Mercer, 1997; Swanson, 1993; Turnbull et al., 1999; Wong, 1991).

Learning disabilities may manifest themselves somewhat differently in elementary and secondary school (J. W. Lerner, 1985). At the elementary level, students with learning disabilities are likely to exhibit poor attention and motor skills and often have trouble acquiring one or more basic skills. As they reach the upper elementary grades, they may also begin to show emotional problems, due at least partly to frustration about their repeated academic failures. In the secondary school grades, difficulties with attention and motor skills may diminish. But at this level, students with learning disabilities may be particularly susceptible to emotional problems. On top of dealing with the usual emotional issues of adolescence (e.g., dating, peer pressure), they must also deal with the more stringent demands of the junior high and high school curriculum. Learning in secondary schools is highly dependent on reading and learning from relatively sophisticated textbooks, yet the average high school student with a learning disability reads at a third- to fifth-grade level and has acquired few if any effective study strategies (Alley & Deshler, 1979; Ellis & Friend, 1991; Heward, 1996). Perhaps for these reasons, adolescents with learning disabilities are often among those students most at risk for failure and dropping out of school (Barga, 1996).

Students with learning disabilities typically have less effective learning and memory skills than their classmates and so may need extra structure and guidance to help them study effectively.

Attention-Deficit Hyperactivity Disorder

Children with **attention-deficit hyperactivity disorder (ADHD)** have either or both of the following characteristics (American Psychiatric Association, 1994; Landau & McAninch, 1993):

- *Inattention.* Children with ADHD may have considerable difficulty focusing and maintaining attention on the task before them; they are easily distracted either by external stimuli or by internal thought processes. Such inattentiveness may manifest itself in behaviors such as daydreaming, difficulty listening to and following directions, frequent and careless mistakes, and an inability to persist at tasks that require sustained mental effort.
- *Hyperactivity and impulsivity.* Children with ADHD may seem to have an excess amount of energy; for instance, they are likely to be fidgety, move around the classroom at inappropriate times, talk excessively, and have difficulty working or playing quietly. In addition, they may show such impulsive behaviors as blurting out answers, interrupting others, and acting without thinking about the potential consequences of behaviors. Such impulsivity may reflect a general inability to inhibit responses to external stimuli (Barkley, 1998).

In addition to inattentiveness, hyperactivity, and impulsivity, students identified as having ADHD may have difficulties with cognitive processing, interpersonal skills, or appropriate classroom behavior (Claude & Firestone, 1995; Gresham & MacMillan, 1997; Grodzinsky & Diamond, 1992; Lorch et al., 1999). Regardless of the specific nature of a child's difficulties, a deficit in executive functioning (the elusive *central executive* that we spoke of earlier) may be at the heart of ADHD (Barkley, 1998).

ADHD is assumed to have a biological and possibly genetic origin (Barkley, 1998; Landau & McAninch, 1993). It seems to run in families, is three times as likely to be identified in boys as in girls, and is more frequently shared by identical twins than by fraternal twins (Conte, 1991; Faraone et al., 1995; Gillis, Gilger, Pennington, & DeFries, 1992). The characteristics associated with ADHD typically last throughout the school years and into adulthood (Claude & Firestone, 1995); perhaps as a result of the difficulties that such characteristics may create in

attention-deficit hyperactivity disorder (ADHD)
Disability (probably biological in origin) characterized by inattention and/or hyperactivity and impulsive behavior.

school, students with ADHD are at greater than average risk for dropping out (Barkley, 1998). But once children are identified as having ADHD, many of them can be helped to control their symptoms through a combination of medication (e.g., Ritalin) and specific instruction to promote more appropriate behavior (Barkley, 1998; Carlson, Pelham, Milich, & Dixon, 1992).

Autism

On the surface, **autism** appears to be more of a disability in social and emotional functioning than in cognitive processing. Probably its most central characteristic is a marked impairment in social interaction: Many children with autism form weak if any emotional attachments to other people and prefer to be alone (Denkla, 1986; Schreibman, 1988). Several other characteristics are also common, including communication impairments (e.g., absent or delayed speech), repetitive behaviors (e.g., continually rocking or waving fingers in front of one's face), narrowly focused and odd interests (e.g., an unusual fascination with watches), and a strong need for a predictable environment (American Psychiatric Association, 1994; Carr et al., 1994; Dalrymple, 1995; Turnbull et al., 1999).

Yet an information processing abnormality may be at the root of autism; in particular, many children with autism appear to have either an undersensitivity or an oversensitivity to sensory stimulation (Sullivan, 1994; Williams, 1996). Temple Grandin, a woman who has gained international prominence as a designer of livestock facilities, reflects on her childhood experiences with autism:

> From as far back as I can remember, I always hated to be hugged. I wanted to experience the good feeling of being hugged, but it was just too overwhelming. It was like a great, all-engulfing tidal wave of stimulation, and I reacted like a wild animal. . . .
>
> Shampooing actually hurt my scalp. It was as if the fingers rubbing my head had sewing thimbles on them. Scratchy petticoats were like sandpaper scraping away at raw nerve endings. . . .
>
> When I was little, loud noises were also a problem, often feeling like a dentist's drill hitting a nerve. They actually caused pain. I was scared to death of balloons popping, because the sound was like an explosion in my ear. Minor noises that most people can tune out drove me to distraction. (Grandin, 1995, pp. 63, 66, 67)

Thus, the abnormal behaviors so commonly associated with autism may reflect a child's attempts to make the environment more tolerable (Carr et al., 1994; Grandin, 1995). Social withdrawal and the desire for a predictable environment both help keep environmental stimulation at a comfortable level. Rocking behaviors, too, can help moderate stimulation, as Grandin explains:

> Rocking made me feel calm. It was like taking an addictive drug. The more I did it, the more I wanted to do it. (Grandin, 1995, p. 45)

Autism is a condition that is almost certainly caused by a brain abnormality (Gillberg & Coleman, 1996). Its origins are often genetic, and it is more commonly seen in males than females (Bristol et al., 1996; Bryson, 1997).

Children and adolescents with autism often show great variability in their cognitive abilities (American Psychiatric Association, 1994). Some have exceptional strengths in visual-spatial skills (Grandin, 1995; Williams, 1996). In a few instances, a child with autism possesses an extraordinary ability (such as exceptional musical talent) that is quite remarkable in contrast to other aspects of mental functioning (Cheatham, Smith, Rucker, Polloway, & Lewis, 1995; Treffert, 1989).

Helping Students with Information Processing Difficulties

Instructional practices and materials for students with learning disabilities, attention-deficit hyperactivity disorder, and autism should, of course, be individualized in accordance with each student's strengths and weaknesses. Yet several strategies are applicable to students with a variety of information processing difficulties:

■ *Help students keep their attention on classroom subject matter.* Many students with information processing difficulties are easily distracted. Therefore, teachers should minimize the presence of other stimuli likely to compete for students' attention, perhaps by making sure

autism
Disability (probably biological in origin) characterized by infrequent social interaction, communication impairments, repetitive behaviors, narrowly focused interests, and a strong need for a predictable environment.

ACCOMMODATING INFORMATION PROCESSING DIFFICULTIES

■ Minimize the presence of distracting stimuli.

A teacher has a student with attention-deficit hyperactivity disorder sit near her desk, away from distractions that classmates may provide; she also encourages the student to keep his desk clear of all objects and materials except those with which he is presently working (Buchoff, 1990).

■ Give students the extra structure they may need to succeed on academic tasks.

A teacher provides a particular format for writing an expository paragraph: one sentence expressing the main idea, followed by three sentences that support the idea and a final, concluding sentence.

■ Look at students' errors for clues about possible processing difficulties.

When a seventh grader spells *refrigerator* as "refegter" and *hippopotamus* as "hep-opoms," her teacher hypothesizes that she has difficulty relating written words to the phonetic sounds they represent.

■ When reading difficulties are evident, minimize dependence on reading materials or provide materials written at a lower-level.

For two high school students reading well below grade level, a teacher finds some supplementary reading materials related to the topics the class is studying; although written for adults, these materials use simpler language than the class textbook. The teacher also meets with the students once a week for verbal explanations of class material and a hands-on exploration of scientific principles.

■ Give students explicit guidance about how to study.

A teacher tells a student, "When you study a new spelling word, it helps if you repeat the letters out loud while you practice writing the word. Let's try it with *house*, the word you are learning this morning. Watch how I repeat the letters—H...O...U...S...E—as I write the word. Now you try doing what I just did."

---

that the classroom is fairly quiet during tasks requiring considerable concentration or by pulling down window shades when other students are playing in the schoolyard. Teachers can also teach their students strategies—keeping one's eyes focused on whoever is speaking, moving to a new location if the current one presents too many distracting sights and sounds, and so on—for maintaining attention on classroom tasks (Buchoff, 1990).

■ *Teach strategies for controlling hyperactivity and impulsivity.* All students, but especially those with information processing difficulties, need regular opportunities to release pent-up energy, such as recess, physical education, and hands-on classroom activities (e.g., Panksepp, 1998). In addition, teachers might give students a "settling-in" time after recess or lunch before asking them to engage in a sedentary activity (Pellegrini & Horvat, 1995); as an example, many elementary teachers begin the afternoon by reading a chapter from a high-interest storybook. Teachers can also teach students to use self-talk as a way of helping them resist the tendency to respond too quickly and impulsively to questions and problems (Meichenbaum & Goodman, 1971).

■ *Analyze students' errors for clues about their processing difficulties.* Students with information processing difficulties are, like anyone else, apt to make errors in responding to questions, problems, and other academic tasks. Rather than think of certain responses simply as being wrong, teachers should scrutinize students' errors for clues about the specific difficulties students are having (J. W. Lerner, 1985). For example, a student who solves a subtraction problem this way

$$\begin{array}{r} 83 \\ -27 \\ \hline 64 \end{array}$$

may be applying an inappropriate strategy (*always subtract the smaller number from the larger one*) to subtraction.

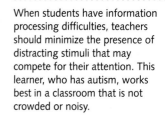

When students have information processing difficulties, teachers should minimize the presence of distracting stimuli that may compete for their attention. This learner, who has autism, works best in a classroom that is not crowded or noisy.

Assessing Students' Information Processing and Metacognitive Skills

OBSERVATION GUIDELINES

CHARACTERISTIC	LOOK FOR	EXAMPLE	IMPLICATION
Attention span	• Ability to stay on task for an age-appropriate period • On-task behavior when distracting stimuli are present	In a fifth-grade "literature circle," a teacher aide and five students discuss Wilson Rawls's *Where the Red Fern Grows*. Four students are attentive throughout the 30-minute discussion, but Ben continually fidgets and looks at what other groups in the classroom are doing.	Monitor students' ability to pay attention in an age-appropriate fashion. If students have exceptional difficulty staying on task, minimize distractions and teach them strategies for focusing their attention more effectively.
Automatization of basic skills	• Retrieval of simple facts in a rapid, effortless fashion • Ability to use simple problem-solving strategies quickly and efficiently	Elena easily solves the problem $$\frac{4}{12} = \frac{x}{36}$$ because she immediately reduces $\frac{4}{12}$ to $\frac{1}{3}$.	Give students numerous opportunities to use and practice essential facts and skills; do so within the context of interesting and motivating activities.
Choice of learning strategies	• Use of rehearsal in the elementary grades • Use of more integrative strategies (e.g., organization, elaboration) in the secondary grades • Flexible use of strategies for different learning tasks	Terry studies each new concept in her high school physics class by repeating the textbook definition aloud three or four times in a row. Later, she can barely remember the definitions she has studied, and she is unable to apply the concepts when trying to solve physics problems.	Show students that their learning difficulties may be due to ineffective strategies, and teach them strategies that can help them learn more successfully.
Self-regulated learning capabilities	• Intentional efforts to keep attention focused on an assigned task • Effective planning and time management • Realistic appraisal of what has and has not been learned	When John has trouble hearing the video that his teacher is showing, he moves to a vacant seat closer to the video screen.	When students fail to complete independent assignments in a timely or thorough manner, provide more structure for subsequent assignments. Gradually remove the structure over time as students become better able to regulate their own learning.
Beliefs about knowledge and learning	• Optimism that knowledge and ability improve with practice and persistence • Striving to understand interrelationships among ideas • Comparing and evaluating various perspectives and theories	Several students are studying for a test on westward migration in North America during the 1800s. Some students focus on interrelationships among events (e.g., demands in Europe for beaverskin hats led to increased fur-trapping along the Platte River). Others make a list of facts from the textbook (e.g., many wagon trains began their trips at St. Louis) and study them in a piecemeal fashion.	Convey the message that mastering a topic is an ongoing, lifelong enterprise that requires effort and persistence. Especially in the secondary grades, convey the message that knowledge about a topic includes an understanding of how different ideas interrelate and a recognition that competing perspectives are not necessarily right or wrong.

Ideally, teachers should look closely at how *all* their students process information. Suggestions about what to look for are presented in the Observation Guidelines table above.

■ *Teach learning and memory strategies.* In comparison with their classmates, students with information processing difficulties use relatively ineffective learning strategies and study skills (Wong, 1991). Thus, teachers must often provide explicit instruction in how students can best learn and study classroom subject matter. For instance, teachers might give students suggestions on how to take notes and then periodically monitor students' notes for accuracy and completeness (Wood & Rosbe, 1985). Teachers might also teach students certain **mnemonics,** or "memory tricks," to help them learn new information (Mastropieri & Scruggs, 1992); for instance, they might suggest *ROY G. BIV* as a way of remembering the colors of the spectrum (red, orange, yellow, green, blue, indigo, violet) or *HOMES* for recalling the five Great Lakes (Huron, Ontario, Michigan, Erie, Superior).

■ *Provide study aids.* In addition to teaching more effective learning strategies, teachers can provide scaffolding that facilitates the sometimes overwhelming task of studying classroom material. For instance, they can distribute study guides that help students identify important ideas (Mastropieri & Scruggs, 1992). They can show how material is organized, perhaps with outlines that enumerate major and subordinate ideas or with graphics that show how key concepts are interrelated (Brigham & Scruggs, 1995; Wood & Rosbe, 1985). They can let students copy the notes of a classmate who is a particularly good note taker (Turnbull et al., 1999).

■ *Keep the classroom schedule and environment relatively predictable.* Some novelty in classroom activities does wonders for maintaining students' interest in academic subject matter (Renninger, Hidi, & Krapp, 1992). But a school day that has surprises around every corner may arouse excessive anxiety in some students, and such anxiety interferes with effective information processing (Eysenck, 1992; Lazarus, 1991). Furthermore, many students with autism find comfort and security in the predictability of their environment. To maintain some sense of predictability in the classroom, teachers might schedule certain activities at the same time each day or on a particular day of each week (Dalrymple, 1995). When there is a change in the schedule (perhaps because of a fire drill or school assembly), they should give students advance warning of the change and indicate when the schedule will be back to normal again (Dalrymple, 1995). And if the class includes one or more students with autism, teachers should change the physical arrangement of their classrooms infrequently if at all.

Students with learning disabilities, ADHD, and autism are not the only ones who have trouble processing and learning information. As a general rule, *children and adolescents process information less effectively than adults do.* Teachers must remember, then, that their students will not always learn classroom material as quickly or effectively as they themselves would. The final case study is a clear example.

CASE STUDY: THE LIBRARY PROJECT

As Jeanne writes this book, she is also supervising several interns who, in the final year of their college teacher education program, are teaching in partnership with experienced middle school teachers. One intern, who is teaching eighth-grade social studies, has assigned her students a month-long group project that involves considerable library research. Midway through the project, she writes the following entry in her journal:

> Within each group, one student is studying culture of the region, one has religion, one has economy, and one government. The point is for the students to become "experts" on their topic in their region. There are a lot of requirements to this assignment. I'm collecting things as we go along because I think a project this long will be difficult for them to organize. . . .
>
> So we spent all week in the library. I collected a minimum of two pages of notes yesterday, which will be a small part of their grade. The one thing that surprised me in our work in the library was their lack of skills. They had such difficulty researching, finding the information they needed, deciding what was important, and organizing and taking notes. As they worked, I walked around helping and was shocked. The librarian had already gotten out all of the appropriate resources. Even after they had the books in front of them, most did not know what to do. For instance, if they were assigned "economy," most looked in the index for that particular word. If they didn't find it, they gave up on the book. After realizing this, I had to start the next day with a brief lesson on researching and cross-referencing. I explained how they could look up *commerce, imports, exports,* and how these would all help them. I was also shocked at how poor their note-taking skills were. I saw a few kids copying paragraphs word for word. Almost none of them understood that notes don't need to be in full sentences. So, it was a long week at the library.

mnemonics
Special memory aid or trick designed to help students learn and remember a particular piece of information.

Next week is devoted to group work and time to help them work on their rough drafts. With the difficulty they had researching, I can imagine the problems that will arise out of turning their notes into papers. (Courtesy of Jessica Jensen)

- Initially, the intern realizes that her students will need some structure to complete the project successfully. In what ways do she and the librarian structure the assignment for the students?
- What specific strategies do the students use as they engage in their library research? How are their strategies less effective than an adult's might be?
- How does the students' prior knowledge (or lack thereof) influence the effectiveness of their strategies?

SUMMARY

Information Processing Theory

Information processing theory focuses on how children receive, think about, mentally modify, and remember information, and on how such cognitive processes change over the course of development. Information processing theorists propose that cognitive capabilities improve with age and experience; such improvements take the form of gradual trends rather than discrete stages. In general, children are less efficient learners than adults are; they have shorter attention spans, a smaller working memory capacity, and a smaller and less integrated knowledge base to which they can relate new information.

Development of Metacognition and Cognitive Strategies

The term *metacognition* refers both to the knowledge that people have about their own cognitive processes and to their intentional use of certain cognitive processes to facilitate learning and memory. Children's metacognitive knowledge and intentional cognitive strategies improve throughout the school years. For instance, children become more proficient in such learning strategies as rehearsal, organization, and elaboration, and they acquire increasingly powerful and effective ways of solving problems. With age, they become more aware of the nature of thinking, learning, and knowledge, and they develop strategies for regulating their own learning.

Theory Theory

Some psychologists propose that growing children gradually construct integrated belief systems (theories) about the biological world, the physical world, and mental events; for instance, they develop a *theory of mind* that encompasses beliefs about how human beings think, feel, and reason. Such theories are not always accurate; to the extent that they include misunderstandings about the world, they may interfere with children's ability to acquire scientifically more sophisticated understandings.

Neo-Piagetian Theories

Neo-Piagetian theories combine elements of Piaget's theory with concepts from information processing theory. Neo-Piagetians reject Piaget's proposal that children acquire a single system of logical operations. Instead, they suggest that children acquire several more specific systems of concepts and thinking skills relevant to particular content domains (e.g., Robbie Case proposed that specific systems develop for social thought, spatial relationships, and number). Neo-Piagetians further suggest that these systems develop in a stagelike manner, with slowly maturing information processing mechanisms (e.g., working memory capacity) setting an upper limit on the complexity of thinking and reasoning skills that can emerge during infancy and childhood.

Exceptionalities in Information Processing

The information processing capabilities of some children are different enough as to require the use of specially adapted instructional practices and materials. Children with learning disabilities have significant difficulties in one or more specific cognitive processes. Children with

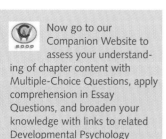

Now go to our Companion Website to assess your understanding of chapter content with Multiple-Choice Questions, apply comprehension in Essay Questions, and broaden your knowledge with links to related Developmental Psychology World Wide Web sites.

attention-deficit hyperactivity disorder (ADHD) have difficulty focusing attention on assigned tasks and/or are unusually hyperactive and impulsive for their age group. Children with autism exhibit a marked impairment in social interaction; oftentimes, their behaviors result from an extreme undersensitivity or oversensitivity to sensory stimulation.

KEY CONCEPTS

information processing theory (p. 153)
sensation (p. 153)
perception (p. 153)
sensory register (p. 153)
working memory (p. 153)
long-term memory (p. 154)
central executive (p. 154)
automatization (p. 157)
knowledge base (p. 158)
symbol (p. 158)
schema (p. 159)
script (p. 159)
sounding (p. 161)
metacognition (p. 163)

cognitive strategy (p. 163)
learning strategy (p. 165)
rehearsal (p. 165)
organization (p. 165)
elaboration (p. 166)
metacognitive awareness (p. 168)
self-regulated learning (p. 170)
comprehension monitoring (p. 171)
co-regulated learning (p. 172)
epistemological beliefs (p. 172)
elaborative interrogation (p. 174)
portfolio (p. 176)

metacognitive scaffolding (p. 177)
theory theory (p. 178)
theory of mind (p. 179)
conceptual change (p. 183)
neo-Piagetian theory (p. 183)
structure (in neo-Piagetian theory) (p. 183)
central conceptual structure (p. 184)
learning disability (p. 189)
attention-deficit hyperactivity disorder (ADHD) (p. 191)
autism (p. 192)
mnemonics (p. 195)

Veronica, age 8

Intelligence

CASE STUDY: GINA

Seventeen-year-old Gina has always been a good student. In elementary school, she consistently achieved straight As on her report cards until finally, in sixth grade, she broke the pattern by getting a B in history. Since then, she has earned a few more Bs, but As continue to dominate her record. Her performance has been highest in her advanced mathematics courses, where she easily grasps the abstract concepts and principles that many of her classmates find difficult to understand.

Gina has other talents as well. She won her high school's creative writing contest 2 years in a row. She has landed challenging roles in her school's drama productions. And as the president of the National Honor Society in her senior year, she has masterfully coordinated a schoolwide peer tutoring program to assist struggling students.

Gina's teachers describe her as a "bright" young woman. Her friends affectionately call her a "brainiac." Test results in her school file bear out their assessments: An intelligence test that she took in junior high school yielded a score of 140, and this year she performed at the 99th percentile on college aptitude tests.

This is not to say that Gina is strong in every arena. She shows little artistic ability in her paintings or clay sculptures. Her piano playing is mediocre despite 5 years of weekly lessons. In athletic events, she has little stamina, strength, or flexibility. She is shy and unsure of herself at social events. And she hasn't earned an A in history since fifth grade, in large part because she studies history ineffectively by simply memorizing people, places, and dates.

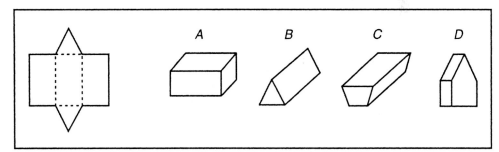

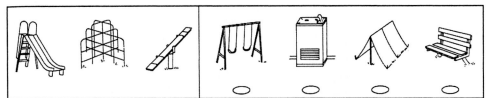

See the slide, the jungle gym and the teeter-totter. Which one belongs with them?

Some school districts, like Gina's, administer general or specific measures of cognitive ability periodically throughout the school years. Such tests typically focus on reasoning and problem-solving skills, perhaps about verbal, mathematical, or spatial material. The top item involves spatial reasoning and might be appropriate for older children or adolescents. The lower item requires children to identify similarities among objects and would be read to children in the primary grades.

Drawings from *Measurement and Evaluation in Psychology and Education,* 6th edition (pp. 243, 251), by R M. Thorndike 1997, Upper Saddle River, NJ: Merrill/Prentice Hall. Reprinted by permission of Pearson Education, Inc. Upper Saddle River, NJ 07458.

As we examined cognitive development in Chapters 4 and 5, we focused primarily on what cognitive abilities and processes are typical for children of various ages. As we address the topic of *intelligence* in this chapter, we focus more on the differences among children in any single age group.

Psychologists don't all agree about what intelligence is. However, many use the term when they are talking about consistently high performance across time and across a variety of tasks. Gina's performance reflects both kinds of consistency: She has earned high marks throughout her school career, and she achieves at high levels in many areas. Yet intelligence is not necessarily a permanent, set-in-concrete characteristic that people either do or do not have. In fact, children's intelligence can, and often does, change with age and experience. Furthermore, children can behave more or less "intelligently" depending on the circumstances.

In this chapter, we consider the nature of intelligence from diverse theoretical perspectives. We look at how intelligence is often measured and how IQ scores are derived. We devote much of the remainder of the chapter to the **psychometric approach** to cognitive development, an approach that focuses on how children's performance on intelligence tests changes over time and how IQ scores are related to other characteristics and behaviors that children exhibit. In the process, we explore controversies about the relative effects of heredity and environment and the origins of group differences in IQ scores. Finally, we consider the two ends of the intelligence continuum: giftedness and mental retardation.

Defining Intelligence

Theorists define and conceptualize intelligence in many different ways, but most agree that it has several distinctive qualities:

- It is *adaptive*, such that it can be used flexibly to respond to a variety of situations and problems.
- It involves *learning ability:* People who are intelligent in particular domains learn new information and behaviors more quickly and easily than people who are less intelligent in those domains.
- It involves the *use of prior knowledge* to analyze and understand new situations effectively.
- It involves the complex interaction and coordination of *many different mental processes.*
- It is *culture-specific.* What is "intelligent" behavior in one culture is not necessarily intelligent behavior in another culture.
  (Laboratory of Human Cognition, 1982; Neisser et al., 1996; Sternberg, 1997; Sternberg & Detterman, 1986)

With these qualities in mind, we offer one possible (but intentionally vague) definition of **intelligence:** the ability to benefit from experiences and thereby modify future behaviors to accomplish new tasks successfully.

For most theorists, intelligence is somewhat distinct from what an individual has actually learned (e.g., as reflected in school achievement). At the same time, intelligent thinking and intelligent behavior inevitably *depend* on prior learning to some degree. The more people know about their environment and about the tasks they need to perform, the more intelligently they can behave.

psychometric approach
Approach to cognitive development that focuses on children's performance on intelligence tests.

intelligence
Ability to modify and adjust one's behaviors in order to accomplish new tasks successfully.

Theoretical Perspectives of Intelligence

Some theorists have suggested that intelligence is a single, general ability that affects performance on many different tasks. Historically, considerable evidence has supported this idea (McGrew et al., 1997; Neisser et al., 1996; Spearman, 1927). Although different measures of intelligence tests yield somewhat different scores, they all correlate with one another: People who score high on one test tend to score high on others as well. Even tests with two different kinds of content (e.g., a verbal test based on knowledge of vocabulary and a nonverbal test based on ability to find patterns in geometric designs) tend to correlate with one another (Brody, 1985; Carroll, 1992; Spearman, 1904).

Yet the correlations are not perfect ones: People who get the highest scores on one test are not always the same ones who get the highest scores on another test. For instance, students who demonstrate exceptional ability in some areas of the curriculum may exhibit only average performance in others (e.g., remember Gina's high performance in mathematics and writing but average performance in art and music). Thus, not all psychologists believe that intelligence is a single entity that people "have" in varying amounts; instead, some propose that people may be more or less intelligent in different situations and on different kinds of tasks.

In this section, we present five theoretical perspectives on the single-entity versus multiple-abilities nature of intelligence. We begin with Charles Spearman's early theory of a general factor (g) in intelligence. Next, we consider Raymond Cattell's distinction between fluid and crystallized intelligence. We then look at how two contemporary theories—Howard Gardner's theory of multiple intelligences and Robert Sternberg's triarchic theory—both portray intelligence as a multidimensional and context-dependent ability. Finally, we look more closely at the role of context as we consider the concept of distributed intelligence.

Spearman's g

In the early 1900s, Charles Spearman (1904, 1927) proposed that intelligence comprises both a single, pervasive reasoning ability (a *general factor*) that is used on a wide variety of tasks and a number of narrow abilities (*specific factors*) involved in executing particular tasks. From Spearman's perspective, people's performance on any given task depends both on the general factor and on any specific factors that the task may involve. To the extent that two tasks or tests tap into the general factor and the same specific factor(s), people's performance on the two will be highly intercorrelated. To the extent that two tasks or tests reflect dissimilar specific factors, the correlation between them will be somewhat lower. For example, measures of various language skills (vocabulary, word recognition, reading comprehension, etc.) are all highly correlated, presumably because they all reflect both general intelligence and verbal ability (a specific factor). A particular measure of verbal ability (e.g., a vocabulary test) will correlate less highly with a measure of mathematical problem solving: The two measures both reflect general intelligence but tap into different specific abilities.

Many contemporary psychologists believe that sufficient evidence supports Spearman's concept of a general factor—often known simply as Spearman's **g**—in intelligence and that the ability to process information quickly may be at its root. Researchers often find substantial correlations between measures of information processing speed (e.g., reaction times to familiar stimuli) and IQ scores (Brody, 1992; Fry & Hale, 1996; Vernon, 1993). For example, children who more quickly learn and remember visual information when they are infants have substantially higher IQ scores when they reach ages 5 to 7 (Brody, 1992; Fagan, 1991; Thompson, Fagan, & Fulker, 1991).

Cattell's Fluid and Crystallized Intelligence

Cattell (1963, 1987) has found evidence for two distinctly different aspects of general intelligence (g). First, people differ in **fluid intelligence** (g_f), their ability to acquire knowledge quickly and thereby to adapt to new situations. Second, people differ in **crystallized intelligence** (g_c), the knowledge and skills they have accumulated from their experiences and schooling. The two aspects of intelligence are more or less relevant to different kinds of tasks. Fluid intelligence relates more to novel tasks, especially those that require rapid decision making and are largely nonverbal in nature. Crystallized intelligence is more important for familiar tasks, especially those that are heavily dependent on language and prior knowledge.

According to Cattell, fluid intelligence is largely the result of inherited biological factors, whereas crystallized intelligence depends on both fluid intelligence and experience and so is influenced by both heredity and environment (Cattell, 1980, 1987). Fluid intelligence peaks in late adolescence and begins to decline in the early 20s. In contrast, crystallized intelligence continues to increase throughout childhood, adolescence, and most of adulthood (Cattell, 1963).

Yet most psychologists (including Spearman and Cattell themselves) have acknowledged that neither a single g factor nor a distinction between g_f and g_c can account for all aspects of intelligent behavior—that more domain-specific abilities play a role as well. Furthermore, Spearman's and Cattell's approaches were almost entirely statistical in nature: Both theorists

g
General factor in intelligence that influences performance in a wide variety of tasks and content domains.

fluid intelligence
Ability to acquire knowledge quickly and thereby adapt readily to new situations.

crystallized intelligence
Knowledge and skills accumulated from prior experience and schooling.

mathematically analyzed the interrelationships among people's scores on a variety of tests of cognitive ability. The two theorists we consider next, while not discounting the value of a statistical approach, have considered other evidence as well, and they have reached somewhat different conclusions about the nature of intelligence.

Gardner's Multiple Intelligences

Howard Gardner acknowledges that a general factor may very well exist in intelligence, but he questions its usefulness in explaining people's performance in particular situations (Gardner, 1995). He proposes that people have several more specific abilities, or *multiple intelligences,* that are relatively independent of one another. Initially, Gardner identified seven distinct intelligences: linguistic, logical-mathematical, spatial, musical, bodily-kinesthetic, interpersonal, and intrapersonal (Gardner, 1983, 1993; Gardner & Hatch, 1990). More recently, he has found evidence for an eighth intelligence: naturalist (Gardner, 1998).

TABLE 6–1   Gardner's Eight Intelligences

TYPE OF INTELLIGENCE	EXAMPLES OF RELEVANT BEHAVIORS
Linguistic Intelligence The ability to use language effectively	• Making persuasive arguments • Writing poetry • Identifying subtle nuances in word meanings
Logical-Mathematical Intelligence The ability to reason logically, especially in mathematics and science	• Solving mathematical problems quickly • Generating mathematical proofs • Formulating and testing hypotheses about observed phenomena[1]
Spatial Intelligence The ability to notice details of what one sees and to imagine and "manipulate" visual objects in one's mind	• Conjuring up mental images in one's mind • Drawing a visual likeness of an object • Making fine discriminations among very similar objects
Musical Intelligence The ability to create, comprehend, and appreciate music	• Playing a musical instrument • Composing a musical work • Having a keen awareness of the underlying structure of music
Bodily-Kinesthetic Intelligence The ability to use one's body skillfully	• Dancing • Playing basketball • Performing pantomime
Interpersonal Intelligence The ability to notice subtle aspects of other people's behaviors	• Reading another's mood • Detecting another's underlying intentions and desires • Using knowledge of others to influence their thoughts and behaviors
Intrapersonal Intelligence Awareness of one's own feelings, motives, and desires	• Discriminating among such similar emotions as sadness and regret • Identifying the motives guiding one's own behavior • Using self-knowledge to relate more effectively with others
Naturalist Intelligence The ability to recognize patterns in nature and differences among natural objects and life-forms	• Identifying members of various species • Classifying natural forms (e.g., rocks, types of mountains) • Applying one's knowledge of nature in such activities as farming, landscaping, or hunting

[1]This example may remind you of Piaget's theory of cognitive development. Many of the stage-relevant characteristics that Piaget described fall within the realm of logical-mathematical intelligence.

Gardner's eight intelligences are described and illustrated in Table 6–1. If we look at this table with the opening case study in mind, we can reasonably conclude that Gina's exceptional talents lie primarily in the linguistic and logical-mathematical intelligences.

Gardner presents some evidence to support the existence of multiple intelligences. For instance, he describes people who are quite skilled in one area (perhaps in composing music) and yet have seemingly average abilities in the other areas. He also points out that people who suffer brain damage sometimes lose abilities that are restricted primarily to one intelligence; for instance, one person might show deficits primarily in language, whereas another might have difficulty with tasks that require spatial reasoning.

According to Gardner, intelligence is reflected somewhat differently in different cultures, depending on how each culture shapes and molds the raw talents of its growing children. For example, in Western culture, spatial intelligence might be reflected in painting, sculpture, or geometry. But among the Kikuyu people in Kenya, it might be reflected in one's ability to recognize every animal within one's own herd of livestock and to distinguish one's own animals from those of other families. Among the Gikwe bushmen of the Kalahari Desert, it might be reflected in the ability to recognize and remember many specific locations over a large area (perhaps over several hundred square miles), identifying each location by the rocks, bushes, and other landmarks found there (Gardner, 1983).

Gardner's perspective offers the possibility that the great majority of children are intelligent in one way or another. Many educators have wholeheartedly embraced such an optimistic view of human potential and propose that all students can successfully master classroom subject matter when instructional methods capitalize on each student's intellectual strengths (e.g., Armstrong, 1994; Campbell, Campbell, & Dickinson, 1998).

In psychological circles, however, reviews of Gardner's theory are mixed. Some psychologists do not believe that Gardner's evidence is sufficiently compelling to support the notion of eight distinctly different abilities (Brody, 1992; Kail, 1998). Others disagree that abilities in specific domains, such as in music or bodily movement, are really "intelligence" per se (Bracken, McCallum, & Shaughnessy, 1999). Many psychologists are simply taking a wait-and-see attitude about Gardner's theory until more research is conducted.

Sternberg's Triarchic Theory

Whereas Gardner focuses on different kinds of intelligence, Robert Sternberg (1984, 1985, 1997, 1998) focuses more on the nature of intelligence itself. Drawing on findings from research on human information processing, Sternberg proposes that intelligent behavior involves an interplay of three factors, all of which may vary from one occasion to the next: (1) the environmental *context* in which the behavior occurs, (2) the way in which one's prior *experiences* are brought to bear on a particular task, and (3) the *cognitive processes* required by that task. These three dimensions are summarized in Figure 6–1.

Role of Environmental Context Sternberg proposes that intelligent behavior involves adaptation: People must modify their responses to deal successfully with specific environmental conditions, modify the environment to better fit their own needs, or select an alternative environment more conducive to success. He also proposes that behavior may be more or less intelligent in different cultural contexts. For example, learning to read is an adaptive response in some cultures yet may be an irrelevant skill in others.

Sternberg has identified three general skills that are particularly adaptive in Western culture. One is *practical problem-solving ability,* such as the ability to identify exactly what the problem is in a particular situation, reason logically about the problem, and generate a multitude of possible problem solutions. A second skill is *verbal ability,* such as the ability to speak and write clearly, develop and use a large vocabulary, and understand and learn from what one reads. A third skill is *social competence,* such as the ability to relate effectively with other human beings, be sensitive to others' needs and wishes, and provide leadership.

Role of Prior Experiences Sternberg proposes that intelligent behavior sometimes involves the ability to deal successfully with a brand-new situation; at other times, it involves the ability to deal with familiar situations rapidly and efficiently. In both cases, an individual's prior experiences play a critical role. When people encounter a new task or problem, they must draw on past experience and consider the kinds of responses that have been effective in similar circumstances.

In Gardner's theory of multiple intelligences, the ability to draw lifelike renditions of three-dimensional objects falls in the domain of spatial intelligence. Art courtesy of Oscar, seventh grade (top), and Daniela, eighth grade (bottom).

FIGURE 6–1 Sternberg's triarchic model of intelligence

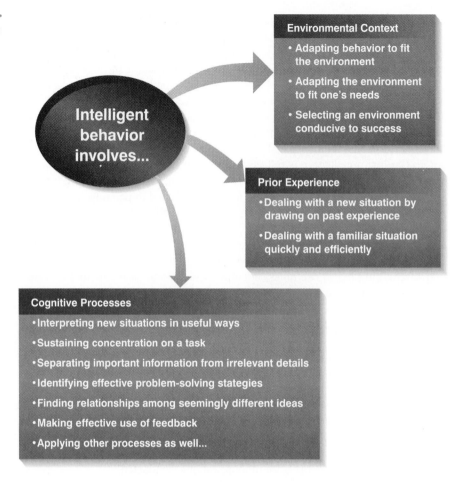

Intelligent behavior involves...

Environmental Context
- Adapting behavior to fit the environment
- Adapting the environment to fit one's needs
- Selecting an environment conducive to success

Prior Experience
- Dealing with a new situation by drawing on past experience
- Dealing with a familiar situation quickly and efficiently

Cognitive Processes
- Interpreting new situations in useful ways
- Sustaining concentration on a task
- Separating important information from irrelevant details
- Identifying effective problem-solving stategies
- Finding relationships among seemingly different ideas
- Making effective use of feedback
- Applying other processes as well...

When they deal with more familiar tasks, basic knowledge and skills related to the task must be sufficiently *automatized* that the task can be completed quickly and effortlessly. As noted in Chapter 5, automatization results from experience—from retrieving certain information and performing certain skills over and over again.

Role of Cognitive Processes In addition to considering how context and prior experience affect behavior, we must also consider how a person thinks about (mentally processes) a particular task or situation. Sternberg proposes that numerous cognitive processes are involved in intelligent behavior: interpreting a new situation in ways that promote successful adaptation, sustaining concentration on a task, separating important and relevant information from unimportant and irrelevant details, identifying possible strategies for solving a problem, finding relationships among seemingly different ideas, making effective use of external feedback about one's performance, and so on. Different cognitive processes are likely to be relevant to different situations, and thus an individual may behave more or less "intelligently" depending on the specific cognitive processes needed at the time.

To date, research neither supports nor refutes the notion that intelligence has the triarchic nature that Sternberg describes; most psychologists are reserving judgment until more evidence has accumulated. At the same time, Sternberg's theory reminds us that a child's ability to behave intelligently may vary considerably, depending on the particular context and specific knowledge, skills, and cognitive processes that a task requires. Some theorists believe that context makes all the difference in the world—a belief that is clearly evident in the concept of distributed intelligence.

Distributed Intelligence

Implicit in our discussion so far has been the assumption that intelligent behavior is something that individuals engage in with little if any help from the objects or people around them. But some theorists point out that people are far more likely to behave intelligently when they have the support of their physical, social, and cultural environments (Pea, 1993; Perkins, 1995; Sternberg & Wagner, 1994). For example, it's easier for many students to solve for x in the equation

$$\frac{7}{25} = \frac{x}{375}$$

if they have pencil and paper, or perhaps even a calculator, with which to work out the problem. Students are more likely to write a convincing persuasive essay if they brainstorm with their peers about possible arguments to make in support of a particular position or opinion about an issue. As we noted in Chapter 4, virtually anyone can perform more difficult tasks when he or she has the support structure, or *scaffolding,* to do so.

This idea that intelligent behavior depends on people's physical, social, and cultural support systems is sometimes referred to as **distributed intelligence.** People can "distribute" their thinking (and therefore think more intelligently) in at least three ways (Pea, 1993; Perkins, 1992, 1995). First, they can use physical objects, and especially technology (e.g., calculators, computers), to handle and manipulate large amounts of information. Second, they can work with other people to explore ideas and solve problems; after all, two heads are usually better than one. Third, they can represent and think about the situations they encounter using the various symbolic systems that their culture provides—for instance, the words, diagrams, charts, mathematical equations, and so on that help them simplify or summarize complex topics and problems.

From this perspective, intelligence is *not* a characteristic that resides "inside" people, nor is it something that could be easily measured and then summarized with a single test score. Instead, it is a highly variable and context-specific ability that virtually anyone can possess when the appropriate support system is available. The concept of distributed intelligence is still in its infancy, however. Much work remains to be done, both in delineating the specific ways in which the environment supports intelligent behavior and in determining how great an effect such support is likely to have.

The five theories just presented provide widely diverging views of the nature of human intelligence. Their differences with respect to the three themes—nature versus nurture, universality versus diversity, and qualitative versus quantitative change—are presented in the Basic Developmental Issues table on the next page. We turn now to a related topic: how various theorists have attempted to *measure* intelligence.

The concept of distributed intelligence reminds us that students often perform more intelligently when they work with others to tackle problems, have symbolic systems such as charts and equations to represent and transform information, and use computers to organize and manipulate data.

Measuring Intelligence

Although psychologists have not been able to pin down exactly what intelligence is, they have been trying to measure it for almost a century. In the early 1900s, school officials in France asked Alfred Binet to develop a way of identifying students who were unlikely to benefit from regular school instruction and would therefore be in need of special education. To accomplish the task, Binet devised a test that measured general knowledge, vocabulary, perception, memory, and abstract thought. He found that students who performed poorly on his test tended to have difficulty performing successfully in the classroom as well.

Binet's test was the earliest version of what we now call an **intelligence test.** Today, intelligence tests are widely used to assess children's cognitive development, with performance on these tests often being summarized as single IQ scores. In the next few pages, we look at several tests of general intelligence and at the derivation of IQ scores. We then consider specific ability tests and assessment of learning potential as two alternative approaches to measuring cognitive ability. Finally, we examine issues of validity and reliability in measuring intelligence.

Tests of General Intelligence

Most intelligence tests in use today have been developed to do the same thing that Alfred Binet's first test was intended to do: identify people with special needs. In many cases, intelligence

distributed intelligence
Thinking facilitated by physical objects and technology, social support, and concepts and symbols of one's culture.

intelligence test
General measure of current cognitive functioning, used primarily to predict academic achievement over the short run.

Contrasting Theories of Intelligence

		BASIC DEVELOPMENTAL ISSUES			
ISSUE	**SPEARMAN'S GENERAL FACTOR (*g*)**	**CATTELL'S FLUID AND CRYSTALLIZED INTELLIGENCE**	**GARDNER'S MULTIPLE INTELLIGENCES**	**STERNBERG'S TRIARCHIC THEORY**	**DISTRIBUTED INTELLIGENCE**
Nature and Nurture 	Spearman did not specifically address the issue of nature versus nurture. Subsequent researchers have found evidence that *g* is probably influenced by both heredity and environment.	Cattell proposed that fluid intelligence is largely the result of inherited factors. Crystallized intelligence is influenced by both heredity (because it depends partly on fluid intelligence) and environmental experiences.	Gardner believes that heredity provides some basis for individual differences in the eight intelligences. However, culture influences the form that each intelligence takes, and formal schooling influences the extent to which each intelligence flourishes.	Sternberg emphasizes the roles of environmental context (e.g., culture) and prior experience in intelligent behavior; thus, his focus is on nurture.	Environmental support mechanisms (physical tools, social interaction, and the symbolic representations of one's culture) influence a person's ability to behave intelligently.
Universality and Diversity	Spearman assumed that the existence of *g* is universal across cultures. However, people vary both in their general intellectual ability and in more specific abilities.	The distinction between fluid and crystallized intelligence is true across cultures. People within a particular culture differ in their fluid and crystallized abilities. In addition, the nature of crystallized intelligence (i.e., what specific knowledge and skills are important) varies from one cultural setting to the next.	According to Gardner, the eight intelligences are products of human evolution and so are universal worldwide. However, any particular intelligence will manifest itself differently in different environments and cultures.	The three factors of the triarchy (context, experience, cognitive processes) are universal. Different cultures may value and require different skills, however, so intelligence may take particular forms in each culture.	The physical, social, and symbolic support mechanisms at one's disposal vary widely from situation to situation and from one cultural group to another.
Qualitative and Quantitative Change	Spearman derived his theory from various tests of cognitive abilities. Implicit in such tests is the assumption that abilities change quantitatively over time.	Cattell, too, based his theory on numerical measures of various abilities. Thus, his emphasis was on quantitative changes in both fluid and crystallized intelligence.	Growth in each intelligence has both quantitative and qualitative elements. For example, in logical-mathematical intelligence, children gain skills in increments (quantitatively) but also acquire increasingly complex (and qualitatively different) abilities.	The effects of relevant prior experiences, more automatized knowledge and skills, and more efficient cognitive processes involve quantitative change. The acquisition of new strategies over time involves qualitative change.	Intelligent behavior is situation-specific and dependent on qualitative differences in context from one occasion to the next.

tests are used as part of a diagnostic battery of tests to determine why certain students are having difficulty in school and whether they require special educational services. In other instances, they are used to identify students with exceptionally high ability who are probably not being challenged by the regular school curriculum and may require more in-depth instruction or more advanced classwork for their cognitive growth.

Intelligence tests typically include a wide variety of questions and problems for students to tackle. The focus is not on what children have specifically been taught in school, but rather on what they have learned and deduced from their general, everyday experiences. Most intelligence tests include measures of deductive reasoning and problem solving. Many include questions involving general knowledge and vocabulary that most people have probably encountered in everyday life at one time or another. Some tests include analogies that tap the ability to recognize similarities among well-known relationships. And some ask students to manipulate concrete objects and analyze pictures and spatial relationships.

To give you a flavor for the nature of intelligence tests, we briefly describe three of them.

Wechsler Intelligence Scale for Children. One widely used intelligence test is the third edition of the *Wechsler Intelligence Scale for Children*, or *WISC-III* (Wechsler, 1991), which is designed for children and adolescents ages 6 to 16. The WISC-III consists of 13 subtests, each involving either verbal responses or object manipulation; examples of items like those on the WISC-III are presented in Figure 6–2. Some subtest scores are combined to obtain a *Verbal IQ* score; others are combined to obtain a *Performance* (i.e., nonverbal) *IQ* score. From the Verbal and Performance scores, a *Full-Scale IQ* score can also be derived.

What do intelligence tests look like? Here are items similar to those found on the verbal and performance portions of the WISC.

Items Similar to Those on Verbal Subtests
- How many wings does a bird have?
- What is the advantage of keeping money in a bank?
- If two buttons cost 15¢, what will be the cost of a dozen buttons?
- In what way are a saw and a hammer alike?

Items Similar to Those on Performance Subtests
- What's missing in this picture?

- Put these pictures in order so they tell a story that makes sense.

- Put these pieces together to make a duck.

FIGURE 6–2 Items similar to those found on the Wechsler Intelligence Scale for Children (WISC-III)

Simulated items similar to those in the *Wechsler Intelligence Scale for Children: Third Edition.* Copyright © 1991 by The Psychological Corporation, a Harcourt Assessment Company. Reproduced by permission. All rights reserved. "Wechsler Intelligence Scale for Children" and "WISC-III" are trademarks of The Psychological Corporation.

Stanford-Binet Intelligence Scale. A second commonly used test is the fourth edition of the *Stanford-Binet Intelligence Scale* (Thorndike, Hagen, & Sattler, 1986). The Stanford-Binet can be used with people ages 2 through adulthood. The individual being assessed is asked to perform a wide variety of tasks, most involving verbal material and responses (for example, defining vocabulary words, finding logical inconsistencies in a story, or interpreting proverbs) but a few involving manipulation of concrete objects (such as cardboard boxes, buttons, or blocks). The Stanford-Binet yields an overall IQ score, plus more specific scores in verbal reasoning, abstract/visual reasoning, quantitative reasoning, and short-term (i.e., working) memory.

Universal Nonverbal Intelligence Test. The WISC-III and Stanford-Binet depend heavily on language; even when tasks involve reasoning about strictly nonverbal, visual material (e.g., see the Performance items in Figure 6–2), the child is given verbal instructions about how to complete the tasks. One recently published instrument, the *Universal Nonverbal Intelligence Test,* or *UNIT* (Bracken & McCallum, 1998), involves no language whatsoever. Designed for children and adolescents ages 5 to 17, the UNIT consists of six subtests involving memory or reasoning regarding visual stimuli (Figure 6–3). Its content (e.g., people, mice, cheese) was chosen from objects and symbols presumed to be universal across all industrialized cultures. Instructions are given entirely through gestures, pantomime, and modeling, and the child responds by either pointing or manipulating objects.

Nonverbal tests such as the UNIT are especially useful for children who have hearing impairments, children who have language-related learning disabilities, and children for whom English is a second language. For instance, children who are deaf and children who have been raised speaking a language other than English perform better on the UNIT than on more traditional language-based intelligence tests (Maller, 2000; McCallum 1999).

IQ Scores In the early 20th century, some psychologists began to calculate scores for intelligence tests by comparing a child's *mental age* (i.e., referring to the age group whose performance was most similar to the child's performance) with his or her chronological age (Stern, 1912; Terman, 1916). The mathematical formula used involved division, and so the resulting score was called an *intelligence quotient,* or **IQ,** score.[1] Even though we still use the term *IQ,* intelligence test scores are no longer based on the old formula. Instead, they are determined by comparing a person's performance on the test with the performance of others in the same age group. Scores near 100 indicate average performance: People with a score of 100 have performed better than half of their age-mates on the test and not as well as the other half. Scores well below 100 indicate below-average performance on the test; scores well above 100 indicate above-average performance.

Figure 6–4 shows the percentage of people getting scores at different points along the scale (e.g., 12.9% get scores between 100 and 105). Notice how the curve is high in the middle and low at both ends. This shape tells us that many more people obtain scores close to 100 than scores very much higher or lower than 100. For example, if we add up the percentages in different parts of Figure 6–4, we find that approximately two-thirds (68%) of individuals in any particular age group score within 15 points of 100 (i.e., between 85 and 115). In contrast, only 2 percent score as low as 70, and only 2 percent score as high as 130. This symmetrical and predictable distribution of scores happens by design rather than by chance; psychologists have created a method of scoring intelligence test performance that intentionally yields such a distribution.[2]

Figure 6–4 does not include scores below 70 or above 130. Such scores are certainly possible but are relatively rare. For instance, Gina, from the opening case study, once obtained a score of 140 on an intelligence test. A score of 140 is equivalent to a percentile rank of 99.4; in other words, only 6 students out of every 1,000 would earn a score this high or higher.

IQ score
Score on an intelligence test determined by comparing one's performance with the performance of same-age peers.

---

[1] Alfred Binet himself objected to the use of intelligence quotients, believing that his tests were too imprecise to warrant such scores. Lewis Terman, an American psychologist, was largely responsible for popularizing the term *IQ* (Montagu, 1999a).

[2] If you have some knowledge of descriptive statistics, you probably recognize Figure 6–4 as a normal distribution. IQ scores are based on a normal distribution with a mean of 100 and, for most tests, a standard deviation of 15. (The Stanford-Binet Intelligence Scale has a standard deviation of 16.)

Symbolic Memory is primarily a measure of short-term visual memory and complex sequential memory for meaningful material. The task is to view a sequence of universal symbols for 5 seconds and then recreate it from memory using the Symbolic Memory Cards.

Spatial Memory is primarily a measure of short-term visual memory for abstract material. The task is to view a pattern of green and/or black dots on a 3 × 3- or 4 × 4-cell grid for 5 seconds and then recreate the pattern from memory using green and black chips on a blank Response Grid.

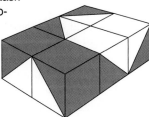

Object Memory is primarily a measure of short-term recognition and recall of meaningful symbolic material. The examinee is presented a randomly arranged pictorial array of common objects for 5 seconds, after which the stimulus page is removed, and a second pictorial array is presented containing all of the previously presented objects and additional objects to serve as foils. The task requires the examinee to identify objects presented in the first pictorial array by placing a response chip on the appropriate pictures.

Cube Design is primarily a measure of visual-spatial reasoning. The task requires the examinee to use two-colored cubes to construct a three-dimensional design that matches a stimulus picture.

Analogic Reasoning is primarily a measure of symbolic reasoning. The task requires the examinee to complete matrix analogies that employ both common objects and novel geometric figures by pointing to one of four multiple choice options.

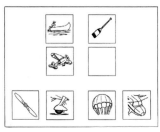

Mazes is primarily a measure of reasoning and planful behavior. The examinee uses paper and pencil to navigate and exit mazes by tracing a path from the center starting point of each maze to the correct exit, without making incorrect decisions en route. A series of increasingly complex mazes is presented.

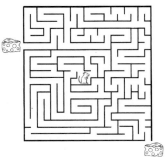

FIGURE 6–3 Items on the Universal Nonverbal Intelligence Test (UNIT)

FIGURE 6–4 Percentage of IQ scores in different ranges

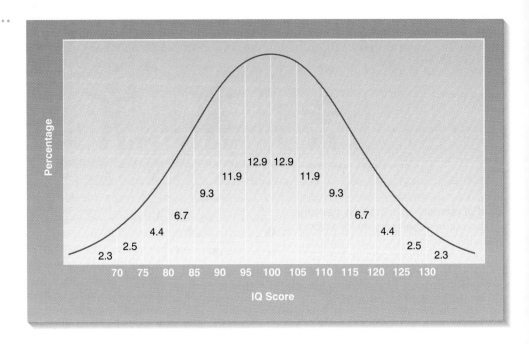

Whenever we use a general intelligence test to estimate a child's cognitive ability and then summarize the child's performance with a single IQ score, we are, to some extent, buying into Spearman's concept of *g*. An alternative approach, using specific ability tests, allows assessment of a child's cognitive capabilities *without* necessarily assuming that intelligence is a single entity.

Specific Ability Tests

Although intelligence tests sometimes yield subscores related to various aspects of reasoning or memory, their primary purpose is to assess overall cognitive functioning. In contrast, **specific ability tests** have been developed to assess particular cognitive abilities. Some of these tests, called *aptitude tests,* are designed to assess students' potential to learn in particular content domains, such as mathematics or auto mechanics. Others focus on specific aspects of cognitive processing (e.g., memory for auditory information, ability to think and reason about spatial relationships) and are often used in identifying children with learning disabilities.

Specific ability tests are more consistent with a multidimensional view of intelligence, such as Spearman's concept of specific abilities or Gardner's concept of multiple intelligences. Nevertheless, they get mixed reviews on whether they predict performance on particular tasks more accurately than general measures of intelligence (Anastasi & Urbina, 1997; McGrew et al., 1997; Neisser et al., 1996).

Assessment of Learning Potential

In recent years, some theorists have suggested an approach that focuses not on assessing existing cognitive abilities but on assessing people's ability to learn in new situations (Feuerstein, 1979; Feuerstein, Feuerstein, & Gross, 1997; Hamers & Ruijssenaars, 1997; Kozulin & Falik, 1995; Lidz, 1997). Such an approach, sometimes called *dynamic assessment* (see Chapter 4), is more consistent with Sternberg's contention that intelligence involves adaptation to new situations and with distributed intelligence theorists' suggestion that intelligent behavior is heavily context-dependent. Measures of learning potential are still in their infancy, but preliminary evidence indicates that they can sometimes provide a more optimistic view of students' abilities than more traditional intelligence tests do (Feuerstein, 1979; Hamers & Ruijssenaars, 1997; Lidz, 1997).

Validity and Reliability in Measures of Intelligence

In Chapter 2, we introduced you to the concepts of validity and reliability. In general, the *validity* of an intelligence test is the extent to which it measures what it is designed to measure. The *reliability* of an intelligence test is the extent to which it yields consistent, dependable scores.

specific ability test
Test designed to assess a specific cognitive skill or the potential to learn and perform in a specific content domain.

To determine the validity of intelligence tests, researchers have focused primarily on predictive validity and construct validity. When they consider the *predictive validity* of an intelligence test, they are concerned with how well test scores correlate with (and so predict) future performance, perhaps school achievement or job performance. When they consider the *construct validity* of an intelligence test, they are concerned with whether or not the test actually measures intelligence. Because the concept of "intelligence" is hard to pin down and, in any case, cannot be directly observed, researchers have used roundabout ways to address construct validity. The fact that scores on various intelligence tests tend to correlate with one another indicates that, to some extent, they are measuring the same thing—a "thing" that researchers assume is intelligence. Furthermore, children's performance on intelligence tests improves as they get older, consistent with the assumption that children do, in fact, become more intelligent with age.

Innumerable research studies have shown that traditional measures of general intelligence, such as the WISC-III and the Stanford-Binet, have both predictive and construct validity. On average, students who get higher scores on these tests do better on standardized achievement tests, have higher school grades, and complete more years of education (Brody, 1997; Gustafsson & Undheim, 1996; Neisser et al., 1996). To a lesser extent, IQ scores also predict people's later performance in the adult workplace (Sternberg, 1996). In addition, children's performance on IQ tests increases with age, and their scores on different tests tend to be quite similar. Because the UNIT has only recently arrived on the scene, we do not yet have data about its long-term predictive powers, but preliminary evidence indicates that it, too, has construct validity and predictive validity for the short run (Farrell & Phelps, 2000; McCallum & Bracken, 1997; Young & Assing, 2000). Many specific ability tests also have some predictive and construct validity (Anastasi & Urbina, 1997; Cohen & Swerdlik, 1999).

To determine the reliability of intelligence tests, researchers look at various indications of consistency, especially the extent to which different items and subtests within a particular test yield similar results for a particular individual (*internal consistency reliability*), the extent to which two different examiners score a child's performance in the same way (*interrater reliability*), and the extent to which the same test yields similar scores on two different occasions (*test-retest reliability*). The WISC-III, Stanford-Binet, and UNIT are highly reliable in these respects, as are most published tests of specific abilities (Anastasi & Urbina, 1997; Cohen & Swerdlik, 1999; Young & Assing, 2000).

Although the idea of assessing learning potential has considerable promise, existing instruments and procedures lack the validity and reliability of more traditional approaches (Reschly, 1997). Accordingly, when practitioners use them to assess children's abilities, they should do so cautiously and *always* within the context of other data.

Most psychologists are reasonably certain that intelligence tests *do* measure intelligence to some degree, and that they measure it in a fairly reliable fashion. Theorists are less certain about whether the scores on such tests primarily reflect children's inherited abilities, on the one hand, or their environments and background experiences, on the other. In the next section, we sort through the data concerning the relative effects of heredity and environment.

Hereditary and Environmental Influences on Intelligence

It is often difficult to separate the relative influences of heredity and environment on human characteristics. People who have similar genetic makeup (e.g., brothers and sisters, parents and their children) typically live in similar environments as well. So when we see similarities in IQ among members of the same family, it is hard to know whether those similarities are due to the genes or to the environments that family members share. Nevertheless, a significant body of research tells us that both heredity and environment affect intelligence, at least as it is reflected in IQ scores.

Evidence for Hereditary Influences

Earlier we mentioned that measures of information processing speed correlate with IQ scores. Speed of processing depends on neurological efficiency and maturation, which are genetically controlled. From this standpoint, then, we have some support for a hereditary basis for intelligence (Perkins, 1995). We find additional evidence in the general observation that children with certain genetic defects (e.g., Down syndrome) have, on average, significantly lower IQ scores than their nondisabled peers (Keogh & MacMillan, 1996). Two additional sources of evidence, twin studies and adoption studies, also indicate that intelligence has a genetic component.

Twin Studies Numerous studies have used monozygotic (identical) twins and dizygotic (fraternal) twins to get a sense of how strongly heredity affects IQ. Because monozygotic twins begin as a single fertilized egg which then separates, they are genetically equivalent human beings. In contrast, dizygotic (fraternal) twins are conceived as two separate fertilized eggs; they share about 50% of their genetic makeup, with the other 50% being unique to each twin. If identical twins have more similar IQ scores than fraternal twins, then we can reasonably suspect that heredity influences intelligence.

Most twins are raised together by the same parent(s) and in the same home; thus, they share similar environments as well as similar genes. Yet even when twins are raised separately (perhaps because they have been adopted and raised by different parents), they typically have similar IQ scores (Bouchard & McGue, 1981; Brody, 1992; Mackintosh, 1998; Plomin & Petrill, 1997). In a review of twin studies, Bouchard and McGue (1981) found these average (median) correlations:

	Correlations of Twins' IQs
Identical twins raised in the same home	.86
Identical twins raised in different homes	.72
Fraternal twins raised in the same home	.60

The correlation of .72 indicates that identical twins raised in different environments nevertheless tend to have very similar IQ scores. In fact, these twins are more similar to each other than are fraternal twins raised in the *same* home.[3]

Adoption Studies Another way to separate the effects of heredity and environment is to compare adopted children with both their adoptive and biological parents. Adopted children share a similar environment with their adoptive parents; they share a similar genetic makeup with their biological parents. When researchers obtain IQ scores for adopted children and for both their biological and adoptive parents, they typically find that the children's IQ scores are more highly correlated with the scores of their biological parents than with the scores of their adoptive parents. In other words, in a group of people who place their infants up for adoption, those with the highest IQs tend to have offspring who, despite being raised by other people, also have the highest IQs. Furthermore, the IQ correlations between adopted children and their biological parents become stronger, and those between the children and their adoptive parents become weaker, as the children grow older, especially during late adolescence (Bouchard, 1997; McGue, Bouchard, Iacono, & Lykken, 1993; Plomin, Fulker, Corley, & DeFries, 1997; Plomin & Petrill, 1997). (If you find this last finding puzzling, we will offer an explanation for it shortly.)

Twin studies and adoption studies do not completely separate the effects of heredity and environment (Wahlsten & Gottlieb, 1997). For example, adopted children have shared at least 9 months' worth of environment—in particular, the 9 months of prenatal development—with their biological mothers. Likewise, monozygotic twins who are raised in separate homes have shared a common prenatal environment. Despite such minor glitches, twin and adoption stud-

Even when identical twins are raised by different families, they typically have similar IQ scores, indicating that intelligence has a biological component. However, twins raised in different homes are somewhat *less* similar than twins raised in the same home, indicating that environment affects intelligence as well.

---

[3]In our own teaching experiences, we have found that some students erroneously interpret the higher correlations as indicating that identical twins have higher intelligence. Such is not the case; the size of the correlations indicates the strength of the relationship, not the level of intelligence.

ies point convincingly to a strong genetic component in intelligence (e.g., Bouchard, 1997; Brody, 1992; Hunt, 1997; Petrill & Wilkerson, 2000).

This is not to say that children are predestined to have an intelligence level similar to that of their biological parents. In fact, most children with high intelligence are conceived by parents of average intelligence rather than by parents with high IQ scores (Plomin & Petrill, 1997). Children's genetic ancestry, then, is hardly a surefire predictor of what their own potential is likely to be. Environment also makes a difference, as we shall see now.

Evidence for Environmental Influences

Numerous sources of evidence converge to indicate that environment has a significant impact on IQ scores. We find some of this evidence in twin studies and adoption studies. Studies of the effects of home environment, early nutrition, early intervention, and formal schooling provide additional support for the influence of environment. Also, a steady increase in performance on intelligence tests over the past few years—known as the Flynn effect—is almost certainly attributable to environmental factors.

Twin Studies and Adoption Studies Revisited Look once again at the IQ correlations for identical twins raised in the same home versus in different homes. The median correlation for twins raised in different homes is .72; that for twins raised in the same home is .86. In other words, twins raised in different homes have less similar IQs than twins raised in the same home. The distinct environments that different families provide *do* have some influence on intellectual development.

Adoption studies, too, indicate that intelligence is not determined entirely by heredity (Capron & Duyme, 1989; Devlin, Fienberg, Resnick, & Roeder, 1995; Waldman, Weinberg, & Scarr, 1994). For instance, in a study by Scarr and Weinberg (1976), some children of poor parents (with unknown IQs) were adopted by middle-class parents with average IQs of 118–121. Others remained with their biological parents. Average IQs of the children in the two groups were as follows:

	Average IQs
Adopted children	105
Nonadopted children	90

Although the adopted children's IQ scores were, on average, lower than those of their adoptive parents, they were about 15 points higher than those of the control group raised by their biological parents.

Effects of Home Environment One likely explanation for the beneficial effects of adoption in studies such as these is that the adoptive parents, who had more financial resources and higher levels of education, may have provided a more stimulating home environment than many of the low-income biological parents would have been able to provide. In fact, stimulating home environments—those in which parents interact frequently with their children, make numerous learning and reading materials available, encourage the development of new skills, use complex linguistic structures in conversation, and so on—are associated with higher IQ scores in children (Bradley & Caldwell, 1984; Brooks-Gunn, Klebanov, & Duncan, 1996; McGowan & Johnson, 1984). Studies of home environment are typically correlational in nature, however, so do not show conclusively that home environment *causes* any observed differences in intelligence. An alternative explanation for the same results is that more intelligent parents provide more stimulating environments *and,* through heredity, produce more intelligent children.

Recently, Segal (2000) took a somewhat different approach in studying the possible effects of home environment on intelligence. She identified 90 sets of "virtual twins": pairs of *un*related children of about the same age (no more than 9 months apart) living in the same home. Some of these "twins" consisted of two adopted children, and others consisted of one adopted and one biological child, but in every case they had shared the same home since their first birthday. Segal found a small positive correlation (.26) between the IQs of these pairs; such a correlation, small as it was, could be attributed only to a common environment (Segal, 2000).

Research indicates that stimulating preschool experiences often increase IQ, at least over the short run.

Effects of Early Nutrition Severe malnutrition, either before birth or during the early years of life, can limit neurological development and thereby have a long-term influence on cognitive development (D'Amato, Chitooran, & Whitten, 1992). Poor nutrition in the early years is associated with lower IQ scores, poorer attention and memory, and lower school achievement (Eysenck & Schoenthaler, 1997; Lozoff, 1989; Miller, 1995; Ricciuti, 1993; Scott-Jones, 1984).

Effects of Early Intervention When children live in impoverished home environments, enriching preschool programs and other forms of early intervention can make a difference. For instance, Head Start and other preschool programs frequently lead to short-term gains in IQ scores (Bronfenbrenner, 1999a; Ramey, 1992; Seitz, Rosenbaum, & Apfel, 1985; Zigler & Finn-Stevenson, 1987). The effects of such programs don't continue indefinitely, however; without follow-up interventions once children reach school age, any advantages in terms of IQ scores diminish over time and may disappear altogether (Bronfenbrenner, 1999a; Campbell & Ramey, 1995; Gustafsson & Undheim, 1996).

We must not be disheartened by such results. For one thing, publicly funded preschool programs such as Head Start often enroll the most economically disadvantaged children in the community. To study the long-term effects of these programs, researchers sometimes have difficulty finding an appropriate control group; for instance, they may compare children who attended the programs with children who, though not attending preschool, grew up in more advantaged circumstances (Schnur, Brooks-Gunn, & Shipman, 1992). Furthermore, early intervention may lead to long-term improvements in areas not reflected in IQ test scores; for instance, in one series of studies, children who attended an intensive daycare program from 3 months until 5 years of age were achieving at higher levels in reading, writing, and mathematics even at ages 12 and 15 (Campbell & Ramey, 1994, 1995). Furthermore, children who attend intensive, academically oriented preschool programs are less likely to need special education services later on, and they are more likely to graduate from high school (Campbell & Ramey, 1995; Royce, Darlington, & Murray, 1983).

Effects of Formal Schooling The very act of attending school leads to small increases in IQ. Students who begin their educational careers early and attend school regularly have higher IQ scores than students who do not. When students must start school later than they would otherwise for reasons beyond their families' control, their IQs are about 5 points lower for every year of delay. Furthermore, children's IQ scores decline slightly over the course of the summer months, when children are not attending school. And other things being equal, students who drop out have lower IQ scores than students who remain in school. For every year of high school not completed, IQ drops an average of 1.8 points (Ceci & Williams, 1997).

The Flynn Effect The last few decades have seen a slow, steady, worldwide increase in people's average performance on IQ tests; this trend is commonly known as the **Flynn effect** (Flynn, 1987, 1999). A similar change has been observed in children's performance on traditional Piagetian tasks (Flieller, 1999). Such improvement is difficult to attribute to heredity because the same gene pool (albeit with an occasional mutation) is passed along from one generation to the next. Instead, psychologists credit better nutrition, better schooling, more enriching and informative stimulation (increased access to television, reading materials, etc.), and other improvements in people's environments (Flieller, 1999; Flynn, 1987; Neisser et al., 1996).

How Nature and Nurture Interact in Their Influence

Clearly, both nature and nurture play a role in the development of intelligence. Some theorists have asked the question, "How much does each of these factors influence IQ?" and have estimated the relative contribution of genetics (the *heritability* of IQ) from the correlations ob-

Flynn effect
Gradual increase in intelligence test performance observed worldwide over the past several decades.

tained in twin and adoption studies (e.g., McGue et al., 1993; Plomin et al., 1997). Such heritability estimates typically attribute at least 40% of intelligence, and often more, to inherited factors (Petrill & Wilkerson, 2000). But other theorists point out that such estimates are derived from populations with limited environmental variability (e.g., the research sample may be comprised largely of middle-income families living in a single culture) and so probably underestimate the role that environmental differences play in intellectual development (e.g., Biesheuvel, 1999; Bronfenbrenner, 1999b; Ceci, Rosenblum, de Bruyn, & Lee, 1997).

Many psychologists believe that it may ultimately be impossible to separate the relative effects of heredity and environment. They suggest that the two combine to influence children's cognitive development and measured IQ in ways that we can probably never disentangle (Bidell & Fischer, 1997; Halpern & LaMay, 2000; Plomin, 1994; Rutter, 1997; Yee, 1995). Theorists have made these general points about how nature and nurture interact as they affect intellectual development:

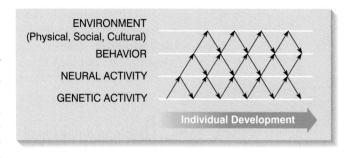

FIGURE 6–5 Bidirectional influences among genetic activity, neural activity, behavior, and environment

From *Individual Development and Evolution: The Genesis of Novel Behavior* (p. 186), by G. Gottlieb, 1992, New York: Oxford University Press. Reprinted with permission.

■ *Genetic expression is influenced by environmental conditions.* Genes require environmental support (e.g., adequate nutrition) to do their work (see Chapter 3). Thus, they are not entirely self-contained, independent "carriers" of developmental instructions; the particular instructions they transmit are influenced by the environments in which they operate (Bidell & Fischer, 1997).

In an extremely impoverished environment—one with a lack of adequate nutrition and little if any stimulation—heredity may have little to say about the extent to which children develop intellectually (Plomin & Petrill, 1997). Yet in an ideal environment—one in which nutrition, parenting practices, and educational opportunities are optimal and age-appropriate—heredity is more likely to have a significant influence on children's IQ scores (Rowe, Jacobson, & Van den Oord, 1999).

■ *Heredity establishes a range rather than a precise figure.* Heredity does not dictate that a child will have a particular IQ score. Instead, it appears to set a *range* of abilities within which children will eventually fall, with the specific level of ability each one achieves depending on his or her specific environmental experiences (Weinberg, 1989). Heredity may also affect how susceptible or impervious a child is to particular environmental influences (Rutter, 1997).

■ *Especially as they get older, children choose their environments and experiences.* Children may actively seek out environmental conditions that match their inherited abilities—a phenomenon known as **niche-picking** (Halpern & LaMay, 2000; Petrill & Wilkerson, 2000; Scarr & McCartney, 1983). For example, children who, genetically speaking, have exceptional quantitative reasoning ability may enroll in advanced mathematics courses, participate in their school's mathematics competitions, delight in tackling mathematical brainteasers, and in other ways nurture their inherited talents. Children with average quantitative ability are less likely to take on such challenges and so have fewer opportunities to develop their mathematical skills. In such circumstances, the relative effects of heredity and environment are difficult to tease apart.

Earlier we mentioned that the IQ correlations between adopted children and their biological parents become *stronger* over time. We now have a possible explanation for this finding. Children gain increasing independence as they get older. Particularly as they reach adolescence, they spend less time in their home environments, and they make more of their own decisions—decisions undoubtedly based, in part, on their natural talents and tendencies (McGue et al., 1993; Petrill & Wilkerson, 2000).

You might think of intelligence as being the result of four factors (Gottlieb, 1992). *Genetic activity* affects *neural activity,* which in turn affects *behavior,* which in turn affects the *environment*. But influence moves in the opposite direction as well: The environment affects behavior, and these two (through stimulation, nutritional intake, physical activity, etc.) affect neural activity and genetic expression. The continuing interplay of genetics, neural activity, behavior, and environment is depicted in Figure 6–5.

niche-picking
Tendency to actively seek out environments that match one's inherited abilities.

Theorists continue to debate the relative influences of heredity and environment on intelligence. From the standpoint of research evidence, the effects of both nature and nurture are well established. Probably a more fruitful course of action for researchers is to examine more closely the specific ways in which the two work together to direct and foster intellectual growth (Bidell & Fischer, 1997; Hunt, 1997; Wahlsten & Gottlieb, 1997).

Developmental Trends in IQ Scores

In one sense, children definitely become more "intelligent" as they develop: They know more, can think in more complex ways, and can solve problems more effectively. However, IQ scores are not based on how much children develop over a period of years; instead, they are based on how well children perform in comparison with their age-mates. On average, then, IQ does not increase with age; by definition, the average IQ score for any age group is 100.

Yet IQ scores do change in two ways over the course of development:

■ *IQ scores become increasingly stable.* Measures of cognitive growth in the first few years of life often have little or no relationship to intelligence in later years (Hayslip, 1994; McCall, 1993; Neisser et al., 1996). "Bright" babies do not necessarily become the brightest fourth graders, and "slow" toddlers may eventually catch up to, or even surpass, their peers. In fact, toddlers and preschoolers often show considerable variability in their test scores from one occasion to the next.

There are at least two reasons for the instability of IQ scores in the early years. First, young children's test performance is often influenced by a variety of unstable and irrelevant factors, including short attention span, misinterpretation of instructions, lack of interest in the test being administered, and so on; in other words, the test scores have lower *reliability* than those of older children and adolescents (Bracken & Walker, 1997; Messick, 1983; Wodtke, Harper, & Schommer, 1989). Second, the nature of items on intelligence tests changes considerably as children grow older. For instance, psychomotor skills (e.g., stacking blocks) typically play a key role in children's performance on infant development tests yet are largely irrelevant to their performance on tests administered in elementary school. The Developmental Trends table on the following page identifies some commonly used indicators of intelligence at different age levels plus additional considerations to keep in mind at each level.

As children progress through the school years, their IQ scores become increasingly stable. Although children continue to develop cognitively, each one's *relative* intelligence in comparison with peers changes less over time (Bloom, 1964; Brody, 1992; Neisser et al., 1996). As an example, look once again at the chapter's opening case study. Gina obtained an IQ score of 140 (equivalent to the 99th percentile) in junior high school and performed at a similar level on college aptitude tests several years later.

Despite this increasing stability, we must remember that IQ scores simply reflect a student's performance on a particular test at a particular time; longitudinal studies indicate that *some* change (often as much as 10 to 20 points' worth, and occasionally even more) can reasonably be expected over the years (McCall, 1993). In fact, the longer the time interval between two administrations of an IQ test, the greater the change in IQ we are likely to see, especially when young children are involved (Bloom, 1964; Humphreys, 1992; McCall, 1993). IQ scores and other measures of cognitive ability often increase over time when children are highly motivated and independent learners and when parents and other adults provide stimulating activities and a variety of reading materials (Echols, West, Stanovich, & Kehr, 1996; Sameroff et al., 1993; Stanovich, West, & Harrison, 1995). Even adults can show noticeable increases in IQ under the right circumstances—for instance, when they pursue advanced training or education (Sticht, Armstrong, Hickey, & Caylor, 1987).

■ *IQ scores become increasingly better predictors of future achievement.* Intelligence tests have greater predictive validity when students are older than when they are younger. Tests given in the preschool and early elementary years—for instance, the school "readiness" tests that are often given to children before they enroll in kindergarten—are often relatively inaccurate estimates of how well children will do in school several years later (Pellegrini, 1998; Sanders, 1997; Wodtke et al., 1989). Accordingly, tests administered in the early years should *not* be used to make long-term predictions about school achievement; they are more appropriately used for screening

Intelligence at Different Age Levels

AGE	WHAT YOU MIGHT OBSERVE	DIVERSITY	IMPLICATIONS
Early Childhood (2–6) 	• Success on test items that involve naming objects, stacking blocks, drawing circles and squares, remembering short lists, and following simple directions • Short attention span, which influences test performance • Variability in test scores from one occasion to the next	• Significant developmental delays in the early years may indicate mental retardation or other disabilities. • On average, children from lower-income families perform at lower levels on measures of cognitive development than children from middle-income families; however, enriching preschool experiences can decrease and occasionally eliminate this difference.	• Use IQ tests primarily to identify significant delays in cognitive development; follow up by seeking appropriate programs for children with such delays. • Do *not* use IQ scores obtained in the early years to predict academic achievement over the long run. • Provide preschool experiences that foster children's language skills, knowledge of numbers and counting, and visual-spatial thinking.
Middle Childhood (6–10) 	• Success on test items that involve defining concrete words, remembering sentences and short sequences of digits, understanding concrete analogies, recognizing similarities among objects, and identifying absurdities in illogical statements • Some consistency in test scores from one occasion to the next • Noticeable differences among students in mastery of classroom subject matter	• Children with mild disabilities (e.g., mild learning disabilities) may perform poorly on some subtests of an intelligence test. • At this age, many intelligence tests become increasingly verbal in nature; thus, proficiency with the English language can significantly affect test performance. • Children from some ethnic minority groups may perform poorly in situations where the test-giver has not established rapport and a sense of trust.	• Individualize instruction to match students' varying abilities to learn classroom topics. • Do *not* assume that poor performance in some areas of the curriculum necessarily indicates limited ability to learn in other areas. • Take children's cultural and linguistic backgrounds into account when interpreting IQ scores.
Early Adolescence (10–14)	• Success on test items that involve defining commonly used abstract words, drawing logical inferences from verbal descriptions, and identifying similarities between opposite concepts • Considerable variability among students in their ability to understand abstract material	• Adolescents from some ethnic minority groups may associate high test performance with "acting White" and so intentionally perform poorly. • Some students who are gifted may try to hide their talents; cultures that stress traditional male and female roles may actively discourage females from achieving at high levels.	• Expect considerable diversity in students' ability to master abstract classroom material, and individualize instruction accordingly. • Make sure that a school's enrichment programs include students from ethnic minority groups; do not rely exclusively on IQ scores when identifying students as gifted (see Observation Guidelines on p. 225).
Late Adolescence (14–18)	• Success on test items that involve defining infrequently encountered vocabulary, identifying differences between similar abstract words, interpreting proverbs, and breaking down complex geometric figures into their component parts • Relative stability in most students' IQ scores • Increasing independence to seek out opportunities consistent with existing ability levels (niche-picking)	• Fears of "acting White" or in other ways appearing "too smart" may continue into the high school years.	• Provide challenging educational activities for students who are gifted. • Encourage bright students from lower-income families to pursue a college education, and help them with the logistics of college applications (e.g., applying for financial aid).

Sources: Brooks-Gunn et al., 1996; Colombo, 1993; David & Rimm, 1998; Luckasson et al., 1992; McLoyd, 1998b; Ogbu, 1994; Terman & Merrill, 1972; Thorndike et al., 1986; Wechsler, 1991.

Educators should never base their expectations for students' achievement solely on intelligence test scores; many students may achieve at higher levels than their IQ scores predict.

children for significant developmental delays that require immediate intervention (Colombo, 1993; Lidz, 1991).

Teachers and other practitioners should remember two additional points about the relationship between intelligence test scores and school achievement. First, intelligence does not necessarily *cause* achievement. Even though students with high IQs typically perform well in school, we cannot say conclusively that their high achievement is actually the result of their intelligence. Intelligence probably does play an important role in school achievement, but many other factors—motivation, quality of instruction, parental support, family income, peer group norms, and so on—are also involved. Second, the relationship between IQ scores and achievement is not a perfect one; there are many exceptions to the rule. For a variety of reasons, some students with high IQ scores do not perform well in the classroom. And other students achieve at higher levels than would be predicted from their IQ scores alone. Educators should never base their expectations for students' achievement solely on intelligence test scores.

Group Differences in Intelligence

By design, intelligence tests reveal individual differences in children's general cognitive ability. But what do these tests reveal about *group* differences? Here we examine research findings related to possible socioeconomic, gender, ethnic, and racial differences in intelligence test performance.

As you read this section, please keep two principles in mind. First, *there is a great deal of individual variability within any group*. We will describe how children of different groups perform on average, yet some children are very different from that "average" description. Second, *there is almost always a great deal of overlap between any two groups*. As an example, consider gender differences in verbal ability. Research studies often find that girls have slightly higher verbal performance than boys (Halpern & LaMay, 2000; Lueptow, 1984; Maccoby & Jacklin, 1974). Yet the difference is typically quite small, with a great deal of overlap between the two groups. Figure 6–6 shows the typical overlap between girls and boys on measures of verbal ability: Notice that many of the boys are better than some of the girls despite the average advantage for girls. Obviously, we could not use such data to make predictions about how *particular* girls and boys would perform in a classroom setting.

Socioeconomic Differences

A person's **socioeconomic status** (often abbreviated as **SES**) encompasses such variables as family income, occupation, and level of education—variables that reflect the individual's general social and economic standing in society. On average, children from low-SES families earn lower IQ scores than children from middle-SES families; they also perform at lower levels on achievement tests, are more likely to be placed in special education programs, and are less likely to graduate from high school (Brooks-Gunn et al., 1996; McLoyd, 1998b). Children who grow up in persistently impoverished conditions are at greatest risk for poor performance in these respects, but even children who endure only short-term poverty suffer to some degree (McLoyd, 1998b).

Several factors probably contribute to differences in IQ and school achievement among socioeconomic groups (McLoyd, 1998b; Miller, 1995). Poor nutrition and health care, both before and after birth, can interfere with maximal neurological development. On average, children of poor families have less cognitive stimulation at home, for many possible reasons. Parents who work long hours (especially single parents) may have little time to spend with their children and may be unable to find or afford high-quality child care; some parents with limited educational backgrounds have never learned much about children's developmental needs (Edwards & Garcia, 1994; Portes, 1996); and the family may, in general, be preoccupied with its survival and physical well-being. Once children begin school, they may lack essential knowledge and skills (e.g., fa-

socioeconomic status (SES)
One's general social and economic standing in society, encompassing such variables as family income, occupation, and level of education.

miliarity with letters and numbers) upon which more advanced learning depends. Their lower school attendance rates, due to frequent health problems, family crises, and changes of residence, further decrease their opportunities for cognitive growth.

In addition, teachers—especially those who have grown up in middle-income families—often have lower academic expectations for children from lower-income homes; as a result, they may give these children less time and attention, fewer opportunities to learn, and less challenging assignments (Alexander, Entwisle, & Thompson, 1987; McLoyd, 1998b; Rosenthal, 1994). Unwittingly, then, teachers may exacerbate any socioeconomic differences in cognitive ability that already exist.

As we have already seen, enriching preschool experiences can boost IQ scores (at least over the short run) and enhance school achievement for children from lower-income families. Programs that teach parents how to provide stimulating activities for their growing children also appear to make a difference (Campbell & Ramey, 1994). And when teachers have high expectations for students from lower-income backgrounds, the students are more likely to perform at high levels (Midgley, Feldlaufer, & Eccles, 1989; Phillips, 1997).

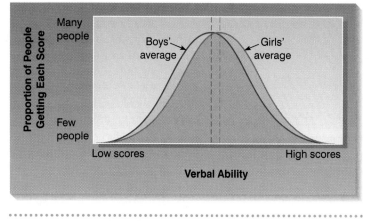

FIGURE 6–6 Typical "difference" between girls and boys in verbal activity

Gender Differences

Males and females are, on average, equivalent in general intellectual ability. Apart from a greater frequency of mental retardation in boys than girls, there are rarely any significant gender differences in IQ scores (Halpern, 1997; Neisser et al., 1996). This finding is at least partly a function of how intelligence tests are developed: As a general rule, test constructors eliminate any test items on which one gender performs better than the other.

Average differences in more specific cognitive abilities are sometimes found but are usually small. For example, females are often slightly better at such verbal tasks as reading and writing (Halpern, 1997; Hedges & Nowell, 1995; Maccoby & Jacklin, 1974). Males typically perform somewhat better on tasks involving visual-spatial thinking, which require people to imagine two- or three-dimensional figures and mentally manipulate them (Eisenberg et al., 1996; Halpern, 1997; Law, Pellegrino, & Hunt, 1993). In any ability differences of this sort, there is typically a great deal of overlap between the two genders.

Some gender differences in specific intellectual abilities may be partly due to subtle biological differences in the brain (Halpern & LaMay, 2000; Neisser et al., 1996; O'Boyle & Gill, 1998). Environmental factors appear to play a role as well. In our society, boys and girls often have distinctly different experiences growing up. For instance, boys are more likely to have toys that require physical manipulation in space (building blocks, model airplanes, footballs, etc.), and such items can foster the development of visual-spatial skills. In contrast, girls are more likely to have dolls, housekeeping items (e.g., dishes, plastic food), and board games—items that are apt to encourage verbal communication with peers (Halpern, 1992; Liss, 1983; Sprafkin, Serbin, Denier, & Connor, 1983). In addition, researchers sometimes observe other patterns of gender differences in particular ethnic groups—for instance, Hispanic girls may demonstrate better visual-spatial ability than Hispanic boys—and such findings weaken the argument for biological differences (Huston, 1983; Schratz, 1978).

In recent years, perhaps because of the push for more equitable educational opportunities, males and females have become increasingly *similar* in the abilities that they demonstrate (Eisenberg et al., 1996; Gustafsson & Undheim, 1996; Jacklin, 1989). For all intents and purposes, teachers should expect boys and girls to have similar academic aptitudes for the various subject areas that make up the school curriculum.

Ethnic and Racial Differences

Some measures of early cognitive functioning in infants reveal no differences among ethnic groups (Fagan & Singer, 1983). However, ethnic and racial differences in intelligence and more specific cognitive abilities appear in the preschool years and persist throughout childhood and adolescence. *On average,* Asian Americans and European Americans outperform African Americans and Hispanic Americans (Brody, 1992; Bruer, 1997; McCallum, 1999; Neisser et al., 1996). In some studies, Asian Americans score at the highest levels of all, outscoring European Americans by 1 to 5 points (Brody, 1992; Flynn, 1991).

Speculations about the source of such differences have prompted considerable debate. In the 1994 book *The Bell Curve,* Richard Herrnstein and Charles Murray used three consistently observed group differences—European American families have higher incomes than African American families, children from upper- and middle-income families have higher IQ scores than children from lower-income families, and European American children have higher IQ scores than African American children—to conclude that European Americans have the genetic advantage over African Americans. As you might suspect, the book generated considerable controversy and a great deal of outrage.

Scholars have poked many holes in *The Bell Curve* (Jacoby & Glauberman, 1995; Marks, 1995; Montagu, 1999b). For instance, they find numerous weaknesses in the research studies and statistical analyses that Herrnstein and Murray described; as one simple example, they remind us that we can never draw conclusions about causation by looking only at correlational studies. They argue that any innate differences in intelligence have not had sufficient time to evolve, nor does it seem logical that some groups would evolve to be less adaptive (i.e., less intelligent) than others. They point out, too, that the very concept of *race,* though widely used to categorize people in our society, has no basis in biology: It is virtually impossible to identify a person's "race" by analyzing his or her DNA.

Most psychologists today believe that environmental factors are largely to blame for ethnic and racial differences in IQ scores. Various theorists have suggested that socioeconomic status, discriminatory practices, cultural bias, and motivation may be involved. Let's look briefly at each of these explanations.

Socioeconomic Status. One likely reason for the lower IQ scores of African American and Hispanic American children is that, on average, these children live in families and neighborhoods with lower incomes than do European American children. Socioeconomic status affects the quality of prenatal and postnatal nutrition, availability of stimulating books and toys, access to educational opportunities, and other environmental factors that are likely to affect intellectual development (Brooks-Gunn et al., 1996; McLoyd, 1998b).

Discriminatory Practices. Even if different ethnic and racial groups had similar economic resources, systematic and long-term discrimination (e.g., exclusion from better schools and jobs, lower expectations for classroom performance) may limit minority children's opportunities for intellectual growth (Ogbu, 1994). Widespread discrimination may cause heredity to have an *indirect* effect on intelligence, in that inherited skin color or other physical characteristics (rather than inherited intellectual potential per se) elicit responses from society that affect intellectual development. Block (1999) offers a helpful analogy:

> Consider a culture in which red-haired children are beaten over the head regularly, but all other children are treated well. This effect will increase the measured heritability of IQ because red-haired identical twins will tend to resemble one another in IQ (because they will both have low IQs) no matter what the social class of the family in which they are raised. The effect of a red-hair gene on red hair is a "direct" genetic effect because the gene affects the color via an internal biochemical process. By contrast . . . the red hair genes affect IQ *indirectly.* (Block, 1999, pp. 466–467, emphasis added)

Cultural Bias. A test has **cultural bias** when one or more of its items either offend or unfairly penalize people of a particular ethnic background, gender, or socioeconomic status, to the point that the test has less predictive and construct validity for those individuals. Some characteristics of intelligence tests may lead certain children to attain scores that do not accurately reflect either their intelligence or their ability to achieve long-term academic or professional success. For instance, many contemporary intelligence tests focus on aspects of "intelligence" (such as abstract thinking) that enable people to succeed in Western, industrialized society; these tests may be less relevant to the demands of other cultures (Miller, 1997; Ogbu, 1994). Lack of familiarity with a test's questions and tasks may also hamper students' ability

cultural bias
Extent to which an assessment instrument offends or unfairly penalizes some individuals because of their ethnicity, gender, or socioeconomic status.

to perform well on the test (Heath, 1989; Neisser et al., 1996). Facility with the English language is a factor as well: Children for whom English is a second language perform relatively poorly on test items that are primarily verbal in nature (Lopez, 1997).

Theorists disagree about whether traditional intelligence tests are culturally biased. Most research studies indicate that IQ scores have similar construct and predictive validity, as well as similar reliability, for different ethnic and racial groups, at least for those whose native language is English (Brown, Reynolds, & Whitaker, 1999). Furthermore, if cultural bias is partly to blame for group differences in IQ, it is certainly not the *only* cause of these differences. The nonverbal UNIT test described earlier was designed specifically to minimize cultural influences on test performance: The UNIT's authors consulted with people from African American, Hispanic American, Asian American, and Native American backgrounds to ensure that the tasks and content were not culturally or racially biased (McCallum, 1999). Ethnic and racial group differences on the UNIT are considerably smaller than the differences seen on more traditional intelligence tests, but there are group differences on the test nonetheless (McCallum, 1999).

Motivation to do well on an intelligence test increases the IQ scores that students earn, especially on group-administered paper-pencil tests.

Motivation. Some children, including many from Asian American and European American backgrounds, put forth maximum effort on assigned school tasks, including intelligence tests (Flynn, 1991; Ogbu, 1994). But others, including many African American and Hispanic American youngsters, may have little motivation to perform well on an intelligence test. Some may give minimal answers (e.g., "I don't know") as a way of shortening a testing session that they find confusing and unsettling (Zigler & Finn-Stevenson, 1992). Others may view school achievement of any sort as a form of "acting White" and therefore as something that interferes with their own sense of cultural identity (Ogbu, 1994).

Undoubtedly, these four factors—socioeconomic status, discriminatory practices, cultural bias, and motivation—have different influences (and in some cases, no influence at all) on how individual children perform on an intelligence test. An encouraging trend is that various ethnic and racial groups have, in recent years, become increasingly *similar* in average IQ. Such a trend can be attributed only to more equitable environmental conditions across our society (Neisser et al., 1996).

Critique of Current Perspectives on Intelligence

The psychological study of intelligence is a virtual mine field of explosive issues: What is it? How should we measure it? How much is it influenced by hereditary (and so presumably immutable) factors? Can enriching experiences significantly improve it? The answers to such questions have major implications not only for educational practice but also for political decision making and social policy.

The questions we've just listed have not yet been definitively answered. We have several additional concerns about contemporary research and practice related to intelligence and intelligence tests:

■ *Research has relied too heavily on traditional intelligence tests.* Most intelligence tests have been designed primarily to identify individuals who may require special educational services. Yet researchers have used intelligence tests for other purposes as well—for instance, to make cross-group comparisons, draw conclusions about the relative effects of heredity and environment in intellectual development, and evaluate the effectiveness of preschool programs for low-income children—without due consideration of the appropriateness of IQ tests for such purposes.

Most intelligence tests are atheoretical in nature: They are comprised of tasks that have been found to predict school achievement rather than tasks that, from a theoretical perspective, reflect the essence of what intelligence might actually be. We do not fault intelligence test authors for this state of affairs. After all, their primary goal is to design instruments that can help educators assess strengths and weaknesses that relate to students' ability to learn in school; it is *not* to help researchers explore the underlying nature of intelligence.

Traditional intelligence tests are probably too limited to help researchers completely answer broad theoretical questions about the origins and development of intelligence. And they certainly don't reflect contemporary views of intelligence—views that portray intelligence as an entity that involves complex cognitive and metacognitive processes and perhaps several relatively independent abilities (Gardner, 1995; Perkins, 1995; Sternberg, 1996). As Robert Sternberg has put it, "there is more to intelligence than IQ" (1996, p. 15).

■ *IQ scores are too often interpreted out of context.* Over the years, the use of intelligence tests in schools has been quite controversial. In earlier decades (as recently as the 1970s), IQ scores were frequently used as the sole criterion for identifying students as having mental retardation. In part as a result of this practice, children from racial and ethnic minority groups were disproportionately represented in special education classes, where it was easy to "write them off" as not having much potential for academic achievement.

Most school psychologists, counselors, and other educational specialists now have sufficient training in psychoeducational assessment to understand that a single IQ score should never warrant a diagnosis of "mental retardation" or any other label. Decisions about special educational placement and services must *always* be based on multiple sources of information about a child. Yet many teachers, and certainly many people in the public at large, seem to view IQ scores as precise measures of permanent characteristics. For instance, we often hear remarks such as "She has an IQ of such-and-such" spoken in much the same matter-of-fact manner as someone might say, "She has brown hair" or "She is very tall."

For many children, IQ scores are reasonably accurate reflections of their current cognitive development and learning potential. But for other children, IQs may be poor summaries of what they can do at present or are likely to do in the future. Educators must be extremely careful not to put too much stock in any single IQ score, particularly when working with students from diverse backgrounds.

■ *Assessment of intelligence in school settings focuses almost exclusively on skills that are valued in mainstream Western culture.* The items found on traditional intelligence tests focus on a limited set of cognitive skills that are valued in mainstream Western, middle-class culture, and particularly in school settings (Sternberg, 1996). Such a bias enhances the tests' predictive validity, because our schools, too, place heavy emphasis on the skills valued in mainstream Western culture.

Yet other cultural and socioeconomic groups value and nurture other abilities that are also beneficial for children's long-term academic and professional success. For example, Mexican American students may show exceptional skill in cooperating with their classmates; cooperation is a valued skill among many Mexican Americans (Abi-Nader, 1993; Okagaki & Sternberg, 1993; Vasquez, 1990). African American students may show particular talent in oral language—more specifically in colorful speech, creative storytelling, or humor (Torrance, 1989). The intelligence of Navajo students may be reflected in their ability to help their family and tribe perform cultural rituals or demonstrate expert craftsmanship (Kirschenbaum, 1989). Ultimately, we can gain a better understanding of children's intellectual abilities only when we broaden the ways in which we *assess* those abilities.

■ *Intelligence tests overlook dispositions and metacognitive strategies as important contributors to intellectual functioning.* Most descriptions and measures of intelligence focus on specific things that a child *can* do (abilities), with little consideration of what a child is *likely* to do (dispositions; Perkins, Tishman, Ritchhart, Donis, & Andrade, 2000). For instance, intelligence tests don't evaluate the extent to which children view a situation from multiple perspectives, examine data with a critical eye, and metacognitively reflect on what they are doing as they tackle everyday tasks and problems, nor do they assess how effectively children engage in self-regulated learning. Yet such qualities are often just as important as intellectual ability in determining success in academic and real-world tasks (Perkins et al., 2000).

■ *Many theorists have placed higher priority on assessing current intelligence than on developing future intelligence.* Implicit in the practice of intelligence testing is the assumption that intelligence is a relatively fixed, and perhaps largely inherited, ability. In our minds, the focus has been entirely too much on sorting children and entirely too little on fostering their development. Fortunately, some psychologists and educators are now calling for a shift in focus from the *assessment* of intelligence to the *development* of intelligence (Boykin, 1994; Council for Exceptional Children, 1995; Nichols & Mittelholtz, 1997; Resnick, 1995). As theorists and researchers gain a better understanding of the nature of intelligence and the environmental factors that promote it, society and schools can, we hope, shift to a more proactive approach, one in which all children are given the opportunities they need to maximize their intellectual growth.

Educational Implications of Theories and Research on Intelligence

Given existing knowledge about the nature and development of intelligence, as well as our concerns about shortcomings in the field, we offer the following suggestions to teachers:

■ *Maintain a healthy skepticism about the accuracy of IQ scores.* Used within the context of other information, IQ scores can, in many cases, provide a general idea of students' current cognitive functioning. Yet IQ scores are rarely dead-on measures of what students can do. For instance, the scores of young children may vary considerably from one testing to the next and have limited predictive validity. And the scores of children from diverse ethnic and linguistic backgrounds are often affected by background experiences, motivation, and proficiency in English.

■ *Remain optimistic about every student's potential.* As you have learned, the environments in which children grow, including their school experiences, have a significant effect on their intellectual development. IQ scores are hardly set in concrete in the early years; they can and often do improve over time. Furthermore, if intelligence is as multifaceted as theorists such as Gardner and Sternberg believe, then different students are likely to be intelligent in different ways. One student may show promise in mathematics, another may be an exceptionally creative writer, a third may be skillful in interpersonal relationships, and a fourth may show talent in art, music, or athletic ability. Finally, intelligence—no matter how we define it—can never be the only characteristic that affects students' academic achievement. Learning strategies, motivation, teacher and parent guidance, and the availability of multiple educational resources also play critical roles in students' ability to succeed in the classroom.

■ *Capitalize on students' unique strengths and abilities.* Gardner's theory in particular encourages teachers to use a variety of approaches to teach classroom subject matter and to build on the diverse abilities that different students may have (Armstrong, 1994; Campbell et al., 1998; Gardner, 1993, 1995). For instance, the following scenario illustrates how some children may learn more effectively when they can use their visual-spatial skills:

> In third grade, Jason loved to build with blocks, legos, toothpicks, popsicle sticks, anything that fit together. During a unit on ancient history, Jason built an object for every culture studied. He fashioned Babylonian ziggurats out of legos, Egyptian pyramids with toothpicks and small marshmallows, the Great Wall of China from miniature clay bricks which he made, the Greek Parthenon from styrofoam computer-packing, Roman bridges out of popsicle sticks and brads, and Mayan temples with molded plastic strips resurrected from an old science kit. While appearing apathetic during most classroom activities, Jason was highly animated during his building projects. History came alive for Jason when he could build the structures of each era and culture studied. (Campbell et al., 1998, p. 79)

Consider, too, how an eighth-grade teacher took advantage of two girls' musical intelligence to teach spelling:

> [B]oth [girls] enjoyed playing the piano. [The teacher] asked the girls to label the piano keys with the letters of the alphabet, so that the girls could "play" the words on their keyboards. Later, on spelling tests, the students were asked to recall the tones and sounds of each word and write its corresponding letters. Not only did spelling scores improve, but the two pianists began thinking of other "sound" texts to set to music. Soon, they performed each classmate's name and transcribed entire sentences. (Campbell et al., 1998, p. 142)

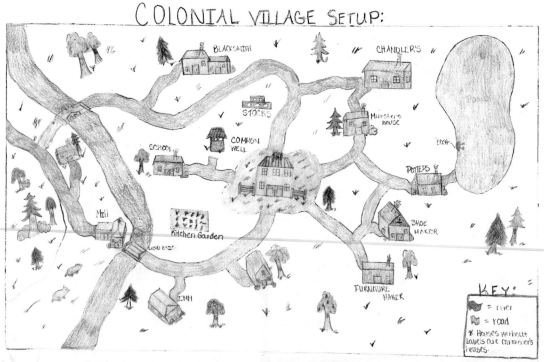

FIGURE 6–7 Examples of how middle school students might use their artistic talents to exhibit their knowledge of colonial life in America.

Drawings courtesy of Jenna and Marianne.

Teachers should consider students' multiple abilities not only when they plan lessons but also when they assess students' achievement. For instance, one of Jeanne's teaching interns, Dan Moulis, gave students in his middle school social studies class several options to demonstrate their knowledge of settlers' life in colonial America. Several students used their artistic talents to depict typical colonial villages; Figure 6–7 presents two of their creations.

Seeing Intelligence in Children's Daily Behavior

OBSERVATION GUIDELINES

CHARACTERISTIC	LOOK FOR	EXAMPLE	IMPLICATION
Oral Language Skills	• Sophisticated vocabulary • Colorful speech • Creative storytelling • Clever jokes and puns	LaMarr entertains his classmates with clever "Your momma's so fat . . ." and "Your momma's so ugly . . ." jokes.	Look for unusual creativity or advanced language development in students' everyday speech.
Learning Ability	• Ability to learn new information quickly • Ability to find relationships among diverse ideas • Excellent memory	As her English class begins reading *Romeo and Juliet,* Meghan suggests that the feud between the Capulets and Montagues bears similarities to the current ethnic conflicts in Eastern Europe.	Make note of situations in which students learn and comprehend new material more quickly than their classmates. Look for creative analogies and interconnections.
Problem-Solving Skills	• Ability to solve challenging problems • Flexibility in applying previously learned strategies to novel situations • Ability to improvise with commonplace objects and materials	A fourth-grade class plans to perform a skit during an upcoming open house. When the children puzzle about how to hang a sheet from the ceiling (to serve as a stage curtain), Jeff suggests that they turn their desks to face the side of the classroom rather than the front. This way, the sheet can be hung from a light fixture that runs the length of the room.	Present unusual tasks and problems for which students have no ready-made strategies.
Cognitive and Metacognitive Strategies	• Use of sophisticated learning strategies • Desire to understand rather than memorize • Effective comprehension monitoring	Shannon, a sixth grader, explains that she learned the countries on South America's west coast (Colombia, Ecuador, Peru, Chile) by creating the sentence, "*Col*in *e*ats *pe*as and *ch*ocolate."	Ask students to explain how they think about and remember classroom subject matter.
Curiosity and Inquisitiveness	• Voracious appetite for knowledge • Tendency to ask a lot of questions • Intrinsic motivation to master challenging subject matter	Alfredo reads every book and article he can find about space; he has a particular interest in black holes.	Find out what students do in their free time, both in and outside of the classroom.
Leadership and Social Skills	• Ability to persuade and motivate others • Exceptional sensitivity to other people's feelings and body language • Ability to mediate disagreements and help others reach reasonable compromises	Gina organizes a schoolwide peer tutoring program.	Observe how students interact with their classmates in cooperative group work and extracurricular activities.

Sources: Clark, 1997; Gottfried, Gottfried, Bathurst, & Guerin, 1994; Lupart, 1995; Maker, 1993; Maker & Schiever, 1989; Perkins, 1995; Torrance, 1989, 1995; Turnbull et al., 1999; Winner, 1997.

■ *Be open-minded about the ways in which students might demonstrate intelligence.* To the extent that intelligence is culture-dependent, intelligent behavior is likely to take different forms in children from different cultural backgrounds (Gardner, 1995; Neisser et al., 1996; Perkins, 1995; Sternberg, 1985). We must not limit our conception of intelligence to students' ability to succeed at traditional academic tasks. The Observation Guidelines table above presents a variety of behaviors that may reflect higher intelligence than children's IQ scores reveal.

■ *Promote more "intelligent" cognitive strategies.* Look back once again at the chapter's opening case study. Gina's relative weakness in history is due largely to her ineffective study strategies. In fact, teachers can promote more effective learning, studying, and problem solving—and thereby promote more intelligent behavior—by teaching students more sophisticated and effective cognitive and metacognitive strategies (Perkins, 1995; Perkins & Grotzer, 1997).

■ *Give students the support they need to think more intelligently.* The notion of distributed intelligence tells us that intelligent behavior should be relatively commonplace when students have the right tools, social groups, and symbolic systems with which to work (Pea, 1993). Rather than ask the question, "How intelligent are my students?" teachers should instead ask themselves, "How can I help my students think as intelligently as possible? What tools, social networks, and symbolic systems can I provide?"

Children and adolescents often differ considerably in the extent to which they display intelligent thinking and behavior. For the most part, teachers can easily accommodate such variability within the context of normal instructional practices. In some cases, however, students' ability levels are so different from those of their peers that students require special educational services to help them maximize their academic achievement. We turn now to exceptionalities in intelligence.

Exceptionalities in Intelligence

No matter how we define or measure intelligence, we find that some children and adolescents show exceptional talent and others show significant cognitive delays relative to their peers. The two ends of the intelligence continuum are commonly known as *giftedness* and *mental retardation*.

Giftedness

Gina, described in the opening case study, is an example of a student who is gifted. More generally, **giftedness** is unusually high ability or aptitude in one or more areas, to the point where special educational services are necessary to help a student meet his or her full potential. Students who are gifted (sometimes called *gifted and talented*) show exceptional achievement or promise in one or more of the following areas:

• General intellectual ability
• Aptitude in a specific academic field
• Creativity
• Visual or performing arts
• Leadership
  (U.S. Department of Education, 1993)

When we try to pin down giftedness more precisely, we find considerable disagreement about how to do so (Carter, 1991; Keogh & MacMillan, 1996). Many school districts identify students as gifted primarily on the basis of general IQ scores, often using 125 or 130 as a cutoff point (Keogh & MacMillan, 1996; Webb, Meckstroth, & Tolan, 1982), but some experts argue that multiple criteria should be applied when determining students' eligibility for special services (Council for Exceptional Children, 1995; Renzulli & Reis, 1986; Sternberg & Zhang, 1995). For instance, one theorist has argued that creativity and task commitment should be considered in addition to IQ scores (Renzulli, 1978). Furthermore, scores on general intelligence tests may be largely irrelevant when identifying students who show exceptional promise in specific academic fields, creativity, the arts, or leadership.

A further complication is that giftedness is likely to take different forms in different cultures. The tendency to rely heavily on traditional intelligence tests for identifying students is probably a key reason that many minority populations are underrepresented in gifted education programs (Harris, 1991; Maker & Schiever, 1989; U.S. Department of Education, Office of Civil Rights, 1993).

giftedness
Unusually high ability in one or more areas, to the point where students require special educational services to help them meet their full potential.

Possible Roots of Giftedness Although giftedness may be partly an inherited character-istic, correlational studies suggest (though do not necessarily prove) that environmental fac-tors may play a significant role as well (Clark, 1997; A. W. Gottfried et al., 1994). For instance, gifted children are more likely to be firstborn or only-born children, who generally have more attention and stimulation from their parents than other children do. They often have many op-portunities to practice and enhance their talents from a very early age, long before they have been identified as being gifted. In fact, children who are gifted are more likely to seek out en-riching opportunities—an example of the *niche-picking* phenomenon described earlier.

In one longitudinal study (A. W. Gottfried et al., 1994), many gifted children showed signs of advanced cognitive and linguistic development beginning at 18 months of age. As is true for Gina in the opening case study, a child's giftedness is often evident throughout the school years. Yet some children may be "late bloomers": Their talents become evident relatively late in the game, perhaps as environmental conditions bring such talents to fruition.

Common Characteristics of Students Who Are Gifted Although gifted students are typically very different from one another in terms of their unique strengths and talents, in gen-eral they learn more quickly and easily, exhibit greater flexibility in ideas and approaches to tasks, and engage in abstract thinking at an earlier age than their classmates (Carter & Ormrod, 1982; Lupart, 1995; Maker, 1993; Winner, 1997). Most students who are gifted have high self-esteem, good social skills, and above-average emotional adjustment (Cornell et al., 1990; A. W. Gottfried et al., 1994). However, a few extremely gifted students may have social or emo-tional difficulties because they are so *very* different from their peers (Keogh & MacMillan, 1996; Winner, 1997).

Many gifted students become bored or frustrated when their school experiences don't pro-vide tasks and assignments that challenge them and help them develop their unique abilities; they may find instruction slow and repetitive of things they already know (Friedel, 1993; Win-ner, 1997). One junior high school student expressed her feelings this way:

> They won't let us learn. . . . What I mean is, they seem to think they have to keep us all together all the time. That means in the subjects I'm good at I can't learn more because I'm always waiting for others to catch up. I guess if I get too far ahead I'll be doing the next year's work, but I can't understand what's wrong with that if that's what I'm ready for. (Feldhusen, Van Winkel, & Ehle, 1996, p. 48)

Recalling Lev Vygotsky's theory of cognitive development from Chapter 4, we could say that gifted students are unlikely to be working within their zone of proximal development if they are limited to the same tasks assigned to other students; thus, they are unlikely to develop more advanced cognitive skills.

As a result of frequent boredom and frustration, some students who are gifted lose interest in school tasks and put in only the minimum effort they need to get by in the classroom (Feldhusen, 1989). In fact, gifted students are among our schools' greatest underachievers: When required to progress at the same rate as their nongifted peers, they achieve at levels far short of their capa-bilities (Carter, 1991; Gallagher, 1991; Reis, 1989). Such underachievement may especially be an issue for female and minority students (Ford, 1996; Nichols & Ganschow, 1992).

Some students try to hide their exceptional talents. They may fear that peers will ridicule them for their high academic abilities and enthusiasm for academic topics, especially at the secondary school level (Covington, 1992; DeLisle, 1984). Girls in particular are likely to hide their talents, especially if they have been raised in cultures that do not value high achievement in females (Covington, 1992; Davis & Rimm, 1998; Nichols & Ganschow, 1992). Gifted Asian Americans, because of cultural traditions of obedience, conformity, and respect for authority, may be reluctant to engage in creative activities and may willingly comply when asked to per-form unchallenging assignments (Maker & Schiever, 1989).

Fostering the Development of Students Who Are Gifted Teachers can foster the spe-cial abilities and talents of gifted students in numerous ways. Following are several strategies that theorists and practitioners recommend:

■ *Provide individualized tasks and assignments.* Even though students who are gifted are a very heterogeneous group, many schools provide the same curriculum and materials for all students they've identified as being gifted. In fact, no single program can meet the specific needs of each and every gifted student. Different students may need special services in very different areas—for example, in mathematics, creative writing, or studio art.

■ *Form study groups of students with similar interests and abilities.* In any school building, there are likely to be several students who have common interests and abilities, and it may sometimes be helpful to pull them together into study groups where they can cooperatively pursue a particular topic or task (Fiedler, Lange, & Winebrenner, 1993; Stanley, 1980). Forming homogeneous study groups has several advantages. First, a single teacher can meet the needs of several students simultaneously. Second, students appear to benefit from increased contact with other students who have similar interests (McGinn, Viernstein, & Hogan, 1980). And third, students are less likely to try to hide their talent and enthusiasm for the subject matter when they work with classmates who share similar ability and motivation (Feldhusen, 1989).

In some cases, a study group may explore a topic with greater depth and more sophisticated analysis than other students do (an *enrichment* approach). For example, in a geometry class, those students who show high ability might be asked to work together on an exceptionally challenging geometric proof. In other cases, a study group may simply move through the standard school curriculum at a more rapid pace (an *acceleration* approach). For example, students reading well above the level of their classmates might be assigned books not ordinarily encountered until more advanced grade levels.

■ *Teach complex cognitive skills within the context of specific subject areas.* Some programs for gifted students have tried to teach complex thought processes, such as logical reasoning or problem solving, as skills totally separate from school subject matter. But this approach tends to have minimal impact on the development of gifted students, and in fact it often focuses on skills that many students have already acquired. Instead, teachers are better advised to teach complex thinking skills within the context of specific topics—for example, reasoning and problem-solving skills in science, or creativity in writing (Linn et al., 1989; Moon, Feldhusen, & Dillon, 1994; Pulos & Linn, 1981; Stanley, 1980).

■ *Provide opportunities for independent study.* Many students who are gifted have advanced learning and metacognitive skills and a strong motivation to learn academic subject matter (Candler-Lotven, Tallent-Runnels, Olivárez, & Hildreth, 1994; Lupart, 1995). Accordingly, independent study in topics of interest may be especially appropriate for these students. When teachers provide opportunities for independent study, however, they should teach students the study habits and research skills necessary to use time and resources effectively.

■ *Encourage students to set high goals for themselves.* Just as gifted students are capable of higher performance in specific areas, so too should they be setting higher goals for themselves in those areas. Teachers should encourage students to aim high, while at the same time reminding them not to expect perfection for themselves (Parker, 1997; Sanborn, 1979). For instance, some students may have given little or no thought to attending college, perhaps because their families have never expected them to pursue higher education; under such circumstances, their teachers might give them the opportunity to visit a college campus and explore possible means of funding a college education (Spicker, 1992).

■ *Seek outside resources.* Any one school building is likely to have students with exceptional potential in so many different areas that no single adult—not even a specialist in gifted education—can reasonably meet all of their needs (Fox, 1979; Stanley, 1980). It is sometimes appropriate to identify suitable *mentors,* or individuals with expertise in a particular area who help students develop their own talent in that area. In other circumstances, outside agencies—for example, laboratories, government offices, private businesses, volunteer community groups, theater groups, and art and videotaping studios—may provide an arena in which students can develop their unique talents (Ambrose, Allen, & Huntley, 1994; Piirto, 1999; Seeley, 1989).

Some students who are gifted also have disabilities—possibly learning disabilities, emotional disorders, or physical challenges. This student's teacher must take both her giftedness and her physical disability into account when planning instruction.

Keep in mind that a student can be gifted and also have a disability. For example, some gifted students have learning disabilities, ADHD, emotional disorders, or physical or sensory challenges. In such situations, teachers must address the students' disabilities as well as their unique gifts when they plan instruction. A few gifted students—for example, those with a limited English background or those who have specific learning disabilities—may even need some training in basic skills (Brown-Mizuno, 1990; Harris, 1991; Udall, 1989).

PROVIDING CHALLENGING ACTIVITIES FOR GIFTED STUDENTS

- Individualize instruction in accordance with students' specific talents.

  A mathematically gifted junior high school student studies calculus via computer-assisted instruction, while a classmate with exceptional reading skills is assigned novels appropriate to his reading level.

- Form study groups of gifted students with similar abilities and interests.

  A music teacher creates, and then provides weekly instruction to, a quartet of exceptionally talented music students.

- Teach complex cognitive skills within the context of specific school topics rather than separately from the standard school curriculum.

  A teacher has an advanced science study group conduct a series of experiments related to a single topic. To promote critical thinking, the teacher gives students several questions they should ask themselves as they conduct these experiments.

- Seek outside resources to help students develop their exceptional talents.

  A student with a high aptitude for learning foreign languages studies Russian at a local university.

Mental Retardation

Children with **mental retardation** show developmental delays in most aspects of their academic and social functioning. A child must exhibit two characteristics before a diagnosis of mental retardation is appropriate (American Association on Mental Retardation, 1992):

- *Significantly below-average general intelligence.* Children and adolescents with mental retardation perform poorly on traditional intelligence tests; their IQ scores are usually no higher than 65 or 70, reflecting performance in the bottom 2 percent of their age group (Keogh & MacMillan, 1996; Turnbull et al., 1999). These individuals show other signs of below-average intelligence as well; for instance, they learn slowly and perform quite poorly on school tasks in comparison with their age-mates, and they show consistently poor achievement across virtually all academic subject areas.
- *Deficits in adaptive behavior.* Low intelligence test scores and poor academic performance are insufficient evidence to classify students as having mental retardation. An additional criterion is a deficit in **adaptive behavior:** Individuals with mental retardation show limitations in *practical intelligence,* or managing the ordinary activities of daily living, and *social intelligence,* or conducting themselves appropriately in social situations. In these respects, children and adolescents with mental retardation often exhibit behaviors typical of individuals much younger than themselves. Specific skills with which they may have difficulty are listed in Figure 6–8.

Possible Roots of Mental Retardation   Mental retardation is often caused by abnormal genetic conditions; for example, most children with Down syndrome have delayed cognitive development. Sometimes mental retardation runs in families, such that many family members' abilities simply fall at the lower end of the normal distribution of intelligence (Kail, 1998).

Yet heredity is not always to blame. Some instances of mental retardation are due to noninherited biological causes, such as severe malnutrition during the mother's pregnancy, oxygen deprivation associated with a difficult birth, or ingestion of lead paint in early childhood (Keogh & MacMillan, 1996; McLoyd, 1998b). Conditions in the home, such as parental neglect or an extremely impoverished and unstimulating home life, may also be at fault (Batshaw & Shapiro, 1997; Feuerstein, 1979; Wagner, 1995a). Undoubtedly as a result of such factors as malnutrition, ingestion of lead, and other environmental hazards, children from poor, inner-city neighborhoods are overrepresented among students who are identified as having mental retardation (U.S. Department of Education, Office of Civil Rights, 1993).

Common Characteristics of Students with Mental Retardation   Children and adolescents with mental retardation show impairments in many aspects of information processing, including attention, working memory, and learning strategies (Butterfield & Ferretti, 1987; Dempster & Corkill, 1999; Turnbull et al., 1999). They have little metacognitive awareness of

mental retardation
Condition marked by significantly below-average general intelligence and deficits in adaptive behavior.

adaptive behavior
Behavior related to daily living skills and appropriate conduct in social situations.

FIGURE 6–8 Adaptive skills considered in identifying people with mental retardation

Derived from the ten adaptive skills described by the American Association on Mental Retardation (1992).

Communication: Skills related to understanding and expressing ideas through spoken and written language and through body language.

Self-care: Skills related to hygiene, eating, dressing, and grooming.

Home-living: Skills related to general functioning at home, including housekeeping, laundry, food preparation, budgeting, and home safety.

Social: Skills related to social interaction, including adhering to social conventions for interaction, helping others, recognizing feelings, forming friendships, controlling impulses, and abiding by rules.

Community use: Skills related to using community resources effectively, including shopping, using local transportation and facilities, and obtaining services.

Self-direction: Skills related to making choices, following a schedule, initiating activities appropriate to the context, completing required tasks, seeking needed assistance, and solving problems.

Health and safety: Skills related to personal health maintenance, basic first aid, physical fitness, basic safety, and sexuality.

Functional academics: Skills acquired in the academic curriculum that have direct application to independent living, such as reading, writing, and basic arithmetic.

Leisure: Skills related to initiating self-chosen leisure and recreational activities based on personal interests, playing socially with others, and abiding by age and cultural norms for activities undertaken.

Work: Skills related to holding a job, including specific job skills, appropriate social behavior, completion of tasks, awareness of schedules, and money management.

how they think and learn, have trouble generalizing the things they learn to new situations, and often exhibit a sense of helplessness about their ability to learn new things (Butterfield & Ferretti, 1987; Seligman, 1975; Turnbull et al., 1999). Their play activities are typical of children much younger than themselves (Hughes, 1998; Malone, Stoneham, & Langone, 1995).

Fostering the Development of Students with Mental Retardation The great majority of children and adolescents with mental retardation attend school, and many of them are capable of mastering a wide variety of academic and vocational skills. Following are several instructional strategies that theorists and practitioners recommend for students with mental retardation:

■ *Pace instruction to ensure a high rate of success.* When working with students who have mental retardation, teachers should pace instruction at a rate commensurate with students' abilities; for example, they might move through topics more slowly, repeat important ideas frequently, and provide numerous opportunities to practice new tasks. Students with mental retardation typically have a long history of failure at academic tasks; hence, they need frequent success experiences to learn that they *can* succeed in school.

■ *Use instructional materials appropriate to students' cognitive abilities.* In many cases, the standard instructional materials for a particular grade level may very well *not* be appropriate for students with mental retardation. Instead, teachers should find reading materials, workbooks, concrete manipulatives, and so on, that are suitable for the learning and reasoning capabilities that individual students currently demonstrate. Materials commonly used for students at lower grade levels are sometimes appropriate, provided that such materials do not appear too "babyish." In other cases, the school district's special education coordinator may be able to recommend appropriate materials.

■ *Provide considerable scaffolding to facilitate effective cognitive processing.* Students with mental retardation typically have little awareness of how to direct and regulate their own learning. So it is often helpful to provide explicit guidance about how to think about classroom material. For instance, teachers can help students focus their attention by using such phrases as "get

MAXIMIZING THE ACHIEVEMENT OF STUDENTS WITH MENTAL RETARDATION

■ Introduce new material at a slower pace, and provide many opportunities for practice.

A teacher gives a student only two new addition facts a week, primarily because any more than two seem to overwhelm him. Every day, the teacher has the student practice writing the new facts and review addition facts learned in previous weeks.

■ Consult with specialists in the school district about appropriate curricular materials and instructional methods.

A teacher asks the school's special education consultant to recommend materials for teaching prereading skills to a nonreading 10-year-old.

■ Explain tasks concretely and in very specific terms.

An art teacher gives a student explicit training in the steps she needs to take at the end of each painting session: (1) Rinse the paintbrush out at the sink, (2) put the brush and watercolor paints on the shelf in the back room, and (3) put the painting on the counter by the window to dry. Initially the teacher needs to remind the student of every step in the process. Eventually, with time and practice, the student carries out the process independently.

■ Give students explicit guidance about how to study.

A teacher tells a student, "When you study a new spelling word, it helps if you repeat the letters out loud while you practice writing the word. Let's try it with *house,* the word you are learning this morning. Watch how I repeat the letters—H...O...U...S...E—as I write the word. Now you try doing what I just did."

■ Give feedback about specific behaviors rather than about general areas of performance.

A teacher tells a student, "You did a good job in science lab this week. You followed my instructions correctly, and you put away the equipment when I asked you to do so."

■ Encourage independence.

A high school teacher teaches a student how to use her calculator to figure out what she needs to pay for lunch every day. The teacher also gives the student considerable practice in identifying the correct bills and coins to use when paying various amounts.

ready," "look," or "listen" (Turnbull et al., 1999). They can give students simple, structured study guides that indicate quite specifically what to focus on when studying (Mastropieri & Scruggs, 1992). They also can teach students a few simple, concrete memory strategies, such as repeating instructions over and over (rehearsal) or physically rearranging a group of items that must be remembered (Fletcher & Bray, 1995; Turnbull, 1974). When students learn such strategies, their learning and academic performance improve (Perkins, 1995).

■ *Include vocational and general life skills in the high school curriculum.* After high school, most students with mental retardation join the adult work force rather than go on to higher education. Accordingly, an important part of any high school curriculum for students with mental retardation is training in general life and work skills. Because of students' limited ability to generalize what they have learned from one situation to another, it is especially important to teach life and work skills in realistic settings—those that closely resemble the situations in which students will find themselves once they leave school (Turnbull et al., 1999).

Although usually a long-term condition, mental retardation is not necessarily a lifelong disability, especially when the presumed cause is environmental rather than genetic (Beirne-Smith, Ittenbach, & Patton, 1998; Landesman & Ramey, 1989). Our final case study illustrates just how much of a difference environment can make.

CASE STUDY: FRESH VEGETABLES

Twelve-year-old Steven had no known genetic or other organic problems but had been officially labeled as having mental retardation based on his low scores on a series of intelligence tests. His prior schooling had been limited to just part of one year in a first-grade classroom in inner-city Chicago. His mother had withdrawn him after a bullet grazed his leg while he was walking to school one morning. Fearing for her son's safety, she would not let him outside the apartment after that, not even to play, and certainly not to walk the six blocks to the local elementary school.

When a truant officer finally appeared at the door one evening five years later, Steven and his mother quickly packed their bags and moved to a small town in northern Colorado. They found residence with Steven's aunt, who persuaded Steven to go back to school. After considering Steven's intelligence and achievement test scores, the school psychologist recommended that he attend a summer school class for students with special needs.

Steven's summer school teacher soon began to suspect that Steven's main problem might simply be a lack of the background experiences necessary for academic success. One incident in particular stands out in her mind. The class had been studying nutrition, and so she had asked her students to bring in some fresh vegetables to make a large salad for their morning snack. Steven brought in a can of green beans. When a classmate objected that the beans weren't fresh, Steven replied, "The hell they ain't! Me and Momma got them off the shelf this morning!"

If Steven didn't know what *fresh* meant, the teacher reasoned, then he might also be lacking many of the other facts and skills on which any academic curriculum is invariably based. She and the teachers who followed her worked hard to help Steven make up for all those years in Chicago during which he had experienced and learned so little. By the time Steven reached high school, he was enrolling in regular classes and maintaining a 3.5 grade-point-average.

Adapted from Jackson & Ormrod (1998).

- Does Steven have mental retardation? Why or why not?
- The school psychologist recommended that Steven be placed in a special class for students with special needs. Was such a class the most appropriate placement for Steven? Why or why not?

SUMMARY

Characterizing Intelligence

Intelligence involves adaptive behavior and may manifest itself differently in different cultures. Some theorists believe that intelligence is a single entity (a general factor, or *g*) that influences students' learning and performance across a wide variety of tasks and subject areas; this belief is reflected in the widespread use of IQ scores as general estimates of academic ability. But other theorists (e.g., Gardner, Sternberg) propose that intelligence consists of many, somewhat independent abilities and therefore cannot be accurately reflected in a single IQ score. There is growing recognition that people are more likely to behave "intelligently" when they have physical, social, and symbolic support systems to help them in their efforts.

Measuring Intelligence

Most intelligence tests have been developed primarily to identify children and adults with special needs (e.g., those who are gifted or have mental retardation). Contemporary intelligence tests include a variety of tasks designed to assess what people have learned and deduced from their everyday experiences. Performance on these tests is usually summarized by one or more IQ scores, which are determined by comparing an individual's performance with the performance of others of the same age. Specific ability tests and measures of learning potential provide alternative ways of assessing intelligence.

Hereditary and Environmental Influences

Studies with twins and adopted children indicate that intelligence may be partly an inherited characteristic. But environmental conditions, including home environment, nutrition, enriching preschool programs, and formal schooling, can also have a significant impact on IQ scores. Heredity and environment interact in their influence, to the point where it may be virtually impossible to separate the relative effects of each on children's intellectual development.

Developmental Trends and Group Differences

Performance on intelligence tests predicts school achievement to some degree, with IQ scores becoming increasingly stable and having greater predictive validity as children grow older. However, individual children's IQ scores may change considerably over time, especially during the early years.

On average, children from low-income families earn lower IQ scores than children from middle-income families. Males and females perform similarly on general tests of intelligence, although slight gender differences are sometimes observed on tests of specific cognitive abilities. Average differences in IQ scores are frequently found among various ethnic and racial groups; environmental factors are probably the primary root of these differences.

Critique of Current Perspectives

Research on intelligence has relied heavily on traditional intelligence tests, which are largely atheoretical in nature, emphasize skills valued in Western culture, and overlook dispositions and metacognitive strategies as important contributors to intellectual performance. Some psychologists and educators are now calling for a shift in focus from the assessment of students' existing intelligence to the development of students' future intelligence.

Educational Implications

Used within the context of other information, intelligence tests can often provide a general idea of students' current cognitive functioning. Yet teachers should remain optimistic about *every* student's potential for intellectual development. They should anticipate that different students will be intelligent in different ways and capitalize on students' unique strengths and abilities to promote learning and achievement. And they should give students the social support and the physical and symbolic tools they need to think more intelligently.

Exceptionalities in Intelligence

Students identified as being gifted show exceptional achievement or promise in general intellectual ability, aptitude in a specific academic field, creativity, leadership, or visual and performing arts. Giftedness may reflect itself differently in different cultures; however, gifted students frequently demonstrate rapid learning, flexibility of ideas, and facility in abstract thinking. Strategies for promoting the achievement of gifted students include forming study groups of students with similar abilities, teaching complex cognitive skills within the context of various academic subject areas, providing opportunities for independent study, and seeking mentors in the outside world.

Mental retardation is characterized by low general intellectual functioning and deficits in adaptive behavior. Strategies for working effectively with students with mental retardation include pacing instruction more slowly than usual, scaffolding cognitive processing, and including vocational and general life skills in the curriculum.

Now go to our Companion Website to assess your understanding of chapter content with Multiple-Choice Questions, apply comprehension in Essay Questions, and broaden your knowledge with links to related Developmental Psychology World Wide Web sites.

KEY CONCEPTS

Drew, age 6

Language Development

CASE STUDY: MARIO

Mario's parents were fluent in both English and Spanish. Although the family lived in rural Vermont, they spoke Spanish almost exclusively at home, in part because Mario's mother found English harsh and unpleasant to the ear. Most of Mario's early exposure to English was in the English-speaking daycare centers and preschools he attended off and on from the time he was 2.

When Mario was 5, his dominant language was Spanish, but he was proficient in English as well. After his first 2 months in kindergarten, his teacher wrote the following in a report to Mario's parents:

> [Mario is] extremely sociable. He gets along fine with all the children, and enjoys school. He is quite vocal. He does not seem at all conscious of his speech. His slight accent has had no effect on his relations with the others. Whenever I ask the class a question, he is always one of the ones with his hand up.
>
> His greatest problem seems to be in the give and take of conversation. Since he always has something to say, he often finds it difficult to wait his turn when others are talking. When he talks, there are moments when you can see his little mind thinking through language—for he sometimes has to stop to recall a certain word in English which he might not have at his finger tips. (Fantini, 1985, p. 28)

The following school year, a speech therapist misperceived Mario's accent to be an articulation problem and so recommended him for speech therapy (Mario's parents refused to give their consent). By the time Mario was 8, any trace of an accent had disappeared from his speech, and his third-grade teacher was quite surprised to learn that he spoke a language other than English at home.

Standardized tests administered over the years attested to Mario's proficiency in English. Before he began kindergarten, his score on a standardized vocabulary test was at the 29th percentile, reflecting performance that, though a little on the low side, was well within an average range. Later, when he took the California Achievement Test in the fourth, sixth, and eighth grades, he obtained scores at the 80th percentile or higher (and mostly above the 90th percentile) on the reading, writing, and spelling subtests. When Mario spent a semester of fifth grade at a Spanish-speaking school in Bolivia, he earned high marks in Spanish as well, with grades of 5 on a 7-point scale in reading, writing, and language usage.

As Mario grew older, however, his vocabulary and written language skills developed more rapidly in English than in Spanish, in large part because his school instruction took place almost exclusively in English. His father described the situation this way:

> [B]y about fifth grade (age ten), he had entered into realms of experience for which he had no counterpart in Spanish. A clear example was an attempt to prepare for a fifth grade test on the topic of "The Industrial Revolution in England and France." It soon became clear that it was an impossibility to try to constrain the child to review materials read and discussed at school—in English—through Spanish. With this incident, [use of English at home] became a fairly well established procedure when discussing other school topics, including science, mathematics, and the like. (Fantini, 1985, p. 73)

Excerpts from *Language Acquisition of a Bilingual Child: A Sociolinguistic Perspective,* by A. E. Fantini, 1985. Clevedon, England: Multilingual Matters. (Available from the SIT Bookstore, School for International Training, Kipling Road, Brattleboro, VT 05302.) Reprinted with permission.

$\mathbb{L}$EARNING A LANGUAGE IS a remarkable accomplishment indeed. At a minimum, it includes acquiring (a) an understanding of what various words mean (and most adults understand many tens of thousands of them), (b) oral-motor skills that enable precise pronunciation, (c) knowledge of innumerable rules for putting words together into meaningful sequences, and (d) awareness of how to speak with others in ways that are considered polite and socially acceptable. Mario's language development was all the more remarkable because he mastered *two* languages instead of one.

In this chapter, we often revisit Mario as we explore the multifaceted nature of human language and its development. As we begin the chapter, we look at several theoretical perspectives on how language develops. We then look at the development of children's first language—their **native language**—and examine the specific linguistic knowledge and skills that emerge during the preschool, elementary, and secondary school years. Later, we look at the effects of bilingualism and consider two approaches to teaching children and adolescents a second language. Finally, we address exceptionalities in language development that may call for individually tailored instructional strategies and materials.

Theoretical Perspectives of Language Development

To understand and use their native language effectively, children must master four basic components of the language: **phonology**, how words sound and are produced; **semantics**, what words mean; **syntax**, how words are combined to form understandable phrases and sentences; and **pragmatics**, how to engage in effective and socially acceptable communication with others. Mastering any one of these components is, from an objective standpoint, an extremely complex and challenging undertaking. Yet within the first 3 or 4 years of life, most children acquire sufficient proficiency in all four areas to carry on productive conversations with those around them. How they accomplish this monumental task in such a short time is one of the great mysteries of child development.

Theorists have offered numerous explanations for how children learn their native language. Here we describe early theories based on modeling and reinforcement plus two more contemporary perspectives: nativism and information processing theory.

Early Theories: Modeling and Reinforcement

Some early theorists suggested that language development comes about largely through modeling: A child imitates the speech that he or she hears other people produce. Imitation must certainly be involved in language development to some extent; otherwise, it would not be possible for all members of a particular social group to pronounce words in the same ways and to use similar grammatical structures. And we do see children occasionally imitating the words, expressions, rhymes, and song lyrics that other people model (Owens, 1996; Peters, 1983). For example, when Mario began attending an English-speaking preschool, he came home using such expressions as "Shut up!" "Don't do dat!" and "Get auta here!" which he had apparently picked up by listening to his classmates (Fantini, 1985, p. 97).

The behaviorist B. F. Skinner (1957) offered another early explanation of language development: Parents and other adults in a child's environment reinforce increasingly more complex language use. Skinner proposed that initially, when infants are uttering a wide variety of speech sounds in a seemingly random fashion, parents respond favorably only to sounds that are used in the family's native language; for example, an English-speaking family is likely to reinforce an "r" sound (which occurs in English speech) but not a rolling "r" (which occurs in Spanish and French but not in English). As the child grows older, the parents begin to reinforce the use of single words, then the use of multiword combinations, and eventually only word combinations that are, from an adult's perspective, grammatically correct.[1]

native language
The first language a child learns.

phonology
The sound system of a language; how words sound and are produced.

semantics
The meanings of words and word combinations.

syntax
Rules used to put words together into sentences.

pragmatics
Strategies and rules for effective and socially acceptable verbal interaction.

---

[1]If you are familiar with B. F. Skinner's theory of operant conditioning, you may recognize this process as being an example of *shaping* desirable behavior over time.

Yet such explanations of language acquisition have not held up under the scrutiny of research and individual case studies. The speech of young children includes many phrases that the people around them neither say nor reinforce (Chomsky, 1959; Cook & Newson, 1996; Lightfoot, 1999). For instance, a child may say "Allgone milk" or "I goed to Grandma's house." In addition, parents usually reinforce their children's statements on the basis of what is factually accurate rather than what is grammatically correct (O'Grady, 1997). For example, in a study by Brown and Hanlon (1970), parents agreed with (i.e., reinforced) sentences such as these:

> Her curl my hair.
> Mama isn't boy, he a girl. (p. 49)

but not sentences such as these:

> There's the animal farmhouse. [The building in question was a lighthouse.]
> And Walt Disney comes on Tuesday. [Disney's television show appeared on Sundays.] (p. 49)

Especially in the toddler and preschool years, but in the elementary and secondary school years as well, the great majority of grammatical errors in children's speech go uncorrected (Bohannon, MacWhinney, & Snow, 1990). Furthermore, children may continue to produce grammatically incorrect sentences even when they get consistent feedback that such sentences need revision. The following dialogue illustrates:

> Child: Nobody don't like me.
> Mother: No, say "nobody likes me."
> Child: Nobody don't like me.
>
> [Eight repetitions of this dialogue]
>
> Mother: No, now listen carefully; say "nobody likes me."
> Child: Oh! Nobody don't likes me. (McNeill, 1966, p. 68)

Yet in other situations, children may learn to use correct grammatical structures even when they receive *no* feedback that they are using these structures correctly (Cromer, 1993).

Thus, children's experiences—the speech they hear and the reinforcement and feedback they receive about their own utterances—seem insufficient to help them acquire an adultlike form of their native language. As a result, many theorists have turned to biology to explain language development, as you will see now.

Nativism

Noam Chomsky (1964, 1965, 1972, 1976) has proposed that growing children have a built-in, biological mechanism—a **language acquisition device**—that enables them to learn many complex aspects of language in a very short time. This mechanism provides a certain amount of "preknowledge" about the nature of language that makes the task of learning language much simpler than it would be if children had to start from scratch. Numerous other theorists share Chomsky's belief that human beings, though certainly not born knowing any *particular* language, nevertheless inherit some predispositions regarding the form that language should take (e.g., Cairns, 1996; Gopnik, 1997; Hirsh-Pasek & Golinkoff, 1996; Lenneberg, 1967; Lightfoot, 1999). Such an approach to language development is generally known as **nativism.**

Nativists have used three major arguments to support their contention that language development has a biological basis. First, the language used in everyday speech is inadequate to allow children to acquire the complex, adultlike language that they eventually *do* acquire. In typical day-to-day conversations, adults often use incomplete sentences, are lax in their adherence to grammatical rules and, when talking to very young children, frequently use artificially short and simple language. In other words, there is a *poverty of the stimulus* in the language children hear (Cook & Newson, 1996; Harris, 1992; Lightfoot, 1999). Second, to communicate effectively, children must derive the underlying rules that govern how words are put together and then use these rules to generate sentences they have never heard before (Chomsky, 1959, 1972; Littlewood, 1984; Pinker, 1993). Third, all children in a particular language community learn essentially the *same* language despite widely differing early childhood experiences and a general lack of systematic instruction in appropriate language use (Cromer, 1993; Littlewood, 1984; Lightfoot, 1999).

language acquisition device
Biologically built-in mechanism hypothesized to facilitate language learning.

nativism
Theoretical perspective that some knowledge is biologically built in and present at birth.

Children's exposure to language influences their language development; for instance, children who watch *Sesame Street* have larger vocabularies (Rice, Huston, Truglio, & Wright, 1990). But children's early linguistic experiences are haphazard and incomplete, leading many developmentalists to propose that human beings have some biologically built-in knowledge about the nature of language.

If human beings do indeed have a built-in language acquisition device, what might such a device include? Most nativists propose that, at a minimum, it includes a **Universal Grammar**, a set of parameters that allow some grammatical structures but exclude other possibilities; thus, children essentially pick from a limited number of options when they learn syntactic rules (Cairns, 1996; Chomsky, 1976; Lightfoot, 1999; O'Grady, 1997). For instance, most (and possibly all) languages seem to have some words that function as nouns and others that function as verbs (O'Grady, 1997; Pinker, 1984; Strozer, 1994). Also, many languages, including those with different origins, have similar rules for forming negatives and asking questions (Chomsky, 1965).

Some nativists suggest that the language acquisition device may contribute to language development in other ways as well. For instance, it may help infants tune in to certain kinds of speech (especially shorter and louder utterances), divide a stream of sound into small segments (e.g., syllables), and identify common patterns in what is heard (Kuhl & Meltzoff, 1997; O'Grady, 1997; Pettito, 1997). It may also include some built-in concepts (e.g., colors such as red, pink, and yellow) that predispose children to categorize their experiences in certain ways; learning the labels for such preexisting concepts is almost certainly an easier task than learning the concepts themselves (Strozer, 1994). And at the most basic level, the language acquisition device may inform children, from a very early age, that there is meaning in speech—that spoken language corresponds directly with specific world events (Hirsh-Pasek & Golinkoff, 1996).

Nativists have not yet come to consensus about the exact nature of the language acquisition device or the precise ways in which it contributes to language development (Hirsh-Pasek & Golinkoff, 1996; O'Grady, 1997). Yet several lines of research converge to support their belief that language *does* have a biological basis:

■ *Babbling is a universal phenomenon in child development.* All infants, even those who are congenitally deaf and so have never heard a human voice, begin to produce speechlike sounds—**babbling**—at about 6 or 7 months of age on average (Kuhl & Meltzoff, 1997; Locke, 1993). Babbling is not necessarily limited to spoken language: Deaf children exposed to sign language often begin to "babble" manually at 7 to 10 months of age (Pettito, 1997).

■ *Children from diverse cultural and linguistic backgrounds tend to reach milestones in language development at similar ages.* For instance, children raised in communities that speak Inuktitut (an Inuit language found in Northern Quebec) and children exposed to sign language from birth make progress in language development (spoken and signed, respectively) similar to that of English-speaking children (Crago, Allen, & Hough-Eyamie, 1997; Pettito, 1997).

■ *Language disabilities often run in families.* Just as the ability to learn language may be inherited, so too might an *impaired* ability to learn it be passed from parents to their children (Cairns, 1996; Gopnik, 1997). For example, a person who, when listening to speech, has difficulty breaking up the series of sounds into meaningful parts may have children who experience the same challenge.

■ *Certain areas of the brain appear to specialize in language functions.* Some language disorders are associated with congenital brain abnormalities or with injuries in certain parts of the brain (Aitchison, 1996; Locke, 1993; Strozer, 1994). People who can comprehend language but do not speak often have damage in *Broca's area,* located in the left frontal cortex of the brain. People who cannot comprehend language but produce meaningless, nonsensical speech often have damage in *Wernicke's area,* a region in the left temporal lobe (see Figure 7–1).

■ *There appear to be sensitive periods in some aspects of language development.* Children who have little or no exposure to language in the early years often have trouble acquiring language even with adequate or enriched language experiences later on (e.g., Curtiss, 1977; Newport, 1990). A frequently cited example is Genie, a girl who was confined to a small, dark room and had little meaningful contact with others until she was 14. Genie subsequently had intensive training in language; although she learned to say and understand many words, her grammar never matured beyond that of a typical 2½-year-old (Curtiss, 1977).

Additional evidence comes from people learning a second language. Typically, people learn how to pronounce a second language flawlessly only if they study it before mid-adolescence or, even better, in the preschool or early elementary years (Bialystok, 1994a; Collier, 1989; Flege,

Universal Grammar
Hypothesized set of parameters within the language acquisition device that allow some grammatical structures but exclude others.

babbling
Universal tendency for human beings to produce speechlike sounds in infancy.

Munro, & MacKay, 1995). Children may also have an easier time mastering a language's various verb tenses and complex aspects of syntax when they are immersed in the language within the first 5 to 10 years of life (Bialystok, 1994a, 1994b; Johnson & Newport, 1989). The effects of age are particularly evident when the second language is syntactically and phonetically very different from the first (Bialystok, 1994a; Strozer, 1994).

Not all research studies yield evidence in support of sensitive periods in language development, however, and some of those that do are methodologically flawed (Bialystok, 1994a). Studies comparing the relative success of various age groups learning a second language yield mixed results; the more sophisticated cognitive abilities of older children and adults may sometimes counterbalance any biological advantage that younger children have (Bialystok, 1994b; Long, 1995; Snow & Hoefnagel-Höhle, 1978).

Because language acquisition involves learning a diverse body of knowledge and skills—including those that are perceptual, psychomotor, and cognitive in nature—there are probably different sensitive periods for different aspects of language development (Bruer, 1999; Locke, 1993). Furthermore, people can learn the vocabulary of a particular language at virtually *any* age (Bruer, 1999). Thus, it may be difficult, perhaps even impossible, to pinpoint a single, specific age range when language is most effectively learned.

FIGURE 7–1 Language specialization centers in the brain. Broca's area (in the left frontal lobe) is involved in speech production. Wernicke's area (in the left temporal lobe) is involved in language comprehension.

Although the evidence for a biological basis for language development is certainly compelling, researchers have yet to obtain indisputable evidence that human beings are truly prewired to acquire language. Furthermore, even if they were able to prove that a language acquisition device exists, such information would not necessarily tell us *how* human beings learn language (Pinker, 1987). Information processing theory better addresses this issue.

Information Processing Theory

Some theorists, while not necessarily denying the role of biology, focus more on the specific cognitive processes that children use as they acquire language and on the environmental events that promote language acquisition. The ideas that these theorists offer vary considerably but are all consistent with the general framework of information processing theory. We can summarize the information processing perspective of language development with several key principles:

■ *Developmental changes in cognitive processes account for many trends observed in children's use and understanding of language.* Information processing theorists propose that children's language development is both propelled and limited by the same mechanisms—attention, working memory, an organized knowledge base, and so on—that influence learning and cognition in general (Bates & MacWhinney, 1987; Marcus, 1996; McDevitt & Ford, 1987; Morgan & Demuth, 1996).

Communicating one's thoughts to others is a complex task indeed. It involves knowledge not only about spoken language but also about appropriate eye contact, gestures, and tone of voice (McDevitt & Ford, 1987). The simple act of conversing would be quite difficult if one had to rely on working memory to keep track of so many skills. Instead, many of those skills (e.g., word pronunciation, syntactic rules) are automatized. In many situations, effective communication is also facilitated by previously developed schemas and scripts (e.g., "Hi, how are you?" "Fine, thanks. How are you?") that occur frequently in social interaction and can be used with little thought or effort.

From an information processing standpoint, attention is essential for language learning (Harris, 1992; Hirsh-Pasek & Golinkoff, 1996). Infants pay attention to human speech and speech-related events from a very early age. For instance, young infants show a strong preference for familiar over unfamiliar voices and will expend considerable effort to hear a familiar voice (Locke, 1993). They are also more likely to look at speakers who use the short, simple, rhythmic language that adults frequently use when talking to young children (Fernald, 1992; Kaplan, Goldstein, Huckeby, & Cooper, 1995). Adults seem to know (perhaps unconsciously) that attention is critical for language learning. Adults in Western cultures often point to the people or objects under discussion when talking with their young children, thereby directing their children's attention (Harris, 1992). And the mother of a young deaf child is most likely to sign to her child when she knows that the child can simultaneously see both her signs and the objects or events she is talking about (Harris, 1992).

■ *Language learning involves hypothesis testing, deductive reasoning, and active construction of a language system.* In the process of acquiring knowledge of their native language, growing children may form hypotheses about the meanings of words and the ways in which words can legitimately be combined into sentences. They then test these hypotheses against the specific linguistic input they hear and eventually pull seemingly correct hypotheses into an integrated set of rules that regulates their understanding and use of language (Atkinson, 1992; Cairns, 1996; Cromer, 1993; Karmiloff-Smith, 1993).

Perhaps as a result of the biologically built-in knowledge about language that nativists describe, children's hypotheses about their language are probably limited to a manageable number of possibilities. Children seem to use deductive reasoning to further limit their hypotheses. We find an example of such deductive reasoning in a study by Au and Glusman (1990). The researchers showed preschoolers a stuffed monkeylike animal with pink horns and consistently referred to the animal as a *mido*. Later, they presented a collection of stuffed animals that included several midos and asked the children to find a *theri* in the set. Although the children had no information to guide their selection, they always chose an animal other than a mido. Apparently they deduced that because the monkeylike animals already had a name, a theri had to be a different kind of animal.

Reasoning also comes into play when children use their knowledge of word meanings to derive syntactic categories—a process known as **semantic bootstrapping** (Bates & MacWhinney, 1987; Pinker, 1984, 1987). The ability to produce syntactically correct sentences requires knowing that different words are used in different ways (as nouns, verbs, adjectives, etc.); thus, young children must have an intuitive sense of various word categories long before they study those categories in school. The meanings of words can provide a basis for categorizing words according to their syntactic functions: People and concrete objects are nouns (and so serve similar functions in sentences), actions are verbs, physical properties and characteristics are adjectives, spatial relationships and directions are prepositions, and so on (Pinker, 1984).

■ *Certain kinds of experiences promote language development.* Although early theories of language acquisition that emphasize the importance of imitation and reinforcement have been left by the wayside, information processing theorists nevertheless propose that certain kinds of experiences, including frequent use of words and direct instruction, *do* promote children's acquisition of language. For instance, in a longitudinal study by Harris (1992), children and their mothers were videotaped in free-play situations from the time the children were 6 months old until they reached 2. Harris found that the children were more likely to say words that their mothers used frequently and that they first used the words in the same contexts as their mothers had.

The adults and older children in a child's life sometimes provide direct instruction in word meanings. In the following case, 5-year-old Kris is playing with her 23-month-old cousin Amy. Kris holds up a stuffed dog:

Kris:	What is it?
Amy:	Doggie.
Kris:	What?
Amy:	Doggie.
Kris:	A doggie, yeah. (Picks up elephant.) What is this?
Amy:	Doggie.
Kris:	What?
Amy:	Baby.
Kris:	(Prompts Amy.) No. Uh—. Uh—.
Amy:	Pig.
Kris:	Uh—. Elephant.
Amy:	Elephant.
Kris:	Yeah elephant.
Amy:	(Touches own foot.) Got my foot.
Kris:	(Picks up tiger.) What's this?

semantic bootstrapping
Using knowledge of word meanings to derive knowledge about syntactic categories.

Amy:	Baby.
Kris:	Tiger. You don't know nothin. You say all baby. (Picks up pig.)
Amy:	Baby.
Kris:	What's this?
Amy:	. . . Piggy.
Kris:	What?
Amy:	Piggy.
Kris:	What is it?
Amy:	Piggy.
Kris:	Pig! Pig. Pig. Say "pig." Say "pig."
Amy:	Oh.
Kris:	Say "pig." Oop. You should a said "pig." (dialogue from Miller, 1982, pp. 74–75; format adapted[2])

Whereas language instruction at home is typically haphazard and superficial at best, language instruction at school is more systematic and in-depth, and there is little doubt that such instruction has a significant impact on children's language development. Later in the chapter, we present numerous suggestions for fostering children's language knowledge and skills in classroom contexts.

Critiquing Theories of Language Development

The Basic Developmental Issues table on the next page summarizes how nativism and information processing theory differ in terms of nature versus nurture, universality versus diversity, and qualitative versus quantitative change. Although, on the surface, the two approaches appear to be incompatible, many theorists embrace aspects of both approaches in their attempts to understand how children acquire proficiency in their native language. For instance, some theorists propose that children learn language by formulating and testing hypotheses about word meanings and syntactic rules (an information processing idea) yet suggest that such hypotheses are limited to those that an inherited language acquisition device allows (a nativist idea). Furthermore, the two theoretical perspectives focus on different aspects of language development, with nativism emphasizing syntactic development and information processing theory often looking more closely at semantic development; thus, it may be quite appropriate to shift from one perspective to another depending on the particular aspect of language development under discussion.

One key source of controversy continues to divide the two approaches, however. Most nativists propose that children inherit a mechanism whose sole function is to facilitate the acquisition of language. In contrast, many information processing theorists believe that language development arises out of more general cognitive abilities—abilities that promote learning and development in a wide variety of domains. To date, this issue is unresolved.

Additional theoretical issues related to language development, although not necessarily central to the nativism–information processing debate, remain unanswered as well. Two that have potential implications for parents and teachers are the following:

■ *Which comes first, language comprehension or language production?* Psychologists studying language development frequently make a distinction between expressive and receptive language skills. **Receptive language** is the ability to understand what one hears and reads; in other words, it involves language *comprehension*. **Expressive language** is the ability to communicate effectively either orally or on paper; in other words, it involves language *production*.

A widely held assumption is that receptive language skills must precede expressive language skills; after all, it seems reasonable that children must understand what words and sentences mean before they use them in their own speech and writing. Yet many theorists don't believe the relationship between receptive and expressive language is so clear-cut (Owens, 1996). Children sometimes use words and expressions whose meanings they don't completely understand. Teresa recalls a 3-year-old girl in her preschool class who talked about the "accoutrements" in her purse, presumably after hearing others use the word in a similar context.

receptive language
Ability to understand the language that one hears or reads.

expressive language
Ability to communicate effectively through speaking and writing.

---

[2]For ease of reading, the original format of some dialogue text has been adapted. Changes were made to spell out speakers' names and to alter the typographic style.

Contrasting Contemporary Theories of Language Development

BASIC DEVELOPMENTAL ISSUES

ISSUE	NATIVISM	INFORMATION PROCESSING THEORY
Nature and Nurture	Children develop language only when they are exposed to the language of others; thus, environmental input is essential. However, the typical everyday speech of a language community is incomplete and error-laden and so, in and of itself, provides an insufficient database from which children can create a complex, flexible language system. Thus, children must rely largely on a biological mechanism that includes predetermined "knowledge" about the nature of language and possibly also includes skills that help them decipher the linguistic code.	Most information processing theorists assume that language learning involves a complex interplay between inherited inclinations and abilities, on the one hand, and experiences that facilitate effective language learning (e.g., attention-getting actions by parents, frequent use of words in simplified contexts) on the other.
Universality and Diversity	Although human languages differ in many respects, most languages have certain things in common (e.g., the use of nouns and verbs). Furthermore, children in different language communities reach milestones in language development at similar ages. Diversity exists primarily in the specific phonological, semantic, and syntactic features of various languages.	Information processing mechanisms that affect language acquisition (e.g., attention, working memory) are universally relevant across cultures. Children's unique language experiences, which differ not only from culture to culture but also from home to home, lead both to differences in the language(s) that children speak and also to differences in children's knowledge of a particular language (e.g., the precise meanings they assign to specific words).
Qualitative and Quantitative Change 	Children often acquire specific syntactic structures in a predictable sequence, with noticeable, stage-like changes in linguistic constructions after each new acquisition (e.g., Dale 1976; O'Grady, 1997).	Many changes in language development—for instance, children's ever-enlarging vocabularies, ongoing refinement of what particular words mean, increasing automaticity in certain skills (e.g., word pronunciation), and expanding working memory capacities (enabling production of longer and more complex sentences)—come about in a trendlike, quantitative fashion.

Although the girl used the word appropriately in this situation, she did not understand all its connotations; in other words, her production exceeded her comprehension.

Ultimately, the development of receptive and expressive language skills probably go hand in hand, with language comprehension facilitating language production and language production also enhancing language comprehension. Definitively declaring that one set of skills precedes the other may be as fruitless as answering "Which came first, the chicken or the egg?"

■ *What role does infant-directed speech play in language development?* Earlier we mentioned that infants seem to prefer the short, simple, rhythmic speech that adults often use when they talk to young children. Such **infant-directed speech** (also called *motherese* or *caretaker speech*) is different from normal adult speech in several ways: It is spoken more slowly and distinctly and at a higher pitch, consists of sentences with few words and simple grammatical structures, has exaggerated shifts in tone that help convey a speaker's message, uses a limited vocabulary, involves frequent repetition, and is generally concerned with objects and events that take place in close temporal and physical proximity to the child (Kuhl & Meltzoff, 1997; Littlewood, 1984). Parents and teachers frequently use such speech when they converse with young children, and they adapt their use of it to the age of the children; for example, preschool teachers use simpler speech with their students than first-grade teachers do (Rondal, 1985).

Logically, infant-directed speech should facilitate language development: Its clear pauses between words, simple vocabulary and syntax, exaggerated intonations, and frequent repetition should make it easier for children to decipher what they hear. The problem with this hypothesis

infant-directed speech
Short, simple, high-pitched speech often used when talking to young children.

is that infant-directed speech is not a universal phenomenon. In some cultures, adults do not think of young children as suitable conversation partners and so speak to them only rarely, if at all; despite these circumstances, the children successfully acquire the language of their community (Heath, 1983; O'Grady, 1997). In the following dialogue, two women (Lillie Mae and Mattie) talk about the health problems of a friend (Miss Lula) while Lillie Mae's 18-month-old son Lem plays with a truck nearby. Notice how Lem is clearly taking in what the two women are saying:

Lillie Mae:	Miz Lula done went to de doctor.
Mattie:	Her leg botherin' her?
Lem:	*(rolling his truck and banging it against a board)* Went to de doctor, doctor leg, Miz Lu Lu Lu, rah, rah, rah.
Lillie Mae:	I reckon so, she was complainin' yesterday 'bout her feet so swelled up she couldn't get no shoes on.
Lem:	*(swishing his truck through the air)* Shoe, shoe, shoe, went to doctor in a shoe, doc, doc, duh, duh, duh, poo-sh, get no shoe. (Heath, 1983, p. 92; reprinted with the permission of Cambridge University Press)

If infant-directed speech isn't essential for language development, what, then, is its purpose? One possibility is simply that it enhances adults' ability to communicate effectively with young children (O'Grady, 1997). After all, many parents interact frequently with their infants and toddlers and undoubtedly want to be understood (e.g., Harris, 1992). Infant-directed speech may also be part of parents' and other adults' attempts to establish and maintain affectionate relationships with children—relationships that should have social and emotional benefits down the road (Trainor, Austin, & Desjardins, 2000).

Trends in Language Development

Children show signs of language development even before they say their first word. When they begin to babble at around 7 months of age, they produce a wide variety of speechlike sounds, but they soon drop the sounds they don't hear in the speech around them (Locke, 1993). In essence, infants first babble in a universal "language" and then later babble only in their native tongue.

On average, children begin using recognizable words sometime around their first birthday, and they are putting these words together by their second birthday. During the preschool years they become capable of forming increasingly longer and more complex sentences. By the time they enroll in elementary school, at 5 or 6 years of age, they use language that seems adultlike in many respects.

Yet throughout the elementary and secondary school years, students learn thousands of new words, and they become capable of comprehending and producing increasingly more complex sentences. They also continue to develop skills related to conversing appropriately with others, and they acquire a better understanding of the nature of language. In the following sections we explore the development of semantics, syntax, listening, speaking, sociolinguistic behavior, and metalinguistic awareness during childhood and adolescence.

Semantic Development

Young children typically say their first word at about 12 months of age, although they have learned the meanings of many words before that time (Harris, 1992; O'Grady, 1997; Tincoff & Jusczyk, 1999). By the time they are 18 months old, many children have 50 words in their expressive vocabularies (O'Grady, 1997). There is considerable variability from child to child, however; for example, Mario did not say his first Spanish word until he was 16 months old, and by his second birthday he was using only 21 words (Fantini, 1985).

At some point during the end of the second year or beginning of the third year, a virtual explosion in word acquisition occurs, with children learning 30 to 50 words a month and, later, as many as 20 new words each day; for instance, Mario was using more than 500 words by the time he was 3 (Fantini, 1985; Harris, 1992; O'Grady, 1997). In the preschool years, children also begin to organize their knowledge of various words into categories, hierarchies (e.g., *dogs* and *cats* are both *animals*), and other interword relationships (Harris, 1992).

When children are 6, their knowledge of words in their language—their **lexicon**—includes 8,000 to 14,000 words, of which they use about 2,600 in their own speech (Carey, 1978). By the sixth grade, children's receptive vocabulary includes, on average, 50,000 words; by high school, it includes approximately 80,000 words (Miller & Gildea, 1987; Nippold, 1988; Owens, 1996). Thus, children learn several thousand new words each year (Nagy, Herman, & Anderson, 1985). The rapid increase in vocabulary throughout childhood and adolescence is especially remarkable when we consider what word knowledge includes: Children must know not only what each word means but also how to pronounce it and how to use it in appropriate contexts (Cairns, 1996).

The dramatic increase in the number of words that children can use and understand is the most obvious aspect of semantic development. Yet several other principles characterize semantic development as well:

■ *Over time, children continue to refine their understandings of words.* Children's initial understandings of words are often fuzzy: The children have a general idea of what certain words mean but define them imprecisely and may use them incorrectly. One common error is **undergeneralization,** in which children attach overly restricted meanings to words, leaving out some situations to which the words apply. For example, Jeanne once asked her son Jeff, then 6, to tell her what an *animal* is. He gave her this definition:

It has a head, tail, feet, paws, eyes, noses, ears, lots of hair.

Like Jeff, young elementary school children often restrict their meaning of *animal* primarily to nonhuman mammals, such as dogs and horses, and insist that fish, birds, insects, and people are *not* animals (Carey, 1985b; Saltz, 1971). We see other examples of undergeneralization in Figure 7–2 and in Cairns' (1996) recollection of an incident with her son Stewart:

[Stewart] had been at nursery school and was now at home, playing on the floor while I graded students' papers. He said, "Mommy, will you be my friend?" I assured him that his mommy was his friend, and went on grading papers. After a few more requests, he became quite insistent . . . he wanted me to sit on the floor with him and work a jigsaw puzzle. It turned out that an older girl had come up to him in nursery school, said, "Stewart, will you be my friend?" and had proceeded to sit on the floor and work a jigsaw puzzle with him. That's what he thought *friend* meant. (Cairns, 1996, pp. 110–111)

Another frequent error is **overgeneralization:** Word meanings are too broad, and so words are applied to situations in which they're not appropriate. Figure 7–2 and the following examples illustrate this phenomenon:

Can't you see? I'm barefoot all over!

I'll get up so early that it will still be late.

Isn't there something to eat in the cupboard? There's only a small piece of cake, but it's middle-aged.
(Chukovsky, 1968, p. 3)

In addition to undergeneralizing and overgeneralizing, children sometimes confuse the meanings of similar words. The following conversation illustrates 5-year-old Christine's confusion between *ask* and *tell:*

Adult:	Ask Eric his last name. [Eric Handel is a classmate of Christine's.]
Christine:	Handel.
Adult:	Ask Eric this doll's name.
Christine:	I don't know.
Adult:	Ask Eric what time it is.
Christine:	I don't know how to tell time.
Adult:	Tell Eric what class is in the library.
Christine:	Kindergarten.
Adult:	Ask Eric who his teacher is.
Christine:	Miss Turner. (dialogue from Chomsky, 1969, p. 55; format adapted)

In a similar manner, young children often confuse comparative words, sometimes interpreting *less* as "more" or thinking that *shorter* means "longer" (Owens, 1996; Palermo, 1974).

lexicon
The words one knows in a particular language.

undergeneralization
Overly restricted meaning for a word, excluding some situations to which the word applies.

overgeneralization
Too broad a meaning for a word, such that it is used in situations to which it doesn't apply.

Undergeneralization   Overgeneralization

FIGURE 7–2 Young children sometimes undergeneralize or overgeneralize word meanings.

■ *Children have difficulty with function words throughout the elementary and middle school years.* Some words play a pivotal role in syntax in that they affect the meanings of other words or the interrelationships among words or phrases within a sentence. Such **function words** include articles (e.g., *a, the*), prepositions (e.g., *before, after*), and conjunctions (e.g., *however, unless*).

Children's mastery of a particular function word typically evolves slowly over a period of several years. For instance, although 3-year-olds can distinguish between the articles *a* and *the*, children as old as 9 are occasionally confused about when to use each one (Owens, 1996; Reich, 1986). Children in the upper elementary and middle school grades have trouble with many conjunctions, such as *but, although, yet, however,* and *unless* (Nippold, 1988; Owens, 1996). As an illustration, consider the following two pairs of sentences:

Jimmie went to school, but he felt sick.

Jimmie went to school, but he felt fine.

The meal was good, although the pie was bad.

The meal was good, although the pie was good.

Even 12-year-olds have trouble identifying the correct sentence in pairs like these, reflecting only a vague understanding of the connectives *but* and *although* (Katz & Brent, 1968). (The first sentence is correct in both cases.)

■ *Understanding of abstract words emerges later than understanding of concrete words.* Words like *but* and *although* may be particularly difficult for elementary school children because their meanings are fairly abstract. If we consider Piaget's proposal that abstract thought doesn't emerge until early adolescence, then we realize that students may not fully understand abstract words until the junior high or high school years. Young children in particular are apt to define words (even fairly abstract ones) in terms of the obvious, concrete aspects of their world (Anglin, 1977; Ausubel, Novak, & Hanesian, 1978). For example, when Jeanne's son Jeff was 4, he defined *summer* as the time of year when school is out and it's hot outside; by the time he was 12, he knew that adults define summer in terms of the earth's tilt relative to the sun—a much more abstract notion.

function word
Word that affects the meanings of other words or the interrelationships among words in a sentence.

■ *Children develop separate lexicons for different languages.* Children have an additional task when they are exposed to two or more languages simultaneously: They must learn which words belong to which language. Yet they appear to accomplish the task with very little difficulty. When Mario first encountered English at his daycare center, he mixed English and Spanish words together as he spoke. He quickly learned to separate the two lexicons, however, and by the time he was 2 years and 8 months old, he was able to speak exclusively in one language or the other and knew which language was appropriate in different contexts (Fantini, 1985).

One particular challenge for Mario—and most likely for any child who learns two different languages in two different environments—was that he would often learn a word in one language but not know its equivalent in the other language. For instance, at home he would sometimes use English words within his Spanish sentences only because he had no other way to express his thoughts. In the following scenario, Mario, age 6, is describing the day's school art project to his mother (English translations are in italics):

Mario:	. . . y después ponemos "cranberries" con "marshmallows" y "pipe cleaner" . . . y una cosa donde vienen las medias de mujer . . . un "pinecone" . . . y después se pone el "glitter" . . . (. . . *and then we put some "cranberries" with "marshmallows" and "pipe cleaner"* . . . *and then the thing (container) in which women's stockings come* . . . *a "pinecone"* . . . *and then you put the "glitter"*. . .)
Mamá:	(interjecting) "Brillo" (*Glitter*)
Mario:	(continuing) . . . y con "glue" . . . [. . . *and with "glue"*. . .]
Mamá:	"Goma" ("*Glue*")
Mario:	. . . y después lo pintas todo "yellow." [. . . *and then you paint it all "yellow."*]
Mamá:	"Amarillo" (*Yellow*) (Fantini, 1985, p. 87)

Mario was fortunate, in that his mother was bilingual and could supply the Spanish equivalents of English words he had encountered at school. Eventually, however, because his schooling was almost entirely in English, Mario's English lexicon far surpassed his Spanish lexicon.

How Children Learn Word Meanings   Children and adolescents learn some words through direct instruction at home and at school. For instance, parents foster toddlers' and preschoolers' semantic development by labeling objects that their children see and by asking such questions as "What is _____?" and "Where is the _____?" while looking at picture books with their children (Dunham, Dunham, & Curwin, 1993; Sénéchal, Thomas, & Monker, 1995). In school, too, explicit instruction in word meanings is beneficial (Fukkink & de Glopper, 1998).

But youngsters probably learn most words by inferring their meaning from the context in which they encounter them (Nippold, 1988; Pinker, 1987; Waxman, 1990). As an example, you can probably learn something about the word *gerk* from reading this statement:

When I arrived at the lab to do my science project, I realized with dismay that I had forgotten to bring my *gerk.*

Although there is not enough information for you to deduce exactly what a *gerk* is, you can reasonably assume that it is (a) a noun, (b) a concrete object, and (c) either helpful or essential for conducting a science project.

Small children—toddlers especially—may need numerous repetitions of a particular word before they understand and use it (Harris, 1992; Peters, 1983). Eventually, however, children become capable of inferring a word's general meaning after only one exposure, a process known as **fast mapping** (Pinker, 1982). Notice how readily you can understand *gerk* if given a little more information:

When I arrived at the lab to do my science project, I realized with dismay that I had forgotten to bring the *gerk* in which I kept my science notes and lab assignments.

With this one statement, you can deduce that a *gerk* must be some sort of container (perhaps a backpack or briefcase) appropriate for carrying important papers.

Over time, children refine their understandings of words through repeated encounters with the words in different contexts and sometimes through direct feedback when they use the words incorrectly (Carey & Bartlett, 1978). In many cases, learning a word's precise meaning

fast mapping
Inferring a word's general meaning after a single exposure.

involves identifying the **defining features** of the concept that the word represents—that is, identifying the characteristics that a particular object or event must exhibit in order to be classified as an instance of that concept. For example, a *circle* must be both round and two-dimensional. *Red* is a term for a certain range of wavelengths of light. People who *walk* are people who stand upright, move their bodies by moving their feet, and have at least one foot on the ground at all times. (If both feet are in the air at once, we are talking instead about *running, skipping, hopping,* or *jumping.*)

Words are most easily learned when they have defining features that are concrete and obvious. Words are harder to learn when their defining features are abstract, subtle, or difficult to pin down. Children, younger ones especially, are often misled by **correlational features**—attributes that are nonessential but frequently present—that are more readily observable than the defining features (Keil, 1989; Mervis, 1987). For example, recall 4-year-old Jeff's belief that *summer* is the time of year when it's hot and school is out; such features are more obvious than summer's defining feature: the earth's tilt relative to the sun. And consider how, 2 years later, Jeff and his older sister Tina defined the word *friend:*

Jeff (age 6):
To play with.

Tina (age 12):
To be your friend and help you in good times and bad times. They're there so you can tell secrets. They're people that care. They're there because they like you. They're people you can trust.

Jeff focused on something he could easily observe—the action of playing. In contrast, Tina, as a 12-year-old, defined a friend as someone "you can trust." Trustworthiness is (in our minds, at least) a defining feature of the word *friend,* but for Jeff, availability for play time was the only consistent feature of *friend* that he observed.

Fostering Semantic Development   Researchers have identified several strategies for how teachers can help their students learn word meanings:

■ *Give definitions.* People learn words more easily when they are told what the defining features are—in other words, when they are given definitions (Merrill & Tennyson, 1977; Tennyson & Cocchiarella, 1986). Definitions are particularly valuable when defining features are abstract or otherwise not obvious. Children can usually learn what a *circle* is and what *red* means even without definitions, because roundness and redness are characteristics that are easily noticed. But the defining features of such words as *polygon* and *fragile* are more subtle; for words like these, definitions can be very helpful. In addition to providing definitions, teachers should also have students define new vocabulary in their own words and use this vocabulary in a variety of contexts.

Children acquire more accurate understandings of words when they see concrete examples.

■ *Provide examples and nonexamples.* People often acquire a more accurate understanding of a word when they are shown several examples (Barringer & Gholson, 1979; Merrill & Tennyson, 1978; Tennyson & Cocchiarella, 1986). Ideally, such examples should be as different from one another as possible so that they illustrate a word's entire range. To illustrate, if teachers limit their examples of *animal* to dogs, cats, cows, and horses, children will understandably draw the conclusion that all animals have four legs and fur (a case of undergeneralization). But if teachers also present goldfish, robins, beetles, earthworms, and people as examples of *animal,* children are more likely to recognize that animals can in fact look very different from one another and that not all of them have legs or fur.

In addition to having examples, students benefit from having *non*examples of a word, particularly those examples that are "near misses" to the word's meaning (Winston, 1973). For instance, to learn what a *salamander* is, a child can be shown such similar animals as snakes and lizards and told that they are "not salamanders." Similarly, when young Jeff is playing with someone who always wants to fight and refuses to share, he can be told, "This boy is not a *friend.*" By presenting nonexamples, including the near misses, teachers minimize the extent to which students are likely to overgeneralize in their use of words.

defining feature
Characteristic that must be present in all instances of a concept.

correlational feature
Characteristic present in many instances of a concept but not essential for concept membership.

■ *Give feedback when students use words incorrectly.* Misconceptions about word meanings (e.g., under- and overgeneralizations) sometimes reveal themselves in students' speech and writing. Astute teachers listen closely not only to what their students say but also to how they say it, and they also look at how students use words in their writing. For instance, a preschooler might mistakenly refer to a rhinoceros as a "hippo," an elementary school student might deny that a square is a rectangle, and a high school student might use the term *atom* when she is really talking about molecules. In such situations, teachers should gently correct the misconceptions, for instance by saying something along these lines: "A lot of people get hippos and rhinoceroses confused, because both of them are large and gray. This animal has a large horn growing out from its nose, so it's a rhinoceros. Let's find a picture of a hippo and look at how the two animals are different."

■ *Encourage students to read as much as possible.* As noted earlier, students probably acquire many more new words through their informal encounters with those words than through formal vocabulary instruction. One way for students to encounter new words is by reading fiction and nonfiction. Avid readers learn many more new words and so have larger vocabularies than do students who read infrequently (Allen, Cipielewski, & Stanovich, 1992; Anderson, Wilson, & Fielding, 1988; Fukkink & de Glopper, 1998; Stanovich, 2000).

Syntactic Development

Which of the following sentences are grammatically correct?

* Growing children need nutritious food and lots of exercise.
* Experience students find to be many junior high school an unsettling.
* Allow class discussions to exchange ideas and perspectives students.
* Schizophrenia often does not appear until adolescence or adulthood.

You undoubtedly realized that the first and last sentences are grammatically correct and that the two middle ones are not. But *how* were you able to tell the difference? Can you describe the specific grammatical rules you used to make your decision?

Rules of syntax—the rules that we use to combine words together into meaningful sentences that express the interrelationships among the words—are incredibly complex (Chomsky, 1972). Much of our knowledge about syntax is at an unconscious level: Although we can produce acceptable sentences and understand the sentences of others, we cannot put our finger on exactly what it is that we *do* know about language that allows us to do these things (Aitchison, 1996).

Children show evidence that they are using simple syntactic rules even when they are putting only two words together as they speak (Cairns, 1996; O'Grady, 1997). For example, their two-word combinations might reflect description ("Allgone sticky"), location ("Sweater chair"), or possession ("Mommy sock"). As children's sentences increase in length, they also increase in syntactic complexity. By the time children reach school age, they have mastered many of the basics of sentence construction (McNeill, 1970; Reich, 1986). Nevertheless, we continue to see some gaps in their syntactic knowledge throughout the elementary school years and often into the secondary school years as well. Following are noteworthy aspects of syntactic development during the school years:

■ *Children learn general rules for word endings before they learn the exceptions.* Knowledge of syntax includes knowledge about when to use word endings (suffixes) such as *-s, -er,* and *-ed.* When children first learn the rules for using suffixes (e.g., that *-s* indicates plural, *-er* indicates a comparison, and *-ed* indicates past tense), they apply these rules indiscriminately, without regard for exceptions. Thus, a child might say "I have two *foots,*" "Chocolate ice cream is *gooder* than vanilla," or "I *goed* to Grandma's house." This phenomenon, known as **overregularization**, is especially common during the preschool and early elementary years. It gradually diminishes as children learn the irregular forms of various words—for instance, as they learn that the plural of *foot* is *feet,* the comparative form of *good* is *better,* and the past tense of *go* is *went* (Cazden, 1968; Marcus, 1996; Siegler, 1994).

Yet most high school students (and, in fact, many adults as well) haven't completely mastered the irregularities of the English language (Marcus, 1996). For instance, as a 16-year-old,

overregularization
Applying a syntactical rule in situations where exceptions to the rule apply.

Jeanne's son Jeff consistently said "I have *broughten* . . . " despite Jeanne's constant reminders to say "I have *brought*. . . . "

■ *Young children rely heavily on word order when they interpret sentences.* Children in the preschool and early elementary years are often misled by the order in which words appear. For instance, many preschoolers seem to apply a general rule that a pronoun refers to the noun that immediately precedes it (O'Grady, 1997). Consider the sentence "John said that Peter washed him." Many 4-year-olds think that *him* refers to *Peter* and so conclude that Peter washed himself. Similarly, kindergartners are likely to have trouble with the sentence "Because she was tired, Mommy was sleeping" because *no* noun appears before *she* (O'Grady, 1997).

We see the influence of word order in other situations as well. In one study (Chomsky, 1969), children were shown a doll with a blindfold over its eyes and asked, "Is this doll easy to see or hard to see?" Children as old as 8 had trouble interpreting the question; they thought that the *doll* was the one doing the "seeing." The following conversation with 6-year-old Lisa illustrates the problem the children had:

Experimenter:	Is this doll easy to see or hard to see?
Lisa:	Hard to see.
Experimenter:	Will you make her easy to see.
Lisa:	If I can get this untied.
Experimenter:	Will you explain why she was hard to see.
Lisa:	(To doll) Because you had a blindfold over your eyes.
Experimenter:	And what did you do?
Lisa:	I took it off. (dialogue from Chomsky, 1969, p. 30; format adapted)

■ *The ability to comprehend passive sentences evolves gradually during the preschool and elementary school years.* Passive sentences frequently confuse young children, who may incorrectly attribute the action described in a sentence to the subject of the sentence—someone who is actually the *recipient* of the action. Consider these two sentences:

The boy is pushed by the girl.

The cup is washed by the girl.

Preschoolers are more likely to be confused by the first sentence—that is, to think that the boy is the one doing the pushing—than by the second sentence (Karmiloff-Smith, 1979). The first sentence has two possible "actors," but the second sentence has only one: Both boys and girls can push someone else, but cups can't wash girls. Complete understanding of passive sentences doesn't appear until sometime around fourth grade (O'Grady, 1997; Owens, 1996; Tager-Flusberg, 1993).

■ *Children can be confused by sentences with multiple clauses.* Word order sometimes leads young children to misinterpret multiple-clause sentences (Clark, 1971; Sheldon, 1974). Consider the sentence "The horse kicked the pig after he jumped over the fence." Children as old as 6 often say that the horse kicked the pig *before* it jumped over the fence, even though the word *after* clearly communicates the opposite sequence (Clark, 1971).

Children begin to produce simple subordinate clauses, such as those that follow and modify nouns (e.g., "This is the toy *that I want*") at about age 4 (Owens, 1996). Sentences with one clause embedded in the middle of another clause are more difficult, particularly if the noun tying the clauses together has a different function in each clause. Consider the sentence "The dog *that was chased by the boy* is angry" (Owens, 1996, p. 382). The dog is the subject of the main clause ("The dog . . . is angry") but the recipient of the action in the embedded clause (". . . [dog] was chased by the boy"). Seventh graders easily understand such sentences, but younger children overrely on word order to interpret them and so may conclude that the boy, rather than the dog, is angry (Owens, 1996).

■ *Knowledge of syntactic rules continues to develop at the secondary level.* In middle school and high school, adolescents learn more subtle aspects of syntax, such as subject-verb and noun-pronoun agreement, correct uses of *that* versus *which* to introduce subordinate clauses, functions of such punctuation marks as colons and semicolons, and so on. They rarely develop such knowledge on their own; instead, most of their syntactic development probably occurs as the result of formal language instruction, especially courses in language arts, English composition, and foreign language.

■ *Multilingual children readily distinguish among the syntactic structures used in different languages.* As Mario simultaneously learned Spanish and English, he also learned which syntactic rules applied to each language. Intrusions from one language to the other occurred infrequently even in the preschool years (he once pluralized the English word *balloon* with the Spanish suffix *-es*, saying "balloones") and disappeared altogether soon after (Fantini, 1985).

How Children Acquire Syntactic Knowledge   Theorists do not yet have a clear understanding of how children learn syntactic rules. However, most theorists believe that syntactic development is largely a constructive and unconscious process, especially in the early years (Aitchison, 1996; Cairns, 1996; Karmiloff-Smith, 1993). Young children typically receive little if any direct instruction about how to form sentences. Instead, they apparently develop their own set of rules through their observations of other people's speech. Corrective feedback from others may be helpful in the process, yet children acquire increasingly sophisticated syntactic structures even without such feedback (Cromer, 1993).

As children develop new rules, they may initially misapply them. The overregularization phenomenon described earlier is a case in point. When children first learn the *-ed* rule for past tense, they sometimes let the rule override the irregular verb forms they already know. Thus, a child who has previously said *I went* may begin to say *I goed* after acquiring the *-ed* rule. Eventually, the child refines the rule to allow for exceptions and so applies it only when appropriate (Dale, 1976; Marcus, 1996).

Formal language arts instruction brings some syntactic knowledge to a conscious level. Beginning in the upper elementary and middle school grades, children often learn to identify the various parts of a sentence (e.g., subject, direct object, prepositional phrase, subordinate clause) about which they acquired intuitive knowledge many years earlier. They also study various verb tenses (e.g., present, past, present progressive) even though they have been using these tenses in their everyday speech for quite some time.

Fostering Syntactic Development   Particularly as they are learning the more complex and subtle aspects of syntax, children and adolescents often benefit from ongoing instruction and practice in the grammatical aspects of the English language. Following are three examples of how teachers can promote students' syntactic development:

■ *Teach irregular forms of verbs and comparative adjectives.* Children do not always hear the standard irregular forms of verbs and adjectives in the everyday speech of people around them. For example, their young playmates may talk about what's *badder* or *worser,* and many adults confuse the past tenses of the verbs *lay* and *lie* (*laid* and *lay,* respectively).

■ *Describe various sentence structures and give students considerable practice in their use.* Having students examine and practice common syntactic structures (active and passive voice, independent and dependent clauses, etc.) has at least two benefits. First, students should be better able to vary their sentence structure as they write—a strategy associated with more sophisticated writing (Byrnes, 1996; Spivey, 1997). Second, learning the labels for such structures (e.g., *passive voice*) in English should help them acquire analogous structures in other languages that they study at a later time.

■ *Provide ample opportunities for students to express their ideas in a relatively "formal" way, both orally and on paper.* As nativists have pointed out, people do not always adhere to syntactic rules in their everyday speech. What's common in casual speech, such as the use of the plural pronoun *they* to refer to a single individual, may be frowned upon in writing. In formal and public situations (e.g., a presentation to a large group, or a letter to the editor of a local newspaper), correct grammar is, in many people's minds, an indication that the speaker or writer is educated and well-informed and is therefore someone to take seriously (Owens, 1996; Purcell-Gates, 1995; Smith, 1998).

Development of Listening Skills

The basic elements of spoken language—the sounds designated as consonants, vowels, and blends—are collectively known as **phonemes**. Phonemes are the smallest units of spoken language that indicate differences in meaning in a particular language. For instance, the word *bite* has three phonemes: a "buh" sound, an "eye" sound, and a "tuh" sound. If we change any one

phonemes
Smallest units of a spoken language that signify differences in meaning.

of these sounds—for instance, if we change *b* to *f* (*fight*), long *i* to long *a* (*bait*), or *t* to *k* (*bike*)—then we get a new word with a different meaning.

In the first few months of life, infants can discriminate among a wide variety of phonemes, including many that they don't hear in the speech around them (Jusczyk, 1995; Werker & Lalonde, 1988). By the time they are a year old, however, they hear only the differences that are important in their own language (Kuhl, Williams, Lacerda, Stevens, & Lindblom, 1992; Werker & Lalonde, 1988). Thus, the sensitive period for learning to differentiate among very similar speech sounds occurs quite early in life. Youngsters quickly begin to ignore phonemic differences that may be important in some languages but are insignificant in their native tongue.

Infants have additional listening abilities that facilitate language acquisition. For instance, 8-month-olds show some ability to divide a continuous stream of speech sounds into individual words (Aslin, Saffran, & Newport, 1998). They also pay more attention to words that they've heard frequently in the past; for instance, Mario showed an early preference to listen to Spanish rather than English (Fantini, 1985; Jusczyk & Aslin, 1995; Saffran, Aslin, & Newport, 1996).

As children move into the preschool, elementary, and secondary school years, their ability to understand what they hear is, of course, closely related to their semantic and syntactic development. The development of listening comprehension skills is also characterized by the following trends:

■ *Young children rely more heavily on context than older children do.* Using various nonverbal contextual clues, children often realize that what a speaker says is different from what the speaker actually means (Donaldson, 1978; Flavell et al., 1993; Paul, 1990). For example, kindergartners may correctly conclude that a teacher who asks "Whose jacket do I see lying on the floor?" is actually requesting the jacket's owner to pick it up and put it where it belongs. Yet young children are sometimes *too* dependent on context for determining the meaning of language, to the point where they don't listen carefully enough to understand a spoken message accurately. They may "hear" what they *think* the speaker means, based on their beliefs about the speaker's intentions, rather than discerning what was actually said.

A study by McGarrigle (cited in Donaldson, 1978) illustrates such misinterpretation. Six-year-olds were shown four cows (two black, two white) and four horses (three black, one white) and asked, "Are there more *cows* or more *black horses*?" (see Figure 7–3). Only 14% correctly answered that there were more cows; most said that there were more black horses. Follow-up questions indicated that the children were interpreting the question as a request to compare only the *black* cows with the black horses. For example, one child defended his incorrect answer this way: "There's more black horses 'cos there's only two black cows" (p. 44). Donaldson (1978) proposed that such findings cast doubt on Piaget's belief that young children cannot classify objects in more than one way at a time. She suggested that, instead, children may merely have difficulty understanding the questions they are asked. You may recall Brian, the 6-year-old in Chapter 4 who was shown a dozen wooden beads (two white and the rest brown) and asked, "Are there more brown beads or more wooden beads?" At this point, we might wonder if Brian's response ("More brown ones") was actually a correct response to the question Brian *thought* the experimenter was asking ("Are there more brown beads or more *white* beads?").

Older children and adolescents consider the context in a somewhat different way, in that they compare a message to the reality of the situation. Such a comparison enables them to

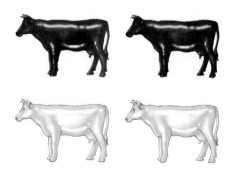
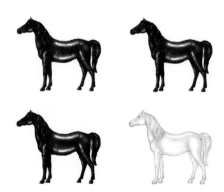

FIGURE 7–3 Are there more cows or more black horses?
After McGarrigle (cited in Donaldson, 1978).

detect sarcasm—to realize that the speaker actually means the exact opposite of what he or she is saying (Capelli, Nakagawa, & Madden, 1990). For instance, they understand that someone who says "Oh, that's just *great!*" in the face of dire circumstances doesn't think the situation is "great" at all.

■ *Young children have an overly simplistic view of what "good listening" is.* Children in the early elementary grades believe that they are good listeners if they simply sit quietly without interrupting the person speaking. Older children (e.g., 11-year-olds) are more likely to recognize that good listening also requires an *understanding* of what is being said (McDevitt, Spivey, Sheehan, Lennon, & Story, 1990).

■ *Elementary school children do not always know what they should do when they don't understand.* In studies by McDevitt (1990; McDevitt et al., 1990), children in grades 1, 3, and 5 were given the following dilemma:

This is a story about a girl named Mary. Mary is at school listening to her teacher, Ms. Brown. Ms. Brown explains how to use a new computer that she just got for their classroom. She tells the children in the classroom how to use the computer. Mary doesn't understand the teacher's directions. She's confused. What should Mary do? (McDevitt, 1990, p. 570)

Some children responded that Mary should ask the teacher for further explanation. But many others said that Mary should either listen more carefully or seek clarification of the procedure from other children. Many children, especially younger ones, apparently believe that it is inappropriate to ask their teacher for help, perhaps because they have previously been discouraged from asking questions in school or at home (McDevitt, 1990; McDevitt et al., 1990). Cultural background plays a role here as well: Children growing up in many Asian and Mexican American communities are reluctant to ask questions because they've been taught that initiating a conversation with an adult is disrespectful (Delgado-Gaitan, 1994; Grant & Gomez, 2001; Trawick-Smith, 2000).

Children in the early elementary grades believe that good listening simply means sitting quietly without interrupting. They don't necessarily understand that listening also means paying attention and understanding what they hear.

■ *Older children and adolescents become increasingly able to find multiple meanings in messages.* As students move into the middle and secondary grades, they become aware that messages may be ambiguous and so have two or more possible meanings (Bearison & Levey, 1977; Nippold, 1988; Owens, 1996). They also become better able to understand **figurative speech,** speech that communicates meaning beyond a literal interpretation of its words. For instance, they understand that idioms are not to be taken at face value—that a person who "hits the roof" doesn't *really* hit the roof and that someone who is "tied up" isn't necessarily bound with rope. They become increasingly adept at interpreting similes and metaphors (e.g., "Her hands are like ice," "That man is the Rock of Gibraltar"). And in the late elementary years, they begin to draw generalizations from proverbs such as "Look before you leap" or "Don't put the cart before the horse." Students' ability to interpret proverbs in a generalized, abstract fashion continues to develop even in the high school years (Owens, 1996).

Although children's ability to understand figurative language depends to some degree on their cognitive maturity, it may also depend on how much children have been exposed to such language. Many inner-city African American communities make heavy use of figurative language, such as similes, metaphors, and hyperbole (intentional overexaggeration), in their day-to-day conversations, jokes, and stories (Hale-Benson, 1986; Ortony, Turner, and Larson-Shapiro, 1985; Smith, 1998). The following anecdote illustrates:

I once asked my mother, upon her arrival from church, "Mom, was it a good sermon?" To which she replied, "Son, by the time the minister finished preaching, the men were crying and the women had passed out on the floor." (Smith, 1998, p. 202)

With such a rich oral tradition, it is not surprising that inner-city African American youth are especially advanced in their ability to comprehend figurative language (Ortony et al., 1985).

Cognitive Factors Influencing the Development of Listening Comprehension Not only does children's ability to understand what they hear depend on their knowledge of word mean-

figurative speech
Speech that communicates meaning beyond a literal interpretation of its words.

PROMOTING LISTENING SKILLS IN YOUNG CHILDREN

■ Discuss the components of good listening.

A first-grade teacher explains to her students that "good listening" involves more than just sitting quietly, that it also involves paying attention and trying to understand what the speaker is saying.

■ Discuss courses of action that children should take when they don't understand a speaker.

A second-grade teacher encourages his students to ask questions whenever they don't understand something he tells them in class.

■ Expect children to listen attentively for only short periods of time.

A kindergarten teacher has learned that most of her students can listen quietly to a speaker for no more than 10 or 15 minutes at a stretch, and he plans his daily classroom activities accordingly.

■ Present only small amounts of information at once.

When a preschool teacher has her class make Valentine's Day cards for their parents or guardians, she describes only one or two steps of the process at a time.

ings and syntax, but it also depends on their general knowledge about the world. For instance, children can better understand a classmate's description of a newly purchased Volkswagen Beetle if they have a schema of what Volkswagen Beetles look like. They can better understand a friend's story about a trip to a fast-food restaurant if they have a script of what such visits typically entail. Children's schemas, scripts, and other knowledge about the world enable them to draw inferences from the things they hear, thus filling in any gaps in the information presented.

Working memory—that part of memory where human beings first hold new information while they mentally process it—influences listening comprehension as well (Anthony, Lonigan, & Dyer, 1996; French & Brown, 1977). Children's ability to understand the things they hear is limited to what they can reasonably hold in working memory. A message that presents too much information in too short a time will be difficult, perhaps even impossible, to understand; in such circumstances, what children hear may, as the saying goes, go in one ear and out the other.

Because young children tend to have a smaller working memory capacity than older children and adults (see Chapter 5), they will be especially limited in their ability to understand and remember what they hear. Preschoolers, for instance, often have trouble remembering and following directions with multiple steps (French & Brown, 1977).

Interpreting messages in nonliteral ways requires abstract thinking and an ability to draw analogies across diverse situations (Owens, 1996; Winner, 1988). Given what we know about when abstract thinking develops, it is hardly surprising that children have difficulty understanding metaphors and proverbs in the preschool and early elementary years.

Promoting Listening Comprehension   Teachers at the preschool and early elementary levels must take into account young children's limited listening comprehension skills when they present information or instructions in an entirely verbal manner (see the Development and Practice feature above). Following are three more general suggestions for teachers at all grade levels:

■ *Adjust the length of verbal presentations to the attention span of the age group, and avoid information overload.* As information processing theory tells us, learners of all ages can understand a message only when they are paying attention, and they can handle only a limited amount of information at a time. Given such limitations, students often benefit from hearing something more than once (e.g., Wasik, Karweit, Burns, & Brodsky, 1998).

■ *Consider children's semantic and syntactic development when you speak, and check frequently to be sure that the children understand.* Using vocabulary and syntactic structures appropriate to the age group is, of course, essential if teachers want their students to understand what they say. Furthermore, rather than assume that their messages are understood, teachers should *make sure* that they are, especially when presenting important information. For example, a teacher might ask questions that assess students' understanding, have students restate ideas in their own words, or have students demonstrate what they've learned through actions or pictures.

■ *Encourage critical listening.* Sometime around the age of 4 to 6, children begin to realize that what people say is not necessarily what is true (Flavell et al., 1993). Yet throughout the elementary and secondary grades, children and adolescents sometimes have difficulty separating fact from fiction in the messages they hear. Children who are taught not to believe everything they hear are more likely to evaluate messages for errors, falsehoods, and ambiguities. For example, when children are reminded that television commercials are designed to persuade them to buy something, they are less likely to be influenced by those commercials (McDevitt, 1990; Roberts, Christenson, Gibson, Mooser, & Goldberg, 1980).

Development of Speaking Skills

As children become more proficient in understanding what other people say, they also become more proficient at expressing their own thoughts, ideas, and wishes. When children first begin to speak, their objective is often to control someone else's behavior. For example, a toddler who yells "Elmo!" may very well be asking a parent to purchase the Elmo doll she sees on a shelf at the toy store. Over the next 2 or 3 years, however, children increasingly use speech to exchange information with others. By age 4, exchanging information appears to be the primary function of oral language (Owens, 1996).

During childhood and adolescence, several trends characterize the development of speaking skills:

■ *Pronunciation continues to develop through the early elementary years.* Children typically do not master all the sounds of the English language until they are about 8 years old (Owens, 1996). During the preschool years, they are likely to have difficulty pronouncing *r* and *th*; for instance, they might say "wabbit" instead of "rabbit" and "dat" instead of "that." Most children have acquired these sounds by the time they are 6, but at this age they may still have trouble with such diphthongs as *str, sl,* and *dr* (Owens, 1996).

Recall Mario's kindergarten teacher referring to Mario's "slight accent." Mario mastered Spanish pronunciation by the time he was 3; a few months later, he could produce many of the additional phonemes required for English. Nevertheless, Spanish phonemes occasionally made their way into Mario's English for several years thereafter, giving his speech a Spanish accent (Fantini, 1985).

■ *As children grow older, their conversations with others increase in length and depth.* Early conversations tend to be short. Most young children are quite willing and able to introduce new topics into a conversation, but they have difficulty maintaining a sustained interchange about any single topic (Owens, 1996). As a result, the things under discussion are likely to change frequently; for instance, a 5-year-old may talk about 50 different topics within a 15-minute period (Brinton & Fujiki, 1984). As children grow older, they can carry on lengthier discussions about a single issue or event, and as they reach adolescence, the content of their conversations becomes increasingly abstract (Owens, 1996).

■ *Children become increasingly able to adapt their speech to the characteristics of their listeners.* As early as age 3, preschoolers use simpler language with toddlers than they do with adults and peers (McDevitt & Ford, 1987; Shatz & Gelman, 1973). Yet preschoolers and elementary school children don't always take their listeners' visual perspectives and prior knowledge into account and so may provide insufficient information for their listeners to understand what they are saying (Glucksberg & Krauss, 1967; McDevitt & Ford, 1987). We can recall numerous occasions when our own children have yelled "What's *this*?" from another room, apparently unaware that we could not possibly see what they were looking at. To some extent, such speech may reflect the preoperational egocentrism that Piaget described. However, it may also be the result of young children's lack of proficiency in precisely describing the objects and events that they are currently experiencing or have previously witnessed (McDevitt & Ford, 1987).

As children grow older, they become increasingly able to take other people's knowledge and perspectives into consideration and so are better able to make their meanings clear; for instance, they give more elaborate explanations to people who they know are unfamiliar with what they are talking about (Sonnenschein, 1988). They also become better able to read the subtle nonverbal signals (e.g., the puzzled brows, the lengthy silences) that indicate that others don't understand what they are saying (McDevitt & Ford, 1987).

■ *Over time, children become more skillful at narratives.* Beginning in the preschool years, children can tell a story, or **narrative**—a sequence of events, either real or fictional, that are logically interconnected (McKeough, 1995; Sutton-Smith, 1986). The following narrative, told by 4-year-old Lucy, is typical:

> Once upon a time there was a girl who lived on a farm with a very good horse and she always rode to the country on the horse and they had a picnic together. (McKeough, 1995, p. 156)

Kindergartners and first graders can often describe a sequence that reflects appropriate ordering of events and includes cause-effect relationships (Kemper, 1984; Kemper & Edwards, 1986; McKeough, 1995). Narratives become increasingly complex during the elementary years: Definite plot lines begin to emerge, as do descriptions of people's thoughts, motives, and emotions (Kemper, 1984; Owens, 1996).

The exact nature of children's narratives varies somewhat from culture to culture. For example, in some African American communities, narratives may include several events that, on the surface, appear to be unrelated yet all contribute to a single underlying message—perhaps providing strategies for avoiding a particular individual or helping one's baby brother (Hale-Benson, 1986; Owens, 1996; Trawick-Smith, 2000). Children from some backgrounds may have little or no exposure to certain kinds of narratives before beginning school (Heath, 1986). For instance, in some working-class Southern communities, children have few if any opportunities to describe events that they alone have experienced; they are more likely to describe events that they have shared with their listeners (Heath, 1986).

■ *Creative and figurative language emerge during the elementary years and continue into adolescence.* Children become increasingly creative in their language use. Elementary school children have widely shared expressions that they use to make choices ("Eenie, meenie, minie, mo"), challenge one another ("I double-dare you"), and establish standards for behavior ("Finders keepers, losers weepers"; Owens, 1996). In inner-city African American communities, creative word play may also appear in the form of **sounding**, playful teasing of one another through exaggerated insults (e.g., "Your momma is so dumb that she climbed over a pane of glass to see what was on the other side"). (Additional examples of sounding appear in the story of Sam, p. 161, in Chapter 5.) Exaggeration (hyperbole) is evident in African American storytelling as well. In the following exchange, 12-year-old Terry and his neighbor Tony begin with a kernel of truth (a cat fight in the neighborhood) and then let their imaginations run wild:

Terry:	Didja hear 'bout Aunt Bess' cat las' night?
Tony:	No, what 'bout dat ol' cat?
Terry:	Dat cat get in a fight.
Tony:	A fight?
Terry:	Yeah, it kilt a dog.
Tony:	Ain't no cat can kill no dog.
Terry:	Dis cat, he kilt a big dog, dat ol' German shepherd stay down by ol' man Oak's place.
Tony:	What'd you do?
Terry:	Me? I kilt a horse.
Tony:	You ain't kilt no horse, (pause) more'n likely a mouse. Where?
Terry:	On Main Street. Yesterday.
Tony:	And you kilt one, for sure?
Terry:	Yea, me 'n dat ol' cat, we built a big fire, stirred it aroun', threw oil in it, got it goin' good, and I rod [*sic*] dat horse right in.
Tony:	Ya did?
Terry:	Yup.
Tony:	I know, it took a while to git de cat outta de fire, 'bout (pause) maybe a week or so, 'n Mr. Rowe [who owns a bicycle shop on Main Street] give us a bicycle, 'n we ride de horse, 'n my friend, Steve, he ride de horse, too, 'n we come back and foun' dat ol' cat done kilt dat big dog.
Terry:	Why?
Tony:	'Cause dat cat say "Wow, I'm de greates', ain't no dog kin git me," (pause) like ain't no fire gonna git *me* (pause) 'n my horse (pause) 'n my bicycle. (Heath, 1983, pp. 183–184; reprinted with the permission of Cambridge University Press)

narrative
A sequence of events, either real or fictional, that are logically interconnected; a story.

sounding
Friendly, playful exchange of insults, common in some African American communities.

The use of figurative language in children's speech emerges during the elementary years and increases in frequency and sophistication during the secondary school years. Adolescents often use metaphors, similes, and phrases with double meanings; they are also likely to use sarcasm to communicate a message opposite from what their words mean literally (Owens, 1996).

■ *Adolescents sometimes use their own teen "dialect" in conversing with one another.* Many adolescents express themselves in ways that are unique to their age group, or perhaps to a small group of friends (Owens, 1996). For example, we think of 12-year-old Tina in the late 1980s, for whom any great occurrence was "radical" or (later) "rad" or (still later) "awesome." We think, too, of Jeanne's son Alex, who at 16 insisted on addressing everyone (including his mother) as "Dude." Such expressions help adolescents establish themselves as belonging to a particular peer group in much the same way that their clothing and hairstyles do (Harris, 1995).

How Children Develop Speaking Skills Although young children occasionally talk to themselves (perhaps, as Vygotsky has suggested, providing a means through which they can more effectively guide their own behavior), most oral language during the preschool years occurs during conversations with other individuals (Owens, 1996). Frequently, preschoolers' conversational partners are adults, who typically guide and control the discussions (Owens, 1996). In their interactions with peers, children can converse more as equal partners. Furthermore, when children assume the roles of "mommy," "teacher," "doctor," or "storekeeper" in play activities, they can experiment with the variety of linguistic styles and jargon that they associate with such roles (Christie & Johnsen, 1983; Nelson, 1986).

During the elementary and secondary school years, experience—in the form of both structured activities (e.g., oral presentations at school) and unstructured interactions (e.g., conversations with friends)—almost certainly continues to play a key role in the development of speaking skills. For instance, the prevalence of word play and figurative language in inner-city African American communities is probably largely responsible for the especially creative speech of the children who grow up in these communities (Ortony et al., 1985; Smith, 1998).

Promoting Speaking Skills To help children and adolescents develop their speaking skills, teachers should, of course, give them many and varied opportunities to speak in class in both structured and unstructured contexts. The following three strategies may also be helpful:

■ *Let students know when something they say is difficult to understand.* People of all ages occasionally have trouble communicating their thoughts clearly to others; young children may have particular difficulty because of their limited ability to consider the knowledge and perspectives of their listeners. Asking questions or expressing confusion when students describe events and ideas ambiguously or incompletely should gradually help them express their thoughts more precisely and take into account what their listeners already do and do not know.

■ *Ask students to tell stories.* Adults often ask questions that encourage children to respond in narrative form (Hemphill & Snow, 1996); for instance, a teacher might ask, "What did you do this weekend?" or "Do you remember what happened the last time someone brought a pet to show-and-tell?" Giving students opportunities to tell narratives—perhaps stories about events in their lives or perhaps fictional creations of their own imaginations—provides a context in which they can practice speaking for sustained periods of time and build on the rich oral traditions of many cultural groups (Hale-Benson, 1986; Hemphill & Snow, 1996; McCarty & Watahomigie, 1998).

The classroom provides an excellent context in which students can develop their speaking skills.

Furthermore, storytelling ability can be enhanced by specific training and practice (McKeough, 1995). Consider how 6-year-old Leanne's ability to tell a story improved over a 2-month period as a result of specific instruction about how to conceptualize and tell stories:

Before instruction:
A girl—and a boy—and a kind old horse. They got mad at each other. That the end. (McKeough, 1995, p. 170)

After instruction:
Once upon a time there was a girl. She was playing with her toys and—um—she asked her mom if she could go outside—to play in the snow. But her mom said no. And then she was very sad. And—and she had to play. So she she[sic] asked her mom if she could go outside and she said yes. She jumped in the snow and she was having fun and she had an idea and she jumped in the snow and she feeled happy. (McKeough, 1995, p. 170)

■ *Encourage creativity in oral language.* Linguistic creativity can be expressed in many ways, such as through stories, poems, songs, rap, jokes, and puns. Such forms of language may not only encourage creative language use but may also help students identify parallels between seemingly dissimilar objects or events—parallels that enable them to construct similes, metaphors, and other analogies.

The playful use of language can have an additional benefit as well. An event in Mario's childhood illustrates:

> Seven-year-old Mario tells his parents a joke that he has heard at school earlier in the day. He relates the joke in English: "What did the bird say when his cage got broken?" His parents have no idea what the bird said, so he tells them, "Cheap, cheap!"
>
> Mario's parents find the joke amusing, so he later translates it for the family's Spanish-speaking nanny: "¿Qué dijo el pájaro cuando se le rompió la jaula?" He follows up with the bird's answer: "Barato, barato." Mario is surprised to discover that the nanny finds no humor in the joke. He knows that he has somehow failed to convey the point of the joke but cannot figure out where he went wrong. (Fantini, 1985, p. 72)

The joke, of course, got lost in translation. The Spanish word *barato* means "cheap" but is not used to indicate the sound that a bird makes ("cheep"). Only several years later did Mario understand that humor that depended on word play would not necessarily translate from one language to another (Fantini, 1985). His eventual understanding of this principle was an aspect of Mario's growing metalinguistic awareness, a concept you will learn more about shortly.

Proficiency in listening to and speaking with others includes knowledge not only about various aspects of language itself, but also about the nonverbal behaviors that one's society deems acceptable for social interaction—behaviors that are often quite different for different cultures. We turn now to an examination of such *sociolinguistic behaviors.*

Development of Sociolinguistic Behaviors

Let's return to a comment Mario's kindergarten teacher made in her report to Mario's parents:

> His greatest problem seems to be in the give and take of conversation. Since he always has something to say, he often finds it difficult to wait his turn when others are talking. (Fantini, 1985, p. 28)

Children's ability to converse successfully with others depends partly on knowledge and skills that have little or nothing to do with language per se. For instance, in mainstream Western culture, children must learn to take turns with other people involved in a conversation; in many situations, it's neither productive nor polite for everyone to talk at once or to interrupt one another. Many children learn that behaviors such as looking a speaker in the eye, smiling, and nodding in agreement are effective ways to show that they are listening and understand what the speaker is saying. They learn to give a greeting (e.g., "Hello") when they first see someone and to end a conversation with some form of sign-off (e.g., "Good-bye"). They learn, too, that the ways that they speak to their peers (e.g., "Shut up!" "Get auta here!") are usually unacceptable when talking to adults.

The social conventions that govern appropriate verbal interaction are called **sociolinguistic behaviors.** Sociolinguistic behaviors fall within the broader domain of *pragmatics,* which

sociolinguistic behaviors
Social and culturally specific conventions that govern appropriate verbal interaction.

includes not only rules of conversational etiquette—taking turns in conversations, saying good-bye when leaving, and so on—but also strategies for initiating conversations, changing the subject, telling stories, and arguing persuasively. All language communities follow general pragmatic rules. For example, children learn quickly that they should temper requests to authority figures with qualifications ("I'm not sure, Mrs. Brown, but I think it's my turn") and appropriate signs of deference ("Mr. Suarez, can I go outside now?").

Children continue to refine their knowledge of pragmatics and sociolinguistic conventions throughout the preschool years and elementary grades (Garvey & Berninger, 1981; Owens, 1996; Warren-Leubecker & Bohannon, 1989); our own observations indicate that this process continues into the middle and high school years as well. Yet children from different cultures often learn different conventions, particularly in matters of etiquette, as you will see now.

Cultural Differences in Sociolinguistic Behaviors Researchers and educators have identified numerous cross-cultural differences in sociolinguistic behaviors. When teachers have been raised in a culture different from that of their students, they sometimes misinterpret students' nonverbal behaviors. For example, some Native American communities believe it unnecessary to say hello or good-bye (Sisk, 1989); when children from those communities fail to extend greetings, their teachers might erroneously conclude that they are being rude. In other Native American communities, children learn that they should rarely express their feelings through facial expressions (Montgomery, 1989); their teachers might easily misinterpret a child's lack of facial expression as an indicator of boredom or disinterest. Following are additional cultural differences that may lead to misunderstandings in classroom settings. These differences are summarized in the Observation Guidelines table on the following page.

■ *Being silent.* Relatively speaking, mainstream Western culture is a chatty one. People often say things to one another even when they have very little to communicate; they make small talk as a way of maintaining interpersonal relationships and filling awkward silences (Irujo, 1988; Trawick-Smith, 2000). But in some cultures, silence is golden; for instance, Brazilians and Peruvians often greet their guests silently, Arabs stop speaking as a way of signaling that they want privacy, and Apaches value silence in general (Basso, 1972; Menyuk & Menyuk, 1988; Trawick-Smith, 2000). Children and adolescents who come from such backgrounds are, of course, likely to behave consistently with their upbringing by saying little in the classroom. Unfortunately, their teachers and classmates may react to their silence by thinking that they are "rude" or "strange" (Menyuk & Menyuk, 1988).

■ *Interacting with adults.* In most Western classrooms, the expectation is that children will speak up when they have comments or questions. Yet children raised in the Yup'ik culture of Alaska are expected to learn primarily by close, quiet observation of adults; they rarely ask questions or otherwise interrupt what adults are doing (Garcia, 1994). In other cultures, children learn very early that they should engage in conversation with adults only when their participation has been directly solicited; this is the case in many Mexican American and Southeast Asian communities, as well as in some African American communities in the southeastern United States (Delgado-Gaitan, 1994; Grant & Gomez, 2001; Ochs, 1982). In fact, children from some backgrounds, including many Puerto Ricans, Mexican Americans, and Native Americans, have been taught that speaking directly and assertively to adults is downright rude, perhaps even rebellious (Delgado-Gaitan, 1994; Hidalgo, Siu, Bright, Swap, & Epstein, 1995; Lomawaima, 1995).

In some cultures, looking an adult in the eye is a sign of respect; in other cultures, it is interpreted as *dis*respect.

■ *Making eye contact.* For many people, looking someone in the eye is a way of indicating that they are trying to communicate or that they are listening intently. But in many African American, Puerto Rican, Mexican American, and Native American cultures, a child who looks an adult in the eye is showing disrespect. Children in such cultures are taught to look down

Identifying Cultural Differences in Sociolinguistic Conventions

OBSERVATION GUIDELINES

CHARACTERISTIC	LOOK FOR	EXAMPLE	IMPLICATION
Talkativeness	• Frequent talking, even about trivial matters, *or* • Silence unless something important needs to be said	When Muhammed abruptly stops talking to his classmates during free time and turns to read his book, his classmates think his action is rude.	Don't interpret a student's sudden or lengthy silence as necessarily reflecting apathy or intentional rudeness.
Style of Interacting with Adults	• Willingness to initiate conversations with adults, *or* • Speaking to adults only when spoken to	Elena is exceptionally quiet in class, and she answers questions only when her teacher directs them specifically at her. At lunch and on the playground, however, she readily talks and laughs with her friends.	Keep in mind that some students won't tell you when they are confused. If you think they may not understand, take them aside and ask specific questions that assess their learning. Provide additional instruction to address any gaps in their understanding.
Eye Contact	• Looking others in the eye when speaking or listening to them, *or* • Looking down or away in the presence of adults	Herman always looks at his feet when his teacher speaks to him.	Don't assume that students aren't paying attention just because they don't look you in the eye.
Personal Space	• Standing quite close to a conversation partner, perhaps touching that person frequently, *or* • Keeping distance between oneself and others when talking with them	Michelle is noticeably uncomfortable when other people touch her.	Give students some personal space during one-on-one interactions. Teach students that what constitutes personal space differs from culture to culture.
Responses to Questions	• Answering questions readily, *or* • Failure to answer even very simple questions	Leah never responds to "What is this?" questions, even when she knows the answers.	Be aware that some students are not used to answering the types of questions that teachers frequently ask. Respect students' privacy when they are reluctant to answer questions about home and family life.
Wait Time	• Waiting several seconds before answering questions, *or* • Not waiting at all, and perhaps even interrupting others	Mario often interrupts his classmates during class discussions.	When addressing a question to the entire class, give students several seconds to think before calling on one student for an answer. When some students interrupt regularly, establish a class procedure (e.g., hand-raising and waiting to be called on) that ensures that all students have a chance to be heard.

in the presence of adults (Gilliland, 1988; Torres-Guzmán, 1998; Trawick-Smith, 2000). The following anecdote shows how a teacher's recognition of this culturally learned behavior can make a difference:

> A teacher [described a Native American] student who would never say a word, nor even answer when she greeted him. Then one day when he came in she looked in the other direction and said, "Hello, Jimmy." He answered enthusiastically, "Why hello Miss Jacobs." She found that he would always talk if she looked at a book or at the wall, but when she looked at him, he appeared frightened. (Gilliland, 1988, p. 26)

■ *Maintaining personal space.* In some cultures, such as in some African American and Puerto Rican communities, people stand close together when they talk and may touch one another frequently (Hale-Benson, 1986; Slonim, 1991). In contrast, European Americans and Japanese Americans tend to keep a fair distance from one another—they maintain some **personal space**—especially if they don't know one another very well (Irujo, 1988; Trawick-Smith, 2000). Teachers must be sensitive to the personal space that children from various cultural backgrounds need to feel comfortable in interactions with others.

■ *Responding to questions.* A common interaction pattern in many Western classrooms is the **IRE cycle:** A teacher *initiates* an interaction by asking a question, a student *responds* to the question, and the teacher *evaluates* the response (Mehan, 1979). Similar cycles are frequently found in parent-child interactions in middle-class European American homes as well; for instance, as we reflect back on our interactions with our own children as toddlers and preschoolers, we can recall many occasions when we asked questions such as "How old are you?" and "What does a cow say?" and praised our children when they answered correctly. But children raised in other environments—for instance, many of those raised in lower-income homes, as well as those raised in some Mexican American, Native American, or Hawaiian communities—are unfamiliar with such question-answer sessions when they first come to school (Losey, 1995). Furthermore, children in some of these cultures, such as those in many Navajo and Hawaiian communities, may feel more comfortable responding to adults' questions as a group rather than interacting with adults one on one (Au, 1980; Miller, 1995).

■ *Answering different kinds of questions.* Consider the following questions:

What's this a picture of?

What color is this?

What's your sister's name?

These questions seem simple enough to answer. But in fact, different cultures teach children to answer different kinds of questions. European American parents frequently ask their children to identify objects and their characteristics. Yet in certain other cultures, parents rarely ask their children questions that they themselves know the answers to (Crago, Annahatak, & Ningiuruvik, 1993; Heath, 1980; Rogoff & Morelli, 1989). For example, parents in some African American communities in the southeastern United States are more likely to ask questions involving comparisons and analogies; rather than asking "What's that?" they may instead ask "What's that like?" (Heath, 1980). Furthermore, children in these same communities are specifically taught *not* to answer questions that strangers may ask about personal and home life (e.g., "What's your name?" "Where do you live?"). Teachers' comments about these children reflect their lack of understanding about the culture from which the children come:

"I would almost think some of them have a hearing problem; it is as though they don't hear me ask a question. I get blank stares to my questions. Yet when I am making statements or telling stories which interest them, they always seem to hear me."

"The simplest questions are the ones they can't answer in the classroom; yet on the playground, they can explain a rule for a ballgame or describe a particular kind of bait with no problem. Therefore, I know they can't be as dumb as they seem in my class." (Heath, 1980, pp. 107–108)

Meanwhile, parents describe the confusion their children are experiencing:

"My kid, he too scared to talk, 'cause nobody play by the rules he know. At home I can't shut him up."

"Miss Davis, she complain 'bout Ned not answerin' back. He says she asks dumb questions she already know about." (Heath, 1980, p. 107)

■ *Waiting and interrupting.* Teachers frequently ask their students questions and then wait for an answer. But exactly how long *do* they wait? The typical **wait time** for many teachers is a second or even less; at that point, they either answer a question themselves or call on another student (Rowe, 1974, 1987). Yet people from some cultures leave lengthy pauses before responding as a way of indicating respect, as this statement by a Northern Cheyenne illustrates:

Even if I had a quick answer to your question, I would never answer immediately. That would be saying that your question was not worth thinking about. (Gilliland, 1988, p. 27)

personal space
Personally and culturally preferred distance between two people during social interaction.

IRE cycle
Teacher-student interaction pattern marked by teacher *initiation*, student *response*, and teacher *evaluation*.

wait time
The length of time a teacher pauses, after either asking a question or hearing a student's comment, before saying something else.

For many cultural groups, then, students are more likely to participate in class and respond to questions when given several seconds to respond (Grant & Gomez, 2001; Mohatt & Erickson, 1981; Tharp, 1989).

In contrast, students from certain other backgrounds, rather than pausing as a way to signal respect, may interrupt teachers or classmates who haven't finished speaking—behavior that many of us might interpret as rudeness. For instance, in some African American, Puerto Rican, and Jewish families, family discourse often consists of several people talking at once; in fact, people who wait for their turn might find themselves being excluded from the discussion altogether (Condon & Yousef, 1975; Farber, Mindel, & Lazerwitz, 1988; Hale-Benson, 1986; Slonim, 1991). And in some Hawaiian communities, an interruption is a sign of personal involvement in the conversation (Tharp, 1989).

How Sociolinguistic Behaviors Develop   Even young infants show turn taking in their "conversations" with others, in that they tend to remain quiet when their parents are talking. This tendency may be essential to language development (Locke, 1993) and so possibly has a biological basis. By and large, however, conversational etiquette and other sociolinguistic behaviors are almost certainly culturally transmitted. Sometimes parents and other family members teach these behaviors directly. In the following interaction between 20-month-old Amy and her mother, Amy burps, and her mother pats her chest:

Mother:	Oh, what do you say?
Amy:	(Touches her throat.) Thank you.
Mother:	No, excuse me.
Amy:	(Touches her throat again.) Excuse me.
Mother:	Excuse me. Yeah. (dialogue from Miller, 1982, p. 100; format adapted)

Teachers, too, often instruct children in desired sociolinguistic behaviors. For instance, Mario once explained to his parents how his kindergarten teacher encouraged students to take turns when speaking in class (we present an English translation):

[A]t school, I have to raise my hand . . . and then wait a long, long time. And then the teacher says: "Now you can speak, Mario," and she makes the other children shut up, and she says, "Mario's speaking now." (Fantini, 1985, p. 83)

Children probably learn many conventions not so much through direct instruction as through copying the behaviors of others. For example, when Jeanne's children were young, they did not require explicit instruction in telephone etiquette. From a very early age they would use polite, "adult" language when talking on the phone, perhaps saying: "I'm sorry but my mother is busy right now. Can I take a message?" We can only assume that they heard their parents give such messages and followed suit.

The feedback that children receive from others (sometimes blatant, sometimes more subtle) may also encourage them to conform to sociolinguistic conventions. For instance, most young children eventually learn that they get along better with their peers when they ask for something nicely ("Can I please have that?") rather than make demands ("Gimme that!"). Older children and adolescents may discover that when they stand too close to others, their conversational partners act uneasy and may even back up to create a more comfortable distance.

Taking Sociolinguistic Differences into Account in the Classroom   When the sociolinguistic behaviors expected at home differ significantly from those expected at school, a sense of confusion, or **culture shock**, can result. Such culture shock can interfere with children's adjustment to the school setting and, ultimately, with their academic achievement as well (Garcia, 1995; Lee & Slaughter-Defoe, 1995; Ogbu, 1992; Phelan, Yu, & Davidson, 1994). Teachers further compound the problem when, interpreting students' behaviors as being unacceptable or otherwise "odd," they jump too quickly to the conclusion that the students are unable or unwilling to make productive contributions to the class (Bowman, 1989; Hilliard & Vaughn-Scott, 1982).

Clearly, teachers must educate themselves about the diverse sociolinguistic patterns they are likely to find in their classrooms so that they don't read unintended messages into students' behaviors. Furthermore, teachers must keep students' varying conversational styles in mind as they

culture shock
Sense of confusion that occurs when one encounters an environment with very different expectations for behavior than those in one's home environment.

Language Skills at Different Age Levels

DEVELOPMENTAL TRENDS

AGE	WHAT YOU MIGHT OBSERVE	DIVERSITY	IMPLICATIONS
Early Childhood (2–6) 	• Rapid advances in vocabulary and syntax • Incomplete understandings of many simple words (e.g., undergeneralization, overgeneralization, confusion between simple comparatives such as *more* vs. *less*) • Frequent overregularization (e.g., *goed, gooder, foots*) • Overdependence on word order and context (instead of syntax) when interpreting messages • Superficial understanding of what "good listening" is • Difficulty pronouncing some phonemes (e.g., *r, th, sl, dr*) • Increasing ability to construct narratives	• Children raised in bilingual environments may show slight delays in language development, but any delays are short-lived and usually not a cause for concern. • Major speech and communication disorders (e.g., abnormal syntactic constructions) reveal themselves in the preschool years.	• Give children corrective feedback when their use of words indicates inaccurate understanding. • Work on simple listening skills (e.g., sitting quietly, paying attention). • Ask follow-up questions to make sure that children accurately understand important messages. • Ask children to construct narratives about recent events (e.g., "Tell me about your camping trip last weekend").
Middle Childhood (6–10) 	• Increasing understanding of temporal words (e.g., *before, after*) and comparatives (e.g., *bigger, as big as*) • Incomplete knowledge of irregular word forms • Literal interpretation of messages (especially before age 9) • Pronunciation mastered by age 8 • Consideration of a listener's knowledge and perspective when speaking • Sustained conversations about concrete topics • Construction of narratives that have plots and cause-effect relationships • Linguistic creativity and word play (e.g., rhymes, word games)	• Minor speech and communication disorders (e.g., persistent articulation problems) become evident. • African Americans often show advanced ability to use figurative language (e.g., metaphor, hyperbole). • Bilingual children are apt to show advanced metalinguistic awareness.	• Teach irregular word forms (e.g., the past tense of *ring* is *rang*, the past tense of *bring* is *brought*). • Use class discussions as a way to explore academic subject matter. • Have students develop short stories that they present orally or in writing. • Encourage jokes and rhymes that capitalize on double meanings and homonyms (i.e., soundalike words). • When articulation problems are evident in the upper elementary grades, consult with a speech-language pathologist.

design classroom lessons and activities. For instance, they might check students' understanding of classroom material by calling for group rather than individual responses or perhaps by having students write their responses on paper. Teachers might also vary the nature of their questions to include the kinds of questions that different students are accustomed to answering at home. And they should allow sufficient wait time—perhaps several seconds—for all students to think about and respond to the questions they pose.

Some children lack the pragmatic skills that are desirable in *any* culture; for instance, we have known children who seemed so insistent on dominating a conversation that no one else could get a word in. When students haven't mastered the basic conventions of conversational etiquette, their peers may find their behavior irritating or strange. A lack of pragmatic skills, then, can seriously interfere with students' relationships with age-mates. It is important for teachers to observe students' pragmatic skills as they interact both with adults and with their classmates and give students guided practice in any skills that may be lacking. If problems persist, students should be evaluated by the school's speech-language pathologist.

AGE	WHAT YOU MIGHT OBSERVE	DIVERSITY	IMPLICATIONS
Early Adolescence (10–14)	• Increasing awareness of the terminology used in various academic disciplines • Ability to understand complex, multiclause sentences • Emerging ability to look beyond literal interpretations; comprehension of simple proverbs • Emerging ability to carry on lengthy conversations about abstract topics • Significant growth in metalinguistic awareness	• Girls are more likely than boys to converse about intimate and confidential matters. • African American teens may bandy insults back and forth in a playful manner. • Adolescents may prefer to use their native dialects even if they have mastered Standard English.	• Begin to use the terminology used by experts in various academic disciplines (e.g., *simile* in language arts, *molecule* in science). • Use classroom debates to explore controversial issues. • Present proverbs and ask students to consider their underlying meanings. • Explore the nature of words and language as entities in and of themselves.
Late Adolescence (14–18)	• Acquisition of many vocabulary words specifically related to various academic disciplines • Subtle refinements in grammar, mostly as a result of formal instruction • Mastery of a wide variety of connectives (e.g., *although, however, nevertheless*) • General ability to understand figurative language (e.g., metaphors, proverbs, hyperbole)	• Boys are apt to communicate their thoughts in a direct and straightforward manner; girls are more likely to be indirect and tactful. • A preference for one's native dialect over Standard English continues into the high school years.	• Consistently use the terminology associated with various academic disciplines. • Distinguish between similar abstract words (e.g., *weather* vs. *climate, velocity* vs. *acceleration*). • Explore complex syntactic structures (e.g., multiple embedded clauses). • Consider the underlying meanings and messages in poetry and fiction. • When students have a native dialect other than Standard English, encourage them to use it in informal conversations and creative writing; encourage Standard English for more formal situations.

Sources: Baker, 1993; Fantini, 1985; Hale-Benson, 1986; McDevitt, 1990; O'Grady, 1997; Ortony et al., 1985; Owens, 1996; Smith, 1998.

Development of Metalinguistic Awareness

Children's **metalinguistic awareness** is their ability to think about the nature of language and reflect on the functions that it serves. For instance, it includes conscious awareness that speech is comprised of smaller units (words, phonemes, etc.), that printed words have one-to-one correspondences to spoken words, and that language is an entity separate from its meaning. It also includes the ability to distinguish between what a person says and what he or she actually means (Yaden & Templeton, 1986).

In the late preschool or early elementary years, children become consciously aware that words are the basic units of language, that spoken words are comprised of phonemes, and that different phonemes tend to be associated with different letters or letter combinations (Tunmer, Pratt, & Herriman, 1984). During the elementary years, children gradually become capable of determining when sentences are grammatically acceptable and when they are not (Bowey, 1986; Hakes, 1980). As they move into upper elementary and middle school, they begin to understand the component parts of speech (nouns, verbs, adjectives, etc.); such growth is almost certainly due, at least in part, to the formal instruction they receive about parts of speech. More sophisticated aspects of metalinguistic awareness, such as recognizing that a word or phrase has multiple meanings, don't emerge until the middle school years and continue to develop throughout adolescence. (The Developmental Trends table above describes some of the characteristics you are likely to see in children's language skills at various age levels.)

metalinguistic awareness
Extent to which one is able to think about the nature of language.

How Children Develop Metalinguistic Awareness   Theoretical accounts of metalinguistic development focus almost exclusively on the effects of experience. One factor that probably promotes metalinguistic awareness is "playing" with language. Children play with language in many ways—through rhymes, chants, jokes, puns, and so on (Christie & Johnsen, 1983; Owens, 1996). Such word play is almost certainly beneficial; for instance, rhymes help students discover the relationships between sounds and letters, and jokes and puns help students discover that words and phrases can have more than one meaning (Bradley & Bryant, 1991; Cazden, 1976; Christie & Johnsen, 1983).

Children's early experiences with books promote metalinguistic awareness as well (Yaden & Templeton, 1986). The very process of reading to children helps them realize that printed language is related to spoken language. In addition, some children's books playfully address the nature of language. An example is *Amelia Bedelia Goes Camping* (Parish, 1985), one of a number of books featuring a rather obtuse maid who takes everything her employers say quite literally. For example, Amelia hits the road with a stick when they say it's time to "hit the road."

Formal language arts instruction further fosters metalinguistic awareness. By exploring parts of speech, various sentence structures, and the like, children and adolescents develop a better understanding of the structure of language. By reading and analyzing poetry and classic literature, they discover a variety of mechanisms—similes, metaphors, symbolism, and so on—that one might use to convey multiple layers of meanings.

Finally, research consistently indicates that knowledge of two or more languages (bilingualism) promotes greater metalinguistic awareness (Diaz & Klingler, 1991; Garcia, 1994; Moran & Hakuta, 1995). By the time Mario was 5, he showed considerable awareness of the nature of language:

> Mario was well aware that things were called in one of several possible ways, that the same story could be retold in another language (he was capable of doing this himself), and he knew that thoughts were convertible or translatable through other forms of expression. He was aware of a variety of codes [languages], not only of Spanish, English and Italian, but also of others like Aymara, French, German, Twi, Japanese, and Quechua. He knew that a code could be varied so as to make it sound funny or to render its messages less transparent, such as in Pig Spanish. . . .
>
> [As Mario grew older,] he became increasingly analytical about the medium which so many take for granted as their sole form of expression. He demonstrated interest, for example, in the multiple meaning of some words (" 'right' means three things"); and in peculiar usages ("Why do you call the car 'she'?"); as well as intuitions about the origins of words (" 'soufflé' sounds French"). (Fantini, 1985, pp. 53–54)

Promoting Metalinguistic Development   The factors that promote metalinguistic awareness—language play, reading experiences, formal instruction, and bilingualism—have obvious implications for classroom practice. Three of them are the following:

■ *Explore multiple meanings through ambiguities, jokes, riddles, and the like.* Having fun with language can be educational as well as entertaining. For example, teachers can ask their students to identify the double meanings of such sentences as these (Wiig, Gilbert, & Christian, 1978):

He is drawing a gun.

This restaurant even serves crabs.

Jokes and riddles provide another vehicle for exploring multiple meanings (Shultz, 1974; Shultz & Horibe, 1974):

Call me a cab.
Okay, you're a cab.

Tell me how long cows should be milked.
They should be milked the same as short ones, of course.

■ *Read literature that plays on the nature of language.* Many children's books capitalize on the idiosyncrasies of language. One of our favorites is *The Phantom Tollbooth* (Juster, 1961), which has considerable fun with word meanings and common expressions. In one scene, the main character (Milo) asks for a square meal and is served (you guessed it) a plate "heaped high with steaming squares of all sizes and colors."

Among the all-time classics in word play are Lewis Carroll's *Alice's Adventures in Wonderland* and *Through the Looking Glass.* The books are packed with whimsical uses of double word meanings, homonyms, and idioms. The following excerpt from *Through the Looking Glass* illustrates:

> "But what could [a tree] do, if any danger came?" Alice asked.
> "It could bark," said the Rose.
> "It says, 'Boughwough!' " cried a Daisy. "That's why its branches are called boughs."

Occasionally Carroll explicitly addresses the nature of language, such as in the following excerpt from *Through the Looking Glass,* which begins with Humpty Dumpty explaining a word he has just used:

> " . . . I meant by 'impenetrability' that we've had enough of that subject, and it would be just as well if you'd mention what you mean to do next, as I suppose you don't mean to stop here all the rest of your life."
> "That's a great deal to make one word mean," Alice said in a thoughtful tone.
> "When I make a word do a lot of work like that," said Humpty Dumpty, "I always pay it extra."

■ *Encourage students to learn a second language.* Promoting metalinguistic awareness is just one of several benefits of learning a second language. In the next section we look more closely at second language learning and bilingualism.

Development of a Second Language

As the adult workplace becomes increasingly international in scope, there is greater need than ever before for children to learn one or more languages in addition to their native tongue. Here we address three issues related to the development of a second language: the optimal timing for second-language learning, the nature of bilingualism, and approaches to teaching a second language.

The Timing of Second-Language Learning

As noted earlier, there may be one or more sensitive periods for learning language, thus making exposure to a language in the first few years of life ideal. Yet research evidence regarding the best time to learn a *second* language is mixed and often tainted by serious methodological problems (Bialystok, 1994b; Hakuta & McLaughlin, 1996; Long, 1995; Newport, 1993). In general, early exposure to a second language is more critical if the second language is very different from the first; for instance, a native English speaker benefits more from an early start in Japanese or Arabic than from an early start in French or German (Bialystok, 1994a; Strozer, 1994). Early exposure is also important for mastering flawless pronunciation of the new language; people who begin studying a language after puberty typically retain an accent no matter how fluent in the language they eventually become (Bialystok, 1994b; Collier, 1989; Long, 1995). Yet any advantage young children may have due to biological "readiness" is probably counterbalanced by the greater cognitive maturity, world knowledge, and metalinguistic sophistication on which adolescents and adults can build as they study a new language (Bialystok, 1994b; Collier, 1989; Long, 1995). People of all ages can acquire proficiency in a second language; there is probably no definitive "best" time to begin.

Although there may be no hard-and-fast sensitive period for learning a second language, beginning second-language instruction in the early years definitely has advantages. For one thing, it appears that learning a second language leads to higher achievement in reading, vocabulary, and grammar (Cunningham & Graham, 1997; Diaz, 1983; Reich, 1986). Instruction in a foreign language also sensitizes young children to the international and multicultural nature of the world in which they live. Children who learn a second language during the elementary school years express more positive attitudes toward people who speak that language, and they are more likely to enroll in foreign language classes in high school (Reich, 1986). Learning a second language can have immediate social benefits as well: In classrooms in which children speak only one of two different languages (perhaps some speaking only English and others speaking only Spanish), instruction in the second language promotes cross-communication and peer interaction (Doyle, 1982).

Bilingualism

Bilingualism is the ability to speak two languages fluently. Bilingual children, like Mario, can switch easily from one language to the other, and they readily distinguish the contexts in which they should use each one (Fantini, 1985).

Some bilingual children have been raised in families in which two languages are spoken regularly. Others have lived for a time in a community where one language is spoken and then moved to a community where a different language is spoken. Still others live in a bilingual society—for example, in Canada (where English and French are spoken), Wales (where English and Welsh are spoken), and certain ethnic neighborhoods in the United States (where a language such as Spanish or Chinese is spoken along with English).

Several decades ago, many theorists believed that bilingual environments were detrimental to children's linguistic and cognitive development. Researchers frequently found bilingual children to have substantially lower IQ scores than monolingual English-speaking children (García, Jiménez, & Pearson, 1998). Unfortunately, their studies typically used, as their "bilingual" samples, children who had recently immigrated to the United States. Thus, the children were not yet proficient in English (they were not truly bilingual) and so performed poorly on intelligence tests as a result (García et al., 1998).

More recent research is far more complimentary. Children raised in bilingual environments from birth or soon thereafter may show some initial delays in language development, and they may occasionally mix the two languages in their early speech. However, by elementary school they have caught up to their monolingual peers and have learned to keep the two languages separate (Baker, 1993; Fantini, 1985; Lanza, 1992). Furthermore, as mentioned earlier, bilingual children show greater metalinguistic sophistication than their monolingual classmates. And, when they are truly fluent in both languages, they tend to perform better in situations requiring complex cognitive functioning—for instance, on intelligence tests and on tasks requiring creativity (Diaz & Klingler, 1991; Garcia, 1994; Moran & Hakuta, 1995).

Being bilingual may also be advantageous from cultural and personal standpoints. In many Native American groups, the ancestral language is important for communicating oral history and cultural heritage and for conducting business within the group; at the same time, adults in the community realize that mastery of spoken and written English is essential for children's long-term success (McCarty & Watahomigie, 1998). Most Puerto Rican children, who will have more educational and professional opportunities if they know English, nevertheless speak Spanish at home, partly as a way of showing respect to their parents and partly as a way of maintaining a sense of cultural identity (Nieto, 1995; Torres-Guzmán, 1998). A high school girl named Marisol put it this way:

> I'm proud of [being Puerto Rican]. I guess I speak Spanish whenever I can. . . . I used to have a lot of problems with one of my teachers 'cause she didn't want us to talk Spanish in class and I thought that was like an insult to us, you know? Just telling us not to talk Spanish, 'cause they were Puerto Ricans and, you know, we're free to talk whatever we want. . . . I could never stay quiet and talk only English, 'cause sometimes, you know, words slip in Spanish. You know, I think they should understand that. (Nieto, 1995, p. 127)

In some cases, being bilingual is the only way children can maintain personal relationships with important people in their lives; for instance, some children are bilingual in English and American Sign Language as a way of communicating effectively with one parent who can hear and another who is deaf (Pettito, 1997).

Approaches to Teaching a Second Language

Children typically learn their native language through the informal and haphazard daily exposure they have to the language; if they are raised in bilingual circumstances (as Mario was), they may learn two languages simultaneously through the same means. When children begin a second language at an older age, perhaps in the middle elementary years or even later, they often learn it more quickly if their language-learning experiences are more structured (Strozer, 1994). But as you may have learned from your own experience, studying a foreign language for one 45-minute period several times a week does not promote rapid mastery. Two more intensive approaches—immersion and bilingual education—are more effective, with each being useful in different situations.

bilingualism
Knowing and speaking two languages fluently.

For English-speaking students who are learning a second language while still living in their native country, total **immersion** in the second language—hearing and speaking it almost exclusively within the classroom—is often the method of choice. Total immersion helps students become proficient in a second language relatively quickly, and any adverse effects of such immersion on achievement in other academic areas appear to be short-lived (Collier, 1992; Genesee, 1985; Thomas, Collier, & Abbott, 1993). But for non-English-speaking students learning English (e.g., children who have recently immigrated to this country), total immersion in English may actually be detrimental. These students do best when instruction in academic subject areas is given in their native language while they are simultaneously taught to speak and write in English. Such **bilingual education** leads to higher overall academic achievement, continuing development of the native language, greater self-esteem, and a better attitude toward school (Garcia, 1995; Snow, 1990; Willig, 1985; Wright & Taylor, 1995; Wright, Taylor, & Macarthur, 2000). Ideally, students in bilingual education gradually move into English-based classes as their English proficiency improves (Krashen, 1996).

Why does immersion work better for some students whereas bilingual education is more effective for others? The relative effectiveness of the two approaches depends on students' proficiency in their native language when they begin second-language instruction; it also depends on whether students have ongoing opportunities to continue developing their first language while they study the second. As you learned in Chapter 4, language development plays several important roles in children's cognitive development: It provides a symbolic means through which children can mentally represent and think about their world (Piaget's theory), promotes social interactions through which children can encounter divergent perspectives (Piaget again), and is the vehicle through which social interactions become internalized into mental processes (Vygotsky's theory). Thus, if instruction in a second language somehow undermines children's development in the first language, it is likely to have deleterious effects on their cognitive development.

Bilingual education programs are especially effective when they encourage skills in students' native language as well as in English.

Immersion programs are typically effective only when students already have a solid foundation in their first language and have regular opportunities to use and enhance their skills in that language; in such circumstances, learning a second language doesn't interfere with cognitive development (Collier, 1989; Krashen, 1996). English-speaking children in this country who are immersed in a second language at school still have many opportunities—at home, with their friends, and in the local community and culture—to continue using and developing their English. In contrast, recent immigrants may have few opportunities outside of their homes to use their native language. If they are taught exclusively in English, they may very well lose proficiency in their native language before developing sufficient proficiency in English, and their cognitive development and academic achievement will suffer in the process. In such cases, bilingual education, which is designed to foster growth in *both* languages, is more likely to promote cognitive as well as linguistic growth (Krashen, 1996; Pérez, 1998; Winsler, Díaz, Espinosa, & Rodriguez, 1999).

Given the many advantages of second-language learning and bilingualism, perhaps educators should begin to think about promoting bilingualism in *all* students (Navarro, 1985; NCSS Task Force on Ethnic Studies Curriculum Guidelines, 1992; Pérez, 1998). Widespread bilingualism would not only promote students' cognitive and linguistic development but also enhance communication, interaction, and interpersonal understanding among students with diverse linguistic and cultural backgrounds (Minami & Ovando, 1995).

Diversity in Language Development

As is true in other developmental domains, children do not all achieve milestones in language development at exactly the same age. For instance, children say their first word, on average, at 12 months of age, but Mario didn't say his first word until 16 months; his first English word appeared considerably later, at age 2½ (Fantini, 1985). In addition to such

immersion
Approach to second-language instruction in which students hear and speak that language almost exclusively within the classroom.

bilingual education
Approach to second-language instruction in which students are instructed in academic subject areas in their native language while simultaneously being taught to speak and write in the second language.

idiosyncratic individual differences, we also see some differences based on children's gender, socioeconomic status, and ethnicity.

Gender Differences

As noted in Chapter 6, research studies often find that females outperform males on tests of verbal ability. This difference is quite small, however, and there is considerable overlap between the two groups (refer to Figure 6–6).

Other studies indicate that there may be qualitative differences in the language that boys and girls use and that these differences persist into adulthood. *On average,* males, who see themselves as information providers, speak more directly and bluntly. In contrast, females, who seek to establish and deepen relationships through their conversations, are more likely to be indirect, tactful, and polite when trying to get their point across (Owens, 1996; Tannen, 1990).

Socioeconomic Differences

In the 1960s and early 1970s, many developmental psychologists proposed that children from lower-income families had an impoverished linguistic environment—that parents with low socioeconomic status (SES) spoke less frequently to their children, used syntactically less complex sentences, and in other ways did less to promote language development than middle-SES parents did. As a result, these psychologists suggested, children growing up in low-SES circumstances acquired less sophisticated language skills than their middle-SES peers (e.g., Bernstein, 1971; Deutsch, 1963; Hunt, 1969).

More recently, however, many theorists have called this *language deficit* idea into question (e.g., Miller, 1982; Portes, 1996). For instance, children growing up in extremely impoverished environments have often been observed to speak quite eloquently about their circumstances (Coles, 1967, 1971a, 1971b, 1977). However, they often speak in dialects other than the **Standard English** that is used in the media and most school systems, and such dialects are sometimes misinterpreted as reflecting incomplete language development. (We will return to the nature of dialects shortly.) Currently, many developmental psychologists believe that the oral language skills of children from low-SES backgrounds are just as advanced as those of their middle-SES peers.

Ethnic Differences

We have already described some of the sociolinguistic behaviors that vary from one ethnic group to another. We have also described the unique narrative styles and creative use of figurative language that are frequently observed in African American communities. Children from various ethnic backgrounds show other language differences as well. Differences in word usage are common; for instance, in the United States and Canada, *corn* refers to a particular kind of grain, whereas in Great Britain, it is often used to refer to grains in general and therefore includes wheat, oats, and so on.

Some languages, especially those spoken by people who are spread over a large geographic area, include grammatical structures used only in particular regions. A **dialect** is a version of a language that shares many syntactic rules with its parent language but also has some syntactic rules unique to itself. Consider the following sentences (Milroy, 1994, p. 157):

It would take you to get there early.

I'm just after my dinner.

If you have been raised in North America, you may not be able to make much sense of them, because they reflect a dialect of English spoken in Northern Ireland. (The two sentences mean, "It's advisable to arrive early" and "I've just finished my dinner," respectively.)

Dialects often include unique ways of pronouncing words as well as unique grammatical structures. For instance, a dialect of English spoken in Jamaica (sometimes called a *patois*) involves pronunciations so different from those of Standard English that residents of North America may understand little of what a native Jamaican says. In China, the same written words usually have the same or similar meanings throughout the country, but their pronunciations may be as different as night and day in various regions (Chang, 1998).

Standard English
Form of English generally considered acceptable in school (as reflected in textbooks, grammar instruction, etc.) and in the media.

dialect
Form of a language characteristic of a particular geographic region or ethnic group.

Some dialects are associated with particular ethnic groups. Perhaps the most widely studied ethnic dialect is **African American English** (also known as *Black English Vernacular,* or simply *Black English*). This dialect, which is actually a group of similar dialects, is used in many African American communities throughout the United States and is characterized by sentences such as these:

He going home.

She have a bike.

He be workin'.

Ask Albert do he know how to play basketball. (Dale, 1976, pp. 274–275)

At one time, researchers believed that the African American dialect represented a less complex form of speech than Standard English and so urged educators to teach students to speak "properly" as quickly as possible. But they now realize that it is, in fact, a very complex language system with its own predictable grammatical rules and its own unique idioms and proverbs, and that it promotes communication and complex thought as readily as Standard English (Dale, 1976; DeLain, Pearson, & Anderson, 1985; Fairchild & Edwards-Evans, 1990).

Many children and adolescents view their native dialect as an integral part of their cultural identity (Garrison, 1989; McAlpine, 1992; Ulichny, 1994). Furthermore, when a local dialect is the language most preferred by residents of a community, it is probably the means through which people can most effectively connect with one another in their day-to-day interactions. At the same time, however, many members of society at large associate higher social status with people who speak Standard English, and they perceive speakers of other dialects in a lesser light (Gollnick & Chinn, 1998; Purcell-Gates, 1995; Smith, 1998). As an example, people who speak African American English are less often hired by employers and, when hired, are offered lower-paying positions (Terrell & Terrell, 1983).

Most experts recommend that all students develop proficiency in Standard English because success in mainstream adult society will be difficult to achieve without such proficiency (e.g., Casanova, 1987; Craft, 1984). At the same time, educators should recognize that other languages and dialects are very effective means of communication in many situations (Fairchild & Edward-Evans, 1990; Garcia, 1995; Lee & Slaughter-Defoe, 1995). For example, although teachers may wish to encourage Standard English in most written work and in formal oral presentations, they might find other dialects quite appropriate in creative writing or informal classroom discussions.

Ideally, children and adolescents from diverse dialectic backgrounds probably function most effectively when they can use both their local dialect and Standard English in appropriate settings (Gollnick & Chinn, 1998; Smith, 1998; Warren & McCloskey, 1993). One teacher of African American children has explained it this way:

I don't want them to be ashamed of what they know but I also want them to know and be comfortable with what school and the rest of society requires. When I put it in the context of "translation" they get excited. They see it is possible to go from one to the other. It's not that they are not familiar with Standard English. . . . They hear Standard English all the time on TV. It's certainly what I use in the classroom. But there is rarely any connection made between the way they speak and Standard English. I think that when they can see the connections and know that they can make the shifts, they become better at both. They're bilingual! (Ladson-Billings, 1994, p. 84)

The group differences we've just described all reflect normal variability in children's oral language skills. We now look at exceptionalities in language development.

Exceptionalities in Language Development

In Chapter 5, we mentioned that some children with learning disabilities have difficulty understanding or remembering what other people say. We mentioned, too, that children with autism may have delayed speech or may not even speak at all. Here we describe possible language difficulties for two additional groups of children: those with speech and communication disorders and those with sensory impairments.

African American English
Dialect of some African American communities that includes some pronunciations, grammatical constructions, and idioms different from those of Standard English.

Speech and Communication Disorders

Some children seem to develop normally in all respects except for language. Children with **speech and communication disorders** (sometimes known as *specific language impairments*) have abnormalities in spoken language or in language comprehension that significantly interfere with their classroom performance. Such disorders may involve problems in one or more of the following areas:

- Articulation (e.g., mispronunciations or omissions of certain sounds)
- Fluency (e.g., stuttering, or an atypical rhythm in speech)
- Syntax (e.g., abnormal syntactic patterns, or incorrect word order)
- Semantics (e.g., difficulty interpreting words that have two or more distinctly different word meanings; consistent use of words with imprecise meanings, such as *thing* or *that*)
- Pragmatics (e.g., talking for a long time without letting anyone else speak)
- Receptive language (e.g., inability to distinguish between different phonemes in other people's speech; difficulty understanding or remembering directions)
  (American Speech-Language-Hearing Association, 1993; Owens, 1996; Turnbull et al., 1999)

Speech and communication disorders are also suspected when children fail to demonstrate age-appropriate language (e.g., a kindergartner who communicates only by pointing and gesturing or a third grader who says, "Him go," instead of, "He's gone"). However, speech patterns that are due to a regional or ethnic dialect and those that are due to a bilingual background do *not* fall within the realm of speech and communication disorders (recall the speech therapist who inappropriately recommended that Mario have speech therapy).

Children with speech and communication disorders sometimes have problems with reading and writing as well as with spoken language (Fey, Catts, & Larrivee, 1995; Johnston, 1997). They may also have personal or social problems as a result of their disability. For instance, they may feel self-conscious and embarrassed when they speak, or they may be reluctant to speak at all (Patton, Blackbourn, & Fad, 1996). Furthermore, if they sound "odd" or are difficult to understand, they may have difficulty making friends, and thoughtless classmates may ridicule them (LaBlance, Steckol, & Smith, 1994; Rice, Hadley, & Alexander, 1993).

Sometimes language disorders are inherited; for instance, they often run in families, and if one identical twin has a disorder, the other is highly likely to have it as well (Gopnik, 1997; Tomblin, 1997). Sometimes the disorders are associated with specific brain abnormalities (Locke, 1993). But in many cases, the exact cause of a speech or communication disorder is unknown (Wang & Baron, 1997).

Adapting Instruction for Students with Speech and Communication Disorders

Typically, trained specialists work with students who have impaired communication skills. Nevertheless, classroom teachers can do several things to help these students:

■ *Encourage regular oral communication.* Because students with speech and communication disorders need as much practice in public speaking as anyone else, their teachers should encourage them to talk in class, provided that doing so does not create exceptional stress for them and that their classmates know how to respond to them with care and compassion.

■ *Listen patiently.* When students have difficulty expressing themselves, their teachers may be tempted to assist them—for example, by finishing their sentences. But students with speech and communication disorders are more likely to make progress when others allow them to complete their own thoughts, no matter how long it takes them to do so. Teachers must learn to listen patiently to students with speech problems, and they must encourage classmates to do likewise.

■ *Ask for clarification when a message is unclear.* When having trouble understanding what students are saying, teachers should repeat the portion they *do* understand and ask students to clarify the rest. Honest feedback helps children learn how well they are communicating (Patton et al., 1996).

■ *Provide guidance about how to converse appropriately with others.* When children lack basic pragmatic skills—for instance, when they dominate a conversation to the point where no one

speech and communication disorders
Category of special needs characterized by abnormalities in spoken language that significantly interfere with students' classroom performance.

HELPING STUDENTS WITH SPEECH AND COMMUNICATION DISORDERS

■ Encourage students to talk, but without forcing them to do so.

A third grader has a noticeable lisp that makes him reluctant to speak in front of many of his classmates. His teacher calls on him only in the context of his advanced reading group, where he feels comfortable expressing himself openly with other group members.

■ Listen patiently.

A high school sophomore stutters badly and often takes longer than most students to complete a sentence. Her teacher listens politely and resists the temptation to finish her sentences for her.

■ Provide instruction in any missing pragmatic skills.

A middle school student is sometimes so tactless and self-centered when she talks to her classmates that most of them avoid her. Her teacher teaches her appropriate conversational skills (e.g., taking turns, listening to what others are saying) in several one-on-one role-playing sessions after school. The teacher also monitors her performance in small-group work in class, where he observes slow but steady progress in her ability to converse effectively with other students.

■ Seek the assistance of a specialist when students show chronic speech and language difficulties.

A fourth-grade teacher realizes that a student's continual mispronunciation of the letter s is not typical for the age group and so seeks the services of the school's speech and language pathologist.

else can participate—they benefit from guided practice and explicit feedback about their conversational skills (Bloom & Lahey, 1978).

Sensory Impairments and Language Development

When children do not have the same access to sensory information that their peers have, they may show delays in language development. For instance, children who have severe visual impairments (e.g., those who are blind) cannot relate what they hear to objects and events around them unless they can perceive those objects and events through sound, touch, or other senses. As a result, they may have more limited semantic knowledge: They simply haven't had as many opportunities to make connections between words and their meanings as sighted children have (Harris, 1992). Their syntactic development is more likely to be on target; for instance, they progress from one-word to two-word "sentences" at about the same time that their age-mates do (Harris, 1992).

Children with hearing impairments are at risk for delays in both the semantic and syntactic aspects of language development, especially if their hearing impairment has been present since birth or occurred early in life (Harris, 1992). Furthermore, children who have been completely deaf from birth or soon thereafter typically need special training to develop proficiency in speaking.

Most children who use a visual language system as their primary mode of communication follow a normal pattern of language development (Harris, 1992; Newport, 1990; Pettito, 1997). As noted earlier in the chapter, even infants who are deaf produce speechlike sounds at about the same age as hearing infants, and those who are regularly exposed to sign language often "babble" with their hands as well (Locke, 1993; Pettito, 1997). When their parents regularly use sign language to communicate with them, children sign their first word at around 18 to 22 months, with multiword phrases following soon thereafter (Pettito, 1997). Like hearing children, children who use sign language appear to actively construct rules for their language, and they refine these rules over time; for instance, the overregularization phenomenon frequently observed in young children's speech is seen in children's sign language as well (Goldin-Meadow & Mylander, 1993; Pettito, 1997).

A case study of BoMee (Wilcox, 1994) illustrates just how much is possible when parents provide a linguistically rich environment through sign language. BoMee was born in Korea 8 weeks prematurely; although she could hear at birth, early illnesses or medications apparently caused profound hearing loss to emerge shortly thereafter. At age 2½, BoMee was adopted by American parents, who communicated with her regularly in sign language. Within a few weeks after BoMee's arrival, they also began to sign their self-talk as a way of "thinking aloud"; for instance, BoMee's mother might sign "What goes next in this recipe?" or "Where are my shoes?" Within a week, BoMee began signing her own self-talk, such as "Where my shoes are?" Soon, self-talk was a regular feature in BoMee's problem-solving activities. On one occasion, BoMee was trying to put a dress on her doll, but the dress was too small. She signed to herself:

> Hmmm, wrong me. This dress fit here? Think not. Hmmm. For other doll here. (Translation: *Hmmm, I'm wrong. Does this dress go on this doll? I don't think so. Hmmm. It goes on this other doll.*) (Wilcox, 1994, p. 119)

BoMee showed other normal linguistic behaviors as well. She simplified her language when she signed to her baby brother. And just as hearing children typically read aloud in the early stages of reading, BoMee signed "out loud" when she began to read.

Like Mario, BoMee may have had an advantage in the development of metalinguistic awareness. She was exposed to both English-based signs and American Sign Language (which has somewhat different vocabulary and syntax) and quickly became bilingual in her knowledge of the two language systems. She understood very early that some people talked and others used sign language. Furthermore, shortly after her third birthday, she appropriately signed "This Little Piggy" in two different ways—in English-based signs and in American Sign Language—to people who understood only one of the two languages. Obviously, children with hearing loss can have very normal cognitive and linguistic development as long as their linguistic environment is appropriate for them.

Making Accommodations for Children with Sensory Impairments When children are blind, specialists teach them to read and write in Braille; when they are deaf, specialists provide training in such communication skills as American Sign Language, finger spelling (alphabetic hand signs), and speechreading (reading lips). Yet many children with major sensory impairments are in general education classrooms for much or all of the school day; thus, much of their learning occurs within the context of regular classroom activities. Following are three strategies teachers should keep in mind for these students:

■ *Communicate the same message through multiple modalities.* Students with normal hearing and vision rely on both auditory information and visual cues—body language, nearby objects and events, and so on—to interpret other people's spoken messages. Therefore, students with impaired vision and those with significant hearing loss get only part of the story, and their ability to understand what is happening around them is often hampered as a result. Teachers must be especially careful to transmit *complete* messages to their students with sensory impairments. They can provide opportunities for visually impaired students to feel objects or in other ways experience topics of discussion—for instance, by having them explore three-dimensional relief maps or globes of various parts of the world (in geography), conduct hands-on experiments (in science), or role-play important historical events (in history). And teachers should present visual equivalents of spoken messages for students with hearing loss—for example, by writing important points on the chalkboard or by illustrating key ideas with pictures and other graphics.

■ *Learn elements of American Sign Language and finger spelling, and teach them to other class members.* Some students with hearing loss, because of their reduced ability to communicate, may feel socially isolated from their teachers and peers. One effective way of opening the lines of communication is for teachers and other class members to gain some competence in American Sign Language and finger spelling. For instance, Jeanne once taught at a middle school where *every* student—those with hearing loss and those without—received some instruction in signing. One girl was totally deaf yet was quite popular with her classmates, and she and her friends could communicate quite easily during class.

■ *Identify and address deficiencies in language skills that may have resulted from students' sensory impairments.* Teachers must be on the lookout for any developmental delays in language that students may have as a result of their sensory impairments. Many of the strategies presented throughout the chapter are quite appropriate for students with limited vision or hearing. In some cases, special educators or other specialists can also provide guidance and assistance in this regard.

The Big Picture: How Language Development Fits into the Larger Scheme of Things

As we have already noted in this and preceding chapters, language development and cognitive development are closely intertwined. Cognitive development is, of course, critical for the development of language: Children can talk only about things that they can first *think* about. But language is equally important for children's cognitive development: It provides a symbolic system by which they can mentally represent external events, enables them to exchange information and perspectives with the people around them, helps them make associations among the various pieces of information they acquire, and (from Vygotsky's perspective) helps them internalize processes that they first experience in a social context.

Language is also critical for social and moral development. Through conversations and confrontations with adults and peers, children learn socially acceptable ways of behaving toward others (see Chapter 13) and, in most cases, eventually establish a set of principles that guide their moral decision making (see Chapter 10).

Finally, mastery of the basic underpinnings of language (i.e., semantics and syntax) and proficiency in the receptive and expressive aspects of spoken language (i.e., listening and speaking) provide the foundation for receptive and expressive skills in *written* language (i.e., reading and writing). We turn to the development of children's literacy skills in the next chapter.

CASE STUDY: BOARDING SCHOOL

Some parts of Alaska are so sparsely settled that building local high schools makes little economic sense. So in some Native American communities, older students are sent to boarding school for their high school education. A high priority for boarding school teachers is to help students master the English language. With this information in mind, consider the following incident:

> Many of the students at the school spoke English with a native dialect and seemed unable to utter certain essential sounds in the English language. A new group of speech teachers was sent in to correct the problem. The teachers worked consistently with the students in an attempt to improve speech patterns and intonation, but found that their efforts were in vain.
>
> One night, the boys in the dormitory were seeming to have too much fun, and peals of laughter were rolling out from under the door. An investigating counselor approached cautiously and listened quietly outside the door to see if he could discover the source of the laughter. From behind the door he heard a voice, speaking in perfect English, giving instructions to the rest of the crowd. The others were finding the situation very amusing. When the counselor entered the room he found that one of the students was speaking. "Joseph," he said, "You've been cured! Your English is perfect." "No," said Joseph returning to his familiar dialect, "I was just doing an imitation of you." "But if you can speak in Standard English, why don't you do it all of the time?" the counselor queried. "I can," responded Joseph, "but it sounds funny, and I feel dumb doing it." (Garrison, 1989, p. 121)

- Why might Joseph prefer his native dialect to Standard English?
- Is Joseph bilingual? Why or why not?
- The counselor told Joseph that he had "been cured." What beliefs about Joseph's native dialect does this statement reflect?

SUMMARY

Theoretical Perspectives

Although modeling, reinforcement, and feedback almost certainly play some role in language development, theories based on such processes cannot adequately account for the fact that most children acquire an extremely complex language system in a very short period of time. *Nativists* propose that young children have a built-in mechanism that facilitates their acquisition of language; this mechanism allows toddlers and preschoolers to construct a complex set of grammatical rules even when the language spoken around them is haphazard and imperfect. In contrast, *information processing theorists* apply general concepts and principles of cognition (e.g., the importance of attention, the limited capacity of working memory) to explain how some aspects of language may develop.

Trends in Language Development

Children and adolescents continue to develop their linguistic knowledge and skills throughout the preschool and school years. For instance, they add several thousand new words to their vocabulary each year. Over time, they rely less on word order and more on syntax to interpret other people's messages, and they can comprehend and produce sentences with increasingly complex syntactic structures. Their conversations with others increase in length, they become better able to adapt the content of their speech to the characteristics of their listeners, and they become more aware of the unspoken social conventions that govern verbal interactions in their culture. They also acquire a growing understanding of the nature of language as an entity in and of itself.

Learning a Second Language

Although research results are mixed with regard to the "best" time to learn a second language, recent research is consistent in indicating that knowing two or more languages enhances achievement in reading and language arts, promotes greater metalinguistic awareness, and fosters multicultural awareness. An *immersion* approach to teaching a second language is effective only when students have ample opportunity to continue developing their native language outside of school; in other situations, *bilingual education* is usually preferable.

Diversity and Exceptionalities in Language Development

Subtle qualitative differences have been observed in the conversational styles of males and females. Various ethnic groups may show differences in sociolinguistic behaviors, storytelling traditions, use of figurative language, and dialects.

Some students have disabilities that affect their language development. Students with *speech and communication disorders* have abnormalities in articulation, fluency, syntax, receptive language, or other aspects of receptive and expressive language that significantly interfere with their classroom performance. Students with hearing impairments and (to a lesser extent) those with visual impairments may have more limited language proficiency because of reduced exposure to language or reduced awareness of the meaningful contexts in which it occurs.

Now go to our Companion Website to assess your understanding of chapter content with Multiple-Choice Questions, apply comprehension in Essay Questions, and broaden your knowledge with links to related Developmental Psychology World Wide Web sites.

KEY CONCEPTS

native language (p. 236)
phonology (p. 236)
semantics (p. 236)
syntax (p. 236)
pragmatics (p. 236)
language acquisition device
  (p. 237)
nativism (p. 237)
Universal Grammar (p. 238)
babbling (p. 238)
semantic bootstrapping
  (p. 240)
receptive language (p. 241)
expressive language (p. 241)
infant-directed speech
  (p. 242)

lexicon (p. 244)
undergeneralization (p. 244)
overgeneralization (p. 244)
function word (p. 245)
fast mapping (p. 246)
defining feature (p. 247)
correlational feature (p. 247)
overregularization (p. 248)
phonemes (p. 250)
figurative speech (p. 252)
narrative (p. 255)
sounding (p. 255)
sociolinguistic behaviors
  (p. 257)
personal space (p. 260)

IRE cycle (p. 260)
wait time (p. 260)
culture shock (p. 261)
metalinguistic awareness
  (p. 263)
bilingualism (p. 266)
immersion (p. 267)
bilingual education (p. 267)
Standard English (p. 268)
dialect (p. 268)
African American English
  (p. 269)
speech and communication
  disorders (p. 270)

Suddenly swerving, seven small swans swam silently southward, seeing six swift sailboats sail slowy seaward.

Laura, age 8

Development of Literacy: Reading and Writing

CASE STUDY: PHYLLIS AND BENJAMIN JONES

Phyllis Jones and her son Benjamin live in a low-income, inner-city, African American neighborhood. Here is their story:

[Phyllis] finished high school and two years of college, and regrets that she did not go farther. She wishes she had "listened to her grandmother" who was "always pushing" her to study; instead, "I did enough just to get by." She is deeply concerned about her son's education, and determined that he will go farther than she did. She is particularly concerned about his learning to read, noting that "without reading, you can't do anything," and that "readers are leaders—I want Benjamin to read and read and read." She has little trust in the local public schools, and is acutely aware of the large numbers of poor black children who fail to learn to read well and who drop out of school: "I guess black people have a tendency to just say 'Oh, I can't do it, I can't do it, I can't do it.' "

Mrs. Jones decided that the only way to be certain that Benjamin would learn to read was to teach him herself. She began buying books for him when he was an infant, and she asked friends and relatives to give him books as Christmas and birthday presents. Before he turned 3, she bought him a set of phonics tapes and workbooks, which she used to conduct regular lessons, helping Benjamin learn to recognize the forms and sounds of letters, combinations of letters, and eventually entire words. She also gave him lessons in letter formation, handwriting, and spelling. When Benjamin was 3, he began attending a Head Start program, while his mother continued to teach him at home. She tried to make these activities "fun for Benjamin." She was pleased with his interest in reading and writing, and sometimes frustrated that he did not learn as quickly as she wanted him to.

Benjamin sometimes pretended to read magazines, newspapers, and books. His mother was gratified by his enthusiasm, commenting on his "reading" of *The Gingerbread Man*, "you can hear the laughter and joy in his voice." But she also told Benjamin he was "not really reading." On one occasion, she pointed to the print in the book Benjamin was pretending to read and said "these are what you read. Someday you will learn to read." Another time she commented, "Benjamin thinks he can read. What he'll do is recite some words from a story and exclaim with great joy 'I can read! I can read!' I explained to him that he isn't reading. Reading is looking at a book and saying the words that are written there. But I say one day he will read—soon, just like Tony [an older friend of Benjamin's]." By the time Benjamin was 4, his mother noted that he knew "all of his alphabet by sight. Praise God!"

When Benjamin turned 4, Mrs. Jones began taking him to a reading program at the storefront church she attended. This program was designed for older children, but she thought he would "pick up something." She also continued to work on reading and writing at home, using index cards to make a card game to teach Benjamin how to write his name. When he was about 4½, Benjamin began sounding out words that he noticed around him, such as "off" and "on." His mother commented, "now he wants to know what everything spells and wants to guess at some of them. He asked me on the bus if E-M-E-R-G-E-N-C-Y spelled 'emergency'." On another occasion, when she picked Benjamin up at Head Start, "he said, 'Guess what we did today? I'll give you a hint—it begins with J. Then he said the word was J-E-M, which was supposed to be 'gym'." His mother was delighted with his interest in reading: "Hurrah! I hope it carries through the rest of his life." By the end of his second year in Head Start, when he had just turned 5, Benjamin could read a number of simple words by sounding them out and had a small sight vocabulary. His mother took great pride in these achievements: "Hallelujah! He can read!"

P HYLLIS KNOWS HOW IMPORTANT reading and writing are for success in the adult world, and so she has provided a foundation that should facilitate Benjamin's reading and writing development in the years to come. Yet other children are not so fortunate. Many students in our public schools never attain the level of literacy they need to participate fully in adult society (Hiebert & Raphael, 1996).

To some extent, children's literacy skills build on their oral language skills. The thousands of words and innumerable syntactic structures that children master in spoken language are basic elements of written language as well. However, written language differs from spoken language in two important ways: It involves a second-order symbol system, and it takes place in a relatively context-free situation.

As noted in Chapter 4, spoken words serve as symbols that enable children to mentally represent and think about objects and events more efficiently. Written words, too, are symbols, but they comprise a **second-order symbol system:** They are symbols that stand for *other* symbols (i.e., they stand for spoken words). To learn to read and write, then, children must learn the relationships between how words sound and are produced in speech, on the one hand, and how they look and are written on paper, on the other. Children must also master nuances of the written symbol system that have no counterparts in spoken language, such as punctuation marks and appropriate uses of upper- and lowercase letters (Dyson, 1986; Liberman, 1998; Paris & Cunningham, 1996).

Spoken language typically occurs in an information-rich context that facilitates communication. People of all ages (and especially young children) often rely on the context to help them understand what they hear, and they frequently use nonverbal cues (gestures, facial expressions, pauses, etc.) to help them convey their meanings when they speak. In contrast, written language is relatively context-free: One person writes something at one time and someone else reads it at a later time, often in a very different location. Writers cannot always anticipate what their readers are likely to know and not know, and readers cannot ask questions if something doesn't make sense. Thus, writers must express themselves more clearly and completely, and readers must rely more heavily on the content of the message itself, than either group would need to do in everyday conversation (Byrnes, 1996; Cameron, Hunt, & Linton, 1996; Nuthall, 1996).

In this chapter, we explore the development of reading and writing throughout childhood and adolescence. We begin by examining three theoretical perspectives of how and why literacy skills develop. We then look at the preliteracy knowledge and behaviors that typically appear in the preschool years (Benjamin's pretend reading is an example) and at the reading and writing skills that emerge in the elementary and secondary grades. Later, we consider how reading and writing development may vary for different genders, socioeconomic levels, and ethnic and linguistic groups, as well as for children with special needs in literacy. Finally, we address the roles that reading and writing play in overall cognitive development.

Theories of Literacy Development

Theorists have proposed a variety of explanations for how reading and writing develop. Many of them reflect one of three general viewpoints: an information processing perspective, a whole-language perspective, or a sociocultural perspective.

The Information Processing Perspective

Information processing theorists believe that reading and writing involve the same general mechanisms (working memory, prior knowledge, cognitive and metacognitive strategies, etc.) that other forms of cognition involve. In addition, most information processing theorists believe that reading and writing are *constructive* processes. Reading is constructive in the sense that people combine what they see on the printed page with their existing knowledge and beliefs to derive meaning from text (Weaver & Kintsch, 1991). Writing is constructive in that good writers must organize their thoughts into a logical sequence and communicate their message in a way that their audience is likely to understand (Bereiter & Scardamalia, 1987; Cameron et al., 1996; Greene & Ackerman, 1995). As children grow older, their ability to con-

second-order symbol system
Set of symbols that stand for other symbols.

struct meaning in both reading and writing improves considerably, in large part because they have an increasing knowledge base—not only about the world in general but also about the general structures and conventions of written language—on which they can draw (Beck, McKeown, Sinatra, & Loxterman, 1991; Benton, 1997; Byrnes, 1996).

From an information processing view, reading and writing can place a considerable strain on people's limited working memory capacities (Benton, 1997; Hall, 1989; McCutchen, 1996; Stanovich, 2000). Reading involves thinking about many things simultaneously, including words and their meanings, syntactic structures, and general knowledge about the subject matter. Writing involves thinking about all of these *plus* thinking about how to communicate effectively and remembering correct spellings, punctuation rules, and other conventions of written language. Until some of these cognitive processes become automatized (i.e., until they occur quickly, efficiently, and with little conscious effort), mature forms of reading and writing are virtually impossible.

Children's reading and writing skills improve as children acquire certain cognitive and metacognitive strategies. For instance, as children grow older, they are more likely to engage in comprehension monitoring—that is, to regularly evaluate their understanding of the author's message—as they read (see Chapter 5). They are also more likely to consider their future audience as they write and then tailor their words, sentence structures, and general message accordingly (Kellogg, 1994; Knudson, 1992; Perfetti & McCutchen, 1987). And in both reading and writing, children become increasingly able to set goals for themselves and to direct their efforts toward achieving those goals (Scardamalia & Bereiter, 1986; Webb & Palincsar, 1996).

You will see the influence of information processing theory throughout our discussions of reading and writing in this chapter. For example, you will see it in our discussion of the importance of *phonological awareness* and *automatization* in word recognition. You will see it in our discussion of *schemas* and *story grammars* in reading comprehension. And it will underlie our depiction of how spelling, composition skills, and metacognitive processes in writing develop.

The Whole-Language Perspective

As noted in Chapter 7, children master the basic components of their native language within the first few years of life. What's especially remarkable about this accomplishment is that they do so with little if any explicit instruction; daily immersion in the language seems to be sufficient for acquiring a sizable vocabulary and learning many of the complexities of syntax. In essence, learning a language is a very natural human process.

Some theorists propose that learning to understand and communicate in written language is, and should be, just as natural a process as learning to understand and communicate in oral language (e.g., Edelsky, Altwerger, & Flores, 1991; Goodman, 1989; Goodman & Goodman, 1979; Weaver, 1990). They argue that children learn reading and writing most effectively by being immersed in a *literate environment*—one with many books, magazines, newspapers, and writing tools—and by engaging in real-life literacy tasks. This view is generally known as the **whole-language perspective.**

Whole-language theorists focus more on the kinds of home and school environments in which literacy can most effectively develop than on the internal, cognitive mechanisms that propel literacy development per se. Within the past two decades, these theorists have been visible and highly influential advocates for teaching reading and writing through authentic activities, such as reading stories and magazine articles, writing letters to relatives, and so on. We summarize research findings about the effectiveness of this approach later in the chapter.

The Sociocultural Perspective

Building on Vygotsky's theory of cognitive development (see Chapter 4), some theorists propose that literacy, like any other cognitive activity, is largely a product of children's social and cultural environments (Green & Dixon, 1996; John-Steiner, Panofsky, & Smith, 1994; Pérez, 1998). When children learn to read and write, they also learn culturally appropriate

Writing involves many things: considering what the reader is likely to know, expressing thoughts coherently, spelling words correctly, adhering to conventions of grammar and punctuation, and so on. Most children and adolescents don't have the working memory capacity to handle all of these tasks simultaneously.

whole-language perspective
Theoretical perspective that proposes that children develop literacy skills most effectively within the context of authentic reading and writing tasks.

ways of achieving their goals through reading and writing (Pérez, 1998). Children learn the purposes of reading by watching their parents and other caregivers engage in such ordinary activities as reading the newspaper, sorting the mail, and consulting the telephone book. They learn the multiple functions of writing when they observe adults making grocery lists, filling out application forms, and communicating with friends through e-mail.

As children grow, they converse frequently with adults and peers about literacy tasks (Panofsky, 1994; Pérez, 1998). At home, they read bedtime storybooks with their parents and occasionally pause to talk about characters and events in the stories. In the elementary grades, they often work with classmates to compose short stories. In high school language arts classes, they discuss possible interpretations of poetry and novels with their teachers and classmates. From a Vygotskian perspective, children gradually *internalize* these social processes, transforming them into their own ways of understanding and producing written language.

In this chapter, the sociocultural perspective will be particularly evident in two places. First, as we discuss early literacy, we describe how parents and teachers can promote literacy development through both the environments they create for children and their interactions with children about written language. Second, as we describe *reciprocal teaching,* we show how teachers can help children and adolescents practice and internalize metacognitive strategies for understanding what they read.

Critiquing Theories of Literacy Development

The three perspectives we've just examined focus on different aspects of literacy development: Information processing theorists address the cognitive processes involved in reading and writing, whole-language theorists describe the kinds of environments in which they believe reading and writing can most effectively emerge, and sociocultural theorists emphasize the social practices that promote literate behavior and thought processes. In one sense, then, the three theories are not necessarily incompatible; in fact, some whole-language theorists believe that their ideas are very much in line with sociocultural ideas (Goodman & Goodman, 1990).

Yet people from different theoretical camps (and, to a lesser extent, people within theoretical camps) do not always agree about the best ways to teach reading and writing. Virtually all theorists believe that authentic reading activities (e.g., reading books, magazines, and newspapers) and authentic writing activities (e.g., writing stories, poems, and personal and business letters) are essential for promoting optimal literacy development. However, whole-language theorists advocate using authentic activities almost exclusively, whereas many information processing theorists suggest that systematic training in basic knowledge and skills (letter-sound relationships, common spelling patterns, etc.) provides fundamental building blocks on which more complex reading and writing processes depend. Throughout the chapter, we consider the effectiveness of these and various other instructional strategies for fostering reading and writing development.

The Basic Developmental Issues table on the next page contrasts the three theoretical perspectives in terms of the basic issues of nature versus nurture, universality versus diversity, and qualitative versus quantitative change. We turn our attention now to trends in the development of literacy, beginning with literacy in the early years.

Literacy in the Early Years

Like Phyllis Jones, many parents place a high priority on reading and writing. These parents promote their children's literacy skills in numerous ways—by providing easy access to reading and writing materials, modeling reading and writing behavior, making frequent trips to the library, talking about the things they've read and written and, more generally, demonstrating that reading and writing are enjoyable activities (McLane & McNamee, 1990; Teale, 1978). But perhaps most importantly, such parents read to their children regularly (Baker, Scher, & Mackler, 1997; Sulzby & Teale, 1991).

Some parents introduce children to books well before their first birthdays, pointing at pictures and labeling the objects they see (Snow & Ninio, 1986). We think back to the books we bought for our own children long before they were walking or talking. Some of these books

Contrasting Perspectives of Literacy Development

BASIC DEVELOPMENTAL ISSUES

ISSUE	INFORMATION PROCESSING PERSPECTIVE	WHOLE-LANGUAGE PERSPECTIVE	SOCIOCULTURAL PERSPECTIVE
Nature and Nurture	The "hardware" of the information processing system (the brain) is, of course, inherited, but well-chosen instructional strategies can promote the cognitive processes essential for reading and writing. Some difficulties with literacy tasks (e.g., dyslexia) may have genetic origins.	Learning to read and write is as natural a process as learning to understand and produce spoken language and so presumably has some biological underpinnings. Authentic literacy activities (e.g., reading books and magazines, writing letters to friends and relatives) optimize literacy development.	The focus is on the social and cultural environments in which children encounter and engage in reading and writing activities. Children learn the purposes of literacy by watching others engage in everyday reading and writing tasks, and their social interactions related to reading and writing become internalized cognitive processes.
Universality and Diversity	Some characteristics of the information processing system (e.g., the limited capacity of working memory) are universal across different environments and cultures. Yet other characteristics (e.g., the specific knowledge stored in long-term memory) are considerably different from one child to the next.	The context in which literacy most effectively develops—an environment in which authentic printed materials and writing implements are prominent and easily available—is universal across cultures. However, children's access to a literate environment varies considerably across cultures; it may also vary across families *within* a culture.	Different cultures use reading and writing for different purposes (and some cultures don't use reading or writing at all), and children's literacy skills vary accordingly.
Qualitative and Quantitative Change 	Many information processing theorists describe general trends in children's reading and writing capabilities over time. But a few (e.g., Bryant, Nunes, & Aidinis, 1999; Chall, 1996; Ehri, 1991; Juel, 1991) propose that certain aspects of reading and writing development may proceed through discernible stages (revealing qualitative change).	Children's proficiency in reading and writing develops in a gradual, continuous fashion.	Children's reading and writing skills emerge gradually over time. Adults initially provide considerable scaffolding for children's efforts and then slowly withdraw this scaffolding as the children become able to read and write independently.

consisted of nothing more than a few plastic or otherwise indestructible pages that depicted a simple item (perhaps a doll, toy truck, cat, or dog) on each page. Although these books hardly had spellbinding plots, they often captured our infants' attention, at least temporarily.

Reading to children may be particularly valuable when parents and other caregivers talk with children about what they are reading together (Panofsky, 1994). Consider the following scenario, in which a mother and her 4-year-old son are reading H. A. Rey's *Curious George Flies a Kite:*

Mother: *George looked into the water. . . . He was so near, maybe he could get it with his hands. George got down as low as he could, and put out his hand.*

Child: Will he fall in dere?

Mother: What?

Child: Will he fall in dere?

Mother: Will he fall in there? I don't know, let's see [turns page]. Oh, you were right! *Splash, into the lake he went. The water was cold and George was cold and wet too. This was no fun at all.*

Child: He shoulda just got his two hands down dere, den put his feet on dere [pointing].

Mother: Yeah, he could have hung on to the dock with his feet, 'cause his feet are like hands, aren't they? (dialogue from Panofsky, 1994, pp. 236–237; format adapted)

Storybook reading in the early years promotes the development of emergent literacy—basic knowledge about written language and literature that provides the foundation for learning how to read and write.

Like this mother, adults often make comments and ask questions that help young children make better sense of a story. For instance, they may label or interpret pictures ("That's a butterfly," "See the tear? He's crying"), identify feelings ("Oh, no!" "He's happy, huh?"), or encourage speculation ("Do you think the fish will like the cake?" "I bet he's scared"; Panofsky, 1994). In doing so, adults engage children in the *social construction of meaning* that we discussed in Chapter 4.

Emergent Literacy

Through their early exposure to reading and writing, children learn many things about written language (Paris & Cunningham, 1996; Pérez, 1998; Weiss & Hagen, 1988). For instance, they learn that

- Print has meaning and conveys information
- Different kinds of printed matter (storybooks, newspapers, telephone books, grocery lists, etc.) serve different purposes
- Spoken language is represented in a consistent way in written language (e.g., particular letters of the alphabet are associated with particular sounds in spoken language)
- Written language includes some predictable elements and conventions (e.g., stories often begin with "Once upon a time," and in the English language, writing proceeds from left to right and from the top of the page to the bottom)

This fundamental knowledge about written language lays a foundation for reading and writing and is known as **emergent literacy.**

Many behaviors of preschool children reflect emergent literacy. Like Benjamin, young children may pretend to read storybooks, speaking in a "storytelling" fashion, turning the pages regularly and, in some cases, recalling part or all of a story from memory (McLane & McNamee, 1990; Sulzby, 1985). They also may correctly identify words that appear in familiar contexts, such as on a stop sign, a cereal box, a soft drink can, or the sign for a fast-food restaurant (Dickinson, Wolf, & Stotsky, 1993; Share & Gur, 1999).

Emergent literacy appears in preschoolers' writing activities as well (Dyson, 1986; McLane & McNamee, 1990; Pérez, 1998). Initially, their attempts at writing may be nothing more than random scribbles. Eventually it may be wavy lines or squiggles written from left to right across the page, perhaps with occasional spaces to indicate where one "word" ends and another begins. Increasingly, their writing assumes letterlike shapes that reflect characteristics of their own language; for example, Arabic preschoolers include many dots in their early pseudowriting, reflecting the prominence of dots in written Arabic (Rowe & Harste, 1986). Figure 8–1 shows two examples of American children's pseudowriting; notice how the older child's writing more closely resembles English letter forms.

Yet preschoolers often don't realize that writing must take a *particular* form to have meaning. For instance, they may scribble something on a page and ask an adult, "What did I write?" (McLane & McNamee, 1990). After a 5-year-old boy named Ashley had written several letterlike shapes on a sheet of paper, an adult asked him, "Tell me about your letters." In a very matter-of-fact manner, Ashley responded, "I don't read 'em; I just write 'em" (Dyson, 1986, p. 205).

For many children, the first word they learn to read and write—perhaps at age 3 or 4—is their own name (Dickinson et al., 1993; McLane & McNamee, 1990; Rowe & Harste, 1986). Yet this accomplishment may initially be a fragile one, as a conversation with 3-year-old Hank illustrates:

emergent literacy
Knowledge and skills that lay a foundation for reading and writing; typically develops in the preschool years from early experiences with written language.

Hank has been successfully writing his name H-A-N-K for several weeks now, although he frequently writes the N upside-down as Ͷ. On one occasion, when an adult asks him to write his name, he writes H-A-K. "Are you done?" the adult asks. Hank replies, "Yep, that N is giving me too much trouble so I decided to leave it out." (Rowe & Harste, 1986, p. 249)

Obviously, Hank has not yet learned something that will be critical for his later reading and writing success: that particular words should always be spelled in the *same* way.

FIGURE 8-1 Two examples of preschoolers' pseudowriting. A 4-year-old boy wrote the letter on the left to his mother and told his teacher it said, "Dear Mommy, from Tommy". A 5-year-old girl wrote the lengthy piece on the right without explaining its meaning.

Writing samples courtesy of Cathy Zocchi.

Effects of Early Literacy Experiences

Researchers consistently find that young children who are read to frequently during the preschool years have more advanced language development (e.g., larger vocabularies), are more interested in reading, and learn to read more easily once they reach elementary school (Sulzby & Teale, 1991; Whitehurst et al., 1994). Associating literacy activities with pleasure may be especially important; for instance, children who enjoy their early reading experiences are more likely to read frequently later on (Baker et al., 1997). In this respect, authentic literacy activities (e.g., reading children's stories) are more beneficial than activities involving drill and practice of isolated skills (e.g., the workbooks Phyllis Jones provided for Benjamin). A heavy focus on drill and practice may lead young children to conclude that reading and writing are tedious tasks (Baker et al., 1997).

By the time they reach school age, some children have more than a thousand hours of reading and writing experience behind them (Adams, 1990; Teale, 1986). Yet for a variety of reasons, other children may have encountered few if any books or other written materials before they begin school (Pérez, 1998). By observing young children as they interact with books and writing materials, preschool teachers can learn a great deal about what the children have and have not learned about the nature of written language; the Observation Guidelines table on the next page offers several ideas about what to look for.

When children's home environments have not given them a preliminary understanding of the nature and purposes of reading and writing, preschool teachers play a critical role in laying the foundation for later literacy development. The "Implication" column of the Observation Guidelines table lists several strategies teachers can use to foster the knowledge and skills of emergent literacy.

Development in Reading

Reading is a complex, multifaceted process that continues to develop throughout the elementary and secondary school years. In kindergarten and first grade (if not before), children begin to identify the specific words they see in print; shortly thereafter, they begin to derive meaning from the printed page. As they get older, they become capable of reading and comprehending increasingly sophisticated and challenging text, and by high school much of their classroom learning depends on their ability to understand and remember what they read.

In the following pages, we explore the development of three important aspects of learning to read—phonological awareness, word recognition, and reading comprehension—and look at Jeanne Chall's description of how reading processes change over the course of childhood and adolescence. We then consider general approaches to reading instruction and more specific strategies for promoting reading development.

OBSERVATION GUIDELINES

CHARACTERISTIC	LOOK FOR	EXAMPLE	IMPLICATION
Attitudes toward Books	• Frequent manipulation and perusal of books • Attentiveness and interest when adults read storybooks • Eagerness to talk about the stories that are read	Martina often mentions the Berenstain Bears books that her father reads to her at home.	Devote a regular time to storybook reading; choose books with colorful pictures and imaginative story lines; and occasionally stop to discuss and interpret events in a story. Make regular trips to the local library; ask parents if they would like to go along (Heath, 1983).
Behaviors with Books	• Correct handling of books (e.g., holding them right side up, turning pages in the appropriate direction) • Pretend reading • Use of picture content or memory of the story to construct a logical sequence of events when pretending to read • Asking "What does this say?" about particular sections of text	Rusty doesn't seem to know what to do with the books in his preschool classroom. He opens them haphazardly and apparently sees nothing wrong with ripping out pages.	If children have had only limited experience with books, occasionally read one-on-one with them. Let them hold the books and turn the pages. Ask them to make predictions about what might happen next in a story.
Word Recognition	• Recognition of product names when they appear in logos and other familiar contexts • Recognition of own name in print	Katherine sees a take-out bag from a local fast-food restaurant and correctly asserts that it says "Burger King."	Prominently label any coat hooks, storage boxes, and other items that belong to individual children. Write children's names in large letters on paper and encourage them to trace or copy the letters. When children are ready, ask them to put their first name (or perhaps its initial letter) on their artwork and other written creations.
Writing Behaviors	• Production of letterlike shapes • Writing in a left-to-right sequence • Ability to write some letters correctly or almost correctly • Ability to write own name	Hank can write his name, but he frequently reverses the *N* and sometimes leaves it out altogether.	Give children numerous opportunities to experiment with writing implements (paper, crayons, markers, pencils, etc.) in both structured tasks and unstructured situations. Provide guidance in forming letters and words when children express an interest in learning how to write them.
Knowledge about the Nature and Purposes of Written Language	• Awareness that specific words are always spelled in the same way • Correct identification of telephone books, calendars, and other reference materials • Pretend writing for particular purposes	When Shakira and Lucie pretend to grocery shop, they write several lines of squiggles on a piece of paper. They say that this is a list of items they need at the store.	Encourage play activities that involve pretend writing (e.g., writing and delivering "letters" to classmates; Hawkins, 1997). Let children see you engaging in a wide variety of reading and writing activities.

Development of Phonological Awareness

Before Benjamin Jones was 3, his mother began teaching him to recognize the shapes and sounds of letters. Letter recognition is a clear prerequisite for learning to read (Adams, 1990; Harris & Giannouli, 1999). Yet learning to recognize all 26 letters of the alphabet in both uppercase and lowercase forms poses a challenge for many children, in part because some letters differ from one another only in their orientation. Thus, young children often have trouble distinguishing between *M* and *W,* and among *b, d, p,* and *q.*

In addition to knowing the letters, children also need to associate those letters with the particular sounds that make up spoken language. A growing body of research indicates that **phonological awareness**—hearing the distinct sounds of which words are comprised—is an important element of successful reading (Foorman, Francis, Fletcher, Schatschneider, & Mehta, 1998; Harris & Hatano, 1999; Stanovich, 2000; Wagner, Torgesen, & Rashotte, 1994). Phonological awareness includes such abilities as these:

- Hearing the specific syllables within words (e.g., hearing "can" and "dee" as separate parts of *candy*)
- Dividing words into discrete phonemes (e.g., hearing the sounds "guh," "ay," and "tuh" in *gate*)
- Blending separate phonemes into meaningful words (e.g., recognizing that, when put together, the sounds "wuh," "eye," and "duh" make *wide*)
- Identifying words that rhyme (e.g., realizing that *cat* and *hat* end with the same sounds)

Phonological awareness evolves gradually in the preschool and early elementary years (Barron, 1998; Goswami, 1999; Lonigan, Burgess, Anthony, & Barker, 1998). Typically it follows this sequence:

1. *Awareness of syllables.* Most children can detect the discrete syllables within words by age 4, well before they begin school and start learning to read (Goswami, 1999; Harris & Giannouli, 1999).
2. *Awareness of onsets and rimes.* Soon after they become aware of the individual syllables in multisyllabic words, children begin to realize that many syllables can be divided into two parts: an **onset** (one or more consonants that precede the vowel sound) and a **rime** (the vowel sound and any consonants that follow it). For example, they can separate *bend* into "buh" and "end" and *spray* into "spruh" and "ay." Most 4- and 5-year-olds show some ability to hear the onsets and rimes that make up word syllables (Goswami, 1998, 1999).
3. *Awareness of individual phonemes.* By the time they are 6 or 7, many children can identify the individual phonemes in spoken words (Goswami, 1999; Owens, 1996). This ability seems to emerge hand in hand with learning to read (Goswami, 1999; Harris & Giannouli, 1999; Perfetti, 1992). Apparently, seeing individual phonemes represented as letters in printed words helps children listen for those phonemes and then hear them as distinct sounds (Ehri & Wilce, 1986).

Specifically teaching children to hear the onsets, rimes, and individual phonemes in words enhances their later reading ability (Bradley & Bryant, 1991; Bus & van IJzendoorn, 1999; Foorman et al., 1998; Murray, 1998; Stanovich, 2000). Phyllis Jones helped Benjamin develop this ability by using phonics workbooks and audiotapes. But probably more effective is promoting phonological awareness within the context of energetic and enjoyable listening, reading, and spelling activities (Muter, 1998). The Development and Practice feature on the nex page presents several useful strategies.

Development of Word Recognition

At age 4, Benjamin can use what he knows about letter-sound relationships to sound out some of the words he sees in his everyday environment. The English language isn't completely dependable when it comes to letter-sound correspondences; for example, the letters *ough* are pronounced quite differently in the words *through, though, bough,* and *rough.* Despite such occasional anomalies, letter-sound correspondences in English are fairly predictable if we consider common letter patterns rather than individual letters (Stanovich, 2000). For instance, the letters *ight* are always pronounced with a long *i* sound and silent *g* and *h* (e.g., *light, might, right*), and the letters *tion* are always pronounced "shun" (e.g., *motion, vacation, intuition*).

When developing readers encounter a word they have never seen before, they may use a variety of **word decoding** skills to determine what the word probably is; more specifically, they may

- Identify the sounds associated with each of the word's letters and then blend the sounds together.

phonological awareness
Ability to hear the distinct sounds within words.

onset
One or more consonant sounds that precede the vowel sound in a syllable.

rime
The vowel sound and any following consonant sounds in a syllable.

word decoding
Identifying an unknown word by using letter-sound relationships, analogies, common letter patterns, and/or semantic and syntactic context.

PROMOTING PHONOLOGICAL AWARENESS AND LETTER RECOGNITION IN YOUNG CHILDREN

■ Read alphabet books that use colorful pictures, amusing poems, or entertaining stories to teach letters and letter sounds.

A preschool teacher shares *The Alphabet Book* (Holtz, 1997) with her group of 4-year-olds. The book has many colorful photographs, each devoted to a different letter. As the children look at the picture for the letter *B*, they delight in identifying the many *B* words they find there—*baby, bottle, block,* and so on.

■ Have children think of words that rhyme.

A kindergarten teacher challenges his students to think of at least five words that rhyme with *break.*

■ Ask children to identify words that begin (or end) with a particular sound or group of sounds.

A first-grade teacher asks, "Who can think of a word that begins with a 'str' sound? For example, *string* begins with a 'str' sound. What are some other words that begin with 'str'?"

■ Say several words and ask students which one begins (or ends) in a different sound.

A second-grade teacher asks, "Listen carefully to these four words: *bend, end, dent,* and *mend.* Which one ends in a different sound than the others? Listen to them again before you decide: *bend, end, dent,* and *mend.*"

■ Show pictures of several objects and ask students to choose the one that begins (or ends) with a different sound from the others.

A kindergarten teacher shows his class pictures of a dog, a door, a wagon, and a dragon. "Three of these things start with the same sound. Which one starts with a *different* sound?"

■ Have students practice writing alphabet letters on paper and representing letters in other ways.

A first-grade teacher has her students make letters with their bodies. For example, one child stands with his arms outstretched like a Y, and two others bend over and clasp hands to form an M.

■ Ask children to create and spell nonsense words using letter-sound relationships.

A class of second graders sings several verses of the song, "I Know an Old Lady Who Swallowed a Fly," substituting a different nonsense word for the word *fly* in each verse. For instance, one verse goes like this:

I know an old lady who swallowed a zwing.
I don't why
She swallowed the zwing.
I guess she'll die (Reutzel & Cooter, 1999, p. 146)

- Think of words they know that are spelled similarly to the unknown word. For instance, a child may notice a similarity between *peak,* a word she doesn't know, and *beak,* a word she has already learned, and simply replace the "buh" sound with "puh." Initially, children make such analogies based on *rimes,* such as *beak–peak* and *cat–hat.* Later, they can draw analogies that cross onset-rime boundaries, such as *beak–bean* and *cat–can* (Goswami, 1999).
- Identify clusters of letters that are typically pronounced in certain ways. For instance, in the common word ending *-ology,* the g is always pronounced "juh," never "guh."
- Use semantic and syntactic context to make an educated guess as to what the word might be. For instance, the word *pint* is pronounced differently than other *-int* words (*hint, mint, squint,* etc.), but a sentence such as *The recipe called for a pint of milk* provides several clues as to its identity.

After encountering a word in print enough times, children no longer need to decode it when they see it; instead, they recognize it immediately and automatically (Adams, 1990; Ehri, 1998).

In the preschool and early elementary years, word recognition abilities typically emerge in the following sequence:

1. Initially (perhaps at age 4), children rely almost entirely on context clues to identify words (Ehri, 1994; Juel, 1991; Share & Gur, 1999). For example, many preschoolers correctly identify the word *stop* when it appears on a red, octagonal sign at the side of the road. They can "read" the word *Cheerios* on a cereal box. They know that a word at a fast-food restaurant is *McDonalds* when the *M* takes the form of the well-known golden arches.

2. Sometime around age 5, children begin to look at one or more features of the word itself; however, they do not yet make connections between how a word is spelled and how it

sounds. Often, they focus on one or two visually distinctive features of a word, using a strategy known as *logographic* or *visual-cue* reading (Ehri, 1991, 1994; Share & Gur, 1999). For example, they see the "tail" hanging down at the end of *dog* or the two "ears" sticking up in the middle of *rabbit* (Ehri, 1991, 1994). Some children remember certain words (such as the various names posted on children's school lockers) by their overall shapes—a strategy known as *visuographic* reading (Share & Gur, 1999).

3. Soon after, children begin to use some of a word's letters for phonetic clues about what the word must be. For example, they might read *box* by looking at the *b* and *x* but ignoring the *o* (Ehri, 1991, 1994).

4. Once children have mastered typical letter-sound relationships, they rely heavily on such relationships as they read (Ehri, 1991, 1994). Doing so allows them to decode such simple words as *cat, bed, Dick,* and *Jane*. However, they have difficulty when they encounter words that violate general pronunciation rules. For instance, using the rule that *ea* is pronounced "ee," they might read *head* as "heed" or *sweater* as "sweeter."

5. As children gain more experience with written language, they develop a reasonable **sight vocabulary**; that is, they recognize a sizable number of words immediately and so no longer need to decode them. At this point, they use not only letter-sound relationships but also word analogies, common spelling patterns, and context to decipher new words (Ehri & Robbins, 1992; Juel, 1991; Owens, 1996; Peterson & Haines, 1992). Most children in the middle elementary grades use multiple strategies to decode unknown words (Owens, 1996).

6. As children continue to read, their recognition of most common words becomes automatized (Adams, 1990; Ehri, 1998; Juel, 1991). Although they do not lose their word decoding skills, they depend on them only infrequently once they reach the middle school and high school grades (Goldsmith-Phillips, 1989; Gough & Wren, 1998).

From an information processing perspective, the mental processes that occur during reading take place in working memory. If children must use their limited working memory capacity to decode individual words, they have little "room" left to understand the overall meaning of what they are reading. It is essential, then, that children eventually automatize their recognition of most words (Adams, 1990; Greene & Royer, 1994; Stanovich, 2000). As you should recall from Chapter 5, automatization develops primarily through practice, practice, and more practice. In some instances—perhaps with beginning readers or with older students who have particular difficulty learning to read (e.g., those with certain learning disabilities)—teachers can sometimes promote automatization by using flashcards of individual words. But probably most effective (and certainly more motivating!) is to encourage students to read as often as possible (Ehri, 1998).

Development of Reading Comprehension

At its most basic level, the term *reading comprehension* means understanding the words and sentences on the page. But for advanced readers, it also means going beyond the page itself: making inferences and predictions, identifying main ideas, detecting an author's assumptions and biases, and so on (Perfetti, 1985).

Children's ability to comprehend what they read is related to, and almost certainly dependent on, their overall language development. For instance, children with larger vocabularies perform better on tests of reading comprehension (Anderson & Freebody, 1981). Their metalinguistic awareness—their knowledge about the nature of language itself—is also a factor in successful reading (Downing, 1986; Tunmer & Bowey, 1984).

Abilities associated with effective reading comprehension emerge and evolve throughout the elementary and secondary school years (and, for many people, into adulthood as well). Several general trends characterize the development of reading comprehension in childhood and adolescence:

■ *Children's growing knowledge base facilitates better reading comprehension.* As they grow older, children become better able to understand what they read, in part because they know more about the topics about which they are reading (Byrnes, 1996; Siegler, 1991). In fact, children's reading comprehension ability at *any* age is influenced by topic knowledge (Lipson, 1983; Pearson,

sight vocabulary
Words that a child can recognize immediately while reading.

Hansen, & Gordon, 1979). In one study, for example, second graders were asked to read a passage about spiders; children who knew a lot about spiders remembered more and drew inferences more readily than their less knowledgeable peers (Pearson et al., 1979).

■ *Children acquire more knowledge about common structures in fictional and nonfictional texts.* Most 5- and 6-year-olds can distinguish between books that tell stories and books that provide information (Field, Labbo, & Ash, 1999). As children get older, they also learn how various kinds of text are typically organized, and such knowledge helps them make better sense of what they read. For instance, they acquire a **story schema** (sometimes called a *story grammar*) that represents the typical components of fictional narratives: They learn that stories usually have a particular *setting* (time and place), one or more *characters* with personalities and motives that influence their actions and reactions, a *plot* that reflects a logical sequence of events, and a *resolution* of a problem or conflict that arises (Graesser, Golding, & Long, 1991; Stein & Glenn, 1979). When a work of fiction is organized in an unusual way (e.g., when it consists of a series of flashbacks), older children use a story schema to rearrange the text's elements into a structure that makes sense (Byrnes, 1996; Stein, 1982; Zwaan, Langston, & Graesser, 1995).

Works of nonfiction also follow predictable structures. For example, persuasive essays frequently begin with a main point and then present evidence to support that point. Academic textbooks use headings and subheadings to indicate key ideas and the general organization of each chapter. As children grow older, they become increasingly able to capitalize on such structures to comprehend what they read (Byrnes, 1996).

When students reach high school, they begin to read text with a critical eye; they no longer take everything they read at face value.

■ *Children become increasingly able to draw inferences from what they read.* Particularly as children reach the upper elementary grades, they become more adept at drawing inferences and better able to learn new information from what they read (Chall, 1996; Paris & Upton, 1976). At the upper elementary level, however, they tend to take the things they read at face value, with little attempt to evaluate them critically and little sensitivity to obvious contradictions (Chall, 1996; Johnston & Afflerbach, 1985; Markman, 1979).

As children reach adolescence and move into the secondary grades, they read written material with a more critical eye (Chall, 1996; Owens, 1996). They begin to recognize that different authors sometimes present different viewpoints on a single issue. They also become more aware of the subtle aspects of fiction—for example, the underlying theme and symbolism of a novel.

The ability to draw inferences seems to be a key factor in children's reading comprehension: Poor readers are less likely to make inferences when they read (Cain & Oakhill, 1998; Oakhill, Cain, & Yuill, 1998). Some poor readers appear to have less working memory capacity, which limits their ability to consider and integrate multiple pieces of information at the same time (Oakhill et al., 1998). In addition, many poor readers don't relate what they read to what they already know about a topic; thus, they are less likely to fill in missing details and thereby make better sense of text (Cain & Oakhill, 1998).

■ *Metacognitive strategies increase in number and sophistication, especially in adolescence.* As children gain more experience with reading, and particularly with reading textbooks and other informational text, they develop a variety of strategies for comprehending written material. For instance, adolescents are better able to identify main ideas than elementary school children are (Byrnes, 1996). High school students are more likely to monitor their comprehension as they read, and also to backtrack (i.e., reread) when they don't understand something the first time, than students in the upper elementary and middle school grades (Garner, 1987; Hacker, 1995). Yet not all adolescents use effective metacognitive reading strategies—identifying main ideas, monitoring comprehension, rereading, and so forth—and those who do not often have considerable difficulty understanding and remembering what they read (Alvermann & Moore, 1991; Hacker, 1995).

Numerous research studies indicate that, with proper instruction and support, children and adolescents can learn to use effective metacognitive strategies and improve their reading comprehension as a result. One effective approach is *reciprocal teaching,* to be described shortly. The Development and Practice feature on the next page presents several additional suggestions.

story schema
Knowledge of the typical elements and sequence of a fictional narrative.

PROMOTING USE OF EFFECTIVE READING COMPREHENSION STRATEGIES

■ Teach reading comprehension skills in all areas of the academic curriculum.

When a health teacher tells his ninth graders to read Chapter 3 of their textbook, he also suggests several strategies they might use to help them remember what they read. For example, as they begin each section of the chapter, they should use the heading to make a prediction as to what the section will be about. At the end of the section, they should stop and consider whether their prediction was accurate (Pressley et al., 1994).

■ Model effective reading strategies.

A girl in a seventh-grade history class reads aloud a passage describing how, during Columbus's first voyage across the Atlantic, many members of the crew wanted to turn around and return to Spain. Her teacher says, "Let's think of some reasons why the crew might have wanted to go home." One student responds, "Some of them might have been homesick." Another suggests, "Maybe they thought they'd never find their way back if they went too far."

■ Encourage students to relate what they are reading to things they already know about the topic.

Children in a third-grade classroom are each reading several books on a particular topic (e.g., dinosaurs, insects, outer space). Before they begin reading a book, their teacher asks them to write answers to three questions: (a) What do you already know about your topic? (b) What do you hope to learn about

your topic? and (c) Do you think what you learn by reading your books will change what you already know about your topic? (Thompson & Carr, 1995).

■ Ask students to identify key elements of the stories they read.

A fourth-grade teacher teaches his students to ask themselves five questions as they read stories: (a) Who is the main character? (b) Where and when did the story take place? (c) What did the main characters do? (d) How did the story end? and (e) How did the main character feel? (Short & Ryan, 1984).

■ Suggest that students create mental images that capture what they are reading (Gambrell & Bales, 1986).

When a high school literature class is reading Nathaniel Hawthorne's *The Scarlet Letter,* the teacher asks her students to close their eyes and imagine what the two main characters, Arthur Dimsdale and Hester Prynne, might look like. She then asks for volunteers to describe their mental images.

■ Scaffold students' early efforts to use complex strategies.

A middle school science teacher asks her students to write summaries of short textbook passages. She gives them four rules to use as they develop their summaries: (1) Identify the most important ideas, (2) delete trivial details, (3) eliminate redundant information, and (4) identify relationships among the main ideas (Rinehart, Stahl, & Erickson, 1986).

As you have discovered, reading is a complex activity that encompasses numerous skills and abilities. Jeanne Chall has synthesized some of the trends in reading development into a series of stages, which we consider now.

Chall's Stages of Reading Development

Chall (1996) has characterized reading development as involving six qualitatively distinct stages. At each stage, children and adolescents acquire new knowledge and skills that provide a foundation for any stages that follow. As we describe the stages, we also list ages and approximate grade levels at which they appear. These ages and grade levels typify reading development in many Western schools at the present time; they do not necessarily apply to other cultural contexts or other historical periods (Chall, 1996).

Stage 0: Prereading (to age 6). Children develop some awareness of word sounds and learn to recognize most letters of the alphabet. They can pretend to read a book and know enough to hold the book right-side up and turn the pages one at a time. However, these prereading activities depend little, if at all, on actual print. (Chall's Stage 0 encompasses the *emergent literacy* described earlier.)

Stage 1: Initial reading, or decoding (ages 6–7, grades 1–2). Children focus on learning letter-sound relationships and gain increasing insight into the nature of English spelling. They depend almost entirely on the printed page as they read; in Chall's words, they are "glued to the print."

Stage 2: Confirmation, fluency, ungluing from print (ages 7–8, grades 2–3).   Children solidify the letter-sound relationships they learned in Stage 1. They automatize their recognition of many common words, become increasingly fluent in their reading, and begin to read silently. Although children now read for meaning, most of what they read confirms what they already know; for instance, they read familiar books and stories but do not yet read textbooks that introduce new ideas.

Stage 3: Reading for learning the new (ages 9–14, grades 4–8 or 9).   Children can now learn new information from the things they read; by the end of Stage 3, reading surpasses listening as a means of acquiring information. Children begin to study the traditional academic content areas (science, history, geography) in earnest and gain much of their knowledge about these subjects from textbooks. They also begin to develop strategies for finding information in chapters, books, and reference materials (looking at headings, consulting indexes, etc.).

Reading materials become increasingly complex, abstract, and unfamiliar during Stage 3, and success at reading and understanding them increasingly relies on children's prior understandings of word meanings and the subject matter. Accordingly, children whose language skills and general world knowledge are relatively limited begin to struggle with reading and learning. This **fourth-grade slump** is often seen in children from low socioeconomic backgrounds, perhaps because they have had less access to reading materials and enriching educational opportunities (museum visits, family travel, etc.) than their more economically privileged classmates (Chall, 1996).

Early in Stage 3, children learn best from reading material that presents a single viewpoint in a clear, straightforward manner, and they typically take what they read at face value. As they reach grades 7 and 8, however, they begin to analyze and think critically about what they read.

Stage 4: Multiple viewpoints (age 14 on, high school).   In high school, teenagers become more skilled readers of textbooks, reference materials, and sophisticated works of fiction. They can now handle reading materials that present multiple points of view, and they can integrate the new ideas they encounter in text with their previous knowledge about a topic.

Stage 5: Construction and reconstruction (age 18 on, college).   Particularly if young people go on to college, they may begin to construct their *own* knowledge and opinions (often at a high level of abstraction) by analyzing, synthesizing, and evaluating what others have written. They also read more purposefully; that is, they may read certain parts of a text but skip other parts to accomplish their goals for reading the text as efficiently as possible. Chall has estimated that fewer than 40% of college students develop their reading skills to a Stage 5 level.

In general, then, as young people move through the elementary and secondary grades, they read with greater fluency and flexibility and become able to read increasingly complex, unfamiliar, and abstract material. As they acquire the skills of new stages, however, they do not necessarily lose previously learned skills. For example, even college students proficient at Stage 5 reading may occasionally relax with a mystery novel that they read in a Stage 2 or Stage 3 fashion (Chall, 1996). The Developmental Trends table on pages 291 and 292 traces the development of reading over the course of childhood and adolescence.

Chall's stages of reading make it clear that different types of reading materials and different instructional techniques are appropriate at different age levels. We look now at general approaches and strategies for promoting children's and adolescents' reading development.

Approaches to Reading Instruction

In the early elementary years, reading instruction focuses on both word recognition and basic comprehension skills, often within the context of reading simple stories (Chall, 1996; Owens, 1996). In the upper elementary and middle school grades, most students have acquired sufficient linguistic knowledge and reading skills to focus almost exclusively on reading comprehension. In the secondary grades, reading instruction typically takes the form of classes in study skills (for textbooks and other nonfiction) and in English and American literature (for fiction).

Throughout most of the 1900s, a *basic-skills* approach to reading instruction predominated in most schools. Within the past 20 years, some teachers have adopted a *whole-language* alternative to reading instruction. In this section, we look at specific teaching practices and research findings related to each of these approaches. We then consider *reciprocal teaching* as an avenue

fourth-grade slump
Tendency for some children (especially those from low-income backgrounds) to experience greater difficulty with reading tasks as they encounter more challenging material in the upper elementary grades.

Reading at Different Age Levels

DEVELOPMENTAL TRENDS

AGE	WHAT YOU MIGHT OBSERVE	DIVERSITY	IMPLICATIONS
Early Childhood (2–6) 	• Use of reading materials in play activities • Increasing knowledge of letters and letter-sound correspondences • Identification of a few words in well-known contexts (e.g., words on commercial products) • Use of a word's distinctive features (e.g., a single letter or overall shape) to read or misread it	• Children who have had little or no exposure to reading before they begin school are apt to have less knowledge about the nature of reading. Some cultures emphasize oral language more than written language. • Lower-income parents are less likely to read either for information or for pleasure. • Some children begin school knowing the alphabet and may have a small sight vocabulary as well. Others may need to start from scratch when learning letters and letter sounds.	• Read to young children using colorful books with high-interest content. • Teach letters of the alphabet through engaging, hands-on activities. • Teach letter-sound correspondences through storybooks, games, rhymes, and enjoyable writing activities. • Encourage children to read words that can be deciphered easily from the contexts in which they appear.
Middle Childhood (6–10) 	• Ability to hear individual phonemes within words • Increasing proficiency in word decoding skills • Growing sight-word vocabulary, leading to greater reading fluency • Beginning of silent reading (at age 7 or 8) • Increasing ability to draw inferences • Tendency to take things in print at face value	• Children with deficits in phonological awareness have a more difficult time learning to read; the strength of this correlation varies from one language to the next. • Children with hearing impairments are less likely to master letter-sound correspondences. • On average, girls develop reading skills earlier than boys. • Children vary widely in their comprehension strategies; some strategies are far more effective than others.	• Explore "families" of words that are spelled similarly. • Assign well-written trade books (e.g., children's paperback novels) as soon as students are able to read and understand them. • Engage students in small-group or whole-class reading discussions. Focus on interpretation, drawing inferences, and speculation. • For students who struggle with reading, explicitly teach phonological awareness and word decoding skills, especially within the context of meaningful reading activities.

(continued)

for promoting reading comprehension. Finally, we identify several more general strategies for fostering reading development in children and adolescents.

Teaching Basic Skills   As you have seen, children often use their knowledge of letter-sound relationships and common spelling patterns to decode unknown words. With age and experience, they acquire sophisticated strategies for understanding and drawing inferences from what they read. Many theorists argue that children learn to read most effectively when teachers teach word decoding and reading comprehension skills in a direct, systematic fashion. For instance, to teach letter-sound relationships, teachers might use phonics exercises (practice in identifying onsets and rimes, blending sounds together to form words, etc.), or they might use basal reading series and other books that emphasize simple words, common letter patterns, and considerable repetition. To teach reading comprehension, teachers might give children instruction and practice in such skills as identifying main ideas and creating summaries (e.g., Oakhill et al., 1998; Rinehart et al., 1986).

Explicit training in basic reading skills appears to facilitate reading development, especially for poor readers (Bradley & Bryant, 1991; Bus & van IJzendoorn, 1999; Foorman et al., 1998; Ross, Smith, Casey, & Slavin, 1995; Schneider, Roth, & Ennemoser, 2000; Stanovich, 2000). Unfortunately, such training sometimes takes the form of tedious exercises that children find dull and boring (Hiebert & Raphael, 1996; Turner, 1995). It does not *have* to be dull and boring, however; with a little creativity, it can be quite engaging and motivating. For example,

DEVELOPMENTAL TRENDS

AGE	WHAT YOU MIGHT OBSERVE	DIVERSITY	IMPLICATIONS
Early Adolescence (10–14)	• Automatized recognition of most common words • Ability to learn new information through reading • Emerging ability to go beyond the literal meaning of text • Emerging metacognitive processes that aid comprehension (e.g., comprehension monitoring, backtracking)	• Adolescents with deficits in phonological awareness continue to lag behind their peers in reading development. • Students who were poor readers in elementary school often continue to be poor readers in adolescence. • Some students (e.g., some with mental retardation) may have excellent decoding skills yet not understand what they read. • Students with sensory challenges may have less general world knowledge that they can use to interpret what they read.	• Assign age-appropriate reading materials in various content areas; give students some scaffolding (e.g., questions to answer) to guide their thinking and learning as they read. • Begin to explore classic works of poetry and literature. • Use reciprocal teaching to promote the reading comprehension skills of poor readers. • Seek the advice and assistance of specialists to help promote the reading skills of low-ability readers.
Late Adolescence (14–18)	• Automatized recognition of many abstract and discipline-specific words • Ability to consider multiple viewpoints about a single topic • Ability to critically evaluate what is read • More sophisticated metacognitive reading strategies	• Poor readers draw few if any inferences from what they read and use few if any effective metacognitive processes. • As classroom learning becomes more dependent on reading textbooks and other written materials, students with reading disabilities may become increasingly frustrated in their attempts to achieve academic success. • Girls are more likely than boys to enroll in advanced language and literature classes.	• Expect that many students can learn effectively from textbooks and other reading materials, but continue to scaffold reading assignments, especially for poor readers. • Encourage students to draw inferences and make predictions from what they read. • Critically analyze classic works of poetry and literature. • Modify reading materials and paper-pencil assessments for students who have poor reading skills.

Sources: Cain & Oakhill, 1998; Chall, 1996; Dryden & Jefferson, 1994; Ehri, 1994; Felton, 1998; Harris & Hatano, 1999; Hedges & Nowell, 1995; Hulme & Joshi, 1998; Johnston & Afflerbach, 1985; McLane & McNamee, 1990; Owens, 1996; Share & Gur, 1999; Trawick-Smith, 2000; Turnbull et al., 1999; Wigfield et al., 1996; Yaden & Templeton, 1986.

Figure 8–2 illustrates how Dr. Seuss's *One Fish Two Fish Red Fish Blue Fish* helps children learn the *-ook* pattern in a way that most young children find highly entertaining.

Whole-Language Instruction As noted earlier, whole-language theorists propose that learning to read is as natural a process as learning to speak. Accordingly, they suggest that children learn to read most effectively by reading authentic materials (children's books, novels, magazines, newspapers, etc.) and especially by reading things they have chosen for themselves (Goodman, 1989; Goodman & Goodman, 1979; Weaver, 1990). Letter-sound relationships, word decoding, and other basic skills are taught solely within the context of real-world reading tasks, and far less time is devoted to instruction of such skills than is true in more traditional reading programs. Instead, students spend a great deal of time writing and talking with their classmates about the things that they have read.

Whole-language instruction has the advantage of engaging children in authentic literacy activities from the very beginning; thus, such an approach may be particularly valuable for children who have had little or no experience with books and other written materials at home (Purcell-Gates, McIntyre, & Freppon, 1995). It may also be more motivating; for instance, in a study with third graders, using children's novels and other trade books and giving students choices about which books to read led to greater interest and persistence in reading (Sheveland, 1994). On the downside, however, phonological awareness is often shortchanged in whole-language classrooms (Juel, 1998; Liberman, 1998; Pressley, 1994).

We took a look.
We saw a Nook.
On his head
he had a hook.
On his hook
he had a book.
On his book
was "How to Cook."

We saw him sit
and try to cook.
He took a look
at the book on the hook.

But a Nook can't read,
so a Nook can't cook.
SO . . .
what good to a Nook
is a hook cook book?

FIGURE 8–2 Dr. Seuss's *One Fish Two Fish Red Fish Blue Fish* teaches common spelling patterns through rhymes and repetition. These two pages give children practice in decoding and recognizing *-ook* words.

From *One Fish Two Fish Red Fish Blue Fish* by Dr. Seuss® & copyright © by Dr. Seuss Enterprises, L.P. 1960, renewed 1988. Reprinted by permission of Random House Children's Books, a division of Random House, Inc.

Numerous research studies have been conducted comparing the effectiveness of whole-language and basic-skills approaches to reading instruction. Studies with kindergartners and first graders find that whole-language approaches are often more effective in promoting emergent literacy—familiarity with the nature and purposes of books, pretend reading, and so on (Purcell-Gates et al., 1995; Sacks & Mergendoller, 1997; Stahl & Miller, 1989). When children must actually *read* text, however, basic-skills approaches—in particular, a focus on developing phonological awareness and knowledge of letter-sound relationships—seem to be superior, especially for children from low socioeconomic backgrounds and for students who show early signs of a reading disability (Adams, 1990; Stahl & Miller, 1989; Stanovich, 2000). Considering such research, many theorists now urge that teachers strike a balance between whole-language activities and basic-skills instruction (Biemiller, 1994; Mayer, 1999; Pressley, 1994).

Reciprocal Teaching As you may recall from our discussion of metacognition in Chapter 5, children and adolescents typically know relatively little about how they can best learn and remember information. As illustrations, here are three high school students' descriptions of how they study a textbook (Brown & Palincsar, 1987, p. 83):

". . . I stare real hard at the page, blink my eyes and then open them—and cross my fingers that it will be right here." [Student points at head.]

"It's easy, if she [the teacher] says study, I read it twice. If she says read, it's just once through."

"I just read the first line in each paragraph—it's usually all there."

None of these students mentions any attempt to understand the information, relate it to prior knowledge, or otherwise think about it in any way, so we might guess that they are *not* engaging in effective learning strategies. In other words, they are not using cognitive processes that should help them store and retain information in long-term memory.

Not only must students learn to read, but they must also read to learn; that is, they must acquire new information from the things they read. When we examine the cognitive processes that good readers (successful learners) often use, especially when reading challenging material, we find strategies such as these (Brown & Palincsar, 1987):

• *Summarizing.* Good readers identify the main ideas—the gist—of what they read.
• *Questioning.* Good readers ask themselves questions to make sure they understand what they are reading; in other words, they monitor their comprehension as they proceed through reading material.

- *Clarifying.* When good readers discover that they don't comprehend something—for example, when a sentence is confusing or ambiguous—they take steps to clarify what they are reading, perhaps by rereading it or making logical inferences.
  - *Predicting.* Good readers anticipate what they are likely to read next, making predictions about the ideas to come.

In contrast, poor readers—those who learn little from textbooks and other reading materials—rarely summarize, question, clarify, or predict. For example, many students cannot adequately summarize a typical *fifth*-grade textbook until high school or even junior college (Brown & Palincsar, 1987; Palincsar & Brown, 1984). Clearly, many students do not easily acquire the ability to read for learning.

In reciprocal teaching, students help one another *read to learn*.

Reciprocal teaching (Brown & Palincsar, 1987; Palincsar & Brown, 1984, 1989) is an approach to teaching reading through which students learn effective reading-to-learn strategies by observing and imitating what their teacher and classmates do. The teacher and several students meet in a group to read a piece of text, occasionally stopping to discuss and process the text aloud. Initially, the teacher leads the discussion, asking questions about the text to promote summarizing, questioning, clarifying, and predicting. Gradually, he or she turns this role over to different students, who then take charge of the discussion and ask one another the same kinds of questions that their teacher has modeled. Eventually, the students can read and discuss a text almost independently of the teacher; they work together to construct its meaning and check one another for comprehension and possible misunderstandings.

As an illustration, following is a reciprocal teaching session for a group of six first graders reading a passage about snowshoe rabbits. In this particular case, the classroom teacher reads the text in small segments (at higher grade levels, the students themselves take turns reading). After each segment, the teacher pauses while students discuss and process the segment. As you read the dialogue, look for examples of summarizing, questioning, clarifying, and predicting (there is at least one instance of each).

The children were reading about the snowshoe rabbit, and it was the 16th day of dialogue. The teacher had just read a segment of text describing the season in which baby rabbits are born and the ways in which the mother rabbit cares for her babies. A student named Kam is the dialogue leader.

Kam:	When was the babies born?
Teacher:	That's a good question to ask. Call on someone to answer that question.
Kam:	Robby? Milly?
Milly:	Summer.
Teacher:	What would happen if the babies were born in the winter? Let's think.

Several children make a number of responses, including: "The baby would be very cold." "They would need food." "They don't have no fur when they are just born."

Kam:	I have another question. How does she get the babies safe?
Kris:	She hides them.
Kam:	That's right but something else. . . .
Teacher:	There is something very unusual about how she hides them that surprised me. I didn't know this.
Travis:	They are all in a different place.
Teacher:	Why do you think she does this?

reciprocal teaching
Approach to teaching reading whereby students take turns asking teacherlike questions of their classmates.

| Milly: | Probably because I heard another story, and when they're babies they usually eat each other or fight with each other. |
| Teacher: | That could be! And what about when that lynx comes? |

Several children comment that that would be the end of all the babies.

Travis:	If I was the mother, I would hide mine, I would keep them all together.
Kris:	If the babies are hidden and the mom wants to go and look at them, how can she remember where they are?
Teacher:	Good question. Because she does have to find them again. Why? What does she bring them?
Milly:	She needs to bring food. She probably leaves a twig or something.
Teacher:	Do you think she puts out a twig like we mark a trail?

Several children disagree and suggest that she uses her sense of smell. One child, recalling that the snowshoe rabbit is not all white in the winter, suggests that the mother might be able to tell her babies apart by their coloring.

Teacher:	So we agree that the mother rabbit uses her senses to find her babies after she hides them. Kam, can you summarize for us now?
Kam:	The babies are born in the summer. . . .
Teacher:	The mother . . .
Kam:	The mother hides the babies in different places.
Teacher:	And she visits them . . .
Kam:	To bring them food.
Travis:	She keeps them safe.
Teacher:	Any predictions?
Milly:	What she teaches her babies . . . like how to hop.
Kris:	They know how to hop already.
Teacher:	Well, let's read and see. (dialogue courtesy of A. Palincsar)

Reciprocal teaching provides a mechanism through which both the teacher and students can model effective reading and learning strategies. Vygotsky's theory of cognitive development is also at work here: Students should eventually *internalize* the processes that they first use in their discussions with others. Furthermore, the structured nature of a reciprocal teaching session scaffolds students' efforts to make sense of the things they read and hear. For example, if you look back at the previous dialogue, you may notice how the teacher models elaborative questions and connections to prior knowledge ("What would happen if the babies were born in the winter?" "Do you think she puts out a twig like we mark a trail?") and provides general guidance and occasional hints about how students should process the passage about snowshoe rabbits ("Kam, can you summarize for us now?" "And she visits them . . ."). Also notice in the dialogue how students support one another in their efforts to process what they are reading; consider this exchange as an example:

Kam:	I have another question. How does she get the babies safe?
Kris:	She hides them.
Kam:	That's right but something else. . . .

Reciprocal teaching has been used successfully with a wide variety of students, ranging from first graders to college students, to teach effective reading and listening comprehension skills (Alfassi, 1998; Campione, Shapiro, & Brown, 1995; Palincsar & Brown, 1989; Rosenshine & Meister, 1994). For example, in an early study of reciprocal teaching (Palincsar & Brown, 1984), six seventh-grade students with a history of poor reading comprehension participated in 20 reciprocal teaching sessions, each lasting about 30 minutes. Despite this relatively short intervention, students showed remarkable improvement in their reading comprehension skills. They became increasingly able to process reading material in an effective manner and to do so independently of their classroom teacher. Furthermore, they generalized their new reading strategies to other classes, sometimes even surpassing the achievement of their classmates (Brown & Palincsar, 1987; Palincsar & Brown, 1984).

General Strategies for Promoting Reading Development Reading is traditionally taught primarily in elementary school. Many middle school and high school teachers assume that their students read well enough to learn successfully from textbooks and other printed materials. As you have seen, such an assumption is not always warranted; even at the high school level, many students have not yet mastered all of the skills involved in reading effectively. Students who are poor readers in elementary school often continue to be poor readers in secondary school (Felton, 1998) and so may be in particular need of ongoing instruction and support in reading.

Several strategies for promoting reading development are applicable to a wide variety of age groups and reading levels:

■ *Use meaningful contexts to teach basic reading skills.* With a little thought, teachers can develop enjoyable activities to teach almost any basic skill. For instance, to promote phonological awareness in young children, teachers might play a game of "Twenty Questions" that begins with a hint such as, "I'm thinking of something in the classroom that begins with the letter *B*." Or they might give children a homework assignment to bring in three objects that begin with the letter *T* and three more that end with *T*.

Because working memory capacity is limited, automatizing word recognition is essential for effective reading comprehension. This is not to say, however, that teachers should postpone teaching reading comprehension until word recognition is automatized. On the contrary, too much focus on words in isolated drill-and-practice activities (e.g., flashcards) can lead young readers to believe that reading is an artificial, boring exercise. Automatization of word recognition probably occurs just as readily (perhaps even more so) in authentic and enjoyable reading activities (Ehri, 1998).

■ *Use high-interest works of literature.* Research consistently indicates that students read more energetically and persistently, use more sophisticated metacognitive strategies, and remember more content when they are interested in what they are reading (Anderson, Shirey, Wilson, & Fielding, 1987; Guthrie et al., 1998; Sheveland, 1994). As much as possible, then, whether teachers are using a whole-language approach or not, they should choose reading materials that are likely to be relevant to students' own lives and concerns, and they should give students some choices in what to read.

■ *Have students work in pairs to help one another with reading.* Students often make considerable gains in reading when they work in pairs in structured reading activities. In one study (Fuchs, Fuchs, Mathes, & Simmons, 1997), 20 second- through sixth-grade classrooms participated in a project called Peer-Assisted Learning Strategies (PALS), designed to foster more effective reading comprehension skills. In each classroom, students were ranked with regard to their reading performance, and the ranked list was divided in two. The first-ranked student in the top half of the list was paired with the first-ranked student in the bottom half of the list, the second student in the top half was paired with the second student in the bottom half, and so on down the line; through this procedure, students who were paired together had moderate but not extreme differences in their reading levels. Each pair read reading material at the level of the weaker reader and engaged in these activities:

• *Partner reading with retell.* The stronger reader read aloud for 5 minutes, then the weaker reader read the same passage of text. Reading something that had previously been read presumably enabled the weaker reader to read the material easily. After the double reading, the weaker reader described the material that the pair had just read.
• *Paragraph summary.* The students both read a passage one paragraph at a time. Then, with help from the stronger reader, the weaker reader tried to identify the subject and main idea of the paragraph.
• *Prediction relay.* Both students read a page of text, and then, with help from the stronger reader, the weaker reader would summarize the text and also make a prediction about what the next page would say. The students would read the following page, then the weaker reader would confirm or disconfirm the prediction, summarize the new page, make a new prediction, and so on.

Such a procedure enabled students in the PALS program (stronger and weaker readers alike) to make significantly greater progress in reading than students who had more traditional reading instruction, even though the amount of class time devoted to reading instruction was similar for both groups. The researchers speculated that the PALS students probably performed better because they had more opportunities to talk about what they were reading, received more frequent feedback about their performance and, in general, were more often encouraged to use effective reading strategies.

■ *Engage students in group discussions about the things they read.* Students often construct meaning more effectively when they discuss what they have read with their classmates. For instance, teachers can form "book clubs" in which students lead small groups of classmates in discussions about specific books (Alvermann, Young, Green, & Wisenbaker, 1999; McMahon, 1992). They can hold "grand conversations" about a particular work of literature, asking students to share their responses to questions with no single right answers—perhaps questions related to interpretations or critiques of various aspects of a text (Eeds & Wells, 1989; Hiebert & Raphael, 1996). They also can encourage students to think about a piece of literature from the author's perspective, posing such questions as "What's the author's message here?" or "Why do you think the author wants us to know about this?" (Beck, McKeown, Worthy, Sandora, & Kucan, 1996).

Even before children are reading books themselves, discussions of storybooks can help them learn that books are to be interpreted and in other ways thought about as well as simply read. For example, in the following dialogue, a kindergarten teacher has just read *Goldilocks and the Three Bears* to her students. Notice how the children quickly move well beyond the bounds of the story itself:

Teacher:	What sort of girl is Goldilocks?
Andrew:	She's curious.
Teacher:	What does "curious" mean?
Andrew:	That you get into trouble.
Charlotte:	She's a robber. She eats food and goes into houses.
Mary Ann:	That's right. She could be a robber. Robbers go into people's houses.
Teacher:	Did she plan on robbing the bears?
Jill:	Yes she did. They forgot to lock the door. The father said, "Don't forget to lock the door."
Janie:	She *is* a robber. She could of stoled their money.
Teddy:	Maybe her parents got killed and she was looking for a house.
Franklin:	She just wanted to go in the house. She wanted to sit in a chair because she was tired from walking too much.
Teacher:	Why was she in the woods?
Jonathan:	Probably she got lost and she was looking for a new house.
Jill:	Or looking for blackberries . . .
Mary Ann:	Maybe she was looking for blackberries and she thought this was the way she always went through the woods, but it wasn't.
Teddy:	Maybe she was cutting down wood.
Clarice:	What if she thinks it's her own house?
Charlotte:	She *did* think it's her own house. She probably has the same furniture.
Karen:	That could happen.
Jeremy:	She went in because of being tired. And when she heard footprints she thought it was her mommy and father. And when she woke up it was the bears. (Paley, 1984, pp. 51–52)

■ *Assign activities that encourage students to interpret what they read through a variety of modalities.* Group discussions are hardly the only mechanisms for fostering interpretation of reading materials. As alternatives, students might perform skits to illustrate stories, write personal letters that one character in a story might send to another character, or create works of art that illustrate the setting or characters of a novel or the underlying meaning of a poem. For example, Figure 8–3 shows how 16-year-old Jeff illustrated Paul Laurence Dunbar's poem *We Wear the Mask* as an assignment for his American literature class.

■ *Encourage reading outside of school.* Reading beyond school walls—for instance, reading during the summer months—probably accounts for a significant portion of children's and adolescents' growth in reading (Hayes & Grether, 1983; Stanovich, 2000). Providing books that students can take home to read or reread (perhaps accompanied by audiotapes) encourages

We Wear the Mask
by Paul Laurence Dunbar

We wear the mask that grins and lies,
It hides our cheeks and shades our eyes,–
This debt we pay to human guile;
With torn and bleeding hearts we smile,
And mouth with myriad subtleties.

Why should the world be overwise,
In counting all our tears and sighs?
Nay, let them only see us, while
We wear the mask.

We smile, but, O great Christ, our cries
To thee from tortured souls arise.
We sing, but oh the clay is vile
Beneath our feet, and long the mile;
But let the world dream otherwise,
We wear the mask!

FIGURE 8–3 Interpreting poetry through art. Jeff's brightly colored painting is the cheerful face ("mask") that its African American owner presents in public. The black face is the flip side of the mask, as viewed by the person wearing it. Depicted in the holes of the mask are a lynching (left eye); a whipping (right eye); an African American woman and a white baby (nostrils), reflecting white owners' rape of slaves; and a slave ship with someone being thrown overboard (mouth).

outside reading and can significantly enhance reading comprehension skills (Koskinen et al., 2000). Visits to the local library can also encourage outside reading. In fact, when planning a library visit, teachers might extend an invitation for parents to accompany the class; in some cases, this may be the first time the parents have ever been to a library (Heath, 1983).

Children and adolescents develop additional insights about both reading and writing when they become authors themselves and when their classmates read what they have written. We turn our attention now to the nature and development of writing and to strategies for helping students become more proficient writers.

Development in Writing

Children exhibit rudimentary forms of writing long before they reach school age, especially if they see those around them writing frequently. Consider what happened when 2½-year-old Rachel first saw her older brother Joshua writing thank-you letters after his sixth birthday:

> Rachel made a series of wavy lines on a piece of paper and told her mother it was a "thank-you letter to Grandma." About six months later, Rachel made letterlike marks on a piece of lined paper and told her mother it said "Dear Grandma and Grandpa. Thank you for the lots of presents. Love, Rachel." She then asked her mother to "get the stuff to mail it to them." A year and a half after this, when Rachel was 4½ and Joshua had recently turned 8, Rachel took a piece of her brother's lined stationery and made neat rows of letters and letterlike shapes (in no apparent order). Then she said to her mother, "I want to write a letter. I have to write a thank-you note to Grandma." She asked, "How do you spell 'Dear Grandma I love my presents'?" Her mother wrote this out for her. Rachel copied "Dear Grandma," then stopped, saying "This is boring," and asked her mother to write the rest. Her mother did, and the finished letter was mailed to her grandmother.[1]

---

[1]Reprinted by permission of the publisher from *Early Literacy* by Joan Brooks McLane and Gillian Dowley McNamee, pp. 42–43, Cambridge, Mass.: Harvard University Press. Copyright © 1990 by Joan Brooks McLane and Gillian Dowley McNamee.

Rachel's early "letters" to her grandparents demonstrated her growing awareness of what writing involves. Even at 2½, she knew that writing progresses from left to right and from the top of the page to the bottom; she also knew that writing conveys a message to someone else. A few months later, she replaced wavy lines with letterlike shapes, reflecting increasing knowledge about the general forms that letters take and, we suspect, maturing psychomotor skills. By the time she was 4½, she could produce the letters of the alphabet and knew that words must be spelled in particular ways.

For adults, writing is, of course, much more than simply putting letters on paper and spelling words correctly. To become skillful writers, growing children must not only master handwriting and spelling but also discover how to communicate their thoughts clearly, learn conventions of capitalization and punctuation, and metacognitively regulate the entire writing effort. In the next few pages, we examine the development of handwriting, spelling, composition skills, written grammar, and metacognitive processes in writing. We then consider several instructional strategies for promoting writing development in children and adolescents.

Development of Handwriting

As early as 18 months of age, children can hold a pencil and scribble randomly on paper (McLane & McNamee, 1990). Their early efforts with pencil and paper are largely exploratory, as they experiment with the kinds of marks they can produce. They "write" by producing scribbles, wavy lines, and pictures; thus, they make little or no distinction between writing and drawing (Graham & Weintraub, 1996; Sulzby, 1986).

With the increasing psychomotor coordination that emerges during the preschool years, children become better able to control their hand movements and so can produce recognizable shapes. By age 4, their writing is clearly different from drawing; for instance, it may consist of wavy lines or connected loops that loosely resemble adults' cursive writing (refer to Figure 8–1). By the time they are 5, children frequently incorporate actual letters and other letterlike forms in the things they write (Graham & Weintraub, 1996).

During the elementary school years, children's handwriting gradually becomes smaller, smoother, and more regular (Graham & Weintraub, 1996). For example, Figure 8–4 shows the changes in Jeff's handwriting from age 4½ to age 9. In the upper elementary grades, children also develop their own unique handwriting styles (Graham & Weintraub, 1996). As an illustration, contrast the cursive writing samples of Tina, Alex, and Jeff in Figure 8–5.

Little if any improvement in handwriting occurs after elementary school, and for some students handwriting quality actually declines during adolescence (Graham & Weintraub,

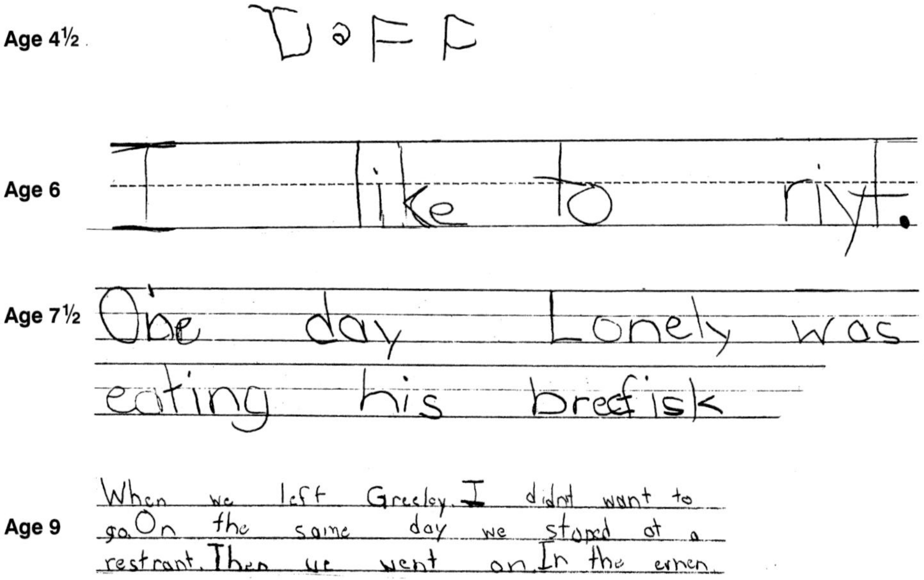

FIGURE 8–4 Changes in Jeff's handwriting from age 4½ to age 9

Age 4½

Age 6

Age 7½

Age 9

Tina

All of a sudden the air became cool and the sky was dark. Sue looked at Paul, Paul looked at Sue.

Alex

Henry delivers newspapers so he doesn't have much time to work on the clubhouse

Jeff

Have a good Mothers days

Sincerely

Jeffrey

1996). Some legibility may be lost because adolescents write more *quickly* than younger children. In fact, rapid, automatized handwriting (or, as an alternative, automatized keyboarding) is an important factor in effective writing (Graham & Weintraub, 1996; Jones & Christensen, 1999).

Development of Spelling

As you might guess, phonological awareness is as important in spelling as it is in reading (Bryant et al., 1999; Griffith, 1991; Lennox & Siegel, 1998). Benjamin Jones showed phonological awareness when, as a 4-year-old, he spelled *gym* as "JEM," thereby representing both the "juh" and "mm" sounds in the word. As children gain greater familiarity with written English, they also take into account common word endings (e.g., most past tense verbs end in *-ed*) and other common letter patterns as they spell (Bryant et al., 1999; Leong, 1998).

Children learn the correct spellings of a few words (such as their names) almost as soon as they learn how to write letters of the alphabet. But they also acquire several general spelling strategies, which typically appear in the following sequence:

1. *Prephonemic spelling.* Beginning writers, including most kindergarten and first graders, often create and use **invented spellings** that may only vaguely resemble actual words. Consider the invented spellings in this kindergartner's creation entitled "My Garden" (note that "HWS" is *house*):

   THIS IS A HWS
   THE SUN
   WL SHIN
   ND MI
   GRDN
   WL GRO (Hemphill & Snow, 1996, p. 192)

Invented spellings typically reflect some but not all of the phonemes in a word; for instance, a child might spell *rabbit* as "RT" (Ferreiro, 1990; Gentry, 1982; Treiman, 1998). Sometimes children use a letter's name for clues about when to use it in a word. As an example, a child might spell *work* as "YRK" because both Y (pronounced "why") and *work* begin with a "wuh" sound (Treiman, 1998).

invented spelling
Children's early and only minimally phonetic attempts at spelling.

HELPING STUDENTS LEARN WORD SPELLINGS

- When engaging young children in authentic writing activities, write a few important words out for them, and give them the correct spellings of any other words they ask for.

  When a kindergarten class makes valentine cards to bring home, the teacher shows the children how *valentine* and *I love you* are spelled.

- Teach common spelling patterns.

  A second-grade teacher asks children to study a list of words that end in an "uff" sound. The list, which includes *puff, muff, stuff, rough, tough,* and *enough,* illustrates two common ways of spelling the sound.

- Teach general spelling rules.

  A fourth-grade teacher teaches his students the rule "*I* before *e* except after *c,* or when pronounced 'ay,' as in *neighbor* and *weigh.*" But he cautions them that the rule is not com-

pletely reliable; for example, the words *either* and *height* are exceptions.

- Encourage older children and adolescents to use dictionaries and computer spell checking programs when they are unsure of how words are spelled.

  After her class completes a writing assignment at the school's computer lab, a seventh-grade teacher shows students how to use the spell-check function in the word processing software. She explains that a spell checker is not completely trustworthy; for example, it won't identify situations in which *they're* has been incorrectly used in place of *there* or *their.*

- Stress the importance of correct spelling for a writer's credibility.

  A high school teacher points out several obvious spelling errors in a story in the local newspaper. He then asks his students to reflect on the impressions that such errors convey about the reporter who wrote the story.

2. *Phonemic spelling.* As children develop greater phonological awareness, they try to represent all of a word's phonemes in their spelling (Beers, 1980; Frith, 1985; Gentry, 1982). For example, "My Garden" includes phonemic spellings of *shine* ("SHIN") and *grow* ("GRO").
3. *Orthographic spelling.* Eventually (perhaps in first or second grade), children begin to consider conventional spelling patterns (Beers, 1980; Bryant et al., 1999; Gentry, 1982). At this point, they use analogies between similar-sounding words—for instance, drawing a parallel between *went* and *sent* or between *nation* and *vacation* (Frith, 1985; Nation & Hulme, 1998). They also apply their increasing knowledge of general spelling rules, such as adding the suffix *-ed* for past tense (Bryant et al., 1999). Thus, they spell the past tense of *pour* as "POURED" (or perhaps "PORED") rather than "POURD." Curiously, many children initially apply the *-ed* rule to irregular verbs (e.g., spelling *felt* as "FELED") and sometimes even to nonverbs (e.g., spelling *soft* as "SOFED"), thus showing the *overregularization* phenomenon described in Chapter 7 (Bryant et al., 1999).
4. *Automatized spelling.* With increasing practice in reading and writing, children learn how various words are actually spelled and can ultimately retrieve many correct spellings quickly and accurately (Rittle-Johnson & Siegler, 1999). Children differ considerably in the extent to which they automatize spelling. Some have mastered most commonly used words by the time they reach the upper elementary grades; others continue to make numerous spelling errors throughout adolescence and into adulthood.

We caution you not to interpret the preceding sequence as a series of discrete stages in spelling development. Instead, children may use a variety of spelling strategies at any single age, and their use of different strategies over time probably resembles the *overlapping waves* phenomenon described in Chapter 5 (Rittle-Johnson & Siegler, 1999). For instance, 6-year-olds and 12-year-olds may both use a sounding-out procedure for words they don't know and automatic retrieval for words they *do* know, but sounding out is a more frequent strategy at age 6 and retrieval is more common at age 12. The Development and Practice feature above describes several strategies for promoting spelling development.

To write effectively and become credible authors, growing children and adolescents must eventually learn the correct spellings of the words they use frequently. (Alternatively, those who have difficulty with spelling, perhaps because of a learning disability, must learn to make regular use of dictionaries and computer spell-check options.) This is not to say, however, that authentic writing tasks should be postponed until after children have learned to spell the words they want to write. On the contrary, many experts urge teachers to engage children in authentic writing tasks even when the children must rely largely on invented spellings to get their thoughts on paper (e.g., Clarke, 1988; Treiman, 1993). Ultimately, the development of children's composition skills—not their knowledge of word spellings—lies at the heart of their ability to write effectively.

Development of Composition Skills

When preschool children engage in early writing activities at home, they often do so with a particular purpose in mind, perhaps to write a letter (recall Rachel's determination to write letters to her grandparents) or label a possession. Only when children enter kindergarten or first grade do most of them begin to write for writing's sake.

Children's earliest compositions are usually narratives: Children write about their personal experiences and create short, fictional stories (Hemphill & Snow, 1996). Expository writing—research reports, persuasive and argumentative essays, and so on—emerges considerably later (Owens, 1996), possibly because teachers typically don't ask for such writing until the upper elementary grades.

The nature and quality of children's and adolescents' writing change in many ways throughout the elementary and secondary school years. Following are four general trends in the development of composition skills:

■ *Children increasingly take their audience into account when they write.* In our discussion of language development in the preceding chapter, we mentioned that children become increasingly able to adapt their speech to the characteristics of their listeners. The same is true for writing: With age and experience, children become better able to envision the audience to whom they are writing and tailor their text accordingly (Kellogg, 1994; Knudson, 1992; Perfetti & McCutchen, 1987).

■ *Children and adolescents develop their topics in greater depth as they grow older.* When children of various ages are asked to write about a particular topic, older ones tend to include more ideas than younger ones do (Scardamalia & Bereiter, 1986). Such growth continues throughout the school years; for instance, when writing persuasive essays, high school students include more arguments than elementary and middle school students do, and 12th graders include more arguments than 9th graders (Knudson, 1992; McCann, 1989).

■ *With age comes an increasing ability to write a cohesive composition.* In the elementary grades, children use few if any devices to tie their compositions together. For instance, they may write a story by beginning with "Once upon a time," listing a sequence of events that lead only loosely to one another, and then ending with "They lived happily ever after" (McLane & McNamee, 1990).

Older children, and especially adolescents, are more capable of analyzing and synthesizing their thoughts when they write, and so they compose more cohesive, integrated texts (McCutchen, 1987; Owens, 1996; Spivey, 1997). As an example, Spivey (1997) gave 6th, 8th, and 10th graders three texts about rodeos (each written by a different author) and asked them to integrate what they learned into a single written description of rodeos. The younger students tended to write in a disconnected, piecemeal fashion, often borrowing phrases or entire sentences from each of the three texts they had read. In contrast, the older students wrote more integrated discussions of what they had learned from the reading materials and made frequent connections among the ideas they had acquired from each resource.

■ *Especially in adolescence, a knowledge-telling approach gradually evolves into a knowledge-transforming approach.* Young writers often compose a narrative or essay simply by writing ideas down in the order in which they think of them. Such an approach is known as **knowledge telling** (Bereiter & Scardamalia, 1987; McCutchen, 1996). As an example, we refer back to Chapter 5's opening case study. In response to the question *How did the United States become a country?* one third grader wrote:

The pilgruns came over in 17 hundreds, when they came over they bilt houses. The Idiuns thout they were mean. Then they came friends, and tot them stuff. Then winter came, and alot died. Then some had babies. So thats how we got here.

knowledge telling
Writing down ideas in whatever order they come to mind, with little regard for communicating the ideas effectively.

With age, experience, and an increasing ability to take the characteristics of potential readers into account, some students begin to conceptualize writing not as a process of putting ideas on paper but instead as a process of presenting ideas in a way that enables their readers to *understand* the ideas. This approach, known as **knowledge transforming,** is illustrated by an eighth grader's response to the question *How did the United States become a country?* (we've left her spelling errors intact):

> We became a country by way of common sense. The inhabitants on American soil thought it rather silly and ridiculus to be loyal to, follow rules and pay taxes to a ruler who has never seen where they live. King George III had never set foot (as far as I know) on American soil, but he got taxes and other things from those who lived here. When America decied to unit and dishonnor past laws and rules, England got angry. There was a war. When we won, drew up rules, and accepted states America was born.
>
> In a more poetic sense, we became a country because of who lived here and what they did. They actions of heros, heroines, leaders, followers, and everyday people made America famous, an ideal place to live. The different cultures and lifestyles made America unique and unlike any other place in the world. If you think about it, it's like visiting the worlds at Epcot in Florida. You can go from country to country without leaving home. (courtesy of Dinah Jackson)

The student's analogy between the United States and Disney World's Epcot Center is knowledge transforming at its finest.

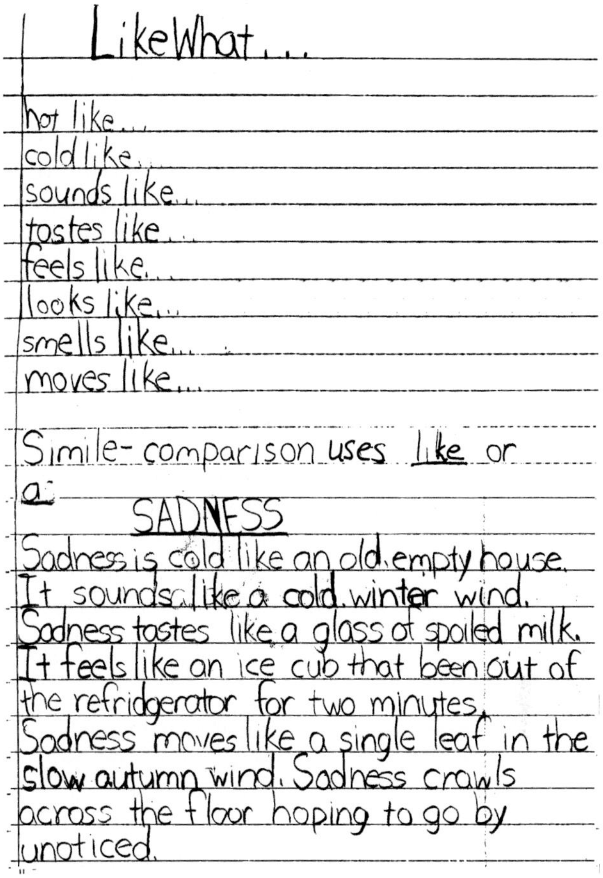
Like What...
hot like...
cold like...
sounds like...
tostes like...
feels like...
looks like...
smells like...
moves like...
Simile- comparison uses like or as
SADNESS
Sadness is cold like an old, empty house. It sounds like a cold winter wind. Sadness tostes like a glass of spoiled milk. It feels like an ice cub that been out of the refridgerator for two minutes. Sadness moves like a single leaf in the slow autumn wind. Sadness crawls across the floor hoping to go by unoticed.

FIGURE 8–6 Teachers can promote students' composition skills by teaching strategies for effectively communicating ideas. Here 11-year-old Charlotte gives a definition of *simile* and lists several examples at the top of the page. She then practices her new skill in a description of sadness.

One reason for knowledge telling (rather than knowledge transforming) in the early years is that most young children, and many adolescents as well, rarely think ahead about what they are going to write (Berninger, Fuller, & Whitaker, 1996; Pianko, 1979). The limited capacity of working memory may also be a factor: Students must consider so many different things (the content, the audience, spelling, grammar, punctuation, handwriting, etc.) when they write that they have little "room" available for thinking creatively about how they can effectively communicate their message (Benton, 1997; Flower & Hayes, 1981; McCutchen, 1996). Teachers can free up some of this capacity by having students address only one aspect of the writing process at a time; for instance, they might ask students to plan and organize their thoughts before they begin writing and ignore the mechanics of writing until after they have written their first draft (Harris & Graham, 1992; Treiman, 1993). To encourage younger children (e.g., first graders) to focus exclusively on the composition process, teachers can ask them to dictate rather than write their stories (McLane & McNamee, 1990; Scardamalia, Bereiter, & Goelman, 1982).

Teachers can also promote knowledge transforming by brainstorming with students about strategies for communicating ideas effectively (e.g., using examples, analogies, graphics, similes, and rhetorical questions) to a particular audience (Chambliss, 1998). Figure 8–6 shows how, as a sixth grader, 11-year-old Charlotte practiced using similes. An additional strategy is to show students examples of how expert writers translate their ideas into a form that readers can easily understand (Byrnes, 1996; Englert, Raphael, Anderson, Anthony, & Stevens, 1991).

Development of Syntax and Grammatical Rules

As children grow older, they use increasingly longer sentences in their writing (Byrnes, 1996). By the time they are 12 or 13, the syntactic structures they use in written work are considerably more complex than those that they use in speech (Gillam & Johnston, 1992).

knowledge transforming
Expressing ideas on paper in a way that a reader can readily understand.

With age, too, comes increasing automatization of punctuation and capitalization rules (Byrnes, 1996).

Providing extensive grammar instruction outside of authentic writing tasks appears to have little effect on the overall quality of students' writing (Berninger et al., 1996; Hillocks, 1989). Nevertheless, a certain amount of systematic instruction in grammatical rules is probably essential. As a society, we are much fussier about adherence to correct grammar in writing than in speaking. The same errors that are readily forgiven in speech—incomplete sentences, lack of agreement between subjects and verbs, and so on—are often interpreted as signs of carelessness or, worse still, ignorance when they appear in writing.

Development of Metacognitive Processes in Writing

In addition to developing handwriting, spelling, composition skills, and knowledge of grammatical rules, children and adolescents must also learn how to focus and regulate their writing efforts. They must consider the nature of the audience for whom they are writing. They must determine the goals they want to achieve in a composition and plan their writing accordingly. They must critically evaluate their work, looking not only for grammatical and spelling errors but also for omissions, ambiguities, logical flaws, and contradictions in meaning. Finally, of course, they must revise their writing to address each of the problems they've identified. All of these mental activities are aspects of the *metacognitive* component of writing.

As noted earlier, children become increasingly capable of taking their audience into account when they write. All too often, however, children and adolescents alike write without giving much thought to who their audience might be. This should not surprise us if we consider that, in most cases, the only person who reads their work is their teacher (Benton, 1997). Students are more likely to write effectively when they are asked to adapt their writing to a particular audience (Burnett & Kastman, 1997; Cameron et al., 1996; Sperling, 1996). For instance, teachers might ask their students to write a letter to children the same age who live in environments very different from their own—perhaps in a large city or in rural farm country (Benton, 1997; Kroll, 1984). Alternatively, teachers might ask students to imagine themselves in particular roles—perhaps as reporters investigating a news story or travelers hoping to spread peace throughout the world (Schneider, 1998). Children as young as 7 or 8 can adapt their writing to different audiences when they understand who those audiences are (Schneider, 1998).

Most children and adolescents also have much to learn about *planning* what and how they are going to write: They rarely set goals for a piece of writing or organize their thoughts before they put pencil to paper (Benton, 1997; Berninger et al., 1996; Pianko, 1979). Here, too, teachers can make a difference by encouraging, or even insisting, that students develop a concrete plan and perhaps one or more goals for writing a short story, essay, research paper, or other composition. In one study, for example, seventh and eighth graders who were studying persuasive writing techniques were taught how to set specific goals for themselves (e.g., to include a certain number of reasons in support of their argument, or to address a particular number of counterarguments). Students who received such training wrote longer and qualitatively better essays than students in a control group (Page-Voth & Graham, 1999).

Finally, elementary and secondary students alike have considerable difficulty identifying problems in their own writing, particularly those related to clarity and cohesiveness (Beal, 1996; Berninger et al., 1996; Fitzgerald, 1987). Many students, younger ones especially, have trouble reading their own writing as another person might read it and so believe they are expressing themselves more clearly than they actually are (Bartlett, 1982; Beal, 1996). As a result, they often don't revise their work unless a teacher or other adult specifically urges them to do so; when they *do* rewrite, they tend to make only small, superficial changes (Beal, 1996; Cameron et al., 1996; Francis & McCutchen, 1994).

Researchers have identified several strategies through which teachers can help their students revise what they've written:

- Schedule in-class time for revising so that students can get assistance as they need it.
- Before students begin rewriting, ask them to list five things they can do to make their writing better.

- Provide questions students should ask themselves as they rewrite (e.g., "Is this confusing?" "Do I need another example here?" "Who am I writing this for?").
- Explicitly teach revision strategies, including adding, deleting, moving, and rewriting text.
- Occasionally have students work in pairs or small groups to help one another revise. (Benton, 1997; Bereiter & Scardamalia, 1987; Cameron et al., 1996; Fitzgerald & Markman, 1987; Graham, MacArthur, & Schwartz, 1995; Graves, 1983; Kish, Zimmer, & Henning, 1994; Webb & Palincsar, 1996)

As you have seen, writing skills change in numerous ways throughout childhood and adolescence. The Developmental Trends table on the next page summarizes the changes in writing seen during the preschool, elementary school, and secondary school years.

General Strategies for Promoting Writing Development

Theorists and practitioners have offered several suggestions for promoting children's and adolescents' writing development:

■ *Assign authentic writing tasks.* By assigning authentic, real-world, personally meaningful writing tasks—writing short stories for classmates, letters to businesses and lawmakers, editorials for the local newspaper, e-mail messages to people in distant locations, and so on—teachers can encourage students to consider the language abilities and prior knowledge of their audience (Benton, 1997; Hiebert & Fisher, 1992; Sugar & Bonk, 1998). Such tasks can also prompt students to set specific goals for writing and to acquire the writing skills they need to achieve those goals.

■ *Give students some choices regarding writing topics.* Students write more frequently, and in a more organized and cohesive fashion, when they are interested in their topic (Benton, 1997; Garner, 1998). For instance, one high school English teacher, who noticed that several very capable students were failing his class because they weren't completing assigned writing tasks, began having his students write about their personal experiences and share them on the Internet with students in other classrooms; the teacher monitored their compositions for vulgar language but imposed no other restrictions. The students suddenly began writing regularly, presumably because they could write for a real audience and could now choose what they wrote about (Garner, 1998).

■ *Scaffold the complex processes involved in writing.* When students initially engage in a particular genre of writing (e.g., creating a summary, writing a persuasive essay), they often benefit from having an explicit structure to follow as they write (Byrnes, 1996; Kellogg, 1994; MacArthur & Ferretti, 1997). Later, teachers can provide **prompts,** short written reminders that help students think about their writing task in the ways that experts do (Englert et al., 1991; Graham & Harris, 1992; Kish et al., 1994). For example, Scardamalia and Bereiter (1985) have used prompts such as the following to help students think more like experts when they write:

"My main point . . ."

"An example of this . . ."

"The reason I think so . . ."

"To liven this up, I'll . . ."

"I can tie this together by . . ."

Scaffolding in self-evaluation and revision processes may also be helpful (De La Paz, Swanson, & Graham, 1998; McCormick, Busching, & Potter, 1992). For example, in a study by De La Paz, Swanson, and Graham (1998), eighth graders with a history of writing difficulties learned the following procedure for evaluating and revising persuasive essays:

First Revision Cycle: Global Evaluation
1. Read the entire paper and choose one of these four evaluations:
   - Ignores obvious point against my ideas
   - Too few ideas
   - Part of the essay doesn't belong with the rest
   - Part of the essay is not in the right order

prompt
An overt reminder about what one can or should do.

Writing at Different Age Levels

DEVELOPMENTAL TRENDS

AGE	WHAT YOU MIGHT OBSERVE	DIVERSITY	IMPLICATIONS
Early Childhood (2–6) 	• Increasing muscular control in writing and drawing • Pseudowriting (e.g., wavy lines, connected loops) in preschool play activities • Ability to write own name (perhaps at age 4) • Ability to write most letters of the alphabet (at age 4 or later) • Invented spellings (at ages 5–6)	• Some children have little if any exposure to written materials at home and so have less knowledge of letters. • Some cultures place greater emphasis on writing than others. • Children who are visually impaired have less awareness of print conventions (left-to-right progression, use of punctuation, etc.).	• Make writing implements (pencils, pens, markers, paper) easily available. • Give children opportunities to write their names and a few other meaningful words. • Have children act out stories they have orally composed.
Middle Childhood (6–10) 	• Gradual increase in smoothness of handwriting; gradual decrease in handwriting size • Increasing use of letter-sound relationships and common letter patterns in spelling • Predominance of narratives in writing • Difficulty identifying problems (especially problems of clarity) in own writing	• Children who are better readers also tend to be better writers, presumably because general language ability provides a foundation for both reading and writing. • Children with deficits in phonological awareness have a more difficult time learning to spell; the strength of this relationship varies from one language to the next. • Girls show higher achievement in writing and spelling beginning in the elementary years. • Children with dyslexia often have poor handwriting skills.	• Engage students in authentic writing activities (e.g., writing letters, creating a class newsletter). • Explore various ways in which particular phonemes and phoneme combinations are spelled in the English language. • Introduce expository forms of writing (e.g., descriptions, lab reports). • Build opportunities for revision into the class schedule; provide suggestions about how children can revise and improve their work.
Early Adolescence (10–14)	• Automatized spelling of most common words • Increasing use of expository forms of writing • Use of longer and more complex syntactic structures • Reluctance to revise unless strongly encouraged to do so	• Some students (e.g., those with learning disabilities) may have exceptional difficulty with handwriting, spelling, and sentence structure.	• When applicable, encourage students to use local dialects in creative writing projects. • Introduce persuasive and argumentative forms of writing. • Give feedback on first drafts, including suggestions on how to improve clarity and cohesiveness. • Give students a specific audience for whom to write.
Late Adolescence (14–18)	• Ability to write about a particular topic in depth • More organized and cohesive essays • Increasing ability to knowledge-transform rather than knowledge-tell • More revisions than at younger ages, but with a focus on superficial rather than substantive problems	• Students with learning disabilities may overemphasize the role of mechanics (spelling, grammatical rules, etc.) in the writing process. • Students from some cultural backgrounds (e.g., those from some East Asian countries) may be reluctant to put their thoughts on paper unless they are confident that they are correct.	• Assign lengthy writing projects; provide considerable guidance about how students can effectively complete them. • Teach specific strategies for organizing and synthesizing ideas. • Show examples of effective writing (e.g., writing that knowledge-transforms rather than knowledge-tells). • When students have language-based learning disabilities, downplay the importance of correct spelling and grammar when evaluating written work; help students acquire strategies for overcoming or compensating for their weaknesses.

Sources: Beal, 1996; Berninger et al., 1996; Byrnes, 1996; Cameron et al., 1996; Dickinson et al., 1993; Dien, 1998; Gentry, 1982; Graham & Weintraub, 1996; Harris & Hatano, 1999; Hedges & Nowell, 1995; Hemphill & Snow, 1996; MacArthur & Graham, 1987; McLane & McNamee, 1990; Rittle-Johnson & Siegler, 1999; Shanahan & Tierney, 1990; Smitherman, 1994; Spivey, 1997; Trawick-Smith, 2000; Turnbull et al., 1995; Yaden & Templeton, 1986.

2. Depending on the evaluation selected, select one of the following strategies:
   - Rewrite something
   - Delete something
   - Add something
   - Move something
3. Execute the strategy selected in step 2. Repeat steps 2 and 3 as many times as necessary.

Second Revision Cycle: Local Evaluations
4. Reread the entire paper and highlight sections that still require revision.
5. For each highlighted section, select one of six evaluations:
   - This one doesn't sound right.
   - This is not what I intended to say.
   - This is an incomplete idea.
   - This is a weak idea.
   - This part is not clear.
   - The problem is ____.
   Fix each problem using one of four strategies: rewrite, delete, add, or move.

Students who learned and followed this procedure revised their work more frequently and effectively and improved the overall quality of their writing (De La Paz et al., 1998).

■ *Encourage students to focus initially on communicating their message clearly and to postpone attention to writing mechanics until final drafts.* Worrying primarily about correct spelling, grammar, and punctuation too early in the composition process may tax working memory and so is likely to be counterproductive.

Unfortunately, the feedback that teachers give students about their writing often focuses more on spelling, grammar, and punctuation than on matters of style, clarity, and cohesiveness (Byrnes, 1996; Covill, 1997), and such feedback may unintentionally give students the message that writing mechanics are the most important ingredient in good writing. Instead, we urge teachers to focus their initial feedback on the overall quality of students' writing and to delay feedback about mechanical errors until relatively late in the game, perhaps as students are polishing up their final drafts.

■ *Use peer groups to promote effective writing skills.* Several studies have shown that when students collaborate on writing projects, they produce longer and more complex texts, revise more, and enhance one another's writing skills (Sperling, 1996; Webb & Palincsar, 1996). Teachers can also ask students to read and respond to one another's work; in the process, students may become better able to examine their own writing from the perspective of potential readers (Benton, 1997; Cameron et al., 1996; Sperling, 1996).

■ *Encourage students to use word processing programs.* Word processing programs encourage students to revise; after all, it is much easier to change words and move sentences when one is working on a computer rather than on paper (Cochran-Smith, 1991; Kellogg, 1994). Word processing may also lessen students' working memory load by taking over some of the mechanical aspects of writing (e.g., checking spelling), thus allowing students to concentrate on the overall quality of writing (Jones & Pellegrini, 1996). As an illustration, consider what the same first grader wrote by hand and by computer (Jones & Pellegrini, 1996):

Students can more effectively revise their writing when they collaborate on a writing project and when they have access to a word processing program.

By hand:
Some busy wut to play boll But thay cnat play Boll Be cus the Big Busys and the grul wit to tale on them (p. 711)

By computer:
The man cooks some soup and he cooks carrots in the soup and the king gives the man a big hat, and the man goes to the house and the man shows the hat cap to the children. (p. 711)

A big difference, wouldn't you say?

■ *Include writing assignments in all areas of the curriculum.* Writing shouldn't be a skill that only elementary teachers and secondary English teachers teach. In fact, writing takes different forms in different disciplines; for instance, writing fiction is very different from writing a science laboratory report, which in turn is very different from writing an analysis of historical documents. Ideally, *all* teachers should teach writing to some degree, and especially at the secondary level, they should teach the writing skills specific to various academic disciplines (Burnett & Kastman, 1997; Sperling, 1996).

Developing Literacy in a Second Language

To some extent, children can apply the reading and writing skills they've learned in one language to literacy tasks in a second language as well (Comeau, Cormier, Grandmaison, & Lacroix, 1999; Krashen, 1996; Pérez, 1998). Children's knowledge of letter-sound relationships in English certainly facilitates their reading and writing in other languages that use the same alphabet. In addition, the strategies children use for deriving meaning from texts written in one language are often equally applicable to texts in a very different language.

Yet some aspects of literacy may be somewhat language-specific (Pérez, 1998). Not all languages use the same left-to-right, top-to-bottom directions that many Western languages do. For instance, writing in most Semitic languages (e.g., Hebrew, Arabic) goes from right to left, and Chinese characters are written in vertical, top-to-bottom columns that begin on the right side of the page and proceed leftward. Word spellings in Semitic languages represent some but not all vowel sounds (e.g., soft "uh" sounds are often omitted), so children raised in Semitic countries may have to fine-tune their phonological awareness to read and spell in English.

Teachers should never assume that when children are learning English as a second language, literacy will follow quickly or easily. If children have been raised in a culture that depends less heavily on reading and writing than our culture does, their literacy skills—perhaps even their knowledge of the potential value and uses of reading and writing—may take several years and considerable experience and guidance to develop (Pérez, 1998).

Diversity in Literacy Development

We often see differences in children's literacy development as a function of their gender, socioeconomic status, and ethnicity. We also see differences in literacy development across languages.

Gender Differences

On average, girls read, write, and spell somewhat better than boys (Feingold, 1993; Hedges & Nowell, 1995). Girls are also more confident than boys about their writing abilities, even when no differences in the actual writing performance of the two groups exist (Pajares & Valiante, 1999). At the high school level, girls are more likely than boys to enroll in advanced language and literature classes (Wigfield et al., 1996). Reasons for such differences have not been actively explored, but we suspect that they are at least partly the result of girls' slightly higher verbal abilities during the school years (see Chapter 6).

Socioeconomic Differences

In general, children from lower-income families come to school with fewer literacy skills than children from middle- and upper-income families; the difference not only persists, but in fact *increases,* over the course of the elementary and secondary school years (Chall, 1996; Jimerson, Egeland, & Teo, 1999; Portes, 1996). Thus, as children from low-income families get older, they fall further and further behind their classmates in reading and writing. To some extent, these socioeconomic differences occur because, on average, children from lower-income families have less access to reading materials (fewer books and magazines, fewer trips to the library, etc.) than children from middle-income families. As children reach the upper elementary grades, their more limited opportunities for enriching educational experiences (travel, trips to zoos and museums, etc.) and less extensive vocabularies may also play a role (recall our earlier discussion of the *fourth-grade slump*).

This is not to say that *all* children from low-income backgrounds are at a disadvantage. As the opening case study illustrates, many low-income parents are fully aware of the importance of reading and writing and so read to their children regularly and in other ways foster literacy development (Jimerson et al, 1999; McLane & McNamee, 1990). Yet many parents at lower socioeconomic levels have little knowledge of how to promote literacy through home reading activities (perhaps because they had few early reading experiences with their own parents). When these parents are taught effective strategies for reading with preschoolers (e.g., labeling and describing the pictures in books, asking questions that stimulate thinking about a story), they have a better understanding of what it means to "Read to your children" (Edwards & Garcia, 1994).

Socioeconomic status is also a predictor of immigrant children's ability to develop literacy in English as a second language, probably for several reasons: Children from middle- and upper-class families typically have a more solid foundation in reading and writing in their native language, greater access to printed materials in English, and parents and other caregivers who can help them with their schoolwork (Krashen, 1996).

Ethnic Differences

Ethnic and cultural groups differ considerably in their emphasis on engaging young children in reading activities. Some African American groups focus more on oral storytelling than on book reading (Trawick-Smith, 2000). Some Native American communities stress art, dance, and oral histories that carry on the group's cultural traditions (Trawick-Smith, 2000).

Writing practices also differ from one group to another. For instance, Vietnamese children may be reluctant to commit their ideas to paper unless they are confident that their ideas are correct and will not be misinterpreted (Dien, 1998). The Yup'ik peoples of northern North America frequently engage in *storyknifing,* whereby they carve symbols and pictures in the mud while simultaneously telling tales about the family's or community's history (deMarrais, Nelson, & Baker, 1994).

People from most ethnic groups in Western society value literacy and see it as essential for children's eventual success in the adult world (Pérez, 1998). Teachers must be sensitive to what students' early language and literacy experiences have been and use them as the foundation for instruction in reading and writing. For example, reading instruction is more effective for native Hawaiian children when they can engage in *overlapping talk* (in which they frequently interrupt one another) as they discuss the stories they are reading; such a conversational style is consistent with their speaking practices at home (Au & Mason, 1981). African American students who use Black English Vernacular at home and with friends write more imaginative narratives when they incorporate this dialect into their writing (Smitherman, 1994). And children and adolescents from all backgrounds will respond more favorably to literature that accurately represents culturally diverse ways of living and thinking (Gollnick & Chinn, 1998).

Cross-Linguistic Differences

Languages differ considerably in the extent to which spelling accurately captures how words are pronounced. Spanish, Portuguese, Italian, German, and Finnish have highly regular and predictable spelling patterns, such that a word's spelling tells a reader exactly how the word is pronounced and its pronunciation tells a writer exactly how it is spelled. English, French, and Greek are less regular, in that some sounds can be represented by two or more different letters or letter combinations. Other languages, such as Chinese and Japanese, do not use an alphabet at all, so that predictable relationships between the forms of spoken and written language are few and far between.[2]

The more regular and predictable a language's letter-sound relationships are, the more easily children learn to read and spell; for instance, Italian and German children learn to read more quickly and easily than English-speaking children do (Harris & Hatano, 1999). In highly regu-

---

[2]Traditionally, Chinese and Japanese are written as *characters* that represent entire syllables rather than individual phonemes. However, children in China, Taiwan, and Japan are often taught one or more alphabetic, phonetic systems for representing their language in writing before they are taught more traditional characters, and such training increases their phonological awareness (e.g., Hanley, Tzeng, & Huang, 1999).

lar languages, knowledge of letter-sound correspondences may be all that children need to decode and spell words accurately; in less regular languages, such as English and French, knowledge of common spelling patterns plays an important role as well (Harris & Hatano, 1999).

Exceptionalities in Reading and Writing Development

To some extent, development of literacy skills goes hand in hand with overall intellectual development. Many (but not all) children who are later identified as intellectually gifted begin to read earlier than their peers, and some read frequently and voraciously (Piirto, 1999; Turnbull et al., 1999). Children with mental retardation learn to read more slowly than their age-mates, and they acquire fewer effective reading strategies. In some instances, they may develop excellent word decoding skills yet understand little or nothing of what they read (Cossu, 1999). Writing development, too, is correlated with general measures of intelligence. Some children who are gifted exhibit extraordinary writing talent, and most children with mental retardation show general delays in their writing skills.

Children with visual or hearing impairments may also be at a disadvantage when learning to read and write. To the extent that their general language development is delayed (see Chapter 7), reading and writing will certainly be affected. In addition, children who are visually impaired cannot see the printed page when caregivers read to them in the early years, and so they know less about the conventions of written language (e.g., the left-to-right progression of words, the use of punctuation) when they begin school (Tompkins & McGee, 1986). Children with hearing impairments who have learned a manual language (e.g., American Sign Language) rather than spoken language cannot capitalize on letter-sound relationships when they learn to read and spell (Andrews & Mason, 1986). Although some of these children may have some phonological knowledge (Alegria, 1998), they nevertheless face a greater challenge than hearing children when, in the process of learning to read and write, they must make connections between the words they use in conversation and the forms that those words take in written language.

General intellectual development and sensory disabilities do not account for all the exceptionalities observed in reading and writing development. Here we look briefly at dyslexia and writing disabilities.

Dyslexia

Some children with learning disabilities have considerable difficulty learning to read; they may have trouble recognizing printed words or have little comprehension of what they read. In their extreme form, such difficulties are known as **dyslexia.** Many theorists believe that dyslexia has biological roots; others propose that some instances of dyslexia may simply reflect the lower end of a normal distribution of specific cognitive abilities (Shaywitz, Escobar, Shaywitz, Fletcher, & Makuch, 1992).

Contrary to popular belief, dyslexia is typically *not* a problem of visual perception, such as reading words or letters backwards (Stanovich, 2000). Instead, most children with reading disabilities appear to have deficits in phonological awareness (Chiappe & Siegel, 1999; Hulme & Joshi, 1998; Morris et al., 1998; Stanovich, 2000; Swanson, Mink, & Bocian, 1999). Others appear to have difficulty automatizing connections between printed words and their meanings (Stanovich, 2000). Some children with reading disabilities may also have general information processing difficulties, such as a smaller working memory capacity or a tendency to process information at a slower-than-average rate (Wimmer, Landerl, & Frith, 1999; Wolf & Bowers, 1999).

Writing Disabilities

dyslexia
Inability to master basic reading skills in a developmentally typical time frame.

dysgraphia
Exceptional difficulty acquiring handwriting skills.

Some children with learning disabilities have problems in handwriting, spelling, or expressing themselves coherently on paper; for instance, children with **dysgraphia** have exceptional difficulty with handwriting. Children with writing disabilities typically focus their writing efforts on addressing mechanical issues (spelling, grammar, etc.), and their ability to communicate effectively in their writing suffers as a result (Graham, Schwartz, & MacArthur,

1993). The quality of their writing improves considerably when the mechanical aspects of writing are minimized (e.g., when they can dictate their stories and other compositions) and when they are given a specific series of steps to follow as they write (Hallenbeck, 1996; MacArthur & Graham, 1987; Sawyer, Graham, & Harris, 1992).

Reading disabilities and writing disabilities are frequently found together. Curiously, however, some children can write words quite accurately yet cannot read the very same words. Cossu (1999) has described several children in Italy who could spell with almost 100% accuracy yet were completely unable to read. On one occasion, a 9-year-old girl correctly wrote a list of 30 two-syllable words but then, when asked to read them immediately afterward, misread every one. For instance, she read *riva* (shore) as *ruota* (wheel), *naso* (nose) as *ago* (needle), and *rospo* (toad) as *fiore* (flower). Apparently, she relied strictly on letter-sound correspondences to spell the words (Italian is a phonetically regular and predictable language) but then could not take advantage of those correspondences to convert printed letters back into speech.

Helping Students with Reading and Writing Disabilities

Ideally, students with reading and writing disabilities receive additional assistance in reading and writing from specialists who have been trained to address their needs. Nonetheless, most of these students attend general education classrooms for most or all of the school day. Following are several strategies that classroom teachers may find helpful in working with these students:

■ *Identify reading and writing problems as early as possible.* If children initially struggle with literacy tasks, they engage in such tasks as little as possible and thereby limit their opportunities for practice, improvement, and automatization of basic skills. The end result is that the gap between their own skills and those of their nondisabled classmates increases considerably over time (Stanovich, 2000).

The typical criterion for identifying children with disabilities in reading or writing is a significant discrepancy between general intelligence level (e.g., as indicated by an IQ score) and performance on reading or writing tasks. Unfortunately, appreciable discrepancies may not appear until the upper elementary grades, at which point the children are so far behind their peers that it is virtually impossible to catch up (Meyer, 2000; Reschly, 1997). Furthermore, to the extent that reading contributes to world knowledge, which in turn affects performance on many intelligence tests (see Chapter 6), then large discrepancies between reading and IQ may never appear (Meyer, 2000).

We urge teachers in the early elementary grades to be on the lookout for signs of reading or writing disabilities in their students. Perhaps the most telling sign will be considerable difficulty in learning letter-sound relationships and applying them effectively in reading and writing tasks. In Figure 8–7, we present a writing sample that indicates a possible weakness in phonological awareness.

■ *Provide explicit training in basic skills.* Although many children learn to read and write quite effectively in whole-language classrooms, children with reading and writing disabilities rarely do so. Instead, children with reading and writing difficulties benefit from deliberate and intensive training in letter recognition, phonological awareness, and word identification strategies (Lovett et al., 2000; Schneider et al., 2000; Stanovich, 2000).

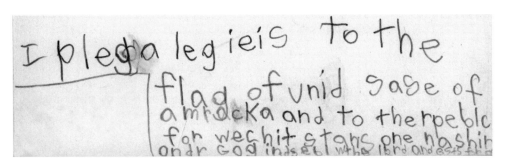

FIGURE 8–7 In this 8-year-old boy's Pledge of Allegiance, many phonemes are not represented; for instance, *United* is spelled "UNID," and *States* is spelled "SASE." If this writing sample is typical of the boy's written work, his third-grade teacher can reasonably guess that he needs work in phonological awareness skills.

■ *Provide technological scaffolding.* Numerous computer programs are available to help students with their reading and writing. For example, some reading software provides assistance when students encounter words that they can't decode and identify; when a student touches an unknown word with a light pen or clicks on it with a mouse, the computer reads the word for the student. And many word processing programs provide assistance with spelling and grammar.

Ideally, students should have whatever scaffolding they need to succeed at reading and writing tasks. Success is far and away the most effective motivator for encouraging students to develop their literacy skills.

Reading and Writing as Facilitators of Cognitive Development

Reading and writing are, of course, valuable in their own right. In addition, reading and writing activities can promote cognitive development more generally. When children and adolescents read regularly, they add to the knowledge base that is so important for helping them interpret and respond to new experiences effectively. Reading also exposes young people to more sophisticated vocabulary than they typically encounter while conversing with others or watching television (Stanovich, 2000).

Writing, too, promotes learning and cognition. For instance, writing about a particular topic enhances students' understanding of the topic (Benton, 1997; Klein, 1999; Konopak, Martin, & Martin, 1990). In addition, various kinds of writing activities may encourage students to engage in and thereby further develop specific cognitive skills, including organization, elaboration, analysis, and critical thinking (Baron, 1987; Greene & Ackerman, 1995; Kellogg, 1994). By assigning writing activities in *all* areas of the school curriculum, then—in science, mathematics, social studies, and so on, as well as in language arts—teachers promote students' development in specific content domains as well as in writing per se.

Our society has a significantly higher literacy rate than it did 50 or 100 years ago (Chall, 1996). Yet even today, many children and adolescents—perhaps because of inherited disabilities or perhaps because of insufficient opportunities and instruction—do not have the reading and writing skills they need to learn effectively in school or to participate fully in adult society. Researchers and practitioners are making great strides in discovering how best to promote literacy development in people of all ages. The final case study illustrates one possible approach.

CASE STUDY: THE TEXAS TUTORING PROGRAM

A group of college students with poor reading skills (their comprehension skills are, on average, similar to those of a typical ninth grader) are tutoring first and second graders who are struggling with reading. The college students meet with their young partners in 45-minute sessions twice a week. They also meet one evening a week to discuss how literacy develops and exchange ideas about possible tutoring activities. At the end of the school year, the college students are reading better than a control group who have attended a regular developmental reading course at the same college, and the first and second graders in the tutoring program are reading better than their untutored classmates (Juel, 1998).

A researcher has videotaped the tutoring sessions. When she analyzes the tapes, she finds several qualities that characterize the most effective tutors. For one thing, they model and scaffold basic reading skills, as the following dialogue illustrates:[3]

| Tutor: | So whenever you see those two letters together, it sounds like "aaaaattt, aaaaaatttt." So what is that? |
| Child: | "Aaaaattt." |

[3]Excerpts from "What Kind of One-on-One Tutoring Helps a Poor Reader?" by C. Juel. In *Reading and Spelling: Development and Disorders,* by C. Hulme & R. M. Joshi (Eds.), 1998, Mahwah, NJ: Erlbaum. Reprinted with permission.

Tutor:	Right, so what word is that?
Child:	At.
Tutor:	Right. So you've got the "at." Let's put a sound on the front of it, okay? What's one of your favorite sounds? I know, it's "ssss."
Child:	"S."
Tutor:	Right. (Puts the letter *s* in front of *at*.) So you go, "ssss"—"at," and put them together. What have you got? You see? You see how that works? "Ssss" plus "at" gives you "sat." What about "m" plus "at"? What does that give you? (Replaces the letter *s* with *m*.)
Child:	"m."
Tutor:	And what is the other part?
Child:	"At."
Tutor:	Put them together. What do you get? You got the "at." You got the "mmmmm" sound. You put them together and what do you get? "Mmmmmaaaaaaat."
Child:	Mat.
Tutor:	Good. (Replaces *m* with *f*.) So you got "f" and "at." Gives you what?
Child:	(Laughs.) Fat.
Tutor:	Right. They come together. You have this word "fffffaaaat." Fat. What do you hear when you say that word *fat?*
Child:	"Ffff."
Tutor:	Right. And the last two?
Child:	"At."
Tutor:	Right. All we did was change the letters, and you change the sound. (Puts up appropriate letters.) "At," then "sssat," then "mmmat," "fat." See? What about "b" plus the "at"?
Child:	Buh. Bat.
Tutor:	Right. You got it. (Juel, 1998, pp. 461–462)

Effective tutors also develop supportive, affectionate relationships with their partners and continually point out that the youngsters are making progress. The following exchange is a typical example:

Tutor:	Hum, so your teacher tells me that you be reading a lot. Is that true? Can you tell? Can you see the improvement in yourself?
Child:	Yeah.
Tutor:	How? How can you see that you've improved? Do you read faster now? Can you sound out words a little bit better than you did before?
Child:	I can sound out words.
Tutor:	I mean you just spelled *tape*. It wasn't up on the board and you could spell it. You spelled it in your head. That's the hardest way to spell things. So that's improvement right there. You could do it without looking. You know all your sounds now . . . so, you're getting better and better every day. Have you been practicing? (Child nods.) See, that's why you're getting better and faster. The more you practice the faster you get. (Juel, 1998, p. 459)

The researcher speculates that because the college students themselves have had difficulty learning to read, they are more aware of specific strategies that their partners can use. One tutor explains it this way:

I had a lot of difficulty in school. My parents were told I was learning disabled. I carry this with me to this day. I found early on that I could learn okay, but usually not in the classroom. I learned early on that my best teachers were my peers, the ones who had just been through the same stuff. They could always explain things better to me than anyone else. I even find this to be true in college. (Juel, 1998, p. 463)

- In this situation, elementary school children who are poor readers benefit from working with older students who are also poor readers. Might children benefit just as much from being tutored by children their own age who are good readers? Why or why not?
- The tutors themselves have improved their reading skills, more so than students who have taken a remedial college reading course. How might you explain their findings?
- The Texas Tutoring Program uses college students as tutors. Might low-reading high school students also be effective tutors in such a program? Why or why not?

Theories of Literacy Development

Information processing theorists propose that reading and writing involve the same mechanisms (attention, working memory, metacognitive strategies, etc.) that are involved in cognition more generally. Whole-language theorists draw parallels between literacy development and oral language development and suggest that children learn to read and write most effectively within the context of authentic literacy activities. Sociocultural theorists apply Vygotsky's ideas to the development of reading and writing and so emphasize culture-specific literacy practices, the importance of conversations with adults, and the gradual internalization of such practices and conversations. The three theoretical perspectives sometimes yield different implications about how children can most effectively learn to read and write.

Early Literacy

When toddlers and preschoolers have multiple and varied experiences with reading and writing materials and activities, they learn a great deal about the nature of written language; for instance, they learn that spoken language is represented in a consistent fashion in written language and that different kinds of printed materials serve different purposes. Such knowledge, known as *emergent literacy,* provides an important foundation for the reading and writing skills that children acquire once they begin school.

Reading Development

Skilled reading involves knowing letter-sound correspondences, recognizing individual letters and entire words quickly and automatically, using context clues to facilitate decoding, constructing meaning from the words on the page, and metacognitively regulating the reading process. Phonological awareness (hearing the distinct sounds within spoken words), word decoding skills, and the automatic recognition of many common words typically develop in the early and middle elementary school years. Reading comprehension and metacognitive strategies continue to develop throughout childhood and adolescence. Strategies for helping students become proficient readers include promoting phonological awareness, giving students many opportunities to read authentic literature, and engaging students in discussions about what they read.

Writing Development

To become skillful writers, children and adolescents must not only master handwriting and spelling but must also discover how to communicate their thoughts clearly; learn conventions of capitalization, punctuation, and syntax; and metacognitively regulate the entire writing effort. Handwriting is usually mastered in the elementary grades, but other aspects of writing continue to develop throughout the school years. Teachers can promote writing development by asking students to clarify their goals for writing and the audience for whom they are writing, organize their thoughts before they begin to write, and focus more on clear communication than on writing mechanics in early drafts. Teachers should assign authentic writing tasks in all areas of the curriculum, scaffold students' initial efforts in various genres of writing, and provide sufficient criteria and feedback to guide students as they revise their written work.

Literacy in a Second Language

To some extent, children can apply the reading and writing skills they've learned in one language to literacy tasks in a second language as well. However, certain aspects of literacy (e.g., the particular sounds that letters represent or the direction in which writing proceeds) may be language-specific.

Diversity and Exceptionalities in Reading and Writing

On average, girls read and write slightly better than boys, and children from middle- and upper-income families have better developed literacy skills than children from lower-income families. Different ethnic groups place greater or less emphasis on literacy activities, and young children's preliteracy skills may vary accordingly. Children who speak languages with phonetically regular and predictable spelling patterns (e.g., Italian or German) learn to read and spell more easily than children who speak less regular languages.

Some children who are intellectually gifted have superior reading and writing skills; children with mental retardation typically show delays in reading and writing. Children with visual or hearing impairments may show delays as well, due either to little familiarity with the conventions of written language (in the case of visual impairments) or less ability to capitalize on letter-sound relationships (in the case of hearing impairments). Some children have reading or writing disabilities despite average or above average intelligence and normal vision and hearing.

Reading and Writing as Facilitators of Cognitive Development

Reading and writing development can promote cognitive development more generally. When children read regularly, they add to the knowledge base (including knowledge of vocabulary) that helps them interpret and respond to their experiences. Various writing activities encourage students to develop such cognitive skills as elaboration, analysis, and critical thinking.

Now go to our Companion Website to assess your understanding of chapter content with Multiple-Choice Questions, apply comprehension in Essay Questions, and broaden your knowledge with links to related Developmental Psychology World Wide Web sites.

KEY CONCEPTS

second-order symbol system (p. 278)
whole-language perspective (p. 279)
emergent literacy (p. 282)
phonological awareness (p. 285)
onset (p. 285)

rime (p. 285)
word decoding (p. 285)
sight vocabulary (p. 287)
story schema (p. 288)
fourth-grade slump (p. 290)
reciprocal teaching (p. 294)
invented spelling (p. 300)

knowledge telling (p. 302)
knowledge transforming (p. 303)
prompt (in facilitating writing) (p. 305)
dyslexia (p. 310)
dysgraphia (p. 310)

Shea, age 9

Personal and Emotional Development

CASE STUDY: MARY

In 1954, Dr. Emmy Werner and her colleagues began a longitudinal study of children born on the island of Kauai, Hawaii. Children in the study faced numerous problems in their early years: They lived in poverty, had parents with mental health problems, received inadequate care, and so on. Despite exposure to numerous risk factors, the majority of these children had *no* serious learning or behavior problems during childhood or adolescence.

Mary was one of these resilient children. Her father was a plantation laborer with only 4 years of formal education. Her mother was seriously overweight and suffered from a variety of medical problems while pregnant with Mary. Nevertheless, Mary's parents were happy about her birth and gave her good care.

At 12 months of age, Mary was described as "easy to deal with," "very active," and a "healthy, alert child who is apparently given much attention." At 22 months, she was an "active, cheerful, energetic, and determined child who showed independence, perseverance, and feminine characteristics, but who also seemed somewhat excitable, distractible, and nervous" (Werner & Smith, 1982, p. 141).

As Mary entered middle childhood, her family environment deteriorated. Her mother had mood swings, suffered from several major illnesses, and was hospitalized twice for emotional disturbance. Mary, too, had her troubles. Her mother reported that, at age 10, Mary had "crying spells and headaches, temper tantrums, and stubborn, contrary behavior" (Werner & Smith, 1982, p. 142).

Later, Mary showed some understanding of her mother's behavior:[1]

> . . . very grumpy—well, she's going through change of life early—every little thing bothers her. She's lonely. My father leaves her a lot and we have our own life. When they're that age, they do get lonely. . . . I used to be blamed for every little thing that my sister did when my parents went out, and when my father went to work, my mother used to hit me and beat me. That's how come I'm not very close to my mother. In a way I used to hate her, but as I got older I understood her better, how she was going through that change of life—but we're not really close. (p. 142)

Her description of her father was more positive and affectionate:

> . . . soft-hearted, very soft-hearted—he cares for our happiness and has always been like that. He's generous, not selfish. I feel very close to him. (p. 142)

As an adolescent, Mary was outgoing, sociable, and concerned with how others perceived her. She believed that she controlled her own destiny—she was not at the mercy of forces beyond her control—and she approached new situations cautiously, typically seeking information before acting. She disliked tension in her interpersonal relationships and avoided conflict whenever possible:

> Me, I don't start fights too much. My mother, she'll go around the house grumbling, until I finally get up to a point where I can't stand it. I can't stand to see a family fighting. Parents shouldn't fight, they should be able to talk things out. (p. 143)

Mary was a good student who scored in the top 25% on achievement tests in high school. Thus, while her family life was often troubled, school was an arena in which she could succeed.

[1]Excerpts from *Vulnerable but Not Invincible: A Longitudinal Study of Resilient Children,* by E. E. Werner and R. S. Smith, 1982, New York: McGraw-Hill. Reprinted 1989, 1998. New York: Adams, Bannister, Cox. Reprinted with permission.

When Mary met with the researchers for the last time, she was 18 and planning to enroll in a community college to prepare for a career in medical or legal secretarial work. She described herself this way:

> If I say how I am, it sounds like bragging—I have a good personality and people like me. I'm not the greedy type—I'm jealous a lot of times, yes. And I don't like it when people think they can run my own life—I like to be my own judge. I know right and wrong, but I feel I have a lot more to learn and go through. Generally, I hope I can make it—I hope. (p. 140)

MARY'S CASE UNDERSCORES THE significance of children's emotional ties to their caregivers. As an adolescent, Mary felt very close to her father but had mixed feelings for her mother. During her infancy, and before her mother's emotional breakdowns, observers found both parents affectionate. It seems likely, then, that Mary initially formed a close emotional bond with her mother but later learned to keep her distance as she encountered instability, irritability, and criticism. In this chapter, we learn about the early attachments children form with their parents, siblings, and other caregivers. We find that these social bonds, when warm and nurturing, give children a secure base from which to explore the world and form later relationships with other people. However, we will also see that healthy social bonds do not ensure good outcomes, nor do weak social bonds guarantee bad ones; intervening social experiences steer the trajectory of later social adjustment.

A second theme in this case, and throughout the chapter as well, is the centrality of emotions in defining experience. Emotions saturate the lives of children, adolescents, and adults. Mary's parents were happy when she was born, and as a young child Mary seemed to thrive on the affection her mother and father gave her. Yet there were indications of negative emotions as well: Mary had crying spells and temper tantrums, and she disliked being blamed for everything. In studying the emotional lives of children, we find that children experience fairly simple, straightforward emotional states early on and then develop more complex feelings that increasingly reflect an understanding of other people's viewpoints. Simple emotions of fear, anger, and happiness in infancy make room for shame, guilt, and pride during early and middle childhood. Children also learn to deal with negative emotions more effectively as they grow older. For instance, Mary's temper tantrums gradually diminished as she learned to channel her anger into other, more productive modes of expression.

Finally, Mary reflected on who she was as an individual. She cast herself in a balanced yet optimistic light. She was concerned that she not appear too conceited, but she perceived herself to have a good personality, to know right from wrong, to be somewhat jealous (though not greedy), and to be receptive to new learning opportunities. In this chapter, we examine how children think about themselves, how they feel about their own worth, and how they evaluate what they can do in life.

The developments we examine in this chapter—attaching to caregivers, effectively expressing and regulating emotions, and constructing a sense of self—are necessary for positive peer interactions, construction of a moral code, healthy family relationships, and the ability to navigate through community and cultural contexts. These assorted social-emotional developments are interrelated, as experiences with peers, family, and the broader cultural community do feed back into how children feel about themselves and how they express their emotions. But we must begin our story somewhere, and it makes sense to start with the very core of children's social-emotional functioning—their first attachments, their emotional expression, and their sense of self.

As you learn about social-emotional development in this and later chapters, we invite you to look for the basic developmental issues we have raised in previous chapters. For instance, attachments, emotions, and understandings of self grow out of the interacting forces of nature and nurture. Their manifestations show some universality and much diversity, and they change in both qualitative and quantitative ways.

Early Attachments

By **attachment** we mean an enduring emotional tie that unites one person to another (Ainsworth, 1973). During infancy and early childhood, attachment to parents and other family members serves an important protective function (Ainsworth, 1963; Bowlby, 1958). Young children use their caregivers as a secure base from which to explore their world. They typically stay close by, and when they do venture out, they routinely return whenever they feel worried or afraid.

In the last few decades, the dominant theoretical perspective on caregiver-infant relationships has been **ethological attachment theory,** a perspective originally suggested by John Bowlby (1951, 1958), fleshed out by Mary Ainsworth (1963, 1973; Ainsworth, Blehar, Waters, & Wall, 1978), and tested and refined by many contemporary psychologists. Ethological attachment theory describes the significance of children's social-emotional bonds with parents in terms of evolutionary function; as such, it is an example of the *evolutionary perspectives* described in Chapter 1. Evolutionary perspectives remind us that human infants, who are unable to feed themselves or protect themselves from harm, must depend on their parents to survive. Parents are biologically predisposed to care for their infants, and infants are biologically programmed to stay close to their parents, especially in times of danger. Infants have many tools at their disposal to maintain this proximity: They can cry, cling, and crawl when distressed, and they can show their affection with snuggles, smiles, and cooing under less stressful conditions.

Initial theorizing about attachment emphasized infants' relationships with their mothers, but contemporary perspectives have been more inclusive of other attachment figures, such as fathers, other family members, and caregivers outside the family. It is becoming increasingly apparent that infants and young children can, and often do, form lasting attachments to a variety of caring individuals.

Evolutionary pressures for adult-child bonding lead us to conclude that attachment is a universal human capacity. Nonetheless, attachment does not happen automatically; rather, it depends squarely on caregivers' capacity to be nurturing and attend to children's welfare (Thompson, 1998). Parents and others who provide sensitive care pick up on infants' signals, drawing inferences about states of discomfort, hunger, fatigue, and so on. They then do what it takes to make things better, perhaps offering bottle or breast, changing a diaper, or giving reassurance. Caregivers also focus on what young children care about and attend to, whether it be the blades of a fan, the rumble of the dryer, the texture of a fabric, or the scent of a flower.

The nature of social-emotional bonds between caregivers and children changes over time. Early on, parents and other caregivers appear to do most of the work. Keep in mind, though, that nature has made infants alluring partners in this social dance; for instance, few parents can resist the chance to cuddle their young babies, and many drop everything to respond to their infants' urgent cries. With time and experience, the relationship changes. Parents increasingly hear the subtle nuances in cries and vocalizations, and infants become more competent participators in social interaction. Face-to-face exchanges evolve from one-sided, parent-directed affairs into two-sided, turn-taking activities. Within their first year, infants show an emerging understanding that they can influence their social world ("If I cry, Daddy comes"; "When I smile, Mommy smiles back"). They also begin to attend to and interpret adults' emotional expressions and associate them with particular contexts ("When I crawl toward the stairs, Mommy looks scared"; "When Grampa drops me off at daycare, he smiles at my teacher").

Attachments are probably most evident when children sense danger, pain, or uncertainty (Bowlby, 1988). An intruding stranger, a stubbed toe, and sheer exhaustion are the kinds of events that send children fleeing to parents or, if they're not yet mobile, crying and thrashing for cuddling and comfort. But attachments reveal themselves under happier circumstances as well. Perhaps you've witnessed the energetic wiggling, cooing, and laughter that a 6-month-old baby shows when a parent walks into the room. It's as if the baby is saying, "Look at me! I'm happy to see you! Come play with me!"

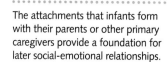

The attachments that infants form with their parents or other primary caregivers provide a foundation for later social-emotional relationships.

attachment
An enduring emotional tie uniting one person to another.

ethological attachment theory
Theoretical perspective that emphasizes the functional importance of caregiver-child bonds in protecting children and giving them a secure base from which to explore their surroundings.

Individual Differences in Attachment

If you look around at young children you know, you may notice variations in how they respond to their parents. Some children are less inclined than others to seek out parents when distressed, and they may have a hard time accepting comfort. Others cling to parents constantly and are reluctant to venture from protective arms. To study such differences in the laboratory, Mary Ainsworth created a mildly stressful situation for 1-year-old infants. First, a mother and her infant were brought to a playroom and left alone. A stranger (a research assistant) soon entered the room and attempted to play with the baby. After 3 minutes, the mother left the room, so that the baby was alone with the stranger. Subsequently, the mother returned and the stranger departed, leaving mother and baby together. Next, mother departed, and baby was alone; the stranger returned at this point. Finally, the mother returned and the stranger departed (Ainsworth et al., 1978). This sequence, commonly known as the *Strange Situation,* has become a classic research tool for assessing attachment in young children.

In the Strange Situation, attention is focused primarily on the child's behavior. Observers rate the child's attempts to seek contact with the mother, the physical proximity of the child to mother, the child's resistance to or avoidance of mother, and the child's apparent level of distress. From such ratings, the child is given one of four classifications:

- Infants who exhibit **secure attachment** seem to use mother as a secure base. When she is present, they actively explore new toys and surroundings. When she returns after leaving the room, they smile at or talk to her, move over to greet her, or in other ways seek proximity with her. About 65% of infants from typical middle-class backgrounds are classified as securely attached (Thompson, 1998).

- Infants who exhibit **insecure-avoidant attachment** fail to greet mother when she comes back and perhaps even look away upon her return. Even before their mother departs, these children appear indifferent to her presence; instead, they go about their business independently, and they are somewhat superficial in their interactions with toys. About 20% of children participating in Strange Situation studies are classified as insecure-avoidant (Thompson, 1998).

- Infants who exhibit **insecure-resistant attachment** seem preoccupied with their mother, but they are not easily comforted during reunions. Even when mother returns, they remain distressed and angry; they may rush to her yet quickly struggle to be released. Insecure-resistant infants comprise about 15% of participants in Strange Situation studies (Thompson, 1998).

- Not part of Ainsworth's original classification, a fourth type—**disorganized and disoriented attachment**—has since been identified (Main & Solomon, 1986, 1990). Infants in this group lack a coherent way of responding to stressful events such as those in the Strange Situation. These infants may be calm and contented one minute yet, without provocation, become angry the next minute. They may interrupt their own actions midstream, for example by crawling toward mother and then suddenly freezing with apprehension. It is difficult to estimate the percentage of children in this category, as it has only recently been identified. It seems safe to say that only a small minority of children would be classified as having a disorganized and disoriented attachment.

Teachers of young children, especially those working in daycare and preschool settings, may occasionally want to make inferences about the quality of children's attachment to parents. Teachers can observe how children and their caregivers typically behave toward one another, recognizing, of course, that "bad days" and unusual events may temporarily disrupt normal patterns of interaction in even the most affectionate of families. In the table that follows, we offer some Observation Guidelines that provide clues about the quality of child-caregiver attachments.

Origins of Attachment Security

What factors lead to different patterns of attachment? Research has shown that the quality of the caregiver-child relationship, the cultural setting, and the child's own behavior each plays a role in the patterns that develop.

secure attachment
Attachment classification in which children use attachment figures as a secure base from which to explore and as a source of comfort in times of distress.

insecure-avoidant attachment
Attachment classification in which children appear somewhat indifferent to attachment figures.

insecure-resistant attachment
Attachment classification in which children are preoccupied with their attachment figures but gain little comfort from them when distressed.

disorganized and disoriented attachment
Attachment classification in which children lack a single coherent way of responding to attachment figures.

Assessing Young Children's Security of Attachment

CHARACTERISTIC	LOOK FOR	EXAMPLE	IMPLICATION
Secure Attachment to Caregivers	• Active, intentional exploration of the environment in the presence of the caregiver • Protest at being separated from a caregiver; ability to be soothed when the caregiver returns • Initial wariness of strangers, with subsequent acceptance if reassured by the caregiver	Luis cries when his father drops him off at daycare in the morning. After a few minutes, he settles down and seeks comfort from a familiar and affectionate daycare provider, who appears to be becoming a target of his attachment as well.	It is natural for young children to resist separation from their parents. Help them establish a routine of saying goodbye in the morning, and give them extra attention during this time. Reassure parents by describing children's daily activities and behaviors, and inform them of how long it takes their children to settle into a relaxed routine after their departure. (Oftentimes parents witness a dramatic protest as they say goodbye, but the distress is usually more short-lived than parents realize.)
Insecure-Avoidant Attachment to Caregivers	• Superficial exploration of the environment • Indifference to a caregiver's departure; failure to seek comfort upon the caregiver's return • Apparent discomfort around strangers, but without an active resistance of their overtures	Jennifer walks around her new preschool with a frown on her face. She parts easily with her mother, and after a short time she seems to settle into her new environment. She glances up and smiles briefly when her mother comes at the end of the day, but she doesn't seem particularly happy about her mother's return.	Independence from parents is often a sign of children's familiarity with daycare or preschool settings. If children seem truly at ease with separation, support their relaxed state by welcoming them in the morning, sending them off warmly in the afternoon, and keeping parents informed of their activities. If children instead appear indifferent to their parents, offer special encouragement to the parents, who may be struggling with issues in their own lives and so find it difficult to invest in their children emotionally. In addition, form your own affectionate relationships with children, with the hopes that such support will lead to secure attachments.
Insecure-Resistant Attachment	• Exceptional clinginess and anxiety when with the caregiver • Agitation and distress at the caregiver's departure; continued crying or fussing after the caregiver returns • Apparent fear of strangers; tendency to stay close to the caregiver in a new situation	Irene tightly clutches her mother's skirt as the two enter the preschool building, and she stays close by as mother signs her in for the morning. She is quite upset when her mother leaves yet finds little comfort in mother's return a few hours later.	If insecure-resistant children appear anxious when they enter a new daycare or preschool setting, give them extra time to part with their parents, and perhaps give them a "comfort" object, such as a teddy bear or blanket from home. Be patient and reassuring as you interact with these children, knowing that such children can eventually form a secure attachment to you.
Disorganized and Disoriented Attachment	• Unpredictable emotional responses (e.g., calmness one moment followed by anger the next, without any obvious provocation) • Tendency to approach a caregiver cautiously and with an appearance of uncertainty, as if wary about the kind of response the caregiver will make	Myles seems lost at school. He arrives hungry, walks aimlessly for some time, and eventually sits to play with blocks. He is aggressive with his peers, and his teacher sees bruises on his arms.	Provide special attention and monitoring to students who seem disorganized and disoriented in their attachment. Be on the lookout for signs of abuse, and be ready to seek advice from authorities. Remember that these children are *not* doomed to serious lifelong problems, and work hard to establish positive, trusting relationships with them.

The quality of the relationship between primary caregivers and their children appears to be the factor that most influences attachment. When caregivers are sensitive and responsive to young children, protect them, and provide for their needs, children are inclined to develop secure attachments (Chisholm, 1996; NICHD Early Child Care Research Network, 1997). With a secure attachment in place, they then feel safe enough to get on with other important matters, such as exploring the physical environment and forming social bonds with other adults and children. Less productive forms of attachment appear to be related to other parenting behaviors (Thompson, 1998). Children with insecure attachments often have parents who either have difficulty caring for them or are unwilling to invest energy in them. Such parents may be struggling with serious emotional issues, may have limited financial resources, or may need to spread their attention among many children. Some children—those who are insecure-avoidant—become independent early on and find creative ways to obtain needed care and comfort from others. Other children—those who are insecure-resistant—cling tenaciously to their caregivers, thereby increasing their chances of gaining access to needed resources. Children with disorganized and disoriented attachments may, in many cases, live with people whose behaviors are unpredictable from one occasion to the next; oftentimes these children are the victims of abuse or maltreatment. These children typically approach their parents slowly and cautiously, unsure if they will get an affectionate response or a punitive one.

Although nonsecure attachment patterns are almost certainly adaptive over the short run, they may be counterproductive over the long run. For instance, children who become demanding and clingy may end up with adequate nourishment and care even under extremely impoverished conditions (DeVries & Sameroff, 1984). Yet they may remain excessively dependent on their parents long after they should be establishing some independence, or they may become overly demanding and competitive with other children (Thompson, 1998).

A second factor affecting the nature of children's attachments is the cultural setting in which they live (Rothbaum, Weisz, Pott, Miyake, & Morelli, 2000). Cultures differ appreciably in their emphasis on a close, exclusive relationship between parents and infants. Here are some examples:

- In some studies with Japanese children, a high proportion of the children have shown behaviors that researchers categorize as reflecting insecure-resistant attachment. Many infants in these studies became quite upset when their mothers left the room, perhaps in part because the Japanese emphasis on physical closeness, intimacy, and strong mother-child bonds leaves children unprepared for separation (Miyake, Chen, & Campos, 1985; Takahashi, 1990). Separation from mother is not a common circumstance in Japan; babysitters are rare, and when mothers leave their children, they often seek the assistance of grandparents (Saarni, Mumme, & Campos, 1998).
- Behaviors consistent with an insecure-resistant attachment classification are also fairly common in Israeli kibbutz–raised infants (Sagi & Lewkowicz, 1987). Infants raised on the kibbutz are accustomed to contact with a small group of children and adults. They rarely see strangers, and adults are suspicious of outsiders. A historical record of unexpected terrorist attacks makes security measures a prudent necessity (Saarni et al., 1998). Infants pick up adults' wary feelings toward strangers, and so, when they encounter a stranger in their midst, they understandably withdraw or communicate distress.
- In northern Germany, many infants display behaviors that, on the surface, would seem to indicate an insecure-avoidant attachment (Grossmann, Grossmann, Huber, & Wartner, 1981). These babies do not fret much when their mothers leave the playroom, nor do they move frantically toward mothers when they return. In northern Germany, infants are regularly left at home alone or outside supermarkets as mothers go about their errands. The time alone is not lengthy, but it happens often enough to be routine. These children seem to understand that their mothers will return shortly and that they can get along just fine in the meantime.

Furthermore, many cultural groups in the United States and elsewhere depend on multiple caregivers, such as aunts, uncles, grandparents, and family friends. Distributing responsibility for child care may have an evolutionary function (Dunbar, 1992; Fisher, Jackson, & Villarruel, 1998). More specifically, the human race has evolved in such a way that children reach out to multiple adults in their community, especially when they have lost their mothers to rampant contagious diseases or other uncontrollable circumstances (Meindl, 1992). In essence, then, cross-cultural data support the value of a tight emotional bond between mother and infant, but having other family and community members stand by as backup has obvious survival value.

A third factor affecting the security of children's attachment is the children themselves (you may recall our discussion of *organismic influences* in Chapter 1). It certainly takes two to form an attachment. Accordingly, children help to strengthen their relationship with parents by reciprocating their affection: snuggling up to them, allowing themselves to be comforted, smiling and rubbing their faces, and so on. Children also contribute to their own attachment security through their unique ways of handling stress and relating to parents. While some children kick up quite a fuss when scared, others are less adamant in their protests. Perhaps those who are prone to be fearful, irritable, anxious, and fussy are more difficult to care for and to interact with, whereas those who are more even-tempered and sociable invite positive interactions. Perhaps, too, mismatches between dispositions of parents and those of children make attachments less smooth. However, available research suggests that differences in infants' behaviors play only a minor role in attachment security (Thompson, 1998). Parents are generally able to be sensitive to a wide range of dispositions and ability levels in children; thus, "fussy" or "difficult" babies are not necessarily destined to become insecure children.

Children's attachments to parents or other caregivers provide the foundation for later social-emotional relationships. With healthy attachments in place, children feel secure and fortified to confront the demons and discomforts of everyday life. Yet some children do not seem able to use the adults in their lives as a source of reassurance. In the next section, we consider the long-term effects of secure and insecure attachment.

Developmental Course of Early Social Ties

As children gain experience with their primary caregivers, they begin to form an internal understanding, or *mental representation,* of what relationships with other people are usually like (Bowlby, 1969/1982, 1973; Ryan, Stiller, & Lynch, 1994). Their understanding of "typical" relationships then influences the kinds of relationships they form with other individuals—particularly with other adults, such as teachers (Ryan et al., 1994). If you've ever visited a preschool, perhaps you know what we're talking about. Some children, curious and affectionate, flock to you with books and puzzles in hand, assuming you will want to join them in their chosen activities (we certainly urge you to do so!). In making these social overtures, children convey their expectations: "Unfamiliar adults are interesting people who will like me and care for me." Such a positive expectation is not universal, however, as you might expect from the attachment literature we've reviewed thus far. A few children may look at you suspiciously, not because they're shy, but because they wonder, "Who are you? What do you want from me? What harm might you cause me?"

Generally speaking, early attachment security is associated with positive long-term outcomes. In Western cultures, children who are securely attached in infancy tend to become relatively independent, empathic, socially competent preschoolers, particularly in comparison with children who are insecurely attached (Kestenbaum, Farber, & Sroufe, 1989; Sroufe, 1983; Vaughn, Egeland, Sroufe, & Waters, 1979). In middle childhood and adolescence, they tend to be self-confident, adjust easily to the school environment, establish productive relationships with teachers and peers, and be motivated to do well at classroom tasks (Elicker, Englund, & Sroufe, 1992; Ryan et al., 1994; Shulman, Elicker, & Sroufe, 1994; Sroufe, Carlson, & Schulman, 1993; Urban, Carlson, Egeland, & Sroufe, 1991). It is important to note, however, that not all of these findings apply to children in non-Western cultures. For instance, in Japan, caregivers encourage dependence on others, reservedness, and avoidance of strangers. Thus, for Japanese children, close and affectionate relationships with caregivers are not as likely to lead to independence and sociability (Rothbaum et al., 2000).

At least two factors may be at the root of the positive outcomes of secure attachment. First, parents who are sensitive to their children's needs during infancy usually continue to be affectionate and responsive as their children grow older; in other words, secure attachments evolve into solid, loving relationships. Second, children with secure attachments form positive expectations about other people, and they take these expectations into new relationships. A self-fulfilling element is at work here: Children expect other people to be trustworthy, and they give second chances to those who initially let them down—actions that feed and sustain healthy emotional ties.

Social-emotional well-being is not necessarily set in stone in infancy, however. Initially, attachment theorists suggested that an infant's early attachment to primary caregivers (especially the mother) sets the tone of all future relationships (e.g., Bowlby, 1973). More recently, however, researchers have discovered that infants often form very different, yet perhaps equally potent, attachments to their mothers and fathers (Bridges, Connell, & Belsky, 1988). Furthermore, as youngsters grow older, their attachments to important peers—perhaps to best friends and, eventually, to romantic partners—may be significantly different from those they have previously formed with their parents (Baldwin, Keelan, Fehr, Enns, & Koh-Rangarajoo, 1996; La Guardia, Ryan, Couchman, & Deci, 2000). To some extent, the strength and quality of their attachments to various other individuals depend on how supportive and responsive those individuals are (La Guardia et al., 2000). Apparently, growing children and adolescents form not one, but several mental representations (perhaps in the form of the mental *schemas* and *scripts* described in Chapter 5) of what interpersonal relationships can sometimes be like (Baldwin et al., 1996).

Stressful life events affect the course of children's attachments. For instance, children who initially form secure attachments to caregivers and then later live through one or more traumatic events (perhaps their parents get divorced, a family member dies or suffers a debilitating illness, or they are physically or sexually abused by a family member) may have difficulty forming attachments as adolescents or adults (Lewis, Feiring, & Rosenthal, 2000; Waters, Merrick, Treboux, Crowell, & Albersheim, 2000; Weinfield, Sroufe, & Egeland, 2000). It is important to note, however, that many children and adolescents maintain their ability to form healthy emotional bonds with others *despite* stressful events in their lives. To illustrate, let's return once again to our opening case study. As an infant, Mary formed a secure attachment to each of her parents. A few years later, her mother's behavior became erratic and occasionally abusive, apparently as the result of an emerging mental illness. Mary's attachment to her mother waned ("we're not really close"), but her attachment to her father remained strong ("I feel very close to him"), and she was sociable and well-adjusted at school.

Educational Implications of Attachment Research

As we have seen, attachments formed during infancy provide the foundation for later social relationships. Nevertheless, this foundation can be rebuilt if it's shaky, and it must occasionally be bolstered if, despite a solid beginning, it later disintegrates in the face of adverse circumstances (Thompson, 1998).

In essence, secure attachment is like a multivitamin: It increases the chances of, but does not guarantee, good health. Conversely, a child with an early insecure attachment may, with help and guidance, become a happy, productive adult. The past *and* the present matter in children's well-being. Based on the existing attachment literature, we formulate these recommendations for teachers:

■ *Cultivate strong relationships with young children in your care.* Although parents and other family members are usually the recipients of children's first attachment bonds, young children often form intensely emotional bonds with daycare providers and preschool teachers as well. Furthermore, high-quality attachments in child-care situations can to some extent compensate for poor parenting (Howes & Ritchie, 1998; NICHD Early Child Care Research Network, 1997). Thus, the recipe for good bonding—sensitive, responsive, and reliable care—is applicable in daycare and school settings as well as at home. By providing consistent warmth and support, teachers can give students needed reassurance to stay on—or get on—the path toward social and emotional well-being.

■ *Acknowledge and encourage multiple attachments.* As children grow older and venture out into the world, they gradually increase the number of social-emotional bonds they form. Children may talk about a variety of people in their lives—brothers and sisters, aunts and uncles, grandparents, neighbors—and invite such individuals to parent-teacher conferences, concerts, and school performances. Teachers and school administrators should acknowledge the importance of these people in children's lives and make them feel welcome at school events.

Unfortunately, some students have few if any supportive, affectionate relationships at home. Such students often have less developed social skills than their more "attached" classmates and so may, in many teachers' eyes, be the most difficult students to love. Yet these students are the ones most in need of affectionate relationships with responsible, dependable adults and peers. In our own experiences working with troubled children, we have found that persistence pays off: Although initial overtures are sometimes rebuffed, a regular, ongoing pattern of kindness, attention, and support eventually fosters relationships of trust and affection with children who may not have believed such relationships were possible. Children benefit, too, from learning more appropriate ways of interacting with their peers; we will offer suggestions for teaching such skills in Chapter 13.

■ *Be alert to signs of maltreatment.* We will discuss child abuse more fully in Chapter 12. For the present, simply note that the attachment literature suggests that abused children may show a disorganized and disoriented attachment pattern, including ambivalent responses to parents and nonproductive social behaviors (e.g., social withdrawal, aggression, or frequent expressions of anger). Teachers who notice such behaviors in children may wish to keep their eyes open for other possible indications of a serious family problem.

■ *When appropriate, seek the assistance of experts.* Children who have serious attachment problems often need the help of a professional therapist (Booth & Koller, 1998; Levy & Orlans, 2000). If students seem unwilling or unable to form emotional bonds with others, teachers should consult with a school psychologist or counselor for guidance about how best to meet the students' needs.

Having bonded with family members and other caregivers, children are ready to take on other social-emotional tasks, such as forming productive relationships with teachers and peers and learning how to treat other people fairly and compassionately. To establish and maintain healthy social relationships, children must be able to "read" other people's emotional cues and express their own emotions appropriately. They must also have a meaningful sense of who they are—where they fit into family and social groups, what is distinctive about them as individuals, and where their strengths and limitations lie. These two areas of development are our focus for the remainder of the chapter.

Emotional Development

Emotions (sometimes referred to as *affect*) are the feelings, both physiological and psychological, that people have in response to events that are personally relevant to their needs and goals. Emotional states energize thinking and acting in ways that are often adaptive to the circumstances (Goleman, 1995; Saarni et al., 1998). For example, if you are being chased by a lion, nature instills you with fear so that you can mobilize energy, focus intently on escape, and run furiously to safety. Stopping to think and reflect on the lion's behavior is *not* an adaptive response; immediately feeling scared and fleeing for your life *is*.

What functions do emotions serve in the classroom? Most of the time, physical survival is not at stake (sadly, we can recall a few tragic exceptions making national headlines in recent years). But even in non-life-threatening situations, emotions are important in guiding behavior. In the following vignettes, we examine some basic emotional states and the kinds of adaptive responses that may grow out of them (Saarni et al., 1998).

- *Happiness.* Paul, age 17, chatters and laughs with his friends during his school's end-of-the-year athletic field day. He is happy about having most of the year's schoolwork behind him and looking forward to his summer job and the paychecks it will bring. Happiness helps people to enjoy life and to seek similar pleasurable experiences.
- *Anger.* Aranya, age 14, sits at her desk frowning, her lips tightly pressed together. She is furious that she wasn't admitted into the elective course, "International Events and Conflicts," which she desperately wanted to take. To make matters worse, her two closest friends did get into the class. Aranya is angry with her teacher, who she thinks dislikes her, and with her mother, who lost the enrollment forms and caused a delay in her request for admission.

emotion
Affective response to an event that is personally relevant to one's needs and goals.

Anger helps people deal with obstacles to their goals, often spurring them to try new tactics and exert pressure. Aranya's anger leads her to think about what she can do to change the situation.

- *Fear.* Tony, age 2½, sits on the mat he has brought from home, eyes wide, body tense. He stares at a poster of a clown on the wall of his preschool classroom. He is afraid of clowns and is particularly anxious at nap time, when the lights are dimmed and the blinds are closed. On this particular day, he becomes downright scared; he runs to his teacher and buries his head in her lap. Fear occurs when people feel threatened and believe that their physical safety and psychological well-being are potentially at stake. Fear motivates people to flee, escape from harm, seek reassurance, and perhaps fight back.

- *Sadness.* Greta, age 15, sits quietly on a bench near her locker. With her head hung low, she rereads the letter from a regional cheerleading organization. She has not been admitted to the prestigious cheerleading summer camp. Since she started high school, cheerleading has given her much joy and satisfaction. People are sad when they realize that they cannot attain a desired goal or when they experience a loss, such as a parent dying or a friend moving to a distant city. Sadness often causes people to reassess their goals: Greta realizes that she can remain on the school's cheerleading squad even though she can't go to cheerleading camp. It also provokes others to be nurturing: When Greta's parents and friends see her tears, they realize how much cheerleading means to her and shower her with affection and reassurance.

- *Disgust.* Norton, age 8, peers at the lunch he has just purchased in the school cafeteria. He wrinkles his nose and averts his gaze from the "tuna melt" on his plate. He doesn't like tuna to begin with, and this particular preparation smells way too "fishy" to him. Disgust occurs when people encounter food, smells, and sights that they sense are contaminating to them. What is "disgusting" is partly in the eye of the beholder, and Norton's tuna melt is probably just fine. Nonetheless, having an aversion response is nature's way of getting people to be wary of substances that are *potentially* troublesome.

- *Anxiety.* Kanesha, age 16, has to give an oral report about the industrial revolution in her history class tomorrow. She has read several books on the topic and thinks she knows quite a bit about it. But she is worried that, when she is standing all by herself in front of the class, she might get so nervous that she will forget everything she wants to say. To make sure that she doesn't look "stupid" in front of her teacher and classmates, she writes the most important ideas on several index cards. She plans to give her report from memory, but she will have the cards as a backup in case she needs them. Anxiety often motivates people to behave in ways that increase their chances of success.

- *Shame.* Luke, age 7, is stunned. He's just had an accident, urinating on the floor. He had felt a bit antsy beforehand but wasn't aware that he needed to go to the bathroom. He doesn't know what to do; his pants are wet, and there is a puddle under his chair. Twenty pairs of eyes are glued on him. How embarrassing! When students feel ashamed, they are aware of other people's standards for behavior and know they have violated these standards. The adaptive function of shame is that it motivates students to try harder. In the short run, they may withdraw and avoid others, but in the long run, they are likely to behave more appropriately. Shame works only when it comes from within; teachers should *never* ridicule students in attempts to shame them. Derisive, hurtful comments don't motivate more responsible behavior; they provoke only anger, withdrawal, and escape.

- *Guilt.* A.J., age 12, regrets bad-mouthing his friend Pete to some other classmates. A.J. had thought his friend was "sucking up" to their teacher, but rather than say something to Pete directly, he instead complained to Tom, Noel, and Isaiah. The other boys promptly teased Pete, taunting "Hey, Petey-Wetey! A.J. says you're the teacher's pet!" A.J. sinks down low in his chair, feeling guilty for what he's said behind Pete's back and for the unanticipated repercussions of his remarks. Guilt occurs when people do something—in this case, betray a friend—that violates their own standards. It leads people to right the wrong, to make things better for the person they've hurt. More generally, it causes people to behave in socially appropriate ways that protect others from harm.

- *Pride.* Jacinda, age 5, is beaming. For the last 20 minutes, she's painstakingly pasted sequins, stars, and feathers onto a mask. Her final product is a fanciful, colorful, delicately adorned creation. She is happy with her work, evident from her ear-to-ear grin. Jacinda looks up at the teacher and her classmates, expecting that others will admire the beauty of her mask. People are proud when they earn others' respect and meet their own goals. Pride fosters continued commitment to behaving appropriately and achieving high standards. It also motivates people to share their accomplishments with others.

In the vignettes just presented, each child's emotional state is a natural, immediate response to a personally meaningful event. Happiness, anger, fear, anxiety, and other emotional responses focus children's attention on important aspects of their lives; they also help children develop new ideas, goals, and plans. Emotions are not just means for venting excess energy; instead, they help students redirect their actions and relationships.

Individual Differences in Emotional Responding

Emotionally, children seem to be different from one another even in early infancy. Some infants are fussy and demanding; others, like Mary in our opening case, are cheerful and easy to care for. Some are fearful and anxious; others actively seek novelty and adventure. Some are quiet and shy; others are more sociable and outgoing. Such differences reflect **temperament**—constitutional ways of responding to emotional events and novel stimulation, as well as ways of regulating impulses (Kagan, 1998; Rothbart & Bates, 1998).

Researchers suspect that cultural differences in temperament result partly from differing approaches to parenting. Many Japanese mothers comfort their infants in a very peaceful and soothing manner—an approach that may partly explain a tendency for Japanese children to be quiet and subdued.

Many aspects of temperament, such as cheerfulness, outgoingness, moodiness, and anxiety, probably have a genetic basis; for example, identical twins reared in different homes often have similar personalities (Henderson, 1982; Rothbart & Bates, 1998; Tellegren, Lykken, Bouchard, & Wilcox, 1988). Yet the genetic basis for temperament is best thought of as only a *predisposition* to behave in a certain way. That predisposition is then molded and modified by experience (Thompson, 1998). For example, temperamentally shy children have more opportunities to interact with other children—and thus are more likely to overcome their shyness—if they attend preschool rather than remain at home until kindergarten or first grade.

Furthermore, parents, teachers, and peers may intentionally cultivate certain ways of responding. In other words, children's emotional responses are the targets of **socialization**—systematic efforts by adults, other children, and institutions (e.g., schools and churches) to prepare youngsters to act in ways their society perceives to be appropriate and responsible. Different cultural groups may socialize children differently, in part by encouraging certain kinds of behaviors (Harwood, Miller, & Irizarry, 1995). For instance, among Navajo Native Americans and in many Middle Eastern societies, it is common for adults to swaddle babies, tightly bundling them in wrapped layers of fabric (Whiting, 1981). Swaddling keeps mothers and their infants near one another, makes it easier for mothers to respond to their infants' cries, and helps infants relax and remain calm in noisy environments (Saarni et al., 1998). In mainstream Western societies, swaddling is not commonly practiced, as many adults believe it engenders passivity. As another example, Japanese parents do much to keep their babies pacified and quiet, in part out of regard for a cultural ideal of harmony and in part out of consideration for neighbors who live on the other side of thin walls. Japanese mothers therefore talk infrequently, speak softly, and gently stroke their babies (Miyake, Campos, Kagan, & Bradshaw, 1986). In contrast, American mothers talk to their infants frequently, often in an expressive and evocative manner, perhaps in an effort to stimulate cognitive development or strengthen the caregiver-infant relationship (e.g., Trainor, Austin, & Desjardins, 2000).

Research on temperamental characteristics suggests some stability over time, such that we can, to some degree, predict children's later personality characteristics and social behaviors from their earlier ones (Caspi, 1998; Kagan, 1998; Rothbart & Bates, 1998). For example, children who are inhibited and fearful as toddlers and preschoolers also tend to become fairly anxious adolescents and adults (Caspi, 1998). Children who freely show negative affect (e.g., irritability, fussiness, frequent anger) in the early years are more likely

temperament
Constitutional ways of responding to emotional events and novel stimulation, and of regulating impulses.

socialization
Systematic efforts by other people and by institutions to prepare youngsters to act in ways deemed by society to be appropriate and responsible.

to show negative affect (e.g., depression, anxiety, aggression) later in life (Caspi, 1998). Such stability is undoubtedly due both to genetic factors and to ongoing, persistent characteristics in children's social environments.

Developmental Changes in Emotional Functioning

As children grow older, they acquire a broader range of emotions; they also become increasingly aware of their own and others' feelings. More specifically, their emotional development is characterized by the following trends:

■ *Children become increasingly sophisticated interpreters of emotions.* From the early days of infancy, children respond to emotional states in others. If you've ever visited an infant daycare center, you may have noticed the **emotional contagion** of babies: When one starts crying, others soon join in with tears of their own (Hatfield, Cacioppo, & Rapson, 1994). In the first year or two of life, children also show the ability to monitor the emotions of others, particularly parents and trusted caregivers. Children who engage in **social referencing** watch their parents' faces, especially in the presence of a novel or puzzling phenomenon (Boccia & Campos, 1989; Sorce, Emde, Campos, & Klinnert, 1985). Creeping to a stand in a slippery bathtub, a toddler may quickly sit when she sees the horrified expression on Mommy's face. Likewise, this same toddler may glance at Daddy's face when a new babysitter enters the house: Is the stranger trustworthy? How does Daddy react to her? Does he seem to recognize her? Is he smiling or frowning?

With age, children become increasingly adept at "reading" people's facial expressions. For instance, when her sons Alex and Connor were 5 and 13, respectively, Teresa asked them to draw pictures of faces showing various emotional expressions. Although she had to give Alex examples of circumstances that might provoke feelings of being "ashamed" and "guilty," both boys found the task to be an easy one. Their drawings, shown in Figure 9–1, indicate clear differentiations among facial expressions that reflect such negative emotions as anger, sadness, fear, disgust, and guilt.

As children grow older, they also become more thoughtful about emotions. As early as age 2 or 3, they talk about emotional states that they and others experience ("Daniel got mad and pushed me"), and they realize that emotions are connected to people's desires ("I'm angry that Kurt ate the last cookie") (Bretherton, Fritz, Zahn-Waxler, & Ridgeway, 1986; Dunn, Bretherton, & Munn, 1987; Wellman, Harris, Banerjee, & Sinclair, 1995). By middle childhood, they realize that their thoughts and interpretations determine how they feel about a particular situation and that other people have different interpretations and, as a result, different feelings ("Arlene feels bad because she thinks I don't like her") (Harris, 1989).

By the upper elementary grades, children begin to realize that emotional expressions do not always reflect people's true feelings (Selman, 1980). For instance, a 9-year-old may observe the smile and cheerful demeanor of his teacher yet know that this teacher just lost her brother to cancer and so is probably very sad. Finally, during the end of middle childhood and the beginning of adolescence, children appreciate that people can have ambivalent feelings toward people and events (Donaldson & Westerman, 1986; Harter & Whitesell, 1989). For instance, a 12-year-old girl may love her father but be angry at him for moving out of the house when her parents divorced; she may like going to see him during custodial visits but not like the feelings of turmoil these visits provoke in her.

■ *Children expand their repertoire of basic emotions to include self-conscious emotions.* Infants seem to be born with a full arsenal of emotional states. Anger, fear, happiness, and disgust are evident from the first days of life; an ability to detect basic emotions in others is present in infancy as well (Caron, Caron, & MacLean, 1988; Emde, Gaensbauer, & Harmon, 1976; Haviland & Lelwica, 1987; Hiatt, Campos, & Emde, 1979; Schwarz, Izard, & Ansul, 1985; Stenberg & Campos, 1990). By preschool age, children also show evidence of **self-conscious emotions,** affective states that reflect awareness of social standards and other people's concerns about adherence to these standards (Lewis, 1993, 1995). Self-conscious emotions include guilt, shame, embarrassment, and pride. Teresa recalls early displays of guilt and shame in both of her sons. As toddlers and preschoolers, the boys would often respond angrily when a misbehavior resulted in their being sent to their rooms or having a privilege taken away. Occa-

emotional contagion
Tendency for infants to cry spontaneously when they hear other infants crying.

social referencing
Observing emotional cues of others and using such cues to interpret the possible implications of an event for oneself.

self-conscious emotion
Affective state that reflects awareness of a community's social standards (e.g., pride, guilt, shame).

FIGURE 9–1 Drawings of basic emotional expressions by Alex (age 5) and Connor (age 13)

sionally they'd swat at her or stomp out of the room in a snit. However, they'd return a few minutes later, scrutinizing her face for signs of sadness and affectionately rubbing her arm as they apologized for their misdeeds.

■ *Children and adolescents gradually learn to regulate their emotions.* **Emotional regulation** (also called *coping*) refers to the strategies children use to manage stressful situations (Brenner & Salovey, 1997). As children grow older, experience a breadth of emotionally significant events, and observe the role models around them, they acquire an increasing number of coping strategies for dealing with difficult situations (Saarni et al., 1998). As an example, they may observe their parents controlling their anger physically yet expressing it verbally: "I'm angry that you said you were going to make dinner and didn't keep your commitment!" They may then use a similar strategy in dealing with peer conflicts: "You said you would meet me at four o'clock but you never showed up. Where *were* you?!" Youngsters who appropriately control and express their emotions are those most likely to be popular with their peers (Fabes et al., 1999).

Children also become better able to appraise the advantages and disadvantages of particular coping strategies. For instance, a 14-year-old may observe a best friend becoming entangled in a fight or an intoxicated neighbor heading for her car with keys in hand; in such circumstances, the teenager quickly identifies a range of possible solutions and considers the potential benefits and risks of each one. As children and adolescents evaluate the various

emotional regulation
Using strategies to manage responses to stressful events (also called *coping*).

Emotional Development | **329**

Despite gains in emotional regulation, adolescents can be more emotionally volatile than younger children, in part because they feel self-conscious about their changing bodies, develop more complex relationships with peers, and have increasing responsibilities both during and after school.

strategies they might use, they seek the social support of others, perhaps by soliciting direct assistance or perhaps by presenting themselves in ways that will gain others' sympathy. In general, younger children are more inclined to go to adults (especially parents, other family members, and teachers) for help and guidance, whereas older children and adolescents are more likely to seek the support of peers (Rossman, 1992).

Sometimes children's appraisals of emotionally charged events enable them to deal directly with a problem—for instance, by confronting a peer. At other times, when they cannot change the situation, they instead try to deal with their emotions. For example, a child might alleviate his anxiety about an upcoming test by reminding himself that he has done well in the past on such examinations.

A final component of emotional regulation is determining when to express emotions publicly. Children gradually learn to curb their emotional reactions to protect themselves and other people (Cole, 1986). For example, many preschoolers realize that they should not reveal their true feelings when disappointed by a gift from a well-meaning relative. They instead conceal their disappointment with a big "thank you," realizing that the relative had good intentions and might be hurt by a more honest reaction ("Does she *really* think I'd wear that hat?").

In the opening case study, Mary had several strategies for coping with troubling events. She entered new situations cautiously, trying to gather more information before committing herself to a particular course of action. She shied away from open conflicts with others, and she kept her distance from her overly critical and punitive mother. As Mary grew older, she became able to put herself in her mother's shoes—for instance, by realizing that her mother was probably lonely and may have been in the midst of early menopause—and this strategy may have made her relationship with mother more tolerable.

■ *Adolescence brings new anxieties and pressures.* Adolescents tend to be more emotionally volatile than younger children: They more often report feeling lonely, embarrassed, or anxious, and they have more extreme mood swings (Arnett, 1999). The hormonal changes that accompany puberty may account for some of this volatility, but environmental factors probably have a more significant effect (Arnett, 1999).

Adolescence ushers in many new situations and problems that children haven't encountered before. As young teenagers undergo rapid, uncontrollable physical changes, they may feel self-conscious and awkward, perhaps even alienated from their own bodies (Rudlin, 1993). As they grow more independent, they may find their own needs and desires conflicting with those of their parents and other authority figures (Arnett, 1999). As peer relationships become more important, their interpersonal problems become an increasing source of anxiety and inner turmoil. School provides additional pressures: Worries about completing homework, getting along with teachers, achieving good grades, and "fitting in" with classmates are common sources of concern for secondary school students (Phelan, Yu, & Davidson, 1994). All of these factors come into play for even the most "normal" of adolescents, but some have additional challenges—perhaps living in poverty, experiencing ongoing family conflict, or being abused by a family member—that they must deal with (Cicchetti & Toth, 1998; Rutter & Garmezy, 1983).

Not surprisingly, then, many (though by no means all) adolescents perceive their lives as being quite stressful, particularly in highly developed Western countries (Arnett, 1999; Masten, Neemann, & Andenas, 1994). They may turn to their peers for understanding and guidance, or perhaps for distraction from their troubles. They may also express their frustrations through poetry and art. For example, early in his senior year of high school, 17-year-old Jeff felt "locked in" by the combined pressures of a demanding course load, impending due dates for college applications, and his role as confidant for several troubled friends. Late one night, he put his schoolwork aside to create the picture shown in Figure 9–2. Because he had trouble drawing human figures, he combined two favorite things—a soft drink and black-and-white cow hide—to represent himself. As you can see, a cage and gigantic boulder hold him in, and so he cannot join in as his peers (represented by other soft drink cans) frolic freely in the distance.

Some adolescents believe that the problems they face exceed their capabilities to cope effectively (Masten et al., 1994). The sad result is that suicide is more common in adolescence than in the earlier years (Durkin, 1995).

Group Differences in Emotional Responding

All children show developmental progression in the expression and control of their emotions. To some degree, their developmental pathways are influenced by their group membership—by their gender, their culture, and their socioeconomic status.

Gender Differences On average, male and female babies tend to be similar in temperament; any gender differences in infancy are subtle and situation-dependent (Eisenberg, Martin, & Fabes, 1996). After the age of 2, however, consistent gender differences begin to emerge. For instance, boys show more anger than girls beginning in the preschool years, and girls more often report feeling sad, fearful, or guilty beginning in the elementary grades (Eisenberg et al., 1996). Girls also respond more negatively to their failures, to the point where their subsequent performance may suffer (Dweck, 1986). As early as elementary school, boys begin to hide their true feelings, oftentimes even from themselves (Eisenberg et al., 1996; Sadker & Sadker, 1994).

Biology may be the source of some gender differences in emotions; for instance, rising hormonal levels at puberty are associated with increases in moodiness and depression in girls, but with aggressiveness and rebelliousness in boys (Buchanan, Eccles, & Becker, 1992; Susman, Inoff-Germain et al., 1987). Yet many theorists suspect that differences in socialization are a more significant cause of gender differences in emotional responding (Durkin, 1995; Eisenberg et al., 1996; Sadker & Sadker, 1994). For instance, parents are more likely to discourage overt anger in daughters than in sons (Birnbaum & Croll, 1984; Malatesta & Haviland, 1982). Parents are apt to discourage sons from expressing emotions yet may encourage daughters to talk about how they are feeling (Block, 1979; Eisenberg et al., 1996). At school, many teachers seem to prefer the passive, compliant nature that girls are more likely to exhibit (Bennett, Gottesman, Rock, & Cerullo, 1993; Pollack, 1998). Witness Pollack's (1998) observations of a fourth-grade classroom:[2]

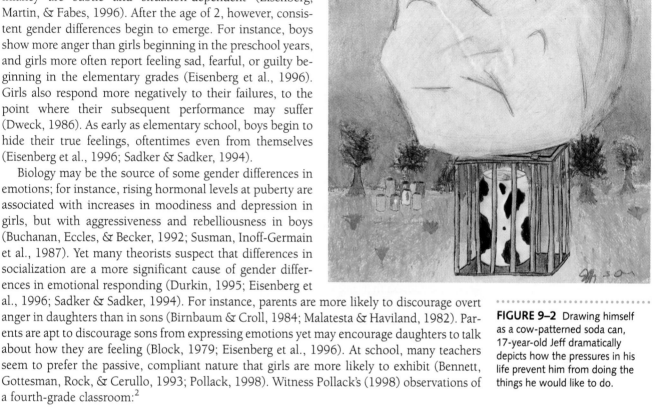

FIGURE 9–2 Drawing himself as a cow-patterned soda can, 17-year-old Jeff dramatically depicts how the pressures in his life prevent him from doing the things he would like to do.

> [O]n several occasions I had observed the fourth-grade class of Ms. Callahan. She was particularly skillful, modern, and warm in her approach, universally beloved by her students. I have every reason to believe that Ms. Callahan was a teacher who would want both boys and girls to derive all they could from the classroom experience.
>
> On this visit, some boys and girls who had been organized into "teams" were working together on a writing project about friendship. Adult volunteers were consultants for these teams and were helping them with their computer skills. I was surprised to see that instead of focusing on the writing project, Ms. Callahan's attention was almost entirely taken up by disciplining the boys. Several lively boys were making a commotion in one corner near the computer. Ms. Callahan cautioned them about making too much noise, and told them to return to their desks and wait their turns. With long faces, the boys meandered across the room and slumped into their seats. A moment later one of the boys could not resist calling out about something. Ms. Callahan gave him a stern second warning. "I don't want to have to caution you again," Ms. Callahan said. "If I do, you're heading for the principal's office."
>
> I had observed the class before, and now I noticed that two of the more creative male students—Robert and Shawn—were not in evidence. I asked Ms. Callahan if they were sick that day.
>
> "No," she explained. "Robert is too excitable for the group process. He's working on an entirely different project." She pointed him out—sitting alone on the floor, tucked out of view, banished from the team endeavor.

---

[2]From *Real Boys: Rescuing Our Sons from the Myths of Boyhood* by William Pollack, copyright © 1998 by William Pollack. Used by permission of Random House, Inc.

"And where's Shawn?" I inquired.

"He was telling inappropriate jokes about Albert Einstein earlier in the day and distracting the entire class. So, he's sitting outside working on his spelling," Ms. Callahan sighed. "Some kids just seem unable to fit into this more quiet team-based teaching."

I wish I had asked her what those jokes about Albert Einstein were, but I was too concerned about her attitude toward these boys. She clearly felt that they could not "fit in" and that they were "unable" to participate appropriately, when I knew (as she did) that these were bright boys with a lot to offer. Although I doubt that Ms. Callahan would agree, I think the prevailing method in class that day was structured around the way girl students prefer to work, and that boys were at a disadvantage. (pp. 240–241)

Cultural Differences Earlier we suggested that temperamental differences in infants may be partly a function of how parents in different cultures care for and respond to their babies. Cultural differences in socialization practices continue throughout childhood and adolescence, resulting in noticeable differences in emotional responding. For instance, in China and Japan, many children are raised to be shy and restrained, whereas in Zambia, smiling and sociability are apt to be the norm (Chen, Rubin, & Sun, 1992; Hale-Benson, 1986; Ho, 1986, 1994; Rothbaum et al., 2000). Many Mexican American parents encourage obedience rather than self-assertiveness (Trawick-Smith, 2000). Girls in India are more likely than British girls to be deferential and controlled, and to hide negative feelings such as anger and sadness, especially in the presence of adults (Joshi & MacLean, 1994).

Socioeconomic Differences Children from lower-income families are more prone to emotional difficulties than children from middle-income families (Caspi, Taylor, Moffitt, & Plomin, 2000; McLoyd, 1998a). Environmental factors are almost certainly to blame for the major portion of these differences. Children living in impoverished circumstances have more than their share of reasons to feel sad, fearful, and angry; for instance, they may not know where their next meal is coming from, and they are more likely to encounter violence and drug addiction in their neighborhoods. Their parents have limited resources (and perhaps limited energy) to address their needs and may apply inconsistent and unpredictable nurturance and discipline (McLoyd, 1998a). Furthermore, many children from low-income backgrounds, particularly those with a history of learning problems, have few if any positive interactions with teachers at school (Clark, 1983).

Teachers, in fact, are in a strategic position to ensure that much goes *right,* rather than wrong, in children's lives. We now consider some strategies that teachers can use to promote their students' emotional development.

Promoting Emotional Development in the Classroom

Emotions are an important part of classroom dynamics, yet many educators are uneasy about how to deal with them, as Sylvester (1995) lamented:

> [W]e know emotion is very important to the educative process because it drives attention, which drives learning and memory. We've never really understood emotion, however, and so don't know how to regulate it in school—beyond defining too much or too little of it as misbehavior and relegating most of it to the arts, PE, recess, and the extracurricular program. (Sylvester, 1995, p. 2)

We propose that teachers can perhaps best promote emotional development if they consider emotional reactions, interpretations, and regulation as *competencies*—that is, as valuable skills that can improve over time. Indeed, some theorists have argued that the ability to interpret and use emotions effectively is a kind of "intelligence" (Bodine & Crawford, 1999; Gardner, 1983; Goleman, 1995). In Chapter 6, we defined intelligence as "the ability to benefit from experiences and thereby modify future behaviors in order to accomplish new tasks successfully." This definition has a practical ring to it: It is action-oriented and conveys the importance of learning from everyday experience. Emotions are clearly action-oriented in that, as we've previously noted, they guide behavior toward personally relevant needs and goals.

People certainly differ from one another in how insightful they are about their own and other individuals' emotions. We invite you to think about "smart" people you know who often do not-so-smart things. Perhaps you can think of academically "bright" classmates who seem to be clueless about other people's thoughts and feelings, insult others without knowing it, and in other ways undermine every attempt to establish productive interpersonal relationships. Smart? In some areas of life, definitely, but in other areas they seem to lack essential skills.

How can emotional competencies be cultivated in the classroom? We offer the following suggestions:

■ *Create an atmosphere of warmth, acceptance, and trust.* Students learn and perform more successfully when they have positive emotions—for instance, when they feel secure, happy, and excited about the subject matter (Boekaert, 1993; Isen, Daubman, & Gorgoglione, 1987; Oatley & Nundy, 1996). And they are more likely to confide in a teacher about troublesome issues if they know that the teacher will continue to like and respect them no matter what they may reveal about themselves in heart-to-heart conversations.

■ *Encourage students to express their feelings.* Children and adolescents can better deal with their feelings when they are aware of what their feelings *are.* Some teachers successfully incorporate discussions about feelings into everyday classroom routines. For example, when Teresa's son Connor was in first grade, his teacher ended each day with "circle time." She asked the children to hold hands and communicate how they felt about their day: one squeeze for happy, two squeezes for sad, three squeezes for bored, and so on. They took turns, and without words, these young students communicated how they felt to their partners, and to the rest of the class, with all eyes glued on the single hand doing the squeezing at the moment. This simple exercise gave the children a chance to reflect on, and then communicate, their basic emotional states.

Some students may, for a variety of reasons, be reluctant to share their feelings so publicly. In such cases, writing about them, perhaps in essays or journals shared only with the teacher, can provide a more confidential alternative. In the essay in Figure 9–3, 10-year-old

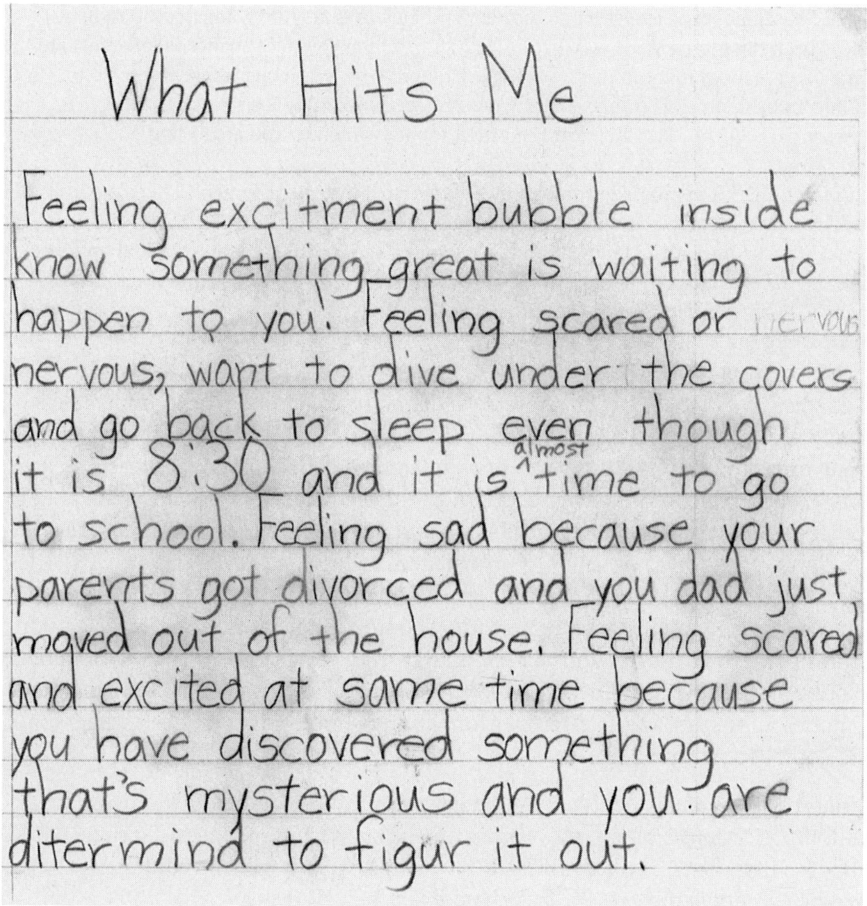

> What Hits Me
>
> Feeling excitment bubble inside know something great is waiting to happen to you. Feeling scared or nervous nervous, want to dive under the covers and go back to sleep even though it is 8:30 and it is almost time to go to school. Feeling sad because your parents got divorced and you dad just moved out of the house. Feeling scared and excited at same time because you have discovered something that's mysterious and you are ditermind to figur it out.

FIGURE 9–3 In this "What Hits Me" essay, 10-year-old Shea describes her experiences with various emotions.

FIGURE 9–4 In this journal entry, 8-year-old Noah reveals his sadness about his parents' recent divorce.

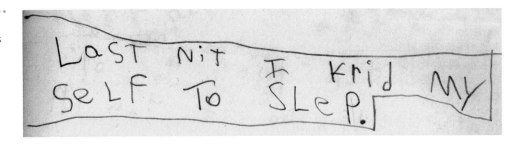

Last Nit I krid My self To Slep.

Shea describes her growing awareness of the various emotions she experiences. In the journal entry in Figure 9–4, 8-year-old Noah—ordinarily a happy, energetic student—reveals how upset he is about his parents' divorce.

■ *Help students become astute observers of others' emotional cues.* Children and adolescents are more successful in their interpersonal relationships when they learn to pick up on the subtle cues that reveal other people's emotional states. As an example, the following classroom discussion between the teacher (T) and various children (C) took place in a third-grade art lesson. The class was beginning to consider possible ways of capturing people's facial expressions on paper.

T: Have you ever noticed that people's faces change depending on how they are feeling?
C: When my mom is mad, her eyes get real skinny and her mouth closes up tight.
C: I can tell when my grandmother is really happy, because her face goes all soft looking.
T: What parts of our faces are important for showing how we feel? Which parts change? How do those parts change?
C: When my little brother gets surprised, his mouth just drops wide open.
C: When I'm scared, my eyes get much rounder and look as if they are going to drop right out.
T: You've been describing some very strong feelings in which your face changes a lot. What are some other feelings that can make your face change? How can it change? . . .
C: If I'm confused, my eyes squint, and my mouth feels all wrinkly.
T: So what parts of your face are most important for showing how you are feeling?
C: Eyes. Mouth.
C: But sometimes if I'm puzzled, my eyebrows go crooked instead of straight.
C: And when my sister smells something bad, her nose twitches. . . .
T: Here are some mirrors. Let's try to imagine some of the feelings we talked about and see how our faces change. Try out two or three very different feelings. How do your eyes change? What happens to your mouth? Do other parts of your face change too? (Smith et al., 1998, pp. 71–72)

■ *Discuss emotions of the characters you study in literature and history.* The innumerable stories that students encounter in the classroom—whether the stories are fiction or nonfiction—provide many opportunities for students to draw inferences about emotional states. We have found in our own experience that even children in the elementary grades are quite able to draw inferences about characters' emotional states and to speculate about how various emotions led to particular courses of action. For instance, in *Frog and Toad Are Friends* (Lobel, 1979), a book for 4- to 8-year-olds, Frog waits impatiently to play with his hibernating friend, Toad, and plays a trick on him to get him up early. The story provides a forum for discussions about friendships, feeling tricked and teased, and sharing feelings with friends (Solomon, Watson, Battistich, Schaps, & Delucchi, 1992). Similarly, the study of history yields many tales of inequities, hostilities, and societal transformations—good fodder for discussions about feelings and coping.

■ *Take cultural differences into account.* As we have seen, some cultures encourage open expression of feelings, whereas others actively *discourage* such expressiveness. Teachers working with children from diverse cultures must continually be mindful of such differences when interpreting the emotional displays (or lack thereof) of their students.

■ *Help students keep their anxiety at a manageable level.* **Anxiety** is an emotional state characterized by worry and apprehension, often about future events with unknown outcomes. Almost all of us feel anxious at one time or another, perhaps when we are performing in public or taking an important test. In such situations, we may experience such physiological symptoms as muscle tension and headaches and may have trouble concentrating on and remembering important information.

Small amounts of anxiety are often beneficial. For instance, anxiety can spur students to take action to make sure undesirable events (e.g., looking "stupid" in front of classmates) don't happen. But many children and adolescents sometimes become excessively anxious, especially when they are taking tests, speaking in public, or in other ways subjecting themselves to the potential evaluation of others.

Teachers can do a variety of things to keep anxiety at a manageable level. For instance, when they assign oral reports, they can encourage students to create index cards or other memory "crutches." Before giving an important test (such as the standardized tests that many school districts require), they can administer a practice test that gives students a general idea of what to expect. And teachers should make sure that in their own classrooms, no single assessment is so important that a student's ultimate success or failure depends on it.

Teachers can serve as exemplary models for staying calm in stressful situations, and they can help relieve students' anxiety by talking through problems in a warm and supportive manner.

■ *Model appropriate ways of dealing with negative emotions.* Students often struggle with how to deal with anger, fear, and sadness and can certainly benefit from seeing adults express their emotions appropriately. Teresa vividly remembers how her fifth-grade teacher expressed anger: Rather than raise her voice, she lowered it to a whisper. Her approach worked quite well: Students sensed her anger and disappointment, responded with concern and guilt, and tried to make amends for their misdeeds. Teachers can enhance the benefits of modeling controlled, honest emotional reactions by explaining what they're doing: "I'm really angry now. Let's talk this out when we've both calmed down"; "I can't believe the School Board cut our budget for new science equipment. I'm going to give the Board a piece of my mind . . . *after* I compose myself."

Some children have such strong emotions that simply talking about feelings and modeling appropriate ways of coping will have limited, if any, effect. We now look at serious emotional problems that some children and adolescents have, as well as at strategies that teachers can use in such situations.

Emotional Problems in Children and Adolescents

In the opening case study, Mary's mother suffered from an "emotional disturbance." Moods fluctuate for everyone—adults and children alike—but some people have more than their share of negative emotional experiences, to the point where such experiences disrupt the quality of their lives and their ability to tackle everyday problems and developmental tasks.

Some emotional problems are manifested in **externalizing behaviors,** behaviors that have direct or indirect effects on other people; examples are aggression, destructiveness, lying, stealing, defiance, and lack of self-control. Others are manifested in **internalizing behaviors,** behaviors that typically affect only the individual who has the problem; examples are depression, anxiety, withdrawal from social interaction, eating disorders, and suicidal tendencies. When distressed, boys are more likely to display externalizing behaviors, such as aggression and destructiveness; girls are more likely to develop internalizing disorders, such as depression and anxiety (Rutter & Garmezy, 1983). Although students with externalizing behaviors are more likely to be referred by teachers for evaluation and possible special services (Kerr & Nelson, 1989), students with internalizing behaviors are often at just as much risk for school failure.

Many emotional problems are believed to result from environmental factors, such as child abuse, inconsistent parenting practices, stressful living conditions, exposure to violence, and family drug or alcohol abuse (Johnson & Friesen, 1993; Patterson, DeBaryshe, & Ramsey, 1989; Shaffer, 1988). At the same time, biological causes, such as heredity,

anxiety
Emotional state characterized by worry and apprehension.

externalizing behavior
Undesirable emotion, behavior, or a combination that affects other people (e.g., aggression, stealing, lack of self-control).

internalizing behavior
Undesirable emotion, behavior, or a combination that primarily affects oneself (e.g., depression, social withdrawal, and suicidal tendencies).

chemical imbalances, brain injuries, and illnesses, may also contribute to emotional and behavioral problems (Hallowell, 1996; Johnson & Friesen, 1993). Overall, it appears that no single factor—biological, psychological, or environmental—accounts for the emergence of serious emotional difficulties, except in extreme conditions (Cicchetti & Toth, 1998). Rather, nature and nurture interact to create problematic emotional conditions for a particular child in a particular cultural setting.

Three emotional-behavioral disorders are fairly common in children and adolescents: depression, anxiety disorder, and conduct disorder. We look at each of these conditions and then formulate some general recommendations for working with students who have ongoing emotional problems.

Depression   People with **depression** feel exceptionally sad, discouraged, and hopeless: they may also feel restless, sluggish, helpless, worthless, or guilty (American Psychiatric Association, 1994; Seligman, 1991). Seriously depressed individuals may have trouble concentrating, lose interest in their usual activities, have little appetite, and have difficulty sleeping (American Psychiatric Association, 1994; Hertel, 1994). In children and adolescents, irritability may be more evident than sadness. Other common characteristics of depression in young people include complaints about physical pain, withdrawal from social relationships, significant substance abuse, and talk of suicide. In a variation of depression, **bipolar disorder** (also known as *manic-depression*), individuals experience periods of extreme elation (*mania*) as well as periods of deep depression.

The specific symptoms of depression vary somewhat from culture to culture. The American Psychiatric Association provides several examples of how depression might manifest itself in different cultures:

> Complaints of "nerves" and headaches (in Latino and Mediterranean cultures), of weakness, tiredness, or "imbalance" (in Chinese and Asian cultures), of problems of the "heart" (in Middle Eastern cultures), or of being "heartbroken" (among Hopi). (American Psychiatric Association, 1994, p. 324)

Many instances of depression and bipolar disorder probably have biological, and possibly genetic, roots (Cicchetti, Rogosch, & Toth, 1997; Griswold & Pessar, 2000). These conditions tend to run in families, are often foreshadowed by temperamental moodiness and insecure attachment, and may reflect chemical imbalances (Cicchetti et al., 1997; Griswold & Pessar, 2000). Yet environmental factors often play a role as well; for instance, the death of a loved one, mental illness or marital conflict in parents, child maltreatment, poverty, inadequate schools, and negative social relationships may bring about or exacerbate depressive symptoms (Cicchetti et al., 1997). When individuals yield to extreme stress with a depressive episode, the event may alter their neurological chemistry, making it more likely for them to suffer another depressive episode in the future (Akiskal & McKinney, 1973; Antelman & Caggiula, 1977; Siever & Davis, 1985).

Before adolescence, depression and bipolar disorder are relatively rare. Their prevalence increases during adolescence; for instance, 5% to 10% of teenagers have one or more major depressive episodes (Cicchetti et al., 1997). During childhood, depression rates are approximately equal for boys and girls, but by age 16, rates are considerably higher for girls than for boys, perhaps because girls are more likely to think about and dwell on their problems (Cicchetti et al., 1997; Eisenberg et al., 1996; Nolen-Hoeksema, 1987).

How might depression emerge in the life of a child? Let's consider Billy, a 5-year-old boy who's just entered kindergarten. His single mother suffers from depression and seems inconsistent in her gestures of affection. She occasionally gives in to his persistent demands, but at other times she vacillates between indifference and anger. When Billy first comes to school, he clings to his mother and is anxious about separating from her. When she does leave, he seems irritable and tired, and he has trouble focusing on activities and interacting with peers. He is not diagnosed with depression for another 10 years, when he shows more classic symptoms—missing school, sleeping irregularly, abusing alcohol, and forecasting his own death to the few friends he has. Billy exemplifies some of the internal vulnerability factors for depression: a possible genetic predisposition (inherited from his mother), uneven temperament, and insecure attachment.

depression
Emotional condition characterized by significant sadness, discouragement, and hopelessness.

bipolar disorder
Condition characterized by cyclical mood swings, including periods of elation (mania) and periods of deep depression.

Suicide is an ever-present risk for youth with serious depression or bipolar disorder. Depressed individuals who contemplate suicide often believe that they face problems they cannot solve or have extreme emotional pain that they wish to end (Miller, 1994). Approximately 15% of individuals with a major depressive disorder die by their own hand (American Psychiatric Association, 1994).

The overwhelming despair and high frequency of suicide that characterize depression make it a condition that educators must take seriously. Through their daily contact with students, teachers have numerous opportunities to observe fluctuations in mood and performance and so are often in a position to spot cases of possible depression in students. (Friends and family, though they may have closer ties to students, may not comprehend how serious a problem is or may possibly even deny its existence.) Teachers will want to offer emotional reassurance to students who appear troubled, but they should consult with principals and school counselors if they suspect serious depression or related emotional disturbance.

Anxiety Disorders In its milder forms, anxiety is a common and very "normal" emotion. But some people, including some children and adolescents, worry excessively and find it difficult to control their worrisome thoughts and feelings; in other words, they have an **anxiety disorder** (American Psychiatric Association, 1994). Children with a *generalized anxiety disorder* tend to worry excessively about a wide variety of things—perhaps including their academic achievement, their performance in sports, and potential catastrophic events such as wars or hurricanes. Some individuals have more specific anxiety disorders—perhaps worrying excessively about gaining weight, having a serious illness, being away from family and home, or feeling embarrassed in public (American Psychiatric Association, 1994).

Anxiety as a trait does tend to run in families, and individuals with anxiety disorders also tend to have biological relatives with other affective disorders, such as major depression (American Psychiatric Association, 1994; Last, Hersen, Kazdin, Francis, & Grubb, 1987). Furthermore, children with anxiety disorders are themselves more susceptible to other emotional difficulties, such as serious depression (Mattison, 1992). There are hints in the research that family environment may play a role in the onset of anxiety disorders, but more investigation is needed in this area (Famularo, Kinscherff, & Fenton, 1992; Mattison, 1992).

Conduct Disorder When children and adolescents display a chronic pattern of externalizing behaviors, they are sometimes identified as having a **conduct disorder.** Youngsters who display a conduct disorder ignore the rights of others in ways that are unusual for their age. Common symptoms include aggression to people and animals (e.g., initiating physical fights, forcing someone into sexual activity, torturing animals), destruction of property (e.g., setting fires, painting graffiti), theft and deceitfulness (e.g., breaking into cars, lying about shoplifting so as not to be caught), and serious violations of rules (e.g., ignoring reasonable curfews, being truant from school) (American Psychiatric Association, 1994).

One or two antisocial acts do not necessarily indicate a serious emotional problem. Conduct disorders are more than a matter of "kids being kids" or "sowing wild oats." Instead, they represent deep-seated and persistent disregard for the rights and feelings of others, as reflected in a *consistent* pattern of antisocial behavior, often beginning in the early elementary years. Youth with conduct disorder tend to see the world through conflict-colored glasses, for example by always assuming that others have hostile intentions toward them (Crick & Dodge, 1994).

Approximately 2% to 6% of school-age youth could be classified as having conduct disorder, with the rates being three or four times higher for boys than for girls (Kazdin, 1997). Particular manifestations of conduct disorder also vary by gender: Boys are more likely to engage in theft and aggression, whereas girls are apt to engage in sexual misbehavior. When boys and girls exhibit conduct disorders in childhood and adolescence, they are also likely to have problems in adulthood, including antisocial behavior and criminal behavior, frequent changes in employment, high divorce rates, little participation in families and community groups, and early death (Kazdin, 1997).

As is true for the emotional disorders we've previously considered, biology may be partly to blame for conduct disorders; for instance, children and adolescents with conduct disorders may have difficulty inhibiting aggressive impulses, perhaps as a result of brain damage

anxiety disorder
Chronic emotional condition characterized by excessive, debilitating worry.

conduct disorder
Chronic emotional condition characterized by lack of concern for the rights of others.

or other neurological abnormalities (Dempster & Corkill, 1999; Gladwell, 1997; Kazdin, 1997). Family environments may be influential as well: Conduct disorders are more common when children's parents provide little love and affection, are highly critical, and unpredictably administer harsh physical punishment (Blackson et al., 1999; DeKlynen, Speltz, & Greenberg, 1998; Kazdin, 1997; Patterson et al., 1989; Webster-Stratton & Hammond, 1999). School environments may further contribute to the problem. Conduct disorders are more frequently observed in situations where teachers have low expectations for students, provide little encouragement or praise for schoolwork, and put little effort into planning lessons (Kazdin, 1997).

Working with Students Who Have Serious Emotional Problems Effective educational programs for students with emotional disorders are usually individualized and tailored to the unique needs of each student. Without such adaptations, schools are difficult places for students with serious emotional problems. As a telling statistic, less than half of these students graduate from high school (Bassett et al., 1996; Koyanagi & Gaines, 1993). Teachers should work closely with psychologists and special education professionals to design specific support systems. In addition, they can consider the following general strategies:

■ *Show an interest in students' well-being.* Many students with emotional disorders have few positive and productive relationships with individuals outside of school, and so their relationships with caring and supportive teachers may become all the more important (Diamond, 1991). The many "little things" teachers do each day—greeting students warmly in the hallway, expressing concern when they seem worried or upset, and lending a ready ear when they want to share their ideas, opinions, feelings, or frustrations—can make a world of difference (Diamond, 1991).

■ *Teach and encourage interpersonal skills.* Many students with emotional problems have difficulty establishing and maintaining friendships (Asher & Coie, 1990; Cartledge & Milburn, 1995; Schonert-Reichl, 1993). Training and practice in effective social skills seem to improve both the interpersonal relationships *and* the emotional functioning of these students (e.g., Gillham, Reivich, Jaycox, & Seligman, 1995). We will look at specific strategies for teaching social skills in our discussion of peer relationships in Chapter 13.

■ *Provide extra structure and support for students who have high levels of anxiety about classroom tasks and activities.* One effective strategy is to communicate expectations for performance in clear and concrete terms; highly anxious students perform better in well-structured classrooms, those in which expectations for academic achievement and social behavior are explicitly laid out (Hembree, 1988; Stipek, 1993; Tobias, 1977). Teachers can also talk with students about specific sources of anxiety, such as separating from parents or giving oral presentations in public. Students often appreciate a teacher's assistance in overcoming their concerns. For instance, a preschool teacher might make it a familiar routine to stand with children at the window to wave goodbye to parents in the morning. A high school teacher might give students the opportunity to give oral presentations to a small group of friends before giving them to the entire class.

Teachers must always be alert for signs that a student is seriously depressed. If they suspect that a student may be contemplating suicide, they should seek trained help immediately.

■ *Be alert for signs that a student may be contemplating suicide.* Seriously depressed students often give signs that they may be thinking about taking their own lives. Such warning signs include the following (Kerns & Lieberman, 1993):

• Sudden withdrawal from social relationships
• Disregard for personal appearance
• A dramatic personality change
• A sudden elevation in mood
• A preoccupation with death and morbid themes
• Overt or veiled threats (e.g., "I won't be around much longer")
• Actions that indicate "putting one's affairs in order" (e.g., giving away prized possessions)

Teachers must take any of these behaviors seriously. They should show genuine caring and concern for potentially suicidal students, and they should also seek trained help, such as from the school psychologist or counselor, *immediately* (McCoy, 1994).

- *Set reasonable limits for behavior.* Even though the misbehaviors that accompany conduct disorders may have a biological basis, children need to learn that certain actions—aggression, destructiveness, stealing, and so on—are simply unacceptable. Establishing rules for appropriate behavior and applying appropriate consequences (e.g., loss of privileges) for infractions provide the structure and guidance that some students need to keep undesirable behaviors in check (Turnbull et al., 1999).

- *Give students a sense that they have some control.* Some students, especially those who consistently defy authority figures, often respond to efforts to control them by behaving even *less* appropriately than they have previously. With such students, it is important that teachers not get into power struggles—situations where only one person "wins" and the other inevitably loses. Instead, teachers might create situations in which students conform to classroom expectations yet also feel that they have some control over what happens to them. For instance, students can learn and apply techniques for observing and monitoring their own actions with the goal of developing more productive classroom behavior (Kern, Dunlap, Childs, & Clark, 1994). They can also be given choices (within reasonable limits) about how to proceed in particular situations (Knowlton, 1995). We will examine such approaches in more depth in Chapter 11.

To some extent, children's emotional well-being is related to how they perceive themselves—for instance, whether they see themselves as capable or incapable of handling life's daily challenges, whether they compare favorably or unfavorably with those around them, and whether they like or dislike the person they see in the mirror. We turn our attention now to children's knowledge, beliefs, and feelings about themselves as human beings.

Development of a Sense of Self

Let's look once again at 18-year-old Mary's description of herself:

> If I say how I am, it sounds like bragging—I have a good personality and people like me. I'm not the greedy type—I'm jealous a lot of times, yes. And I don't like it when people think they can run my own life——I like to be my own judge. I know right and wrong, but I feel I have a lot more to learn and go through. Generally, I hope I can make it—I hope. (Werner & Smith, 1982, p. 140)

Like Mary, children and adolescents often have very definite beliefs and feelings about themselves. The term **self-concept** refers to the beliefs that people have about themselves, their personal attributes, and their strengths and weaknesses. Mary's self-concept included her reflection that she was likeable, independent, and prone to jealousy. **Self-esteem** is based on the judgments and feelings students have of their capabilities and worth. Mary seemed to have positive feelings about herself—so much so that she thought she might come across as "bragging."[3]

Children and adolescents tend to have an overall, general feeling of self-worth: They believe either that they are good, capable individuals or that they are somehow inept and unworthy (Harter, 1990a; Marsh & Craven, 1997). At the same time, they are usually aware that they have both strengths and weaknesses—that they do some things well and other things poorly (Harter, Whitesell, & Junkin, 1998; Marsh & Craven, 1997; Wigfield, 1994). Consider 9-year-old Shea's *Song of Myself,* presented in Figure 9–5. Note the multiplicity of domains that Shea addresses; for instance, she says, "I am kind, responsible, pretty, smart; I think, plan, help, research. . . ."

By the time they reach adolescence, young people have distinctly differing beliefs about themselves in at least eight domains: cognitive competence, behavioral conduct, physical appearance, romantic appeal, positive regard from peers, relationships with close friends, athletic competence, and job performance (Harter, Whitesell, & Junkin, 1998). They view some

self-concept
Beliefs that people have about themselves, their characteristics, and their abilities.

self-esteem
Feelings that people have about their own capabilities and self-worth.

---

[3]Theorists often have difficulty distinguishing between *self-concept* and *self-esteem,* as the two constructs clearly overlap (Hart, 1988; Marsh & Craven, 1997; Wigfield & Karpathian, 1991). In general, however, they tend to use *self-concept* to refer to cognition (beliefs, theories) about the self and *self-esteem* to refer to affect (emotions).

FIGURE 9–5 Shea's *Song of Myself*. Shea and her classmates were given "stems" to guide their writing (e.g., "Above me . . . ," "I feel . . . ," "I am . . . ," "I dream . . .").

Song of Myself

I am Shea
Above me are the bright colored leaves on the trees
Below me are seeds waiting to become flowers next spring
Before me are years to come full of new things to be learned
Behind me are memories I've forgotten
All around me are my friends lending me a helping hand
I see children having fun
I smell the sweet scent of flowers
I hear the birds talking to each other
I feel the fur of a helpless baby bunny
I move like wind as I run through the grass
I am old like the planets who have been here from the beginning
I am young like a seed waiting to sprout
I am the black of a panda's patches
I am the gold of the sun
I am the green of a cat's eye
I am the many colors of the sunset
I am a parrot, kangaroo, tiger, turtle
I am kind, responsible, pretty, smart
I think, plan, help, research
I give ideas to people that need them
I fear lightning
I believe that we all are equal
I remember my dreams
I dream of bad things as well as the good
I do not understand why some people pollute the Earth
I am Shea, a child of honesty
May I walk in peace

FIGURE 9–5 Shea's *Song of Myself*. Shea and her classmates were given "stems" to guide their writing (e.g., "Above me . . . ," "I feel . . . ," "I am . . . ," "I dream . . .").

of these domains as being more important than others, and their proficiency in domains that they think *are* important has a greater influence on their overall sense of self-worth (Bender, 1997; Harter, Whitesell, & Junkin, 1998; Marsh & Craven, 1997).

Especially as they get older, individuals may even have differing beliefs about themselves regarding specific tasks and situations *within* a particular domain. For instance, Jeanne doesn't perceive herself to be a very good athlete—she's not very strong, and she has little endurance—but she knows that she's a proficient racquetball player (when she and Teresa lived in the same city, she routinely beat Teresa at racquetball). Teresa doesn't perceive herself to be a good athlete either, but she is a fairly decent runner (she wishes Jeanne would join her in a running race). Children, too, develop these kinds of refined ideas about their skills within any domain, such as athletics or academics: They are good at some things and not so good at others.

When we talk about people's self-beliefs at this level of specificity, we are often talking about their **self-efficacy**—their beliefs about whether they are capable of achieving certain goals or outcomes (e.g., Bandura, 1982, 1994). Students' expectations about their probable success or failure at particular tasks influence their choices of tasks, their effort and persistence, and (in part as a result of their effort and persistence) their *actual* success or failure (Bandura, 1982).

self-efficacy
Belief that one is capable of executing certain behaviors or reaching certain goals in a particular task or domain.

(Judging from what you've learned about self-efficacy, who do you think would be more likely to initiate a racquetball game, Jeanne or Teresa?)

Students' self-perceptions are important factors influencing behavior and achievement in school: Students tend to behave in ways that are consistent with their beliefs about themselves and their expectations for future success or failure (Pintrich & Garcia, 1994; Yu, Elder, & Urdan, 1995). For instance, those who believe that they are capable of high academic achievement are more likely to pay attention in class, use effective learning strategies, seek out challenges, and persist in the face of difficulty (Eccles, Wigfield, & Schiefele, 1998; Meyer, Turner, & Spencer, 1994; Zimmerman & Bandura, 1994). In contrast, those who believe they are "poor students" are likely to misbehave in class, study infrequently or not at all, ignore homework assignments, and avoid taking difficult subjects. Along a similar vein, students who see themselves as friendly and likable are apt to seek the company of their classmates and to run for student council, whereas those who believe they are disliked by classmates may keep to themselves or perhaps even act with hostility and aggression toward their peers. Students with a high sense of physical competence will go out for extracurricular athletics, whereas those who see themselves as total klutzes probably will not. More generally, students who have positive beliefs about themselves in particular domains or tasks are those most likely to succeed in those domains (Assor & Connell, 1992; Ma & Kishor, 1997; Marsh & Yeung, 1998; Pajares, 1996).

Factors Influencing the Development of Self-Perceptions

Several factors affect the development of children's self-concepts and self-esteem. Perhaps most influential is children's *own past behaviors and performance.* We noted earlier that children's beliefs about themselves influence the ways in which they behave. Yet the reverse is true as well: To some extent, children's self-concepts and self-esteem depend on how successfully they have behaved in the past (Damon, 1991; Marsh, 1990a). Children are more likely to believe they have an aptitude for mathematics if they have been successful in previous math classes, to believe that they are capable athletes if they have been victorious in athletic competitions, or to believe that they are likable individuals if they have been able to establish and maintain friendly peer relationships.

In addition, the *behaviors of other people,* both adults and peers, play a crucial role in the development of students' self-concepts (Durkin, 1995; Harter, 1983b, 1988; Hartup, 1989). How other individuals behave toward a child communicates their evaluations of the child and their beliefs about his or her worth as a person. For example, parents who accept their children as they are and treat their children's concerns as important are likely to have children with positive self-concepts and high self-esteem. Parents who punish their children for the things they cannot do, without also praising for things done well, are likely to have children with low self-esteem (Harter, 1983b). Teacher behaviors have an impact as well; for example, the relative proportion of positive and negative feedback that teachers give influences students' expectations for future academic success (e.g., Little, Oettingen, Stetsenko, & Baltes, 1995). And students' classmates communicate information about their social competence through a variety of behaviors—for example, by seeking out their companionship or by ridiculing them in front of others. Some adolescents are especially preoccupied with peers' approval, basing their own sense of self-worth largely on what peers think of them (Harter, Stocker, & Robinson, 1996).

Given the preceding discussion, you might predict that praising children should always lead to a higher self-concept and that criticizing children should inevitably lead to a lower one. As it turns out, the effects of praise and criticism are not so simple (Parsons, Kaczala, & Meece, 1982; Stipek, 1996). For instance, when adults praise children for successes on *easy* tasks, children may conclude that they are not capable of handling anything more difficult. Conversely, when adults criticize children's performance on difficult tasks, they may, in the process, communicate the message that the children *can* succeed on such challenges. The key factor appears to be the *expectations* that adults communicate through their statements and actions. When parents and teachers communicate high expectations and offer support and encouragement for the attainment of challenging goals, children tend to have more positive self-concepts (Eccles, Jacobs, Harold-Goldsmith, Jayaratne, & Yee, 1989; Harris & Rosenthal, 1985).

So far our discussion has focused primarily on the effects of children's experiences—that is, on environment—in the development of their self-perceptions. Yet biology also has its say, albeit indirectly. For one thing, inherited temperamental predispositions and physical and intellectual capabilities contribute to children's successes in social, athletic, and academic pursuits. Furthermore, physical appearance is a highly influential factor in the self-esteem of people of all ages (Harter, 1998); for instance, adults respond differently to children (even to infants!) depending on their perceived physical attractiveness (Langlois, 1981; Maccoby & Martin, 1983). And children with disabilities—conditions that usually have biological roots—report less positive self-concepts, on average, than their nondisabled peers (e.g., Harter, Whitesell, & Junkin, 1998).

Developmental Trends in Children's Self-Concepts

Children's and adolescents' physical, cognitive, and social capabilities change with age, and their perceptions of themselves shift accordingly. Yet we see several other age-related changes in children's self-concepts as well:

■ *Self-concepts become increasingly abstract.* Young children tend to define themselves in terms of external and concrete characteristics. As they grow older, they begin to define themselves more in terms of internal and abstract characteristics (Harter, 1983a, 1988; Livesley & Bromley, 1973; Rosenberg, 1986). For example, Jeanne once asked her three children to describe themselves. Their responses were as follows:

Jeff (age 6):
I like animals. I like making things. I do good in school. I'm happy. Blue eyes. Yellow hair. Light skin.

Alex (age 9):
I have brown hair, brown eyes. I like wearing short-sleeved shirts. My hair is curly. I was adopted. I was born in Denver. I like all sorts of critters. The major sport I like is baseball. I do fairly well in school. I have a lizard, and I'm going to get a second one.

Tina (age 12):
I'm cool. I'm awesome. I'm way cool. I'm 12. I'm boy crazy. I go to Brentwood Middle School. I'm popular with my fans. I play viola. My best friend is Lindsay. I have a gerbil named Taj. I'm adopted. I'm beautiful.

Notice how Jeff and Alex mostly talked about how they looked, how they behaved, and what they liked. In contrast, Tina described more abstract qualities—cool, awesome, boy crazy, popular, beautiful—that she had apparently derived from many specific, concrete experiences over time. (Appropriately, her list of self-descriptors did not include "modest.")

■ *Self-concepts become both increasingly differentiated and increasingly integrated.* As children grow older, they make increasingly finer distinctions among various aspects of themselves (Harter, 1983a; Rosenberg, 1986). Eventually, they also pull these distinctions together into an integrated conception of who they are (Harter, 1988). Somewhere around age 15, they identify aspects of their self-definitions that are potentially contradictory and then develop higher-level understandings that resolve such contradictions (Harter, 1988). For instance, they may resolve their perceptions of being both "cheerful" and "depressed" into a realization that they are "moody," or they may explain their inconsistent behaviors in different situations by concluding that they are "flexible" or "open-minded" (Harter, 1988).

■ *Children increasingly base their self-assessments on comparisons with peers.* Young children (e.g., second graders) tend to base their self-evaluations largely on their own improvement over time. Older children (e.g., sixth graders) are more likely to consider how well classmates are performing when they evaluate their own capabilities (Marsh, 1990b; Nicholls, 1984; Pintrich & Schunk, 1996). Thus, at the middle and secondary school levels especially, students who think they are doing better than others are likely to develop a relatively positive self-concept, whereas those who think they perform less well are likely to develop a more negative self-concept.

■ *With age, self-concepts become more stable.* Children with the most positive self-concepts in the early years also tend to have the most positive self-concepts in later years. Conversely, students who think poorly of themselves in elementary school also tend to have lower self-esteem in high school (Marsh & Craven, 1997; O'Malley & Bachman, 1983; Savin-Williams & Demo, 1984). As children get older, their self-perceptions become increasingly stable, probably for several reasons. First, as mentioned earlier, people usually behave in ways that are consistent with what they believe about themselves, so their behaviors are likely to produce reactions from others that confirm their self-concepts. Second, people tend to seek out information that confirms what they already believe about themselves: Those with positive self-concepts are more likely to seek out positive feedback, whereas those with negative self-concepts may actually look for information about their weaknesses and limitations (Epstein & Morling, 1995; Swann, 1997). Third, people seldom put themselves in situations where they believe they won't succeed, thereby eliminating any possibility of discovering that they *can* succeed. For example, if a teenager believes he is a poor athlete and so refuses to go out for the baseball team, he may never learn that, in fact, he has the potential to become a skillful player. And fourth, many outside factors that contribute to one's self-concept—for example, parental behaviors, socioeconomic circumstances, and one's physical attractiveness—usually remain relatively stable throughout childhood (O'Malley & Bachman, 1983).

This is *not* to say that once children acquire low self-concepts, they will always think poorly of themselves. Quite the contrary can be true, particularly when circumstances change significantly—for instance, when, after a history of failures, children begin experiencing regular success (Marsh & Craven, 1997). We will look at specific strategies for enhancing children's and adolescents' self-concepts a bit later in the chapter.

Development of the Self Across Childhood and Adolescence

The developmental trends just listed reflect gradual changes in the nature of self-concepts over time. Yet we also see qualitative differences among preschoolers, elementary students, middle schoolers, and high school students. We now look at unique aspects of self-perceptions at four age levels: early childhood, middle childhood, early adolescence, and late adolescence.

Early Childhood (Ages 2–6)   Most young children have positive self-concepts, to the point where they may believe they are more capable than they actually are (Flavell et al., 1993; Paris & Cunningham, 1996). They probably make such overestimations because they base their self-assessments on their improvement in various activities over time, rather than on a comparison to age-mates. A small amount of overconfidence is probably beneficial for children's development, in that it motivates children to try and to persist at new and challenging tasks (Bjorklund & Green, 1992; Pintrich & Schunk, 1996).

Not all young children are so naively optimistic, however. Some quickly become pessimists in the face of failure. For instance, in a series of studies by Carol Dweck and her colleagues, preschoolers, kindergartners, and first graders worked on several picture puzzles that were either unsolvable (the pieces didn't fit together) or too difficult to complete in the time provided. Later, when the children were given a second opportunity to work on these puzzles, some chose to do so, but others preferred to work on puzzles they had already completely successfully. Of these "nonpersisting" youngsters, many showed signs of *learned helplessness*—a belief that their efforts would simply not pay off for them (Burhans & Dweck, 1995). (We will revisit the phenomenon of learned helplessness in Chapter 11.)

Middle Childhood (Ages 6–10)   Research indicates that children's self-concepts sometimes drop soon after they begin elementary school (Harter, 1990a; Stipek, 1981), probably as a result of the many new academic and social challenges that school presents. Elementary school gives children many occasions to compare their performance with that of peers, and so their self-assessments gradually become more realistic (Hart, 1988; Paris & Cunningham, 1996; Wigfield, 1994). Yet this comparative approach inevitably creates "winners" and "losers." Children who routinely find themselves at the bottom of the heap must do some fancy footwork to keep their self-esteem intact. Often, they focus on performance areas in which they excel (e.g., sports, social relationships, or hobbies) and discount areas that give them trouble (e.g., "Reading is dumb"). Perhaps because they have so many domains and experiences to consider as they look for strengths in their own performance, most children maintain fairly high and stable self-esteem during the elementary school years (Wigfield & Eccles, 1994).

Early Adolescence (Ages 10–14) Another drop in self-concept occurs at about the time that students move from elementary school to junior high school; this drop is especially pronounced for girls (Eccles & Midgley, 1989; Marsh, 1990b; Sadker & Sadker, 1994; Simmons & Blyth, 1987; Wigfield & Eccles, 1994). The physiological changes that occur with puberty may be a factor: Students' self-concepts depend increasingly on their beliefs about their appearance and their popularity, yet boys and girls alike tend to think of themselves as being somewhat less attractive once they reach adolescence (Cornell et al., 1990; Hart, 1988; Harter, 1990a; Harter, Whitesell, & Junkin, 1998). The changing school environment probably also has a negative impact. Traditional junior high schools often differ from elementary schools in several ways (Eccles & Midgley, 1989). For one thing, students don't have the opportunity to form the close-knit, supportive relationships with teachers that many of them had in elementary school. Students may also discover that their school grades are based more on competitive criteria—that is, on how well they perform in comparison with their classmates. Furthermore, at a time when they probably have an increased need for close friendships, students may find themselves in classes with many people they don't know.

With all of these unsettling changes occurring simultaneously, it is not surprising that we see a temporary drop in young adolescents' self-perceptions. Fortunately, with the advent of the *middle school* concept, many school districts now take great pains to ease students' transition into a more socially complex and academically challenging secondary school environment. For instance, large schools may split up the student body into smaller and more intimate "clusters" of perhaps 60–90 students, and many schools provide explicit guidance in the skills and habits necessary for self-regulated learning. Once students have successfully adjusted to their changing school environment, most adolescents enjoy positive self-concepts and general mental health (Durkin, 1995; Nottelmann, 1987; Powers, Hauser, & Kilner, 1989; Wigfield & Eccles, 1994).

Yet in early adolescence, two new phenomena appear. First, many young adolescents believe that, in any social situation, everyone else's attention is focused squarely on them (Elkind, 1981a; Lapsley, 1993; Ryan & Kuczkowski, 1994). This self-centered aspect of the adolescent self-concept is sometimes called the **imaginary audience.** Because they believe themselves to be the center of attention, teenagers (girls especially) are often preoccupied with their physical appearance and are quite critical of themselves, assuming that everyone else is going to be equally observant and critical. Extreme sensitivity to embarrassment, when coupled with inadequate social skills, can lead some adolescents to respond with undue violence when their peers insult or verbally attack them (Lowry, Sleet, Duncan, Powell, & Kolbe, 1995).

A second noteworthy phenomenon in early adolescence is the **personal fable:** Young teenagers often believe themselves to be completely unlike anyone else (Elkind, 1981a; Lapsley, 1993). For instance, they often think that their own feelings are completely unique—that those around them have never experienced such emotions. Hence, they may insist that no one else, least of all parents and teachers, can possibly know how they feel. Furthermore, they may have a sense of invulnerability and immortality, believing that they are not susceptible to the normal dangers of life. Thus, many adolescents take seemingly foolish risks, such as driving at high speeds, experimenting with drugs and alcohol, or having unprotected sexual intercourse (Arnett, 1995; DeRidder, 1993; Packard, 1983; Thomas, Groër, & Droppleman, 1993).

imaginary audience
Belief that one is the center of attention in any social situation.

personal fable
Belief that one is completely unlike other people, cannot be understood, and is impervious to danger.

A frequently observed phenomenon in early adolescence is the *personal fable:* Young teenagers often believe that they are completely unique, to the point where no one else—least of all their parents and teachers—can possibly understand their thoughts and feelings.
Zits by Jerry Scott and Jim Borgman. Reprinted with special permission of King Features Syndicate.

The development of both the imaginary audience and personal fable may to some extent reflect students' changing cognitive abilities during the adolescent years. Elkind (1981a) has proposed that both the imaginary audience and the personal fable are a function of the *formal operational egocentrism* that Piaget described (see Chapter 4). More specifically, young adolescents have difficulty distinguishing between their own perspectives on the world and those of others and so assume that because their *own* thoughts are focused on themselves, everyone else's thoughts must be focused on them as well. Yet researchers have found no correlation between measures of youngsters' formal thinking capabilities and measures of the imaginary audience and personal fable (Lapsley, 1993; Lapsley, Milstead, Quintana, Flannery, & Buss, 1986). An alternative explanation is that the two phenomena serve adaptive purposes as young adolescents strive for increasing independence from their families. The personal fable—in particular, the sense of invulnerability—may encourage young people to venture out into the world and try new things (Bjorklund & Green, 1992; Lapsley, 1993). At the same time, the imaginary audience keeps them "connected" to their larger social context, so that they are continually considering how others might judge their actions (Lapsley, 1993; Ryan & Kuczkowski, 1994). Whatever the origins of these phenomena, they appear to peak in early adolescence and then slowly decline (Lapsley, 1993; Lapsley, Jackson, Rice, & Shadid, 1988).

Late Adolescence (Ages 14–18) As their worlds broaden in the teenage years, young people have a greater variety of social experiences and so are apt to get conflicting messages about their characteristics and capabilities (Hart, 1988). The result is that their self-concepts may include contradictory views of themselves (Harter, 1990b; Wigfield, Eccles, & Pintrich, 1996). As they reach high school age, they begin to wrestle with such contradictions and, with luck, eventually establish a sense of **identity**—a self-constructed definition of who they are, what things they find important, and what goals they want to accomplish in life.

Membership in groups—perhaps informal cliques at school, organized clubs or teams, ethnic neighborhoods, and the community at large—often plays a key role in adolescents' identities (Durkin, 1995; Lave & Wenger, 1991; Trawick-Smith, 2000; Wigfield et al., 1996). Not only do such groups help teenagers define who they are, but they also endorse values and goals that teenagers may adopt for themselves.

Before adolescents achieve a true sense of their adult identity, most need considerable time to explore their various options for careers, political beliefs, religious affiliations, and so on. Marcia (1980) has observed four distinct patterns of behavior that may characterize the status of an adolescent's search for identity:

- *Identity diffusion.* The adolescent has made no commitment to a particular career path or ideological belief system. Possibly there has been some haphazard experimentation with

identity
People's self-constructed definition of who they are, what they find important, and what goals they want to accomplish in life.

Emotional and Personal Development at Different Age Levels

DEVELOPMENTAL TRENDS

AGE	WHAT YOU MIGHT OBSERVE	DIVERSITY	IMPLICATIONS
Early Childhood (2–6) 	• Desire to be close to parents when afraid, hurt, or uncertain • Wide variety of emotions (e.g., happiness, sadness, fear, anger, disgust) • Emergence of self-conscious emotions (e.g., pride, shame, guilt) • Only a rudimentary sense of one's unique characteristics, talents, and weaknesses • Optimism about what academic and physical tasks can be accomplished	• Children vary in the number of close attachments they form, the extent to which they find reassurance in these attachment figures, and their responses to strangers. Some cling tightly to caregivers, others venture confidently to explore new environments and check out strangers. • Children vary in how they express their emotions. Some are very controlled, especially in masking anger and sadness. Others are more expressive.	• Realize that young children may initially be cautious or fearful in a new classroom environment; they will become more confident as they begin to form attachments to their teachers. • Be patient in establishing relationships with young children; some may form attachments quickly, but others make take several weeks or months before they begin to trust adults outside the home. • Teach appropriate ways of handling negative emotions. For example, encourage children to "use their words" rather than physically pushing and hitting when angry or frustrated.
Middle Childhood (6–10) 	• Increasing number of emotional bonds with teachers and peers • Increasing ability to regulate emotions • Increasing tendency to base self-perceptions of ability on how others perform • Generally positive self-concept in most children	• Children are affected by major family disruptions (e.g., divorce of parents, death or illness of a family member). Such risk factors may provide opportunities for social-emotional growth, but they often undermine children's sense of well-being and security, at least temporarily. • Some children have strong role models for emotional regulation (e.g., a parent may work out negative feelings in productive ways, resolve conflicts with others constructively, etc.). • Different children derive their sense of self-worth from different arenas—perhaps from social relationships, academic performance, or physical accomplishments.	• Incorporate discussions of emotional states into the curriculum; for example, address the feelings of characters in literature and history. • Model appropriate ways of expressing feelings. • Praise children for their talents and accomplishments in numerous areas (e.g., in physical activities, social relationships, and specific academic subjects).

particular roles or beliefs, but the individual has not yet embarked on a serious exploration of issues related to self-definition.

- *Foreclosure.* The adolescent has made a firm commitment to an occupation and/or a particular set of beliefs. The choices have been based largely on what others (especially parents) have prescribed, without an earnest exploration of other possibilities.
- *Moratorium.* The adolescent has no strong commitment to a particular career or set of beliefs but is actively exploring and considering a variety of professions and ideologies. In essence, the individual is undergoing an **identity crisis.**
- *Identity achievement.* The adolescent has previously gone through a period of moratorium and emerged with a clear choice regarding occupation and/or commitment to particular political or religious beliefs.

Perhaps the ideal situation is to proceed through moratorium, a period of searching and experimentation that may continue into early adulthood, before finally settling on a clear identity (Berzonsky, 1988; Marcia, 1988). Foreclosure—identity choice *without* prior exploration—rules

identity crisis
Period during which an individual actively struggles to choose a course in life.

AGE	WHAT YOU MIGHT OBSERVE	DIVERSITY	IMPLICATIONS
Early Adolescence (10–14)	• Frequent fluctuations in mood, partly as a result of hormonal changes • Careful regulation of emotions (e.g., hiding joy about a good grade in order to appear "cool" to peers) • Possible temporary drop in self-concept after the transition to middle school or junior high • Preoccupation with appearance (often reflected in conformity in dress, behavior, etc.) • Increased risk taking, accompanied by a sense of invulnerability	• Adolescents differ in the extent to which they strive to conform to gender stereotypes. • Drops in self-esteem, when sizable and not followed by a rebound, can signal a serious problem. • Some serious emotional problems, such as depression and bipolar disorder, first appear during adolescence. • Some students tend to internalize their stresses (e.g., experiencing depression or anxiety); other respond with externalizing behaviors (e.g., being violent, breaking the law).	• Be a willing and supportive "ear" when students want to share concerns or anxieties. • Keep in mind that some moodiness is normal in the middle school grades. However, talk with parents and trained professionals (e.g., the school psychologist or counselor) about your concerns for the emotional well-being of students who seem especially troubled. • To help students discover that not everyone views the world as they do, plan activities in which they can express their opinions and perspectives.
Late Adolescence (14–18)	• Seeking of intimacy with same-sex and opposite-sex peers • Decrease in the self-consciousness evident in early adolescence • Wrestling with identity issues: Who am I? What do I believe? How do I fit into society?	• Adolescents differ in the extent to which they focus on dating and intimacy. • Some adolescents willingly accept the professional goals and ideologies that their parents offer. Others engage in more soul-searching and exploration as they strive to develop their identity. • Minority youth are more likely than European American youth to reflect on how their ethnic status plays a role in their identity.	• Provide opportunities for students to work closely together on classroom assignments. • Explore diverse belief systems. • Provide service learning and mentoring opportunities that allow adolescents to try on a variety of occupational "hats."

out potentially more productive alternatives, and identity diffusion leaves youth without a clear sense of direction in life.

Even as high school students move rapidly toward independence and self-reliance, their attachment to family members—especially parents—continues to play a significant role in their personal development. Adolescents who have strong emotional bonds with their parents tend to have higher self-esteem and function at more mature levels (Josselson, 1988; Ryan & Lynch, 1989). Such bonds are not overly restrictive or protective, however; parents best foster their children's personal growth by gradually releasing the apron strings as their offspring gain competence (Lapsley, 1993; Ryan & Lynch, 1989). Adolescents who feel alienated from (i.e., have little sense of attachment to) their parents are susceptible to the opinions of others for a longer period of time (i.e., the imaginary audience persists) and have more difficulty establishing a sense of identity (i.e., they are identity-diffused) (Josselson, 1988; Marcia, 1988; Ryan & Kuczkowski, 1994).

In the Developmental Trends table above, we summarize the general course of development of emotions and sense of self across the four age ranges. Keep in mind, however, that such development is characterized by considerable diversity. We now look at group differences in children's and adolescents' sense of self.

Group Differences in Representations of the Self

We have already seen several examples of diversity in children's self-perceptions. For instance, some preschoolers are more optimistic about their own capabilities than others, and adolescents with close attachments to their parents have higher self-esteem than adolescents without such close emotional bonds. To some extent, children's and adolescents' self-perceptions are a function of their group membership. Here we consider research findings related to gender, ethnicity, and cultural background.

Gender Differences   As children grow older, their understandings of gender become increasingly sophisticated, and this trend has implications for their self-concepts and behaviors. During their toddler and preschool years, children show a rudimentary understanding of gender. For instance, they realize that there are two sexes, can label them, and know that they personally are either girl or boy (Etaugh, Grinnell, & Etaugh, 1989; Fagot & Leinbach, 1989). But it takes several years for them to appreciate that this state is permanent—in other words, that boys do not become girls if they grow their hair long and wear ribbons, nor do girls become boys if they cut their hair short and wear boys' clothes (Bem, 1989; DeLisi & Gallagher, 1991; Emmerich, Goldman, Kirsh, & Sharabany, 1977; Slaby & Frey, 1975). With this developing concept of gender, young children watch the world around them for further clues about the distinctions between what is "male" and what is "female," and they are especially attentive to role models of their own gender.

During middle childhood, friendships are largely dictated by gender: Although boys may have friends who are girls, and vice versa, children usually prefer same-sex companions. Furthermore, by defining themselves as "boy" or "girl," children tend to choose activities and exhibit behaviors that their society deems to be "gender-appropriate." For example, girls are more concerned about their appearance, but also less satisfied with it, beginning in middle childhood (Maloney, McGuire, & Daniels, 1988; Stein, 1996). Of course, there are individual differences in how strictly children adhere to sex-role stereotypes. **Androgynous** individuals show both feminine and masculine attributes; for instance, they might be nurturing and sensitive with friends (stereotypically "feminine" characteristics) yet assertive and independent in classroom activities (stereotypically "masculine" characteristics) (Bem, 1977). Children, adolescents, and adults who relax the sex-role boundaries seem to be fairly well adjusted, perhaps because they have more choices in the standards by which they evaluate themselves and because others respond favorably to their wide range of skills and dispositions (Piche & Plante, 1991; Williams & D'Alessandro, 1994).

With the onset of puberty, being "male" or "female" takes on an entirely new meaning. Many young adolescents show an upsurge in gender-specific interests (Galambos, Almeida, & Petersen, 1990). For example, at age 13, Teresa's son Connor displayed a newfound interest in American football—definitely a rough and "manly" sport—and so joined the middle school football team. Also during adolescence, earlier interests may begin to dwindle, particularly if they are emblematic of the opposite sex. For example, both of us recall having mixed feelings about mathematics in adolescence. Although math was something we were clearly good at, we thought of it as a "masculine" domain that would somehow make us look less feminine. (Fortunately, our interest rekindled in college, where we felt more free to "be ourselves" and not conform to sex-role stereotypes.) Even girls who have grown up in more recent and "open-minded" decades than we did tend to have less interest and self-confidence in subject areas that are traditionally "masculine"—notably mathematics, science, and sports (Binns, Steinberg, Amorosi, & Cuevas, 1997; Chandler & Goldberg, 1990; Middleton, 1999; Rowe, 1999; Wigfield et al., 1996).

As young people continue to define themselves throughout childhood and adolescence, they integrate their ideas about gender into their core concepts of self. For instance, they determine how well they measure up to ideal gender roles. If their characteristics and behaviors approximate these ideals, they feel good about themselves, especially if they strongly value being a "manly" man or "womanly" woman. If they don't measure up, their self-concepts and self-esteem may suffer (Harter, 1998).

Children and adolescents learn about and adhere to gender roles through several mechanisms. Biology clearly has some influence. The brain is permanently marked "male" or "female" during prenatal development; for example, a part of the forebrain known as the *hypothalamus* is shaped somewhat differently in boys and girls (Arnold & Gorski, 1984). Sex differences in the brain become more prominent during adolescence, because circulating hormones activate gender-specific structures that have previously remained rather quiet (Ruble & Martin, 1998). As noted earlier, in boys these rising hormones are associated with increased aggression—a stereotypically "male" characteristic (Susman, Inoff-Germain et al., 1987).

Girls who value being feminine and boys who value being masculine integrate such ideas about gender into their self-concepts.

androgyny
Tendency to have some characteristics that are stereotypically "female" (e.g., nurturance) and others that are stereotypically "male" (e.g., assertiveness).

But perhaps more importantly, children and adolescents are socialized to conform to sex roles: Family, peers, and the broader community reinforce them for "staying within bounds" and punish them (e.g., by ridicule or exclusion) when they violate accepted gender roles (Pipher, 1994; Ruble & Martin, 1998). For example, a boy who cries after breaking his arm may be called a "sissy," and a girl who excels in mathematics might be teased for being a "math geek." Agents of socialization affect gender differentiation in concepts ("Nurses are almost always women"), self-perceptions ("Like most girls, I'm no good at auto mechanics"), preferences ("I'm a boy, so I like trucks"), and behaviors ("Can I borrow your lipstick?") (Ruble & Martin, 1998).

Finally, gender roles are intensified by children's own thinking and desire to fit into society's structure (Ruble & Martin, 1998). Children help to socialize themselves initially by constructing an understanding of gender as a stable attribute: It doesn't change from day to day, and it doesn't depend on clothing or hairstyle. In addition, they develop mental representations, or schemas, for "what boys do" and "what girls do" (Bem, 1981; Martin, 1991; Martin & Halverson, 1981). With such understandings in place, children are motivated to interpret the world through the lens of gender. They stay vigilant about gender-related roles in their social world and to some degree are motivated to be boylike or girl-like, as the following recollection from Benita Balegh illustrates:

> I was one of seven girls in a family of eight children. The son was like "Big Son," because he was the answer to my parents' prayers and the rest of us—we didn't quite make it.
>
> In our home we had to defer to this boy and, of course, to my father. When my father and my brother would come home, everybody would stand around to serve them, to do anything we could to gain their favor. . . .
>
> It was OK, even feminine, not to be good in math. It was even cute. And so I locked myself out of a very important part of what it is to be a human being, and that is to know all of oneself. I just locked that part out because I didn't think that was an appropriate thing for me to do. . . . [But] it was not OK for the men to not do well in math. It was *not* OK for them to not take calculus. It was not manly. . . .
>
> Another thing that affected me greatly happened when I went to a foreign country. One day I decided that I was going to build a sandbox for my little boy. I went in to get the wood and they told me, "Oh, no! You cannot buy wood. You have to have your husband's permission before you can purchase wood." That was a very big shock to me. But it was a shock that helped me see the insidiousness of what had happened to me in the beginning. And it helped me to open my eyes. When I came back to my country I was very intolerant of what I had swallowed hook, line, and sinker. (Benita Balegh, in Weissglass, 1998, p. 160)

Benita's reluctance to speak her mind is not a problem for all girls, nor is it a problem *only* for girls. Also, when it does appear, it is not always a general trait; for instance, some youth may be reticent in classrooms yet be quite vocal with friends and family (Harter, Waters, Whitesell, & Kastelic, 1998).

In broaching the topic of male-female differences, we don't mean to imply that the two sexes are entirely different, nor do we wish to communicate that the sexes are blandly uniform. In fact, there is *substantial* variation in both groups on all psychological characteristics. Finally, our discussion of gender and self-representations would be remiss if we did not recognize the unique dilemmas faced by students who are homosexual and bisexual in orientation. These students face the added challenge of forming an integrated self-concept and maintaining high self-esteem when they face rampant rejection in society at large and, sadly, occasional rejection from family and peers. Gay and lesbian youngsters who have close relationships with their parents and families tend to have more positive identities and to disclose their orientation ("come out") sooner than those with poor relationships (Beaty, 1999). We will explore the topic of sexual orientation in greater detail in Chapter 13.

Ethnic and Cultural Differences Many children and adolescents from ethnic and racial minority groups have positive self-concepts and high general self-esteem. In fact, researchers often find that, on average, minority youth have more favorable self-perceptions than European American youth (Cooper & Dorr, 1995; Spencer & Markstrom-Adams, 1990; Stevenson, Chen, & Uttal, 1990; van Laar, 2000). Given that members of minority groups are often the victims of prejudice and discrimination in our society, this finding seems quite puzzling, yet theorists have offered possible explanations for it. First, widespread prejudice and discrimination—though certainly not attitudes and practices that we advocate—may, in a backhanded way, actually enhance the self-concepts of some youngsters, who take credit for their successes (they worked hard for them and/or have exceptional talent) but blame outside factors for their failures (others are biased against them and are preventing them from getting ahead) (van Laar, 2000).

A second possible explanation is that some ethnic groups encourage children to take pride in the accomplishments of their families or communities, rather than in their own, individual achievements (Harrison, Wilson, Pine, Chan, & Buriel, 1990; Olneck, 1995; Pang, 1995; Trawick-Smith, 2000). Such groups often encourage a strong **ethnic identity,** an awareness of one's membership in the group and willingness to adopt certain behaviors characteristic of that group. A strong sense of ethnic or racial identity and pride often helps youth from minority groups deal with the racist behaviors of others (McAdoo, 1985; Spencer & Markstrom-Adams, 1990). Consider this statement by Eva, an African American high school student:

> I'm proud to be black and everything. But, um, I'm aware of, you know, racist acts and racist things that are happening in the world, but I use that as no excuse, you know. I feel as though I can succeed. . . . I just know that I'm not gonna let [racism] stop me. . . . Being black is good. I'm proud to be black but you also gotta face reality. And what's going on, you know, black people are not really getting anywhere in life, but I know I will and I don't know—I just know I will. Well, I'm determined to . . . and with God's help, you can't go wrong. (Way, 1998, p. 257)

Not all minority youth identify strongly with their ethnic and cultural backgrounds, however (Phinney, 1989). The strength of their ethnic identity will inevitably depend, in part, on the extent to which their families nurture it and the extent to which they want to assimilate into mainstream society (Dien, 1998; Thornton, Chatters, Taylor, & Allen, 1990).

Another important factor affecting the self-concepts and self-esteem of children and adolescents from ethnic minority groups is the treatment they receive in classrooms. Consider Rogelio López del Bosque's recollection of his first day at an American school in the 1950s:

> As I walked into the school with my sister, I remember smiling with pride and full of that desire to learn. Now that I recall, my sister gave me a sense of security. She had been directed by my Mom to take me to school the first day. (Mom did not feel she could do it herself since she spoke Spanish.) I was ready, and I know my family was proud. My parents were probably very happy that I was the last of 13 children to finally go to school.
>
> Shortly after arriving in the classroom and meeting the teacher, I recall vividly learning that I was no longer going to be called by my name, Rogelio. I was given a new name. I thought it was part of being in school.
>
> Of course, I found out later that the name Rogelio was too difficult for the teacher to pronounce. There was something wrong with me. So my name had to be changed. This was the beginning of my feeling different.
>
> Was there something wrong with my name? It really did not matter. This was what schools did, and it would help me learn—so I thought. I rationalized: Big deal, my Mom does not even call me Rogelio. She calls me "Rogelito." So on my first day of school, I was given a new name so I would fit in with everyone else and I would be ready to learn.
>
> Little did I know that the excitement of that first day of school would soon change to discomfort. I really could not identify exactly what I was feeling. But something was not right.
>
> During my years of school, I experienced low expectations and hostile attitudes on the part of some teachers, administrators, and other students. I had difficulty assimilating into this unfamiliar environment. Continuously, I was made aware that speaking Spanish had bad consequences. I was also told many times that I should not speak Spanish because I used an incorrect form. Was the language I learned at home inferior? I had learned to express my love, desires, and fears in that language. Of course, my parents must have been a very bad influence by teaching me such language, this Tex-Mex. . . .
>
> Like all children, there were so many qualities that I brought with me to school that were valuable. I was eager to learn, eager to please, and eager to do a good job and feel right just like everyone. Instead, like so many other students with similar backgrounds, I was made to feel wrong, unintelligent, and inferior. My whole person was in jeopardy. (López del Bosque, 2000, pp. 3–4)

Although most teachers today are more aware of the need to acknowledge and respect students' ethnic and cultural backgrounds, we have, in our own experience, occasionally seen teachers whose behaviors are as condescending and demeaning as Rogelio's teacher was. At the other

ethnic identity
Awareness of one's membership in a particular ethnic or cultural group, and willingness to adopt certain behaviors characteristic of that group.

Emotional and Personal Characteristics of Children and Adolescents

ISSUE	ATTACHMENT TO CAREGIVERS	EMOTIONAL STATES AND REGULATION	DEVELOPMENT OF THE SELF
Nature and Nurture	Young human beings are biologically predisposed to form close social-emotional bonds with their parents and other primary caregivers, but they are more likely to form attachments to such individuals when they are treated in a socially sensitive and responsible fashion. Parents, in turn, are by nature predisposed to care for their offspring, but they learn specific ways of caring for their children from other family members and from the community and culture in which they live.	The full range of emotions is made possible by human genetic instructions; the brain is wired to experience anger, joy, fear, and so on. Genetic factors also affect individual differences in temperament (e.g., activity level, irritability, and characteristic ways of responding to new stimuli). Nurture affects the specific ways in which emotions are expressed. Children learn to control their expression of negative emotional responses in part from observing other people within their culture and in part from practicing various ways of dealing with their own emotional experiences. Some children who are maltreated or have parents who are emotionally depressed cope in counterproductive ways, yet others show considerable resilience in the face of negative emotional experiences.	The capacities to reflect on oneself as a social agent and to think about how other people view oneself are species-specific and so seem to have a genetic basis. These capacities are not fully functioning at birth, however; rather, they develop with experience and social input. Temperamental predispositions interact with experience and feedback from others to become the fodder for self-reflection (e.g., "I'm always getting in trouble at school") and influence self-concept and self-esteem.
Universality and Diversity	The predisposition to form close social-emotional bonds is probably universal. Moreover, socially sensitive care is the universal trigger for forming emotional attachments. However, not all children form secure attachments to their caregivers, and different environments place differing demands on children. For example, being clingy and demanding may help infants who live in an environment with scarce resources. Similarly, being able to negotiate multiple relationships may enhance adjustment when children are exposed to numerous caregivers during the early years.	All children experience such basic emotions as happiness, sadness, anger, and fear. The tendency for emotional states to energize particular kinds of responses (e.g., fleeing in response to fear) is also universal. But substantial diversity is present in how children regulate their emotions (e.g., when trying to conceal their true feelings). Some children are more likely than others to respond to situations in a positive, "upbeat" fashion.	Self-concept seems to be universal as a multidimensional construct; that is, all children see themselves as good at some things and not so good at other things. The trend toward increasing self-reflection also appears to be universal. But children differ in the particular domains in which they think they are strong and weak, as well as in the importance that they attach to each domain. Gender differences and cultural differences are seen in self-concepts and self-esteem, but there is also considerable variability *within* each gender and cultural group.

(continued)

extreme are well-meaning teachers who take great pains to give positive feedback to students from minority backgrounds, to the point where the feedback greatly overrates students' actual performance and gives little information about areas in which students need to continue refining their skills (Little et al., 1995; Paris & Cunningham, 1996). In our minds, this state of affairs may not be much of an improvement over how things were in López del Bosque's day. Ideally, educators should help students of all ethnic and cultural backgrounds acquire the knowledge, skills, and abilities they need to achieve genuine successes both in the classroom and in the outside world. Such successes will lead to high yet accurate self-concepts.

At this point, we should step back and reconsider what we've learned related to the three basic themes of nature versus nurture, universality versus diversity, and qualitative versus quantitative change. The Basic Developmental Issues table above summarizes how these

Emotional and Personal Characteristics of Children and Adolescents *(continued)*

ISSUE	ATTACHMENT TO CAREGIVERS	EMOTIONAL STATES AND REGULATION	DEVELOPMENT OF THE SELF
Qualitative and Quantitative Change	The development of attachments largely reflects quantitative change: Children gradually become more active in guiding interactions with their parents, initiating conversations and other exchanges, taking "turns" to keep interactions going, and so on. Qualitative change occurs when young children, who have previously met strangers with no protest, suddenly display "stranger anxiety." During this phase, they are anxious around people they do not know and show a clear preference for their attachment figures.	Children gradually gain knowledge and skills for assessing other people's emotional states. By watching facial expressions, listening to tone of voice, and drawing inferences from behaviors, children learn how others express and control emotions. They also become increasingly reflective about their own emotional states. However, the emergence of self-conscious emotions (pride, shame, guilt, etc.) represents a qualitative change in development. As children become more aware of family and societal standards, they learn to apply these standards to their own actions, are motivated (usually) to adhere to them, and feel shameful or guilty when they have violated them.	Changes in self-esteem are most often quantitative, increasing as children learn new skills and master more complex tasks but occasionally decreasing as children face major transitions in their lives. In the early years, children use self-improvement as a gauge for evaluating their performance, but beginning in middle childhood they begin to compare their performance to that of their peers—a shift that reflects qualitative change.

For positive self-concepts and high self-esteem, students need numerous opportunities to achieve success, perhaps in academic activities, in interpersonal relationships, or on the athletic field.

themes surface not only in the development of the self but also in the formation of attachments and emotional development. We turn now to strategies for enhancing students' sense of self in the classroom.

Enhancing Students' Sense of Self

The interplay between self-concept and behavior can create a vicious downward spiral: A low self-concept leads to less productive behavior, which leads to fewer successes, which perpetuates the low self-concept. Yet simply telling students that they are "good" or "smart" or "popular" is unlikely to make much of a dent in poor self-perceptions (Damon, 1991; Marsh & Craven, 1997; Pajares, 1996). Furthermore, vague, abstract statements such as "You're special" have little meaning in the concrete realities of young children (McMillan, Singh, & Simonetta, 1994). The following strategies are more likely to be effective:

■ *Promote success on academic, social, and physical tasks.* Success experiences are far and away the most powerful catalysts for the development of positive self-concepts and high self-esteem (Damon, 1991; Marsh & Craven, 1997). Thus, teachers should gear assignments to students' developmental levels and cognitive capabilities—for instance, by making sure that students have already mastered any necessary prerequisite knowledge and skills.

Yet success at very *easy* activities is unlikely to have much of an impact. Mastering the significant challenges in life—the hard-won successes that come only with effort, and perhaps with persistence in the face of obstacles—brings more enduring and resilient self-perceptions (Dweck, 1986; B. Lerner, 1985). Thus, teachers are most likely to bolster students' self-concepts when they assign challenging tasks and provide the structure and support (the scaffolding) that students need to accomplish those tasks successfully. They should also help students keep the little "failures" along the way in perspective: Mistakes

ENHANCING STUDENTS' EMOTIONAL WELL-BEING AND SENSE OF SELF

■ Communicate a genuine interest in students' welfare.

When a student is visibly teary-eyed during class, her teacher invites her to take a walk during lunchtime. The student describes the trouble she is having making friends at her new school, and she and her teacher develop a plan to address the problem.

■ Promote success on classroom tasks.

A high school teacher provides a format (scaffolding) for writing an expository paragraph: a sentence expressing the main idea, three sentences that support that idea, and a concluding sentence.

■ Hold reasonably high expectations for students' performance.

A junior high swimming coach encourages students to come out for the swim team regardless of past experience. She works as closely with newcomers as with experienced swimmers so that all team members can improve.

■ Give positive feedback for students' accomplishments. Accompany negative feedback with the message that students can improve.

The same swimming coach tells a student, "Your crawl stroke has really improved. Your timing on the butterfly is a bit off; let's work on that today."

■ Give students opportunities to examine and try out a variety of adultlike roles.

A first-grade teacher develops a list of classroom chores, such as getting a hot-lunch count, delivering messages to the main office, and feeding the class goldfish and rabbit. He assigns these chores to students on a rotating basis.

■ Learn about the domains of performance most important to individual students.

A fifth-grade teacher asks his students to write an essay about the school activities that they like most and least. He makes sure his students have frequent opportunities to engage in their favorite activities and compliments them when they do especially well in their areas of interest.

are an inevitable yet very temporary part of learning anything new (Clifford, 1990; Eccles & Wigfield, 1985).

■ *Focus students' attention on their own improvement rather than on how others are performing.* Students are likely to be optimistic about their chances of success if they see that, yes, they are making progress and gaining increasing expertise. They are unlikely to have much optimism if they see that their own performance doesn't measure up to that of their peers (Deci & Ryan, 1992; Krampen, 1987; Stipek, 1996). To help students develop positive self-concepts, then, teachers should minimize competition and other situations in which students might compare themselves unfavorably with classmates.

■ *Give constructive and encouraging feedback.* In part because of the frequent feedback children and adolescents get from others, their self-perceptions are usually similar to how others perceive them (Harter, 1990a; Shaffer, 1988). For example, students' beliefs about their academic ability are similar to their classroom teachers' beliefs about their intelligence and aptitude. Their beliefs about their physical ability are correlated with the perceptions of their physical education teachers. And their sense of their own competence in social situations is likely to be a reflection of their actual popularity with peers.

Obviously, teachers are going to promote more positive self-concepts if they acknowledge and praise students' accomplishments. At the same time, teachers' feedback should reflect fairly accurate assessments of what students currently can and cannot do; thus, it must inevitably include criticism as well as praise (Marsh, 1990b; Parsons, Kaczala, & Meece, 1982; Stipek, 1996). If teachers provide only praise—and particularly if they provide highly inflated evaluations of students' performance—then students will be unaware of areas that need improvement (Little et al., 1995; Paris & Cunningham, 1996). In fact, occasional criticism can actually bolster students' self-concepts and self-esteem *if* it communicates an expectation that students can do better and *if* it provides guidance about how to improve (Pintrich & Schunk, 1996).

■ *Consider the unique needs of girls and boys.* Many children and adolescents may place little value on characteristics and abilities that they think are more "appropriate" for members of the opposite sex. In addition, they may place *too much* value on qualities they think they need to be "feminine" or "manly." Thus, some teenage girls may strive for impossible standards of physical beauty; some teenage boys may worry that they are maturing too slowly and lack the height and build of some of their classmates.

With these points in mind, teachers should probably use somewhat different tactics in nurturing the self-concepts of girls and boys. For example, they might want to help girls identify realistic standards by which to judge themselves and (given girls' propensity to react more negatively to failures) encourage them to pat themselves on the back for their many successes, even those (and perhaps *especially* those) in traditionally "male" domains such as science and mathematics. But boys, too, have special needs (it's our opinion, in fact, that there is entirely too little literature on the needs of boys). Boys are often brought up to believe that they should be manly, aggressive, and "tough," and that they should hide any self-doubts and feelings of inadequacy. Accordingly, teachers may want to take special pains to acknowledge boys' "softer" sides—perhaps their compassion, gentleness, or skill in interacting with small children—and to communicate that childhood and adolescence are times for trying new activities, developing new skills, and inevitably making a few mistakes along the way.

As you can see, teachers can do many things to promote positive, healthy self-concepts. What seems to be particularly critical is that students succeed in areas that are important to *them*. We should note, however, that the popular educational literature often overrates positive self-concepts and high self-esteem as targets for educational enhancement (Harter, 1998). Certainly we want students to feel good about themselves, but we also want them to study hard, learn a lot, and get along with peers. Promoting healthy representations of self can be valuable, but it needs to take place in a meaningful educational context and not interfere with other instructional objectives for students. We encourage our readers to consider the recommendations in the Development and Practice feature in this section, as well as to formulate implications for the specific age level of students they plan to teach.

As we've explored the topics of attachment, emotional development, and development of the self, we've found that different age groups have different priorities. For instance, forming attachments is a major focus in infancy, whereas establishing a personal identity is a particular concern during adolescence. Erik Erikson has synthesized some of these age-specific issues into a life-span perspective of personal and emotional development. His theory is the final topic of the chapter.

A Life-Span Approach to Personal and Emotional Development: Erikson's Theory

Erikson (1963, 1972) outlined eight developmental periods, or **psychosocial stages,** to characterize the course of personal and emotional development. He proposed that human beings tackle a different developmental task or dilemma at each stage and that their achievements at that stage have lifelong implications. Here we describe his eight stages and relate them to concepts we have previously considered.

Trust Versus Mistrust (Infancy) According to Erikson, infants' primary developmental task is to learn whether or not they can trust other people to satisfy their basic needs. A child's parents and other primary caregivers play a key role here. When caregivers can be depended on to feed a hungry stomach, change an uncomfortable diaper, and provide physical affection at regular intervals, an infant learns *trust*—that others are consistently dependable and reliable. When caregivers ignore the infant's needs, are inconsistent in attending to them, or are even abusive, the infant may instead learn *mistrust*—that the world is an undependable, unpredictable, and possibly dangerous place.

Erikson's notion of trust aligns closely with the secure attachment we spoke of earlier. His notion of mistrust is more reflective of insecure attachment and, even more so, disorganized and disoriented attachment. But, as you may recall from our discussion of attachment, young children form attachments with other people besides their primary caregivers. Furthermore, throughout their development they continue to have many opportunities to form trusting relationships with others.

psychosocial stages
In Erikson's theory, eight periods of life that involve age-related tasks or dilemmas.

Autonomy Versus Shame and Doubt (Toddler Years) As toddlers gain increased muscular coordination and the mobility that accompanies crawling and walking, they become capable of satisfying some of their own needs. They are learning to feed themselves, wash and dress themselves, and use the bathroom. When parents and other caregivers encourage self-sufficient behavior, toddlers develop *autonomy,* a sense of being able to handle many problems on their own. But when caregivers demand too much too soon, refuse to let children perform tasks of which they are capable, or ridicule early attempts at self-sufficiency, children may instead develop *shame and doubt* about their ability to handle the problems they encounter.

Erikson's concept of autonomy is reminiscent of an idea we considered earlier—that securely attached children are more willing to venture out on their own and explore their environment. His concepts of shame and doubt suggest the beginnings of self-conscious emotions and a poor self-concept.

Initiative Versus Guilt (Preschool Years) If all goes well, children spend their infancy and toddler years learning to trust others and to construct a sense of autonomy: The world is a good place, people love them, and they can make things happen. With these important lessons under their belts, children are ready to face Erikson's third psychosocial stage. With their growing independence, preschoolers begin to get their own ideas about the activities they want to pursue; for example, they may undertake simple art projects, make houses and roadways in the sandbox, or play "house" with other children. When parents and preschool teachers encourage and support such efforts, children develop *initiative*—independence in planning and undertaking activities. When adults discourage such activities, children may instead develop *guilt* about their needs and desires.

Drawing on a concept we considered earlier, we could say that children with high self-efficacy—those who are confident that they can achieve desired goals—are more likely to initiate challenging tasks that will benefit their long-term development. And adults, through the messages they communicate about children's capabilities, play a key role in fostering high self-efficacy.

Industry Versus Inferiority (Elementary School Years) When they reach elementary school, children are expected to master many new skills, and they soon learn that they can gain the recognition of adults through their academic assignments, art projects, athletic accomplishments, and so on. When children are allowed and encouraged to make and do things and when they are praised for their accomplishments, they begin to demonstrate *industry*—a pattern of working hard, persisting at lengthy tasks, and putting work before pleasure. But when children are ridiculed or punished for their efforts or when they find that they cannot meet their teachers' and parents' expectations for performance, they may develop feelings of *inferiority* about their own abilities.

Earlier we discovered that children in the lower elementary grades define themselves largely in terms of concrete, observable characteristics such as physical appearance, behaviors, and the like. In Chapter 4, we learned that elementary school children often have difficulty with abstract ideas. It makes sense, then, that children in this age range should derive satisfaction from concrete, observable accomplishments.

Identity Versus Role Confusion (Adolescence) As they make the transition from childhood to adulthood, adolescents begin to wrestle with the questions of who they are and how they will eventually fit into the adult world. Initially, they are likely to experience some *role confusion*—mixed ideas and feelings about the specific ways in which they will fit into society—and may experiment with a variety of behaviors and activities (e.g., tinkering with cars, baby-sitting for neighbors, engaging in extracurricular activities at school, affiliating with particular political or religious groups). According to Erikson, most adolescents eventually achieve a sense of *identity* regarding who they are and where their lives are headed.

As you may have noticed, Erikson's concept of identity is very similar to Marcia's concept of identity achievement, and his concept of role confusion should remind you of Marcia's concepts of identity diffusion and moratorium. Such parallels are hardly a coincidence. In fact, Marcia used Erikson's theory of psychosocial development as a springboard for his own work on adolescent identity.

Intimacy Versus Isolation (Young Adulthood) Once people have established their identities, they are ready to make commitments to one or more other individuals. They become capable of engaging in *intimacy*—that is, they form close, reciprocal relationships with others (e.g., through marriage, partnerships, or close friendships) and willingly make the sacrifices and compromises that such relationships require. When people cannot form these intimate relationships (perhaps because of their reluctance or inability to forego the satisfaction of their own needs), then a sense of *isolation* may result.

Generativity Versus Stagnation (Middle Age) During middle age, the primary developmental task is one of contributing to society and helping to guide future generations. When an individual makes a contribution during this period, perhaps by raising a family or by working toward the betterment of society, a sense of *generativity*—a sense of productivity and accomplishment—results. In contrast, an individual who is self-centered and unable or unwilling to help society move forward develops a feeling of *stagnation,* a dissatisfaction with the relative lack of production.

Integrity Versus Despair (Retirement Years) According to Erikson, the final developmental task is a retrospective one. Individuals look back on their lives and accomplishments. They develop feelings of contentment and *integrity* if they believe that they have led a happy, productive life. They may instead develop a sense of *despair* if they look back on a life of disappointments and unachieved goals.

Critiquing Erikson's Theory

Erikson's stages nicely summarize some of the ideas we've presented in this chapter. Yet the stages are probably not completely accurate descriptions of what happens at each age period, in part because they ignore the very important role that culture plays in personal and emotional development. For example, many cultures intentionally discourage autonomy, initiative, and self-assertiveness in young children, sometimes as a way of protecting them from the very real dangers of their environments (Chen et al., 1992; Harwood et al., 1995; Powell, 1983). Furthermore, Erikson believed that most people achieve a sense of identity by the end of adolescence. But more recent evidence indicates that, even by the high school years, only a small minority of students have begun to think seriously about the eventual role they will play in society and the lifelong goals they wish to pursue (Archer, 1982; Durkin, 1995; Marcia, 1988). Also problematic is the fact that Erikson based his stages on studies of *men.* For many women, a focus on intimacy occurs simultaneously with, and in some cases may even precede, a focus on identity (Josselson, 1988).

Perhaps a useful perspective to take on Erikson's theory is one similar to the stance we advocated for Piaget's theory in Chapter 4: The eight psychosocial stages provide a general idea of the ages at which various issues in personal and emotional development are likely to emerge. Nevertheless, considerable flexibility and diversity are present in these timelines.

The importance of children's emotions and self-perceptions will continue to be evident as we explore the development of social understanding and morality in Chapter 10 and motivation in Chapter 11. For now, however, we use our closing case study to consider how emotions and self-perceptions influence classroom behavior.

CASE STUDY: THE GIRLY SHIRT

Eight-year-old Tim caused quite a disruption in class this morning. His teacher, Amy Fox, isn't quite sure what caused the disruption, and so she is meeting with Tim while the other students are at lunch so she can better understand what happened.

Ms. Fox:	Things got out of control in class this morning, didn't they, Tim?
Tim:	I guess they did.
Ms. Fox:	Tell me what happened.
Tim:	John and Steven were teasing me about my shirt. They really made me mad.
Ms. Fox:	They were teasing you about your *shirt?* What did they say?
Tim:	That it's too pink. That it's a "girly" color.
Ms. Fox:	Really? I don't think it's too "girly" at all. In fact, I rather like that color on you. But anyway, you say the boys teased you about it. What did you do then?
Tim:	I yelled at them. Then when you gave me that dirty look, they kept on laughing, and so I kept on yelling.

Ms. Fox:	I see. John and Steven were certainly wrong to tease you about your clothes. I'll speak to them later. But right now I'm concerned about how you reacted to the situation. You were so loud that the class couldn't possibly continue with the lesson.
Tim:	I know. I'm sorry.
Ms. Fox:	I appreciate your apology, Tim. And I'd like to make sure that the next time someone hurts your feelings—maybe intentionally, maybe not—you don't blow up the way you did today. Let's come up with a plan for how you might keep your temper under better control.

- In what way does John's and Steven's behavior reflect the process of *socialization?* What effect might their behavior have on Tim's self-concept?
- Considering what you have learned about trends in emotional development, is Tim's reaction typical for his age?
- What kind of plan might be effective in helping Tim control his anger?

SUMMARY

Early Attachments

Early attachments are close and enduring social-emotional bonds that form between infants and their caregivers. Sensitive and responsive nurturance provides the necessary catalyst for the formation of attachments, but children also contribute by returning their caregivers' affection. Secure attachments in the early years are predictive of positive social-emotional outcomes later on. Yet attachments manifest themselves somewhat differently in different cultures, and the nature of people's attachments can and often does change over time.

Emotional Development

Emotions are universally seen in all cultures, and they seem to have an adaptive function. Individual differences in emotional functioning appear to be the result of both biology (e.g., temperament, gender-specific hormones) and environment (e.g., socialization by parents, peers, and culture). Emotions develop in several ways; for instance, children and adolescents become increasingly able to regulate their emotions in ways that are both socially acceptable and personally effective. Dealing with students' emotions is an important part of teaching, and in fact teachers can do many things to promote students' emotional development. Teachers need to be especially alert to the needs of students with serious and chronic emotional needs (depression, anxiety disorders, conduct disorders).

Development of the Self

Children develop a perception of who they are (self-concept) and have feelings about their worthiness (self-esteem). As they encounter various successes and failures, and as other people continue to give them feedback about their performance and worth, they develop increasingly complex understandings of themselves, and such self-perceptions influence their behavior and achievement at school. Most children and adolescents enjoy positive self-concepts and high self-esteem, but temporary declines are often seen at major transition points (e.g., when children begin elementary school and then again when they move on to secondary school). In childhood, the focus is largely on learning what one can and cannot do; in adolescence, the focus shifts to the formation of an identity—a sense of who one is and what course one's life will take. Teachers can most effectively foster positive self-concepts not by telling students that they are "good" or "smart," but rather by helping them succeed at challenging academic, social, and physical tasks.

Erikson's Theory

Erikson proposed that eight stages (the first beginning in infancy and the last occurring in old age) describe the evolution of people's personal and emotional functioning. There are similarities between how Erikson described the stages and what other theorists have learned about attachment, self-concept, and identity. However, some psychologists argue that Erikson's theory does not accurately describe emotional development in some cultures, nor does it adequately account for the interplay of identity and intimacy.

 Now go to our Companion Website to assess your understanding of chapter content with Multiple-Choice Questions, apply comprehension in Essay Questions, and broaden your knowledge with links to related Developmental Psychology World Wide Web sites.

KEY CONCEPTS

attachment (p. 319)
ethological attachment theory (p. 319)
secure attachment (p. 320)
insecure-avoidant attachment (p. 320)
insecure-resistant attachment (p. 320)
disorganized and disoriented attachment (p. 320)
emotion (p. 325)
temperament (p. 327)

socialization (p. 327)
emotional contagion (p. 328)
social referencing (p. 328)
self-conscious emotion (p. 328)
emotional regulation (p. 329)
anxiety (p. 335)
externalizing behavior (p. 335)
internalizing behavior (p. 335)
depression (p. 336)
bipolar disorder (p. 336)
anxiety disorder (p. 337)

conduct disorder (p. 337)
self-concept (p. 339)
self-esteem (p. 339)
self-efficacy (p. 340)
imaginary audience (p. 344)
personal fable (p. 344)
identity (p. 345)
identity crisis (p. 346)
androgyny (p. 348)
ethnic identity (p. 350)
psychosocial stages (p. 354)

Dustin, age 14

Social Understanding and Moral Development

CASE STUDY: TOM

For a 13-year-old, Tom is remarkably insightful about social problems within his society. Although members of his immediate family have advocated and modeled tolerance for people from all walks of life, he is frustrated by the racial and religious prejudice he sees in his extended family and among his peers:

[1]My father told me to make all kinds of friends. If you don't get friends—it's the same with adults—you are always cranky and mad.

. . . [My father] made a love-match to a Catholic [my mother] against his parents' will. My grandmother, she's still mad. My father is different from all his other brothers. Maybe it came from the time he went for my mother.

. . . My uncle thinks prejudice against Russians is unfair, but he makes my cousins prejudiced. My cousins keep talking against Jews, and Catholics, too. But my father tells them they should save up and be so smart. Once he made them scramble for pennies to tease them out of it! That's what kids do to Jews! Prejudice, it's really painful. People can really just hate. I can't believe how people hate others, and I don't understand it. . . .

. . . I think the main problem causing racism is people just don't want to associate. . . . They don't care that much. We put people together in the schools, and it's a lot better than white and black separate, but still nobody really tries. Especially in the high school; my brother tells me about that. I've seen here in junior high that more kids don't like black kids than before, and they don't try to make them feel better any more. They used to, in sixth grade. Now they go off, the blacks by themselves, so what can you do? Well, I get models and make them with Tim because we were friends in sixth. You got to care. Some Indians are starving, and people don't care. Even right here in the U.S. We gotta put money in that. I read the paper, and I see nobody knows what's going on. You gotta change the system of forgetting poor people, first of everything. (Davidson & Davidson, 1994, pp. 88–90)

Yet Tom has considerable optimism that a democratic society has the means to make societal conditions more equitable for people from diverse backgrounds:

It's important to consider what laws should be made. It is laws that make a nation, because people would otherwise go by their own thoughts, and there could be no cooperation, no society, no progress. Cooperation makes progress. It would be better if the whole world could work on laws, but the way it is, nations do. If you don't have taxes, you can't have good education. You have to have money provided. If you put something in, you get something out. Then educated people can work on the laws, to make them more fair, and to see why they have to pay taxes. It's the main thing not to be rich, as an ideal, not to beat out the other guys, but just to live, and to preserve all life.

. . . It gets more selfish as you get older. Maybe you get a job and you're busy. Then you kind of forget the things you wanted to do for somebody. That's why I want to be a politician—to do all the projects I want to do, to change things. (Davidson & Davidson, 1994, p. 90)

[1]Excerpts from *Changing Childhood Prejudice: The Caring Work of the Schools* by Florence H. Davidson and Miriam M. Davidson. Copyright © 1994 by Florence H. Davidson and Miriam M. Davidson. Reproduced with permission of Greenwood Publishing Group, Inc., Westport, CT.

T OM IS DEEPLY CONCERNED about the rights and welfare of his fellow human beings. He voices disdain for unjustified prejudices and for the widespread indifference to those in need, but he tries to understand how people might acquire their biases and self-centeredness ("Maybe you get a job and you're busy. Then you kind of forget the things you wanted to do for somebody," Davidson & Davidson, 1994, p. 90). He believes that society has an obligation to care for those who live in poverty and expresses optimism that by becoming a politician, he can "do all the projects I want to do, to change things" (p. 90).

Tom's advanced social understandings and desire to make the world a better place provide us with a positive, hopeful context in which to introduce the concepts of this chapter. We look first at children's and adolescents' social understandings—for instance, the characteristics and qualities they notice in other people, the inferences they make about others' feelings and motives, the conclusions they draw about particular social groups, and the theories they construct about such broad social institutions as government and private industry. We then consider children's and adolescents' moral development—their continuing growth in their sense of right and wrong, concern for the rights of others, and commitment to caring for those less fortunate than themselves.

Schools and classrooms provide key contexts in which young people acquire their social knowledge and moral beliefs. Accordingly, at several points in the chapter we offer suggestions for how teachers can nurture the development of productive perspectives about society and morality.

Social Understanding

Tom is thoughtful about the internal mental life of other people. When family members and classmates behave in disturbing ways, he considers possible underlying causes for their actions. He ruminates over how they respond to events ("People can really just hate," Davidson & Davidson, 1994, p. 89) and the experiences that might have led to certain behavior patterns ("My uncle . . . makes my cousins prejudiced," p. 89). Occasionally he remains puzzled ("I can't believe how people hate others, and I don't understand it," p. 89). He is clearly constructing his own informal theories about the people around him (recall our discussion of *theory theory* in Chapter 5) but continues to revise and refine these theories as he acquires new evidence.

Children and adolescents think a lot about social matters and use the fruits of their social thinking to fine-tune their interpersonal skills and relationships. In this section of the chapter, we explore such social understandings. We look first at *social cognition,* including the ways in which children and adolescents interpret other people's actions and the specific information processing mechanisms that may underlie such interpretations. We then consider *social perspective taking,* the ability to look at situations from another's viewpoint. Later, we consider how children supplement their inferences about people's internal states with deliberations on the broader social world, including government, the worlds of industry and commerce, and the unequal distribution of income and prejudicial treatment of certain groups of people. Finally, we offer suggestions for enhancing children's and adolescents' social understandings in classroom settings.

Social Cognition

As someone who is currently studying child development, you undoubtedly find children and adolescents to be fascinating creatures. Youngsters share this fascination about others. While you're wondering about them, they're wondering about you and, perhaps even more intently, about one another. Children and adolescents spend much of their mental energy engaged in **social cognition**, thinking about people (including themselves) and society (Fiske & Taylor, 1991).

Social cognition is such an important topic that we've integrated it into several chapters of the book, albeit under different labels. In Chapter 9, we discussed children's developing beliefs about themselves—about who they are, what they stand for, and where they hope to go in life. This is social cognition turned inward, applied to the self. Social cognition about the

social cognition
Thinking about people, self, and society.

self can also be found in students' beliefs about their own abilities and talents. In Chapter 11, we will show that these beliefs are influential in children's activity choices, persistence, and other aspects of motivation.

Turned outward, social cognition helps children make sense of social relationships and institutions. You may recall our discussion of attachment in Chapter 9: Secure attachments predispose children to trust others; insecure attachments make them wary and suspicious. As you will see in Chapter 13, children also develop understandings about other close relationships, such as friendships. And in Chapter 12, we will examine the beliefs that parents have about children in general and about the purposes that schools and education should serve.

We've also introduced concepts from social cognition into our discussion of cognition itself. As an example, recall the concept of *theory of mind*, described in Chapter 5. By middle childhood, children know that the mind can be wrong: They may realize that they have been duped by a peer, or they may hear classmates presenting interpretations of a poem or a novel that differ from the interpretation that they themselves have constructed.

Social cognition, then, is a robust theme that can be found in many developmental "places." It is in this chapter, however, that we put it under the microscope, sharpening the lens on how children and adolescents think about people. We begin with two fundamental elements of social cognition, **person perception,** the recognition and interpretation of others' physical features, behaviors, and internal psychological states, and **social information processing**, the mental processes involved in understanding and responding to social events.

Person Perception How do children perceive other people? To make this question meaningful, we ask you to imagine a simple event:

> A man walks into a room with a sad look on his face. He comes in, stumbles a bit, then sits at a table beside a young boy, smiles, picks up a cookie, takes a bite, drinks from a glass of milk, and then puts the half-filled glass on the table.

How might children interpret this vignette? We can speculate about how responses might vary across the age levels.

Early childhood (ages 2–6). From their earliest days, children perceive people to be different from inanimate objects: They expect people to be active, expressive, and responsive. Infants look away or become downright huffy when adults stay motionless in front of them (Tronick, Als, & Adamson, 1979). At age 2, children spontaneously use words that refer to people's mental states—for instance, saying "Mommy want lunch" or "Billy feel sad" (Bretherton & Beeghly, 1982; Dunn, 1988). In the case of our vignette, we would expect preschoolers to perceive the man as engaging in a series of intentional, goal-driven actions, even though the children would not use such words. For instance, they might say that the man is "hungry" or that he "wants" to sit near the boy.

Middle childhood (ages 6–10). In the elementary school years, children recognize that people have psychological qualities but tend to zero in on concrete, observable features. In responding to our vignette, they would probably first focus on behaviors and appearance; for instance, they might mention that the man sits down and eats a cookie and that the boy is wearing a soccer uniform (Hart & Damon, 1986; Livesley & Bromley, 1973; Newman, 1991; Oppenheimer & de Groot, 1981). As they get older, children increasingly address psychological characteristics, such as being friendly, grouchy, or bossy; for instance, they might suggest that the man is a father who is tired after a hard day at work (Barenboim, 1981). Elementary-age children are also aware that people sometimes hide their true emotions (see Chapter 9); thus, children might speculate that the man is sad from his day at work but trying to be happy and friendly for the benefit of his son.

Early adolescence (ages 10–14). Young adolescents turn to person perception with a passion. When describing people, they continue to offer information about appearance and general background information, such as a person's age, gender, religion, or school affiliation (Livesley & Bromley, 1973). Thus, we might learn that the man, who appears to be a father, sits down with a young boy, who may be his son. Their interpretation might include multiple motivations: Perhaps the father has missed his son during the day *and* is hungry since it has been a long time since lunch. Especially notable during early adolescence is the dramatic increase in inferences

person perception
Recognition and interpretation of people's basic characteristics, including their physical features, behaviors, and internal psychological states.

social information processing
Series of cognitive steps applied to understanding of, and responding to, social events.

about psychological states: We may hear about a boy who is lonely and hungry and a father who is frustrated with his job but finds comfort in his family.

Late adolescence (ages 14–18). Older adolescents, who can draw on a rich knowledge base derived from numerous social experiences, become more skillful at drawing inferences about people's psychological characteristics, intentions, and needs (Eisenberg, Carlo, Murphy, & Van Court, 1995; Paget, Kritt, & Bergemann, 1984). Furthermore, they are more attuned to the complex dynamics that influence behavior (Flanagan & Tucker, 1999). For instance, an older teen might speculate that the man in the vignette had been troubled by other interpersonal relationships (perhaps with his wife or boss), tried to drown his sorrows at a local bar (his drunken state explains his stumble upon entering the room), and now wants to hide his despair and inebriation from his son.

Social Information Processing Social information processing is, in many respects, similar to the more general information processing we described in Chapter 5. For example, it involves selecting and paying *attention* to certain stimuli, making sense of those stimuli through *elaboration, storing* and *organizing* what one has learned in long-term memory, and *retrieving* previously acquired information and beliefs on relevant occasions. Dodge (1986) has proposed that people go through five steps when they encounter, interpret, and respond to specific social situations. To give life to Dodge's model, let's imagine an extension to our earlier vignette:

> A man walks into a room with a sad look on his face. He comes in, stumbles a bit, sits at a table beside a young boy, smiles, picks up a cookie, takes a bite, drinks from a glass of milk, and then puts the half-filled glass on the table. The boy looks up at the man, smiles, and knocks over the milk. The milk spills and splashes onto the man's shirt. The man gets up quickly, walks over to the sink, and finds a kitchen rag. He brushes off his shirt and then cleans up the wet table.

If we were to videotape such a scenario, children would, from Dodge's perspective, engage in the following cognitive processes in their efforts to understand and respond to it (note that we describe these processes within the context of concepts presented in Chapter 5):

1. *Encoding.* The children would attend to particular aspects of people's appearance and behavior and then store such information in working memory. We suspect that children would be most attentive to the spilled milk segment, with its noisy and fast-moving features.
2. *Representation.* The children would interpret the social phenomena they observed; that is, they would elaborate on the information they've obtained given what they have already learned about human nature. Considering their preliminary ideas of what's going on, they would search for other relevant information in the scenario that might confirm or contradict their interpretations. For instance, they might wonder: Why did the man stumble? Was spilling the milk an accident, or did the boy do it on purpose? What will the boy do now? Using the social cues in the situation, as well as their own knowledge and beliefs about how people typically behave, they might formulate some tentative answers to such questions.
3. *Response search.* Events that are personally relevant call for a response. Children draw on their past experiences to decide how to handle their social dilemmas; that is, they retrieve potentially useful responses from long-term memory. For example, if we asked our child viewers what they would do if the boy spilled milk all over *them*, they might suggest a variety of possibilities—perhaps including patiently cleaning up the spill or retaliating against the "aggressor"—with their specific suggestions depending on their prior social experiences.
4. *Response decision.* Once they've retrieved alternative responses, children need to weigh the benefits and drawbacks of each solution. If the boy spilled milk on them, what would they gain and lose from cleaning up the mess? What would they gain and lose from retaliating? In some cases, children may ponder various alternatives for some time; in other cases, they may reach their conclusion quickly, with very little forethought.
5. *Enactment.* In real-life situations, once they've settled on a course of action, children enact the response and observe its effects. For example, if they clean up the mess (and perhaps ask the boy to be more careful), they might find that they maintain a productive relation-

ship with him. If, instead, they retaliate, they might find themselves embroiled in an escalating argument.

As you can see, then, Dodge's model is not confined to perception of and response to immediate social stimuli; it also draws on memories of past social events and actions and incorporates deliberation and decision making.

The social information processing model has spawned much research and has been an especially useful perspective for describing exceptionally aggressive children (Crick & Dodge, 1996; Lochman & Dodge, 1994, 1998; Schwartz et al., 1998; Zelli, Dodge, Lochman, & Laird, 1999). Children who are overly aggressive tend to attribute aggressive intentions to others, often mistakenly; for instance, they would quickly conclude that the boy in our vignette spilled the milk as a premeditated, hostile act. Aggressive children's thinking may be different in other ways as well; for instance, they may have a bigger arsenal of aggressive actions to pull from their behavioral repertoire, and they are likely to perceive their aggressive behaviors as justified and effective (e.g., the boy should be "taught a lesson"). We will look at the nature and possible roots of aggression more closely in Chapter 13.

Social Perspective Taking

To truly understand and get along with other people, recognizing others' physical and psychological characteristics and identifying appropriate responses to their actions is not enough. Children must also be able to step into other people's shoes—that is, to look at the world from other viewpoints. In the opening case, Tom tries to understand why, in his mind, people become increasingly selfish as they get older: "Maybe you get a job and you're busy. Then you kind of forget the things you wanted to do for somebody" (Davidson & Davidson, 1994, p. 90). Such **social perspective taking** helps children make sense of actions that might otherwise be puzzling and choose responses that are most likely to achieve desired results and maintain positive interpersonal relationships. We begin our examination of social perspective taking by looking at Robert Selman's classic theory.

By learning to appreciate the perspectives of others, children and adolescents become increasingly effective in interpersonal situations.

Development of Perspective Taking: Selman's Theory Consider the following situation:

Holly's Dilemma

Holly is an 8-year-old girl who likes to climb trees. She is the best tree climber in the neighborhood. One day while climbing down from a tall tree she falls off the bottom branch but does not hurt herself. Her father sees her fall. He is upset and asks her to promise not to climb the trees any more. Holly promises.

Later that day, Holly and her friends meet Sean. Sean's kitten is caught up in a tree and cannot get down. Something has to be done right away or the kitten may fall. Holly is the only one who climbs trees well enough to reach the kitten and get it down, but she remembers her promise to her father. . . .

Does Holly know how Sean feels about the kitten?
Does Sean know why Holly cannot decide whether or not to climb the tree? . . .

What does Holly think her father will think of her if he finds out?
Does Holly think her father will understand why she climbed the tree? (Selman & Byrne, 1974, p. 805)

To answer these questions, you must look at the situation from the perspectives of three different people: Sean, Holly, and Holly's father.

By presenting situations like the "Holly" story and asking children to view them from various perspectives, Robert Selman (1980; Selman & Schultz, 1990) found that with age, children show an increasing ability to take the perspective of others. He described a series of five levels that characterize the development of perspective taking. Selman's levels, and some ways in which they may manifest themselves, are presented in the Observational Guidelines table that follows.

social perspective taking
Imagining what someone else is thinking or feeling.

Using Selman's Levels to Assess Students' Social Perspective Taking

OBSERVATION GUIDELINES

CHARACTERISTIC	LOOK FOR	EXAMPLE	IMPLICATION
Level 0: Egocentric Perspective Taking	• Awareness that people are different in physical ways (e.g., gender, appearance) • Little if any awareness that people are also different in psychological ways (e.g., thoughts, feelings); assumption that other people share one's thoughts and feelings • Indignant responses when other people express differing views	Four-year-old Andrea assumes that her preschool classmates know about her fear of heights. So she expresses surprise and indignation when Rose and Molly ask her to join them in going down the slide.	Encourage students to share their unique perspectives about simple topics. For example, read a story to preschoolers and then ask them to describe how they each felt about various story characters' actions. Point out the variability in the children's opinions ("Isn't it wonderful how much we can learn from hearing all these different ideas?").
Level 1: Subjective Perspective Taking	• Realization that other people have thoughts and feelings different from one's own • Overly simplistic perceptions of others' perspectives • Tendency to equate people's outward expressions (e.g., smiles) with their internal feelings	Eight-year-old Li-Wen realizes that her friend Tony is sad about his grandfather's death. However, she does not fully appreciate the depth of his sorrow, nor does she understand his simultaneous relief that the grandfather's physical suffering has ended.	Acknowledge students' perceptiveness in detecting the unique perspectives of others. Extend their understanding by pointing out the complex feelings that people sometimes have.
Level 2: Second-Person, Reciprocal Perspective Taking	• Realization that others may have mixed and possibly contradictory feelings about a situation • Understanding that people may feel differently from what their behaviors indicate and that people sometimes do things they didn't intend to do	Eleven-year-old Pablo understands that his friend Mark may have misgivings about his decision to experiment with inhalants at a friend's house. Pablo hears Mark bragging but senses some reservations in Mark's tone of voice and body language.	Help students to make sense of the complex motivations that guide people's actions. Communicate the legitimacy of mixed feelings ("I bet you're excited *and* sad about your move to a new school").
Level 3: Third-Person, Mutual Perspective Taking	• Ability to not only see a situation from one's own and another's perspectives but also to look at a two-person relationship from a distance (i.e., as an outsider might) • Appreciation of the need to satisfy both oneself and another simultaneously • Understanding of the advantages of cooperation, compromise, and trust	Two high-school freshmen, Jasmine and Alethea, discover that they've both arranged a homecoming party for the same night. They learn that they've sent invitations to numerous mutual friends as well as to each other. Since they were both looking forward to hosting a party, they discuss options for rescheduling one or both of the parties.	Acknowledge students' respect for the rights of others as they pursue their own needs and goals. Help students brainstorm alternative strategies when they have trouble identifying ways for everyone to "win" in certain situations.
Level 4: Societal, Symbolic Perspective Taking	• Recognition that people are a product of their environment—that past events and present circumstances contribute to personality and behavior • Understanding that people are not always aware of why they act as they do • Emerging comprehension of the true complexity of human behaviors, thoughts, and emotions	In their high school psychology course, Jerome and Keith are preparing a joint oral report on strategies of social persuasion. They find magazine advertisements that are geared toward adolescents and discuss possible images and feelings that advertisers are trying to invoke.	Initiate class discussions of psychological motives, perhaps within the context of studying historical events in a history class or works of poetry and fiction in a literature class. For example, encourage students to identify the varying motives that may have converged to affect a character's decisions in a classic work of literature.

Sources: Based on Selman, 1980; Selman & Schultz, 1990.

According to Selman, most preschoolers are incapable of taking anyone else's perspective (they are at Level 0); thus, we see the preoperational egocentrism that Piaget described (see Chapter 4). But by the time children reach the primary grades, most have begun to realize that people have different thoughts and feelings as well as different physical features (Level 1). They view someone else's perspective as a relatively simplistic, one-dimensional entity, however; for example, another person is simply happy, sad, or angry. Furthermore, they tend to equate behavior with feelings: A happy person will smile, a sad person will pout or cry, and so on. Their interpretations of someone else's actions are also overly simplistic, as this scenario illustrates:

> Donald is a new student in a second-grade classroom. A group of boys in the class openly ridicule his unusual hairstyle and shun him at lunch and on the playground. After school, one of the boys makes a cruel remark about Donald's hair, and Donald responds by punching him. The boys decide that Donald is a "mean kid."

The boys at Donald's new school are interpreting his behavior in a simplistic, Level 1 fashion. They do not yet appreciate the many feelings that Donald may be experiencing: anxiety about a new school and community, shame about a hairstyle that was "cool" at his previous school, and frustration at his inability to make new friends.

As they approach the upper elementary grades, children are likely to show signs of Level 2 perspective taking. They now know that other people can have mixed, conflicting feelings about a situation. They also realize that people may feel differently from what their behaviors indicate—that they may try to hide their true feelings. At this point, too, children recognize the importance of intentions: They understand that people may do things that they didn't really want or intend to do. For example, Level 2 children would be more likely to appreciate Donald's predicament and to understand that his aggressive behavior might reflect something other than a mean streak. They might also recognize that Donald's punch was an unintended reaction to a thoughtless insult.

In middle and secondary school, most individuals are at Selman's two highest levels of perspective taking, in which they are able to take an "outsider's" perspective of interpersonal relationships. Children and adolescents at Levels 3 and 4 appreciate the need to satisfy both oneself and another simultaneously and therefore understand the advantages of cooperation, compromise, and trust. Not surprisingly, then, friendships become relationships of mutual sharing and support beginning in middle and junior high school (more on this point in Chapter 13). Additional aspects of perspective taking emerge at Level 4: Teenagers begin to recognize that an individual's behavior is likely to be influenced by many factors—including one's thoughts, feelings, present circumstances, and past events—and that other people are not always aware of why they act as they do. Level 4 perspective taking, then, relies on understanding the true complexity of human behaviors, thoughts, and emotions.

Other theorists have offered additional insights about children's perspective-taking abilities. First, as we have already seen, young children appear able to consider how other people think and feel about things, even if they do not always exercise this ability; thus, they are not as egocentric as Piaget and Selman proposed. For example, in their communication, children appear to be truly other-oriented the majority of the time; that is, they listen to what other people say, respond appropriately, and take into account how their listeners might be thinking and feeling (Garvey & Horgan, 1973; Mueller, 1972; Rubin & Pepler, 1995). Furthermore, researchers have looked more closely at several aspects of social perspective taking, including awareness of intentionality, recursive thinking, and the role of empathy.

Awareness of Intentionality   Under the auspices of their work on children's theory of mind, developmentalists have examined children's comprehension of **intentionality**—their beliefs about whether someone performs an action purposefully or accidentally. As an example, consider the following conversation between 2½-year-old Adam and his mother:

Adam:	Why she write dat name?
Mother:	Because she wanted to.
Adam:	Why she wanted to?
Mother:	Because she thought you'd like it.
Adam:	I don't want to like it. (Wellman, Phillips, & Rodriquez, 2000, p. 908)

intentionality
Engaging in an action congruent with one's purpose or goal.

FIGURE 10–1 Which boy wants to swing? Astington (1991) used such drawings to assess young children's understanding of intention.

From "Intention in the Child's Theory of Mind," by J. W. Astington. In *Children's Theories of Mind* (p. 168), by C. Moore & D. Frye, 1991, Hillsdale, NJ: Erlbaum. Reprinted with permission of Lawrence Erlbaum Associates.

In this brief conversation, Adam's discussion of wanting and not wanting reveals an emerging awareness that both he and others have specific desires, and his "why" question reveals his assumption that the unnamed female had a particular purpose in mind when she wrote "dat name."

By their first birthday, infants seem to have some understanding that people often act in a goal-directed fashion, and by age 2 they have a rudimentary sense of what people's intentions might be in certain situations (Dunn, 1988; Woodward & Sommerville, 2000). In the years that follow, children frequently make inferences about whether or not people mean to do something (recall our spilled milk illustration), and their ability to make accurate inferences improves with age. For example, in one study, Astington (1991) showed 3- to 5-year-old children a series of pairs of pictures (Figure 10–1 provides an example) and then asked questions such as "Which boy thinks he'll swing?" and "Which boy would like to swing?" (Astington, 1991, p. 167). The majority of the 5-year-old children pointed to the child preparing to engage in the behavior in question; few of the 3-year-olds answered correctly. More generally, it appears that children gradually learn the multiple cues (e.g., people's facial expressions, the content of people's speech, and the consistency of people's actions) that help them draw conclusions about what people intend to do and whether their behaviors reflect such intentions (Astington, 1991; Rotenberg, Simourd, & Moore, 1989; Smith, 1978; Wellman et al., 2000).

Recursive Thinking Researchers have found that the capacity for social perspective taking expands in specific ways during adolescence. Courtesy of their expanding cognitive abilities, memory capacity, and social awareness, older children and adolescents increasingly appreciate people's perspectives *recursively* (Oppenheimer, 1986; Perner & Wimmer, 1985). That is, they can think about what other people might be thinking about them and eventually can reflect on other people's thoughts about themselves through multiple iterations (e.g., "You think that I think that you think. . ."). This is not to say that adolescents, or adults for that matter, always use this capacity. In fact, thinking only about one's own perspective, without regard for those of others, is a common phenomenon in the adolescent years (e.g., recall our discussion of the *imaginary audience* and *personal fable* in Chapter 9). Thus, teachers and other adults may often need to remind teenagers to consider *why* others might reasonably think and behave as they do.

Role of Empathy Emotions sometimes complement cognitive processes in social perspective taking (Eisenberg, Losoya, & Guthrie, 1997; Feshbach, 1997; Hoffman, 1998; Zahn-Waxler & Smith, 1992). In particular, **empathy** involves experiencing the same feelings as someone else, perhaps someone in pain or distress (Damon, 1988; Eisenberg, 1982; Hoffman, 1991). Empathy seems to play a central role in children's desire to "do the right thing," that is, to behave morally, as we shall discover later in the chapter. It is also a key factor in children's prosocial behaviors (see Chapter 13).

empathy
Experiencing the same feelings as someone else, especially someone in pain or distress.

Children show some signs of empathy by age 2 or 3: They may look concerned when some-one else is in distress and try to give comfort and assistance (Lamb & Feeny, 1995; Lennon & Eisenberg, 1987; Zahn-Waxler & Radke-Yarrow, 1982; Zahn-Waxler, Radke-Yarrow, Wagner, & Chapman, 1992). Empathy continues to develop throughout childhood, and often into ado-lescence as well (Eisenberg, 1982). In early childhood, children are empathic primarily toward people they know, such as friends and classmates. But by the late elementary school years, chil-dren may also begin to feel empathy for complete strangers—perhaps for the poor, the home-less, or those living in war-torn nations (Damon, 1988; Hoffman, 1991).

As you can see, then, children show an early disposition to take into account how others perceive, interpret, and emotionally respond to events. Initially, this disposition is superficial, fragile, and undependable. Over time, it becomes increasingly complex and insightful, and in adolescence, it includes the ability to consider numerous viewpoints recursively. The growing capacity for social perspective taking does not ensure that young people will always apply it, however, as even older adolescents (adults as well, in fact) do not necessarily consider other people's perspectives and feelings in particular social settings.

Conceptions of Society

Individual people are objects of children's analysis, but so are *groups* of people—families, schools, crowds, community associations, corporate organizations, and governments. Chil-dren gradually develop **conceptions of society,** beliefs about the nature, structure, and op-eration of social institutions (Furth, 1980). As with many conceptual developments, chil-dren first apply personalized and concrete notions to the task of understanding various parts of society and then gradually transform their ideas into more comprehensive and abstract models (Furth, 1980). Notice the parallel to our earlier descriptions of developmental trends in person perception and social perspective taking: There is a common shift from concrete to abstract representations.

We now look more closely at children's conceptions about several aspects of their society, including social conventions, neighborhoods and communities, political systems, and eco-nomic systems. We then consider the role that experience plays in such conceptions.

Conceptions of Social Conventions By the time children are 6 or 7, they are aware that society has certain rules and conventions regarding acceptable and unacceptable behaviors (Turiel, 1983). For instance, they know that in our society, people are expected to wear clothes in public and that children should show deference to adult authority figures. They know, too, that certain actions, such as picking one's nose or using obscene language in class, are frowned upon and often lead to social sanctions.

In the early elementary grades, children believe that social conventions should be fol-lowed for their own sake. As they grow older, however, they become more aware of the im-portance of such conventions for maintaining a cohesive society (Turiel, 1983). As an ex-ample, imagine that a boy named Peter calls his teacher by her first name. Children and adolescents almost invariably say that such behavior is inappropriate, but they offer differ-ing explanations about *why* it is inappropriate. Let's consider how three boys analyzed the situation (Turiel, 1983):

John (age 6)
John: [He shouldn't have called the teacher by her first name] because what the teacher tells you, you have to obey and it is being nice to call someone what they want to be called. . . . Because he or she is pretty important.

Bruce (age 11)
Bruce: Wrong, because the principal told him not to. Because it was a rule. It was one of the rules of the school.
Adult: And why does that make it wrong to call a teacher by his first name?
Bruce: Because you should follow the rules.
Adult: Do you think if there wasn't a rule, that it would be wrong—or would it be right to call teachers by their first names?
Bruce: Right. Because if there wasn't a rule, it wouldn't matter. . . . It wouldn't matter what they called her if there wasn't a rule.

conceptions of society
Beliefs about the nature, structure, and operation of social institutions.

Richard (age 17)

Richard: I think he was wrong, because you have to realize that you should have respect for your elders and that respect is shown by addressing them by their last names.

Adult: Why do you think that shows respect?

Richard: Informally, you just call any of your friends by their first names, but you really don't have that relation with a teacher. Whereas with parents too, you call them Mom and Dad and it's a different relation than the other two.

Adult: What if Peter thought it didn't make any difference what you called people, that you could still respect them no matter what you called them?

Richard: I think he'd have to realize that you have to go along with the ways of other people in your society. . . .
(dialogues from Turiel, 1983, pp. 107, 108, 110; format adapted)

Generally speaking, 6- and 7-year-olds (like John) believe that people should follow rules and conventions in large part because authority figures tell them they must do so. In contrast, 10- and 11-year-olds (like Bruce) believe that one should follow rules and conventions simply because they exist, even though they recognize that rules and conventions are somewhat arbitrary. By late adolescence (e.g., at ages 14 to 16), young people realize that conventions help society function more smoothly; for instance, Richard says "you have to go along with the ways of other people in your society" (Kurtines, Berman, Ittel, & Williamson, 1995; Turiel, 1983).

Conceptions of Neighborhoods and Communities For children, "society" is initially what they see close to home in their neighborhoods and communities. Although parents define neighborhoods in terms of physical blocks and boundaries that children can safely navigate, children conceptualize their neighborhoods more as social networks with friends and other neighbors (Bryant, 1985; Burton & Price-Spratlen, 1999). Furthermore, children learn many things about their neighbors that parents do not necessarily know, as the following conversation among Sharelle and Kenya (both age 9) and Dante (age 7) illustrates:

Sharelle: I been knowing ever since I was five about what be going on in our neighborhood . . . about rules and who makes them . . . about when you can be outside and when you can't . . . My momma didn't teach me, huh Kenya, you showed me.

Kenya: Yeah, I learned it from sugababe, now we got the little rookie Dante to teach.

Dante: I'm getting an understanding but I'm gon keep it on the down low. We can't tell old people everything. (Burton & Price-Spratlen, 1999, p. 86)

Sharelle, Kenya, and Dante share a physical environment with adults, but the two generations have different sets of social experiences and so have constructed their own views of social reality.

Children's perceptions of their neighborhoods and communities seem to affect some aspects of their social-emotional development, such as how fearful they become (Garbarino, Kostelny, & Dubrow, 1991a; van Andel, 1990). Neighborhoods and communities vary considerably in how supportive they are as environments for young people, and children quickly become attuned to potential dangers to their physical and psychological safety (Bryant, 1985; Gephart, 1997). To illustrate this point, we present the story of Candida, a girl who grew up in Nicaragua:

Candida grew up on a *finca*, a farm in the country with trees, cows, and chickens. For several years fighting had been occurring in her region. After some of the teenagers in the region were kidnapped by Contras, Candida's father sent some of his older children to live in another village that was safer. One day, when Candida was nine years old, she went out with her father and mother to milk the cows. A group of Contras ambushed and kidnapped all three of them. Candida was separated from her parents and taken away by the Contras. She was held for five months during which time she learned the Contra life: stealing food from houses and carrying supplies while the Contras moved about.

She shuddered as she told us about being forced to watch as the Contras stripped a kidnapped man naked, and then slit his throat with a knife. Afterward, she was given his clothes to wear.

Some of the Contras tried to rape her. An older Contra intervened, claiming that she already belonged to him. He kept her as his "mascot" and protected her from the others. Candida stated that two other kidnapped girls with her had not been so lucky. One was chosen to be the "wife" of the leader, and the other girl was continually raped. (Garbarino, Kostelny, & Dubrow, 1991b, pp. 92–93)[2]

---

[2]From *No Place to Be a Child: Growing Up in a War Zone,* by J. Garbarino, K. Kostelny, & N. Dubrow, 1991, Lexington, MA: Lexington Books. Copyright © 1991 by Lexington Books. Reprinted by permission of Jossey-Bass, Inc., a subsidiary of John Wiley & Sons, Inc.

Candida finally escaped from the Contras; she learned that her parents had been killed but reunited with surviving members of her family. She did not speak for a year after being adopted by her father's cousin, and she had frequent nightmares. Eventually, she gathered her resolve and learned to cope, in part by laboring for a better world:

> Sixteen now, she is known as the *solidad*, the one who is not yet married. She told us she had more important things on her agenda. Sure, she has boyfriends, but she plans to become a civil engineer. She excels in school, especially at math, and has finished six grades in less than three years. She had the opportunity to study abroad—government policy dictates that war orphans are entitled to the best education—but she preferred to study in Nicaragua and stay with her family. She is very active in politics and is very proud that she could vote in the elections. While she hopes there won't be more war, she will join the struggle if necessary. (Garbarino et al., 1991b, p. 93; see footnote 2)

Candida has firsthand knowledge of a brutal and ruthless society. Her interest in politics has grown naturally out of her desire to embrace higher values and work toward a better society (Garbarino et al., 1991b). Candida is hardly alone in her experience with dangerous social environments; we will see other examples in our discussions of abusive families in Chapter 12, aggressive relationships in Chapter 13, and poverty in Chapter 14. For now, though, let's pick up on Candida's interest in political participation.

Conceptions of Political Systems Although most children and adolescents do not encounter an immediate social environment as terrifying as Candida's, many still yearn for a more humane world, and such longing may feed an interest in political systems. Recall Tom's concerns about the plight of poor people in our introductory case: He was determined to improve the living conditions of those around him and envisioned a political career to make this happen. Many young people are, like Tom and Candida, naturally motivated to learn about political participation and the structure of government.

What might political participation mean to young people? Flanagan and Faison (2001) identify several competencies, understandings, and dispositions that children and adolescents might acquire:

- *Civic literacy:* Knowledge about community affairs, political processes, and the ways in which citizens become informed and promote change
- *Civic skills:* Abilities that enable achievement of group goals, including speaking in public, listening to others, taking others' perspectives, contacting public officials, and leading and organizing a group
- *Civic attachment:* Emotional connection with a community and the belief that one can make a difference in community affairs

Family discussions about controversial political issues foster young people's civic understandings and commitments (Chaffee & Yang, 1990). Teachers and other school personnel are influential as well—for instance, by conducting discussions about current events and by providing opportunities for participation in student government and community service (Chapman, Nolin, & Kline, 1997; Niemi & Junn, 1998). Furthermore, many schools promote an appreciation for the value and benefits of democracy. Reflecting on their own research, Flanagan and Faison write:

> We have found that, to the extent that a civic ethos describes the climate at school, students are more likely to believe that America is a just society where equal opportunity is the rule. The ethos to which we refer is one in which teachers insure that all students are treated equally. Not only do teachers hold the same high standards for and respect the ideas of all students, but they insist that students listen to and respect one another as well. And, if there are instances of intolerance or bullying, the teacher intervenes to stop the incivility. Note that by tolerance we are not referring to apathy or indifference. Students are encouraged to develop their own opinions. They are not asked to agree with one another, only to respect one another's rights to self-determination. (Flanagan & Faison, 2001, pp. 4–5)

Many young people envision and yearn for a more humane world.

Conceptions of Economic Systems We get a sense of children's conceptions of the world of industry and commerce from a study by Berti and Bombi (1988). These researchers interviewed 120 Italian children, ages 4 to 13, who lived in Marghera, an industrialized city near Venice. In the following excerpts (translated from Italian), an interviewer asks children about factories. We begin with Mara (age 4½):

Adult: Have you ever seen a factory?
Mara: No.
Adult: Do you know what the word "factory" means?
Mara: No.
Adult: What work does your father do?
Mara: He goes to Venice.
Adult: And when he gets there what does he do?
Mara: Works with his friends.
Adult: What does he do when he works?
Mara: My mother gives him money.
Adult: Does he need money to work?
Mara: Yes.
Adult: What does he do with it?
Mara: Because then there is water and he goes fishing. (dialogue from Berti & Bombi, 1988, p. 139; reprinted with the permission of Cambridge University Press)

Mara's ignorance of factories is typical of the youngest children (ages 4 and 5) that Berti and Bombi interviewed. In contrast, children ages 6 to 10 were generally able to describe some of the activities that take place in factories. In the following interview, Mauro (age 8½) shows some understanding of the employment hierarchy but struggles with issues related to ownership of property:

Adult: Whose are the toys which they make in the factory?
Mauro: They take them to the shops and sell them.
Adult: Who takes them?
Mauro: The workers.
Adult: But do the dolls belong to the workers or to the boss?
Mauro: The boss, I think.
Adult: You don't seem very convinced?
Mauro: I'm not really.
Adult: Why not?
Mauro: Because it's the workers who make them.
Adult: Why don't the workers keep them?
Mauro: Because they have to sell them. (dialogue from Berti & Bombi, 1988, p. 143; reprinted with the permission of Cambridge University Press)

The oldest children, ages 12 and 13, differentiated between bosses, who supervised the workers, and owners, who owned property in the business. In the final interview, we hear from Alessandro (age 12½):

Adult: Does the factory belong to someone?
Alessandro: Of course, small factories though: Montedison for instance doesn't belong to a single person. I think it belongs to a lot of people.
Adult: Why do you think that?
Alessandro: Because it's impossible that one man could have such a big industry. There would have to be lots of people. On the other hand a small factory which makes furniture or shoes has a single owner.
Adult: Why couldn't there be just a single owner for the big factory?
Alessandro: Because he would have to have an enormous amount of money to keep all those workers.
Adult: What do the owners do?
Alessandro: They have to maintain contacts with the middlemen, so that if someone wanted a certain type of shoe they would send their representatives around to show them theirs. . . . I think they would sit in an office with lots of telephones.
Adult: They wouldn't supervise the workers?
Alessandro: No.
Adult: Whose are the things which they make in the factory?

Alessandro:	They must belong to the owner, who sells them to someone, who then sells them to someone else who has a shop.
Adult:	How come these things belong to the owner?
Alessandro:	Because he pays the workers who do this particular job.
Adult:	Does the owner own everything in the factory, the sheds, the machines?
Alessandro:	If they're partners one owns a half, if there's only one he is the owner of it all.
Adult:	And if they're partners?
Alessandro:	They have to divide it, one has a piece of the shed, another one another piece, another one another piece and so on. (dialogue from Berti & Bombi, 1988, pp. 143–144; reprinted with the permission of Cambridge University Press)

Berti's and Bombi's interviews reveal a developmental progression toward more complete and systematic understandings of factories, production, and trade. Children become increasingly knowledgeable; for instance, with time and experience, they encounter and master such concepts as *bosses, owners,* and *middlemen*. Furthermore, they uncover anomalies in their own thinking, which motivate them to seek more information (recall Piaget's concept of *disequilibrium*, described in Chapter 4). Children who start to question parts of the system become receptive to learning more about complex operations (e.g., What *do* banks do with the money that people deposit? Is it fair that some people get paid more than others?; Furth, 1980; Jahoda, 1979).

Social Experiences and Conceptions of Society Developmental changes in children's conceptions of society are partly the result of advancements in cognitive abilities, but social experiences (or the lack thereof) play a role as well. Many children have little if any direct contact with social institutions, limiting opportunities for learning about them. For instance, most children don't work, don't get paid, and don't pay bills. Instead, they try to understand the larger social world by applying whatever knowledge they do have, extrapolating from their close relationships, and using their current reasoning skills. For instance, at about age 4, Teresa's son Connor asked for a credit card for his birthday (he didn't get one). At age 5, her son Alex watched his father paying bills and spontaneously observed, "I get it! The money goes round and round!" Teresa didn't probe him at the time (contents of her oven took priority), but she did make a mental note of his earnest attempts to figure out the elusive system of money.

When children have more direct contact with the world of work, they become knowledgeable about commerce and trade at an earlier age. For example, in a study by Jahoda (1983), two adults interviewed children from Harare, a township in Zimbabwe that was made up of mostly low-income families. The children's parents either were actively involved in selling goods (some were small traders who purchased items for resale; others were farmers who grew their own produce for sale) or not involved in selling goods. The two adults performed simple sales transactions in front of the children using props such as boxes of pens, biscuits, and balloons; the boxes were labeled with prices. The interviewers then asked them how much the customer paid for the item, how much the shop had to pay the supplier for the item, and what happened to the money in the cash register at the end of the day. In interpreting the children's responses, Jahoda noted whether they understood that the shopkeeper paid the supplier less than the customer paid the shopkeeper and considered their explanations for the differing amounts.

Jahoda found that children whose parents were actively involved in selling and were somewhat involved in selling themselves had a more accurate understanding of profit than children whose families were not regularly involved in sales. Furthermore, Jahoda compared his sample to the performance of English, Scottish, and Dutch children in previous investigations (Furth, 1980; Jahoda, 1979, 1982). The children from Zimbabwe outperformed their European counterparts, presumably because their personal experiences with trading and their frequent exposure to adults' discussions about trading led them to develop an understanding of profit and the mechanisms needed to ensure it. Even those African children who came from nonselling families outperformed the European children, perhaps because the African children grew up in a culture in which trading was a frequent topic of conversation.

Another factor that affects children's conceptions of economic systems is their family's financial circumstances. In a study with 7- to 13-year-olds in England, France, and the United States, Emler and colleagues explored children's judgments about the fairness of income inequalities (Emler, Ohana, & Dickinson, 1990). The researchers asked the children questions about the kinds of salaries that people earned in different professions (i.e., doctor, teacher, bus driver, street cleaner) and the fairness of having some people make more money than others. Across samples, children from lower-income families were more likely than children from middle-income families to say that it would be better to pay people in different types of jobs the same salary. With age came an increasing understanding of why some people have higher salaries than others. Whereas 10- and 11-year-olds mentioned social contributions (how much people help others in their jobs) and the amount of effort a job requires, older participants (12- to 15-year-olds) also mentioned that years of education and possession of certain skills contributed to income level. In addition, those older participants who came from middle-income backgrounds gave more complex justifications for income differences, suggesting that they accepted the legitimacy of such differences.

Social-Cognitive Bias and Prejudice

Although young people acquire advanced social cognitive processes and considerable knowledge about their social world, they do not always make use of such things, in part because they frequently lack the time and inclination to engage in careful, rational, and methodical thinking (Cialdini, 2001; Kahneman, 2000; Thaler, 2000). In fact, people of all ages regularly use mental shortcuts, or **social-cognitive biases,** to make their dealings with their complex social world more efficient and manageable (Brenner, Koehler, Liberman, & Tversky, 1996; Tversky & Kahneman, 1990). For example, people may uncritically accept what an authority figure says, expect that a single action reflects a person's typical behavior (rather than an exception), or believe that expensive items are invariably of higher quality than inexpensive items. Let's consider some illustrations:

- Walking down a busy city street, Heidi manages to avoid bumping into other people. She gives minimal attention to the faces she passes, consumed as she is by her own thoughts. Usually, other pedestrians have no special meaning for her. However, if she doesn't look up, she's likely to miss her best friend, who's approaching on the other side of the street.
- Gerry watches the unhappy man in our earlier spilled milk vignette. He jumps to the conclusion that the man is *always* angry; in other words, he overgeneralizes his one observation into expectations that the bad temper is a stable trait.
- In her favorite clothing store, Roberta notices two similar blouses, one for $19.99 and the other for $29.99. She decides to purchase the more expensive one, believing it to be prettier and more durable. In reality, the two blouses are the same, with one incorrectly marked.

Many social-cognitive biases are a minor nuisance—they lead to small distortions in thinking—but don't cause grave harm. Yet some social biases *do* have serious consequences. For instance, people occasionally make hasty judgments about other people based on group membership (e.g., gender, ethnicity, sexual orientation, religious affiliation). In other words, they respond on the basis of a **stereotype,** a rigid, simplistic, and erroneous characterization of a particular group. Often, people have stereotypes that encompass a host of negative attributes (e.g., "stingy," "lazy," "promiscuous") and lead them to exhibit negative attitudes, feelings, and behaviors—that is, **prejudice**—toward a particular group. Recall our introductory case: Tom's uncle and cousins made derogatory remarks about Jewish and Catholic people, and classmates shunned Tim because he was African American.

The roots of stereotypes and prejudice lie in the natural tendency of human beings to categorize their experiences. In their first few years, children learn that people belong to different groups, such as boys, girls, "blacks," and "whites"; for example, many preschoolers can identify members of various ethnic groups (Aboud, 1988, 1993). As children are forming these social categories, they tend to favor their own group and to expect undesirable characteristics and behaviors from members of other groups, especially if the different groups are in competition with one another (Black-Gutman & Hickson, 1996; Harris, 1995; Powlishta, 1995; Wilder & Shapiro, 1989).

To some degree, stereotypes and prejudice decrease as children move through the elementary school grades (Carter, Detine-Carter, & Benson, 1995; Davidson, 1976; Martin, 1989; Powlishta, Serbin, Doyle, & White, 1994). This decline is probably due to children's increasing ability to see the limits of social categories; for instance, they begin to realize that people

social-cognitive bias
Mental shortcuts in thinking about social phenomena.

stereotype
Rigid, simplistic, and erroneous characterization of a particular group.

prejudice
Exhibiting negative attitudes, feelings, and behaviors toward particular individuals because of their membership in a specific group.

who share membership in a category (e.g., "girls") may be similar in some ways but very different in others.

Although advancements in cognitive abilities work to reduce stereotypes and prejudice, other factors may work to maintain or strengthen them, and some children show an increase in prejudice as they reach early adolescence (Black-Gutman & Hickson, 1996). Children whose parents make racist jokes within earshot or restrict playmates to peers of similar backgrounds are more likely to exhibit prejudice against certain ethnic groups (Ashmore & DelBoca, 1976). Stereotypical images in the media may contribute as well. For example, children who watch a lot of television are more likely to have stereotypical views of males and females, perhaps because television shows more often than not depict males as strong and aggressive and females as weak and passive (Huston et al., 1992; Kimball, 1986; Signorielli & Lears, 1992).

Stereotypes and prejudice are concerns to many educators, who observe the harmful effects on students' self-esteem and interpersonal interactions. By adolescence, and probably before, students who are victims of prejudice are aware that they are treated unfairly (Phinney & Tarver, 1988; Taylor, Casten, Flickinger, Roberts, & Fulmore, 1994). Over time they acquire a variety of strategies for coping with prejudice and discrimination; for instance, they may become more assertive, try harder in social situations, withdraw from competition, or seek the social support of family and friends (Major & Schmader, 1998; Miller & Myers, 1998; Swim, Cohen, & Hyers, 1998). Such strategies may or may not be effective, however, as people who are daily victims of prejudice are more likely to become ill or depressed (Allison, 1998).

Clearly, the detrimental effects of prejudice make it an important target for classroom intervention. In fact, schools and classrooms provide optimal environments for advancing young people's social cognitive processes more generally. We look now at strategies for enhancing children's and adolescents' social understandings.

Enhancing Children's Social Understandings

The theories and research findings we've just reviewed have numerous implications for classroom practice. We offer the following suggestions for fostering greater understanding of people and society:

■ *Talk about psychological phenomena in age-appropriate ways.* Teachers frequently talk about their own thoughts and feelings and speculate about what other people (students, school administrators, figures in historical and current events, fictional characters, etc.) might be thinking and feeling. In doing so, they almost certainly enhance students' appreciation for the complex internal lives of fellow human beings. Teachers should, of course, try to gear their comments to students' cognitive and linguistic capabilities. For instance, at the preschool level, it may be helpful to label another person's feelings as "sadness," "disappointment," or "anger" (Chalmers & Townsend, 1990; Wittmer & Honig, 1994). Furthermore, preschool teachers usually talk about simple, straightforward thoughts and emotions ("Are you *sad* that your mom had to go to work today?" "Paula is *hoping* you'll join her in the blocks corner"). But at the high school level, students have sufficient cognitive and social reasoning capabilities to consider abstract and complex psychological qualities (e.g., being *passive aggressive* or having an inner *moral compass*) and to speculate about people's feelings in catastrophic circumstances (e.g., the bombing of Hiroshima and Nagasaki in World War II; Yeager et al., 1997).

At the same time, teachers can encourage students to think "one level up" in terms of Selman's levels of perspective taking. For example, preschool teachers may often want to point out how classmates' feelings differ from students' own (Level 1). Elementary school teachers can discuss situations in which students may have mixed feelings or want to hide their feelings—situations such as going to a new school, trying a difficult but enjoyable sport for the first time, or celebrating a holiday without a favorite family member present (Level 2). Middle school and secondary school teachers can explore aspects of psychology, so that students begin to understand the many ways in which people are a product of their environments (Level 4).

■ *Provide opportunities for students to encounter multiple, and often equally legitimate, perspectives.* The sociodramatic play of early childhood is a virtual breeding ground for training in social perspective training (Rubin & Pepler, 1995). Such play has numerous benefits for cognitive and social-emotional development (see Chapters 4 and 13), but for now we note that

PROMOTING SOCIAL UNDERSTANDINGS

■ Ask students to share their perceptions and interpretations with one another.

A kindergarten teacher finds several children arguing over how Serena tripped and fell during their game of tag; meanwhile, Serena has run away from the group and is crying. The teacher comforts Serena and then asks her to join the other children. She asks the children for their varying perspectives on what happened and suggests that each of them may be partly right. She then urges them to be more careful when they play running games, as it is easy for children to bump one another accidentally in such activities.

■ Ask students to consider the perspectives of people they don't know.

A sixth-grade teacher prepares his class for the arrival of a new student, first by discussing the feelings of uncertainty, apprehension, and loneliness that the student is likely to have and then by helping the class identify steps it can take to make the student feel at home. Later in the day, during a discussion of a recent earthquake in South America, the teacher asks his students to imagine how people must feel when they lose their home and possessions so quickly and don't know whether their loved ones are dead or alive.

■ Bring representatives and artifacts from social institutions to the classroom.

A third-grade teacher invites people in a variety of professions (e.g., in industry, retail, social service, government) to talk about what they do in their jobs and how they contribute to the community's productivity and well-being.

■ Encourage students to look for the individual differences that exist within groups of people who share a particular attribute, such as ethnic heritage, gender, or religious affiliation.

A high school history teacher asks his students to notice women's varying attitudes and behaviors during the early struggles for women's voting rights.

■ Combat prejudice.

At a middle school faculty meeting, teachers and administrators establish a policy prohibiting jokes and other remarks that disparage members of a particular group. When the teachers meet with their homeroom groups the following morning, they describe the policy, explain what *stereotype* and *prejudice* mean, identify the counterproductive effects such biases can have, and state emphatically that they will enforce the new policy at all times.

children engaged in pretend play must work hard to determine how their play partners are conceiving various pretend roles and activities. Throughout the elementary and secondary school grades, teachers can engage students in group discussions about complex or controversial topics and in group projects that require coordination of varying skills and talents; such activities inevitably expose students to diverse perspectives, perhaps including those of different genders, races, cultures, religions, and political belief systems. And teachers at all grade levels can elicit students' varying perspectives on the unplanned incidents and conflicts—the accidental spilled milk, the disputes about playground equipment, the derogatory ethnic jokes, and so on—that arise.

■ *Be especially attuned to the interpretations and misinterpretations of students with cognitive and social-emotional disabilities.* Children with certain disabilities (e.g., attention-deficit hyperactivity disorder, autism, mental retardation) often have particular difficulty drawing accurate inferences from others' behaviors and body language (Gray & Garaud, 1993; Leffert, Siperstein, & Millikan, 1999; Milch-Reich, Campbell, Pelham, Connelly, & Geva, 1999). For example, children with autism less frequently share a single focus of attention with other people: They are less apt to notice where a parent is looking and follow the parent's gaze toward an object (Charman et al., 1997; Sigman, Kasari, Kwon, & Yirmiya, 1992). Children with autism also do not often engage in sociodramatic play and may have limited understandings of how other people's minds and emotions work (Baron-Cohen, 1993; Hobson, 1993; Hughes,

Students at all grade levels benefit from hearing a variety of perspectives.

1998). Children with certain disabilities, then, may need considerable teacher guidance and support in their efforts to make sense of others' thoughts, feelings, and intentions.

■ *Bring students to the world of work, commerce, and government.* Children gain considerable knowledge about how their society functions from field trips to the post office, bank, police station, local government offices, and so on, particularly when such trips involve a behind-the-scenes view of the daily activities of such institutions. Field trips have an additional benefit as well, in that they provide a mechanism for involving parents and other family members in children's school activities (more about family involvement in Chapter 12).

■ *Bring society's institutions into the classroom.* In preschool and kindergarten settings, teachers can bring assorted props (e.g., supplies from a pizza restaurant, hardware store, hair salon, or veterinary clinic) to extend children's fantasies in pretend play (Ferguson, 1999). In the elementary and secondary grades, teachers might ask students to set up a market economy (e.g., producing, selling, and buying goods), create a student government to make classroom decisions, or establish a classroom courthouse to try mock cases. (Teresa recalls how, during a presidential election, 5-year-old Alex's kindergarten teacher demonstrated the voting process by having the children mark ballots about their preferred type of cookie, chocolate chip or oatmeal. Chocolate chip won, hands down.) Furthermore, students of all ages can learn from community members who visit the classroom to describe their day-to-day activities in the workforce.

■ *Examine inequities in society's systems.* Older students, especially those from low-income families, may struggle with inequities in income and living conditions, and their teachers may be able to help them make sense of such inequities. As Flanagan and Faison (2001) put it, "to promote democracy youth need to know the full story, not just the 'good parts' of history. If they appreciate that history and politics are controversial, they may see the importance of taking a stand and of adding their voice to the debate" (Flanagan & Faison, 2001, p. 3).

■ *Work to break down stereotypes and prejudice.* Teachers can address negative stereotypes and prejudice in a variety of ways. First of all, they should use curriculum materials that portray all groups in a positive light—for example, selecting textbooks, works of fiction, and videotapes that portray people of diverse ethnic backgrounds as legitimate participants in mainstream society rather than as exotic "curiosities" that live in a strange and separate world. Teachers should be particularly vigilant in screening out materials that portray members of minority groups in an overly simplistic, romanticized, exaggerated, or otherwise stereotypical way (Banks, 1994; Boutte & McCormick, 1992; Ladson-Billings, 1994; Pang, 1995).

A second important strategy is to encourage students to see people as *individuals*—as human beings with their own unique strengths and weaknesses—rather than as members of particular groups. For instance, teachers might point out how dramatic the differences among members of any single group usually are (García, 1994; Lee & Slaughter-Defoe, 1995; Spencer & Markstrom-Adams, 1990). But even more effective is to increase interpersonal contacts among people from diverse groups (and ideally create a sense that "we are all in this together"), perhaps through cooperative group activities, multischool community service projects, or pen pal relationships with students from distant locations (Devine, 1995; Dovidio & Gaertner, 1999; Koeppel & Mulrooney, 1992; Ramsey, 1995).

Finally, teachers must challenge stereotypes and prejudicial attitudes whenever they encounter them. For example, when a student talks about "lazy migrant workers," a teacher might respond by saying, "That's a common stereotype, Bill. I wonder where it came from? Migrant workers are often up working before dawn and picking produce until dusk. And many of them take up other demanding jobs when the growing season is over." Notice how the teacher confronts the "lazy migrant worker" stereotype tactfully and matter-of-factly and does not assume that Bill's remark has malicious intent. Students often thoughtlessly repeat the prejudicial remarks of others, and playing on their interest in appearing tolerant and open-minded may be more effective than chastising them for attitudes they have not carefully thought through (Dovidio & Gaertner, 1999).

Children's understandings of other people and the broader social world feed into their increasing ability to consider others' rights and needs—that is, these understandings feed into their increasing sense of morality. We turn to the nature of moral development now.

Moral Development

The term **morality** refers to a general set of standards about right and wrong and encompasses such traits as honesty, compassion, and respect for other people's rights and needs. Immoral behaviors involve actions that are unfair, cause physical or emotional harm, or violate the rights of others. In the opening case, we saw a young adolescent with a strong sense of what was morally right—an internal compass that he used to direct his own course of action and judge other people's conduct. Tom expressed an abhorrence for prejudice against people of other religions and races and a commitment to working for a more compassionate society.

Families, schools, and social relationships are highly influential in young people's moral development. Tom's strong moral convictions developed, at least in part, out of the lessons he received at home. Some lessons were positive ones: His father taught him to "make all kinds of friends" and modeled religious tolerance by marrying a Catholic despite other family members' protests. Tom's negative experiences contributed to his moral development as well: The bigotry he observed in his extended family and classmates only strengthened his determination to combat intolerance and injustice.

In some instances, however, the negative influences may overpower the positive ones. Consider the case of Lun Cheung, who in seventh grade joined a gang in New York's Chinatown and was soon embroiled in a world of extortion, violence, and murder:

> [3]Lun had come to America from Hong Kong at age four, but unlike many immigrants, his family had not fled deprivation. They had lived in Hong Kong on the largesse of a grandfather, Lun's father studying to become an engineer, his mother remaining at home to rear five children. It was only for the children that the Cheungs left all that was certain and comfortable. Their first place in New York was a two-room tenement, and making the rent was a full-time ordeal. Lun's mother sewed in a garment factory, while his father cooked in a Chinese restaurant. Without a mother to manage the household, Lun's three older brothers assigned him the chores, insisting that labor elevated the soul, wrapping their bullying in Confucian cloaks. No longer was Lun's father the stable force he had been. As year after year he continued cooking, and abandoned his dreams of engineering, a withheld rage corroded him from the inside out. Sometimes he sat and looked at the portrait of his college class from Hong Kong, and complained that he had never wanted to leave. Sometimes he threw plates and broke mirrors. Eventually, he committed himself to a psychiatric hospital, to which he returned many times, often for periods of months.
>
> Between a troubled father, overbearing brothers, and a mother straining to hold her fissioning family intact, Lun discovered his sole refuge on the streets. He had a friend in seventh grade who served alongside his father in the Ghost Shadows, one of Chinatown's two dominant gangs. First inducted a year earlier at age twelve, Lun's friend drove his own Pontiac Firebird and carried $800 in cash instead of lunch money. When the boy invited Lun to join the Ghost Shadows, Lun felt honored and pleased. There were no oaths or rituals, Lun would later remember, only the warning, "Join another gang and we'll kill you."
>
> The threat was anything but idle. The Chinatown gangs in one ten-month period of 1977 slew thirty innocents and rivals, using guns and bats and meat cleavers alike. They ran protection and gambling, sold women and drugs. When so moved, they marched into movie houses or wedding receptions to relieve the attendees of their wallets and jewels. At the top, the gangs worked in tandem with entrenched Chinese organized crime syndicates; at the bottom, they drew on boys like Lun—teenagers born in Hong Kong, unhinged at home, bored in school, craving status and excitement and money.
>
> Lun started his career as the junior partner in a three-man extortion firm. The ring was responsible for Mott Street, a few bustling blocks of curio shops, restaurants, and herbal medicine shops, the place any guidebook would direct a tourist to experience "the real Chinatown." Lun stood rear guard as the leader demanded money, cursing each shopkeeper's ancestors. A small business was assessed $150 a month, a large one $400. Owners who refused to pay were beaten, and for those who persisted, the leader packed a .38. Lun also served as a watchman outside basement gambling parlors, and one night while he was on duty, he saw several Ghost Shadows attack a rival gangster, bludgeoning him with a lead pipe until his head cracked like a melon. (Freedman, 1990, pp. 303–304)

morality
General set of standards about right and wrong.

---

[3]Pages 303–4 from *Small Victories* by Samuel G. Freedman. Copyright © 1990 by Samuel G. Freedman. Reprinted by permission of HarperCollins Publishers, Inc.

378 | Chapter Ten / Social Understanding and Moral Development

By the time English teacher Jessica Siegel had Lun in her high school journalism class, he was, fortunately, no longer a member of the gang. In an autobiography that Ms. Siegel asked her students to write, Lun explained why and how he was finally able to break free from gang life:

[4][I]n the tenth grade, as he told Jessica in his autobiography, he was jumped and beaten senseless and his best friend Steve was killed. Another friend, this one a gang member, accidentally killed himself while cleaning his gun. Lun's parents sent him to Hong Kong that summer, where he boarded with cousins and vowed to straighten his ways. He returned in the fall to a hard, dull, legitimate life, doing his homework, working as a cashier, and choosing new friends. . . . He watched from the sidelines as the police splintered the Ghost Shadows with dozens of arrests, and he was relieved to see temptation sent to prisons far away. (Freedman, 1990, p. 304)

At last report, Lun was a second-semester freshman at Brooklyn College, off to a good start toward making a more productive contribution to society.

What circumstances influence young people's ability to behave in a respectful, compassionate, and in other ways *moral* manner toward their fellow human beings? In Lun Cheung's case, a traumatic incident—the murder of his best friend—was an important turning point. In most cases, however, moral development is nurtured by an accumulation of many seemingly minor experiences: observing moral behavior (as Tom saw in his father), bickering with siblings and classmates about what's "fair," being chastised by a parent for hurting someone's feelings, seeing sadness on another's face, wrestling with moral issues in the classroom, and so on.

In the pages that follow, we consider the multidimensional nature of moral development. We first look at how various researchers have approached the study of moral development and at general developmental trends in moral reasoning and behavior. We then consider Lawrence Kohlberg's theory of moral reasoning and the factors that affect moral development. Finally, we examine diversity in moral development and identify strategies that teachers can use to promote moral development in the classroom.

Approaches to the Study of Moral Development

Developmentalists have approached moral development from several angles. Many have focused on how families and communities socialize children to behave in morally acceptable ways. Others have focused instead on children's interpretations and reasoning (i.e., their cognition) about moral issues. Still others have emphasized the emotions (e.g., empathy, shame) that accompany morally "right" and "wrong" behaviors. Let's look more closely at each of these approaches.

Focus on Socialization Conceivably, moral development has a genetic basis. Some evolutionary theorists have speculated that moral behaviors—helping people in need, showing respect for other people's possessions, and so on—hold social groups together and so increase the likelihood that the human species will survive and reproduce (Cosmides & Tooby, 1989; Wright, 1994). Nevertheless, most psychologists assume that environmental factors play a more significant role in moral development. For example, numerous aspects of Lun Cheung's environment (overbearing siblings, regular contact with gang members, monetary rewards for illicit activities, etc.) almost certainly contributed to his immoral behaviors during early adolescence.

Some theorists have proposed that moral development is primarily a process of **internalization**: Growing children increasingly adopt and take ownership of their society's rules and values regarding acceptable behavior. Such internalization occurs largely as a result of socialization, whereby parents and other members of the society model appropriate behaviors, reward children for behaving in a similarly appropriate manner, and punish behaviors deemed to be harmful, inconsiderate, or in other ways morally wrong.

One early theorist stressing the importance of early experiences on moral development was Sigmund Freud (e.g., 1959). Freud proposed that, at birth, children are motivated primarily to satisfy their own instinctual urges, especially urges related to sex and aggression (recall our description of psychodynamic perspectives in Chapter 1). Yet parents and other members of society insist that the children follow certain expectations for behavior, and such expectations

internalization
Adopting society's rules and values about acceptable behavior as one's own.

---

[4]Page 304 from *Small Victories* by Samuel G. Freedman. Copyright © 1990 by Samuel G. Freedman. Reprinted by permission of HarperCollins Publishers, Inc.

Over time, children increasingly internalize their society's rules and conventions for behavior. What rules and conventions does this artist have in mind?

Art by Jessica, 6th grade.

are often in conflict with what children instinctually want to do. Sometime between ages 3 to 6, Freud suggested, children develop a conscience, or *superego,* that enables them to resist their biological impulses. They do so in large part by *identifying* with the same-sex parent and assuming that parent's values regarding appropriate behavior.

More recently, other theorists have, like Freud, described moral development as a process of being socialized by parents and other caregivers and eventually taking on the moral behaviors and values that the preceding generation espouses (e.g., Blasi, 1995; Burton & Kunce, 1995; Peláez-Nogueras & Gewirtz, 1995; Skinner, 1971). We will see the influence of this approach later in the chapter as we consider *induction* and *modeling* as factors affecting moral development.

Focus on Cognition   The processes of socialization and internalization do not totally account for the phenomena observed in moral development. Children and adolescents don't always take adults' standards for behavior at face value (Harris, 1998; Turiel, 1998). In fact, some are quite critical of how the preceding generation behaves and insist on behaving differently; recall Tom's disdain for his grandmother's and uncle's attitudes about Catholics and Jews. Furthermore, young people acquire considerable flexibility in their moral decision making: They apply varying moral standards in different circumstances, depending on their interpretation of each situation and the likely outcomes of their actions (Grusec & Goodnow, 1994). Theorists who take a cognitive approach place much of the responsibility for moral development on children themselves, rather than on the adults in children's lives.

Many developmentalists who focus on cognitive processes have suggested that, through interactions with adults and peers, children gradually construct their *own* moral beliefs and values. One early theorist taking this approach was Jean Piaget, whose theory of cognitive development is described in Chapter 4. Piaget proposed that, over time, children construct increasingly complex and flexible understandings of "good" and "bad" behavior. For instance, in the early elementary years, children believe that behaviors that are "bad" or "naughty" are those that cause serious damage or harm. By the upper elementary grades, however, children consider people's motives and intentions when evaluating behaviors. As an illustration of this change, consider the following situations:

A. A little boy who is called John is in his room. He is called to dinner. He goes into the dining room. But behind the door there was a chair, and on the chair there was a tray with fifteen cups on it. John couldn't have known that there was all this behind the door. He goes in, the door knocks against the tray, bang go the fifteen cups, and they all get broken!

B. Once there was a little boy whose name was Henry. One day when his mother was out he tried to get some jam out of the cupboard. He climbed up on to a chair and stretched out his arm. But the jam was too high up and he couldn't reach it and have any. But while he was trying to get it he knocked over a cup. The cup fell down and broke. (Piaget, 1932/1960, p. 118)

A 6-year-old child, whom we'll call "Susan," evaluates the two boys' misdeeds this way (she initially refers to the 15 cups as "plates"):

Adult: Are those children both naughty, or is one not so naughty as the other?
Susan: Both just as naughty.
Adult: Would you punish them the same?
Susan: No. The one who broke fifteen plates.
Adult: And would you punish the other one more, or less?
Susan: The first broke lots of things, the other one fewer.
Adult: How would you punish them?
Susan: The one who broke the fifteen cups: two slaps. The other one: one slap. (dialogue from Piaget, 1932/1960, p. 121; format adapted)

In contrast, 9-year-old "Greta" takes the boys' motives into account:

Adult: Which of these two silly things was naughtiest, do you think?
Greta: The one where he tried to take hold of a cup was [the silliest] because the other boy didn't see [that there were some cups behind the door]. He saw what he was doing.
Adult: How many did he break?
Greta: One cup.
Adult: And the other one?
Greta: Fifteen.
Adult: Then which one would you punish most?
Greta: The one who broke one cup.
Adult: Why?
Greta: He did it on purpose. If he hadn't taken the jam, it wouldn't have happened. (dialogue from Piaget, 1932/1960, p. 125; format adapted)

After interviewing children about a variety of situations—causing damage, telling lies, stealing someone else's possessions, playing games, and so on—Piaget proposed that children's moral reasoning undergoes qualitative changes over time. For preschoolers, "good" behavior consists of obeying adults and other authority figures. Around age 5, children begin to judge what is good and appropriate based on established *rules* for behavior. At this point, they see rules as firm and inflexible, as dictates to be obeyed without question (Piaget called this rule-based morality **moral realism**). Sometime around age 8 or 9, children begin to recognize that rules are created primarily to help people get along and can be changed if everyone agrees to the change.

Researchers have found that Piaget was not always accurate about when various aspects of moral reasoning emerge; for instance, many preschoolers recognize that certain behaviors (e.g., pushing others or damaging their property) are wrong even if an adult assures them that such behaviors are acceptable (Nucci & Turiel, 1978; Tisak, 1993; Turiel, 1983). However, many developmentalists find value in Piaget's notion that children construct their own standards for moral behavior—often as a result of having discussions with adults and peers—rather than taking moral guidelines unaltered from those around them (Davidson & Youniss, 1995; Kohlberg, 1984; Kurtines et al., 1995; Turiel, 1998). Furthermore, they acknowledge that development of children's moral understandings depends considerably on advancing cognitive capabilities, such as perspective taking and abstract thought (Eisenberg, 1995; Kohlberg, 1969; Kurtines et al., 1995). You will find an example of a constructivist approach to moral development in Lawrence Kohlberg's theory of moral reasoning, to be described shortly.

Focus on Emotions   Some theorists have focused not on the cognitions, but on the emotions, involved in moral reasoning and behavior. For instance, Sigmund Freud and several other early theorists (Aronfreed, 1976; Parke & Walters, 1967) argued that children tend to behave in a morally appropriate manner primarily because behaving otherwise elicits considerable *anxiety*. More recently, theorists have proposed that several "feel-good" emotions—especially *love, attachment, sympathy,* and *empathy*—entice children to engage in moral behaviors, and "feel-bad" emotions—*shame* and *guilt* as well as anxiety—discourage them from indulging in immoral ones (Damon, 1988; Hoffman, 1991; Kagan, 1984; Turiel, 1998). For example, children are more likely to engage in **prosocial behavior**—that is, to behave more for another's benefit than for one's own—if they feel empathy for the person in need (Eisenberg, 1995). They also are more

moral realism
Viewing rules for behavior as firm and inflexible, as having a life of their own separate from the purposes they serve.

prosocial behavior
Action intended to benefit another, without regard for one's own needs.

Contrasting Approaches to the Study of Moral Development

BASIC DEVELOPMENTAL ISSUES			
ISSUE	FOCUS ON SOCIALIZATION	FOCUS ON COGNITION	FOCUS ON EMOTIONS
Nature and Nurture	Emphasis is on nurture: Theorists consider the ways in which members of society (and especially parents) model and encourage moral behavior and values, as well as the strategies people use to discourage immoral activities.	Specific experiences (e.g., conflicts with peers, encounters with moral dilemmas) influence the views of morality that children construct. Children's ability to think abstractly about moral issues depends on their cognitive development, which may be partly constrained by biological maturation.	The various emotions that underlie moral behavior have a biological basis, but the extent to which children associate them with particular moral actions is determined by experience and learning.
Universality and Diversity	The process of socialization is universal, as are many of the techniques (e.g., modeling, rewards, punishments) that adults use to socialize children. However, different cultures, and to some extent different families within each culture, socialize different moral beliefs and behaviors.	The general sequence through which children progress as they acquire moral reasoning capabilities is presumed to be universal across cultures. Not all individuals progress through the entire sequence, however, and the specific moral ideals that children construct may be somewhat culture-specific.	Love, empathy, shame, guilt, and other emotions associated with moral behavior are universal across cultures. However, children's feelings about various behaviors differ, depending on their prior experiences. Some children (e.g., many of those identified as having conduct disorders) show deficits in the emotions typically associated with immoral actions.
Qualitative and Quantitative Change 	Children's increasing conformity to society's standards for behavior is presumed to be predominantly quantitative in nature.	Children and adolescents progress through a series of qualitatively different stages in moral reasoning.	Emotions such as shame, guilt, and empathy increase in a quantitative fashion in the early years. Empathy also shows qualitative change, progressing from a very superficial understanding of other people's needs in the preschool and early elementary years to a true appreciation for the plights of others in adolescence. Some adolescents move to yet another level, showing empathy for entire groups of people (including many that they do not know) as well as individuals in their immediate environments.

likely to repair any damage that their thoughtless actions have caused if they feel guilty about what they have done (Eisenberg, 1995; Narváez & Rest, 1995).

Increasingly, developmentalists are including *both* cognition and emotion in their explanations of moral development and behavior (e.g., Gibbs, 1995; Narváez & Rest, 1995; Turiel, 1998). For example, Nancy Eisenberg's theory of prosocial reasoning proposes that children's judgments about prosocial behavior are dependent on their ability to empathize with other people (we describe her theory in Chapter 13). Developmentalists also acknowledge that, to some extent, children base their moral standards on those of their families, communities, and cultures. For instance, as you will see shortly, people of different cultures acquire somewhat different ideas about morality—a finding that can only be explained if one acknowledges the role of socialization in moral development.

Clearly, then, all three of the approaches just considered make a contribution to our understanding of moral development. We summarize and contrast the three approaches in the Basic Developmental Issues table above. We turn now to general trends in the development of morality.

Developmental Trends in Morality

Researchers have uncovered several developmental trends that characterize children's moral reasoning and behavior:

■ *Children begin using internal standards to evaluate behavior at a very early age.* Children distinguish between what's "good" and "bad" and what's "nice" and "naughty" as early as 19 months of age (Lamb & Feeny, 1995). Many early theorists, including Freud and Piaget, believed that young children base their decisions about right and wrong exclusively on what adults tell them to do and not do and on which behaviors adults reward and punish. Young children certainly do try out a wide variety of behaviors to see how their parents and other caregivers will respond, but they begin to apply their *own* standards for behavior as early as age 2 (Dunn, 1987, 1988; Kim & Turiel, 1996; Lamb, 1991; Laupa, 1994; Smetana, 1981; Tisak, 1993). By age 4, most understand that causing harm to another person is wrong even if an authority figure tells them otherwise. As an example, Laupa (1994) described several hypothetical school situations to 4- and 5-year-olds:

1. Two children are on the playground and want to go down the slide. They disagree as to who should go first. A person comes along and tells them which child should go first and which one should go second.
2. Some children can't decide where to sit during snack time. A person comes along and tells them where to sit.
3. Two children are fighting on the playground. A person comes along and tells them that they should stop fighting.
4. Two children are fighting on the playground. A person comes along and tells them that it's OK for them to keep fighting.

For these situations, the person in the story who gave the instructions varied among four possibilities:

- An adult with authority (a teacher)
- An adult without authority (a lady from across the street)
- A peer with authority (a teacher's helper)
- A peer without authority (another child on the playground)

After each situation, Laupa asked, "Is it all right for her to tell them that?" and "Should they do what she tells them to do?" (p. 10). As a general rule, the children were more likely to accept a teacher's instructions than those of a teacher's helper, but they were more likely to accept the instructions of a helper (a peer with authority) than those of a lady from across the street. (Most did not put much stock in what a child *without* authority had to say.) Thus, both adult status and authority status entered into children's decisions to abide by someone else's instructions. Laupa found an exception to this general pattern in the situations involving fighting, which had the potential to cause physical harm: The children were much more likely to obey a peer authority or adult nonauthority who said to *stop* fighting than to obey a teacher who said that it was OK to continue fighting.

■ *Children increasingly distinguish between moral transgressions and conventional transgressions.* Society discourages some actions because they cause damage or harm, violate human rights, or run counter to basic principles of equality, freedom, or justice. Such actions are **moral transgressions.** Society discourages other actions because, although not unethical, they violate widely held understandings about how one should behave (e.g., you should never talk back to your parents or burp at the dinner table). These actions are **conventional transgressions** that interfere with society's ability to run smoothly (recall our earlier discussion of social conventions). Social transgressions are usually culturally defined; for instance, although burping is frowned upon in mainstream Western culture, people in some cultures burp at the table to compliment their host. In contrast, many moral transgressions are universal across cultures.

Children learn about the "wrongness" of moral and conventional transgressions in different ways. Consider the following scenarios (Laupa & Turiel, 1995):

A number of nursery school children are playing outdoors. There are some swings in the yard, all of which are being used. One of the children decides that he now wants to use a swing. Seeing

moral transgression
Action that causes damage or harm or in some other way infringes on the needs and rights of others.

conventional transgression
Action that violates society's general guidelines (often unspoken) for socially acceptable behavior.

that they are all occupied, he goes to one of the swings, where he pushes the other child off, at the same time hitting him. The child who has been pushed is hurt and begins to cry. (p. 461)

Children are greeting a teacher who has just come into the nursery school. A number of children go up to her and say "Good morning, Mrs. Jones." One of the children says, "Good morning, Mary." (p. 461)

In the first scenario, the child who pushes his peer gets immediate feedback that he has caused harm and distress: The child cries and is clearly injured. In the second scenario, the child who calls a teacher by her first name may get verbal feedback that such behavior is unacceptable but will not see any concrete evidence of harm. Sometimes children get *no* feedback that they have violated social conventions, in part because some conventions are situation-specific (e.g., at the Cambridge Friends School in Massachusetts, everyone—children, teachers, administrators—is on a first-name basis with everyone else). When adults do respond to conventional transgressions, they typically respond differently than they do to moral transgressions. For instance, they are more likely to use physical punishment (e.g., a spanking) for moral infringements than for conventional ones (Catron & Masters, 1993). And when adults explain what children have done wrong, they focus on other people's needs and rights for moral transgressions ("You've really hurt Megan's feelings by your unkind remark") but emphasize rules and the need for social order for conventional violations ("We always use our 'indoor' voices when speaking in class"; Chilamkurti & Milner, 1993; Nucci & Nucci, 1982b; Nucci & Turiel, 1978; Smetana, 1989).

Children show a similar distinction in how they react to their peers' transgressions (Nucci & Nucci, 1982a, 1982b; Turiel, 1983). They talk about possible injury or injustice in the case of moral transgressions, as the following observation on a playground illustrates:

Two boys have forcibly taken a sled away from a younger boy and are playing with it. A girl who was watching says to the boys, "Hey, give it back, assholes. That's really even odds, the two of you against one little kid." The girl pulls the sled away from one of the older boys, pushes him to the ground, and hands the sled back to the younger boy. He takes the sled and the incident ends. (Nucci & Nucci, 1982a, p. 1339)

In contrast, children talk about the importance of rules and norms in the case of conventional transgressions. For instance, if a 7-year-old boy sees another child spitting on the grass, he might admonish the child, "You're not supposed to spit" (Nucci & Nucci, 1982a, p. 1339).

Even preschoolers have some understanding that not all actions are wrong in the same way, and that some misbehaviors—those that violate moral conventions—are more serious than others (Nucci & Weber, 1995; Smetana, 1981; Smetana & Braeges, 1990; Turiel, 1983). Their sensitivity to violations of social conventions is minimal in early childhood but increases throughout the elementary school years (Nucci & Nucci, 1982b; Nucci & Turiel, 1978; Turiel, 1983).

Initially, children distinguish between moral and conventional transgressions only for situations with which they have had personal experience (e.g., a boy bullying children on the playground vs. a girl eating dinner with her fingers). By the time they are 9, they make the distinction even for unfamiliar situations (Davidson, Turiel, & Black, 1983; Laupa & Turiel, 1995).

Yet children and adults do not always agree about which behaviors constitute moral transgressions, which ones fall into the conventional domain, and which ones fall into a third category of personal choice. For instance, adolescents typically think of their friends as a matter of personal choice: They have a right to hang out with whomever they want. But their parents view their children's selection of friends as potentially having moral implications (Smetana & Asquith, 1994). For instance, friends influence teenagers' choices about whether to spend leisure time productively or inappropriately (recall

Students and teachers sometimes disagree about whether and why certain actions are wrong.

Lun Cheung's moral decline once he started hanging out with the wrong crowd). Furthermore, whereas adults typically view drug use as a moral transgression, teenagers often think it is totally acceptable as long as it doesn't harm other people (Berkowitz, Guerra, & Nucci, 1991).

- *Children's understanding of fairness evolves throughout early and middle childhood.* The ability to share with others depends on children's sense of **distributive justice,** their beliefs about what constitutes people's fair share of a valued commodity (food, toys, recreational time, etc.). Children's notions of distributive justice appears to proceed through several levels (Damon, 1977, 1980). In the preschool years, children's beliefs about what's fair are based on their own needs and desires; for instance, it would be perfectly "fair" to give oneself a large handful of candy and give others smaller amounts. In the early elementary grades, children base their judgments about fairness on strict equality: A desired commodity is divided into equal portions. Sometimes around age 8, children begin to take merit and special needs into account; for instance, children who contribute more to a group's efforts should reap a greater portion of the group's rewards, and people who are exceptionally poor might be given more resources than others.

- *Emotions related to moral behavior develop in early and middle childhood.* As you have learned, certain emotions accompany and may spur moral behavior. Some of these emotions emerge gradually as children grow older. By the time children reach the middle elementary grades, most of them occasionally feel **shame:** They feel embarrassed or humiliated when they fail to meet the standards for moral behavior that parents and teachers have set for them (Damon, 1988). Shortly thereafter, they sometimes experience **guilt**—a feeling of discomfort when they know that they have caused someone else pain or distress (Damon, 1988; Hoffman, 1991). Both shame and guilt, though unpleasant in nature, are thought to be important motivators for moral and prosocial actions (you may recall our description of shame and guilt as *self-conscious emotions* in Chapter 9).

  Shame and guilt emerge when children believe they have done something wrong. In contrast, *empathy* motivates moral and prosocial behavior even in the absence of wrongdoing; as you learned earlier, empathy emerges in early childhood but continues to develop in scope through middle childhood and adolescence. Empathy is especially likely to promote moral and prosocial behavior when it leads to **sympathy,** whereby children not only assume another person's feelings but also have concerns for the individual's well-being (Eisenberg & Fabes, 1991; Turiel, 1998).

- *Children increasingly take circumstances into account in their evaluation of behavior.* Recall from our earlier discussion how Susan and Greta judged the two boys who broke cups. Six-year-old Susan thought the boy who broke 15 cups was naughtier: Her suggested punishment for him was two slaps, whereas the boy who broke one cup needed only one slap. In contrast, 9-year-old Greta thought the boy who broke the single cup was naughtier because his intentions were less admirable: He was trying to take some jam during his mother's absence. As children get older, they are more likely to take motives and other situational factors into account in their moral judgments and decision making (Piaget, 1932/1960; Thorkildsen, 1995; Turiel, 1998). For example, children and adolescents are more likely to think of lying as immoral if it causes someone else harm than if it has no adverse effect—that is, if it is just a "white lie" (Turiel, Smetana, & Killen, 1991). And although most American adolescents endorse such civil liberties as freedom of speech and freedom of religion in principle, they recognize that such liberties must sometimes be restricted to protect others from harm (Helwig, 1995).

  In general, children and adolescents become increasingly able to reason flexibly and abstractly about moral issues as they grow older. Lawrence Kohlberg has proposed a series of stages that capture some of the changes in their reasoning over time. We look at his theory now.

Development of Moral Reasoning: Kohlberg's Theory

Consider the following situation:

> In Europe, a woman was near death from a rare form of cancer. There was one drug that the doctors thought might save her, a form of radium that a druggist in the same town had recently discovered. The druggist was charging $2,000, ten times what the drug cost him to make. The sick woman's husband, Heinz, went to everyone he knew to borrow the money, but he could only get together about half of what the drug cost. He told the druggist that his wife was dying and asked him to sell it cheaper or let him pay later. But the druggist said no. So Heinz got desperate and broke into the man's store to steal the drug for his wife. (Kohlberg, 1984, p. 186)

distributive justice
Beliefs about what constitutes people's fair share of a valued commodity.

shame
Feeling of embarrassment or humiliation after failing to meet the standards for moral behavior that others have set.

guilt
Feeling of discomfort when one knows that he or she has caused someone else pain or distress.

sympathy
Feeling of sorrow or concern about another's problems or distress.

Should Heinz have stolen the drug? What would you have done if you were Heinz? Which is worse, stealing something that belongs to someone else or letting another person die a preventable death, and why?

The story of Heinz and his dying wife is an example of a **moral dilemma**—a situation for which there is no clear-cut right or wrong solution. Lawrence Kohlberg presented a number of moral dilemmas to people of various ages and asked them to propose solutions for each one. Following are three boys' solutions to Heinz's dilemma (we have given the boys' fictitious names so that we can refer to them again later):

Andrew (a fifth grader):
Maybe his wife is an important person and runs a store, and the man buys stuff from her and can't get it any other place. The police would blame the owner that he didn't save the wife. He didn't save an important person, and that's just like killing with a gun or a knife. You can get the electric chair for that. (Kohlberg, 1981, pp. 265–266)

Blake (a high school student):
If he cares enough for her to steal for her, he should steal it. If not he should let her die. It's up to him. (Kohlberg, 1981, p. 132)

Charlie (a high school student):
In that particular situation Heinz was right to do it. In the eyes of the law he would not be doing the right thing, but in the eyes of the moral law he would. If he had exhausted every other alternative I think it would be worth it to save a life. (Kohlberg, 1984, pp. 446–447)

Each student offers a different reason to justify why Heinz should steal the lifesaving drug. Andrew bases his decision on the possible advantages and disadvantages of stealing or not stealing the drug for Heinz alone; he does not consider the perspective of the dying woman at all. Likewise, Blake takes a very self-serving view, proposing that the decision to either steal or not steal the drug depends on how much Heinz loves his wife. Only Charlie considers the value of human life in justifying why Heinz should break the law.

After obtaining hundreds of responses to moral dilemmas, Kohlberg proposed that the development of moral reasoning is characterized by a series of stages (e.g., Colby, Kohlberg, Gibbs, & Lieberman, 1983; Kohlberg, 1963, 1984). These stages, as in any stage theory, form an invariant sequence: An individual progresses through them in order, without skipping any. Each stage builds upon the foundation laid by earlier stages but reflects a more integrated and logically consistent set of moral beliefs than those before it.

Kohlberg grouped his stages into three *levels* of morality—the preconventional, conventional, and postconventional levels. These levels, and the stages within them, are summarized in the Observation Guidelines table on the facing page. (We omit Stage 6, for a reason you will discover shortly.) Let's look at each level and stage more closely.

Level I: Preconventional Morality   We see preconventional morality in preschool children, most elementary school students (especially those in the primary grades), some middle and junior high school students, and a few high school students (Colby & Kohlberg, 1984; Reimer, Paolitto, & Hersh, 1983). Preconventional reasoning is the earliest and least mature form of moral reasoning, in that the individual has not yet adopted or internalized society's conventions regarding what is morally right or wrong. The preconventional person's judgments about the morality of behavior are determined primarily by the consequences of those behaviors. Behaviors that lead to rewards and pleasure are "right"; behaviors that lead to punishment are "wrong." Preconventional individuals will obey people who have control of rewards and punishments; they will not necessarily obey people without control over such consequences.

Stage 1: Punishment-avoidance and obedience.   Stage 1 individuals (including fifth grader Andrew) make moral decisions based on what they think is best for themselves, without considering the needs or feelings of other people. For these individuals, the only wrong behaviors are ones that will be punished. Stage 1 individuals follow rules of behavior that are established by people more powerful than themselves, whether these people are parents, teachers, or stronger peers. But they may disobey rules if they think that they can

moral dilemma
Situation in which there is no clear-cut answer regarding the morally correct thing to do.

Assessing Students' Moral Reasoning in Terms of Kohlberg's Theory

OBSERVATION GUIDELINES

CHARACTERISTIC	LOOK FOR	EXAMPLE	IMPLICATION
Level I: Preconventional Morality			
Stage 1: Punishment-Avoidance and Obedience	• Preoccupation with one's own needs; lack of concern about the needs of others • Obedience of more powerful individuals • Focus on external consequences of behavior	Jane will do whatever she can get away with. For instance, she has no qualms about stealing things from classmates' backpacks if she knows she won't get caught in the process.	Tell students the consequences for appropriate and inappropriate classroom behavior, and apply those consequences consistently. Accompany any consequences for inappropriate behavior with explanations of how students have caused harm or violated others' rights.
Stage 2: Exchange of Favors	• Some recognition of others' needs • Some reciprocity ("You scratch my back, I'll scratch yours") • Focus on external consequences of behavior	Sean and Matt have an ongoing agreement that Sean will do the math homework, Matt will do the science homework, and they'll copy each other's work as they ride the bus to school each morning.	Provide the same opportunities for all students and in other ways make things as fair as possible.
Level II: Conventional Morality			
Stage 3: Good Boy/Good Girl	• Focus on pleasing others, especially authority figures • Concern about maintaining interpersonal relationships through sharing, trust, and loyalty • Consideration of one's intentions in evaluating behavior	Cara volunteers to help serve meals at the local soup kitchen every Tuesday afternoon because Kirsten, the most popular girl in her class, also works at the soup kitchen on Tuesdays.	Communicate appreciation when students behave morally or prosocially; communicate disapproval when students disregard others' needs or violate others' rights.
Stage 4: Law and Order	• Taking guidelines for appropriate behavior from society at large rather than from specific authority figures • Perception of rules as inflexible entities to be obeyed without question • Strong sense of duty to obey rules	In a high school history class, several students insist that every able-bodied male adult has a duty to serve his country in times of war regardless of his personal beliefs about war.	Have students study the processes through which government officials establish new laws and repeal laws that are no longer useful. Conduct class discussions about situations in which changing laws or, if necessary, breaking them may be morally appropriate.
Level III: Postconventional Morality			
Stage 5: Social Contract	• Recognition that rules are socially constructed entities that maintain the general social order • Understanding that rules can be modified if a change would better serve society	A committee of students and faculty members examines the pros and cons of allowing students to smoke on school grounds. After interviewing more than 100 people at school and in the community, the committee eventually decides that establishing a smoking area would not be in the best interest of the school as a whole.	At the high school level, begin to talk with students about such abstract principles as equality, justice, and human rights, and identify situations in which a society's laws or conventions might be counterproductive.

avoid punishment in doing so. In a nutshell, individuals in Stage 1 will do anything if they can get away with it.

Stage 2: Exchange of favors. Individuals in Stage 2 (which Kohlberg has often called the *instrumental-relativist* stage) are beginning to recognize that others have needs just as they do. They sometimes address the needs of others by offering to exchange favors ("You scratch my back, and I'll scratch yours"), but they usually try to get the better end of the bargain. To Stage 2 individuals, being "fair" means that everybody gets the same opportunities or the same amount of whatever is being handed out. Teachers might hear "That's not fair!" from Stage 2 students who think they're being shortchanged.

Like Stage 1 individuals, Stage 2 individuals focus on the physical consequences of behavior, rather than on abstract, less observable consequences. For example, if a boy at this stage is thinking about insulting a classmate, he may refrain from doing so if he thinks that the classmate will beat him up, but the thought that the insult might hurt the classmate's feelings will not be a deterrent. Kohlberg classified Blake's response to the Heinz dilemma as a Stage 2 response. Blake is beginning to recognize the importance of saving someone else's life, but the decision to do so ultimately depends on whether or not Heinz loves his wife; in other words, it depends on *his* feelings alone.

In the elementary years, many students begin to follow basic rules even without adult supervision.

Level II: Conventional Morality A few older elementary school students, some middle and junior high school students, and many high school students exhibit conventional morality (Colby & Kohlberg, 1984; Reimer et al., 1983). Conventional morality is characterized by an acceptance of society's conventions concerning right and wrong: The individual obeys rules and follows society's norms even when there is no reward for obedience and no punishment for disobedience. Adherence to rules and conventions is somewhat rigid; a rule's appropriateness or fairness is seldom questioned.

Stage 3: Good boy/good girl. Stage 3 individuals look primarily to the people they know, and especially to authority figures (e.g., parents, teachers, popular classmates), for guidance about what is right and wrong. Stage 3 individuals want to please others and gain their approval; they like being told that they are a "good boy" or a "good girl." They are also concerned about maintaining interpersonal relationships through sharing, trust, and loyalty. For example, they believe in the Golden Rule ("Treat others as you would like to be treated") and in the importance of keeping promises and commitments.

Stage 3 individuals can put themselves in another person's shoes and consider the perspectives of others in making decisions. They also acknowledge that someone's intentions must be considered in determining guilt or innocence. For instance, 9-year-old Greta, who judged the boy who broke one cup to be naughtier than the boy who broke 15 cups because the former "did it on purpose," has apparently reached Stage 3.

Stage 4: Law and order. Stage 4 individuals look to society as a whole, rather than just to the people they know, for guidelines (conventions) about what is right and wrong. They know that rules are necessary for keeping society running smoothly and believe that it is their "duty" to obey them. They see these rules as set in concrete, however; they do not yet recognize that it may occasionally be more morally justifiable to break laws (perhaps those legitimating racial segregation or interfering with basic human rights) than to follow them. Nor do they recognize that, as society's needs change, rules should be changed as well.

Level III: Postconventional Morality Postconventional morality is rarely observed in students before they reach college, and in fact most people never reach this level of moral reasoning at all (Colby & Kohlberg, 1984; Reimer et al., 1983; Snarey, 1995). Postconventional individuals have developed their own set of abstract principles to define what actions are morally right and wrong—principles that typically include such basic human rights as life, liberty, and justice. Postconventional individuals obey rules consistent with their own abstract principles of morality, and they may *disobey* rules inconsistent with such principles.

Stage 5: Social contract. Stage 5 individuals view rules that are determined through a democratic process as a *social contract,* an agreement among many people about how everyone should behave. They think of rules as being useful mechanisms that maintain the general social order and protect individual human rights, rather than as absolute dictates that must be obeyed simply because they are "the law." They also recognize the flexibility of rules; rules that no longer serve society's best interests can and should be changed. We see a glimmer of Stage 5 reasoning in Tom's statements in the opening case study:

> You gotta change the system. . . . [E]ducated people can work on the laws, to make them more fair, and to see why they have to pay taxes. It's the main thing not to be rich, as an ideal, not to beat out the other guys, but just to live, and to preserve all life. (Davidson & Davidson, 1994, p. 90)

We find a clearer example in Charlie's response to the Heinz dilemma:

> In the eyes of the law he would not be doing the right thing, but in the eyes of the moral law he would. If he had exhausted every other alternative I think it would be worth it to save a life. (Kohlberg, 1984, pp. 446–447)

Stage 6: Universal ethical principle. Kohlberg (1984) described Stage 6 as an ideal stage that few people ever reach (hence our reason for omitting it in the Observation Guidelines table). This stage represents adherence to a few abstract, universal principles that transcend specific norms and rules for behavior. Such principles typically include respect for human dignity and basic human rights, the belief that all people are truly equal, and a commitment to justice and due process. Stage 6 individuals answer to a strong inner conscience, rather than to authority figures or concrete laws, and they willingly disobey laws that violate their own ethical principles. Martin Luther King Jr.'s "Letter from a Birmingham Jail," excerpted here, illustrates Stage 6 reasoning:

> One may well ask, "How can you advocate breaking some laws and obeying others?" The answer lies in the fact that one has not only a legal but a moral responsibility to obey just laws. One has a moral responsibility to disobey unjust laws, though one must do so openly, lovingly and with a willingness to accept the penalty. An individual who breaks a law that conscience tells him is unjust, and accepts the penalty to arouse the conscience of the community, is expressing in reality the highest respect for law. An unjust law is a human law not rooted in eternal law and natural law. A law that uplifts human personality is just; one which degrades human personality is unjust. (King, 1965, cited in Kohlberg, 1981, pp. 318–319)

Factors Influencing Progression Through Kohlberg's Stages As you undoubtedly just noticed, children and adolescents at any particular age do not necessarily reason at the same level and stage. Educators are likely to see the greatest variability in high school students, some of whom may show Stage 4 reasoning while others are still reasoning at Stage 1. Why do students of the same age sometimes show very different stages of moral reasoning? Kohlberg suggested that two aspects of Piaget's theory—his stages of cognitive development and his concept of disequilibrium—affect progression to more advanced stages of moral reasoning.

Stage of cognitive development. Kohlberg proposed that moral reasoning is somewhat dependent on Piaget's stages of cognitive development (Kohlberg, 1976). Postconventional morality, because it involves reasoning with abstract principles, cannot occur until an individual has acquired formal operational thought. Even conventional morality probably requires formal operational abilities, in that understanding the interplay between *law* and *order* entails thinking about abstract ideas. Thus, conventional and postconventional levels of moral reasoning do not usually appear until adolescence. At the same time, progression to an advanced stage of cognitive development does not guarantee equivalent moral development; for example, it is quite possible to be formal operational in logical reasoning but preconventional in moral reasoning. In other words, Kohlberg maintained that cognitive development is a *necessary but insufficient* condition for moral development to occur.

Disequilibrium. As you should recall from Chapter 4, Piaget proposed that children progress to a higher stage of cognitive development when they experience *disequilibrium*— when they realize that their knowledge and schemes do not adequately explain the events around them. Because disequilibrium is an uncomfortable feeling, children are motivated to reorganize their thoughts and ideas into a more complex and better integrated system, one that better accounts for their experiences.

Kohlberg proposed that a similar process promotes moral development. Individuals become increasingly aware of the weaknesses of a particular stage of moral reasoning, especially when their moral judgments are challenged by people reasoning at the next higher stage (e.g., a Stage 3 student who agrees to let a popular cheerleader copy his homework may begin to question his decision if a Stage 4 student argues that the cheerleader would learn more by doing her *own* homework). By struggling with such challenges and with moral dilemmas, individuals begin to restructure their thoughts about morality and so gradually move from one stage to the next.

What Research Tells Us About Kohlberg's Stages Many research studies of moral development have followed on the heels of Kohlberg's theory. Some research supports Kohlberg's sequence of stages: Generally speaking, people seem to progress through the stages in the order Kohlberg proposed, and they don't regress (i.e., go backwards) to lower levels (Colby & Kohlberg, 1984; Reimer et al., 1983; Walker & Taylor, 1991). At the same time, Kohlberg acknowledged that people are not always completely in one stage: Their moral thought usually reflects a particular stage, but they also show occasional instances of reasoning in the two surrounding stages. Furthermore, young children are not as authority-oriented as Kohlberg thought; as you learned in our discussion of developmental trends, many preschoolers know that it is wrong to fight (and possibly hurt someone else) even if an authority tells them otherwise.

Kohlberg's theory has been criticized because it focuses on moral *thinking* rather than on moral *behavior*. Generally speaking, people who exhibit higher stages of moral reasoning do behave more morally as well (Bear & Richards, 1981; Blasi, 1980; Reimer et al., 1983). For example, students at the higher stages are less likely to cheat or make prejudicial remarks about others, more likely to help people in need, and more likely to disobey orders that would cause harm to another individual (Davidson, 1976; Kohlberg, 1975; Kohlberg & Candee, 1984; Miller, Eisenberg, Fabes, & Shell, 1996). However, researchers typically find only moderate relationships between moral reasoning and moral behavior, probably because nonmoral considerations (e.g., "How much will I be inconvenienced if I help someone in need?" "Will other people like me better if I participate in this public service project?") often enter into moral decision making (Eisenberg, 1987; Turiel, 1983). Obviously, then, Kohlberg's theory cannot give us the total picture of how morality develops.

The Developmental Trends table on the facing page summarizes much of what we have learned about the nature of social cognition and moral development at different age levels. We now consider factors that appear to promote moral development.

Factors Affecting Moral Development

As you have seen, children and adolescents in the early stages of moral development make behavior choices based largely on the consequences they anticipate for their actions. Yet it does little good to lecture young people about morally appropriate behavior (Damon, 1988), and attempts at "character education" are fraught with difficulties (Higgins, 1995; Turiel, 1998).[5] Several other conditions *do* seem to make a difference in the development of moral reasoning and behavior: use of reasons, interactions with peers, models of moral and prosocial behavior, and moral issues and dilemmas. We look at each of these in turn.

---

[5] Some prominent members of our society (e.g., some politicians, religious leaders, and newspaper columnists) suggest that society is in a sharp moral decline and urge parents and educators to impose appropriate moral traits (honesty, integrity, loyalty, responsibility, etc.) through lectures at home and in school, as well as through firm control of children's behavior. Several problems arise with such an approach, however: (a) These traits are difficult to define precisely (e.g., at what point does integrity become stubbornness?); (b) people do not always agree about which traits are most important to nurture; and (c) there is little evidence to indicate that firm control of children's behavior is sufficient to inculcate a particular set of values (Higgins, 1995; Turiel, 1998). Furthermore, the assumption that previous generations were more morally righteous than the present generation of youth remains unsubstantiated (Turiel, 1998).

Social Understanding and Morality at Different Age Levels

DEVELOPMENTAL TRENDS

AGE	WHAT YOU MIGHT OBSERVE	DIVERSITY	IMPLICATIONS
Early Childhood (2–6) 	• Emerging awareness of other people's mental and emotional states • Minimal ability to take others' perspectives, yet with some signs of empathy for people in distress • Preoccupation with one's own needs over the needs of others • Little or no knowledge of social institutions • Growing awareness that some behaviors are morally wrong, but with a tendency to define "right" and "wrong" behaviors in terms of their consequences for oneself	• Preschoolers who have had few positive interactions with peers may have trouble sharing and cooperating with others. • Experiences with the outside world (e.g., with parents' places of business) affect children's knowledge of social institutions.	• Talk frequently about various people's thoughts, feelings, perspectives, and needs. • Bring social institutions into the classroom, for instance by providing props that enable children to role-play numerous professions in their sociodramatic play.
Middle Childhood (6–10) 	• Increasing awareness of other people's psychological characteristics, but with limited understanding of the complexity of others' mental states • Recognition that other people's thoughts and feelings are different from one's own • Increasing empathy for unknown individuals who are suffering or in need • Knowledge of social conventions for appropriate behavior • Recognition that people should strive to meet others' needs as well as their own; growing appreciation for the importance of cooperation and compromise • Appearance of shame and guilt for moral wrongdoings	• Some children consistently misinterpret peers' thoughts and motives (e.g., by interpreting accidents as deliberate attempts to hurt them). • Some cultures place greater emphasis on ensuring individuals' rights and needs, while others place greater value on the welfare of the community as a whole. • Children whose parents explain why certain behaviors are unacceptable show more advanced moral development. • Many children with certain disabilities (e.g., ADHD, autism, mental retardation) have difficulty making inferences about people's motives and intentions and accurately interpreting people's actions.	• Assist students in their attempts to resolve interpersonal conflicts by asking them to consider one another's perspectives and to develop a solution that addresses everyone's needs. • Talk about how school rules enable the classroom to run more smoothly. • Explain how students can meet their own needs while helping others (e.g., when asking students to be "reading buddies" for younger children, explain that doing so will help them become more fluent readers).

(continued)

Use of Reasons Although it is important to impose consequences for immoral or antisocial behaviors, punishment by itself often focuses children's attention primarily on their own hurt and distress (Hoffman, 1975). Adults are more likely to promote children's moral development when they focus children's attention on the hurt and distress that their behaviors have caused *others*. For example, a teacher might describe how a behavior harms someone else either physically ("Having your hair pulled the way you just pulled Mai's can really be painful") or emotionally ("You probably hurt John's feelings when you call him names like that"). A teacher might also show children how they have caused someone else inconvenience ("Because you ruined Marie's jacket, her parents are making her work around the house to earn the money for a new one"). Still another approach is to explain someone else's perspective, intention, or motive ("This science project you've just ridiculed may not be as fancy as yours, but I know that Michael spent many hours working on it and is quite proud of what he's done").

Giving children reasons that certain behaviors are unacceptable is known as **induction** (Hoffman, 1970, 1975). The consistent use of induction in disciplining children, particularly

induction
Explaining why a certain behavior is unacceptable, often with a focus on the pain or distress that someone has caused another.

Moral Development | **391**

DEVELOPMENTAL TRENDS

AGE	WHAT YOU MIGHT OBSERVE	DIVERSITY	IMPLICATIONS
Early Adolescence (10–14)	• Interest in other people's internal mental states and feelings; recognition that people may have multiple and possibly conflicting motives and emotions • Tendency to think of rules and conventions as standards that should be followed for their own sake • Interest in pleasing others	• Some students with social-emotional problems (e.g., those with conduct disorders) show deficits in empathy for others. • Children's religious beliefs (e.g., their beliefs in an afterlife) influence their judgments about morality. • Violence-prone children and adolescents often believe that hitting another is reasonable retribution for unjust actions.	• Conduct class discussions that require students to look at a controversial issue from multiple perspectives. • When disciplining students for moral transgressions, explain how their behaviors have hurt another or in some other way jeopardized another's rights; providing such reasons is especially important for students with deficits in empathy and moral reasoning. • Involve students in group projects that will benefit their school or community.
Late Adolescence (14–18)	• Recognition that people are products of their environment and that past events and present circumstances influence personality and behavior • Ability to think recursively about one's own and others' thoughts • Understanding that rules and conventions help society run more smoothly • Increasing concern about doing one's duty and abiding by the rules of society as a whole rather than simply pleasing certain people	• Some students continue to reason at Kohlberg's preconventional level. Those who continue to focus on their own needs, with little regard for the needs of others, are more likely to exhibit antisocial behavior. • A small minority of high school students consider abstract principles rather than society's rules when choosing a moral course of action. • Adolescents who engage in delinquent activities tend to have less advanced moral reasoning.	• Do not tolerate ethnic jokes or other remarks that show prejudice toward a particular group. • Talk about other people's complex (and sometimes conflicting) motivations in class, perhaps while discussing historical events or works of fiction. • Give students a political voice in making school decisions.

Sources: American Psychiatric Association, 1994; Astor, 1994; Barenboim, 1981; Berti & Bombi, 1988; Chandler & Moran, 1990; Damon, 1988; Dunn, 1988; Flanagan & Faison, 2001; Gibbs, 1995; Gray & Garaud, 1993; Hoffman, 1975, 1991; Juvonen, 1991; Kohlberg, 1984; Kurtines et al., 1995; Lamb & Feeny, 1995; Leffert et al., 1999; Livesley & Bromley, 1973; Milch-Reich et al., 1999; Oppenheimer, 1986; Perner & Wimmer, 1985; Rushton, 1980; Schonert-Reichl, 1993; Selman, 1980; Selman & Schultz, 1990; Shweder, Mahapatra, & Miller, 1987; Snell & Janney, 2000; Triandis, 1995; Turiel, 1983, 1998; Zahn-Waxler, Radke-Yarrow, et al., 1992.

when accompanied by *mild* punishment for misbehavior, appears to promote compliance with rules as well as the development of such prosocial characteristics as empathy, compassion, and altruism (Baumrind, 1971; Brody & Shaffer, 1982; Hoffman, 1975; Maccoby & Martin, 1983; Rushton, 1980).

In our discussion of families in Chapter 12, we describe different parenting styles and their potential effects on children's social-emotional development. As you will discover when you read that chapter, induction is an integral part of *authoritative parenting,* a style characterized by emotional warmth coupled with high standards and expectations for behavior. Authoritative parenting appears to promote moral development: Children become more sensitive to others' needs and are more willing to accept responsibility for their wrongdoings (Damon, 1988; Eisenberg, 1995; Hoffman, 1975).

Interactions with Peers Children learn many lessons about morality in their interactions, both congenial and conflict-ridden, with other children. For instance, group play activities bring up issues related to sharing, cooperation, and negotiation (Damon, 1981, 1988; Turiel, 1998). Conflicts between siblings and playmates frequently arise as a result of physical harm, disregard for another's feelings, mistreatment of possessions, and so on (Dunn & Munn, 1987; Killen & Nucci, 1995). To resolve their interpersonal conflicts successfully, children must begin to look at situations from other children's perspectives, show consideration for other children's feelings and possessions, and attempt to satisfy other children's needs in addition to their own (Killen & Nucci, 1995).

Models of Moral and Prosocial Behavior Children are more likely to exhibit moral and prosocial behavior when they see other people behaving in morally appropriate ways. For example, when parents are generous and show concern for others, their children tend to do likewise (Rushton, 1980). Yet by the same token, when children see their peers cheating, they themselves are more likely to cheat (Sherrill, Horowitz, Friedman, & Salisbury, 1970). Television, too, provides both prosocial and antisocial models for children. When children watch television shows that emphasize prosocial behavior (e.g., *Barney & Friends* or *Mister Rogers' Neighborhood*), they are more likely to exhibit prosocial behavior themselves; when they see violence on television, they, too, are more likely to be violent (Eron, 1980; Hearold, 1986; Rushton, 1980.) (We examine the effects of television in more detail in Chapter 14.)

Moral Issues and Dilemmas Kohlberg proposed that children develop morally when they are challenged by moral dilemmas they cannot adequately deal with at their current stage of moral reasoning. Research confirms his belief: Discussions of controversial topics and moral issues appear to promote the transition to more advanced moral reasoning and increased perspective taking, especially when children are exposed to a higher stage of moral reasoning than their own (Berkowitz & Gibbs, 1985; DeVries & Zan, 1996; Power, Higgins, & Kohlberg, 1989; Schlaefli, Rest, & Thoma, 1985).

The four factors we've just described—use of reasons, interactions with peers, models of moral behavior, and moral issues and dilemmas—will be present to a greater or lesser extent, and will also take varying forms, in different children's experiences. Not surprisingly, then, children show considerable diversity in the moral values and behaviors that they acquire. We look at diversity in moral development next.

> Giving children reasons about why specific rules are necessary and holding them accountable for their transgressions can help promote their moral development.

Diversity in Moral Development

As you have seen, students' moral reasoning is partly a function of their age: Older children and adolescents exhibit more sophisticated judgments about moral issues than younger children. Yet even those within a particular age group can hold widely varying beliefs; for instance, some adolescents show reasoning consistent with Kohlberg's Stage 4 while others reason in a Stage 1 fashion.

As the case of Lun Cheung so poignantly illustrates, moral values and behaviors are also influenced by the neighborhood in which young people live. Lun's decision to leave the gang may have been partly prompted by his summer with his cousins in Hong Kong: Adolescents' delinquent behaviors decrease when they move from neighborhoods with high delinquency rates to neighborhoods with little or no delinquency (Harris, 1998). Religious affiliation is related to moral reasoning as well (Narvaez, Getz, Rest, & Thoma, 1999), although a direct cause-effect relationship has not been established.

Most research addressing diversity in moral development has focused on either gender differences or cultural background. We now look at findings in each of these areas.

Gender Differences As you have learned, Kohlberg developed his stages of moral reasoning after studying how people responded to hypothetical moral dilemmas. But consider this quirk in his research: Subjects in his early studies were exclusively males (Kohlberg, 1963). When he eventually began to interview young adults of both genders, he found that females reasoned, on average, at Stage 3, whereas males were more likely to reason at Stage 4 (Kohlberg & Kramer, 1969).

Carol Gilligan (1982, 1987; Gilligan & Attanucci, 1988) has raised concerns about Kohlberg's findings, proposing that Kohlberg's theory does not adequately describe female moral development. More specifically, Kohlberg's stages emphasize issues of fairness and justice but omit other aspects of morality, especially compassion and caring for those in need, that Gilligan suggests are more characteristic of the moral reasoning and behavior of females. She argues that females are socialized to stress interpersonal relationships and to take responsibility for the well-being of others to a greater extent than males; therefore, females develop a morality that emphasizes a greater concern for others' welfare. The following dilemma can elicit either a **justice orientation** that Gilligan says characterizes male morality or a **care orientation** that characterizes female morality:

The Porcupine Dilemma

A group of industrious, prudent moles have spent the summer digging a burrow where they will spend the winter. A lazy, improvident porcupine who has not prepared a winter shelter approaches the moles and pleads to share their burrow. The moles take pity on the porcupine and agree to let him in. Unfortunately, the moles did not anticipate the problem the porcupine's sharp quills would pose in close quarters. Once the porcupine has moved in, the moles are constantly being stabbed. The question is, what should the moles do? (Meyers, 1987, p. 141, adapted from Gilligan, 1985)

According to Gilligan, males are more likely to look at this situation in terms of someone's rights being violated. For example, they might point out that the burrow belongs to the moles, and so the moles can legitimately throw the porcupine out. If the porcupine refuses to leave, some may argue that the moles are well within their rights to kill him. In contrast, females are more likely to show compassion and caring when dealing with the dilemma. For example, they may suggest that the moles simply cover the porcupine with a blanket; this way, his quills won't annoy anyone and everyone's needs will be met (Meyers, 1987).

Gilligan has suggested that a morality of care proceeds through three stages. At the first stage, children are concerned exclusively about their own needs, mostly to ensure their own survival. At the second stage, they show concern for people who are unable to care for themselves, including infants and the elderly. At the third and final stage, they recognize the interdependent nature of personal relationships and extend compassion and care to all human beings (Gilligan, 1977, 1982).

Gilligan raises a good point: Males and females are often socialized quite differently, as you discovered in Chapter 9. Furthermore, by including compassion for other human beings as well as consideration for their rights, she broadens our conception of what morality is (Durkin, 1995; Walker, 1995). Yet critics have found several shortcomings in Gilligan's theory. Gilligan provides only the most general explanation of how gender differences emerge (and has not empirically tested it) and no explanation at all about how children might move from one stage to the next (Turiel, 1998; Walker, 1995). Her early studies involved only small samples of college women discussing a single issue, abortion, which is clouded by women's views on whether an unborn fetus is a living human being (Turiel, 1998). An additional problem is that the women's responses were analyzed in an arguably superficial, subjective fashion; the absence of a systematic coding scheme raises concerns about the validity and reliability of Gilligan's findings (Turiel, 1998; Walker, 1995).

More to the point, however, is that most research studies do not find major gender differences in moral reasoning (Eisenberg et al., 1996; Nunner-Winkler, 1984; Walker, 1991). Minor differences (usually favoring females) sometimes emerge in early adolescence but disappear by late adolescence (Basinger, Gibbs, & Fuller, 1995; Eisenberg et al., 1996). Furthermore, males and females typically incorporate both justice and care into their moral reasoning, applying different orientations (sometimes one, sometimes the other, sometimes both) to different moral problems (Johnston, 1988; Rothbart, Hanley, & Albert, 1986; Smetana, Killen, & Turiel, 1991; Walker, 1995). Such findings are sufficiently compelling that Gilligan herself has acknowledged that both justice and care orientations are frequently seen in males and females alike (Brown, Tappan, & Gilligan, 1995; Gilligan & Attanucci, 1988).

The culture people grow up in also helps determine how they incorporate issues of justice and care into their moral reasoning. We now look more closely at what cross-cultural research tells us about moral development.

Cultural Differences Different cultural groups have somewhat different standards about what constitute right and wrong behaviors. Following are several examples:

- In our culture, lying to avoid facing repercussions for inappropriate behavior is considered wrong, but it is a legitimate way of saving face in many other cultures (Triandis, 1995).

justice orientation
Focus on individual rights in moral decision making.

care orientation
Focus on nurturance and concern for others in moral decision making.

- Some cultures emphasize the importance of being considerate of other people (e.g., "Please be quiet so that your sister can study"), whereas others emphasize the importance of tolerating inconsiderate behavior (e.g., "Please try not to let your brother's radio bother you when you study"; Fuller, 2001; Grossman, 1994).

- Whereas many people in North America and western Europe espouse the belief that all people should have equal rights, traditionally the culture of India has supported hierarchical power structures in which some people have more rights than others. For instance, people are designated as members of various social classes (*castes*), and members of higher castes avoid touching those in lower ones for fear of becoming soiled or polluted (Shweder et al., 1987).

- Many European Americans aspire to an egalitarian system for men and women. In contrast, many Hindu people in India believe that a woman's obedience to her husband is integral to the moral order, and so a husband is justified in beating his wife if she doesn't obey (Shweder et al., 1987). Furthermore, Hindu religious beliefs dictate rigid adherence to gender roles:

    Women do not plough the land. They can go to the field, sow the plants, arrange the plants in a row, but they may not plough. People will not let her plough because if she does, Laxmi [the goddess of wealth] will leave her house. If she touches the ploughing iron, something bad will happen. There may be an earthquake or the hills may split into pieces. Something will be destroyed—the oxen, houses, something. (Shweder & Miller, 1985, p. 48)

- Most people in Western culture believe that social conventions (e.g., table manners, forms of greeting, modes of dress) have little relevance to morality. In certain other cultures, however, some social conventions are of paramount importance, in that they are thought to affect relatives' souls or success in the afterlife (Shweder et al., 1987). For instance, in the Hindu culture of India, a son who eats a chicken the day after his father's death will jeopardize his father's salvation (Shweder & Miller, 1985).

A cross-cultural study by Miller and Bersoff (1992) provides an example of how cultural differences sometimes enter into children's and adolescents' moral decision making. These researchers presented several moral dilemmas to third graders, seventh graders, and undergraduate students in both the United States and India. An American version of one dilemma was as follows (Indian names and an Indian city were used in the Indian version):

    Ben planned to travel to San Francisco in order to attend the wedding of his best friend. He needed to catch the very next train if he was to be on time for the ceremony, as he had to deliver the wedding rings.
    However, Ben's wallet was stolen in the train station. He lost all of his money as well as his ticket to San Francisco.
    Ben approached several officials as well as passengers at the train station and asked them to loan him money to buy a new ticket. But, because he was a stranger, no one was willing to lend him the money he needed.
    While Ben was sitting on a bench trying to decide what to do next, a well-dressed man sitting next to him walked away for a minute. Ben noticed that the man had left his coat unattended. Sticking out of the man's coat pocket was a train ticket to San Francisco. . . . He also saw that the man had more than enough money in his coat pocket to buy another train ticket. (Miller & Bersoff, 1992, p. 545)

Participants were asked to choose one of two solutions to the problem and to explain their reasoning. One solution placed priority on individual rights and justice; the other placed priority on caring for others (Miller & Bersoff, 1992):

    Ben should not take the ticket from the man's coat pocket—even though it means not getting to San Francisco in time to deliver the wedding rings to his best friend. (p. 545)

    Ben should go to San Francisco to deliver the wedding rings to his best friend—even though it means taking the train ticket from the other man's coat pocket. (p. 545)

Indian participants almost always chose caring solutions over justice solutions. Some American participants also chose caring solutions, but many others put higher value on preserving individual rights.

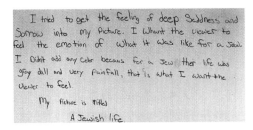

FIGURE 10–2 Students' moral beliefs influence their interpretations of and reactions to school subject matter. Here Cody tries to imagine and capture the feelings of Jewish people during World War II in a seventh-grade unit on the Holocaust.

Additional support for cultural differences comes from cross-cultural studies of Kohlberg's stages. Although progression through Kohlberg's Stages 1 through 4 appears to be universal across many cultures, Stage 5 is observed in modern, urbanized societies—which place high priority on justice and the rights of individuals—more often than in more traditional ones (Snarey, 1995).

Cultural differences almost certainly affect the degree to which children, boys and girls alike, acquire justice or care orientations toward morality (Markus & Kitayama, 1991; Miller, 1997; Shweder, Much, Mahapatra, & Park, 1997; Triandis, 1995). At the same time, we must be careful not to overgeneralize about differences in moral reasoning across cultural groups. In fact, virtually all cultures place value on *both* individual rights and concern for others (Turiel, 1998; Turiel, Killen, & Helwig, 1987). Furthermore, moral decision making within any culture is often situation-specific, calling for justice in some situations, compassion in other situations, and a balance between the two in still others (Turiel, 1998; Turiel et al., 1987).

Promoting Moral Development in the Classroom

Students' beliefs about moral and immoral behavior—about what's right and wrong—affect their actions at school and in the classroom. For example, teachers will see fewer infractions of school and classroom rules when students recognize the importance of following such rules, fewer instances of theft or violence when students respect the property and safety of their classmates, and fewer cases of cheating when students believe that cheating is morally unacceptable.

Students' beliefs about morality also affect how they think about and understand the topics they study in school. For instance, students' moral values are likely to influence their reactions when, in history, they read descriptions of the slave trade during pre–Civil War America or the Holocaust during World War II (see Figure 10–2). Their sense of human dignity may enter in when they read the anti-Semitic statements that some characters in Shakespeare's *The Merchant of Venice* make about a Jewish money-lender. And the importance of fairness and respect for the rights of others certainly come into play in any discussions about good sportsmanship on the athletic field. Students simply cannot avoid moral issues as they study school subject matter and get involved in school activities.

Teachers play a significant role in the moral development of their students (Pollard, Kurtines, Carlo, Dancs, & Mayock, 1991; Rushton, 1980). Consider the teacher who prepares a class for the arrival of a new student, first by discussing the feelings of uncertainty, apprehension, and loneliness that the student is likely to have, and then by helping the class identify steps it can take to make the student feel at home. This teacher is encouraging perspective taking and setting the stage for students to behave prosocially toward the newcomer. Now consider the teacher who ignores incidents of selfishness and aggression in class and on the playground, perhaps using the rationale that students should always work things out among themselves. This teacher is doing little to promote students' social and moral growth and in fact may inadvertently be sending students the message that antisocial behavior is quite acceptable.

Drawing from the theories and research findings previously presented, we offer the following recommendations for teachers:

■ *Clarify which behaviors are acceptable and which are not, and help students understand the reasons for various regulations and prohibitions.* Teachers must make it clear that some behaviors

PROMOTING MORAL DEVELOPMENT

■ Talk about reasons why some behaviors are inappropriate, emphasizing the harm or inconvenience that those behaviors have caused.

A second-grade teacher explains to Sarah that because she has thoughtlessly left her chewing gum on Margaret's chair, Margaret's mother must now pay to have Margaret's new pants professionally cleaned. The teacher, Sarah, and Margaret work out an arrangement through which Sarah can make amends for the inconvenience and expense to Margaret and her family.

■ Model appropriate moral and prosocial behavior.

A junior high school teacher mentions that he will be working in the annual canned food drive on Saturday and asks if any of his students would like to help.

■ Incorporate moral issues and dilemmas into classroom discussions.

When discussing the Vietnam War, a high school history teacher mentions that many young men in the United States avoided the draft by going to Canada. She asks her students to decide whether they think such behavior was appropriate and to explain their reasoning.

■ Remember that standards for what is moral and immoral differ somewhat from one culture to another.

A teacher sees a student inadvertently knock a classmate's jacket off its hook. The teacher mentions the incident to the student, but he denies that he had anything to do with the fallen jacket. Remembering that in this student's culture, lying is an acceptable way of saving face, the teacher doesn't chastise the student; instead, she asks him to do her the "favor" of returning the jacket to its hook. A short time later, she engages her class in a conversation about the importance of being careful around other people's belongings.

(e.g., hitting, pushing, insulting, bringing weapons to school) will not be acceptable under any circumstances. They should also explain that some behaviors may be quite appropriate in certain situations yet *in*appropriate in others. For example, copying a classmate's work is permissible when a student is learning but is unacceptable (it constitutes fraud) during tests and other assessments of what a student has already learned (Thorkildsen, 1995).

Teachers should accompany any disciplinary actions or discussions of rules with explanations about why certain behaviors cannot be tolerated, with a particular emphasis on potential or actual physical or psychological harm (recall our earlier discussion of *induction*). For example, a preschool teacher might say, "If we throw the blocks, someone may get hurt. Jane can come back to the block area when she is ready to use the blocks for building" (Bronson, 2000, p. 206). Similarly, an elementary school teacher might remind students, "We walk when we are in line so nobody gets bumped or tripped" (Bronson, 2000, p. 205). Teachers might also ask students to describe to one another exactly how they feel about particular misbehaviors directed toward them or to speculate about how they would feel in a situation where someone else has been victimized (Doescher & Sugawara, 1989; Hoffman, 1991).

■ *Expose students to numerous models of moral behavior.* Teachers teach by what they do as well as by what they say. When teachers model compassion and consideration of the feelings of others, such behaviors are likely to rub off on students. When they are instead self-centered and place their own needs before those of others, their students may follow suit.

Teachers can expose their students to additional models of moral behavior as well. For instance, they might invite public servants or members of charitable organizations to talk with their students about the many intangible rewards of community service work. Teachers can also make use of models of moral behavior found in literature. For example, in Harper Lee's *To Kill a Mockingbird,* set in the highly segregated and racially charged Alabama of the 1930s, a lawyer defends an obviously innocent African American man who is charged with murder; in doing so, he exemplifies a willingness to fight for high moral principles in the face of strong social pressure to hang the man for the crime (Ellenwood & Ryan, 1991).

■ *Engage students in discussions about social and moral issues.* Social and moral issues often arise at school. Sometimes these issues relate to inappropriate student behaviors that occur in most classrooms at one time or another (e.g., cheating, plagiarism, theft, interpersonal conflicts). For instance, Kohlberg and his colleagues (e.g., Higgins, 1995; Power, Higgins, &

Kohlberg, 1989) have recommended a practice known as a **just community,** whereby students and teachers hold regular "town meetings" to discuss issues of fairness and justice and establish rules for appropriate behavior. Meetings are democratic, with students and teachers alike having one vote apiece, and the will of the majority is binding. As an example, consider how a just community at one high school (the Cluster School in Cambridge, Massachusetts) dealt with a stealing incident:

> Nine dollars was taken during a class from someone's purse, and no one would admit to taking the money. A community meeting was convened to discuss the theft. One group of students came to the meeting with a proposal that each member of the school should chip in fifteen cents to make up for the nine dollars stolen from the girl's purse. Phyllis, a girl from this group, offered an elaborate rationale for reimbursing the stolen money. "It's everyone's fault that she don't have no money. It was stolen because people just don't care about the community. Everybody should care that she got her money stolen, (and therefore) we decided to give her money back to her."
>
> Not everyone agreed with the proposal. Bob was worried that if they adopted the proposal, "then anyone can say I lost ten dollars."
>
> Jill asked, "How do you know whether to believe someone who says her money has been stolen?"
>
> Bob and Jill both thought the fault lay not with the community but with the girl for having left her pocketbook unattended. "She gives you a chance to steal it; if you had it in your arms (length), wouldn't you be thinking about stealing it?"
>
> In response, Phyllis reiterated her point. She began with the assumption that Cluster ought to be a community and its members ought to trust one another. If people could not be trusted, it was the group's failure, and they would have to pay for the fault. Some staff members and students both pointed out that the community should put pressure on the guilty party to return the money. The community adopted a compromise. "If the money is not returned anonymously by a certain date, everyone will be assessed fifteen cents." This combined proposal was voted in and in fact proved effective. The person who stole the money eventually admitted it and was given a schedule of repayment. Even though the girl who stole the money only repaid a portion, this incident ended stealing in the Cluster School. A certain level of group trust had been established based on a sense of the group as a true community. There were no thefts in the school in the three years after that meeting. (Higgins, 1995, pp. 67–68)

Case studies such as the one just presented suggest that just communities not only decrease immoral behaviors but also promote more advanced moral reasoning. For instance, Higgins (1995) reported that after two years of using the just-community model, students at the Cluster School showed an increased understanding of how their own actions impacted others, gained a sense of responsibility for one another's well-being, and were more likely to reason at Kohlberg's Stages 3 and 4.

Sometimes moral issues also appear in course content. For instance, an English class might debate whether Hamlet was justified in killing Claudius to avenge the murder of his father. A social studies class might wrestle with how a capitalist society can encourage free enterprise while at the same time protecting the rights of citizens and the ecology of the environment. A science class might discuss the ethical issues involved in using laboratory rats to study the effects of cancer-producing agents.

Teachers can do several things to ensure that classroom discussions about moral issues promote students' moral development (Reimer et al., 1983). First, they can provide a trusting and nonthreatening classroom atmosphere in which students feel free to express their ideas without censure or embarrassment. Second, they can help students identify all aspects of a dilemma, including the needs and perspectives of the various individuals involved. Third, they can help students explore their reasons for thinking as they do—that is, to clarify and examine the principles that their moral judgments reflect.

■ *Challenge students' moral reasoning with slightly more advanced reasoning.* Teachers are more likely to create disequilibrium regarding moral issues (and thus to foster moral growth) when they present moral arguments one stage above the stage at which students are currently reasoning—for instance, when they present "law and order" logic (Stage 4) to a student who is concerned primarily about gaining the approval of others (Stage 3). If they present a moral argument that is too much higher than the student's current stage, then the student is unlikely to understand and remember what the teacher is saying (e.g., Narvaez, 1998) and so unlikely to experience disequilibrium.

just community
Approach to classroom decision making in which students and teachers meet regularly to address issues of fairness and justice and then reach decisions in a democratic manner.

■ *Expose students to diverse viewpoints about moral issues.* Children may get some inkling of varying cultural perspectives in their daily interactions with peers ("You're always telling lies" "You'll go to hell" "You dishonor your family"). Teachers can expand on and make sense of such beginning lessons by including discussions of culture and morality in the school curriculum. For example, they can introduce a variety of moral perspectives through the literature, folklore, and historical accounts of other countries.

Furthermore, teachers should encourage students to think about moral dilemmas from the perspective of various domains, that is, to consider the extent to which a dilemma involves care, justice, convention, or personal choice (Nucci & Weber, 1991). For example, although classmates who deface their school building with graffiti might believe that they are engaging in creative self-expression (personal choice), they are also breaking a rule (convention), disregarding other students' rights to study and learn in a clean and attractive setting (justice), and thumbing their nose to the needs of those around them (care).

In the various perspectives of social understanding and moral reasoning we've considered in this chapter, we find a common thread: a gradual progression away from self-centeredness toward increased awareness of the perspectives and needs of others and an increased desire to help fellow human beings. In Chapter 11 we'll consider some of the motives that underlie children's desires to interact with and help others, and in Chapter 13 we'll look more closely at the development of prosocial behavior.

CASE STUDY: JOAN

Researcher Hans Furth asks 6-year-old Joan for her views about obedience to authority figures:

Dr. Furth:	If a teacher tells you to do something, do you have to do it?
Joan:	Yes, that's part of learning. . . . If you didn't, like if the teacher said, "Get out your little red number book," and you didn't, you'd have to go in the corner. . . .
Dr. Furth:	Do you have to do something if your mummy tells you to?
Joan:	Yes, because it's part of, your mummy loves you, and a child has to love your mother, mummy and, if you don't do what you're told, get a smack, and then your mummy won't love you; well, she will love you, but she will have to be horrible to you for a day; like send you into the corner, and you'd get upset, and would do more horrible things.
Dr. Furth:	Um, so what do you do about it? How can you stop doing more horrible things?
Joan:	By forgetting . . . all about it the next day.
Dr. Furth:	How do you know about that, and about mummy loving you, and?
Joan:	'Cos, it just comes in my mind. . . .
Dr. Furth:	If a friend tells you to do something, do you have to do it?
Joan:	No—yes, well, sometimes you have to do it, if you're—yes, you have to do it, because that's part of being friends.
Dr. Furth:	What—tell me some more.
Joan:	Part of being friends, and then, if you don't do what the child, your friend, wants you to do, then you lose friends. (dialogue from Furth, 1980, p. 119; format adapted)

- What beliefs does Joan have about why she should obey her teacher and mother? How might you use Kohlberg's theory to understand her thinking?
- Applying what you've read about moral development in this chapter, predict how Joan's beliefs might change over the school years.
- What kinds of social experiences at school might affect Joan's beliefs about authority and morality?

SUMMARY

Social Understanding

As children grow older, they become increasing attuned to and interested in the mental life of those around them. They gradually learn that people have thoughts, feelings, and motives different from their own and that such thoughts, feelings, and motives can be complex and at times contradictory. They also become increasingly skilled in taking the perspectives of those around them: They can imagine how other people must think and feel and begin to empathize with those who are suffering or in need. To some degree, such social cognition encompasses elements of cognition more generally; for instance, it involves storing information about social events in working memory, expanding (elaborating) on such events using one's existing knowledge base, and retrieving possible responses from long-term memory.

Young people's conceptions of their society reflect a similar progression toward more complex, comprehensive, and abstract views. With age, children and adolescents gain greater awareness of social conventions as a means of helping their society function more smoothly and cohesively, and they become increasingly knowledgeable about their society's political and economic foundations. Often accompanying such advancements in social cognition, however, are faulty, nonproductive inclinations in thinking about others, such as stereotypes and prejudice.

Schools and classrooms are important contexts in which children and adolescents develop their social cognitive skills. Teachers can promote students' acquisition of such skills in numerous ways, for instance by exposing them to multiple and equally legitimate perspectives about controversial issues, conducting class discussions about inequities in society's institutions, and confronting inaccurate and counterproductive stereotypes.

Moral Development

Moral reasoning encompasses a complex array of understandings and dispositions. From a young age, children make distinctions between moral transgressions (those that cause harm or trespass on others' rights) and social transgressions (those that violate culture-specific social norms). As children move through the elementary grades, they gain an increasing understanding of fairness and an increasing capacity to feel shame and guilt about moral wrongdoings. Lawrence Kohlberg has suggested that moral reasoning progresses from an initial preoccupation with addressing one's own needs (in early and middle childhood) to greater concern for pleasing others and obeying rules (in adolescence) and then possibly to a commitment to abstract principles of right and wrong (in late adolescence or adulthood if at all). Teachers can promote students' moral development by explaining why certain behaviors are unacceptable (in that they cause harm or distress to another or jeopardize another's rights and needs), introducing students to numerous models of moral and prosocial behavior, engaging students in discussions about moral issues and dilemmas, and exposing them to diverse and slightly more advanced moral perspectives.

Now go to our Companion Website to assess your understanding of chapter content with Multiple-Choice Questions, apply comprehension in Essay Questions, and broaden your knowledge with links to related Developmental Psychology World Wide Web sites.

KEY CONCEPTS

social cognition (p. 362)
person perception (p. 363)
social information processing
   (p. 363)
social perspective taking
   (p. 365)
intentionality (p. 367)
empathy (p. 368)
conceptions of society (p. 369)
social-cognitive bias (p. 374)

stereotype (p. 374)
prejudice (p. 374)
morality (p. 378)
internalization (p. 379)
moral realism (p. 381)
prosocial behavior (p. 381)
moral transgression (p. 383)
conventional transgression
   (p. 383)

distributive justice (p. 385)
shame (p. 385)
guilt (p. 385)
sympathy (p. 385)
moral dilemma (p. 386)
induction (p. 391)
justice orientation (p. 394)
care orientation (p. 394)
just community (p. 398)

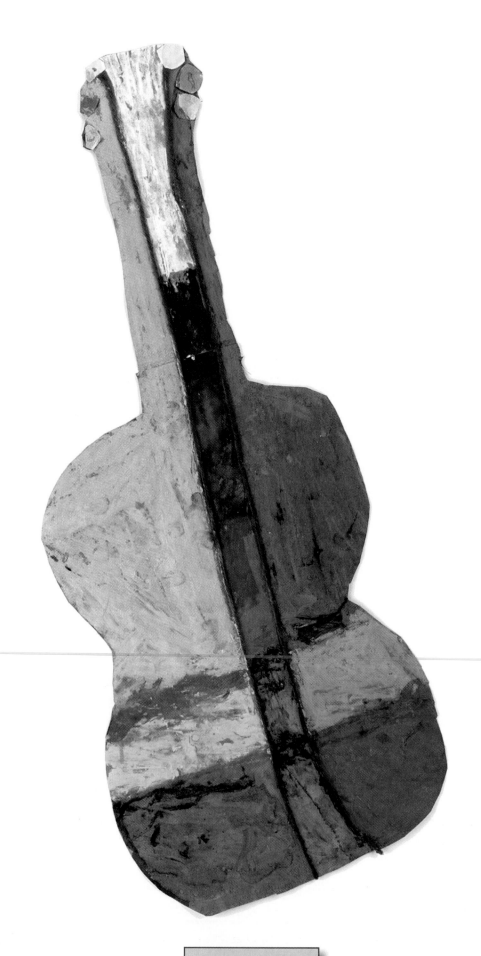

William, age 7

Development of Motivation and Self-Regulation

CASE STUDY: MAKING KITES

Ms. Keany[1] teaches a mathematics class for fifth and sixth graders who have a history of poor performance in math. She has recently shown her class how concepts in geometry relate to aerodynamics, emphasizing that the size and shape of an object affect the ease with which it can fly. As a follow-up to the lesson, she asks her students to experiment with a variety of sizes and shapes of kites and then to design a kite using what they have learned.

The kite project lasts several days. A researcher observes the class throughout the project and interviews the children afterward. She finds that different children take very different approaches to the task and have widely varying perspectives about it. For instance, a girl named Sara approaches the task as a scientist might: She seems keenly interested in creating an aerodynamic kite design and realizes that doing so will take time and patience. She redesigns her kite three times to make it as aerodynamic as possible. After the project, she summarizes her results:

> . . . I wasn't completely successful, because I had a few problems. But I realized that most scientists, when they try experiments, well, they're not always right. . . . [I]f I can correct myself on [errors] then I don't really mind them that much. I mean, everybody learns from their mistakes. I know I do. . . . I think mistakes are actually good, to tell you the truth. . . .
>
> When I had my test flights, the shape flew really, really well, and I was going to stick with that shape. . . . I had no doubts because I knew that I could really do it; I knew I could put this together really well, 'cause I had a lot of confidence in myself. (Meyer, Turner, & Spencer, 1997, pp. 511–512)

Unlike Sara, Amy sticks with a single kite design throughout the project even though she has trouble getting her kite to fly. Later, Amy tells the researcher:

> I knew from the start what shape I wanted. Once I had the materials it was very easy to make the kite. . . . [T]here wasn't enough wind for the kites to fly. (Meyer et al., 1997, pp. 510, 513)

The researcher asks Amy how important the project was to her and whether she ever takes risks at school. She responds:

> I feel lazy because I don't like to make challenges for myself, to make goals. I just like to do it as I go along, not make goals or challenges. . . . I like to do well for [the teacher] and my parents, and myself, I guess. . . . [I]f it doesn't affect my grade, whether I do this or not, if I totally fail and do everything wrong, if it doesn't affect my grade, then I'll [take risks]. (pp. 510, 512)

Had her kite flown, how might Amy have explained it? Amy tells the researcher that it would probably have been "beginner's luck" (Meyer, Turner, & Spencer, 1994, 1997).

---

[1]Although the case is real, "Ms. Keany" is a pseudonym.

S ARA IS WILLING TO experiment and make mistakes so that she can construct the best kite possible, whereas Amy prefers an easier, though less successful, course of action. Sara finds satisfaction in her own accomplishments, whereas Amy seems more interested in pleasing her teacher and parents. Sara attributes her successful kite to her own effort and ability, whereas Amy concludes that her failure was due to poor weather conditions and suspects that any success on the task would have been a matter of luck. All of these differences illustrate aspects of *motivation* that we consider in this chapter.

In general, **motivation** energizes, directs, and sustains behavior; it gets people moving, points them in a particular direction, and keeps them going. We usually see it reflected in a certain amount of *personal investment* in particular activities, as exemplified by the time and effort that Sara puts into creating her kite.

Virtually all children and adolescents are motivated in one way or another. One may be keenly interested in the subject matter being taught and so may seek out challenging coursework, participate actively in classroom discussions, complete assignments diligently, and earn high marks on classroom assignments. Another may be more concerned about the social side of school, interacting with classmates frequently, participating in extracurricular activities almost every day, and perhaps running for a student government office. Still another may be focused on athletics, excelling in physical education classes, playing or watching sports most afternoons and weekends, and working out daily in hopes of making the soccer team next year. And yet another, perhaps because of an undetected learning disability, poor social skills, or a seemingly uncoordinated body, may be interested primarily in *avoiding* academics, social situations, or athletic activities.

Sometimes children and adolescents are motivated **intrinsically**—by factors within themselves or inherent in the task they are performing. For example, they may engage in an activity because it gives them pleasure, helps them develop a skill they think is important, or seems the ethically and morally right thing to do. At other times, they are motivated **extrinsically**—by factors external to themselves and unrelated to the task they are performing. For example, they may want the good grades, money, or glory that particular activities and accomplishments bring.

Over the years, psychologists have looked at motivation and its development from a variety of angles. In the upcoming sections, we consider four general approaches to the study of motivation: the behaviorist, social cognitive, trait, and cognitive perspectives. After comparing and critiquing these perspectives, we draw from all of them to make suggestions for fostering children's and adolescents' motivation in the classroom. Later, we pull ideas from three of the four perspectives to gain an understanding of how children become increasingly able to direct and regulate their own behavior. Finally, we look at how the overall classroom environment contributes to motivation and learning.

motivation
State that energizes, directs, and sustains behavior.

intrinsic motivation
Internal desire to perform a particular task.

extrinsic motivation
Motivation promoted by factors external to the individual and unrelated to the task being performed.

behaviorism
Theoretical perspective in which behavior is described and explained in terms of specific stimulus-response relationships.

operant conditioning
Explanation of behavior change in which a response increases in frequency as a result of being followed by reinforcement.

reinforcer
Consequence of a response that leads to an increased frequency of that response.

Behaviorist Perspectives of Motivation

Behaviorism emphasizes the influence of environmental conditions on people's behaviors. In particular, behaviorist theorists look at the specific *stimuli* people encounter and the *responses* they make as a result of those stimuli. Hence, behaviorism is sometimes called *stimulus-response theory* or, more simply, *S-R theory.*

Without question, the best-known behaviorist theory is the late B. F. Skinner's theory of **operant conditioning** (e.g., 1953, 1968). Skinner proposed that people's behaviors are largely influenced by the consequences that result from those behaviors. In particular, he proposed that responses that are followed by certain kinds of consequences are more likely to be made again. Consequences that lead to an increase in behavior—consequences that are usually (though not always) pleasant—are known as **reinforcers.**

From Skinner's perspective, children behave primarily to obtain reinforcing outcomes, and many of the behaviors they exhibit are those that have been reinforced in the past. For instance, Peter might practice the piano regularly if his parents continually praise him for his efforts. Sally might throw frequent temper tantrums if she's learned that her tantrums are the only way she can get special toys or privileges. Mike might misbehave in class if doing so gains him the attention of his teacher and classmates. The last of these examples illustrates an important point: Reinforcers are not always what we would typically think of as "rewards." The attention Mike gets for his misbehavior may seemingly be unpleasant—Mike's teacher may scold him for acting out, or his classmates might shake their heads in disgust—but if Mike's misbehaviors increase as a result, then the negative attention is indeed a reinforcer.

So far, we have been talking about **positive reinforcement**, in which the consequence involves *getting* something—perhaps parental praise, a toy, or teacher attention. On some occasions, reinforcement instead involves *getting rid of* something. A child might misbehave, procrastinate, or complain of a stomachache to escape or avoid unpleasant situations. For instance, Jeanne confesses that as a junior high school student, she often stayed home "sick" as a way of avoiding tests she wasn't prepared for. The phenomenon in which a behavior increases because it enables a person to escape or avoid a particular event is known as **negative reinforcement.**

B. F. Skinner focused primarily on the effects of reinforcement. Yet many behaviorists believe that a second kind of consequence—punishment—affects people's behavior as well. Behaviorist researchers have found that punishment of undesirable responses, especially when combined with reinforcement of desired responses, can produce lasting improvements in children's behavior (e.g., Hall, Axelrod, Foundopoulos, Shellman, Campbell, & Cranston, 1971; Walters & Grusec, 1977). For example, some teachers and therapists of children with serious behavioral problems award points (reinforcement) for desired behaviors and take away points (punishment) for inappropriate ones; at the end of the day, the children can exchange the points they've accumulated for small toys or privileges. Taking away previously earned points for unacceptable behavior (a strategy called *response cost*) can be quite effective in bringing about behavior change (O'Leary & O'Leary, 1972). Many other forms of punishment are ineffective, however, particularly those that model aggression or inflict physical or psychological harm (Davis & Thomas, 1989; Straus, 2000; Walker & Shea, 1995).

Trends in Children's Responses to Reinforcers

Behaviorists have observed developmental changes in children's responses to reinforcers:

■ *With age, secondary reinforcers become increasingly influential.* Young infants are concerned primarily with stimuli that satisfy physiological needs: food, drink, warmth, physical affection[2], and so on. Consequences that satisfy physiological needs are called **primary reinforcers.** But over time, children begin to associate certain other stimuli with primary reinforcers. For example, a child might learn that praise from mother often comes with a special candy treat or discover that a good grade frequently leads to a hug from father. Through such associations, consequences such as praise, good grades, money, and attention (sometimes even in the form of a scolding) become reinforcing in their own right: They become **secondary reinforcers.**

Secondary reinforcers are far more common in classrooms than primary reinforcers. Yet teachers must remember that secondary reinforcers are *learned* reinforcers, and not all students have learned to appreciate them. Although most students will probably respond positively to such consequences as praise or a good grade, a few students may not.

■ *Children soon learn that some responses are reinforced only occasionally.* With experience, children discover that reinforcers don't necessarily follow every response that they make. For example, a preschooler may learn that he has to ask his mother for a cookie several times

---

[2]In the 1950s, Harry Harlow raised rhesus monkeys in complete isolation from other monkeys (including their mothers). In their cages, infant monkeys had two surrogate "mothers": (a) a wire-mesh cylinder with a wooden head and (b) a softer, cuddlier terry-cloth cylinder with a more monkeylike head. A bottle of infant formula was consistently attached to one of the mothers. Regardless of which mother provided the nourishment, the monkeys spent considerable time cuddling against the terry-cloth mother and developed an obvious emotional attachment to "her" (Harlow, 1959; Harlow & Harlow, 1962). Such results suggest that monkeys (and probably other primates as well) have a biological need for physical cuddling.

positive reinforcement
Consequence that brings about the increase of a behavior through the presentation (rather than removal) of a stimulus.

negative reinforcement
Consequence that brings about the increase of a behavior through the removal (rather than presentation) of a stimulus.

primary reinforcer
Stimulus that satisfies a basic physiological need.

secondary reinforcer
Stimulus that becomes reinforcing over time through its association with another reinforcer.

Children are more likely to persist at difficult tasks when they discover that their responses do not always lead to success—in other words, when they are reinforced only intermittently.

before Mom relents and gives him one, and a high school student may learn that she has to practice a particular gymnastic skill over and over before she earns the praise of her coach. Whenever a response is reinforced only occasionally, with some occurrences of the response going unreinforced, **intermittent reinforcement** is at work. Children who are intermittently reinforced for their behaviors often learn to persist in the face of disappointment and failure.

■ *Children become increasingly able to delay gratification.* In his theory of operant conditioning, Skinner proposed that a reinforcer is most effective when it is presented immediately after a child has made a desired response. Consistent with Skinner's proposal, research indicates that immediate reinforcement *is* more effective than delayed reinforcement in classroom settings (Kulik & Kulik, 1988).

Yet as children get older, they become better able to **delay gratification:** They can forego small, immediate rewards for the larger rewards that their long-term efforts are likely to bring down the road (e.g., Green, Fry, & Myerson, 1994; Rotenberg & Mayer, 1990; Vaughn, Kopp, & Krakow, 1984). A 3-year-old is likely to choose a small toy she can have *now* over a larger and more attractive toy she can't have until tomorrow. An 8-year-old is more willing to wait a day or two for the more appealing item. Many adolescents can delay gratification for weeks at a time. For instance, as a 16-year-old, Jeanne's son Jeff worked long hours stocking shelves at the local grocery store (hardly a rewarding activity!) to earn enough money to pay half the cost of a $400-a-night limousine for the junior prom.

Some children and adolescents are better able to delay gratification than others, and those who do are less likely to yield to temptation, more carefully plan their future actions, and achieve at higher levels in academic settings (Durkin, 1995; Shoda, Mischel, & Peake, 1990; Veroff, McClelland, & Ruhland, 1975). However, even 4- and 5-year olds can learn to delay gratification for a few hours if their teachers tell them that rewards for desired behaviors (such as sharing toys with other children) will be coming later in the day (Fowler & Baer, 1981). Teaching children effective waiting strategies enhances children's ability to delay gratification as well. For instance, in a study by Binder, Dixon, and Ghezzi (2000), three preschoolers with ADHD were asked to choose between a small immediate reward (half of a cookie) and a larger delayed one (a whole cookie). Initially, the three children were interested only in immediate gratification: They always chose the smaller cookie. But when they learned strategies for passing the time during a delay period (either by focusing their attention on another task or by reminding themselves "If I wait a little longer, I will get the bigger one"), they became increasingly able to resist the immediate temptation of the half cookie and hold out for the whole one.

Although the study just described brings mental processes (e.g., reminding oneself "If I wait a little longer . . . ") into the picture, behaviorists focus largely on children's behaviors and give little thought to cognition. As you will see now, another perspective of motivation—social cognitive theory—considers what children think as well as what they do.

intermittent reinforcement
Reinforcing a response only occasionally, with some occurrences of the response going unreinforced.

delay of gratification
Foregoing small immediate rewards for larger, more delayed ones.

social cognitive theory
Theoretical perspective that focuses on the roles of observation and modeling in learning and motivation.

Social Cognitive Perspectives of Motivation

Social cognitive theory (also called *social learning theory*) focuses on the role that observation and modeling play in children's learning and development: Children learn many new behaviors by watching and imitating those around them (Bandura, 1977, 1986). Social cognitive theory also emphasizes the importance of self-efficacy and expectations as factors in motivation (Bandura, 1982, 1986; Schunk, 1989).

By and large, social cognitive theorists focus more on general principles of learning and motivation than on how learning and motivation change over time. Thus, it will be more helpful to talk about general principles that characterize social cognitive perspectives of motivation than about developmental trends per se.

General Principles of Motivation

Key among social cognitive principles of motivation are these:

■ *Children are more likely to behave in ways that they expect will bring about desirable consequences.* From a behaviorist perspective, the previous consequences of certain behaviors (previous reinforcements and, for some theorists, previous punishments as well) have a direct effect on children's present behavior. In contrast, social cognitive theorists argue that children's *expectations* of *future* consequences have a greater influence on their behavior choices. Past consequences obviously affect their expectations for future consequences, but present circumstances play a role as well. For example, 5-year-old Sam may have learned that at home, whining and complaining have usually gotten him what he's wanted. When he begins school, he may quickly discover that whining and complaining are frowned upon and rarely yield satisfactory results; in fact, his negative attitude may result in a lack of playmates at recess. Sam may soon discover, perhaps on his own or perhaps with his teacher's guidance, that other behaviors are more likely to lead to positive consequences such as teacher approval and attention from peers.

■ *Children imitate some people more frequently than others.* Social cognitive theorists have found some consistency in the types of models that children are most likely to imitate (Bandura, 1986; Rosenthal & Bandura, 1978). Effective models typically exhibit one or more of the following characteristics:

- *Competence.* Children typically imitate people who do something well, not those who do it poorly. For instance, they will imitate the basketball skills of a professional basketball player rather than those of the class klutz. They will wear clothes similar to those of a popular classmate rather than those of a peer who is socially isolated.
- *Prestige and power.* Children often imitate people who are famous or powerful. Some effective models—a world leader, a renowned athlete, a popular rock star—are famous at a national or international level. The prestige and power of other models—a head cheerleader, the captain of the high school hockey team, a gang leader—may be limited to a more local environment.
- *"Gender-appropriate" behavior.* Children are more likely to imitate models whom they believe are behaving appropriately for their own gender (with different children defining *gender appropriate* somewhat differently). For example, many girls and boys limit their academic choices and career aspirations to subjects and professions they believe are "for women" or "for men." Some girls may shy away from careers in mathematics, which they see as too "masculine." Some boys may not take keyboarding (typing) because they perceive it to be a secretarial skill, and most secretaries are women. Exposure to numerous examples of people in nontraditional careers (e.g., female mathematicians and engineers, male secretaries and nurses) can help broaden children's perceptions as to what behaviors are gender appropriate.

■ *Children's expectations are influenced by what happens to others as well as by what happens to themselves.* Children are more likely to engage in certain behaviors when they see other people reinforced for those behaviors; they are less likely to exhibit behaviors for which they have seen others punished. These phenomena are known as **vicarious reinforcement** and **vicarious punishment,** respectively. For example, by watching the consequences that their classmates experience, children might learn that being elected to class office brings status and popularity, that acting out in class gets the teacher's attention, or that unsportsmanlike conduct on the playing field leads to being benched during the next game.

■ *Children are more likely to undertake activities for which they have high self-efficacy.* In Chapter 9 we introduced the concept of *self-efficacy:* one's beliefs about whether one is achieving certain goals or outcomes. Children are more likely to choose an activity, exert considerable effort in performing it, and persist in the face of failure when they have high self-efficacy for that activity (Bandura, 1982, 1994). For example, Lucinda is more likely to work hard on a homework assignment if she has had success with similar assignments at school, and Marcus is more likely to try out for the school basketball team if he has successfully competed against his neighbors in pickup games at the local recreation center. In the opening case study, Sara

vicarious reinforcement
Phenomenon in which a person increases a certain response after seeing another person reinforced for that response.

vicarious punishment
Phenomenon in which a person decreases a certain response after seeing another person punished for that response.

reveals a high sense of self-efficacy about building a kite: "I had no doubts because I knew that I could really do it; I knew I could put this together really well" (Meyer et al., 1997, p. 512).

Children's self-efficacy beliefs are not entirely the result of their own successes and failures, however. Watching others, especially peers, has an effect as well (Schunk & Hanson, 1985; Schunk, Hanson, & Cox, 1987). When children see others of similar age and ability successfully accomplish a task, they are more likely to believe that they, too, can accomplish it. For instance, in one study (Schunk & Hanson, 1985), elementary school children having trouble with subtraction were given 25 subtraction problems to complete. Children who had seen another student successfully complete the problems got an average of 19 correct, whereas those who saw a teacher complete the problems got only 13 correct, and those who saw no model at all solved only 8.

Both behaviorists and social cognitive theorists focus largely on the kinds of experiences (reinforcement, punishment, observation of others, etc.) that influence children's motivation, and they assume that the principles and trends they've identified apply to most or all children. In contrast, trait theorists focus on ways in which children are often quite different from one another.

Trait Perspectives of Motivation

Trait theorists propose that people have a variety of motives and varying levels of each one. For example, children may differ in the extent to which they seek out friendly relationships with others (reflecting their *need for affiliation*), want others to praise them for what they do (reflecting their *need for approval*), and want to do well in school (reflecting their need for achievement, or *achievement motivation*). Let's briefly look at each of these.

Need for Affiliation

Some theorists have proposed that people of all ages have a fundamental need to feel socially connected and secure the love and respect of others; in other words, they have a **need for relatedness** (Connell, 1990; Connell & Wellborn, 1991). For many school-age children and adolescents, this need may be reflected in the high priority they put on socializing with friends, often at the expense of getting their schoolwork done (Doyle, 1986; Wigfield, Eccles, Mac Iver, Reuman, & Midgley, 1991).

Yet children and adolescents differ in the extent to which they desire and actively seek out friendly relationships with others; in other words, they differ in their **need for affiliation.** For example, Jeanne's daughter Tina has always been a very social creature; the thought of spending more than a couple of hours alone horrifies her. In contrast, Jeff, although he enjoys the companionship of others, is often quite content to spend an afternoon creating a Bart Simpson cartoon on the computer or designing the "executive mansion" in which, so he tells his parents, he intends to live some day.

Children's and adolescents' needs for affiliation are reflected in the kinds of choices they make at school (Boyatzis, 1973; French, 1956; Wigfield et al., 1996). For example, students with a low need for affiliation may prefer to work alone, whereas students with a high need more often prefer to work in small groups. When choosing work partners, students with a low affiliation need are apt to choose classmates whom they believe to be competent at the assigned task; students with a high affiliation need are apt to choose their friends even if these friends are relatively incompetent. In high school, students with a low need for affiliation are likely to choose a class schedule that meets their own interests and ambitions, whereas students with a high need for affiliation are more likely to choose one that enables them to be with their friends.

Need for Approval

In the opening case study, Amy explains that "I like to do well for [the teacher] and my parents, and myself, I guess" (Meyer et al., 1997, p. 512). It appears that Amy works on classroom tasks primarily to please her teacher and parents. Pleasing *herself* (intrinsic motivation) is almost an afterthought.

The **need for approval** is a strong desire to gain the acceptance and positive judgments of other people (Igoe & Sullivan, 1991; Juvonen & Weiner, 1993; Urdan & Maehr, 1995). Chil-

trait theory
Theoretical perspective focusing on stable individual differences in human behavior.

need for relatedness
Fundamental human need to feel socially connected and secure the love and respect of others.

need for affiliation
Consistent tendency in some individuals to seek out friendly relationships with others.

need for approval
Consistent desire in some individuals to gain the acceptance and positive judgments of others.

ADDRESSING SOCIAL NEEDS IN THE CLASSROOM

- Have students work together on some learning tasks.

  A high school history teacher incorporates classroom debates, small-group discussions, and cooperative learning tasks into every major unit of her courses.

- Continually communicate the message that you like and respect your students.

  A middle school teacher tells a student that he saw her dancing troupe's performance at the local mall over the weekend. "I had no idea you were so talented," he says. "How many years have you been studying dance?"

- Give frequent praise to students who have a high need for approval.

  Several students in a second-grade class have difficulty staying on task during independent

assignments. Their teacher has found that they are more likely to stay on task when she praises them for doing so.

- Praise students privately when being a high achiever is not socially acceptable among peers.

  While reading a stack of short stories that his students have written, a high school English teacher discovers that one of his students—a young woman who, he knows, is quite concerned about looking "cool" in front of her classmates—has written a particularly creative story. On the second page of her story (where the student's classmates won't be likely to see what he has written), he writes, "This is great work, Megan! I think it's good enough to enter into the state writing contest. I'd like to meet with you before or after school some day this week to talk more about the contest."

dren with a high need for approval are overly concerned with pleasing others and tend to give in easily to group pressure, for fear that they might otherwise be rejected (Crowne & Marlowe, 1964; Wentzel & Wigfield, 1998). Whereas their classmates might engage in a school task for the pleasure that success at the task brings, children with a high need for approval tend to engage in the task primarily to please their teacher and will persist at it only as long as their teacher praises them for doing so (Harter, 1975; Rose & Thornburg, 1984).

In the early years, children are most apt to seek the approval of adults, such as parents and teachers. As they get older, and especially as they move into adolescence, they are usually more interested in gaining the approval of their peers (Juvonen & Weiner, 1993; Urdan & Maehr, 1995). Culture can influence the relative value children and adolescents place on adult versus peer approval, however; for instance, many teenagers from Asian cultures highly value the approval of adult authority figures (e.g., Dien, 1998).

Teachers cannot ignore the high needs for affiliation and approval that many students bring to the classroom. On the contrary, students are more academically successful when they feel that their teachers and peers like and respect them and when they have a sense of belonging in the classroom community (Goodenow, 1993; Ladd, 1990). The Development and Practice feature above suggests several ways in which teachers can simultaneously promote academic achievement and satisfy students' social needs.

Achievement Motivation

Of the various needs that children might have, most research has focused on the need for achievement, more often called **achievement motivation.** Achievement motivation is the need for excellence for its own sake, without regard for any external rewards that accomplishments might bring (e.g., Atkinson & Feather, 1966; McClelland, Atkinson, Clark, & Lowell, 1953; Veroff et al., 1975). Children with high achievement motivation seek out challenging tasks that they know they can accomplish with effort and persistence. They rarely rest on their laurels; instead, they set increasingly higher standards for excellence as their current standards are met (Eccles, Wigfield, & Schiefele, 1998; Veroff et al., 1975).

In its earliest conceptualization, achievement motivation was thought to be a general characteristic that people exhibit consistently in a variety of tasks across many domains. More recently, however, many theorists have proposed that this need may instead be somewhat specific to particular tasks and occasions (e.g., Dweck & Elliott, 1983; Stipek, 1996; Wigfield, 1997). Theorists are also beginning to explain achievement motivation in terms of specific cognitive factors that influence the choices students make and the tasks they

achievement motivation
Need for excellence for its own sake, without regard for any external rewards that one's accomplishments might bring.

pursue. Thus, explanations of achievement motivation have shifted away from a "trait" approach to a more cognitive approach. We now look at what contemporary cognitive perspectives of motivation encompass.

Cognitive Perspectives of Motivation

Within the last two or three decades, psychologists have radically changed their approach to the study of motivation and its development. Talk of physiological needs has largely gone by the wayside. Concrete, external reinforcers play less of a role in theoretical conceptions of how children behave. And interest in global needs that may vary from one child to another (achievement motivation, need for approval, etc.) is diminishing.

Most theorists now describe human motivation as being a function of human cognition—as involving inquisitiveness, goal-setting, development of interests in specific topics, and so on. They point out that motivation *affects* cognition as well; for instance, children who are intrinsically motivated to learn something are more likely to pay attention and engage in effective learning strategies (Eccles & Wigfield, 1985; Pintrich, Marx, & Boyle, 1993; Voss & Schauble, 1992).

Some cognitive theorists further propose that motivation, rather than being a relatively permanent characteristic that children carry around inside of them, is largely a function of the particular context in which children find themselves; this phenomenon is sometimes called **situated motivation** (Graham & Weiner, 1996; Paris & Turner, 1994; Rueda & Moll, 1994). In classrooms, many factors influence motivation; among these are the kinds of instructional materials that a teacher uses (whether they are interesting, challenging, relevant to students' needs, and so on), the extent to which students must compete with one another, and the ways in which students are evaluated (Boykin, 1994; Paris & Turner, 1994; Stipek, 1996).

Cognitive theorists have gone in many directions in their explorations of human motivation. Here we focus on development in three areas: intrinsic motivation, goals, and attributions.

Development of Intrinsic Motivation

Most of the research on intrinsic motivation has focused on motivation for learning and achievement in school settings, and so we, too, limit our focus accordingly. Intrinsic motivation related to academic pursuits goes by various names, such as *need for achievement, achievement motivation, motivation to learn,* and *mastery orientation.* These concepts, though not identical from a theoretical standpoint, overlap considerably, and so we lump them together under the more general term *intrinsic motivation* for purposes of our discussion.

The Observation Guidelines table that follows lists several common indicators of intrinsic motivation. Students who are intrinsically motivated to learn and master classroom subject matter are more likely to use effective learning strategies (e.g., elaboration) when they read, listen, and study (Pintrich & Schrauben, 1992; Schiefele, 1996; Voss & Schauble, 1992). Not surprisingly, then, they achieve at higher levels than students who are extrinsically motivated (Flink, Boggiano, Main, Barrett, & Katz, 1992; Gottfried, 1990; Schiefele, Krapp, & Winteler, 1992).

Cognitive theorists have offered a variety of explanations regarding the nature of intrinsic motivation. For instance, different theorists have suggested that intrinsic motivation may involve one or more of the following:

- *Curiosity.* As you should recall from Chapter 4, Jean Piaget proposed that children are naturally curious about their world and actively seek out information to help them understand and make better sense of it (e.g., Piaget, 1952b).
- *Need for cognitive consistency.* Piaget also suggested that a key factor driving a child's learning and development is *disequilibrium,* an inconsistency between new information and what the child already believes to be true. According to Piaget, disequilibrium causes mental discomfort and spurs the child to integrate, reorganize, or in some cases replace existing schemes to accommodate to the new information. Like Piaget, some contemporary psychologists believe that human beings have an innate need for consistency and coherence among the things they learn (e.g., Bronson, 2000).

situated motivation
Phenomenon in which aspects of one's immediate environment enhance one's motivation to learn particular things or behave in particular ways.

Identifying Aspects of Intrinsic Motivation

OBSERVATION GUIDELINES

CHARACTERISTIC	LOOK FOR	EXAMPLE	IMPLICATION
Inquisitiveness	• Eagerness to explore and learn • Frequent and thoughtful questions • Lack of concern about external rewards for learning	Jamie likes to take small appliances apart to see how they work.	Pique students' curiosity with puzzling situations, unusual phenomena, and opportunities to explore the physical world.
Long-term Interests	• Consistent selection of a particular topic when choices are given • Frequent initiation of activities in a particular domain	Whenever his class goes to the school library, Connor looks for books about military battleships or aircraft.	Relate classroom subject matter to students' interests and needs. Give them occasional choices about the topics they study and write about.
Sense of Competence	• Obvious pleasure in mastering tasks • Willingness to tackle challenging topics and activities • Willingness to take risks and make mistakes	Luana delights in trying to solve the brainteasers that her math teacher occasionally assigns for extra credit.	Give students the academic support they need to succeed at challenging tasks. Use evaluation procedures that encourage risk taking and allow for occasional mistakes.
Effective Learning Strategies	• Focus on making sense of subject matter, rather than on rote memorization of facts • Persistence in trying to solve difficult problems and understand complex ideas	At home, Mark reads an assigned chapter about how mountains are formed. He finds the geography book's description of folded mountains confusing and so asks his teacher about them in class the next day.	In both instruction and assessment activities, emphasize genuine understanding and integration of the subject matter, rather than rote memorization of isolated facts.

- *Interest.* Theorists typically distinguish between two kinds of interest (Alexander & Jetton, 1996; Hidi & Anderson, 1992; Krapp, Hidi, & Renninger, 1992). **Situational interest** is evoked by something in the environment—something that is perhaps new, unusual, or surprising. In contrast, **personal interest** resides within the individual; people tend to have personal preferences about the topics they pursue and the activities in which they engage. Situational interests are transitory and highly dependent on environmental circumstances, whereas personal interests are relatively stable over time. For instance, during the elementary school years, Jeanne's son Alex often showed temporary (situational) interest in exciting events (e.g., going to the circus, camping in the mountains). Yet his passion (personal interest) was for reptiles: He regularly hunted for garter snakes in the neighborhood, had a series of geckos and iguanas as pets, and often borrowed books about dinosaurs and lizards from the local library.
- *Value.* Another important factor in intrinsic motivation is **value**: Children must believe that there are direct or indirect benefits in performing a task (Dweck & Elliott, 1983; Feather, 1982; Wigfield & Eccles, 1992). Some activities are valued because they are associated with certain personal qualities; for example, a boy who wants to be smart and thinks that smart people do well in school will place a premium on academic success. Other activities have high value because they are seen as means to a desired goal; for example, much as she detested mathematics, Jeanne's daughter Tina struggled through four years of high school math classes because many colleges require that much math. Still other activities are valued simply because they bring pleasure and enjoyment (Eccles & Wigfield, 1985; Eccles [Parsons], 1983).
- *Competence.* Some theorists propose that an important source of intrinsic motivation is an innate need to feel *competent*—to believe that one can deal effectively with one's environment (Bronson, 2000; Deci & Ryan, 1992; White, 1959). The need for competence may

situational interest
Interest evoked temporarily by something in the environment.

personal interest
Long-term interest about a particular topic or activity.

value
Belief that an activity has direct or indirect benefits.

PROMOTING INTRINSIC MOTIVATION

■ Pique students' curiosity.

In a lesson on vacuums, a middle school science teacher places a peeled hard-boiled egg on the neck of an empty bottle and points out that it is just a little too big to slide into the bottle. She removes the egg and places some crumpled paper inside the bottle. She sets the paper on fire and then sets the egg on top of the bottle once again. Her students watch in amazement as the egg is slowly sucked into the bottle.

■ Capitalize on students' personal interests.

A high school nutrition teacher has his students research the fat content and nutritional value of their favorite junk foods.

■ Plan activities involving fantasy and make-believe.

A second-grade teacher has students work in small groups to act out various scenes from a book they've been reading.

■ Help students see value in learning school subject matter.

A high school history teacher focuses her lessons on the impact that events in history have had on current social and political practices. In her tests and other assessments, she emphasizes student's ability to apply what they have learned rather than their knowledge of specific names, dates, and places.

■ Provide opportunities for students to make choices.

A middle school language arts teacher lets his students choose among four possibilities for their next book. Over the next several weeks, he meets weekly with the students reading each book to discuss their interpretations and reactions.

■ Show students that success is within their grasp.

A fifth-grade teacher asks students to write a five-page research paper on a topic of their choice. Realizing that five pages seem like a lot to 10- and 11-year-olds, he spreads the assignment out over several weeks and breaks it into small, easily accomplishable pieces. He also teaches the students how to type their papers on the computer and illustrate them using images they've scanned.

■ Give students some control over classroom assignments and activities.

A high school mathematics teacher tells her students, "I know you can't always do your homework the same day I assign it. Let's talk about some reasonable due dates for your assignments so that you have enough time to do them and yet we don't get behind in our schedule of topics for the year."

have evolutionary significance: It pushes children to develop ways of dealing more effectively with environmental conditions and thus increases their chances of survival (White, 1959). Furthermore, children's beliefs about their competence at particular tasks and activities (referred to as *self-efficacy* by social cognitive theorists but as **sense of competence** by some cognitive theorists) influence the choices that they make and their persistence in the face of difficulty.

• *Self-determination.* Some theorists suggest that intrinsic motivation is more likely when children have a **sense of self-determination,** a belief that they have some choice and control regarding the things they do and the direction their lives take (Deci & Ryan, 1985, 1992). For instance, a child who thinks "I *want* to do this" or "I'd *find it valuable* to do that" has a high sense of self-determination. In contrast, a child who thinks "I *must* do this" or "*My teacher wants* me to do this" is thinking that someone or something else is directing the course of events.

As you can see, then, intrinsic motivation may stem from a variety of sources. Its multifaceted nature allows teachers to foster it in numerous ways, as is evident in the Development and Practice feature above.

Developmental Trends in Intrinsic Motivation   Researchers have identified several trends in intrinsic motivation over the course of childhood and adolescence:

■ *As children get older, they become less optimistic about their capabilities.* Children are more intrinsically motivated to perform tasks they think they can do well. Most 4- to 6-year-olds are overly confident about their ability to perform various tasks; for instance, most first graders

sense of competence
Belief that one can deal effectively with a particular aspect of one's environment.

sense of self-determination
Belief that one has some choice and control regarding the future course of one's life.

rank themselves as being one of the best readers in their class (Eccles et al., 1998; Nicholls, 1979). As they move through the elementary grades, however, they can better recall their past successes and failures, and they become increasingly aware of how their performance compares with that of their classmates (Eccles et al., 1998; Feld, Ruhland, & Gold, 1979). Presumably as a result of these changes, they become less confident, though probably more realistic, about what they can and cannot do.

■ *As children grow older, their interests become increasingly stable and dependent on existing ability levels.* In the early years, interests are largely situational in nature: Children are readily attracted to novel, attention-getting stimuli. By the middle to upper elementary grades, however, children acquire specific interests—perhaps in reptiles, ballet, or outer space—that persist over a period of time (Eccles et al., 1998; Nagy, 1912). By and large, children form interests in activities that they can do well and that are stereotypically associated with their gender and social class (Gottfredson, 1981; Wigfield, 1994).

■ *Choices gradually shift from those based on personal interest to those based on usefulness.* In the elementary grades, children choose activities primarily because they perceive them as interesting and enjoyable. In contrast, adolescents in high school increasingly choose activities because of their utilitarian value for achieving long-term goals (Wigfield, 1994).

For many students, intrinsic motivation for learning academic subject matter declines after elementary school. What are some reasons why this occurs?

■ *Intrinsic motivation for learning school subject matter declines during the school years.* Young children are often eager and excited to learn new things at school. But sometime between grades 3 and 9, children become less intrinsically motivated, and more *extrinsically* motivated, to learn and master school subject matter (Harter, 1992). Their intrinsic motivation may be especially low when they make the often anxiety-arousing transition from elementary to secondary school (Eccles & Midgley, 1989).

This decline in intrinsic motivation for academic subject matter is probably due to several factors. As students move through the grade levels, they are increasingly reminded of the importance of good grades (extrinsic motivators) for promotion, graduation, and college admission, and evidence mounts to suggest that they are not necessarily "at the top of the heap" in comparison with their peers (Harter, 1992). Furthermore, they become more cognitively able to set and strive for long-term goals and begin to evaluate school subjects in terms of their relevance to such goals, rather than in terms of their intrinsic appeal. And they may grow increasingly impatient with overly structured, repetitive activities (Battistich, Solomon, Kim, Watson, & Schaps, 1995). The following interview with high school student Alfredo illustrates this last point:

Alfredo: I could do my work. And when I do it, it's always—I always get a good grade for it. It's like when I'm in school, I don't know, me and [my friend] starts talking to me. You know, I'm ready to talk and start laughing.
Adult: So then you don't pay attention? Do you think your classes are interesting?
Alfredo: Some of them are. But some of them are boring. You go to the same class everyday and you just do the same type of work every day. Like biology, I like [this] class. She's about the only one I like. And last year I had the same problem. The only class I liked last year was science. . . . We used to do different things every day . . . but like classes like Reading, you go inside, read a story with the same person every day. That's boring.
Adult: That's boring? So will you just not show up?
Alfredo: No, I'll go but I won't do nothing sometimes. (dialogue from Way, 1998, p. 198; format adapted)

■ *Over time, children internalize the motivation to perform some activities.* So far we have implied that intrinsic and extrinsic motivation represent an either-or state of affairs. In fact, there is a third possibility. With age and experience, children and adolescents gradually adopt behaviors that other people value, without regard for any external consequences that such behaviors may bring. This phenomenon is called **internalized motivation.**

Deci and Ryan (1995) have described four stages through which internalized motivation may evolve:

1. *External regulation.* The child is motivated to behave (or *not* to behave) in certain ways based primarily on the external consequences that will follow behaviors; in other words, the child is extrinsically motivated. For instance, children at this stage may do schoolwork primarily to avoid being punished for poor grades, and they are likely to need a lot of prodding to get their work done.

2. *Introjection.* The child behaves in particular ways to gain the approval of others; for example, a child may willingly complete an easy, boring assignment as a means of gaining the teacher's approval. At the introjection stage, we see some internal pressure to behave in particular ways; for instance, children may feel guilty when violating certain standards or rules for behavior. However, they do not fully understand the rationale behind such standards and rules; instead, their primary motive is protecting their sense of competence.

3. *Identification.* The child now sees certain behaviors as being personally important or valuable. Children at this stage value learning and academic success for their own sake, perceive assigned classroom tasks as being essential for helping them learn, and so need little prodding to get their work done.

4. *Integration.* The child has fully accepted the desirability of certain behaviors and has integrated them into an overall system of motives and values. For example, a child at this stage might have acquired a keen interest in science as a career goal; if so, we are likely to see that interest reflected in many things the child does on a regular basis.

Deci and Ryan have suggested that three conditions promote the development of internalized motivation (e.g., Ryan, Connell, & Grolnick, 1992):

- *A warm, responsive, and supportive environment.* Within such an environment, children feel a sense of relatedness to, and regard for, important other people (e.g., parents, teachers) in their lives.
- *Some degree of autonomy.* Caregivers exert no more control over children's behavior than necessary, as a way of maximizing children's sense of self-determination. As children grow older and become capable of making appropriate decisions, they gain increasing autonomy and independence.
- *Appropriate guidance and structure.* The environment provides information about expected behaviors and why they're important, and the consequences of inappropriate behaviors are clearly spelled out.

Fostering the development of internalized motivation, then, involves a delicate balancing act between giving children sufficient opportunities for experiencing self-determination and providing some guidance about appropriate behavior. In a sense, parents, teachers, and other influential adults scaffold desired behaviors at first, gradually reducing their support as the learner exhibits desired behaviors more easily and frequently.

Development of Goals

Many contemporary psychologists believe that human beings are purposeful by nature: People set goals for themselves and choose courses of action that they think will help them achieve those goals (e.g., Dweck & Elliott, 1983; Kaplan, 1998; Locke & Latham, 1994). Some goals (e.g., "I want to finish reading my dinosaur book") are short-term and transitory; others (e.g., "I want to be a paleontologist") are long-term and relatively enduring. Students' goals influence both the extent to which they actively engage themselves in school learning tasks and the kinds of learning strategies they use as they read and study (Anderman & Maehr, 1994; Nolen, 1996; Winne & Marx, 1989).

Children and adolescents typically have a wide variety of goals: Doing well in school, being popular among classmates, gaining recognition for accomplishments, defeating others in competitive events, earning money, finding a long-term mate, and having children are just a few of the many possibilities. Yet among their many goals are certain **core goals** that drive

internalized motivation
Adoption of behaviors that others value, without regard for the external consequences of such behaviors.

core goal
Long-term goal that drives much of what a person does.

Many young children are concerned with mastery goals, such as learning to read. Older children become increasingly concerned with performance goals, such as looking cool in front of peers.

much of what they do (Schutz, 1994). For instance, students who attain high levels of academic achievement typically make classroom learning a high priority; students who achieve at lower levels are often more concerned with social relationships (Wentzel & Wigfield, 1998; Wigfield et al., 1996).

Here we look at research findings related to *mastery and performance goals* and *career goals.* We then consider how children and adolescents often try to coordinate multiple goals.

Mastery and Performance Goals Let's return once again to the opening case study. Sara is primarily concerned with constructing a kite that flies well and redesigns it three times so that it is aerodynamically effective. She doesn't mind the occasional stumbling blocks she encounters: "I mean everybody learns from their mistakes. I know I do" (Meyer et al., 1997, p. 511). In contrast, Amy sticks with her initial kite design, one that is easy to make but never gets off the ground. She says that she is primarily concerned with pleasing her teacher and parents, acknowledges that she rarely takes risks at school if a good grade is at stake, and then adds, "I feel lazy because I don't like to make challenges for myself, to make goals. I just like to . . . do it as I go along, not make goals or challenges" (p. 510).

Both girls want to do well in school but for different reasons. Sara has a **mastery goal:** She wants to acquire new knowledge and skills related to kites and their construction, and to do so she must inevitably make a few mistakes. Amy has a **performance goal:** She wants to look good and receive favorable judgments from others and so tries to avoid mistakes if at all possible (e.g., Ames, 1992; Dweck & Elliott, 1983; Nicholls, 1984).[3]

To the extent that children have mastery goals, they engage in the very activities that will help them learn: They pay attention in class, are more likely to process information in ways that promote long-term memory storage, and learn from their mistakes. Furthermore, they have a healthy perspective about learning, effort, and failure: They realize that learning is a process of trying hard and continuing to persevere even after temporary setbacks (Anderman & Maehr, 1994; Dweck & Elliott, 1983).

Children who have performance goals may be so concerned about how they appear to others that they stay away from challenging tasks that would best help them master new skills (Dweck, 1986; Urdan, 1997). Furthermore, because they may exert only the minimal effort needed to achieve desired performance outcomes, they may learn only a fraction of what their teachers can offer them (Brophy, 1987).[4]

---

[3]You may sometimes see the term *learning goal* or *task involvement* used instead of *mastery goal* and the term *ego involvement* used instead of *performance goal* (e.g., Dweck & Elliott, 1983; Nicholls, 1984).

[4]Some theorists distinguish between *performance-approach goals* (seeking positive judgments) and *performance-avoidance* or *work-avoidance goals* (avoiding negative judgments or tasks that might result in such judgments). Children with performance-approach goals may take on challenging tasks to show others how competent they are. Those with performance- or work-avoidance goals are those most likely to avoid tasks and activities that will maximize their learning and development (Kaplan, 1998; Urdan, 1997).

mastery goal
Desire to acquire additional knowledge or master new skills.

performance goal
Desire to look good and receive favorable judgments from others.

Cognitive Perspectives of Motivation | **415**

Mastery and performance goals are not necessarily mutually exclusive; on many occasions, children are likely to have *both* kinds of goals at the same time (Anderman & Maehr, 1994). However, we do see a developmental trend in the relative prevalence of the two types of goals. Young children seem to be primarily concerned with mastery goals. By the time they reach second grade, however, they begin to show signs of having performance goals as well, and such goals become increasingly prominent as they move into middle and secondary school (Eccles & Midgley, 1989; Elliot & McGregor, 2000; Nicholls, Cobb, Yackel, Wood, & Wheatley, 1990). The greater emphasis on performance goals at older ages is probably due both to children's increasing awareness of how their performance compares with that of their peers and to the increasing emphasis that middle school and secondary school teachers place on grades and other forms of formal evaluation (Eccles et al., 1998; Nicholls et al., 1990).

Career Goals Many children include career goals among their long-term goals. Young children set such goals with little thought and change them frequently; for instance, a 6-year-old may want to be a firefighter one week and a professional baseball player the next. By late adolescence, many (though by no means all) have reached some tentative and relatively stable decisions about the career paths they want to pursue (Marcia, 1980).

In general, boys set higher aspirations for themselves than girls do, especially in domains that are stereotypically masculine (Deaux, 1984; Durkin, 1987; Lueptow, 1984). Even preschoolers are aware that men and women tend to hold different kinds of jobs: doctors, police officers, and truck drivers are usually men, whereas nurses, teachers, and secretaries are usually women. By the time children reach elementary school, they have formed definite stereotypes about the careers that are appropriate for males and females, and these gender stereotypes influence their own career aspirations (Deaux, 1984; Kelly & Smail, 1986). As they move into the secondary school years, they are more likely to recognize that both males and females can hold virtually any job; nevertheless, they continue to aspire to careers consistent with male and female stereotypes (Smith & Russell, 1984). Girls also tend to choose careers that they believe will not interfere with their future roles as wives and mothers; in so doing, they limit their aspirations even further (Eccles [Parsons], 1984).

Females are making some headway in this area; for example, girls growing up now are more likely to have career plans than girls a generation or two ago (e.g., King, 1989). Nevertheless, many girls—especially those in some ethnic groups—continue to aspire only to traditional female roles (Durkin, 1995; Olneck, 1995; S. M. Taylor, 1994).

Coordinating Multiple Goals Most children and adolescents simultaneously have numerous goals toward which they are striving, and they take a variety of approaches to try to juggle their goals. Sometimes they find activities that allow them to achieve several goals simultaneously; for instance, they may satisfy both academic and social goals by forming a study group to prepare for a test. But in other situations, they may believe they have to abandon one goal to satisfy another (McCaslin & Good, 1996; Phelan et al., 1994). For example, students who want to do well in school may choose *not* to perform at their best so that they can maintain relationships with peers who don't value academic achievement. Students with mastery goals in particular subject areas may find that the multiple demands of school coerce them into focusing on performance goals (e.g., getting good grades) rather than studying the subject matter as thoroughly as they'd like. Brian, a junior high school student, expresses his ambivalence about striving for performance goals over mastery goals:

> I sit here and I say, "Hey, I did this assignment in five minutes and I still got an A+ on it." I still have a feeling that I could do better, and it was kind of cheap that I didn't do my best and I still got this A. . . . I think probably it might lower my standards eventually, which I'm not looking forward to at all. . . . I'll always know, though, that I have it in me. It's just that I won't express it that much. (Thomas & Oldfather, 1997, p. 119)

Teachers' instructional strategies and grading practices influence the extent to which students have mastery goals and successfully juggle such goals with their social goals and performance goals. For example, students are more apt to strive for mastery goals when their assignments entice them to learn new skills (thus encouraging a focus on mastery), when they have occasional group projects (thus helping them meet their social goals), and when evaluation criteria allow for risk taking and mistakes (thus helping them meet their performance goals). Students are *unlikely* to strive for mastery goals when classroom assignments ask little of them (consider Brian's concern about low standards), when teachers insist that students compete with one another for resources or high test scores, and when any single failure has a significant impact on final grades.

Development of Attributions

In the opening case study, Amy cannot get her kite to fly. Even though she has put little effort into designing and constructing the kite, she chalks up her failure to insufficient wind and speculates that a successful kite would have been a matter of luck. In contrast, Sara, who creates a more aerodynamic kite, takes ownership of both her success ("I knew that I could really do it") and her little failures along the way ("I mean, everybody learns from their mistakes. I know I do" [Meyer et al., 1997, p. 511]).

The various causal explanations that people have for their successes and failures are **attributions** (e.g., Dweck, 1986; Weiner, 1986). Children form a variety of attributions about the causes of classroom events; they draw conclusions (possibly accurate, possibly not) about why they do well or poorly on tests and assignments, why they are popular with their classmates or have trouble making friends, why they are skilled athletes or total klutzes, and so on. They may attribute their school successes and failures to such factors as aptitude or ability (how smart or proficient they are), effort (how hard they tried), other people (how well the teacher taught or how much their classmates like them), task difficulty (how easy or hard something is), luck, mood, illness, fatigue, or physical appearance. Such attributions differ from one another along at least three dimensions (Weiner, 1984, 1986):

- *Internal versus external.* Children may attribute the causes of events to factors within themselves (*internal* things) or to factors outside themselves (*external* things). Sara's attributions are clearly internal, whereas Amy's are external.
- *Stable versus unstable.* Children may believe either that events are due to *stable* factors, which probably won't change much in the near future, or to *unstable* factors, which can vary from one occasion to the next. Sara attributes her success to her own, relatively stable ability ("I knew that I could really do it"). In contrast, Amy's explanations of "not enough wind" and "beginner's luck" are based on unstable factors that change unpredictably.
- *Controllable versus uncontrollable.* Children may attribute events to *controllable* factors, which they can influence and change, or to *uncontrollable* factors, which they cannot influence. Sara clearly sees herself in control of her success ("I knew I could put this together really well, 'cause I had a lot of confidence in myself"), whereas Amy of course has no control over bad weather conditions or a lucky break.

When children attribute their successes and failures to stable factors, they expect their future performance to be similar to their current performance: Successful children anticipate that they will continue to succeed, and unsuccessful children believe that they will always fail. In contrast, when children attribute their successes and failures to *unstable* factors, their current success rate has less influence on their expectations for future success (Dweck, 1978; Weiner, 1986). The most optimistic children—those who have the highest expectations for future success—are the ones who attribute their successes to stable factors such as innate ability and their failures to unstable but controllable factors such as lack of effort or inappropriate strategies (Schunk, 1990; Weiner, 1984).

When children believe that their failures are due to their own lack of effort and that, furthermore, they *do* have the ability to succeed if they work hard enough, they are likely to try harder and persist longer in future situations (Dweck, 1975; Feather, 1982; Weiner, 1984). But when they instead attribute failure to a lack of innate ability (they couldn't do it even if they tried), they give up easily and sometimes can't even perform tasks they have previously accomplished successfully (Dweck, 1978; Eccles [Parsons], 1983).

Developmental Trends in Attributions Researchers have observed several trends in the development of attributions:

■ *Children are increasingly able to distinguish among various attributions.* Up until age 5 or 6, children don't have a clear understanding of the differences among the possible causes—

attribution
Belief about the cause of one's success or failure.

effort, ability, luck, task difficulty, and so on—of their successes and failures (Eccles et al., 1998; Nicholls, 1990). Especially troublesome is the distinction between effort and skill, which they gradually get a better handle on over time (Nicholls, 1990):

- At about age 6, children begin to recognize that effort and ability are separate qualities. At this point, they believe that people who try hardest are those who have the greatest ability, and that effort is the primary determiner of successful outcomes.
- At about age 9, children begin to understand that effort and ability often compensate for one another, that people with less ability may have to exert greater effort to achieve the same outcome as their more able peers. They do not apply this distinction consistently, however.
- At about age 13, adolescents clearly differentiate between effort and ability. They realize that people differ both in their inherent ability to perform a task and in the amount of effort they exert on a task. They also realize that ability and effort can often compensate for each other but that a lack of ability sometimes precludes success no matter how much effort a person puts forth.

As children gain an increasing grasp on the distinction between effort and ability, they may also develop one of two general beliefs about the nature of ability (Dweck & Leggett, 1988). Some children form an *entity view,* thinking that ability is something over which they have little control. Others instead form an *incremental view,* thinking that, with effort and perseverance, they can gain greater ability over time. Children with an incremental view are more likely to have mastery goals and to seek out challenges as a way of enhancing their ability to accomplish various tasks (Dweck & Leggett, 1988).

■ *With age, children are more likely to attribute their successes and failures to ability rather than to effort.* In the elementary grades, children tend to attribute their successes to effort and hard work; therefore, they are usually relatively optimistic about their chances for success and so may work harder when they fail. By adolescence, however, they attribute success and failure more to ability—something that often appears to be fairly stable and beyond their control. At this point, effort becomes a sign of low ability: Someone who has to exert a great deal of effort to accomplish a task doesn't have "what it takes" to be successful (Covington, 1992; Nicholls, 1990; Paris & Cunningham, 1996). Probably for this reason, students in the secondary grades are more discouraged by their failures than students in the elementary grades (Eccles & Wigfield, 1985; Pressley, Borkowski, & Schneider, 1987).

This trend to attribute success and failure increasingly to ability rather than effort has been observed primarily in Western cultures. Adolescents from Asian backgrounds often attribute their academic achievement to effort, perhaps because many Asian parents actively nurture such a belief (Hess, Chih-Mei, & McDevitt, 1987; Lillard, 1997; Peak, 1993).

Some researchers have found gender differences in children's attributions for success and failure. More specifically, they have observed that boys are more likely to attribute their successes to a fairly stable ability and their failures to lack of effort, thus having the attitude that *I know I can do this.* Girls show the reverse pattern: They attribute their successes to effort and their failures to lack of ability, believing that *I don't know whether I can keep on doing it, because I'm not very good at this type of thing.* Such differences, which can appear even when boys' and girls' previous levels of achievement are equivalent, are more frequently observed in stereotypically male domains such as mathematics and sports (Eccles & Jacobs, 1986; Fennema, 1987; Stipek, 1984; Vermeer, Boekaerts, & Seegers, 2000).

■ *As they get older, children and adolescents become more aware of the reactions that different attributions elicit.* Teachers are often sympathetic and forgiving when children fail because of something beyond their control (illness, lack of ability, etc.) but frequently get angry when children fail simply because they didn't try very hard. By the time children reach fourth grade, most of them are aware of this fact and so may verbalize attributions that are likely to elicit a favorable reaction (Juvonen, 2000). For instance, a student who knows very well that she did poorly on an assignment because she didn't put forth her best effort may distort the truth, telling her teacher that she "doesn't understand this stuff" or that she "wasn't feeling well."

Children also become more adept at tailoring their attributions for the ears of their classmates. Generally speaking, fourth graders believe that their peers value diligence and hard work, and so they are likely to tell their classmates that they did well on an assignment because they worked hard. By eighth grade, however, many students believe that their peers will disapprove of those who exert much effort on academic tasks, and so they often prefer to convey the impression that they *aren't* working very hard—for instance, that they "didn't study very much" for an important exam (Juvonen, 2000).

■ *Children gradually develop predictable patterns of attributions and expectations for their future performance.* Some children and adolescents develop a general sense of optimism that they can master new tasks and succeed in a variety of endeavors. They attribute their accomplishments to their own ability and effort and have an *I can do it* attitude known as a **mastery orientation.** Others, either unsure of their chances for success or else convinced that they cannot succeed, begin to display a growing sense of futility about their chances for future success. They have an *I can't do it* attitude known as **learned helplessness.**

Even though individuals with a mastery orientation and those with learned helplessness may have equal ability initially, those with a mastery orientation behave in ways that lead to higher achievement over the long run: They set ambitious goals, seek challenging situations, and persist in the face of failure. Individuals with learned helplessness behave very differently: Because they underestimate their own ability, they set goals they can easily accomplish, avoid the challenges that are likely to maximize their learning and growth, and respond to failure in counterproductive ways that almost guarantee future failure as well (Dweck, 1986; Peterson, 1990; Seligman, 1991).

Even 4-year-olds can develop learned helplessness about a particular task if they consistently encounter failure when attempting it (Burhans & Dweck, 1995). As a general rule, however, children younger than 8 rarely exhibit learned helplessness, perhaps because they still believe that success comes largely from their own efforts (Eccles et al., 1998; Paris & Cunningham, 1996). By early adolescence, feelings of helplessness are more common: Some middle schoolers believe they cannot control what happens to them and are at a loss for strategies about how to avert future failures (Paris & Cunningham, 1996; Peterson, Maier, & Seligman, 1993).

Students of color are more likely than Caucasian students to develop a sense of learned helplessness about their ability to achieve academic success (Graham, 1989; Holliday, 1985). Racial prejudice may be one factor here: Students begin to believe that, because of the color of their skin, they have little chance of success no matter what they do (Sue & Chin, 1983; van Laar, 2000).

Origins of Attributions Why do different children attribute the same events to different causes? For instance, why does one believe that a failure is merely a temporary setback due to low effort, whereas another sees the same failure as evidence of lack of ability and an ominous sign of more failures to come, and still another places blame on a teacher's capricious, unpredictable actions?

To some degree, children's attributions are the result of their previous success and failure experiences (Covington, 1987; Hong, Chiu, & Dweck, 1995). Those who usually succeed when they give a task their best shot are likely to believe that success is due to internal factors such as effort or high ability. Those who frequently fail despite their best efforts are likely to believe that success is due to something beyond their control—perhaps to an ability they don't possess or to such external factors as luck or a teacher's arbitrary evaluations.

The things for which children are reinforced and punished may also play a role in the formation of attributions. Generally speaking, children are more apt to attribute events to internal, controllable causes when adults reinforce their successes but don't punish their failures. Conversely, children are more likely to make external attributions when adults punish failures and ignore successes (Katkovsky, Crandall, & Good, 1967).

Adults further influence children's attributions through the messages they communicate, in either what they do or what they say, about how *they* interpret children's successes and failures. For example, when teachers criticize and express anger about students' poor performance, they convey the message that students have the ability to master the task and simply aren't trying hard enough. But when teachers express pity for the same performance, they communicate their belief that students' low ability is the reason for failure (Graham, 1997; Pintrich & Schunk, 1996; Weiner, 1984). Frequent praise is often a message that students' successes are due to effort; however, by praising students for *easy* tasks, teachers may simultaneously convey the message that success wasn't expected—in other words, that students have low ability (Graham, 1990, 1991; Schunk, 1989; Stipek, 1996).

mastery orientation
General belief that one is capable of accomplishing challenging tasks, accompanied by the intent to master such tasks.

learned helplessness
General belief that one is incapable of accomplishing tasks and has little or no control of the environment.

Motivation at Different Age Levels

DEVELOPMENTAL TRENDS

AGE	WHAT YOU MIGHT OBSERVE	DIVERSITY	IMPLICATIONS
Early Childhood (2–6) 	• Preference for small, immediate rewards over larger, delayed ones • Overconfidence about one's ability to perform novel tasks • Rapidly changing, situation-dependent interests • Focus on obtaining the approval of adults more than that of peers • Focus on mastery (rather than performance) goals • Little understanding of the reasons for successes and failures	• Differences in need for affiliation are evident as early as the preschool years. • Children who begin school without basic knowledge of colors, shapes, letters, or numbers may see obvious differences between their own abilities and those of more knowledgeable peers, setting the stage for low self-evaluations.	• Praise (or in some other way reinforce) desired behaviors as soon as they occur. • Provide a wide variety of potentially interesting toys, puzzles, and equipment.
Middle Childhood (6–10) 	• Increasing ability to delay gratification • Increasing awareness of how one's performance compares with that of peers; more realistic assessment about one's abilities • Emergence of performance goals in addition to mastery goals • Increasing distinction between effort and ability as possible causes of success and failure; tendency to attribute successes to hard work	• Students with a history of learning problems (e.g., those with learning disabilities) have less intrinsic motivation to learn academic subject matter. • Girls who are gifted may be reluctant to do their best because of concerns about appearing unfeminine or surpassing their classmates. • Students of color and students with disabilities are those most likely to develop learned helplessness about their ability to achieve academic success.	• Communicate that *all* students can master basic knowledge and skills in academic subject matter. • Focus students' attention on the progress they are making, rather than on how their performance compares to that of their classmates. • Stress the importance of learning for the intrinsic pleasure that it brings; downplay the importance of grades.

A study by Barker and Graham (1987) illustrates the effects that teacher comments can have on children's attributions. Children ages 4 to 12 watched a videotape depicting two boys either solving single-digit math problems at the blackboard or throwing balls through a large hoop in the gymnasium; the two tasks appeared to be easy ones for the boys to accomplish. Some children saw a videotape in which both boys succeeded; the teacher praised one boy (e.g., "Great job!") but gave the other only neutral feedback (e.g., "Correct"). Other children saw a videotape in which the two boys failed at their task; one was criticized for his failure (e.g., "What's the matter with you? That's not the right answer!") and the other was given neutral feedback (e.g., "No, not quite").

The children were subsequently asked to rate the two boys for either intelligence (for the math problem videos) or throwing ability (for the ball-throwing videos) on a 5-point scale. Of the children who saw the two boys succeed, most younger ones (4- and 5-year-olds) concluded that the boy praised for his success had higher ability, whereas most older ones (11- and 12-year-olds) concluded that the praised boy had *lower* ability. Of the children who saw the two boys fail, the younger ones deduced that the boy criticized for his failure had lower ability, whereas older children thought he had *higher* ability. As children get older, then, they are increasingly apt to interpret praise for easy success as a sign of low ability and interpret blame for failure on an easy task as an indication of high ability.

The Developmental Trends table above draws from the four theoretical perspectives just considered to summarize developmental trends in motivation; it also describes some of the diversity that emerges at various age levels. We now step back and take a more critical look at each perspective.

AGE	WHAT YOU MIGHT OBSERVE	DIVERSITY	IMPLICATIONS
Early Adolescence (10–14)	• Declining sense of competence, often accompanying the transition to middle school or junior high • Increasing interest in social activities; increasing concern about gaining approval of peers • Decline in intrinsic motivation to learn school subject matter • Increasing motivation to learn and achieve in stereotypically gender-appropriate domains • Increasing focus on performance goals	• Girls are more likely than boys to have a high need for affiliation. • Many girls believe that demonstrating high achievement may interfere with popularity. • Adolescents from some ethnic groups (e.g., those from many Asian countries) continue to place high value on teacher approval. • On average, students from lower socioeconomic backgrounds show lower achievement motivation than students from middle and upper socioeconomic backgrounds. • Some students develop a sense of learned helplessness about achieving academic success.	• Evaluate students on the basis of how well they are achieving instructional objectives, not on how well their performance compares with that of their classmates. • Incorporate social activities, in which students collaborate in learning classroom subject matter, into the weekly schedule. • Assign cooperative group projects that allow students to display their unique talents and thereby contribute to the overall success of the group. • When students exhibit a pattern of consistent failure, provide the support they need to begin achieving success regularly.
Late Adolescence (14–18)	• Ability to postpone immediate pleasures for long-term rewards • Increasing stability of interests and priorities • Increasing focus on the utilitarian value of activities • Tendency to attribute successes and failures more to ability than to effort • Some tentative decisions about careers	• Girls work harder on school assignments, and are also more likely to graduate, than boys. • Students from Asian cultures often attribute their successes and failures to effort rather than ability. • Many students have career aspirations that are stereotypically gender appropriate; this is especially true for girls in ethnic groups that hold rigid expectations for how males and females should behave. • Students from low socioeconomic groups have lower long-term aspirations and are at greater risk for failure and dropping out of school.	• Point out the relevance of academic subject matter for students' long-term goals. • Allow students to pursue personal interests within the context of particular academic domains. • Provide opportunities for students to explore various careers and occupations.

Sources: Bell, 1989; Block, 1983; Cooper & Dorr, 1995; Deaux, 1984; Deshler & Schumaker, 1988; Dien, 1998; Durkin, 1995; Dweck, 1986; Eccles & Midgley, 1989; Eccles et al., 1998; Graham, 1989; Green et al., 1994; Halpern, 1992; Harter, 1992; Jacobsen, Lowery, & DuCette, 1986; Juvonen, 2000; Lillard, 1997; McCall, 1994; Nicholls, 1990; Pajares & Valiante, 1999; Paris & Cunningham, 1996; Peak, 1993; Peterson, 1990; Portes, 1996; Rotenberg & Mayer, 1990; Sadker & Sadker, 1994; Schultz & Switzky, 1990; Seligman, 1991; Vaughn et al., 1984; Wigfield et al., 1991.

Critiquing Theories of Motivation

Each of the theoretical perspectives we've considered in this chapter has its merits and its drawbacks. Behaviorism's most important contribution probably lies in its implications for changing children's behavior. Planned and systematic uses of reinforcement for desired responses, perhaps in conjunction with a carefully chosen punishment for unacceptable behavior, are often highly effective in treating serious behavior problems; furthermore, they often work in situations where other approaches have failed (e.g., O'Leary & O'Leary, 1972; Rimm & Masters, 1974; Smith & Schloss, 1998). Yet by themselves, behaviorist views are too limited to explain all the nuances of human motivation. For example, they cannot explain why some children and adolescents seek out challenging situations (brainteasers, puzzling phenomena, etc.) that have

Contrasting Theories of Motivation

ISSUE	BEHAVIORIST PERSPECTIVES	SOCIAL COGNITIVE PERSPECTIVES	TRAIT PERSPECTIVES	COGNITIVE PERSPECTIVES
Nature and Nurture	Behaviorists suggest that early reinforcers satisfy biological needs. However, they emphasize the environmental conditions that increase and decrease the frequencies of various responses.	Social cognitive theorists focus on experiences (e.g., past successes and failures) and environmental conditions (e.g., the presence of competent and prestigious models) that encourage and discourage certain behaviors.	Trait theorists focus on individual differences in people's needs and motives but with little concern about the origins of such differences. For the most part, then, they ignore the nature/nurture question.	Cognitive theorists propose that certain needs (e.g., needs for competence and self-determination) are shared by all human beings and so probably have a biological basis. The specific ways in which people address those needs are often influenced by environmental conditions (culture, parental upbringing, etc.).
Universality and Diversity	Basic principles of reinforcement and punishment are universally shared. Furthermore, most of these principles apply not only to human beings but to other species as well. However, any particular consequence may have different effects on different individuals.	Some phenomena (e.g., observing and imitating others' behaviors, developing beliefs about one's self-efficacy for various tasks) are universal. However, specific manifestations of these phenomena vary from one person to the next (e.g., different people imitate different models and have varying levels of self-efficacy for particular tasks).	By definition, trait theories focus on individual differences—that is, on the diversity that exists among people.	A few basic needs (e.g., the need for self-determination) are universal across the human race. However, their manifestations frequently vary across ages, genders, and ethnic groups.
Qualitative and Quantitative Change	Reinforcement and punishment influence the frequency (quantity) of the behaviors they follow; as the consequences for particular behaviors change over time, so, too, will the frequency of the behaviors change.	Self-efficacy increases or decreases in a quantitative fashion as a result of success and failure experiences.	Achievement motivation, need for affiliation, and other needs may either increase or decrease (in a quantitative fashion) with development.	Emphasis is on qualitative differences among individuals but on quantitative changes over time.

no obvious external benefits and why others even put their lives in jeopardy for the thrill of riding a roller coaster or racing at lightning speed down the highway.

Trait theorists have made us aware of the variety of needs that children and adolescents have, and their research has yielded surveys and tests that are useful in assessing such needs. But, although they have pinned down some of the broad motivational differences that exist among children, they help us very little in explaining why and how those differences emerge as children develop.

Social cognitive and cognitive perspectives fill some of the voids in behaviorist and trait perspectives. For instance, they do explain why people often seek out challenging situations: Successfully meeting a challenge enhances one's self-efficacy and sense of competence. They also explain why some children have higher levels of achievement motivation than others: Prior experiences influence children's self-efficacy and sense of competence; and present circumstances can create disequilibrium, foster beliefs about an activity's value, and affect children's feelings of self-determination. However, cognitive approaches to motivation have been criticized for largely ignoring motivation's emotional components (Eccles et al., 1998). Furthermore, at the present time, they don't yet form a cohesive picture of the nature and development of motivation. Instead, they are like pieces of a jigsaw puzzle: They sometimes interlock and sometimes do not, and many of the pieces are missing from the box.

The Basic Developmental Issues table on the facing page contrasts the four theoretical perspectives with regard to nature versus nurture, universality versus diversity, and qualitative versus quantitative change. We now draw from all four as we offer suggestions for classroom practice.

Fostering Motivation in the Classroom

Students process school subject matter more effectively when they are intrinsically rather than extrinsically motivated.

Effective teachers motivate their students in a variety of ways. For instance, they design and conduct interesting lessons, hold students to reasonable expectations for performance, show a genuine concern for students' learning and well-being in one-on-one and group interactions, and assess achievement through meaningful tests and assignments. The theories and principles we've just presented yield the following recommendations for classroom practice:

■ *Focus on strategies that promote intrinsic (rather than extrinsic) motivation.* As behaviorists have pointed out, extrinsic reinforcers—praise, good grades, points, and so on—often bring about desired changes in behavior. Yet such reinforcers have some disadvantages. Although they provide a source of extrinsic motivation, they can undermine students' *intrinsic* motivation, especially when students perceive them to be controlling, manipulative, or in some other way limiting their freedom and sense of self-determination (Deci & Ryan, 1987). Furthermore, they may communicate the message that classroom tasks are unpleasant chores (why else would a reinforcer be necessary?), rather than activities to be carried out and enjoyed for their own sake (Hennessey, 1995; Stipek, 1993). Ideally, teachers should focus students' attention *not* on the external consequences of their efforts (good grades, teacher and parent approval, etc.) but on the internal pleasures—the feelings of enjoyment, satisfaction and pride—that academic accomplishments bring.

■ *Use extrinsic reinforcers when necessary.* There may be occasions when, despite teachers' best efforts, students will have little interest in acquiring certain knowledge or skills critical for their later success in life. In such situations, teachers may have to provide extrinsic reinforcers—grades, free time, special privileges—to encourage learning. How can teachers use such reinforcers without diminishing students' sense of self-determination? For one thing, they can use reinforcers such as praise to communicate information and enhance students' self-efficacy and sense of competence (Deci, 1992; Ryan, Mims, & Koestner, 1983); consider these statements as examples:

• "Your description of the main character in your short story makes her come alive."
• "This poster clearly states the hypothesis, method, results, and conclusions of your science project. Your use of a bar graph makes the differences between your treatment and control groups easy to see and interpret."

Teachers may also want to encourage *self-reinforcement*—a strategy we will examine shortly in our discussion of self-regulation.

■ *Expose students to successful models with characteristics and backgrounds similar to their own.* As social cognitive theorists have shown us, students are more likely to have high self-efficacy for a task if they have seen people similar to themselves achieve success at the task. Oftentimes, the most effective models are students of the same or a similar age (Schunk & Hanson, 1985; Schunk et al., 1987). But adults, too, can be effective models, especially if they have characteristics and backgrounds similar to students' own. For instance, students of ethnic minority groups benefit from observing successful minority adults, and students with disabilities become more optimistic about their own futures when they meet adults successfully coping with and overcoming their own disabilities (Pang, 1995; Powers, Sowers, & Stevens, 1995).

■ *Minimize comparisons and competition among students; instead, focus students' attention on their own improvement.* Inevitably, there are more losers than winners in competitive situations where students are pitted against one another, and many students lose even when they exert considerable effort. They quite logically reach the conclusion that effort is not enough—that some sort of natural ability is the critical ingredient for success (Ames, 1984; Nicholls, 1984; Stipek, 1993). They see themselves as lacking that elusive ability and become pessimistic about their prognosis for future success. Thus, teachers should encourage students to focus more on their own improvement—improvement that indicates that hard work does make a difference—than on how well their performance compares with that of their peers (Deci & Ryan, 1992; Stipek, 1996).

■ *Encourage students to shoot for specific goals.* Children (younger ones especially) often have trouble conceptualizing a "future" that is abstract and perhaps many years down the road. Breaking that distant future into a number of more immediate "futures" that children can strive for in specific ways makes long-term goals both more concrete and achievable (e.g., Bandura, 1981; Schunk, 2000). For instance, a teacher might suggest that students read a certain number of storybooks at home each week or try to master a certain number of uppercase or lowercase cursive letters by the end of each month.

As students reach adolescence, their increasing capacity for abstract thought allows them to envision and work toward long-term goals—perhaps making a varsity sports team, gaining admission to a prestigious college, or having a career in journalism. Yet many students (e.g., many females, members of ethnic minority groups, and students from low-income families) set their sights lower than they need to, curbing their long-term academic and career aspirations. Teachers must not only encourage such students to aim high but also convince them that high goals are worthwhile and achievable. For instance, when encouraging girls to consider stereotypically masculine career paths, teachers might provide examples of women who have led successful and happy lives in those careers. When encouraging students from low-income families to think about going on to college, they might make arrangements for students to apply for scholarships and talk with college financial aid officers about how people with limited resources can pay for a college education.

■ *Focus students' attention on mastery goals as well as (ideally even more than) performance goals.* Many common teaching practices promote performance goals rather than mastery goals. Grading on a curve, reminding students that they need to get good grades if they want to go to college, rewarding high achievers with honor roll status—all of these strategies, though undoubtedly well intended, encourage students to focus their attention more on "looking good" than on learning (Thomas & Oldfather, 1997; Wentzel & Wigfield, 1998). When teachers instead point out how school subject matter will be useful in the future, show students that they are making progress, and acknowledge that effective learning requires exerting effort and making mistakes, they are emphasizing mastery goals that will help students focus on understanding and gaining command of subject matter (Anderman & Maehr, 1994; Graham & Weiner, 1996; Meece, 1994). Focusing attention on mastery goals, especially when those goals have relevance for students' long-term success, may be especially beneficial for students from diverse ethnic backgrounds and students at risk for dropping out of school (Garcia, 1992; Kaplan & Maehr, in press; Wlodkowski & Ginsberg, 1995).

■ *Downplay the seriousness of failures.* Students are more apt to accept responsibility for their mistakes if teachers don't make a big deal of them. For instance, teachers can give students numerous opportunities to improve assignments and overall class grades (Ames, 1992). In some instances, they may also find it appropriate to focus students' attention on the *processes* they use to tackle assignments and solve problems, rather than on the final outcome of their efforts (Stipek & Kowalski, 1989). For example, a teacher may occasionally give an assignment with instructions like these:

It doesn't matter at all how many you get right. In fact, these problems are kind of hard. I'm just interested in learning more about what [you] think about while [you're] working on problems like these. I want you to focus on the problem and just say out loud whatever you're thinking while you're working—whatever comes into your head. (Stipek & Kowalski, 1989, p. 387)

■ *Give encouraging messages about the causes of students' successes and failures.* Cognitive theorists often recommend that teachers attribute students' past successes partly to a relatively stable ability and partly to such controllable factors as effort and learning strategies. In this way, they provide assurance that students "have what it takes" to succeed but remind them that continued success also requires hard work. When identifying possible causes for students' failures, however, teachers should focus primarily on effort and learning strategies—attributions that are internal, unstable, and controllable. Following are some examples:

- "You've done very well. Obviously you're good at this, and you've been trying very hard to get better."
- "Your project shows a lot of talent and a lot of hard work."
- "The more you practice, the better you will get."
- "Perhaps you need to study a little bit more next time. Let's talk about how you might also need to study a little differently."

When students' failures are consistently attributed to lack of effort or ineffective learning strategies, rather than to low ability or uncontrollable external factors, and when new strategies or increased effort do in fact produce success, then students work harder, persist longer in the face of failure, and seek help when they need it (Dweck & Elliott, 1983; Eccles & Wigfield, 1985; Graham, 1991).

■ *Help students learn that some successes come only with considerable effort and perseverance.* Once teachers know that their students have a high sense of competence about the subject matter in question, they may occasionally want to assign tasks that students can accomplish successfully only if they exert considerable time and mental effort. In doing so, teachers can promote **learned industriousness:** Students will begin to realize that they can succeed at some tasks only with effort, persistence, and well-chosen strategies (Eisenberger, 1992; Winne, 1995a).

■ *Maintain students' sense of self-determination when describing rules and giving instructions.* Virtually any classroom needs a few rules and procedures to ensure that students act appropriately and classroom activities run smoothly. Furthermore, teachers must often impose guidelines and restrictions about how students carry out their assignments. The trick is to present these rules, procedures, guidelines, and restrictions without communicating the message that teachers want to control every aspect of classroom life (thereby undermining students' sense of self-determination). Instead, teachers should present them as *information*—for instance, as conditions that can help students accomplish classroom objectives (Deci, 1992; Koestner, Ryan, Bernieri, & Holt, 1984).

An experiment by Koestner and colleagues (1984) illustrates how simple differences in wording can affect students' sense of self-determination and intrinsic motivation. First and second graders were asked to paint a picture of a house they would like to live in. The children were given the materials they needed—a paintbrush, a set of watercolor paints, two sheets of paper, and several paper towels—and then told some rules about how to proceed. For some children (the controlling-limits condition), restrictions described things that they could and couldn't do, as follows:

Before you begin, I want to tell you some things that you will have to do. They are rules that we have about painting. You have to keep the paints clean. You can paint only on this small sheet of paper, so don't spill any paint on the big sheet. And you must wash out your brush and wipe it with a paper towel before you switch to a new color of paint, so that you don't get the colors all mixed up. In general, I want you to be a good boy (girl) and don't make a mess with the paints. (Koestner et al., 1984, p. 239)

For other children (the informational-limits condition), restrictions were presented as information, like this:

Before you begin, I want to tell you some things about the way painting is done here. I know that sometimes it's really fun to just slop the paint around, but here the materials and room need to be

learned industriousness
Recognition that one can succeed at some tasks only with effort, persistence, and well-chosen strategies.

kept nice for the other children who will use them. The smaller sheet is for you to paint on, the larger sheet is a border to be kept clean. Also, the paints need to be kept clean, so the brush is to be washed and wiped in the paper towel before switching colors. I know that some kids don't like to be neat all the time, but now is a time for being neat. (Koestner et al., 1984, p. 239)

Each child was allowed 10 minutes of painting time. The experimenter then took the child's painting to another room, saying he would return in a few minutes. As he departed, he placed two more sheets of paper on the child's table, saying, "You can paint some more on this piece of paper, if you like, or if you want you can play with the puzzles over on that table" (p. 239). In the experimenter's absence, the child was surreptitiously observed, and painting time was measured. Children in the informational-limits condition spent more time painting (so were apparently more intrinsically motivated to paint) than did their counterparts in the controlling-limits condition, and their paintings were judged to be more creative.

Following are additional examples of how teachers might describe rules or give instructions in an informational rather than controlling manner:

- "We can make sure everyone has an equal chance to speak and be heard if we listen without interrupting and if we raise our hands when we want to contribute to the discussion."
- "I'm giving you a particular format to follow when you do your math homework. If you use this format, it will be easier for me to find your answers and figure out where and how you are running into difficulty."

■ *Tailor your motivational strategies to individual students' needs and motives.* As behaviorists point out, different reinforcers are more or less effective for different individuals. In addition, trait theorists remind us that students vary considerably in their needs for affiliation and approval. Teachers must take such diversity into account whenever they consider motivational strategies to use either with an entire class or with particular students. For example, public praise may be highly reinforcing to many students yet be the "kiss of death" to someone who wants to maintain his social status in a low-achieving peer group. Likewise, the opportunity to study in small groups may be highly motivating for students with a high need for affiliation yet have little appeal to those who cherish their time alone.

■ *Be especially attentive to the needs of students at risk.* **Students at risk** are students with a high probability of failing to acquire the minimum academic skills necessary for success in the adult world. Many of them drop out before high school graduation; many others graduate without basic skills in reading or mathematics (National Assessment of Educational Progress, 1985; Slavin, 1989). Such individuals are often ill-equipped to make productive contributions to their families, communities, or society at large.

Some students at risk have identified special educational needs, such as learning disabilities. Others may have cultural backgrounds that don't mesh easily with the dominant culture at school. Still others may come from home environments in which academic success is neither supported nor encouraged.

Students at risk come from all socioeconomic levels, but children of poor, single-parent families are especially likely to leave school before high school graduation (Steinberg, Blinde, & Chan, 1984). Boys are more likely to drop out than girls, and African Americans, Hispanics, and Native Americans are more likely to drop out than European American students (Miller, 1995; Roderick & Camburn, 1999). Students at greatest risk for dropping out are those whose families speak little or no English and whose own knowledge of English is also quite limited (Steinberg et al., 1984). In addition, students at risk typically have some or all of the following characteristics:

- A history of poor academic achievement, appearing as early as third grade (Garnier, Stein, & Jacobs, 1997; Lloyd, 1978)
- Limited learning strategies and self-regulated learning skills (Belfiore & Hornyak, 1998; Steinberg et al., 1984)
- Emotional and behavioral problems, including low self-esteem, disruptive behavior, drug use, and criminal activities (Garnier et al., 1997; Jozefowicz, Arbreton, Eccles, Barber, & Colarossi, 1994; U.S. Department of Education, 1992)
- Lack of psychological attachment to school (e.g., little engagement in extracurricular activities) and decreasing involvement in school over time (Finn, 1989; Jozefowicz et al., 1994; Rumberger, 1995)

students at risk
Students who have a high probability of failing to acquire the minimal academic skills necessary for success in the adult world.

Although students at risk for academic failure are a diverse group of individuals with a diverse set of needs, teachers and other school personnel can do many things to help them succeed and stay in school:

- Identify them as early as possible, ideally in the elementary school grades, and begin to address their academic and social-emotional needs
- Make the curriculum relevant to their lives and needs
- Engage their interest with stimulating activities
- Communicate high expectations for academic success
- Acknowledge past learning problems but provide the time and resources necessary to help them overcome those problems
- Encourage and facilitate participation in athletic programs, extracurricular activities, and student government
- Involve them in school policy and management decisions
  (Alderman, 1990; Finn, 1989; Garibaldi, 1992; Lee-Pearce, Plowman, & Touchstone, 1998; Murdock, 1999; Pogrow & Londer, 1994; Ramey & Ramey, 1998)

Most of these strategies are beneficial for *all* students, but they are especially critical for students at risk. As you will discover in our discussion of *resiliency* in Chapter 14, teachers' efforts can make a world of difference in the lives of such students.

The strategies we've just presented focus on how *teachers* can better meet students' needs. The topic we turn to now—self-regulation—focuses on how growing children can begin to meet their *own* needs.

Development of Self-Regulation

People of all ages have a greater sense of self-determination, and so are more intrinsically motivated, when they can make choices about what they do and so can, to some extent, direct the course of their lives. Doing these things effectively involves **self-regulation,** which includes such capabilities as these:

- *Goal setting:* Identifying and striving for valued, self-chosen goals
- *Impulse control:* Resisting sudden urges to engage in forbidden or counterproductive behaviors
- *Emotional control:* Expressing emotions in a socially appropriate manner and controlling them in ways that facilitate goal attainment
- *Delaying gratification:* Putting off small, immediate rewards in anticipation of larger rewards at a later time
- *Self-regulated learning:* Directing and monitoring one's own attention and learning strategies in ways that promote effective cognitive processing

As you learned in Chapter 5, students who regulate their own learning are more academically successful than those who do not. Self-regulation is important in social relationships as well: Children who can control their emotions and behaviors have better social skills and are more popular among their peers (Bronson, 2000; Fabes et al., 1999; Patrick, 1997).

With age and experience, most children and adolescents become increasingly self-regulating in virtually every aspect of their lives—for instance, in their adherence to rules and regulations, in their interactions with peers, and in their academic pursuits. Ideally, young people should be almost entirely self-regulating once they finish their schooling: They must be able to make wise choices that enable them to achieve their goals and make productive contributions to society.

We considered self-regulated learning in our discussion of cognitive development in Chapter 5. Here we look more generally at the nature and development of self-regulation. After surveying several theoretical perspectives, we examine developmental trends in self-regulation and conditions that foster its development. We then identify several strategies for promoting self-regulatory behavior in classroom settings.

self-regulation
Setting standards and goals for oneself and engaging in behaviors that lead to the accomplishment of those standards and goals.

Theories of Self-Regulation

Theorists have taken a variety of approaches to studying self-regulation and its development. Their explanations fall into three of the perspectives we considered earlier: behaviorist, social cognitive, and cognitive.

Behaviorist Approaches From a behaviorist perspective, behavior is initially controlled entirely by environmental stimuli (e.g., external reinforcement and punishment). Over time, and perhaps with explicit training, people learn strategies for changing and controlling their own behavior. For instance, Belfiore and Hornyak (1998) have proposed that to be self-regulating, children must learn two kinds of responses: *target responses* (the behaviors they need to be more successful) and *self-management responses* (behaviors they can use to control their target responses). For example, if a child wants to learn to keep appointments (a target response), he might learn to leave a reminder note on the kitchen counter the day of the appointment (a self-management response).

Belfiore and Hornyak have applied this perspective to teaching adolescents how to regulate themselves in an after-school homework program; the target response in this case was *homework completion*. At the end of the regular school day, students reported to a particular classroom in the school building, where they would find their homework assignments on a shelf. They learned to follow the checklist depicted in Figure 11–1 and to check off steps that they had completed. They also learned to administer **self-reinforcement**: They gave themselves a reward (e.g., they allowed themselves to play a board game or spend time on the computer) whenever they had completed the checklist. Furthermore, they learned problem-solving strategies to use when they encountered difficulties (e.g., asking a teacher for assistance when they couldn't find the materials for an assignment). Initially, a teacher monitored whether the checklist reflected the homework completed; eventually, such monitoring was no longer necessary. Furthermore, the self-imposed extrinsic reinforcers became less critical; the sense of accomplishment the students felt about completing their homework became a sufficient reinforcer (Belfiore & Hornyak, 1998).

The checklist in Figure 11–1 might strike you as a set of steps that should be obvious to anyone. In fact, although many children and adolescents develop a similar list of steps on their own and so have little difficulty completing their homework, others need explicit guidance to acquire such a self-regulating system.

FIGURE 11–1 Daily checklist for homework completion

From "Operant Theory and Application to Self-Monitoring in Adolescents" by P. J. Belfiore and R. S. Hornyak, 1998. In *Self-Regulated Learning: From Teaching to Self-Reflective Practice* (p. 190), by D. H. Schunk & B. J. Zimmerman (Eds.), New York: Guilford Press. Copyright 1998 by Guilford Press. Reprinted with permission.

STUDENT: _____ DATE: _____

SUBJECT AREA: _____ GRADE: _____

TEACHER: _____

STEPS TO FOLLOW	YES	NO	NOTES
1. Did I turn in yesterday's homework?			
2. Did I write all homework assignments in my notebook?			
3. Is all homework in homework folder?			
4. Are all my materials to complete homework with me?			
5. BEGIN HOMEWORK?			
6. Are all homework papers completed?			
7. Did someone check homework to make sure it was completed?			
8. After checking, did I put all homework back in folder?			
9. Did I give this paper to teacher?			

self-reinforcement
Self-imposed pleasurable consequence for a desired behavior.

Social Cognitive Approaches Several social cognitive theorists (e.g., Schunk & Zimmerman, 1997; Zimmerman & Kitsantas, 1999) have suggested that the acquisition of self-regulation in any particular domain proceeds through four levels:

1. *Observational level.* The child watches a behavior being performed. The person exhibiting the behavior (the model) explains what he or she is doing and encourages the child to learn the behavior.
2. *Imitative level.* The child imitates the behavior, and the model provides guidance, feedback, and positive reinforcement. As the child becomes more proficient, guidance, feedback, and reinforcement are gradually phased out.
3. *Self-controlled level.* The child can perform the behavior without the model present but relies largely on his or her memory for what the model did and tries to match it as closely as possible. The child now engages in self-reinforcement (perhaps self-praise, perhaps something more tangible) to sustain the activity.
4. *Self-regulated level.* The child can now perform the behavior flexibly and adapt it readily to changing circumstances. The child may occasionally seek out an expert's guidance to fine-tune the behavior but is in other respects working independently of how others have previously demonstrated it. The child uses three strategies to guide performance:
   • *Self-observation:* Paying attention to specific aspects of the behavior being executed
   • *Self-judgment:* Comparing current performance against external standards
   • *Self-reaction:* Evaluating the performance as being acceptable or unacceptable
   At this point, too, motivation is entirely intrinsic: The enhanced feelings of self-efficacy (competence) are sufficient to sustain the behavior.

Many educators have successfully applied ideas of social cognitive theory to help children and adolescents become more self-regulating. You will see the influence of social cognitive theory in our discussion of *self-monitoring* and *self-evaluation* a bit later in the section.

Cognitive Approaches As you learned in Chapter 4, Lev Vygotsky proposed that children gradually internalize social interactions into mental processes, often through a process of *self-talk.* By talking themselves through new and challenging situations, children begin to guide and direct their own behavior in much the same way that adults have previously guided them. At about age 6 or 7, such self-talk "goes underground" to become *inner speech*; in other words, children *think* (rather than talk) themselves through situations (Vygotsky, 1962). Many contemporary theorists believe that self-talk and its gradual internalization play a major role in the development of self-regulation (e.g., Berk, 1994; Schimmoeller, 1998). You will see the influence of these concepts in our upcoming discussion of *self-instructions.*

Contemporary information processing theorists have described additional cognitive processes that enable people to direct and monitor their own learning and behavior (e.g., Kuhl, 1985; Menec & Schonwetter, 1994). Terms such as *metacognition* and *learning strategies* (see Chapter 5) originated in information processing theory and clearly imply self-regulation in thinking, learning, and performance.

From an information processing perspective, self-regulation encompasses such processes as these:

• Focusing attention on appropriate objects and events
• Selecting appropriate information to store in memory
• Identifying appropriate learning strategies to remember the information
• Controlling emotions (e.g., anxiety) so that they don't interfere with successful learning and performance
• Maintaining motivation to persist at an activity
• Choosing or creating an environment (e.g., going to the library to study) that facilitates all of the above (Kuhl, 1985)

These processes emerge slowly throughout childhood and adolescence. For example, as you discovered in Chapter 5, young children are easily distracted by objects and events unrelated to the task at hand; thus, they seem to have little control over their own attention. Furthermore, children initially have few if any effective learning strategies. They acquire an ability to direct their attention and increasingly sophisticated strategies as they proceed to higher grade levels and more difficult subject matter.

Over time, children become increasingly able to regulate their own behaviors and emotions. As a first grader, Brenda (*top*) can probably resist many temptations but must occasionally be reminded about how to behave, and she may often reveal her feelings when she is angry or upset. As a seventh grader, Palet (*bottom*) regularly behaves in accordance with accepted social standards, and she is able to control her emotions in public most of the time.

Developmental Trends in Self-Regulation

Young children have considerable difficulty controlling their own behavior. For instance, parents often complain about the "terrible twos," the period between the second and third birthdays when children are mobile enough to get into almost anything, have few if any scruples about what they should and shouldn't do, and put up quite a fuss when they don't get their own way.

Self-regulation of actions, thoughts, and emotions requires several capabilities that are, in toddlers and other young children, only beginning to emerge. First, self-regulation requires an ability to inhibit certain behaviors and cognitions, and this ability is partly a function of neurological development (Dempster & Corkill, 1999; Schore, 1994). Second, to the extent that self-regulation involves self-talk, it requires sufficient language skills to accurately represent actions and events (Bronson, 2000). Third, self-regulation requires a number of cognitive mechanisms and processes—memory for past events, the ability to anticipate the consequences of future actions, an understanding of why various emotions have been aroused, and so on—that become increasingly powerful and effective with age (Bronson, 2000; Eccles et al., 1998).

Researchers have identified at least three ways in which children's self-regulatory capabilities change over time:

■ *External rules and restrictions gradually become internalized.* Children can comply with simple requests and restrictions by the time they are 12 to 18 months old (Kaler & Kopp, 1990; Kopp, 1982). As they become increasingly verbal, they begin to use self-talk to prevent themselves from engaging in prohibited behaviors even when caregivers are absent; for instance, a toddler may say "no" or "can't" to herself as she begins to reach for an electric outlet (Kochanski, 1993). By age 3 or 4, children are acquiring flexible strategies for regulating their own behavior in accordance with adult rules and prohibitions. For example, if they are asked to wait for a short time (e.g., 15 minutes), they might invent games or sing to themselves to pass the time more quickly (Mischel & Ebbesen, 1970). If a playmate has an enticing toy, they may turn away and engage in an alternative activity as a way of lessening the temptation to grab the toy (Kopp, 1982). Children who have such strategies are better able to resist temptation than children who do not (Mischel, Shoda, & Rodriguez, 1989).

During the elementary and secondary school years, children and adolescents increasingly take ownership of society's rules and regulations. Deci and Ryan (1995) have proposed that this ownership proceeds through the process of internalization of motivation that we described earlier. The first sign of internalization (the *introjection* stage) is evident when children feel some internal pressure (e.g., guilt) to comply with rules and regulations. Later (at the *identification* stage), children start to perceive rules and other desired behaviors to be important or valuable to them personally. Finally (at the *integration* stage), rules and regulation become an integral part of children's self-concepts. At this point, a teenage girl might define herself as being "generous" or "compassionate" and so strive to behave in ways consistent with her self-definition.

■ *Emotional reactions become more restrained.* Toddlers have little control of their emotions; for instance, they may throw a temper tantrum if they don't get what they want or become physically aggressive if events make them frustrated or angry (Bronson, 2000; Kopp, 1992). In the preschool years, children's interactions with age-mates typically increase in frequency and duration, and so they must learn to control their emotions and behaviors sufficiently to get along with their peers (e.g., they must refrain from hitting and biting). By the early elementary grades, children become better able to view situations from other people's perspectives (see Chapter 10), and so they temper their emotional reactions in accordance with how they expect others to react (Bronson, 2000). As they move through the grade levels, they become increasingly able to vent their emotions appropriately, largely as a result of their experience in interacting with peers (Barkley, 1997).

■ *Self-evaluation becomes more frequent.* Infants and young toddlers do not seem to evaluate their own performance, nor do they show much concern about how others evaluate it. In contrast, 2-year-olds often seek adults' approval for their actions (Stipek, Recchia, & McClintic, 1992). Sometime around age 3, children show the first signs of *self*-evaluation; for instance, they look happy when they're successful and sad when they fail (Heckenhausen, 1984, 1987).

As children move into elementary school, they show a marked increase in their own self-awareness (Bronson, 2000). Their teachers give them frequent information about their academic performance, and their classmates often let them know in no uncertain terms about the appropriateness of their social behavior. Such feedback allows them to develop criteria by which they can more accurately judge their own actions. As their ability for self-reflection grows and they become increasingly concerned about others' perceptions, especially in adolescence, they look more closely at their own behavior and evaluate it in line with how they think others will judge it (Dacey & Kenny, 1994).

Despite such improvements, many adolescents continue to lack the basic self-regulating behaviors they need for success in secondary school. Consider the case of Anna who, in her first semester of high school, earned mostly Ds and failed her science class. She explains her poor performance this way:

> In geography, "he said the reason why I got a lower grade is 'cause I missed one assignment and I had to do a report, and I forgot that one." In English, "I got a C . . . 'cause we were supposed to keep a journal, and I keep on forgetting it 'cause I don't have a locker. Well I do, but my locker partner she lets her cousins use it, and I lost my two books there. . . . I would forget to buy a notebook, and then I would have them on separate pieces of paper, and I would lose them." And, in biology, "the reason I failed was because I lost my folder . . . it had everything I needed, and I had to do it again, and, by the time I had to turn in the new folder, I did, but he said it was too late . . .' cause I didn't have the folder, and the folder has everything, all the work . . . That's why I got an F." (Roderick & Camburn, 1999, p. 305)

Anna's constant absentmindedness indicates that she still has a long way to go in gaining control of her own learning and achievement.

Conditions That Promote Self-Regulation

In Chapter 12, we discuss *parenting styles*, general patterns of behavior that parents use to nurture and guide their children. We briefly describe one parenting style here, as it relates to our discussion of self-regulation. In **authoritative parenting,** parents and other caregivers establish, justify, and consistently enforce standards for acceptable behavior while also showing emotional warmth, considering children's rights and needs, and including children in decision making. An authoritative environment, whether it be at home or at school, appears to promote intrinsic motivation and self-regulation (Baumrind, 1989; Bronson, 2000; Eccles et al., 1998; Reeve, Bolt, & Cai, 1999). In other words, parents and teachers who have warm and supportive relationships with children, set reasonable boundaries for behavior, and take everyone's needs into consideration create the conditions in which children learn to make appropriate choices and work toward productive goals.

Adults promote self-regulation in another way as well: by modeling self-regulating behaviors (Bronson, 2000; Schunk & Swartz, 1993). For example, in a classic study by Bandura and Mischel (1965), fourth and fifth graders watched adult models make a series of choices between small, immediate rewards and more valuable, delayed ones (e.g., plastic chess pieces available that day vs. wooden ones that they could have in 2 weeks). Some models chose the immediate rewards (e.g., saying "Chess figures are chess figures. I can get much use out of the plastic ones right away," p. 701). Others chose the delayed rewards (e.g., saying "The wooden chess figures are of much better quality, more attractive and will last longer. I'll wait two weeks for the better ones," p. 701). Immediately after they had observed the models, and also on a second occasion 4 or 5 weeks later, the children themselves were asked to choose between small, immediate rewards and larger, delayed ones (e.g., a small plastic ball now or a much larger one in 2 weeks). The children were more likely to delay gratification if they had seen the model do likewise.

Children and adolescents are also more likely to become self-regulating when they have age-appropriate opportunities for independence (Feldman & Wentzel, 1990; Silverman &

authoritative parenting
Parenting style characterized by emotional warmth, high expectations and standards for behavior, consistent enforcement of rules, explanations of the reasons behind these rules, and the inclusion of children in decision making.

Ragusa, 1990). They are most likely to benefit from such opportunities when they are taught the skills they need to direct their own behaviors productively and successfully overcome any challenges they encounter (Belfiore & Hornyak, 1998).

Promoting Self-Regulation in the Classroom

Students will be self-regulating only when they are intrinsically motivated to accomplish certain goals. To encourage self-regulation, then, teachers must also encourage intrinsic motivation—for example, by creating conditions in which students have high self-efficacy and can maintain their sense of self-determination (Bronson, 2000). With this caveat in mind, we offer the following suggestions for classroom practice:

■ *Create an orderly and somewhat predictable classroom environment.* Students are in a better position to make wise choices and direct their activities appropriately when they have a reasonable structure to follow, know what to expect in the hours and days ahead, and can reasonably anticipate that certain behaviors will yield certain outcomes (e.g., Bronson, 2000). Communicating guidelines for classroom behavior, establishing regular routines for completing assignments, identifying the locations of items that students may need during the day (glue, hole punches, dictionaries, atlases, etc.)—all of these strategies help students work productively with minimal guidance from adults.

■ *Provide age-appropriate opportunities for independence.* Older children and adolescents need frequent opportunities to make their own decisions and direct their own activities. Independent assignments, computer-based instruction, group projects, and the like are clearly beneficial for these age groups, particularly when the activities are structured sufficiently that students know how to proceed and understand the expectations for their performance.

Although young children inevitably require some adult supervision to keep them safe, they, too, benefit from having some independence. However, their teachers must anticipate problems that are likely to arise when children make their own decisions; the teachers can then take steps to help children make good choices. For instance, preschool and kindergarten teachers might create a few rules for taking turns and sharing materials, designate certain areas of the classroom for messy activities (e.g., painting, working with clay), and put potentially dangerous objects out of reach (Bronson, 2000).

Children with mental and physical disabilities may be in particular need of opportunities for independence, as adults often monitor their behavior and well-being fairly closely (Sands & Wehmeyer, 1996). Such opportunities should, of course, be appropriate for the children's capabilities. For example, a teacher might ask a student with mental retardation to take the daily attendance sheet to the office but remind her that as soon as she has done so, she should return immediately to class (Patton et al., 1996). Or a teacher might give a student who is blind a chance to explore the classroom before other students have arrived, locating various objects in the classroom (wastebasket, pencil sharpener, etc.) and identifying distinctive sounds (e.g., the buzz of a wall clock) that will help the student get his bearings (Wood, 1989).

■ *Provide help when, but only when, students really need it.* Being self-regulating doesn't necessarily always mean doing something independently; it also involves knowing when assistance is needed and seeking it out (Karabenick & Sharma, 1994). Teacher assistance then often provides the scaffolding that students need to succeed at new and challenging tasks. Accordingly, teachers should welcome any reasonable requests for help or guidance and not convey the message that students are "dumb" or bothersome for asking (Newman & Schwager, 1992).

Yet sometimes students, especially young children, ask for help when they actually just want company or attention. For instance, if a 4-year-old asks for help on a puzzle, an astute preschool teacher might, after watching the child work at the puzzle, say, "I don't think you need help with this. But I can keep you company for a few minutes if you'd like" (Bronson, 2000).

■ *To guide behavior, use suggestions and rationales more frequently than direct commands.* Students are more likely to internalize guidelines for their behavior when adults make suggestions about how to accomplish goals successfully and provide a rationale for why some behaviors are unacceptable (Bronson, 2000; Hoffman, 1975). Figure 11–2 shows how Michael Gee, a

MY BROAD GOALS

- Plan and implement a balanced curriculum.
- Help students develop a repertoire of skills and styles of working (open-ended assignments/discrete assignments; collaboration/individual).
- Get students engaged in mental activity; emphasize learning and being a strategic thinker.
- Help students to be both organized and flexible, deal with a schedule, and set priorities for time and things done.

DISCIPLINE

Overarching Golden Rule
Treat others as you would like to be treated.

BASIC RULES

1. Be responsible for your own actions.
2. Use work time for school work; use recess time for play.
3. Appreciate other people; respect the rights of others.
4. Make your behavior appropriate for the situation.

I try to be fair and not play favorites. Everyone is valued and respected. I run the classroom to take care of everyone. The focus is on correcting the behaviors that need correcting so that we develop habit patterns of behavior that serve instructional goals.

My appeal: You've been taught at home for years how to behave. You have a good head—now use it.

Typical fifth-grade problems:

1. Cliques and excluding others—being angry at lunch, friends again after school. A problem especially with the girls.
2. Silliness and not setting boundaries for appropriate behavior, such as bringing recess into the classroom. A problem especially with the boys.
3. Too much undirected talk, talk across desks and across the room, especially during transition times.
4. Restroom problems—talking loudly in the hallways, messing around and loitering in the restrooms.
5. Whininess and sneakiness. Talk to me honestly and openly about problems.
6. "Romance" (going-with) talk or teasing. These are absolutely not allowed in the classroom.

FIGURE 11–2
A fifth-grade teacher's goals and expectations. In this handout, Michael Gee describes his expectations for students' behavior and encourages age-appropriate self-regulation.

Adapted with the permission of Michael Gee, Barrington Elementary School, Columbus, Ohio.

fifth-grade teacher in Columbus, Ohio, encouraged self-regulation using a handout that explained his expectations for behavior. The handout, distributed during an open house at school, also gave parents important information about how Gee conducted his classroom.

Consistent with what we have learned about cognitive development, younger children respond more favorably to suggestions that are concrete rather than abstract. As an example, to avoid incidents of bumping and pushing in the cafeteria, teachers at one school asked students to imagine that they had "magic bubbles" around them. They could keep their bubbles from popping if they kept a safe distance between themselves and others. This simple strategy resulted in fewer behavior problems at lunchtime (Sullivan-DeCarlo, DeFalco, & Roberts, 1998).

■ *Teach specific self-management skills.* Many research studies indicate that children and adolescents become more self-regulating when they learn specific strategies for controlling and evaluating their own behavior. Such strategies include the following:

- **Self-monitoring.** Students aren't always aware of how frequently they do something wrong or how *in*frequently they do something right. To help them attend to these things,

self-monitoring
Process of observing and recording one's own behavior.

teachers can ask them to observe and record their own behavior. Such self-focused observation and recording often brings about significant improvements in students' academic and social behaviors (Harris, 1986; Mace & Kratochwill, 1988; Webber, Scheuermann, McCall, & Coleman, 1993).

- **Self-instructions.** Sometimes students simply need a reminder about how to respond in particular situations. By teaching them how to talk themselves through these situations, teachers give them a means through which they remind *themselves* about appropriate actions, thereby helping them to control their own behavior. Such a strategy is often effective in helping students with poor impulse control (Casey & Burton, 1982; Meichenbaum, 1985; Yell, Robinson, & Drasgow, 2001).

- **Self-evaluation.** Both at home and in school, students' behaviors are frequently judged by others—by their parents, teachers, classmates, and so on. But to become self-regulating, students must eventually learn to judge their own behavior. For instance, teachers might have students complete self-assessment instruments that show them what to look for in their evaluations (Paris & Ayres, 1994). At the secondary level (and perhaps even sooner), students should also play a role in identifying the criteria by which their performance can most appropriately be evaluated.

The Development and Practice feature on the next page illustrates these and other self-management skills. Teachers must, of course, monitor students' ability to use them and make adjustments accordingly. For instance, students with ADHD tend to have more success with self-monitoring and self-evaluation than with self-instructions; even so, they often need teacher monitoring and reinforcement as well to develop and maintain appropriate behaviors (Barkley, 1998).

Up to this point, we have focused on specific strategies that teachers can use to address growing children's motives and needs and to promote their self-regulation. We now look at more general issues related to motivation and the overall classroom environment.

Effects of the Classroom Environment

Mary dropped out of school after her junior year. In an interview, she explains why:

Mary:	. . . These public schools are filled with violence and things. You know, people getting shot in the next classroom. It is not an environment for learning, you know what I mean. I just wasn't gonna risk my life to go to school. To me it wasn't that important.
Interviewer:	What do you think about the actual education, putting aside the violence, what did you think about the actual school?
Mary:	In these public schools? Well, by the time they got the rowdy class to sit down, the period was over.
Interviewer:	You just felt like it was pointless?
Mary:	Yeah. I was like going to school to take your life in hand, to set there and have them try to get the class together and once they did, it was time to leave. It was just like, this is wasting my time as well as the teacher's. . . . There was another thing—I knew a lot of people in this school, I had a lot of friends. I had friends who would just bring you down, I'll tell you that much. . . . You know it would be like, "Oh, well, we can cut this class today. We can always make it up tomorrow." But there's always—there's never a tomorrow. . . . "We'll cut class today. We'll go to class tomorrow. We'll cut class the next day." It's endless and it's useless 'cause you're just wasting the teacher's time and your own. (dialogue from Way, 1998, p. 200; format adapted)

Mary describes three important characteristics of a productive classroom environment. First, the classroom should be a place where students feel physically and psychologically safe. Second, teacher and students should be focused on important instructional objectives—not on disruptive behavior—for most of the school day. And third, students should believe that their classmates are interested in learning and achieving, such that they do not, as Mary puts it, "bring you down."

In this section, we look at how educators can create a classroom and school environment that enables students to focus effectively on learning and, in the process, fosters their cogni-

self-instructions
Instructions that people give themselves as they perform a complex behavior.

self-evaluation
Judging one's own performance or behavior in accordance with predetermined criteria.

TEACHING SELF-MANAGEMENT SKILLS

- Have students observe and record their own behavior.

  When a student has trouble staying on task during class activities, her teacher asks her to stop and reflect on her behavior every 10 minutes (with the aid of an egg timer) and determine whether she was doing what she was supposed to be doing during each interval. The student uses the checklist shown below to record her observations.

  Within a couple of weeks, the student's on-task behavior has noticeably improved.

- Teach students instructions they can give themselves to remind them of what they need to do.

  A teacher helps a student control his impulsive behavior on standardized multiple-choice tests by having him mentally say to himself as he reads each question: "Read the entire question. Then look at each answer carefully and decide whether it is correct or incorrect. Then choose the answer that seems *most* correct."

- Encourage students to evaluate their own performance.

  A science teacher asks students to evaluate the lab reports they have written the day before and gives them a list of criteria to use as they do so. For the first few reports, she assigns grades not on the basis of how well students have completed their reports but instead on how accurately they have *evaluated* their reports.

- Teach students to reinforce themselves for appropriate behavior.

  A teacher helps students develop more regular study habits by encouraging them to make a favorite activity—for example, shooting baskets, watching television, or calling a friend on the telephone—contingent on completing their homework first.

- Provide strategies that students can use to solve interpersonal problems.

  A teacher teaches his students a sequence to follow when they find themselves in a conflict with a classmate: *Identify* the source of the conflict, *listen* to each other's perspectives, *verbalize* each other's perspectives, and *develop* a solution that provides a reasonable compromise.

Self-Observation Record for _____Karen_____

Every ten minutes, put a mark to show how well you have been staying on task.

+   means you were almost always on task
1/2   means you were on task about half the time
–   means you were hardly ever on task

9:00-9:10	9:10-9:20	9:20-9:30	9:30-9:40	9:40-9:50	9:50-10:00
+	+	–	+	1/2	–
10:00-10:10	10:10-10:20	10:20-10:30	10:30-10:40	10:40-10:50	10:50-11:00
1/2	–	recess		+	1/2
11:00-11:10	11:10-11:20	11:20-11:30	11:30-11:40	11:40-11:50	11:50-12:00

---

tive, personal, and social development. We first consider the role of schools in socializing children and adolescents to behave in acceptable ways in the adult world. We then examine the effects of classroom climate and teacher expectations on students' social-emotional well-being and academic achievement. Finally, we consider how teachers and students can create a *sense of community* in which they work together to maximize all students' learning and development.

The Role of Schools in Socialization

Beginning early in their lives, most children learn that there are certain things that they can or should do and other things that they definitely should not do. For example, many parents teach their toddlers not to hit other children, first-grade teachers ask their students to sit and listen quietly when someone else is speaking, and high school teachers expect their students to turn in homework assignments on time. Such efforts to teach children and adolescents how to behave appropriately in their society are collectively known as **socialization.**

Most children learn their earliest lessons about society's expectations from their parents, who teach them personal hygiene, table manners, rudimentary interpersonal skills (e.g., saying "please" and "thank you"), and so on. Yet teachers become equally important **socialization agents** once children reach school age. For example, teachers typically expect and encourage behaviors such as these:

- Behaving in an orderly fashion
- Showing respect for authority figures
- Controlling impulses
- Following instructions
- Completing assigned tasks in a timely manner
- Working independently
- Helping and cooperating with classmates
- Striving for academic excellence

When behaviors expected of students at school differ from those expected at home, children may become confused, nonproductive, and sometimes even resistant (Hess & Holloway, 1984). In other words, they may experience some **culture shock** when they first enter school.

Teachers' expectations for behavior—often unstated—are sometimes known as the **hidden curriculum** of the classroom (Anyon, 1988; Chafel, 1997; Jackson, 1988). An additional aspect of the hidden curriculum is the message that teachers communicate about the nature of academic learning and academic subject matter (Anyon, 1988; Chafel, 1997; Doyle, 1983). Unfortunately, this message often portrays schoolwork as memorizing facts, getting the right answer, doing tasks in a particular way and, in general, getting things done as quickly as possible. Understandably, students have little reason to feel intrinsically motivated under such circumstances and may passively or actively resist, as the following dialogue between a teacher and several students illustrates:

Teacher:	I will put some problems on the board. You are to divide.
Child:	We got to divide?
Teacher:	Yes.
Several children:	(*Groan*) Not again, Mr. B., we done this yesterday.
Child:	Do we put the date?
Teacher:	Yes. I hope we remember we work in silence. You're supposed to do it on white paper. I'll explain it later.
Child:	Somebody broke my pencil. (*Crash*—a child falls out of his chair.)
Child:	(*repeats*) Mr. B., somebody broke my *pencil*!
Child:	Are we going to be here all morning? (Anyon, 1988, p. 367)

In this situation, the teacher presents math problems merely as "things that need to be done," and the children clearly have little interest in the assignment.

Effects of Classroom Climate

The dialogue just presented is troublesome in two additional ways as well. First, the teacher communicates a message of control ("You are to divide. . . . You're supposed to do it on white paper") that probably undermines students' sense of self-determination. Second, the teacher comes across as aloof and unconcerned about students' needs. More generally, the teacher's remarks seem to create a cold, nonnurturing classroom climate that is hardly conducive to students' learning.

By **classroom climate**, we mean the overall psychological environment of the classroom. From our earlier discussions of motivation and self-regulation, we can derive several general principles concerning the classroom climate in which students are most likely to thrive:

socialization
Systematic efforts by other people and by institutions to prepare youngsters to act in ways deemed by society to be appropriate and responsible.

socialization agents
People who play a key role in preparing youngsters to act in ways deemed by society to be appropriate and responsible.

culture shock
Sense of confusion that occurs when people encounter a culture with very different expectations for behavior than the expectations with which they have been raised.

hidden curriculum
Unstated norms and beliefs that underlie teachers' treatment of academic subject matter and expectations for student behavior.

classroom climate
General psychological atmosphere of the classroom.

- Teachers communicate genuine caring, respect, and support for students.
- Students feel both physically and psychologically safe; for instance, they know that they can make mistakes without being ridiculed by their teacher or classmates.
- Teachers adopt an authoritative approach to instruction and classroom management, setting clear guidelines for behavior but, in the process, also considering students' needs and involving students in decision making.
- Teachers provide some order and structure to guide classroom assignments and procedures.
- Teachers give students opportunities to engage in appropriate self-chosen and self-directed activities.

Teachers should help students see their schoolwork as activities that enable them to achieve important knowledge and skills, not just as things to "get done."

Classrooms that reflect these principles are, in general, highly productive ones: Students have higher self-esteem, are better behaved, have a mastery orientation toward their schoolwork, and achieve at higher levels (Davis & Thomas, 1989; deCharms, 1984; Roderick & Camburn, 1999; Wentzel, 1999; Wentzel & Wigfield, 1998).

Such classrooms may be particularly beneficial for students growing up in impoverished home environments (Diamond, 1991; Levine & Lezotte, 1995). Many students from low-income neighborhoods are exposed to crime and violence nearly every day; their world may be one in which they can rarely control the course of events. A classroom that is dependable and predictable can engender a sense of self-determination that is difficult to come by elsewhere; hence, it can be a place to which they look forward to coming each day.

Contrasting Elementary and Secondary Classroom Environments Elementary school classrooms are often very warm, nurturing ones in which teachers get to know 20 or 30 students very well and so are in an ideal position to foster each student's cognitive, personal, and social development. As students make the transition to secondary school, they simultaneously encounter many changes in the nature of their schooling:

- The school is larger and has more students.
- Students have several teachers at a time, and each teacher has many students. Teacher-student relationships are therefore more superficial and less personal than they were in elementary school.
- There is more whole-class instruction, with less individualized instruction that takes into account each student's particular needs.
- Competition among students (e.g., for popular classes and spots on an athletic team) is more common.
- Students have more independence and responsibility for their own learning; for instance, they sometimes have relatively unstructured assignments to be accomplished over a 2- or 3-week period, and they must take the initiative to seek help when they are struggling.
- Standards for assigning grades are more rigorous, so students may earn lower grades than they did in elementary school. Grades are often assigned on a comparative basis, with only the highest-achieving students getting As and Bs. (Eccles & Midgley, 1989; Roderick & Camburn, 1999; Wentzel & Wigfield, 1998; Wigfield et al., 1996)

Furthermore, previously formed friendships can be disrupted as students move to new (and sometimes different) schools. And, of course, students are also dealing with the physiological changes that accompany puberty and adolescence.

For many students, all these changes lead to decreased confidence, lower self-esteem, and considerable anxiety. Students develop less positive attitudes about school and academic subjects and show less intrinsic motivation to learn. Focus on social relationships increases, academic achievement drops, and some students become emotionally disengaged from the school environment—a disengagement that may eventually result in dropping out of school (Eccles & Midgley, 1989; Urdan & Maehr, 1995; Wigfield et al., 1996). Urban youth (especially males and minorities) are particularly at risk for making a rough transition from elementary to secondary school. For instance, in one recent study, 42% of students in the Chicago public schools failed at least one major course in the first semester of 9th grade. By 10th grade, 50% had failed at least one course (Roderick & Camburn, 1999).

The concept of *middle school* was developed to ease the transition to secondary school (e.g., Kohut, 1988; Lounsbury, 1984). In principle, middle schools are designed to accommodate the unique needs of preadolescents and early adolescents, including their anxieties about more demanding academic expectations, the changing nature of their social relationships, and their own rapidly maturing bodies. Ideally, middle schools give attention to students' personal, emotional, and social development as well as to academic achievement and are attuned to students' individual differences and unique academic needs. They teach learning and study skills that help students move toward increasing independence as learners. At many middle schools, teams of four or five teachers work with a subset of the student population (perhaps 75 to 125 students per team), coordinating activities and exchanging information about how particular students are progressing. Such strategies often ease the transition to a secondary school format; even so, many young adolescents have considerable difficulty adjusting to a middle school setting (Eccles et al., 1998; Roderick & Camburn, 1999).

Students who make a smooth transition to a secondary school environment are more likely to be successful there and, as a result, are more likely to graduate from high school (Roderick & Camburn, 1999; Wigfield et al., 1996). The Development and Practice feature on the next page suggests several strategies for teachers at the middle school and high school levels.

Teacher Expectations: A Self-Fulfilling Prophecy?

As we have seen, teachers invariably have expectations for how their students should perform, both academically and socially, in the classroom. But many also form expectations about how students *are likely* to perform. Teachers typically draw conclusions about their students relatively early in the school year, forming opinions about each one's strengths, weaknesses, and potential for academic success. In many instances, teachers size up their students fairly accurately: They know which ones need help with reading skills, which ones have short attention spans, and so on. But even the best teachers occasionally make inaccurate assessments. For instance, teachers often underestimate the abilities of students who

- Are physically unattractive (Ritts, Patterson, & Tubbs, 1992)
- Misbehave frequently in class (Bennett, Gottesman, Rock, & Cerullo, 1993)
- Speak in dialects other than Standard English (Bowie & Bond, 1994; McLoyd, 1998b)
- Are members of low-income communities (Knapp & Woolverton, 1995; McLoyd, 1998b)
- Are recent immigrants (Nieto, 1995; Olneck, 1995)

Teachers frequently treat their students in ways consistent with their expectations for those students. For example, when teachers have high expectations for students' performance, they create a warmer classroom climate, interact with students more frequently, provide more opportunities for students to respond, and give more positive feedback; they also present more course material and more challenging topics. In contrast, when teachers have low expectations for certain students, they offer fewer opportunities for speaking in class, ask easier questions, give less feedback about students' responses, and present few if any challenging assignments (Babad, 1993; Good & Brophy, 1994; Graham, 1990; Harris & Rosenthal, 1985; Rosenthal, 1994).

Treating students differently based on their perceived ability is not necessarily a bad thing; for example, a teacher who expects a student to have difficulty learning to read, perhaps because the students' parents are illiterate, may spend extra time with the student to develop basic reading skills (Goldenberg, 1992; Good & Brophy, 1994). Yet when teacher behaviors consistently communicate an expectation of poor performance, students may begin to see themselves as others see them and perform accordingly (Eccles [Parsons], 1983; Yee & Eccles, 1988). Many theorists believe that teacher expectations lead to a **self-fulfilling prophecy**, in which students learn and achieve at the levels their teachers expect of them.

How much do teacher expectations affect students' classroom performance and overall academic growth? Research on this topic yields mixed results (Eccles et al., 1998; Goldenberg, 1992; Rosenthal, 1994). Some research indicates that girls, students from low-income families, and students from ethnic minority groups are more susceptible to teacher expectations than European American boys (Graham, 1990; Jussim, Eccles, & Madon, 1996). Teacher expectations also appear to have a greater influence in the early elementary school years (grades

self-fulfilling prophecy
Phenomenon in which a teacher's expectations for students' performance directly or indirectly bring about that level of performance.

EASING THE TRANSITION TO MIDDLE AND SECONDARY SCHOOL

■ Provide a means through which every student can feel part of a small, close-knit group.

In September, a ninth-grade math teacher establishes *base groups* of three or four students who provide support and assistance for one another throughout the school year. At the beginning or end of every class period, the teacher gives the groups 5 minutes to help one another with questions and concerns about daily lessons and homework assignments.

■ Find time to meet one-on-one with every student.

Early in the school year, while his classes are working on a variety of cooperative learning activities, a middle school social studies teacher schedules individual appointments with each of his students. In these meetings, he searches for common interests that he and his students share and encourages the students to seek him out whenever they need help with academic or personal problems. Throughout the semester, he continues to touch base with his students (often during lunch or before or after school) to see how they are doing.

■ Teach students the skills they need to be successful independent learners.

After discovering that many of her students have little idea of how to take effective notes in class, a high school science teacher distributes a daily "notes skeleton" that guides them through the note-taking process that day. For instance, before a lesson on the various diseases associated with poor nutrition, she distributes a sheet like the one shown.

As the year progresses, she reduces the specific nature of these handouts; by the end of the

school year, the handouts simply have four sections—"Topic of the Lesson," "Definitions," "Important Ideas," and "Examples"—that students fill in as they take notes.

■ Assign grades on the basis of mastery (not on comparisons with peers), and provide reasonable opportunities for improvement.

A junior high school language arts teacher requires students to submit two drafts of every essay and short story he assigns; he gives them the option of submitting additional drafts as well. He judges students' compositions on four criteria: cohesiveness, word usage, grammar, and spelling. He explains and illustrates each of these criteria and gives ample feedback on every draft that students turn in.

```
Topic: DIET AND DISEASES

Scurvy:
    Caused by: _____
    Symptoms: _____
    _____

Rickets:
    Caused by: _____
    Symptoms: _____
    _____

Beriberi:
    Caused by: _____
    Symptoms: _____
    _____

Anemia:
    Caused by: _____
    Symptoms: _____
    _____
```

1 and 2) and in the first year of secondary school—in other words, at times when students are entering new and unfamiliar school environments (Jussim et al., 1996; Raudenbush, 1984; Weinstein et al., 1995).

Being Optimistic About Students' Performance A characteristic consistently found in effective schools is high expectations for student performance (Phillips, 1997; Roderick & Camburn, 1999). Even if students' initial academic performance is low, teachers must remember that cognitive abilities and skills can and do change over time, especially when environmental conditions are conducive to such change. The following strategies can help teachers maintain a sense of optimism about what students can accomplish over the course of the school year:

■ *Learn more about students' backgrounds and home environments.* Teachers are most likely to develop low expectations for students' performance when they have rigid stereotypes about students from certain ethnic or socioeconomic groups (McLoyd, 1998b; Snow, Corno, & Jackson, 1996). And such stereotypes are often the result of ignorance about students' home environments and cultures (Alexander, Entwisle, & Thompson, 1987). Education is the key here:

Teachers must learn as much as they can about students' backgrounds and local communities. When they have a clear picture of students' families, activities, habits, and values, they are far more likely to think of their students as *individuals*—each with a unique set of talents and skills—than as stereotypical members of a particular group.

■ *Collaborate with colleagues to maximize academic success on a schoolwide basis.* Teachers are more likely to have high expectations for students when they are confident in their own ability to help students achieve academic and social success (Ashton, 1985; Weinstein et al., 1995). Consider the case of one inner-city high school. For many years, teachers at the school believed that their low-achieving students, most of whom were from low-income families, were simply unmotivated to learn. They also saw themselves, their colleagues, and school administrators as being ineffective and uninvested in helping these students succeed. To counteract such tendencies, the school faculty held regular 2-hour meetings in which they

- Read research related to low-achieving and at-risk students
- Explored various hypotheses as to why their students were having difficulty
- Developed, refined, and evaluated innovative strategies for helping their students succeed
- Established a collaborative atmosphere in which, working together, they could take positive action

Such meetings helped the teachers form higher expectations for students' achievement and a better understanding of what they themselves could do to help the students achieve (Weinstein et al., 1995).

Creating a Sense of Community in Classrooms and Schools

Earlier we suggested that teachers minimize competitive situations. Competitions among *groups* of students can be effective motivators if all groups have equal ability and if the final outcome is determined more by student effort than by uncontrollable factors (Stipek, 1996). Under most circumstances, however, competitive events are counterproductive: They focus students' attention on performance (rather than mastery) goals, decrease students' self-efficacy and sense of competence, and increase the likelihood that students will attribute their failures to low ability (Ames, 1984; Deci & Ryan, 1992; Nicholls, 1984; Spaulding, 1992).

Cooperative classrooms, in which students work *with* and *for* one another rather than *against* one another, are more motivating and productive learning environments, largely because they increase the likelihood that students will be successful (Ames, 1984; Deci & Ryan, 1985). Cooperative classrooms appear to be especially beneficial for girls (Eccles, 1989; Inglehart, Brown, & Vida, 1994) and for students from ethnic minority groups that value group achievements over individual conquests (Grant & Gomez, 2001; Miller, 1995; Suina & Smolkin, 1994).

Classrooms as Communities Many experts encourage teachers to create a **sense of community** in the classroom—a sense that teachers and students have shared goals, respect and support one another's efforts, and believe that everyone makes an important contribution to classroom learning (Emmer, Evertson, Clements, & Worsham, 1994; Hom & Battistich, 1995; Kim, Solomon, & Roberts, 1995; Lickona, 1991). Several strategies can help create a sense of classroom community:

- Soliciting students' ideas and opinions, and incorporating them into classroom discussions and activities
- Creating mechanisms through which students can help make the classroom run smoothly and efficiently (e.g., assigning various "helper" roles to students on a rotating basis)
- Emphasizing such prosocial values as sharing and cooperation
- Providing opportunities for students to help one another (e.g., by asking, "Who has a problem that someone else might be able to help you solve?")
- Providing public recognition of students' contributions to the overall success of the classroom
(Emmer et al., 1994; Kim et al., 1995; Lickona, 1991)

sense of community
Widely shared feeling that teacher and students have common goals, are mutually respectful and supportive of one another's efforts, and believe that everyone makes an important contribution to classroom learning.

When students share a sense of community, they are more likely to exhibit prosocial behavior, stay on task, express enthusiasm about classroom activities, and achieve at high levels. Furthermore, a sense of classroom community is associated with lower rates of disruptive classroom behavior, truancy, violence, and drug use (Hom & Battistich, 1995; Kim et al., 1995).

Some theorists suggest that one way to create this sense of community is to transform the classroom into a **community of learners** in which teacher and students actively and cooperatively work to help one another learn (Brown & Campione, 1994; Campione et al., 1995; Rogoff, Matusov, & White, 1996). A classroom that operates as a community of learners is likely to have characteristics such as these:

- All students are active participants in classroom activities.
- Discussion and collaboration among two or more students are common occurrences and play a key role in learning.
- Diversity in students' interests and rates of progress are expected and respected.
- Students and teacher coordinate their efforts at helping one another learn; no one has exclusive responsibility for teaching others.
- Everyone is a potential resource for the others; different individuals are likely to serve as resources on different occasions, depending on the topics and tasks at hand. (In some cases, students may "major" in a particular topic and thereby become local "experts" on that topic.)
- The teacher provides some guidance and direction for classroom activities, but students may also contribute to such guidance and direction.
- Constructive questioning and critique of one another's work is commonplace.
- The process of learning is emphasized as much as, and sometimes more than, the finished product.
(Brown & Campione, 1996; Campione et al., 1995; Rogoff, 1994; Rogoff et al., 1996)

Researchers have not yet systematically compared the academic achievement of communities of learners to the achievement of more traditional classrooms; however, case studies indicate that classes structured as communities of learners have some positive effects. For one thing, these classes appear to promote relatively sophisticated cognitive processes for extended periods of time (Brown & Campione, 1994). They are also highly motivating; for instance, students often insist on going to school even when they are ill, and they are disappointed when summer vacation begins (Rogoff, 1994). Finally, such classrooms create an environment in which teachers can meet students' needs for affiliation at the very same time that they encourage mastery goals and an intrinsic motivation to learn classroom subject matter. One eighth-grade English teacher described her experiences with a community of learners this way:

> The classroom became . . . like a dining-room table, where people could converse easily about books and poems and ideas. I would watch my students leave the classroom carrying on animated conversations about which book was truly Robert Cormier's best, why sequels are often disappointing, which books they planned to reread or pack into their trunks for summer camp. Books became valuable currency, changing hands after careful negotiation: "Okay, you can borrow Adams's *So Long and Thanks for All the Fish* (Pocket), but you have to lend me the first two books in the Xanth series." The shelves neatly lined with class sets of books gradually gave way to a paperback library, stocked with books donated by students and their families, bonus copies from book clubs, and books I ordered with my budgeted allotment each year. (Moran, 1991, pp. 439)

Schools as Communities Ideally, teachers should not only create a sense of community within their individual classrooms but also create an overall sense of community within their schools (Battistich et al., 1995; Battistich, Solomon, Watson, & Schaps, 1997; Brown & Campione, 1994). In schools that operate as true communities, students get the same message from all school personnel: that everyone is working together to help students become informed, successful, and productive citizens, and that students can and should help one another as well. When teachers and other school personnel communicate an overall sense of school community, students have more positive attitudes toward school, are more motivated to achieve at high levels, and exhibit more prosocial behavior, and students from diverse backgrounds are more likely to interact with one another. Furthermore, teachers have higher

community of learners
Classroom in which teacher and students actively and cooperatively work to help one another learn.

expectations for students' achievement and a greater sense of self-efficacy about their own teaching effectiveness (Battistich et al., 1995, 1997).

School environments clearly play a significant role in children's and adolescents' motivation to achieve academic success and become productive, caring citizens. Schools are not the only environments that nurture (or in some cases stifle) motivation and appropriate behavior, however. Families, peers, and broader environmental contexts—cultural practices, socioeconomic conditions, neighborhood support, messages in the media, and so on—play equally important roles. We consider such influences in the next three chapters.

CASE STUDY: DERRIKA

In a study conducted in the Chicago public schools, Roderick and Camburn (1999) investigated the academic progress of students who had recently made the transition from relatively small elementary or middle schools to much larger high schools. Many students in their research sample experienced considerable difficulty making the transition from eighth to ninth grade, as the case of Derrika illustrates:

> Derrika liked to be challenged and felt her eighth-grade teachers cared and made her work. Derrika entered high school with plans to go to college and felt that her strong sense of self would get her through: "Nobody stops me from doing good because I really wanna go to college . . . Nobody in my family's been to college . . . so I want to be the first person to go to college and finish."
>
> Derrika began having problems in eighth grade. Despite average achievement scores and previously high grades, she ended eighth grade with a C average and failed science. In high school, her performance deteriorated further. At the end of the first semester, Derrika received Fs in all her major subjects, had 20 absences, almost 33 class cuts for the last two periods of the day, and had been suspended for a food fight. Derrika is vague in explaining her performance, except for biology, in which she admits, "I don't never get up on time." She feels that her elementary school teachers were better because, "If you don't want to learn, they are going to make you learn," while her current teachers think, "If you fail, you just fail. It ain't our fault. You're the one that's dumb." (Roderick & Camburn, 1999, p. 304)

- Given what you've learned about the development of motivation and self-regulation, how might you explain Derrika's sudden academic difficulties beginning in the eighth grade?
- To what factors did Derrika's elementary school teachers apparently attribute any academic failures that she had? To what factors do her high school teachers attribute her failures?
- What strategies might a teacher use to help Derrika get back on the road to academic success?

SUMMARY

Motivation

Motivation energizes, directs, and sustains behavior. It can be either intrinsic (emanating from characteristics within a person or inherent in the task being performed) or extrinsic (emanating from factors external to both the person and the task). Children who are intrinsically motivated to learn school subjects are more likely to pay attention and engage in effective learning strategies than children who are extrinsically motivated.

Behaviorists propose that the sources of motivation come largely from the consequences (e.g., rewards, punishments) that result from people's behaviors. As children develop, they work more for such reinforcers as praise, attention, and good grades than for reinforcers that satisfy basic physiological needs. They also learn that some behaviors are reinforced only occasionally, and they become increasingly able to delay gratification.

Social cognitive theorists propose that by observing the consequences of their own and others' behaviors, children form expectations about the future consequences that various responses are likely to bring. Children often imitate other people and are especially likely to imitate models whom they see as competent, prestigious, powerful, and "gender appropriate."

Trait theorists propose that some motives and needs vary considerably from one person to the next. For instance, some children have a high need for affiliation, in that they want to spend much of their time interacting with others (especially peers), whereas other children have a much lower need for affiliation. Children also differ in their needs for approval from adults and peers. With age comes an increasing need to gain the approval and affection of peers, often paired with a drop in the need for the approval and affection of adults.

Cognitive theorists focus on the nature of the mental phenomena (interests, goals, attributions, etc.) involved in motivation. They propose that intrinsic motivation is a multifaceted entity; for example, depending on the situation, it may involve curiosity, a need for cognitive consistency, interest in particular topics, or a perception that a particular skill has relevance for one's long-term goals. Cognitive theorists also suggest that children and adolescents have numerous goals (goals related to academic achievement, social relationships, future careers, etc.) and differing degrees of success in coordinating multiple goals. They argue, too, that children and adolescents attribute successes and failures to a variety of possible causes, and such explanations influence future behaviors.

Each of the four perspectives contributes to our understanding of children's motivation and its development, and each has implications for classroom practice. For instance, behaviorists suggest that extrinsic reinforcers (attention, praise, special privileges) are sometimes necessary to bring about desired behavior change. Social cognitive theorists emphasize the importance of exposing students to good role models who have characteristics and backgrounds similar to students' own. Trait theorists remind us that different students may require different motivational strategies; for example, some students will enjoy and benefit from group projects more than others. Cognitive theorists suggest that teachers encourage students to shoot more for mastery goals (where the focus is on learning) than for performance goals (where the focus is on appearance). In addition, teachers should communicate the belief that successes and failures are more a function of effort and learning strategies—temporary factors over which students have considerable control—than of natural ability—a more permanent entity over which students have very little control.

Development of Self-Regulation

With age and experience, most children and adolescents become increasingly able to regulate and direct their own behavior and learning. They internalize the rules and restrictions that adults have imposed, more effectively control their emotional reactions, and can evaluate their own performance with increasing accuracy. Nevertheless, most high school students do not regulate their own behaviors as effectively as adults do. Adults promote self-regulation through authoritative parenting, establishing definite guidelines for behavior while also attending to children's needs, listening to children's ideas and perspectives, and providing a reasonable rationale for any requests. Adults also model self-regulating behaviors and give children age-appropriate opportunities for independence.

Effects of the Classroom Environment

Schools play a major role in the socialization of children and adolescents: Teachers expect and encourage certain behaviors at school that parents and other caregivers may or may not require at home. Through their *own* behaviors (e.g., the extent to which they give guidelines for behavior, communicate caring and concern, and provide justifications for requests), teachers create a particular climate (psychological atmosphere) that may either foster or impede children's classroom productivity. Furthermore, teachers form particular expectations about how individual students are likely to perform, and such expectations may, by affecting how teachers interact with students, lead to a self-fulfilling prophecy.

Classrooms and schools in which most students learn effectively are cooperative rather than competitive ones. Effective teachers create a sense of community in which teachers and students have shared goals, respect and support one another's efforts, and believe that everyone makes an important contribution to classroom learning. A sense of community may be especially important for students who are at risk for academic failure.

Now go to our Companion Website to assess your understanding of chapter content with Multiple-Choice Questions, apply comprehension in Essay Questions, and broaden your knowledge with links to related Developmental Psychology World Wide Web sites.

motivation (p. 404)

intrinsic vs. extrinsic
motivation (p. 404)

behaviorism (p. 404)

operant conditioning (p. 404)

reinforcer (p. 404)

positive reinforcement (p. 405)

negative reinforcement (p. 405)

primary reinforcer (p. 405)

secondary reinforcer (p. 405)

intermittent reinforcement
(p. 406)

delay of gratification (p. 406)

social cognitive theory (p. 406)

vicarious reinforcement
(p. 407)

vicarious punishment (p. 407)

trait theory (p. 408)

need for relatedness (p. 408)

need for affiliation (p. 408)

need for approval (p. 408)

achievement motivation
(p. 409)

situated motivation (p. 410)

situational interest (p. 411)

personal interest (p. 411)

value (p. 411)

sense of competence (p. 412)

sense of self-determination
(p. 412)

internalized motivation (p. 414)

core goal (p. 414)

mastery goal (p. 415)

performance goal (p. 415)

attribution (p. 417)

mastery orientation (p. 419)

learned helplessness (p. 419)

learned industriousness
(p. 425)

students at risk (p. 426)

self-regulation (p. 427)

self-reinforcement (p. 428)

authoritative parenting (p. 431)

self-monitoring (p. 433)

self-instructions (p. 434)

self-evaluation (p. 434)

socialization (p. 436)

socialization agents (p. 436)

culture shock (p. 436)

hidden curriculum (p. 436)

classroom climate (p. 436)

self-fulfilling prophecy (p. 438)

sense of community (p. 440)

community of learners (p. 441)

Noah, age 10

Families

CASE STUDY: CEDRIC AND BARBARA JENNINGS

Cedric Lavar Jennings is a senior at Ballou High School, an inner-city school in Washington, D.C. Throughout his school career, his grades have been exemplary, and he has recently learned that he has been accepted at Brown University for the following year.

Cedric and his mother Barbara are very close. They have been a family of two since Cedric was born. They live in a lower-income neighborhood on 16th Street, where crack cocaine dealers regularly do business at both ends of the block and gunshots are frequent background noise at night. Despite such an environment, Cedric has flourished, in large part because of his mother's support. Not only is he a high achiever, but he is also a very likeable young man with a strong moral code.

One night in January, Barbara and Cedric attend the Parent-Teacher-Student Association (PTSA) meeting at Ballou. After the meeting, they go to Cedric's homeroom, where Ms. Wingfield, the homeroom teacher, is handing out first-semester grade reports. Cedric is appalled to discover a B on his grade sheet. In *A Hope in the Unseen,* Suskind (1998) reports what happens next:

"I got a B in physics! I can't believe it."

He begins ranting about the cheating in his class, about how he thinks a lot of other kids cheated. . . . Barbara remembers that he mentioned something about this a week ago—but she dismissed the whole matter.

Squeezed into a school desk next to him, she wants to tell Cedric that it doesn't matter. None of it. Some small hubbub about cheating and grades is meaningless now that he's been admitted to Brown, the top college acceptance of any Ballou student in years.

But, of course, he knows all that, too. And the more dismissive her look, the more rabid he becomes. Then she gets it: it's about her watching over him, defending him, always being there. ". . .I mean, what are *we* going to do?!" he shouts at the end of his furious soliloquy about what's right and fair and just.

She's up. "Well, Lavar [she usually calls him by his middle name], we'll just have to go have a word with that teacher." A second later, they're stomping together through the halls, headed for the physics classroom of an unsuspecting Mr. Momen. They find that he is alone. He turns and offers greetings as they enter, but Cedric launches right in—the whole diatribe, offered with added verve from his rehearsal with his mom.

Mr. Momen, a wry, sometimes sarcastic man in his mid-forties, mournfully shakes his head, a helmet of gray-flecked hair. "Cedric, you got a B for the marking period," he says in precise, accented English. "The test for you is irrefutable. The curve says yours is a B, and that, for you, is a B for the marking period. So, okay. That's it, yes?"

"But kids are cheating! You leave the room and they open the book. Lots of them. You don't know what goes on. You shouldn't leave the room, that's when it starts. It ends up that I get penalized 'cause I won't cheat."

"Cedric, stop. I can't, myself, accuse all of them of cheating," says Mr. Momen, shrugging.

Barbara watches the give-and-take, realizing that the teacher has artfully shoved Cedric into a rhetorical corner by placing her son's single voice against the silent majority—his word against theirs.

Years of practice at this have taught her much: choose your words meticulously and then let them rumble up from some deep furnace of conviction. "My son doesn't lie," she says, like an oracle, "not about something like this."

The silent majority vanishes. She stands, straight and motionless, a block of granite. Momen looks back at her, eye to eye. Soon, the silence becomes unbearable. He's forced to move. "I guess he could take a retest I make for him," he says haltingly. "It will be a hard test, though, that I will make for you, Cedric."

"Fine," says Barbara, closing the deal. "Thank you, Mr. Momen. We can go now," she says. Once they're in the hallway, she whispers to Cedric, "You *will* be getting an A on that test, Lavar. You understand?" She doesn't expect an answer.

After a week of ferocious study, Cedric does get his A on the special test—scoring 100—and an A for the marking period. He brings home the paper and lays it on the dining room table, like a prize, a trophy.

Barbara looks at it for a moment. "On the next stop, you know you'll be on your own. I won't be there to come to the rescue," she says, feeling as though a clause of their partnership has expired.

"Well, then," he says a little tersely, tapping the paper once with his index finger, "I guess this paper is sort of your diploma." (pp. 113–115)

From *A Hope in the Unseen* by Ron Suskind, copyright © 1998 by Ron Suskind. Used by permission of Broadway Books, a division of Random House, Inc.

LIKE BARBARA JENNINGS, MOST parents give their children not only love but also guidance, encouragement, emotional support, and material resources. Families are structured environments with unequal distributions of power: By and large, parents call the shots. In the process, they teach children how to behave and what kind of person to become. As the opening case demonstrates, however, influence within families is a two-way street. Barbara's initial reaction to Cedric's B in physics is to let the matter drop, because in the long run, the B will in no way affect her son's academic and career success. Yet Cedric, outraged by the unfairness of the situation, spurs her into action on his behalf.

One of the challenges parents face is to guide their children in safe and constructive directions while also allowing increasing independence as the children gain competence. In all cultures, most parents slowly loosen the apron strings over time, until eventually their offspring are making their own decisions and choosing their own courses of action. For example, Barbara Jennings comes to Cedric's assistance when his teacher grades him unfairly, but she also tells him, "On the next stop, you know you'll be on your own."

In this chapter we examine families, including their nature, structure, and influences. We explore diversity in how families express affection, discipline their children, and prepare them for school. Much of this diversity represents healthy variation, although, as you will discover, some family environments compromise children's growth and well-being. In the final section of the chapter, we consider how school personnel can forge productive partnerships with parents to better promote children's and adolescents' academic progress and social-emotional development.

Socialization in the Family

The family is at the center of most children's lives. It is essentially a "headquarters" from which children get the love, guidance, support, and resources they need to tackle life's many tasks and challenges (Garbarino & Abramowitz, 1992a).

Families take many forms. Here we use the term **family** to refer to an adult or group of adults (perhaps a single parent, a husband-and-wife pair, an unmarried couple, grandparents, or foster parents) caring for children for many years and guiding the children in such a way that they can eventually take on adult roles and responsibilities (Reiss, 1980).

In Chapter 9, we introduced the concept of *socialization*—the systematic efforts of adults, peers, and institutions to prepare growing children to act in ways that society perceives to be appropriate and responsible. Parents, and often other family members as well, typically play a major role in socializing children; in other words, they serve as **socialization agents.** As such, they pass along the knowledge and values of their society, encourage culturally approved ways of behaving, and insist that children assume increasing responsibility for their own (and perhaps others') welfare. Family members are, of course, not the only socialization agents in the community. Teachers, counselors, neighbors, youth organizations, religious groups, and local social agencies can also be important influences in the socialization of growing children.

family
One or more adults caring for offspring for a significant portion of their childhood.

socialization agents
People who play a key role in preparing children and adolescents to act in ways deemed by society to be appropriate and responsible.

As socialization agents, parents and other adults have many strategies at their disposal (Damon, 1988). They describe, teach, and model proper ways of behaving in various situations. They reward appropriate behaviors and punish inappropriate ones. They arrange for children to gain certain kinds of information and experiences and steer them clear of less productive ones. And by nurturing close emotional bonds with children, they enhance children's motivation to comply with rules and requests.

Other socialization agents also have profound effects on children, even though society does not always sanction their efforts. Many people (e.g., friends, classmates, rock stars, sports figures) and the general media (e.g., films, television shows and commercials, magazines, computer games, Internet sites) transmit ideas that influence children's behaviors, attitudes, and lifestyle choices. Some of these messages are similar to those that parents and other caregivers offer; others are in direct conflict with what caring adults think is best for children.

Yet the various socialization influences on children are not simple or direct. Children do not passively become what their parents and others want them to be. Instead, they actively seek out information about their social world and their place in it. They also filter the advice they hear, choose role models to imitate, adjust standards for behavior, and reject actions and values that are inconsistent with their own ideas of who they are and should be. Thus, children are active participants in their own socialization. Some theorists use the term **self-socialization** when describing the active thinking and decision making in which children, adolescents, and young adults engage while learning how to behave and participate appropriately in their culture (Deutsch, Ruble, Fleming, & Brooks-Gunn, 1988; Durkin, 1995; Lewis, 1991).

The decisions that children make about which individuals and sources of information to trust depend on their own developmental levels and life experiences. Parents loom large in the lives of infants, toddlers, and preschoolers. Peers become increasingly important as children grow and develop, not necessarily replacing parents but certainly offering compelling models of how to dress, which music to listen to, and how to spend leisure time. Despite the increasing influence of peers, parents typically remain strong sources of support and persuasion, especially with respect to core values. Most young people continue to see their relationships with parents and other family members as important and valuable throughout adolescence (Cauce, Mason, Gonzales, Hiraga, & Liu, 1994; Furman & Buhrmester, 1992; Neubauer, Mansel, Avrahami, & Nathan, 1994).

Some developmental researchers have worked to characterize and understand the dynamic interplay between children and their families and other socialization agents. In the process, they have tried to identify the truly significant patterns of relationships within families. Who influences whom? In what ways do parents affect children, and in what ways do children sway parents? Are parents' influences on children based on genetic transmission, social processes, or some combination of forces? Within the context of such questions, several theoretical perspectives have emerged to help define the basic ways in which families support children's development.

Theoretical Perspectives on Family Socialization

Developmental theorists have used at least four theoretical perspectives to describe and explain how family members influence and socialize one another. These varying perspectives have emerged, in part, because different groups of theorists focus on distinct features of family systems: children's and parents' observable behaviors (social-cognitive perspectives), children's thinking (cognitive-developmental perspectives), genetic foundations and evolutionary pressures (biological perspectives), and the ways in which family and community members interact as a complex whole to support children's growth (ecological systems perspectives).

Social-Cognitive Perspectives From a social-cognitive perspective (e.g., Bandura, 1986), parents and other family members influence children through the specific experiences they arrange for children to observe and participate in. They also reward children for desirable responses and punish them for undesirable ones. And they serve as powerful role models, indirectly communicating messages about appropriate behaviors through the actions that they themselves exhibit.

self-socialization
The active thinking and decision making in which children engage as they learn how to behave and participate appropriately in their culture.

Children, in turn, closely attend to and remember what other people do and say. Children and adolescents have a remarkable capacity for observation and imitation, as the following examples illustrate:

- A 3-year-old boy pushes his plastic lawn mover across the lawn while puckering his lips to produce the "brrmmm brrmmm" sounds of his parents' mower.
- A 6-year-old girl sits next to her father and peruses one of her storybooks while her dad reads the newspaper.
- A 14-year-old boy adopts his mother's excessive drinking habits, befriending peers who provide easy access to alcoholic beverages at social gatherings.

Through their experiences and observations, children also develop expectations about the likely consequences of their behaviors. For example, a 4-year-old may hear her mother commending an older brother for writing a thank-you note to Grandma and then follow suit without being asked (recall the example of Rachel in Chapter 8).

Children and adolescents do not imitate everything they observe, however. From the behaviors they see other family members exhibit, as well as from the positive and negative consequences that result from their own and others' actions, children develop a growing sense of what actions are "right" and "wrong" and begin to abide by their own standards for behavior (Bandura, 1986). For example, in the opening case study, Cedric wouldn't cheat on his physics exam even though his classmates were cheating. As an 18-year-old, Cedric had long since determined that cheating was inappropriate behavior despite the desirable consequences (good grades) that it might bring.

Cognitive-Developmental Perspectives From a cognitive-developmental perspective (e.g., see Piaget's theory of cognitive development in Chapter 4 and Kohlberg's theory of moral development in Chapter 10), children largely control and direct their *own* development. They energetically labor to understand their environment by exploring objects, tinkering with ideas, acquiring increasingly sophisticated ways of thinking, and combining various actions and procedures into complex forms of problem solving.

Cognitive developmentalists downplay the role of families, teachers, and other possible socialization agents. Piaget did acknowledge that discussions and conflicts with peers are critical for helping children learn to see situations from other people's perspectives, and Kohlberg proposed that children may progress in their moral reasoning when they encounter moral arguments at one stage above their own. By and large, however, cognitive developmentalists have devoted little attention to how families transmit particular behaviors, skills, ideas, and values. Instead, children must themselves be cognitively ready for change when they encounter ideas that contradict their current ways of thinking, and when they show major developmental advances, they themselves take credit for the gain.

Some theorists have argued that the cognitive-developmental perspective is a lopsided view of children's development that neglects the important influences of meaningful social interactions (e.g., Chandler, 1982; Durkin, 1995). Yet the basic cognitive-developmentalist idea that children construct their own understandings and reasoning capabilities has withstood vigorous criticism (Brainerd, 1996; Flavell, 1996) and needs to be integrated into our thinking about how families do and do not influence children. More specifically, there are limits to what parents and other family members can explicitly "teach" a child at any given time: Their efforts will have little or no effect on a child's thinking or behavior if the child is not cognitively ready for change. Teresa recalls a relevant example involving her son Alex, then 2. Teresa's husband and older son Connor taught Alex to answer "Two" to questions such as "How old are you?" "What's one plus one?" "What's the square root of four?" and "What's the cube root of eight?" Despite Alex's consistently correct responses, his understanding of mathematics progressed not one iota throughout the "training."

The cognitive-developmental perspective encourages us to distinguish between areas of development that are and are not likely to benefit from family interactions. Basic logical reasoning capabilities—object permanence, conservation, classification, and so on—may undergo fairly predictable developmental changes in a wide variety of family experiences. Other developmental changes—including knowledge of specific subject areas, development of social skills, and acquisition of certain standards for academic achievement and acceptable behavior—may be more responsive to family influences.

The cognitive-developmental perspective, on balance, does offer guidance about how family members can best foster children's development (Kohlberg, 1969; Maccoby, 1980). Ideally, families should provide a rich physical, social, and intellectual environment in which children can explore physical phenomena, practice emerging skills, exchange ideas, and encounter challenging concepts and beliefs. What does not work is intellectual "force-feeding," which is likely to promote only anxiety or rote responding (e.g., saying "Two" to every question), rather than meaningful developmental change.

From an evolutionary perspective, parents' tendency to protect their children from danger enhances the likelihood that the species will survive, reproduce, and flourish. Art by Rachel, age 10.

Biological Perspectives   From a biological perspective, families are highly influential agents in children's development. For one thing, of course, parents give their children life. In the process, they pass along common human traits, such as the ability to produce and understand language, manual dexterity and talent with tools, a predisposition to form social relationships, and a tendency to observe and imitate others. But parents also give their children a unique genetic heritage. For instance, Teresa's older son Connor is in some respects very much like his father, in that he is good-humored and socially outgoing. From Teresa's side of the family, Connor has inherited a tendency to be unusually tall (his mother and aunts stand 5'8" or 5'9" and his uncles are 6'0" or taller). In other ways, though, Connor is like neither of his parents; as an example, he has a fascination with historical events that far exceeds that of either of his parents. Individual differences arise out of a complex interplay of genetics, exposure to hormones, and personal experiences (Bjorklund, 1997).

Biological perspectives also tend to portray family life and children's development in terms of evolutionary pressures and adaptations. As do all living species, human beings organize their lives around physical survival and sexual reproduction—activities that ensure the long-term success of the species (Darwin, 1859). The species evolves when individuals who have certain characteristics adapt successfully to the environment and have families of their own, while those not possessing such characteristics do not survive to have offspring (Bjorklund, 1997; Cairns, 1983; Charlesworth, 1992; Dixon & Lerner, 1992).

Within the context of families, evolutionary pressures are seen in the length of childhood: Compared to the offspring of many other animal species, human children remain dependent on parents and other caregivers for a long time. This period allows children many opportunities to learn the ways of their culture (Bruner, 1972; Leaky, 1994). When sheltered from adult responsibilities, children playfully learn how to use tools, relate to others, and practice adult roles (mommies and daddies, hunters, basket weavers, teachers, firefighters, etc.). Evolutionary pressures are also evident in the emotional bonds that form between parents and children and in the moral conscience that motivates parents to meet their children's needs (see the discussion of attachment in Chapter 9). An evolutionary perspective even explains how parent-adolescent conflicts may ultimately be beneficial for development and so may have an adaptive function. When adolescents regularly butt heads with their parents, they spend less time at home and more time with their peers; in the process, they develop increasing independence and self-reliance, thereby easing their transition to adulthood (Steinberg, 1993).

Ecological Systems Perspectives   From an ecological systems framework, family influences on children are strong but are also part of a larger, complex set of environmental contexts that affect children's development. As an example, we describe Bronfenbrenner's ecological systems theory (Bronfenbrenner, 1979, 1989, 1993). In Bronfenbrenner's view, the family operates as a *social system,* a structure of individuals who interact regularly in defined roles. Some of these roles are fairly predictable based on culture, generation, and gender. For instance, in most North American and European families with school-aged children, parents rather than children make decisions about important family matters, such as where the family will live and what schools the children will attend. Other, more specific roles develop over time. For example, one child with academic successes or athletic prowess might emerge as the family "star," and another might become a scapegoat blamed for all the family's problems.

Two or more family members may form *subsystems,* perhaps in the form of longstanding alliances or animosities. For example, two brothers may occasionally rebel against their "unfair" parents, solidifying their connections to each another ("We don't like Mom, right?"), or a mother and daughter might unite against a harsh and punitive father. Alternatively, two parents might both be so consumed with the health of a chronically ill daughter that they neglect their relationship to each other (Bowen, 1978).

From Bronfenbrenner's perspective, the family is also a *nested system* within several larger environmental and community systems. The *microsystem* consists of children's experiences in their immediate surroundings. In daycare centers, schools, and the neighborhood, children develop relationships with and are influenced by a variety of adults and peers. Children also influence these other individuals by virtue of their personalities, interests, and behaviors. For instance, a boy fascinated with how automobiles work may spend time with adult neighbors who tinker with car engines and welcome his assistance with their maintenance projects. A girl who teaches foul language to neighborhood children may find herself restricted from future contact with those children and subsequently have fewer opportunities for interaction with peers. Children's social supports within the microsystems (e.g., their relationships with friends, neighbors, and extended family members) may be particularly important when parents work outside the home or have limited energy and resources. Far too often, however, children's microsystems are too weak to support optimal development in the absence of strong family nurturance (Garbarino & Abramowitz, 1992b).

The various microsystems in children's lives (their neighborhoods, schools, etc.) form a connected network known as the *mesosystem.* Children are more likely to thrive when families and schools maintain regular and productive communication—for instance, when parents know what is happening at school through newsletters and parent-teacher meetings and when parents and teachers respect and trust one another. When links between important socialization agents are strong and positive, children perform better academically (Garbarino, 1981). Unfortunately, connections within the mesosystem are not always productive; for instance, the encounter between Barbara Jennings and Cedric's physics teacher might have led to a shouting match, or a less assertive mother might have been reluctant to confront the teacher about his unfair grading practices.

Another layer within Bronfenbrenner's hierarchy of systems is the *exosystem,* which includes individuals and institutions that influence children's microsystems even though their actual contact with children is minimal. Examples of entities within the exosystem include parents' work settings, public support systems (e.g., social service agencies), health and fitness clubs, and parents' extended families and friends. Exosystems can offer tremendous indirect support to children through the direct support they offer parents. As working mothers, we can relate personally to the impact of the wider exosystem. With children, husbands, homes, and full-time jobs, we must work hard to keep things in balance. It helps that we have work schedules with some flexibility and that we've been able to reduce our working hours over the summer, when our children require more care and supervision. When our children were young, we had ready access to excellent daycare centers. Both of our families have benefited from the support we've received from extended family members and good friends, who've occasionally looked after our children when we've had other commitments, swapped stories with us about the trials and tribulations of their own families and work lives, and entertained us with meals and recreation. Without such support systems, the stresses of daily living might have become overwhelming. Instead, because we have been socially and emotionally bolstered by others, we have been able to provide better social and emotional environments for our children.

At a still broader level, exosystems exist within the context of cultural belief systems and behavior patterns, or *macrosystems.* Macrosystems include far-reaching social events, such as war and social strife, general migration from inner-city settings into suburban and rural areas, and cultural values and practices (e.g., an emphasis on self-reliance vs. dependence on others, or an intolerance for racism and sexism vs. acceptance of such behaviors). For example, children's moral development seems to depend somewhat on the form of government in the countries in which they live: Children who grow up in democratic societies (those in which diverse viewpoints are acceptable and federal and local laws protect individual needs and rights) are

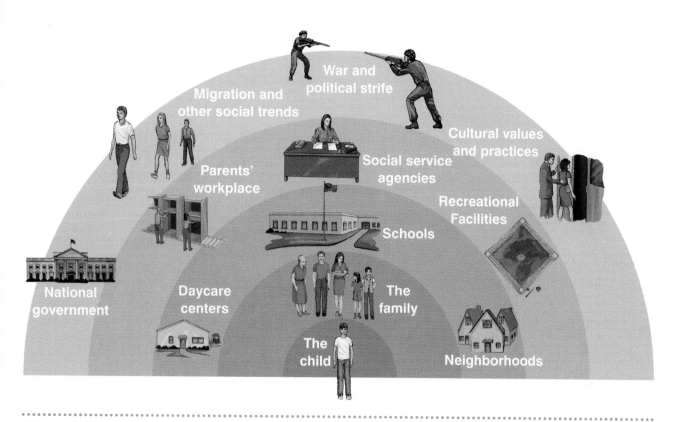

FIGURE 12–1 A systems view of family socialization. Many systems affect families and the children within them. The influences of some are direct and easily seen. The influences of others are more indirect and subtle, in that they affect the larger environment within which the family operates.

more likely to listen to the viewpoints of peers and adults, and less likely to conform to adult authority, than children who grow up in totalitarian regimes (Garbarino & Bronfenbrenner, 1976). Children who grow up in war zones or amongst terrorists are in some cases more likely to seek revenge for wrongdoing but in other cases may actively pursue peaceful resolutions (Garbarino, Kostelny, & Dubrow, 1991). Children's development is hindered when social events and patterns in the larger macrosystem limit adults' ability to care for children and guide them in productive directions (Garbarino & Abramowitz, 1992c).

The various systems just described are hardly static; they are *changing systems*. For instance, as children develop, a parent's role shifts from one of constant care and observation to one of looser and more distant nurturance and surveillance. When children first become mobile as toddlers, they must be watched constantly, prevented from experimenting with dangerous objects and substances, kept from wandering in the street, and so on. As they grow older, they begin to internalize rules and guidelines for behavior and acquire a better understanding of what actions may threaten their well-being. By adolescence, they need relatively little adult supervision; often, they simply keep their parents informed about their activities and whereabouts (Maccoby, 1984). Parents, too, undergo developmental transformations and other changes across the lifespan. Changes in parents' occupational status, economic security, emotional well-being, and physical health all have an impact on children's day-to-day experiences.

An ecological systems framework reminds us that families do not operate in isolation from the larger environmental context in which they exist. Neighborhoods, school systems, local communities, national governmental structures, and cultural milieus all have a significant influence, either direct or indirect, on family members' ability to function effectively and thereby support children's cognitive, emotional, and social development. We illustrate the ecological systems perspective in Figure 12–1.

Integrating Perspectives of Family Socialization The Basic Developmental Issues table that follows summarizes the theoretical perspectives just described in terms of nature versus nurture, universality versus diversity, and qualitative versus quantitative change. In some respects, the

BASIC DEVELOPMENTAL ISSUES

ISSUE	SOCIAL-COGNITIVE PERSPECTIVES	COGNITIVE-DEVELOPMENTAL PERSPECTIVES	BIOLOGICAL PERSPECTIVES	ECOLOGICAL SYSTEMS PERSPECTIVES
Nature and Nurture	Focus is on the experiences that parents arrange for children, including the behaviors they model and the consequences they impose for desirable and undesirable actions.	Children actively try to make sense of their experiences within their families. Children's conceptual understandings of physical and social phenomena, which are limited by their cognitive maturation, influence the extent to which they can interpret and benefit from their parents' messages.	Evolutionary pressures dictate that nature and nurture interact in children's development. Significant biological foundations (nature) are present in species-specific patterns, such as in the intense emotional bonds that usually form between parents and their young. Families also care for their dependent children over a lengthy period (nurture), a pattern that probably evolved to allow children time to learn the complex knowledge and skills of their society. Natural pressures also encourage humans to be social beings, with families functioning as key social partners, teachers, and protectors.	Focus is on environmental factors that affect family functioning. Families provide central and pivotal support systems for children, but they are embedded in and affected by broader community and societal resources and networks. Children are active agents within the family, eliciting certain kinds of responses from others based on their own characteristics and actions.
Universality and Diversity	Because families differ in the specific behaviors they model, reward, and punish, considerable diversity in children's behaviors is to be expected.	The sequences of many aspects of cognitive and moral development are assumed to be universal across societies and cultures. However, family interactions provide experiences and viewpoints that encourage children and adolescents to revise their thinking in particular directions.	Universality is present in many aspects of family functioning: Children form intense and enduring relationships with other family members in the first few years of life, learn the ways of the world from them during middle childhood, and begin to separate from family ties during adolescence. Yet families are composed of individuals with vastly different genetic predispositions. Furthermore, human beings' capacity to develop cultural values and practices and to transmit them from one generation to the next results in considerable diversity in social norms and beliefs.	Universality is present in a general sense, in that neighborhoods, communities, and broader societal conventions influence all children and families. Yet different children grow within the context of different family configurations and community networks. Children also contribute to their own family systems through their unique characteristics, interests, and demands.

different perspectives present contradictory views about families' influences on children's development. For example, from a social-cognitive perspective, children acquire moral behaviors by observing appropriate role models, receiving rewards for good behavior and punishment for wrongdoing, and gradually internalizing standards and expectations. From a cognitive-developmental perspective, however, moral development occurs as children construct internal understandings of

ISSUE	SOCIAL-COGNITIVE PERSPECTIVES	COGNITIVE-DEVELOPMENTAL PERSPECTIVES	BIOLOGICAL PERSPECTIVES	ECOLOGICAL SYSTEMS PERSPECTIVES
Qualitative and Quanitative Change	Changes in children's lives tend to occur in trendlike, quantitative forms. Through training from parents and others, children gradually become more responsible for their own behavior.	Significant qualitative transformations occur in children's thinking, largely as a result of children's ongoing restructuring of their understandings of the physical and social environments.	Families support both qualitative and quantitative changes. For example, children's interest and knowledge about sexual activity may increase in a slow, quantitative fashion during childhood, as reflected in the questions children ask and the answers they receive from parents, peers, and others. The nature of their interest may change qualitatively during adolescence, at which point parents may or may not continue to be supportive.	The systems in which a child grows up (the family, the neighborhood, various social agencies, etc.) and their interconnections may change in a qualitative fashion over time, thereby impacting how effectively family members can nurture and support children.

right and wrong and then make active and ongoing attempts to modify and restructure these understandings to incorporate new experiences and viewpoints.

Without dismissing such contradictions, we believe that each of these perspectives offers valuable insights into family functioning, processes, and influences and adds to our understanding of how families socialize children and adolescents. We urge our readers not to adopt one perspective to the exclusion of the others. For example, a cognitive-developmental approach that focuses solely on children's own understandings and motives neglects parents' active attempts to guide children's thinking and shape their behaviors. The social-cognitive perspective, which focuses primarily on situational variables, overlooks influential biological factors (e.g., enduring temperamental differences of various family members) and the broader social and cultural milieus in which children and adolescents grow. Ultimately, we need all four perspectives to adequately account for the power and limits of family influences on children.

Diversity in the Socialization of Children

Regardless of their theoretical perspective, most developmentalists acknowledge that considerable diversity exists in how families socialize their children. Here we describe children's gender, cultural environment, and family size as possible sources of diversity.

Gender Differences In most cultures, parents and other important individuals in children's lives socialize girls and boys somewhat differently. For instance, in Western countries, parents are more likely to encourage their daughters to engage in stereotypically feminine behaviors (e.g., playing with dolls, helping other people) and to encourage their sons to undertake stereotypically masculine activities (e.g., playing with blocks, engaging in rough-and-tumble play) (Bornstein et al., 1999; Lytton & Romney, 1991). Parents also tend to assign household chores based on traditional male and female roles; for example, they ask their daughters to wash dishes and clean the house but ask their sons to mow the lawn and take out the garbage (Eisenberg et al., 1996; McHale, Bartko, Crouter, & Perry-Jenkins, 1990). And parents are more likely to enroll their sons, rather than their daughters, in competitive sports programs and programs for gifted students (Eccles, Wigfield, & Schiefele, 1998).

Yet children themselves are often willing partners in such gender-specific socialization. Considerable *self-socialization* is at work even in the preschool years. In early childhood, children learn that the world is divided up into boys (males) and girls (females) and that they themselves fall into one of these two groups. Soon after, they learn that this honor of boyhood or girlhood is bestowed on them indefinitely; henceforth, they show great interest in the activities of boys and girls, men and women, daddies and mommies and in so doing begin to construct an understanding of the typical characteristics and behaviors for their gender. By the time children are 3, many of their play activities conform to traditional gender stereotypes (Langlois & Downs, 1980). Furthermore, their peers respond negatively (especially to boys) when they exhibit behaviors traditionally associated with the opposite sex (Levy, Taylor, & Gelman, 1995). Children also begin to view the world with gender-colored glasses, for example, by remembering a female physician as a "nurse" and a male nurse as a "doctor" (Carter & Levy, 1988; Liben & Signorella, 1993).

After developing a general sense of traits and activities that are "for girls" and "for boys," children focus more and more on activities they deem to be suitable for their gender and learn less about activities that are seemingly unsuitable (Martin, 1991; Martin & Halverson, 1987). For example, many boys can recite the names and functions of different kinds of trucks yet know very little about the kinds of dolls available at the toy store. As children soak up societal stereotypes, they may adamantly reject their parents' attempts to be egalitarian and flexible in the toys and activities made available to them.

Cultural Differences In some ethnic groups, such as those in many Hispanic, Native American, and Asian communities, obligation to family is especially important. Children raised in these cultures are likely to feel responsibility for their family's well-being and a strong sense of loyalty to other family members; children also go to great lengths to please their parents (Abi-Nader, 1993; Garcia, 1994; Hidalgo, Siu, Bright, Swap, & Epstein, 1995). Such cultures place a high premium on cooperation within social groups and may actively discourage the focus on competition and individual needs that characterizes mainstream culture in North America (Hollins, 1996; Okagaki & Sternberg, 1993).

Some ethnic traditions in families help children develop especially strong coping skills. African American families in particular often show positive attributes that sustain children in difficult environmental conditions, such as high unemployment and poverty. For example, strong bonds with extended family members may help African American children resist the negative influences of peer pressure (Giordano, Cernkovich, & DeMaris, 1993). Strict disciplinary strategies may communicate the importance of following family rules immediately and exactly when the surrounding communities are harsh and violent (Kelley, Power, & Wimbush, 1992; Willis, 1992). Deep religious convictions fostered in the home can also help children deal with life's stresses (McCreary, Slavin, & Berry, 1996).

In most cultures in Western countries, parents value school achievement and encourage their children to do well in school (Banks & Banks, 1995; Delgado-Gaitan, 1992; Duran & Weffer, 1992; Hossler & Stage, 1992; Yee, 1992). Yet the specific form that such encouragement takes may differ from one cultural group to another. Many Asian American parents transmit the belief that high academic achievement comes only with considerable effort and persistence, and they insist on such effort and persistence from their children (Hess, Chang, & McDevitt, 1987). In many Latino cultures, being well educated (*bien educato*) does not solely refer to a good formal education; it also refers to being successful in social situations and showing respect to others (Okagaki & Sternberg, 1993; Parke & Buriel, 1998). In some very traditional Native American and Polynesian communities, children are expected to excel in art, dance, and other aspects of their culture more so than in such academic pursuits as reading or mathematics (Kirschenbaum, 1989; Reid, 1989; Wise & Miller, 1983).

Effects of Family Size Socialization processes play out somewhat differently depending on family size. In larger families, children have more role models to choose from, and subsystems within the family are more likely to develop. Children in large families are more likely to acquire altruistic behaviors (e.g., helping others, taking care of younger siblings), especially when it is clear that their contributions are essential to the overall welfare of the family (Whiting & Whiting, 1975). Yet in smaller families (such as in Barbara and Cedric Jennings' family of two), family members often form more close-knit and intimate relationships (Falbo, 1992).

Not only does family size affect socialization but so, too, does the way in which the family is structured. In the following section, we explore various family configurations and their influence on children's and adolescents' development.

Family Structures

As society has changed over time, the nature of families has changed as well. For instance, in 1830, almost 70% of children in the United States lived on farms in two-parent families (Hernandez, 1997). Children in farming families fed the chickens, milked the cows, harvested crops, and in other ways were vital contributors to their family's economic well-being. Today, fewer than 5% of children live on family farms (Hernandez, 1997). Most instead live in urban and suburban neighborhoods and have little involvement in their parents' livelihoods. Furthermore, children are less likely to live in a traditional two-parent family than was true in the early 1800s. Consider these statistics for American children in 1995 (Hernandez, 1997):

Nearly 1 in 4 students, on average, grows up in a family headed by a single mother.

- 56% lived with both biological parents
- 14% lived either with a biological parent and a stepparent or with adoptive parents
- 23% lived in a mother-only family
- 3% lived in a father-only family
- 4% had no parent residing in the home

The number of children raised in mother-only families has shown a particularly big jump in recent years. Whereas 6% to 8% lived with single (divorced, separated, or never-married) mothers in the 1940s and 1950s, 23% did so in 1995 (Hernandez, 1997).

By **family configuration**, we mean the particular members of a family and their interrelationships. Some family configurations involve a father employed outside the home and a mother working full-time at home to care for the children and tend to household matters. But most family configurations are quite different from this traditional pattern; perhaps they involve two working parents, a single parent, a gay or lesbian parent couple, foster parents, or extended family members (e.g., grandparents, aunts, or uncles) raising children.

Many youngsters experience significant changes in their family configurations over the course of childhood or adolescence, perhaps as a result of parental separation, divorce, remarriage, or death. Consider Theo, a girl born to a teen mother in Baltimore in the mid-1960s:

> Theo lived for two years with her mother and grandmother before her parents started living together. When she was three, they married; but her father moved out just before her sixth birthday. When Theo was eight, her mother started living with Robbie, who became like a stepfather to Theo until he moved out when she was fifteen. Throughout her childhood, Theo has continued to see her biological father on an occasional basis, although these visits have become more and more irregular. After Robbie left, he, too, continued to visit Theo and her half-brother, who was his biological child. Still another surrogate father lived with Theo for a brief time after her quasi-stepfather Robbie moved out, but this relationship was short-lived and of little consequence. (Furstenberg & Cherlin, 1991, pp. 12–13)

What was Theo's family configuration? Clearly, she experienced several. As various father figures moved in and out of her life, Theo faced ongoing challenges: She needed to form and renegotiate her relationships with each man, and she undoubtedly had to deal with the emotional upheavals in her mother's life as well as in her own.

Families with Mothers and Fathers

Having both a mother and a father is *not* an essential condition for normal development (Silverstein & Auerbach, 1999). Yet mothers and fathers often play different and complementary roles in raising and caring for children. Mothers typically spend more time in physical caregiving responsibilities (feeding, bathing, changing diapers, scheduling doctors' appointments, etc.) and display more affection (e.g., kisses, hugs, smiles) toward their children (Belsky, Gilstrap, & Rovine, 1984; Hossain & Roopnarine, 1994; Parke & Tinsley, 1987). Mothers also spend more time engaging their children in visual games such as peek-a-boo, playing with toys with them, and reading to them (Parke & Tinsley, 1981). In a wide range of cultures,

family configuration
The particular members of a family and their interrelationships.

A 5-year-old boy drew this picture of his traditional two-parent family: (*clockwise, from right*) his father, himself, his mother, and his older brother. Also included are the family goldfish and the family's house and driveway.

mothers overwhelmingly assume primary responsibility for the hands-on care of young children (Engle & Breaux, 1998).

In contrast, fathers are more likely to engage their infants in active physical play, and they may be particularly instrumental in helping children get along with people outside the family (Bridges et al., 1988; Engle & Breaux, 1998; Lamb, 1976; Pettit, Brown, Mize, & Lindsey, 1998). Although fathers typically defer to mothers in basic caregiving activities, they are quite competent and sensitive in feeding, bathing, and nurturing their children when they do take on these responsibilities (Lamb, 1976; Lamb, Frodi, Hwang, Frodi, & Steinberg, 1982).

In many societies, fathers become more involved as children grow older; for instance, they may gradually take over the role of disciplinarian (Engle & Breaux, 1998). Fathers may also function as influential role models for boys during adolescence, helping their sons expand their images of a "man" to include subtle characteristics such as sensitivity and dependability in addition to more stereotypical masculine characteristics such as strength and aggression (Munroe & Munroe, 1992).

In addition to their individual influences, mothers and fathers affect children through the nature of their relationship with each other. When children live with two parents, they may gain valuable lessons in cooperation, role negotiation, problem solving, conflict resolution and, ideally, effective group functioning (McHale & Rasmussen, 1998). When parents have a healthy relationship, they tend to have good relationships with their children as well and shower their children with signs of affection (Dube, Julien, Lebeau, & Gagnon, 2000; Ward & Spitze, 1998). Children of happily married couples tend to perceive their lives as enjoyable and satisfying, and when they reach adulthood, they are generally able to establish intimacy with their own partners (Feldman, Gowen, & Fisher, 1998; Gohm, Oishi, Darlington, & Diener, 1998). In contrast, when parents are frequently embroiled in conflict, their interactions with their children are often tense, and they may lose their ability to discipline consistently (Almeida, Wethington, & Chandler, 1999; Belsky, 1981; Hetherington & Clingempeel, 1992). Marital conflict is associated with assorted problems in children and adolescents, including higher rates of externalizing behaviors (e.g., physical aggression) and internalizing behaviors (e.g., depression and anxiety), as well as long-term difficulties in trusting others and maintaining intimate relationships (Forehand, Biggar, & Kotchick, 1998; Hetherington et al., 1999; Tallman, Gray, Kullberg, & Henderson, 1999; Webster-Stratton & Hammond, 1999).

Attachment research indicates that children typically form strong emotional bonds with both of their parents. On average, children who are securely attached to both parents show better social and emotional adjustment (e.g., they have better social skills, display greater empathy toward others, show fewer signs of depression, and are less likely to abuse alcohol and drugs) than children who are securely attached to one parent but insecurely attached to the other (Constantina, 1998; Lamb, 1976; Main & Weston, 1981; Rohner, 1998).

Children who begin life in two-parent families do not necessarily remain in that situation throughout childhood and adolescence. We look now at how children fare during and following the divorce of their parents.

Families Realigned Through Divorce

Once an infrequent occurrence, divorce is now fairly commonplace. The United States has the highest divorce rate in the world—marriages end in divorce for about half of all couples aged 25 to 40—but divorce rates in European countries have also soared since the mid-1960s (Cherlin & Furstenberg, 1988; Norton & Moorman, 1987).

For children, the divorce of parents is not a single event but instead a series of occurrences, and each one demands adjustment. Ongoing marital friction often precedes a divorce; in fact, couples who divorce rarely do so suddenly (Furstenberg & Cherlin, 1991). When parents have serious marital conflicts, they tend to be less available for their children, show less affection, and be inconsistent in their expectations and demands. Despite such warning signs, children are sometimes caught off guard when their parents decide to divorce (Wallerstein & Kelly, 1980). Earlier trial separations may have been accompanied by assurances that "Mommy still loves Daddy" or "We're trying to work things out," so children may be several steps behind their parents when the decision is made to divide the family unit. Children may be left anxious and uncertain, unable to imagine a family structure that does not include both parents. Consumed with their own anger and bewilderment, parents may not be able to offer their children adequate explanations and reassurances.

The first year after divorce seems to be particularly difficult for parents and children alike (Hetherington, Cox, & Cox, 1978). Divorced couples may continue to squabble over finances and child-raising responsibilities. As they try to cope with feelings of stress or depression, either or both may have difficulty managing all the tasks involved in maintaining an organized household, including shopping, cooking, cleaning, paying bills, and monitoring children's activities and homework (Wallerstein & Kelly, 1980). Financial setbacks can further complicate the picture. Women more often serve as the custodial parent but tend to earn smaller wages than men. Parents who previously owned a house may have to sell it, and so, on top of everything else, children must move to new (and inevitably smaller) quarters and lose the proximity and support of many friends and neighbors (Furstenberg & Cherlin, 1991; Harris, 1998).

As divorcing parents begin to establish separate households, children may only slowly learn where they will live and the circumstances under which they will see and talk with each parent. Such arrangements may change over time as well, especially if the two parents have difficulty maintaining an amicable postmarital relationship. One parent may withdraw from the children and former spouse altogether and eventually invest, both emotionally and financially, in a new life and perhaps a new family. Thus, one unfortunate consequence of some divorces is that children lose intimate contact with one of their parents, in most cases their father (Furstenberg & Cherlin, 1991).

Although some divorced fathers gradually withdraw over time, this trend is by no means universal. Many fathers actively seek joint custody arrangements after their divorce (Thompson, 1994). Others continue to maintain contact with their children through regular visits, particularly when they continue to live nearby (Thompson, 1994). Sometimes noncustodial fathers redefine their roles with their children, perhaps becoming fun-loving companions (e.g., taking regular trips to the movies, amusement parks, etc.) rather than nurturers and disciplinarians (Asmussen & Larson, 1991).

Every family experiencing divorce is unique, but some general factors appear to affect children's adjustment to the change. Divorce is sometimes more difficult for boys than girls, especially when mothers assume custody, do not remarry, and establish negative and coercive ways of interacting with their sons (Hetherington, 1988, 1989). Divorce can be particularly overwhelming for young children, who may erroneously believe that their own naughty behavior provoked their parents to separate and who may harbor unrealistic hopes for eventual reconciliation (Fausel, 1986; Wallerstein, 1984). Although older children and adolescents usually find their parents' divorce quite painful, most cope reasonably well with the change, at least over the long run, especially if they have easygoing temperaments and age-appropriate social skills (Forehand et al., 1991; Hetherington, Bridges, & Insabella, 1998). Nevertheless, about 25% of adolescents from divorced families subsequently have some difficulty establishing social and emotional independence and intimate relationships with peers (Hetherington et al., 1998). Children's and adolescents' adjustment to divorce is especially difficult when conflicts between divorcing or divorced parents are drawn out and acrimonious (Johnston, 1994), when the parent assuming primary custody has difficulty meeting their needs (Hetherington, 1999a), or when they live through more than one marital breakup (Hetherington et al., 1998).

Some conditions bolster children in their efforts to adjust to a divorce. Children are more likely to adjust positively when parents and teachers maintain affectionate relationships with them, hold firm and consistent expectations for their behavior, and willingly listen to their concerns and opinions (Hetherington, 1988, 1989; Hetherington & Clingempeel 1992). Children who have support from family and friends weather a divorce more successfully than those who are socially isolated (Hetherington et al., 1998). And, of course, children are more likely to come out on top when divorced parents establish reasonably productive relationships with each other and can agree on expectations and disciplinary measures (Hetherington et al., 1978).

In a few cases, divorce is actually beneficial for children's development. Some children rise to the occasion, comforting parents and siblings, filling in as needed around the house, and in other ways acquiring adultlike behaviors. Furthermore, a peaceful, single-parent home may be infinitely preferable to a household in which two parents engage in continual, intense bickering or in which one parent is abusive or irresponsible (Grych & Finchman, 1997).

Families Headed by Single Parents

The U.S. Census Bureau estimates that almost half of the children born in the United States have spent or will spend some part of their childhood in a single-parent household (Garbarino & Abramowitz, 1992b). If trends for divorce and single-parent childbearing continue, this figure may soon increase to 60% (Furstenberg & Cherlin, 1991). Most single-parent families are headed by women, but 13%–14% of them are headed by men (Hernandez, 1997; Hetherington & Stanley-Hagan, 1997).

Compared to two-parent families, single-parent families experience unique challenges. Single parents, mothers and fathers alike, express reservations about their ability to "do it all"—to juggle children, home, and work responsibilities (Thompson, 1994). Unless they have the support of extended family members, neighbors, or friends, single parents have particular difficulty coping when they are tired, sick, or emotionally taxed, and they may be unable to offer children the rich range of roles, activities, and relationships that are likely to maximize children's development (Garbarino & Abramowitz, 1992b).

Generally, though, single-parent families cope well, particularly if they have a reasonable standard of living and the support of a stable network of family and friends (Harris, 1998). In fact, the simpler structure of single-parent families provides some advantages: Children are shielded from intense conflict between parents, may observe their custodial parent showing strong coping skills, and can enjoy the intimacy of a small family. Consider what Cedric Jennings wrote in his application to Brown University:

> [B]eing a black male in a single parent home is sometimes tough without that male figure to help in the growing process. But I thank God for my loving mother. I even see some of my peers that have a mother and father, but are heading in the wrong direction. Some of them are into drug-dealing and others try to be "cool" by not doing good in school and not going to classes. But my mother has instilled so many positive values in me it would be hard to even try to get on the wrong track. (Suskind, 1998, p. 107)[1]

Blended Families

The majority of divorced parents eventually remarry. When they do, they and their children become members of a **blended family,** a family in which an original parent-and-children family structure expands to include a new parent figure and any children for which he or she has custody. Approximately 1 out of every 5 married couples with children under the age of 18 lives in a "step" or blended family (Furstenberg & Cherlin, 1991).

As is true for all family configurations, children in blended families experience unique benefits and challenges. A new adult may bring additional income to the family and can help with household duties and child care. Children can forge relationships with a new parent figure and, possibly, new brothers and sisters. Yet children may feel that they must now share their parent's time and affections with a new spouse. They may believe, too, that the new stepparent is interfering with a possible reunion of the divorced parents and that by showing affection to the stepparent, they are being disloyal to their nonresident parent (Papernow, 1988). For a family to blend successfully, it must establish its own identity and traditions. It must decide how to spend money, divide household chores, prepare and serve meals, and celebrate holidays. It must also develop productive ways of expressing and resolving conflicts and agree upon rules and disciplinary techniques. In essence, the family must learn, very quickly, how to *act* like a family.

Although children from divorced and blended families are at somewhat higher risk for personal, social, and academic problems, in fact most children eventually adjust quite successfully to a blended family situation (Dawson, 1991; Furstenberg & Cherlin, 1991;

blended family
Family created when one parent-child(ren) family structure combines with another parent figure and any children in his or her custody.

---

[1]From *A Hope in the Unseen* by Ron Suskind, copyright © 1998 by Ron Suskind. Used by permission of Broadway Books, a division of Random House, Inc.

Hetherington et al., 1998). In one survey of blended families, 91% of parents and 81% of children reported a large amount of sharing in their family; 78% of parents and 66% of children described family relationships as close; and 67% of parents and children stated that family life was relaxed (Furstenberg, Nord, Peterson, & Zill, 1983). Relationships between stepparents and stepchildren are not always as close and affectionate as those between biological parents and children, and stepparents may have greater difficulty disciplining their stepchildren (Furstenberg et al., 1983; Hetherington et al., 1999). Yet in many instances stepparents soon become important parts of children's lives. In Figure 12–2, we present 9½-year-old Shea's Mother's Day poem to her stepmother Ann, who at that point had been a family member for about 3 years.

MOM is WOW

She is great at hide-and-seek
She takes me to look at an antique
I get to see her three times a week

MOM is WOW

She helped teach me multiplication
She encourages my imagination
She is involved when it comes to participation

MOM is WOW

She's a great stepmom, I guarantee
She lets us watch Disney TV
She is an important part of the family tree

MOM is WOW

No matter what, she is never late
If I have a question, she will demonstrate
When it comes to stepmoms, she's great

MOM is WOW

Adoption

Approximately 2 out of every 100 children in the United States are adopted (Zill, 1985). Half of these adoptions involve a child's relatives or stepparents; the other half are arranged through social services agencies, adoption agencies, attorneys, and other intermediaries (Stolley, 1993). Birth mothers who place their infants up for adoption are often young, single women from middle- or upper-income two-parent families who support the decision; women who choose to keep and parent their infants are more likely to come from lower-income, single-parent families (Stolley, 1993).

The last few decades have seen several changes in adoption practices (Center for the Future of Children, 1993). One growing practice is *open adoption,* in which the birth mother (and perhaps also the birth father) choose and meet the adopting family. Another is *international adoption,* whereby orphaned or relinquished children living in one country are adopted by families in another country. Furthermore, many adoption agencies now allow greater diversity in the people they deem to be suitable adoptive parents; the result is an increasing number of adoptive parents among single, older, gay, lesbian, and lower-income adults.

In recent years, international adoptions have become increasingly common. Many adoptive parents encourage their children to learn about their native cultures as well as the cultures of their adoptive homelands.

Although adopted children are at slightly greater risk for emotional, behavioral, and academic problems than children raised by their biological parents, the great majority of adopted children thrive and grow up to be well-adjusted individuals (Brodzinsky, 1993). Adoptive children seem to cope best when family members talk openly about the adoption yet provide the same love and nurturance that they would offer any biological offspring.

Foster Care

In *foster care,* children are placed with families through a legal but temporary arrangement. As of 1992, 429,000 children in the United States were in foster care, representing an increase of 53% since 1987 (McKenzie, 1993). Tragically, parental substance abuse has been a major factor in the recent increase in the number of children in foster care.

Many children in foster care are available for adoption. However, because most adoptive parents prefer adopting newborn infants, foster children often become "the children who wait" (McKenzie, 1993). Thus, their living arrangements are interminably temporary, with frequent shifts from one family to another. Such a transitory existence is particularly detrimental when children have already faced other challenges, perhaps neglect, abuse, abandonment, or early exposure to drugs or HIV when living with their biological parents.

Fortunately, some children in foster care are eventually adopted, sometimes by their foster parents and sometimes by other adults who are willing or eager to adopt older children. If these children have not had a history of stable, consistent, and loving care, they may be angry or irritable and may have trouble forming close emotional ties with their adoptive parents. Furthermore, foster children, including those who are adopted later on, have a higher-than-average need for special services either within or outside of school. Fortunately, many parents who adopt older children with special needs have had previous experience as foster parents and become skilled parents and effective advocates for their children (McKenzie, 1993).

Other Family Configurations

Our discussion of family configurations has not been an exhaustive list; some children experience unique variations on these configurations or live in other family configurations altogether. For instance, a growing number of children live with gay or lesbian parents. (As we write this book, Jeanne's daughter Tina is a teaching intern in a first-grade class in which 4 of the 15 students have two gay or lesbian parents.) Children who have gay and lesbian parents are as intelligent and well adjusted as other children, and the majority grow up to be heterosexual adults (Bailey, Bobrow, Wolfe, & Mikach, 1995; Faks, Filcher, Masterpasqua, & Joseph, 1995; Golombok & Tasker, 1996; Patterson, 1992).

In many cultural groups, especially among people of color, grandparents and other extended family members (perhaps aunts and uncles) assume central roles in the lives of children and may even serve as primary caregivers (Harrison et al. 1990; Stack & Burton, 1993). Many children of poor, single teenage mothers live with their grandmothers either in addition to or instead of with their mothers. Grandmothers tend to be less punitive and more responsive to children's needs than teen mothers are, and children have more economic stability, show greater self-reliance, and seem better able to resist engaging in drug abuse or vandalism (Chase-Lansdale, Brooks-Gunn, & Zamsky, 1994; Taylor & Roberts, 1995; Wilson, 1989). In some cultures, male members of the extended family serve as primary father figures for children (Engle & Breaux, 1998). For example, in Botswana, the mother's brother may play the role of father, and in Vietnam, an older male relative, such as a grandfather, may assume fatherly responsibilities.

Some children spend considerable time in a **cohabiting family**, in which a parent has an intimate but nonmarital partner living in the home (e.g., recall the case of Theo presented earlier). In 1995, almost 4 million cohabiting couples lived in the United States, and 80% of them were age 25 or older (U.S. Bureau of the Census, 1996). Cohabiting couples who have children are more likely to maintain a long-term relationship than couples without children (Wu, 1995). Little is known about the experiences of children with cohabiting parents, however. Like children in other family configurations, children with cohabiting parents probably adjust more favorably if their family circumstances are relatively stable and if both adults in the household establish and maintain warm, nurturant, and consistent relationships with them.

Educators and other professionals working with young people must remember that children's families, no matter how configured, are central features of children's lives. Yet we urge our readers not to jump to conclusions about children based on the particular family environments in which they live. Two-parent families are easily overromanticized as being the ideal situation (Furstenberg & Cherlin, 1991). In fact, there are many poorly functioning two-parent families, as well as many strong single-parent families who, like Barbara and Cedric Jennings, are sustained by friends, neighbors, extended family, and other community members. What undoubtedly matters most is not the *structure* of the family but the *relationships* that are formed within the family unit (Hetherington & Stanley-Hagan, 1999).

Educational Implications of Diverse Family Structures

Regardless of how they are structured, children's families are an integral part of who children are—and also who they perceive themselves to be—as human beings. The following recommendations suggest several ways in which teachers can both acknowledge and convey respect for the diversity of family structures that exist in today's society:

■ *When assigning activities that relate to students' family members, make them flexible enough to be relevant to a wide variety of family circumstances.* School activities and assignments sometimes involve doing something with, for, or about one or more family members. For instance, preschool classes sometimes invite parents for breakfast or lunch. In the elementary grades, children sometimes make cards for Mother's Day and Father's Day. In high school biology classes, students may be asked to trace the occurrence of dominant and recessive traits (e.g., brown eyes and blue eyes) in several generations of their family. Such tasks, though well intended, may disenfranchise students whose family circumstances (e.g., grandparent caregivers, single or same-sex parents, adoption by nonbiological parents) don't fit the traditional mold. With a little creativity, teachers can easily broaden such activities and assignments so that they accommodate students' diverse family structures. For instance, when Shea composed the Mother's Day card for her stepmother (Figure 12–2), her teacher gave her sufficient time to create that card in addition to the one she created for her mother. And consider the biology teacher who wants students to study the effects of heredity on various physical characteristics: Rather than singling out adopted children by giving them an alternative assignment, the teacher can be more inclusive by presenting data on several generations of a hypothetical biological family that *all* class members can analyze.

■ *Model and encourage acceptance of diverse family structures.* Occasionally students taunt or tease classmates from nontraditional families; for instance, gay and lesbian parents often worry that their children will be ridiculed because of their parents' sexual orientation (Hare, 1994). At the preschool and elementary levels, teachers can counteract such thoughtless behaviors by

cohabiting family
Family in which a parent and child(ren) live with the parent's nonmarital partner.

reading stories about children from a variety of family configurations and by frequently expressing the view that families are formed in many ways. At the secondary grades, students tend to be more informed and accepting about diverse family structures; nevertheless, teachers should keep an ear open for, and emphatically discourage, any derogatory comments about classmates' family circumstances.

It is important, too, to acknowledge the very central roles that extended family members (e.g., grandparents) play in many students' lives. Teachers and other school personnel should make room for and welcome such individuals to school open houses, student plays and concerts, parent-teacher groups, and other school events.

■ *Be especially supportive when children are undergoing major family transitions.* Many events can change a child's family configuration, including divorce, remarriage, departure of a parent's non-marital partner, death of a family member, or movement from one foster family to another. In each case, one or more old relationships may end, and one or more new relationships may begin. Children's and adolescents' adjustment to any major family transitions may take considerable time, and their feelings are likely to be ambivalent and somewhat changeable from one day to the next, underscoring the need for broad-based support from teachers and other caregivers for several months or perhaps even longer (Hetherington, 1999b). Other family members are likely to appreciate kind words and understanding as well, especially in the early weeks.

We urge educators to be especially proactive in reaching out to students who are living in foster care. Such children may be emotionally overburdened and have trouble asking for the assistance and comfort they need. Furthermore, they may have profound academic and social needs and may sometimes engage in behaviors that challenge even the most experienced of teachers. Nevertheless, foster children almost invariably benefit from a stable classroom environment, clear and consistent expectations for behavior, and their teachers' ongoing personal support.

Family Influences on Children

Parents and other family members have a powerful impact on children's lives. In this section we look at how typical parent behaviors (i.e., *parenting styles*) and parent employment affect children's cognitive and social-emotional development. We also look at how other family members, especially grandparents and siblings, affect children's social-emotional growth and well-being. Later, we consider the ways in which families nurture children's academic achievement—in other words, the ways in which families function as little "schoolhouses." Finally, we identify risk factors that affect families and can potentially lead to maltreatment of children.

Parenting Styles

Parents worldwide tend to be fairly warm and responsive to their children but also moderately demanding of them (Rohner & Rohner, 1981). However, parents differ dramatically in how warm and sensitive they are, on the one hand, and how controlling and demanding they are, on the other. Warmth and sensitivity to children's needs are, without doubt, qualities that should benefit children. The effects of control are not so straightforward. Excessive control may hinder children's ability to make choices, learn from mistakes, and develop a sense of competence and self-efficacy. Yet too little control may leave children without goals, a willingness to adhere to rules and conventions, or internalized standards for socially mature behavior.

The general patterns of behavior that parents use to nurture and guide their children—the affection they exhibit, their expectations for children's behavior, their methods of discipline, and so on—are known as **parenting styles.** In a series of landmark studies, Diana Baumrind and her colleagues investigated interpersonal relationships and disciplinary styles in families with preschool-aged children (Baumrind, 1967, 1971, 1980, 1989, 1991). Through interviews and observations, Baumrind (1967) classified parents as exhibiting one of three styles: authoritarian, authoritative, and permissive.

In **authoritarian parenting,** parents expect complete and immediate compliance. They neither negotiate expectations nor provide reasons for their requests ("Clean your room because I told you to—and I mean *now!*). Authoritarian parents also tend to be somewhat cool, aloof, and punitive with their children, and they expect children to act maturely at a young

parenting style
General pattern of behaviors that a parent uses to nurture and guide his or her children.

authoritarian parenting
Parenting style characterized by strict expectations for behavior and rigid rules that children are expected to obey without question.

age. Baumrind found that children of authoritarian parents had social-emotional difficulties, in that they were withdrawn, mistrusting, and unhappy. Other researchers have found that these children have low self-esteem, little self-reliance, and poor social skills, and in some cases they are overly aggressive with others (Coopersmith, 1967; Lamborn, Mounts, Steinberg, & Dornbusch, 1991; Maccoby & Martin, 1983; Simons, Whitbeck, Conger, & Conger, 1991).

In **authoritative parenting,** parents seek mature behavior from their children as well, but they do so in a warmer manner that incorporates give-and-take, explanations for why rules should be followed (recall our discussion of *induction* in Chapter 10), and respect for children's viewpoints ("OK, maybe you don't need to sort through your backpack *every* night, but we should come up with a schedule that prevents you from losing assignments and allows us to know what's going on at school. Can we both agree to every Wednesday and Saturday?"). Children of authoritative parents seemed to be the most well-adjusted children in Baumrind's studies. They appeared mature, friendly, energetic, self-confident in tackling new tasks, and able to resist distractions. Subsequent work has found that these children exhibit high self-esteem, considerable self-reliance, and good social skills; furthermore, they achieve at high levels academically, are well-behaved at school, and adjust more successfully to family trauma (Coopersmith, 1967; Dekovic & Janssens, 1992; Dornbusch, Ritter, Leiderman, Roberts, & Fraleigh, 1987; Hetherington & Clingempeel, 1992; Lamborn et al., 1991; Loeb, Horst, & Horton, 1980; Steinberg, Elmen, & Mounts, 1989). Such positive effects continue into the college years, where students who have enjoyed authoritative parenting show better adjustment, earn higher grades, and are more likely to persist at difficult tasks (Strage & Brandt, 1999).

In **permissive parenting,** parents wield little control over their children. Children act on their impulses with minimal parental restraint ("Fine. Just ignore what I say!"). In Baumrind's analysis, children of permissive parents appeared least competent overall. These children were immature, demanding and dependent on parents and, not surprisingly, disobedient when their parents did ask them to do something they did not want to do. Other investigators have found that these children have difficulty in school, are aggressive with peers, and engage in delinquent activities as adolescents (Lamborn et al., 1991; Pulkkinen, 1982).

In Baumrind's classification, a single emotional orientation—whether warm or indifferent—did not emerge for the permissive style. Since her initial work, however, other researchers have distinguished two groups of parents who exert few demands for mature behavior: (a) those who are reasonably caring but lax in their efforts to guide and control children and (b) those who are inattentive or indifferent to their children's needs for affection (Maccoby & Martin, 1983). Baumrind's original permissive parents probably fit the first scenario, in that they were more indulgent than indifferent. Permissive parents are nurturing and affectionate, but they relinquish decisions to children (even fairly young ones) about when to go to bed, what chores (if any) to do around the house, and what curfews to abide by.

The second scenario reflects what researchers have called **uninvolved parenting.** Like permissive parents, uninvolved parents make few demands on their children, but they also respond to their children in an uncaring and rejecting manner. Children of uninvolved, indifferent parents show problems related to school achievement, emotional control, tolerance for frustration, and adolescent delinquency (Lamborn et al., 1991; Simons, Robertson, & Downs, 1989). When parental neglect is extreme, it becomes a form of maltreatment, which we examine in more detail later in the chapter.

The four parenting styles just described have implications for teachers, whose students have been influenced by the affection and structure they've received at home. Table 12–1 summarizes and illustrates the four styles and offers suggestions for classroom teachers.

Which parenting style appears most effective in promoting children's social, emotional, and intellectual development? Theorists and researchers have almost unanimously chosen the authoritative style. An authoritative style may have positive influences for several reasons. First, parents convey the message that children must live up to appropriate standards but at the same time are valued family members with important needs and perspectives; such a message almost certainly enhances children's self-esteem. Second, by providing the reasons behind rules, parents help children focus on the consequences of their actions for themselves and others and so help them understand and internalize society's rules and customs (Hess & McDevitt, 1984). Third, by being caring and sensitive, authoritative parents create a peaceful, secure environment and thereby instill in their children a desire to

authoritative parenting
Parenting style characterized by emotional warmth, high expectations and standards for behavior, consistent enforcement of rules, explanations regarding the reasons behind these rules, and the inclusion of children in decision making.

permissive parenting
Parenting style characterized by emotional warmth but few expectations or standards for children's behavior.

uninvolved parenting
Parenting style characterized by a lack of emotional support and a lack of standards regarding appropriate behavior.

TABLE 12–1 Parenting Styles

PARENTING STYLE	DESCRIPTION	CHILDREN'S TYPICAL CHARACTERISTICS	EXAMPLE	IMPLICATION
Authoritarian Parenting	Parents convey relatively little emotional warmth, hold high expectations for their children's behaviors, establish rules of behavior without regard for children's needs, expect rules to be obeyed without question, and allow little give-and-take in parent-child discussions.	• Unhappy • Anxious • Low in self-confidence • Lacking initiative • Dependent on others • Lacking in social skills and altruistic behaviors • Coercive in dealing with others • Defiant	A third-grade girl hovers around her peers on the playground. She alternates between barking orders (which the others ignore) and retreating to be on her own.	When students display characteristics consistent with an authoritarian home, adopt an authori*tative* style in the classroom, showing emotional warmth, soliciting students' perspectives on classroom rules and procedures, and focusing on the reasons why certain behaviors are unacceptable. Keep in mind that authoritarian parenting styles at home may be adaptive in some cultural settings and in economically impoverished neighborhoods.
Authoritative Parenting	Parents provide a loving, supportive home environment, hold high expectations and standards for their children's behavior, enforce household rules consistently, explain why some behaviors are acceptable and others are not, and include children in family decision making.	• Happy • Self-confident • Curious • Independent and self-reliant • Well-behaved at school • Effective social skills • Likable • Respectful of others • Successful in school	During a middle-school parent-teacher conference, a father looks directly at his daughter and asks her why she has been disruptive in class recently and what she thinks she should do to improve her behavior.	When students display characteristics consistent with an authoritative home, employ a similar style at school, giving them input into classroom decision making and explaining the reasons for your expectations and actions. Provide age-appropriate opportunities for independent activities and decision making.

reciprocate with similar behaviors (Lewis, 1981; Sroufe & Fleeson, 1986). Finally, children may generalize the give-and-take of an authoritative household to their own negotiations with peers and authority figures and so cultivate greater social sensitivity and skill. In classrooms and on the playground, children of authoritative parents know that rules exist for a reason, exceptions are sometimes possible, and everyone has a right to voice an opinion. Authoritative parenting predicts healthy peer relationships in children and may be particularly beneficial with children who are resistant to following rules and so are difficult to manage (Hinshaw, Zupan, Simmel, Nigg, & Melnick, 1997).

Factors Affecting Use of Parenting Styles With all the good news about authoritative parenting, why don't all parents use it? One reason is that the ways in which parents express their affection and discipline their children are culturally defined. Children of authoritative parents appear well-adjusted, in part, because they fit well with ideal roles defined in Western cultures: They listen respectfully to others, follow rules at a reasonably young age, try to be independent, and strive for academic achievement. But control and warmth are expressed differently in different cultures, and particular parenting styles may be suited to values and customs that parents endorse. As an example of cultural variation, children of very controlling (and so apparently "authoritarian") Asian American parents do quite well in school (Chao, 1994; Dornbusch et al., 1987; Lin & Fu, 1990). In many Asian American families, high demands for obedience are made within the context of a close, supportive mother-child relationship (Chao, 1994). Furthermore, principles of Confucianism teach children that parents are always right and that obedience and emotional restraint are essential for family harmony (Chao, 1994).

PARENTING STYLE	DESCRIPTION	CHILDREN'S TYPICAL CHARACTERISTICS	EXAMPLE	IMPLICATION
Permissive Parenting	Parents provide a loving, supportive home environment, hold few expectations or standards for their children's behavior, rarely punish inappropriate behavior, and allow their children to make many of their own decisions (e.g., about eating, bedtime).	• Selfish • Unmotivated • Dependent on others • Demanding of attention • Disobedient • Impulsive	A high school student expects his teacher to immediately grade a class research paper he turned in a month late.	When students display characteristics consistent with a permissive home, be warm but firm about expectations for behavior and consistently apply rewards for obedience and sanctions for disobedience. Explain the reasons why certain behaviors are unacceptable, focusing on their potential impact on self and others.
Uninvolved Parenting	Parents provide little if any emotional support for their children, hold few expectations or standards for their children's behavior, have little interest in their children's lives, and seem overwhelmed by their own problems.	• Disobedient • Demanding • Low in self-control • Low in tolerance for frustration • Lacking long-term goals	A kindergarten child has a difficult time adjusting to school, appears angry during class activities, and impulsively rips the pages out of a book she doesn't like.	When students display characteristics consistent with the home of uninvolved parents, be firm in expectations for behavior and administration of consequences, but do so in a way that conveys caring, concern, and respect for students' needs and rights. Explain why some behaviors are not in students' best interest and so will not be tolerated.

Sources: Baumrind, 1971, 1989; Dekovic & Janssens, 1992; Lamborn et al., 1991; Maccoby & Martin, 1983; Simons et al., 1991; Steinberg, 1993; Steinberg et al., 1989.

A second reason that an authoritative parenting style is not universal is that the contexts of parents' lives do not always foster it. Parents may have learned different decision-making styles in the workplace and in the home environments in which they themselves grew up. Furthermore, economic hardship, career pressures, marital discord, and other family stresses may seep into parents' interactions with children (Katz & Gottman, 1991; Russell & Russell, 1994). For instance, when parents live in neighborhoods where danger potentially lurks around every corner, such as in some inner-city neighborhoods, parents may better serve their children by being very strict and directive about activities (Hale-Benson, 1986; McLoyd, 1998b). In some cases, the stresses of impoverished financial resources become so overwhelming as to limit parents' ability to enjoy their children's companionship and seek their children's ideas about family rules (Bronfenbrenner, Alvarez, & Henderson, 1984). Communicating high standards for behavior and negotiating rules with children take considerable energy and resolve—perhaps more energy and resolve than some people under various types of stress can manage.

Children's temperaments affect parenting styles as well. For instance, children with mild temperaments may elicit calm and reasoned behavior from parents, whereas more spirited, irritable, or rebellious children may provoke parents to clamp down firmly on frequent misbehavior (Eisenberg & Fabes, 1994; Harris, 1995, 1998; Scarr, 1993). Developmental psychologist Judith Harris (1998) has described her experiences with her own two children:[2]

> I . . . reared a pair of very different children. My older daughter hardly ever wanted to do anything that her father and I didn't want her to do. My younger daughter often did. Raising the first was easy; raising the second was, um, interesting. . . .

_____

[2]Reprinted with the permission of The Free Press, a Division of Simon & Schuster, Inc., from *The Nurture Assumption: Why Children Turn Out the Way They Do* by Judith Rich Harris. Copyright © 1998 by Judith Rich Harris.

. . . How can you treat two children both the same when they *aren't* the same—when they do different things and say different things, have different abilities and different personalities? . . .

. . . I would have been pegged as a permissive parent with my first child, a bossy one with my second. . . .

. . . My husband and I seldom had hard-and-fast rules with our first child; generally we didn't need them. With our second child we had all sorts of rules and none of them worked. Reason with her? Give me a break. Often we ended up taking the shut-your-mouth-and-do-what-you're-told route. That didn't work either. In the end we pretty much gave up. Somehow we all made it through her teens. (Harris, 1998, pp. 26, 48)

Not only are parents often inconsistent from one child to the next, but they are sometimes inconsistent in how they interact with any single child. In particular, parents may exert considerable control about certain aspects of a child's behavior yet be quite permissive in other domains (Costanzo & Fraenkel, 1987). For instance, in raising their three children, Jeanne and her husband consistently held high expectations for academic performance and prosocial behavior; they were more lax about making sure the children completed household chores or arrived home in time for dinner. Such inconsistencies in parenting style probably reflect the fact that parents feel more strongly about certain behaviors than others (Costanzo & Fraenkel, 1987).

Now that we have made a case for the benefits of authoritative parenting, we must back up a bit and tell you that parenting styles do not appear to have a *strong* effect on children's personalities and social-emotional well-being (Maccoby & Martin, 1983; Weiss & Schwartz, 1996). In fact, children appear to thrive with parents who exhibit a wide variety of parenting styles, provided that their homes aren't severely neglectful or abusive: Most parents provide "good-enough" homes that promote children's social-emotional growth (Harris, 1995, 1998; Lykken, 1997; Scarr, 1992).

Furthermore, research on the potential effects of parenting styles is almost exclusively correlational in nature, so that true cause-effect relationships are very difficult to establish.[3] An alternative explanation for correlations between parents' ways of interacting with their children, on the one hand, and children's personalities and behaviors, on the other, is that parents who treat their children well have well-behaving children not because they use effective parenting styles but because the parents pass along good-behavior genes to their children (Harris, 1995, 1998). Developmental researchers still have a long way to go in teasing apart the relative effects of heredity and environment (and their interactions) in family dynamics.

Effects of Parent Employment

In 1940, only 10% of children lived with a mother who was employed outside the home; by 1990, almost 60% had mothers who were so employed (Hernandez, 1997). When we consider school-age children, the number is even higher; for instance, in 1995, nearly 75% of mothers of school-age children were in the workforce (U.S. Bureau of the Census, 1995). One implication of this trend is that, in comparison with earlier times, children spend less time supervised directly by their parents. Parents rely on a range of backup systems, including daycare, after-school programs, and the good will of friends and extended family members. Sometimes parents have little choice but to let their children tend to their own needs for a few hours. Such **self-care** was often the only option for Barbara and Cedric Jennings:

One day in late August, after Cedric and Barbara trolled a few thrift stores, they began walking the streets on all sides of the apartment. Barbara spoke to Cedric in careful, measured words. "You're gonna be a big kindergartner next week. And I got to be going back to get a job, when you're at school. Now, walking back from school, I don't want you to be talking to anyone, understand?"

He nodded, picking up on her seriousness. Then she squatted next to him, so their faces were side by side, and she pointed across the street. "See that man over there?" she said firmly. "He's a drug dealer. He sometimes asks kids to do things. Don't ever talk to him. He's a friend of the devil." Block by block, corner by corner they went, until she'd pointed out every drug dealer for five blocks in either direction. Later that night, she slowly explained the daily drill. After school, he would walk by himself to the apartment, double lock the door, and immediately call her—the number would be taped by the phone. And, along the way, he would talk to no one.

---

self-care
Taking care of one's own needs (cooking, doing chores, etc.) before or after school while parents are at work.

[3]If you have read Chapter 2, then you should recall that only *experimental studies* can conclusively demonstrate cause-effect relationships, and such studies are logistically impractical and ethically questionable as a means of studying the effects of children's home environments.

The first day of school arrived. She'd bought him an outfit specially for the day: blue slacks and a white shirt. She walked him over to Henry T. Blow Elementary, which was just behind their apartment.

"Here, I got something for you." She took from her purse a fake gold chain with a key on one end and put it around his neck.

"This, so you won't lose it."

"Ma," he said, already conscious of his appearance, "can I wear it underneath?"

She nodded, and he slipped it inside the crew neck of his white shirt. Years later, he would recall that dangling key—the metal cold against his smooth chest—and think ruefully about how exhilarating it felt: a first, cool breeze of freedom. (Suskind, 1998, p. 32)[4]

Many children come home to an empty house or apartment after school and tend to their own needs until their parents finish work.

Like Cedric, many children care for themselves after (and sometimes before) school while their parents are working. Many children in self-care (who are sometimes known as *latchkey children*) do well: They check in with parents by phone, make themselves a snack, do chores, and start their homework. Others become fearful and lonely (Long & Long, 1982) or may "care" for themselves unwisely, perhaps by participating in risky activities, partaking in alcohol and other mind-altering substances, or spending long hours playing video games or watching television. Self-care arrangements appear more effective when parents explain safety procedures, convey expectations for behavior when home alone, and monitor children's activities by phone (Galambos & Maggs, 1991; Steinberg, 1986). (We will explore self-care in more depth in Chapter 14.)

Parents' employment influences children's development in a very different way as well. In the workplace, parents encounter certain kinds of decision-making practices—perhaps collaborative decisions that consider the needs of everyone, on the one hand, or top-down "Do what I tell you" mandates, on the other—and such practices filter down to the home front (Crouter, 1994; Kohn, 1977). Middle-income jobs often require a fair amount of consultation with others, and people employed in such positions typically have a fair amount of autonomy and opportunity for independent decision making. Lower-income jobs more often place demands for punctuality and compliance to prespecified routines. Parents in both income groups seem to prepare their children to fit into existing income tracks, with middle-income parents valuing self-direction in their children and lower-income parents seeking immediate conformity to authority.

Through their employment, parents also serve as effective role models for their children, in that they are responsible, working citizens who are presumably contributing to the greater good of society. Girls whose mothers are employed outside the home are more likely to perceive women as having numerous career options and rewarding lives (Williams & Radin, 1993). Daughters also seem to develop their own career aspirations in part from watching their mothers' professional accomplishments. Work can interfere with effective parenting, however, especially when job pressures elevate stress levels at home and when parents must work excessively long hours (Moorehouse, 1991).

Influences of Grandparents

Many grandparents have the luxury of maintaining warm and loving relationships with their grandchildren while leaving issues of behavior control and discipline to the parents. Such nonjudgmental relationships can be quite beneficial for children. For example, child psychiatrist Arthur Kornhaber noticed that one of his patients, a boy named Billy, was typically very hyperactive but was "more relaxed, less agitated, and less impulsive" with his grandmother (Kornhaber, 1996, p. 1). Dr. Kornhaber made some observations:

What happened between Billy and his grandmother that transformed his behavior? Was Billy aware of how differently he behaved in the presence of his grandmother? I decided to find out. During our next session I asked him to draw a picture of his family and tell me about his drawing. Billy drew his family as a three-layered pyramid. He was on top, running after a football. His

---

[4]From *A Hope in the Unseen* by Ron Suskind, copyright © 1998 by Ron Suskind. Used by permission of Broadway Books, a division of Random House, Inc.

Grandparents are important parts of many children's lives.

parents were underneath, in the center layer, watching him play, and "saying how well he played." On the bottom of the pyramid Billy placed his grandparents, looking up at him adoringly. "They are watching me play football and are happy that I am happy," Billy explained, "and my parents are happy because I am a good football player."

Although he didn't know it, and I wasn't totally aware of it at the time, Billy had put his finger on an important difference in the way parents and grandparents love their children. His grandparents were happy that he was joyful; his parents were pleased because he was performing well. The former is love without condition, the latter is tinged with approval for performance. (Kornhaber, 1996, p. 2)

Not all children are as fortunate as Billy, however. Although some grandparents have close, meaningful relationships with their grandchildren, others are distant pen pals or even completely absent (Kornhaber, 1996).

Grandparents aren't always able to choose their level of involvement in grandchildren's lives. When parents divorce, grandparents on the noncustodial parent's side of the family may be completely shut out of their grandchildren's lives. Yet in other circumstances (e.g., when a child's parents are neglectful, imprisoned, or incapacitated by illness or substance abuse), grandparents become primary caregivers for their grandchildren (Burton, 1992; Minkler & Roe, 1992). Grandparents often take on the responsibility with mixed feelings: Although they are grateful for the close and intimate relationships they can have with their grandchildren, they also worry about the limited energy and financial resources they have to raise another generation and regret the lifestyle changes that their new parenting responsibilities require (Cox, 2000; Kornhaber, 1996).

Influences of Siblings

Over the past 150 years, the size of American families has dropped considerably. For instance, in 1865, 82% of adolescents lived in families with five or more children; by 1930, 57% of adolescents lived in families with three or fewer children. Within that same 65-year period, the average (median) number of siblings for adolescents dropped from 7.3 to 2.6 children (Hernandez, 1997).

For many children, siblings are an important part of family life. Children are often deeply attached to their siblings and rely on them for comfort when anxious or upset (Bank, 1992; Stewart, 1983). In our society, older siblings often assume caretaking responsibilities for young children when their parents go shopping or do brief errands; in many other societies, older children are the primary caregivers for their younger brothers and sisters for a significant part of the day (Parke & Buriel, 1998; Weisner & Gallimore, 1977). Furthermore, older siblings serve as role models (e.g., this is how you ask your parents to buy you something) and playmates for younger children (Barr, 1999). They may also teach young children new skills (e.g., tying shoes), although they are less likely to be patient tutors than parents (Perez-Granados & Callanan, 1997). At school, teachers can certainly take advantage of the close-knit relationships with siblings that some of their students enjoy. For instance, in times of family crisis (e.g., a beloved grandparent dying or a parent going to prison), students may appreciate contact with siblings during the school day, perhaps on the playground, in the lunchroom, or in the nurse's office.

Sibling relationships are not always constructive ones, however. Resentment may brew if one child feels slighted by a parent who appears to favor another (Brody, Stoneman, & McCoy, 1994). Children may also feel jealous or displaced when, with age, their siblings increasingly form friendships outside the family circle (Dunn, 1996). In addition, parents and other adults often compare children within a family, and some children may consistently come up short ("Why can't you get good grades like your sister Lucy?"). In response to such comparisons, children sometimes carve their own niches in the family and perhaps in the larger social sphere as well (e.g., "I'm the musician in the family; my brother is the athlete"; Huston, 1983).

Children's individual family experiences depend somewhat on their birth order—that is, on whether they were born first, second, or somewhere later down the line. Older children tend to have a slight advantage academically, perhaps because of the exclusive time they had with their parents before any brothers or sisters came along (Zajonc & Mullally, 1997). Younger children show greater skill in interacting with peers, perhaps as a result of experience in negotiating daily with older siblings and learning how to outmaneuver the older children to gain parental attention and family resources (Dunn, 1984; Miller & Maruyama, 1976). Even preschool-age siblings discuss their wants and desires with one another, and such discussions may help promote the perspective taking we spoke of in Chapter 10 (Dunn, 1993; Perner, Ruffman, & Leekam, 1994; Ruffman, Perner, Naito, Parkin, & Clements, 1998).

Yet sibling relationships are not essential for healthy development. **Only children**—children without brothers or sisters—are often stereotyped as spoiled and egotistical, but research patterns on their adjustment are complimentary. On average, only children perform well in school and enjoy particularly close relationships with their parents (Falbo, 1992; Falbo & Polit, 1986).

Families as Little Schoolhouses

In a sense, families are little "schoolhouses" for children. Through their families, children learn about people, the world, and future opportunities. These lessons color children's understandings and interpretations of events, social relationships, tasks, and expectations at school: Should authority figures be feared, respected, or befriended? What are books used for? Is intellectual curiosity valued? Will I go to college? What careers might I pursue?

Family Influences on Children's Achievement Often, children acquire the foundations for school tasks and subject matter at home; for instance, they learn basic purposes and patterns of language, reading materials, art, music, computer technology, and scientific and mathematical thinking (Hess & Holloway, 1984; Scott-Jones, 1991; also see the section "Emergent Literacy" in Chapter 8). To some degree, these important lessons occur before children ever set foot in a formal classroom. When children do enter school, their parents, guardians, and siblings continue to offer ways to think about schooling—how to behave, what goals to strive for, how hard to try, what to do in the face of obstacles, and so on. Increasingly, parents also influence children by consciously selecting a school for them from a myriad of choices, including public schools, private schools, charter schools, home schooling, or schools that embody particular cultural values, such as African-centered education (Madhubuti & Madhubuti, 1994).

Many parents deliberately prepare their children for academic endeavors. Some parents, especially those who are well educated and financially comfortable, immerse their children in highly verbal and technologically rich environments that include sophisticated language, stimulating books and toys, and age-appropriate computer programs. They also encourage their children to explore their environments through manipulation of complex objects, engagement in exploratory play activities, and trips to museums and other educationally enriching sites. Numerous studies indicate that richer home environments and experiences are associated with more advanced cognitive, linguistic, and academic development (Bradley & Caldwell, 1984; Brooks-Gunn et al., 1996; Ericsson & Chalmers, 1994; Gottfried et al., 1994; Hart & Risley, 1995; Hess & Holloway, 1984; Jimerson et al., 1999; McGowan & Johnson, 1984). Keep in mind, however, that these studies are typically correlational rather than experimental and so do not show conclusively that academically rich home environments have a direct influence on cognitive development.

Parents almost certainly nurture their children's classroom performance in another way as well: by modeling particular ways of engaging in academic tasks and subject matter (e.g., Bandura, 1986). (This idea should remind you of the social-cognitive perspective of socialization described earlier.) As one example, children are better readers when their parents read

only child
A child without siblings.

MY FATHER

Choosing my idol was very easy for me. It was easy for me because of how successful he is now and where he came from. In Ireland in the mid Fifties my idol was born. He was born to a poor family. His father was a company sergeant in the Irish army. His father volunteered for the United Nations and went all the way to the Congo to maintain peace. He was injured in an attack on the Leopoldville airforce base in the Congo. . . .

My idol lived in a two-bed room apartment on the military grounds. His Mom stayed home to look after him and his sister. My idol worked very hard in school. He made good choices. While some of his friends were playing soccer he was working hard and studying. Now after all that hard work he is a Dean of Education. He has two excellent children (especially the older one). He is my Father.

My dad got as far as he is in many ways. The one he thinks is the most important thing in getting him the furthest in life is the fact that his parents every night made him study and do homework. Sometimes he did not like having to do all the homework because he missed out on the fun. Now he says it is the education that got him so far. All of his friends would walk by his house and have a good time and ask him if he could come out. . . . He says that I should do my homework before friends and do it right because an education is very important. Without a good education you cannot do much.

After working hard in secondary (high) school, he got a scholarship to go to college. Without the scholarship he could not have gone to college because his family could not afford to send him. Going to college was a big deal because not many Catholics at that time in that country went to college. College would be a big responsibility for him. He also made a choice to go to a predominately Protestant college, even though he was a Catholic. One consequence of this was that the Christian Brothers (teachers) in his high school were mad at him. He persevered and attended Trinity College Dublin.

In college he joined the rowing club. Rowing had many consequences for him. He made new friends, traveled the country, and became very fit. Another consequence for him was that he would be very tired after rowing. Sometimes he and his friends were so tired they couldn't ride their bikes home from practice. They would have to walk! He was very persistent. He also ran on the cross-country team. These sports could have affected him and his grades but he studied hard. He said that, "you have to have priorities." He had a responsibility to his grades. He got a degree in psychology.

What have I learned from my Dad's experiences? He came from a poor background to be very successful. From his background you could not have predicted his job or his success (or how wonderful his children are). What were the keys to his success? He studied hard, had goals and priorities, and was persistent. If I could do something similar I would probably study as hard as I could. Also I would try as hard as he did in school. He is trying to teach me the same values and work ethic. I would like to have his values. However, sometimes it's hard for me to devote time to studying. There's lots of distractions, especially friends, Nintendo, and sports. I'm trying my best.

frequently at home (Hess & McDevitt, 1989). The composition in Figure 12–3 describes what 13-year-old Connor learned from his father about hard work and schooling. Connor had been asked to "Write an essay describing your idol" as part of an interdisciplinary unit on choices and responsibilities.

Family Involvement in Children's Education In the opening case study, Barbara Jennings intervened when Cedric unfairly received a B from his physics teacher. Barbara was involved in her son's education in other ways as well: She regularly attended parent-teacher-student meetings, made sure Cedric did his homework, and helped him with his assignments whenever she had the knowledge and skills to do so. Parents and other family members are more likely to become involved in children's education when they believe that (a) their involvement is necessary or important, (b) they can exert a positive influence on their children's educational achievement, and (c) school personnel want their involvement (Clark, 1983; Hoover-Dempsey & Sandler, 1997; Lareau, 1989).

Generally speaking, family involvement in children's education is a good thing (Hoover-Dempsey & Sandler, 1997). Parents and other family members may do a variety of things at home related to children's learning and activities at school; for instance, they might discuss school activities, assist with homework (or at least nag children to do it), lavish praise or give feedback about in-class projects and assignments, and confer with teachers on the telephone about children's classroom performance and progress. Some parents also contribute to the activities and success of their children's schools as a whole, perhaps by helping to chaperone field trips, participating in fund-raising activities, or serving on parent advisory boards. Students whose parents are involved in school activities have better attendance records, higher achievement, and more positive attitudes toward school than students whose parents are not actively involved; this difference exists even when the prior school performance of both groups of students has been the same (Chavkin, 1993; Eccles & Harold, 1993; Epstein, 1996; Hoover-Dempsey & Sandler, 1997; Jimerson et al., 1999). Students with actively involved parents are also more likely to graduate from high school (Rumberger, 1995).

Naturally, not all parent involvement is constructive (Hoover-Dempsey & Sandler, 1997). One can imagine assistance that is ill suited to children's developmental needs, such as parents insisting that their average-ability second grader do advanced algebra at home "for fun" or hovering over a high school student while he completes his homework assignments, thereby taking from him an opportunity to develop self-regulatory skills. Granting such exceptions, it is still the case that, in general, active parent involvement predicts good academic outcomes for children.

As teachers quickly discover, some parents eagerly and actively participate in their children's education, whereas other parents have little or no involvement. Numerous factors account for such differences, including parents' work schedules and other obligations, child-care responsibilities, health and energy levels, access to transportation, and emotional well-being. A few parents seem to have little interest in their children's welfare (see the earlier discussion of uninvolved parenting). Other parents believe that they are unwelcome at school or unlikely to make a difference in their children's academic progress (Carr, 1997; Hoover-Dempsey & Sandler, 1997). Later in the chapter we consider numerous strategies for encouraging such parents to become more involved in their children's schooling.

Taking Cultural Differences into Account In Chapter 4, we introduced the idea of an *apprenticeship* as a mechanism through which adults gradually teach children new skills. Across all cultures, children serve as apprentices to their parents; as such, they are slowly and steadily guided toward fuller participation in adult activities and practices (Rogoff, 1990). Individual cultures and family legacies determine what tools and procedures children are exposed to, whether they are explicitly taught or instead learn from observation and eavesdropping, and how early they take on particular responsibilities.

When teachers are not familiar with the cultural norms of their students' families, values and practices that are nourished on the home front may be misconstrued at school. Consider the child who is taught at home to be docile, respectful, and conforming in interactions with adults. A teacher who expects lively and talkative behavior from students may incorrectly interpret the child's behaviors as reflecting a lack of motivation, intelligence, or social skills. Consider, too, the child who is taught at home that cooperation and helping others are more important than individual achievement. A teacher who expects all students to work independently on classroom assignments may, upon seeing the child help a classmate during "independent seatwork time," erroneously conclude that the child is cheating.

Students are most likely to succeed at school when teaching strategies in the classroom are similar to those used at home. An example of instruction that builds on families' cultural practices is the Kamehameha Elementary Education Program, or KEEP (Au, 1997; Tharp & Gallimore, 1988). Designed to enhance the educational achievement of ethnic-minority Hawaiian children who are risk for academic failure, the KEEP program is organized around activity centers, at which teachers strive to offer activities that appropriately challenge each student's existing cognitive capabilities. All children attend "Center One," which focuses on reading and language development; they then rotate through other centers designed to meet the students' varying backgrounds and talents. Teachers adjust their instructional style to match the communication styles that children and their families use at home. For example, cooperation and harmony are central cultural values in the Hawaiian community; consistent with such values, the teachers assemble small groups of children and encourage them to cooperate on assignments (Jordan, 1981; Weisner, Gallimore, & Jordan, 1988). In addition, the teachers try to match the children's customary conversational style:

> The group discussion pattern for Hawaiian children's instructional conversations is characterized by rapid-fire responses, liveliness, mutual participation, interruptions, over-lapping volunteered speech, and joint narration. Children build on one another's responses to create a pattern of "group speech." Teachers in the KEEP lessons do not require the children to speak one at a time, but allow them to cooperate with one another to frame answers to questions. (Tharp & Gallimore, 1988, p. 151)

Developing culturally compatible teaching practices requires considerable familiarity with the cultural practices of students and their families. Teachers can learn a great deal about such practices by discussing local customs and values with parents and other family members, as well as by becoming active participants in (and open-minded observers of) the day-to-day, nonacademic activities of the local community.

Risk Factors in Families

As you have seen, "good" families—those that foster children's physical, cognitive, and social-emotional development—come in a wide variety of packages. Not all parents and other caregivers provide optimal environments for children, however. Some have such limited financial resources that they cannot afford adequate food, housing, or medical care. Others are so overwhelmed by crises in their own lives (marital conflict, loss of employment, life-threatening illness, etc.) that they have little time or energy to devote to their children. Still others, including many uninvolved parents, suffer from serious psychological problems (e.g., depression or schizophrenia) or have immersed themselves in a self-destructive lifestyle of alcohol or drug abuse.

Some children successfully rise above such environments to become productive, well-adjusted adults. For example, a child may be able to adjust to a parent's mental illness if other family members are affectionate and dependable. (You saw one instance of this situation in the opening case study about Mary in Chapter 9.) We will look at the conditions that promote such *resiliency* in Chapter 14.

Unfortunately, many other children suffer long-term consequences of unhealthy family environments. For example, when parents have psychological problems, such as chronic mental illness, children show difficulties in adjustment and may themselves exhibit externalizing behaviors, such as aggression, or internalizing behaviors, such as anxiety or depression (McHale & Rasmussen, 1998; Zahn-Waxler, Mayfield, Radke-Yarrow, McKnew, Cytryn, & Davenport, 1988). The more family stresses children are exposed to, the more vulnerable they appear to become (Sameroff, Seifer, Barocas, Zax, & Greenspan, 1987). As Garbarino and Abramowitz (1992c) aptly put it, "Risk accumulates in the child's life like a poison" (p. 22).

The most serious consequence of an unhealthy family environment is, of course, *child maltreatment*. Maltreatment takes four major forms (English, 1998; Thompson & Wyatt, 1999). **Neglect** occurs when caregivers fail to provide food, clothing, shelter, health care, or basic affection and do not adequately supervise children's activities. Caregivers engage in **physical abuse** when they intentionally cause physical harm to children, perhaps by kicking, biting, shaking, or punching them. If spanking causes serious bruises or injuries, it, too, is considered physical abuse. Caregivers engage in **sexual abuse** when they seek sexual gratification from children through acts such as genital contact or pornography. They engage in **emotional abuse** when they consistently ignore, isolate, reject, denigrate, or terrorize children or when they corrupt children by encouraging them to engage in substance abuse or criminal activity. Sadly, some parents and other caregivers submit children to more than one form of abuse, as one woman's recollection illustrates:

> My father used to do the weirdest things to me. I hate him. He was in the navy, back in the war and stuff like that. I guess he picked up weird things like that. He used to put me in the corner and put a bag over my head and every time he'd walk by he'd kick me—just like a dog. My mom

neglect
Failure to provide the basic necessities for children's health, safety, and emotional well-being.

physical abuse
Intentionally causing physical harm to another.

sexual abuse
Seeking sexual gratification from a child or adolescent.

emotional abuse
Ongoing pattern of total disregard for children's feelings and social and moral behaviors (e.g., isolating, terrorizing, or corrupting children).

Most caregivers who abuse their children suffer from serious psychological problems.

told me once he put a tick on my stomach and let the tick suck my blood. Things like that— really gross, things that a father would never do to their (sic) daughter. He'd stick toothpicks up my fingernails until it would bleed. [Did he sexually abuse you, too?] Oh, yeah. When I was six. Had to get me to the hospital. I had twenty stitches. I just can't talk about it. (Belenky, Clinchy, Goldberger, & Tarule, 1986, p. 159)

The perpetrators of child maltreatment are, in most cases, individuals who themselves suffer serious psychological problems. They tend to have low self-esteem and to be anxious, depressed, aggressive, and impulsive (National Research Council, 1993b; Thompson & Wyatt, 1999). Some suffer from emotional illness; others have serious substance abuse problems (Kienberger-Jaudes, Ekwo, & Van Voorhis, 1995; Thompson & Wyatt, 1999). Many have little or no contact with or support from family or friends and so are socially and emotionally isolated (Thompson & Wyatt, 1999). Some abusive parents are quite naive about children's development and hold unrealistic expectations about what their children should be able to do (English, 1998). As an example, two staff members at a preschool reported the following incident:

It was time to go to the yard, and . . . Donna B. made mud pies and puddles. I then saw her bringing Timmie over. He was crying. Donna later told the reason why he cried. . . . He was playing in some water and spilled it on his shirt. Sister Donna said he was crying because he was going to get another beating from his father for having his shirt wet.

. . . I was trying to reassure and comfort Timmie who was sobbing quietly but convulsively when his sister Donna walked near and pulled up Timmie's shirt to show me his badly lacerated and still bloody-raw back. "He cry 'cause he father goin' give him 'nother beatin' for gettin' wet." (Hawkins, 1997, pp. 194–195)

The children most likely to be maltreated are those who are very young (premature infants are especially at risk), those who have disabilities, and those who are temperamentally difficult (English, 1998; Little, 2000b; Sullivan & Knutson, 1998; Thompson & Wyatt, 1999). In some cases, maltreated children suffer the ultimate consequence: death. More often, however, they survive but suffer lasting physical and psychological effects (English, 1998; Emery & Laumann-Billings, 1998; Leiter & Johnsen, 1997; Thompson & Wyatt, 1999). Infants without adequate nutrition may experience permanent retardation of their physical growth. Neglected toddlers have difficulty trusting others and forming healthy relationships with peers and adults (a finding consistent with our discussion of attachment in Chapter 9). When they reach school age, children who have been abused and neglected tend to do poorly in school and have high absentee rates; they are also more likely to experience emotional problems, commit crimes (e.g., shoplifting), and engage in alcohol and substance abuse. Children who endure sexual abuse may become infected with sexually transmitted diseases. Physically abused children are more likely than nonabused children to become aggressive themselves, have poor social skills, and show little or no empathy for the distress of others.

In the United States, almost a million children are documented as being abused or neglected every year (Larner, Stevenson, & Behrman, 1998). The actual incidence of child maltreatment is certainly much higher: Many instances of maltreatment are never reported to authorities; many others lack sufficient evidence to substantiate charges filed against the perpetrators.

Educators and others working with children and adolescents must, by law, contact proper authorities (e.g., Child Protective Services) when they suspect child abuse or neglect. Mandatory reporting laws for professionals who suspect abuse might give the impression that maltreated children, once identified, will be protected. On the contrary, an overload of cases and ambivalence about the responsibilities of the Child Protective Services system leave many children and families isolated and vulnerable (Larner et al., 1998). Teachers can find additional information and support services for victims of family maltreatment through the National Child Abuse Hotline (1-800-4-A-CHILD) or the Website for Childhelp USA (http://www.childhelpusa.org).

Fortunately, the overwhelming majority of parents and other caregivers do *not* neglect or abuse children. In fact, they make children's welfare one of their highest priorities (often attending to their children's needs before their own), and their influences on children's development are predominantly positive. But as we mentioned earlier, influences within families go in both directions: from parents to children *and* from children to parents. We look now at the possible influences that children have on other family members.

The Other Side of the Coin: Children's Influences on Families

A common misconception about socialization is that it is a one-way process—that children change but their parents do not. This misconception probably endures because children do change in many ways as they grow older, and their parents are often their most visible teachers about the ways of the world and society. Yet while children listen to their parents' guidance, advice, and expectations, they also make their wants and needs known, often quite emphatically (recall Cedric's outraged response to his B in physics: ". . . what are *we* going to do?!"). Through their own requests, demands, and actions, children influence parents' and other family members' behaviors.

We have already seen how children influence parents' parenting styles through their temperaments and dispositions: Temperamentally easy children elicit authoritative parenting behaviors, whereas temperamentally more difficult ones may elicit a more authoritarian approach. Children also influence parents and other family members through their unique talents and interests. For instance, when Jeanne's daughter Tina joined a soccer team, the family spent many Saturdays traveling to various athletic fields in eastern Colorado to watch her play. When Jeanne's son Alex encouraged her to take an undergraduate art history class with him when he was a high school senior, together they developed a more intense and informed appreciation for a wide variety of art forms.

Furthermore, children may alter the emotional climate of the family, sometimes for the better and sometimes not. Children who are successful at school, on the playing field, or in social situations often evoke feelings of joy and pride in other family members. Those who don't meet parents' expectations for performance may cause disappointment, frustration, or anger. Some children are the source of considerable emotional stress for parents; for instance, parents (especially mothers) of children with serious disabilities report high levels of stress, especially if they have little help from their spouses in caring for the children's needs (Little, 2000a; Mahoney, O'Sullivan, & Robinson, 1992).

To some degree, children's influences on other family members arise out of dispositions and talents that they have inherited from their parents—a fact that complicates the question of who is influencing whom. For example, a father with an extensive vocabulary and superior verbal reasoning may genetically endow his daughter with similar talents. As her verbal skills blossom, the young girl pleads with her parents to read to her, explain the meanings of challenging words, and discuss complex ideas. On the surface, her parents promote their daughter's verbal abilities through their actions, and undoubtedly they do. But their daughter also influences them, instigating her own opportunities for learning. And inciting the requests she makes for verbal input is an inborn, genetically supported talent (Scarr, 1992, 1993).

Despite such genetic factors, some of children's influences on parents clearly have environmental origins. A compelling example comes from the field of political socialization (M. McDevitt & Chaffee, 1998). In a quasi-experimental study,[5] approximately half of all class-

---

[5]You may wish to revisit the discussion of quasi-experimental designs in Chapter 2. In this case, the study was quasi-experimental in that students were not randomly assigned to the treatment group (which had the citizenship curriculum) or control group (which had no citizenship curriculum); instead, students participated in Kids Voting USA if their schools chose to implement the curriculum. The curriculum and control schools did not differ on any of the demographic variables measured, such as ethnicity or socioeconomic status.

rooms in San Jose, California, participated in "Kids Voting USA," a program in citizenship education for students from kindergarten through grade 12, and the other half served as a control group. Students in the program learned about voting and citizenship during the 3 months prior to the 1994 election. The researchers then interviewed 456 students (some from the treatment group, some from the control group) and one parent from each of the students' families. Apparently, the students in the Kids Voting USA program brought their knowledge and excitement about politics home with them. Compared to students in the control group, they discussed politics more frequently at home, and apparently as a result, their parents began to pay more attention to the news, talked more frequently about politics, and gained greater knowledge and formed stronger opinions about candidates and political issues. The researchers collected additional data from the parents 2 years later and found that the 3-month program's effects on parents' interest in news and politics were still evident. In this case, knowledge and interest "trickled up" from children to parents, with effects being particularly strong in families of limited income. The researchers suggested that, to some extent, educating children about citizenship can indirectly provide a "second chance" for *parents* to become informed participatory citizens.

Family influences go both ways. Just as parents influence their children's behavior, so, too, do children's characteristics and actions influence their parents' behavior.

The Reciprocal Nature of Family Influences

Families influence children, and children influence families; together, family members comprise a *dynamic system* of interrelationships (recall our earlier discussion of ecological systems theory). Increasingly, developmentalists are recognizing that the socialization of children involves *reciprocal influences,* whereby children and their parents simultaneously affect one another's behaviors and so mutually create the environment in which they all live. Reciprocal influences are evident in parent-child interactions from the very beginning of the relationship (Bell, 1988). As any parent of an infant can attest, babies are not quiet, idle creatures. They demand attention, comfort, and sustenance by crying, thrashing their arms and legs, and in other ways making their dissatisfaction known. But they also coo, chatter, and lure their parents into contact in a most disarming manner. A mother intent on vacuuming the family room cannot resist the antics of her 6-month-old who wiggles, chatters, establishes eye contact, and smiles at her. She turns off the vacuum and joins the fun. A father puts the newspaper down as his 12-month-old climbs onto his legs and offers him a bite of his cookie and a book to read. The two of them end up wrestling on the floor. In these and other ways, children contribute immensely to the formation and growth of their relationship with their parents. They respond in predictable ways, reward their parents' attention with laughter or imitation, protest their parents' absence, and in other ways tell their parents that what the parents do matters to them (Bell, 1988).

Reciprocal influences launched in infancy continue to unfold as children grow and develop. Through play, games, and other social interactions, preschoolers and their parents take turns imitating and responding to one another (Kohlberg, 1969). As children get older, they and their parents continue to respond to one another, cueing off one another's actions. The following scenario illustrates how one person's behavior often prompts another to act:

> Shakira walks in the door, unloading her groceries, purse, and briefcase onto the counter. Exhausted, she looks up to see her husband, Marvin, preparing dinner. Her 7-year-old daughter, Florence, is cutting pictures from an old magazine, while 3-year-old Tyrone assembles a block tower on the kitchen floor.
>
> Marvin greets Shakira with a kiss, then reminds her that Florence has soccer practice shortly and that they need to give Tyrone his medicine. He looks up from chopping vegetables and notices Shakira's expression. "You OK, hon?"
>
> "I had a terrible day," Shakira answers. "I never had time for lunch, and I've got a ferocious headache. And remind me to tell you later about our staff meeting." Marvin hands her a carrot stick and encourages her to take a rest. She sags onto the sofa.
>
> Tyrone looks up from his blocks and asks, "You got a headache, Mommy? Can I rub your head?" Marvin observes the gesture of sympathy and smiles. Shakira gestures to Tyrone to come to her. "Tell me about your day, Ty. Did you play with Isaiah?" Tyrone climbs on her

lap, patting her head. Florence wanders over and asks if she's coming to the soccer game. "I might be able to go after all," Shakira sighs.

In this scenario, family members respond to a mother's distress. During the short course of the interaction, the four family members maintain their own interests and objectives but at the same time are influenced by one another. During pivotal points in the incident, family members respond to Shakira's distress with understanding and comfort. The father sets a positive tone, but the children also take their own initiatives. One can imagine an entirely different dynamic here, with Marvin insisting that Shakira take over the dinner preparation and the children making their own demands or squabbling between themselves. During a less calm day when the children were cranky or the father had encountered his own difficulties at work, or under the circumstances of an unstable marriage, the event might have unfolded quite differently. Let's consider another scenario, then, when reciprocal influences manifest themselves in a less productive manner:

> Fourteen-year-old Ross storms into his parents' room. "Mom, where are my jeans?" His mother Judith is talking to a friend on the telephone. "I'm on the phone, Ross. Come back in a minute."
>
> Ross stands his ground and repeats the question more loudly. "Where are my jeans?!"
>
> Judith says goodbye to her friend and returns Ross's gaze. "Ross, that was rude. I was talking to Betty and you interrupted. Find your own jeans. Come back when you're ready to show some respect. Now get out of my room!"
>
> Ross, agitated, mocks his mother, "Out of my room! Out of my room!" He kicks the bedroom door as he walks out.
>
> "Get back here and apologize!" Judith demands.
>
> "Fat chance!" Ross shouts back. "If you weren't so busy gabbing to your friends all the time, you'd have time to take care of your family for a change."
>
> "Ross, you get back here and apologize or you're grounded for a month! Now!"
>
> Ross scowls, comes back to her room, kicks the door again—harder this time—and declares, "Grounded! Hah! I'm going to Bill's house. His family knows how to be civil."

In this case of reciprocal influences, things go from bad to worse. The interaction between Ross and his mother starts off on the wrong foot and deteriorates from there. Notice how the initial requests are ineffective (Ross does not find the jeans, and his mother does not get any more time on the phone). Subsequently, both mother and son escalate their demands. Judith seeks compliance and an apology and tries to curtail Ross's privileges. Ross resorts to disrespectful mocking, physical aggression, and blatant disobedience. With each overture, Judith and Ross get angrier, intensify their demands, and try to coerce each other with aversive tactics. Such coercive exchanges are common among some troubled families (Patterson & Reid, 1970).

For good and for bad, then, reciprocal influences saturate interactions between parents and their children. Before long, parents and children alike fall into habitual ways of responding to one another. Yet both parents and children grow and change, often in response to people and events outside the family context, and their relationships continue to be redefined over time.

Our emphasis thus far has been largely on how *behaviors* (of parents, children, and other family members) influence family dynamics and children's developmental progress. Yet *cognitions* affect family life as well, as you will discover in the next section.

A Look Inside: How Parents Conceptualize Childhood

How parents act toward and socialize their children is, in part, a function of their beliefs about their children—as well as about children more generally—and the visions they have for their children's future accomplishments. In this section, we examine a range of ideas that parents hold about children and childhood, examine literature on how parents acquire these ideas, and consider situations in which parents' beliefs might be quite different from those of teachers.

Diversity in Parents' Conceptions

Some parents view childhood as a time of innocence to be cherished; others may instead view it as a period of selfish desires and uncivilized urges. Some see childhood as a useless period that should be grown out of as quickly as possible, whereas others may intentionally insulate their children from adult responsibilities (Goodnow & Collins, 1990). Such beliefs inevitably affect parents' approaches to childrearing, expectations for children's behavior, and disciplinary practices.

Parents differ, too, in the underlying goals they have for their children. LeVine (1974, 1988) has hypothesized that parents' goals for children are somewhat hierarchical in nature (Figure 12–4). Their most basic goal is their children's sheer survival. In harsh conditions (e.g., in times of war or famine), survival is parents' predominant concern; they place less priority on culturally defined ideals, such as being responsible, pious, polite, or tidy ("I don't talk nice to my kids when I'm worrying that they might get killed by some slug. I demand that they come straight home from school!"). If parents feel reasonably certain that their children are safe from violent assaults and devastating diseases, they are freer to think about economic prospects ("He'll never get rich with his art, but he can always fall back on his computer skills"). With basic survival and economic needs assured, parents may be more attentive to intellectual and social characteristics that their culture values ("What a smart little guy my 3-year-old is. Ask him to name the planets!"). In reality, parents can probably juggle a range of concerns simultaneously, and lower- or higher-level concerns may float into consciousness at unpredictable times (Goodnow & Collins, 1990). To illustrate, parents in poor and distressed families, for whom we would predict concerns about survival and economic subsistence, may still concentrate on nurturing their children's emotional and social development (e.g., Richman, Miller, & Solomon, 1988). Conversely, parents whose children are usually healthy may still fret over survival, for instance by having their children immunized against serious diseases and taking precautions to remove chemicals and other impurities from the drinking water.

Parents also may differ in what they personally expect to gain from their children (Goodnow & Collins, 1990). Because you are reading this book, we are guessing that you have children in your life now or hope to have them in your life sometime in the not-too-distant future, perhaps as a parent, a teacher, or some other professional involved in child care or social services. Take a moment to consider your own reasons for wanting to have or work with children. We suspect that many of our readers want opportunities to cherish children, enjoy their companionship, delight in their antics and, by helping to nurture and guide the next generation, gain a sense of personal fulfillment and accomplishment. But there are other reasons to have children. For some people, bearing or fathering a child may give them "adult" status and, in some cultures, prestige.

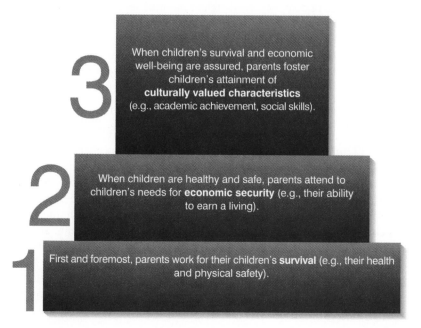

FIGURE 12–4 Hierarchical nature of parents' goals for children.
After LeVine, 1974, 1988.

3 When children's survival and economic well-being are assured, parents foster children's attainment of **culturally valued characteristics** (e.g., academic achievement, social skills).

2 When children are healthy and safe, parents attend to children's needs for **economic security** (e.g., their ability to earn a living).

1 First and foremost, parents work for their children's **survival** (e.g., their health and physical safety).

A Look Inside: How Parents Conceptualize Childhood | **479**

Other people have children either as a matter of custom or under pressure from family and friends. Still others want a person in their lives who can give them unconditional love (Coley & Chase-Lansdale, 1998) or can care for them in later years (L. W. Hoffman, 1988). In some cases, a couple may hope that having a child will strengthen a faltering marriage or relationship or may conceive a child as an unintentional consequence of sexual activity.

Origins of Parents' Conceptions About Children and Childhood

The range of ideas that parents have about children and childhood leads us to wonder how parents acquire these ideas to begin with. Mostly, parents' conceptions of children and childhood spring from the people around them—that is, from family, friends, people in the media, and so on—and from the specific culture in which they live (Goodnow & Collins, 1990; Hess, Chih-Mei, & McDevitt, 1987). A recent investigation by Okagaki and Frensch (1998) provides a concrete illustration of cultural influences on parents' beliefs. Okagaki and Frensch compared the expectations of three groups of parents living in northern California: Asian Americans, Latino Americans, and European Americans. Of the three groups, Asian American parents held the highest expectations for their children's educational attainment; on average, these parents hoped that their children would not only attend college but also obtain a graduate or professional degree. Asian American parents were also the least satisfied when their children earned grades lower than an A. Latino American parents were most likely to want to monitor their children's activities at school, and they placed high priority on the development of desired personal characteristics, such as conformity (e.g., showing respect to adults, obeying teachers) and autonomy (e.g., making decisions on one's own, working through problems by oneself). European American parents had the most confidence that they personally had the knowledge and skills necessary to help their children succeed in school.

Culture also influences parents' beliefs about the purposes of education and about what a "good education" involves. For some immigrant families, and particularly for parents of Mexican descent, education means not only academic achievement but also acquisition of the social and moral practices needed in one's journey along the *buen camino de la vida,* or "good path of life" (Dunbar, Azmitia, & Brown, 1999). Yet some parents from other cultural backgrounds, especially those from Southeast Asian countries, may think of education almost exclusively in terms of academic achievement and view less academic endeavors—sports, dramatic productions, field trips, and so on—as "play" activities that should be used primarily as rewards for hard work (Kang-Ning, 1981).

Personal experience is another, though probably less influential, source of parents' conceptions about children (Goodnow & Collins, 1990). Parents may formulate hypotheses ("With all the love and attention I give my daughter, she's bound to become a supernatural wonder"), collect data ("No matter what I do or say, my daughter has little regard for other family members' needs or feelings and is particularly mean-spirited toward her brother"), and revise their expectations ("I guess children are less influenced by parents than I first thought, or maybe I've been too easy on her"). Some evidence indicates that parents do, in fact, form and change their beliefs in response to experience. For instance, Holden (1988) found that parents and nonparents differed in the ways they interpreted an infant's crying and in the amount and types of information they sought about the cause of the crying.

When parents do use cultural messages and personal experiences in forming their conceptualizations, they do not necessarily do so systematically or rationally (Goodnow & Collins, 1990). Parents (like all human beings) may entertain two inconsistent beliefs at the same time without acknowledging or wrestling with the inconsistency. For example, a parent may believe that children should be responsible for their own "stuff" yet continually pick up after a son or daughter to minimize household clutter. Furthermore, parents (again, like all human beings) work hard to protect their own self-image. Most parents are fiercely invested in their relationships with their children, are quite mindful of their own hard work in caring for and nurturing their children, and see their children's performance as reflections of their own competence. Accordingly, they may blame others—oftentimes teachers—when their children have academic or social difficulty at school.

Parents often take shortcuts in forming their beliefs and expectations. They sometimes use existing stereotypes to develop impressions of their children's abilities; for instance, the common (though erroneous) belief that "boys are better at math than girls" may color their assessment of the actual mathematical abilities of their sons and daughters (Dunton, McDevitt, & Hess, 1988; Parsons, Adler, & Kaczala, 1982). Parents are also selective in the advice they use from experts. In a vivid illustration, Cohen (1981) examined the beliefs of English mothers who had recently moved to a new housing development. These mothers formed a discussion group, reading and analyzing books that offered advice for nurturing children's development. They accepted advice to emphasize play and discovery while their children were small but ignored the experts' advice to use meaningful learning experiences rather than rote memorization to teach academic skills in later years. For example, although the experts advised a focus on concrete manipulatives to teach basic mathematical concepts and skills, many mothers supplemented this approach by introducing traditional multiplication tables in the upper elementary grades, thinking that by doing so they would increase the children's chances for doing well on the selective entrance exams required by the "better" secondary schools (Cohen, 1981). When it came to the guidance of the experts, then, the mothers took some and left some, depending on their own beliefs and understandings about their children's learning and development.

Contrasting Parents' and Educators' Perspectives

In school settings, parents' perspectives about their children, about childhood in general, and about education are perhaps most obvious when they differ considerably from educators' perspectives. Consider the following vignettes and the contrasting viewpoints they reflect:

- Jane Schmidt is the single mother of 7-year-old Samuel. In the mind of Samuel's teacher, Rita, Jane is not very cooperative. Rita is concerned because Samuel has not acquired some of the basic skills in reading and mathematics that most of his second-grade classmates have mastered. She suspects that Samuel might catch up with the other children if he would only do the practice activities she sends home with him every night. But Jane rarely insists that Samuel do his homework. From Rita's perspective, Jane is overindulgent and permissive. From Jane's perspective, Samuel is working to his capacity and needs time after school for sports, play, and relaxation. "We should let kids enjoy their childhood," Jane tells Rita.
- John and Elaine Rodriguez, parents of 10-year-old Tara, remain silent during parent-teacher conferences. Tara's fifth-grade teacher, Norman, is frustrated about their apparent disinterest in Tara's progress. In fact, John and Maria are deeply concerned about Tara's school performance. Wanting to show their daughter's teacher complete respect, they refrain from idle chatter or questions that might appear to challenge his authority.
- Katherine Martin telephones Colleen, the advisor of a junior high school cheerleading squad, to express her anger that her 13-year-old daughter, Pearl, has been cut from the squad because of failing grades. In the course of the conversation, Colleen expresses her concerns about Pearl's health. "Your daughter is seriously underweight and doesn't seem to have much energy," Colleen says. "There's nothing wrong with being slender," Katherine responds. "I'd rather she be too thin than too fat."
- Elliott, a high school art teacher, encourages his students to create original paintings, pottery, and sculptures. In an informal discussion at an evening meeting, several parents ask why their children are not getting direct instruction in artistic form and technique, and one particularly vocal father argues that originality is not possible until students have mastered basic skills. Elliott explains that he tries to teach skills within the context of specific projects but wants the students to develop unique visions for their own creations. Again the father insists that imagination is not possible until some level of technical expertise is mastered.

In these vignettes, teachers encountered parents who viewed children and education differently than they did. It is all too easy for teachers to fall into the trap of thinking "I'm right, so they must be wrong." Before teachers jump to such a conclusion, they should remember that many beliefs about children, childhood, and education are just that—*beliefs*—and are not necessarily right or wrong but merely different.

Parents and teachers sometimes hold conflicting beliefs as a result of differences in their educational or cultural backgrounds. For instance, the father who argued with Elliott about the relative value of systematic instruction versus less systematic exploration in art education may himself have had considerable formal training in artistic techniques and believed that he benefited from them.[6] Yet even when parents and teachers share similar backgrounds, they may have been exposed to different ideas and belief systems through their families, communities, and the media. Furthermore, they see the same children in different settings (home vs. school) and draw on different knowledge bases as they interpret children's performance and behavior.

To some degree, parents and teachers must have similar understandings about children and teaching practices if they are to work cooperatively to maximize students' growth and development (e.g., Churchill, 1999). Yet it is rarely productive for teachers to try to convince parents to change their beliefs about children and education. (For one thing, parents are sometimes right!) An alternative approach is for parents and teachers to share their perspectives about development and instruction, as well as their objectives for the children in their care. When teachers take the time to build rapport and credibility with parents, they may also be in a good position to offer information and suggestions based on what they have learned through their experiences, coursework, and professional reading. (For instance, Katherine Martin may be unaware that eating disorders are becoming increasingly common in adolescent girls and might account for Pearl's thinness.) In the final section of the chapter, we consider strategies through which teachers can establish and maintain productive working relationships with parents and other family members.

Educational Partnerships with Families

Families are where it all starts for children. Parents and other caregivers serve as teachers, cheerleaders, nursemaids, managers and, when things go wrong, psychotherapists and parole officers. When children begin some form of schooling—whether in preschool, kindergarten, or first grade—effective teachers get parents and other important family members (e.g., grandparents, older siblings) actively involved in school life and children's learning (Davis & Thomas, 1989; Epstein, 1996; Levine & Lezotte, 1995). Ideally, relationships between teachers and family members are partnerships in which everyone collaborates to promote students' long-term development and learning (Hidalgo et al., 1995). Such a relationship may be especially important when teachers are working with students from diverse cultural backgrounds or with students who have special educational needs (Hidalgo et al., 1995; Salend & Taylor, 1993; Turnbull et al., 1999).

Most parents and other primary caregivers ultimately want what's best for their children. Yet many do not participate actively in their children's schooling; some do not even attend parent-teacher conferences, school open houses, or other events designed specifically for family members. Often, parents are actively involved when their children are in elementary school but increasingly withdraw as their children move to the middle and secondary school grade levels (Epstein, 1996; Finders & Lewis, 1994; Roderick & Camburn, 1999).

Before jumping too quickly to the conclusion that some parents are *uninterested* in their children's education, teachers must realize that there are several possible reasons why parents might be reluctant to make or maintain contact with educators (Chavkin, 1993; Finders & Lewis, 1994; Hidalgo et al., 1995; Lareau, 1987; Salend & Taylor, 1993). Some may have an exhausting work schedule or lack adequate child care. Others may have difficulty communicating in English. Still others may believe that it's inappropriate to bother teachers with questions about their children's progress or to offer information as to why their children are having difficulty. A few may simply have had bad experiences with school when they themselves were children. One father put it this way:

> They expect me to go to school so they can tell me my kid is stupid or crazy. They've been telling me that for three years, so why should I go and hear it again? They don't do anything. They just tell me my kid is bad.

---

[6]For example, teachers in China and Japan typically provide considerable training in artistic techniques even in the elementary grades; teachers in Western countries are much less likely to do so (Case, Okamoto, et al., 1996).

See, I've been there. I know. And it scares me. They called me a boy in trouble but I was a troubled boy. Nobody helped me because they liked it when I didn't show up. If I was gone for the semester, fine with them. I dropped out nine times. They wanted me gone. (Finders & Lewis, 1994, p. 51)

A good first step in getting families more involved in children's education is to get a sense of children's family configurations and relationships, as well as the neighborhoods and cultural contexts in which the families live. Teachers are more likely to establish productive partnerships when they accommodate the diverse structures that families are likely to take: If Grandma is a child's primary caregiver, then she, in addition to the child's parent(s), should be invited to a parent-teacher conference. Teachers should also consider a family's cultural background; for instance, although most Chinese American parents are deeply concerned about their children's education, they may be reluctant to seek out teachers because they're unfamiliar with procedures for scheduling appointments or may think it inappropriate to question the judgment of school personnel (Hidalgo et al., 1995). The Observation Guidelines table on the next two pages lists characteristics that teachers might consider in their efforts to better understand their students' family environments.

Communicating with Families

Effective communication is at the heart of any partnership. Accordingly, we urge teachers to keep in regular contact with families about the progress that students are making, not only academically but socially and emotionally as well. Parents and other caregivers appreciate hearing about children's accomplishments, and they deserve to know about behaviors that are consistently interfering with children's learning and achievement. In fact, when lines of communication between teachers and parents are regularly used, information can run both ways: from teacher to family *and* from family to teacher. For instance, family members often provide insights about behaviors, habits, and customs at home that yield ideas about how better to teach and motivate children.

Teachers have several commonly used forms of communication at their disposal:

- *Parent-teacher conferences.* In most school districts, formal parent-teacher conferences are scheduled one or more times a year; additional conferences are scheduled if requested by either a teacher or a parent. In many schools, teachers invite students to join parent-teacher conferences. By doing so, they increase parents' attendance at the conference, encourage students to reflect on their own academic progress, and make it likely that each participant leaves the meeting with a shared understanding of the student's progress and the steps to be taken next.
- *Written communication.* Written communication can take a variety of forms. For example, it can be a regularly scheduled report card that documents a student's academic progress. It can be a quick, informal note or postcard acknowledging a significant accomplishment. Or it can be a general newsletter describing noteworthy classroom activities. These forms of written communication let parents know what is happening at school and also convey teachers' intentions to stay in touch on an ongoing basis.
- *Telephone conversations.* Telephone calls are useful when issues require immediate attention. Teachers might call a parent to express their concern when a student's behavior deteriorates unexpectedly and without apparent provocation. But they might also call to express their excitement about an important step forward that a student has made. Parents, too, should feel free to call teachers. Keep in mind that many parents are at work during the school day; hence, it is often helpful for teachers to take calls at home during the early evening hours.
- *E-mail and Web sites.* Increasingly, educators are finding that they can maintain regular contact with some parents electronically—for instance, by sending e-mail messages and creating classroom Web pages that list class activities and assignments. Such strategies, of course, can only be used when teachers and parents have access to computer resources. For this reason, teachers should use electronic forms of communication *only* when students' families have made it clear that they use computers regularly to transmit and seek information.
- *Parent discussion groups.* In some instances, teachers may want to assemble a group of parents to discuss issues of mutual concern. For example, they might use such a group as a

Identifying Family Structures and Processes

OBSERVATION GUIDELINES

CHARACTERISTIC	LOOK FOR	EXAMPLE	IMPLICATION
Family Configuration	• Single vs. multiple caregivers • Presense or absence of siblings • Extended family members living in the home • Nonrelatives living in the home • Children's attachments to and relationships with other family members	Alexis has a chronic kidney disease, and its periodic flare-ups cause her to be fatigued and irritable. In times of reduced health, she finds great comfort in being with her older sister in the school yard and at lunch. Alexis's teachers have observed her close relationship with her sister and provide opportunities for them to touch base when she's not well.	Accept families as legitimate educational partners, regardless of their form. Include extended family members (especially those who appear to be regular caregivers) at school functions. Give students time to be with siblings in times of personal or family crisis.
Cultural Background	• Language(s) spoken at home • Children's loyalty to and sense of responsibility for other family members • Children's attitudes toward cooperation and competition • Children's and parents' communication styles (whether they make eye contact, ask a lot of questions, are open about their concerns, etc.)	Carlos is very quiet and reserved in class. He willingly follows instructions and classroom rules and in other ways shows that he wants to do well in school. However, he rarely seeks his teacher's help when he runs into difficulty, even though she has encouraged him to do so. Instead, he often asks his cousin (a classmate) for assistance.	Remember that most students and parents are interested in academic achievement despite what their behaviors may lead you to conclude. Adapt instructional styles to students' preferred ways of interacting and communicating. Consider how families' cultural knowledge and skills might enrich the classroom curriculum.
Family's Economic Structure and Well-being	• Presence of a family business (e.g., farm, cottage industry) that requires children's involvement • Children in self-care for several hours after school • Older children and adolescents with part-time jobs (e.g., grocery store work, paper routes) • Parental unemployment	April completes several chores on the family farm before going to school each morning. She keeps ongoing records about the weight and general health of three calves born last year. She constructs charts to show their progress as a project for her seventh-grade science class.	Take students' outside work commitments into account when assigning homework. For example, give students at least 2 days to complete short assignments and at least a week for longer ones. Be flexible about due dates when students are important contributors to their family's economic well-being.

sounding board to choose among topics for the classroom curriculum, or perhaps to make decisions about assigning controversial yet potentially valuable works of literature. Alternatively, they might want to use a discussion group as a mechanism through which all participants can share ideas about how best to promote students' academic, personal, and social development.

Whatever the form communication may take, several strategies enhance the likelihood of its effectiveness:

■ *Involve both parents whenever possible and appropriate.* Whenever both parents are actively involved in a student's life—whether they live in the same household or not—teachers should try to get to know both parents and show respect for the role that each plays in the student's development and education. All too often, fathers are left out of the picture when it comes to teacher-parent communication, yet in today's society fathers tend to be more involved in their children's education than their own fathers were with them (Tamis-LeMonda & Cabrera, 1999).

■ *Take parents' work schedules and other commitments into account.* Some parents have considerable flexibility in their work schedules and may be able to come to a parent-teacher conference or meeting during the school day. But many others are not so fortunate, especially if they work in lower-paying positions. If educators want to maximize parents' involvement in

CHARACTERISTIC	LOOK FOR	EXAMPLE	IMPLICATION
Parenting Styles	• Parents' apparent warmth or coldness toward their children • Parents' expectations for their children's behavior and performance • Parents' concerns about their children's needs • Parents' willingness to discuss issues and negotiate solutions with their children • Possible effects of children's temperaments and dispositions on parents' disciplinary styles	At a parent-teacher conference, Julia's parents express their exasperation about trying to get Julia to do her homework. "We've tried everything—reasoning with her, giving ultimatums, offering extra privileges for good grades, punishing her for bad grades—but nothing seems to work. She'd rather hang out with her friends all day than crack open a textbook."	Acknowledge that most parents have their children's best interests at heart and use disciplinary methods they have seen others model. Recognize that parents often adapt their parenting styles to children's dispositions and temperaments. At the same time, model an authoritative style (e.g., show sensitivity to students' needs, give reasons for your requests) in your own interactions with students.
Disruptive Influences	• Change in family membership (e.g., as a result of death, divorce, remarriage, or cohabitation) • Change of residence • Physical or mental illness in parents or other family members • Parental alcoholism or substance abuse	Justin has had trouble concentrating since his parents' divorce, and he no longer shows much enthusiasm for class activities.	Show heightened care and compassion for students undergoing a significant family transition, and offer yourself as a willing listener if students would like to talk. Realize that some families may return to healthy functioning with short-term support from family and friends, but others may be in turmoil for lengthy periods. Seek the assistance of a school psychologist or counselor when students do not rebound quickly.
Maltreatment	• Frequent injuries, usually attributed to "accidents" • Age-inappropriate sexual knowledge or behavior • Extreme withdrawal, anxiety, or depression • Untreated medical or dental needs • Chronic hunger • Poor hygiene and grooming • Lack of warm clothing in cold weather	Michael often has bruises on his arms and legs, which his mother says are the result of a "blood problem." He had a broken collar bone in October, and now, 4 months later, he arrives with a broken arm and a black eye. "I fell down the stairs," he explains, but refuses to talk further about the mishap.	Immediately report any signs of child maltreatment to the school counselor or principal. Contact Child Protective Services for advice about additional courses of action.

their children's education, then, they may sometimes have to schedule meetings in the early morning or evening hours.

■ *Establish rapport.* Although some parents feel quite confident and comfortable when they talk with teachers, others may be anxious, uncertain, or distrustful. Teachers can do many little things to improve rapport. For instance, using friendly body language (smiling, offering a handshake) and presenting an interested and upbeat demeanor (asking a lot of questions, displaying a sense of humor) can help teachers communicate that they can be trusted and that parents' ideas and opinions have value.

■ *Be a listener as well as a talker.* Most parents want to be heard rather than just "talked at" (Hoover-Dempsey & Sandler, 1997), yet some may be reluctant to voice their perspectives without some encouragement. Teachers can often encourage their input by asking specific questions ("What kinds of books does Jason like to read at home?" "What might we do to make sure Melina does her homework every night?") and assuring them that they should feel free to call whenever they have questions or concerns.

■ *Remember that most parents view their children's behavior as reflections of their own competence.* Parents typically feel proud when their children are successful in school. But they may respond to their children's academic failures or behavior problems in a variety of ways. Some respond with embarrassment, shame, or anger that their children's performance does not reflect favorably on them. Others deny that their "angels" could possibly be doing anything wrong and instead place blame on the teacher for any academic or social shortcomings. More generally, parents, like all human beings, tend to deal with negative feedback in ways that protect their self-esteem. Teachers are more likely to have productive parent-teacher discussions if they acknowledge that children's temperamental differences are often beyond parents' control and that, if everyone works as a team, they all might be able to remedy students' classroom difficulties.

■ *Be alert for possible philosophical and cultural differences.* As you have seen, parents have varying beliefs about children, childhood, and education, and such beliefs are likely to color their interpretations of their children's performance and the effectiveness of a teacher's instructional strategies. Furthermore, their cultural backgrounds may influence their communication styles—whether they make eye contact, whether they are willing to speak their minds, and so on. Teachers are more likely to communicate effectively with parents if they are on the lookout for perspectives and customs very different from their own. For instance, teachers can ask for parents' explanations of any difficulties children may be having in school performance or adjustment. And they should not assume that parents who are quiet and unassertive during conferences and other discussions lack interest in their children's school success.

When conferring with parents about problematic classroom behaviors, teachers should keep in mind that people from different cultural groups sometimes have radically different ideas about how children should be disciplined. For example, many Chinese American parents believe that Western schools are too lenient in their attempts to correct inappropriate behavior (Hidalgo et al., 1995). In some Native American and Asian cultures, a child's misbehaviors may be seen as bringing shame on the family or community; thus, a common disciplinary strategy is to ignore or ostracize the child for an extended period of time (Pang, 1995; Salend & Taylor, 1993). As teachers confer with parents from cultures different from their own, they should listen with an open mind to the viewpoints expressed and try to find common ground on which to develop strategies for helping students acquire productive classroom behavior (Salend & Taylor, 1993).

■ *Accommodate language and literacy differences.* When a student's parents speak a language other than English, educators will, of course, want to include in any parent-teacher conversations someone who can converse fluently with the parents in their native tongue (and ideally, someone whom the parents trust). They should also have newsletters and other written messages translated.

None of the communication strategies just described will, in and of itself, guarantee a successful working relationship with parents. Parent-teacher conferences and parent discussion groups typically occur infrequently. Written communication is ineffective with parents who have limited literacy skills. And, of course, not everyone has a telephone. Despite these individual problems, effective teachers find ways to stay in touch and exchange ideas with all of their students' families (e.g., see the Development and Practice feature on the next page). Ideally, educators want not only to communicate with parents, but to get them actively involved in school activities as well.

Getting Families Actively Involved in School Activities

Many students at both the elementary and secondary school levels report that they wish their families were more involved in school activities (Epstein, 1996). Furthermore, parents who believe their children's schools want them to be involved have more positive views about the schools (Dauber & Epstein, 1993). Ideally, family involvement should be important and meaningful, with a two-way communication of ideas and strategies (Epstein, 1996; Hoover-Dempsey & Sandler, 1997).

Parents and other family members typically become involved in school activities only when they have a specific invitation to do so and when they know that school personnel

MAKING CLASSROOMS FAMILY-FRIENDLY

■ Recognize the significance of families in children's lives.

A first-grade teacher asks students to bring in a photograph of themselves and their families to post on a bulletin board labeled "My Family and Me."

■ Acknowledge the strengths of families' varying backgrounds.

When planning a lesson on the history of farming in Colorado, a middle school social studies teacher asks a mother if she would be willing to talk about her own childhood experiences as a member of an immigrant family that harvested crops every summer.

■ Use a variety of formats to communicate with parents.

A fourth-grade teacher works with the children in his class to produce a monthly newsletter for parents. Two versions of the newsletter are created, one in English and one in Spanish.

■ Tell parents about children's many strengths, even when communicating information about their shortcomings.

A teacher talks on the phone with the parents of one of her students. She describes several areas in which the student has made

considerable progress but also asks for advice about strategies that might help him stay on task and be more careful in his work.

■ Be sensitive to parents' concerns about the limits of their influence.

A high school teacher talks with worried parents of a 16-year-old girl who has begun smoking and possibly experimenting with illegal drugs. Thinking about the girl's keen interest in photography, the teacher seeks an opening in an after-school photography club, with hopes that the companionship of more academically oriented peers might get her back on the right track.

■ Encourage all parents and guardians to get involved in school activities.

A high school principal sends home a book of "coupons" with assorted activities that parents and other family members might do to help the school (e.g., tutoring in the classroom, chaperoning field trips, baking goodies for a school open house, serving on the parent-teacher advisory group, participating in fund-raising activities). She accompanies the book with a letter expressing her hope that all parents will return a coupon to sign up for at least one activity for the year.

---

genuinely want them to be involved (Carr, 1997; Epstein, 1996; Hoover-Dempsey & Sandler, 1997). For example, teachers might invite family members to a classroom skit in the evening or request parents' help with a school fundraiser on a Saturday afternoon. Teachers might seek volunteers to help with field trips, special projects, or individual tutoring during the school day. And they should certainly use family members as resources to enrich the multicultural perspective of the community in which they work (Minami & Ovando, 1995).

Yet some parents, especially those from minority groups, may believe that invitations are not directed specifically at them. Consider this parent's perspective:

Effective teachers get students' families actively involved in school activities. These mothers are helping out at the school-sponsored carnival.

The thing of it is, had someone not walked up to me and asked me specifically, I would not hold out my hand and say, "I'll do it." Same thing here. You get parents here all the time, black parents that are willing, but maybe a little on the shy side and wouldn't say I really want to serve on this subject. You may send me the form, I may never fill the form out. Or I'll think about it and not send it back. But you know if that principal, that teacher, my son's math teacher called and asked if I would. . . . (Carr, 1997, p. 2)

Experts have offered numerous suggestions for getting families more involved in children's schooling. In particular, teachers might

• Invite not only parents but also other important family members (e.g., grandparents, aunts, uncles) to participate in school activities, especially if a student's cultural background is one that places high value on the extended family (Hidalgo et al., 1995; Salend & Taylor, 1993)

- Find out what family members do exceptionally well (e.g., woodworking, cooking, calligraphy, storytelling) and ask them to share their talents with the class (Finders & Lewis, 1994)
- Identify individuals (e.g., bilingual parents) who can translate for those who speak little or no English (Finders & Lewis, 1994)
- Include parent advisory groups that offer suggestions and concerns about school curriculum and practices (Epstein, 1996)
- Use parents as liaisons with other community agencies and institutions (e.g., businesses, universities) that can support students' learning and development (Epstein, 1996)
- Provide opportunities for parents and other family members to volunteer for jobs that don't require them to leave home (e.g., to be someone whom students can call when unsure about homework assignments; Sanders, 1996)

Supporting Families' Efforts at Home

One obvious way in which parents and other family members support children's learning and development on the home front is by assisting with homework assignments. Yet parents vary considerably in their ability to help in this regard. For instance, in 1995, approximately 17% of American children had mothers who had not graduated from high school, 35% had mothers who had graduated from high school but had not attended college, 29% had mothers who attended college but did not complete a degree, and 20% had mothers who had completed a college degree (Hernandez, 1997). Thus, many mothers (and presumably many fathers as well) lack the knowledge and skills necessary to help with homework, especially when their children are in high school. At the upper grade levels, then, teachers should limit students' homework assignments to things they can do with little or no help from adults (Cooper, 1989).

Even when parents have had limited education themselves, they are often quite willing and able to help children master basic skills in such areas as reading, spelling, and mathematics. However, they may sometimes need guidance about how to do so effectively (Edwards & Garcia, 1994; Portes, 1996). As an example, in a study by Edwards and Garcia (1994), low-income mothers were shown several strategies for reading books to their young children, including pointing to and talking about the pictures in the books, asking questions to improve and monitor the children's comprehension, and encouraging the children to draw inferences and make predictions. Learning such strategies enabled the mothers to more effectively nurture their children's emergent literacy skills.

Just as parents often assist teachers in the job of fostering children's academic development, so, too, can teachers assist parents in the job of fostering children's development more generally. On average, teachers have more training in child development and instructional methodologies than parents do, and parents often welcome information about developmental trends and effective childrearing strategies. Teachers should not preach to parents about such matters, but they can certainly provide suggestions about strategies that might work at home, perhaps at parent-teacher conferences or in regular newsletters and fliers sent home (see Figure 12–5 for an example of a flier for middle school parents). Developmental issues that are often of interest and concern to parents are presented in the Developmental Trends table that follows.

Adolescent Development

Eleven . . . is a time of breaking up, of discord and discomfort. Gone is the bland complaisance of the typical ten-year-old. Eleven is a time of loosening up, of snapping old bonds, of trial and error as the young child tests the limits of what authority will and will not permit.

Louise Bates Ames, Ph.D.
Your Ten- to Fourteen-Year-Old
Gesell Institute of Human Development

To understand your adolescent, you need to consider . . .
. . . the child's basic individuality.
. . . what is expected of anyone of his or her particular age level.
. . . what environment your child finds himself or herself in.

Eleven-year-olds can be . . .
egocentric,
energetic,
always "loving" or "hating";

as well as . . .
not as cooperative or accepting as in the past
more angry than in the past
inattentive
hungry all the time
more interested in the clothes they wear
(but not in cleaning them!)
uncertain
more apt to cry
fearful
rebellious
very interested and involved in family activities

FIGURE 12–5
Teachers can be valuable sources of information about child and adolescent development. In this flier for parents, middle school teacher Erin Miguel describes several common characteristics of young adolescents.
Reprinted with permission of Erin Miguel, Jones Middle School, Columbus, Ohio.

Topics of Concern to Parents of Children and Adolescents at Different Age Levels

DEVELOPMENTAL TRENDS

AGE	TOPICS	DIVERSITY	IMPLICATIONS
Early Childhood (2–6) 	**Physical Development** • Ensuring children's basic safety (e.g., protecting them from street traffic and household chemicals) • Helping children with self-care routines (e.g., dressing, brushing teeth, bathing) • Finding appropriate outlets for physical play activities **Cognitive Development** • Responding to children's incessant questions • Channeling curiosity into constructive activities • Reading stories and in other ways promoting a foundation for literacy • Offering age-appropriate forms of cognitive enrichment • Preparing for the transition to formal schooling **Social-Emotional Development** • Curbing temper tantrums and in other ways dealing with temperamentally "difficult" children • Promoting sharing with siblings and peers; addressing conflicts • Forming relationships with new caregivers in daycare and preschool	• Some parents, worrying about their children's safety, are exceptionally reluctant to leave them in the care of others. • Low-income families have little or no discretionary income with which to purchase books and provide opportunities for cognitive enrichment. • Some kindergartners and first graders have had little or no prior experiences with other children; for instance, they may be only children or may not have previously attended daycare or preschool. • Some parents (especially those from higher-income, professional backgrounds) may overdo efforts to maximize their children's cognitive development, giving children too many intellectually challenging activities and too few chances to relax and play.	• Suggest possible approaches to teaching young children about self-care habits, social skills, and impulse control. • Keep parents regularly informed about their children's progress in both academic and social skills. • Provide books and other stimulating materials that parents can check out and use at home. • When highly educated parents seem overly concerned about maximizing their children's cognitive development, suggest literature (e.g., John Bruer's *The Myth of the First Three Years*) that encourages a balance between stimulation and recreation.
Middle Childhood (6–10) 	**Physical Development** • Fostering healthy eating habits • Using safety equipment (e.g., seatbelts in the car, helmets for cycling or skateboarding) • Establishing exercise routines and curbing sedentary pursuits (e.g., television, video games) **Cognitive Development** • Helping children acquire habits and expectations for their academic work • Promoting mastery of basic academic skills • Enhancing children's education through family involvement and outings **Social-Emotional Development** • Giving children increasing independence and responsibility (e.g., getting up on time, going to school without supervision, doing homework) • Monitoring interactions with siblings and playmates • Fostering an appreciation for financial prudence • Instilling desirable moral behaviors (e.g., honesty, fairness)	• Some parents may be overly stressed from work responsibilities. • Some neighborhoods have few if any playgrounds or other places where children can safely play. • Children's special talents and interests influence their choices of activities outside the home.	• Obtain and distribute literature about safety habits from local police, fire departments, and pediatricians' offices. • Provide resource materials (perhaps through a parent library in the classroom) that parents can use to assist their children with academic subject matter. • Encourage parents' involvement in school activities and parent-teacher groups. • Suggest facilities and programs in the community (e.g., youth soccer leagues, scout organizations) that provide free or inexpensive opportunities for after-school recreation and skill development.

(continued)

Topics of Concern to Parents of Children and Adolescents at Different Age Levels *(continued)*

DEVELOPMENTAL TRENDS

AGE	TOPICS	DIVERSITY	IMPLICATIONS
Early Adolescence (10–14)	**Physical Development** • Recognizing and dealing with early stages of puberty • Encouraging physical fitness • Affording adequate clothing during periods of rapid growth **Cognitive Development** • Supporting school-based changes in expectations for academic performance • Sympathizing with young adolescents who envision a better world **Social-Emotional Development** • Showing sensitivity to self-consciousness about appearance • Accommodating requests for more leisure time with peers • Dealing with increased conflict as adolescents seek greater autonomy in decision making • Renegotiating parent-child relationships	• Children differ markedly in the age at which they begin puberty. • Different families have different decision-making styles. • Some parents may have considerable difficulty untying the apron strings to allow their children greater independence. • Parent-teenager conflicts are rare in some cultures, especially in those that cultivate respect for elders (e.g., many Asian cultures). • Some young teens may have little or no access to safe and appropriate recreational facilities. • Peer groups encourage varying behaviors and values.	• Identify and inform parents about age-appropriate athletic and social programs in the community. • Collaborate with colleagues and teachers to establish a homework hotline through which students can get ongoing support and guidance for home assignments. • Share with parents your impressions about reasonable expectations for independence and responsibility for their children.
Late Adolescence (14–18)	**Physical Development** • Keeping track of teenagers' whereabouts • Encouraging high school students to maintain realistic schedules that allow adequate sleep • Fretting about driving safety • Concern about possible use of alcohol and drugs **Cognitive Development** • Encouraging youth to persist with increasingly challenging academic subject matter • Understanding adolescents' increasing capacity for logical and systematic thinking • Expanding adolescents' knowledge of employment prospects and college requirements **Social-Emotional Development** • Worrying about the loss of parental control over teenagers' social activities • Finding a reasonable balance between supervision and independence • Monitoring adolescents' part-time jobs	• Families differ in their knowledge of, and experiences with, higher education; some may be unable to counsel their children about options in postsecondary education. • Alcohol and drugs are readily available in any community, but their use is more frequent and socially acceptable in some neighborhoods and communities than in others. • Some parents refuse to believe that their children may be engaged in serious health-compromising behaviors, even when faced with considerable evidence. • Parents differ in the extent to which they condone and encourage teenagers' part-time employment.	• Provide information about possible careers and educational opportunities after high school; include numerous options, including part-time and full-time vocational programs, community colleges, and four-year colleges and universities. • Suggest ways in which young adolescents can maintain regular contact with their families when they are away from home for lengthy periods (e.g., by making regular phone calls home).

Sources: Collins, 1990; Maccoby, 1980, 1984; Montemayor, 1982; Mortimer, Shanahan, & Ryu, 1994; Paikoff & Brooks-Gunn, 1991; Pipher, 1994; Warton & Goodnow, 1991; Youniss, 1983.

Home visits are a widely used way of supporting parents' efforts at home, especially with young children (Gomby, Culross, & Behrman, 1999). Existing home visiting programs have a variety of objectives, though typically they focus on educating parents about children's needs, providing information and support to help parents nurture their children's development, and preventing problems such as neglect or abuse. Home-visiting programs work quite well with some parents but not so well with others. For instance, some parents do not want strangers in their homes (Salend & Taylor, 1993). Others, though more willing, may frequently miss appointments and group meetings (Gomby et al., 1999). To make home visits maximally effective, educators and other child-care professionals should present themselves as warm, friendly, and nonjudgmental; make an effort to establish rapport with parents and other family members; and offer concrete, practical suggestions about how to foster children's development and well-being.

In the United States, Project Head Start offers one model of how educators can help low-income parents become actively involved in their children's preschool education both at school and at home (Seefeldt, Denton, Galper, & Younoszai, 1999; Sissel, 2000; Washington & Bailey, 1995). Although Head Start programs differ somewhat from one community to the next, parent involvement is typically encouraged in several ways:

- Parents are welcome at school any time and given a specific place in which they might convene.
- Parents receive materials and suggestions for working with their children on educational tasks.
- Adult education classes are offered on such topics as parenting, nutrition, and health.
- Access to social services and adult literacy services is provided.
- Monthly family dinners are held at school.
- Parents are involved in planning for children's transition from the program to kindergarten or first grade.
- When employment opportunities within the program open up, parents are given preference for any positions for which they are qualified.

Such strategies appear to foster parents' views of themselves as important educators for their children and assure them that they can, in fact, enhance their children's academic abilities (Seefeldt et al., 1999; Washington & Bailey, 1995). Ongoing involvement in Head Start programs can also enhance parents' confidence about their *own* learning abilities. For example, a group of fathers at one Head Start program in New York City decided to work together in preparing for and seeking meaningful employment. They studied together to become sanitation engineers, took the required examination, and began getting jobs in their newly chosen profession (Washington & Bailey, 1995). Other parents, after working as staff members in Head Start classrooms, eventually go on to get credentials or degrees in early childhood education (Washington & Bailey, 1995).

As you can see, then, helping children sometimes means *helping parents help their own children*. Furthermore, *helping parents help themselves* (e.g., providing opportunities to acquire new job skills) indirectly helps children by giving other family members more self-confidence and economic stability. As the ecological systems perspective reminds us, there are both direct and indirect routes to nurturing children's development. Undoubtedly, the most productive indirect route is through children's families.

CASE STUDY: FOUR-YEAR-OLD SONS

A common behavior in preschoolers is to ask a lot of *why* questions. Consider how the following two mothers of 4-year-old boys interpret their sons' incessant questioning. Elizabeth describes her son Charles as

> . . . mouthing off; just always mouthing off. Whenever I say anything to him, he asks me "Why?" Like I say we're going to the store and he says "Why?" Or I tell him "Don't touch the bug 'cuz it's dead" and he says "Why?" Like he's just trying to get me mad by never listening to me. He never accepts what I say. He mouths off all the time instead of believing me. It's like he just wants to tease me. You know, he tests me. (Belenky, Bond, & Weinstock, 1997, pp. 129–130).

In contrast, Joyce describes her son Peter this way:

> Well, you know, he's got such an active mind, always going; like he's never satisfied with just appearances—he's always trying to figure out how things tick, why they do. So if I ask him to do

something or tell him to do something, he's always asking why. He really wants to understand what's the goal—what's the purpose—how come? He's really trying to piece the world all together . . . and understand it all. It's wonderful. Or if I say, "We're going to the store," he wants to know why. He's real interested in figuring out how one thing leads to another. It's great, because sometimes he helps me realize that I haven't really thought through why I'm saying what I am. And so we do think it through. (p. 130).

- How do the two mothers interpret their sons' questions differently? How might their beliefs about children prompt these different interpretations? How might their interpretations help us to predict their disciplinary styles?
- How might the lives of these women and their families differ more globally? In other words, what would you expect their educational backgrounds to be? What kinds of life stresses might each experience?
- What kinds of educational opportunities would these mothers create at home for their children? What might teachers do to encourage each mother's involvement at school?

SUMMARY

Socialization in the Family

Families are complex social structures that have both immediate and lasting impacts on children and adolescents. Youngsters are not passive recipients of their families' socialization efforts, however; instead, they actively seek out, interpret, and filter the messages they get from others. Furthermore, just as children and adolescents are influenced by their parents and siblings, so, too, do they influence these other family members and the overall dynamics of the family environment.

Four theoretical viewpoints help us to understand how families affect children's development. Social-cognitive perspectives consider the specific experiences (role models, consequences for behavior, etc.) that parents and other family members provide for children. Cognitive-developmental perspectives describe the ways in which children's ability to interpret and respond to their environments changes with age. Biological perspectives focus on parents' genetic influences on children and on the ways in which family relationships and practices have survival value and so have probably evolved with the species. Ecological systems perspectives look at families as complex systems of relationships that exist within larger systems and support structures. In some respects the four perspectives offer conflicting views of families, yet each contributes to our understanding of how families and children influence one another.

How children are socialized depends somewhat on their gender, cultural group membership, and family configuration. For example, many families ask boys and girls to perform household chores consistent with gender stereotypes. Some cultural groups encourage competition, whereas others encourage a more cooperative spirit. Children in large families are more likely to acquire altruistic behaviors, particularly when their contributions are essential to the family's welfare.

Family Structures

Families come in many forms, including two-parent families, single-parent families, blended families, adoptive families, foster families, cohabiting families, and numerous variations on these structures. Many young people experience one or more changes in their family structure (e.g., as a result of divorce, remarriage, or death of a parent) at some point during their childhood or adolescence. Individual family configurations all offer unique benefits and challenges for children, but ultimately the quality of family relationships is more important than the structure of the family per se.

Family Influences on Children

Parents influence children's development through the ways in which they show affection, establish rules and expectations, and discipline children (i.e., through their general parenting styles) and through the instruction, experiences, and resources they offer to promote cognitive growth. Parents may also affect children's development through their employment outside the home; for instance, working mothers may have to leave their children in self-care during the after-school hours yet may encourage their daughters to have high career aspirations. Other family members influence children's development as well. Grandparents can be sources of unconditional love, and siblings can provide nurturance, instruction, and emotional support.

Most families provide safe and nurturing environments for children. However, some families maltreat children, either by neglecting them or by subjecting them to physical, sexual, or emotional abuse. Such maltreatment may have long-term effects on children's physical, cognitive, and social-emotional development. Often, the perpetrators of child maltreatment suffer from serious emotional problems themselves.

Children's Influences on Families

Through their own temperaments, personalities, interests, and behaviors, children influence other family members' behaviors and the general emotional climate of the family. Ultimately, educators must think of each student's family as a *dynamic system* that changes over time as a result of both the complexity of interpersonal relationships within it and the external environmental conditions that either support or undermine its effectiveness.

Parents' Beliefs About Children

Parents' beliefs about their children's abilities, the nature of childhood in general, and the purposes of education affect their expectations, disciplinary practices, and approval or disapproval of teachers' instructional strategies. Such beliefs arise in part out of widely held cultural values and assumptions and in part out of parents' personal experiences. Parents and teachers are more likely to work cooperatively toward common goals for students if they share similar beliefs about children and education.

Partnerships with Families

Effective partnerships with families rest squarely on good communication. Educators have several common methods of communication with families at their disposal but should also try to get parents actively involved in their children's education both at school and at home. Furthermore, teachers can be valuable sources of information to parents about how to support children's development more generally.

Now go to our Companion Website to assess your understanding of chapter content with Multiple-Choice Questions, apply comprehension in Essay Questions, and broaden your knowledge with links to related Developmental Psychology World Wide Web sites.

KEY CONCEPTS

family (p. 448)
socialization agents (p. 448)
self-socialization (p. 449)
family configuration (p. 457)
blended family (p. 460)
cohabiting family (p. 463)
parenting style (p. 464)

authoritarian parenting (p. 464)
authoritative parenting (p. 465)
permissive parenting (p. 465)
uninvolved parenting (p. 465)

self-care (p. 468)
only child (p. 471)
neglect (p. 474)
physical abuse (p. 474)
sexual abuse (p. 474)
emotional abuse (p. 474)

Artists: Lisia, Alyssa, Emmett, Ismael, Kit, Eric, Corey, Lisa, Humberto, Michael, Peggy, Keturah, Ama, Naomi, Mike. Supervising Artist: Jon Tran.

Interpersonal Relationships

CASE STUDY: AQEELAH, KELLY, AND JOHANNA

Aqeelah, Johanna, and Kelly had been close friends since elementary school. The three came from diverse ethnic and religious backgrounds: Aqeelah was an African American Muslim, Johanna was half Puerto Rican and half Jewish, and Kelly was an Irish Catholic. The girls lived in a racially and ethnically mixed suburban New Jersey community that seemed proud of its cultural diversity and integrated school system.

Yet as Tamar Lewin (2000) reported in *The New York Times,* other forces conspired to split the girls apart. In ninth grade, peers began pressuring them to declare loyalty to a single ethnic group:

> "[I]t's really confusing this year," [Aqeelah] said. "I'm too white to be black, and I'm too black to be white. If I'm talking to a white boy, a black kid walks by and says, 'Oh, there's Aqeelah, she likes white boys.' And in class, these Caucasian boys I've been friends with for years say hi, and then the next thing they say is, 'Yo, Aqeelah, what up?' as if I won't understand them unless they use that kind of slang. Or they'll tell me they really like 'Back That Thing Up' by Juvenile. I don't care if they like a rapper, but it seems like they think that's the only connection they have with me.
> "Last year this stuff didn't bother me, but now it does bother me, because some of the African-American kids, joking around, say I'm an Oreo."

Johanna and Kelly were surprised by her pain; they had not heard this before. But they did sense her increasing distance from them.

> "It's like she got lost or something," Kelly said. "I never see her."

Aqeelah had always been the strongest student of the three, the only one in a special math class, one rung above honors. But by winter, she was getting disappointing grades, especially in history, and beginning to worry about being moved down a level. Math was not going so well either, and so she dropped track to focus on homework. She was hoping to make the softball team, and disappointed that neither of her friends was trying out. "I'll never see you," she complained. (Lewin, 2000, p. 19)

Aqeelah did see less of Kelly and Johanna that year. Kelly and Johanna remained close, but Aqeelah spent more time with a family friend, another African American girl. Aqeelah felt a loss for her old friends:

> "I don't know why I don't call Johanna or Kelly," she said. "They'll always have the place in my heart, but not so much physically in my life these days. It seems like I have no real friends this year. You know how you can have a lot of friends, but you have no one? Everyone seems to be settled in their cliques and I'm just searching. And the more I get to know some people, the more I want to withdraw. I'm spending a lot more time with my family this year." (Lewin, 2000, pp. 19–20)

Excerpts from "Growing Up, Growing Apart: Fast Friends Try to Resist the Pressure to Divide by Race," by T. Lewin, June 25, 2000, *The New York Times.* Copyright © 2000 by the New York Times Co. Reprinted by permission.

PEERS ARE A POWERFUL force in children's and adolescents' lives. Close friends often provide companionship and emotional support for one another, and they acknowledge and value one another's individual strengths and talents. Furthermore, friends and nonfriends alike send regular messages about what behaviors are acceptable and what behaviors are not. Many of these messages are beneficial for children's long-term development; for instance, a child whose thoughtless remarks bring a classmate to tears learns a basic lesson about tact and diplomacy. Other messages from peers are not necessarily in young people's best interests, however; for instance, the students who called Aqeelah an "Oreo" were essentially telling her that it was inappropriate for her to associate with people outside her racial group.

In this chapter, we examine children's and adolescents' interpersonal behaviors, with a particular emphasis on their relationships with age-mates. We first explore theoretical perspectives and research findings regarding the development of interpersonal behaviors, both productive ones (such as prosocial behavior) and counterproductive ones (such as aggression). We then look more closely at the nature of peer relationships, such as friendships, cliques, and gangs. Finally, we consider the nature and development of romantic relationships and sexuality. Throughout the chapter, we identify strategies that teachers can use to promote social skills and productive peer relationships in classroom settings.

Development of Interpersonal Behaviors

As children grow older, they acquire an increasing repertoire of **social skills,** strategies they use to interact effectively with others. Yet they vary considerably in their social competence. Some are courteous, know how to initiate and sustain conversations, and regularly cooperate and share with peers. Others are less skilled; for instance, they may be anxious and uncertain in social situations and so keep to themselves, or they may shout, call names (e.g., Oreo), use physical aggression, and in other ways alienate their age-mates. As you might guess, children's and adolescents' social skills affect the number and quality of friendships that they have (Dishion, Andrews, & Crosby, 1995; Gottman, 1983; Rose & Asher, 1999).

Children develop social skills largely through experience and practice with peers and adults. For instance, when preschoolers engage in fantasy play, they must continually communicate, negotiate, and compromise regarding the course of events (Gottman, 1986b). When they cannot effectively resolve their conflicts, their activities may quickly disintegrate. Consider what happens when two 4-year-old girls disagree as they begin to play house:

> D: I'm the mommy.
> J: Who am I?
> D: Um, the baby.
> J: Daddy.
> D: Sister.
> J: I wanna be the daddy.
> D: You're the sister.
> J: Daddy.
> D: You're the *big* sister!
> J: Don't play house. I don't want to play house. (Gottman, 1983, p. 57)

Children also learn social skills by observing the behaviors of those around them. For instance, children's parents may model a variety of interpersonal behaviors—perhaps being upbeat, agreeable, and concerned about others' needs and rights, on the one hand, or hostile and aggressive, on the other (Dodge, Pettit, Bates, & Valente, 1995; Nix et al., 1999; Putallaz & Heflin, 1986).

Cognitive factors, such as personal goals and interpretations of others' behaviors, affect children's social competence as well. For example, children respond differently to situations such as this one:

> You and your friend just finished playing a board game. You had fun playing the game because you got to pick the game and it is your favorite. You really want to play the same game again, but your friend doesn't want to and says its her [or his] turn to play. (Rose & Asher, 1999, p. 73)

social skills
Strategies that people use to
interact effectively with others.

Children who are most interested in preserving the friendship in such a situation (e.g., "I would be trying to stay friends," "I would be trying to be fair") tend to have more friends than children who are primarily concerned with addressing their own needs (e.g., "I would be trying to keep my friend from pushing me around," "I would be trying to get back at my friend"; Rose & Asher, 1999, p. 71). As another example, adolescents who interpret any unwillingness or refusal on the part of another (e.g., "Do you want to go skating with me on Saturday?" "No, I can't. I'm busy on Saturday") as a sign of personal rejection are more likely to be aggressive in their interactions with others and have greater difficulty in their romantic relationships (Downey, Bonica, & Rincón, 1999; Downey, Lebolt, Rincón, & Freitas, 1998).

Two kinds of interpersonal behaviors—prosocial behavior and aggression—have been the subject of considerable research, and so we focus on them in the pages that follow. Later, we examine how children's and adolescents' interpersonal behaviors vary as a function of age and group membership.

Prosocial and Aggressive Behavior

Prosocial behavior is an action taken to benefit another person, such as helping, sharing, comforting, or showing empathy. **Aggressive behavior** is an action intentionally taken to hurt another person either physically (e.g., by hitting, shoving, or fighting) or psychologically (e.g., by embarrassing, insulting, or ostracizing). Curiosity about prosocial and aggressive tendencies in human beings, and in children more specifically, has spawned countless research studies and numerous theoretical explanations. Collectively, this body of work reveals that although prosocial behavior and aggression are at opposite ends of a helping-versus-hurting continuum, each probably has both hereditary and environmental origins. Here we look at the effects of heredity and environment and at basic principles and trends that characterize the development of prosocial and aggressive behavior.

Hereditary Influences   From an evolutionary perspective, both prosocial and aggressive tendencies have enabled human beings to survive and flourish (Coie & Dodge, 1998; Hoffman, 1981; Lorenz, 1966). Prosocial behavior promotes group cohesion, is critical for childrearing, and helps people survive in harsh conditions. For example, if you help your younger cousin by dressing her wounds, offering her water, and carrying her back to camp, you may prolong her life. When she becomes an adult and has her own children, she will pass along some of the genes that the two of you share. Prosocial behavior may also have played a role in our ancestors' mate selection: Females may have overlooked the chest-pounding king of the jungle in favor of more socially sensitive men. Aggression, too, though antisocial in nature, increases the chances of survival. Squabbling and warfare cause people to spread apart (thereby increasing their chances of finding adequate food and other essential resources), and in times of battle the strongest members of the species are those most likely to survive and give birth to future generations.

An evolutionary perspective of the hereditary roots of prosocial and aggressive behaviors is, of course, speculative at best. Twin studies provide more convincing evidence that such behaviors have genetic origins: Monozygotic (identical) twins tend to be more similar than dizygotic (fraternal) twins with respect to altruistic behavior, empathy for others, and aggression (Ghodsian-Carpey & Baker, 1987; Matthews, Batson, Horn, & Rosenman, 1981; Plomin et al., 1993; Rushton, Fulkner, Neal, Nias, & Eysenck, 1986; Zahn-Waxler, Robinson, & Emde, 1992). Furthermore, children's aggressive behavior may be partly determined by their temperaments, which tend to be fairly stable over time and often have a genetic basis (see Chapters 3 and 9). Some children show high levels of negative emotion beginning in early infancy, in that they are more irritable, impulsive, angry, and fearful than other infants (Matheny, 1989). In one study, children's temperaments at 6 months predicted their mothers' reports of behavior problems at age 3 (Bates, Maslin, & Frankel, 1985).

Environmental Influences   Environmental variables have their say in the development of prosocial and aggressive behavior as well. One particularly influential factor is the presence of prosocial and aggressive models in children's lives. For instance, children who observe sympathetic and generous models tend to be more helpful than those without such models (Elliott & Vasta, 1970; Owens & Ascione, 1991; Wilson, Piazza, & Nagle, 1990; Yarrow, Scott, &

prosocial behavior
Action intended to benefit another, without regard for one's own needs.

aggressive behavior
Action intentionally taken to hurt another, either physically or psychologically.

Waxler, 1973). People who are especially prosocial tend to have parents and other role models who've frequently acted with compassion, often despite personal sacrifice or risk (Oliner & Oliner, 1988; Rosenhan, 1970). For instance, rescuers of Jews in Nazi Europe before and during World War II perceived their parents as being people who regularly demonstrated strong moral convictions (London, 1970; Oliner & Oliner, 1988).

Just as prosocial models increase prosocial behavior, so, too, do aggressive models—whether they be actual adults or peers in children's lives or fictional characters in the media—engender more aggressive behavior (Bandura, 1973; Eron, 1980; Kellam, 1990). In a classic study (Bandura, Ross, & Ross, 1961), preschoolers were taken, one at a time, to a playroom containing a variety of toys and were seated at a table where they could draw pictures. Some of the children then observed an adult (an aggressive model) enter the room and engage in numerous aggressive behaviors toward an inflatable punching doll, including kicking the doll in the air, straddling it and hitting it over the head with a wooden mallet, and making statements like "Pow!" "Kick him," and "Punch him in the nose." Other children instead observed an adult (a nonaggressive model) come in and play in a constructive way with building blocks. Still other children saw no model while they were in the playroom. The children were then led to another room where they were mildly frustrated: Just as they began to play with some very attractive and entertaining toys, the toys were taken away from them. Finally, the children were taken to a third room in which both nonaggressive and aggressive toys (including the inflatable punching doll and wooden mallet) were present; their behaviors were recorded and coded for aggressive content by observers on the other side of a one-way mirror. Children who had seen the aggressive model were clearly the most aggressive of the three groups, and in fact they mimicked many of the same behaviors that they had seen the aggressive model display (e.g., straddling the doll and hitting it with the mallet). Children who had seen a nonaggressive model were even less aggressive than the no-model group. Models, then, can have an influence either way: Aggressive models are likely to increase aggression in children, and nonaggressive models are likely to decrease aggression.

Reinforcement plays a role as well. Over the short run, children engage in more prosocial behavior when they are reinforced (e.g., with candy or praise) for such behavior (Bryan, Redfield, & Mader, 1971; Eisenberg, Fabes, Carlo, & Karbon, 1992; Rushton & Teachman, 1978). However, such tangible rewards appear to be counterproductive over the long run, perhaps because children begin to perform prosocial actions to benefit themselves ("I gave her some of my candy because I knew Dad would give me an even bigger treat later for being so generous") rather than to express sympathy or genuine altruism (Eisenberg & Fabes, 1998; Fabes, Fultz, Eisenberg, May-Plumee, & Christopher, 1989; Szynal-Brown & Morgan, 1983). Aggressive behavior is often reinforced through the outcomes it brings about, in that it may enable children to gain desired objects or opportunities or to get revenge for perceived wrongdoings against themselves (Coie & Dodge, 1998; Crick & Dodge, 1996; Lochman, Wayland, & White, 1993). Sadly, some children are reinforced by the expressions of alarm and pain in their victims, perhaps because they gain a sense of power when they see someone else squirm (Bandura, 1991).

Finally, the general social and cultural contexts in which children are raised affect their prosocial and aggressive tendencies. For instance, children are more likely to imitate their parents' prosocial behaviors when parents exhibit an authoritative parenting style—when they are warm and loving, hold high standards for behavior, and explain why certain behaviors are unacceptable (Eisenberg, 1995; Eisenberg & Fabes, 1998; M. L. Hoffman, 1988). Children also tend to be more prosocial when their parents (mothers as well as fathers) have work obligations outside the home and so give them numerous responsibilities (e.g., taking care of younger siblings) to help keep the household going (Whiting & Whiting, 1975).

In contrast, some environments seem to be breeding grounds for aggression. For instance, frequent physical punishment at home appears to foster more aggression and other antisocial behavior in children (Straus, 2000; also see Chapter 12). Furthermore, some cultures teach children that aggression is an appropriate means of resolving conflicts or maintaining one's honor (Cohen & Nisbett, 1994; Staub, 1995). Environments also increase the probability of aggression when they induce negative feelings, thoughts, and memories (Berkowitz, 1989, 1993). For instance, children who live in poverty tend to be more aggressive than their peers, perhaps because their parents live in more stressful conditions and are more coercive and less

- Recent data from large-scale nationwide surveys and from police records of reported crimes reveal that almost 1 of every six 12- to 17-year-olds is the victim of at least one theft or other property crime every year. More than half of these crimes occur on school grounds. Furthermore, about 40% of crimes involving serious physical aggression occur at school rather than elsewhere. African American students and students living in urban areas are especially at risk for being the victims of criminal activity (Finkelhor & Ormrod, 2000).
- In a national survey of high school students, 36% of respondents reported being in a physical fight in the past year, 26% reported carrying a weapon in the past 30 days, and 10% had carried a weapon *at school* during that time period (Brener, Simon, Krug, & Lowry, 1999).
- In 1996, 5% of high school seniors reported that they had been injured with a weapon at school within the past 12 months, and 12% reported being injured without a weapon (Kaufman et al., 1999).
- During the 1996–1997 academic year, 10% of public schools reported at least one serious violent crime (e.g., murder, rape, suicide, attack with a weapon, robbery) to a law enforcement agency. Almost half of public schools (47%) reported a lesser crime (e.g., vandalism, fighting without a weapon) during the same period (Kaufman et al., 1999) .
- During the 1993–1994 academic year, 12% of elementary and secondary teachers were threatened with injury by a student, and 4% were physically attacked (Kaufman et al., 1999).
- In 1995, 9% of students ages 12–19 years avoided at least one place at school because of fear for their personal safety (Kaufman et al., 1999).

effective with them as a result (Guerra, Huesmann, Tolan, Van Acker, & Eron, 1995). Yet children from all walks of life encounter serious aggression and violence to some degree (Bell & Jenkins, 1993; Fingerhut, Ingram, & Feldman, 1992; Garbarino, 1995; Mazza & Overstreet, 2000; Osofsky, 1995; Rosenberg, O'Carroll, & Powell, 1992). Figure 13–1 illustrates the prevalence of physical aggression and violence in American society today.

Development of Prosocial Behavior Even infants respond to the distress of others, in that they often begin to cry when they hear other infants crying, and toddlers make feeble attempts to comfort people who seem to be unhappy or in pain (Simner, 1971; Zahn-Waxler, Radke-Yarrow et al., 1992). Young preschoolers occasionally exhibit such prosocial behaviors as helping, nurturing, and sharing, although their efforts are limited by minimal knowledge of what they can specifically do to help (Farver & Branstetter, 1994; Lamb, 1991). As a general rule, children behave more prosocially as they grow older; for example, they become increasingly generous (Eisenberg, 1982; Rushton, 1980). The Developmental Trends table on the next page describes common prosocial behaviors at various age levels.

Age, of course, is not the only variable that determines whether children and adolescents act prosocially. Youngsters who show higher stages of moral reasoning are more apt to exhibit moral and prosocial behavior (see the discussion of Kohlberg's theory in Chapter 10). Several additional factors are reflected in the following general principles:

- *Greater perspective-taking ability, empathy, and sympathy are associated with more prosocial behavior.* Children and adolescents are more likely to help someone else when they can look at a situation from the other person's perspective and have empathy and sympathy[1] for the person's plight (Eisenberg, 1995; Miller, et al., 1996; Underwood & Moore, 1982). Sympathy, a genuine concern for the person's well-being, is probably the most influential factor (Batson, 1991; Eisenberg & Fabes, 1998).

Early signs of perspective taking and empathy, in the form of concerned facial expressions, appear at age 2 or even earlier (Zahn-Waxler, Radke-Yarrow, et al., 1992), but true

---

[1]As noted in Chapter 10, *empathy* involves experiencing the same emotions as someone else, perhaps someone in pain or distress. *Sympathy* involves experiencing another's emotions *plus* feeling sorrow or concern about the person's plight.

Prosocial Behavior at Different Age Levels

DEVELOPMENTAL TRENDS

AGE	WHAT YOU MIGHT OBSERVE	DIVERSITY	IMPLICATIONS
Early Childhood (2–6) 	• Attempts to comfort those in distress, especially people whom children know well • Ineffective strategies for helping others in distress (e.g., crying, smiling, walking away, possibly even hitting a crying child) • Some sharing with others, especially familiar caregivers, beginning in the second year • Emerging concerns about possession and ownership, thereby limiting the inclination to share	• Children who have warm, sensitive parents more frequently comfort others. • Children from large families tend to be more prosocial than those from smaller ones.	• Allow children to give comfort when they can. • Model sympathetic responses; explain what you are doing and why you are doing it. • Recognize that young children's selfish and territorial behaviors are part of normal development.
Middle Childhood (6–10) 	• Increasing ability to care for younger children (e.g., feeding, clothing, doctoring scraped knees) • Increasing ability to take another's perspective, enabling more appropriate care and comfort to those in distress • General increase in the desire to help others as an objective in and of itself	• Children whose parents value prosocial behavior are more likely to value it as well and to have genuine concern for others. • Some children may act prosocially primarily to please adults or gain rewards.	• Alert children to the needs of others, and encourage them to see such needs as a reason for providing assistance. • Draw attention to a comforted child's relief when another child helps ("Look how much better Sally feels now that you've shared your snack with her"). • Use prosocial adjectives (e.g., "kind," "helpful") when praising altruistic behavior ("Brendan, you're always willing to help others. What a considerate young man you are!").
Early Adolescence (10–14)	• Growing ability to contribute to the maintenance of home and school environments • Emerging ability to serve as responsible caregivers of younger children • Tendency to believe that distressed individuals (e.g., the homeless) are entirely to blame for their own fate	• Some young adolescents are accustomed to sharing household responsibilities, whereas others are not. • Some young adolescents feel self-conscious about offering assistance even when concerned about others' welfare.	• Actively involve students in helping to maintain their school environment. • Let students know that giving, sharing, and caring for others are high priorities. • Encourage adolescents to think about how society's laws and practices affect people in need (e.g., the poor, the sick, the elderly).
Late Adolescence (14–18)	• Growing ability to assess the psychological characteristics of others and identify effective ways of providing comfort and assistance • Increasing ability to understand that people in any single category comprise a heterogeneous group (e.g., people may be homeless because they've lost their jobs, been the victims of natural disasters, are addicted to drugs or alcohol, etc.) • Belief that society has an obligation to help others in need	• Some teenagers are optimistic about what government and politicians can do to help people in need; others are more cynical. • Despite the stereotype that females are more empathic than males, young men are sometimes more active in helping others than young women (Eagly & Crowley, 1986).	• Encourage community service work to engender feelings of commitment to helping others. Ask students to reflect on their experiences through group discussions or written essays. • Assign autobiographies and other literature that depict individuals who have actively worked to help others.

Sources: Bar-Tal, Raviv, & Leiser, 1980; Burleson & Kunkel, 1995; Eagly & Crowley, 1986; Eisenberg & Fabes, 1998; Farver & Branstetter, 1994; Flanagan, 1995; Grusec & Redler, 1980; Hay, 1979; Hoffman, 1975; Krebs & Van Hesteren, 1994; Torney-Purta, 1990; West & Rheingold, 1978; Whiting & Whiting, 1975; Yates & Youniss, 1996; Youniss & Yates, 1999; Zahn-Waxler, Radke-Yarrow, et al., 1992.

concern for others' needs probably emerges only gradually over time. Nancy Eisenberg and her colleagues (Eisenberg, 1982; Eisenberg et al., 1995; Eisenberg, Lennon, & Pasternack, 1986) have identified five levels, reflecting different degrees of empathy and sympathy, that can help us predict how children at different ages are likely to behave in situations that call for altruism and other prosocial behaviors:

1. *Hedonistic orientation.* Most preschoolers and many younger elementary school students show little or no interest in helping others unless they can meet their own needs in the process. They are most likely to behave prosocially toward another person when they like that person and believe they will probably get something in return.
2. *Superficial needs-of-others orientation.* Some preschoolers and many elementary school students show some concern for others' physical and emotional needs and may express willingness to help another person even at personal sacrifice to themselves. Yet their concern lacks true understanding of, or empathy for, the other person's perspective. For example, a child might say "He's hungry" or "She needs this" without further explanation.
3. *Stereotyped, approval-focused orientation.* Some elementary and secondary students advocate prosocial behavior on the grounds that it's the "right" thing to do and that they will be better liked or appreciated if they help. However, they hold limited and stereotypical views of what "good" and "bad" people do. For example, a child may explain that "It's nice to help out" or "She'll be my friend if I help her."
4. *Empathic orientation.* A few elementary students and many secondary students express true empathy for another person's situation and a willingness to help other people based on those empathic feelings. Furthermore, they seem genuinely concerned with the well-being of another person and are able to perceive a situation from that person's perspective. For instance, they might say "I know just how she feels" or "I'd feel badly if I didn't help him because then he'd be in pain."
5. *Internalized values orientation.* A small minority of high school students express internalized values about helping other people—values that reflect concern for equality, dignity, human rights, and the welfare of society as a whole. These individuals maintain their self-respect by behaving in accordance with such values. For instance, they might say "I couldn't live with myself if I didn't help out" or "It's the responsibility of all of us to help one another whenever we can."

Children tend to act in more prosocial ways as they grow older; for example, they become increasingly empathic with age.

These five levels are not true *stages,* in that children and adolescents do not necessarily progress through them in a sequential or universal fashion. Instead, children may reason at two or more different levels during any particular time period (Eisenberg, Miller, Shell, McNalley, & Shea, 1991). Generally speaking, however, children and adolescents show increasing use of the upper levels, and less frequent use of lower ones, as they grow older (Eisenberg et al., 1995).

■ *Children tend to behave more prosocially when they feel responsible for another's welfare.* Youngsters are more likely to help people they know well (e.g., siblings and friends) than strangers, apparently because they have a greater sense of responsibility for people they know (Costin & Jones, 1992). They are also more likely to help another person if that individual has previously helped them (Berkowitz, 1968; Dreman, 1976; Levitt, Weber, Clark, & McDonnell, 1985). Guilt is involved in feelings of responsibility as well: Children are more likely to be helpful when they feel guilty about having caused another person pain or distress (Eisenberg, 1995).

■ *Children are more likely to help those whose misfortunes they perceive to be uncontrollable.* In Chapter 11, we described the explanations, or *attributions,* that children often have for their own successes and failures. But children (and adults, too) tend to form attributions about *others'* successes and failures as well. When children believe that others have brought misfortunes upon themselves (perhaps because of carelessness or a lack of effort), they are often reluctant to help. Their willingness to act prosocially increases when they believe that a person's troubles have occurred as a result of an accident, disability, or other uncontrollable circumstances (Eisenberg & Fabes, 1998; Graham, 1997).

> Dear Diary,
>
> Today there was a tragedy at school! Two people are now no longer with us. All because one person decided to bring a gun to school. This isn't fair to the parents, friends, and relitives of those people who died. My best friend is now gone. How could this happen? Why?
>
> anonymous

FIGURE 13–2 Occasionally, physical aggression at school has tragic consequences.

■ *Children weigh the costs and benefits of helping others and make their decisions accordingly.* Children are more likely to behave prosocially if the costs of doing so are inconsequential. For instance, they are more likely to share a snack if it's one that they don't particularly care for (Eisenberg & Shell, 1986). They are also more apt to be helpful if they believe that any significant costs involved are outweighed by the benefits of acting prosocially (Eisenberg et al., 1995; Eisenberg & Fabes, 1998). For instance, they are more likely to help if they believe the person will later return the favor (Eisenberg, Fabes, Schaller, Carlo, & Miller, 1991; Peterson, 1980). In some situations, of course, the benefits of prosocial actions are strictly internal: A feeling of personal satisfaction about helping someone else may more than make up for any loss of time or convenience.

Sometimes, of course, children believe that *aggression* yields more benefits than prosocial actions. We turn now to trends and principles that characterize the development of aggressive behavior.

Development of Aggressive Behavior Aggression takes many forms. Sometimes it involves physical violence, such as hitting, pushing, fighting, or the use of weapons (Figure 13–2). But at other times, the pain inflicted is psychological, such as when people tease, insult, ridicule, or spread malicious gossip about others. Aggression among children and adolescents occurs more frequently at school, particularly in locations where adult supervision is minimal (e.g., hallways, parking lots), than at any other location (Astor, Meyer, & Behre, 1999; Finkelhor & Ormrod, 2000).

Researchers have identified two distinct groups of aggressive children and adolescents (Crick & Dodge, 1996; Poulin & Boivin, 1999; Vitaro, Gendreau, Tremblay, & Oligny, 1998). Those who engage in **proactive aggression** deliberately aggress against someone else as a means of obtaining desired goals. Those who engage in **reactive aggression** respond aggressively to frustration or provocation. As you will discover shortly, youngsters who display the two types of aggression have somewhat different characteristics. Those who exhibit proactive aggression are most likely to have difficulty maintaining friendships with others (Poulin & Boivin, 1999).

Earlier we cited evidence that aggressive tendencies are partly the result of genetics, and so it should not surprise you to learn that aggression has a biological basis. For instance, high levels of the male hormone testosterone are correlated with high levels of aggression in adults (Archer, 1991). The causal nature of this relationship is somewhat unclear: Although different individuals have genetically influenced tendencies to produce greater or lesser amounts of testosterone, acting aggressively can also, in and of itself, lead to an increase in testosterone level (Coie & Dodge, 1998). The relative amounts of certain neurotransmitters (chemicals involved in transmitting messages from one neuron to another in the brain; see Chapter 3) also influence aggression: They determine whether children inhibit their initial impulses, on the one hand, or respond immediately to any annoyance or provocation, on the other (Coie & Dodge, 1998). In some cases, individuals who display heightened aggression have neurological deficits, such as a head injury resulting in damage to the frontal lobe, an area of the brain involved in the planning and control of behavior (Pennington & Bennetto, 1993; Raine & Scerbo, 1991).

Perhaps in part because some individuals are biologically predisposed to be more aggressive than others, children's aggressive tendencies remain somewhat stable over time. That is, those who are aggressive when they are young tend to be more aggressive in later years as well (Eron, 1980; Kupersmidt & Coie, 1990; Ladd & Burgess, 1999; Stattin & Magnusson, 1989). Furthermore, children who display proactive (but not reactive) aggression are at increased risk for engaging in delinquent activities later on (Vitaro et al., 1998). Generally speaking, however, aggressive behaviors decline in frequency throughout childhood and adolescence, especially as youngsters develop more effective ways of interacting with others and resolving conflicts (Cairns, Cairns, Neckerman, Ferguson, & Gariépy, 1989; Coie & Dodge, 1998; Loeber, 1982). Additional developmental changes in aggression are described in the Developmental Trends table that follows.

proactive aggression
Deliberate aggression against another as a means of obtaining a desired goal.

reactive aggression
Aggressive response to frustration or provocation.

Aggression at Different Age Levels

DEVELOPMENTAL TRENDS

AGE	WHAT YOU MIGHT OBSERVE	DIVERSITY	IMPLICATIONS
Early Childhood (2–6) 	• Displays of anger when desires are thwarted, especially in younger children; increasing ability to inhibit angry responses with age • Aggressive struggles with peers over possessions • Decrease in physical aggression and increase in verbal aggression (between ages 2 and 4) • Higher rates of aggression when children first get to know one another; eventually they work out their differences and establish dominance hierarchies (i.e., leaders and followers)	• Some children have "difficult" temperaments (e.g., they are easily angered and distressed) and are more likely to act aggressively toward peers. • Children with language delays are more likely to exhibit physical aggression (Richman, Stevenson, & Graham, 1982). • On average, boys are more physically aggressive than girls.	• Encourage young children to use their words rather than their fists. • Acknowledge any gentle, controlled, and constructive responses to frustration or provocation. • Comfort the victims of aggression, and administer appropriate consequences for the perpetrators. Be sure to explain why aggressive behavior cannot be tolerated. • Reassure parents that aggressive behavior is fairly common in preschoolers, but offer strategies for promoting prosocial behavior and discouraging aggression.
Middle Childhood (6–10) 	• Decrease in overt physical aggression, but with an increase in more covert antisocial behaviors (e.g., cheating, lying, stealing) • Awareness of others' hostile intentions ("She meant to do that")	• Some children become highly aggressive in the elementary grades. • Some children frequently engage in *relational aggression*, gossiping about others and excluding them from friendship groups. • Some children (more boys than girls) display ongoing conduct problems (defiance, aggression, temper tantrums). Children with conduct disorders may instigate fights, use weapons, vandalize buildings, or set fires.	• Do not tolerate physical aggression or bullying. Make sure students understand rules for behavior, and follow through with established procedures when students are aggressive. • Keep your eyes open for children who seem to be the frequent victims of others' aggression, and help them form productive relationships with peers. • Communicate with parents about effective disciplinary strategies (e.g., through newsletters or evening parent groups).

(continued)

Researchers have identified several general principles that can better help us understand the nature and causes of aggression in children and adolescents:

■ *Some forms of verbal aggression are common and appear to serve a social function.* Teasing one another is a common way of initiating conversation or showing affection, especially in early adolescence (B. B. Brown, 1999; Gottman & Mettetal, 1986). And gossip provides a means whereby children and adolescents alike can explore one another's beliefs and priorities; it may also help them establish an emotional bond—a sense of *we-ness*—that unites them against a common "enemy" (Gottman, 1986a, 1986b; Gottman & Mettetal, 1986). As an example, consider how two middle school students use gossip about their teachers to get to know each other better:

A: I have a dumb teacher. She goes, "Well, I'd like to try your muffins but I have no sense of taste." I'm going [*makes a disgusted face*].

B: [*Giggle.*]

A: I mean you could tell by her clothes that she had no sense of taste . . . [*Later.*] Yeah, my teacher she shows the dumbest movies. We, Friday we saw a movie about how bread gets moldy. She wants to teach us all about, um, calories and stuff and she's so fat you can tell she needs to learn more than us.

B: [*Giggle.*]

A: There's not a fat person in the class, except for the teacher.

B: [*Giggle.*] About the most sophisticated foreign language teacher we have is our French teacher.

AGE	WHAT YOU MIGHT OBSERVE	DIVERSITY	IMPLICATIONS
Early Adolescence (10–14)	• Decline in physical aggression • Frequent teasing and taunting of peers • Occasional sexual harassment and hazing	• Some young adolescents engage in criminal behaviors, such as forced sex or other violent crimes. • Adolescents in some families and neighborhoods have easy access to weapons and regular exposure to violent role models.	• Supervise students' between-class and after-school activities; make it clear that physical aggression is not acceptable on school grounds. • Enforce prohibitions against bringing weapons to school. • Initiate programs that have been shown to reduce school aggression (e.g., peer mediation programs).
Late Adolescence (14–18)	• For many, less motivation to engage in aggressive behavior, often as a result of forming intimate relationships or securing stable employment • Possible increase in risky behaviors and aggressive activities, especially for some boys	• Boys are more likely to be arrested for criminal offenses than girls (Snyder, Finnegan, Nimick, Sickmund, & Tierney, 1987). In late adolescence, serious crimes continue to increase for boys but level off for girls; boys' crimes decrease after age 18 (Elliott, 1994). • On average, students who live in poor, violent neighborhoods are more apt to become aggressive. • Substance use and sexual activity increase the probability of aggression.	• Give students reasons for optimism about making a living in the work world (e.g., arrange for mentorships or internships with local businesspeople or government officials), in part as a way to steer them away from criminal activities. • Continually show students how classroom subject matter relates to their personal goals and equips them to deal constructively with the demands of the outside world. • Work cooperatively with law enforcement and social service agencies in efforts to curtail aggression and crime in your community.

Sources: B. B. Brown, 1999; Cairns, 1979; Coie & Dodge, 1998; Crick & Grotpeter, 1995; Dodge, 1980; Elliott, 1994; Hartup, 1974; Hay & Ross, 1982; Jenkins, Bax, & Hart, 1980; Jersild & Markey, 1935; Jessor, Donovan, & Costa, 1991; Kagan, 1981; Ladd & Burgess, 1999; Lahey, Loeber, Quay, Frick, & Grimm, 1992; Loeber, 1982; Loeber & Hay, 1993; Loeber, Lahey, & Thomas, 1991; Loeber & Schmaling, 1985; Mischel, 1974; Richman et al., 1982; Rutter, 1989; Snyder et al., 1987; Stenberg, Campos, & Emde, 1983; Strayer & Trudel, 1984; Thomas, Chess, & Birch, 1968; Wenar, 1972.

A: I can't stand it.

B: Oh, and she's always going, I say, "Hi, Miss Rickey" and she goes, "Bonjour" *[giggles]*.

A: *[Giggle.]*

B: I was walking down steps and I almost fell. I was cracking up. I was going, "OK, whatever you say."

A: Ours is a mean French teacher and she goes, OK I was, I was writing a note to my friend, and she goes, "Are you doing your homework?" And I go, "No" and she goes, "Ah, ah, ah." You know, I mean I can't take this little kid stuff.

B: It's so pitiful to see the teachers.

A: Uh huh. (Gottman & Mettetal, 1986, p. 214; reprinted with the permission of Cambridge University Press)

■ *Aggressive children often have deficits in perspective-taking, empathy, and moral judgment.* Children and adolescents who are highly aggressive tend to get low scores on measures of perspective-taking ability, empathy, and moral reasoning (Chandler, 1973; Damon & Hart, 1988; Marcus, 1980). The ways in which aggressive youths often justify their aggression reveal their disengagement from the feelings and rights of others. For instance, they may rationalize violent acts by focusing on their own reputations ("I'm the Man"), comparing their behaviors to more severe violations ("I never shot anyone with a gun"), describing what they're doing in euphemistic terms ("I gotta teach Billy a lesson"), deflecting personal responsibility

("I was just doing what Dad does"), or dehumanizing victims with derogatory labels ("She's a dumb-ass prude"; Coie & Dodge, 1998).

■ *Aggressive children often misinterpret social cues.* Virtually any social situation provides clues about people's motives and intentions. Although some social cues are straightforward, others are not. For instance, if one child bumps into another, it is not always clear whether the child intended to cause harm. In such ambiguous situations, aggressive children and adolescents often perceive hostile intent in others' behaviors. This **hostile attributional bias** of aggressive children has been observed in numerous studies (Erdley, Qualey, & Pietrucha, 1996; Graham & Hudley, 1994; Graham, Hudley, & Williams, 1992; Guerra & Slaby, 1989; Juvonen, 1991; Katsurada & Sugawara, 1998; Lochman & Dodge, 1994). It is especially prevalent in children who are prone to *reactive* aggression (Crick & Dodge, 1996).[2]

■ *Many aggressive children have poor social problem–solving skills.* Imagine yourself in an 8-year-old's shoes encountering the following situation:

> Pretend one day that one of the adults came in with a plate of candy bars. There was just enough for each kid to have one candy bar and another kid in the group took two candy bars leaving none for you. (Schwartz et al., 1998, p. 440)

Aggressive children often have limited ability to generate effective solutions to such social dilemmas; for instance, they are apt to think that hitting, shoving, or barging into the middle of a game are perfectly acceptable behaviors (Lochman & Dodge, 1994; Neel, Jenkins, & Meadows, 1990; Schwartz et al., 1998; Shure & Spivack, 1980). And those who display high rates of *proactive* aggression are more likely than their nonaggressive peers to anticipate that aggressive action will yield positive results—for instance, that it will enhance their status (Anderson, 1990; Dodge, Lochman, Harnish, Bates, & Pettit, 1997; Hart, Ladd, & Burleson, 1990; Pellegrini & Bartini, 2000).

■ *Aggressive children may have different priorities than nonaggressive children.* Many people, children and adults alike, have a high need for affiliation; in other words, they actively seek out friendly relationships with others (see Chapter 11). For most young people, establishing and maintaining such relationships is a high priority. For aggressive youngsters, however, more self-centered goals—perhaps seeking revenge or gaining power and dominance—often take precedence (Crick & Dodge, 1996; Erdley & Asher, 1996; Lochman et al., 1993; Pellegrini, Bartini, & Brooks, 1999).

■ *Aggressive children often think aggression is appropriate behavior.* Many aggressive youngsters believe that violence and other forms of aggression are acceptable ways of resolving conflicts and retaliating for others' misdeeds (Astor, 1994; Boldizar, Perry, & Perry, 1989; Erdley et al., 1996; Zelli et al., 1999). For example, in a study by Astor (1994), children with a history of violent behavior (e.g., throwing rocks at others, hitting classmates with objects, engaging in fist fights, in one case beating up a substitute teacher) and nonaggressive children were given situations that described unprovoked and provoked acts of aggression. The following scenarios are examples:

Unprovoked aggression
Josh and Mark are brothers. One day Mark was playing in the yard. He was running across the yard and fell down and hurt himself. He was really mad. He turned around and saw Josh. He hit Josh on the head. Josh looked upset and walked away. (Astor, 1994, p. 1057)

Provoked aggression
Jack and Ron are brothers. One day after school, they were both playing in the backyard of their apartment. After a few minutes of playing Jack started teasing and calling Ron bad names. So Ron punched Jack in the stomach and face. Jack got hurt and cried a lot. (Astor, 1994, p. 1058)

The children, aggressive and nonaggressive alike, believed that unprovoked acts of aggression were morally wrong. Furthermore, the nonaggressive children believed that physical aggression in response to psychological harm (e.g., teasing, name calling) was also morally unacceptable—that physical harm was a far more serious offense than psychological harm. In contrast, the violent children gave equal weight to the seriousness of physical and psychological aggression

---

[2]Within the context of Dodge's (1986) social information processing theory (see Chapter 10), hostile attributions are made during the *representation* phase.

hostile attributional bias
Tendency to interpret others' behaviors (especially ambiguous ones) as reflecting aggressive or hostile motives.

and believed that physical aggression was appropriate retaliation for psychological abuse. Astor speculated that the violent children may have been the recipients of considerable psychological aggression in their own lives and perceived it to be as painful as physical aggression.

■ *Some children show a pattern of bullying behavior, often directed at particular victims.* Researchers have found that some youngsters (**bullies**) direct considerable aggression toward particular children, or *victims* (Patterson, Littman, & Bricker, 1967; Pellegrini et al., 1999; Schwartz, Dodge, Pettit, & Bates, 1997). Some victims rarely retaliate or in other ways stand up for themselves; others are prone to reactive aggression (Schwartz et al., 1997; Schwartz et al., 1998). Children who are chronic bullies tend to be hyperactive, to overreact to accidents and other unfortunate incidents, to be relatively unpopular, and to believe that bullying behavior will enhance their status with peers (Pellegrini & Bartini, 2000; Pellegrini et al., 1999). Victims are often children who are immature, anxious, socially withdrawn, and friendless (some also have disabilities) and so are relatively defenseless against more powerful aggressors (Hodges, Malone, & Perry, 1997; Juvonen, Nishina, & Graham, 2000; Little, 2000c; Schwartz, McFadyen-Ketchum, Dodge, Pettit, & Bates, 1999). Those victims who respond with reactive aggression are often the victims of aggression and abuse at home as well as at school (Schwartz et al., 1997).

In the Basic Developmental Issues table on the facing page, we contrast prosocial behavior and aggression in terms of nature versus nurture, universality versus diversity, and qualitative versus quantitative change. We now look more generally at how children's interpersonal behaviors change over time.

Interpersonal Behaviors at Different Ages

Throughout the lifespan, people continue to develop and refine strategies for interacting effectively with others. But most strategies are acquired in the first two decades of life, in childhood and adolescence. Each of the four developmental periods we've considered throughout the book—early childhood, middle childhood, early adolescence, and late adolescence—offers new lessons and new opportunities for growth in social skills.

Early Childhood (Ages 2–6) Two-year-olds already have a few rudimentary social skills. When they were infants, they probably learned to respond appropriately when other infants pointed, babbled, or smiled at them (Eckerman, 1979; Mueller & Silverman, 1989). As toddlers, they may have offered one another toys and imitated one another, creating a sharing focus: I do this, and you do that, then I follow you, then you follow me, and so on (Howes, 1992; Howes & Matheson, 1992). Their developing language in the second year, as well as games with older children and adults (e.g., peek-a-boo, pat-a-cake), permitted increasingly sustained and meaningful exchanges (Bronson, 1981).

With the capacity for coordinating attention with others well underway by age 2, young children increasingly interact with their age-mates, particularly within the context of play activities. In a classic study, Mildred Parten (1932) carefully observed the behaviors of forty 2- to 5-year-old children who attended a preschool at the University of Minnesota. From her observations, she identified six categories of behavior in preschoolers, five of which involve play:

- *Unoccupied behavior.* Children fail to engage in a particular activity or interact with another individual. They may wander around the room or remain stationary, simply sitting or staring into space.
- *Solitary play.* Children sit absorbed with their own playthings. Other children are in the same room but might as well be on another planet: The children neither communicate with one another nor acknowledge one another's existence.
- *Onlooker behavior.* Children watch others who are engaged in play activities but make no social overtures. For instance, a child may quietly watch another child build a tower with wooden blocks.
- *Parallel play.* Children play quietly side by side. Although they may do similar things, they do not talk much with one another.
- *Associative play.* Children play together, sharing objects and talking a little. They may pass objects back and forth and make occasional comments on what they are doing.
- *Cooperative play.* Children actively coordinate their activities, swapping toys, taking on defined roles, and in other ways keeping an interaction going.

bully
Child who repeatedly pesters and humiliates other children, with a particular focus on certain victims.

Contrasting Prosocial Behavior and Aggression

BASIC DEVELOPMENTAL ISSUES

ISSUE	PROSOCIAL BEHAVIOR	AGGRESSION
Nature and Nurture	The capacity for prosocial behavior appears to be a natural, inborn human characteristic, but individual children have unique genetic endowments (e.g., temperaments) that affect such prosocial behavior. Prosocial behavior is nurtured by role modeling, specific instruction and feedback, and other environmental supports.	The capacity for aggression has a biological basis and is to some degree inherited. Aggressiveness in individual children is influenced by temperamental dispositions, hormone levels, and neurological structures in the brain. Yet the social environment powerfully influences how children express their aggressive impulses. Parents and other caregivers may treat children harshly and punitively and in other ways model (and possibly even encourage) aggressive behavior; such actions can lead to aggression and conduct problems at school.
Universality and Diversity	The capacity for prosocial behavior is universal in the human species; furthermore, people in most cultures become increasingly prosocial as they get older. Significant diversity exists in the extent to which various cultural groups encourage prosocial activities (e.g., sharing, nurturing), as well as in children's exposure to adults who model prosocial behavior and articulate a commitment to care for people in need.	Aggressive behavior is universal in human beings. Some general developmental sequences in aggressive expression, such as a gradual shift from physical aggression to more verbal aggression, may also be universal. Substantial diversity is present in the ways that children and adolescents express aggression, in the amount of aggression young people encounter in their daily environments, and in the extent to which cultural groups condone aggression as a way of resolving conflict.
Qualitative and Quantitative Change	Qualitative changes may occur in students' understanding of why helping others is important and valuable; for instance, young children often give help primarily to gain rewards or approval, whereas older children and adolescents are more likely to have a genuine concern for those in need. Quantitative increases occur in children's knowledge of effective prosocial strategies and in their ability to carry out such strategies.	Qualitative change is seen in the shift from physical aggression to verbal aggression. Furthermore, although young children may grab or hit other children to obtain desired toys, they don't necessarily intend to hurt their peers; in contrast, older children may become more deliberately hostile and hurtful in their actions toward others. The degree to which children and adolescents display aggressive behavior changes quantitatively with development. The frequency of aggression is often low in infancy, increases in early childhood, and decreases during middle childhood. For a minority, it increases again during adolescence, after which it usually decreases, especially as young adults take on conventional adult responsibilities and form intimate relationships with mates.

Sources: Coie & Dodge, 1998; Eisenberg & Fabes, 1998.

Parten concluded that children progress through a defined sequence of play—beginning with unoccupied behavior, moving through the categories, and eventually developing cooperative play—all the while becoming more social in their exchanges.

To some extent, Parten was right: Children do become increasingly interactive and cooperative in their play activities as they grow older (Gottman, 1983; Howes & Matheson, 1992). Yet younger and older preschoolers alike exhibit all five categories of play; thus, later forms do not completely replace earlier ones (Howes & Matheson, 1992). Furthermore, parallel play, though seemingly nonsocial, appears to have a definite social function: Children use it as a way to learn more about other children's interests and to initiate conversations (Bakeman & Brownlee, 1980; Rubin, Bukowski, & Parker, 1998).

Such qualifications aside, Parten rightly elevated cooperative play to an advanced state. The imagination and social coordination that characterize cooperative play make it a stellar achievement of early childhood. In one form of cooperative play, **sociodramatic play,** children assume complementary imagined roles and carry out a logical sequence of actions. In the following

sociodramatic play
Play in which children take on assumed roles and act out a scenario of events.

scenario, we see Eric and Naomi, long-time friends who've assumed the roles of husband "Bob" and wife "Claudia." Naomi is making plans to go shopping:

N: I'm buying it at a toy store, to buy Eric Fisher a record 'cause he doesn't have a . . .
E: What happened to his old one?
N: It's all broken.
E: How did it get all broken?
N: Ah, a robber stealed it, I think. That's what he said, a robber stealed it.
E: Did he see what the action was? You know my gun is in here, so could you go get my gun? It's right over there, back there, back there, not paper . . . did you get it?
N: Yes, I found the robbers right in the closet.
E: Good, kill 'em.
N: I killed em.
E: Already?
N: Yes, so quick they can't believe it.
E: Well, Claudia, you can call me Bob everytime, Claudia . . . (Gottman, 1986b, p. 191; reprinted with the permission of Cambridge University Press)

In Chapter 4, we considered the ways in which play, especially sociodramatic play, fosters cognitive development. Yet sociodramatic play and other forms of cooperative play promote social development as well. More specifically, successful cooperative play requires children to hone their social skills in the following ways:

■ *Children learn more about other people's perspectives.* For children to play successfully together, they must learn a great deal about one another's ideas, interests, and wishes (Göncü, 1993; Gottman, 1986b; Howes, 1992). They also get practice in establishing **intersubjectivity,** that is, in sharing understandings and finding common ground (Göncü, 1993; Gottman, 1983; Mueller & Brenner, 1977). Preschoolers exhibit a variety of strategies that show an appreciation for one another's perspectives. For instance, they may voice approval for one another's actions ("That's pretty"), express sympathy and support ("Don't worry about that, it'll come off"), and exchange witticisms ("How do you do this stupid thing?" "You do it in a stupid way?"; Gottman, 1983, p. 58).

■ *Children learn how to coordinate their actions and perspectives.* When two children play together cooperatively, they must often take turns, share objects, and in other ways consider what their playmate is doing. They must also agree on individual roles ("I'll be the warrior" "OK, I'll be the chief"), props ("The log can be our base"), and rules and guidelines that govern actions ("We'll let Frances play, but she has to be the horse"; Garvey, 1990; Howes & Matheson, 1992). And underneath it all, they must agree to share certain fantasies—a phenomenon known as **social pretense** (Rubin et al., 1998).

Young children often enter into activities that require cooperation and coordination slowly and carefully, particularly when they don't know one another very well (Gottman, 1983). Notice how two 4-year-olds, playing together for the first time, increasingly coordinate their activities with Play-Doh:

J: I got a fruit cutter plate.
D: Mine's white.
J: You got white Play-Doh and this color and that color.
D: Every color. That's the colors we got. . . .
D: I'm putting pink in the blue.
J: Mix pink.
D: Pass the blue.
J: I think I'll pass the blue. . . .
D: And you make those for after we get it together, OK?
J: 'Kay.
D: Have to make these.
J: Pretend like those little roll cookies, too, OK?
D: And make, um, make a, um, pancake, too.
J: Oh rats. This is a little pancake.
D: OK. Make, make me, um, make two flat cookies. Cause I'm, I'm cutting any, I'm cutting this. My snake. . . .
J: You want all my blue?

intersubjectivity
Interaction between two or more social partners who share a common frame of reference, or interpretation of events.

social pretense
Ability to share internal fantasies with a social partner.

508 | Chapter Thirteen / Interpersonal Relationships

D: Yes. To make cookies. Just to make cookies, but we can't mess the cookies all up.
J: Nope. . . .
D: Put this the right way, OK? We're making supper, huh?
J: We're making supper. Maybe we could use, if you get white, we could use that, too, maybe.
D: I don't have any white. Yes, we, yes I do.
J: If you got some white, we could have some, y'know. (Gottman, 1983, pp. 56–57)

As children grow older, they more readily coordinate their play activities, particularly when they know one another well. In the following scenario, Teresa's son Alex (age 5) and his long-time friend Davis (age 6) have just jointly completed a drawing (Figure 13–3). As they worked on the picture, they continually listened to each other, built on each other's ideas, and drew from their many past experiences together (e.g., playing "chemistry" with vinegar, baking soda, food coloring, and dirt in the backyard). The result was a mutually agreed-upon effort:

Teresa: What do you call your picture?
Alex: It's like a robot house.
Davis: A robot chemistry house.
Alex: Yeah, it's a robot house that keeps chemistry in it and people.
Davis: We tour other people in it.
Alex: Yeah, like Connor and Mom and Dad, and our fish.
Davis: Yeah, and like my Mom and Dad and Jacob [brother] and Sydney [cat].
Alex: Yeah. This is our chemistry lab.
Davis: That [pointing at green object on bottom] is a spaceship made out of green. This [pointing at blue object at top] is fire coming out of chemistry.
Alex: This [pointing to object in black at top left] is our helicopter. This [black swirling lines] is our trails.
Davis: This is our trails. We just walk around and get exercise. It's shaped to look like a robot to scare bad guys.
Alex: I need to make wheels [draws three enclosed circles toward bottom].

FIGURE 13–3 Alex (age 5) and Davis (age 6) drew this picture together, sharing fantasies that guided their drawing.

■ *Children learn how to ask for what they want.* As children gain experience with their peers, they become increasingly skillful and polite in making requests of others (Parkhurst & Gottman, 1986). Directives are common among younger preschoolers (e.g., "Give me the red one" "You hafta . . ."), whereas 5- and 6-year-olds are more likely to use hints and suggestions ("Have you got . . . ?" "Let's . . ." "Would you like . . ."; Parkhurst & Gottman, 1986, p. 329).

■ *Children develop strategies for resolving conflicts.* Cooperative play is a fertile training ground for developing social problem–solving and conflict-resolution skills (Göncü, 1993; Gottman, 1986b; Howes, 1992). For instance, children may haggle and eventually compromise about roles in sociodramatic play ("I want to be the Mommy, you're the baby" "No, you were the Mommy last time; it's *my* turn" "OK, but next time I get to be the Mommy"). And when they discover that they cannot reach agreement, they often return to an activity at which they have previously played more harmoniously (Gottman, 1983). Nevertheless, even older preschoolers sometimes cooperate more successfully when adults help them iron out their difficulties (Mize, Pettit, & Brown, 1995; Parke & Bhavnagri, 1989).

Because cooperative play requires so many skills, it does not, of course, burst on the scene fully formed. Children have to work hard at it (fortunately, it's a sufficiently entertaining enterprise that they don't mind the effort). With time and practice, children become increasingly proficient; for example, they develop new strategies for finding common ground, engage in longer episodes of sociodramatic play, and construct increasingly elaborate roles and story lines (Göncü, 1993; Rubin et al., 1998). By the time they reach the early elementary grades, they are ready to take on new challenges in their interpersonal relationships.

Middle Childhood (Ages 6–10) Life becomes much more social in middle childhood. Any single day is filled with countless interactions with family members, teachers, classmates, and other individuals of all ages (Barker & Wright, 1951). This complex social world provides many opportunities to interact with age-mates. At ages 6 through 12, children spend about 40% of their waking hours with peers, approximately twice as much time as they did in early childhood (Zarbatany, Hartmann, & Rankin, 1990).

FIGURE 13–4 In 10-year-old Jacob's drawing, a child and his friend argue but then come to a mutually acceptable solution.

During middle childhood, children become increasingly attuned to other people's psychological characteristics—their personalities, emotions, and so on (see Chapter 10). They also become increasingly aware that, in the company of peers, certain ways of behaving are acceptable and others are not (Gottman & Mettetal, 1986; Harris, 1998). In a gossip session, 8-year-olds Erica and Mikaila reveal their shared belief that tattling on others is inappropriate:

E: Katie's just a . . .
M: Tattletale.
E: Yeah, she tells on everything.
M: Yeah. (Gottman & Mettetal, 1986, p. 206; reprinted with the permission of Cambridge University Press)

With their growing awareness of other people's opinions, children become more eager and able to behave in socially acceptable ways; they also become more concerned about equitably resolving conflicts and preserving friendships (Hartup, 1996; Newcomb & Bagwell, 1995). In Figure 13–4, 10-year-old Jacob reveals his awareness that arguing with friends can be unpleasant but that disputes often can be resolved to everyone's satisfaction. Not all attempts to resolve conflicts are successful, of course. Most children discover that such strategies as sulking ("I'm going home!"), threatening ("I'm never gonna play with you again!"), and hitting ("Take that!") rarely work. Through experimentation with a variety of strategies and through their growing capacity for perspective taking and empathy, most children become increasingly proficient at maintaining amicable relationships with their peers.

By the elementary school years, much of children's time is spent *without* the direct supervision of adults. When parents and teachers are not hovering nearby, children tend to sort things out for themselves, not only in dealing with disagreements but also in choosing and directing activities. Unlike younger children, who get together in groups of two or three to engage in free-flowing fantasy and pretense, elementary school children often convene in larger groups and choose games and other activities that have established rules, such as verbal contests (e.g., "Twenty Questions," "I Spy"), board games, and team sports (Corsaro, 1985; Hartup, 1984). In fact, rules take on a certain immutable quality: They are permanent fixtures that cannot be altered by whim, and failure to follow them constitutes cheating—a serious breach from what is good and civilized. In the following conversation with 10-year-old Ben, an adult asks if it would be possible to change the rules in a game of marbles. Ben agrees (somewhat unwillingly) that he could formulate new rules but has serious concerns about their legitimacy:

Ben: [I]t would be cheating.
Adult: But all your pals would like to [play with the new rule], wouldn't they?
Ben: Yes, they all would.
Adult: Then why would it be cheating?
Ben: Because I invented it: it isn't a rule! It's a wrong rule because it's outside of the rules. A fair rule is one that is in the game.
Adult: How does one know if it is fair?
Ben: The good players know it.
Adult: And suppose the good players wanted to play with your rule?
Ben: It wouldn't work. Besides they would say it was cheating.
Adult: And if they all said that the rule was right, would it work?
Ben: Oh, yes, it would. . . . But it's a wrong rule!
Adult: But if they all said it was right how would anyone know that it was wrong?
Ben: Because when you are in the square it's like a garden with a fence, you're shut in [so that if the shooter stays inside the square, you are "dished"].
Adult: And suppose we draw a square like this [we draw a square with a break in one of the sides, like a fence broken by a door]?
Ben: Some boys do that. But it isn't fair. It's just for fun for passing the time.
Adult: Why?
Ben: Because the square ought to be closed.

Adult:	But if some boys do it, is it fair or not?
Ben:	It's both fair and not fair.
Adult:	Why is it fair?
Ben:	It is fair for waiting [for fun].
Adult:	And why is it not fair?
Ben:	Because the square ought to be closed.
Adult:	When you are big, suppose everyone plays that way, will it be right or not?
Ben:	It will be right then because there will be new children who will learn the rule.
Adult:	And for you?
Ben:	It will be wrong.
Adult:	And what will it be "really and truly"?
Ben:	It will really be wrong. (dialogue from Piaget, 1932/1960, p. 55; format adapted)

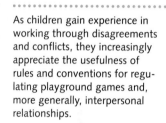

Children learn a great deal from participating in rule-governed games. For instance, they discover how to use rules to their own advantage ("If I put another house on Boardwalk, you have to pay me double the amount next time you land on it"), how to form alliances with other children ("I'll run behind him, and then you pass me the ball way over his head"), and how to deal with ambiguous situations ("It was *in!*" "Are you kidding? It was *out!*" "OK, it's out, but next time *I* get to decide"). Occasional bickering aside, the predominance of rule-governed activities in middle childhood seems to reflect children's growing motivation to learn and abide by the rules of society (DeVries, 1997).

As children gain experience in working through disagreements and conflicts, they increasingly appreciate the usefulness of rules and conventions for regulating playground games and, more generally, interpersonal relationships.

Early Adolescence (Ages 10–14) Once children reach puberty, they rely increasingly on their peers for emotional support as well as recreation (Levitt, Guacci-Franco, & Levitt, 1993; Ryan et al., 1994). Furthermore, many young adolescents, girls especially, begin to reveal their innermost thoughts to others, and more often to peers rather than adults (Basinger et al., 1995; Levitt et al., 1993). In fact, such **self-disclosure** is usually a key ingredient in close friendships (Gottman, 1986a).

Even as their tendency for self-disclosure increases, young adolescents become increasingly self-conscious about what others might think of them. Recall our discussion of the *imaginary audience* in Chapter 9: Adolescents often overestimate other people's interest in their appearance and behavior. This heightened concern for how others evaluate them can lead them to be quite conforming—that is, to rigidly imitate their peers' choices in dress, music, slang, and behavior. By looking and sounding like others, they may feel that they better fit in with their classmates (Hartup, 1983; Owens, 1996). Young adolescents encourage others to conform as well, perhaps by teasing or insulting those who stand out as different (recall how some African American students called Aqeelah an Oreo for her friendships with Caucasians). Such **peer pressure** has its greatest effects during the junior high school years; adolescents who have weaker emotional bonds to their families seem to be especially vulnerable (Berndt, Laychak, & Park, 1990; Erwin, 1993; Ryan & Lynch, 1989; Urdan & Maehr, 1995).

Although peer pressure is certainly a factor in teenagers' desire to conform, their internal motivation to fit in is probably a stronger determinant (recall our discussion of *self-socialization* in Chapter 12). A desire to be part of the "in" crowd drives many to do foolish things, as one student reveals:

There's all this crap about being accepted into a group and struggling and making an effort to make friends and not being comfortable about your own self-worth as a human being. You're trying very hard to show everyone what a great person you are, and the best way to do that is if everyone else is drinking therefore they think that's the thing to do, then you might do the same thing to prove to them that you have the same values that they do and therefore you're okay. At the same time, the idea of peer pressure is a lot of bunk. What I heard about peer pressure all the way through school is that someone is going to walk up to me and say, "Here, drink this and you'll be cool." It wasn't like that at all. You go somewhere and everyone else would be doing it and you'd think, "Hey, everyone else is doing it and they seem to be having a good time—now why wouldn't I do this?" In that sense, the preparation of the powers that be, the lessons that they tried to drill into me, they were completely off. They had no idea what we are up against. (Lightfoot, 1992, p. 240)

self-disclosure
Revealing information about oneself to another.

peer pressure
Tactics used to encourage some behaviors and discourage others in age-mates.

Young adolescents also have a tendency to categorize other people; for instance, they may pigeonhole their classmates into such groups as "brains," "jocks," "skaters," and "geeks" (Harris, 1995; Pipher, 1994). Divisions along racial lines increase as well. Recall how Aqeelah's long-time Caucasian friends suddenly began using African American slang when they spoke to her ("Yo, Aqeelah, what up?") and assumed that, because she was African American, she would like rap music. With this trend toward racial categorization, young teens are also more likely to segregate into racial groups, much to Aqeelah's, Kelly's, and Johanna's dismay. For example, when Johanna had a birthday party in eighth grade, most of her friends spent the entire evening in two groups—blacks and whites—with one group hanging out and dancing in the basement and the other standing outside and talking (Lewin, 2000).

In their desire to fit in with peers, teenagers sometimes seem to lead double lives, displaying one set of behaviors with their families and an entirely different set of behaviors at school (Harris, 1998). For instance, if they believe that their classmates view high academic achievement as uncool, they might do their homework faithfully at home each night yet feign disinterest in classroom activities, disrupt class with jokes or goofy behaviors, and express surprise at receiving high grades (Brown, 1993; Covington, 1992). Many adolescents have trouble reconciling their different sides and may feel as if they are continually hiding their true selves (Brown et al., 1995; Harter, Bresnick, Bouchey, & Whitesell, 1997; Harter, Waters, & Whitesell, 1997).

Late Adolescence (Ages 14–18) Older adolescents spend almost half of their waking hours interacting with friends and classmates (Csikszentmihalyi, 1995). They spend relatively little time with adults and *very* little time exclusively with an adult, such as a parent or teacher (Csikszentmihalyi, 1995; Csikszentmihalyi & Larson, 1984).

Whereas young adolescents seem to split themselves into two or more separate selves, older adolescents strive to recombine those selves into an adult *identity* (see Chapter 9), and they often use their peers as a forum for self-exploration and self-understanding (Gottman & Mettetal, 1986). For example, in the following dialogue, two girls struggle with their beliefs about premarital sexual intercourse as they discuss one girl's recent breakup with her boyfriend, Randy:

A: [*joking*] I think you should take Randy to court for statutory rape.
B: I don't. I'm to the point of wondering what "that kind of girl" . . . I don't know about the whole scene.
A: The thing is . . .
B: It depends on the reasoning. And how long you've been going out with somebody.
A: Yeah, I'm satisfied with my morals.
B: As long as you're satisfied with your morals, that's cool.
A: Yeah, but other people . . .
B: And I'm pretty, I'm pretty sturdy in mine.
A: Yeah [*giggle*], I know that. Mine tend to bend too easily. (Gottman & Mettetal, 1986, p. 218; reprinted with the permission of Cambridge University Press)

Older adolescents' greater capacity for abstract thought may allow them to think of other people more as unique individuals and less as members of specific categories, and they become increasingly aware of the characteristics they share with people from diverse backgrounds. Perhaps as a result, ties to specific peer groups dissipate, hostilities between groups soften, and young people become more flexible about the people with whom they associate (Brown, Eicher, & Petrie, 1986; Gavin & Furman, 1989; Larkin, 1979; Shrum & Cheek, 1987). For example, at Columbia High School (the school that Aqeelah, Johanna, and Kelly attended), students of different ethnic and racial backgrounds mingled freely again by the time they were seniors. Makita, a recent graduate of the school, explains:

"Senior year was wonderful, when the black kids and the white kids got to be friends again, and the graduation parties where everyone mixed. . . . It was so much better." (Lewin, 2000, p. 20)

But social maturity is a long time in the making. Whereas high school seniors have far more sophisticated social skills than do preschoolers or fifth graders, most have not completely mastered the tact and courtesy so essential for resolving delicate interpersonal matters. For example, they may occasionally show intolerance for other people's weaknesses or yell crude or insulting remarks in a moment of anger. Furthermore, many older adolescents continue to engage in the high-risk behaviors that some peers seem to endorse (Csikszentmihalyi & Larson, 1984).

Overall, then, what stands out about late adolescence is how vital peer relationships are. Parents, grandparents, aunts and uncles, teachers, and other adults continue to be important, but peers are the social partners of choice. As young people spend an increasing amount of time with their age-mates, they create the social experiences they need to launch themselves into the challenging world of adults. Soon they will need skills in inferring others' intentions, forming intimate relationships, raising the next generation, and dealing with people who are inclined to hurt or manipulate them. The social experiences of late adolescence prepare young people for many of these later experiences, although new social challenges will, of course, continue to present themselves throughout adulthood.

Group Differences in Interpersonal Behaviors

We have already seen how interpersonal behaviors change with age. Yet such behaviors also differ as a function of children's and adolescents' gender, cultural background, and special educational needs.

Gender Differences   Researchers and educators alike frequently see gender differences in children's play activities (Gallahue & Ozmun, 1998; Gottman, 1986b; Paley, 1984). In sociodramatic play, girls tend to enact scenarios that are relatively calm and sedate (e.g., playing house or school), whereas boys often introduce elements of adventure and danger (e.g., playing cops and robbers or engaging in intergalactic battles). Boys are more active even in relatively sedentary activities; for instance, if their teachers asks them to sit down and draw, they may "animate . . . volcanoes and space wars with exploding noises, as if they have jumped inside the pictures" (Paley, 1984, p. 5). Boys' higher activity levels are also seen in their greater preference for large outdoor spaces, where they can run, throw balls, and chase one another (Frost et al., 1998).

Preschoolers of both genders tend to relate to one another primarily through their activities. As they grow older, however, boys continue to place high priority on activities, but girls increasingly devote their time to talking—for instance, sharing personal concerns, telling secrets, and seeking emotional support (Berndt, 1992; Jones & Dembo, 1989; McCallum & Bracken, 1993; Ryan et al., 1994). In general, girls tend to be more affiliative: They form closer and more intimate relationships with others (Block, 1983). Girls also seem to be more sensitive to the subtle, nonverbal messages (the body language) that other people give them (Block, 1983; Deaux, 1984). Some researchers have found that girls have a slight advantage in perspective-taking ability and prosocial behavior; other researchers have found the two groups to be similar in these respects (Basinger et al., 1995; Eisenberg et al., 1996; Zahn-Waxler, Radke-Yarrow, et al., 1992).

The gender difference found most consistently in research studies is in *physical aggression:* Beginning in the preschool years, boys are more physically aggressive than girls (Collaer & Hines, 1995; Eagly, 1987; Gropper & Froschl, 1999; Loeber & Stouthamer-Loeber, 1998). This greater male inclination toward physical aggression is probably the result of both biological factors (as noted earlier, testosterone has been linked with aggressive behavior) and socialization (parents are more likely to allow aggression in sons than in daughters; Collaer & Hines, 1995; Condry & Ross, 1985; Eisenberg et al., 1996; Erdley et al., 1996). However, girls are often just as aggressive as boys in more subtle and less physical ways—for example, by tattling, gossiping, and snubbing their peers (Bjorkqvist, Osterman, & Kaukiainen, 1992; Brodzinsky, Messer, & Tew, 1979; Crick & Grotpeter, 1995; Loeber & Stouthamer-Loeber, 1998).

Boys also tend to be more assertive than girls. For example, in mixed-sex work groups, they are more likely to dominate activities and take charge of needed equipment, and they are more likely to get their way when group members disagree (Jovanovic & King, 1998). Such assertiveness may be nurtured in same-sex activity groups over the years, as boys' friendships typically involve more conflict and competition than girls' friendships do (Eisenberg et al., 1996). In contrast, girls are more likely to acquiesce to others' wishes, perhaps because they value group harmony more than boys do and so make frequent small concessions to keep the peace (Becker, 1986; Miller, Danaher, & Forbes, 1986).

Cultural Differences Children may have more or fewer opportunities to interact with peers, depending on the culture in which they grow up. Unlike in North America, where most children come into frequent contact with age-mates at an early age, children in some cultures stay close to home and play primarily with parents and siblings, at least until they reach school age (Whiting & Edwards, 1988). Children whose primary language is different from that of the larger society in which they live (e.g., as is true for non-English-speaking immigrants to an English-speaking country) also have limited opportunities to interact with age-mates (Doyle, 1982; Trawick-Smith, 2000).

To some degree, different cultural groups also model and teach different interpersonal behaviors. For instance, children in China are encouraged to be shy; those in Israel are encouraged to be assertive (Chen, Rubin, & Li, 1995; Krispin, Sternberg, & Lamb, 1992). Smiling is a sign of agreement and friendliness in almost any cultural group, but in a few cultures (e.g., in some Japanese American families), it may also indicate embarrassment (Eckman, 1972). Sociolinguistic behaviors, or appropriate ways of acting when talking with others, also differ from culture to culture (see Chapter 7).

Cultures differ, too, in how strongly they encourage competitive or cooperative behavior with others. In North America, many people see competition as healthy and growth producing (e.g., parents may enter their children in dance contests, high school teachers sometimes grade on a curve), and children are more likely to be praised for their individual achievements than for group success. In contrast, many other cultures (e.g., most Asian and Hispanic societies) place a high premium on loyalty, trust, cooperation, and prosocial behavior (Durkin, 1995; Greenfield, 1994a; Smith & Bond, 1994; Triandis, 1995).

Students with Special Needs On average, children and adolescents who have been identified as gifted have good social skills, although a few whose intellectual talents are highly advanced sometimes have difficulty in their interpersonal relationships because they are so *very* different from their peers (Gottfried, Fleming, & Gottfried, 1994; Keogh & MacMillan, 1996; Winner, 1997). Those with mental retardation typically have social skills similar to much younger children (DuPaul & Eckert, 1994; Greenspan & Granfield, 1992). Youngsters with chronic emotional and behavioral problems (e.g., conduct disorders) often have difficulty making and keeping friends, usually because of deficits in social problem solving and other social skills (Asher & Coie, 1990; Cartledge & Milburn, 1995; DuPaul & Eckert, 1994). And some (but by no means all) youngsters with information processing difficulties, including most who have autism and some who have learning disabilities or ADHD, show less advanced social understanding and interpersonal skills than their nondisabled peers (e.g., Greenspan & Granfield, 1992; Milch-Reich, Campbell, Connelly, & Geva, 1999). In the following section, we offer suggestions for helping such children, and in fact for helping *all* children, develop more effective interpersonal behaviors.

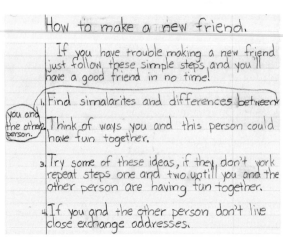

FIGURE 13–5 In this writing assignment, 9-year-old Mariel lists four strategies that her teacher has suggested for making a new friend.

Fostering Effective Interpersonal Skills

As complex social settings rich in peer contacts, schools and classrooms are one of the major contexts in which social skills develop (Deutsch, 1993; Elliott & Busse, 1991). Following are several strategies for helping children and adolescents acquire effective interpersonal behaviors at school:

■ *Teach specific social skills and social problem–solving strategies.* Through their frequent interactions with peers and adults, many young people acquire effective social and prosocial behaviors on their own. Nevertheless, many others—perhaps because of limited opportunities to interact with age-mates, a disability, or poor role models at home—know little about how to initiate conversations, exchange compliments, offer emotional support, or in other ways establish and maintain rewarding interpersonal relationships (e.g., Patrick, 1997). Furthermore, some lack productive strategies for solving social problems; for example, they may barge into a game without asking or respond to any provocation with aggression.

Teachers and other adults can teach many effective interpersonal behaviors both through explicit verbal instructions (e.g., see Figure 13–5) and through encouraging and modeling de-

PROMOTING SOCIAL SKILLS AND PROSOCIAL BEHAVIOR

■ Have students role-play specific strategies.

A counselor who is working with several very shy and socially isolated high school students teaches them several ways to initiate and maintain conversations with others. "One thing you might do," he says, "is give a compliment about something you like about a person. Then you can follow up with a question to get the person talking. For example, you might say, 'I really liked what you said about protecting the rainforests in class the other day. I didn't realize how quickly the earth's rain forests were being destroyed. Have you read a lot about the topic?' " After describing several additional strategies, the counselor has the students work in pairs to practice each one.

■ Ask students to brainstorm approaches to solving social dilemmas.

A middle school teacher presents this situation to his class: "Imagine that one of your classmates comes up to you and asks if she can copy your homework. You don't want to let her do it—after all, she won't learn what her teacher wanted her to learn by copying someone else's work—but you also don't want to make her angry or upset. How might you refuse her request while also keeping her friendship?"

■ Encourage students to think carefully before acting in difficult situations.

A third-grade teacher finds that several of her students react impulsively to any provocation; for instance, they might hit or yell at a classmate who unintentionally brushes them while walking past their desks. The teacher teaches the students four steps to follow in such situations: (a) *Think* about what just happened, (b) *list* three different ways to respond, (c) *predict* what might happen for each response, and (d) *choose* the best response.

■ Give concrete feedback about effective and ineffective interpersonal behaviors.

During a cooperative learning activity, a high school teacher notices that the members of one cooperative group are getting increasingly angry. After listening to their conversation for a minute or two, the teacher reminds them, "As we agreed yesterday, it's OK to criticize ideas, but it's *not* OK to criticize people."

■ Communicate your concern for students who are hurt, and enlist the support of other students in caring for them.

A preschool teacher sympathizes with a child who has skinned his knee. She brings out the first aid kit and asks another child to find a bandage as she applies the antiseptic.

■ Recognize students' good deeds.

When a teacher notices a student helping a classmate who doesn't understand an assignment, she comments, "Thank you for helping Amanda, Jack. You're always ready to lend a hand!"

■ Communicate the message that prosocial behavior is desirable.

A middle school teacher asks students to look for prosocial and self-serving behaviors in the novels they are reading. He voices approval for characters who are altruistic and encourages the students to observe how other characters exploit or harm those around them.

■ Arrange for students to participate in service activities in the school or community.

A high school requires all of its students to complete 25 hours of service to the school district each year. Students can meet this requirement in numerous ways, for instance by serving meals in the cafeteria, participating in a school fund-raising drive, painting a mural on the gymnasium wall, or reading to "buddies" at the local elementary school.

sired behaviors. Such instruction is especially likely to be effective when students have opportunities to practice their newly learned skills (perhaps through role playing) and when they receive concrete feedback about how they are doing (Elliott & Busse, 1991; Schloss & Smith, 1994; Vaughn, 1991; Zirpoli & Melloy, 1993). The Development and Practice feature above describes several strategies teachers might use.

At the same time, teachers must be careful that they are not *too* directive as they guide students toward more productive interpersonal behaviors. Children sometimes benefit from their own trial and error with various social strategies. Following is one elementary teacher's perspective on the advantages of letting children learn some social lessons on their own:

Before, when problems came up, I think I was very quick to intervene. Certainly, I asked the kids involved to express themselves "very briefly" about what had happened. But I was quick to judge, to comment, to advise, and to try to reconcile them, for instance, by saying, "Well, now you must be friends." Thus, the students themselves were not active in the problem solution. It was usually

I who found the solutions and I who controlled the situation. Now I am not as quick to intervene. I ask the children to stop and think, and to express themselves about what happened, and I withdraw more and listen to them. Certainly it is more effective if they themselves face and solve the problems. Then the solution and the whole experience are more likely to stay with them. (Adalbjarnardottir & Selman, 1997, p. 421)

■ *Plan cooperative activities.* When students participate in cooperative games, rather than in competitive ones, their aggressive behaviors toward one another decrease (Bay-Hinitz, Peterson, & Quilitch, 1994). In cooperative learning activities, they can learn and practice help-giving, help-seeking, and conflict-resolution skills while developing a better sense of justice and fairness toward their classmates (Damon, 1988; Lickona, 1991; Webb & Farivar, 1994). Furthermore, cooperative tasks that require a number of different skills and abilities foster an appreciation for the various strengths that students with diverse backgrounds are likely to contribute (Cohen, 1994; Cohen & Lotan, 1995). Yet virtually any "cooperative" approach to instruction (cooperative learning, peer tutoring, reciprocal teaching) may help students begin to recognize that, despite the obvious diversity among them, they are ultimately more similar to one another than they are different (Schofield, 1995). Cooperative activities are usually most successful when students have a structure to follow as they conduct their business (e.g., when each group member is given a specific role to perform) and are given some guidelines about appropriate group behavior (Cohen, 1994; Schofield, 1995; Webb & Palincsar, 1996).

■ *Label appropriate behaviors as they occur.* Teachers can heighten students' awareness of effective social skills by identifying and praising behaviors that reflect those skills (Vorrath, 1985; Wittmer & Honig, 1994). For example, a teacher might say, "Thank you for *sharing* your art materials so unselfishly" or "I think that you two were able to write a more imaginative short story by *cooperating* on the project." Some researchers have found, too, that describing children as having desirable characteristics (helpfulness, generosity, empathy, etc.) has beneficial effects (Mills & Grusec, 1989). For example, 8-year-olds who are told, "You're the kind of person who likes to help others whenever you can," are more likely to share their belongings with others at a later date (Grusec & Redler, 1980).

■ *Ask students to consider the effects their behaviors might have.* Children are more likely to behave prosocially when they are given reasons why certain behaviors are unacceptable (see the discussion of *induction* in Chapter 10). More generally, children are more likely to exhibit effective interpersonal behaviors and inhibit *in*effective ones when they think about the consequences of their behaviors, either actual past consequences or possible future consequences (Guerra & Slaby, 1990; Rushton, 1980). For example, a teacher might say, "I'm sure you didn't mean to hurt Jamal's feelings, but he's pretty upset about what you said. Why don't you think about what you might do or say to make him feel better?"

■ *Develop a peer mediation program.* Elementary and secondary students alike benefit from **mediation training,** in which they learn how to intervene effectively in classmates' interpersonal disputes (Deutsch, 1993; Johnson, Johnson, Dudley, Ward, & Magnuson, 1995; Schrumpf, Crawford, & Usadel, 1991). For example, in an experiment involving several second- through fifth-grade classes (Johnson et al., 1995), children were trained to help their peers resolve conflicts by asking the opposing sides to:

1. Define the conflict (the problem)
2. Explain their own perspectives and needs
3. Explain the *other* person's perspectives and needs
4. Identify at least three possible solutions to the conflict
5. Reach an agreement that addresses the needs of both parties

mediation training
Teaching students how to mediate conflicts among classmates by asking opposing sides to express their differing viewpoints and then working together to identify a reasonable resolution.

The students took turns serving as mediator for their classmates, so that each student had a chance to practice resolving the conflicts of others. At the end of the training program, the students more frequently resolved their *own* interpersonal conflicts in ways that addressed the needs of both parties, and they were less likely to ask for adult intervention, than students in an untrained control group. Similarly, in a case study involving adolescent gang members (Sanchez & Anderson, 1990), students were given mediation training and were asked to be responsible for mediating gang-related disputes. After only one month of training, rival gang members were exchanging friendly greetings in the corridors, giving one another the "high five" sign, and interacting at lunch; meanwhile, gang-related fights virtually disappeared from the scene.

■ *Make it clear that aggressive behavior—whether it involves physical or psychological harm to others—is unacceptable on school grounds.* Most schools have firm rules against physical aggression at school. Furthermore, in the United States, federal laws make it illegal to carry weapons on school grounds. Yet behaviors that cause psychological harm—malicious gossip, prejudicial remarks, sexual harassment, intimidation, ostracism, and so on—can also make school an unpleasant environment for many students (e.g., Juvonen et al., 2000). In fact, as noted earlier, some children perceive psychological harm to be just as painful as physical harm (Astor, 1994).

Unfortunately, simply establishing clear prohibitions against aggression and imposing appropriate consequences on those who violate such prohibitions are not always enough. Some children and adolescents have a history of aggressive behavior, perhaps as a result of neurological deficits or harsh and punitive parenting, and may require planned intervention to help them acquire more prosocial interpersonal behaviors. Strategies such as the following are often effective with chronically aggressive students:

- Teaching effective social skills
- Teaching more effective ways of resolving conflicts and solving interpersonal problems
- Teaching strategies for anger control (e.g., self-talk)
- Increasing students' ability to look at situations from others' perspectives
- Encouraging more advanced moral reasoning
- Fostering more accurate interpretation of others' behaviors, body language, and other nonverbal social cues (e.g., teaching students to distinguish between intentional and unintentional actions)
  (Crick & Dodge, 1996; Graham, 1997; Guerra & Slaby, 1990; Henrich, Brown, & Aber, 1999; Hughes, 1988; Iannotti, 1978; Sasso, Melloy, & Kavale, 1990)

One final way to foster interpersonal skills is to help students make friends and in other ways get to know their classmates better. Friends and other peer relationships play an important—many theorists would say *critical*—role in social-emotional development. In the next section, we look at the nature of peer relationships in childhood and adolescence.

Peer Relationships

Throughout the book we have seen many ways in which adults, especially parents and teachers, affect children's and adolescents' development. **Peers,** or people of approximately the same age and social status, make equally important contributions to development, especially in the social-emotional domain. In the next few pages, we look at the unique functions of peer relationships, consider the factors that affect

For most children and adolescents, peers are a primary source of companionship and recreation.

Art courtesy of Madison, age 7.

popularity and social isolation, and examine the nature of close friendships and larger social groups (e.g., cliques, gangs). Finally, we offer recommendations for supporting peer relationships at school.

Functions of Peer Relationships

In young people's minds, peers serve primarily as companions—as sources of amusement, excitement, and pleasure (Asher & Parker, 1989; Ginsberg, Gottman, & Parker, 1986). Most children and adolescents actively seek out peers, and play groups are observed universally around the world (Harris, 1995). In fact, for many children and adolescents, interacting with friends is more important than completing classroom assignments (Brown, 1993; Doyle, 1986).

peers
Individuals of approximately the same age and ability level.

From a developmental standpoint, peer relationships serve additional functions as well:

■ *Peers provide partners for practicing existing social skills and trying out new ones.* When children and adolescents interact with their peers, they enter social exchanges on a more or less equal footing: No single individual has absolute power or authority over the others. In their attempts to satisfy their own needs while also maintaining productive relationships with others, they acquire skills in perspective taking, persuasion, negotiation, compromise, and emotional control (Creasey, Jarvis, & Berk, 1998; Gottman, 1986b; Sutton-Smith, 1979). They make occasional social blunders in their experimentation with newly emerging skills, but usually without the sanctions that parents and other adults might impose (Vandenberg, 1978).

■ *Peers socialize one another.* Children and adolescents socialize one another in several ways (Erwin, 1993; Ginsburg et al., 1986; Harris, 1998; Ryan, 2000). They define options for leisure time, perhaps playing jump rope in a vacant lot, getting together in a study group, or smoking cigarettes on the corner. They offer new ideas and perspectives, perhaps demonstrating how to do an "Ollie" on a skateboard or presenting potent arguments for becoming a vegetarian. They serve as role models and provide standards for acceptable behavior, showing what is possible, what is admirable, what is cool; even toddlers imitate one another to some extent (Eckerman & Didow, 1996). They reinforce one another for acting in ways deemed appropriate for their age, gender, ethnic group, and cultural background. And they sanction one another for stepping beyond acceptable bounds, perhaps through ridicule (recall how Aqeelah was taunted in the opening case), gossip, or ostracism.

■ *Peers contribute to a sense of identity.* Association with a particular group of peers helps children and adolescents decide who they are and who they want to become (see Chapter 9). For instance, when Jeanne's son Alex was in middle school, he and his friends were avid skateboarders and spent long hours at a local skateboard ramp practicing and refining their technique. Alex proudly labeled himself as a "skater" and wore the extra-large T-shirts and wide-legged pants that conveyed such an identity.

In addition to deriving identity from their solidarity with a particular group of peers, children and adolescents also compare themselves to their peers and observe how their own characteristics (physical appearance, athletic prowess, school achievement, etc.) make them unique. The result of such comparisons is that, particularly in adolescence and young adulthood, young people increasingly look *inward* at their own characteristics, rather than *outward* toward their peers, to get a handle on who they are as individuals.

■ *Peers help one another make sense of their lives.* Recall the earlier conversation in which two girls (one of whom had just broken up with her boyfriend) shared their views about premarital intercourse. Growing up brings many confusing, ambiguous, and troubling events, and peers help one another sort through them. By sharing and critiquing one another's ideas, perspectives, beliefs, and values, children and adolescents construct increasingly complex and perceptive understandings of the world around them, reflecting the *social construction of meaning* we spoke of in Chapter 4.

■ *Peers provide emotional and social support.* Youngsters often seek comfort from peers when they are anxious or upset; for instance, preschoolers are more willing to explore a new environment if familiar playmates are nearby (Asher & Parker, 1989; Ginsburg et al., 1986; Wentzel, 1999). Peers provide social support as well; for example, children who have one or more good friends are less likely to be victimized by bullies (Ginsburg et al., 1986; Pellegrini & Bartini, 2000; Schwartz et al., 1999). Although some youngsters adjust quite successfully on their own, as a general rule children and adolescents who have peers to turn to in times of trouble or stress have higher self-esteem, fewer emotional problems (e.g., depression), and higher school achievement (Buhrmester, 1992; Guay, Boivin, & Hodges, 1999; Levitt et al., 1999; Ryan et al., 1994).

Popularity and Social Isolation

Popularity among peers has definite advantages. By and large, when children and adolescents believe that their classmates accept and like them, they achieve at higher levels, have higher self-esteem, are happier at school, exhibit fewer problem behaviors, and have better attendance records (Guay et al., 1999; Harter, 1996; Reese & Thorkildsen, 1999; Wentzel, 1999).

Yet we have to be clear about the qualities represented by the term *popularity*. When researchers ask children to identify classmates they would most like to do something with, they don't necessarily choose those whom they and their teachers perceive to be the most popular members of the student body (Lafontana & Cillessen, 1998; Parkhurst & Hopmeyer, 1998). This finding is consistent with the seemingly self-contradictory comment that Jeanne's daughter Tina often made as a junior high school student: "No one likes the popular kids." Tina was talking about students who, in her eyes, had a dominant social status at school (perhaps they were star athletes or members of a prestigious social group) but were often aggressive or stuck-up. When we talk about **popularity** here, however, we are describing students who are well liked, kind, and trustworthy—students who may or may not hold obvious high-status positions (Parkhurst & Hopmeyer, 1998). Children who are popular in this way typically have good social skills; for instance, they know how to initiate and sustain conversations, are sensitive to the subtle social cues that others give them, and adjust their behaviors to changing circumstances. They also tend to be quite prosocial; for instance, they are more likely to help, share, cooperate, and empathize with others (Caprara, Barbaranelli, Pastorelli, Bandura, & Zimbardo, 2000; Crick & Dodge, 1994; Wentzel & Asher, 1995).

In addition to asking children whom they would most like to do something with, researchers often ask them to identify classmates whom they would *least* like to do something with. Those who are frequently selected are known as **rejected children.** Rejected children often have poor social skills (e.g., they may continually try to draw attention to themselves); they may also be impulsive and disruptive in the classroom (Asher & Renshaw, 1981; Pellegrini et al., 1999; Putallaz & Heflin, 1986). Many (but not all) aggressive children are also rejected, probably in part because they place higher priority on acquiring objects and gaining power over others than on establishing and maintaining congenial interpersonal relationships (Dodge, Bates, & Pettit, 1990; Ladd & Burgess, 1999; Patrick, 1997).

Researchers have identified a third group of children as well. **Neglected children** are those whom classmates rarely select as someone they would either most like or least like to do something with (Asher & Renshaw, 1981). Neglected children tend to be quiet and keep to themselves. Some prefer to be alone, others may simply not know how to go about making friends, and still others may be quite content with the one or two close friends that they have (Guay et al., 1999; Rubin & Krasnor, 1986). Having "neglected" status is often only a temporary situation; students whom researchers categorize as neglected at one time are not always the ones so categorized in follow-up assessments.

Not all children and adolescents fall neatly into one of these three categories. Some are **controversial,** in that some of their classmates really like them and others really *don't* like them. Still others are, for lack of a better name, known simply as *average* children, in that some classmates like them and others don't, but without the intensity of feelings shown for popular, rejected, or controversial children. In the Observation Guidelines table on the next page, we present common characteristics of popular, rejected, neglected, controversial, and average children.

Probably more important than popularity, however, is the quality of young people's close friendships. We look now at the nature of friendships in childhood and adolescence.

Friendships

Healthy friendships come in many forms. Some are brief liaisons; others last a lifetime. Some are relatively casual; others are deep and intimate. Some children and adolescents have many friends; others invest steadfastly in a few close ones.

Three qualities make **friendships** distinct from other kinds of peer relationships:

- *They are voluntary relationships.* Children and adolescents often spend time with peers strictly through happenstance: Perhaps they ride the same school bus, are members of the same class, or join the same sports team. In contrast, they *choose* their friends. Two or more youngsters remain friends as long as they continue to enjoy one another's company and can successfully resolve their differences.

- *They are powered by shared routines and customs.* Friends find activities that are mutually meaningful and enjoyable, and over time they acquire a common set of experiences that enable them to share certain perspectives on life (Gottman, 1986b; Suttles, 1970). As a result, they can easily communicate about many topics. For instance, children talk, smile,

popular children
Children whom many peers like and perceive to be kind and trustworthy.

rejected children
Children whom many peers identify as being unfavorable social partners.

neglected children
Children whom peers rarely select as someone they would either most like or least like to do something with.

controversial children
Children whom some peers really like and other peers strongly dislike.

friendship
Peer relationship that is voluntary and reciprocal and includes shared routines and customs.

Estimating Children's Social Acceptance Among Peers

OBSERVATION GUIDELINES

CHARACTERISTIC	LOOK FOR	EXAMPLE	IMPLICATION
"Popular" Children	• Good social and communication skills • Sensitivity and responsiveness to others' wishes and needs • Willingness to assimilate into ongoing activities • Signs of leadership potential	On the playground before school, 8-year-old Daequan moves easily from one group to another. Before joining a conversation, he listens to what others are saying and is careful to add an appropriate comment. He doesn't draw much attention to himself but is well liked by most of his classmates.	Use popular students as leaders when trying to change other students' behavior. For example, when starting a recycling program, ask a well-regarded student to help get the program off the ground.
"Rejected" Children	• For some, high rates of aggression; for others, immature, anxious, or impulsive behavior • Disruptive behavior in class • Unwillingness of other children to play or work with them	Most children dislike 10-year-old Terra. She frequently calls her classmates insulting nicknames, threatens to beat them up, and noisily intrudes into their private conversations.	Help rejected students learn basic social skills, such as how to join a conversation. Place them in cooperative groups with students who are likely to be sensitive and accepting. If students are aggressive, follow through with appropriate consequences and teach self-regulatory strategies to help students keep their impulses in check (see Chapter 11). Publicly compliment all students (including those who are rejected) about the things they do well.
"Neglected" Children	• Tendency to be relatively quiet; little or no disruptive behavior • Fewer than average interactions with classmates, but possible friendships with one or two peers • For some, anxiety about interacting with others • Possible temporary nature of "neglected" status (this classification is not stable over time)	Fourteen-year-old Sedna is initially shy and withdrawn at her new school. Later in the year, however, she seems to be happier and more involved in school activities.	Identify group activities in which neglected students might feel comfortable and be successful. Arrange situations in which shy students with similar interests can get to know one another.
"Controversial" Children	• Acceptance by some peers, rejection by others • Possibly aggressive and disruptive in some situations yet helpful, cooperative, and socially sensitive in others	Thirteen-year-old Marcus can be disruptive, obnoxious, and manipulative, but his charm and sunny personality lead many classmates to forgive his transgressions.	Let controversial students know in no uncertain terms when their behaviors are in appropriate, but acknowledge their effective social skills as well.
"Average" Children	• Tendency to be liked by some students but disliked by others • Average interpersonal skills (e.g., average levels of prosocial behavior and aggression) • Ability to find a comfortable social niche	Five-year-old Joachim doesn't draw much attention to himself. He's made a few friends in kindergarten and seems to get along fairly well with them, but he sometimes has conflicts with others.	Help average children refine their emerging social skills. Be sensitive and responsive to the occasional signs of rejection by others.

Sources: Coie & Dodge, 1988; Coie & Kupersmidt, 1983; Dodge, 1983; Dodge, Coie, & Brakke, 1982; Dodge, Schlundt, Schocken, & Delugach, 1983; Newcomb & Bukowski, 1984; Newcomb, Bukowski, & Pattee, 1993; Putallaz & Gottman, 1981; Rubin et al., 1998.

and laugh more often with friends than with nonfriends; they also engage in more complex fantasy play (Parker, 1986).

- *They are reciprocal relationships.* Friends spend time with one another and address one another's needs (Epstein, 1986; Rubin et al., 1998). But how they feel about one another, rather than what they do with or for one another, is arguably the primary basis of the friendship. Friends generally perceive their relationship to be deeper than the activities they share or the material goods and services they exchange.

We see such qualities in the three-way friendship depicted in our opening case study. In addition to going to school together, Aqeelah, Johanna, and Kelly shared many common routines (e.g., they regularly attended meetings of the Martin Luther King Association) and cared deeply for one another (Lewin, 2000). Over time, as they developed diverging interests, it became more difficult for the girls to sustain their friendship. Aqeelah was disappointed when she learned that Johanna and Kelly were not going out for the softball team with her: Without common activities, they might grow apart.

Friends play a role in social-emotional development that goes beyond that of peer relationships more generally. Because friends have an emotional investment in their relationship, they work hard to look at a situation from one another's point of view and to resolve any disputes that threaten to separate them; as a result, they develop increased perspective-taking and conflict resolution skills (Basinger et al., 1995; DeVries, 1997). Furthermore, friends often provide the emotional support that helps children and adolescents cope with stressful events (Berndt & Keefe, 1995; Ginsburg et al., 1986). In the writing sample in Figure 13–6, 7-year-old Jessica reveals her emerging understanding of the importance of friends in her life.

Close friends tend to be similar in age and are usually of the same sex and race (Hartup, 1992; Kovacs, Parker, & Hoffman, 1996; Roopnarine, Lasker, Sacks, & Stores, 1998). Cross-sex friendships are most common in the preschool years (e.g., recall 4-year-olds Eric and Naomi in their roles as "Bob" and "Claudia"), but some older children and adolescents have close friends of the opposite sex as well (Gottman, 1986b; Kovacs et al., 1996). Cross-race friendships (such as that of Aqeelah, Johanna, and Kelly) are most often seen when the number of available peers is relatively small, as might occur in small classes or rural communities (Hallinan & Teixeria, 1987; Roopnarine et al., 1998).

Characteristics of Friendships at Different Ages   Years ago, Jeanne asked her three children, "What are friends for?" Here are their responses (you previously encountered two of these in Chapter 7):

Jeff (age 6):   To play with.

Alex (age 9):   Friends can help you in life. They can make you do better in school. They can make you feel better.

Tina (age 12):   To be your friend and help you in good times and bad times. They're there so you can tell secrets. They're people that care. They're there because they like you. They're people you can trust.

Like Jeff, young children describe friends primarily as recreational companions and potential sources of shared playthings; thus, their understandings of friendship are relatively superficial and concrete. As they reach the upper elementary grades, they, like Alex, begin to articulate that friends can help and depend on one another. Adolescents, like Tina, describe increasingly more intimate friendships as they start to share their innermost secrets and dreams (Berndt, 1992; Damon, 1977; Gottman & Mettetal, 1986; Jones & Dembo, 1989; Youniss, 1980).

Such developmental trends in children's descriptions of friendships notwithstanding, even friendships in early childhood reflect some degree of mutual dependence and trust, as reflected in young children's enjoyment of one another's company and their ability to coordinate their actions and make occasional compromises. As we look more closely at the nature of friendships during the four developmental periods, we will see how friendships grow in complexity and stability and how they increasingly reflect such characteristics as loyalty, trust, and intimacy.

Today Miranda walked me to school and she is going to walk me back. Miranda is my best friend we met egether afther lunch. Miranda is teching me lots of things she the best friend any boty cuold have.

FIGURE 13–6 Seven-year-old Jessica recognizes the value of a good friend.

Early childhood (ages 2–6). Primitive friendships emerge in the first year or two of life. Toddlers respond differently to familiar and unfamiliar children: They are more likely to make social overtures, carry on complex interactions, and display positive emotions with children that they know (Howes, 1988). For example, when Teresa's son Connor was less than a year old, he became friends with Patrick, another child at his daycare center. The two boys established familiar play routines, often laughing and chasing one another as they crawled around the room. Although they weren't yet speaking, and they certainly didn't swap secrets, they were clearly attuned to each other's behaviors. After they moved on to separate elementary schools, they occasionally called one another to arrange play sessions and sleepovers. Even as adolescents, they still communicate, albeit less often.

In the preschool years, children build on the rudimentary relationships of infancy. Well into early childhood, children enrich their social interactions with friends through their language, fantasy, and play. For instance, when 3- and 4-year-olds interact with familiar peers (rather than with strangers), they are more likely to offer social greetings and carry on a conversation, engage in more complex play, and exhibit better social skills (Charlesworth & LaFreniere, 1983; Doyle, 1982; Hinde, Titmus, Easton, & Tamplin, 1985).

Of course, early friendships also provide opportunities for disagreements, arguments, and even physical aggression (Hartup & Laursen, 1991). Such disputes can be quite heated, but young children are motivated to solve them. When they have conflicts with nonfriends, preschoolers often stand firm; when they have conflicts with friends, they are more inclined to negotiate, compromise, or withdraw (Hartup, Laursen, Stewart, & Eastenson, 1988). Thus, young children seem to have different motives in their conflicts with nonfriends and friends. From an unfamiliar child, they want their toys back and their dignity reaffirmed; they may also want that ill-tempered upstart out of sight! Although children may be angry with friends, they want to restore communication and good feelings. In the process of working through conflicts with friends, then, they begin to acquire an important skill: asserting themselves while still maintaining productive relationships.

Middle childhood (ages 6–10). During the elementary school years, children continue to act differently with friends than with peers who are not friends. For example, they are more likely to express and regulate their feelings (important capabilities described in Chapter 9) and to understand the other's emotional states (Newcomb & Bagwell, 1995; Newcomb & Brady, 1982). In times of conflict, they strive to identify an equitable resolution and preserve the relationship (Hartup, 1996; Newcomb & Bagwell, 1995). At this age, friends develop a sense of loyalty to one another, and many of them, girls especially, use self-disclosure as an important strategy for maintaining a friendship (Buhrmester, 1996; Diaz & Berndt, 1982).

Friendships are often more stable in middle childhood than in earlier years (Berndt & Hoyle, 1985). Children don't choose friends because they just happen to live in the same apartment building, attend the same preschool, or have parents who are friends. They become more deliberate in selecting their playmates and are usually attracted to peers who have similar interests and styles of behavior (Rubin, Lynch, Coplan, Rose-Krasnor, & Booth, 1994). For example, a child who is energetic and high-spirited and another who is more quiet and sedate are each likely to seek a companion with a similar disposition. Youngsters in this age range typically choose friends of their own sex, perhaps in part because same-sex peers are more likely to be behaviorally compatible; for instance, boys are more likely than girls to enjoy rough-and-tumble play (Gottman, 1986b; Kovacs et al., 1996; Maccoby, 1990).

Close friendships in the elementary and middle school years are typically between children of the same sex.

Art courtesy of Andres, age 10.

Early adolescence (ages 10–14). Differences in relationships between friends and nonfriends intensify during early adolescence (Basinger et al., 1995; Parker & Gottman, 1989). Many young adolescents let down their guard and reveal their weaknesses and vulnerabilities to close friends, even as they may try to maintain a demeanor of competence and self-confidence in front of most other age-mates. They begin to confront feelings of possessiveness and jealousy about friends, and after age 11 the number of close friends slowly declines (Rubin et al., 1998). Gradually, young adolescents learn that friendships don't have to be exclusive—that they are not necessarily jeopardized when one friend spends time with other people—and that friends are more likely to grow by having relationships with many individuals (Rubin et al., 1998). Thus, many friendship pairs gradually converge into larger groups, such as cliques (more about these shortly).

Late adolescence (ages 14–18). Older adolescents tend to be quite selective in their choice of friends (Epstein, 1986). Gone are the days when they run out of fingers as they count off their "close" friends. Instead, they tend to nurture relationships with a few friends that they keep for some time, perhaps throughout their lives, and having such friendships enhances their self-esteem (Berndt, 1992; Berndt & Hoyle, 1985).

Many friendships in late adolescence are enriched with self-disclosure, intimacy, and loyalty (Buhrmester, 1996; Newcomb & Bagwell, 1995). Older teenagers frequently turn to friends for emotional support in times of trouble or confusion, and they are likely to engage in lengthy discussions about personal problems and possible solutions (Asher & Parker, 1989; Buhrmester, 1992; Parker & Gottman, 1989; Seltzer, 1982). In the process, they often discover that they aren't as unique as they once thought, thereby poking holes in the *personal fable* we spoke of in Chapter 9 (Elkind, 1981a). For such reasons, friendships become especially important during the teenage years (Csikszentmihalyi, 1995; Wigfield et al., 1996).

Most children and adolescents interact regularly with, and clearly enjoy the company of, many peers besides their close friends. We look now at the nature of their larger social groups.

Larger Social Groups

In middle childhood, children enter elementary school and gain increasing ability to travel independently in their neighborhoods. As a result of such changes, they come into contact with a greater number of peers, and many begin to form larger social groups that regularly fraternize (Eisenberg et al., 1996; Gottman & Mettetal, 1986). Initially, such groups are usually comprised of a single sex, but in adolescence they often include both boys and girls (Gottman & Mettetal, 1986; Harris, 1995).

Children's and adolescents' social groups vary considerably in size, function, and character. However, many have the following attributes:

■ *Group members share a common culture.* The group develops a general set of rules (often unspoken), expectations, and interpretations—a **peer culture**—that influences how group members behave (Davidson & Youniss, 1995; Harris, 1998; Knapp & Woolverton, 1995). This shared culture gives group members a sense of community, belonging, and identity. It also entices them to adopt the group's shared norms and values, that is, to *self-socialize* (Gottman & Mettetal, 1986; Kindermann, 1993). Other group members encourage such conformity as well, both by reinforcing behaviors that are appropriate in the eyes of the group and by discouraging behaviors that are not (Clasen & Brown, 1985; Dishion, Spracklen, Andrews, & Patterson, 1996).

Fortunately, many children's and adolescents' peer groups embrace productive and prosocial behaviors such as honesty, fairness, cooperation, academic achievement, and a sense of humor (Damon, 1988; Kindermann, 1993; McCallum & Bracken, 1993). Many others, however, encourage less worthy pursuits, such as aggression and violence, and discourage scholastic endeavors, perhaps by making fun of "brainy" students or endorsing such behaviors as cheating, cutting class, and skipping school (Berndt, 1992; Brown, 1993; Knapp & Woolverton, 1995; Lowry et al., 1995).

Peer groups are particularly influential in matters of style—for example, in dress, music, and social activities. Parents, teachers, and other significant adults continue to be influential in most young people's views about education, morality, religion, and careers (Harris, 1998; Hartup, 1983; Sewald, 1986). It's important to note, too, that many young people actively think about and evaluate what their peers ask them to do; they rarely accept anyone's suggestions without question (Brown, 1990).

■ *Group members have a sense of unity as a group.* Once children or adolescents gel as a group, they prefer other group members over nonmembers, and they develop feelings of loyalty to individuals within the group. In some cases, they also develop feelings of hostility and rivalry toward

peer culture
General set of rules, expectations, and interpretations that influence how members of a particular peer group behave.

members of other groups (Harris, 1995, 1998; Sherif, Harvey, White, Hood, & Sherif, 1961). Such feelings toward *out-groups* are particularly intense when two or more groups must actively compete for status or resources, as rival athletic teams and adolescent gangs often do.

■ *Dominance hierarchies emerge within the group.* When children's groups continue for any length of time, a pecking order, or **dominance hierarchy,** gradually evolves (Harris, 1998; Strayer, 1991). Some group members rise to the top, leading the way and making decisions for the entire group. Other group members are followers rather than leaders: They look to those around them for guidance about how to behave and assume lesser roles in the group's activities. Sometimes these less dominant individuals find unique niches within the group, perhaps becoming the clown, daredevil, or brain of the group.

Social groups become a particularly prominent feature of children's social worlds once they reach puberty. Researchers have described three group phenomena during the adolescent years: cliques, subcultures, and gangs.

Cliques Cliques are moderately stable friendship groups of perhaps 3 to 10 individuals, and such groups provide the setting for most voluntary social interactions (Crockett, Losoff, & Peterson, 1984; Epstein, 1986; Kindermann, McCollom, & Gibson, 1996). Clique boundaries tend to be fairly rigid and exclusive (some people are "in," others are "out"), and membership in various cliques affects social status and dominance with peers (Wigfield et al., 1996). In early adolescence, cliques are usually comprised of a single sex; in later adolescence, cross-sex cliques become increasingly common (Epstein, 1986).

Although most middle school and high school students have friends, a smaller number of them belong to cliques (Epstein, 1986). Thus, the emergence of cliques in early adolescence heightens young people's concerns about acceptance and popularity (Gavin & Furman, 1989). Young adolescents wonder about their social standing: "Who likes me?" "Will I be popular at my new school?" "Why didn't Sal invite me to his party?" When they occasionally leave one clique to join another (perhaps more prestigious) one, they may engender feelings of betrayal, hurt, and jealousy in the friends they leave behind (Kanner, Feldman, Weinberger, & Ford, 1987; Rubin et al., 1998).

Subcultures Some adolescents affiliate with a well-defined **subculture,** a group that resists a powerful dominant culture by adopting a significantly different way of life (Epstein, 1998). Such a group may be considerably larger than a clique, and it does not always have the tight-knit cohesiveness and carefully drawn boundaries of a clique. Instead, it is defined by common values, beliefs, and behavior patterns. Some subcultures are relatively benign; for instance, a middle school skateboarders' culture may simply espouse a particular mode of dress. Other subcultures, such as those that endorse racist and antisemitic behaviors (e.g., skinheads) and those that practice Satanic worship and rituals, are more worrisome (Clark, 1992).

Adolescents are more likely to affiliate with subcultures when they feel alienated from the dominant culture (perhaps that of their school or that of society more generally) and want to distinguish themselves from it in some way (Clark, 1992; Harris, 1998). They also tend to develop subcultures when they are pessimistic or apathetic about their future (Epstein, 1998). For example, some subcultures within racial minority groups discourage "acting white"—that is, displaying behaviors endorsed by the dominant European American culture (Brown, 1993; Ogbu, 1992). Individuals in these subcultures, especially boys, find little value in doing well at traditional academic tasks, which represent the culture from which they want to distance themselves (Graham, Taylor, & Hudley, 1998; Ogbu, 1992). Consider what happened to professional basketball player Kareem Abdul-Jabbar when, as a 9-year-old, he enrolled in a new, predominantly African American school:

> I got there and immediately found I could read better than anyone in the school. . . . When the nuns found this out they paid me a lot of attention, once even asking me, a fourth grader, to read to the seventh grade. When the kids found this out I became a target. . . . I got all A's and was hated for it; I spoke correctly and was called a punk. I had to learn a new language simply to be

Some adolescent subcultures, like this one, are distinguished by relatively superficial characteristics, such as hairstyle or mode of dress. Other subcultures that endorse dangerous or antisocial behaviors are more worrisome.

dominance hierarchy
Relative standing of group members in terms of such qualities as leadership and popularity.

clique
Moderately stable friendship group of perhaps 3 to 10 members.

subculture
Group that resists the ways of the dominant culture and adopts its own norms for behavior.

able to deal with the threats. I had good manners and was a good little boy and paid for it with my hide. (Abdul-Jabbar & Knobles, 1983, p. 16)

In his classmates' eyes, Abdul-Jabbar was, by reading so well, endorsing the value system of mainstream European American society; in doing so, he was betraying the members of an African American subculture.

Gangs A **gang** is a cohesive social group characterized by initiation rites, distinctive colors and symbols, ownership of a specific territory, and feuds with one or more rival groups (Campbell, 1984). Gangs have well-defined dominance hierarchies, with specific roles defined for each member (Campbell, 1984). Typically, they are governed by strict rules for behavior, with stiff penalties for breaking them.

Historically, gangs in the United States originated out of conflicts among immigrant ethnic groups (e.g., recall the case of Lun Cheung in Chapter 10). Yet gangs have grown in number in recent decades, especially in lower-income inner-city areas (Parks, 1995). They have also become increasingly violent, in part as a result of greater drug use and access to more effective weapons (Parks, 1995).

Adolescents (and sometimes children as well) affiliate with gangs for a variety of reasons (Campbell, 1984; Clark, 1992; Parks, 1995; Simons, Whitbeck, Conger, & Conger, 1991). Some do so as a way of demonstrating their loyalty to their family, friends, or neighborhood. Some seek the status and prestige that gang membership brings. Some have poor academic records and see the gang as an alternative arena in which they might be successful and gain recognition for their accomplishments. Gangs also promise financial rewards through criminal activities. Many members of gangs have had troubled relationships with their families, or they have been consistently rejected by peers, and so they turn to street gangs or other deviant subcultures to get the emotional support they can find nowhere else.

Historically, gangs have been dominated by young men, but young women have become increasingly active (Parks, 1995). In an in-depth case study of three gangs in New York, Campbell (1984) found that female gang members fit no single stereotype. Some joined a gang for a relatively short time, hoping to liberate a beloved boyfriend from the organization. Some joined a gang in a passing adolescent phase but quickly realized that long-term membership would be a dead-end street, perhaps leading to life "in a grubby apartment, taking the children upstate on a bus every weekend to visit their father in prison" (Campbell, 1984, p. 7). Many others enjoyed the excitement and intrigue of the gang: "They like sharp clothes, loud music, alcohol, and soft drugs. They admire toughness and verbal 'smarts' " (Campbell, 1984, pp. 7–8).

In some instances, gang members endorse prosocial behaviors, but benevolent gang activities are rarely acknowledged by the media (Campbell, 1984). As one gang member put it:

> The press mention that we exist or whatever, but usually if a club does something good in the neighborhood, we don't get it in the papers. Sometimes, if there was a gang member saving a person from a building, from a fire, or saving somebody's life in a holdup, that's not going to come out in the papers. But if they were doing the opposite, actually doing the act, like [setting] the fire or robbing a person, then that would come out in the papers. In other words, the press doesn't want to let the people know that we have a good thing on our side, they just want to make us look like a bunch of savage animals and things like that. (Campbell, 1984, p. 251)

Yet generally speaking, gangs do more harm than good: They have high levels of violent and criminal activity, making them a matter of great concern to law enforcement officers, political figures, and educators.

Schools are one of the primary contexts in which children and adolescents make friends— or perhaps learn that they *can't* make friends—and in other ways develop beliefs about their ability to establish productive relationships with peers. Yet teachers and other school personnel do not necessarily have to leave students' experiences with their peers to chance. On the contrary, they can do many simple things to ensure that students have positive experiences with peers and find a few classmates with whom to develop a mutually rewarding companionship. We look now at some strategies for doing so.

gang
Cohesive social group characterized by initiation rites, distinctive colors and symbols, territorial orientation, and feuds with rival groups.

Supporting Peer Relationships at School

One obvious way to support positive peer interactions is to teach social skills to students who seem to have few effective ones (see the Development and Practice feature "Promoting Social Skills and Prosocial Behavior" on p. 515). But even when students are able to relate effectively with one another, many of them interact almost exclusively within small, close-knit groups, and a few others remain socially isolated. For example, students often divide themselves along ethnic lines when they eat lunch and interact in the school yard (Schofield, 1995). Immigrant students rarely interact with long-term residents (Olneck, 1995). And students with special needs are often poorly accepted or even rejected by their classmates (Cook & Semmel, 1999; Gresham & MacMillan, 1997; Morrison, Furlong, & Smith, 1994; Yude, Goodman, & McConachie, 1998).

Teachers are in an excellent position to broaden the base of students' social interactions. Intervention is particularly important for students who are rejected by their peers, in part because their tendency to alienate others leaves them few opportunities to develop the social skills they so desperately need, and so they are often very lonely and unhappy (Bullock, 1993; Coie & Cillessen, 1993). Hence we offer the following suggestions:

■ *Set up situations in which students can form new friendships.* Having a single close friend frequently offsets the more general peer rejection that a relatively unpopular student may experience (Guay et al., 1999; Pérez, 1998). Furthermore, when students make friends with high-achieving students, they are more likely to value school achievement themselves (Kindermann, 1993; Kindermann et al., 1996). Teachers can do many simple things to encourage students to get to know one another, and particularly to get to know high-achieving classmates. They can arrange situations that encourage students to work or play cooperatively with their classmates; for example, they can develop structured cooperative learning activities in which all group members must share equal responsibility or provide play equipment that requires the participation of several students (Banks, 1994; Martin, Brady, & Williams, 1991; Slavin, 1990; Schofield, 1995).[3] They can assign partners to students with special needs, and such partners can provide assistance when needed, perhaps reading to a student with a visual impairment, signing to a student with hearing loss, tutoring a student with a learning disability, or taking notes for a student with a physical impairment. Even the very simple practice of giving students assigned seats in class and then occasionally changing those assignments increases the number of friends that they make (Schofield, 1995).

■ *Minimize or eliminate barriers to social interaction.* Students are less likely to interact with their classmates when there are physical, linguistic, or social barriers to doing so. For example, Jeanne recalls a junior high girl who could not negotiate the cafeteria steps with her wheelchair and so always ended up eating lunch alone. Obviously, teachers must be on the lookout for any physical impediments to the mobility of students with special needs and campaign for the removal of such obstacles. They can also teach groups of students who speak different languages (including American Sign Language, with which many students with hearing loss communicate) some basic vocabulary and simple phrases in one another's native tongues. And they must actively address the prejudices and tensions that sometimes separate diverse ethnic groups (see Chapter 10).

■ *Encourage and facilitate participation in extracurricular activities.* Extracurricular activities provide additional opportunities for students to interact and work cooperatively with a wide range of classmates (Genova & Walberg, 1984; Phelan et al., 1994; Schofield, 1995). (Such activities also help to keep them out of trouble, as noted in Chapters 3 and 14.) Adult coaches and advisors must be careful, however, that no single group of students dominates in membership or leadership in any particular activity (Sleeter & Grant, 1999). For some students, schools may need to make special arrangements for after-school transportation (Schofield, 1995).

■ *Develop nondisabled students' understanding of students with special needs.* Nondisabled students sometimes feel resentment or anger about inappropriate behaviors that they believe a

---

[3]Teachers will need to closely supervise any cooperative groups that include a student with poor social skills, helping the student behave appropriately and modeling effective ways for other group members to respond to antisocial behaviors.

classmate with special needs should be able to control (Juvonen, 1991; Juvonen & Weiner, 1993). For example, they are less likely to be tolerant of students with cognitive difficulties or emotional and behavioral disorders than they are of students with obvious physical disabilities (Madden & Slavin, 1983; Ysseldyke & Algozzine, 1984). Teachers must help nondisabled students understand the difficulties that classmates may have as a result of a disability. At the same time, teachers can, perhaps through the paired or small-group activities they arrange, show nondisabled students that their peers with disabilities have many of the same thoughts, feelings, and desires as anyone else their age (Staub, 1998).

■ *Help change the reputations of formerly antisocial students.* Unfortunately, students' bad reputations often live on long after their behavior has changed for the better. Even after students show dramatic improvements in social behavior, their classmates may continue to dislike and reject them (Bierman, Miller, & Staub, 1987; Juvonen & Hiner, 1991; Juvonen & Weiner, 1993). For example, in the case of formerly aggressive students, the perception of many classmates is "once a bully, always a bully." So when teachers work to improve the behaviors of antisocial students, they must work to improve their reputations as well—for example, by placing them in structured cooperative learning groups where they can use their newly developed social skills or by encouraging their active involvement in extracurricular activities. In one way or another, teachers must help students show their peers that they have changed and are worth getting to know better.

■ *Encourage a general feeling of respect for others.* Teachers who effectively promote friendships among diverse groups of students are often those who convey a consistent message over and over again: All members of the school community deserve respect as human beings (Turnbull, Pereira, & Blue-Banning, 2000). Fernando Arias, a high school vocational education teacher, has put it this way:

> In our school, our philosophy is that we treat everybody the way we'd like to be treated. . . . Our school is a unique situation where we have pregnant young ladies who go to our school. We have special education children. We have the regular kids, and we have the drop-out recovery program . . . we're all equal. We all have an equal chance. And we have members of every gang at our school, and we hardly have any fights, and there are close to about 300 gangs in our city. We all get along. It's one big family unit it seems like. (Turnbull et al., 2000, p. 67)

■ *Be a backup system when relationships with peers aren't going well.* Disruptions in peer relationships—perhaps because of interpersonal conflicts or a best friend's relocation to a distant city—are often a source of serious emotional distress (Wentzel, 1999). Warm, supportive teachers can lessen the pain in such circumstances, and their ongoing gestures of affection and support can bolster the spirits of students who, for whatever reasons, have no close friends (Guay et al., 1999; Wentzel, 1999). Such overtures of caring and goodwill may be especially important for students who have little support at home and might otherwise turn to deviant subcultures or gangs to gain attention and affection (Parks, 1995).

So far we have limited our discussion to platonic peer relationships, or those relationships that are social, emotional, and perhaps cognitive, but rarely physical. In the final section of the chapter, we consider the nature of romantic relationships and the development of sexuality.

Romantic Relationships and Sexuality

Even preschoolers show considerable awareness of, as well as interest in, romantic relationships. Many, especially those living in traditional two-parent families, believe that getting married and having children is a normal, perhaps inevitable, part of growing up. They sometimes act out their fantasies and emerging understandings about romance in their sociodramatic play, as this episode involving Eric and Naomi (previously observed planning a shopping trip and killing robbers in the closet) illustrates:

E: Hey, Naomi, I know what we can play today.
N: What?
E: How about, um, the marry game. You like that.
N: Marry?

Most preschoolers are very aware of and curious about courtship and marriage. Here Teresa's son Alex (age 5) depicts his image of his parents getting married. He created the drawing at school during a period when he and his classmates were especially fascinated with engagements and weddings.

E: How about baker or something? How about this. Marry you? OK, Naomi, you want to pretend that?

N: Yes.

E: OK, Naomi, do you want to marry me?

N: Yeah.

E: Good, just a minute, Naomi, we don't have any marry place.

N: We could pretend this is the marry place.

E: Oh, well, pretend this, ah, there'll have to be a cake.

N: The wedding is here first.

E: OK, but listen to this, we have to have a baby, oh, and a pet.

N: This is our baby.

E: And here's our pet, a bunny. Watch how much he can hop.

N: [*Laughs, shrieks.*] He did it again! (Gottman, 1986b, p. 157; reprinted with the permission of Cambridge University Press)

Consistent with what we have learned about cognitive abilities at this age, young children's understandings of courtship and marriage are superficial and concrete. For example, in the preceding scenario, the children focus on having a "marry place" and wedding cake; jumping the gun a bit, they also make sure they have a baby and family pet.

As children grow older, they become increasingly aware of the romantic nature of many adult relationships. For instance, prior to puberty, some children practice courtship behaviors (Elkind, 1981b). Girls may vie for the attention of boys, use cosmetics, and choose clothing and hairstyles that make them look older. Boys, meanwhile, may flaunt whatever manly airs they can muster. Both sexes pay close heed to the romantic activities of those around them and absorb the many romantic images they see in the media (Connolly & Goldberg, 1999; Larson, Clore, & Wood, 1999).

As they reach adolescence, romance is increasingly on young people's minds and a frequent topic of conversation (Brown, Feiring, & Furman, 1999). The biological changes associated with puberty usher in romantic and sexual desires (Larson et al., 1999). Furthermore, in most Western cultures, social pressures mount to tempt, perhaps even push, young adolescents into dating and some degree of sexual activity (Larson et al., 1999; Miller & Benson, 1999).

Romantic relationships in adolescents have numerous benefits. From adolescents' own perspective, being one half of a couple addresses needs for companionship, affection, and security and may significantly enhance social status with peers (Collins & Sroufe, 1999; Furman & Simon, 1999; Miller & Benson, 1999). Yet such relationships also promote social-emotional development, in that they provide opportunities for young people to experiment with new interpersonal behaviors, acquire new social skills, and examine previously unexplored aspects of their own being (Furman & Simon, 1999). Young adolescents' early ventures into cross-sex relationships are often awkward and unskilled: When 12-year-old Connor received his first telephone call from a girl, his response was "Huh? I gotta go." With time and experience, however, many become adept at capturing and maintaining the interest and affections of potential or actual romantic partners.

At the same time, romantic involvements can wreak havoc with adolescents' emotions (Larson et al., 1999). As noted in Chapter 9, adolescents have more extreme mood swings than younger children or adults, and such instability is sometimes due to the excitement and frustrations of being romantically involved (or perhaps *not* involved) with another. The emotional highs and lows that come with romance—the roller coaster ride between exhilaration and disappointment—can cloud judgment and interfere with accurate information processing and reality testing (Larson et al., 1999). Romantic breakups can lead to severe depression and deficits in motivation; in a play on the term *post-traumatic stress syndrome,* some theorists have called this phenomenon "postromantic distress syndrome" (Larson et al., 1999).

Fortunately, most adolescents enter the world of romance slowly and cautiously (B. B. Brown, 1999; Connolly & Goldberg, 1999). Initially, their romances often exist more in their minds than in reality, as the following conversation between two young teenagers illustrates:

A: How's Lance [*giggle*]? Has he taken you to a movie yet?

B: No. Saw him today but I don't care.

A: Didn't he say anything to you?

B: Oh . . .

A: Lovers!
B: Shut up!
A: Lovers at first sight! [*Giggle.*]
B: [*Giggle.*] Quit it! (Gottman & Mettetal, 1986, p. 210; reprinted with the permission of Cambridge University Press)

Young adolescents' romantic thoughts may also involve crushes for people who are out of reach—perhaps favorite teachers, movie idols, or rock stars (B. B. Brown, 1999; Miller & Benson, 1999). At the same time, however, any unspoken prohibitions against affiliating with members of the opposite sex are fading, and so interactions with opposite-sex peers increase (B. B. Brown et al., 1999; Miller & Benson, 1999). Eventually, many adolescents broaden their interpersonal worlds in two ways: by dating and experiencing sexual intimacy. Some of them also wrestle with new feelings about members of their own sex. Let's look more closely at developmental phenomena related to dating, sexual intimacy, and sexual orientation.

Dating

Dating is a developmental milestone for young people. It represents something new, a marker of adult status. Dating behaviors do have antecedents, however. Research suggests that teenagers bring their prior social experiences with family and friends into relationships with romantic partners (Bigelow, Tesson, & Lewko, 1999; Collins & Sroufe, 1999; Leaper & Anderson, 1997). For instance, adolescents who have formed secure attachments to family members are more likely to have successful dating experiences, perhaps because they have greater self-confidence, better social skills, and more experience with deep, enduring emotional relationships. Adolescents who have grown up in an authoritative family (recall the discussion of authoritative parenting in Chapter 12) are accustomed to a balanced give-and-take in decision making and may use this same style with romantic partners, negotiating what movie to see, which party to attend, and so on. Conversely, teens who have repeatedly seen violence in their home lives may bring physical aggression into disagreements with dating partners, hitting, pushing, or in other ways violating them (Wolfe & Wekerle, 1997); they may also tolerate and rationalize aggressive behavior from partners ("He didn't mean it" "She was drunk" "He'll outgrow it").

In the middle school years, young adolescents' forays into coupleship may initially consist of little more than being identified as a couple in the eyes of peers. For instance, in their seventh-grade year, Jeanne's daughter Tina and her friends often talked about their various "boyfriends." Although the girls described themselves as "going out" with this boy or that, in fact they never actually dated any of them. Eventually, however, most venture out on actual dates with one or more peers.

In general, beginning to date has more to do with social expectations than with the onset of puberty (Collins & Sroufe, 1999; Dornbusch et al., 1981; Miller & Benson, 1999). If adolescents have friends who are dating, odds are that they will also begin to date. Early dating partners are often chosen because of their physical attractiveness or social status, and dating relationships tend to be short-lived and involve only superficial interaction (B. B. Brown, 1999; Collins & Sroufe, 1999; Downey et al., 1999).

As teenagers move into the high school years, some begin to form more long-term, intimate relationships (B. B. Brown, 1999; Connolly & Goldberg, 1999). At this point, their choices of dating partners depend more on personality characteristics and compatibility, and peers' judgments are less influential. Relationships become more intense, sometimes stealing time away from other, more platonic friendships. And usually, such relationships lead to varying degrees of sexual intimacy.

Sexual Intimacy

For many adolescents, sexual intimacy goes hand in hand with, and is a natural outgrowth of, long-term romantic relationships (Graber, Britto, & Brooks-Gunn, 1999; Miller & Benson, 1999). For many others, however, it is something that should be saved for the "right moment," or perhaps for after marriage. And for some, sexual intimacy is an activity completely separate from romantic involvement; rather, it may be a means of enhancing one's image and social status with peers, exploring one's sexual orientation, or gaining another's attention and affection (Collins & Sroufe, 1999; Diamond, Savin-Williams, & Dubé, 1999).

The capacity for sexual arousal is present in both sexes before puberty (Conn & Kanner, 1940; Langfeldt, 1981). Children and preadolescents occasionally look at or touch one another in private places and play games (e.g., strip poker) that have sexual overtones (Dornbusch et al., 1981; Katchadourian, 1990). Except in cases of sexual abuse, however, sexuality before adolescence lacks the erotic features present in later development.

Sexual maturation is, like dating, a sign of adulthood and a harbinger of intimacies and pleasures to come. Even so, no one knows how best to handle adolescent sexuality—not parents, not teachers, and certainly not adolescents themselves (Katchadourian, 1990). Many adults ignore the topic, assuming (or perhaps hoping) it's not yet relevant for adolescents. Even teenagers who have good relationships with their parents have few chances to talk about sex (Brooks-Gunn & Furstenberg, 1990; Leite, Buoncompagno, Leite, & Mergulhao, 1995). When parents and teachers do broach the topic of sexuality, they often raise it in conjunction with *problems*, such as irresponsible behavior, substance abuse, disease, and unwanted pregnancy.

Adolescents, meanwhile, must come to terms with their emerging sexuality, either on their own or in collaboration with trusted peers. They must learn to accept their changing bodies, cope with unanticipated new feelings of sexual arousal and desire, and try to reconcile the conflicting messages they get from various sources—home, school, religious groups, peers, the media—about whether and under what circumstances varying degrees of sexual intimacy are appropriate (Brooks-Gunn & Paikoff, 1993).

Their early sexual experiences often add to the confusion; consider these varying recollections about a first kiss (Alapack, 1991):

> "It felt so smooth. I walked home on cloud nine immensely pleased with myself. Finally I had something to boast about. Mission accomplished!" (p. 58)

> "The experience was so gentle that I was in awe. I walked back to my cabin on weak knees. My girlfriends told me I was blushing furiously. I felt lightheaded, but oh so satisfied." (p. 58)

> "I found myself mentally stepping back, thinking: 'no rockets, fireworks, music or stars.' I had to fake enjoyment, humor him. But I felt nothing! Later I sat on my bed and contemplated becoming a nun!" (p. 60)

> "He kissed me violently and pawed me over. When I started to cry, he let me go . . . I didn't want it to count. I wanted to wipe it off as I rubbed off the saliva. I couldn't. It couldn't be reversed; I couldn't be unkissed again. And the moisture, I could feel it, smell it, even though it was wiped. It made me nauseous. I felt like I was going to throw up." (p. 62)

These varied accounts have little in common, except perhaps a common sense of discovery. Other first sexual experiences also reflect such variability. Some teens are moved by tenderness and shared pleasure, but others are disappointed or even repulsed.

Most adolescents add gradually to their repertoire of sexual behaviors. Typically, they initiate actual sexual intercourse (in teenage lingo, they "go all the way") only after several years of experience with less intimate contacts (DeLamater & MacCorquodale, 1979; Udry, 1988). The experience is usually a positive one for boys, but many girls have mixed feelings, sometimes even regret (Carns, 1973; Sorensen, 1983).

In the United States, the trend has been for first intercourse to occur at younger ages. In the 1940s, fewer than 10% of 16-year-old European American girls had tried intercourse; by 1988, almost half had tried it (Hofferth & Hayes, 1987; Kinsey, Pomeroy, & Martin, 1948). Average ages for first intercourse vary as a function of gender (boys lose their virginity sooner than girls), socioeconomic status, and ethnicity, reflecting group differences in peer group and cultural norms about what behaviors are acceptable when (Goodson, Evans, & Edmundson, 1997; Miller & Benson, 1999; U.S. Department of Health and Human Services, 1998). In some societies, men are lauded for their sexual conquests, perhaps even as women are encouraged to remain chaste until marriage. In other cultures, it is rare for high school students to be sexually active, in part because dating couples are regularly accompanied by an adult chaperone (B. B. Brown et al., 1999). Early and frequent sexual activity is also associated with alcohol and drug use (Cooper & Orcutt, 1997).

Sexual Orientation

By **sexual orientation**, we mean the particular sex(es) to which an individual is romantically and sexually attracted. A small but sizable percentage of adolescents find themselves sexually attracted to their own sex either instead of or in addition to the opposite sex. Although it has been difficult to establish precise figures, researchers have estimated that 5% to 10% of the adult population may be gay, lesbian, or bisexual (Durby, 1994; Patterson, 1995).

Sexual orientation does not appear to be a voluntary decision: Some adolescents actively try to ignore or stifle what they perceive to be deviant urges, and intensive treatments to convert homosexual adults into heterosexual ones have been largely unsuccessful (Gabard, 1999; Halderman, 1991). The exact causes of sexual orientation remain elusive, however. Some evidence for a genetic component comes from twin studies: Monozygotic (identical) twins are more similar in their sexual orientation than dizygotic (fraternal) twins (Bailey & Pillard, 1997; Gabard, 1999). Nevertheless, even monozygotic twins are not always similar. For male twins, if one is homosexual, the other has a 50–50 chance of being so; for female twins, the probability is a bit lower. Some researchers have observed subtle differences between homosexual and heterosexual individuals in certain brain structures, and still others have found that varying levels of androgens (male hormones) during prenatal development affect sexual orientation in animals (Bailey & Pillard, 1997; Money, 1987). Yet such biological variables may be the result of environmental rather than genetic influences (Dickemann, 1995; Money, 1987, 1988). At this point, many theorists suspect that both genetic and environmental factors are involved in determining sexual orientation (Byne, 1997; De Cecco & Parker, 1995; Money, 1988; Savin-Williams & Diamond, 1997).

In some cultures, homosexuality is considered to be well within the bounds of acceptable behavior. For instance, on certain islands in the South Pacific, 9- to 19-year-old boys live together in a single large house at the center of their village. They participate in numerous homosexual activities, and *not* participating is considered deviant (Herdt, 1981; Money, 1987). In most Western societies, however, homosexual acts are disparaged, and people who are gay, lesbian, or bisexual encounter considerable misunderstanding, prejudice, and discrimination (Patterson, 1995).

Many homosexual and bisexual young people recall feeling "different" from peers in their childhood days (Anderson, 1994; Savin-Williams, 1995). Adolescence is a particularly confusing time for them, as they struggle to form an identity while feeling different and isolated from peers (Morrow, 1997; Patterson, 1995). When their attractions to same-sex peers become stronger, they may initially work hard to ignore or discount such feelings. At an older age, they may begin to accept some aspects of their homosexuality, and later still, they may "come out" and identify fully and openly with other gay and lesbian individuals.

Yet they often find the road to self-acceptance to be a rocky one, and anger, depression, and suicidal thoughts are common along the way (Elia, 1994; Patterson, 1995). Adolescents with a homosexual or bisexual orientation are frequently harassed by peers and occasionally the victims of hate crimes (Friend, 1993; Savin-Williams, 1995). When the topic of homosexuality comes up in the school curriculum, it is usually within the context of acquired immune deficiency syndrome (AIDS) and other risks; more often, it is not discussed at all. One 17-year-old student recalls:

> I don't remember any formal discussion of homosexuality in school. In fact, it's really surprising to me that we didn't discuss it. My required eleventh grade health class, come to think of it, covered everything but it. We did condoms, sex, teen pregnancy, suicide, eating disorders, every kind of cancer—you name it, we did it. But nothing on homosexuality. (Malinsky, 1997, p. 40)

Under such circumstances, gay, lesbian, and bisexual youths often feel "silent, invisible, and fearful" (Harris, 1997, p. xxi), and a higher than average proportion drop out of school (Elia, 1994). Furthermore, some school personnel offer little in the way of comfort. A young woman named Elise describes what happened when she shared her homosexuality with her high school counselor:

> I came out to my counselor in my freshman year in high school. I've told this story over and over because it cracks me up but it's also very scary. It's just that she told me first of all not to confuse being gay with masturbation. Uh, which confused me. I wasn't confused before [laughs] but I was

sexual orientation
Particular sex(es) to which an individual is romantically and sexually attracted.

after that. She said, "Don't let your gay friends pressure you into it." At this point in time I knew I was gay; I recognized that fact but I didn't have any gay friends. Nobody's pressuring me into it; I don't know any gay people—that's why I'm upset. "Don't make a decision like this until you're at least 18." . . . I was in there saying I'm gay, not I think I'm gay . . . I believe if I had not been secure in already recognizing who I was and very strong-minded . . . that would have probably pushed me back in the closet. If this wasn't misinformation. . . ." (Herr, 1997, p. 59)

While drawing attention to the negative experiences of many gay and lesbian adolescents, we must also point out that most are psychologically and socially healthy (Savin-Williams, 1989). Moreover, many gain considerable social and emotional support from their parents, teachers, counselors, and peers. For example, Elise's mother was more understanding than her counselor had been and eventually put Elise in touch with a local support group. Elise found long-sought contact with other gay and lesbian adolescents to be very reassuring:

> I was so happy to realize that—oh wow, it's very difficult to describe the feeling—realizing, feeling completely completely alone and then realizing that other people know exactly where you're at or what you're going through. I mean it was amazing. (Herr, 1997, p. 60)

Regardless of adolescents' sexual orientation, their sexuality is an important and sometimes all-consuming concern. We now look at some ways in which teachers and other school personnel can help teenagers come to terms with their changing bodies and feelings.

Addressing Sexuality Issues in the Classroom

When students reach puberty, romance saturates the school environment. Students become preoccupied with who harbors secret yearnings for whom, whether the objects of desire reciprocate the affection, and which classmates have progressed to various points along the continuum of sexual exploration. Teachers often find this undercurrent of romantic desire distracting, yet they cannot prevent students from growing up or squash the instincts that energize students' bodies. So what can teachers do? We offer the following suggestions:

- *Remember how you felt as an adolescent.* If romance was not a part of your own adolescence, we suspect that you longed for it or found yourself fantasizing about a particular someone. If you dated occasionally or frequently, the depth of sentiments from your first experiences undoubtedly left a trace (we wager you can remember your first date, first kiss, first rejection). Distracting as they might be, romantic desires are a natural, healthy part of coming-of-age.

- *Expect diversity in students' romantic relationships.* Students' romantic activities will, to some degree, reflect the cultural norms of the surrounding community. Yet within any given culture, individual differences are sizable. Some students attract a series of steady admirers, whereas others may be inexperienced in, possibly even indifferent to, the world of romance. And a small percentage of students will have yearnings for members of their own sex.

Teenagers are most likely to share their questions and concerns about romantic issues when teachers are clearly understanding, open-minded, and supportive about such issues.

- *Make information about human sexuality easily available.* A conventional attitude has been that education about "the birds and the bees" is the prerogative of parents and has no place in the schools. Thus, as noted in Chapter 3, if sex education is a part of the school curriculum at all, it focuses on the biological aspects of sexual intercourse and procreation and offers little information to help teens make sense of their conflicting thoughts and feelings about sex and romance. Furthermore, students' participation in a sex education curriculum usually requires their parents' approval, and many parents are loathe to give it. Less controversial alternatives are to let students know that school counselors, nurses, and other support personnel are always willing to talk with students about matters of sexuality (and to listen to their concerns with an open mind) and to make literature about a variety of sexuality issues readily available at the school library. (For related suggestions, see the sections "Sexual Activity" and "Addressing Health-Compromising Behaviors" in Chapter 3.)

FIGURE 13–7 Example of how educators might describe sexual harassment in language that students understand

Originally appeared as "Stop Sexual Harassment in Schools," by N. Stein, May 18, 1993, *USA Today.* Copyright 1993 by Nan Stein. Reprinted with permission of the author.

SEXUAL HARASSMENT: IT'S NO JOKE!

■ **Sexual harassment is unwanted and unwelcomed sexual behavior** which interferes with your right to get an education or to participate in school activities. In school, sexual harassment may result from someone's words, gestures or actions (of a sexual nature) that make you feel uncomfortable, embarassed, offended, demeaned, frightened, helpless or threatened. If you are the target of sexual harassment, it may be very scary to go to school or hard to concentrate on your school work.

■ **Sexual harassment can happen once, several times, or on a daily basis.**

■ **Sexual harassment can happen any time and anywhere** in school—in hallways or in the lunchroom, on the playground or the bus, at dances or on field trips.

■ **Sexual harassment can happen to anyone!** Girls and boys both get sexually harassed by other students in school.

■ **Agreement isn't needed.** The target of sexual harassment and the harasser do not have to agree about what is happening; sexual harassment is defined by the girl or boy who is targeted. The harasser may tell you that he or she is only joking, but if their words, gestures or actions (of a sexual nature) are making you uncomfortable or afraid, then you're being sexually harassed. You do not have to get others, either your friends, teachers or school officials, to agree with you.

■ **No one has the right to sexually harass another person!** School officials are legally responsible to guarantee that all students, you included, can learn in a safe environment which is free from sexual harassment and sex discrimination. If you are being sexually harassed, your student rights are being violated. Find an adult you trust and tell them what's happening, so that something can be done to stop the harassment.

■ **Examples of sexual harassment in school:**
  - touching, pinching, and grabbing body parts
  - being cornered
  - sending sexual notes or pictures
  - writing sexual graffiti on desks, bathroom walls or buildings
  - making suggestive or sexual gestures, looks, jokes, or verbal comments (including "mooing," "barking" and other noises)
  - spreading sexual rumors or making sexual propositions
  - pulling off someone's clothes
  - pulling off your own clothes
  - being forced to kiss someone or do something sexual
  - attempted rape and rape

REMEMBER: SEXUAL HARASSMENT IS SERIOUS AND AGAINST THE LAW!

■ *Work to create a supportive environment for all students.* To adults, the romantic bonds and breakups of adolescents often seem trivial, but they may be a source of considerable stress and emotional volatility for teenagers. For instance, students may feel deep humiliation after rejection from an elusive suitor or a profound sense of loss as a long-term relationship ends (Kaczmarek & Backlund, 1991). In such situations, teachers and other school personnel can help students sort through their feelings and look forward with optimism to brighter days and new opportunities ahead (Larson et al., 1999).

In addition, educators must make sure that students with diverse sexual orientations feel welcome, respected, and safe at school (Morrow, 1997). They may also need to confront misconceptions in some of their colleagues: Creating a climate that is tolerant of sexual diversity is not likely to increase the number of students who are gay and lesbian. What it may do, however, is keep them in school.

Peer Relationships at Different Age Levels

AGE	WHAT YOU MIGHT OBSERVE	DIVERSITY	IMPLICATIONS
Early Childhood (2–6) 	• Increasing frequency and complexity of peer interactions as children gain experience with age-mates • Variability in styles of play (sometimes solitary, sometimes parallel, sometimes cooperative) • Ability to approach and watch a peer and then initiate conversation • Increase in complexity of socio-dramatic play, which provides practice in communication and negotiation • Agreement on roles and willingness to take turns in play activities (ages 4–6)	• Children who know their classmates or have had earlier positive experiences with peers may be more socially oriented than children who are new to the group or have previously had negative experiences with peers. • Temperament affects children's interactive style. Some children may be drawn to peers yet have trouble controlling their emotions (e.g., they may be aggressive and disruptive). • Children who have insecure attachments to parents and other family members may be less knowledgeable about how to interact sensitively and may not expect kindness from others (Bretherton & Waters, 1985). • Children with language delays may have more difficulty interacting with peers effectively.	• Help shy children gain entry into group activities, especially if they have previously had limited social experiences. • Let children bring one or two items from home (e.g., favorite snuggly toys for nap time) and maintain ownership of their possessions, but remind them of the need to take turns and share school toys and equipment. • When necessary, help children resolve interpersonal conflicts, but encourage them to identify solutions that benefit everyone and let them do as much of the negotiation as possible. • Help children deal with anger and conflict constructively so that they learn strategies for maintaining productive interpersonal relationships.
Middle Childhood (6–10) 	• Increase in time spent with peers; greater concern about being accepted by peers • Tendency to assemble in larger groups than in early childhood • Less need for adult supervision than in early childhood • Decline of pretend play and rough-and-tumble play over middle childhood (pretend play may continue in private, where there are unlikely to be social sanctions against it) • Less physical aggression, but more verbal aggression (e.g., threats, insults) than in earlier years • Increase in gossip, as children show concern over who are their friends and enemies • Some social exclusiveness, with friends being reluctant to have others join in their activities • Predominance of same-sex friendships (especially after age 7)	• Boys tend to play in larger groups than girls. • Some children are temperamentally cautious and timid; they may stand at the periphery of groups and show little social initiative. • Some children are actively rejected by their peers, perhaps because they are perceived as odd or have poor social skills. • Bullying and other forms of victimization emerge during middle childhood. Bullies are aggressive, show little self-control, and tend to seek victims who are insecure, anxious, and isolated.	• Supervise children's peer relationships from a distance, intervene when needed to defuse an escalating situation. Identify ways to resolve conflicts that ensure everyone's welfare and rights. • Help isolated and rejected children join games, work groups, and lunch groups, and teach them skills for interacting effectively with classmates. • Teach aggressive students more productive ways to solve conflicts with peers.

sexual harassment
Form of discrimination in which a target individual perceives other's actions or statements to be hostile, humiliating, or offensive, especially related to physical appearance or sexual matters.

■ *Educate students about what sexual harassment is and why it is prohibited.* **Sexual harassment** is any action that a target can reasonably construe as being hostile, humiliating, or sexually offensive (Sjostrom & Stein, 1996). It is a form of discrimination and, as such, is prohibited by federal and state laws. Sexual harassment can be a problem at the late elementary, middle school, and high school levels, and students must know that it will not be tolerated. For instance, they should be informed that under no circumstances can they degrade one another, either in words or in actions,

AGE	WHAT YOU MIGHT OBSERVE	DIVERSITY	IMPLICATIONS
Early Adolescence (10–14) 	• Variety of contexts (e.g., competitive sports, extracurricular activities, parties) used as opportunities to see and interact with peers • Increased concern about acceptance and popularity among peers • Fads and conformity in dress and communication styles in peer groups • Same-sex cliques, often restricted to members of a single ethnic group • Increasing intimacy, self-disclosure, and loyalty among friends • New interest in members of the opposite sex; for gay and lesbian youths, interest in the same sex takes on new dimensions • For some, initiation of dating, often within the context of group activities	• Some young adolescents are very affiliative and socially outgoing; others are more quiet and reserved. • Some young adolescents hold tenaciously to childhood interests, such as dolls or Lego blocks. • Some young adolescents (especially boys) become involved in gangs and other delinquent social activities. • A few young adolescents are sexually active. • A small percentage begin to construct an identity as a gay or lesbian individual.	• Make classrooms and schools friendly, affirming places for all students. Do not tolerate name calling, ethnic slurs, or sexual harassment. • Provide appropriate places for students to "hang out" before and after school. Identify mechanisms (e.g., cooperative learning groups, public service projects) through which students can fraternize productively as they work toward academic or prosocial goals. Give students sufficient structure that they can work together effectively. • On some occasions, decide which students will work together in groups; on other occasions, let students choose their own work partners. • Sponsor structured after-school activities (e.g., in sports, music, or academic interest areas).
Late Adolescence (14–18) 	• Emerging understanding that relationships with numerous peers do not necessarily threaten close friendships • Increasing dependence on friends for advice and emotional support; however, adults remain important in such matters as educational choices and career goals • Less cliquishness toward the end of high school; greater tendency to affiliate with larger, less exclusive crowds • Increasing amount of time spent in mixed-sex groups • Many social activities unsupervised by adults • Emergence of committed romantic couples, especially in the last two years of high school	• Some teenagers have parents who continue to monitor their whereabouts; others have little adult supervision. • Adolescents' choice of friends and social groups affect their pastimes, risk-taking behaviors, and attitudes about schoolwork. Some adolescents, known as thrill-seekers, actively seek out risky activities. • Teens who find themselves attracted to same-sex peers face additional challenges in constructing their adult identities; some are prone to anger, depression, or suicidal thoughts, especially if others are not understanding and accepting.	• In literature and history, assign readings with themes of psychological interest to adolescents (e.g., loyalty among friends, self-disclosure of feelings and vulnerability). • Be alert to the specific peer groups with which students are associating. If they associate with troubled students who may discourage academic achievement or prosocial behavior, encourage them to join extracurricular activities and in other ways make them feel an integral part of the school community. • Sponsor school dances and other supervised social events that give adolescents opportunities to socialize in safe and wholesome activities.

Sources: Baumeister & Senders, 1989; Bigelow, 1977; Bretherton & Waters, 1985; Buhrmester, 1996; Coie & Dodge, 1998; Eder, 1985; Epstein, 1986; Furman & Buhrmester, 1992; Garvey, 1974, 1990; Göncü, 1993; Kindermann et al., 1996; Leaper, 1994; O'Brien & Bierman, 1987; Olweus, 1993a, 1993b; Patterson, 1995; Rubin et al., 1998; Rubin, Coplan, Fox, & Calkins, 1995; Selman & Schultz, 1990; Shrum & Cheek, 1987; Teasley & Parker, 1995; Youniss & Smollar, 1985; Zarbatany et al., 1990.

about physical characteristics or sexual orientation. An example of a description of sexual harassment, appropriate for students at varying grade levels, appears in Figure 13–7 on page 533.

■ *Make appropriate referrals when necessary.* Teachers in middle school, junior high, and high school settings occasionally hear more than they anticipated about students' personal lives, including stories about the unexpected consequences of precocious sexual adventures. For instance, students may tell teachers they are pregnant, have a pregnant girlfriend, or suspect they've contracted a sexually transmitted disease. Teachers need to be prepared to make immediate referrals to school counselors and other support personnel, who can offer guidance and support and encourage students to talk with their parents and other family members.

In this chapter, we've seen many changes in young people's social skills and peer relationships over the course of childhood and adolescence. In the Developmental Trends table on pp. 534–535, we summarize key characteristics of interpersonal relationships during the four developmental periods of early childhood, middle childhood, early adolescence, and late adolescence and offer additional suggestions for teachers. In the following, final chapter of the book, we go beyond family and peers to look at the larger contexts in which young people grow up.

CASE STUDY: AARON AND COLE

Aaron and Cole became friends when they were both students in Mr. Howard's fifth-grade class. Whereas Aaron was in most respects a typical fifth grader, Cole had significant developmental delays. Special educator Debbie Staub (1998) summed up both his special educational needs and his strengths as follows:

> Cole has limited expressive vocabulary and uses one- or two-word sentences. He does not participate in traditional academic tasks, although he is included with his typically developing schoolmates for the entire school day. Cole has a history of behavioral problems that have ranged from mild noncompliance to adult requests to serious aggressive and destructive behavior such as throwing furniture at others. In spite of his occasional outbursts, however, it is hard not to like him. Cole is like an eager toddler who finds wonder in the world around him. The boys he has befriended in Mr. Howard's class bring him great joy. He appreciates their jokes and harmless teasing. Cole would like nothing better than to hang out with his friends all day, but if he had to choose just one friend, it would be Aaron. (p. 76)

Aaron and Cole remained close until Cole moved to a group home 30 miles away at the beginning of seventh grade. Throughout their fifth- and sixth-grade years, Aaron was both a good friend and a caring mentor to Cole.

> Without prompting from adults, Aaron helped Cole with his work, included him at games at recess, and generally watched out for him. Aaron also assumed responsibility for Cole's behavior by explaining to Cole how his actions affected others. The following excerpt from a classroom observation illustrates Aaron's gentle way with Cole: "Cole was taking Nelle's [a classmate's] things out of her bag and throwing them on the floor. As soon as Aaron saw, he walked right over to Cole and started talking to him. He said, 'We're making a new rule—no being mean.' Then he walked with Cole to the front of the room and told him to tell another boy what the new rule was. Cole tapped the boy's shoulder to tell him but the boy walked away. Cole looked confused. Aaron smiled and put his hand on Cole's shoulder and told him, 'It's okay. Just remember the rule.' Then he walked Cole back to Nelle's stuff and quietly asked Cole to put everything back." (Staub, 1998, pp. 77–78)

But Aaron, too, benefited from the friendship, as his mother explained: "Our family has recently gone through a tough divorce and there are a lot of hurt feelings out there for everyone. But at least when Aaron is at school he feels good about being there and I think a big reason is because he has Cole and he knows that he is an important person in Cole's life" (Staub, 1998, pp. 90–91).

Dr. Staub observed that, despite their developmental differences, the boys' relationship was in many respects a normal one:

> I asked Mr. Howard once, "Do you think Cole's and Aaron's friendship looks different from others' in your class?" Mr. Howard thought for a moment before responding, "No, I don't think it looks that different. Well, I was going to say one of the differences is that Aaron sometimes tells Cole to be quiet, or 'Hey Cole, I gotta do my work!' But I don't know if that is any different than what he might say to Ben leaning over and interrupting him. I think I would say that Aaron honestly likes Cole and it's not because he's a special-needs kid." (Staub, 1998, p. 78)

Excerpts from *Delicate Threads: Friendships Between Children with and Without Special Needs in Inclusive Settings,* by D. Staub, 1998, Bethesda, MD: Woodbine House. Reprinted with permission.

- In what way did the friendship promote each boy's social-emotional development?
- Was the boys' friendship a reciprocal one? Why or why not?

SUMMARY

Development of Interpersonal Behaviors

Children and adolescents continue to acquire and refine social skills (e.g., cooperation, negotiation, conflict resolution) throughout the elementary and secondary grades, and school provides one important context in which such skills develop. Most become increasingly prosocial over the years, propelled in part by their growing capacity for perspective taking and empathy. Some degree of aggression (especially verbal aggression) is common; however, a few youngsters display troublesome levels of physical or psychological aggression and may require planned interventions to teach them more effective social skills, as well as to make the school environment safer and more comfortable for classmates.

Both prosocial behavior and aggression appear to have genetic roots, but environmental factors (e.g., parenting styles, exposure to prosocial and aggressive models) also play a role in their development.

Peer Relationships

Peers serve important functions in social-emotional development. Not only do they offer companionship and pleasure, but they also provide a context for practicing social skills, help one another make sense of social experiences, and influence one another's habits and ideas. Peer relationships change systematically over childhood and adolescence; for instance, activities tend to shift from pretend play to structured group games and then, in adolescence, to social activities within cliques and (in high school) larger, mixed-sex groups. Friendships are especially important, in that they provide social and emotional support, motivation to resolve conflicts in mutually satisfying ways, and eventually, emotional intimacy.

Romantic Relationships and Sexuality

Although preschoolers and elementary school children are well aware that romantic relationships are common among teenagers and adults, young people do not appreciate the full significance of romance and sexuality until they reach adolescence. As they go through puberty, they must come to terms with their changing bodies, sexual drives, and increasing sexual attraction to some of their peers. Romances, either actual or imagined, can wreak havoc with teenagers' emotions, which in turn may affect their behavior and achievement at school. Some adolescents experiment with sexual intimacy with only limited information about the potential risks of doing so, and others must wrestle with sexual feelings about members of their own sex. Such changes require sensitivity, understanding and, in many cases, support on the part of teachers and other school personnel.

Now go to our Companion Website to assess your understanding of chapter content with Multiple-Choice Questions, apply comprehension in Essay Questions, and broaden your knowledge with links to related Developmental Psychology World Wide Web sites.

KEY CONCEPTS

social skills (p. 496)
prosocial behavior (p. 497)
aggressive behavior (p. 497)
proactive aggression (p. 502)
reactive aggression (p. 502)
hostile attributional bias
  (p. 505)
bully (p. 506)
sociodramatic play (p. 507)
intersubjectivity (p. 508)

social pretense (p. 508)
self-disclosure (p. 511)
peer pressure (p. 511)
mediation training (p. 516)
peers (p. 517)
popular children (p. 519)
rejected children (p. 519)
neglected children (p. 519)
controversial children
  (p. 519)

friendship (p. 519)
peer culture (p. 523)
dominance hierarchy
  (p. 524)
clique (p. 524)
subculture (p. 524)
gang (p. 525)
sexual orientation (p. 530)
sexual harassment (p. 534)

Artists: Antonio, Gabe, Awurama, Agapito, Nikia, Alyssa, Jon. Supervising Artists: Heidi Schork and Teig Grennan.

Growing Up in Context

CASE STUDY: THE NEW SCHOOL

In *The Dreamkeepers,* Gloria Ladson-Billings (1994) describes her childhood experiences as an African American student in the American public schools. In the following excerpt, she describes what it was like to change schools—and simultaneously to change cultures—when she began seventh grade:

> I was sent to an integrated junior high school that was not in my neighborhood. I describe it as "integrated" rather than "desegregated" because no court mandates placed black children there. I was there because my mother was concerned about the quality of our neighborhood school.
>
> There were a handful of African American students in my seventh-grade class, but I knew none of them. They lived in a more affluent neighborhood than I did. Their parents had stable blue collar or white collar jobs. They had gone to better-equipped elementary schools than I had. The white students were even more privileged. Their fathers had impressive jobs as doctors, lawyers—one was a photojournalist. Most of their mothers were homemakers. In contrast, my mother and father both worked full-time. My father often even worked two jobs, yet we still lived more modestly than most of my classmates did.
>
> In seventh grade I learned what it means to be competitive. In elementary school my teachers did not seem to make a big deal out of my academic achievements. They encouraged me but did not hold me up as an example that might intimidate slower students. Although I suspect I was a recipient of a kind of sponsored mobility—perhaps because my mother always sent me to school neat and clean and with my hair combed—I don't think this preferential treatment was obvious to the other students. But in my new surroundings the competition was very obvious. Many of my white classmates made a point of showing off their academic skills. Further, their parents actively lent a hand in important class assignments and projects. For example, one boy had horrible penmanship. You could barely read what he scrawled in class, but he always brought in neatly typed homework. I asked him once if he did the typing and he told me his mother typed everything for him. She also did the typing of his cousin, who was also in our class and had beautiful penmanship. The teachers often commented on the high quality of these typed papers.
>
> I had come from a school where children learned and produced together. This competitiveness, further encouraged by the parents, was new to me. I could attempt to keep up with this unfair competition and "act white" or I could continue to work my hardest and hope I could still achieve.

From *The Dreamkeepers: Successful Teachers of African American Children* (pp. 11–12), by G. Ladson-Billings, 1994, San Francisco: Jossey-Bass. Copyright © 1994 by Jossey-Bass, Inc., Publishers. Reprinted by permission of Jossey-Bass, Inc., a subsidiary of John Wiley & Sons.

OR THE OTHER STUDENTS at Gloria's new school, the focus on individual talents and accomplishments was a way of life that everyone took for granted. For Gloria herself, such a focus was out of sync with that of her previous schools, where children worked cooperatively toward common goals. Gloria's encounter with new and unsettling values and assumptions illustrates just one of the innumerable ways in which culture permeates children's everyday experiences.

In preceding chapters, we have often considered the role that culture plays in human development. In this chapter we look more generally at culture as a broad social environment, or *context,* in which children and adolescents grow. We look at other contexts as well, including historical events, religious affiliation, socioeconomic status, neighborhoods and communities, and the media. As we examine such contexts, we consider their effects on children's development and their implications for classroom practice.

Culture and Ethnicity

By **culture,** we mean the behaviors and belief systems that characterize a social group. A community's cultural heritage provides an ongoing framework in which its members decide what is true, good, healthy, rational, and normal (Shweder et al., 1998).

Notice that this definition of culture includes both *behaviors* and *beliefs.* Cross-cultural differences in behavior—customs, traditions, and everyday practices—are often fairly concrete and easily observed. For instance, various cultural groups exhibit differences in meal practices (what, how, and with whom they eat), division of responsibility in families (who makes decisions about financial purchases, who disciplines the children, who prepares dinner and cares for the house, etc.), and social practices (with whom parents converse and children play). Cultural practices are also frequently seen in how people mark children's increasing age and responsibility. In some cultures, specific rituals and ceremonies mark an abrupt passage from childhood to adulthood. In others, such as in many Western societies, numerous small events mark a more gradual transition from "child" to "adolescent" to "adult," perhaps including acquisition of a driver's license, graduation from high school, a first intimate sexual experience, or eligibility to vote in national elections.

Belief systems, though not as obvious as behaviors, are an equally important part of a group's cultural heritage. As examples, consider the following ideas:

- Babies are innocent at birth.
- As children grow, they should become increasingly self-reliant and independent.
- If people want something, they should say so.
- Some competition among individuals is healthy and productive.

Such beliefs are among the core ideas of mainstream Western culture (Hollins, 1996; Shweder et al., 1998). Yet they are not universally held across cultures. For example, some cultural groups believe that infants are far from innocent—that, instead, they are born with inappropriate impulses that must be eradicated (Shweder et al., 1998). And as we saw in the opening case study, not all groups value competition. In the United States, people of European American descent tend to be relatively competitive, whereas people in ethnic minority groups tend to be more cooperative (Dien, 1998; Hollins, 1996; Webb & Palincsar, 1996).

The two bookends of culture—behaviors and beliefs—are closely related, in that common practices often stem from particular beliefs about what is true, healthy, or appropriate. For example, most European American parents have their children sleep in rooms separate from their own, justifying this practice with assertions that it provides nighttime privacy for adults and fosters independence in children (Shweder et al., 1998). Yet in other cultures, children sleep with their parents, and people justify such co-sleeping arrangements with as much vigor as European Americans rationalize separate sleeping arrangements. For instance, Japanese parents may say, "I value and want to promote interdependency and feelings of closeness and solidarity among members of the family" and "I know that co-sleeping will help children overcome feelings of distance and separation from members of the family who are older or of a

culture
Behaviors and belief systems that characterize a social group and provide a framework for how group members decide what is normal and appropriate.

different sex" (Shweder et al., 1998, p. 873). Oriya Hindu parents offer a different explanation for the same practice: "I highly value children as members of the family" and "I know that children are fragile, vulnerable, and needy and therefore should not be left alone and unprotected during the night" (Shweder et al., 1998, p. 873).

Ultimately, culture is the essence of what makes a community meaningful for children. To a large extent, it determines the ideas and values that children acquire, the tools and actions that they master, and the adult roles to which they aspire. It identifies the problems that are worth solving and provides specific strategies for solving them. And it guides the development of language and communication skills, expression and regulation of emotions, and formation of a sense of self.

Membership in a particular racial group is not always a good indication of children's ethnic identity.

Ethnicity and Race

The concepts *culture* and *ethnicity* overlap, but the term *ethnicity* refers to membership in a particular group. More specifically, **ethnicity** refers to a group of individuals with the following characteristics:

- Its roots either precede the creation of or are external to the country in which it resides; for example, it may be comprised of people of the same race, national origin, or religious background.
- It has a common set of values, beliefs, and behaviors that influence the lives of its members.
- Its members share a sense of "peoplehood" and interdependence, a feeling that their lives are intertwined. (Au, 1993; Fisher et al., 1998; NCSS Task Force on Ethnic Studies Curriculum Guidelines, 1992)

Sometimes members of a particular race are considered to be an ethnic group; for instance, in earlier chapters we have sometimes spoken of African Americans, Caucasians (using the term *European Americans*), or Asian Americans. The term *race* generally refers to a group of people who share certain physical similarities, such as skin color or the shape of the eyes, that have a genetic basis (Fisher et al., 1998). However, as noted in Chapter 6, race is not defined simply by biology: We cannot pinpoint a person's race by analyzing DNA. Furthermore, racial categories are fuzzy at best, and many individuals can claim ancestry from more than one racial group.

We prefer the term *ethnicity* over *race* because the former label emphasizes important cultural dimensions without connoting that differences arise out of biological factors. Certainly ethnicity and race are sometimes related. For instance, many people in North America who are "white" (Caucasian) share common experiences and assumptions: They are part of a dominant class system and, courtesy of their common European ancestors, have somewhat similar cultural viewpoints; for instance, they tend to place high value on self-reliance and competition. Likewise, many "black" North Americans show common language patterns (see the discussion of African American English in Chapter 7). Yet the correlations are hardly perfect; for instance, some black people in North America align themselves with their African heritage, others identify more closely with their Hispanic roots, and still others trace their recent ancestry to Caribbean nations.

Yet *ethnicity*, too, is a broad descriptor with limited utility. Consider the terms *Hispanic* and *Latino/Latina*. The term *Hispanic* refers to any Spanish-speaking individual and includes people from Spain, Mexico, Central and South American countries, and Spanish-speaking Caribbean nations; it may also include Portuguese-speaking people of Portugal and Brazil. The terms *Latino* and *Latina* (for males and females, respectively) are more frequently limited to people whose origins are Central and South America (Fisher et al., 1998). When such broad categories are used, they obscure the tremendous variation that exists within groups. For example, *Hispanic American* includes people of Mexican origin living in the southwestern states, those of Puerto Rican origin living in the northeastern states, and those of Cuban origin living in Florida.

Finally, even within a single ethnic group in which people have similar cultural origins, significant individual and family differences exist in personalities, political beliefs, educational

ethnicity
Membership in a group of people with a common set of values, beliefs, and behaviors. The group's roots either precede the creation of, or are external to, the country in which the group resides.

Characterizing Culture and Ethnicity

BASIC DEVELOPMENTAL ISSUES

ISSUE	CULTURE AND ETHNICITY
Nature and Nurture	Culture and ethnicity, as reflected in people's language patterns, social hierarchies, interpersonal behaviors, chosen professions, priorities, and so on, are constructed by social groups and so are entirely environmental in origin. Nature is present across the species in some of children's yearnings, such as their desires to form attachments and other social relationships and to master the language of their community. Individual children's inherited temperaments and talents may influence the particular ways in which they manifest the teachings of their culture. Furthermore, racial heritage, which is genetic in origin, sometimes influences the particular cultural and ethnic groups with which children identify.
Universality and Diversity	All cultural and ethnic groups prescribe certain behaviors and belief systems for their members. However, the specific behaviors and beliefs prescribed differ widely from one group to another. In multicultural countries, such as the United States, ethnic groups differ further in the opportunities each has within the dominant society; for example, some groups experience discrimination in housing, jobs, and educational opportunities. Additional diversity in behaviors and beliefs may exist *within* a particular group. Both between-group and within-group diversity have implications for educators, who must be sensitive to cultural differences yet not form rigid stereotypes of particular groups.
Qualitative and Quantitative Change	Some cultures and ethnic groups view development in terms of abrupt qualitative changes; for instance, rituals that signify passage from childhood to adulthood may be accompanied by an immediate and drastic change in young people's roles in the community and in others' expectations for their performance. Other cultures and ethnic groups view development as a series of smaller, more gradual steps—for instance, by allowing gradually increasing responsibility and independence.

accomplishments, and so on. Children and adults manifest their ethnic beliefs and values, and avail themselves of different opportunities, in different ways depending on their particular talents, interests, and family circumstances. For example, in a culture with strong obligations to family, one grown child may show this characteristic by sending home money, another may do repairs around the house, and another may simply visit his or her parents whenever possible.

The Basic Developmental Issues table above characterizes culture and ethnicity in terms of nature versus nurture, universality versus diversity, and qualitative versus quantitative change. We now look more closely at the kinds of diversity we are likely to see among children of different ethnic groups.

Contrasting Children's Ethnic Worlds

Cultural and ethnic differences often reveal themselves in the ways that adults instruct and nurture children. For instance, in the opening case study, we saw differing emphases on cooperation versus competition in schools in different ethnic neighborhoods of a single American city. Following are three additional examples of cultural and ethnic differences:

- When mothers from European American backgrounds ask their children "where" questions, they typically focus on physical objects and tools ("Where's your book? Look, I see it near your blanket!"; Mundy-Castle, 1974). But in the Wolof culture in Senegal, Africa, mothers use "where" questions to teach their children about social relationships (Rabain-Jamin, 1994). For instance, a mother asks 6-month-old Karjata, "Karjata . . . Where is Malik's sister? . . . Here is Umar's sister. . . . Where is Bokar's mother? . . . Where is Demba's mother? . . . One mustn't hurt someone's mother!" (Rabain-Jamin, 1994, pp. 150–151).
- In most Western schools, teachers depend heavily on interactive verbal lessons to teach information and skills. In contrast, many Native American communities have a tradition

of nonparticipatory observational learning, in which children intently watch adults in their daily occupations (pottery, weaving, etc.) and the adults give only occasional explanations about what they are doing. Many Native American children are also encouraged to listen without interruption to lengthy stories and to create mental images of the legendary characters and events that the stories depict (Tharp, 1994).

- In Western countries, young children may have many experiences interacting with age-mates, but they typically do so under the supervision of adults. In contrast, Nso children, who live in the Bamenda Grassfields of Cameroon, spend considerably more time with other children than with adults. For instance, numerous Nso children ranging in age from 1½ to 6 or 7 might play together under the supervision of two older girls, who are perhaps 8 to 10 years old (Nsamenang & Lamb, 1994).

Most children seem to adjust well, despite the significantly different childrearing practices of the cultures and ethnic environments into which they are born or adopted.

You might wonder *why* ethnic environments are so different from one another. Particularly influential in shaping cultural practices are the natural resources and jobs available to the majority of people in the society (Kim & Choi, 1994). Let's return to the Nso people of Cameroon, where older children supervise younger ones for much of the day. Encouraging early social competence and shared responsibilities is typical of rural agricultural groups that are comprised of large, close-knit families (Nsamenang & Lamb, 1994). Such a pattern is less adaptive in migratory tribes living in jungles, mountains, and deserts (Barry, Child, & Bacon, 1959). Tribes facing uncertain and inhospitable environments need distinct skills to survive: They must pull up roots frequently to search for food and water, and they socialize their children to be assertive, venturesome, and self-reliant (Barry et al., 1959). To some extent, then, ethnic culture is an outgrowth of the history of a people and the adaptations the group has made to minimize hardships, increase physical comfort and well-being, and maintain social harmony.

Ethnicity, Immigration, and Social Change

Cultural and ethnic differences often become salient when people move from one cultural environment to another—for instance, when they immigrate to a new country. In the United States, immigrant families arrive from many countries, most frequently from Mexico, Central and South America, and Asia (Board on Children and Families, Commission on Behavioral and Social Sciences and Education, National Research Council, & Institute of Medicine, 1995). With immigration come increases in the number and diversity of children in the public schools. By 2010, more than 20% of the U.S. school-age population will probably be children of immigrants (Board on Children and Families et al., 1995; Fix & Passel, 1994).

When families move from one culture to another, they often find that they are not embraced as full, privileged participants in their new setting. In the United States, for instance, public anxiety arises from misperceptions that most immigrants come into the country illegally (not true) and that they take jobs away from native citizens (not supported by the data; Board on Children and Families et al., 1995; Fix & Passel, 1994). Such anti-immigrant sentiments have led to legislation that limits immigrants' access to public services in the schools and elsewhere. For instance, as you learned in Chapter 7, most immigrant children achieve at higher levels in bilingual education programs than in English-only classes (see Chapter 7). Yet federal expenditures for bilingual education, adjusted for inflation, declined 48% during the 1980s, despite a 50% increase in the size of the population with limited English proficiency (Board on Children and Families et al., 1995).

Acculturation, Assimilation, and Bicultural Orientation   When different cultural groups exist in the same region, the two groups interact and learn about one another (Fisher et al., 1998). As people participate in the customs and take on the values of a new culture, **acculturation** occurs. For different individuals, acculturation takes different forms:

- **Assimilation.** Some people totally embrace the values and customs of the new culture, giving up their original cultural identity in the process (LaFromboise, Hardin, Coleman, & Gerton, 1993). For instance, the Irish and German groups who migrated to the United States in the early decades of the 20th century have been largely assimilated into mainstream American culture; the only obvious signs of their cultural backgrounds are their

acculturation
Taking on the customs and values of a new culture.

assimilation
Totally embracing a new culture, abandoning one's previous culture in the process.

Irish and German surnames. Assimilation is typically a very gradual process that occurs over several generations (Delgado-Gaitan, 1994).

- **Selective adoption.** Immigrants may acquire some of the customs of the new culture while retaining certain customs of their homeland. Cafeteria style, they choose the traditions they like and disregard those they dislike. For instance, Naomi Padilla, a Mexican American woman who lived next door to Jeanne for several years, enjoyed many American customs (e.g., celebrating the Fourth of July) yet every day made flour tortillas for her family in much the same way that her mother had made tortillas in Mexico.

- **Rejection.** Sometimes people move to a new culture without taking on any of their new community's cultural practices (Kim & Choi, 1994). Complete rejection of a new culture is probably possible only when an individual has little need to interact with people in that culture on a regular basis. For example, a Mexican American colleague of ours had her elderly mother living with her for many years. The mother learned little English and rarely ventured outside the home except in the company of her daughter, and so her Mexican customs and beliefs remained intact throughout the many years that she lived in the United States.

- **Bicultural orientation.** Some people retain their original culture yet also acquire the beliefs and master the practices of their new culture, and they readily adjust their behaviors to fit the particular contexts in which they find themselves (Hong, Morris, Chiu, & Benet-Martínez, 2000). For example, we think of Midori and Saori, the two daughters of an American father and Japanese mother who once worked with us at the University of Northern Colorado. The girls were born and raised in the United States, but they often lived with their maternal grandparents in Japan during the summer. Midori and Saori were fluent not only in two languages (English and Japanese) but also in both American and Japanese cultural practices, and they expertly adapted their speech and behaviors to the countries in which they were living at any particular time.

Sometimes two or more forms of acculturation can be seen in a single immigrant family. For example, imagine that a Vietnamese family, the Huongs, moves to a culturally diverse neighborhood in Los Angeles. Mr. and Mrs. Huong may show selective adoption of some American cultural practices (e.g., learning American business practices so that they can operate a restaurant) while retaining many of their Vietnamese traditions both in their restaurant and at home. The Huong children, whose classmates hail from a variety of ethnic backgrounds, may develop a bicultural orientation, such that they are equally comfortable at school and at home and know appropriate ways of behaving (showing respect, making requests, etc.) in each setting. When Mrs. Huong's elderly mother comes for a summer visit, she may reject all aspects of American culture—for instance, complaining about the high rates of crime and violence in downtown Los Angeles, the unhealthy food offered at fast-food restaurants, and the video games that preoccupy her grandchildren.

At one time, total assimilation was considered to be the optimal situation for immigrants and other ethnic minority citizens, at least in the United States. The route to success was presumed to be one of diving headfirst into a "melting pot," in which people of diverse backgrounds became increasingly similar. More recently, however, researchers have discovered that when young immigrants give up their family's cultural traditions, they are at greater risk for dangerous behaviors, such as using alcohol and drugs, having unprotected sex, and engaging in criminal activities (Caetanno, 1987; Gilbert & Cervantes, 1986; Neff, Hoppe, & Perea, 1987; Vega, Gil, Warheit, Zimmerman, & Apospori, 1993; Ventura & Tappel, 1985). Children and adolescents who reject traditional cultural values often find themselves in conflict with their parents and may lack the strong positive values they need to resist temptation (Fisher et al., 1998).

Increasingly, the idea that the United States is a melting pot is giving way to the idea that it can be more productively thought of as a "mosaic" of cultural and ethnic pieces that all legitimately contribute to the greater good of society (Fisher et al., 1998). Immigrant children and adolescents appear to adjust most successfully when they learn certain aspects of their new culture while also retaining aspects of their original culture—that is, when they show a pattern of either selective adoption or bicultural orientation. For instance, adolescent immigrants who maintain allegiance to traditional values enjoy close, unstressed relationships with their parents and support from extended family and community members. As a general rule, they do well in school, have few be-

selective adoption
Assuming some customs of a new culture while also retaining some customs of one's previous culture.

rejection
Refusing to learn or accept any customs and values found within a new cultural environment.

bicultural orientation
Ability to behave in accordance with two different cultural frameworks in appropriate contexts.

havioral or mental health problems, and express high life satisfaction (Fisher et al., 1998; Fuligni, 1998; Kim & Choi, 1994). Those who adjust most successfully tend to be children of middle- and upper-class families that place high value on education and on family members' responsibility for one another (Fuligni, 1998).

Developmental Issues for Children from Diverse Cultural Backgrounds

When children come from cultural backgrounds different from mainstream culture, they must not only tackle normal developmental tasks—mastering language, learning about the physical world, refining social skills, and so on—but face additional challenges as well. Many develop coping mechanisms to help them deal with such challenges. Nevertheless, their school performance is not always on a par with their classmates from the majority group. In this section, we look at each of these issues: developmental challenges, coping mechanisms, and school performance.

Children of diverse ethnic backgrounds often adjust well when they have a bicultural orientation—when they remain knowledgeable about their ethnic heritage but also master the customs of mainstream society.

Developmental Challenges for Ethnic Minority Children As already noted in both this and previous chapters, children from diverse cultural backgrounds have different kinds of experiences, and such experiences may lead to very different kinds of knowledge, beliefs, and habits. In some cases, of course, children from different countries and ethnic backgrounds speak different languages. Yet other significant differences may exist as well. For instance, some African cultures make little use of numbers and measurement in day-to-day activities, and so their children master few fundamentals of traditional Western mathematics (Gay & Cole, 1967; Posner, 1982; Saxe & Posner, 1983). In many minority groups in the United States, parents rarely engage their children in the question-answer sessions ("What does a doggie say?" "Wuff" "That's right! A dog says, 'Ruff, ruff'") that are seen in many European American homes and in most American classrooms (Losey, 1995; Miller, 1995). When the knowledge and skills learned at home are different from those that teachers expect, children are at a decided disadvantage in the classroom.

Children whose cultural backgrounds are different from those of their teachers and classmates may also have different beliefs about what constitutes acceptable behavior. The following incident reported by a preschool teacher illustrates:

> Sarah signaled me that she felt faint. I rose and started toward Pedro. Suddenly I saw what Sarah had seen: around his neck, punched for stringing like mittens, were the two bloody ears of a deer. I had seconds to recover and speak. Grasping the psychiatrist's technique of reaching for the obvious, I asked, "Someone in your family, Pedro, has been deer hunting?"
>
> "Yup," he said, "my dad."
>
> Trying not to look too closely, I removed the strung ears, saying I would hang them where they would be safe, high above an out-of-the-way blackboard. With Sarah pale and off to the side and Pedro center stage, I sat on the floor with the children and invited Pedro to give us some details. With relish he did so, although briefly. The other children and I listened in rapt silence.
>
> I had recently learned one small fact about Alaskan Indian caribou hunting, so I felt I could ask Pedro if his mother did the butchering, the cutting up for roasts and steaks. "Yup," he answered, and we were launched on a discussion of the meat and its distribution. It would go to friends and family, primarily to the latter. Cousin Timmy showed us with his hands how big a roast would come to his family. (This was in response to a mistake I had made in assuming cousin Timmy's family might get a half. "No," corrected Pedro, "only a roast.") (Hawkins, 1997, pp. 329–330)

In Pedro's eyes, the deer ears were tokens of his father's skill as a hunter, and so he wore them with pride. Yet a teacher less sensitive to cultural differences might have rebuffed or in some other way punished Pedro for his "disgusting" behavior.

Another challenge that many families and children from minority groups face is *discrimination*, inequitable treatment as a result of their group membership. For example, data on home mortgages suggest that discrimination against African Americans and Hispanic Americans occurs across all income levels (Fisher et al., 1998). Likewise, African Americans and Hispanic Americans have, on average, lower-paying jobs than European Americans and are underrepresented in managerial positions and professional occupations (Federal Glass Ceiling Commission, 1995). And of adolescents who use or sell drugs, African Americas are more likely than European Americans to get caught and have to contend with the juvenile justice system (Fisher et al., 1998).

When ethnic minority families have little discretionary income and limited options as to where they can live, their children end up in schools that are poorly funded, inadequately equipped and staffed, and overcrowded (Fisher et al., 1998; Portes, 1996). For example, Cedric Jennings, the African American high school student introduced at the beginning of Chapter 12, had considerable difficulty in his first year at Brown University; his inner-city high school had simply not prepared him for the rigors of a challenging college curriculum (Suskind, 1998). (The story has a happy ending: With effort and perseverance, Cedric graduated with his class in 1999.)

Coping Mechanisms How do children and adolescents from ethnic minority group backgrounds deal with such challenges? One way is to develop a strong **ethnic identity,** or an awareness of membership in a particular group and a willingness to adopt certain behaviors characteristic of that group. A strong sense of ethnic identity often helps young people cope with racism and other forms of discrimination (McAdoo, 1985; Spencer & Markstrom-Adams, 1990).

Children and adolescents develop a sense of ethnic identity out of the gamut of messages they receive from families, peers, their community, and the media. For instance, they may hear tales of their ancestors' struggles and victories in a discriminatory setting, and they may see media portrayals of their ethnic group in particular roles—perhaps as leaders and trailblazers for humane causes or, alternatively, as violent and deviant troublemakers (Fisher et al., 1998). The different messages children hear and see are not always consistent, and so children may initially struggle to form a coherent set of beliefs about their cultural group. Eventually, many ethnic minority youth begin to reject messages from mainstream society that demean their own ethnic culture (Phinney, 1990).

A second way in which many young people cope with the challenges of minority group membership is to develop a **cultural frame of reference,** a particular way of perceiving and interpreting the cultural differences between their own group and the dominant group of their society. John Ogbu (1994) has used this concept to explain why some minority cultural and ethnic groups enjoy greater success in mainstream society than others. Central to the notion of cultural frame of reference is the way in which an ethnic minority group became a part of its host country. **Voluntary minority groups** are people who have moved to a new country with hopes of economic well-being and political freedom, as well as the descendents of such individuals. **Involuntary minority groups** are people who became members of the new country against their will (through slavery, conquest, or colonization), as well as their descendants. Examples of involuntary minorities include African Americans and Native Hawaiians in the United States, the Burakumin and Koreans in Japan, and the Maori in New Zealand.

Voluntary and involuntary minorities alike face discrimination in the dominant society but tend to interpret such discrimination differently. In the United States, voluntary minorities often see their situation in the new country as being better than the environment from which they have come. They generally have confidence that they can succeed in their new country once they master English and learn the skills they need to acquire better-paying jobs. They are likely to place great emphasis on education and teach their children the importance of studying hard and obeying school rules. In contrast, involuntary minorities in the United States compare their own circumstances to those of majority group members and realize that they enjoy fewer economic, social, and political benefits. They are likely to interpret their menial jobs and high unemployment rates as being the result of long-term discrimination by the white majority. They tend not to trust the public schools to educate their children with the same quality and commitment afforded children from European American backgrounds.

Because they perceive their difficulties to be the result of widespread discrimination, people in involuntary minority groups often establish clear psychological boundaries between themselves and the host society that has not equitably shared its resources with them. More specifically, they develop an **oppositional frame of reference** in which they intentionally reject the values and practices of the dominant group. As an example, many African Americans use words and grammatical structures that are rarely if ever heard outside of their own com-

ethnic identity
Awareness of one's membership in a particular ethnic or cultural group and willingness to adopt certain behaviors characteristic of that group.

cultural frame of reference
Particular way of perceiving and interpreting the cultural differences between one's own group and the dominant group of one's society.

voluntary minority group
People who have moved to a new country with hopes of economic well-being and political freedom, plus the descendents of such individuals.

involuntary minority group
People who have become members of a new country against their will, plus the descendants of such individuals.

oppositional frame of reference
Establishment of clear psychological boundaries between one's own group and the dominant culture of the society, and rejection of the dominant group's values and practices.

munities (again recall our discussion of African American English in Chapter 7). Ogbu (1994) suggests that such language reflects an oppositional frame of reference in that it provides a concrete way for people to maintain some distance from mainstream culture. In fact, African American children often experience considerable social pressure to remain "different" from the mainstream. For instance, those who speak in a Standard English dialect (that used in the media and most school systems; see Chapter 7) are often accused by other African Americans of "acting white" (Luster, 1992). Behaving in accordance with common practices and values of the mainstream culture (e.g., getting good grades, competing against classmates at school) is also a sign that one is acting white; recall Gloria Ladson-Billings's concern about being too competitive in the opening case study.

School Performance   Despite the challenges they face, many children and adolescents from diverse cultural and ethnic backgrounds manage to hold their own in the classroom. On average, children of immigrant families—families that Ogbu would, by and large, classify as *voluntary* minorities—perform as well academically and stay in school longer than native-born children of similar income backgrounds; children of Asian families and those of highly educated parents are especially successful (Davenport et al., 1998; Flynn, 1991; Fuligni, 1998; McDonnell & Hill, 1993). Such is not the case for all ethnic groups, however. African Americans and Native Americans—two groups that Ogbu would classify as involuntary minorities—and Mexican Americans have historically performed at lower levels in the classroom than their classmates of European descent (Miller, 1995). Furthermore, students in these three groups are more likely to be identified as having special educational needs and to drop out prior to graduation (Portes, 1996; Rumberger, 1995; U.S. Department of Education, Office of Civil Rights, 1993).

The lower school achievement of members of some ethnic minority groups appears to be the combined result of several factors, including the environmental stresses associated with chronic economic hardship, limited access to good schools and other educational opportunities, and (in the case of recent immigrants from non-English-speaking countries) language barriers (McLoyd, 1998b; Stevenson et al., 1990). Furthermore, some students, if they continually encounter teachers who hold low expectations for their achievement, develop a sense of learned helplessness about their ability to perform in the classroom (Graham, 1989; Holliday, 1985).

In any ethnic minority group, some children and adolescents do extremely well in the classroom despite the many challenges they face. Furthermore, teachers have many strategies at their disposal to help students from diverse ethnic backgrounds achieve academic success. We consider such strategies now.

Taking Culture and Ethnicity into Account in the Classroom

In the United States, students in public school classrooms are increasingly coming from ethnic minority backgrounds (Hernandez, 1997). Between 1900 and 1970, 85%–89% of American children were from European ("white") backgrounds, but in 1995 only 69% were from such backgrounds. Researchers have estimated that by 2050, the U.S. school population will be 28% Hispanic, 20% African-American non-Hispanic, 10% Asian and Pacific Islander, and 1% Native American (Hernandez, 1997). In other words, in schools, "minority" youngsters will soon be the majority.

Many teachers work quite effectively with students from cultural backgrounds different from their own. Typically, they use strategies such as those we offer here:

■ *Adapt your teaching strategies to the practices, belief systems, and values of students' cultural groups.* Some teachers, in an effort to treat everyone equitably, try to be "color blind" in their treatment of students. But in fact, teachers are most effective in teaching children and adolescents with diverse backgrounds when they tailor their classroom practices to those backgrounds (Diller, 1999; Kottler, 1997; Pérez, 1998; Weiner, 1999). Consider Ed, a man of European American descent who is just beginning his first year teaching in a classroom of Native American children. Two researchers enter Ed's classroom:

It is our first visit to Ed's room, and we have just finished introducing ourselves to the children. Ed turns to the class and tells them to introduce themselves to us. No one speaks. Ed calls on one of the children to begin. The boy is almost inaudible; we lean forward to hear better. The next

ACCOMMODATING CULTURAL AND ETHNIC DIFFERENCES

■ Educate yourself about the cultures in which students have been raised.

A teacher moves from the East Coast to western New Mexico to teach at a school on the Navajo Nation. One evening he accepts an invitation to have dinner with several of his students and their families, all of whom are dining together at one family's home. During his visit, the teacher discovers why his students are always interrupting one another and completing one another's sentences: Their parents converse in a similar manner and seem to enjoy the spontaneity that such conversations allow (Jackson & Ormrod, 1998).

■ Think about how cultural beliefs and practices serve adaptive functions for students.

Early in the school year, a teacher notices that few of her students are willing to answer her questions in class, even though it is clear in their written work that they know the answers. She discovers that bringing attention to oneself is not appropriate in their culture and so modifies her instructional practices to allow for group responses.

■ Build on students' background experiences.

A teacher asks a class of inner-city African American students to vote on their favorite rap song. She puts the words to the song on an overhead transparency and asks students to translate each line for her. In doing so, she shows students how their local dialect and Standard English are interrelated and gives them a sense of pride about being "bilingual" (Ladson-Billings, 1994).

■ Use curriculum materials that represent all ethnic groups in a positive and competent light.

A history teacher peruses a history textbook to make sure that it portrays all ethnic groups in a nonstereotypical manner. He supplements the text with readings that highlight the important roles that members of various ethnic groups have played in history.

■ Provide opportunities for students of different backgrounds to get to know one another better.

For a cooperative learning activity, a middle school teacher forms groups that integrate students from various neighborhoods and ethnic groups.

■ Expose students to successful models from various ethnic backgrounds.

A high school teacher invites several successful professionals from minority groups to speak with her class about their careers. When some students seem especially interested in one or more of these careers, she arranges for the students to spend time with the professionals in their workplaces.

child is the same. None of the children makes eye contact with us, although they are glancing at one another. Finally, the last child has finished. Ed, sensing the same discomfort that we have, addresses the children, "Gee, maybe next time I should have you introduce each other. Maybe that would work better." (Suina & Smolkin, 1994, p. 125)

As a newcomer to the Pueblo community in which the children live, Ed has not yet learned all the nuances of the Pueblo culture, but he is at least aware that he has in some way violated the children's cultural norms. He will soon discover that Pueblo children believe it is inappropriate to single themselves out and will accommodate that belief in his instructional strategies.

Some cultural differences—such as variations in dress, hairstyles, food preferences, and eating practices—are readily apparent. Others are less visible; for instances, rules about how to interact in a social group and how to respond to authority figures are rarely articulated. Teachers unfamiliar with such unspoken rules may easily misunderstand their students' most basic actions. For example, in many African American and Hawaiian communities, interrupting a speaker shows social engagement ("I'm 'with' you, I'm interested"), yet members of many other ethnic groups consider interruptions to be rude (Gottlieb, 1964; Irvine, 1990; Tharp, 1994).

Teachers become increasingly aware of the practices and beliefs of their students' cultural and ethnic groups if they participate in local community activities and converse regularly with community members (McCarty & Watahomigie, 1998; Smith, 1998). In the process, they also discover that virtually any group has certain traditions and values that have proven effective in sustaining the group. For example, the Latin American value of *familism* establishes strong feelings of respect and responsibility among a child's family members. The strong multigenerational kinship networks among many African American families give children close family support from multiple, loving caregivers.

In the Observation Guidelines table on page 259 of Chapter 7, we presented examples of cultural differences in sociolinguistic conventions. Additional examples of diverse cultural practices and beliefs and specific strategies that teachers can use to accommodate such diversity are presented in the Observation Guidelines table on the next page. At the same time, teachers must be careful not to overgeneralize: Students of any background are a diverse group, and their specific behaviors, attitudes, and educational needs will vary considerably depending on their individual experiences and circumstances.

As teachers consider how they might adapt classroom instruction to fit the cultural backgrounds of their students, they can find some guidance in the educational literature. For instance, Madhubuti and Madhubuti (1994) describe African-centered schools in which group learning activities play a key role, African and African American history and traditions are incorporated into the curriculum, and African American role models are regularly invited into the classroom. Extensive evaluation data are not yet available on the achievement of students in African-centered schools, but preliminary data indicate that some African American students achieve at higher levels in these schools than in more traditional schools (Bakari, 2000). Other educators offer additional recommendations for working with African American students. In particular, they suggest that teachers acknowledge students' feelings of inequity and disenfranchisement regarding their education, describe the struggles and contributions of students' ancestors, and conduct class discussions about how, together, they can all work toward a better society (Asante, 1991; Beauboeuf-LaFontant, 1999; Ladson-Billings, 1994; Mitchell, 1998).

■ *Consider how your own beliefs, values, and biases may potentially interfere with your ability to teach in a culturally sensitive manner.* Teachers, too, have beliefs and attitudes that are a product of the specific cultural environments—mainstream or minority—in which they have grown up. Like all human beings, teachers are likely to favor their own beliefs and attitudes and, particularly for those in the dominant culture, see these beliefs and attitudes as the way things "should" be (Miller & Goodnow, 1995). They then use their own culturally based concepts and assumptions to interpret other people's actions (Hong et al., 2000). This bias helps them interpret events quickly in ways that may be appropriate within the context of their own culture but may lead them astray when it comes to understanding people from other cultures. For instance, middle-income European American teachers may judge low-income African American students as having lower maturity and social competence than middle-income European American students even when the two groups of students are similar (Alexander et al., 1987). They are also more likely to attribute low achievement in ethnic minority students to problems in students' families than to problems in the schools, such as racist behaviors of peers, ethnic stereotypes in curriculum materials, or discrimination in special education placements (Kailin, 1999).

Furthermore, although very few teachers intentionally discriminate against students based on the color of their skin (Sleeter & Grant, 1999), teachers' actions often perpetuate group differences. Some teachers tend to call on and praise students who are European American, male, and middle class more than other students (Jackson & Cosca, 1974; Sadker & Sadker, 1988). Other teachers rarely modify or individualize instruction for students with diverse needs; instead, they present instruction in a take-it-or-leave-it manner (Sleeter & Grant, 1999).

As educators have begun to learn about the many ways in which cultural differences affect students' classroom performance, many have become increasingly motivated to help students from diverse backgrounds achieve academic success. Yet considerable naivete remains. In a study of teacher education students' attitudes toward working with African American students (Bakari, 2000), many prospective teachers expressed willingness to teach such students, for instance agreeing with such statements as "I would enjoy the opportunity to motivate African American students" and "I feel personally invested in helping African American children achieve." However, they less often agreed with statements that reflected sensitivity to African American perspectives, such as "I respect African American culture" and "African American literature is important when teaching African American children to read." Clearly, culturally sensitive teaching requires more than giving lip service to cultural diversity; it also requires a genuine commitment to modifying instruction in ways that enable students from diverse cultural backgrounds to achieve their full academic potential.

Identifying Cultural Practices and Beliefs

OBSERVATION GUIDELINES

CHARACTERISTIC	LOOK FOR	EXAMPLE	IMPLICATION
Individualism (characteristic of many European American groups)	• Independence, assertiveness, and self-reliance • Eagerness to pursue individual assignments and tasks • Willingness to compete against others • Pride in one's own accomplishments	When given the choice of doing a science fair project either by herself or with a partner, Melissa decides to work alone. She is thrilled when she earns a third-place ribbon.	Provide some time for independent work, and accommodate students' individual achievement levels. Give feedback about personal accomplishments, but do so in private rather than in front of classmates.
Collectivism (characteristic of many African American, Asian, Hispanic, and Native American groups)	• Willingness to depend on others • Emphasis on group accomplishments over individual achievements • Preference for cooperative rather than competitive tasks • Concern about bringing honor to one's family • Strong sense of loyalty to other family members	Tsusha is a talented and hardworking seventh grader. She is conscientious about bringing home her graded work assignments to show her parents, but she appears embarrassed and self-conscious when she is praised in front of her classmates at school.	Stress group progress and achievement more than individual gains. Make frequent use of cooperative learning activities.
Behavior toward authority figures	• Looking down in the presence of an authority figure (common in many Native American, African American, Mexican American, and Puerto Rican children) *vs.* looking an authority figure in the eye (common in many children of European American descent) • Observing an adult quietly (an expectation in some Native American and some Hispanic groups) *vs.* asking questions when one doesn't understand (common in many European American groups)	A Native American student named Jimmy never says a word, and in fact often looks frightened, when his teacher looks him in the eye and greets him each morning. One day, the teacher looks in another direction and says, "Hello, Jimmy" as he enters the classroom. "Why hello Miss Jacobs," he enthusiastically responds (Gilliland, 1988, p. 26).	Recognize that different cultures show respect for authority figures in different ways; don't misinterpret lack of eye contact or a nonresponse as an indication of disinterest or disrespect.

■ *Include various cultural perspectives as an integral part of the curriculum.* Textbooks and other instructional materials almost invariably reflect the cultural biases of their authors. For example, when Sleeter and Grant (1991) analyzed American textbooks for students in grades 1 through 8, they found that the following themes, though rarely stated overtly, permeated many texts:

> The United States is the land of wealth and opportunity; it is open to all who try; anyone can get what he works for.
>
> American history flowed from Europe to the east coast of North America; from there it flowed westward.
>
> American culture is of European origin; Europe is the main source of worthwhile cultural achievements.
>
> National ideals are (and should be) individual advancement, private accumulation, rule by the majority as well as by market demand, loyalty to the U.S. government, and freedom of speech.
>
> Some social problems existed in the past, but they have been solved.
>
> Most problems society faces have technical solutions, for which science and math offer the best keys.
>
> Americans share consensus about most things; differences are individual and can be talked out. . . .

OBSERVATION GUIDELINES

CHARACTERISTIC	LOOK FOR	EXAMPLE	IMPLICATION
Cognitive tools	• Focus on the abstract properties of objects and ideas (common in many European American communities) • Preference for personal anecdotes about objects and events (common in some Native American and African American groups)	A fourth-grade teacher asks students to categorize a collection of rocks and minerals and guess how they were formed and where they came from. Francisco talks about volcanos and sandstone, whereas Seymour groups specimens based on which ones look similar to those in his grandmother's rock garden.	When presenting academic subject matter, refer both to abstract concepts and ideas and to objects and experiences in students' everyday lives.
Valued activities	• Hopes for high achievement in traditional academic areas (common in many cultural groups in Western countries) • Devaluing of school achievement as representative of white culture (evident in some students from involuntary minority groups) • Expectations for excellence in culture-specific activities, such as art or dance (often seen in traditional Native American and Polynesian communities)	Clarence is obviously a very bright young man, but he shows considerable ambivalence about doing well in his high school classes. He often earns high marks on quizzes and tests, but he rarely participates in class discussions or turns in homework assignments.	Show how academic subject matter relates to students' lives. Acknowledge students' achievement in nonacademic as well as academic pursuits. Allow students to keep their accomplishments confidential from classmates so that they can maintain credibility with peers who don't value school achievement.
Conceptions of time	• Concern for punctuality and acknowledgment of deadlines for assignments (common for many students of European descent) • Lack of concern for specific times and schedules (observed in some Hispanic and Native American communities)	Lucy is often late for school. Her parents are very diligent about coming to parent-teacher conferences but do not always arrive at the time the teacher has scheduled.	Encourage punctuality as a way of enhancing students' long-term success in mainstream Western society. At the same time, recognize that not all students are especially concerned about clock time when they first begin school. Be flexible when some parents seem to disregard strict schedules.

Sources: Banks & Banks, 1995; Basso, 1984; Garcia, 1994; Garrison, 1989; Gilliland, 1988; Grant & Gomez, 2001; Heath, 1983; Irujo, 1988; Kirschenbaum, 1989; Losey, 1995; McAlpine & Taylor, 1993; Miller, 1995; Ogbu, 1994; Reid, 1989; Shweder et al., 1998; Tharp, 1994; Torres-Guzmán, 1998; Trawick-Smith, 2000; Triandis, 1995.

Other places in the world may have poverty and problems, but the United States does not; [America] tend[s] to solve other nations' problems.

America is basically White, middle-class, and heterosexual; wealthy White men are the world's best thinkers and problem solvers, and they usually act in the best interests of everyone. (Sleeter & Grant, 1999, p. 117)

As you read the list of themes, you undoubtedly found some (e.g., the "ideal" of individual advancement) that conflict with the values of certain cultural groups and others (e.g., the belief that Americans share consensus about most things) that fly in the face of what you know to be true from your own experiences.

As the United States increasingly becomes the multicultural mosaic we spoke of earlier, it is essential that classroom curricula, methods, and implicit messages reflect such diversity. Sleeter and Grant (1999) have described five different forms that instruction about diverse cultures may take (see Table 14–1). These five approaches differ on several dimensions, including the nature of their attempts to eradicate oppression and the comprehensiveness with which they study multiple cultural groups or, conversely, focus on a single group's characteristics and needs.

True multicultural education is not limited to cooking ethnic foods, celebrating Cinco de Mayo, or studying famous African Americans during Black History Month—strategies

TABLE 14–1   Five Possible Frameworks for Teaching Students About Diverse Cultures

FRAMEWORK	DESCRIPTION	EXAMPLE	STRENGTHS AND WEAKNESSES
Educators using a cultural difference model	Teachers concentrate on ways that students learn, students' natural patterns of speaking and listening, and potential bridges between what students already know and what they need to learn. They choose instructional strategies to match students' needs and integrate culturally relevant material into the curriculum.	Ms. Vanderbilt, a Head Start teacher in Chicago, plans a field trip for her preschoolers to the Art Institute, where they will pay special attention to three French painters.	Differences among students are acknowledged as real and legitimate, and cultural practices are integrated into daily lessons. However, the approach can be detrimental if it stereotypes groups, trivializes profound cultural differences, or ignores individual differences. Furthermore, the burden rests largely on children from diverse backgrounds to assimilate into the classroom, and the forces of oppression are not challenged.
Educators using a human relations approach	Teachers try to help students from different backgrounds get along, establish common ground, and mediate conflicts. They promote positive feelings among diverse groups, encourage students to show tolerance for one another's differences, and address stereotypes.	After a series of ethnic slurs among school children, Mrs. Wilson suggests that the school put up bulletin boards that emphasize the similarity of people from different backgrounds, the value of brotherhood and sisterhood, and the need to respect others.	Students are encouraged to accept students who are different from themselves. However, the approach has been criticized for its failure to address academic achievement directly and for being too simplistic about why discrimination and inequality exist. It may also encourage students to act pleasantly toward one another while not confronting poverty, racism, homophobia, and sexism.
Educators inspired by single-group studies	Teachers study the histories, experiences, and needs of specific groups, such as women, African Americans, students with disabilities, and gay men and lesbian women. They make a point to display practices, beliefs, and accomplishments from identified groups.	Mr. Ricardo wonders why his school's curriculum doesn't give more attention to the perspectives of Hispanic cultures. When he teaches his students about the battle at the Alamo, he presents the view of a Mexican general who is putting down a revolt against the Mexican government instead of the typical American perspective of fallen heroes.	Students may learn a considerable amount about a particular cultural group. However, the approach has been criticized for promoting cultural separatism and for not preparing students adequately in academic knowledge needed for mainstream settings. Also, if materials are adapted to be consistent with the perspective of a single group, students do not learn about other groups' beliefs and practices.

that Ladson-Billings (1994) calls a "foods and festivals" approach. Rather, **multicultural education** includes the perspectives and experiences of numerous cultural groups—and also those of both men and women, people of varying sexual orientations, and people with disabilities—on a regular basis (Banks, 1995; García, 1995; Hollins, 1996; NCSS Task Force on Ethnic Studies Curriculum Guidelines, 1992). Following are examples of what teachers might do:

- In history, look at wars and other major events from diverse perspectives (e.g., the Spanish perspective of the Spanish-American War, the Japanese perspective of World War II, Native American groups' perspectives of the pioneers' westward migration in North America).
- In social studies, consider such issues as discrimination and oppression.
- In literature, present the work of minority authors and poets.
- In art, consider the creations and techniques of artists from around the world.
- In music, teach songs from many cultures and nations.
- In physical education, teach games or folk dances from other countries and cultures.
  (Asai, 1993; Boutte & McCormick, 1992; Casanova, 1987; Cottrol, 1990; Freedman, 2001; Koza, 2001; NCSS Task Force on Ethnic Studies Curriculum Guidelines, 1992; Pang, 1995; Sleeter & Grant, 1999; Ulichny, 1994)

multicultural education
Education that includes the perspectives and experiences of numerous cultural groups on a regular basis.

FRAMEWORK	DESCRIPTION	EXAMPLE	STRENGTHS AND WEAKNESSES
Educators adhering to general principles of multicultural education	Teachers promote the strength and value of cultural diversity, human rights and respect for all people, alternative life choices, social justice and equal opportunity, and equity in power among groups. They ensure that the curriculum includes diverse perspectives and contributions, use cooperative learning strategies, and include all students in extracurricular activities. They seek not only to integrate students from diverse backgrounds into the classroom but also to make significant changes in society.	Three teachers attend a three-day multicultural institute. The institute gives them an opportunity to develop lesson plans enriched by diverse cultural perspectives. But they also decide to work together with other teachers in the school to develop a schoolwide plan to increase the multicultural focus of the curriculum.	The approach promotes respect for diverse viewpoints; furthermore, it is inclusive and proactive. However, some critics argue that it does not foster the skills and knowledge students need to assimilate into a dominant culture or succeed in mainstream institutions. Others argue that the approach dilutes attention to specific groups (e.g., students with disabilities) and that students are not taught how to get along with others. Still others complain that the general emphasis on culture diverts attention from poverty, the powerlessness of groups, and the need for social justice.
Educators teaching in a multicultural and reconstructionist fashion	Teachers use approaches similar to those listed above for multicultural education but give more attention to identifying and eradicating injustice. They organize the curriculum around current social issues (e.g., sexism, discrimination against people with disabilities). They ask students to be active and responsible citizens, to become familiar with the workings of oppression, and to participate in community projects that strive for social justice.	Several teachers plan a school project in which students will investigate the closing of a local county hospital. Students will study how different branches of the city government affect policy and how the mayor, members of the city council, and community factions bargain and compromise. Students will also study how race predicts voting patterns. The teachers encourage students to work together, making sure they are integrated across lines of race, gender, and class.	This model is comprehensive along many fronts, and it works to combat injustice directly. Critics wonder if schools, as instruments of society, can effectively redesign the existing social world order. They also raise concerns about students' ability and motivation to think critically about questions of social injustice.

Source: Based on distinctions and vignettes outlined in Sleeter and Grant (1999).

As teachers and students explore various cultures, they should look for commonalities as well as differences. For example, they might study how various cultural groups celebrate the beginning of a new year, discovering that "out with the old and in with the new" is a common theme among many such celebrations (Ramsey, 1987). At the secondary level, classes might explore issues that adolescents of all cultures face: gaining the respect of elders, forming trusting relationships with peers, and finding a meaningful place in society (Ulichny, 1994). One important goal of multicultural education should be to communicate that, underneath it all, people are more alike than different.

■ *Communicate and foster respect for diverse cultures and ethnic groups.* In addition to taking students' cultural backgrounds into account when planning and carrying out instruction, teachers should convey the message that diverse cultural perspectives all have merit and value. They should select curriculum materials that represent all cultural groups in a positive and competent light—for instance, by choosing textbooks, works of fiction, and videotapes that portray people of varying ethnic backgrounds as legitimate participants in mainstream society rather than as exotic "curiosities" who live in a separate world from everyone else. Teachers should also avoid or modify curriculum materials that portray members of minority groups in an overly simplistic, romanticized, exaggerated, or otherwise stereotypical fashion (Banks, 1994; Boutte & McCormick, 1992; Pang, 1995).

Students gain further respect for different cultures when they have positive interactions with people from backgrounds different from their own. For instance, in culturally heterogeneous schools, teachers might promote friendships among students from different groups by using cooperative learning activities, teaching basic words and phrases in other students' native languages, and encouraging schoolwide participation in extracurricular activities. In culturally homogeneous schools, teachers might take students, either physically or vicariously, beyond school boundaries—perhaps engaging them in community service projects for a particular ethnic group or finding penpals in a distant location.

Teaching respect for diverse cultural perspectives does not necessarily mean that "anything goes" or that there are no moral judgments to be made. For instance, teachers and students do not necessarily need to embrace a culture in which some people's basic human rights are blatantly violated. It does mean, however, that teachers and students alike try to understand another cultural group's behaviors within the context of that culture's beliefs and assumptions (Cohen, 1998). Ultimately, any culturally sensitive classroom must espouse such democratic ideals as human dignity, equality, and justice in addition to tolerance for diverse points of view (Cottrol, 1990; NCSS Task Force on Ethnic Studies Curriculum Guidelines, 1992; Sleeter & Grant, 1999).

Cultural ideas and practices do not stay the same over time. Instead, the core beliefs that people hold and the ways in which they socialize their children change with history. We now turn to historical events as additional contexts in which children develop.

Historical Events

In the field of child and adolescent development, **history** means large-scale events that bring about social change, including war, famine, prosperity, technological advances, and communication with other societies. Historical events dramatically affect the socialization of children and adolescents, but their effects are tempered by gender, birth order, religious background, and family income (Levi & Schmitt, 1997). Consider the following contexts for young people during various periods in European history:

- In ancient Rome, young men often entered into military service, where they were socialized to curb their impulses and comply with the commands of their leaders. As a mass of foot soldiers acting in unity, they were strong; as individuals acting on their own, they had little power (Fraschetti, 1997).
- In the Middle Ages, adolescence was a time of agitation and disorder, and young people frequently violated the laws of society and religion (Crouzet-Pavan, 1997).
- In medieval Spain, age 10 marked the transition from childhood to adulthood for girls, and marriages of 10- to 12-year old girls were common (Horowitz, 1997).
- In 17th century Italy, firstborn sons of aristocratic families inherited their family's fortunes. Other young men were expected to remain celibate; many of them did not marry, and one in three entered religious orders. Many young women also remained single and celibate. Younger daughters were more likely to marry than older ones, as their families had had a longer time in which to assemble substantial collections of household goods (dowries) to entice potential husbands (Ago, 1997).

Such specific destinies for young people required distinct socialization patterns. Think about how the "right stuff" would vary for adolescents preparing to serve in the military, marry at a young age, or enter a religious order. To adapt to particular positions and life circumstances, young people had to internalize certain values. For instance, young Spanish girls who agreed to marry a spouse of their parents' choosing were undoubtedly socialized to accept their parents' decisions without question.

Consider the opportunities and liabilities that modern times offer young people. In our complex and increasingly international society, economic, political, and social conditions can change quickly. In the current booming economy, our own children have many more opportunities and resources—school trips to France and Spain, handheld calculators that quickly graph complex algebraic formulas, access to a wealth of information on the World Wide Web—than we ourselves had as children in the 1950s and 1960s. Yet change is not always for the better. With a stock market collapse or unexpected layoffs at a parent's workplace, a family's financial well-being can deteriorate into ruin overnight. During times of political upheaval and civil war, children may suddenly find themselves orphaned and homeless.

history
Large-scale events that bring about significant social change.

Historical events do not influence all children in the same way. For instance, war, economic collapses, and other traumatic circumstances often affect older children and adolescents more intensely than toddlers and preschoolers (Baltes et al., 1980). Teresa's two sons provide an illustration. On the first anniversary of the disaster at Columbine High School, in which two Colorado high school students shot and killed 12 of their classmates and one of their teachers, 12-year-old Connor was reluctant to attend school, as were many of his classmates. In comparison, 5-year-old Alex knew nothing of the event and so showed no signs of fear or concern.

When children and adolescents personally experience traumatic historical events, such as war or violence, they initially respond in a disorganized fashion (perhaps appearing stunned or detached) and have trouble comprehending and believing what has happened. Later, they cycle through intense emotions such as anger, sadness, and depression (Casarez-Levison, 2000). Teachers cannot assume that students who have recently experienced trauma or upheaval will rebound quickly. In fact, teachers can be invaluable in helping students try to make sense of a tragedy and providing comfort and stability.

Even when students are not themselves affected by significant historical events, teachers can easily incorporate such events into the curriculum. For instance, a natural disaster affecting a nearby region (e.g., an earthquake or hurricane) provides a chance for students to organize fund-raisers and in other ways provide support to those who have suffered losses. When students become actively involved in such altruistic activities, they are more likely to see themselves and their potential contributions to society in a positive light.

Religious Affiliation

For many children and adolescents, religious affiliation provides another influential context for development, in that it imbues everyday events with meaning and purpose. Fighting with your brother? God wants us to get along. Suffering from asthma? Seek out a healer. Dad lost his job? We pray for God's guidance. Grandpa died last week? He's joined the great oneness of spirits. A victim of oppression? Come to church for comfort. Confused? Read the Bible, the Koran, the writings of Malcolm X, the scriptures of Buddha, the philosophy of Confucius, or one of many other sources of spiritual inspiration.

In an average week, 43% of adults in the United States attend a church or synagogue, and a larger percentage have religious beliefs that influence their daily behaviors (Bezilla, 1993; Gallup, 1996). Of those who have a religious preference, the great majority of U.S. citizens align with a denomination of Christianity (e.g., they are Protestant, Roman Catholic, Eastern Orthodox, Latter Day Saint) or Judaism (e.g., they are Orthodox, Reform, Conservative). (Gollnick & Chinn, 1998).

Religion affects the roles that people adopt as marital partners, the ways in which they raise their children, and the expectations they have for school curricula; it is also correlated with the moral judgments they make (Narvaez, Getz, Rest, & Thoma, 1999). For growing children and adolescents, religion is a factor in dress and appearance, social activities, choice of friends, smoking, and alcohol consumption (Gollnick & Chinn, 1998). Children's religious affiliations (or lack thereof) may also affect their relationships with peers. For instance, members of mainstream religious groups occasionally harass members of small religious sects (e.g., Jehovah's Witnesses, Children of God, the Unification Church) and children of atheistic parents (Gollnick & Chinn, 1998). And some families and organizations regularly articulate anti-Semitic, anti-Muslim, or anti-Catholic sentiments.

Dear Mr. Lincoln,

you were a great presadent. I'm glad you freed the slaves is it fun up there in hevin

Yours truly,

Jared

As 7-year-old Jared's letter to Abraham Lincoln illustrates, religious beliefs infiltrate many children's interpretations of the world.

Fowler's Stages of Faith

James Fowler (1981) has proposed that religious development occurs in a predictable sequence. Initially, the trust that infants establish with parents predisposes them to accept their parents' beliefs and preachings related to religion. As children grow older, they try to make sense of these beliefs and preachings in accordance with their current knowledge and cognitive abilities. Drawing from the theories of Jean Piaget, Erik Erikson, and Lawrence Kohlberg (see Chapters 4, 9, and 10, respectively) and from interviews with children and adolescents, Fowler has proposed the following *stages of faith*.

Stage 1: intuitive-projective faith. In early childhood (i.e., during Piaget's preoperational stage), children apply an active imagination to construct their own interpretations of religious ideas and symbols. Because they have difficulty taking other people's perspectives (in Piaget's terminology, they are *egocentric*), they assume that their own views are the *only* views and therefore are accurate ones. In the following interview, 6-year-old Freddy illustrates intuitive-projective faith in his description of a powerful God:

Interviewer:	When you do something bad, does God know?
Freddy:	Yes, He spreads all around the world in one day.
Interviewer:	He does? How does he do that?
Freddy:	He does 'cause he's smart.
Interviewer:	He's smart? How does he get all around the world in one day?
Freddy:	Uh—he can split or he can be like a God.
Interviewer:	He can split into a lot of things?
Freddy:	Yeah. (Fowler, 1981, p. 128)[1]

Stage 2: mythic-literal faith. In middle childhood (i.e., during Piaget's concrete operations stage), children continue in their efforts to make sense of religion, but they now strive for logical coherence in their understandings. Such reasoning is evident in an interview with 10-year-old Millie:

Interviewer:	. . . [T]ell me now why you think there are people here in the world. Are they here for any purpose?
Millie:	There—well, if there wasn't any people in the world, who would keep God company?
Interviewer:	Is that why people are here?
Millie:	I don't know, but that question just popped into my mind. How—how would God keep busy?
Interviewer:	And what does God do with people?
Millie:	He—he makes the people. He tries to give them good families. And he, he, um, made the world. He made trees and everything. If you didn't have trees you wouldn't have books. And if you didn't—like he made the whole world, which has a lot of beauty and that makes up things. Like rocks make metals and some kinds of rocks make metal. (Fowler, 1981, p. 138)[2]

Religious ideas in mythic-literal faith reflect the heavy dependence on concrete reality that characterizes thinking during middle childhood. Consider what Millie says when the interviewer asks her to describe what God looks like:

Millie:	. . .I imagine that he's an old man with a white beard and white hair wearing a long robe and that the clouds are his floor and he has a throne. And he has all these people and there's angels around him. And there's all the good people, angels and—and um, cupids and that he has like—I guess I—he has a nice face, nice blue eyes. (Fowler, 1981, p. 138)[3]

By and large, children in middle childhood unquestioningly accept the religious doctrines and practices that their parents and others pass down to them, and the concrete aspects of their religion are far more salient than the abstract—and ultimately more central—qualities. Nine-year-old Noah describes himself as both Jewish and Christian primarily because his mother and father are, respectively, Jewish and Christian; in Figure 14–1, he focuses on the very concrete advantages (presents!) of his affiliations.

> I think I'm going to have a good time, on winter break. Hopefully I'm going to get Christmas presents, I'm going to eat dinner with my friend, on Christmas day.
> I'm also going to get Hannkah presents. I spend Hannkah, with my mom because she is Jewish,
> I am glad I'm Jewish and Christian because I get more presents. Now I know I'm going to have a good winter break.

FIGURE 14–1 In middle childhood, children's notions of religion are fairly concrete. Here 9-year-old Noah conceptualizes Christmas and Hanukkah as a time for getting presents.

[1]–[5]Five excerpts from *Stages of Faith: The Psychology of Human Development and the Quest for Meaning* by James W. Fowler. Copyright © 1981 by James W. Fowler. Reprinted by permssion of HarperCollins Publishers, Inc.

Stage 3: synthetic-conventional faith. In adolescence (i.e., during Piaget's formal operations stage), abstract understandings about religion become increasingly possible. Initially, however, adolescents have difficulty distinguishing between concrete religious symbols and the abstract meanings that they represent, and they do not seriously examine or question the beliefs that others have passed along to them. In the following interview, 15-year-old Linda reveals an abstract notion of God as well as an acceptance of what her parents have told her:

Interviewer: Linda, when you say you *know* what you believe in . . . can you try to trace *how* you came to know what you believe in?

Linda: I guess religion. I've always gone to church and everything. And my parents, they always guided me. . . . They've always taught me that God's always there and, you know, he's the only way that you can really make it. . . . You depend upon him and I really believe in him and, you know how they say God talks in many mysterious ways? Well, in a sense he's told me lots of times . . . I really think that he's led me to where I am today. 'Cause lots of times I've just thought the world is just, you know, I just don't feel anything. But then that morning I'll just have a feeling that . . . I guess there is Somebody, you know?

Interviewer: What do you think God is?

Linda: God is different to a lot of people. . . . I don't exactly go by the Bible. I think you should try to make the world . . . you should try to make people happy and at the same time enjoy yourself, you know? In a good kind way. . . (Fowler, 1981, pp. 155–156)[4]

According to Fowler, many young people stop at Stage 3: Although they may make minor adjustments to what others have told them (e.g., Linda acknowledges that she doesn't completely "go by the Bible"), by and large they accept their religious legacy. But other adolescents eventually become uncomfortable with what they've been told, as the next stage illustrates.

Stage 4: individuative-reflective faith. In the late teens or early 20s, some young people critically examine their religious beliefs and assumptions. They place their religion within its historical context and begin to understand how it has been shaped by many social, political, and economic factors over the years. Thus, individuative-reflective faith is characterized by a more analytic attitude and more conscious decision making about one's own beliefs. Sixteen-year-old Brian, whom Fowler classified as still being in Stage 3, nevertheless is beginning to show signs of the critical attitude that characterizes individuative-reflective faith:

Interviewer: It bothers you, this sense of the unknown about what happens at death?

Brian: Right, because it's unexplainable. We only make up what we feel is the answer. Just take that. Maybe the answer is something that no one can grasp because no one is really smart enough or it's something completely beyond our conceptions of being able to grasp what life is about and something like that. It makes me think quite a bit; I don't know about anyone else, but not being able to grasp an idea—it's physically impossible to grasp that idea—really bothers me and makes me think about it. (Fowler, 1981, pp. 160–161)[5]

Some evidence is consistent with Fowler's belief that adolescents take a critical stance toward religion: The vast majority of teenagers (90%) report that they pray, but only 25% report they are highly confident in organized religion (Gallup & Poling, 1980). Furthermore, some teens who are inquisitive yet insecure may be attracted to small "cult" religions in which extensive training programs convert and persuade new members (Swope, 1980). Overall, religious development during adolescence appears to be related to other changes, such as an increasing capacity for abstract reasoning and emotional vulnerabilities (Elkind, 1978; Pipher, 1994).

Fowler has suggested that a few adults also progress through one or two additional stages (*conjunctive faith* and *universalizing faith*), in which they develop increasingly abstract and integrated understandings and an unwaivering commitment to their beliefs. Details of these stages are beyond the scope of this book, as teachers are unlikely to see them in school-age children and adolescents.

As you think about Fowler's stages, keep in mind that he based them on three theories that do not necessarily provide airtight explanations of child and adolescent development (see the critiques of Piaget, Erikson, and Kohlberg in Chapters 4, 9, and 10). Furthermore, his interviews with children were limited (Fowler does not say how many he interviewed) and apparently restricted to those raised in Christian, Jewish, and Unitarian homes; thus, his stages of faith do not necessarily characterize the religious development of children around the world.

Religion in Schools

Religion is a positive guiding force in many students' lives. It is ironic, then, that religious affiliations can be a source of problems in the classroom (Gollnick & Chin, 1998). Some children make inappropriate remarks based on their own religious beliefs or those of their classmates ("The Bible says homosexuality is a sin!" "Mei-Chang's a Buddhist. How weird!" "Those kids in the Bible Club are Jesus Freaks."). And families' diverse beliefs can create controversies about appropriate curriculum and reading materials (Should evolution or biblical creationism be taught? Should sex education take place at school or home?).

In the United States, the First Amendment to the Constitution requires that matters of church and state be separate. Public school teachers can certainly discuss various religions within the context of curricula about history, culture, or other appropriate academic topics. But they should not incorporate religious ideas or practices into classroom activities in any way that shows preference for one religion over another, or even a preference for religion over atheism. Nevertheless, we acknowledge religion as an important diversity issue for children and their families, and ask our readers to consider the following suggestions:

■ *Become aware of the religious diversity that exists in the community in which you work.* Teachers and other school personnel should think about religious holidays and observances whenever they schedule parent-teacher meetings, class plays, and other events. They must certainly avoid giving preferential treatment to students from religious (or nonreligious) backgrounds similar to their own.

■ *Foster a climate of religious tolerance in the classroom.* Just as teachers foster respect for diverse cultural backgrounds, so, too, should they foster respect for diverse religious beliefs. If they are to work effectively in adult society, students must learn that many religious persuasions have value and that their nation guarantees citizens' right to religious freedom. Many school districts have specific policies that prohibit any name-calling that denigrates others' religious beliefs, practices, and affiliations.

■ *Work with school administrators to cultivate productive communication with families about controversial curriculum issues.* Parents and other community members are often involved in making decisions about the content of the curriculum in the public schools, and some have strong religious convictions about whether certain content (e.g., creationism, birth control) should be included. Crafting a reasonable compromise when people hold firmly to disparate religious doctrines often takes hard work from teachers and administrators, but with open minds and a willingness to listen, it *can* be done.

Socioeconomic Status

When Gloria Ladson-Billings enrolled in an integrated junior high school far from her own neighborhood, she noticed a clear difference between the jobs and income levels of her classmates' parents and those of her own mother and father. Together, people's occupations, income, and educational levels reflect their **socioeconomic status** (**SES**). A family's socioeconomic status—whether high-SES, middle-SES, or low-SES—gives us a sense of their standing in the community: how much flexibility they have in where they live and what they buy, how much influence they have on political decision making, what educational opportunities they can offer their children, and so on. When we have spoken of "middle-income" versus "low-income" families and children in previous chapters, we have essentially been talking about socioeconomic status.

On average, students from low-SES backgrounds achieve at lower levels than students from middle-SES backgrounds, and the gap between the two groups widens as students move through the grade levels (Jimerson et al., 1999; McLoyd, 1998b; Miller, 1995). Low-SES students also exhibit more frequent and severe behavior problems at school and are more likely

socioeconomic status (SES)
One's general social and economic standing in society, encompassing such variables as family income, occupation, and education level.

to drop out prior to high school graduation (McLoyd, 1998b; Nichols, Ludwin, & Iadicola, 1998; Rumberger, 1995). It is important to stress, however, that other factors—for instance, children's activities and abilities and the guidance and support they get from their parents—are far more predictive of children's academic accomplishments than is socioeconomic status per se (Hoover-Dempsey & Sandler, 1997; Jimerson et al., 1999; McLoyd, 1998b; Seaton et al., 1999; Walberg & Paik, 1997). For instance, Gloria Ladson-Billing achieved considerable success (she holds a Ph.D. from Stanford University and is now a college professor) despite growing up poor, as have many others. Her parents' decision to send her to a high-quality junior high school and her own motivation and abilities proved to be more important than her parents' socioeconomic status.

Children and adolescents in low-income neighborhoods may have fewer choices for recreation than their more economically advantaged peers.

Low-income families are a diverse lot. They range from families who must carefully watch their budgets but can afford life's basic necessities to families who live in abject poverty. In the following sections we look at the effects of poverty on children's development, discover how some children successfully meet the challenges of an economically impoverished environment, and identify strategies for working with students from low-income families.

Poverty

Ideally, it's what you do, not what you have, that matters. But this generalization may not hold for the truly needy. Families in poverty have so very little that they have few options as to what they can do for their children. And there are many more children living in poverty than most people realize. In 1995, *1 out of every 5* children living in the United States was classified as poor (Hernandez, 1997; Lewit, Terman, & Behrman, 1997).

In addition to being alarmingly high, poverty rates are disproportionate across ethnic groups: African American, Native American, and Hispanic children are far more likely to be poor than children from European American backgrounds (McLoyd, 1998a; Sidel, 1996). Yet we must be careful not to overgeneralize, as poor people come from all walks of life:

> Poor . . . are young, they are middle-aged, and they are old. They are from rural Maine and Mississippi, from New York, Detroit, and Los Angeles, from small towns in the Midwest, from the mining towns of Appalachia, and from the suburban communities that ring the major cities. They are married, divorced, separated, widowed, and never married. They are from all backgrounds— white, African-American, Latina, Asian-American, Native American, and many others on whom the Census Bureau does not keep detailed data. They are full-time workers, part-time workers, the unemployed and the underemployed. They are high school dropouts and high school graduates; some have attended college, some have even completed college. (Sidel, 1996, p. 65)

Poverty is a brief experience for some and an ongoing way of life for others. One in three children spends at least one year in poverty before reaching adulthood (Center for the Future of Children, 1997). Sadly, 5% of children—1 in 20—spend 10 years or more in poverty (Center for the Future of Children, 1997). Low income during the preschool years is more predictive of low rates of high school completion than is low income during later childhood and adolescence (Baydar, Brooks-Gunn, & Furstenberg, 1993; Brooks-Gunn & Duncan, 1997; Center for the Future of Children, 1997; Duncan, Yeung, Brooks-Gunn, & Smith, 1998).

Risk Factors Associated with Poverty Along with the normal challenges associated with physical, cognitive, and social-emotional development, children and adolescents living in poverty face several additional challenges:

- *Poor nutrition and health care.* Some children are poorly fed and have little access to adequate health care; as a result, they may suffer from malnutrition and other chronic health problems (Center for the Future of Children, 1997; Miller, 1995). Children who experience severe malnutrition either prenatally or in the first few years of life tend to have lower IQ scores, poorer attention and memory, and lower school achievement (D'Amato et al., 1992; Morgan & Gibson, 1991; Ricciuti, 1993).
- *Inadequate housing.* Many children live in very tight quarters, perhaps sharing one or two rooms with several other family members. For instance, teacher Frances Hawkins

describes what often happened when her inner-city Boston preschoolers played with a dollhouse:

> When we furnished the dollhouse, the children would move all the furniture into one room. It was an "apartment" house to them. They knew no other. (Hawkins, 1997, p. 180)

Some children have no place to live at all, except, perhaps, the family car or a homeless shelter. Children of homeless families often have health problems, low self-esteem, a short attention span, poor language skills, and inappropriate behaviors (Coe, Salamon, & Molnar, 1991; McLoyd, 1998b; Pawlas, 1994). Some may be reluctant to come to school because they lack bathing facilities and presentable clothing (Gollnick & Chinn, 1998).

- *Gaps in background knowledge.* Teachers typically assume that children have had certain kinds of experiences before they begin school—for instance, that they have been read to, have seen many kinds of animals at farms or zoos, and have had ample opportunities to explore their physical environment. Yet some children who live in extreme poverty miss out on such foundational experiences (Case, Okamoto, et al., 1996; McLoyd, 1998b). As an example, Frances Hawkins reports how her inner-city preschoolers behaved when she gave them a chance to play with toy boats in a tub of water:

> Children *shoved* the boats along. Impatient with the slow floating motion—not familiar with the way things move in water, or just natural impatience with slowness?. . .
>
> As our understanding of how and where these children lived fell into place, we realized that the chance even to use water, to play with water, was rare. One kitchen, one bath—not always in working order—was normal in a house for three, four, or five families to share. (Hawkins, 1997, p. 187)

Furthermore, when children move frequently from one school to another—as many homeless children do—they miss some of the early school experiences so essential to their success in later grades (Pawlas, 1994).

- *Increased probability of disabling conditions.* Children who live in poverty are more likely to have physical, mental, or social-emotional disabilities (McLoyd, 1998b; U.S. Department of Education, 1997). In some cases, such disabilities are the result of poor nutrition (in the womb or later), exposure to lead paint, and other environmental hazards; in other cases, they may be due to harsh and inconsistent parenting (Brooks-Gunn & Duncan, 1997; McLoyd, 1998b).
- *Emotional stress.* Children function less effectively when they are under stress, and many poor families live in chronically stressful conditions (Maccoby & Martin, 1983; Trueba, 1988). The lack of financial resources is one obvious source of anxiety; children may wonder where their next meal is coming from or how long the landlord will wait before evicting them for not paying the rent. The preponderance of single-parent homes among low-SES families is another factor; a single parent may be overwhelmed with worries about supporting the family (Scott-Jones, 1984). In addition, poor children are more likely to be subjected to maltreatment by parents and other adults and to encounter violent crimes in their neighborhoods (Center for the Future of Children, 1997; McLoyd, 1998b; Thompson & Wyatt, 1999).
- *Lower quality schools.* In the opening case, Gloria Ladson-Billings attended a high school in another part of town because her mother had concerns about the quality of the neighborhood school. Schools in low-income neighborhoods and communities are often poorly funded and equipped, and they have high teacher turnover rates. Furthermore, some teachers at these schools have lower expectations for students—and so offer a less demanding curriculum, assign less homework, and set lower standards for performance—than tends to be true for teachers of middle-SES students (McLoyd, 1998b; Murdock, 1999; Portes, 1996).
- *Public misconceptions and disdain.* People from economically more advantaged backgrounds often have mixed feelings toward low-SES families: They may feel some pity yet simultaneously believe that poor people are responsible for their own misfortunes, perhaps because of laziness, promiscuity, or overdependence on social welfare programs (Chafel, 1997; McLoyd, 1998a; Sidel, 1996). Agents in social service and federal programs who work with poor families sometimes share these conflicted feelings and may come across

to the people they serve as uncaring and punitive (McLoyd, 1998a). Teachers of lower-income children—especially those from upper- and middle-income backgrounds—often have such biases as well, particularly when they have limited knowledge of students' families and cultures (Alexander et al., 1987; McLoyd, 1998b).

Such challenges make it difficult for children and adolescents to hold much optimism for their future. In Jonathan Kozol's *Amazing Grace,* a teenager named Maria describes her feeling of being ignored by a more affluent society:

> It's not like, "well, these babies just aren't dying fast enough," Maria says. "Let's figure out a way to kill some more." It's not like that at all. It's like—I don't know how to say this. . . . If you weave enough bad things into the fibers of a person's life—sickness and filth, old mattresses and other junk thrown in the streets and other ugly ruined things, and ruined people, a prison here, sewage there, drug dealers here, the homeless people over there, then give us the very worst schools anyone could think of, hospitals that keep you waiting for ten hours, police that don't show up when someone's dying, take the train that's underneath the street in the good neighborhoods and put it up above where it shuts out the sun, you can guess that life will not be very nice and children will not have much sense of being glad of who they are. (Kozol, 1995, pp. 39–40)

Many children and adolescents find the challenges of abject poverty so overwhelming that they engage in behaviors—dropping out of school, abusing drugs and alcohol, participating in criminal activities—that create further problems. Yet the great majority of children and adolescents from poor families do well *despite* the adversities they face: They work hard in school, graduate from high school, and may even go on to college (Bell-Scott & Taylor, 1989; Children's Defense Fund, 1991; Nieto, 1995). In essence, they appear to be relatively *resilient* to life's hardships.

Resiliency

Although children who live in poverty have less reason to be optimistic about their future than their more economically advantaged peers, in fact a great number of them set their sights on a better life. For example, in 1992, although high school seniors from low-income families were less likely to aspire to college than students from middle- or high-income families, 92% of them did plan to go to college either immediately after graduation or within a few years' time (National Center for Education Statistics, 1999a).

The term **resiliency** refers to the ability of many children and adolescents to beat the odds and succeed in school and in life despite exceptional hardships such as poverty or parental maltreatment. Resilient youngsters develop characteristics and coping skills that help them rise above their adverse circumstances. As a group, they have likable personalities, positive self-concepts, strong motivation to succeed, and high yet realistic goals. They believe that success comes with hard work, and their bad experiences serve as constant reminders of the importance of getting a good education (English, 1998; Masten & Coatsworth, 1998; McMillan & Reed, 1994; Werner, 1995).

Resilient youngsters usually have one or more individuals in their lives whom they trust and know they can turn to in difficult times (English, 1998; Masten & Coatsworth, 1998; Thompson & Wyatt, 1999; Werner, 1995). Such individuals may be family members, neighbors, or school personnel; for example, resilient students may mention teachers who have taken a personal interest in them and been instrumental in their school success (McMillan & Reed, 1994; Paris & Cunningham, 1996). Consider how one teacher, Mr. Taylor, took an interest in Cedric Jennings, the inner-city high school student introduced in Chapter 12 (Suskind, 1998):

> [6]Mr. Taylor . . . has personally invested in Cedric's future since the student appeared in his tenth grade chemistry class—back then, Cedric was a sullen ninth grader who had just been thrown out of biology for talking back to the teacher and needed somewhere to go. Taylor let him sit in, gave him a few assignments that the older kids were doing, and was soon marveling at flawless A papers. Taylor took Cedric for an after-school dinner at Western Sizzlin', and they were suddenly a team.

---

[6]From *A Hope in the Unseen* by Ron Suskind, copyright © 1998 by Ron Suskind. Used by permission of Broadway Books, a division of Random House, Inc.

resiliency
Ability of some children and adolescents to thrive and achieve despite adverse environmental conditions.

In the last two years, Taylor has offered his charge a steady stream of extra-credit projects and trips, like a visit last month with scientists at the National Aeronautics and Space Administration. He challenges Cedric with elaborate intellectual puzzles, withholding praise and daring the pupil to vanquish his theatrical doubting with a real display of intellectual muscle. It's call and response, combative but productive. (p. 6)

Mr. Taylor also offered frequent words of encouragement, especially when Cedric encountered classmates' taunts that he was a "nerd" or acting white:

[7]"You see, Cedric, you're in a race, a long race. . . . You can't worry about what people say from the sidelines. They're already out of it. You, however, are still on the track. You have to just keep on running. . . . (pp. 6–7)

Working with Students from Low-Income Families

Teaching students from low-income families can be challenging, but it can also be highly rewarding. In fact, teachers who want to "make a difference" in children's lives are most likely to do so in schools that serve students from low-SES backgrounds. But to be effective, teachers must be committed to their profession, hold high expectations for students' achievement, think creatively about how they can make the most of limited school equipment and resources, and show a contagious enthusiasm for their subject matter (Anderson & Pellicer, 1998; Ogden & Germinario, 1988). Experts offer the following recommendations:

■ *Identify and build on students' strengths.* When teachers concentrate on students' weaknesses, students become easily discouraged and may soon resign themselves to the idea that their efforts in the classroom will be largely in vain. In contrast, thinking about what's *right* with children can generate optimism, enthusiasm, and a definite commitment to learning on the part of teachers and students alike. Although many students from lower-SES backgrounds lag behind their classmates in such basic academic skills as reading, writing, and computation, they nevertheless bring strengths to the classroom. For example, they may have strong social and leadership skills. They are often clever at improvising with everyday objects (Torrance, 1995). If they work part-time to help their families make ends meet, they may have a good understanding of the working world. If they are children of single, working parents, they may know far more than their classmates about cooking, cleaning house, and taking care of younger siblings (Whiting & Edwards, 1988). If financial resources have been particularly scarce, they may know firsthand what it is like to be hungry for days at a time or to live in an unheated apartment in the winter; they may therefore have a special appreciation for basic human needs and true empathy for victims of war or famine around the world. In some areas, then, students who have grown up in poverty may have more knowledge and skills than their more economically advantaged peers. Furthermore, students who are willing to talk about the challenges they've faced can sensitize their classmates to the serious inequities that currently exist in our society.

When teachers provide opportunities for students to build on their strengths, they increase the likelihood that students will be successful and have enhanced self-efficacy (Masten & Coatsworth, 1998). One elementary school established a singing group, called the "Jazz Cats," for low-income fourth and fifth graders (Jenlink, 1994). The group rehearsed regularly, performed at a variety of community events, and enjoyed considerable visibility for its talent. The group members clearly thrived on their success and recognition, as one teacher observed:

I can't think of any of the Jazz Cats that at one time or another during one of their performances— that you don't see a big smile come across their faces, whether it's during the performance or afterwards . . . that kind of look of happiness and satisfaction at what they did. (Jenlink, 1994, p. 21)

The success of the program extended far beyond music: Many group members exhibited increased self-esteem, improvement in other school subjects, and greater teamwork and leadership skills (Jenlink, 1994). One student's mother reported on the difference she saw in her daughter after being in Jazz Cats:

---

[7]From *A Hope in the Unseen* by Ron Suskind, copyright © 1998 by Ron Suskind. Used by permission of Broadway Books, a division of Random House, Inc.

Abbey has completely turned around. . . . She's not shy to ask questions anymore. . . . I think the Jazz Cats have helped her with the idea that everything will work its way out. So she doesn't seem to be this angry, quiet little girl any more. She wants to be very loving, very outspoken. (Jenlink, 1994, p. 20)

■ *Create a sense of community.* In Chapter 11, we described the importance of creating a *sense of community* in schools and classrooms—a sense that teachers and students have shared goals, respect and support one another's efforts, and believe that everyone makes an important contribution. The caring, camaraderie, respect, and support of teachers and classmates may be especially important for students from low-income backgrounds (Anderson & Pellicer, 1998; Downey, 2000). Teachers can create a community spirit among students in a variety of ways: They can assign classroom chores on a rotating basis, use cooperative learning activities, involve students in cross-grade tutoring, and encourage everyone's participation in extracurricular activities (Downey, 2000). Above all, teachers must convey the message that they deeply care not only about students' academic performance but also about students' physical, social, and emotional well-being; they must also provide the encouragement and support students need to succeed both inside and outside of the classroom (Masten & Coatsworth, 1998; McMillan & Reed, 1994; Werner, 1995).

■ *Establish clear and consistent expectations for students' behavior.* For all students, and especially those who have had more than their share of life's challenges and assaults, knowing what's expected is important. But it's not enough to ask for "responsibility" or "respect for others." Instead, teachers should describe their expectations in clear, concrete terms (Downey, 2000). For instance, when finishing lunch in the cafeteria, students might be asked to "Empty the napkins and leftovers into the trash bin, put the trays and dishes on the counter, and go quietly outside." When working in cooperative groups, students might be reminded that "Everyone needs to participate in the discussions and contribute to the group project" and "It's OK to find fault with ideas, but it's *not* OK to find fault with people." Ideally, teachers should convey such expectations in an informational, rather than controlling, manner (see Chapter 11).

■ *Place a high priority on developing reading skills.* Many students from low-SES backgrounds have poor reading skills, in part because their families may not have the skills or resources to teach their children literacy basics at home (see Chapter 8). Yet reading proficiency seems to be a fundamental cornerstone on which many resilient students build their later successes (Downey, 2000; Lee, Winfield, & Wilson, 1991; Werner, 1993). It is important to identify and address any deficiencies in emergent literacy or reading skills early in the game, ideally in the preschool years or early elementary grades (Chall, 1996).

■ *Show the relevance of school activities and subject matter to students' lives and needs.* Finding meaningfulness and personal relevance in classroom activities and subject matter is important for any student (see Chapter 11), but it may be especially critical for students from low-SES backgrounds (Anderson & Pellicer, 1998; Lee-Pearce, Plowman, & Touchstone, 1998).

■ *Communicate high expectations for students' success.* Students from low-SES backgrounds often do not expect much of themselves in terms of academic achievement. Furthermore, they typically have lower aspirations for their higher education and possible careers (Knapp & Woolverton, 1995; Taylor, 1994). Yet teachers can communicate a can-do attitude and back up the message by offering the extra support students may need to achieve ambitious goals. Offering help sessions for challenging classroom material, finding low-cost academic enrichment programs available during the summer, and helping students fill out applications for college scholarships are just a few of the forms that such support might take.

■ *Make sure students' basic needs are met.* Schools in low-income neighborhoods are often actively involved in making sure students are well fed (e.g., through free or reduced-cost breakfast and lunch programs) and adequately clothed (e.g., through local "jackets for kids" programs). Yet some very poor children attend schools in more affluent neighborhoods, and teachers must be alert for indications that they need assistance in meeting basic needs.

■ *Have compassion for parents' circumstances.* Virtually all parents, including those living in extreme poverty, want their children to do well in school (Stevenson et al., 1990). Yet many do not have the the financial resources, the emotional energy, or the educational background to help their children achieve academic success (e.g., in the opening case study, Gloria Ladson-Billings could not bring in the neatly typed papers that some of her classmates did). It's all too easy for teachers to find fault with parents—to think that parents are shirking their obligations to their children—when in fact parents may be doing all that they possibly can. In many cases, a visit to students' homes or neighborhoods can give teachers a better understanding of the life challenges that students and their families face (Belle, 1984; Hawkins, 1997). Ultimately, teachers work more effectively with parents when they strive to work in partnership with students' parents, rather than when they place blame for what parents may or may not have done (see Chapter 12).

■ *Seek out good role models for students.* Students from low-income neighborhoods encounter fewer good role models than students from more economically advantaged neighborhoods (Torrance, 1995). Students are more likely to be optimistic about their future when they meet—and ideally establish close, trusting relationships with—people from their neighborhood or community who have succeeded despite limited financial resources. Close relationships with adults through community "big brother" and "big sister" programs provide another source of positive role models (Masten & Coatsworth, 1998).

Not only do children's neighborhoods and communities offer potential role models, but they also assist in children's development more generally. We turn now to the numerous ways in which neighborhoods and communities serve as yet another context for development.

Art by Marsalis, age 7½

Neighborhoods and Communities

Children's experiences can be very, very different from one community to the next, and even within distinct neighborhoods in a single community. Neighborhoods and communities influence children's development in several ways:

■ *They affect the peer group with whom children come into contact.* Children spend a great deal of time close to home, often within hollering distance when they are young, and within easy reach by bicycle, car, bus, or subway as they grow older. Occasionally children maintain long-distance friendships by telephone or the Internet, but such friendships usually supplement, rather than replace, face-to-face contact with age-mates in the local community.

As you should recall from Chapter 13, peer groups play a key role in children's development: They foster the development of social skills, provide companionship and social support, and help children and adolescents make sense of their lives. However, when social problems such as unemployment, violence, and drug use are prevalent and saturate young people's immediate peer groups, then peers foster social deviance and despair (Crane, 1991; Harris, 1998). In fact, when children and adolescents move from high-crime neighborhoods to more law-abiding ones, their behavior sometimes improves dramatically. Consider Larry Ayuso, a 16-year-old New York City resident with low grades and heavy involvement in crime and drugs:

Art by James, age 13

As children gain increasing mobility with age, their neighborhoods expand. Marsalis stays very close to home, but James can easily travel a mile or more on his bicycle.

Three of his friends had died in drug-related homicides. He was headed for high school dropout and a life (or death) of crime when he was rescued by a program that takes kids out of urban ghettos and puts them somewhere else—somewhere far away. Larry ended up in a small town in New Mexico, living with a middle-class . . . family. Two years later he was making A's and B's, averaging 28 points a game on his high school basketball team, and headed for college. (Harris, 1998, p. 212)[8]

[8]Reprinted with the permission of The Free Press, a Division of Simon & Schuster, Inc., from *The Nurture Assumption: Why Children Turn Out the Way They Do* by Judith Rich Harris. Copyright © 1998 by Judith Rich Harris.

CONSIDERING THE CONTEXTS IN WHICH CHILDREN ARE GROWING UP

■ Discuss current events in class.

A high school history teacher compares a recent riot in a nearby city to class conflicts in industrial England and contemporary ethnic conflicts in Eastern Europe and the Middle East. Students discuss their fears and concerns about the riot and try to consider the perspectives of all parties involved.

■ Be neutral, inclusive, and respectful regarding students' religious practices.

A third-grade teacher encourages her students to bring in items that show how they will celebrate various holidays during the winter months. Students bring in decorations and religious symbols related to Christmas, Kwanzaa, Hanukkah, and the winter solstice.

■ Work closely with families of low-income children to ensure their academic success.

A teacher working in a low-socioeconomic neighborhood regularly invites parents and guardians to participate in class and school events. He learns about the goals that family members have for their children, arranges for child-care during meetings and conferences, and becomes familiar with community services that families may find helpful.

■ Establish close relationships with local neighborhoods and communities.

A high school teacher encourages all of her students to engage in local community service projects. Students choose from a wide range of possibilities, including neighborhood cleanups, reading sessions with preschoolers at the library, volunteer work at a food bank or soup kitchen, and visits to a nursing home.

■ *They affect choices for recreation.* Children and adolescents make decisions about how to spend their spare time based largely on what opportunities and resources are convenient and affordable. Recreational opportunities in the local neighborhood are especially important for children from low-income families, who rarely travel far from home (Elliott et al., 1996).

■ *They tell children what society expects them to be as adults.* The activities in which local adults engage—whether productive employment and community volunteerism, on the one hand, or drug trafficking and gang affiliation, on the other—tell youngsters what behaviors are normal and desirable. For instance, when a high percentage of adults in a neighborhood have stable and high-status jobs, children are more likely to stay in school and aspire to similar types of employment (Jencks & Mayer, 1990).

■ *They offer formal support to families through agencies and institutions.* As we discovered in our discussion of ecological systems theory in Chapter 12, neighborhoods and communities comprise the larger social systems within which families operate. Many agencies and institutions within the local community—schools, health clinics, social service agencies, criminal justice systems, homeless shelters, and so on—support families' ongoing efforts to help children grow into productive adults.

■ *They provide informal social support systems.* The informal supportive connections families make within their neighborhood and community indirectly affect, and often enhance, the lives of children. For example, community members may occasionally supervise children's activities, model and offer advice on effective parenting strategies, inform parents about employment opportunities and educational resources, and provide the emotional support that family members sometimes need in times of trouble and stress (Cochran, 1993; McLoyd, 1990; Simons, Lorenz, Wu, & Conger, 1993).

Neighborhoods and communities are most likely to foster children's development when community members know and respect one another and work cooperatively to solve local problems (Sampson & Groves, 1989). When there is little sense of community—for example, when people move into and out of the neighborhood frequently, or when people of various ethnic groups mistrust one another—crime rates increase, and children and adolescents are more likely to fall into delinquent behavior (Sampson & Groves, 1989).

Types of Communities

Neighborhoods and communities do not exist in isolation from the broader social landscape; instead, each is nested within a particular geographical location. Furthermore, each has a particular density of inhabitants. People in urban communities live in close proximity to one another; those in rural environments often live quite a distance from one another. Here we look briefly at the potential advantages and disadvantages of living in urban, rural, and suburban communities. Keep in mind that the descriptions of the three types of communities are generalizations. Individual urban, rural, and suburban communities show great variation, influenced by the characteristics of the region in which they are located and their proximity to other types of communities. In densely populated states, for example, the demarcation between what is urban, rural, or suburban is often blurred.

Urban Communities   A large city provides many sources of enrichment for young people. For instance, most major cities have ongoing events and resources related to music, art, drama, science, sports, and diverse cultures. But children's daily lives in urban communities are influenced by their family's financial status. Some families can afford to make choices about where they live and which schools their children attend, but many others must choose among less desirable alternatives.

Tragically, many inner-city neighborhoods are fraught with serious problems, including poverty, drugs, violence, crime, and racial segregation (Massey & Denton, 1993). Not surprisingly, these problems seep into schools. For instance, secondary school principals in inner-city public schools are more likely than their counterparts in rural and suburban schools to see poverty, inadequate academic skills, student apathy, and lack of parent involvement as serious problems affecting their schools (National Center for Education Statistics, 1999b). Undoubtedly because of such problems, many people in the public at large hold negative stereotypes of inner-city youths—especially those from ethnic and racial minority groups—and often think of these youngsters as being violent, drug-addicted, uneducated, and dependent on welfare (Gibbs, 1985; Way, 1998). In reality, many young people living in the inner city steer clear of delinquent activities, graduate from high school, find jobs or pursue higher education, and live productive lives (Price & Clarke-McLean, 1997; Way, 1998).

Rural Communities   Families who live in rural settings, particularly farming communities, often foster a cooperative spirit and strong work ethic (Garcia, 1994; Reynolds, 1999). For instance, farm families tend to structure chores and jobs so that all family members contribute to the family's economic livelihood. Furthermore, farm families often drop their own work to help other families with such activities as chopping wood and harvesting crops. Some rural neighbors also exchange produce and handmade goods and in the process deepen their community ties and sense of social obligation.

Although a rural environment offers many advantages for growing children and adolescents, its limited recreational activities can be problematic for some, who may seek excitement and variety through unproductive activities. For instance, school principals in rural areas and small towns are more likely than principals in central cities and suburban areas to identify student alcohol abuse as a serious problem (National Center for Education Statistics, 1999b).

Historically, members of rural communities have been actively involved in local schools, perhaps volunteering to organize social gatherings or help with school maintenance. Rural communities frequently have a limited budget for children's schooling, and so several communities may join forces to create large, consolidated school districts. In a consolidated school, students have access to more educational resources than they might otherwise, but some may need to travel many miles to attend school each day and so have limited opportunity to participate in extracurricular activities or in other ways socialize with classmates after school hours. Furthermore, parents may feel little connection to, or investment in, a distant school operated by teachers they do not know (National Center for Education Statistics, 1999b).

Suburban Communities   On average, families in suburban communities have higher incomes than those who live in inner cities or rural areas, and so schools are often better funded. In some people's minds, a suburban community is the "ideal" environment for growing children: There is easy access to the educational and cultural resources of the big city, yet everyone has a bit of backyard and a bit of privacy.

Yet economic resources are not equally distributed in suburban communities, and not all young people have an optimistic outlook about their chances for future success (Gaines, 1991). Furthermore, some children and adolescents in wealthier communities may reject their less financially advantaged classmates, especially if those classmates don't adhere to unspoken rules for acceptable behavior. Developmental psychologist Judith Harris (1998) describes such rejection in her own childhood:

> We moved around a lot, those early years, and several times I was taken out of a classroom in the middle of the school year and put into another one, but I had no trouble making new friends. My high spirits and outgoing nature made me popular with my peers, both boys and girls.
>
> Then we moved once more—as usual, after the school year had begun—and everything changed. I found myself the youngest and smallest child, and one of the few who wore glasses, in a fourth-grade classroom in a snooty suburb in the Northeast. The other girls were sophisticated little ladies, interested in hairstyles, proud of their pretty clothes. I wasn't like them, and they didn't like me.
>
> My family remained in that place for four years, and they were the worst four years of my life. I went to school each day with children from my neighborhood, but not one of them would play with me or talk to me. If I dared to say anything to them, it was ignored. Pretty soon I gave up trying. Within a year or two I went from being active and outgoing to being inhibited and shy. My parents knew nothing of this—they saw no major changes in my behavior at home. The only thing that changed, as far as they were concerned, was that I was spending a lot of time reading. Too much time, in their opinion. (Harris, 1998, pp. 146–147)[9]

Harris's experience is not unusual; regardless of the setting in which children live—whether urban, rural, or suburban—frequent moves from one community to another can disrupt peer relationships and support networks. Yet frequent mobility is becoming more and more a normal part of life in Western society. For example, in 1994, approximately one in six children had moved to a new home within the last year (Hernandez, 1997). Children who move frequently are at risk both academically and socially, in part because the frequent transition from one school to another often leaves gaps in their basic knowledge and skills and in part because they have little continuity in their peer support group (Harris, 1998; Knutson & Mantzicopoulos, 1999).

Considering Community Ties in the Classroom

"It takes a village to raise a child." This old African proverb is right on the mark: Children's development is fostered not only by family members and teachers but also by neighbors and community members. We urge teachers to capitalize on the resources in their towns and cities, and also to encourage students to give back to their communities, as the following ideas suggest:

■ *Build a sense of community at the school site.* Most parents and other caregivers need ongoing social and emotional support from others who have children. Parent-teacher meetings, evening concerts and plays, and school suppers (serving spaghetti, chili, or other easy-to-prepare dishes) give parents a chance to connect with one another and compare notes about their children's progress and problems. Such gatherings may also give family members an opportunity to interact with local government officials, school board members, law enforcement officers, and other public figures in the community.

■ *Take active measures to integrate new children and families into the classroom and school community.* As our earlier example of the girl who moved to the "snooty" suburb illustrates, children's transitions to new schools are not always easy. School personnel are often among the first community members new residents meet. A few simple gestures—perhaps finding a group of boys or girls with whom a new student can eat lunch, inviting a new parent to help with a class fund-raiser, or scheduling a class potluck dinner to welcome the new family—can make a world of difference in helping the newcomers feel at home and begin to establish social ties in the community.

■ *Honor the accomplishments of local citizens.* Successful adults from the local community provide valuable role models for all children and may be especially important for students whose daily lives bring them into regular contact with deviant activities and lifestyles. In a few

---

[9]Reprinted with the permission of The Free Press, a Division of Simon & Schuster, Inc., from *The Nurture Assumption: Why Children Turn Out the Way They Do* by Judith Rich Harris. Copyright © 1998 by Judith Rich Harris.

cases, conversations between students and successful citizens may even lead to productive mentoring relationships or apprenticeships (see Chapter 4) outside of school.

■ *Bring your own outside activities into the classroom.* Some teachers have particular hobbies and service roles in the community that they can bring to school. As one simple example, Julia Devereaux, a teacher of children from low-income families and also a Girl Scout leader, reported: "I just bring all of the membership information here and tell the girls how wonderful scouting can be. Frankly, by the time I describe the sleepovers—over-night camping—and the skating part, everyone says they want to be in the troop."[10]

■ *Get students involved in community service projects.* Students often feel more connected to their community when, in some small way, they contribute to the community's overall well-being. Members of a school or classroom might conduct a neighborhood cleanup, volunteer in a nursing home or in a hospital pediatric ward, serve as readers at the local library, or raise funds to benefit community causes (Ladson-Billings, 1994). For example, the city of Boston sponsors an after-school program called the Mural Crew, in which groups of teenagers replace graffiti on buildings with large-scale murals. Since 1991, adolescents in the program have created more than 60 public works of art. One of the murals, shown at the beginning of the chapter, appears in more detail in Figure 14–2.

Community Support for Children's Care and Development

Neighborhood and community support for children is often most evident during the times that children are not attending school: throughout the day during the infant and preschool years and before and after school hours in later years. Here we look at three forms that such support might take—daycare, preschools, and after-school programs for older children and adolescents—as well as at the potential role of friends and neighbors when children take care of themselves before or after school. We also consider the potential risks and benefits of part-time employment for adolescents.

Daycare Many young children are in **daycare**, in the care of people other than their parents, for a significant portion of the work week. Mothers' increasing employment outside the

daycare
Care of children by nonparental adults for a significant portion of the workweek.

---

[10]From *The Dreamkeepers: Successful Teachers of African American Children* (pp. 64–65), by G. Ladson-Billings, 1994, San Francisco: Jossey-Bass. Copyright © 1994 by Jossey-Bass, Inc., Publishers. Reprinted by permission of Jossey-Bass, Inc., a subsidiary of John Wiley & Sons.

home and the rise of single-parent families have contributed to the use of daycare in many Western countries. For example, in the United States, the majority of infants are regularly cared for by someone other than their mothers or fathers, and more than two-thirds of children under age 4 are routinely cared for by a nonparent (Lamb, 1998). Most infants are cared for in home settings, either their own or those of a daycare provider. As children get older, however, attendance at child-care centers becomes more common (Kisker, Hofferth, Phillips, & Farguhar, 1991; Lamb, 1998).

Many people have raised concerns about the potentially negative effects of daycare on young children's social-emotional and cognitive development. By and large, however, daycare appears to be a positive experience for most children. Following are some key research findings:

■ *Daycare does not undermine children's attachment to their parents.* Many social commentators lament the trend for an increasing number of infants to be apart from their mothers during the day and suggest that nonparental care compromises the infant-mother bond. (Curiously, the same critics appear to think it quite natural for fathers to be off at work.) Research on quality daycare has largely invalidated their concerns. Only when attachment relationships are already vulnerable—for instance, when mothers are insensitive and nonresponsive to their infants' needs—do young children in daycare display insecure attachment to parents (Lamb, 1998).

Infants frequently become attached to their daycare providers, especially when caregivers are stable, warm, sensitive, and actively involved in infants' care (Barnas & Cummings, 1994; Raikes, 1993). Furthermore, mothers who are emotionally depressed or otherwise ill-prepared for the task of parenting may actually help their children form secure attachments to them by placing them in daycare. To illustrate, in a study of infants with depressed mothers, Cohn, Campbell, and Ross (1991) found a positive correlation between the number of hours that the infants spent in daycare and their security of attachment to their mothers.

■ *High-quality daycare can enhance cognitive and linguistic development for some children.* High-quality infant care seems to be especially beneficial for children's development when their alternative is a home environment that is not stimulating or challenging (Lamb, 1998; Ramey, 1992; Scarr, 1997). Its benefits have been observed primarily for children from low-income families; daycare seems to have minimal effects, either positive or negative, on the cognitive development of children from middle- and upper-income homes (Scarr, 1998).

■ *Experience in daycare may help children develop social skills and independence.* Children who have high-quality daycare experiences are more likely to be socially competent (Field, 1991; Field, Masi, Goldstein, Perry, & Parl, 1988; Howes, 1988; Scarr, 1998; Scott-Little & Holloway, 1992). Daycare may also foster self-confidence and self-reliance; for instance, in a study with 8-year-old Swedish children, those who had had out-of-home care as infants appeared to their teachers to be more persistent and independent, as well as less anxious, than those who did not have this experience (Andersson, 1989).

■ *Exposure to daycare at a young age may increase aggression and noncompliance slightly.* Some data suggest that children who have been exposed to daycare as infants are somewhat more aggressive and noncompliant than their peers. However, these effects are not always seen, and when they are, they are quite small for high-quality care (Bagley, 1989; Clarke-Stewart, 1989; DiLalla, 1998; Hegland & Rix, 1990). The long-term impact of such effects is not known, although there is some evidence that any overly aggressive behaviors decrease over time (Clarke-Stewart, 1989). It may be that children in daycare settings learn more quickly to stand up for their own rights and needs—in other words, they become more *assertive*—and that researchers and teachers misinterpret their assertiveness as aggression or noncompliance (Hegland & Rix, 1990). As children learn more effective ways of interacting with their peers over time, inappropriate forms of assertiveness should diminish.

■ *Quality matters.* Researchers have tried to assess the quality of daycare programs in two ways. *Structural measures* include such objective indices as caregivers' training and experience, child-caregiver ratios, staff turnover, and number and complexity of toys and equipment (Lamb, 1998; Sims, Hutchins, & Taylor, 1997). For instance, the Panel on Child Care Policy of the National Research Council (1991) recommends the following child-caregiver ratios: 4:1

for children under age 2; between 4:1 and 6:1 for 2-year-olds; between 5:1 and 10:1 for 3-year-olds; and between 7:1 and 10:1 for 4- and 5-year-olds. *Process measures* of quality, which address the nature of children's social and cognitive experiences in a daycare setting, include measures of child-caregiver relationships, child-peer interactions, and developmentally appropriate activities (Harms & Clifford, 1980; Sims et al., 1997).

As you can imagine, process measures are not as straightforward or concrete as structural measures, yet they are almost certainly more informative indicators of daycare quality (Sims et al., 1997). At the same time, different children may have higher- or lower-quality experiences in a single daycare setting, depending on their temperaments, cultural backgrounds, and ways in which they interact with particular teachers (Dahlberg et al., 1999; Sims et al., 1997). As you can see, then, the "quality" of any single daycare program may be impossible to pin down, as it is likely to vary from one child to the next.

Child-care settings that work well often have close ties with the communities in which they operate. We find an example in a statement written by the Meadow Lake Tribal Council of northern Saskatchewan, Canada:

> The First Nations of the Meadow Lake Tribal Council believe that a child care program developed, administered and operated by their own people is a vital component to their vision of sustainable growth and development. It impacts every sector of their long-term plans as they prepare to enter the twenty-first century. It will be children who inherit the struggle to retain and enhance the people's culture, language and history; who continue the quest for economic progress for a better quality of life; and who move forward with a strengthened resolve to plan their own destiny. (Dahlberg et al., 1999, p. 168)

The First Nations people did not readily accept the "best practices" for daycare that Canadian governmental authorities offered them. Instead, the tribal council decided to work with the School of Child and Youth Care at the University of Victoria, which agreed that the tribal council should direct its own daycare planning. Eventually, the council designed a program that considered research on child development, advice from elders in the community, *and* traditional practices, such as use of cradle boards to tightly hold swaddled infants. The result was a high-quality program that integrated local cultural values and practices into child-care activities and also revitalized the community by reaffirming traditional values and ceremonies (Dahlberg et al., 1999).

Most of the research on daycare has been conducted at relatively high-quality sites. Consequently, we do not have adequate information about the outcomes of daycare that is emotionally cold, punitive, or overpopulated. We suspect, however, that low-quality daycare—"care" in which children are inadequately nurtured, stimulated, and supervised—may seriously tax children's resiliency, especially when children's home environments are equally nonnurturing. Daycare can be of benefit only when it addresses children's immediate physical and emotional needs and when it includes toys and activities designed to foster children's cognitive and social development.

Preschools and Compensatory Education High-quality preschool environments routinely have positive effects on children's intellectual growth and may be particularly beneficial for children from low-SES backgrounds (Lamb, 1998; McLoyd, 1998a; Ramey & Ramey, 1998; Scarr, 1998). Accordingly, legislators and educators have joined forces to create preschools that give young children of low-income families important foundational knowledge and skills. Such **compensatory education** typically combines a preschool educational program with other supports for children and their families, such as basic medical care, social services, and guidance in parenting skills.

In the United States, the best-known model of compensatory education is Project Head Start. Established under federal legislation, Head Start was designed for 3- to 5-year-old low-income children and their families. Since 1965, it has served more than 13 million children, many of them from single-parent homes. A typical Head Start program includes early childhood education (preschool), health screening and referrals, mental health services, nutrition education, family support services, and considerable parent involvement in decision making (McLoyd, 1998a; Washington & Bailey, 1995).

Numerous research studies have been conducted on the effectiveness of Head Start and similar compensatory education programs. The short-term effects of such programs on children's

compensatory education
Preschool program designed to foster basic academic skills in children whose home environments may not nurture such skills.

cognitive development are clear—children score higher on measures of cognitive ability and achieve at higher levels in school—but such gains often disappear by the upper elementary grades (Lee, Brooks-Gunn, Schnur, & Liaw, 1990; McKey et al., 1985; McLoyd, 1998b; Ramey & Ramey, 1998). Other long-term benefits have been observed, however: Low-income children who attend Head Start or similar preschool programs are less likely to require special educational services and are more likely to graduate from high school than similar children who have no preschool experience (Lazar, Darlington, Murray, Royce, & Snipper, 1982; McLoyd, 1998a; Schweinhart & Weikart, 1983; Washington & Bailey, 1995). Longer and more intensive programs (e.g., 2 or more years of full-time preschool rather than a single year of part-time schooling), as well as programs in which teachers are well trained and parents are actively involved, yield the greatest benefits (Ramey & Ramey, 1998; Ripple, Gilliam, Chanana, & Zigler, 1999).

Anecdotal evidence also attests to the potential benefits of compensatory education, as illustrated in the following testimonials from Head Start graduates (Mills, 1998):

- Tami Torres is an award-winning boutique owner and community volunteer in Merced, California. She reflects back on her own childhood: "I knew we were poor. I didn't know everybody else was" (Mills, 1998, pp. 170–171). At age 5, she lived below the poverty level, "still loving life," due in part to the care and guidance she received in Head Start. "I am a prime example of why we need the federal Head Start Program" (p. 171).
- Pancho Mansera is a machinist in Santa Maria, California. As an adult, he went to night school to earn his high school diploma, and he now regularly helps his four children do their homework. Through the services of Head Start, he was diagnosed with a treatable thyroid condition. He says that Head Start "gave me a second chance in life. I started living like a normal kid" (p. 163).
- Rachel Jones is a journalist specializing in children's issues. One of 10 children, Rachel remembers going to bed hungry, "longing for the luxury of the hot dogs or Sloppy Joes they served at Head Start and kindergarten" (p. 172). Concerned about the fate of social programs for families, Jones reflects: "[W]hen I think of the smiles, the loving support, the hopeful, helpful moments doled out in a warm, bustling school basement 30 years ago, I know I'd gladly pay an extra dollar of taxes to provide Head Start to someone else's child" (pp. 172–173).

Given the generally positive effects of compensatory education, it is unfortunate that not all needy children are served. In fact, only 30% of eligible 3- to 5-year-old children participate in Head Start (McLoyd, 1998a).

Some educators suggest that quality care and education should be more universally available and start much earlier than age 3. Accordingly, one model program, the Carolina Abecedarian Project, offers services to children of poor families beginning in infancy (Campbell & Ramey, 1994, 1995; Horacek, Ramey, Campbell, Hoffman, & Fletcher, 1987). In one longitudinal experimental study of the program's effectiveness, children were randomly divided into four groups:

1. Those who attended a full-time preschool program from 4 months to 5 years of age
2. Those who received supplementary academic support in the early elementary grades, from age 5 through age 8
3. Those who both attended the preschool program and had supplementary academic support in the early elementary grades
4. Those who participated in neither program (the control group)

Children in all four groups received nutrition and health services, but children in the three treatment groups received educational enrichment as well. The preschool program (for Groups 1 and 3) was designed to stimulate children's motor, cognitive, language, and social skills; beginning at age 3, it also included activities to foster basic prereading and mathematical skills. The supplementary support during the early elementary years (for Groups 2 and 3) involved the services of a resource teacher, who regularly visited the children's homes and provided educational activities tailored to individual needs. Early intervention had a significant effect on cognitive development: Children who attended the preschool program earned higher IQ scores from age 1½ until age 15, and they were less likely to require special educational services, than those who had no early intervention. The effects of the latter, school-age intervention were positive but weaker than the effects of the early childhood intervention.

Other programs supporting children in the early elementary years have been instituted as well (e.g., Reynolds, 1994; Zigler & Muenchow, 1992). Although such programs appear to have positive effects, evaluations of them often lack the tight experimental controls (e.g., random assignment to groups) that make conclusions about cause-effect relationships possible. Increasingly, however, educators are discovering that children make the most progress when interventions begin early (ideally in infancy) and continue throughout the school years. We agree with other educators that it is virtually impossible to inoculate children against impoverished living conditions with just a short intervention (Ramey & Ramey, 1998; Washington & Bailey, 1995).

In considering the potential benefits of compensatory education, educators from middle- and upper-income backgrounds must be careful not to think of children from lower-SES neighborhoods as necessarily being "disadvantaged" or "deprived," nor should they conceptualize compensatory education as providing the "enrichment" that children lack (Bruer, 1999). In fact, children from low-income families often have a great deal of stimulation and many enriching experiences at home. What they lack may simply be *certain kinds* of knowledge and skills—for instance, in language, literacy, mathematics and, later on, perhaps in study skills and reading comprehension—that they need for academic success.

Art by Brandon, age 11.

Effective after-school programs typically offer a variety of activities in which students can pursue their individual interests and develop their unique talents.

Before- and After-School Programs Another way in which neighborhoods and communities contribute to young people's development is through the programs they offer before and after school and during the summer—the clubs, sports leagues, dance and martial arts lessons, scout troops, and so on. Many of these programs are located at public recreation facilities, youth centers, private businesses, and community members' homes. For example, many national organizations (e.g., the YMCA, Boys and Girls Clubs of America, National 4-H Council, and National Association of Police Athletic Leagues) sponsor activities designed to meet the developmental needs of a variety of age levels; such groups also build skills, foster teamwork, and bring young people into regular contact with positive role models (Chaiken, 1998).

Other before- and after-school programs take place on school grounds. At the middle school and secondary level, most of these take the form of *extracurricular activities*, such as clubs and athletic teams. At the elementary level, many take the form of **extended-day programs** that provide supervision, academic support, and recreational activities for children of working parents. With financial aid from federal, state, and local agencies, schools are opening their doors earlier in the morning and closing them later at night, and they are increasingly making their facilities available to students and families on weekends and during the summer (Dryfoos, 1999).

More than 25% of before- and after-school programs are located in school buildings (Dryfoos, 1999). Many are offered by schools themselves; many others are offered by community-based organizations (Dryfoos, 1999; National Center for Education Statistics, 1997). In some cases, schools form partnerships with other community groups to unify services in "community hubs" on school grounds. In one model (the CoZi Schools), school-based centers offer home visits to parents of children from birth to age 3, all-day child care for preschoolers ages 3 to 5, before- and after-school care and vacation care for school-age children, support and education for family members (e.g., home visits, referrals to community services), assistance with nutritional and health needs, and mental health services (Finn-Stevenson & Stern, 1996; Stern & Finn-Stevenson, 1999).

A growing body of research indicates that participation in after-school programs fosters children's cognitive and social-emotional development. For instance, extended-day programs for elementary students can lead to more positive feelings about school, better school attendance, higher school grades and achievement test scores, better classroom behavior, greater conflict resolution skills, and decreased tension with other family members at home (Charles A. Dana Center, 1999; Dryfoos, 1999; Vandell & Pierce, 1999). Summer school programs that focus on remedial or accelerated learning also appear to leave positive marks on students' academic

extended-day program
Before- and after-school programs that provides supervision, academic enrichment, and recreation for children of working parents.

knowledge and skills (Cooper, Charlton, Valentine, & Muhlenbruck, 2000).

Nonacademic programs, too, have clear benefits. For instance, high school students who participate in their school's extracurricular activities are more likely to achieve at high levels and graduate from high school, and they are less likely to smoke, use alcohol or drugs, join gangs, engage in criminal activities, or become teenage parents (Biddle, 1993; Cooper, Valentine, Nye, & Lindsay, 1999; Donato et al., 1997; Eppright, Sanfacon, Beck, & Bradley, 1998; Zill, Nord, & Loomis, 1995). Joining a club or team at school may also give students a productive peer group with which to associate and identify and indirectly promote greater attachment to school (H. Cooper et al., 1999; Zill et al., 1995). High school sports programs may have additional advantages, in that they can foster a team spirit and a willingness to work hard, perform under pressure, and handle wins and losses constructively (Danish, Nellen, & Owens, 1996). And community service projects provide an opportunity for **service learning**, in which children and adolescents gain new knowledge and skills and increased self-confidence while assisting other people or in other ways contributing to the betterment of their community (Sheckley & Keeton, 1997; Stukas, Clary, & Snyder, 1999).

After-school service learning activities foster new skills and enhance self-esteem while also encouraging young people to make productive contributions to their communities.

Effective after-school programs typically have several characteristics (Kerewsky & Lefstein, 1982; Lefstein & Lipsitz, 1995):

- A variety of activities, including recreation, academic and cultural enrichment, and pursuit of individual interests
- Meaningful participation, perhaps through service learning activities in which students practice new skills while giving back to their neighborhoods or communities
- Opportunities for success, perhaps in domains where students have previously unrecognized talents
- Positive interactions with others, through which students form friendships with peers and find appropriate role models or mentors in adults
- Structure and clear limits, with students' active participation in planning and rule setting

In addition, *cultural sensitivity,* while important in all educational settings, is especially so in after-school settings, as students who do not feel welcome will likely opt out of attendance (Cooper, Denner, & Lopez, 1999).

It is important to note that many studies of extracurricular and other after-school activities are correlational in nature, and so it is difficult to determine that participation in them actually *causes* the possible effects that we've listed. An alternative explanation is that students who actively participate in after-school programs are different from those who don't. For example, students who join clubs and athletic teams might be those who feel more positively about their school and who would be unlikely to smoke, use alcohol, or engage in criminal activity even if they didn't join such groups. Despite such misgivings, the potential—and, we suggest, *likely*—benefits of after-school programs certainly merit some investment of time, energy, and financial resources until social scientists sort through causal forces with more certainty.

Self-Care Learning to take care of oneself is a natural part of development. Choosing clothes, getting dressed, preparing snacks and simple meals, deciding what to do with free time, and avoiding dangerous situations are essential developmental tasks. Accordingly, as children grow older, parents, teachers, and other caregivers give them increasing autonomy in tending to their own needs. Children do not always act responsibly when the reigns are loosened, but eventually most do learn to make decisions that assure their safety and physical well-being.

Questions arise, however, about the age at which children can safely engage in **self-care,** looking after themselves before or after school while their parents are away from home. Most parents and child development experts think that the preschool years are too early, yet one in a hundred preschoolers is left alone regularly (Kerrebrock & Lewitt, 1999). Small as this proportion may seem, it indicates that tens of thousands of American preschoolers are frequently left home by themselves.

Self-care is more prevalent once children reach school age. Two national surveys indicate that approximately 12% of children ages 5 to 12 care for themselves at least once a week; this

service learning
Activity that promotes learning and skill development through volunteerism or community service.

self-care
Taking care of one's own needs (cooking, doing chores, etc.) before or after school while parents are at work or otherwise away from home.

Neighborhoods and Communities | 573

figure may underestimate the actual percentage, however, as parents are often reluctant to admit that they leave their children unattended (Kerrebrock & Lewitt, 1999). By adolescence, some self-care is common (Medrich & Marzke, 1991).

Why do parents leave their children unattended? Many work, cannot afford after-school care, have children who resist having babysitters or attending daycare centers, or are unaware of other options (Belle, 1999). While at work, many parents worry: What do their children really do in their absence? Are they safe? Is it legal to leave them alone? As one single-mother mother with an 8-year-old at home put it, "All I do after 3:00 is worry" (Belle, 1999, p. 52).

Parents do have reason to worry about leaving their children home alone. In caring for themselves, young children are not always safety-minded. They may put themselves at risk by leaving a hot stove unattended, opening the door to strangers, getting into fights with siblings, and in other ways making poor decisions. (At age 12, Teresa's son Connor once took a nap while babysitting his 5-year-old brother.) Older children and adolescents, who have greater mobility in the community, face additional temptations in the form of unhealthful or illegal activities with unsupervised age-mates. For instance, about half of all juvenile crime takes place after school hours, between 2:00 P.M. and 8:00 P.M. (Fox & Newman, 1997; Sickmund, Snyder, & Poe-Yamagata, 1997).

Correlational studies indicate that self-care may have some negative effects (yet remember that correlational studies do not conclusively show cause-effect relationships). On average, children who spend considerable time in self-care in the early elementary grades show poorer academic performance and social skills, as well as more behavior problems, than children who are more closely supervised in the early years (Pettit, Laird, Bates, & Dodge, 1997; Vandell & Posner, 1999). Studies addressing the potential impact of self-care have not always found negative effects, however (Vandell & Shumow, 1999). Some children may, in fact, *benefit* from caring for themselves, in that they have an opportunity to develop self-regulatory skills such as establishing a self-care routine, buckling down to do homework without parental prodding, and cooperating with siblings to complete household chores.

Children are more likely to succeed in self-care when their parents maintain regular contact with them about their activities and whereabouts (Galambos & Maggs, 1991; Goyette-Ewing, in press; Pettit, Bates, Dodge, & Meece, 1999; Steinberg, 1986). They are more likely to negotiate the challenges of self-care when they are socially outgoing and emotionally well-adjusted and when they can take minor frustrations in stride (Goyette-Ewing & Knoebber, 1999).

Although children and adolescents in self-care are ostensibly on their own, in fact neighborhood and community contexts influence the success of such arrangements. For instance, some residential areas may include many caring adults who are at home during the day and keep an eye on their younger neighbors, whereas other areas may offer the company of only drug dealers and adolescent gangs during the daytime hours. Although any neighborhood offers potential dangers for unsupervised children and adolescents, low-income urban neighborhoods are particularly prone to them. Thus, children from low-income families who engage in self-care for part of the day often feel afraid and socially isolated (Long & Long, 1982; Marshall, White, Keefe, & Marx, 1999; Zill, 1983). Furthermore, they are more likely than unattended children from high-income families to show aggression and delinquent behavior in later years (Meece, Colwell, and Pettit, 1999).

Community agencies provide valuable backup services for children who arrive home before their parents do. For instance, homework hotlines, often staffed by parents or other volunteers, offer assistance when children encounter difficulty with classroom assignments. Phone calls to police stations, poison control centers, and 911 can bring rapid assistance or advice when emergencies arise.

Part-time Employment Particularly in the high school years, many adolescents take on part-time jobs in their local communities. Such jobs have both advantages and disadvantages, as the following interview with 17-year-old Jeremy illustrates:

Adult: You've been working at the local grocery store for almost 2 years now. In what ways has it been worthwhile?

Jeremy: Oh, lots of ways. Real-world experience. The money, of course. Interaction with people, both customers and coworkers, in a setting other than school.

ENHANCING STUDENTS' BEFORE- AND AFTER-SCHOOL EXPERIENCES

■ Help children navigate transitions between school and daycare.

After school, a kindergarten teacher walks out with children to make sure that each one successfully connects with family members or car pool drivers, gets on the appropriate bus, or begins walking home.

■ Inform parents and guardians about out-of-school programs in your area.

At a parent-teacher-student conference, a middle school teacher describes clubs and sports programs at school, as well as recreational opportunities in the local community.

■ Sponsor after-school clubs at your school.

A high school Spanish teacher organizes a Hispanic Cultures Club after school. She encourages students to speak only in Spanish but allows them to choose their own group activities—possibly cooking, discussing Spanish literature, or translating the school newsletter into Spanish.

■ Be explicit about students' homework assignments, and provide sufficient support and guidance to allow students to complete them independently.

When a high school mathematics teacher gives homework assignments, she also cross-references each assignment to the textbook pages that provide explanations for the concepts and problems in question.

■ Encourage parents to set limits on their children's television viewing and to watch and talk about TV programs with their children.

In a newsletter to students and their families, a third-grade teacher includes "TV Tips" that outline the educational uses and benefits of television.

	It broadens my network of connections with other people. Development of social skills, teamwork, leadership skills.
Adult:	Is there a downside to working while you're still in school?
Jeremy:	Sometimes it's hard to get everything done, in schoolwork and in personal stuff I have to do. Also, sometimes it conflicts with other activities I'd rather do.
Adult:	Has it been a good experience overall?
Jeremy:	Definitely. I have more friends and acquaintances because of it. I have more real-world experience. I feel I'm better prepared for going off to college or another job.

At the time of this interview, Jeremy had a 3.1 grade-point-average in a challenging high school curriculum, maintained a good relationship with his parents, was active in French Club and service activities at school, and went skiing with a friend every Saturday—all while working about 15 hours a week as a cashier at the grocery store.

Not all teens juggle the multiple demands of work, school, home, and a social life as successfully as Jeremy, however. Research on the potential effects of students' employment and work experience has been somewhat inconclusive, perhaps in part because group averages mask the effects that individual teenagers' ability levels, temperaments, and inclinations are likely to have. Many employed adolescents learn to be responsible: They get to work on time, adhere to required procedures and standards of the job, and use their wages judiciously. However, employment can also adversely affect adolescents' grade-point-averages, decrease their attachment to school, and increase high-risk behaviors such as substance abuse (Charner & Fraser, 1988; Steinberg, Brown, Cider, Kaczmarek, & Lazzaro, 1988). Limiting work commitments to a maximum of 15 to 20 hours per week seems to minimize the possibility for such negative effects (Mortimer, Finch, Seongryeol, Shanahan, & McCall, 1993; Steinberg et al., 1988).

As you have seen in the last few pages, people and institutions in the immediate neighborhood and community have numerous influences, both positive and negative, on children's development and well-being. In fact, people across the nation and even across the world can influence growing children. The *media*—television, films, popular music, books, newspapers, and so on—provide one means through which they do so. The media are the final context for development that we consider in this chapter.

The Media

Television, films, radio, music, books, magazines, computers, the Internet—all of these give children and adolescents many options for entertainment, education, and communication. Such media permeate young people's lives both inside and outside of formal school settings.

To some extent, children's minds are shaped by the messages that the media present. For instance, persuasive advertisements may influence their activities and eating habits; we recall our own children (and ourselves many years earlier) being absolutely certain that they (or we) would just *die* if they (we) didn't acquire a particular toy, game, breakfast cereal, or soft drink. Furthermore, children encounter certain social messages quite routinely in the television shows, books, and magazines they peruse and in the song lyrics they listen to. Some of these messages (e.g., "Treat your neighbor as you yourself would like to be treated," "Every citizen should vote") are certainly beneficial, in that they promote prosocial behavior, citizenship, and other responsible actions, but others (e.g., "Violence resolves interpersonal conflicts," "Sexual promiscuity is safe and commonplace") give tacit approval to behaviors that are not in children's and adolescents' best interests. The media may also convey or perpetuate stereotypes about particular groups of people. For instance, television shows often cast members of racial minority groups in bad-guy roles and portray female characters as weak and passive, and academic textbooks more often portray men than women engaging in math and science (Eisenberg et al., 1996; Huston et al., 1992).

Yet children's and adolescents' own actions and thoughts mediate the effects that communication technologies and other media are likely to have. For example, most young people have considerable choice about the television programs they watch and actively interpret the content they view (Huston & Wright, 1998). As a high school student, Jeanne's son Jeff was an avid viewer of *The Simpsons,* an animated cartoon series that depicts a decidedly dysfunctional American family. Jeff certainly did not model Homer Simpson's alcoholic tendencies, Bart Simpson's delinquent activities, or Krusty the Clown's inappropriate interactions with children; he merely laughed at the characters' antics and found pleasure in the show's biting social and political commentary.

In this section we review research related to two forms of media: television and computers. We then consider some things that teachers can do to take advantage of the benefits that the media have to offer.

Television

On average, television viewing time increases rapidly during early childhood, continues to increase in middle childhood and early adolescence (reaching a peak of almost 4 hours a day), and then declines gradually after about age 14 (Comstock, 1991; Medrich, Roizen, Rubin, & Buckley, 1982; Timmer, Eccles, & O'Brien, 1985). Children vary greatly in their television viewing habits, however: Some are glued to their TV sets for several hours a day while others rarely if ever watch television.

Television's increasing prominence in daily life has led many parents, teachers, and social activists to wonder about its possible negative effects on children and adolescents. They voice concerns not only about the graphic depictions of violence and sexual activity but also about the sheer number of hours that children spend watching TV. Consider this episode in Chris Zajac's fifth-grade classroom:

> One Monday morning Chris asked Jimmy what time he went to bed last night. Jimmy, whose eyes looked glassy, with little bags beneath them, said he didn't know. Well, said Chris, what time did the last show he watched on TV begin?
> Jimmy said eleven-thirty.
> "Eleven-thirty?" she cried.
> Yeah, said Jimmy, but it was special, a really good movie called *Cobra.*
> Mrs. Zajac had just started in on her usual speech about bedtimes, the I-don't-care-what-show-it-was-eleven-thirty's-too-late-even-Mrs.-Zajac-can't-stay-up-*that*-late lecture, when from the class rose several other voices.
> "I saw that!"
> "Yeah, bro, that was fresh!"

"Remember that part where the guy . . ."

"This is what I'm up against," said Chris, slowly turning her head from one child to the other to make sure each got to see her stupefied look. (Kidder, 1989, pp. 40–41)

In the following sections we look both at television's possible negative effects and at its potential benefits for children's development.

What Harm Does Television Do and *Not* Do? Researchers have found that, over all, television viewing is not necessarily a bad thing but that certain kinds of programs can have detrimental effects. Let's examine several common questions about the effects of television and the answers that emerge from the research.

■ *Does television take time away from more productive activities?* Apparently not. In fact, the activities that seem most displaced by television are going to the movies and listening to the radio (Huston & Wright, 1998). Contrary to many people's assumptions, television does not interfere directly with time that would otherwise be spent reading. In the United States, leisure reading time averages about 15 minutes per day, an amount that has remained constant since 1945 (Neuman, 1991).

■ *Does television interfere with academic achievement?* For most children, no. Synthesizing the results of numerous studies, Huston and Wright (1998) concluded that watching television does not significantly interfere with school achievement, except at very high levels of exposure—for instance, when students watch TV more than 4 hours a day or more than 30 hours a week, as some of Chris Zajac's students apparently did. *Extensive* television viewing may also inhibit the development of reading skills, although other factors—such as family background, exposure to print, and time spent doing homework—are far more influential factors in reading development (Huston & Wright, 1998; Ritchie, Price, & Roberts, 1987).

■ *Does television stifle imagination and breed mental passivity?* Not for most children. Contrary to public perceptions, children do not become "lumps on a log" when viewing television. They actively interpret programs, can identify underlying themes, and show good recall for what they've seen (Huston & Wright, 1998). Nor does television automatically dampen children's imagination and creativity. However, the content of the programs they watch does seem to influence their imagination. In particular, children who watch a lot of violence on television engage in less fantasy play than children who view little or no violence (Van der Voort & Valkenburg, 1994).

■ *Does television make children distractible?* Again, not really. Many educators believe that television's quick pace and frequent change of topics impair children's ability to attend thoughtfully and patiently to classroom lessons. However, there is no systematic evidence to support this assertion (Huston & Wright, 1998). For example, children who watch *Sesame Street,* which consists of many short segments, have been generally perceived by teachers to adjust well to the classroom setting (Wright & Huston, 1995).

■ *Do children mistake television for reality?* Perhaps television's most negative impact resides in the content of its messages. Television often portrays people in ways that are arguably inappropriate. Television characters have been described as aggressive, stereotyped in gender and ethnic roles, and sexually active with partners they know only casually and with whom they do not use protective measures (Huston & Wright, 1998; Signorielli & Lears, 1992).

Children and adolescents do show some understanding that television's social world is artificial. For instance, adolescents in grades 8 through 12 understand that sexual behavior on television does not mirror sexual behavior in everyday life (Silverman-Watkins & Sprafkin, 1983). They realize that the probability of having sex with someone one has just met is higher on television than in real life and that the negative consequences of unprotected sexual activity (e.g., an unwanted pregnancy or contraction of a sexually transmitted disease) are rarely shown on TV. Despite such understandings, children and adolescents can still be influenced by television's social content, especially when they are heavy viewers (Huston & Wright, 1998).

■ *Does television lead to more aggression?* Although research results have not been 100% consistent, the general picture they paint makes us pause. Repeated exposure to violent acts on television seems to make children more aggressive, and it may be particularly harmful to those already predisposed to be aggressive (Andison, 1977; Eron, 1980; Hearold, 1986; Paik & Comstock, 1994; Van der Voort & Valkenburg, 1994; Wood, Wong, & Chachere, 1991). In other words, young children inclined to solve conflicts in physically aggressive ways may choose to watch programs that are particularly violent in content, and they become even more aggressive after viewing televised violence. Realistic violence seems to be more influential than the violence depicted in cartoons, though the latter appears to have an effect as well (Huston & Wright, 1998).

How Can Television Benefit Children? With its engaging combination of visual and auditory stimuli, television has tremendous potential for positively impacting children's learning and development (Comstock, 1991; Huston & Wright, 1998). It can be effective in teaching basic skills, knowledge of current and historical events, understanding and problem solving in science and mathematics, and appreciation for literature, music, drama, and art. It can also promote greater awareness of the practices, language, and music of diverse cultures. For example, *Sesame Street* helps children learn their letters and numbers (Comstock, 1991; Huston & Wright, 1998). *Barney & Friends* promotes understanding of emotions, manners, nature, health, and cultural differences (D. G. Singer & Singer, 1994; J. L. Singer & Singer, 1994). *Reading Rainbow* piques interest in children's literature (RMC Research Corporation, 1989). Other programs have been found to enhance knowledge and attitudes about science and mathematics (Bennett, Debold, & Solan, 1991; Chen, 1984; Hall, Esty, & Fisch, 1990).

Unfortunately, the vast majority of content on commercial television is *not* educational; those segments that do have educational value most often focus on natural and social science (Neapolitan & Huston, 1994). Furthermore, most families do little to steer children toward educational programming. In fact, parents rarely monitor or guide their children's viewing, nor do they sit down and watch television with their children (Comstock, 1991; Huston & Wright, 1998). Parents can use V-chip technology, as well as editing devices, to screen unwanted content, but few take advantage of this service. (Teresa confesses that her son Connor, then 12, showed *her* how to use the V-chip system).

Although television is rarely used in schools and daycare centers (Huston & Wright, 1998), it *can* be used productively in educational settings. For example, the benefits of watching *Barney & Friends* are greatest when preschool teachers plan classroom activities that build on what children learn from the program (D. G. Singer & Singer, 1994; J. L. Singer & Singer, 1994). Some distributors of educational programs offer suggestions for lesson plans and supplementary curriculum materials that complement what children see on television.[11]

Teachers must choose their selections carefully, however. One controversial program is *Channel One,* a program broadcast directly to middle and high schools that consists of 10 minutes of news and 2 minutes of advertisements (Huston & Wright, 1998; Wartella, 1995). Students seem to gain knowledge of current events, but the advertisements influence their preferences for commercial products and may encourage them to become more avid consumers (Brand & Greenberg, 1994).

In industrialized societies, another medium is gaining increasing prominence in many children's lives and, we suspect, is partly replacing television as a source of both entertainment and information. That medium is the computer.

Computers and the Internet

Personal computers and their progeny seem to be just about everywhere these days—in homes, schools, preschools, libraries, shopping malls, airports, and even coffee shops. Computer technologies are changing the ways that adults communicate, make decisions, spend money, and entertain themselves. Children and adolescents follow suit and in many cases actually lead the pack.

One form of computer technology—video games—is a popular source of entertainment among American youth, especially boys between 5 and 12 (Huston & Wright, 1998). Video game systems can be found in many homes, and youngsters spend many hours clutching a

---

[11]For examples, check out the following Websites: PBS (http://www.pbs.org), Discovery Channel (http://school.discovery.com), and Nickelodeon (http://www.teachers.nick.com).

controller as they engage in virtual karate matches, motorcycle races, and explorations of mythical environments. Although these games may foster sensorimotor and spatial-visual skills (Greenfield, 1994b), those with violent content may desensitize children to violence and increase aggressive behavior (Cocking & Greenfield, 1996; Gailey, 1993; Irwin & Gross, 1995). Some social critics worry that video games are replacing social play, but it has been our observation as parents that children remain very social in their use of video games: They often share games with friends, watch one another in (virtual) action, compete with or against one another using two or more controllers, and eventually move on to other forms of recreation.

Other uses of the computer are more beneficial than video games, however (Huston & Wright, 1998). Many computer programs make challenging cognitive demands and require considerable planning and strategy (Greenfield, 1994b). They can also be highly motivating. For instance, when her son Alex was 4, Teresa would routinely find him on the computer when she picked him up at his daycare center, and Alex would insist on finishing what he was doing before they went home. Computers have an additional advantage in that, unlike television, communication goes two ways (not only from computer to child, but also from child to computer), and so children can see the immediate effects of their actions. However, such interactivity does not always enhance learning, as the images and sounds that the computer produces may captivate children more than the academic skills that program writers intend for them to master (Huston & Wright, 1998).

To date, little research has been conducted on the effects of young people's use of Internet communication and resources. Considerable anecdotal evidence indicates that children and adolescents use the Internet both for beneficial academic and social purposes (e.g., finding data on the World Wide Web for research papers, keeping in touch with friends through e-mail messages) and for ventures into controversial and forbidden terrain (e.g., surfing racist Websites, downloading pornographic images). Thus, computers and the Internet are a mixed bag:

> The new technologies, like television itself, have been exploited to deliver entertainment of questionable taste and value at considerable cost to children and profit to the industry. The vast educational and prosocial potentials of the media have been touched, sampled, proved valuable, but not yet developed to even a fraction of that potential. (Huston & Wright, 1998, p. 1027)

Educational Implications of Mass Media and Computers

Television, computers, and other media have tremendous potential for educating children. You may hope, as we do, that corporate sponsors of television programming will increasingly support programs that are educational as well as captivating. In addition, we offer the following suggestions:

■ *Encourage parents to regulate and monitor their children's television viewing.* At school meetings and in newsletters home, teachers can encourage parents to set specific TV-viewing goals for their children. For instance, if parents find their children watching television 4 or more hours a day, they might want to set a 2-hour limit. Parents also may find it helpful and informative to watch television with their children. In the process, they can discover how their children interpret what they watch and provide a reality check when characters and story lines consistently violate norms for appropriate behavior ("Do you think people should really insult one another like that?").

■ *Teach critical viewing skills.* In the classroom, teachers can teach students how to watch television and surf the Internet with a critical eye. Preschool teachers can help young children understand that television commercials are designed to persuade them to buy toys and hamburgers. Teachers of older children and adolescents may point out more subtle advertising ploys, such as the use of color, images (e.g., sexual symbols), and endorsements by famous actors and athletes. As students begin to use the Internet for classroom activities, teachers should give guidance for evaluating the quality of information on the World Wide Web (e.g., data provided by government agencies and well-known nonprofit organizations are fairly reliable, but opinion pieces on someone's personal home page may not be). And for any medium—television, computers, books, magazines, and so on—teachers can help students become more aware and critical of stereotypes and negative portrayals of men and women, ethnic groups, and various professions.

Growing Up in Context at Different Age Levels

DEVELOPMENTAL TRENDS

AGE	WHAT YOU MIGHT OBSERVE	DIVERSITY	IMPLICATIONS
Early Childhood (2–6) 	• Strong motivation to learn the physical tools of one's culture (e.g., writing implements, computers) • Emerging but rudimentary understandings of gender and ethnic differences and of variations in religious practice • For many children, attendance at group child-care or home-care settings	• Children differ in their prior knowledge- and skill-building experiences (e.g., storybook reading, visits to zoos and museums, travel to distant places). • Children celebrate holidays and birthdays differently depending on their families' cultural backgrounds. • Some children need extra reassurance from child-care providers when saying good-bye to parents in the morning.	• Show respect for diverse backgrounds and perspectives (e.g., talk about the "holiday season" rather than Christmas). • Identify and build on the strengths that children from various cultural, religious, and socioeconomic backgrounds are likely to have. • Provide age-appropriate access to various media (books, computer programs, etc.).
Middle Childhood (6–10) 	• Increasing interest about people's differing cultural and religious beliefs and practices. • Increasing responsibility in decision making and self-care.	• Some children are more understanding and respectful than others of classmates' backgrounds and income levels. • Some children can care for themselves responsibly, whereas others do not know or follow basic safety guidelines.	• Model and encourage respect for diverse practices and beliefs. • Incorporate multiple perspectives into the curriculum (e.g., in literature, history, music, art). • Provide a variety of activities and after-school programs so that all students can find enrichment and success in at least one activity.

■ *Use televised movies and computer programs that build on instructional units at school.* When chosen wisely, television programs and videos can often make classroom content more concrete and understandable. For instance, when Teresa and a group of sixth and seventh graders read George Bernard Shaw's play *Pygmalion* during a "Great Books" discussion, they often struggled to decipher certain characters' dialect. Afterward, the group watched segments of *My Fair Lady,* a movie based on the play, and found the dialect much easier to understand. Furthermore, the play's and movie's different endings provoked considerable discussion.

■ *Increase students' familiarity and comfort with computers.* Although many middle- and upper-income families now have personal computers, most lower-income families cannot afford them. But as we look to the future, we anticipate that computer expertise, including Internet use, will be increasingly critical for *everyone's* success in the adult world. Teachers at all levels and in all subject areas can find ways to incorporate computers and the Internet into classroom lessons and activities. For instance, a preschool teacher might teach children how to play computer games that give practice in basic skills in prereading and arithmetic. An elementary school teacher might show students how to track the path of a hurricane using government weather maps. A high school physical education teacher might provide Internet Web sites where students can find rules and regulations for soccer, basketball, or racquetball.

■ *Encourage use of a wide range of media.* Television is the primary medium, and in some cases the *only* medium, through which many children and adolescents gain news and information about their region and country. Ideally, students should learn to use the many other media available to them—not only the Internet but also books, newspapers, and newsmagazines—to gain the knowledge and skills they will need in the adult world.

AGE	WHAT YOU MIGHT OBSERVE	DIVERSITY	IMPLICATIONS
Early Adolescence (10–14)	• Increasing identification with a particular ethnic group • Increasing ability to care for oneself; increasing independence from adult supervision • More time spent watching television and playing video games than in early or middle childhood	• Members of minority groups are more likely than members of the mainstream culture to form a strong ethnic identity (Phinney, 1989). • Some members of minority groups may see academic achievement in a negative light (i.e., as acting white). • With their increasing independence, some young adolescents come into contact with deviant adults and peers in their neighborhoods. • Some students have few constructive after-school activities and resources in their neighborhoods.	• Stress the relevance of school subject matter for people from all backgrounds. • Let young adolescents make choices about some of their activities in after-school groups (Eccles, 1999). • Let young adolescents help establish goals and rules for their after-school clubs and programs. • Make regular use of newspaper and newsmagazine articles when exploring classroom topics.
Late Adolescence (14–18)	• Increasing opportunities to explore the community and nearby cities independently of parents and other family members • Gradual decline in television viewing • Greater skill in accessing and exploring the Internet	• Some teenagers participate regularly in community activities (e.g., employment, public service activities); others rarely venture far from home in the after-school hours. • Students differ considerably in their knowledge about and access to computers.	• Collaborate with community agencies to offer opportunities for career exploration and public service. • Encourage students to use online sources to supplement rather than replace libraries and other traditional sources of information.

Effects of Context: The Big Picture

The contexts in which children grow—their immediate families, their neighborhoods, their communities and cultural groups, and the world at large—affect children in different ways, depending on children's personalities, talents, and abilities, as well as on their developmental levels. The Developmental Trends table above illustrates some of the ways that children in different age groups may respond to the various contexts in which they find themselves.

One theme that has pervaded the book, and especially this chapter, is the considerable diversity that exists in children's thoughts, beliefs, behaviors, and needs. A related theme, most prominent in this chapter, is the inequity in the resources and opportunities available to different children. Some children and their families enjoy considerable freedom and choice in the neighborhoods in which they live, in the educational and recreational activities of which they can partake, and in the schools that the children attend. Others have fewer choices and encounter significant challenges: possibly poverty, discrimination, maltreatment, or neglect.

How can educators make sense of the profound differences that characterize students' lives? Like all human beings, teachers have a tendency to see their own way of living as being normal and appropriate and to see departures from this lifestyle as being aberrant or inferior. For instance, they may perceive a student who frequently interrupts others as being "rude," when in fact the student is simply eager to get involved in discussions. They may think of a student who rarely completes homework as "lazy," when actually the student wishes she could finish her assignments but doesn't have the knowledge, skills, and outside resources to do so. They may perceive the student in shabby clothes to be "neglected," when in reality the student is a resilient young man successfully rising to meet and overcome the exceptional challenges of poverty.

Theorists and researchers, too, impose their cultural biases on their exploration and interpretation of children's behavior and the contexts in which children grow. With few exceptions, developmentalists focus on the experiences and developmental trends of middle-income, European and American children and portray such children's behaviors and accomplishments as being the norm. When we read about ethnic minority children in the research literature, we learn a great deal about risk factors but all too little about strengths and resiliency.

Overcoming the biases and ways of thinking inherent in one's own culture is not easy. Yet it is essential if teachers and other practitioners are going to offer maximally beneficial experiences and support for growing children and adolescents. Teaching in a developmentally appropriate fashion means, ultimately, communicating a message of hope and optimism to *all* children and adolescents.

CASE STUDY: FRANK

In *Angela's Ashes,* Frank McCourt (1996) describes what it was like to be a small child in Ireland dealing with hunger, cold, inadequate housing, health problems, an alcoholic father, and an overwhelming sense of personal responsibility for his family.

[12]I wish I could swing up into the sky, up into the clouds. I might be able to fly around the whole world and not hear my brothers, Oliver and Eugene, cry in the middle of the night anymore. My mother says they're always hungry. She cries in the middle of the night, too. She says she's worn out nursing and feeding and changing and four boys is too much for her. She wishes she had one little girl all for herself. She'd give anything for one little girl. . . . (p. 22)

My mother tells me all the time, Never, never leave that playground except to come home. But what am I to do with the twins bawling with the hunger in the pram? I tell Malachy I'll be back in a minute. I make sure no one is looking, grab a bunch of bananas outside the Italian grocery shop and run down Myrtle Avenue, away from the playground, around the block and back to the other end where there's a hole in the fence. We push the pram to a dark corner and peel the bananas for the twins. There are five bananas in the bunch and we feast on them in the dark corner. The twins slobber and chew and spread banana over their faces, their hair, their clothes. I realize then that questions will be asked. Mam will want to know why the twins are smothered in bananas, where did you get them? I can't tell her about the Italian shop on the corner. I will have to say, A man. . . . (p. 32)

Dad and Mam lay at the head of the bed, Malachy and I at the bottom, the twins wherever they could find comfort. Malachy made us laugh again. Ye, ye, ye, he said, and oy oy oy, and then fell asleep. Mam made the link hink hink snore sound that told us she was sleeping. In the moonlight I could look up the length of the bed and see Dad still awake and when Oliver cried in his sleep Dad reached for him and held him. Whishst, he said. Whisht.

Then Eugene sat up, screaming, tearing at himself. Ah, ah, Mommy, Mommy. Dad sat up. What's up son? Eugene went on crying and when Dad leaped up from the bed and turned on the gaslight we saw the fleas, leaping, jumping, fastened to our flesh. We slapped at them and slapped but they hopped from body to body, hopping, biting. We tore at the bites till they bled. We jumped from the bed, the twins crying, Mam moaning. . . . (p. 59)

I'm seven, eight, nine going on ten and still Dad has no work. He drinks his tea in the morning, signs for the dole at the Labour Exchange, reads the papers at the Carnegie Library, goes for his long walks far into the country. If he gets a job at the Limerick Cement Company or Rank's Flour Mills he loses it in the third week. He loses it because he goes to the pubs on the third Friday of the job, drinks all his wages and misses the half day of work on Saturday morning. . . . (p. 145)

You never know when you might come home and find Mam sitting by the fire chatting with a woman and a child, strangers. Always a woman and a child. Mam finds them wandering the streets and if they ask, Could you spare a few pennies, Miss? Her heart breaks. She never has money so she invites them home for tea and a bit of friend break and if it's a bad night she'll let them sleep by the fire on a pile of rags in the corner. The bread she gives them always means less for us and if we complain she says there are always people worse off and we can surely spare a little from what we have. (p. 273)

Having read these descriptions of Frank's childhood, you may wonder what transformed a poor child into the witty and successful author that Frank has become. What kind of education did Frank have? Did he have warm and sympathetic teachers? Did they help him build his confidence? We peek back into his school experiences looking for answers.

Mr. O'Neill is the master in the fourth class at school. We call him Dotty because he's small like a dot. He teaches in the one classroom with a platform so that he can stand above us and threaten us with his ash plant and peel his apple for all to see. The first day of school in September he writes on

[12]Extracts reprinted with the permission of Scribner, a Division of Simon & Schuster, Inc., from *Angela's Ashes* by Frank McCourt. Copyright © 1996 by Frank McCourt.

the blackboard three words which are to stay there for the rest of the year, Euclid, geometry, idiot. Now, repeat after me, Anyone who doesn't understand the theorems of Euclid is an idiot. Of course we all know what an idiot is because that's what the masters keep telling us we are.

Brendan Quigley raises his hand. Sir, what's a theorem and what's a Euclid?

We expect Dotty to lash at Brendan the way all masters do when you ask them a question but he looks at Brendan with a little smile. Ah, now, here's a boy with not one but two questions. What is your name, boy?

Brendan Quigley, sir.

This is a boy who will go far. Where will he go, boys?

Far, sir.

Indeed and he will. The boy who wants to know something about the grace, elegance and beauty of Euclid can go nowhere but up. In what direction and no other can this boy go, boys?

Up, sir.

Without Euclid, boys, mathematics would be a poor doddering thing. Without Euclid we wouldn't be able to go from here to there. Without Euclid the bicycle would have no wheel. Without Euclid St. Joseph could not have been a carpenter for carpentry is geometry and geometry is carpentry. Without Euclid this very school could never have been built. (McCourt, 1996, pp. 151–152)

- In what ways were daily hardship, poverty, and injustice part of Frank's education? How are Frank's experiences similar to what you've read in this chapter about children who live in poverty?
- How might Frank have used his peers as a source of social support?
- Frank eventually became a successful author. From what you learned about resiliency in this chapter, how might you explain his success?

SUMMARY

Culture and Ethnicity

Children's cultural heritage helps them to derive meaning from their interactions with their physical and social worlds. Membership in a particular cultural or ethnic group gives them values, beliefs, and traditions that influence their daily behaviors both in and outside of school; it may also become an important part of children's sense of identity. Depending on the circumstances, children from minority groups may embrace mainstream culture, find a workable balance between their own roots and mainstream practices, or reject mainstream ideals.

History

The significant social and political events that occur during childhood and adolescence affect children's knowledge, skills, motives, attitudes, priorities, and goals. War, peace, famine, prosperity, the destructive forces of nature, technological advances—these and many other aspects of history influence children's development from one generation to the next, and from one region of the world to another.

Religious Affiliation

Religion, like culture, helps children impose meaning on their lives. Initially, children's religious beliefs are quite concrete in nature but in other ways tend to be similar to those of their parents. Adolescents form more abstract notions and begin to question the religious ideas and practices that their elders have handed down to them.

Socioeconomic Status

Economic well-being affects the availability of many resources and influences families' decisions about where they live and what schools their children will attend. Children whose families live in poverty face numerous challenges, possibly including poor nutrition and health care, inadequate housing, gaps in background knowledge, increased risk for physical and mental disabilities, emotional stress, low-quality schools, and public misconceptions and disdain. Nevertheless, many children and adolescents are resilient to such environmental insults (particularly if they have one or more supportive people in their lives) and grow to be successful, productive adults.

Neighborhoods and Communities

Neighborhoods and communities affect children directly in the role models and peer groups they provide, as well indirectly in the social and emotional support they offer families. Neighborhoods and communities contribute in significant ways to children's care and development—for instance, in the daycare centers, preschools, after-school programs, and employment opportunities they provide and in the agencies, hotlines, and other services they offer.

The Media

Many children and adolescents spend a good deal of their after-school hours watching television and playing or working on the computer. Television, computers, and other media have considerable potential for fostering children's cognitive development, but their benefits have not yet been fully realized.

Now go to our Companion Website to assess your understanding of chapter content with Multiple-Choice Questions, apply comprehension in Essay Questions, and broaden your knowledge with links to related Developmental Psychology World Wide Web sites.

KEY CONCEPTS

culture (p. 540)
ethnicity (p. 541)
acculturation (p. 543)
assimilation (p. 543)
selective adoption (p. 544)
rejection (of a new culture) (p. 544)
bicultural orientation (p. 544)
ethnic identity (p. 546)
cultural frame of reference (p. 546)

voluntary minority group (p. 546)
involuntary minority group (p. 546)
oppositional frame of reference (p. 546)
multicultural education (p. 552)
history (p. 554)
socioeconomic status (SES) (p. 558)

resiliency (p. 561)
daycare (p. 568)
compensatory education (p. 570)
extended-day program (p. 572)
service learning (p. 573)
self-care (p. 573)

GLOSSARY

accommodation Dealing with a new event by either modifying an existing scheme or forming a new one.

acculturation Taking on the customs and values of a new culture.

achievement motivation Need for excellence for its own sake, without regard for any external rewards that one's accomplishments might bring.

action research Systematic study of an issue or problem in one's own situation, with the goal of bringing about more productive outcomes as a result of the research.

actual developmental level Extent to which one can successfully perform a task independently.

adaptation Developmental process of responding to the environment in an increasingly effective manner.

adaptive behavior Behavior related to daily living skills and appropriate conduct in social situations.

addiction Physical and psychological dependence on a substance, such that increasing quantities must be taken to produce a desired effect and withdrawal produces adverse physiological and psychological effects.

African American English Dialect of some African American communities that includes some pronunciations, grammatical constructions, and idioms different from those of Standard English.

aggressive behavior Action intentionally taken to hurt another, either physically or psychologically.

alleles Genes located at the same point on corresponding (paired) chromosomes and related to the same physical characteristic.

androgyny Tendency to have some characteristics that are stereotypically "female" (e.g., nurturance) and others that are stereotypically "male" (e.g., assertiveness).

anorexia nervosa Eating disorder in which a person, in an attempt to be thin, eats little or nothing for weeks or months and seriously jeopardizes health.

anxiety Emotional state characterized by worry and apprehension.

anxiety disorder Chronic emotional condition characterized by excessive, debilitating worry.

apprenticeship Situation in which a person works intensively with an expert to learn how to accomplish complex tasks.

assimilation In Piaget's theory, dealing with a new event in a way that is consistent with an existing scheme (Ch. 4). Also, a form of acculturation that involves totally embracing a new culture, abandoning one's previous culture in the process (Ch. 14).

attachment An enduring emotional tie uniting one person to another.

attention-deficit hyperactivity disorder (ADHD) Disability (probably biological in origin) characterized by inattention and/or hyperactivity and impulsive behavior.

attribution Belief about the cause of one's success or failure.

authentic activity Classroom activity similar to one that a student might encounter in the outside world.

authoritarian parenting Parenting style characterized by strict expectations for behavior and rigid rules that children are expected to obey without question.

authoritative parenting Parenting style characterized by emotional warmth, high expectations and standards for behavior, consistent enforcement of rules, explanations of the reasons behind these rules, and the inclusion of children in decision making.

autism Disability (probably biological in origin) characterized by infrequent social interaction, communication impairments, repetitive behaviors, narrowly focused interests, and a strong need for a predictable environment.

automatization Process of becoming able to respond quickly and efficiently while mentally processing or physically performing certain tasks.

axon Armlike part of a neuron that sends information to other neurons.

babbling Universal tendency for human beings to produce speechlike sounds in infancy.

behavioral learning perspective Theoretical perspective that focuses on environmental stimuli and learning processes that lead to developmental change.

behaviorism Theoretical perspective in which behavior is described and explained in terms of specific stimulus-response relationships.

bicultural orientation Ability to behave in accordance with two different cultural frameworks in appropriate contexts.

bilingual education Approach to second-language instruction in which students are instructed in academic subject areas in their native language while simultaneously being taught to speak and write in the second language.

bilingualism Knowing and speaking two languages fluently.

bipolar disorder Condition characterized by cyclical mood swings, including periods of elation (mania) and periods of deep depression.

blended family Family created when one parent-child(ren) family structure combines with another parent figure and any children in his or her custody.

bulimia Eating disorder in which a person, in an attempt to be thin, eats a large amount of food and then purposefully purges it from the body by vomiting or taking laxatives.

bully Child who repeatedly pesters and humiliates other children, with a particular focus on certain victims.

canalization Tight genetic control of a particular aspect of development.

care orientation Focus on nurturance and concern for others in moral decision making.

causal-comparative study Research study in which relationships are identified between existing conditions in children's lives and one or more aspects of the children's behavior.

central conceptual structure Integrated network of concepts and cognitive processes that forms the basis for much of one's thinking, reasoning, and learning in specific content domains.

central executive Component of the human information processing system that oversees the flow of information throughout the system.

chromosome Rodlike structure that resides in the nucleus of every cell of the body and contains genes that guide growth and development.

class inclusion Recognition that something simultaneously belongs to a particular category and to one of its subcategories.

classroom climate General psychological atmosphere of the classroom.

clinical method Procedure whereby a researcher probes a child's reasoning about a task or problem, tailoring questions to what the child has previously said or done.

clique Moderately stable friendship group of perhaps 3 to 10 members.

codominance Situation in which the two genes of an allele pair, though not identical, both have some influence on the characteristic they affect.

cognition The various mental activities in which a person engages.

cognitive apprenticeship Mentorship in which a teacher and a student work together on a challenging task and the teacher suggests ways to think about the task.

cognitive development Systematic changes in reasoning, concepts, memory, and language.

cognitive-developmental perspective Theoretical perspective that focuses on qualitative changes in thinking processes over time.

cognitive strategy Specific mental process that people use to acquire or manipulate information.

cohabiting family Family in which a parent and child(ren) live with the parent's nonmarital partner.

community of learners Classroom in which teacher and students actively and cooperatively work to help one another learn.

compensatory education Preschool program designed to foster basic academic skills in children whose home environments may not nurture such skills.

comprehension monitoring Process of checking oneself to make sure one understands what one is learning.

conceptions of society Beliefs about the nature, structure, and operation of social institutions.

conceptual change Revising one's knowledge and understanding of a topic in response to new information about the topic.

conduct disorder Chronic emotional condition characterized by lack of concern for the rights of others.

conservation Realization that if nothing is added or taken away, amount stays the same regardless of any alterations in shape or arrangement.

constructivism Theoretical perspective proposing that learners construct a body of knowledge from their experiences, rather than absorbing knowledge at face value.

control group A group of participants in a research study who do not receive the treatment under investigation; often used in an experimental study.

controversial children Children whom some peers really like and other peers strongly dislike.

conventional transgression Action that violates society's general guidelines (often unspoken) for socially acceptable behavior.

core goal Long-term goal that drives much of what a person does.

co-regulated learning Process through which a teacher and learner share responsibility for directing various aspects of the learning process.

correlation Extent to which two variables are related to each other, such that when one variable increases, the other either increases or decreases in a somewhat predictable fashion.

correlational feature Characteristic present in many instances of a concept but not essential for concept membership.

correlational study Research study that explores relationships among variables.

correlation coefficient A statistic that indicates the nature of the relationship between two variables.

cortex Part of the forebrain that houses conscious thinking processes (executive functions).

cross-sectional study Research study in which the performance of individuals at different ages is compared.

crystallized intelligence Knowledge and skills accumulated from prior experience and schooling.

cultural bias Extent to which an assessment instrument offends or unfairly penalizes some individuals because of their ethnicity, gender, or socioeconomic status.

cultural frame of reference Particular way of perceiving and interpreting the cultural differences between one's own group and the dominant group of one's society.

culture Behaviors and belief systems that characterize a social group and provide a framework for how group members decide what is normal and appropriate.

culture shock Sense of confusion that occurs when one encounters an environment with very different expectations for behavior than those in one's home environment.

daycare Care of children by nonparental adults for a significant portion of the workweek.

deductive reasoning Drawing a logical inference about something that must be true given other information that has already been presented as true.

defining feature Characteristic that must be present in all instances of a concept.

delay of gratification Foregoing small immediate rewards for larger, more delayed ones.

dendrite Branchlike part of a neuron that receives information from other neurons.

depression Emotional condition characterized by significant sadness, discouragement, and hopelessness.

development Systematic, age-related changes in physical and psychological functioning.

developmentally appropriate practice Adapting instructional practices and materials to the age, characteristics, and developmental progress of students.

dialect Form of a language characteristic of a particular geographic region or ethnic group.

differentiation An increase from general to more specific functioning over the course of development.

disequilibrium State of being unable to explain new events in terms of existing schemes.

disorganized and disoriented attachment Attachment classification in which children lack a single coherent way of responding to attachment figures.

distributed intelligence Thinking facilitated by physical objects and technology, social support, and concepts and symbols of one's culture.

distributive justice Beliefs about what constitutes people's fair share of a valued commodity.

diversity Characteristics and developmental progressions that differ from one individual to another.

dizygotic twins Twins that began as two separate zygotes and so are as genetically similar as two siblings conceived and born at different times.

DNA Short for deoxyribonucleic acid, a double-helix shaped "ladder" of four chemicals that specifies how to build specific proteins that direct growth and developmental change.

dominance hierarchy Relative standing of group members in terms of such qualities as leadership and popularity.

dominant gene Gene that overrides any competing instructions in an allele pair.

dynamic assessment Examining how a student's knowledge or reasoning may change as a result of learning or performing a specific task.

dysgraphia Exceptional difficulty acquiring handwriting skills.

dyslexia Inability to master basic reading skills in a developmentally typical time frame.

ecological and socio-historic perspectives Theoretical perspectives that focus on the social and cultural systems in which human beings grow and develop.

egocentric speech Speaking without taking the perspective and knowledge of the listener into account.

elaboration Using prior knowledge to expand on new information and thereby learn it more effectively.

elaborative interrogation Study strategy in which students develop and answer questions designed to promote elaboration of new material.

emergent literacy Knowledge and skills that lay a foundation for reading and writing; typically develops in the preschool years from early experiences with written language.

emotion Affective response to an event that is personally relevant to one's needs and goals.

emotional abuse Ongoing pattern of total disregard for children's feelings and social and moral behaviors (e.g., isolating, terrorizing, or corrupting children).

emotional contagion Tendency for infants to cry spontaneously when they hear other infants crying.

emotional regulation Using strategies to manage responses to stressful events (also called coping).

empathy Experiencing the same feelings as someone else, especially someone in pain or distress.

epistemological beliefs Beliefs regarding the nature of knowledge and knowledge acquisition.

equilibration Movement from equilibrium to disequilibrium and back to equilibrium; a process that promotes the development of increasingly complex forms of thought and knowledge.

equilibrium State of being able to explain new events in terms of existing schemes.

ethnic identity Awareness of one's membership in a particular ethnic or cultural group and willingness to adopt certain behaviors characteristic of that group.

ethnicity Membership in a group of people with a common set of values, beliefs, and behaviors. The group's roots either precede the creation of, or are external to, the country in which the group resides.

ethological attachment theory Theoretical perspective that emphasizes the functional importance of caregiver-child bonds in protecting children and giving them a secure base from which to explore their surroundings.

evolutionary perspective Theoretical perspective that focuses on inherited behavior patterns that enhance the survival and reproduction of the species.

executive functions Conscious thinking processes within the brain (e.g., reasoning, communicating, decision making).

experimental study Research study in which a researcher manipulates one aspect of the environment (a treatment), controls other aspects of the environment, and assesses the treatment's effects on participants' behavior.

expressive language Ability to communicate effectively through speaking and writing.

extended-day program Before- and after-school programs that provides supervision, academic enrichment, and recreation for children of working parents.

externalizing behavior Undesirable emotion, behavior, or a combination that affects other people (e.g., aggression, stealing, lack of self-control).

extrinsic motivation Motivation promoted by factors external to the individual and unrelated to the task being performed.

family One or more adults caring for offspring for a significant portion of their childhood.

family configuration The particular members of a family and their interrelationships.

fast mapping Inferring a word's general meaning after a single exposure.

figurative speech Speech that communicates meaning beyond a literal interpretation of its words.

fine motor skills Small, precise movements of particular parts of the body, especially the hands.

fluid intelligence Ability to acquire knowledge quickly and thereby adapt readily to new situations.

Flynn effect Gradual increase in intelligence test performance observed worldwide over the past several decades.

forebrain Part of the brain responsible for complex thinking, emotions, and motivation.

formal operational egocentrism Inability of an individual in Piaget's formal operations stage to separate one's own abstract logic from the perspectives of others and from practical considerations.

fourth-grade slump Tendency for some children (especially those from low-income backgrounds) to experience greater difficulty with reading tasks as they encounter more challenging material in the upper elementary grades.

friendship Peer relationship that is voluntary and reciprocal and includes shared routines and customs.

function word Word that affects the meanings of other words or the interrelationships among words in a sentence.

g General factor in intelligence that influences performance in a wide variety of tasks and content domains.

gang Cohesive social group characterized by initiation rites, distinctive colors and symbols, territorial orientation, and feuds with rival groups.

gene Basic unit of genetic instruction in a living cell.

germ cell Cell that, in humans, contains 23 rather than 46 chromosomes; a male germ cell (sperm) and a female germ cell (ovum) join at conception.

giftedness Unusually high ability in one or more areas, to the point where students require special educational services to help them meet their full potential.

glial cell Cell in the brain or other part of the nervous system that provides structural or functional support for one or more neurons; also called neuroglia.

goal-directed behavior Planful behavior intended to bring about an anticipated outcome.

gross motor skills Large movements of the body that permit locomotion around the environment.

growth spurt Rapid increase in height and weight during puberty.

guilt Feeling of discomfort when one knows that he or she has caused someone else pain or distress.

hidden curriculum Unstated norms and beliefs that underlie teachers' treatment of academic subject matter and expectations for student behavior.

hindbrain Part of the brain controlling the basic physiological processes that sustain survival.

history Large-scale events that bring about significant social change.

hostile attributional bias Tendency to interpret others' behaviors (especially ambiguous ones) as reflecting aggressive or hostile motives.

identity People's self-constructed definition of who they are, what they find important, and what goals they want to accomplish in life.

identity crisis Period during which an individual actively struggles to choose a course in life.

imaginary audience Belief that one is the center of attention in any social situation.

immersion Approach to second-language instruction in which students hear and speak that language almost exclusively within the classroom.

inclusion Practice of educating all students, including those with severe and multiple disabilities, in neighborhood schools and general education classrooms.

individual constructivism Theoretical perspective that focuses on how people construct meaning from events without the assistance of others.

induction Explaining why a certain behavior is unacceptable, often with a focus on the pain or distress that someone has caused another.

infant-directed speech Short, simple, high-pitched speech often used when talking to young children.

information processing perspective Theoretical perspective that focuses on the precise nature of human cognitive processes.

information processing theory Theoretical perspective that focuses on the specific ways in which people mentally think about ("process") the information they receive.

inner speech "Talking" to oneself mentally rather than aloud.

insecure-avoidant attachment Attachment classification in which children appear somewhat indifferent to attachment figures.

insecure-resistant attachment Attachment classification in which children are preoccupied with their attachment figures but gain little comfort from them when distressed.

integration An increasing coordination of body parts over the course of development.

intelligence Ability to modify and adjust one's behaviors in order to accomplish new tasks successfully.

intelligence test General measure of current cognitive functioning, used primarily to predict academic achievement over the short run.

intentionality Engaging in an action congruent with one's purpose or goal.

intermittent reinforcement Reinforcing a response only occasionally, with some occurrences of the response going unreinforced.

internalization In Vygotsky's theory, the gradual evolution of external, social activities into internal, mental activities (Ch. 4). In moral development, adopting society's rules and values about acceptable behavior as one's own (Ch. 10).

internalized motivation Adoption of behaviors that others value, without regard for the external consequences of such behaviors.

internalizing behavior Undesirable emotion, behavior, or a combination that primarily affects oneself (e.g., depression, social withdrawal, and suicidal tendencies).

intersubjectivity Interaction between two or more social partners who share a common frame of reference, or interpretation of events.

interview Data collection technique that obtains self-report data through face-to-face conversation.

intrinsic motivation Internal desire to perform a particular task.

invented spelling Children's early and only minimally phonetic attempts at spelling.

involuntary minority group People who have become members of a new country against their will, plus the descendants of such individuals.

IQ score Score on an intelligence test determined by comparing one's performance with the performance of same-age peers.

IRE cycle Teacher-student interaction pattern marked by teacher initiation, student response, and teacher evaluation.

just community Approach to classroom decision making in which students and teachers meet regularly to address issues of fairness and justice and then reach decisions in a democratic manner.

justice orientation Focus on individual rights in moral decision making.

knowledge base One's knowledge about specific topics and the world in general.

knowledge telling Writing down ideas in whatever order they come to mind, with little regard for communicating the ideas effectively.

knowledge transforming Expressing ideas on paper in a way that a reader can readily understand.

language acquisition device Biologically built-in mechanism hypothesized to facilitate language learning.

learned helplessness General belief that one is incapable of accomplishing tasks and has little or no control of the environment.

learned industriousness Recognition that one can succeed at some tasks only with effort, persistence, and well-chosen strategies.

learning disability Significant deficit in one or more cognitive processes, to the point where special educational services are required.

learning strategy Specific mental process used in acquiring new information.

left hemisphere Left side of the cortex; largely responsible for sequential reasoning and analysis, especially in right-handed people.

legitimate peripheral participation A child's early and somewhat limited involvement in adult activities.

level of potential development Extent to which one can successfully execute a task with the assistance of a more competent individual.

lexicon The words one knows in a particular language.

life-span perspective Theoretical perspective that looks at developmental patterns from conception until death.

longitudinal study Research study in which the performance of a single group of people is tracked over a long period of time.

long-term memory Component of memory that holds knowledge and skills for a relatively long time.

mastery goal Desire to acquire additional knowledge or master new skills.

mastery orientation General belief that one is capable of accomplishing challenging tasks, accompanied by the intent to master such tasks.

maturation Genetically controlled changes that occur over the course of development.

maturational perspective Theoretical perspective that emphasizes genetically guided unfolding of developmental structures, neurological organizations, and motor abilities.

mediated learning experience   Discussion between an adult and a child in which the adult helps the child make sense of an event they have mutually experienced.

mediation training   Teaching students how to mediate conflicts among classmates by asking opposing sides to express their differing viewpoints and then working together to identify a reasonable resolution.

menarche   First menstrual period in an adolescent female.

mental retardation   Condition marked by significantly below-average general intelligence and deficits in adaptive behavior.

metacognition   Knowledge and beliefs about one's own cognitive processes, as well as efforts to regulate those cognitive processes to maximize learning and memory.

metacognitive awareness   Extent to which one is able to reflect on the nature of one's own thinking processes.

metacognitive scaffolding   Supportive technique that guides students in their use of metacognitive strategies.

metalinguistic awareness   Extent to which one is able to think about the nature of language.

midbrain   Part of the brain that coordinates communication between the hindbrain and forebrain.

mnemonics   Special memory aid or trick designed to help students learn and remember a particular piece of information.

monozygotic twins   Twins that began as a single zygote and so share the same genetic makeup.

moral dilemma   Situation in which there is no clear-cut answer regarding the morally correct thing to do.

moral realism   Viewing rules for behavior as firm and inflexible, as having a life of their own separate from the purposes they serve.

moral transgression   Action that causes damage or harm or in some other way infringes on the needs and rights of others.

morality   General set of standards about right and wrong.

motivation   State that energizes, directs, and sustains behavior.

multicultural education   Education that includes the perspectives and experiences of numerous cultural groups on a regular basis.

multiple classification   Recognition that objects may belong to several categories simultaneously.

myelinization   The growth of a fatty sheath around neurons that allows them to transmit messages more quickly.

narrative   A sequence of events, either real or fictional, that are logically interconnected; a story.

native language   The first language a child learns.

nativism   Theoretical perspective that some knowledge is biologically built in and present at birth.

naturalistic study   Research study in which individuals are observed in their natural environment.

nature   Effects of heredity and genetically controlled maturational processes on development.

need for affiliation   Consistent tendency in some individuals to seek out friendly relationships with others.

need for approval   Consistent desire in some individuals to gain the acceptance and positive judgments of others.

need for relatedness   Fundamental human need to feel socially connected and secure the love and respect of others.

negative reinforcement   Consequence that brings about the increase of a behavior through the removal (rather than presentation) of a stimulus.

neglect   Failure to provide the basic necessities for children's health, safety, and emotional well-being.

neglected children   Children whom peers rarely select as someone they would either most like or least like to do something with.

neo-Piagetian theory   Theoretical perspective that combines elements of both Piaget's theory and information processing theory and portrays cognitive development as involving a series of distinct stages.

neuron   Cell that transmits information to other cells; also called nerve cell.

neurotransmitter   Chemical substance through which one neuron sends a message to another neuron.

niche-picking   Tendency to actively seek out environments that match one's inherited abilities.

nurture   Effects of environmental conditions on development.

obesity   Condition in which a person weighs at least 20% more than what is optimal for good health.

object permanence   Realization that objects continue to exist even after they are removed from view.

observation   Data collection technique whereby a researcher carefully observes and documents the behaviors of participants in a research study.

only child   A child without siblings.

onset   One or more consonant sounds that precede the vowel sound in a syllable.

operant conditioning   Explanation of behavior change in which a response increases in frequency as a result of being followed by reinforcement.

operation   In Piaget's theory, an organized and integrated system of thought processes.

oppositional frame of reference   Establishment of clear psychological boundaries between one's own group and the dominant culture of the society, and rejection of the dominant group's values and practices.

organismic influences   Characteristics and behaviors of human beings that influence later development.

organization   Finding interrelationships among pieces of information as a way of learning them more effectively.

overgeneralization   Too broad a meaning for a word, such that it is used in situations to which it doesn't apply.

overregularization   Applying a syntactical rule in situations where exceptions to the rule apply.

parenting style   General pattern of behaviors that a parent uses to nurture and guide his or her children.

peer culture   General set of rules, expectations, and interpretations that influence how members of a particular peer group behave.

peer pressure   Tactics used to encourage some behaviors and discourage others in age-mates.

peers   Individuals of approximately the same age and ability level.

perception   Cognitive interpretation of stimuli that the body has sensed.

performance goal   Desire to look good and receive favorable judgments from others.

permissive parenting   Parenting style characterized by emotional warmth but few expectations or standards for children's behavior.

person perception   Recognition and interpretation of people's basic characteristics, including their physical features, behaviors, and internal psychological states.

personal fable   Belief that one is completely unlike other people, cannot be understood, and is impervious to danger.

personal interest   Long-term interest about a particular topic or activity.

personal space   Personally and culturally preferred distance between two people during social interaction.

phonemes   Smallest units of a spoken language that signify differences in meaning.

phonological awareness   Ability to hear the distinct sounds within words.

phonology   The sound system of a language; how words sound and are produced.

physical abuse   Intentionally causing physical harm to another.

physical development   Physical and neurological growth and age-related changes in motor skills.

polygenic inheritance   Situation in which many genes combine in their influence on a particular characteristic.

popular children   Children whom many peers like and perceive to be kind and trustworthy.

portfolio   Systematic collection of a student's work over a lengthy period of time.

positive reinforcement   Consequence that brings about the increase of a behavior through the presentation (rather than removal) of a stimulus.

pragmatics   Strategies and rules for effective and socially acceptable verbal interaction.

prejudice   Exhibiting negative attitudes, feelings, and behaviors toward particular individuals because of their membership in a specific group.

preoperational egocentrism   Inability of a child in Piaget's preoperational stage to view situations from another person's perspective.

primary reinforcer   Stimulus that satisfies a basic physiological need.

proactive aggression   Deliberate aggression against another as a means of obtaining a desired goal.

prompt   An overt reminder about what one can or should do.

prosocial behavior   Action intended to benefit another, without regard for one's own needs.

psychodynamic perspective   Theoretical perspective that focuses on how early experiences affect social and personality development.

psychometric approach   Approach to cognitive development that focuses on children's performance on intelligence tests.

psychosocial stages In Erikson's theory, eight periods of life that involve age-related tasks or dilemmas.

puberty Physiological changes that occur during adolescence and lead to reproductive maturation.

qualitative change Relatively dramatic developmental change that reflects considerable reorganization or modification of functioning.

qualitative research Research study in which the data collected are largely nonnumerical.

quantitative change Developmental change that involves a series of minor, trendlike modifications.

quantitative research Research study in which the data collected are predominantly numerical.

quasi-experimental study Research study in which one or more experimental treatments are administered but in which random assignment to groups is not possible.

questionnaire Data collection technique that obtains self-report data through a paper-pencil inventory.

reactive aggression Aggressive response to frustration or provocation.

receptive language Ability to understand the language that one hears or reads.

recessive gene Gene that influences growth and development only if the other gene in the allele pair is identical to it (and so also recessive).

reciprocal teaching Approach to teaching reading whereby students take turns asking teacherlike questions of their classmates.

reflex An automatic response to a particular kind of stimulation.

rehearsal Attempt to learn and remember information by repeating it over and over.

reinforcer Consequence of a response that leads to an increased frequency of that response

rejected children Children whom many peers identify as being unfavorable social partners.

rejection Refusing to learn or accept any customs and values found within a new cultural environment.

reliability Extent to which a data collection technique yields consistent, dependable results—results that are only minimally affected by temporary and irrelevant influences.

resiliency Ability of some children and adolescents to thrive and develop despite adverse environmental conditions.

right hemisphere Right side of the cortex; largely responsible for simultaneous processing and synthesis, especially in right-handed people.

rime The vowel sound and any following consonant sounds in a syllable.

rough-and-tumble play Playful physical "fighting" typical in early and middle childhood.

sample The specific participants in a research study; their performance is often assumed to indicate how a larger population of individuals would perform.

scaffolding Support mechanism, provided by a more competent individual, that helps a child successfully perform a task within his or her zone of proximal development.

schema Organized and internalized body of knowledge about a specific topic.

scheme In Piaget's theory, an organized group of similar actions or thoughts.

schizophrenia Psychiatric condition characterized by irrational ideas and disorganized thinking.

script Schema that involves a predictable sequence of events related to a common activity.

secondary reinforcer Stimulus that becomes reinforcing over time through its association with another reinforcer.

second-order symbol system Set of symbols that stand for other symbols.

secure attachment Attachment classification in which children use attachment figures as a secure base from which to explore and as a source of comfort in times of distress.

selective adoption Assuming some customs of a new culture while also retaining some customs of one's previous culture.

self-care Taking care of one's own needs (cooking, doing chores, etc.) before or after school while parents are at work or otherwise away from home.

self-concept Beliefs that people have about themselves, their characteristics, and their abilities.

self-conscious emotion Affective state that reflects awareness of a community's social standards (e.g., pride, guilt, shame).

self-disclosure Revealing information about oneself to another.

self-efficacy Belief that one is capable of executing certain behaviors or reaching certain goals in a particular task or domain.

self-esteem Feelings that people have about their own capabilities and self-worth.

self-evaluation Judging one's own performance or behavior in accordance with predetermined criteria.

self-fulfilling prophecy Phenomenon in which a teacher's expectations for students' performance directly or indirectly bring about that level of performance.

self-instructions Instructions that people give themselves as they perform a complex behavior.

self-monitoring Process of observing and recording one's own behavior.

self-regulated learning Directing and regulating one's own cognitive processes in order to learn successfully.

self-regulation Setting standards and goals for oneself and engaging in behaviors that lead to the accomplishment of those standards and goals.

self-reinforcement Self-imposed pleasurable consequence for a desired behavior.

self-report Data collection technique whereby participants are asked to describe their own characteristics and performance.

self-socialization The active thinking and decision making in which children engage as they learn how to behave and participate appropriately in their culture.

self-talk Talking to oneself as a way of guiding oneself through a task.

semantic bootstrapping Using knowledge of word meanings to derive knowledge about syntactic categories.

semantics The meanings of words and word combinations.

sensation Physiological detection of stimuli in the environment.

sense of community Widely shared feeling that teacher and students have common goals, are mutually respectful and supportive of one another's efforts, and believe that everyone makes an important contribution to classroom learning.

sense of competence Belief that one can deal effectively with a particular aspect of one's environment.

sense of self-determination Belief that one has some choice and control regarding the future course of one's life.

sensitive period A period in development when certain environmental experiences have a more pronounced influence than is true at other times.

sensory register Component of memory that holds incoming information in an unanalyzed form for a very brief time (2–3 seconds or less).

service learning Activity that promotes learning and skill development through volunteerism or community service.

sexual abuse Seeking sexual gratification from a child or adolescent.

sexual harassment Form of discrimination in which a target individual perceives other's actions or statements to be hostile, humiliating, or offensive, especially related to physical appearance or sexual matters.

sexual orientation Particular sex(es) to which an individual is romantically and sexually attracted.

shame Feeling of embarrassment or humiliation after failing to meet the standards for moral behavior that others have set.

sight vocabulary Words that a child can recognize immediately while reading.

situated motivation Phenomenon in which aspects of one's immediate environment enhance one's motivation to learn particular things or behave in particular ways.

situational interest Interest evoked temporarily by something in the environment.

situative perspective Theoretical perspective that cognitive abilities are tied to the specific contexts in which they have been acquired.

social cognition Thinking about people, self, and society.

social-cognitive bias Mental shortcuts in thinking about social phenomena.

social cognitive theory Theoretical perspective that focuses on the roles of observation and modeling in learning and motivation.

social constructivism Theoretical perspective that focuses on people's collective efforts to impose meaning on the world.

social-emotional development Systematic changes in emotional, social, and moral functioning.

social information processing Series of cognitive steps applied to understanding of, and responding to, social events.

socialization Systematic efforts by other people and by institutions to prepare youngsters to act in ways deemed by society to be appropriate and responsible.

socialization agents People who play a key role in preparing children and adolescents to act in ways deemed by society to be appropriate and responsible.

social perspective taking Imagining what someone else is thinking or feeling.

social pretense Ability to share internal fantasies with a social partner.

social referencing Observing emotional cues of others and using such cues to interpret the possible implications of an event for oneself.

social skills Strategies that people use to interact effectively with others.

sociocognitive conflict Encountering and having to wrestle with ideas and viewpoints different from one's own.

sociocultural perspective Theoretical perspective emphasizing the importance of society and culture for promoting cognitive development.

sociodramatic play Play in which children take on assumed roles and act out a scenario of events.

socioeconomic status (SES) One's general social and economic standing in society, encompassing such variables as family income, occupation, and education level.

sociolinguistic behaviors Social and culturally specific conventions that govern appropriate verbal interaction.

sounding Friendly, playful exchange of insults, common in some African American communities.

specific ability test Test designed to assess a specific cognitive skill or the potential to learn and perform in a specific content domain.

speech and communication disorders Category of special needs characterized by abnormalities in spoken language that significantly interfere with students' classroom performance.

spermarche First ejaculation in an adolescent male.

stage A period of development characterized by a particular way of behaving or thinking.

stage theory Theory that describes development as involving a series of qualitatively distinct changes, with these changes occurring in the same sequence for everyone.

Standard English Form of English generally considered acceptable in school (as reflected in textbooks, grammar instruction, etc.) and in the media.

standards General statements specifying the knowledge and skills that students should achieve and the characteristics that their accomplishments should reflect.

stereotype Rigid, simplistic, and erroneous characterization of a particular group.

story schema Knowledge of the typical elements and sequence of a fictional narrative.

structure In neo-Piagetian theory, a specific system of concepts and thinking skills that influence thinking and reasoning in a particular content domain.

students at risk Students who have a high probability of failing to acquire the minimal academic skills necessary for success in the adult world.

subculture Group that resists the ways of the dominant culture and adopts its own norms for behavior.

symbol Mental entity that represents an external object or event, often without reflecting its perceptual and behavioral qualities.

symbolic thought Ability to represent and think about external objects and events in one's mind.

sympathy Feeling of sorrow or concern about another's problems or distress.

synapse Junction between two neurons.

synaptic pruning A universal process in brain development whereby many synapses formed earlier wither away, especially if they have not been used frequently.

synaptogenesis A universal process in brain development whereby many new synapses appear, typically in the first 3½ years of life.

syntax Rules used to put words together into sentences.

temperament Constitutional ways of responding to emotional events and novel stimulation, and of regulating impulses.

test Instrument designed to assess knowledge, understandings, abilities, or skills in a consistent fashion across individuals.

theory Organized system of principles and explanations regarding a particular phenomenon.

theory of mind Child's integrated beliefs about the existence and nature of thought.

theory theory Theoretical perspective proposing that children construct increasingly integrated and complex understandings of physical and mental phenomena.

trait theory Theoretical perspective focusing on stable individual differences in human behavior.

undergeneralization Overly restricted meaning for a word, excluding some situations to which the word applies.

uninvolved parenting Parenting style characterized by a lack of emotional support and a lack of standards regarding appropriate behavior.

Universal Grammar Hypothesized set of parameters within the language acquisition device that allow some grammatical structures but exclude others.

universality Characteristics and developmental progressions shared by virtually all human beings.

validity Extent to which a data collection technique actually assesses what it is intended to assess.

value Belief that an activity has direct or indirect benefits.

vicarious punishment Phenomenon in which a person decreases a certain response after seeing another person punished for that response.

vicarious reinforcement Phenomenon in which a person increases a certain response after seeing another person reinforced for that response.

voluntary minority group People who have moved to a new country with hopes of economic well-being and political freedom, plus the descendents of such individuals.

wait time The length of time a teacher pauses, after either asking a question or hearing a student's comment, before saying something else.

whole-language perspective Theoretical perspective that proposes that children develop literacy skills most effectively within the context of authentic reading and writing tasks.

word decoding Identifying an unknown word by using letter-sound relationships, analogies, common letter patterns, and/or semantic and syntactic context.

working memory Component of memory that enables people to actively think about and process a small amount of information.

zone of proximal development (ZPD) Range of tasks that one cannot yet perform independently but can perform with the help and guidance of others.

zygote Cell formed when a male sperm joins with a female ovum; it is essentially the "start" of a new human being.

REFERENCES

Abdul-Jabbar, K., & Knobles, P. (1983). *Giant steps: The autobiography of Kareem Abdul-Jabbar.* New York: Bantam.

Abi-Nader, J. (1993). Meeting the needs of multicultural classrooms: Family values and the motivation of minority students. In M. J. O'Hair & S. J. Odell (Eds.), *Diversity and teaching: Teacher education yearbook I.* Fort Worth, TX: Harcourt Brace Jovanovich.

Aboud, F. E. (1988). *Children and prejudice.* Oxford, England: Blackwell.

Aboud, F. E. (1993). The developmental psychology of racial prejudice. *Transcultural Psychiatric Research Review, 30,* 229–242.

Adalbjarnardottir, S., & Selman, R. L. (1997). "I feel I have received a new vision": An analysis of teachers' professional development as they work with students on interpersonal issues. *Teaching and Teacher Education, 13,* 409–428.

Adams, G. R., Gullotta, T. P., & Markstrom-Adams, C. (1994). *Adolescent life experiences* (3rd ed.). Pacific Grove, CA: Brooks/Cole.

Adams, M. J. (1990). *Beginning to read: Thinking and learning about print.* Cambridge, MA: MIT Press.

Adams, R. J. (1987). An evaluation of color preference in early infancy. *Infant Behavior and Development, 10,* 143–150.

Ago, R. (1997). Young nobles in the age of absolutism: Paternal authority and freedom of choice in seventeenth-century Italy. In G. Levi & J. C. Schmitt (Eds.), *A history of young people in the west: Vol. 1. Ancient and medieval rites of passage* (C. Naish, Trans.; pp. 283–322). Cambridge, MA: Belknap Press of Harvard University Press.

Ainsworth, M. D. S. (1963). The development of infant-mother interaction among the Ganda. In B. M. Foss (Ed.), *Determinants of infant behavior* (Vol. 2, pp. 67–104). New York: Wiley.

Ainsworth, M. D. S. (1973). The development of infant-mother attachment. In B. Caldwell & H. Ricciuti (Eds.), *Review of child development research* (Vol. 3, pp. 1–94). Chicago: University of Chicago Press.

Ainsworth, M. D. S., Blehar, M. C., Waters, E., & Wall, S. (1978). *Patterns of attachment.* Hillsdale, NJ: Erlbaum.

Aitchison, J. (1996). *The seeds of speech: Language origin and evolution.* Cambridge, England: Cambridge University Press.

Akiskal, H. S., & McKinney, W. T. (1973). Depressive disorders: Toward a unified hypothesis. *Science, 162,* 20–29.

Alapack, R. (1991). The adolescent first kiss. *Humanistic Psychologist, 19,* 48–67.

Alderman, M. K. (1990). Motivation for at-risk students. *Educational Leadership, 48*(1), 27–30.

Alegria, J. (1998). The origin and functions of phonological representations in deaf people. In C. Hulme & R. M. Joshi (Eds.), *Reading and spelling: Development and disorders.* Mahwah, NJ: Erlbaum.

Alessi, N. E., Krahn, D., Brehm, D., & Wittekindt, J. (1989). Prepubertal anorexia nervosa and major depressive disorder. *Journal of the American Academy of Child and Adolescent Psychiatry, 28,* 380–384.

Alexander, K., Entwisle, D., & Thompson, M. (1987). School performance, status relations, and the structure of sentiment: Bringing the teacher back in. *American Sociological Review, 52,* 665–682.

Alexander, P. A., Graham, S., & Harris, K. R. (1998). A perspective on strategy research: Progress and prospects. *Educational Psychology Review, 10,* 129–154.

Alexander, P. A., & Jetton, T. L. (1996). The role of importance and interest in the processing of text. *Educational Psychology Review, 8,* 89–121.

Alfassi, M. (1998). Reading for meaning: The efficacy of reciprocal teaching in fostering reading comprehension in high school students in remedial reading classes. *American Educational Research Journal, 35,* 309–332.

Allen, L., Cipielewski, J., & Stanovich, K. E. (1992). Multiple indicators of children's reading habits and attitudes: Construct validity and cognitive correlates. *Journal of Educational Psychology, 84,* 489–503.

Alley, G., & Deshler, D. (1979). *Teaching the learning disabled adolescent: Strategies and methods.* Denver, CO: Love.

Allison, K. W. (1998). Stress and oppressed social category membership. In J. K. Swim & C. Stangor (Eds.), *Prejudice: The target's perspective* (pp. 149–170). San Diego, CA: Academic Press.

Almeida, D. M., Wethington, E., & Chandler, A. L. (1999). Daily transmission of tensions between marital dyads and parent-child dyads. *Journal of Marriage and the Family, 61,* 49–61.

Alvermann, D. E., & Moore, D. W. (1991). Secondary school reading. In R. Barr, M. L. Kamil, P. B. Mosenthal, & P. D. Pearson (Eds.), *Handbook of reading research* (Vol. II). New York: Longman.

Alvermann, D. E., Young, J. P., Green, C., & Wisenbaker, J. M. (1999). Adolescents' perceptions and negotiations of literacy practices in after-school read and talk clubs. *American Educational Research Journal, 36,* 221–264.

Ambrose, D., Allen, J., & Huntley, S. B. (1994). Mentorship of the highly creative. *Roeper Review, 17,* 131–133.

American Association on Mental Retardation. (1992). *Mental retardation: Definition, classification, and systems of supports* (9th ed.). Washington, DC: Author.

American Psychiatric Association (1994). *Diagnostic and statistical manual of mental disorders* (4th ed.). Washington, DC: Author.

American Speech-Language-Hearing Association (1993). Definitions of communication disorders and variations. *ASHA, 35*(Suppl. 10), 40–41.

Ames, C. (1984). Competitive, cooperative, and individualistic goal structures: A cognitive-motivational analysis. In R. Ames & C. Ames (Eds.), *Research on motivation in education: Vol. 1. Student motivation.* San Diego, CA: Academic Press.

Ames, C. (1992). Classrooms: Goals, structures, and student motivation. *Journal of Educational Psychology, 84,* 261–271.

Anastasi, A., & Urbina, S. (1997). *Psychological testing* (7th ed.). Upper Saddle River, NJ: Prentice Hall.

Anderman, E. M., & Maehr, M. L. (1994). Motivation and schooling in the middle grades. *Review of Educational Research, 64,* 287–309.

Anderson, D. A. (1994). Lesbian and gay adolescents: Social and developmental considerations. *The High School Journal, 77* (1,2), 13–19.

Anderson, E. (1990). *Streetwise: Race, class, and change in an urban community.* Chicago: University of Chicago Press.

Anderson, J. C. (1983). *The architecture of cognition.* Cambridge, MA: Harvard University Press.

Anderson, J. R., Reder, L. M., & Simon, H. A. (1997). Situative versus cognitive perspectives: Form versus substance. *Educational Researcher, 26*(1), 18–21.

Anderson, L. W., & Pellicer, L. O. (1998). Toward an understanding of unusually successful programs for economically disadvantaged students. *Journal of Education for Students Placed at Risk, 3,* 237–263.

Anderson, R. C., Shirey, L., Wilson, P., & Fielding, L. (1987). Interestingness of children's reading materials. In R. Snow & M. Farr (Eds.), *Aptitude, learning, and instruction: III. Conative and affective process analyses.* Hillsdale, NJ: Erlbaum.

Anderson, R. C., Wilson, P. T., & Fielding, L. G. (1988). Growth in reading and how children spend their time outside of school. *Reading Research Quarterly, 23,* 285–303.

Anderson, R. G., & Freebody, P. (1981). Vocabulary knowledge. In J. T. Guthrie (Ed.), *Comprehension and teaching: Research reviews.* Newark, DE: International Reading Association.

Andersson, B. E. (1989). Effects of public day care: A longitudinal study. *Child Development, 60,* 857–866.

Andison, F. S. (1977). TV violence and viewer aggression: Accumulation of study results 1956–1976. *Public Opinion Quarterly, 41,* 314–331.

Andrews, J. F., & Mason, J. M. (1986). Childhood deafness and the acquisition of print concepts. In D. B. Yaden, Jr., & S. Templeton (Eds.), *Metalinguistic awareness and beginning literacy: Conceptualizing what it means to read and write.* Portsmouth, NH: Heinemann.

Anglin, J. M. (1977). *Word, object, and conceptual development.* New York: Norton.

Antelman, S., & Caggiula, A. (1977). Norepinephrine-dopamine interactions and behavior. *Science, 195,* 646–651.

Anthony, J. L., Lonigan, C. J., & Dyer, S.M. (1996, April). *The development of reading comprehension: Listening comprehension or basic language processes?* Paper presented at the annual meeting of the American Educational Research Association, New York.

Anyon, J. (1988). Social class and the hidden curriculum of work. In G. Handel (Ed.), *Childhood socialization.* New York: Aldine de Gruyter.

Archer, J. (1991). The influence of testosterone on human aggression. *British Journal of Psychology, 82,* 1–28.

Archer, S. L. (1982). The lower age boundaries of identity development. *Child Development, 53,* 1551–1556.

Arcus, D. M. (1991). *Experiential modification of temperamental bias in inhibited and uninhibited children.* Unpublished doctoral dissertation, Harvard University, Cambridge, MA.

Armstrong, T. (1994). *Multiple intelligences in the classroom.* Alexandria, VA: Association for Supervision and Curriculum Development.

Arnett, J. (1995). The young and the reckless: Adolescent reckless behavior. *Current Directions in Psychological Science, 4,* 67–71.

Arnett, J. J. (1999). Adolescent storm and stress, reconsidered. *American Psychologist, 54,* 317–326.

Arnold, A. P., & Gorski, R. A. (1984). Gonadal steroid induction of structural sex differences in the central nervous system. *Annual Review of Neuroscience, 7,* 413–442.

Aronfreed, J. (1976). Moral development from the standpoint of a general psychological theory. In T. Lickona (Ed.), *Moral development and behavior: Theory, research, and social issues* (pp. 54–69). New York: Holt, Rinehart & Winston.

Artman, L., & Cahan, S. (1993). Schooling and the development of transitive inference. *Developmental Psychology, 29,* 753–759.

Asai, S. (1993). In search of Asia through music: Guidelines and ideas for teaching Asian music. In T. Perry & J. W. Fraser (Eds.), *Freedom's plow: Teaching in the multicultural classroom.* New York: Routledge.

Asante, M. K. (1991). Afrocentric curriculum. *Educational Leadership, 24*(4), 28–31.

Asher, S. R., & Coie, J. D. (Eds.). (1990). *Peer rejection in childhood.* Cambridge, England: Cambridge University Press.

Asher, S. R., & Parker, J. G. (1989). Significance of peer relationship problems in childhood. In B. H. Schneider, G. Attili, J. Nadel, & R. P. Weissberg (Eds.), *Social competence in developmental perspective.* Dordrecht, Netherlands: Kluwer.

Asher, S. R., & Renshaw, P. D. (1981). Children without friends: Social knowledge and social skill training. In S. R. Asher & J. M. Gottman (Eds.), *The development of children's friendships* (pp. 273–296). Cambridge, England: Cambridge University Press.

Ashmore, R., & DelBoca, F. (1976). Psychological approaches. In P. A. Katz (Ed.), *Elimination of racism.* New York: Pergamon.

Ashton, P. (1985). Motivation and the teacher's sense of efficacy. In C. Ames & R. Ames (Eds.), *Research on motivation in education: Vol. 2. The classroom milieu.* San Diego, CA: Academic Press.

Aslin, R. N. (1993). Perception of visual direction in human infants. In C. E. Granrud (Ed.), *Visual perception and cognition in infancy.* Hillsdale, NJ: Erlbaum.

Aslin, R. N., Saffran, J. R., & Newport, E. L. (1998). Computation of conditional probability statistics by 8-month-old infants. *Psychological Science, 9,* 321–324.

Asmussen, L., & Larson, R. (1991). The quality of family time among adolescents in single-parent and married-parent families. *Journal of Marriage and the Family, 53,* 1021–1030.

Assor, A., & Connell, J. P. (1992). The validity of students' self-reports as measures of performance affecting self-appraisals. In D. H. Schunk & J. L. Meece (Eds.), *Student perceptions in the classroom.* Hillsdale, NJ: Erlbaum.

Astington, J. W. (1991). Intention in the child's theory of mind. In C. Moore & D. Frye (Eds.), *Children's theories of mind* (pp. 157–172). Hillsdale, NJ: Erlbaum.

Astington, J. W., & Pelletier, J. (1996). The language of mind: Its role in teaching and learning. In D. R. Olson & N. Torrance (Eds.), *The handbook of education and human development: New models of learning, teaching and schooling* (pp. 593–619). Cambridge, MA: Blackwell.

Astor, R. A. (1994). Children's moral reasoning about family and peer violence: The role of provocation and retribution. *Child Development, 65,* 1054–1067.

Astor, R. A., Meyer, H. A., & Behre, W. J. (1999). Unowned places and times: Maps and interviews about violence in high schools. *American Educational Research Journal, 36,* 3–42.

Atkinson, J. W., & Feather, N. T. (Eds.). (1966). *A theory of achievement motivation.* New York: Wiley.

Atkinson, M. (1992). *Children's syntax: An introduction to principles and parameters theory.* Oxford, England: Blackwell.

Attie, I., & Brooks-Gunn, J. (1989). Development of eating problems in adolescent girls: A longitudinal study. *Developmental Psychology, 25,* 70–79.

Attie, I., Brooks-Gunn, J., & Petersen, A. (1990). A developmental perspective on eating disorders and eating problems. In M. Lewis & S. M. Miller (Eds.), *Handbook of developmental psychopathology* (pp. 409–420). New York: Plenum Press.

Atwater, E. (1996). *Adolescence.* Upper Saddle River, NJ: Prentice Hall.

Au, K. H. (1980). Participation structures in a reading lesson with Hawaiian children: Analysis of a culturally appropriate instructional event. *Anthropology and Education Quarterly, 11,* 91–115.

Au, K. H. (1993). *Literacy instruction in multicultural settings.* Fort Worth, TX: Harcourt Brace Jovanovich.

Au, K. H. (1997). A sociocultural model of reading instruction: The Kamehameha Elementary Education Program. In S. A. Stahl & D. A. Hayes (Eds.), *Instructional models in reading* (pp. 181–202). Mahwah, NJ: Erlbaum.

Au, K. H., & Mason, J. (1981). Social organizational factors in learning to read: The balance of rights hypothesis. *Reading Research Quarterly, 17,* 115–152.

Au, T. K., & Glusman, M. (1990). The principle of mutual exclusivity in word learning: To honor or not to honor? *Child Development, 61,* 1474–1490.

Ausubel, D. P., Novak, J. D., & Hanesian, H. (1978). *Educational psychology: A cognitive view* (2nd ed.). New York: Holt, Rinehart & Winston.

Babad, E. (1993). Teachers' differential behavior. *Educational Psychology Review, 5,* 347–376.

Bagley, C. (1989). Aggression and anxiety in daycare graduates. *Psychological Reports, 64,* 250.

Bailey, J. M., Bobrow, D., Wolfe, M., & Mikach, S. (1995). Sexual orientation of adult sons of gay fathers. *Developmental Psychology, 31,* 124–129.

Bailey, J. M., & Pillard, R. C. (1997). The innateness of homosexuality. In M. R. Walsh (Ed.), *Women, men, and gender: Ongoing debates* (pp. 184–187). New Haven, CT: Yale University Press.

Baillargeon, R. (1994). How do infants learn about the physical world? *Current Directions in Psychological Science, 3,* 133–140.

Bakari, R. (2000). The development and validation of an instrument to measure preservice teachers' attitudes toward teaching African American students. Unpublished doctoral dissertation, University of Northern Colorado, Greeley.

Bakeman, R., & Brownlee, J. R. (1980). The strategic use of parallel play: A sequential analysis. *Child Development, 51,* 873–878.

Baker, C. (1993). *Foundations of bilingual education and bilingualism.* Clevedon, England: Multilingual Matters.

Baker, L., Scher, D., & Mackler, K. (1997). Home and family influences on motivations for reading. *Educational Psychologist, 32,* 69–82.

Baker-Ward, L., Ornstein, P. A., & Holden, D. J. (1984). The expression of memorization in early childhood. *Journal of Experimental Child Psychology, 37,* 555–575.

Baldwin, M. W., Keelan, J. P. R., Fehr, B., Enns, V., & Koh-Rangarajoo, E. (1996). Social-cognitive conceptualization of attachment working models: Availability and accessibility effects. *Journal of Personality and Social Psychology, 71,* 94–109.

Baltes, P. B., Reese, H. W., & Lipsitt, L. P. (1980). Life-span developmental psychology. *Annual Review of Psychology, 31,* 65–110.

Bandura, A. (1973). *Aggression: A social learning analysis.* Englewood Cliffs, NJ: Prentice Hall.

Bandura, A. (1977). *Social learning theory.* Upper Saddle River, NJ: Prentice Hall.

Bandura, A. (1981). Self-referent thought: A developmental analysis of self-efficacy. In J. Flavell & L. Ross (Eds.), *Social cognitive development: Frontiers and possible futures.* Cambridge, England: Cambridge University Press.

Bandura, A. (1982). Self-efficacy mechanism in human agency. *American Psychologist, 37,* 122–147.

Bandura, A. (1986). *Social foundations of thought and action: A social cognitive theory.* Englewood Cliffs, NJ: Prentice Hall.

Bandura, A. (1991). Social cognitive theory of moral thought and action. In W. M. Kurtines & J. L. Gewirtz (Eds.), *Handbook of moral behavior and development: Vol. 1. Theory.* Hillsdale, NJ: Erlbaum.

Bandura, A. (1994). *Self-efficacy: The exercise of control.* New York: Freeman.

Bandura, A., & Mischel, W. (1965). Modification of self-imposed delay of reward through exposure to live and symbolic models. *Journal of Personality and Social Psychology, 2,* 698–705.

Bandura, A., Ross, D., & Ross, S. A. (1961). Transmission of aggression through imitation of aggressive models. *Journal of Abnormal & Social Psychology, 63,* 575–582.

Bank, S. (1992). Remembering and reinterpreting sibling bonds. In F. Boer & J. Dunn (Eds.), *Children's sibling relationships: Developmental and clinical issues.* Hillsdale, NJ: Erlbaum.

Banks, J. A. (1994). *An introduction to multicultural education.* Needham Heights, MA: Allyn & Bacon.

Banks, J. A. (1995). Multicultural education: Historical development, dimensions, and practice. In J. A. Banks & C. A. M. Banks (Eds.), *Handbook of research on multicultural education.* New York: Macmillan.

Banks, J. A., & Banks, C. A. M. (Eds.). (1995). *Handbook of research on multicultural education.* New York: Macmillan.

Barenboim, C. (1981). The development of person perception in childhood and adolescence: From behavioral comparisons to psychological constructs to psychological comparisons. *Child Development, 52,* 129–144.

Barga, N. K. (1996). Students with learning disabilities in education: Managing a disability. *Journal of Learning Disabilities, 29,* 413–421.

Barker, G. P., & Graham, S. (1987). Developmental study of praise and blame as attributional cues. *Journal of Educational Psychology, 79,* 62–66.

Barker, R. G., & Wright, H. F. (1951). *One boy's day: A specimen record of behavior.* New York: Harper & Brothers.

Barkley, R. A. (1997). *ADHD and the nature of self-control.* New York: Guilford Press.

Barkley, R. A. (1998). *Attention-deficit hyperactivity disorder: A handbook for diagnosis and treatment* (2nd ed.). New York: Guilford Press.

Barnas, M. V., & Cummings, E. M. (1994). Caregiver stability and toddlers' attachment-related behaviors towards caregivers in day care. *Infant Behavior and Development, 17*(2), 141–147.

Baron, J. B. (1987). Evaluating thinking skills in the classroom. In J. B. Baron & R. J. Sternberg (Eds.), *Teaching thinking skills: Theory and practice.* New York: Freeman.

Baron-Cohen, S. (1993). From attention-goal psychology to belief-desire psychology: The development of a theory of mind and its dysfunction. In S. Baron-Cohen, H. Tager-Flusberg, & D. Cohen (Eds.), *Understanding other minds: Perspectives from autism* (pp. 59–82). Oxford, England: Oxford University Press.

Barr, H. M., Streissguth, A. P., Darby, B. L., & Sampson, P. D. (1990). Prenatal exposure to alcohol, caffeine, tobacco, and aspirin: Effects on fine and gross motor performance in 4-year-old children. *Developmental Psychology, 26,* 339–348.

Barr, R. (1999, April). *The role of siblings in the development of imitation.* Paper presented at the biennial meeting of the Society for Research in Child Development, Albuquerque, NM.

Barringer, C., & Gholson, B. (1979). Effects of type and combination of feedback upon conceptual learning by children: Implications for research in academic learning. *Review of Educational Research, 49,* 459–478.

Barron, R. W. (1998). Proto-literate knowledge: Antecedents and influences on phonological awareness and literacy. In C. Hulme & R. M. Joshi (Eds.), *Reading and spelling: Development and disorders.* Mahwah, NJ: Erlbaum.

Barry, H., III, Child, I. L., & Bacon, M. K. (1959). Relations of child training to subsistence economy. *American Anthropologist, 61,* 51–63.

Bar-Tal, D., Raviv, A., & Leiser, T. (1980). The development of altruistic behavior: Empirical evidence. *Developmental Psychology, 16,* 516–524.

Bartlett, E. J. (1982). Learning to revise: Some component processes. In M. Nystrand (Ed.), *What writers know: The language, process, and structure of written discourse.* New York: Academic Press.

Barton, K. C., & Levstik, L. S. (1996). "Back when God was around and everything": Elementary children's understanding of historical time. *American Educational Research Journal, 33,* 419–454.

Basinger, K. S., Gibbs, J. C., & Fuller, D. (1995). Context and the measurement of moral judgment. *International Journal of Behavioral Development, 18,* 537–556.

Bassett, D. S., Jackson, L., Ferrell, K. A., Luckner, J., Hagerty, P. J., Bunsen, T. D., & MacIsaac, D. (1996). Multiple perspectives on inclusive education: Reflections of a university faculty. *Teacher Education and Special Education, 19,* 355–386.

Basso, K. (1972). To give up on words: Silence in western Apache culture. In P. Giglioli (Ed.), *Language and social context.* New York: Penguin Books.

Basso, K. H. (1984). Stalking with stories: Names, places, and moral narratives among the Western Apache. In E. M. Bruner & S. Plattner (Eds.), *Text, play and story: The construction and reconstruction of self and society* (pp. 19–55). Washington, DC: American Ethnological Society.

Bates, E., & MacWhinney, B. (1987). Competition, variation, and language learning. In B. MacWhinney (Ed.), *Mechanisms of language acquisition.* Hillsdale, NJ: Erlbaum.

Bates, J. E., Maslin, C. A., & Frankel, K. A. (1985). Attachment security, mother-child interaction, and temperament as predictors of behavior problem ratings at age three years. In L. Bretherton & E. Waters (Eds.), Growing points of attachment theory and research. *Monographs of the Society for Research in Child Development, 50*(1/2, Serial No. 209).

Batshaw, M. L., & Shapiro, B. K. (1997). Mental retardation. In M. L. Batshaw (Ed.), *Children with disabilities* (4th ed.). Baltimore: Brookes.

Batson, C. D. (1991). *The altruism question: Toward a social-psychological answer.* Hillsdale, NJ: Erlbaum.

Battistich, V., Solomon, D., Kim, D., Watson, M., & Schaps, E. (1995). Schools as communities, poverty levels of student populations, and students' attitudes, motives, and performance: A multilevel analysis. *American Educational Research Journal, 32,* 627–658.

Battistich, V., Solomon, D., Watson, M., & Schaps, E. (1997). Caring school communities. *Educational Psychologist, 32,* 137–151.

Bauer, P. J., & Dow, G. A. (1994). Episodic memory in 16- and 20-month-old children: Specifics not generalized, but not forgotten. *Developmental Psychology, 30,* 403–417.

Baumeister, R. F., & Senders, P. S. (1989). Identity development and the role of structure of children's games. *Journal of Genetic Psychology, 150,* 19–37.

Baumrind, D. (1967). Child care practices anteceding three patterns of preschool behavior. *Genetic Psychology Monographs, 75,* 43–88.

Baumrind, D. (1971). Current patterns of parental authority. *Developmental Psychology Monographs, 4*(1, Pt. 2).

Baumrind, D. (1980). New directions in socialization research. *American Psychologist, 35,* 639–652.

Baumrind, D. (1989). Rearing competent children. In W. Damon (Ed.), *Child development today and tomorrow.* San Francisco: Jossey-Bass.

Baumrind, D. (1991). Parenting styles and adolescent development. In R. Lerner, A. C. Petersen, & J. Brooks-Gunn (Eds.), *The encyclopedia of adolescence.* New York: Garland Press.

Baydar, N., Brooks-Gunn, J., & Furstenberg, F. F., Jr. (1993). Early warning signs of functional illiteracy: Predictors in childhood and adolescence. *Child Development, 64*(3), 815–829.

Bay-Hinitz, A. K., Peterson, R. F., & Quilitch, H. R. (1994). Cooperative games: A way to modify aggressive and cooperative behaviors in young children. *Journal of Applied Behavior Analysis, 27,* 435–446.

Beal, C. R. (1996). The role of comprehension monitoring in children's revision. *Educational Psychology Review, 8,* 219–238.

Bear, G. G., & Richards, H. C. (1981). Moral reasoning and conduct problems in the classroom. *Journal of Educational Psychology, 73,* 644–670.

Bearison, D., & Levey, L. (1977). Children's comprehension of referential communication: Decoding ambiguous messages. *Child Development, 48,* 716–720.

Bearison, D. J. (1998). Pediatric psychology and children's medical problems. In W. Damon (Editor-in-Chief), I. E. Sigel & K. A. Renninger (Vol. Eds.), *Handbook of child psychology: Vol. 4. Child psychology in practice* (5th ed., pp. 635–711). New York: Wiley.

Beatty, B. (1996). Rethinking the historical role of psychology in educational reform. In D. R. Olson & N. Torrance (Eds.), *The handbook of education and human development: New models of learning, teaching and schooling* (pp. 100–116). Cambridge, MA: Blackwell.

Beaty, J. J. (1998). *Observing development of the young child* (4th ed.). Upper Saddle River, NJ: Merrill/Prentice Hall.

Beaty, L. A. (1999). Identity development of homosexual youth and parental and familial influences on the coming out process. *Adolescence, 34,* 597–601.

Beauboeuf-LaFontant, T. (1999). A movement against and beyond boundaries: "Politically relevant teaching" among African American teachers. *Teachers College Record, 100*(4), 702–723.

Beck, I. L., McKeown, M. G., Sinatra, G. M., & Loxterman, J. A. (1991). Revising social studies text from a text-processing perspective: Evidence of improved comprehensibility. *Reading Research Quarterly, 26,* 251–276.

Beck, I. L., McKeown, M. G., Worthy, J., Sandora, C. A., & Kucan, L. (1996). Questioning the author: A yearlong classroom implementation to engage students with text. *The Elementary School Journal, 96,* 385–414.

Becker, B. J. (1986). Influence again: An examination of reviews and studies of gender differences in social influence. In J. S. Hyde & M. C. Linn (Eds.), *The psychology of gender differences: Advances through meta-analysis.* Baltimore: Johns Hopkins University Press.

Beers, J. W. (1980). Developmental strategies of spelling competence in primary school children. In E. H. Henderson & J. W. Beers (Eds.), *Developmental and cognitive aspects of learning to spell: A reflection of word knowledge.* Newark, DE: International Reading Association.

Begg, I., Anas, A., & Farinacci, S. (1992). Dissociation of processes in belief: Source recollection, statement familiarity, and the illusion of truth. *Journal of Experimental Psychology: General, 121,* 446–458.

Beirne-Smith, M., Ittenbach, R., & Patton, J. R. (1998). *Mental retardation* (5th ed.). Upper Saddle River, NJ: Merrill/Prentice Hall.

Belenky, M. F., Bond, L. A., & Weinstock, J. S. (1997). *A tradition that has no name: Nurturing the development of people, families, and communities.* New York: Basic Books.

Belenky, M. F., Clinchy, B. M., Goldberger, N. R., & Tarule, J. M. (1986). *Women's ways of knowing: The development of self, voice, and mind.* New York: Basic Books.

Belfiore, P. J., & Hornyak, R. S. (1998). Operant theory and application to self-monitoring in adolescents. In D. H. Schunk and B. J. Zimmerman (Eds.), *Self-regulated learning: From teaching to self-reflective practice.* New York: Guilford Press.

Bell, C. C., & Jenkins, E. J. (1993). Community violence and children on Chicago's southside. *Psychiatry, 56,* 46–55.

Bell, L. A. (1989). Something's wrong here and it's not me: Challenging the dilemmas that block girls' success. *Journal for the Education of the Gifted, 12,* 118–130.

Bell, N., Grossen, M., & Perret-Clermont, A. (1985). Sociocognitive conflict and intellectual growth. In M. W. Berkowitz (Ed.), *Peer conflict and psychological growth.* San Francisco: Jossey-Bass.

Bell, R. Q. (1988). Contributions of human infants to caregiving and social interaction. In G. Handel (Ed.), *Childhood socialization* (pp. 103–122). New York: Aldine de Gruyter.

Belle, D. (1984). Inequality and mental health: Low income and minority women. In L. Walker (Ed.), *Women and mental health policy* (pp. 135–150). Beverly Hills, CA: Sage.

Belle, D. (1999). *The after-school lives of children: Alone and with others while parents work.* Mahwah, NJ: Erlbaum.

Bell-Scott, P., & Taylor, R. L. (1989). Introduction: The multiple ecologies of black adolescent development. *Journal of Adolescent Research, 4*(2), 119–124.

Belsky, J. (1981). Early human experience: A family perspective. *Developmental Psychology, 17,* 3–23.

Belsky, J., Gilstrap, B., & Rovine, M. (1984). The Pennsylvania Infant and Family Development Project, I: Stability and change in mother-infant and father-infant interaction in a family setting at one, three, and nine months. *Child Development, 55,* 692-705.

Bem, S. L. (1977). On the utility of alternative procedures for assessing psychological androgyny.

Journal of Consulting and Clinical Psychology, 45, 196–205.

Bem, S. L. (1981). Gender schema theory: A cognitive account of sex typing. Psychological Review, 88, 354–364.

Bem, S. L. (1989). Genital knowledge and gender constancy in preschool children. Child Development, 60, 649–662.

Bender, T. A. (1997). Assessment of subjective well-being during childhood and adolescence. In G. D. Phye (Ed.), Handbook of classroom assessment: Learning, achievement, and adjustment. San Diego, CA: Academic Press.

Bennett, D. T., Debold, E., & Solan, S. V. (1991, April). Children and mathematics: Enjoyment, motivation, and Square One TV. Paper presented at the biennial meeting of the Society for Research in Child Development, Seattle, WA.

Bennett, R. E., Gottesman, R. L., Rock, D. A., & Cerullo, F. (1993). Influence of behavior perceptions and gender on teachers' judgments of students' academic skill. Journal of Educational Psychology, 85, 347–356.

Benton, S. L. (1997). Psychological foundations of elementary writing instruction. In G. D. Phye (Ed.), Handbook of academic learning: Construction of knowledge. San Diego, CA: Academic Press.

Bereiter, C., & Scardamalia, M. (1987). The psychology of written composition. Hillsdale, NJ: Erlbaum.

Bergin, D. A. (1996, April). Adolescents' out-of-school learning strategies. Paper presented at the annual meeting of the American Educational Research Association, New York.

Berk, L. E. (1994). Why children talk to themselves. Scientific American, 271, 78–83.

Berk, L. E. (1997). Child development (4th ed.). Boston: Allyn & Bacon.

Berk, L. E., & Spuhl, S. T. (1995). Maternal interaction, private speech, and task performance in preschool children. Early Childhood Research Quarterly, 10, 145–169.

Berkowitz, L. (1968). Responsibility, reciprocity, and social distance in help giving: An experimental investigation of English social class differences. Journal of Experimental Social Psychology, 4, 46–63.

Berkowitz, L. (1989). Frustration-aggression hypothesis: Examination and reformulation. Psychological Bulletin, 106, 59–73.

Berkowitz, L. (1993). Towards a general theory of anger and emotional expression: Implications of the cognitive-neoassociationist perspective for the analysis of anger and other emotions. In R. W. Wyer, Jr., & T. K. Srull (Eds.), Advances in social cognition: Vol. 6. Perspectives on anger and emotion (pp. 1–45). Hillsdale, NJ: Erlbaum.

Berkowitz, M. W., & Gibbs, J. C. (1985). The process of moral conflict resolution and moral development. In M. W. Berkowitz (Ed.), Peer conflict and psychological growth. San Francisco: Jossey-Bass.

Berkowitz, M. W., Guerra, N., & Nucci, L. (1991). Sociomoral development and drug and alcohol abuse. In W. M. Kurtines & J. L. Gewirtz (Eds.), Moral behavior and development: Vol. 3. Application. Hillsdale, NJ: Erlbaum.

Berndt, T. J. (1992). Friendship and friends' influence in adolescence. Current Directions in Psychological Science, 1, 156–159.

Berndt, T. J., & Hoyle, S. G. (1985). Stability and change in childhood and adolescent friendships. Developmental Psychology, 21, 1007–1015.

Berndt, T. J., & Keefe, K. (1995). Friends' influence on adolescents' adjustment to school. Child Development, 66, 1312–1329.

Berndt, T. J., Laychak, A. E., & Park, K. (1990). Friends' influence on adolescents' academic achievement motivation: An experimental study. Journal of Educational Psychology, 82, 664–670.

Berninger, V. W., Fuller, F., & Whitaker, D. (1996). A process model of writing development across the life span. Educational Psychology Review, 8, 193–218.

Bernstein, B. (1971). Class codes and control: Vol. 1. Theoretical studies toward a sociology of language. London: Routledge & Kegan Paul.

Bertenthal, B. I., & Campos, J. J. (1987). New directions in the study of early experience. Child Development, 58, 560–567.

Berti, A. E., & Bombi, A. S. (1988). The child's construction of economics. Cambridge, England: Cambridge University Press.

Berzonsky, M. D. (1988). Self-theorists, identity status, and social cognition. In D. K. Lapsley & F. C. Power (Eds.), Self, ego, and identity: Integrative approaches (pp. 243–261). New York: Springer-Verlag.

Best, D. L., & Ornstein, P. A. (1986). Children's generation and communication of mnemonic organizational strategies. Developmental Psychology, 22, 845–853.

Bezilla, R. (Ed.). (1993). Religion in America. Princeton, NJ: Princeton Religion Research Center.

Bialystok, E. (1994a). Representation and ways of knowing: Three issues in second language acquisition. In N. C. Ellis (Ed.), Implicit and explicit learning of languages. London: Academic Press.

Bialystok, E. (1994b). Towards an explanation of second language acquisition. In G. Brown, K. Malmkjær, A. Pollitt, & J. Williams (Eds.), Language and understanding. Oxford, England: Oxford University Press.

Bibace, R., & Walsh, M. E. (1981). Children's conceptions of illness. In R. Bibace & M. E. Walsh (Eds.), New directions for child development: Children's conceptions of health, illness, and bodily functions (pp. 31–48). San Francisco: Jossey-Bass.

Biddle, S. J. (1993). Children, exercise and mental health. International Journal of Sport Psychology, 24, 200–216.

Bidell, T. R., & Fischer, K. W. (1997). Between nature and nurture: The role of human agency in the epigenesis of intelligence. In R. J. Sternberg & E. L. Grigorenko (Eds.), Intelligence, heredity, and environment (pp. 193–242). Cambridge, England: Cambridge University Press.

Biemiller, A. (1994). Some observations on beginning reading instruction. Educational Psychologist, 29, 203–209.

Bierman, K. L., Miller, C. L., & Stabb, S. D. (1987). Improving the social behavior and peer acceptance of rejected boys: Effect of social skill training with instructions and prohibitions. Journal of Consulting and Clinical Psychology, 55, 194–200.

Biesheuvel, S. (1999). An examination of Jensen's theory concerning educability, heritability and population differences. In A. Montagu (Ed.), Race and IQ (expanded ed.; pp. 108–121). New York: Oxford University Press.

Bigelow, B. J. (1977). Children's friendship expectations: A cognitive developmental study. Child Development, 48, 246–253.

Bigelow, B. J., Tesson, G., & Lewko, J. H. (1999). The contextual influences of sibling and dating relations on adolescents' personal relations and their close friends, dating partners, and parents: The Sullivan-Piaget-Hartup hypothesis considered. In J. A. McLellan & M. J. V. Pugh (Eds.), The role of peer groups in adolescent social identity: Exploring the importance of stability and change. New directions for child and adolescent development (No. 84, pp. 71–86). San Francisco: Jossey-Bass.

Bijeljac-Babic, R., Bertoncini, J., & Mehler, J. (1993). How do 4-day-old infants categorize multisyllable utterances? Developmental Psychology, 29, 711–721.

Binder, L. M., Dixon, M. R., & Ghezzi, P. M. (2000). A procedure to teach self-control to children with attention deficit hyperactivity disorder. Journal of Applied Behavior Analysis, 33, 233–237.

Binns, K., Steinberg, A., Amorosi, S., & Cuevas, A. M. (1997). The Metropolitan Life survey of the American teacher 1997: Examining gender issues in public schools. New York: Louis Harris and Associates.

Birnbaum, D. W., & Croll, W. L. (1984). The etiology of children's stereotypes about sex differences in emotionality. Sex Roles, 10, 677–691.

Bivens, J. A., & Berk, L. E. (1990). A longitudinal study of the development of elementary school children's private speech. Merrill-Palmer Quarterly, 36, 443–463.

Bjorklund, D. F. (1987). How age changes in knowledge base contribute to the development of children's memory: An interpretive review. Developmental Review, 7, 93–130.

Bjorklund, D. F. (1997). In search for a metatheory for cognitive development (or, Piaget is dead and I don't feel so good myself). Child Development, 68, 144–148.

Bjorklund, D. F., & Brown, R. D. (1998). Physical play and cognitive development: Integrating activity, cognition, and education. Child Development, 69, 604–606.

Bjorklund, D. F., & Coyle, T. R. (1995). Utilization deficiencies in the development of memory strategies. In F. E. Weinert & W. Schneider (Eds.), Research on memory development: State of the art and future directions. Hillsdale, NJ: Erlbaum.

Bjorklund, D. F., & Green, B. L. (1992). The adaptive nature of cognitive immaturity. American Psychologist, 47, 46–54.

Bjorklund, D. F., & Jacobs, J. W. (1985). Associative and categorical processes in children's memory: The role of automaticity in the development of organization in free recall. Journal of Experimental Child Psychology, 39, 599–617.

Bjorklund, D. F., Schneider, W., Cassel, W. S., & Ashley, E. (1994). Training and extension of a memory strategy: Evidence for utilization deficiencies in high- and low-IQ children. Child Development, 65, 951–965.

Bjorkqvist, K., Osterman, K., & Kaukiainen, A. (1992). The development of direct and indirect aggressive strategies in males and females. In K. Bjorkqvist & P. Niemala (Eds.), Of mice and women: Aspects of female aggression. San Diego, CA: Academic Press.

Black-Gutman, D., & Hickson, F. (1996). The relationship between racial attitudes and social-cognitive development in children: An Australian study. Developmental Psychology, 32, 448–456.

Blackson, T. C., Butler, T., Belsky, J., Ammerman, R. T., Shaw, D. S., & Tarter, R. E. (1999). Individual traits and family contexts predict sons' externalizing behavior and preliminary relative risk ratios for conduct disorder and substance use disorder outcomes. Drug & Alcohol Dependence, 56(2), 115–131.

Blakemore, C. (1976). The conditions required for the maintenance of binocularity in the kitten's visual cortex. Journal of Physiology, 261, 423–444.

Blasi, A. (1980). Bridging moral cognition and moral action: A critical review of the literature. Psychological Bulletin, 88, 593–637.

Blasi, A. (1995). Moral understanding and the moral personality: The process of moral integration. In W. M. Kurtines & J. L. Gewirtz (Eds.), *Moral development: An introduction.* Boston: Allyn & Bacon.

Block, J. H. (1979). Another look at sex differentiation in the socialization behaviors of mothers and fathers. In J. Sherman & F. L. Denmark (Eds.), *Psychology of women: Future of research.* New York: Psychological Dimensions.

Block, J. H. (1983). Differential premises arising from differential socialization of the sexes: Some conjectures. *Child Development, 54,* 1335–1354.

Block, N. (1999). How heritability misleads about race. In A. Montagu (Ed.), *Race and IQ* (expanded ed.; pp. 444–486). New York: Oxford University Press.

Bloom, B. S. (1964). *Stability and change in human characteristics.* New York: Wiley.

Bloom, L., & Lahey, M. (1978). *Language development and language disorders.* New York: Wiley.

Blyth, D. A., Simmons, R. G., & Zakin, D. F. (1985). Satisfaction with body image for early adolescent females: The impact of pubertal timing within different school environments. *Journal of Youth and Adolescence, 14,* 207–225.

Board on Children and Families, Commission on Behavioral and Social Sciences and Education, National Research Council, & Institute of Medicine. (1995). Immigrant children and their families: Issues for research and policy. *The Future of Children, 5,* 72–89.

Boccia, M., & Campos, J. J. (1989). Maternal emotional signals, social referencing, and infants' reactions to strangers. In N. Eisenberg (Ed.), *New directions for child development* (Vol. 44, pp. 25–49). San Francisco: Jossey-Bass.

Bodine, R. J., & Crawford, D. K. (1999). *Developing emotional intelligence: A guide to behavior management and conflict resolution in schools.* Champaign, IL: Research Press.

Boekaert, M. (1993). Being concerned with well-being and with learning. *Educational Psychologist, 28,* 149–167.

Bogin, B. (1988). *Patterns of human growth.* Cambridge, England: Cambridge University Press.

Bohan, J. S. (1995). *Re-placing women in psychology: Readings toward a more inclusive history* (2nd ed.). Dubuque, IA: Kendall/Hunt.

Bohannon, J. N., MacWhinney, B., & Snow, C. (1990). No negative evidence revisited: Beyond learnability, or who has to prove what to whom. *Developmental Psychology, 26,* 221–226.

Boldizar, J. P., Perry, D. G., & Perry, L. C. (1989). Outcome values and aggression. *Child Development, 60,* 571–579.

Booth, P. B., & Koller, T. J. (1998). Training parents of failure-to-attach children. In J. M. Briesmeister & C. E. Schaefer (Eds.), *Handbook of parent training: Parents as co-therapists for children's behavior problems* (2nd ed., pp. 308–342). New York: Wiley.

Bornstein, M. H., Haynes, O. M., Pascual, L., Painter, K. M., & Galperin, C. (1999). Play in two societies: Pervasiveness of process, specificity of structure. *Child Development, 70,* 317–331.

Botvin, G. J., & Scheier, L. M. (1997). Preventing drug abuse and violence. In D. K. Wilson, J. R. Rodrigue, & W. C. Taylor (Eds.), *Health-promoting and health-compromising behaviors among minority adolescents* (pp. 55–86). Washington, DC: American Psychological Association.

Bouchard, T. J., Jr. (1997). IQ similarity in twins reared apart: Findings and responses to critics. In R. J. Sternberg & E. L. Grigorenko (Eds.), *Intelligence, heredity, and environment* (pp. 126–160). Cambridge, England: Cambridge University Press.

Bouchard, T. J., & McGue, M. (1981). Familial studies of intelligence: A review. *Science, 212,* 1056.

Boutte, G. S., & McCormick, C. B. (1992). Authentic multicultural activities: Avoiding pseudomulticulturalism. *Childhood Education, 68*(3), 140–144.

Bowen, M. (1978). *Family therapy in clinical practice.* New York: Jason Aaronson.

Bowey, J. (1986). Syntactic awareness and verbal performance from preschool to fifth grade. *Journal of Psycholinguistic Research, 15,* 285–308.

Bowie, R., & Bond, C. (1994). Influencing future teachers' attitudes toward Black English: Are we making a difference? *Journal of Teacher Education, 45*(2), 112–118.

Bowlby, J. (1951). *Maternal care and mental health.* Geneva, Switzerland: World Health Organization.

Bowlby, J. (1958). The nature of the child's tie to his mother. *International Journal of Psycho-Analysis, 39,* 350–373.

Bowlby, J. (1969/1982). *Attachment and loss: Vol. 1. Attachment* (2nd ed.). New York: Basic Books.

Bowlby, J. (1973). *Attachment and loss: Vol. 2. Separation: Anxiety and anger.* New York: Basic Books.

Bowlby, J. (1988). *A secure base: Parent-child attachment and healthy human development.* New York: Basic Books.

Bowman, B. T. (1989). Educating language-minority children: Challenges and opportunities. *Phi Delta Kappan, 71,* 118–120.

Boyatzis, R. E. (1973). Affiliation motivation. In D. C. McClelland & R. S. Steele (Eds.), *Human motivation: A book of readings.* Morristown, NJ: General Learning Press.

Boykin, A. W. (1994). Harvesting talent and culture: African-American children and educational reform. In R. J. Rossi (Ed.), *Schools and students at risk: Context and framework for positive change.* New York: Teachers College Press.

Bracken, B. A., & McCallum, R. S. (1998). *Universal Nonverbal Intelligence Test.* Itasca, IL: Riverside.

Bracken, B. A., McCallum, R. S., & Shaughnessy, M. F. (1999). An interview with Bruce A. Bracken and R. Steve McCallum, authors of the Universal Nonverbal Intelligence Test (UNIT). *North American Journal of Psychology, 1,* 277–288.

Bracken, B. A., & Walker, K. C. (1997). The utility of intelligence tests for preschool children. In D. P. Flanagan, J. L. Genshaft, & P. L. Harrison (Eds.), *Contemporary intellectual assessment: Theories, tests, and issues* (pp. 484–502). New York: Guilford Press.

Bradley, L., & Bryant, P. (1991). Phonological skills before and after learning to read. In S. A. Brady & D. P. Shankweiler (Eds.), *Phonological processes in literacy.* Hillsdale, NJ: Erlbaum.

Bradley, R. H., & Caldwell, B. M. (1984). The relation of infants' home environments to achievement test performance in first grade: A follow-up study. *Child Development, 55,* 803–809.

Brain Injury Association. (1999). *Kids' corner.* Retrieved from the World Wide Web: http://www.biausa.org/national.htm.

Brainerd, C. J. (1996). Piaget: A centennial celebration. *Psychological Science, 7*(4), 191–195.

Brand, J. E., & Greenberg, B. S. (1994). Commercials in the classroom: The impact of Channel One advertising. *Journal of Advertising Research, 34,* 18–27.

Bredekamp, S. (Ed.). (1987). *Developmentally appropriate practice in early childhood programs serving children from birth through age 8.* Washington, DC: National Association for the Education of Young Children.

Brener, N. D., Simon, T. R., Krug, E. G., & Lowry, R. (1999). Recent trends in violence-related behaviors among high school students in the United States. *Journal of the American Medical Association, 282,* 440–446.

Brenner, E. M., & Salovey, P. (1997). Emotion regulation during childhood: Developmental, interpersonal, and individual considerations. In P. Salovey & D. J. Sluyter (Eds.), *Emotional development and emotional intelligence: Educational implications* (pp. 168–195). New York: Basic Books.

Brenner, L. A., Koehler, D. J., Liberman, V., & Tversky, A. (1996). Overconfidence in probability and frequency judgments: A critical examination. *Organizational Behavior and Human Decision Processes, 65*(3), 212–219.

Bretherton, I., & Beeghly, M. (1982). Talking about internal states: The acquisition of an explicit theory of mind. *Developmental Psychology, 18,* 906–921.

Bretherton, I., Fritz, J., Zahn-Waxler, C., & Ridgeway, D. (1986). Learning to talk about emotions: A functionalist perspective. *Child Development, 57,* 529–548.

Bretherton, I., & Waters, E. (Eds.). (1985). Growing points in attachment theory and research. *Monographs of the Society for Research in Child Development, 50*(Serial No. 209).

Bridges, L. J., Connell, J. P., & Belsky, J. (1988). Similarities and differences in infant-mother and infant-father interaction in the Strange Situation: A component process analysis. *Developmental Psychology, 24,* 92–100.

Brigham, F. J., & Scruggs, T. E. (1995). Elaborative maps for enhanced learning of historical information: Uniting spatial, verbal, and imaginal information. *Journal of Special Education, 28,* 440.

Brinton, B., & Fujiki, M. (1984). Development of topic manipulation skills in discourse. *Journal of Speech and Hearing Research, 27,* 350–358.

Bristol, M. M., Cohen, D. J., Costello, E. J., Denckia, M., Eckberg, T. J., Kallen, R., Kraemer, H. C., Lord, C., Maurer, R., McIlvane, W. J., Minsher, N., Sigman, M., & Spence, M. A. (1996). State of the science in autism: Report to the National Institutes of Health. *Journal of Autism and Developmental Disorders, 26,* 121–154.

Britt, M. A., Rouet, J-F., Georgi, M. C., & Perfetti, C. A. (1994). Learning from history texts: From causal analysis to argument models. In G. Leinhardt, I. L. Beck, & C. Stainton (Eds.), *Teaching and learning in history.* Hillsdale, NJ: Erlbaum.

Brodal, P. (1992). *The central nervous system: Structure and function.* New York: Oxford Press.

Brody, G. H., & Shaffer, D. R. (1982). Contributions of parents and peers to children's moral socialization. *Developmental Review, 2,* 31–75.

Brody, G. H., Stoneman, Z., & McCoy, J. K. (1994). Forecasting sibling relationships in early adolescence from child temperament and family processes in middle childhood. *Child Development, 65,* 771–784.

Brody, N. (1985). The validity of tests of intelligence. In B. B. Wolman (Ed.), *Handbook of intelligence.* New York: Wiley.

Brody, N. (1992). *Intelligence.* New York: Academic Press.

Brody, N. (1997). Intelligence, schooling, and society. *American Psychologist, 52,* 1046–1050.

Brodzinsky, D. M. (1993). Long-term outcomes in adoption. *The Future of Children, 3*(1), 153–166.

Brodzinsky, D. M., Messer, S. M., & Tew, J. D. (1979). Sex differences in children's expression and control of fantasy and overt aggression. *Child Development, 50,* 372–379.

Bronfenbrenner, U. (1979). *The ecology of human development: Experiments by nature and design.* Cambridge, MA: Harvard University Press.

Bronfenbrenner, U. (1989). Ecological systems theory. In R. Vasta (Ed.), *Annals of child development* (Vol. 6, pp. 187–251). Greenwich, CT: JAI Press.

Bronfenbrenner, U. (1993). The ecology of cognitive development: Research models and fugitive findings. In R. H. Wozniak & K. W. Fischer (Eds.), *Development in context* (pp. 3–44). Hillsdale, NJ: Erlbaum.

Bronfenbrenner, U. (1999a). Is early intervention effective? Some studies of early education in familial and extra-familial settings. In A. Montagu (Ed.), *Race and IQ* (expanded ed.; pp. 343–378). New York: Oxford University Press.

Bronfenbrenner, U. (1999b). Nature with nurture: A reinterpretation of the evidence. In A. Montagu (Ed.), *Race and IQ* (expanded ed.; pp. 153–183). New York: Oxford University Press.

Bronfenbrenner, U., Alvarez, W. F., & Henderson, C. R., Jr. (1984). Working and watching: Maternal employment status and parents' perceptions of their three-year-old children. *Child Development, 55,* 1362–1379.

Bronfenbrenner, U., Kessel, F., Kessen, W., & White, S. (1986). Toward a critical social history of developmental psychology: A propaedeutic discussion. *American Psychologist, 41,* 1218–1230.

Bronson, M. B. (2000). *Self-regulation in early childhood: Nature and nurture.* New York: Guilford Press.

Bronson, W. C. (1981). Toddlers' behaviors with agemates: Issues of interaction, cognition, and affect. *Monographs of Infancy, 1,* 127.

Brook, J. S., Brook, D. W., Gordon, A. S., Whiteman, M., & Cohen, P. (1990). The psychological etiology of adolescent drug use: A family interactional approach. *Genetic Psychology Monographs, 116,* (No. 2).

Brookhart, S. M., & Freeman, D. J. (1992). Characteristics of entering teacher candidates. *Review of Educational Research, 62,* 36–60.

Brooks-Gunn, J. (1989). Pubertal processes and the early adolescent transition. In W. Damon (Ed.), *Child development today and tomorrow* (pp. 155–176). San Francisco: Jossey-Bass.

Brooks-Gunn, J., & Duncan, G. J. (1997). The effects of poverty on children. *The Future of Children: Children and Poverty, 7*(2), 55–71.

Brooks-Gunn, J., & Furstenberg, F. F. (1990). Coming of age in the era of AIDS: Puberty, sexuality, and contraception. *Milbrank Quarterly, 68* (Suppl 1), 59–84.

Brooks-Gunn, J., Klebanov, P. K., & Duncan, G. J. (1996). Ethnic differences in children's intelligence test scores: Role of economic deprivation, home environment, and maternal characteristics. *Child Development, 67,* 396–408.

Brooks-Gunn, J., & Paikoff, R. L. (1992). Changes in self-feelings during the transition toward adolescence. In H. R. McGurk (Ed.), *Childhood social development: Contemporary perspectives* (pp. 63–97). Hillsdale, NJ: Erlbaum.

Brooks-Gunn, J., & Paikoff, R. L. (1993). "Sex is a gamble, kissing is a game": Adolescent sexuality and health promotion. In S. G. Millstein, A. C. Petersen, & E. O. Nightingale (Eds.), *Promoting the health of adolescents: New directions for the twenty-first century* (pp. 180–208). New York: Oxford University Press.

Brophy, J. E. (1987). Synthesis of research on strategies for motivating students to learn. *Educational Leadership, 45*(2), 40–48.

Brown, A. L., & Campione, J. C. (1994). Guided discovery in a community of learners. In K. McGilly (Ed.), *Classroom lessons: Integrating cognitive theory and classroom practice.* Cambridge, MA: MIT Press.

Brown, A. L., & Campione, J. C. (1996). Psychological theory and the design of innovative learning environments: On procedures, principles, and systems. In L. Schauble & R. Glaser (Eds.), *Innovations in learning: New environments for education.* Mahwah, NJ: Erlbaum.

Brown, A. L., & Palincsar, A. S. (1987). Reciprocal teaching of comprehension strategies: A natural history of one program for enhancing learning. In J. Borkowski & J. D. Day (Eds.), *Cognition in special education: Comparative approaches to retardation, learning disabilities, and giftedness.* Norwood, NJ: Ablex.

Brown, A. L., & Palincsar, A. S. (1989). Guided, cooperative learning and individual knowledge acquisition. In L. B. Resnick (Ed.), *Knowing, learning, and instruction: Essays in honor of Robert Glaser.* Hillsdale, NJ: Erlbaum.

Brown, A. L., Susser, E. S., Butler, P. D., Andrews, R. R., Kauffman, C. A., & Gorman, J. M. (1996). Neurobiological plausibility of prenatal nutritional deprivation as a risk factor for schizophrenia. *Journal of Nervous and Mental Disease, 184*(2), 71–85.

Brown, B. (1999). Optimizing expression of the common human genome for child development. *Current Directions in Psychological Science, 8,* 37–41.

Brown, B. B. (1990). Peer groups and peer culture. In S. S. Feldman & G. R. Elliott (Eds.), *At the threshold: The developing adolescent* (pp. 171–196). Cambridge, MA: Harvard University Press.

Brown, B. B. (1993). School culture, social politics, and the academic motivation of U.S. citizens. In T. M. Tomlinson (Ed.), *Motivating students to learn: Overcoming barriers to high achievement.* Berkeley, CA: McCrutchan.

Brown, B. B. (1999). "You're going out with *who?*" Peer group influences on adolescent romantic relationships. In W. Furman, B. B. Brown, & C. Feiring (Eds.), *The development of romantic relationships in adolescence* (pp. 291–329). Cambridge, England: Cambridge University Press.

Brown, B. B., Eicher, S. A., & Petrie, S. (1986). The importance of peer group ("crowd") affiliation in adolescence. *Journal of Adolescence, 9,* 73–96.

Brown, B. B., Feiring, C., & Furman, W. (1999). Missing the love boat: Why researchers have shied away from adolescent romance. In W. Furman, B. B. Brown, & C. Feiring (Eds.), *The development of romantic relationships in adolescence* (pp. 1–16). Cambridge, England: Cambridge University Press.

Brown, J. D., & Siegel, J. D. (1988). Exercise as a buffer of life stress: A prospective study of adolescent health. *Health Psychology, 7,* 341–353.

Brown, J. S., Collins, A., & Duguid, P. (1989). Situated cognition and the culture of learning. *Educational Researcher, 18*(1), 32–42.

Brown, L. M., Tappan, M. B., & Gilligan, C. (1995). Listening to different voices. In W. M. Kurtines & J. L. Gewirtz (Eds.), *Moral development: An introduction.* Boston: Allyn & Bacon.

Brown, R., & Hanlon, C. (1970). Derivational complexity and order of acquisition in child speech. In J. R. Hayes (Ed.), *Cognition and the development of language.* New York: Wiley.

Brown, R. D., & Bjorklund, D. F. (1998). The biologizing of cognition, development, and education: Approach with cautious enthusiasm. *Educational Psychology Review, 10,* 355–373.

Brown, R. T., Reynolds, C. R., & Whitaker, J. S. (1999). Bias in mental testing since *Bias in Mental Testing.* *School Psychology Quarterly, 14,* 208–238.

Brownell, M. T., Mellard, D. F., & Deshler, D. D. (1993). Differences in the learning and transfer performance between students with learning disabilities and other low-achieving students on problem-solving tasks. *Learning Disabilities Quarterly, 16,* 138–156.

Brown-Mizuno, C. (1990). Success strategies for learners who are learning disabled as well as gifted. *Teaching Exceptional Children, 23*(1), 10–12.

Bruer, J. T. (1997). Education and the brain: A bridge too far. *Educational Researcher, 26*(8), 4–16.

Bruer, J. T. (1999). *The myth of the first three years: A new understanding of early brain development and lifelong learning.* New York: Free Press.

Bruner, J. S. (1972). The nature and uses of immaturity. *American Psychologist, 27,* 687–708.

Bruni, M. (1998). *Fine-motor skills in children with Down syndrome: A guide for parents and professionals.* Bethesda, MD: Woodbine House.

Bryan, J. H., Redfield, J., & Mader, S. (1971). Words and deeds concerning altruism and subsequent reinforcement power of the model. *Child Development, 42,* 1501–1508.

Bryant, A. L., & Zimmerman, M. A. (1999, April). *Adolescent substance use and school apathy: A developmental perspective examining motivational, peer, and family factors.* Paper presented at the Biennial Meeting of the Society for Research in Child Development, Albuquerque, NM.

Bryant, B. K. (1985). *The neighborhood walk: Sources of support in middle childhood.* Chicago: University of Chicago Press.

Bryant, P., Nunes, T., & Aidinis, A. (1999). Different morphemes, same spelling problems: Cross-linguistic developmental studies. In M. Harris & G. Hatano (Eds.), *Learning to read and write: A cross-linguistic perspective.* Cambridge, England: Cambridge University Press.

Bryson, S. E. (1997). Epidemiology of autism: Overview and issues outstanding. In D. J. Cohen & F. R. Volkmar (Eds.), *Handbook of autism and pervasive developmental disorders* (2nd ed.). New York: Wiley.

Buchanan, C. M. (1991). Pubertal status in early adolescent girls: Relations to moods, energy, and restlessness. *Journal of Early Adolescence, 11*(2), 185–200.

Buchanan, C. M., Eccles, J. S., & Becker, J. B. (1992). Are adolescents the victims of raging hormones: Evidence for activational effects of hormones on moods and behaviors at adolescence. *Psychological Bulletin, 111*(1), 62–107.

Buchoff, T. (1990). Attention deficit disorder: Help for the classroom teacher. *Childhood Education, 67*(2), 86–90.

Bugental, D. B., & Goodnow, J. J. (1998). Socialization processes. In W. Damon (Editor-in-Chief) and N. Eisenberg (Vol. Ed.), *Handbook of child psychology: Vol. 3. Social, emotional, and personality development* (5th ed., pp. 389–462). New York: Wiley.

Buhrmester, D. (1992). The developmental courses of sibling and peer relationships. In F. Boer and J. Dunn (Eds.), *Children's sibling relationships: Developmental and clinical issues.* Hillsdale, NJ: Erlbaum.

Buhrmester, D. (1996). Need fulfillment, interpersonal competence, and the developmental contexts of friendship. In W. M. Bukowski, A. F. Newcomb, & W. W. Hartup (Eds.), *The company they keep: Friendship during childhood and adolescence* (pp. 158–185). New York: Cambridge University Press.

Bullock, J. R. (1993). Children's loneliness and their relationships with family and peers. *Family Relations, 42,* 46–49.

Burhans, K. K., & Dweck, C. S. (1995). Helplessness in early childhood: The role of contingent worth. *Child Development, 66,* 1719–1738.

Burleson, B. R., & Kunkel, A. W. (1995, March). *Socialization of emotional support skills in childhood: The influence of parents and peers.* Paper presented at the biennial meeting of the Society for Research in Child Development, Indianapolis, Indiana.

Burnett, R. E., & Kastman, L. M. (1997). Teaching composition: Current theories and practices. In G. D. Phye (Ed.), *Handbook of academic learning: Construction of knowledge.* San Diego, CA: Academic Press.

Burton, L. M. (1992). Black grandparents rearing children of drug addicted parents: Stressors, outcomes, and social service needs. *The Gerontologist, 32*(6), 744–751.

Burton, L. M., & Price-Spratlen, T. (1999). Through the eyes of children: An ethnographic perspective on neighborhoods and child development. In A. S. Masten (Ed.), *Cultural processes in child development. The Minnesota Symposia on Child Psychology, 29,* 77–96. Mahwah, NJ: Erlbaum.

Burton, R. V., & Kunce, L. (1995). Behavioral models of moral development: A brief history and integration. In W. M. Kurtines & J. L. Gewirtz (Eds.), *Moral development: An introduction.* Boston: Allyn & Bacon.

Bus, A. G., & van IJzendoorn, M. H. (1999). Phonological awareness and early reading: A meta-analysis of experimental training studies. *Journal of Educational Psychology, 91,* 403–414.

Bush, P. J., Zuckerman, A. E., Taggert, V. S., Theiss, P. K., Peleg, E. O., & Smith, S. A. (1989). Cardiovascular risk factor prevention in Black school children: The 'Know Your Body' evaluation project. *Health Education Quarterly, 16,* 215–227.

Butler, D. L., & Winne, P. H. (1995). Feedback and self-regulated learning: A theoretical synthesis. *Review of Educational Research, 65,* 245–281.

Butterfield, E. C., & Ferretti, R. P. (1987). Toward a theoretical integration of cognitive hypotheses about intellectual differences among children. In J. G. Borkowski & J. D. Day (Eds.), *Cognition in special children: Approaches to retardation, learning disabilities, and giftedness.* Norwood, NJ: Ablex.

Byne, W. (1997). Why we cannot conclude that sexual orientation is primarily a biological phenomenon. *Journal of Homosexuality, 34,* 73–80.

Byrnes, J. P. (1996). *Cognitive development and learning in instructional contexts.* Boston: Allyn & Bacon.

Caetanno, R. (1987). Acculturation and drinking patterns among U.S. Hispanics. *British Journal of Addiction, 82,* 789–799.

Cain, K., & Oakhill, J. (1998). Comprehension skill and inference-making ability: Issues of causality. In C. Hulme & R. M. Joshi (Eds.), *Reading and spelling: Development and disorders.* Mahwah, NJ: Erlbaum.

Cairns, H. S. (1996). *The acquisition of language* (2nd ed.). Austin, TX: Pro-Ed.

Cairns, R. B. (1979). *Social development: The origins and plasticity of interchanges.* San Francisco: Freeman.

Cairns, R. B. (1983). The emergence of developmental psychology. In W. Kessen (Ed.) & P. H. Mussen (Series Ed.), *Handbook of child psychology: Vol. 1. History, theory, and methods* (pp. 41–102). New York: Wiley.

Cairns, R. B., Cairns, B. D., Neckerman, H. J., Ferguson, L. L., & Gariépy, J.-L. (1989). Growth and aggression: 1. Childhood to early adolescence. *Developmental Psychology, 25,* 320–330.

Calfee, R. C., & Masuda, W. V. (1997). Classroom assessment as inquiry. In G. D. Phye (Ed.), *Handbook of classroom assessment: Learning, achievement, and adjustment.* San Diego, CA: Academic Press.

Cameron, C. A., Hunt, A. K., & Linton, M. J. (1996). Written expression as recontextualization: Children write in social time. *Educational Psychology Review, 8,* 125–150.

Campbell, A. (1984). *The girls in the gang: A report from New York City.* New York: Basil Blackwell.

Campbell, D. T., & Stanley, J. C. (1963). Experimental and quasi-experimental designs for research on teaching. In N. L. Gage (Ed.), *Handbook of research on teaching* (pp. 171–246). Chicago: Rand McNally.

Campbell, D. W., Eaton, W. O., McKeen, N. A., & Mitsutake, G. (1999, April). *The rise and fall of motor activity: Evidence of age-related change from 7 to 14 years.* Paper presented at the biennial meeting of the Society for Research in Child Development, Albuquerque, NM.

Campbell, F. A., & Ramey, C. T. (1994). Effects of early intervention on intellectual and academic achievement: A follow-up study of children from low-income families. *Child Development, 65,* 684–698.

Campbell, F. A., & Ramey, C. T. (1995). Cognitive and school outcomes for high-risk African-American students at middle adolescence: Positive effects of early intervention. *American Educational Research Journal, 32,* 742–772.

Campbell, L., Campbell, B., & Dickinson, D. (1998). *Teaching and learning through multiple intelligences* (2nd ed.). Boston: Allyn & Bacon.

Campione, J. C., Shapiro, A. M., & Brown, A. L. (1995). Forms of transfer in a community of learners: Flexible learning and understanding. In A. McKeough, J. Lupart, & A. Marini (Eds.), *Teaching for transfer: Fostering generalization in learning.* Mahwah, NJ: Erlbaum.

Campos, R., Antunes, C. M., Raffaelli, M., Halsey, N., Ude, W., Greco, M., Greco, D., Ruff, A., Rolf, J., & Street Youth Study Group. (1994). Social networks and daily activities of street youth in Belo Horizonte, Brazil. *Child Development, 65,* 319–330.

Candler-Lotven, A., Tallent-Runnels, M. K., Olivýrez, A., & Hildreth, B. (1994, April). *A comparison of learning and study strategies of gifted, average-ability, and learning-disabled ninth grade students.* Paper presented at the annual meeting of the American Educational Research Association, New Orleans, LA.

Capelli, C. A., Nakagawa, N., & Madden, C. M. (1990). How children understand sarcasm: The role of context and intonation. *Child Development, 61,* 1824–1841.

Caplow, T., Bahr, H. M., Chadwick, B. A., Hill, R., & Williamson, M. H. (1982). *Middletown families.* Minneapolis: University of Minnesota Press.

Caprara, G. V., Barbaranelli, C., Pastorelli, C., Bandura, A., & Zimbardo, P. G. (2000). Prosocial foundations of children's academic achievement. *Psychological Science, 11,* 302–306.

Capron, C., & Duyme, M. (1989). Assessment of effects of socio-economic status on IQ in a full cross-fostering study. *Nature, 340,* 552–554.

Carey, S. (1978). The child as word learner. In M. Halle, J. Bresnan, & G. Miller (Eds.), *Linguistic theory and psychological reality.* Cambridge, MA: MIT Press.

Carey, S. (1985a). Are children fundamentally different kinds of thinkers and learners than adults? In S. F. Chipman, J. W. Segal, & R. Glaser (Eds.), *Learning and thinking skills: Vol. 2. Research and open questions.* Hillsdale, NJ: Erlbaum.

Carey, S. (1985b). *Conceptual change in childhood.* Cambridge, MA: MIT Press.

Carey, S., & Bartlett, E. (1978). Acquiring a single new word. *Papers and Reports on Child Language Development, 15,* 17–29.

Carlson, C. L., Pelham, W. E., Milich, R., & Dixon, J. (1992). Single and combined effects of methylphenidate and behavior therapy on the classroom performance of children with attention deficit hyperactivity disorder. *Journal of Abnormal Child Psychology, 20,* 213–232.

Carlson, N. R. (1999). *Foundations of physiological psychology.* Boston: Allyn & Bacon.

Carns, D. (1973). Talking about sex: Notes on first coitus and the double sexual standard. *Journal of Marriage and the Family, 35,* 677–688.

Caron, A. J., Caron, R. F., & MacLean, D. J. (1988). Infant discrimination of naturalistic emotional expressions: The role of face and voice. *Child Development, 59,* 604–616.

Carr, A. A. (1997, March). *The participation "race": Kentucky's site based decision teams.* Paper presented at the annual meeting of the American Educational Research Association, Chicago.

Carr, E. G., Levin, L., McConnachie, G., Carlson, J. I., Kemp, D. C., & Smith, C. E. (1994). *Communication-based intervention for problem behavior: A user's guide for producing positive change.* Baltimore: Brookes.

Carr, M., & Schneider, W. (1991). Long-term maintenance of organizational strategies in kindergarten children. *Contemporary Educational Psychology, 16,* 61–72.

Carraher, T. N., Carraher, D. W., & Schliemann, A. D. (1985). Mathematics in the streets and in the schools. *British Journal of Developmental Psychology, 3,* 21–29.

Carroll, J. B. (1992). Cognitive abilities: The state of the art. *Psychological Science, 3,* 266–270.

Carter, D. B., & Levy, G. D. (1988). Cognitive aspects of early sex-role development: The influence of gender schemas on preschoolers' memories and preferences for sex-typed toys and activities. *Child Development, 59,* 782–792.

Carter, D. E., Detine-Carter, S. L., & Benson, F. W. (1995). Interracial acceptance in the classroom. In H. C. Foot, A. J. Chapman, & J. R. Smith (Eds.), *Friendship and social relations in children* (pp. 117–143). New Brunswick: Transaction Publishers.

Carter, K. R. (1991). Evaluation of gifted programs. In N. Buchanan & J. Feldhusen (Eds.), *Conducting research and evaluation in gifted education: A handbook of methods and applications.* New York: Teachers College Press.

Carter, K. R., & Ormrod, J. E. (1982). Acquisition of formal operations by intellectually gifted children. *Gifted Child Quarterly, 26,* 110–115.

Cartledge, G., & Milburn, J. F. (1995). *Teaching social skills to children and youth: Innovative approaches* (3rd ed.). Needham Heights, MA: Allyn & Bacon.

Casanova, U. (1987). Ethnic and cultural differences. In V. Richardson-Koehler (Ed.), *Educator's* handbook: A research perspective. White Plains, NY: Longman.

Casarez-Levison, R. (2000, April). *In the aftermath of the Columbine tragedy: An exploration of the psychological dimensions of victimization in school settings.* Paper presented at the annual meeting of the American Educational Research Association, New Orleans.

Case, R. (1985). *Intellectual development: Birth to adulthood.* Orlando, FL: Academic Press.

Case, R., & Edelstein, W. (1993). *The new structuralism in cognitive development: Theory and research on individual pathways.* Basel, Switzerland: Karger.

Case, R., & Okamoto, Y., in collaboration with Griffin, S., McKeough, A., Bleiker, C., Henderson, B., & Stephenson, K. M. (1996). The role of central conceptual structures in the development of children's thought. *Monographs of the Society for Research in Child Development, 61*(1–2, Serial No. 246).

Case, R., Okamoto, Y., Henderson, B., & McKeough, A. (1993). Individual variability and consistency in cognitive development: New evidence for the existence of central conceptual structures. In R. Case & W. Edelstein (Eds.), *The new structuralism in cognitive development: Theory and research on individual pathways.* Basel, Switzerland: Karger.

Case-Smith, J. (1996). Fine motor outcomes in preschool children who receive occupational therapy services. *American Journal of Occupational Therapy, 50*(1), 52–61.

Casey, W. M., & Burton, R. V. (1982). Training children to be consistently honest through verbal self-instructions. *Child Development, 53,* 911–919.

Caspi, A. (1998). Personality development across the life course. In W. Damon (Editor-in-Chief) & N. Eisenberg (Vol. Ed.), *Handbook of child psychology: Vol. 3. Social, emotional, and personality development* (5th ed., pp. 311–388). New York: Wiley.

Caspi, A., Taylor, A., Moffitt, T. E., & Plomin, R. (2000). Neighborhood deprivation affects children's mental health: Environmental risks identified in a genetic design. *Psychological Science, 11,* 338–342.

Catania, J. A., Coates, T. J., Stall, R., Turner, H., Peterson, J., Hearst, N., Dolcini, M. M., Hudes, E., Gagnon, J., Wiley, J., & Groves, R. (1992). Prevalence of AIDS-related risk factors and condom use in the United States. *Science, 258,* 1101–1106.

Catron, T. F., & Masters, J. C. (1993). Mothers' and children's conceptualizations of corporal punishment. *Child Development, 64,* 1815–1828.

Cattell, R. B. (1963). Theory of fluid and crystallized intelligence: A critical experiment. *Journal of Educational Psychology, 54,* 1–22.

Cattell, R. B. (1980). The heritability of fluid, g_f, and crystallised, g_c, intelligence, estimated by a least squares use of the MAVA method. *British Journal of Educational Psychology, 50,* 253–265.

Cattell, R. B. (1987). *Intelligence: Its structure, growth, and action.* Amsterdam: North-Holland.

Cauce, A. M., Mason, C., Gonzales, N., Hiraga, Y., & Liu, G. (1994). Social support during adolescence: Methodological and theoretical considerations. In F. Nestemann & K. Hurrelmann (Eds.), *Social networks and social support in childhood and adolescence.* Berlin, Germany: Aldine de Gruyter.

Cazden, C. (1976). Play with language and metalinguistic awareness: One dimension of language experience. In J. Bruner, A. Jolly, & K. Sylva (Eds.), *Play: Its role in development and evolution.* New York: Basic Books.

Cazden, C. B. (1968). The acquisition of noun and verb inflections. *Child Development, 39,* 433–448.

Ceci, S. J., & Roazzi, A. (1994). The effects of context on cognition: Postcards from Brazil. In R. J. Sternberg & R. K. Wagner (Eds.), *Mind in context: Interactionist perspectives on human intelligence.* Cambridge, England: Cambridge University Press.

Ceci, S. J., Rosenblum, T., de Bruyn, E., & Lee, D. Y. (1997). A bio-ecological model of intellectual development: Moving beyond h^2. In R. J. Sternberg & E. L. Grigorenko (Eds.), *Intelligence, heredity, and environment* (pp. 303–322). Cambridge, England: Cambridge University Press.

Ceci, S. J., & Williams, W. M. (1997). Schooling, intelligence, and income. *American Psychologist, 52,* 1051–1058.

Center for the Future of Children. (1993). Overview and major recommendations: Adoption. *The Future of Children, 3*(1), 4–16.

Center for the Future of Children. (1997). Executive Summary: Children and Poverty, *The Future of Children, 7*(2), 1–7.

Cerella, J., & Hale, S. (1994). The rise and fall in information-processing rates over the life span. *Acta Psychologia, 86,* 109–197.

Chafel, J. A. (1991). The play of children: Developmental processes and policy implications. *Child & Youth Care Forum, 20,* 115–132.

Chafel, J. A. (1997). Schooling, the hidden curriculum, and children's conceptions of poverty. *Social Policy Report: Society for Research in Child Development, 11*(1), 1–18.

Chaffee, S. H., & Yang, S. M. (1990). Communication and political socialization. In O. Ichilov (Ed.), *Political socialization, citizenship, education, and democracy* (pp. 137–157). New York: Teachers College Press.

Chaiken, M. R. (1998). Tailoring established afterschool programs to meet urban realities. In D. S. Elliot & B. A. Hamburg (Eds.), *Violence in American schools: A new perspective* (pp. 348–375). New York: Cambridge University Press.

Chalfant, J. C. (1989). Learning disabilities: Policy issues and promising approaches. *American Psychologist, 44,* 392–398.

Chall, J. S. (1996). *Stages of reading development* (2nd ed.) Fort Worth, TX: Harcourt, Brace.

Chalmers, J., & Townsend, M. (1990). The effects of training in social perspective taking on socially maladjusted girls. *Child Development, 61,* 178–190.

Chambliss, M. J. (1994). Why do readers fail to change their beliefs after reading persuasive text? In R. Garner & P. A. Alexander (Eds.), *Beliefs about text and instruction with text.* Hillsdale, NJ: Erlbaum.

Chambliss, M. J. (1998, April). *Children as thinkers composing scientific explanations.* Paper presented at the annual meeting of the American Educational Research Association, San Diego, CA.

Champagne, A. B., & Bunce, D. M. (1991). Learning-theory-based science teaching. In S. M. Glynn, R. H. Yeany, & B. K. Britton (Eds.), *The psychology of learning science.* Hillsdale, NJ: Erlbaum.

Chan, C., Burtis, J., & Bereiter, C. (1997). Knowledge building as a mediator of conflict in conceptual change. *Cognition and Instruction, 15,* 1–40.

Chandler, M. (1982). Social cognition and social structure. In F. C. Serafica (Ed.), *Social cognitive development in context.* New York: Guilford Press.

Chandler, M., & Boyes, M. (1982). Social-cognitive development. In B. Wolman (Ed.), *Handbook of developmental psychology.* Upper Saddle River, NJ: Prentice Hall.

Chandler, M., & Moran, T. (1990). Psychopathy and moral development: A comparative study of delinquent and nondelinquent youth. *Development and Psychopathology, 2,* 227–246.

Chandler, M. J. (1973). Egocentrism and antisocial behavior: The assessment and training of social perspective-taking skills. *Developmental Psychology, 9,* 326–332.

Chandler, T. J. L., & Goldberg, A. D. (1990). The academic All-American as vaunted adolescent role-identity. *Sociology of Sport Journal, 7,* 287–293.

Chang, J.-M. (1998). Language and literacy in Chinese American communities. In B. Pérez (Ed.), *Sociocultural contexts of language and literacy.* Mahwah, NJ: Erlbaum.

Chao, R. K. (1994). Beyond parental control and authoritarian parenting style: Understanding Chinese parenting through the cultural notion of training. *Child Development, 65,* 1111–1119.

Chapman, C., Nolin, M., & Kline, K. (1997). *Student interest in national news and its relation to school courses* (NCES 97–970). Washington, DC: U.S. Department of Education, National Center for Education Statistics.

Charles A. Dana Center. (1999). *Hope for urban education: A study of nine high-performing, high-poverty, urban elementary schools.* Washington, DC: U.S. Department of Education, Planning and Evaluation Service.

Charlesworth, W. R. (1992). Charles Darwin and developmental psychology: Past and present. *Developmental Psychology, 28,* 5–16.

Charlesworth, W. R., & LaFreniere, P. (1983). Dominance, friendship, and resource utilization in preschool children's groups. *Ethology and Sociobiology, 4,* 175–186.

Charman, T., Swettenham, J., Baron-Cohen, S., Cox, A., Baird, G., & Drew, A. (1997). Infants with autism: An investigation of empathy, pretend play, joint attention, and imitation. *Developmental Psychology, 33,* 781–789.

Charner, I., & Fraser, B. S. (1988). *Youth and work: What we know, what we don't know, what we need to know.* Washington, DC: Commission on Work, Family, and Citizenship. (ERIC Document Service No. ED 292 980)

Chase-Lansdale, P. L., & Brooks-Gunn, J. (1994). Correlates of adolescent pregnancy and parenthood. In C. B. Fisher & R. M. Lerner (Eds.), *Applied developmental psychology* (pp. 207–236). New York: McGraw-Hill.

Chase-Lansdale, P. L., Brooks-Gunn, J., & Zamsky, E. S. (1994). Young African-American multigenerational families in poverty: Quality of mothering and grandmothering. *Child Development, 65,* 373–393.

Chasnoff, I. J., Burns, K. A., Burns, W. J., & Schnoll, S. H. (1986). Prenatal drug exposure: Effects on neonatal and infant growth and development. *Neurobehavioral Toxicology & Teratology, 8*(4), 357–362.

Chassin, L., Curran, P. J., Hussong, A. M., & Colder, C. R. (1996). The relation of parent alcoholism to adolescent substance use: A longitudinal follow-up study. *Journal of Abnormal Psychology, 105,* 70–80.

Chavez, A., Martinez, C., Soberanes, B. (1995). Effects of early malnutrition on late mental and behavioral performance. *Developmental Brain Dysfunction, 8*(2–3), 90–102.

Chavkin, N. F. (Ed.). (1993). *Families and schools in a pluralistic society*. Albany: State University of New York Press.

Cheatham, S. K., Smith, J. D., Rucker, H. N., Polloway, E. A., & Lewis, G. W. (1995, September). Savant syndrome: Case studies, hypotheses, and implications for special education. *Education and Training in Mental Retardation*, 243–253.

Chen, J.-Q., Krechevsky, M., & Viens, J. (1998). *Building on children's strengths: The experience of Project Spectrum*. New York: Teachers College Press.

Chen, M. (1984). *A review of research on the educational potential of 3-2-1 Contact: A children's TV series on science and technology*. New York: Children's Television Workshop.

Chen, X., Rubin, K. H., & Li, Z. (1995). Social functioning and adjustment in Chinese children. *Developmental Psychology, 31*, 531–539.

Chen, X., Rubin, K. H., & Sun, Y. (1992). Social reputation and peer relationships in Chinese and Canadian children: A cross-cultural study. *Child Development, 63*, 1336–1343.

Cherlin, A. J., & Furstenberg, F. F., Jr. (1988, September). The changing European family: Lessons for the American reader. *Journal of Family Issues, 9*, 291–297.

Chi, M. T. H. (1978). Knowledge structures and memory development. In R. S. Siegler (Ed.), *Children's thinking: What develops?* Hillsdale, NJ: Erlbaum.

Chiappe, P., & Siegel, L. S. (1999). Phonological awareness and reading acquisition in English- and Punjabi-speaking Canadian children. *Journal of Educational Psychology, 91*, 20–28.

Chilamkurti, C., & Milner, J. S. (1993). Perceptions and evaluations of child transgressions and disciplinary techniques in high- and low-risk mothers and their children. *Child Development, 64*, 1801–1814.

Children's Defense Fund. (1991). *Preventing adolescent pregnancy: What schools can do*. Washington, DC: Author.

Chinn, C. A., & Brewer, W. F. (1993). The role of anomalous data in knowledge acquisition: A theoretical framework and implications for science instruction. *Review of Educational Research, 63*, 1–49.

Chisholm, J. S. (1996). The evolutionary ecology of attachment organization. *Human Nature, 1*, 1–37.

Chomsky, C. S. (1969). *The acquisition of syntax in children from 5 to 10*. Cambridge, MA: MIT Press.

Chomsky, N. (1959). [Review of B. F. Skinner's *Verbal behavior*]. *Language, 35*, 26–58.

Chomsky, N. (1964). *Current issues in linguistic theory*. The Hague, Netherlands: Mouton.

Chomsky, N. (1965). *Aspects of the theory of syntax*. Cambridge, MA: MIT Press.

Chomsky, N. (1972). *Language and mind* (enlarged ed.). San Diego, CA: Harcourt Brace Jovanovich.

Chomsky, N. (1976). *Reflections on language*. London: Temple Smith.

Christie, J. F., & Johnsen, E. P. (1983). The role of play in social-intellectual development. *Review of Educational Research, 53*, 93–115.

Chu, Y.-W. (2000). *The relationships between domain-specific self-concepts and global self-esteem among adolescents in Taiwan*. Unpublished doctoral dissertation, University of Northern Colorado, Greeley.

Chugani, H. T. (1998). Biological bases of emotions: Brain systems and brain development. *Pediatrics, 102*(5 Suppl. E), 1225–1229.

Chukovsky, K. (1968). *From two to five* (M. Morton, Trans.). Berkeley: University of California Press.

Churchill, S. L. (1999, April). *Parent and teacher agreement on child and parenting behaviors as a predictor of child outcomes*. Paper presented at the biennial meeting of the Society for Research in Child Development, Albuquerque, NM.

Cialdini, R. B. (2001). *Influence: Science and practice*. Boston: Allyn & Bacon.

Cicchetti, D., & Garmezy, N. (1993). Prospects and promises in the study of resilience. *Development and Psychopathology, 5*, 497–502.

Cicchetti, D., Rogosch, F. A., & Toth, S. L. (1997). Ontogenesis, depressotypic organization, and the depressive spectrum. In S. S. Luthar, J. A. Burack, D. Cicchetti, & J. R. Weisz (Eds.), *Developmental psychopathology: Perspectives on adjustment, risk, and disorder* (pp. 273–313). Cambridge, England: Cambridge University Press.

Cicchetti, D., & Toth, S. L. (1998). Perspectives on research and practice in developmental psychopathology. In W. Damon (Editor-in-Chief), I. E. Sigel, & K. A. Renninger (Vol. Eds.), *Handbook of child psychology: Vol. 4. Child psychology in practice* (5th ed., pp. 479–583). New York: Wiley.

Clark, B. (1997). *Growing up gifted* (5th ed.). Upper Saddle River, NJ: Merrill/Prentice Hall.

Clark, C. C. (1992). Deviant adolescent subcultures: Assessment strategies and clinical interventions. *Adolescence, 27*(106), 283–293.

Clark, E. V. (1971). On the acquisition of the meaning of "before" and "after." *Journal of Verbal Learning and Verbal Behavior, 10*, 266–275.

Clark, R. M. (1983). *Family life and school achievement: Why poor Black children succeed or fail*. Chicago: University of Chicago Press.

Clarke, L. K. (1988). Invented versus traditional spelling in first graders' writings: Effects on learning to spell and read. *Research in the Teaching of English, 22*, 281–309.

Clarke-Stewart, K. A. (1989). Infant day care: Maligned or malignant? *American Psychologist, 44*, 266–273.

Clasen, D. R., & Brown, B. B. (1985). The multidimensionality of peer pressure in adolescence. *Journal of Youth and Adolescence, 14*, 451–468.

Claude, D., & Firestone, P. (1995). The development of ADHD boys: A 12-year follow-up. *Canadian Journal of Behavioural Science, 27*, 226–249.

Clifford, M. M. (1990). Students need challenge, not easy success. *Educational Leadership, 48*(1), 22–26.

Clinchy, E. (1994). Higher education: The albatross around the neck of our public schools. *Phi Delta Kappan, 75*, 744–751.

Cochran, M. (1993). Personal networks in the ecology of human development. In M. Cochran, M. Larner, D. Riley, L. Gunnarsson, & C. R. Henderson, Jr. (Eds.), *Extending families: The social networks of parents and their children* (pp. 1–33). New York: Cambridge University Press.

Cochran-Smith, M. (1991). *The making of a reader*. Norwood, NJ: Ablex.

Cochran-Smith, M., & Lytle, S. (1993). *Inside out: Teacher research and knowledge*. New York: Teachers College Press.

Cocking, R. R., & Greenfield, P. M. (1996). Introduction. In P. M. Greenfield & R. Cocking (Eds.), *Interacting with video* (pp. 3–7). Norwood, NJ: Ablex.

Coe, J., Salamon, L., & Molnar, J. (1991). *Homeless children and youth*. New Brunswick, NJ: Transaction.

Cohen, D., & Nisbett, R. E. (1994). Self-protection and the culture of honor: Explaining Southern violence. *Personality and Social Psychology Bulletin, 20*, 551–567.

Cohen, E. G. (1994). Restructuring the classroom: Conditions for productive small groups. *Review of Educational Research, 64*, 1–35.

Cohen, E. G., & Lotan, R. A. (1995). Producing equal-status interaction in the heterogeneous classroom. *American Educational Research Journal, 32*, 99–120.

Cohen, G. (1981). Culture and educational achievement. *Harvard Educational Review, 51*, 270–285.

Cohen, M. N. (1998). Culture, not race, explains human diversity. *The Chronicle of Higher Education*, April 17.

Cohen, M. R. (1997). Individual and sex differences in speed of handwriting among high school students. *Perceptual and Motor Skills, 84*(3, Pt. 2), 1428–1430.

Cohen, R. J., & Swerdlik, M. E. (1999). *Psychological testing and assessment*. Mountain View, CA: Mayfield.

Cohn, J. F., Campbell, S. B., & Ross, S. (1991). Infant response in the still-face paradigm at 6 months predicts avoidant and secure attachment at 12 months. *Development and Psychopathology, 3*, 367–376.

Coie, J. D., & Cillessen, A. H. N. (1993). Peer rejection: Origins and effects on children's development. *Current Directions in Psychological Science, 2*, 89–92.

Coie, J. D., & Dodge, K. A. (1988). Multiple sources of data on social behavior and social status. *Child Development, 59*, 815–829.

Coie, J. D., & Dodge, K. A. (1998). Aggression and antisocial behavior. In W. Damon (Editor in Chief) & N. Eisenberg (Vol. Ed.), *Handbook of child psychology: Vol. 3. Social, emotional, and personality development* (pp. 779–862). New York: Wiley.

Coie, J. D., Dodge, K. A., Terry, R., & Wright, V. (1991). The role of aggression in peer relations: An analysis of aggression episodes in boys' play groups. *Child Development, 62*, 812–826.

Coie, J. D., & Kupersmidt, J. (1983). A behavioral analysis of emerging social status in boys' groups. *Child Development, 54*, 1400–1416.

Colby, A., & Kohlberg, L. (1984). Invariant sequence and internal consistency in moral judgment stages. In W. M. Kurtines & J. L. Gewirtz (Eds.), *Morality, moral behavior, and moral development*. New York: Wiley.

Colby, A., Kohlberg, L., Gibbs, J., & Lieberman, M. (1983). A longitudinal study of moral judgment. *Monographs of the Society for Research in Child Development, 48*(1–2, Serial No. 200).

Cole, M., & Schribner, S. (1977). Cross-cultural studies of memory and cognition. In R. V. Kail & J. W. Hagen (Eds.), *Perspectives on the development of memory and cognition*. Hillsdale, NJ: Erlbaum.

Cole, N. S. (1990). Conceptions of educational achievement. *Educational Researcher, 19*(3), 2–7.

Cole, P. (1986). Children's spontaneous control of facial expression. *Child Development, 57*, 1309–1321.

Coles, R. (1967). *Children of crisis: Vol. 1. A study of courage and fear*. Boston: Little, Brown.

Coles, R. (1971a). *Children of crisis: Vol. 2. Migrants, sharecroppers, mountaineers*. Boston: Little, Brown.

Coles, R. (1971b). *Children of crisis: Vol. 3. The south goes north*. Boston: Little, Brown.

Coles, R. (1977). *Children of crisis: Vol. 4. Eskimos, Chicanos, Indians*. Boston: Little, Brown.

Coley, R. L., & Chase-Lansdale, P. L. (1998). Adolescent pregnancy and parenthood. *American Psychologist, 53*, 152–166.

Coll, C. G., Crnic, K., Lamberty, G., Wasik, B. J., Jenkins, R., García, H. V., & McAdoo, H. P. (1996). An integrative model for the study of developmental competencies in minority children. *Child Development, 67,* 1891–1914.

Collaer, M. L., & Hines, M. (1995). Human behavioral sex differences: A role for gonadal hormones during early development? *Psychological Bulletin, 118,* 55–107.

Collier, V. (1989). How long? A synthesis of research on academic achievement in a second language. *TESOL Quarterly, 23,* 509–523.

Collier, V. P. (1992). The Canadian bilingual immersion debate: A synthesis of research findings. *Studies in Second Language Acquisition, 14,* 87–97.

Collingwood, T. R. (1997). *Helping at-risk youth through physical fitness programming.* Champaign, IL: Human Kinetics.

Collins, A., Brown, J. S., & Newman, S. E. (1989). Cognitive apprenticeship: Teaching the crafts of reading, writing, and mathematics. In L. B. Resnick (Ed.), *Knowing, learning, and instruction: Essays in honor of Robert Glaser.* Hillsdale, NJ: Erlbaum.

Collins, W. A. (1990). Parent-child relationships in the transition to adolescence: Continuity and change in interaction, affects, and cognition. In R. Montemayor, G. Adams, & T. Gullota (Eds.), *Advances in adolescent development* (Vol. 2). Beverly Hills, CA: Sage.

Collins, W. A., & Sroufe, L. A. (1999). Capacity for intimate relationships: A developmental construction. In W. Furman, B. B. Brown, & C. Feiring (Eds.), *The development of romantic relationships in adolescence* (pp. 125–147). Cambridge, England: Cambridge University Press.

Colombo, J. (1993). *Infant cognition: Predicting later intellectual functioning.* Newbury Park, CA: Sage.

Comeau, L., Cormier, P., Grandmaison, É., & Lacroix, D. (1999). A longitudinal study of phonological processing skills in children learning to read in a second language. *Journal of Educational Psychology, 91,* 29–43.

Comstock, G., with H. Paik. (1991). *Television and the American child.* San Diego, CA: Academic Press.

Condon, J. C., & Yousef, F. S. (1975). *An introduction to intercultural communication.* Indianapolis, IN: Bobbs-Merrill.

Condry, J. C., & Ross, D. F. (1985). Sex and aggression: The influence of gender label on the perception of aggression in children. *Child Development, 56,* 225–233.

Conn, J., & Kanner, L. (1940). Spontaneous erections in childhood. *Journal of Pediatrics, 16,* 237–240.

Connell, J. P. (1990). Context, self, and action: A motivational analysis of self-system processes across the life span. In D. Cicchetti & M. Beeghly (Eds.), *The self in transition: Infancy to childhood.* Chicago: University of Chicago Press.

Connell, J. P., & Wellborn, J. G. (1991). Competence, autonomy, and relatedness: A motivational analysis of self-system processes. In M. R. Gunnar & L. A. Sroufe (Eds.), *Self processes and development: The Minnesota Symposia on Child Psychology* (Vol. 23). Hillsdale, NJ: Erlbaum.

Connolly, J., & Goldberg, A. (1999). Romantic relationships in adolescence: The role of friends and peers in their emergence and development. In W. Furman, B. B. Brown, & C. Feiring (Eds.), *The development of romantic relationships in adolescence* (pp. 266–290). Cambridge, England: Cambridge University Press.

Consortium for Longitudinal Studies. (1983). *As the twig is bent: Lasting effects of preschool programs.* Hillsdale, NJ: Erlbaum.

Constantina, N. (1998). Adolescents' perceived attachment to parents and its relationship to depression. *Dissertation Abstracts International: Section B. The Sciences and Engineering, 58*(12–B), June, 6870.

Conte, R. (1991). Attention disorders. In B. Y. L. Wong (Ed.), *Learning about learning disabilities.* San Diego, CA: Academic Press.

Cook, B., & Semmel, M. (1999). Peer acceptance of included students with disabilities as a function of severity of disability and classroom composition. *Journal of Special Education, 33*(10), 50–62.

Cook, V., & Newson, M. (1996). *Chomsky's universal grammar: An introduction* (2nd ed.). Oxford, England: Blackwell.

Cooper, C. R., Denner, J., & Lopez, E. M. (1999, Fall). Cultural brokers: Helping Latino children on pathways toward success. *The Future of Children: When School Is Out, 9,* 51–57.

Cooper, H. (1989). Synthesis of research on homework. *Educational Leadership, 47*(3), 85–91.

Cooper, H., Charlton, K., Valentine, J. C., & Muhlenbruck, L. (2000). Making the most of summer school: A meta-analytic and narrative review. *Monographs of the Society for Research in Child Development, 65*(1, Serial No. 260).

Cooper, H., & Dorr, N. (1995). Race comparisons on need for achievement: A meta-analytic alternative to Graham's narrative review. *Review of Educational Research, 65,* 483–508.

Cooper, H., Valentine, J. C., Nye, B., & Lindsay, J. J. (1999). Relationships between five after-school activities and academic achievement. *Journal of Educational Psychology, 91,* 369–378.

Cooper, M. L., & Orcutt, H. K. (1997). Drinking and sexual experience on first dates among adolescents. *Journal of Abnormal Psychology, 106,* 191–202.

Coopersmith, S. (1967). *The antecedents of self-esteem.* San Francisco: Freeman.

Copeland, R. W. (1979). *How children learn mathematics: Teaching implications of Piaget's research* (3rd ed.). New York: Macmillan.

Cornell, D. G., Pelton, G. M., Bassin, L. E., Landrum, M., Ramsay, S. G., Cooley, M. R., Lynch, K. A., & Hamrick, E. (1990). Self-concept and peer status among gifted program youth. *Journal of Educational Psychology, 82,* 456–463.

Corsaro, W. A. (1985). *Friendship and peer culture in the early years.* Norwood, NJ: Ablex.

Cosmides, L., & Tooby, J. (1989). Evolutionary psychology and the generation of culture: II. Case study: A computational theory of social exchange. *Ethology and Sociobiology, 10,* 51–97.

Cossu, G. (1999). The acquisition of Italian orthography. In M. Harris & G. Hatano (Eds.), *Learning to read and write: A cross-linguistic perspective.* Cambridge, England: Cambridge University Press.

Costanzo, P. R., & Fraenkel, P. (1987). Social influence, socialization, and the development of social cognition: The heart of the matter. In N. Eisenberg (Ed.), *Contemporary topics in developmental psychology* (pp. 190–215). New York: Wiley.

Costin, S. E., & Jones, D. C. (1992). Friendship as a facilitator of emotional responsiveness and prosocial interventions among young children. *Developmental Psychology, 28,* 941–947.

Cota-Robles, S., & Neiss, M. (1999, April). *The role of puberty in non-violent delinquency among Anglo-American, Hispanic, and African American boys.* Paper presented at the Biennial Meeting of the Society for Research in Child Development, Albuquerque, NM.

Cottrol, R. J. (1990). America the multicultural. *American Educator, 14*(4), 18–21.

Council for Exceptional Children. (1995). *Toward a common agenda: Linking gifted education and school reform.* Reston, VA: Author.

Covill, A. E. (1997, March). *Students' revision practices and attitudes in response to surface-related feedback as compared to content-related feedback on their writing.* Paper presented at the annual meeting of the American Educational Research Association, Chicago.

Covington, M. V. (1987). Achievement motivation, self-attributions, and the exceptional learner. In J. D. Day & J. G. Borkowski (Eds.), *Intelligence and exceptionality.* Norwood, NJ: Ablex.

Covington, M. V. (1992). *Making the grade: A self-worth perspective on motivation and school reform.* Cambridge, England: Cambridge University Press.

Cox, C. B. (2000). *Empowering grandparents raising grandchildren.* New York: Springer.

Craft, D. H. (1995). Visual impairments and hearing losses. In J. P. Winnick (Ed.), *Adapted physical education and sport* (2nd ed., pp. 143–166). Champaign, IL: Human Kinetics.

Craft, M. (1984). Education for diversity. In M. Craft (Ed.), *Educational and cultural pluralism.* London: Falmer Press.

Crago, M. B., Allen, S. E. M., & Hough-Eyamie, W. P. (1997). Exploring innateness through cultural and linguistic variation. In M. Gopnik (Ed.), *The inheritance and innateness of grammars.* New York: Oxford University Press.

Crago, M. B., Annahatak, B., & Ningiuruvik, L. (1993). Changing patterns of language socialization in Inuit homes. *Anthropology and Education Quarterly, 24,* 205–223.

Crane, J. (1991). The epidemic theory of ghettos and neighborhood effects on dropping out and teenage childbearing. *American Journal of Sociology, 64,* 32–41.

Creasey, G. L., Jarvis, P. A., & Berk, L. E. (1998). Play and social competence. In O. N. Saracho & B. Spodek (Eds.), *Multiple perspectives on play in early childhood education.* Albany: State University of New York Press.

Crick, N. R., & Dodge, K. A. (1994). A review and reformulation of social information-processing mechanisms in children's social adjustment. *Psychological Bulletin, 115,* 74–101.

Crick, N. R., & Dodge, K. A. (1996). Social information-processing mechanisms in reactive and proactive aggression. *Child Development, 67,* 993–1002.

Crick, N. R., & Grotpeter, J. K. (1995). Relational aggression, gender, and social-psychological adjustment. *Child Development, 66,* 710–722.

Crockett, L., Losoff, M., & Peterson, A. C. (1984). Perceptions of the peer group and friendship in early adolescence. *Journal of Early Adolescence, 4,* 155–181.

Cromer, R. F. (1993). Language growth with experience without feedback. In P. Bloom (Ed.), *Language acquisition: Core readings.* Cambridge, MA: MIT Press.

Crouter, A. (1994). Processes linking families and work: Implications for behavior and development in both settings. In R. D. Parke & S. G. Killam (Eds.), *Exploring family relationships with other social contexts.* Hillsdale, NJ: Erlbaum.

Crouzet-Pavan, E. (1997). A flower of evil: Young men in medieval Italy. In G. Levi & J. C. Schmitt (Eds.), *A history of young people in the west: Vol. 1. Ancient and medieval rites of passage* (pp. 173–221). (C. Naish, Trans.) Cambridge, MA: Belknap Press of Harvard University Press.

Crowne, D. P., & Marlowe, D. (1964). *The approval motive: Studies in evaluative dependence.* New York: Wiley.

Csikszentmihalyi, M. (1995). Education for the twenty-first century. *Daedalus, 124*(4), 107–114.

Csikszentmihalyi, M., & Larson, R. (1984). *Being adolescent: Conflict and growth in the teenage years.* New York: Basic Books.

Cunningham, T. H., & Graham, C. R. (1997, March). *Increasing native English vocabulary recognition through Spanish immersion: Cognate transfer from foreign to first language.* Paper presented at the annual meeting of the American Educational Research Association, Chicago.

Curtiss, S. (1977). *Genie: A psycholinguistic study of a modern-day "wild child."* New York: Academic Press.

Dacey, J., & Kenny, M. (1994). *Adolescent development.* Madison, WI: William C. Brown.

Dahlberg, G., Moss, P., & Pence, A. (1999). *Beyond quality in early childhood education and care: Postmodern perspectives.* London: Falmer Press.

Dale, P. S. (1976). *Language development: Structure and function* (2nd ed.). New York: Holt, Rinehart & Winston.

Dalrymple, N. J. (1995). Environmental supports to develop flexibility and independence. In K. A. Quill (Ed.), *Teaching children with autism: Strategies to enhance communication and socialization.* New York: Delmar.

D'Amato, R. C., Chitooran, M. M., & Whitten, J. D. (1992). Neuropsychological consequences of malnutrition. In D. I. Templer, L. C. Hartlage, & W. G. Cannon (Eds.), *Preventable brain damage: Brain vulnerability and brain health.* New York: Springer.

Damon, W. (1977). *The social world of the child.* San Francisco: Jossey-Bass.

Damon, W. (1980). Patterns of change in children's social reasoning: A two-year longitudinal study. *Child Development, 51,* 1010–1017.

Damon, W. (1981). Exploring children's social cognitions on two fronts. In J. M. Flavell & L. Ross (Eds.), *Social cognitive development: Frontiers and possible futures* (pp. 154–175). Cambridge, England: Cambridge University Press.

Damon, W. (1984). Peer education: The untapped potential. *Journal of Applied Developmental Psychology, 5,* 331–343.

Damon, W. (1988). *The moral child: Nurturing children's natural moral growth.* New York: Free Press.

Damon, W. (1991). Putting substance into self-esteem: A focus on academic and moral values. *Educational Horizons, 70*(1), 12–18.

Damon, W., & Hart, D. (1988). *Self-understanding in childhood and adolescence.* New York: Cambridge University Press.

DanceSafe (2000a). *What is LSD?* Oakland, CA: Author. Retrieved from the World Wide Web: http://www.dancesafe.org/lsd.html

DanceSafe (2000b). *What is Speed?* Oakland, CA: Author. Retrieved from the World Wide Web: http://www.dancesafe.org/speed.html

Daniel, W. F., & Yeo, R. A. (1994). Accident proneness and handedness. *Biological Psychiatry, 35*(7), 499.

Danish, S. J., Nellen, V. C., & Owens, S. S. (1996). Teaching life skills through sport: Community based programs for adolescents. In J. V. Raalte & B. W. Brewer (Eds.), *Exploring sport and exercise psychology* (pp. 205–225). Washington, DC: American Psychological Association.

Danner, F. W., & Day, M. C. (1977). Eliciting formal operations. *Child Development, 48,* 1600–1606.

Darling-Hammond, L. (1995). Inequality and access to knowledge. In J. A. Banks & C. A. M. Banks (Eds.), *Handbook of research on multicultural education.* New York: Macmillan.

Darwin, C. (1859). *On the origin of species by means of natural selection, or, the preservation of favored races in the struggle for life.* London: John Murray.

Dauber, S. L., & Epstein, J. L. (1993). Parents' attitudes and practices of involvement in inner-city elementary and middle schools. In N. F. Chavkin (Ed.), *Families and schools in a pluralistic society* (pp. 53–71). Albany: State University of New York Press.

Davenport, E. C., Jr., Davison, M. L., Kuang, H., Ding, S., Kim, S., & Kwak, N. (1998). High school mathematics course-taking by gender and ethnicity. *American Educational Research Journal, 35,* 497–514.

Davidson, F. H. (1976). Ability to respect persons compared to ethnic prejudice in childhood. *Journal of Personality and Social Psychology, 34,* 1256–1267.

Davidson, F. H., & Davidson, M. M. (1994). *Changing childhood prejudice: The caring work of the schools.* Westport, CT: Bergin & Garvey.

Davidson, P., Turiel, E., & Black, A. (1983). The effect of stimulus familiarity on the use of criteria and justification in children's social reasoning. *British Journal of Developmental Psychology, 1,* 49–65.

Davidson, P., & Youniss, J. (1995). Moral development and social construction. In W. M. Kurtines & J. L. Gewirtz (Eds.), *Moral development: An introduction.* Boston: Allyn & Bacon.

Davis, G. A., & Rimm, S. B. (1998). *Education of the gifted and talented* (4th ed.). Boston: Allyn & Bacon.

Davis, G. A., & Thomas, M. A. (1989). *Effective schools and effective teachers.* Needham Heights, MA: Allyn & Bacon.

Dawson, D. A. (1991). Family structure and children's health and well-being: Data from the 1988 National Health Interview Survey on Child Health. *Journal of Marriage and the Family, 53,* 573–584.

Deal, L. W., Gomby, D. S., Zippiroli, L., & Behrman, R. E. (2000). Unintentional injuries in childhood: Analysis and recommendations. *Future of Children, 10*(1), 4–22.

Deaux, K. (1984). From individual differences to social categories: Analysis of a decade's research on gender. *American Psychologist, 39,* 105–116.

De Cecco, J. P., & Parker, D. A. (1995). The biology of homosexuality: Sexual orientation or sexual preference. *Journal of Homosexuality, 28,* 1–27.

deCharms, R. (1984). Motivation enhancement in educational settings. In R. Ames & C. Ames (Eds.), *Research on motivation in education: Vol. 1. Student motivation.* Orlando, FL: Academic Press.

Deci, E. L. (1992). The relation of interest to the motivation of behavior: A self-determination theory perspective. In K. A. Renninger, S. Hidi, & A. Krapp (Eds.), *The role of interest in learning and development.* Hillsdale, NJ: Erlbaum.

Deci, E. L., & Ryan, R. M. (1985). *Intrinsic motivation and self-determination in human behavior.* New York: Plenum Press.

Deci, E. L., & Ryan, R. M. (1987). The support of autonomy and the control of behavior. *Journal of Personality and Social Psychology, 53,* 1024–1037.

Deci, E. L., & Ryan, R. M. (1992). The initiation and regulation of intrinsically motivated learning and achievement. In A. K. Boggiano & T. S. Pittman (Eds.), *Achievement and motivation: A social-developmental perspective.* Cambridge, England: Cambridge University Press.

Deci, E. L., & Ryan, R. M. (1995). Human autonomy: The basis for true self-esteem. In M. H. Kernis (Ed.), *Efficacy, agency, and self-esteem.* New York: Plenum Press.

De Corte, E., Greer, B., & Verschaffel, L. (1996). Mathematics teaching and learning. In D. C. Berliner & R. C. Calfee (Eds.), *Handbook of educational psychology.* New York: Macmillan.

DeKlynen, M., Speltz, M. L., & Greenberg, M. T. (1998). Fathering and early onset of conduct problems: Positive and negative parenting, father-son attachment, and the marital context. *Clinical Child & Family Psychology Review, 1*(1), 3–28.

Dekovic, M., & Janssens, J. M. (1992). Parents' child-rearing style and child's sociometric status. *Developmental Psychology, 28,* 925–932.

DeLain, M. T., Pearson, P. D., & Anderson, R. C. (1985). Reading comprehension and creativity in black language use: You stand to gain by playing the sounding game! *American Educational Research Journal, 22,* 155–173.

DeLamater, J., & MacCorquodale, P. (1979). *Premarital sexuality: Attitudes, relationships, behavior.* Madison: The University of Wisconsin Press.

De La Paz, S., Swanson, P. N., & Graham, S. (1998). The contribution of executive control to the revising by students with writing and learning difficulties. *Journal of Educational Psychology, 90,* 448–460.

Delgado-Gaitan, C. (1992). School matters in the Mexican-American home: Socializing children to education. *American Educational Research Journal, 29,* 495–513.

Delgado-Gaitan, C. (1994). Socializing young children in Mexican-American families: An intergenerational perspective. In P. M. Greenfield & R. R. Cocking (Eds.), *Cross-cultural roots of minority child development* (pp. 55–86). Hillsdale, NJ: Erlbaum.

DeLisi, R., & Gallagher, A. M. (1991). Understanding of gender stability and constancy in Argentinian children. *Merrill-Palmer Quarterly, 37,* 483–502.

DeLisle, J. R. (1984). *Gifted children speak out.* New York: Walker.

DeLoache, J. S., Cassidy, D. J., & Brown, A. L. (1985). Precursors of mnemonic strategies in very young children's memory. *Child Development, 56,* 125–137.

DeLoache, J. S., Miller, K. F., & Rosengren, K. S. (1997). The credible shrinking room: Very young children's performance with symbolic and non-symbolic relations. *Psychological Science, 8,* 308–313.

DeLoache, J. S., & Todd, C. M. (1988). Young children's use of spatial categorization as a mnemonic strategy. *Journal of Experimental Child Psychology, 46,* 1–20.

deMarrais, K. B., Nelson, P. A., & Baker, J. H. (1994). Meaning in mud: Yup'ik Eskimo girls at play. In J. L. Roopnarine, J. E. Johnson, & F. H. Hooper (Eds.), *Children's play in diverse cultures.* Albany, NY: SUNY Press.

Dempster, F. N., & Corkill, A. J. (1999). Interference and inhibition in cognition and behavior: Unifying themes for educational psychology. *Educational Psychology Review, 11,* 1–88.

Denkla, M. B. (1986). New diagnostic criteria for autism and related behavioral disorders: Guidelines for research protocols. *Journal of the American Academy of Child Psychiatry, 25,* 221–224.

DeRidder, L. M. (1993). Teenage pregnancy: Etiology and educational interventions. *Educational Psychology Review, 5,* 87–107.

Derry, S. J. (1996). Cognitive schema theory in the constructivist debate. *Educational Psychologist, 31,* 163–174.

Deshler, D. D., & Schumaker, J. B. (1988). An instructional model for teaching students how to learn. In J. L. Graden, J. E. Zins, & M. J. Curtis (Eds.), *Alternative educational delivery systems: Enhancing instructional options for all students.* Washington, DC: National Association of School Psychologists.

Deutsch, F. M., Ruble, N., Fleming, A., & Brooks-Gunn, J. (1988). Information-seeking and maternal self-definition during the transition to motherhood. *Journal of Personality and Social Psychology, 55*(3), 420–431.

Deutsch, M. (1993). Educating for a peaceful world. *American Psychologist, 48,* 510–517.

Deutsch, M. P. (1963). The disadvantaged child and the learning process. In A. H. Passow (Ed.), *Education in depressed areas.* New York: Teachers College Press.

DeVault, G., Krug, C., & Fake, S. (1996, September). Why does Samantha act that way: Positive behavioral support leads to successful inclusion. *Exceptional Parent,* 43–47.

Devine, P. G. (1995). Prejudice and out-group perception. In A. Tesser (Ed.), *Advanced social psychology.* New York: McGraw-Hill.

Devlin, B., Fienberg, S. E., Resnick, D. P., & Roeder, K. (1995). Galton redux: Intelligence, race, and society: A review of "The Bell Curve: Intelligence and Class Structure in American Life." *American Statistician, 90,* 1483–1488.

DeVries, M. W., & Sameroff, A. J. (1984). Culture and temperament: Influences on infant temperament in three East-African societies. *American Journal of Orthopsychiatry, 54,* 83–96.

DeVries, R. (1997). Piaget's social theory. *Educational Researcher, 26*(2), 4–17.

DeVries, R., & Zan, B. (1996). A constructivist perspective on the role of the sociomoral atmosphere in promoting children's development. In C. T. Fosnot (Ed.), *Constructivism: Theory, perspectives, and practice.* New York: Teachers College Press.

Diagram Group, The. (1983). *The human body on file.* New York: Facts on File.

Diamond, L. M., Savin-Williams, R. C., & Dub?, E. M. (1999). Sex, dating, passionate friendships, and romance: Intimate peer relations among lesbian, gay, and bisexual adolescents. In W. Furman, B. B. Brown, & C. Feiring (Eds.), *The development of romantic relationships in adolescence* (pp. 175–210). Cambridge, England: Cambridge University Press.

Diamond, M., & Hopson, J. (1998). *Magic trees of the mind.* New York: Dutton.

Diamond, S. C. (1991). What to do when you can't do anything: Working with disturbed adolescents. *Clearing House, 64,* 232–234.

Diaz, R. M. (1983). Thought and two languages: The impact of bilingualism on cognitive development. In E. W. Gordon (Ed.), *Review of research in education* (Vol. 10). Washington, DC: American Educational Research Association.

Diaz, R. M., & Berndt, T. J. (1982). Children's knowledge of best friend: Fact or fancy? *Developmental Psychology, 18,* 787–794.

Diaz, R. M., & Klingler, C. (1991). Toward an explanatory model of the interaction between bilingualism and cognitive development. In E. Bialystok (Ed.), *Language processing in bilingual children.* Cambridge, England: Cambridge University Press.

Dickemann, M. (1995). Wilson's panchreston: The inclusive fitness hypothesis of sociobiology reexamined. *Journal of Homosexuality, 28,* 147–183.

Dickinson, D., Wolf, M., & Stotsky, S. (1993). Words move: The interwoven development of oral and written language. In J. B. Gleason (Ed.),

The development of language. Boston: Allyn & Bacon.

Dien, T. (1998). Language and literacy in Vietnamese American communities. In B. Pérez (Ed.), *Sociocultural contexts of language and literacy.* Mahwah, NJ: Erlbaum.

DiLalla, E. F. (1998). Daycare, child, and family influences on preschoolers' social behaviors in a peer play. *Child Study Journal, 28,* 223–244.

Diller, D. (1999). Opening the dialogue: Using culture as a tool in teaching young African American children. *The Reading Teacher, 52,* 820–828.

diSessa, A. A. (1996). What do "just plain folk" know about physics? In D. R. Olson & N. Torrance (Eds.), *The handbook of education and human development: New models of learning, teaching, and schooling.* Cambridge, MA: Blackwell.

Dishion, T. J., Andrews, D. W., & Crosby, L. (1995). Antisocial boys and their friends in early adolescence: Relationship characteristics, quality, and interactional process. *Child Development, 66,* 139–151.

Dishion, T. J., Spracklen, K. M., Andrews, D. W., & Patterson, G. R. (1996). Deviancy training in male adolescents' friendships. *Behavior Therapy, 27,* 373–390.

Dixon, R. A., & Lerner, R. M. (1992). A history of systems in developmental psychology. In M. H. Bornstein & M. E. Lamb (Eds.), *Developmental psychology: An advanced textbook* (3rd ed., pp. 3–58). Hillsdale, NJ: Erlbaum.

Dodge, K. A. (1980). Social cognition and children's aggressive behavior. *Child Development, 51,* 162–170.

Dodge, K. A. (1983). Behavioral antecedents of peer social status. *Child Development, 54,* 1386–1399.

Dodge, K. A. (1986). A social information processing model of social competence in children. In M. Perlmutter (Ed.), *Minnesota symposia on child psychology: Vol. 18. Cognitive perspectives in children's social and behavioral development.* Hillsdale, NJ: Erlbaum.

Dodge, K. A., Bates, J. E., & Pettit, G. S. (1990). Mechanisms in the cycle of violence. *Science, 250,* 1678–1683.

Dodge, K. A., Coie, J. D., & Brakke, N. P. (1982). Behavior patterns of socially rejected and neglected preadolescents: The role of social approach and aggression. *Journal of Abnormal Child Psychology, 10,* 389–410.

Dodge, K. A., Lochman, J. E., Harnish, J. D., Bates, J. E., & Pettit, G. S. (1997). Reactive and proactive aggression in school children and psychiatrically impaired chronically assaultive youth. *Journal of Abnormal Psychology, 106,* 37–51.

Dodge, K. A., Pettit, G. S., Bates, J. E., & Valente, E. (1995). Social information processing patterns partially mediate the effect of early physical abuse on later conduct problems. *Journal of Abnormal Psychology, 104,* 632–643.

Dodge, K. A., Schlundt, D. G., Schocken, I., & Delugach, J. D. (1983). Social competence and children's social status: The role of peer group entry strategies. *Merrill-Palmer Quarterly, 29,* 309–336.

Doescher, S. M., & Sugawara, A. I. (1989). Encouraging prosocial behavior in young children. *Childhood Education, 65,* 213–216.

Dole, J. A., Duffy, G. G., Roehler, L. R., & Pearson, P. D. (1991). Moving from the old to the new: Research on reading comprehension instruction. *Review of Educational Research, 61,* 239–264.

Donaldson, M. (1978). *Children's minds.* New York: Norton.

Donaldson, S. K., & Westerman, M. A. (1986). Development of children's understanding of ambivalence and causal theories of emotion. *Developmental Psychology, 22,* 655–662.

Donato, F., Assanelli, D., Chiesa, R., Poeta, M. L., Tomansoni, V., & Turla, C. (1997). Cigarette smoking and sports participation in adolescents: A cross-sectional survey among high school students in Italy. *Substance Use and Misuse, 32,* 1555–1572.

Dornbusch, S. M., Carlsmith, J. M., Gross, R. T., Martin, J. A., Jennings, D., Rosenberg, A., & Duke, P. (1981). Sexual development, age, and dating: A comparison of biological and social influences upon one set of behaviors. *Child Development, 52,* 179–185.

Dornbusch, S. M., Ritter, P. L., Leiderman, P. H., Roberts, D. F., & Fraleigh, M. J. (1987). The relation of parenting style to adolescent school performance. *Child Development, 58,* 1244–1257.

Dovidio, J. F., & Gaertner, S. L. (1999). Reducing prejudice: Combating intergroup biases. *Current Directions in Psychological Science, 8,* 101–105.

Downey, G., Bonica, C., & Rinc-n, C. (1999). Rejection sensitivity and adolescent romantic relationships. In W. Furman, B. B. Brown, & C. Feiring (Eds.), *The development of romantic relationships in adolescence* (pp. 148–174). Cambridge, England: Cambridge University Press.

Downey, G., Lebolt, A., Rinc-n, C., & Freitas, A. L. (1998). Rejection sensitivity and children's interpersonal difficulties. *Child Development, 69,* 1074–1091.

Downey, J. (2000, March). *The role of schools in adolescent resilience: Recommendations from the literature.* Paper presented at the International Association of Adolescent Health, Washington, DC.

Downing, J. (1986). Cognitive clarity: A unifying and cross-cultural theory for language awareness phenomena in reading. In D. B. Yaden, Jr., & S. Templeton (Eds.), *Metalinguistic awareness and beginning literacy: Conceptualizing what it means to read and write.* Portsmouth, NH: Heinemann.

Doyle, A. (1982). Friends, acquaintances, and strangers: The influence of familiarity and ethnolinguistic background on social interaction. In K. H. Rubin & H. S. Ross (Eds.), *Peer relationships and social skills in childhood* (pp. 229–252). New York: Springer-Verlag.

Doyle, W. (1983). Academic work. *Review of Educational Research, 53,* 159–199.

Doyle, W. (1986). Classroom organization and management. In M. C. Wittrock (Ed.), *Handbook of research on teaching* (3rd ed.). New York: Macmillan.

Dreman, S. B. (1976). Sharing behavior in Israeli school children: Cognitive and social learning factors. *Child Development, 47,* 186–194.

Dryden, M. A., & Jefferson, P. (1994, April). *Use of background knowledge and reading achievement among elementary school students.* Paper presented at the annual meeting of the American Educational Research Association, New Orleans, LA.

Dryfoos, J. G. (1999, Fall). The role of the school in children's out-of-school time. *The Future of Children: When School Is Out, 9,* 117–134.

Dube, E. F. (1982). Literacy, cultural familiarity, and "intelligence" as determinants of story recall. In U. Neisser (Ed.), *Memory observed: Remembering in natural contexts.* San Francisco: Freeman.

Dube, M., Julien, D., Lebeau, E., & Gagnon, I. (2000). Marital satisfaction of mothers and the quality of daily interaction with their adolescents. *Canadian Journal of Behavioural Science, 32*(1), 18–28.

Duit, R. (1991). Students' conceptual frameworks: Consequences for learning science. In S. M. Glynn, R. H. Yeany, & B. K. Britton (Eds.), *The psychology of learning science*. Hillsdale, NJ: Erlbaum.

Dunbar, N. D., Azmitia, M., & Brown, J. R. (1999, April). *Mexican-descent parents' beliefs and guidance strategies for their adolescent children's paths in life*. Paper presented at the biennial meeting of the Society for Research in Child Development, Albuquerque, NM.

Dunbar, R. (1992). Mating and parental care. In S. Jones, R. Martin, D. Pilbeam, & S. Bunney (Eds.), *Cambridge encyclopedia of human evolution* (pp. 150–154). Cambridge, England: Cambridge University Press.

Duncan, G. J., Yeung, W. J., Brooks-Gunn, J., & Smith, J. R. (1998). How much does childhood poverty affect the life chances of children? *American Sociological Review, 63*(3), 406–423.

Duncan, P. D., Ritter, P. L., Dornbusch, S. M., Gross, R. T., & Carlsmith, J. M. (1985). The effects of pubertal timing on body image, school behavior, and deviance. *Journal of Youth and Adolescence, 14*, 227–235.

Dunham, P. J., Dunham, F., & Curwin, A. (1993). Joint-attentional states and lexical acquisition at 18 months. *Developmental Psychology, 29*, 827–831.

Dunn, J. (1984). *Sisters and brothers*. Cambridge, MA: Harvard University Press.

Dunn, J. (1987). The beginnings of moral understanding: Development in the second year. In J. Kagan & S. Lamb (Eds.), *The emergence of morality in young children* (pp. 91–112). Chicago: University of Chicago Press.

Dunn, J. (1988). *The beginnings of social understanding*. Cambridge, MA: Harvard University Press.

Dunn, J. (1993). Social interaction, relationships, and the development of causal discourse and conflict management. *European Journal of Psychology of Education, 8*, 391–401.

Dunn, J. (1996). Sibling relationships and perceived self-competence: Patterns of stability between childhood and early adolescence. In A. J. Sameroff & M. M. Haith (Eds.), *The five to seven year shift* (pp. 253–270). Chicago: University of Chicago Press.

Dunn, J., Bretherton, I., & Munn, P. (1987). Conversations about feeling states between mothers and their young children. *Developmental Psychology, 23*, 132–139.

Dunn, J., & Munn, P. (1987). Development of justification in disputes with mother and sibling. *Developmental Psychology, 23*, 791–798.

Dunton, K. J., McDevitt, T. M., & Hess, R. D. (1988). Origins of mothers' attributions about their daughters' and sons' performance in mathematics in sixth grade. *Merrill-Palmer Quarterly, 34*, 47–70.

DuPaul, G. J., & Eckert, T. L. (1994). The effects of social skills curricula: Now you see them, now you don't. *School Psychology Quarterly, 9*, 113–132.

Duran, B. J., & Weffer, R. E. (1992). Immigrants' aspirations, high school process, and academic outcomes. *American Educational Research Journal, 29*, 163–181.

Durand, V. M. (1998). *Sleep better: A guide to improving sleep for children with special needs*. Baltimore: Brookes.

Durby, D. D. (1994). Gay, lesbian, and bisexual youth. In T. DeCrescenzo (Ed.), *Helping gay and lesbian youth: New policies, new programs, new practice* (pp. 1–37). New York: The Haworth Press.

Durkin, K. (1987). Social cognition and social context in the construction of sex differences. In M. A. Baker (Ed.), *Sex differences in human performance*. Chichester, England: Wiley.

Durkin, K. (1995). *Developmental social psychology: From infancy to old age*. Cambridge, MA: Blackwell.

Dweck, C. S. (1975). The role of expectations and attributions in the alleviation of learned helplessness. *Journal of Personality and Social Psychology, 31*, 674–685.

Dweck, C. S. (1978). Achievement. In M. E. Lamb (Ed.), *Social and personality development*. New York: Holt, Rinehart & Winston.

Dweck, C. S. (1986). Motivational processes affecting learning. *American Psychologist, 41*, 1040–1048.

Dweck, C. S., & Elliott, E. S. (1983). Achievement motivation. In E. M. Hetherington (Ed.), *Handbook of child psychology: Vol. 4. Socialization, personality, and social development* (4th ed.). New York: Wiley.

Dweck, C. S., & Leggett, E. L. (1988). A social-cognitive approach to motivation and personality. *Psychological Review, 95*, 256–273.

Dyson, A. H. (1986). Children's early interpretations of writing: Expanding research perspectives. In D. B. Yaden, Jr., & S. Templeton (Eds.), *Metalinguistic awareness and beginning literacy: Conceptualizing what it means to read and write*. Portsmouth, NH: Heinemann.

Eacott, M. J. (1999). Memory for the events of early childhood. *Current Directions in Psychological Science, 8*, 46–49.

Eagly, A. H. (1987). *Sex differences in social behavior: A social-role interpretation*. Hillsdale, NJ: Erlbaum.

Eagly, A. H., & Crowley, M. (1986). Gender and helping behavior: A meta-analytic review of the social psychological literature. *Psychological Bulletin, 100*, 283–308.

Eaton, W. O., & Enns, L. R. (1986). Sex differences in human motor activity level. *Psychological Bulletin, 100*, 19–28.

Eccles, J. (1999, Fall). The development of children ages 6 to 14. *The Future of Children: When School Is Out, 9*, 30–44.

Eccles, J. S. (1989). Bringing young women to math and science. In M. Crawford & M. Gentry (Eds.), *Gender and thought: Psychological perspectives*. New York: Springer-Verlag.

Eccles, J. S., & Harold, R. D. (1993). Parent-school involvement during the early adolescent years. *Teachers College Record, 94*, 568–587.

Eccles, J. S., & Jacobs, J. E. (1986). Social forces shape math attitudes and performance. *Signs: Journal of Women in Culture and Society, 11*, 367–380.

Eccles, J. S., Jacobs, J., Harold-Goldsmith, R., Jayaratne, T., & Yee, D. (1989, April). *The relations between parents' category-based and target-based beliefs: Gender roles and biological influences*. Paper presented at the Society for Research in Child Development, Kansas City, MO.

Eccles, J. S., & Midgley, C. (1989). Stage-environment fit: Developmentally appropriate classrooms for young adolescents. In C. Ames & R. Ames (Eds.), *Research on motivation in education: Vol. 3. Goals and cognition*. San Diego, CA: Academic Press.

Eccles, J. S., & Wigfield, A. (1985). Teacher expectations and student motivation. In J. B. Dusek (Ed.), *Teacher expectancies*. Hillsdale, NJ: Erlbaum.

Eccles, J. S., Wigfield, A., & Schiefele, U. (1998). Motivation to succeed. In W. Damon (Editor-in-Chief) & N. Eisenberg (Vol. Ed.), *Handbook of child psychology: Vol. 3. Social, emotional, and personality development* (5th ed.). New York: Wiley.

Eccles (Parsons), J. S. (1983). Expectancies, values, and academic behaviors. In J. T. Spence (Ed.), *Achievement and achievement motivation*. San Francisco: Freeman.

Eccles (Parsons), J. S. (1984). Sex differences in mathematics participation. In M. Steinkamp & M. Maehr (Eds.), *Women in science*. Greenwich, CT: JAI Press.

Echols, L. D., West, R. F., Stanovich, K. E., & Kehr, K. S. (1996). Using children's literacy activities to predict growth in verbal cognitive skills: A longitudinal investigation. *Journal of Educational Psychology, 88*, 296–304.

Eckerman, C. O. (1979). The human infant in social interaction. In R. Cairns (Ed.), *The analysis of social interactions: Methods, issues, and illustrations* (pp. 163–178). Hillsdale, NJ: Erlbaum.

Eckerman, C. O., & Didow, S. M. (1996). Nonverbal imitation and toddlers' mastery of verbal means of achieving coordinated action. *Developmental Psychology, 32*, 141–152.

Eckman, P. (1972). Universals and cultural differences in facial expressions of emotion. In J. K. Cole (Ed.), *Nebraska symposium on motivation*. Lincoln: University of Nebraska Press.

Edelman, M. W. (1993, March). Investing in our children: A struggle for America's conscience and future. *USA Today, 121*(2574), 24–26.

Edelsky, C., Altwerger, B., & Flores, B. (1991). *Whole language: What's the difference?* Portsmouth, NH: Heinemann.

Eden, G. F., Stein, J. F., & Wood, F. B. (1995). Verbal and visual problems in reading disability. *Journal of Learning Disabilities, 28*, 272–290.

Eder, D. (1985). The cycle of popularity: Interpersonal relations among female adolescents. *Sociology of Education, 58*, 154–165.

Edmundson, P. J. (1990). A normative look at the curriculum in teacher education. *Phi Delta Kappan, 71*, 717–722.

Edwards, P. A., & Garcia, G. E. (1994). The implications of Vygotskian theory for the development of home-school programs: A focus on storybook reading. In V. John-Steiner, C. P. Panofsky, & L. W. Smith (Eds.), *Sociocultural approaches to language and literacy: An interactionist perspective*. Cambridge, England: Cambridge University Press.

Eeds, M., & Wells, D. (1989). Grand conversations: An explanation of meaning construction in literature study groups. *Research in the Teaching of English, 23*, 4–29.

Ehri, L. (1991). Development of the ability to read words. In P. D. Pearson (Ed.), *Handbook of reading research* (2nd ed.). New York: Longman.

Ehri, L. (1994). Development of the ability to read words: Update. In R. B. Ruddell, M. R. Ruddell, & H. Singer (Eds.), *Theoretical models and processes of reading* (4th ed.). Newark, DE: International Reading Association.

Ehri, L. C. (1998). Word reading by sight and by analogy in beginning readers. In C. Hulme & R. M. Joshi (Eds.), *Reading and spelling: Development and disorders*. Mahwah, NJ: Erlbaum.

Ehri, L. C., & Robbins, C. (1992). Beginners need some decoding skill to read words by analogy. *Reading Research Quarterly, 27*, 12–27.

Ehri, L. C., & Wilce, L. S. (1986). The influence of spellings on speech: Are alveolar flaps /d/ or /t/?. In D. B. Yaden, Jr., & S. Templeton (Eds.), *Metalinguistic awareness and beginning literacy:*

Conceptualizing what it means to read and write. Portsmouth, NH: Heinemann.

Eisenberg, N. (1982). The development of reasoning regarding prosocial behavior. In N. Eisenberg (Ed.), *The development of prosocial behavior.* New York: Academic Press.

Eisenberg, N. (1987). The relation of altruism and other moral behaviors to moral cognition: Methodological and conceptual issues. In N. Eisenberg (Ed.), *Contemporary topics in developmental psychology* (pp. 165–189). New York: Wiley.

Eisenberg, N. (1995). Prosocial development: A multifaceted model. In W. M. Kurtines & J. L. Gewirtz (Eds.), *Moral development: An introduction.* Boston: Allyn & Bacon.

Eisenberg, N. (1998). Introduction. In W. Damon (Editor-in-Chief) & N. Eisenberg (Vol. Ed.), *Handbook of child psychology: Vol. 3. Social, emotional, and personality development* (5th ed., pp. 1–24). New York: Wiley.

Eisenberg, N., Carlo, G., Murphy, B., & Van Court, N. (1995). Prosocial development in late adolescence: A longitudinal study. *Child Development, 66,* 1179–1197.

Eisenberg, N., & Fabes, R. A. (1991). Prosocial behavior: A multimethod developmental perspective. In M. S. Clark (Ed.), *Review of personality and social psychology* (Vol. 2, pp. 34–61). Newbury Park, CA: Sage.

Eisenberg, N., & Fabes, R. A. (1994). Mothers' reactions to children's negative emotions: Relations to children's temperament and anger behavior. *Merrill-Palmer Quarterly, 40,* 138–156.

Eisenberg, N., & Fabes, R. A. (1998). Prosocial development. In W. Damon (Editor-in-Chief), & N. Eisenberg (Vol. Ed.), *Handbook of child psychology: Vol. 3. Social, emotional, and personality development* (pp. 701–778). New York: Wiley.

Eisenberg, N., Fabes, R. A., Carlo, G., & Karbon, M. (1992). Emotional responsivity to others: Behavioral correlates and socialization antecedents. In N. Eisenberg & R. A. Fabes (Eds.), *New directions in child development* (No. 55, pp. 57–73). San Francisco: Jossey-Bass.

Eisenberg, N., Fabes, R. A., Schaller, M., Carlo, G., & Miller, P. A. (1991). The relations of parental characteristics and practices to children's vicarious emotional responding. *Child Development, 62,* 1393–1408.

Eisenberg, N., Lennon, R., & Pasternack, J. F. (1986). Altruistic values and moral judgment. In N. Eisenberg (Ed.), *Altruistic emotion, cognition, and behavior.* Hillsdale, NJ: Erlbaum.

Eisenberg, N., Losoya, S., & Guthrie, I. K. (1997). Social cognition and prosocial development. In S. Hala (Ed.), *The development of social cognition. Studies in developmental psychology* (pp. 329–363). Hove, England: Psychology Press/Erlbaum.

Eisenberg, N., Martin, C. L., & Fabes, R. A. (1996). Gender development and gender effects. In D. C. Berliner & R. C. Calfee (Eds.), *Handbook of educational psychology.* New York: Macmillan.

Eisenberg, N., Miller, P. A., Shell, R., McNalley, S., & Shea, C. (1991). Prosocial development in adolescence: A longitudinal study. *Developmental Psychology, 27,* 849–857.

Eisenberg, N., & Shell, R. (1986). Prosocial moral judgment and behavior in children: The mediating role of cost. *Personality and Social Psychology Bulletin, 12,* 426–433.

Eisenberger, R. (1992). Learned industriousness. *Psychological Review, 99,* 248–267.

Elia, J. P. (1994). Homophobia in the high school: A problem in need of a resolution. *Journal of Homosexuality, 77*(1), 177–185.

Elicker, J., Englund, M., & Sroufe, L. A. (1992). Predicting peer competence and peer relationships in childhood from early parent-child relationships. In R. D. Parke & G. W. Ladd (Eds.), *Family-peer relationships: Modes of linkage* (pp. 77–106). Hillsdale, NJ: Erlbaum.

Elkind, D. (1978). Understanding the young adolescent. *Adolescence, 13,* 127–134.

Elkind, D. (1981a). *Children and adolescents: Interpretive essays on Jean Piaget* (3rd ed.). New York: Oxford University Press.

Elkind, D. (1981b). *The hurried child: Growing up too fast too soon.* Reading, MA: Addison-Wesley.

Elkind, D. (1984). *All grown up and no place to go.* Reading, MA: Addison-Wesley.

Ellenwood, S., & Ryan, K. (1991). Literature and morality: An experimental curriculum. In W. M. Kurtines & J. L. Gewirtz (Eds.), *Moral behavior and development: Vol. 3. Application.* Hillsdale, NJ: Erlbaum.

Elliot, A. J., & McGregor, H. A. (2000, April). Approach and avoidance goals and autonomous-controlled regulation: Empirical and conceptual relations. In A. Assor (Chair), *Self-determination theory and achievement goal theory: Convergences, divergences, and educational implications.* Symposium conducted at the annual meeting of the American Educational Research Association, New Orleans, LA.

Elliott, D. J. (1995). *Music matters: A new philosophy of music education.* New York: Oxford University Press.

Elliott, D. S. (1994). Serious violent offenders: Onset, developmental course, and termination— The American Society of Criminology 1993 Presidential Address. *Criminology, 32,* 1–21.

Elliott, D. S., Wilson, W. J., Huizinga, D., Sampson, R. J., Elliott, A., & Rankin, B. (1996). The effects of neighborhood disadvantage on adolescent development. *Journal of Research in Crime and Delinquency, 33,* 389–426.

Elliott, R., & Vasta, R. (1970). The modeling of sharing: Effects associated with vicarious reinforcement, symbolization, age, and generalization. *Journal of Experimental Child Psychology, 10,* 8–15.

Elliott, S. N., & Busse, R. T. (1991). Social skills assessment and intervention with children and adolescents. *School Psychology International, 12,* 63–83.

Ellis, E. S., & Friend, P. (1991). Adolescents with learning disabilities. In B. Y. L. Wong (Ed.), *Learning about learning disabilities.* San Diego, CA: Academic Press.

Ember, C. R., & Ember, M. (1994). War, socialization, and interpersonal violence. *Journal of Conflict Resolution, 38,* 620–646.

Emde, R., Gaensbauer, T., & Harmon, R. (1976). *Emotional expression in infancy: A biobehavioral study* (Psychological Issues, Vol. 10, No. 37). New York: International Universities Press.

Emery, R. E., & Laumann-Billings, L. (1998). An overview of the nature, causes, and consequences of abusive family relationships. *American Psychologist, 53,* 121–135.

Emler, N., Ohana, J., & Dickinson, J. (1990). Children's representations of social relations. In G. Duveen & B. Lloyd (Eds.), *Social representations and the development of knowledge* (pp. 47–69). Cambridge, England: Cambridge University Press.

Emmer, E. T., Everston, C. M., Clements, B. S., & Worsham, M. E. (1994). *Classroom management for secondary teachers* (3rd ed.). Needham Heights, MA: Allyn & Bacon.

Emmerich, W., Goldman, K. S., Kirsch, B., & Sharabany, R. (1977). Evidence of a transitional phase in the development of gender constancy. *Child Development, 48,* 930–936.

Engle, P. L., & Breaux, C. (1998). Fathers' involvement with children: Perspectives from developing countries. *Social Policy Report: Society for Research in Child Development, 12*(1), 1–21.

Englert, C. S., Raphael, T. E., Anderson, L. M., Anthony, H. M., & Stevens, D. D. (1991). Making strategies and self-talk visible: Writing instruction in regular and special education classrooms. *American Educational Research Journal, 28,* 337–372.

English, D. J. (1998). The extent and consequences of child maltreatment. *The Future of Children: Protecting Children from Abuse and Neglect, 8*(1), 39–53.

Eppright, T. D., Sanfacon, J. A., Beck, N. C., & Bradley, S. J. (1998). Sport psychiatry in childhood and adolescence: An overview. *Child Psychiatry and Human Development, 28,* 71–88.

Epstein, J. A., Botvin, G. J., Diaz, T., Toth, V., & Schinke, S. P. (1995). Social and personal factors in marijuana use and intentions to use drugs among inner city minority youth. *Journal of Developmental and Behavioral Pediatrics, 16,* 14–20.

Epstein, J. L. (1983). Longitudinal effects of family-school-person interactions on student outcomes. *Research in Sociology of Education and Socialization, 4,* 101–127.

Epstein, J. L. (1986). Friendship selection: Developmental and environmental influences. In E. Mueller & C. Cooper (Eds.), *Process and outcome in peer relationships* (pp. 129–160). New York: Academic Press.

Epstein, J. L. (1996). Perspectives and previews on research and policy for school, family, and community partnerships. In A. Booth & J. F. Dunn (Eds.), *Family-school links: How do they affect educational outcomes?* Mahwah, NJ: Erlbaum.

Epstein, J. S. (1998). Introduction: Generation X, youth culture, and identity. In J. S. Epstein (Ed.), *Youth culture: Identity in a postmodern world.* Malden, MA: Blackwell.

Epstein, L. H. (1990). Behavioral treatment of obesity. In E. M. Stricker (Ed.), *Handbook of behavioral neurobiology: Vol. 10. Neurobiology of food and fluid intake* (pp. 61–73). New York: Plenum Press.

Epstein, L. H., Wing, R. R., & Valoski, A. (1985). Childhood obesity. *Pediatric Clinics of North America, 32,* 363–379.

Epstein, S., & Morling, B. (1995). Is the self motivated to do more than enhance and/or verify itself? In M. H. Kernis (Ed.), *Efficacy, agency, and self-esteem.* New York: Plenum Press.

Erdley, C. A., & Asher, S. R. (1996). Children's social goals and self-efficacy perceptions as influences on their responses to ambiguous provocation. *Child Development, 67,* 1329–1344.

Erdley, C. A., Qualey, L. L., & Pietrucha, C. A. (1996, April). *Boys' and girls' attributions of intent and legitimacy of aggression beliefs as predictors of their social behavior.* Paper presented at the annual meeting of the American Educational Research Association, New York.

Ericsson, K. A., & Chalmers, N. (1994). Expert performance: Its structure and acquisition. *American Psychologist, 49,* 725–747.

Erikson, E. H. (1963). *Childhood and society* (2nd ed.). New York: Norton.

Erikson, E. H. (1972). Eight ages of man. In C. S. Lavatelli & F. Stendler (Eds.), *Readings in child behavior and child development.* San Diego, CA: Harcourt Brace Jovanovich.

Eron, L. D. (1980). Prescription for reduction of aggression. *American Psychologist, 35,* 244–252.

Eron, L. D. (1987). The development of aggressive behavior from the perspective of a developing behaviorism. *American Psychologist, 42,* 435–442.

Erwin, P. (1993). *Friendship and peer relations in children.* Chichester, England: Wiley.

Etaugh, C., Grinnell, K., & Etaugh, A. (1989). Development of gender labeling: Effect of age of pictured children. *Sex Roles, 21,* 769–773.

Eysenck, H. J., & Schoenthaler, S. J. (1997). Raising IQ level by vitamin and mineral supplementation. In R. J. Sternberg & E. L. Grigorenko (Eds.), *Intelligence, heredity, and environment* (pp. 363–392). Cambridge, England: Cambridge University Press.

Eysenck, M. W. (1992). *Anxiety: The cognitive perspective.* Hove, England: Erlbaum.

Fabes, R. A., Eisenberg, N., Jones, S., Smith, M., Guthrie, I., Poulin, R., Shepard, S., & Friedman, J. (1999). Regulation, emotionality, and preschoolers' socially competent peer interactions. *Child Development, 70,* 432–442.

Fabes, R. A., Fultz, J., Eisenberg, N., May-Plumlee, T., & Christopher, F. S. (1989). The effect of reward on children's prosocial motivation: A socialization study. *Developmental Psychology, 25,* 509–515.

Fagan, J. F. (1991). The paired-comparison paradigm and infant intelligence. In A. Diamond (Ed.), *The development and neural bases of higher cognitive functions.* New York: New York Academy of Sciences.

Fagan, J. F., & Singer, L. T. (1983). Infant recognition memory as a measure of intelligence. In L. P. Lipsitt (Ed.), *Advances in infancy research* (Vol. 2). Norwood, NJ: Ablex.

Fagot, B. I., & Leinbach, M. D. (1989). Gender-role development in young children: From discrimination to labeling. *Developmental Review, 13,* 205–224.

Fahrmeier, E. D. (1978). The development of concrete operations among the Hausa. *Journal of Cross-Cultural Psychology, 9,* 23–44.

Fairchild, H. H., & Edwards-Evans, S. (1990). African American dialects and schooling: A review. In A. M. Padilla, H. H. Fairchild, & C. M. Valadez (Eds.), *Bilingual education: Issues and strategies.* Newbury Park, CA: Sage.

Faks, D. K., Filcher, I., Masterpasqua, E., & Joseph, G. (1995). Lesbians choosing motherhood: A comparative study of lesbian and heterosexual parents and their children. *Developmental Psychology, 31,* 105–114.

Falbo, T. (1992). Social norms and the one-child family: Clinical and policy implications. In F. Boer & J. Dunn (Eds.), *Children's sibling relationships* (pp. 71–82). Hillsdale, NJ: Erlbaum.

Falbo, T., & Polit, D. (1986). A quantitative review of the only child literature: Research evidence and theory development. *Psychological Bulletin, 100,* 176–189.

Famularo, R., Kinscherff, R., & Fenton, T. (1992). Psychiatric diagnoses of maltreated children: Preliminary findings. *Journal of the American Academy of Child and Adolescent Psychiatry, 31,* 863–867.

Fantini, A. E. (1985). *Language acquisition of a bilingual child: A sociolinguistic perspective.* Clevedon, England: Multilingual Matters. (Available from the SIT Bookstore, School for International Training, Kipling Road, Brattleboro, VT 05302)

Faraone, S. V., Biederman, J., Chen, W. J., Milberger, S., Warburton, R., & Tsuang, M. T. (1995). Genetic heterogeneity in attention-deficit hyperactivity disorder (ADHD): Gender, psychiatric comorbidity, and maternal ADHD. *Journal of Abnormal Psychology, 104,* 334–345.

Farber, B., Mindel, C. H., & Lazerwitz, B. (1988). The Jewish American family. In C. H. Mindel, R. W. Habenstein, & R. Wright (Eds.), *Ethnic families in America: Patterns and variations.* New York: Elsevier.

Farrar, M. J., & Goodman, G. S. (1992). Developmental changes in event memory. *Child Development, 63,* 173–187.

Farrell, M. M., & Phelps, L. (2000). A comparison of the Leiter-R and the Universal Nonverbal Intelligence Test (UNIT) with children classified as language impaired. *Journal of Psychoeducational Assessment, 18,* 268–274.

Farver, J. A. M., & Branstetter, W. H. (1994). Preschoolers' prosocial responses to their peers' distress. *Developmental Psychology, 30,* 334–341.

Fausel, D. F. (1986). Loss after divorce: Helping children grieve. *Journal of Independent Social Work, 1*(1), 39–47.

Feather, N. T. (1982). *Expectations and actions: Expectancy-value models in psychology.* Hillsdale, NJ: Erlbaum.

Federal Glass Ceiling Commission. (1995). *Good for business: Making full use of the nation's human capital. The environmental scan.* Washington, DC: U.S. Government Printing Office.

Fein, G. G. (1979). Play and the acquisition of symbols. In L. Katz (Ed.), *Current topics in early childhood education.* Norwood, NJ: Ablex.

Feingold, A. (1993). Cognitive gender differences: A developmental perspective. *Sex Roles, 29,* 91–112.

Feist, J., & Brannon, L. (1989). *An introduction to behavior and health.* Belmont, CA: Wadsworth.

Feld, S., Ruhland, D., & Gold, M. (1979). Developmental changes in achievement motivation. *Merrill-Palmer Quarterly, 25,* 43–60.

Feldhusen, J. F. (1989). Synthesis of research on gifted youth. *Educational Leadership, 26*(1), 6–11.

Feldhusen, J. F., Van Winkle, L., & Ehle, D. A. (1996). Is it acceleration or simply appropriate instruction for precocious youth? *Teaching Exceptional Children, 28*(3), 48–51.

Feldman, S. S., Gowen, L. K., & Fisher, L. (1998). Family relationships and gender as predictors of romantic intimacy in young adults: A longitudinal study. *Journal of Research on Adolescence, 8*(2), 263–286.

Feldman, S. S., & Wentzel, K. R. (1990). The relationship between parental styles, sons' self-restraint, and peer relations in early adolescence. *Journal of Early Adolescence, 10,* 439–454.

Feldman, S. S., & Wood, D. N. (1994). Parents' expectations for preadolescent sons' behavioral autonomy: A longitudinal study of correlates and outcomes. *Journal of Research on Adolescence, 4*(1), 45–70.

Felton, R. H. (1998). The development of reading skills in poor readers: Educational implications. In C. Hulme & R. M. Joshi (Eds.), *Reading and spelling: Development and disorders.* Mahwah, NJ: Erlbaum.

Fennema, E. (1987). Sex-related differences in education: Myths, realities, and interventions. In V. Richardson-Koehler (Ed.), *Educators' handbook: A research perspective.* White Plains, NY: Longman.

Ferguson, C. J. (1999). Building literacy with child-constructed sociodramatic play centers. *Dimensions of Early Childhood, 27,* 23–29.

Fernald, A. (1992). Human maternal vocalizations to infants as biologically relevant signals: An evolutionary perspective. In J. Barkow, L. Cosmides, & J. Tooby (Eds.), *Evolutionary psychology and the generation of culture.* New York: Oxford University Press.

Ferreiro, E. (1990). Literacy development: Psychogenesis. In Y. M. Goodman (Ed.), *How children construct literacy.* Newark, DE: International Reading Association.

Feshbach, N. (1997). Empathy: The formative years—Implications for clinical practice. In A. C. Bohart & L. S. Greenberg (Eds.), *Empathy reconsidered: New directions for psychotherapy* (pp. 33–59). Washington, DC: American Psychological Association.

Feuerstein, R. (1979). *The dynamic assessment of retarded performers: The Learning Potential Assessment Device, theory, instruments, and techniques.* Baltimore: University Park Press.

Feuerstein, R. (1980). *Instrumental enrichment: An intervention program for cognitive modifiability.* Baltimore: University Park Press.

Feuerstein, R. (1990). The theory of structural cognitive modifiability. In B. Z. Presseisen (Ed.), *Learning and thinking styles: Classroom interaction.* Washington, DC: National Education Association.

Feuerstein, R., Feuerstein, R., & Gross, S. (1997). The Learning Potential Assessment Device. In D. P. Flanagan, J. L. Genshaft, & P. L. Harrison (Eds.), *Contemporary intellectual assessment: Theories, tests, and issues* (pp. 297–313). New York: Guilford Press.

Feuerstein, R., Klein, P. R., & Tannenbaum, A. (Eds.). (1991). *Mediated learning experience: Theoretical, psychosocial, and learning implications.* London: Freund.

Fey, M. E., Catts, H., & Larrivee, L. (1995). Preparing preschoolers for the academic and social challenges of school. In M. E. Fey, J. Windsor, & S. F. Warren (Eds.), *Language intervention: Preschool through elementary years.* Baltimore: Brookes.

Fiedler, E. D., Lange, R. E., & Winebrenner, S. (1993). In search of reality: Unraveling the myths about tracking, ability grouping and the gifted. *Roeper Review, 16*(1), 4–7.

Field, D. (1987). A review of preschool conservation training: An analysis of analyses. *Developmental Review, 7,* 210–251.

Field, S. L., Labbo, L. D., & Ash, G. E. (1999, April). *Investigating young children's construction of social studies concepts and the intersection of literacy learning.* Paper presented at the annual meeting of the American Educational Research Association, Montreal, Canada.

Field, T. (1991). Quality infant daycare and grade school behavior and performance. *Child Development, 62,* 863–870.

Field, T., Masi, W., Goldstein, D., Perry, S., & Parl, S. (1988). Infant daycare facilitates preschool behavior. *Early Childhood Research Quarterly, 3,* 341–359.

Field, T., Woodson, R., Greenberg, R., & Cohen, D. (1982). Discrimination and imitation of facial expressions by neonates. *Science, 218,* 179–81.

Finders, M., & Lewis, C. (1994). Why some parents don't come to school. *Educational Leadership, 51*(8), 50–54.

Fingerhut, L. A., Ingram, D. D., & Feldman, J. J. (1992). Firearm and nonfirearm homicide among persons 15 through 19 years of age: Differences by level of urbanization, United States, 1979 through 1989. *Journal of the American Medical Association, 267,* 3048–3053.

Finkelhor, D., & Ormrod, R. (2000, December). *Juvenile victims of property crimes.* Washington, DC: U.S. Department of Justice, Office of Justice Programs, Office of Juvenile Justice and Delinquency Prevention.

Finn, J. D. (1989). Withdrawing from school. *Review of Educational Research, 59,* 117–142.

Finn-Stevenson, M., & Stern, B. (1996). CoZi: Linking early childhood and family support services. *Principal, 75*(5), 6–10.

Fischer, K. W., & Bidell, T. (1991). Constraining nativist inferences about cognitive capacities. In S. Carey & R. Gelman (Eds.), *The epigenesis of mind: Essays on biology and cognition*. Hillsdale, NJ: Erlbaum.

Fischer, K. W., Knight, C. C., & Van Parys, M. (1993). Analyzing diversity in developmental pathways: Methods and concepts. In R. Case & W. Edelstein (Eds.), *The new structuralism in cognitive development: Theory and research on individual pathways*. Basel, Switzerland: Karger.

Fisher, C. B., & Brone, R. J. (1991). Eating disorders in adolescence. In R. M. Lerner, A. C. Petersen, & J. Brooks-Gunn (Eds.), *Encyclopedia of adolescence* (Vol. 1). New York: Garland.

Fisher, C. B., Jackson, J. F., & Villarruel, F. A. (1998). The study of African American and Latin American children and youth. In W. Damon (Editor-in-Chief) & R. M. Lerner (Vol. Ed.), *Handbook of child psychology: Vol. 1. Theoretical models of human development* (5th ed., pp. 1145–1207). New York: Wiley.

Fisher, J. D., & Fisher, W. A. (1992). Changing AIDS-risk behavior. *Psychological Bulletin, 111*, 455–474.

Fiske, S. T., & Taylor, S. E. (1991). *Social cognition* (2nd ed.). New York: McGraw-Hill.

Fitzgerald, J. (1987). Research on revision in writing. *Review of Educational Research, 57*, 481–506.

Fitzgerald, J., & Markman, L. R. (1987). Teaching children about revision in writing. *Cognition and Instruction, 41*, 3–24.

Fivush, R., Haden, C., & Adam, S. (1995). Structure and coherence of preschoolers' personal narratives over time: Implications for childhood amnesia. *Journal of Experimental Child Psychology, 60*, 32–56.

Fix, M., & Passel, J. S. (1994, May). *Immigration and immigrants: Setting the record straight*. Washington, DC: Urban Institute.

Flanagan, C. (1995, March). *Adolescents' explanations for poverty, unemployment, homelessness, and wealth*. Paper presented at the biennial meeting of the Society for Research in Child Development, Indianapolis, Indiana.

Flanagan, C. A., & Faison, N. (2001). Youth civic development: Implications of research for social policy and programs. *Social Policy Report of the Society for Research in Child Development, 15*(1), 1–14.

Flanagan, C. A., & Tucker, C. J. (1999). Adolescents' explanations for political issues: Concordance with their views of self and society. *Developmental Psychology, 35*, 1198–1209.

Flannery, D. J., Vazsonyi, A. T., Torquati, J., & Fridrich, A. (1994). Ethnic and gender differences in risk for early adolescent substance use. *Journal of Youth and Adolescence, 23*, 195–213.

Flavell, J. H. (1963). *The developmental psychology of Jean Piaget*. New York: Van Nostrand Reinhold.

Flavell, J. H. (1994). Cognitive development: Past, present, and future. In R. D. Parke, P. A. Ornstein, J. J. Rieser, & C. Zahn-Waxler (Eds.), *A century of developmental psychology* (pp. 569–587). Washington, DC: American Psychological Association.

Flavell, J. H. (1996). Piaget's legacy. *Psychological Science, 7*(4), 200–203.

Flavell, J. H., Friedrichs, A. G., & Hoyt, J. D. (1970). Developmental changes in memorization processes. *Cognitive Psychology, 1*, 324–340.

Flavell, J. H., Green, F. L., & Flavell, E. R. (1995). Young children's knowledge about thinking.

Monographs of the Society for Research in Child Development, 60(1, Serial No. 243).

Flavell, J. H., Green, F. L., Flavell, E. R., & Lin, N. T. (1999). Development of children's knowledge about unconsciousness. *Child Development, 70*, 396–412.

Flavell, J. H., Miller, P. H., & Miller, S. A. (1993). *Cognitive development* (3rd ed.). Upper Saddle River, NJ: Prentice Hall.

Flege, J. E., Munro, M. J., & MacKay, I. R. A. (1995). Effects of age of second-language learning on the production of English consonants. *Speech Communication, 16*(1), 1–26.

Fletcher, K. L., & Bray, N. W. (1995). External and verbal strategies in children with and without mild mental retardation. *American Journal on Mental Retardation, 99*, 363–475.

Flexibility in teaching: An excursion into the nature of teaching and training (pp. 59–71). New York: Longman.

Flieller, A. (1999). Comparison of the development of formal thought in adolescent cohorts aged 10 to 15 years (1967–1996 and 1972–1993). *Developmental Psychology, 35*, 1048–1058.

Flink, C., Boggiano, A. K., Main, D. S., Barrett, M., & Katz, P. A. (1992). Children's achievement-related behaviors: The role of extrinsic and intrinsic motivational orientations. In A. K. Boggiano & T. S. Pittman (Eds.), *Achievement and motivation: A social-developmental perspective*. Cambridge, England: Cambridge University Press.

Flower, L. S., & Hayes, J. R. (1981). A cognitive process theory of writing. *College Composition and Communication, 32*, 365–387.

Flynn, J. R. (1987). Massive IQ gains in 14 nations: What IQ tests really measure. *Psychological Bulletin, 101*, 171–191.

Flynn, J. R. (1991). *Asian Americans: Achievement beyond IQ*. Hillsdale, NJ: Erlbaum.

Flynn, J. R. (1999). Searching for justice: The discovery of IQ gains over time. *American Psychologist, 54*, 5–20.

Folds, T. H., Footo, M., Guttentag, R. E., & Ornstein, P. A. (1990). When children mean to remember: Issues of context specificity, strategy effectiveness, and intentionality in the development of memory. In D. F. Bjorklund (Ed.), *Children's strategies: Contemporary views of cognitive development*. Hillsdale, NJ: Erlbaum.

Foorman, B. R., Francis, D. J., Fletcher, J. M., Schatschneider, C., & Mehta, P. (1998). The role of instruction in learning to read: Preventing reading failure in at-risk children. *Journal of Educational Psychology, 90*, 37–55.

Forbes, M. L., Ormrod, J. E., Bernardi, J. D., Taylor, S. L., & Jackson, D. L. (1999, April). *Children's conceptions of space, as reflected in maps of their hometown*. Paper presented at the annual meeting of the American Educational Research Association, Montreal.

Ford, D. Y. (1996). *Reversing underachievement among gifted black students*. New York: Teachers College Press.

Ford, M. E. (1997). Developmental psychology. In H. J. Walberg & G. D. Haertel (Eds.), *Psychology and educational practice*. Berkeley, CA: McCrutchan.

Forehand, R., Biggar, H., & Kotchick, B. A. (1998). Cumulative risk across family stressors: Short- and long-term effects for adolescents. *Journal of Abnormal Child Psychology, 26*(2), 119–128.

Forehand, R., Wierson, M., Thomas, A. M., Fauber, R., Armistead, L., Kempton, T., & Long, N. (1991). A short-term longitudinal examination of young adolescent functioning following divorce:

The role of family factors. *Journal of Abnormal Child Psychology, 19*, 97–111.

Forgey, M. A., Schinke, S., & Cole, K. (1997). School-based interventions to prevent substance use among inner-city minority adolescents. In D. K. Wilson, J. R. Rodrigue, & W. C. Taylor (Eds.), *Health-promoting and health-compromising behaviors among adolescents* (pp. 251–267). Washington, DC: American Psychological Association.

Fowler, J. W. (1981). *Stages of faith: The psychology of human development and the quest for meaning*. San Francisco: Harper & Row.

Fowler, S. A., & Baer, D. M. (1981). "Do I have to be good all day?" The timing of delayed reinforcement as a factor in generalization. *Journal of Applied Behavior Analysis, 14*, 13–24.

Fox, J. A., & Newman, S. A. (1997, September). *After-school programs or after-school crime*. Washington, DC: Fight crime: Invest in kids.

Fox, L. H. (1979). Programs for the gifted and talented: An overview. In A. H. Passow (Ed.), *The gifted and the talented: Their education and development. The seventy-eighth yearbook of the National Society for the Study of Education*. Chicago: University of Chicago Press.

Francis, M., & McCutchen, D. (1994, April). *Strategy differences in revising between skilled and less skilled writers*. Paper presented at the annual meeting of the American Educational Research Association, New Orleans, LA.

Frank, A. (1967). *The diary of a young girl* (B. M. Mooyaart-Doubleday, Trans.). New York: Doubleday.

Fraschetti, A. (1997). Roman youth. In G. Levi & J. C. Schmitt (Eds.), *A history of young people in the west: Vol. 1. Ancient and medieval rites of passage* (C. Naish, Trans.; pp. 51–82). Cambridge, MA: Belknap Press of Harvard University Press.

Freedman, K. (2001). The social reconstruction of art education: Teaching visual culture. In C. A. Grant & M. L. Gomez, *Campus and classroom: Making schooling multicultural* (2nd ed.). Upper Saddle River, NJ: Merrill/Prentice Hall.

Freedman, S. G. (1990). *Small victories: The real world of a teacher, her students, and their high school*. New York: Harper & Row.

French, E. G. (1956). Motivation as a variable in work partner selection. *Journal of Abnormal and Social Psychology, 53*, 96–99.

French, L., & Brown, A. (1977). Comprehension of "before" and "after" in logical and arbitrary sequences. *Journal of Child Language, 4*, 247–256.

Freud, S. (1959). *Collected papers*. New York: Basic Books.

Friedel, M. (1993). *Characteristics of gifted/creative children*. Warwick, RI: National Foundation for Gifted and Creative Children.

Friend, M., & Davis, T. L. (1993). Appearance-reality distinction: Children's understanding of the physical and affective domains. *Developmental Psychology, 29*, 907–914.

Friend, R. A. (1993). Choices, not closets: Heterosexism and homophobia in schools. In L. Weis & M. Fine (Eds.), *Beyond silenced voices: Class, race, and gender in United States schools* (pp. 209–235). Albany, NY: SUNY Press.

Frith, U. (1985). Beneath the surface of surface dyslexia. In K. E. Patterson, J. C. Marshall, & M. Coltheart (Eds.), *Surface dyslexia: Neuropsychological and cognitive studies of phonological reading*. London: Routledge & Kegan Paul.

Frost, J. L., Shin, D., & Jacobs, P. J. (1998). Physical environments and children's play. In O. N. Saracho & B. Spodek (Eds.), *Multiple per-*

spectives on play in early childhood education. Albany: State University of New York Press.

Fry, A. F., & Hale, S. (1996). Processing speed, working memory, and fluid intelligence. *Psychological Science, 7,* 237–241.

Fuchs, D., Fuchs, L. S., Mathes, P. G., & Simmons, D. C. (1997). Peer-assisted learning strategies: Making classrooms more responsive to diversity. *American Educational Research Journal, 34,* 174–206.

Fukkink, R. G., & de Glopper, K. (1998). Effects of instruction in deriving word meanings from context: A meta-analysis. *Review of Educational Research, 68,* 450–469.

Fuligni, A. J. (1998). The adjustment of children from immigrant families. *Current Directions in Psychological Science, 7,* 99–103.

Fuller, M. L. (2001). Multicultural concerns and classroom management. In C. A. Grant & M. L. Gomez, *Campus and classroom: Making school multicultural* (pp. 109–134). Upper Saddle River, NJ: Merrill/Prentice Hall.

Furman, W., & Buhrmester, D. (1992). Age and sex differences in perceptions of networks and personal relationships. *Child Development, 63,* 103–115.

Furman, W., & Simon, V. A. (1999). Cognitive representations of adolescent romantic relationships. In W. Furman, B. B. Brown, & C. Feiring (Eds.), *The development of romantic relationships in adolescence* (pp. 75–98). Cambridge, England: Cambridge University Press.

Furstenberg, F. F. Jr., & Cherlin, A. J. (1991). *Divided families: What happens to children when parents part.* Cambridge, MA: Harvard University Press.

Furstenberg, F. F. Jr., Nord, C., Peterson, J. L., & Zill, N. (1983). The life course of children and divorce: Marital disruption and parental conflict. *American Sociological Review, 48,* 656–668.

Furth, H. G. (1980). *The world of grown-ups: Children's conceptions of society.* New York: Elsevier.

Gabard, D. L. (1999). Homosexuality and the Human Genome Project: Private and public choices. *Journal of Homosexuality, 37,* 25–51.

Gailey, C. W. (1993). Mediated messages: Gender, class, and cosmos in home video games. *Journal of Popular Culture, 27*(1), 81–97.

Gaines, D. (1991). *Teenage wasteland: Suburbia's dead end kids.* New York: Pantheon.

Galambos, N. L., Almeida, D. M., & Petersen, A. C. (1990). Masculinity, femininity, and sex role attitudes in early adolescence: Exploring gender intensification. *Child Development, 61,* 1905–1914.

Galambos, N. L., & Maggs, J. L. (1991). Out-of-school care of young adolescents and self-reported behavior. *Developmental Psychology, 27,* 644–655.

Galambos, S. J., & Maggs, J. L. (1991). Children in self-care: Figures, facts and fiction. In J. V. Verner & N. L. Galambos (Eds.), *Employed mothers and their children* (pp. 131–157). New York: Garland Press.

Gallagher, J. J. (1991). Personal patterns of underachievement. *Journal for the Education of the Gifted, 14,* 221–233.

Gallahue, D. L., & Ozmun, J. C. (1998). *Understanding motor development: Infants, children, adolescents, adults.* Boston: McGraw-Hill.

Gallimore, R., & Tharp, R. (1990). Teaching mind in society: Teaching, schooling, and literate discourse. In L. C. Moll (Ed.), *Vygotsky and education: Instructional implications and applications of sociohistorical psychology.* Cambridge, England: Cambridge University Press.

Gallistel, C. R., Brown, A. L., Carey, S., Gelman, R., & Keil, F. C. (1991). Lessons from animal learn-ing for the study of cognitive development. In S. Carey & R. Gelman (Eds.), *The epigenesis of mind: Essays on biology and cognition* (pp. 3–36). Hillsdale, NJ: Erlbaum.

Gallup, G. H., Jr. (1996). *Religion in America.* Princeton, NJ: Princeton Religious Research Center.

Gallup, G. H., Jr., & Poling, D. (1980). *The search for America's faith.* New York: Abington.

Gambrell, L. B., & Bales, R. J. (1986). Mental imagery and the comprehension-monitoring performance of fourth- and fifth-grade poor readers. *Reading Research Quarterly, 21,* 454–464.

Garbarino, J. (1981). *Successful schools and competent students.* Lexington, MA: Lexington Books.

Garbarino, J. (1995). The American war zone: What children can tell us about living with violence. *Developmental and Behavioral Pediatrics, 16,* 431–435.

Garbarino, J., & Abramowitz, R. H. (1992a). The family as a social system. In J. Garbarino (Ed.), *Children and families in the social environment* (pp. 72–98). New York: Aldine de Gruyter.

Garbarino, J., & Abramowitz, R. H. (1992b). Sociocultural risk and opportunity. In J. Garbarino (Ed.), *Children and families in the social environment* (pp. 35–70). New York: Aldine de Gruyter.

Garbarino, J., & Abramowitz, R. H. (1992c). The ecology of human development. In J. Garbarino (Ed.), *Children and families in the social environment* (pp. 11–33). New York: Aldine de Gruyter.

Garbarino, J., & Bronfenbrenner, U. (1976). The socialization of moral judgment and behavior in cross-cultural perspective. In T. Lickona (Ed.), *Moral development and behavior.* New York: Holt, Rinehart & Winston.

Garbarino, J., Kostelny, K., & Dubrow, N. (1991a). What children can tell us about living in danger. *American Psychologist, 46*(4), 376–383.

Garbarino, J., Kostelny, K., & Dubrow, N. (1991b). *No place to be a child: Growing up in a war zone.* Lexington, MA: Lexington Books.

García, E. E. (1992). "Hispanic" children: Theoretical, empirical, and related policy issues. *Educational Psychology Review, 4,* 69–93.

García, E. E. (1994). *Understanding and meeting the challenge of student cultural diversity.* Boston: Houghton Mifflin.

García, E. E. (1995). Educating Mexican American students: Past treatment and recent developments in theory, research, policy, and practice. In J. A. Banks & C. A. M. Banks (Eds.), *Handbook of research on multicultural education.* New York: Macmillan.

García, G. E., Jiménez, R. T., & Pearson, P. D. (1998). Metacognition, childhood bilingualism, and reading. In D. J. Hacker, J. Dunlosky, & A. C. Graesser (Eds.), *Metacognition in educational theory and practice.* Mahwah, NJ: Erlbaum.

Gardner, H. (1983). *Frames of mind: The theory of multiple intelligences.* New York: Basic Books.

Gardner, H. (1993). *Multiple intelligences: The theory in practice.* New York: Basic Books.

Gardner, H. (1995). Reflections on multiple intelligences: Myths and messages. *Phi Delta Kappan, 77,* 200–209.

Gardner, H. (1998, April). *Where to draw the line: The perils of new paradigms.* Paper presented at the annual meeting of the American Educational Research Association, San Diego, CA.

Gardner, H., & Hatch, T. (1990). Multiple intelligences go to school: Educational implications of the theory of multiple intelligences. *Educational Researcher, 18*(8), 4–10.

Gardner, H., Torff, B., & Hatch, T. (1996). The age of innocence reconsidered: Preserving the best of the progressive traditions in psychology and education. In D. R. Olson & N. Torrance (Eds.), *The handbook of education and human development: New models of learning, teaching and schooling* (pp. 28–55). Cambridge, MA: Blackwell.

Garibaldi, A. M. (1992). Educating and motivating African American males to succeed. *The Journal of Negro Education, 61*(1), 4–11.

Garner, R. (1987). Strategies for reading and studying expository texts. *Educational Psychologist, 22,* 299–312.

Garner, R. (1998). Epilogue: Choosing to learn or not-learn in school. *Educational Psychology Review, 10,* 227–237.

Garnier, H. E., Stein, J. A., & Jacobs, J. K. (1997). The process of dropping out of high school: A 19-year perspective. *American Educational Research Journal, 34,* 395–419.

Garrison, L. (1989). Programming for the gifted American Indian student. In C. J. Maker & S. W. Schiever (Eds.), *Critical issues in gifted education: Vol. 2. Defensible programs for cultural and ethnic minorities.* Austin, TX: Pro-Ed.

Garvey, C. (1974). Some properties of social play. *Merrill-Palmer Quarterly, 20,* 163–180.

Garvey, C. (1990). *Play.* Cambridge, MA: Harvard University Press.

Garvey, C., & Berninger, G. (1981). Timing and turn taking in children's conversations. *Discourse Processes, 4,* 27–59.

Garvey, C., & Horgan, R. (1973). Social speech and social interaction: Egocentrism revisited. *Child Development, 44,* 562–568.

Gathercole, S. E., & Hitch, G. J. (1993). Developmental changes in short-term memory: A revised working memory perspective. In A. F. Collins, S. E. Gathercole, M. A. Conway, & P. E. Morris (Eds.), *Theories of memory.* Hove, England: Erlbaum.

Gavin, L. A., & Fuhrman, W. (1989). Age differences in adolescents' perceptions of their peer groups. *Developmental Psychology, 25,* 827–834.

Gay, G. (1993). Building cultural bridges: A bold proposal for teacher education. *Education and Urban Society, 25*(3), 285–299.

Gay, J., & Cole, M. (1967). *The new mathematics and an old culture.* New York: Holt, Rinehart & Winston.

Gelman, R. (1972). Logical capacity of very young children: Number invariance rules. *Child Development, 43,* 75–90.

Gelman, R., & Baillargeon, R. (1983). A review of some Piagetian concepts. In J. H. Flavell & E. M. Markman (Eds.), *Handbook of child psychology: Vol. 3. Cognitive development.* New York: Wiley.

Genesee, F. (1985). Second language learning through immersion: A review of U.S. programs. *Review of Educational Research, 55,* 541–561.

Genova, W. J., & Walberg, H. J. (1984). Enhancing integration in urban high schools. In D. E. Bartz & M. L. Maehr (Eds.), *Advances in motivation and achievement: Vol. 1. The effects of school desegregation on motivation and achievement.* Greenwich, CT: JAI Press.

Gentry, R. (1982). An analysis of the developmental spellings in *Gnys at Wrk. The Reading Teacher, 36,* 192–200.

Gephart, M. (1997). Neighborhoods and communities as contexts for development. In J. Brooks-Gunn, G. J. Duncan, & J. L. Aber (Eds.), *Neighborhood poverty: Context and consequences for children* (Vol. 1, pp. 1–43). New York: Russell Sage Foundation Press.

Gesell, A. (1923). *The preschool child.* New York: Houghton Mifflin.

Gesell, A. (1928). *Infancy and human growth.* New York: Macmillan.

Gesell, A. (1929). The guidance nursery of the Yale Psycho-Clinic. In *Twenty-eighth yearbook of the National Society for the Study of Education.* Chicago: University of Chicago Press.

Ghodsian-Carpey, J., & Baker, L. A. (1987). Genetic and environmental influences on aggression in 4- to 7-year-old twins. *Aggressive Behavior, 13,* 173–186.

Gibbs, J. C. (1995). The cognitive developmental perspective. In W. M. Kurtines & J. L. Gewirtz (Eds.), *Moral development: An introduction.* Boston: Allyn & Bacon.

Gibbs, J. T. (1985). City girls: Psychosocial adjustment of urban black adolescent females. *Sage, 2*(2), 28–36.

Giedd, J. N., Blumenthal, J., Jeffries, N. O., Castellanos, F. X., Liu, H., Zijdenbos, A., Paus, T., Evans, A. C., & Rapoport, J. L. (1999). Brain development during childhood and adolescence: A longitudinal MRI study. *Nature Neuroscience, 2,* 861–863.

Giedd, J. N., Blumenthal, J., Jeffries, N. O., Rajapakse, J. C., Vaituzis, A. C., Liu, H., Berry, Y. C., Tobin, M., Nelson, J., & Castellanos, F. X. (1999). Development of the human corpus callosum during childhood and adolescence: A longitudinal MRI study. *Progress in Neuro-Psychopharmacology and Biological Psychiatry, 23,* 571–588.

Giedd, J. N., Jeffries, N. O., Blumenthal, J., Castellanos, F. X., Vaituzis, A. C., Fernandez, T., Hamburger, S. D., Liu, H., Nelson, J., Bedwell, J., Tran, L., Lenane, M., Nicolson, R., & Rapoport, J. L. (1999). Childhood-onset schizophrenia: Progressive brain changes during adolescence. *Biological Psychiatry, 46,* 892–898.

Gilbert, M. J., & Cervantes, R. (1986). Patterns and practices of alcohol use among Mexican Americans: A comprehensive review. *Hispanic Journal of Behavioral Sciences, 8,* 1–60.

Gillam, R. B., & Johnston, J. R. (1992). Spoken and written language relationships in language/learning-impaired and normal achieving school-age children. *Journal of Speech and Hearing Research, 35,* 1303–1315.

Gillberg, I. C., & Coleman, M. (1996). Autism and medical disorders: A review of the literature. *Developmental Medicine and Child Neurology, 38,* 191–202.

Gillham, J. E., Reivich, K. J., Jaycox, L. H., & Seligman, M. E. P. (1995). Prevention of depressive symptoms in schoolchildren: Two-year follow-up. *Psychological Science, 6,* 343–351.

Gilligan, C. (1977). In a different voice: Women's conceptions of self and of morality. *Harvard Educational Review, 47,* 481–517.

Gilligan, C. (1982). *In a different voice: Psychological theory and women's development.* Cambridge, MA: Harvard University Press.

Gilligan, C. F. (1985, March). Keynote address. Conference on Women and Moral Theory, Stony Brook, NY.

Gilligan, C. F. (1987). Moral orientation and moral development. In E. F. Kittay & D. T. Meyers (Eds.), *Women and moral theory.* Totowa, NJ: Rowman & Littlefield.

Gilligan, C. F., & Attanucci, J. (1988). Two moral orientations. In C. F. Gilligan, J. V. Ward, & J. M. Taylor (Eds.), *Mapping the moral domain: A contribution of women's thinking to psychological theory and education.* Cambridge, MA: Center for the Study of Gender, Education, and Human Development (distributed by Harvard University Press).

Gilliland, H. (1988). Discovering and emphasizing the positive aspects of the culture. In H. Gilliland & J. Reyhner (Eds.), *Teaching the native American.* Dubuque, IA: Kendall/Hunt.

Gillis, J. J., Gilger, J. W., Pennington, B. F., & DeFries, J. C. (1992). Attention deficit disorder in reading-disabled twins: Evidence for a genetic etiology. *Journal of Abnormal Child Psychology, 20,* 303–315.

Ginsberg, D., Gottman, J. M., & Parker, J. G. (1986). The importance of friendship. In J. M. Gottman & J. G. Parker (Eds.), *Conversations of friends: Speculations on affective development* (pp. 3–48). Cambridge, England: Cambridge University Press.

Ginsburg, M. B., & Newman, M. K. (1985). Social inequalities, schooling, and teacher education. *Journal of Teacher Education, 36*(2), 49–54.

Giordano, P. C., Cernkovich, S. A., & DeMaris, A. (1993). The family and peer relations of black adolescents. *Journal of Marriage and the Family, 55,* 277–287.

Gladwell, M. (1997, Feb. 24 and Mar. 3). Crime and science: Damaged. *The New Yorker.*

Glick, J. (1975). Cognitive development in cross-cultural perspective. In F. Horowitz (Ed.), *Review of child development research* (Vol. 4). Chicago: University of Chicago Press.

Glucksberg, S., & Krauss, R. M. (1967). What do people say after they have learned to talk? Studies of the development of referential communication. *Merrill-Palmer Quarterly, 13,* 309–316.

Glynn, S. M., Yeany, R. H., & Britton, B. K. (1991). A constructive view of learning science. In S. M. Glynn, R. H. Yeany, & B. K. Britton (Eds.), *The psychology of learning science.* Hillsdale, NJ: Erlbaum.

Gohm, C. L., Oishi, S., Darlington, J., & Diener, E. (1998). Culture, parental conflict, parental marital status, and the subjective well-being of young adults. *Journal of Marriage & the Family, 60*(2), 319–334.

Goldberg, E., & Costa, L. D. (1981). Hemisphere differences in the acquisition and use of descriptive systems. *Brain and Language, 14,* 144–173.

Goldenberg, C. (1992). The limits of expectations: A case for case knowledge about teacher expectancy effects. *American Educational Research Journal, 29,* 517–544.

Goldin-Meadow, S. (1997). When gestures and words speak differently. *Current Directions in Psychological Science, 6,* 138–143.

Goldin-Meadow, S., & Mylander, C. (1993). Beyond the input given: The child's role in the acquisition of language. In P. Bloom (Ed.), *Language acquisition: Core readings.* Cambridge, MA: MIT Press.

Goldsmith-Phillips, J. (1989). Word and context in reading development: A test of the interactive-compensatory hypothesis. *Journal of Educational Psychology, 81,* 299–305.

Goleman, D. (1995). *Emotional intelligence.* New York: Bantam Books.

Gollnick, D. M., & Chinn, P. C. (1998). *Multicultural education in a pluralistic society* (5th ed.). Upper Saddle River, NJ: Merrill/Prentice Hall.

Golombok, S., & Tasker, F. (1996). Do parents influence the sexual orientation of their children? Findings from a longitudinal study of lesbian families. *Developmental Psychology, 32,* 3–11.

Gomby, D. S., Culross, P. L., & Behrman, R. E. (1999). Home visiting: Recent program evaluations—Analysis and recommendations. *The Future of Children. Home Visiting: Recent Program Evaluations, 9*(1), 4–26.

Göncü, A. (1993). Development of intersubjectivity in the dyadic play of preschoolers. *Early Childhood Research Quarterly, 8,* 99–116.

Good, T. L., & Brophy, J. E. (1994). *Looking in classrooms* (6th ed.). New York: Harper Collins.

Good, T. L., McCaslin, M. M., & Reys, B. J. (1992). Investigating work groups to promote problem solving in mathematics. In J. Brophy (Ed.), *Advances in research on teaching: Vol. 3. Planning and managing learning tasks and activities.* Greenwich, CT: JAI Press.

Goodenow, C. (1993). Classroom belonging among early adolescent students: Relationships to motivation and achievement. *Journal of Early Adolescence, 13*(1), 21–43.

Goodman, K. S. (1989). Whole-language research: Foundations and development. *Elementary School Journal, 90,* 207–221.

Goodman, K. S., & Goodman, Y. M. (1979). Learning to read is natural. In L. B. Resnick & P. A Weaver (Eds.), *Theory and practice of early reading* (Vol. 1). Hillsdale, NJ: Erlbaum.

Goodman, Y. M., & Goodman, K. S. (1990). Vygotsky in a whole-language perspective. In L. C. Moll (Ed.), *Vygotsky and education: Instructional implications and applications of sociohistorical psychology.* Cambridge, England: Cambridge University Press.

Goodnow, J. J., & Collins, W. A. (1990). *Development according to parents: The nature, sources, and consequences of parents' ideas.* East Sussex, England: Erlbaum.

Goodson, P., Evans, A., & Edmundson, E. (1997). Female adolescents and onset of sexual intercourse: A theory-based review of research from 1984 to 1994. *Journal of Adolescent Health, 21,* 147–156.

Goodwin, A. L. (1997). Multicultural stories: Preservice teachers' conceptions of and responses to issues of diversity, *Urban Education, 32*(1), 117–145.

Gopnik, M. (Ed.). (1997). *The inheritance and innateness of grammars.* New York: Oxford University Press.

Gortmaker, S. L., Dietz, W. H., Sobol, A. M., & Wehler, C. A. (1987). Increasing pediatric obesity in the United States. *American Journal of Diseases of Children, 141,* 535–540.

Goswami, U. (1998). Rime-based coding in early reading development in English: Orthographic analogies and rime neighborhoods. In C. Hulme & R. M. Joshi (Eds.), *Reading and spelling: Development and disorders.* Mahwah, NJ: Erlbaum.

Goswami, U. (1999). The relationship between phonological awareness and orthographic representation in different orthographies. In M. Harris & G. Hatano (Eds.), *Learning to read and write: A cross-linguistic perspective.* Cambridge, England: Cambridge University Press.

Gottfredson, L. S. (1981). Circumscription and compromise: A developmental theory of occupational aspirations. *Journal of Counseling Psychology Monograph, 28,* 545–579.

Gottfried, A. E. (1990). Academic intrinsic motivation in young elementary school children. *Journal of Educational Psychology, 82,* 525–538.

Gottfried, A. E., Fleming, J. S., & Gottfried, A. W. (1994). Role of parental motivational practices in children's academic intrinsic motivation and achievement. *Journal of Educational Psychology, 86,* 104–113.

Gottfried, A. W., Gottfried, A. E., Bathurst, K., & Guerin, D. W. (1994). *Gifted IQ: Early developmental aspects.* New York: Plenum Press.

Gottlieb, D. (1964). Teaching and students: The views of Negros and white teachers. *Sociology of Education, 37,* 345–353.

Gottlieb, G. (1991). Experiential canalization of behavioral development: Theory. *Developmental Psychology, 27,* 4–13.

Gottlieb, G. (1992). *Individual development and evolution: The genesis of novel behavior.* New York: Oxford University Press.

Gottman, J. M. (1983). How children become friends. *Monographs of the Society for Research in Child Development, 48*(3, Serial No. 201).

Gottman, J. M. (1986a). The observation of social process. In J. M. Gottman & J. G. Parker (Eds.), *Conversations of friends: Speculations on affective development* (pp. 51–100). Cambridge, England: Cambridge University Press.

Gottman, J. M. (1986b). The world of coordinated play: Same- and cross-sex friendship in young children. In J. M. Gottman & J. G. Parker (Eds.), *Conversations of friends: Speculations on affective development* (pp. 139–191). Cambridge, England: Cambridge University Press.

Gottman, J. M., & Mettetal, G. (1986). Speculations about social and affective development: Friendship and acquaintanceship through adolescence. In J. M. Gottman & J. G. Parker (Eds.), *Conversations of friends: Speculations on affective development* (pp. 192–237). Cambridge, England: Cambridge University Press.

Gough, P. B., & Wren, S. (1998). The decomposition of decoding. In C. Hulme & R. M. Joshi (Eds.), *Reading and spelling: Development and disorders.* Mahwah, NJ: Erlbaum.

Gould, S. J. (1977). *Ontogeny and phylogeny.* Cambridge, MA: Harvard University Press.

Goyen, T. A., Lui, K., & Woods, R. (1998). Visual-motor, visual-perceptual, and fine-motor outcomes in very-low-birthweight children at 5 years. *Developmental Medicine and Child Neurology, 40*(2), 76–81.

Goyette-Ewing, M. (in press). Children's after school arrangements: A study of self-care and developmental outcomes. *Journal of Prevention and Intervention in the Community.*

Goyette-Ewing, M., & Knoebber, K. (1999, April). *Outcomes of self-care for third graders three years later: Who is at risk?* Paper presented at the biennial meeting of the Society for Research in Child Development, Albuquerque, NM.

Graber, J. A., Britto, P. R., & Brooks-Gunn, J. (1999). What's love got to do with it? Adolescents' and young adults' beliefs about sexual and romantic relationships. In W. Furman, B. B. Brown, & C. Feiring (Eds.), *The development of romantic relationships in adolescence* (pp. 364–395). Cambridge, England: Cambridge University Press.

Graesser, A., Golding, J. M., & Long, D. L. (1991). Narrative representation and comprehension. In R. Barr, M. L. Kamil, P. Mosenthal, & P. D. Pearson (Eds.), *Handbook of reading research* (Vol. II). New York: Longman.

Graham, S. (1989). Motivation in Afro-Americans. In G. L. Berry & J. K. Asamen (Eds.), *Black students: Psychosocial issues and academic achievement.* Newbury Park, CA: Sage.

Graham, S. (1990). Communicating low ability in the classroom: Bad things good teachers sometimes do. In S. Graham & V. S. Folkes (Eds.), *Attribution theory: Applications to achievement, mental health, and interpersonal conflict.* Hillsdale, NJ: Erlbaum.

Graham, S. (1991). A review of attribution theory in achievement contexts. *Educational Psychology Review, 3,* 5–39.

Graham, S. (1997). Using attribution theory to understand social and academic motivation in African American youth. *Educational Psychologist, 32,* 21–34.

Graham, S., & Harris, K. R. (1992). Self-regulated strategy development: Programmatic research in writing. In B. Y. L. Wong (Ed.), *Contemporary intervention research in learning disabilities: An international perspective.* New York: Springer-Verlag.

Graham, S., & Hudley, C. (1994). Attributions of aggressive and nonaggressive African-American male early adolescents: A study of construct accessibility. *Developmental Psychology, 30,* 365–373.

Graham, S., Hudley, C., & Williams, E. (1992). Attributional and emotional determinants of aggression among African-American and Latino young adolescents. *Developmental Psychology, 28,* 731–740.

Graham, S., MacArthur, C., & Schwartz, S. (1995). Effects of goal setting and procedural facilitation on the revising behavior and writing performance of students with writing and learning problems. *Journal of Educational Psychology, 87,* 230–240.

Graham, S., Schwartz, S. S., & MacArthur, C. A. (1993). Knowledge of writing and the composing process, attitude toward writing, and self-efficacy for students with and without learning disabilities. *Journal of Learning Disabilities, 26,* 237–249.

Graham, S., Taylor, A. Z., & Hudley, C. (1998). Exploring achievement values among ethnic minority early adolescents. *Journal of Educational Psychology, 90,* 606–620.

Graham, S., & Weiner, B. (1996). Theories and principles of motivation. In D. C. Berliner & R. C. Calfee (Eds.), *Handbook of educational psychology.* New York: Macmillan.

Graham, S., & Weintraub, N. (1996). A review of handwriting research: Progress and prospects from 1980 to 1994. *Educational Psychology Review, 8,* 7–87.

Grandin, T. (1995). *Thinking in pictures and other reports of my life with autism.* New York: Random House.

Grant, C. A., & Gomez, M. L. (2001). *Campus and classroom: Making schooling multicultural* (2nd ed.). Upper Saddle River, NJ: Merrill/Prentice Hall.

Graves, D. (1983). *Writing: Teachers and children at work.* Portsmouth, NH: Heinemann.

Gray, C., & Garaud, J. D. (1993). Social stories: Improving responses of students with autism with accurate social information. *Focus on Autistic Behavior, 8,* 1–10.

Green, J., & Dixon, C. (1996). Language of literacy dialogues: Facing the future or reproducing the past. *Journal of Literacy Research, 28,* 290–301.

Green, L., Fry, A. F., & Myerson, J. (1994). Discounting of delayed rewards: A life-span comparison. *Psychological Science, 5,* 33–36.

Greene, B. A., & Royer, J. M. (1994). A developmental review of response time data that support a cognitive components model of reading. *Educational Psychology Review, 6,* 141–172.

Greene, S., & Ackerman, J. M. (1995). Expanding the constructivist metaphor: A rhetorical perspective on literacy research and practice. *Review of Educational Research, 65,* 383–420.

Greenfield, P. M. (1994a). Independence and interdependence as developmental scripts: Implications for theory, research, and practice. In P. M. Greenfield & R. R. Cocking (Eds.), *Cross-cultural roots of minority child development.* Hillsdale, NJ: Erlbaum.

Greenfield, P. M. (1994b). Video games as cultural artifacts. *Journal of Applied Developmental Psychology, 15,* 3–11.

Greenhoot, A. F., Ornstein, P. A., Gordon, B. N., & Baker-Ward, L. (1999). Acting out the details of a pediatric check-up: The impact of interview condition and behavioral style on children's memory reports. *Child Development, 70,* 363–380.

Greeno, J. G. (1997). On claims that answer the wrong questions. *Educational Researcher, 26*(1), 5–17.

Greenough, W. T., Black, J. E., & Wallace, C. S. (1987). Experience and brain development. *Child Development, 58,* 539–559.

Greenspan, S., & Granfield, J. M. (1992). Reconsidering the construct of mental retardation: Implications of a model of social competence. *American Journal of Mental Retardation, 96,* 442–453.

Gregg, M., & Leinhardt, G. (1994, April). Constructing geography. Paper presented at the annual meeting of the American Educational Research Association, New Orleans, LA.

Gresham, F. M., & MacMillan, D. L. (1997). Social competence and affective characteristics of students with mild disabilities. *Review of Educational Research, 67,* 377–415.

Gribov, I. (1992). Creativity and brain hemispheres: Educational implications. *European Journal for High Ability, 3*(1), 6–14.

Griffin, S., Case, R., & Capodilupo, A. (1995). Teaching for understanding: The importance of the central conceptual structures in the elementary mathematics curriculum. In A. McKeough, J. Lupart, & A. Marini (Eds.), *Teaching for transfer: Fostering generalization in learning.* Mahwah, NJ: Erlbaum.

Griffin, S. A., Case, R., & Siegler, R. S. (1994). Rightstart: Providing the central conceptual prerequisites for first formal learning of arithmetic to students at risk for school failure. In K. McGilly (Ed.), *Classroom lessons: Integrating cognitive theory and classroom practice.* Cambridge, MA: MIT Press.

Griffith, P. L. (1991). Phonemic awareness helps first graders invent spellings and third graders remember correct spellings. *Journal of Reading Behavior, 23,* 215–233.

Griffore, R. J. (1981). *Child development: An educational perspective.* Springfield, IL: Charles C Thomas.

Griswold, K. S., & Pessar, L. F. (2000). Management of bipolar disorder. *American Family Physician, 62,* 1343–1356.

Grodzinsky, G. M., & Diamond, R. (1992). Frontal lobe functioning in boys with attention-deficit hyperactivity disorder. *Developmental Neuropsychology, 8,* 427–445.

Gropper, N., & Froschl, M. (1999, April). *The role of gender in young children's teasing and bullying behavior.* Paper presented at the annual meeting of the American Educational Research Association, Montreal.

Gross, R. T., & Duke, P. M. (1980). The effect of early versus late physical maturation in adolescent behavior. *Pediatric Clinics of North America, 27,* 71–77.

Grossman, H. L. (1994). *Classroom behavior management in a diverse society.* Mountain View, CA: Mayfield.

Grossmann, K. E., Grossmann, K., Huber, F., & Wartner, U. (1981). German children's behavior toward their mothers at 12 months and their father at 18 months in Ainsworth's Strange Situation. *International Journal of Behavioral Development, 4,* 157–181.

Grotpeter, J. K., & Crick, N. R. (1996). Relational aggression, overt aggression, and friendship. *Child Development, 67,* 2328–2338.

Grusec, J. E., & Goodnow, J. J. (1994). Impact of parental discipline methods on the child's internalization of values: A reconceptualization of current points of view. *Developmental Psychology, 30,* 4–19.

Grusec, J. E., & Redler, E. (1980). Attribution, reinforcement, and altruism. *Developmental Psychology, 16,* 525–534.

Grych, J. H., & Finchman, F. D. (1997). Children's adaptation to divorce: From description to explanation. In S. A. Wolchik & I. N. Sandler (Eds.), *Handbook of children's coping: Linking theory to intervention* (pp. 159–193). New York: Plenum Press.

Guay, F., Boivin, M., & Hodges, E. V. E. (1999). Social comparison processes and academic achievement: The dependence of the development of self-evaluations on friends' performance. *Journal of Educational Psychology, 91,* 564–568.

Guerra, N. G., Huesmann, L. R., Tolan, P. H., Van Acker, R., & Eron, L. D. (1995). Stressful events and individual beliefs as correlates of economic disadvantage and aggression among urban children. *Journal of Consulting and Clinical Psychology, 63,* 518–528.

Guerra, N. G., & Slaby, R. G. (1989). Evaluative factors in social problem solving by aggressive boys. *Journal of Abnormal Child Psychology, 17,* 277–289.

Guerra, N. G., & Slaby, R. G. (1990). Cognitive mediators of aggression in adolescent offenders: 2. Intervention. *Developmental Psychology, 26,* 269–277.

Gustafsson, J., & Undheim, J. O. (1996). Individual differences in cognitive functions. In D. C. Berliner & R. C. Calfee (Eds.), *Handbook of educational psychology.* New York: Macmillan.

Guthrie, B. J., Caldwell, C. H., & Hunter, A. G. (1997). Minority adolescent female health: Strategies for the next millennium. In D. K. Wilson, J. R. Rodrigue, & W. C. Taylor (Eds.), *Health-promoting and health-compromising behaviors among minority adolescents* (pp. 153–171). Washington, DC: American Psychological Association.

Guthrie, J. T., Cox, K. E., Anderson, E., Harris, K., Mazzoni, S., & Rach, L. (1998). Principles of integrated instruction for engagement in reading. *Educational Psychology Review, 10,* 177–199.

Guttmacher, S., Lieberman, L., Ward, D., Freudenberg, N., Radosh, A., & DesJarlais, D. (1997). Condom availability in New York City public high schools: Relationships to condom use and sexual behavior. *American Journal of Public Health, 87,* 1427–1433.

Hacker, D. J. (1995, April). *Comprehension monitoring of written discourse across early-to-middle adolescence.* Paper presented at the annual meeting of the American Educational Research Association, San Francisco.

Haenan, J. (1996). Piotr Gal'perin's criticism and extension of Lev Vygotsky's work. *Journal of Russian and East European Psychology, 34*(2), 54–60.

Hagen, J. W., & Stanovich, K. G. (1977). Memory: Strategies of acquisition. In R. V. Kail, Jr. & J. W. Hagen (Eds.), *Perspectives on the development of memory and cognition.* Hillsdale, NJ: Erlbaum.

Haight, W. L., & Miller, P. J. (1993). *Pretending at home: Early development in a sociocultural context.* Albany, NY: SUNY Press.

Hakes, D. T. (1980). *The development of metalinguistic abilities in children.* Berlin, Germany: Springer-Verlag.

Hakuta, K., & McLaughlin, B. (1996). Bilingualism and second language learning: Seven tensions that define the research. In D. C. Berliner &

R. C. Calfee (Eds.), *Handbook of educational psychology.* New York: Macmillan.

Halderman, D. C. (1991). Sexual orientation conversion therapy for gay men and lesbians: A scientific examination. In J. C. Gonsiorek & J. D. Weinrich (Eds.), *Homosexuality: Research implications for public policy* (pp. 149–160). Newbury Park, CA: Sage.

Hale-Benson, J. E. (1986). *Black children: Their roots, culture, and learning styles.* Baltimore: Johns Hopkins University Press.

Halford, G. S. (1989). Cognitive processing capacity and learning ability: An integration of two areas. *Learning and Individual Differences, 1,* 125–153.

Hall, E. R., Esty, E. T., & Fisch, S. M. (1990). Television and children's problem-solving behavior: A synopsis of an evaluation of the effects of Square One TV. *Journal of Mathematical Behavior, 9,* 161–174.

Hall, G. S. (1904). *Adolescence.* New York: Appleton-Century-Crofts.

Hall, R. V., Axelrod, S., Foundopoulos, M., Shellman, J., Campbell, R. A., & Cranston, S. S. (1971). The effective use of punishment to modify behavior in the classroom. *Educational Technology, 11*(4), 24–26.

Hall, W. S. (1989). Reading comprehension. *American Psychologist, 44,* 157–161.

Hallenbeck, M. J. (1996). The cognitive strategy in writing: Welcome relief for adolescents with learning disabilities. *Learning Disabilities Research and Practice, 11,* 107–119.

Hallinan, M. T., & Teixeria, R. A. (1987). Opportunities and constraints: Black-white differences in the formation of interracial friendships. *Child Development, 58,* 1358–1371.

Hallowell, E. (1996). *When you worry about the child you love.* New York: Simon and Schuster.

Halpern, D. F. (1992). *Sex differences in cognitive abilities* (2nd ed.). Hillsdale, NJ: Erlbaum.

Halpern, D. F. (1997). Sex differences in intelligence: Implications for education. *American Psychologist, 52,* 1091–1102.

Halpern, D. F., & LaMay, M. L. (2000). The smarter sex: A critical review of sex differences in intelligence. *Educational Psychology Review, 12,* 229–246.

Hamburg, D. A. (1992). *Children of urban poverty: Approaches to a critical American problem* (Report of the President, 1992). New York: Carnegie Corporation.

Hamers, J. H. M., & Ruijssenaars, A. J. J. M. (1997). Assessing classroom learning potential. In G. D. Phye (Ed.), *Handbook of academic learning: Construction of knowledge.* San Diego, CA: Academic Press.

Hamill, P. V., Drizd, T. A., Johnson, C. L., Reed, R. B., Roche, A. F., & Moore, W. M. (1979). Physical growth: National Center for Health Statistics percentiles. *American Journal of Clinical Nutrition, 32,* 607–629.

Hammer, D. (1994). Epistemological beliefs in introductory physics. *Cognition and Instruction, 12,* 151–183.

Hanley, J. R., Tzeng, O., & Huang, H.-S. (1999). Learning to read Chinese. In M. Harris & G. Hatano (Eds.), *Learning to read and write: A cross-linguistic perspective.* Cambridge, England: Cambridge University Press.

Hare, J. (1994). Concerns and issues faced by families headed by a lesbian couple. *Families in Society, 43,* 27–35.

Harlow, H. F. (1959). Love in infant monkeys. *Scientific American, 200,* 68–74.

Harlow, H. F., & Harlow, M. K. (1962). Social deprivation in monkeys. *Scientific American, 207,* 137–146.

Harms, T., & Clifford, R. M. (1980). *The early childhood environment rating scale.* New York: Teachers College Press.

Harris, C. R. (1991). Identifying and serving the gifted new immigrant. *Teaching Exceptional Children, 23*(4), 26–30.

Harris, J. R. (1995). Where is the child's environment? A group socialization theory of development. *Psychological Review, 102,* 458–489.

Harris, J. R. (1998). *The nurture assumption: Why children turn out the way they do.* New York: Free Press.

Harris, K. R. (1986). Self-monitoring of attentional behavior versus self-monitoring of productivity: Effects of on-task behavior and academic response rate among learning disabled children. *Journal of Applied Behavior Analysis, 19,* 417–423.

Harris, K. R., & Graham, S. (1992). Self-regulated strategy development: A part of the writing process. In M. Pressley, K. R. Harris, & J. T. Guthrie (Eds.), *Promoting academic competence and literacy in school.* San Diego, CA: Academic Press.

Harris, M. (1992). *Language experience and early language development: From input to uptake.* Hove, England: Erlbaum.

Harris, M., & Giannouli, V. (1999). Learning to read and spell in Greek: The importance of letter knowledge and morphological awareness. In M. Harris & G. Hatano (Eds.). *Learning to read and write: A cross-linguistic perspective.* Cambridge, England: Cambridge University Press.

Harris, M., & Hatano, G. (Eds.). (1999). *Learning to read and write: A cross-linguistic perspective.* Cambridge, England: Cambridge University Press.

Harris, M. B. (1997). Preface: Images of the invisible minority. In M. B. Harris (Ed.), *School experiences of gay and lesbian youth: The invisible minority* (pp. xiv–xxii). Binghamton, NY: Harrington Park Press.

Harris, M. J., & Rosenthal, R. (1985). Mediation of interpersonal expectancy effects: 31 meta-analyses. *Psychological Bulletin, 97,* 363–386.

Harris, P. L. (1989). *Children and emotion: The development of psychological understanding.* Oxford, England: Basil Blackwell.

Harrison, A. O., Wilson, M. N., Pine, C. J., Chan, S. Q., & Buriel, R. (1990). Family ecologies of ethnic minority children. *Child Development, 61,* 347–362.

Hart, B., & Risley, T. R. (1995). *Meaningful differences in the everyday experiences of young American children.* Baltimore: Brookes.

Hart, C. H., Ladd, G. W., & Burleson, B. (1990). Children's expectations of the outcomes of social strategies: Relations with sociometric status and maternal disciplinary styles. *Child Development, 61,* 127–137.

Hart, D. (1988). The adolescent self-concept in social context. In D. K. Lapsley & F. C. Power (Eds.), *Self, ego, and identity: Integrative approaches* (pp. 71–90). New York: Springer-Verlag.

Hart, D., & Damon, W. (1986). Developmental trends in self-understanding. *Social Cognition, 4*(4), 388–407.

Harter, S. (1975). Mastery motivation and the need for approval in older children and their relationship to social desirability response tendencies. *Developmental Psychology, 11,* 186–196.

Harter, S. (1983a). Children's understanding of multiple emotions: A cognitive-developmental approach. In W. F. Overton (Ed.), *The relationship between social and cognitive development*. Hillsdale, NJ: Erlbaum.

Harter, S. (1983b). Developmental perspectives on the self-system. In P. M. Mussen (Series Ed.) & E. M. Hetherington (Vol. Ed.), *Handbook of child psychology: Vol. 4. Socialization, personality, and social development* (4th ed.). New York: Wiley.

Harter, S. (1988). The construction and conservation of the self: James and Cooley revisited. In D. K. Lapsley & F. C. Power (Eds.), *Self, ego, and identity: Integrative approaches* (pp. 43–69). New York: Springer-Verlag.

Harter, S. (1990a). Causes, correlates, and the functional role of global self-worth: A life-span perspective. In R. J. Sternberg & J. Kolligian, Jr. (Eds.), *Competence considered*. New Haven, CT: Yale University Press.

Harter, S. (1990b). Processes underlying adolescent self-concept formation. In R. Montemayer, G. R. Adams, & T. P. Gullotta (Eds.), *From childhood to adolescence: A transitional period?* Newbury Park, CA: Sage.

Harter, S. (1992). The relationship between perceived competence, affect, and motivational orientation within the classroom: Processes and patterns of change. In A. K. Boggiano & T. S. Pittman (Eds.), *Achievement and motivation: A social-developmental perspective*. Cambridge, England: Cambridge University Press.

Harter, S. (1996). Teacher and classmate influences on scholastic motivation, self-esteem, and level of voice in adolescents. In J. Juvonen & K. Wentzel (Eds.), *Social motivation: Understanding children's school adjustment*. New York: Cambridge University Press.

Harter, S. (1998). The development of self-representations. In W. Damon (Editor-in-Chief) & N. Eisenberg (Vol. Ed.), *Handbook of child psychology: Vol. 3. Social, emotional, and personality development* (5th ed., pp. 553–617). New York: Wiley.

Harter, S. (1999). *The construction of the self*. New York: Guilford Press.

Harter, S., Bresnick, S., Bouchey, H., & Whitesell, N. R. (1997). The development of multiple role-related selves during adolescence. *Development and Psychopathology, 9*, 835–853.

Harter, S., Stocker, C., & Robinson, N. S. (1996). The perceived directionality of the link between approval and self-worth: The liabilities of a looking glad self-orientation among young adolescents. *Journal of Research on Adolescence, 6*, 285–308.

Harter, S., Waters, P. L., & Whitesell, N. R. (1997). Lack of voice as a manifestation of false self-behavior among adolescents: The school setting as a stage upon which the drama of authenticity is enacted. *Educational Psychologist, 32*, 153–173.

Harter, S., Waters, P. L., Whitesell, N. R., & Kastelic, D. (1998). Level of voice among female and male high school students: Relational context, support, and gender orientation. *Developmental Psychology, 34*, 892–901.

Harter, S., & Whitesell, N. R. (1989). Developmental changes in children's understanding of single, multiple, and blended emotion concepts. In C. Saarni & P. Harris (Eds.), *Children's understanding of emotion* (pp. 81–116). Cambridge, England: Cambridge University Press.

Harter, S., Whitesell, N. R., & Junkin, L. J. (1998). Similarities and differences in domain-specific

and global self-evaluations of learning-disabled, behaviorally disordered, and normally achieving adolescents. *American Educational Research Journal, 35*, 653–680.

Hartmann, D. P., & George, T. P. (1999). Design, measurement, and analysis in developmental research. In M. H. Bornstein & M. E. Lamb (Eds.), *Developmental psychology: An advanced textbook* (4th ed., pp. 125–195). Mahwah, NJ: Erlbaum.

Hartup, W. W. (1974). Aggression in childhood: Developmental perspectives. *American Psychologist, 29*, 336–341.

Hartup, W. W. (1983). Peer relations. In P. H. Mussen (Ed.), *Handbook of child psychology: Vol. IV. Socialization* (4th ed.). New York: Wiley.

Hartup, W. W. (1984). The peer context in middle childhood. In A. Collins (Ed.), *Development during middle childhood: The years from six to twelve*. Washington, DC: National Academy Press.

Hartup, W. W. (1989). Social relationships and their developmental significance. *American Psychologist, 44*, 120–126.

Hartup, W. W. (1992). Friendships and their developmental significance. In H. McGurk (Ed.), *Contemporary issues in childhood social development*. London: Routledge.

Hartup, W. W. (1996). The company they keep: Friendships and their developmental significance. *Child Development, 67*, 1–13.

Hartup, W. W., & Laursen, B. (1991). Relationships as developmental contexts. In R. Cohen & W. A. Siegel (Eds.), *Context and development* (pp. 253–279). Hillsdale, NJ: Erlbaum.

Hartup, W. W., Laursen, B., Stewart, M. I., & Eastenson, A. (1988). Conflict and the friendship relations of young children. *Child Development, 59*, 1590–1600.

Harwood, R. L., Miller, J. G., & Irizarry, N. L. (1995). *Culture and attachment: Perceptions of the child in context*. New York: Guilford Press.

Hatano, G., & Inagaki, K. (1991). Sharing cognition through collective comprehension activity. In L. B. Resnick, J. M. Levine, & S. D. Teasley (Eds.), *Perspectives on socially shared cognition*. Washington, DC: American Psychological Association.

Hatano, G., & Inagaki, K. (1993). Desituating cognition through the construction of conceptual knowledge. In P. Light and G. Butterworth (Eds.), *Context and cognition: Ways of learning and knowing*. Hillsdale, NJ: Erlbaum.

Hatano, G., & Inagaki, K. (1996). Cognitive and cultural factors in the acquisition of intuitive biology. In D. R. Olson & N. Torrance (Eds.), *The handbook of education and human development: New models of learning, teaching, and schooling*. Cambridge, MA: Blackwell.

Hatfield, E., Cacioppo, J. T., & Rapson, R. L. (1994). *Emotional contagion*. Cambridge, England: Cambridge University Press.

Hattie, J., Biggs, J., & Purdie, N. (1996). Effects of learning skills interventions on student learning: A meta-analysis. *Review of Educational Research, 66*, 99–136.

Haviland, J. M., & Lelwica, M. (1987). The induced affect response: 10-week-old infants' responses to three emotional expressions. *Developmental Psychology, 23*, 97–104.

Hawkins, F. P. L. (1997). *Journal with children: The autobiography of a teacher*. Niwot: University Press of Colorado.

Hay, D. F. (1979). Cooperative interactions and sharing between very young children and their parents. *Developmental Psychology, 15*, 647–653.

Hay, D. F., & Ross, H. S. (1982). The social nature of early conflict. *Child Development, 53*, 105–113.

Hayes, C. D., & Hofferth, S. L. (1987). *Risking the future: Adolescent sexuality, pregnancy, and childbearing* (Vol. 2). Washington, DC: National Academy Press.

Hayes, D. P., & Grether, J. (1983). The school year and vacations: When do students learn? *Cornell Journal of Social Relations, 17*(1), 56–71.

Hayslip, B., Jr. (1994). Stability of intelligence. In R. J. Sternberg (Ed.), *Encyclopedia of human intelligence* (Vol. 2). New York: Macmillan.

Hearold, S. (1986). A synthesis of 1,043 effects of television on social behavior. In G. Comstock (Ed.), *Public communication and behavior* (Vol. 1). New York: Academic Press.

Heath, S. (1986). Taking a cross-cultural look at narratives. *Topics in Language Disorders, 7*(1), 84–94.

Heath, S. B. (1980). Questioning at home and at school: A comparative study. In G. Spindler (Ed.), *The ethnography of schooling: Educational anthropology in action*. New York: Holt, Rinehart & Winston.

Heath, S. B. (1983). *Ways with words: Language, life, and work in communities and classrooms*. Cambridge, England: Cambridge University Press.

Heath, S. B. (1989). Oral and literate traditions among black Americans living in poverty. *American Psychologist, 44*, 367–373.

Heckenhausen, H. (1984). Emergent achievement behavior: Some early developments. In J. Nicholls (Ed.), *Advances in achievement motivation*. Greenwich, CT: JAI Press.

Heckenhausen, H. (1987). Emotional components of action: Their ontogeny as reflected in achievement behavior. In D. Girlitz & J. F. Wohlwill (Eds.), *Curiosity, imagination, and play*. Hillsdale, NJ: Erlbaum.

Hedges, L. V., & Nowell, A. (1995). Sex differences in mental test scores, variability, and numbers of high-scoring individuals. *Science, 269*, 41–45.

Hegland, S. M., & Rix, M. K. (1990). Aggression and assertiveness in kindergarten children differing in day care experiences. *Early Childhood Research Quarterly, 5*, 105–116.

Helwig, C. C. (1995). Adolescents' and young adults' conceptions of civil liberties: Freedom of speech and religion. *Child Development, 66*, 152–166.

Hembree, R. (1988). Correlates, causes, effects, and treatment of test anxiety. *Review of Educational Research, 58*, 47–77.

Hemphill, L., & Snow, C. (1996). Language and literacy development: Discontinuities and differences. In D. R. Olson & N. Torrance (Eds.), *The handbook of education and human development: New models of learning, teaching, and schooling*. Cambridge, MA: Blackwell Publishers.

Henderson, N. D. (1982). Human behavior genetics. *Annual Review of Psychology, 33*, 403–440.

Hennessey, B. A. (1995). Social, environmental, and developmental issues and creativity. *Educational Psychology Review, 7*, 163–183.

Henrich, C. C., Brown, J. L., & Aber, J. L. (1999). Evaluating the effectiveness of school-based violence prevention: Developmental approaches. *Social Policy Report, Society for Research in Child Development, 8*(3), 1–17.

Henshaw, S. K. (1997). Teenager abortion and pregnancy statistics by state, 1992. *Family Planning Perspectives, 29*, 115–122.

Herdt, G. H. (1981). *Guardians of the flutes: Idioms of masculinity*. New York: McGraw-Hill.

Hernandez, D. J. (1997). Child development and the social demography of childhood. *Child Development, 68*, 149–169.

Herr, K. (1997). Learning lessons from school: Homophobia, heterosexism, and the construction of failure. In M. B. Harris (Ed.), *School experiences of gay and lesbian youth: The invisible minority* (pp. 51–64). Binghamton, NY: Harrington Park Press.

Herrnstein, R. J., & Murray, C. (1994). *The bell curve: Intelligence and class structure in American life.* New York: Free Press.

Hertel, P. T. (1994). Depression and memory: Are impairments remediable through attentional control? *Current Directions in Psychological Science, 3,* 190–193.

Hess, E. H. (1958). "Imprinting" in animals. *Scientific American, 198*(3), 81–90.

Hess, R. D., Chang, C. M., & McDevitt, T. M. (1987). Cultural variations in family beliefs about children's performance in mathematics: Comparisons among People's Republic of China, Chinese-American, and Caucasian-American families. *Journal of Educational Psychology, 79,* 179–188.

Hess, R. D., Chih-Mei, C., & McDevitt, T. M. (1987). Cultural variations in family beliefs about children's performance in mathematics: Comparisons among People's Republic of China, Chinese-American, and Caucasian-American families. *Journal of Educational Psychology, 79,* 179–188.

Hess, R. D., & Holloway, S. D. (1984). Family and school as educational institutions. In R. D. Parke, R. N. Emde, H. P. McAdoo, & G. P. Sackett (Eds.), *Review of child development research* (Vol. 7). *The family* (pp. 179–222). Chicago: University of Chicago Press.

Hess, R. D., & McDevitt, T. M. (1984). Some cognitive consequences of maternal intervention techniques: A longitudinal study. *Child Development, 55,* 2017–2030.

Hess, R. D., & McDevitt, T. M. (1989). Family. In E. Barnouw (Ed.), *International encyclopedia of communications.* New York: Oxford University Press.

Hetherington, E. M. (1988). Family relations six years after divorce. In E. M. Hetherington & R. D. Parke (Eds.), *Contemporary readings in child psychology.* New York: McGraw-Hill.

Hetherington, E. M. (1989). Coping with family transitions: Winners, losers, and survivors. *Child Development, 60,* 1–14.

Hetherington, E. M. (1999a). Should we stay together for the sake of the children? In E. M. Hetherington et al. (Eds.), *Coping with divorce, single parenting, and remarriage: A risk and resiliency perspective* (pp. 93–116). Mahwah, NJ: Erlbaum.

Hetherington, E. M. (1999b). Social capital and the development of youth from nondivorced, divorced and remarried families. In C. W. Andrew & L. Brett (Eds.), *The Minnesota Symposia on Child Psychology: Vol. 30. Relationships as developmental contexts* (pp. 177–209). Mahwah, NJ: Erlbaum.

Hetherington, E. M., Bridges, M., & Insabella, G. M. (1998). What matters? What does not? Five perspectives on the association between marital transitions and children's adjustment. *American Psychologist, 53,* 167–184.

Hetherington, E. M., & Clingempeel, W. G. (1992). Coping with marital transitions: A family systems perspective. *Monographs of the Society for Research in Child Development, 57*(2–3, Serial No. 227).

Hetherington, E. M., Cox, M., & Cox, R. (1978). The aftermath of divorce. In J. H. Stevens, Jr., & M. Matthews (Eds.), *Mother-child father-child relationships.* Washington, DC: National Association for the Education of Young Children.

Hetherington, E. M., Henderson, S. H., Reiss, D., Anderson, E. R., Bridges, M., Chan, R. W., Insabella, G. M., Jodl, K. M., Kim, J. E., Mitchell, A. S., O'Connor, T. G., Skaggs, M. J., & Taylor, L. C. (1999). Adolescent siblings in stepfamilies: Family functioning and adolescent adjustment. *Monographs of the Society for Research in Child Development, 64*(4, Serial No. 259).

Hetherington, E. M., & Stanley-Hagan, M. M. (1997). The effects of divorce on fathers and their children. In M. E. Lamb (Ed.), *The role of the father in child development* (pp. 191–211). New York: Wiley.

Hetherington, E. M., & Stanley-Hagan, M. M. (1999). Stepfamilies. In M. E. Lamb (Ed.), *Parenting and child development in "nontraditional" families* (pp. 137–159). Mahwah, NJ: Erlbaum.

Heuwinkel, M. K. (1998). *An investigation of preservice teachers' interactive assessment of student understanding in a traditional program and a professional development school.* Unpublished doctoral dissertation, University of Northern Colorado, Greeley.

Heward, W. L. (1996). *Exceptional children: An introduction to special education* (5th ed.). Upper Saddle River, NJ: Merrill/Prentice Hall.

Hiatt, S., Campos, J., & Emde, R. (1979). Facial patterning and infant emotional expression: Happiness, surprise, and fear. *Child Development, 50,* 1020–1035.

Hickey, D. T. (1997). Motivation and contemporary socio-constructivist instructional perspectives. *Educational Psychologist, 32,* 175–193.

Hickey, T. L., & Peduzzi, J. D. (1987). Structure and development of the visual system. In P. Salapatek & L. Cohen (Eds.), *Handbook of infant perception: Vol. 1. From sensation to perception.* New York: Academic Press.

Hidalgo, N. M., Siu, S., Bright, J. A., Swap, S. M., & Epstein, J. L. (1995). Research on families, schools, and communities: A multicultural perspective. In J. A. Banks & C. A. M. Banks (Eds.), *Handbook of research on multicultural education.* New York: Macmillan.

Hidi, S., & Anderson, V. (1992). Situational interest and its impact on reading and expository writing. In K. A. Renninger, S. Hidi, & A. Krapp (Eds.), *The role of interest in learning and development.* Hillsdale, NJ: Erlbaum.

Hiebert, E. H., & Fisher, C. W. (1992). The tasks of school literacy: Trends and issues. In J. Brophy (Ed.), *Advances in research on teaching: Vol. 3: Planning and managing learning tasks and activities.* Greenwich, CT: JAI Press.

Hiebert, E. H., & Raphael, T. E. (1996). Psychological perspectives on literacy and extensions to educational practice. In D. C. Berliner & R. C. Calfee (Eds.), *Handbook of educational psychology.* New York: Macmillan.

Higgins, A. (1995). Educating for justice and community: Lawrence Kohlberg's vision of moral education. In W. M. Kurtines & J. L. Gewirtz (Eds.), *Moral development: An introduction.* Boston: Allyn & Bacon.

Higgins, A. T., & Turnure, J. E. (1984). Distractibility and concentration of attention in children's development. *Child Development, 55,* 1799–1810.

Hill, J. P., Holmbeck, G. N., Marlow, L., Green, T. M., & Lynch, M. E. (1985). Menarchal status and parent-child relations in families of seventh-grade girls. *Journal of Youth and Adolescence, 14,* 301–316.

Hilliard, A., & Vaughn-Scott, M. (1982). The quest for the minority child. In S. G. Moore & C. R. Cooper (Eds.), *The young child: Reviews of research* (Vol. 3). Washington, DC: National Association for the Education of Young Children.

Hillier, L., Hewitt, K. L., & Morrongiello, B. A. (1992). Infants' perception of illusions in sound localization: Reaching to sounds in the dark. *Journal of Experimental Child Psychology, 53,* 159–179.

Hillocks, G. (1989). Synthesis of research on teaching writing. *Educational Leadership, 44,* 71–82.

Hinde, R. A., Titmus, G., Easton, D., & Tamplin, A. (1985). Incidence of "friendship" and behavior with strong associates versus non-associates in preschoolers. *Child Development, 56,* 234–245.

Hinshaw, S. P., Zupan, B. A., Simmel, C., Nigg, J. T., & Melnick, S. (1997). Peer status in boys with and without Attention-Deficit Hyperactivity Disorder: Predictions from overt and covert antisocial behavior, social isolation, and authoritative parenting beliefs. *Child Development, 68,* 880–896.

Hirsh-Pasek, K., & Golinkoff, R. M. (1996). *The origins of grammar: Evidence from early language comprehension.* Cambridge, MA: MIT Press.

Hirsh-Pasek, K., Hyson, M., & Rescorla, L. (1990). Academic environments in preschool: Do they pressure or challenge young children? *Early Education and Development, 1*(6), 401–423.

Ho, D. Y. F. (1986). Chinese pattern of socialization: A critical review. In M. H. Bond (Ed.), *The psychology of Chinese people.* Oxford, England: Oxford University Press.

Ho, D. Y. F. (1994). Cognitive socialization in Confucian heritage cultures. In P. M. Greenfield & R. R. Cocking (Eds.), *Cross-cultural roots of minority child development.* Hillsdale, NJ: Erlbaum.

Hobson, R. P. (1993). *Autism and the development of mind.* London: Erlbaum.

Hodges, E., Malone, J., & Perry, D. (1997). Individual risk and social risk as interacting determinants of victimization in the peer group. *Developmental Psychology, 32,* 1033–1039.

Hofer, B. K., & Pintrich, P. R. (1997). The development of epistemological theories: Beliefs about knowledge and knowing and their relation to learning. *Review of Educational Research, 67,* 88–140.

Hofferth, S. L., & Hayes, C. D. (Eds.). (1987). *Risking the future: Adolescent sexuality, pregnancy, and childbearing,* (Vol. II). Washington, DC: National Academy of Sciences Press.

Hoffman, L. W. (1988). Cross-cultural differences in childrearing goals. In R. A. LeVine, P. M. Miller, & M. M. West (Eds.), *Parental behavior in diverse societies* (pp. 99–122). San Francisco: Jossey-Bass.

Hoffman, M. L. (1970). Moral development. In P. H. Mussen (Ed.), *Carmichael's manual of child psychology* (Vol. 2). New York: Wiley.

Hoffman, M. L. (1975). Altruistic behavior and the parent-child relationship. *Journal of Personality and Social Psychology, 31,* 937–943.

Hoffman, M. L. (1981). Is altruism part of human nature? *Journal of Personality and Social Psychology, 40,* 121–137.

Hoffman, M. L. (1988). Moral development. In M. H. Bornstein & M. E. Lamb (Eds.), *Developmental psychology: An advanced textbook* (2nd ed.). Hillsdale, NJ: Erlbaum.

Hoffman, M. L. (1991). Empathy, social cognition, and moral action. In W. M. Kurtines & J. L. Gewirtz (Eds.), *Moral behavior and development: Vol. 1. Theory.* Hillsdale, NJ: Erlbaum.

Hoffman, M. L. (1998). Varieties of empathy-based guilt. In J. Bybee (Ed.), *Guilt and children* (pp. 91–112). San Diego, CA: Academic Press.

Hogan, K. (1997, March). *Relating students' personal frameworks for science learning to their cognition in collaborative contexts.* Paper presented at the annual meeting of the American Educational Research Association, Chicago.

Holden, G. W. (1988). Adults' thinking about a child-rearing problem: Effects of experience, parental status, and gender. *Child Development, 59,* 1623–1632.

Holliday, B. G. (1985). Towards a model of teacher-child transactional processes affecting black children's academic achievement. In M. B. Spencer, G. K. Brookins, & W. R. Allen (Eds.), *Beginnings: The social and affective development of black children.* Hillsdale, NJ: Erlbaum.

Hollins, E. R. (1996). *Culture in school learning: Revealing the deep meaning.* Mahwah, NJ: Erlbaum.

Holtz, L. T. (1997). *The alphabet book.* London: DK Publishing.

Hom, A., & Battistich, V. (1995, April). *Students' sense of school community as a factor in reducing drug use and delinquency.* Paper presented at the annual meeting of the American Educational Research Association, San Francisco.

Hong, Y., Chiu, C., & Dweck, C. S. (1995). Implicit theories of intelligence: Reconsidering the role of confidence in achievement motivation. In M. H. Kernis (Ed.), *Efficacy, agency, and self-esteem.* New York: Plenum Press.

Hong, Y., Morris, M. W., Chiu, C., & Benet-Mart'nez, V. (2000). Multicultural minds: A dynamic constructivist approach to culture and cognition. *American Psychologist, 55,* 709–720.

Hoover-Dempsey, K. V., & Sandler, H. M. (1997). Why do parents become involved in their children's education? *Review of Educational Research, 67,* 3–42.

Horacek, H., Ramey, C., Campbell, F., Hoffman, K., & Fletcher, R. (1987). Predicting school failure and assessing early intervention with high-risk children. *American Academy of Child and Adolescent Psychiatry, 26,* 758–763.

Horgan, D. (1990, April). *Students' predictions of test grades: Calibration and metacognition.* Paper presented at the annual meeting of the American Educational Research Association, Boston.

Horowitz, E. (1997). The worlds of Jewish youth in Europe, 1300–1800. In G. Levi & J. C. Schmitt (Eds.), *A history of young people in the west: Vol. 1. Ancient and medieval rites of passage* (C. Naish, Trans.; pp. 83–119). Cambridge, MA: Belknap Press of Harvard University Press.

Hossain, Z., & Roopnarine, J. L. (1994). African American fathers' involvement with infants: Relationship to their functioning style, support, education, and income. *Infant Behavior and Development, 17,* 175–184.

Hossler, D., & Stage, F. K. (1992). Family and high school experience influences on the postsecondary educational plans of ninth-grade students. *American Educational Research Journal, 29,* 425–451.

Howes, C. (1988). The peer interactions of young children. *Monographs of the Society for Research in Child Development, 53*(1, Serial No. 217).

Howes, C. (1992). *The collaborative construction of pretend.* Albany: State University of New York Press.

Howes, C., & Matheson, C. C. (1992). Sequences in the development of competent play with peers: Social and social-pretend play. *Developmental Psychology, 28,* 961–974.

Howes, C., & Ritchie, S. (1998). Changes in child-teacher relationships in a therapeutic preschool program. *Early Education and Development, 9,* 411–422.

Hubel, D., & Wiesel, T. (1965). Binocular interaction in striate cortex of kittens reared with artificial squint. *Journal of Neurophysiology, 28,* 1041–1059.

Hughes, F. P. (1998). Play in special populations. In O. N. Saracho & B. Spodek (Eds.), *Multiple perspectives on play in early childhood education* (pp. 171–193). Albany: State University of New York Press.

Hughes, J. N. (1988). *Cognitive behavior therapy with children in schools.* New York: Pergamon.

Hulme, C., & Joshi, R. M. (Eds.). (1998). *Reading and spelling: Development and disorders.* Mahwah, NJ: Erlbaum.

Humphreys, A. P., & Smith, P. K. (1987). Rough-and-tumble play, friendship, and dominance in school children: Evidence for continuity and change with age. *Child Development, 58,* 201–212.

Humphreys, L. G. (1992). What both critics and users of ability tests need to know. *Psychological Science, 3,* 271–274.

Hunt, D. E. (1981). Teachers' adaptation: "Reading" and "flexing" to students. In B. R. Joyce, C. C. Brown, & L. Peck (Eds.), *Flexibility in teaching: An excursion into the nature of teaching and training* (pp. 59–71). New York: Longman.

Hunt, E. (1997). Nature vs. nurture: The feeling of *vujà dé.* In R. J. Sternberg & E. L. Grigorenko (Eds.), *Intelligence, heredity, and environment* (pp. 531–551). Cambridge, England: Cambridge University Press.

Hunt, E., Streissguth, A. P., Kerr, B., & Olson, H. C. (1995). Mothers' alcohol consumption during pregnancy: Effects on spatial-visual reasoning in 14-year-old children. *Psychological Science, 6,* 339–342.

Hunt, J. M. V. (1969). *The challenge of incompetence and poverty.* Urbana: University of Illinois Press.

Hussong, A., Chassin, L., & Hicks, R. (1999, April). *The elusive relation between negative affect and adolescent substance use: Does it exist?* Paper presented at the Biennial Meeting of the Society for Research in Child Development, Albuquerque, NM.

Huston, A. C. (1983). Sex typing. In E. M. Hetherington (Ed.), *Handbook of child psychology: Vol. 4. Socialization, personality, and social development* (4th ed., pp. 387–467). New York: Wiley.

Huston, A. C., Donnerstein, E., Fairchild, H., Feshbach, N. D., Katz, P. A., Murray, J. P., Rubenstein, E. A., Wilcox, B. L., & Zuckerman, D. (1992). *Big world, small screen: The role of television in American society.* Lincoln: University of Nebraska Press.

Huston, A. C., & Wright, J. C. (1998). Mass media and children's development. In W. Damon (Editor-in-Chief), I. E. Sigel, & K. A. Renninger (Vol. Eds.), *Handbook of child psychology: Vol. 4. Child psychology in practice* (5th ed., pp. 999–1058). New York: Wiley.

Huttenlocher, P. R. (1993). Morphometric study of human cerebral cortex development. In M. H. Johnson (Ed.), *Brain development and cognition: A reader.* Cambridge, MA: Blackwell.

Iannotti, R. J. (1978). Effects of role-taking experiences on role-taking, empathy, altruism, and aggression. *Developmental Psychology, 14,* 119–124.

Igoe, A. R., & Sullivan, H. (1991, April). *Gender and grade-level differences in student attributes related to school learning and motivation.* Paper presented at the annual meeting of the American Educational Research Association, Chicago.

Inglehart, M., Brown, D. R., & Vida, M. (1994). Competition, achievement, and gender: A stress theoretical analysis. In P. R. Pintrich, D. R. Brown, & C. E. Weinstein (Eds.), *Student motivation, cognition, and learning: Essays in honor of Wilbert J. McKeachie.* Hillsdale, NJ: Erlbaum.

Inhelder, B., & Piaget, J. (1958). *The growth of logical thinking from childhood to adolescence* (A. Parsons & S. Milgram, Trans.). New York: Basic Books.

Interagency Forum on Child and Family Statistics (1999). *America's children: Key national indicators of well-being, 1999.* Washington, DC: U.S. Government Printing Office. Retrieved from the World Wide Web: http://www.ChildStats.gov/ac1999/highlight.asp

Irujo, S. (1988). An introduction to intercultural differences and similarities in nonverbal communication. In J. S. Wurzel (Ed.), *Toward multiculturalism: A reader in multicultural education.* Yarmouth, ME: Intercultural Press.

Irvine, J. (1990). *Black students and school failure: Policies, practices, and prescriptions.* New York: Greenwood Press.

Irwin, C. E., Jr., & Millstein, S. G. (1992). Biopsychosocial correlates of risk-taking behaviors during adolescence: Can the physician intervene? *Journal of Adolescent Health Care, 7*(Suppl. 6), 82S–96S.

Irwin, R. A., & Gross, A. M. (1995). Cognitive tempo, violent video games, and aggressive behavior in young boys. *Journal of Family Violence, 10,* 337–350.

Isen, A., Daubman, K. A., & Gorgoglione, J. M. (1987). The influence of positive affect on cognitive organization: Implications for education. In R. E. Snow & M. J. Farr (Eds.), *Aptitude, learning and instruction: Vol. 3. Cognitive and affective process analysis.* Hillsdale, NJ: Erlbaum.

Jacklin, C. N. (1989). Female and male: Issues of gender. *American Psychologist, 44,* 127–133.

Jackson, D. L., & Ormrod, J. E. (1998). *Case studies: Applying educational psychology.* Upper Saddle River, NJ: Merrill/Prentice Hall.

Jackson, G., & Cosca, C. (1974). The inequality of educational opportunity in the Southwest: An observational study of ethnically mixed classrooms. *American Educational Research Journal, 11,* 219–229.

Jackson, P. W. (1988). The daily grind. In G. Handel (Ed.), *Childhood socialization.* New York: Aldine de Gruyter.

Jacobsen, B., Lowery, B., & DuCette, J. (1986). Attributions of learning disabled children. *Journal of Educational Psychology, 78,* 59–64.

Jacobsen, L. K., Giedd, J. N., Berquin, P. C., Krain, A. L., Hamburger, S. D., Kumra, S., & Rapoport, J. L. (1997). Quantitative morphology of the cerebellum and fourth ventricle in childhood-onset schizophrenia. *American Journal of Psychiatry, 154,* 1663–1669.

Jacobsen, L. K., Giedd, J. N., Castellanos, F. X., Vaituzis, A. C., Hamburger, S. D., Kumra, S., Lenane, M. C., & Rapoport, J. L. (1997). Progressive reduction of temporal lobe structures in childhood-onset schizophrenia. *American Journal of Psychiatry, 155,* 678–685.

Jacoby, R., & Glauberman, N. (Eds.). (1995). *The bell curve debate: History, documents, opinions.* New York: Random House.

Jahoda, G. (1979). The construction of economic reality by some Glaswegian children. *European Journal of Social Psychology, 9,* 115–127.

Jahoda, G. (1982). The development of ideas about an economic institution: A cross-national replication. *British Journal of Social Psychology, 21,* 337–338.

Jahoda, G. (1983). European "lag" in the development of an economic concept: A study in Zimbabwe. *British Journal of Developmental Psychology, 1*(2), 113–120.

Jalongo, M. R., Isenberg, J. P., & Gerbracht, G. (1995). *Teachers' stories: From personal narrative to professional insight.* San Francisco: Jossey-Bass.

James, W. T. (1890/1950). *The principles of psychology.* New York: Dover.

Jencks, C. M., & Mayer, S. (1990). The social consequences of growing up in a poor neighborhood: A review. In M. McGreary & L. Lynn (Eds.), *Concentrated urban poverty in America.* Washington, DC: National Academy.

Jenkins, S., Bax, M., & Hart, H. (1980). Behavior problems in preschool children. *Journal of Child Psychology and Psychiatry, 21,* 5–18.

Jenlink, C. L. (1994, April). *Music: A lifeline for the self-esteem of at-risk students.* Paper presented at the annual meeting of the American Educational Research Association, New Orleans, LA.

Jersild, A. T., & Markey, F. U. (1935). Conflicts between preschool children. *Child Development Monographs.*

Jessor, R., & Jessor, S. L. (1977). *Problem behavior and psychosocial development: A longitudinal study of youth.* San Diego, CA: Academic Press.

Jessor, R., Donovan, J. E., & Costa, F. M. (1991). *Beyond adolescence: Problem behavior and young adult development.* New York: Academic Press.

Jimerson, S., Egeland, B., & Teo, A. (1999). A longitudinal study of achievement trajectories: Factors associated with change. *Journal of Educational Psychology, 91,* 116–126.

Joe, J. R. (1994). Revaluing Native-American concepts of development and education. In P. M. Greenfield & R. R. Cocking (Eds.), *Cross-cultural roots of minority child development* (pp. 107–113). Hillsdale, NJ: Erlbaum.

Johnson, D. W., Johnson, R., Dudley, B., Ward, M., & Magnuson, D. (1995). The impact of peer mediation training on the management of school and home conflicts. *American Educational Research Journal, 32,* 829–844.

Johnson, H. C., & Friesen, B. (1993). Etiologies of mental and emotional disorders in children. In H. Johnson (Ed.), *Child mental health in the 1990s: Curricula for graduate and undergraduate.* Washington, DC: U.S. Department of Health and Human Services.

Johnson, J. S., & Newport, E. L. (1989). Critical period effects in second language learning: The influence of maturational state on acquisition of English as a second lanuage. *Cognitive Psychology, 21,* 60–99.

Johnson, M. H., & Morton, J. (1991). *Biology and cognitive development: The case of face recognition.* Oxford, England: Blackwell.

John-Steiner, V., & Mahn, H. (1996). Sociocultural approaches to learning and development: A Vygotskian framework. *Educational Psychologist, 31,* 191–206.

John-Steiner, V., Panofsky, C. P., & Smith, L. W. (Eds.). (1994). *Sociocultural approaches to language and literacy: An interactionist perspective.* Cambridge, England: Cambridge University Press.

Johnston, D. K. (1988). Adolescents' solutions to dilemmas in fables: Two moral orientations—two problem solving strategies. In C. Gilligan, J. V. Ward, J. M. Taylor, & B. Bardige (Eds.), *Mapping the moral domain: A contribution of women's thinking to psychological theory and*

education (pp. 49–71). Cambridge, MA: Harvard University Press.

Johnston, J. R. (1994). High-conflict divorce. *The Future of Children: Children and Divorce, 4*(1), 164–182.

Johnston, J. R. (1997). Specific language impairment, cognition and the biological basis of language. In M. Gopnik (Ed.), *The inheritance and innateness of grammars.* New York: Oxford University Press.

Johnston, L. D., O'Malley, P. M., & Bachman, J. G. (2000). *The Monitoring the Future national results on adolescent drug use: Overview of key findings, 1999.* Bethesda, MD: National Institute on Drug Use. Retrieved from the World Wide Web: http://www.monitoringthefuture.org/pubs/keyfindings.pdf

Johnston, L. D., O'Malley, P. M., Bachman, J. G., & Schulenberg, J. E. (1999). *Cigarette brand preferences among adolescents* (Monitoring the Future Occasional Paper 45). Ann Arbor: University of Michigan Institute for Social Research. Retrieved from the World Wide Web: http://www.isr.umich.edu/src/mtf/occpaper45/paper.html

Johnston, P., & Afflerbach, P. (1985). The process of constructing main ideas from text. *Cognition and Instruction, 2,* 207–232.

Jones, D., & Christensen, C. A. (1999). Relationship between automaticity in handwriting and students' ability to generate written text. *Journal of Educational Psychology, 91,* 44–49.

Jones, G. P., & Dembo, M. H. (1989). Age and sex role differences in intimate friendships during childhood and adolescence. *Merrill-Palmer Quarterly, 35,* 445–462.

Jones, H. F. (1949). Adolescence in our society. In *Anniversary Papers of the Community Service Society of New York: The family in a democratic society* (pp. 70–82). New York: Columbia University Press.

Jones, I., & Pellegrini, A. D. (1996). The effects of social relationships, writing media, and microgenetic development on first-grade students' written narratives. *American Educational Research Journal, 33,* 691–718.

Jordan, C. (1981). The selection of culturally compatible teaching practices. *Educational Perspectives, 20,* 16–19.

Joshi, M. S., & MacLean, M. (1994). Indian and English children's understanding of the distinction between real and apparent emotion. *Child Development, 65,* 1372–1384.

Josselson, R. (1988). The embedded self: I and Thou revisited. In D. K. Lapsley & F. C. Power (Eds.), *Self, ego, and identity: Integrative approaches* (pp. 91–106). New York: Springer-Verlag.

Jovanovic, J., & King, S. S. (1998). Boys and girls in the performance-based science classroom: Who's doing the performing? *American Educational Research Journal, 35,* 477–496.

Jozefowicz, D. M., Arbreton, A. J., Eccles, J. S., Barber, B. L., & Colarossi, L. (1994, April). *Seventh grade student, parent, and teacher factors associated with later school dropout or movement into alternative educational settings.* Paper presented at the annual meeting of the American Educational Research Association, New Orleans, LA.

Juel, C. (1991). Beginning reading. In R. Barr, M. Kamii, P. Mosenthal, & P. D. Pearson (Eds.), *Handbook of reading research* (Vol. II). New York: Longman.

Juel, C. (1998). What kind of one-on-one tutoring helps a poor reader? In C. Hulme & R. M. Joshi (Eds.), *Reading and spelling: Development and disorders.* Mahwah, NJ: Erlbaum.

Jusczyk, P. W. (1995). Language acquisition: Speech sounds and phonological development. In J. L.

Miller & P. D. Eimas (Eds.), *Handbook of perception and cognition: Vol. 11. Speech, language, and communication.* Orlando, FL: Academic Press.

Jusczyk, P. W., & Aslin, R. N. (1995). Infants' detection of the sound patterns of words in fluent speech. *Cognitive Psychology, 29,* 1–23.

Jussim, L., Eccles, J., & Madon, S. (1996). Social perception, social stereotypes, and teacher expectations: Accuracy and the quest for the powerful self-fulfilling prophecy. In L. Berkowitz (Ed.), *Advances in experimental social psychology.* New York: Academic Press.

Juster, N. (1961). *The phantom tollbooth.* New York: Random House.

Juvonen, J. (1991). Deviance, perceived responsibility, and negative peer reactions. *Developmental Psychology, 27,* 672–681.

Juvonen, J. (2000). The social functions of attributional face-saving tactics among early adolescents. *Educational Psychology Review, 12,* 15–32.

Juvonen, J., & Hiner, M. (1991, April). *Perceived responsibility and annoyance as mediators of negative peer reactions.* Paper presented at the annual meeting of the American Educational Research Association, Chicago.

Juvonen, J., Nishina, A., & Graham, S. (2000). Peer harassment, psychological adjustment, and school functioning in early adolescence. *Journal of Educational Psychology, 92,* 349–359.

Juvonen, J., & Weiner, B. (1993). An attributional analysis of students' interactions: The social consequences of perceived responsibility. *Educational Psychology Review, 5,* 325–345.

Kaczmarek, M. G., & Backlund, B. A. (1991). Disenfranchised grief: The loss of an adolescent romantic relationship. *Adolescence, 26,* 253–259.

Kagan, D. (1992). Implications of research on teacher belief. *Educational Psychologist, 27,* 65–90.

Kagan, J. (1981). *The second year: The emergence of self-awareness.* Cambridge, MA: Harvard University Press.

Kagan, J. (1984). *The nature of the child.* New York: Basic Books.

Kagan, J. (1998). Biology and the child. In W. Damon (Editor-in-Chief) & N. Eisenberg (Vol. Ed.), *Handbook of child psychology.: Vol. 3. Social, emotional, and personality development* (5th ed., pp. 177–235). New York: Wiley.

Kahl, B., & Woloshyn, V. E. (1994). Using elaborative interrogation to facilitate acquisition of factual information in cooperative learning settings: One good strategy deserves another. *Applied Cognitive Psychology, 8,* 465–478.

Kahneman, D. (2000). Preface. In D. Kahneman, & A. Tversky (Eds.). *Choices, values, and frames* (pp. ix–xvii). New York: Russell Sage Foundation.

Kail, R. (1990). *The development of memory in children* (3rd ed.). New York: Freeman.

Kail, R. (1993). The role of a global mechanism in developmental change in speed of processing. In M. L. Howe & R. Pasnak (Eds.), *Emerging themes in cognitive development: Vol. 1. Foundations.* New York: Springer-Verlag.

Kail, R. V. (1998). *Children and their development.* Upper Saddle River, NJ: Prentice Hall.

Kail, R., & Park, Y. (1994). Processing time, articulation time, and memory span. *Journal of Experimental Child Psychology, 57,* 281–291.

Kailin, J. (1999). How white teachers perceive the problem of racism in their schools: A case study in "liberal" Lakeview. *Teachers College Record, 100*(4), 724–750.

Kaler, S. R., & Kopp, C. B. (1990). Compliance and comprehension in very young toddlers. *Child Development, 61,* 1997–2003.

Kang-Ning, C. (1981). Education for Chinese and Indochinese. *Theory into Practice, 20*(1), 35–44.

Kanner, A. D., Feldman, S. S., Weinberger, D. A., & Ford, M. E. (1987). Uplifts, hassles, and adaptational outcomes in early adolescents. *Journal of Early Adolescence, 7,* 371–394.

Kaplan, A. (1998, April). *Task goal orientation and adaptive social interaction among students of diverse cultural backgrounds.* Paper presented at the annual meeting of the American Educational Research Association, San Diego, CA.

Kaplan, A., & Maehr, M. L. (in press). Enhancing the motivation of African American students: An achievement goal theory perspective. *Journal of Negro Education.*

Kaplan, P. S., Goldstein, M. H., Huckeby, E. R., & Cooper, R. P. (1995). Habituation, sensitization, and infants' responses to motherese speech. *Developmental Psychobiology, 28,* 45–57.

Kapp-Simon, K., & Simon, D. J. (1991). Meeting the challenge: Social skills training for teens with special needs. *Connections: The Newsletter of the National Center for Youth and Disabilities, 2*(2), 1–5.

Karabenick, S. A., & Sharma, R. (1994). Seeking academic assistance as a strategic learning resource. In P. R. Pintrich, D. R. Brown, & C. E. Weinstein (Eds.), *Student motivation, cognition, and learning: Essays in honor of Wilbert J. McKeachie.* Hillsdale, NJ: Erlbaum.

Kardash, C. A. M., & Howell, K. L. (1996, April). *Effects of epistemological beliefs on strategies employed to comprehend dual-positional text.* Paper presented at the annual meeting of the American Educational Research Association, New York.

Karmiloff-Smith, A. (1979). Language development after five. In P. Fletcher & M. Garman (Eds.), *Language acquisition: Studies in first language development.* Cambridge, England: Cambridge University Press.

Karmiloff-Smith, A. (1993). Innate constraints and developmental change. In P. Bloom (Ed.), *Language acquisition: Core readings.* Cambridge, MA: MIT Press.

Karpov, Y. V., & Haywood, H. C. (1998). Two ways to elaborate Vygotsky's concept of mediation: Implications for instruction. *American Psychologist, 53,* 27–36.

Katchadourian, H. (1990). Sexuality. In S. S. Feldman & G. R. Elliott (Eds.), *At the threshold: The developing adolescent* (pp. 330–351). Cambridge, MA: Harvard University Press.

Katkovsky, W., Crandall, V. C., & Good, S. (1967). Parental antecedents of children's beliefs in internal-external control of reinforcements in intellectual achievement situations. *Child Development, 38,* 765–776.

Katsurada, E., & Sugawara, A. I. (1998). The relationship between hostile attributional bias and aggressive behavior in preschoolers. *Early Childhood Research Quarterly, 13,* 623–636.

Katz, E. W., & Brent, S. B. (1968). Understanding connectives. *Journal of Verbal Learning and Verbal Behavior, 7,* 501–509.

Katz, L. F., & Gottman, J. M. (1991). Marital discord and child outcomes: A social psychophysiological approach. In J. Garber & K. A. Dodge (Eds.), *The development of emotion regulation and dysregulation.* Cambridge, England: Cambridge University Press.

Katz, L. G. (1999a). *Another look at what young children should be learning.* Champaign, IL: ERIC Clearing-house on Elementary and Early Childhood Education (ERIC Document Reproduction Service No. ED 430 735).

Katz, L. G. (1999b, November). *Current perspectives on education in the early years: Challenges for the new millennium.* Paper presented at the Annual Rudolph Goodridge Memorial Lecture, Barbados, West Indies. (ERIC Document Reproduction Service No. ED 437 212).

Kaufman, P., Chen, X., Choy, S. P., Chandler, K. A., Chapman, C. D., Rand, M. R., & Ringel, C. (1999). Indicators of school crime and safety, 1998. *Education Statistics Quarterly, 1*(1), 42–45.

Kaye, K. (1982). *The mental and social life of babies: How parents create persons.* Chicago: University of Chicago Press.

Kazdin, A. E. (1997). Conduct disorder across the life-span. In S. S. Luthar, J. A. Burack, D. Cicchetti, & J. R. Weisz (Eds.), *Developmental psychopathology: Perspectives on adjustment, risk, and disorder* (pp. 248–272). Cambridge, England: Cambridge University Press.

Kearins, J. M. (1981). Visual spatial memory in Australian aboriginal children of desert regions. *Cognitive Psychology, 13,* 434–460.

Keating, D. P. (1996a). A grand theory of development. In R. Case & Y. Okamoto, in collaboration with S. Griffin, A. McKeough, C. Bleiker, B. Henderson, & K. M. Stephenson. The role of central conceptual structures in the development of children's thought. *Monographs of the Society for Research in Child Development, 61*(1, Serial No. 246).

Keating, D. P. (1996b). Habits of mind for a learning society: Educating for human development. In D. R. Olson & N. Torrance (Eds.), *The handbook of education and human development: New models of learning, teaching and schooling* (pp. 461–481). Cambridge, MA: Blackwell.

Kedesdy, J. H., & Budd, K. S. (1998). *Childhood feeding disorders: Biobehavioral assessment and intervention.* Baltimore: Brookes.

Keeney, T. J., Canizzo, S. R., & Flavell, J. H. (1967). Spontaneous and induced verbal rehearsal in a recall task. *Child Development, 38,* 953–966.

Keil, F. C. (1987). Conceptual development and category structure. In U. Neisser (Ed.), *Concepts and conceptual development: Ecological and intellectual factors in categorization.* Cambridge, England: Cambridge University Press.

Keil, F. C. (1989). *Concepts, kinds, and cognitive development.* Cambridge, MA: MIT Press.

Keil, F. C. (1991). Theories, concepts, and the acquisition of word meaning. In S. A. Gelman & J. P. Byrnes (Eds.), *Perspectives on language and thought: Interrelations in development.* Cambridge, England: Cambridge University Press.

Keil, F. C., & Silberstein, C. S. (1996). Schooling and the acquisition of theoretical knowledge. In D. R. Olson & N. Torrance (Eds.), *The handbook of education and human development: New models of learning, teaching, and schooling.* Cambridge, MA: Blackwell.

Kellam, S. G. (1990). Developmental epidemiological framework for family research on depression and aggression. In G. R. Patterson (Ed.), *Depression and aggression in family interaction* (pp. 11–48). Hillsdale, NJ: Erlbaum.

Kelley, M. L., Power, T. G., & Wimbush, D. D. (1992). Determinants of disciplinary practices in low-income Black mothers. *Child Development, 63,* 573–582.

Kellogg, R. (1967). *The psychology of children's art.* New York: CRM–Random House.

Kellogg, R. T. (1994). *The psychology of writing.* New York: Oxford University Press.

Kelly, A., & Smail, B. (1986). Sex stereotypes and attitudes to science among eleven-year-old children. *British Journal of Educational Psychology, 56,* 158–168.

Kelly, J. A. (1995). *Changing HIV risk behavior: Practical strategies.* New York: Guilford Press.

Kelly, J. A., Murphy, D. A., Sikkema, K. J., & Kalichman, S. C. (1993). Psychological interventions to prevent HIV infection are urgently needed. *American Psychologist, 48,* 1023–1034.

Kemper, S. (1984). The development of narrative skills: Explanations and entertainments. In S. Kuczaj (Ed.), *Discourse development: Progress in cognitive development research.* New York: Springer-Verlag.

Kemper, S., & Edwards, L. (1986). Children's expression of causality and their construction of narratives. *Topics in Language Disorders, 7*(1), 11–20.

Kenneth, K., Smith, P. K., & Palermiti, A. L. (1997). Conflict in childhood and reproductive development. *Evolution and Human Behavior, 18,* 109–142.

Keogh, B. K., & MacMillan, D. L. (1996). Exceptionality. In D. C. Berliner & R. C. Calfee (Eds.), *Handbook of educational psychology.* New York: Macmillan.

Kerewsky, W., & Lefstein, L. M. (1982). Young adolescents and their community: A shared responsibility. In L. M. Lefstein et al. (Eds.), *3:00 to 6:00 P.M.: Young adolescents at home and in the community.* Carrboro, NC: Center for Early Adolescence.

Kern, L., Dunlap, G., Childs, K. E., & Clark, S. (1994). Use of a classwide self-management program to improve the behavior of students with emotional and behavioral disorders. *Education and Treatment of Children, 17,* 445–458.

Kerns, L. L., & Lieberman, A. B. (1993). *Helping your depressed child.* Rocklin, CA: Prima.

Kerr, M. M., & Nelson, C. M. (1989). *Strategies for managing behavior problems in the classroom* (2nd ed.). Upper Saddle River, NJ: Merrill/Prentice Hall.

Kerrebrock, N., & Lewitt, E. M. (1999). Children in self-care. *The Future of Children: When School Is Out, 9,* 151–160.

Kestenbaum, R., Farber, E. A., & Sroufe, L. A. (1989). Individual differences in empathy among preschoolers: Relation to attachment history. In N. Eisenberg (Ed.), *Empathy and related emotional responses* (New Directions for Child Development, No. 44; pp. 51–64). San Francisco: Jossey-Bass.

Kidder, T. (1989). *Among schoolchildren.* New York: Avon Books.

Kienberger-Jaudes, R., Ekwo, E., & Van Voorhis, J. (1995). Association of drug abuse and child abuse. *Child Abuse and Neglect, 19*(5), 531–543.

Killen, M., & Nucci, L. P. (1995). Morality, autonomy, and social conflict. In M. Killen & D. Hart (Eds.), *Morality in everyday life: Developmental perspectives* (pp. 52–86). Cambridge, England: Cambridge University Press.

Kim, D., Solomon, D., & Roberts, W. (1995, April). *Classroom practices that enhance students' sense of community.* Paper presented at the annual meeting of the American Educational Research Association, San Francisco.

Kim, J. M., & Turiel, E. (1996). Korean and American children's concepts of adult and peer authority. *Social Development, 5,* 310–329.

Kim, U., & Choi, S. H. (1994). Individualism, collectivism, and child development: A Korean perspective. In P. M. Greenfield & R. R. Cocking (Eds.), *Cross-cultural roots of minority child development* (pp. 227–257). Hillsdale, NJ: Erlbaum.

Kimball, M. M. (1986). Television and sex-role attitudes. In T. M. Williams (Ed.), *The impact of television.* New York: Academic Press.

Kindermann, T. A. (1993). Natural peer groups as contexts for individual development: The case of children's motivation in school. *Developmental Psychology, 29,* 970–977.

Kindermann, T. A., McCollam, T. L., & Gibson, E., Jr. (1996). Peer networks and students' classroom engagement during childhood and adolescence. In J. Juvonen & K. R. Wentzel (Eds.), *Social motivation: Understanding children's school adjustment.* Cambridge, England: Cambridge University Press.

King, A. (1994). Guiding knowledge construction in the classroom: Effects of teaching children how to question and how to explain. *American Educational Research Journal, 31,* 338–368.

King, A., Staffieri, A., & Adelgais, A. (1998). Mutual peer tutoring: Effects of structuring tutorial interaction to scaffold peer learning. *Journal of Educational Psychology, 90,* 134–152.

King, A. J. C. (1989). Changing sex roles, lifestyles and attitudes in an urban society. In K. Hurrelmann & U. Engel (Eds.), *The social world of adolescents: International perspectives.* New York: Aldine de Gruyter.

Kinsey, A. C., Pomeroy, W. B., & Martin, C. E. (1948). *Sexual behavior in the human male.* Philadelphia: Saunders.

Kirschenbaum, R. J. (1989). Identification of the gifted and talented American Indian student. In C. J. Maker & S. W. Schiever (Eds.), *Critical issues in gifted education: Vol. 2. Defensible programs for cultural and ethnic minorities.* Austin, TX: Pro-Ed.

Kish, C. K., Zimmer, J. W., & Henning, M. J. (1994, April). *Using direct instruction to teach revision to novice writers: The role of metacognition.* Paper presented at the annual meeting of the American Educational Research Association, New Orleans, LA.

Kisker, E., Hofferth, S., Phillips, D., & Farguhar, E. (1991). *A profile of child care settings: Early education and care in 1990.* Princeton, NJ: Mathematica Policy Research.

Klassen, T. P., MacKay, J. M., Moher, D., Walker, A., & Jones, A. L. (2000). Community-based injury prevention interventions. *The Future of Children, 10*(1), 83–110.

Klein, P. D. (1999). Reopening inquiry into cognitive processes in writing-to-learn. *Educational Psychology Review, 11,* 203–270.

Knapp, M. S., & Woolverton, S. (1995). Social class and schooling. In J. A. Banks & C. A. M. Banks (Eds.), *Handbook of research on multicultural education.* New York: Macmillan.

Knowlton, D. (1995). Managing children with oppositional behavior. *Beyond Behavior, 6*(3), 5–10.

Knudson, R. E. (1992). The development of written argumentation: An analysis and comparison of argumentative writing at four grade levels. *Child Study Journal, 22,* 167–181.

Knutson, D. J., & Mantzicopoulos, P. Y. (1999, April). *Contextual factors of geographic mobility and their relation to the achievement and adjustment of children.* Paper presented at the annual meeting of the American Educational Research Association, Montreal.

Kochanski, G. (1993). Toward a synthesis of parental socialization and child temperament in early development of conscience. *Child Development, 64,* 325–347.

Koeppel, J., & Mulrooney, M. (1992). The Sister Schools Program: A way for children to learn about cultural diversity—when there isn't any in their school. *Young Children, 48*(1), 44–47.

Koestner, R., Ryan, R. M., Bernieri, F., & Holt, K. (1984). Setting limits in children's behavior: The differential effects of controlling versus informational styles on intrinsic motivation and creativity. *Journal of Personality, 52,* 233–248.

Kohlberg, L. (1963). Moral development and identification. In H. W. Stevenson (Ed.), *Child psychology: 62nd yearbook of the National Society for the Study of Education* (pp. 277–332). Chicago: University of Chicago Press.

Kohlberg, L. (1969). Stage and sequence: The cognitive-developmental approach to socialization. In D. A. Goslin (Ed.), *Handbook of socialization theory and research* (pp. 347–480). Chicago: Rand McNally.

Kohlberg, L. (1975). The cognitive-developmental approach to moral education. *Phi Delta Kappan, 57,* 670–677.

Kohlberg, L. (1976). Moral stages and moralization: The cognitive-developmental approach. In T. Lickona (Ed.), *Moral development and behavior: Theory, research, and social issues.* New York: Holt, Rinehart & Winston.

Kohlberg, L. (1981). *The philosophy of moral development: Moral stages and the idea of justice.* San Francisco: Harper & Row.

Kohlberg, L. (1984). *The psychology of moral development: The nature and validity of moral stages.* San Francisco: Harper & Row.

Kohlberg, L., & Candee, D. (1984). The relationship of moral judgment to moral action. In W. M. Kurtines & J. L. Gewirtz (Eds.), *Morality, moral behavior, and moral development.* New York: Wiley.

Kohlberg, L., & Kramer, R. (1969). Continuities and discontinuities in childhood and adult moral development. *Human Development, 12,* 93–120.

Kohlberg, L., & Mayer, R. (1972). Development as the aim of education. *Harvard Educational Review, 42,* 449–496.

Kohn, M. L. (1977). *Class and conformity* (2nd ed.). Chicago: University of Chicago Press.

Kohut, S., Jr. (1988). *The middle school: A bridge between elementary and high schools* (2nd ed.). Washington, DC: National Education Association.

Kolb, B., & Fantie, B. (1989). Development of the child's brain and behavior. In C. R. Reynolds & E. F. Janzen (Eds.), *Handbook of clinical child neuropsychology* (pp. 17–40). New York: Plenum Press.

Konopak, B. C., Martin, S. H., & Martin, M. A. (1990). Using a writing strategy to enhance sixth-grade students' comprehension of content material. *Journal of Reading Behavior, 22,* 19–37.

Kopp, C. B. (1982). Antecedents of self-regulation: A developmental perspective. *Developmental Psychology, 18,* 199–214.

Kopp, C. B. (1992). Emotional distress and control in young children. In N. Eisenberg & R. A. Fabes (Eds.), *Emotion and its regulation in early development.* San Francisco: Jossey-Bass.

Korkman, M., Autti-Raemoe, I., Koivulehto, H., & Granstroem, M. L. (1998). Neuropsychological effects at early school age of fetal alcohol exposure of varying duration. *Child Neuropsychology, 4*(3), 199–212.

Kornhaber, A. (1996). *Contemporary grandparenting.* Thousand Oaks, CA: Sage.

Koskinen, P. S., Blum, I. H., Bisson, S. A., Phillips, S. M., Creamer, T. S., & Baker, T. K. (2000). Book access, shared reading, and audio models: The effects of supporting the literacy learning of linguistically diverse students in school and at home. *Journal of Educational Psychology, 92,* 23–36.

Kottler, J. A. (1997). *What's really said in the teachers' lounge: Provocative ideas about cultures and classrooms.* Thousand Oaks, CA: Corwin Press.

Kovacs, D. M., Parker, J. G., & Hoffman, L. W. (1996). Behavioral, affective, and social correlates of involvement in cross-sex friendship in elementary school. *Child Development, 67,* 2269–2286.

Koyanagi, C., & Gaines, S. (1993). *All systems failure: An examination of the results of neglecting the needs of children with serious emotional disturbance.* Alexandria, VA: National Mental Health Association.

Koza, J. E. (2001). Multicultural approaches to music education. In C. A. Grant & M. L. Gomez, *Campus and classroom: Making schooling multicultural* (2nd ed.). Upper Saddle River, NJ: Merrill/Prentice Hall.

Kozol, J. (1995). *Amazing grace: The lives of children and the conscience of a nation.* New York: Crown Publishers.

Kozulin, A., & Falik, L. (1995). Dynamic cognitive assessment of the child. *Current Directions in Psychological Science, 4,* 192–196.

Kraemingk, K., & Paquette, A. (1999). Effects of prenatal alcohol exposure on neuropsychological functioning. *Developmental Neuropsychology, 15*(1), 111–140.

Krampen, G. (1987). Differential effects of teacher comments. *Journal of Educational Psychology, 79,* 137–146.

Krapp, A., Hidi, S., & Renninger, K. A. (1992). Interest, learning, and development. In K. A. Renninger, S. Hidi, & A. Krapp (Eds.), *The role of interest in learning and development.* Hillsdale, NJ: Erlbaum.

Krashen, S. D. (1996). *Under attack: The case against bilingual education.* Culver City, CA: Language Education Associates.

Krebs, D. L., & Van Hesteren, F. (1994). The development of altruism: Toward an integrative model. *Developmental Review, 14,* 103–158.

Krebs, P. L. (1995). Mental retardation. In J. P. Winnick (Ed.), *Adapted physical education and sport* (2nd ed., pp. 93–109). Champaign, IL: Human Kinetics.

Kreutzer, M. A., Leonard, C., & Flavell, J. H. (1975). An interview study of children's knowledge about memory. *Monographs of the Society for Research in Child Development, 40*(1, Serial No. 159).

Krispin, O., Sternberg, K. J., & Lamb, M. E. (1992). The dimensions of peer evaluation in Israel: A cross-cultural perspective. *International Journal of Behavioral Development, 15,* 299–314.

Kroll, B. M. (1984). Audience adaptation in children's persuasive letters. *Written Communication, 1,* 407–427.

Kruger, A. C., & Tomasello, M. (1996). Cultural learning and learning culture. In D. R. Olson & N. Torrance (Eds.), *The handbook of education and human development: New models of learning, teaching and schooling* (pp. 369–387). Cambridge, MA: Blackwell.

Kuhl, J. (1985). Volitional mediators of cognition-behavior consistency: Self-regulatory processes and actions versus state orientation. In J. Kuhl & J. Beckmann (Eds.), *Action control: From cognition to behavior.* Berlin, Germany: Springer-Verlag.

Kuhl, P. K., & Meltzoff, A. N. (1997). Evolution, nativism and learning in the development of language and speech. In M. Gopnik (Ed.), *The inheritance and innateness of grammars.* New York: Oxford University Press.

Kuhl, P. K., Williams, K. A., Lacerda, F., Stevens, K. N., & Lindblom, B. (1992). Linguistic experience alters phonetic perception in infants by 6 months of age. *Science, 255,* 606–608.

Kuhn, D. (1997). Constraints or guideposts? Developmental psychology and science education. *Review of Educational Research, 67,* 141–150.

Kuhn, D., Amsel, E., & O'Loughlin, M. (1988). *The development of scientific thinking skills.* San Diego, CA: Academic Press.

Kuhn, D., & Phelps, E. (1982). The development of problem-solving strategies. In H. Reese (Ed.), *Advances in child development and behavior* (Vol. 17). New York: Academic Press.

Kuhn, D., Shaw, V., & Felton, M. (1997). Effects of dyadic interaction on argumentative reasoning. *Cognition and Instruction, 15,* 287–315.

Kulberg, A. (1986). Substance abuse: Clinical identification and management. *Pediatrics Toxicology, 33*(2), 325–361.

Kulik, J. A., & Kulik, C. C. (1988). Timing of feedback and verbal learning. *Review of Educational Research, 58,* 79–97.

Kunzinger, E. L., III (1985). A short-term longitudinal study of memorial development during early grade school. *Developmental Psychology, 21,* 642–646.

Kupersmidt, J. B., & Coie, J. D. (1990). Preadolescent peer status, aggression, and school adjustment as predictors of externalizing problems in adolescence. *Child Development, 61,* 1350–1362.

Kurtines, W. M., Berman, S. L., Ittel, A., & Williamson, S. (1995). Moral development: A co-constructivist perspective. In W. M. Kurtines & J. L. Gewirtz (Eds.), *Moral development: An introduction.* Boston: Allyn & Bacon.

Kurtines, W. M., & Gewirtz, J. L. (Eds.). (1991). *Moral behavior and development: Vol. 2. Research.* Hillsdale, NJ: Erlbaum.

LaBlance, G. R., Steckol, K. F., & Smith, V. L. (1994). Stuttering: The role of the classroom teacher. *Teaching Exceptional Children, 26*(2), 10–12.

Laboratory of Human Cognition. (1982). Culture and intelligence. In R. J. Sternberg (Ed.), *Handbook of human intelligence.* Cambridge, England: Cambridge University Press.

Ladavas, E. (1988). Asymmetries in processing horizontal and vertical dimensions. *Memory and Cognition, 16*(4), 377–382.

Ladd, G. W. (1990). Having friends, keeping friends, making friends, and being liked by peers in the classroom: Predictors of children's early school adjustment? *Child Development, 61,* 1081–1100.

Ladd, G. W., & Burgess, K. B. (1999). Charting the relationship trajectories of aggressive, withdrawn, and aggressive/withdrawn children during early grade school. *Child Development, 70,* 910–929.

Ladson-Billings, G. (1994). *The dreamkeepers: Successful teachers of African American children.* San Francisco: Jossey-Bass.

Lafontana, K. M., & Cillessen, A. H. N. (1998). The nature of children's stereotypes of popularity. *Social Development, 7,* 301–320.

LaFromboise, T., Hardin, L., Coleman, K., & Gerton, J. (1993). Psychological impact of biculturalism: Evidence and theory. *Psychological Bulletin, 114,* 395–412.

La Guardia, J. G., Ryan, R. M., Couchman, C. E., & Deci, E. L. (2000). Within-person variation in security of attachment: A self-determination theory perspective on attachment, need fulfillment, and well-being. *Journal of Personality and Social Psychology, 79,* 367–384.

Lahey, B., Loeber, R., Quay, H. C., Frick, P. J., & Grimm, J. (1992). Oppositional defiant and conduct disorders: Issues to be resolved for DSM-IV.

Journal of the American Academy of Child and Adolescent Psychiatry, 31, 539–546.

Lamb, M. E. (1976). Interactions between eight-month-old children and their fathers and mothers. In M. E. Lamb (Ed.), *The role of the father in child development* (pp. 307–327). New York: Wiley.

Lamb, M. E. (1998). Nonparental child care: Context, quality, correlates, and consequences. In W. Damon (Editor-in-Chief), I. E. Sigel, & K. A. Renninger (Vol. Eds.), *Handbook of child psychology* (Vol. 4, pp. 73–133). New York: Wiley.

Lamb, M. E., Frodi, A. M., Hwang, C. P., Frodi, M., & Steinberg, J. (1982). Mother- and father-infant interactions involving play and holding in traditional and non-traditional Swedish families. *Developmental Psychology, 18,* 215–221.

Lamb, S. (1991). First moral sense: Aspects of and contributions to a beginning morality in the second year of life. In W. M. Kurtines & J. L. Gewirtz (Eds.), *Handbook of moral behavior and development: Vol. 2. Research.* Hillsdale, NJ: Erlbaum.

Lamb, S., & Feeny, N. C. (1995). Early moral sense and socialization. In W. M. Kurtines & J. L. Gewirtz (Eds.), *Moral development: An introduction.* Boston: Allyn & Bacon.

Lamborn, S. D., Mounts, N. S., Steinberg, L., & Dornbusch, S. M. (1991). Patterns of competence and adjustment among adolescents from authoritative, authoritarian, indulgent, and neglectful families. *Child Development, 62,* 1049–1065.

Lampert, M. (1990). When the problem is not the question and the solution is not the answer: Mathematical knowing and teaching. *American Educational Research Journal, 27,* 29–64.

Landau, S., & McAninch, C. (1993). Young children with attention deficits. *Young Children, 48*(4), 49–58.

Landesman, S., & Ramey, C. (1989). Developmental psychology and mental retardation: Integrating scientific principles with treatment practices. *American Psychologist, 44,* 409–415.

Lane, D. M., & Pearson, D. A. (1982). The development of selective attention. *Merrill-Palmer Quarterly, 28,* 317–337.

Lange, G., & Pierce, S. H. (1992). Memory-strategy learning and maintenance in preschool children. *Developmental Psychology, 28,* 453–462.

Langfeldt, T. (1981). Sexual development in children. In M. Cook & K. Howells (Eds.), *Adult sexual interest in children.* London: Academic Press.

Langlois, J. H. (1981). Beauty and the beast: The role of physical attractiveness in the development of peer relations and social behavior. In S. S. Brehm, S. M. Kassin, & F. X. Gibbons (Eds.), *Developmental social psychology: Theory and research* (pp. 47–63). New York: Oxford University Press.

Langlois, J. H., & Downs, A. C. (1980). Mothers, fathers, and peers as socialization agents of sex-typed play behaviors in young children. *Child Development, 51,* 1237–1247.

Lanza, E. (1992). Can bilingual two-year-olds code-switch? *Journal of Child Language, 19,* 633–658.

Lapsley, D. K. (1993). Toward an integrated theory of adolescent ego development: The "new look" at adolescent egocentrism. *American Journal of Orthopsychiatry, 63,* 562–571.

Lapsley, D. K., Jackson, S., Rice, K., & Shadid, G. (1988). Self-monitoring and the "new look" at the imaginary audience and personal fable: An

ego-developmental analysis. *Journal of Adolescent Research, 3,* 17–31.

Lapsley, D. K., Milstead, M., Quintana, S., Flannery, D., & Buss, R. (1986). Adolescent egocentrism and formal operations: Tests of a theoretical assumption. *Developmental Psychology, 22,* 800–807.

Lareau, A. (1987). Social class differences in family-school relationships: The importance of cultural capital. *Sociology of Education, 60,* 73–85.

Lareau, A. (1989). *Home advantage: Social class and parental intervention in elementary education.* New York: Falmer Press.

Larkin, R. W. (1979). *Suburban youth in cultural crisis.* New York: Oxford University Press.

Larner, M. B., Stevenson, C. S., & Behrman, R. E. (1998). Protecting children from abuse and neglect: Analysis and recommendations. *The Future of Children: Protecting Children From Abuse and Neglect, 8*(1), 4–22.

Larson, R. W., Clore, G. L., & Wood, G. A. (1999). The emotions of romantic relationships: Do they wreak havoc on adolescents? In W. Furman, B. B. Brown, & C. Feiring (Eds.), *The development of romantic relationships in adolescence* (pp. 19–49). Cambridge, England: Cambridge University Press.

Last, C. G., Hersen, M., Kazdin, A. E., Francis, G., & Grubb, H. J. (1987). Psychiatric illness in the mothers of anxious children. *American Journal of Psychiatry, 144,* 1580–1583.

Laupa, M. (1994). "Who's in charge?" Preschool children's concepts of authority. *Early Childhood Research Quarterly, 9,* 1–17.

Laupa, M., & Turiel, E. (1995). Social domain theory. In W. M. Kurtines & J. L. Gewirtz (Eds.), *Moral development: An introduction.* Boston: Allyn & Bacon.

Lautrey, J. (1993). Structure and variability: A plea for a pluralistic approach to cognitive development. In R. Case & W. Edelstein (Eds.), *The new structuralism in cognitive development: Theory and research on individual pathways.* Basel, Switzerland: Karger.

Lave, J. (1991). Situating learning in communities of practice. In L. B. Resnick, J. M. Levine, & S. D. Teasley (Eds.), *Perspectives on socially shared cognition.* Washington, DC: American Psychological Association.

Lave, J. (1993). Word problems: A microcosm of theories of learning. In P. Light and G. Butterworth (Eds.), *Context and cognition: Ways of learning and knowing.* Hillsdale, NJ: Erlbaum.

Lave, J., & Wenger, E. (1991). *Situated learning: Legitimate peripheral participation.* Cambridge, England: Cambridge University Press.

Law, D. J., Pellegrino, J. W., & Hunt, E. B. (1993). Comparing the tortoise and the hare: Gender differences and experience in dynamic spatial reasoning tasks. *Psychological Science, 4,* 35–40.

Lazar, I., Darlington, R., Murray, H., Royce, J., & Snipper, A. (1982). Lasting effects of early education: A report from the Consortium for Longitudinal Studies. *Monographs of the Society for Research in Child Development, 47*(2–3, Serial No. 195).

Lazarus, R. S. (1991). *Emotion and adaptation.* New York: Oxford University Press.

Leakey, R. (1994). *The origin of humankind.* New York: Basic Books.

Leaper, C. (1994). Exploring the consequences of gender segregation on social relationships. In C. Leaper (Ed.), *Childhood gender segregation: Causes and consequences* (pp. 67–86). San Francisco: Jossey-Bass.

Leaper, C., & Anderson, K. J. (1997). Gender development and heterosexual romantic relationships during adolescence. In S. Shulman & W. A. Collins (Eds.), Romantic relationships in adolescence: Developmental perspectives. *New directions for child development* (No. 78, pp. 85–103). San Francisco: Jossey-Bass.

Lee, C. D., & Slaughter-Defoe, D. T. (1995). Historical and sociocultural influences on African and American education. In J. A. Banks & C. A. M. Banks (Eds.), *Handbook of research on multicultural education.* New York: Macmillan.

Lee, S. (1985). Children's acquisition of conditional logic structure: Teachable? *Contemporary Educational Psychology, 10,* 14–27.

Lee, V., Brooks-Gunn, J., Schnur, E., & Liaw, F. (1990). Are Head Start effects sustained? A longitudinal follow-up comparison of disadvantaged children attending Head Start, no preschool, and other preschool programs. *Child Development, 61,* 495–507.

Lee, V. E., Winfield, L. F., & Wilson, T. C. (1991). Academic behaviors among high-achieving African American students. *Education and Urban Society, 24*(1), 65–86.

Lee-Pearce, M. L., Plowman, T. S., & Touchstone, D. (1998). Starbase-Atlantis, a school without walls: A comparative study of an innovative science program for at-risk urban elementary students. *Journal of Education for Students Placed at Risk, 3,* 223–235.

Leffert, J. S., Siperstein, G. N., & Millikan, E. (1999). *Social perception and strategy generation: Two key social cognitive processes in children with mental retardation.* Paper presented at the biennial meeting of the Society for Research in Child Development, Albuquerque, NM.

Lefstein, L. M., & Lipsitz, J. (1995). *3:00 to 6:00 P.M.: Programs for young adolescents.* Minneapolis, MN: Search Institute.

Lehman, D. R., & Nisbett, R. E. (1990). A longitudinal study of the effects of undergraduate training on reasoning. *Developmental Psychology, 26,* 952–960.

Leinhardt, G. (1994). History: A time to be mindful. In G. Leinhardt, I. L. Beck, & C. Stainton (Eds.), *Teaching and learning in history.* Hillsdale, NJ: Erlbaum.

Leite, R. M. C., Buoncompagno, E. M., Leite, A. C. C., & Mergulhao, E. A. (1995). Psychosexual characteristics of male university students in Brazil. *Adolescence, 30,* 363–380.

Leiter, J., & Johnsen, M. C. (1997). Child maltreatment and school performance declines: An event-history analysis. *American Educational Research Journal, 34,* 563–589.

Lenneberg, E. H. (1967). *Biological foundations of language.* New York: Wiley.

Lennon, R., & Eisenberg, N. (1987). Gender and age differences in empathy and sympathy. In N. Eisenberg & J. Strayer (Eds.), *Empathy and its development* (pp. 195–217). New York: Cambridge University Press.

Lennon, R., Eisenberg, N., & Carroll, J. L. (1983). The assessment of empathy in early childhood. *Journal of Applied Developmental Psychology, 4,* 295–302.

Lennox, C., & Siegel, L. S. (1998). Phonological and orthographic processes in good and poor spellers. In C. Hulme & R. M. Joshi (Eds.), *Reading and spelling: Development and disorders.* Mahwah, NJ: Erlbaum.

Leong, C. K. (1998). Strategies used by 9- to 12-year-old children in written spelling. In C. Hulme & R. M. Joshi (Eds.), *Reading and spelling: Development and disorders.* Mahwah, NJ: Erlbaum.

Leont'ev, A. N. (1981). *Problems of the development of mind.* Moscow: Progress.

Lerner, B. (1985). Self-esteem and excellence: The choice and the paradox. *American Educator, 9*(4), 10–16.

Lerner, J. W. (1985). *Learning disabilities: Theories, diagnosis, and teaching strategies* (4th ed.). Boston: Houghton Mifflin.

Lerner, R. M. (1989). Developmental contextualism and the life-span view of person-context interaction. In M. Bornstein & J. S. Bruner (Eds.), *Interaction in human development* (pp. 217–239). Hillsdale, NJ: Erlbaum.

Levi, G., & Schmitt, J. C. (1997). Introduction: Paternal authority and freedom of choice in seventeenth-century Italy. In G. Levi & J. C. Schmitt (Eds.), *A history of young people in the west: Vol. 1. Ancient and medieval rites of passage* (C. Naish, Trans.; pp. 1–11). Cambridge, MA: Belknap Press of Harvard University Press.

Levine, D. U., & Lezotte, L. W. (1995). Effective schools research. In J. A. Banks & C. A. M. Banks (Eds.), *Handbook of research on multicultural education.* New York: Macmillan.

LeVine, R. A. (1974). Parental goals: A cross-cultural view. *Teachers College Record, 76*(2), 226–239.

LeVine, R. A. (1988). Human parental care: Universal goals, cultural strategies, individual behavior. In R. A. LeVine, P. M. Miller, & M. M. West (Eds.), *Parental behavior in diverse societies* (pp. 5–12). San Francisco: Jossey-Bass.

Levitt, M. J., Guacci-Franco, N., & Levitt, J. L. (1993). Convoys of social support in childhood and early adolescence: Structure and function. *Developmental Psychology, 29,* 811–818.

Levitt, M. J., Levitt, J. L., Bustos, G. L., Crooks, N. A., Santos, J. D., Telan, P., & Silver, M. E. (1999, April). *The social ecology of achievement in pre-adolescents: Social support and school attitudes.* Paper presented at the annual meeting of the American Educational Research Association, Montreal.

Levitt, M. J., Weber, R. A., Clark, M. C., & McDonnell, P. (1985). Reciprocity of exchange in toddler sharing behavior. *Developmental Psychology, 21,* 122–123.

Levy, G. D., Taylor, M. G., & Gelman, S. A. (1995). Traditional and evaluative aspects of flexibility in gender roles, social conventions, moral rules, and physical laws. *Child Development, 66,* 515–531.

Levy, T. M., & Orlans, M. (2000). Attachment disorder and the adoptive family. In T. M. Levy et al. (Eds.), *Handbook of attachment interventions* (pp. 243–259). San Diego, CA: Academic Press.

Lewin, B., Siliciano, P., & Klotz, M. (1997). *Genes VI.* Oxford, England: Oxford University.

Lewin, T. (2000, June 25). Growing up, growing apart: Fast friends try to resist the pressure to divide by race. *The New York Times,* pp. 1, 18–20.

Lewis, C. (1981). The effects of firm control: A reinterpretation of findings. *Psychological Bulletin, 90,* 547–563.

Lewis, M. (1991). Self-knowledge and social influence. In M. Lewis & S. Feinman (Eds.), *Social influences and socialization in infancy: Vol. 6. Genesis of behavior* (pp. 111–134). New York: Plenum Press.

Lewis, M. (1993). Self-conscious emotions: Embarrassment, pride, shame, and guilt. In M. Lewis & J. Haviland (Eds.), *The handbook of emotions* (pp. 563–573). New York: Guilford Press.

Lewis, M. (1995). Embarrassment: The emotion of self-exposure and evaluation. In J. Tangney & K. Fischer (Eds.), *Self-conscious emotions: The psychology of shame, guilt, embarrassment and pride* (pp. 198–218). New York: Guilford Press.

Lewis, M., Feiring, C., & Rosenthal, S. (2000). Attachment over time. *Child Development, 71,* 707–720.

Lewit, E. M., Terman, D. L., & Behrman, R. E. (1997). Children and poverty: Analysis and recommendations. *The Future of Children: Children and Poverty, 7,* 4–24.

Liben, L. S., & Downs, R. M. (1989). Understanding maps as symbols: The development of map concepts in children. In H. W. Reese (Ed.), *Advances in child development and behavior* (Vol. 22). San Diego, CA: Harcourt Brace Jovanovich.

Liben, L. S., & Signorella, M. L. (1993). Gender-schematic processing in children: The role of initial interpretations of stimuli. *Developmental Psychology, 29,* 141–149.

Liberman, A. M. (1998). Why is speech so much easier than reading and writing?. In C. Hulme & R. M. Joshi (Eds.), *Reading and spelling: Development and disorders.* Mahwah, NJ: Erlbaum.

Lickona, T. (1991). Moral development in the elementary school classroom. In W. M. Kurtines & J. L. Gewirtz (Eds.), *Moral behavior and development: Vol. 3. Application.* Hillsdale, NJ: Erlbaum.

Lidz, C. S. (1991). Issues in the assessment of preschool children. In B. A. Bracken (Ed.), *The psychoeducational assessment of preschool children* (2nd ed., pp. 18–31). Boston: Allyn & Bacon.

Lidz, C. S. (1997). Dynamic assessment approaches. In D. P. Flanagan, J. L. Genshaft, & P. L. Harrison (Eds.), *Contemporary intellectual assessment: Theories, tests, and issues* (pp. 281–296). New York: Guilford Press.

Light, J. G., & Defries, J. C. (1995). Comorbidity of reading and mathematics disabilities: Genetic and environmental etiologies. *Journal of Learning Disabilities, 28,* 96–106.

Light, P., & Butterworth, G. (Eds.). (1993). *Context and cognition: Ways of learning and knowing.* Hillsdale, NJ: Erlbaum.

Lightfoot, C. (1992). Constructing self and peer culture: A narrative perspective on adolescent risk taking. In L. T. Winegar & J. Valsiner (Eds.), *Children's development within social context: Vol. 2. Research and methodology* (pp. 229–245). Hillsdale, NJ: Erlbaum.

Lightfoot, D. (1999). *The development of language: Acquisition, change, and evolution.* Malden, MA: Blackwell.

Lillard, A. (1999). Developing a cultural theory of mind: The CIAO approach. *Current Directions in Psychological Science, 8,* 57–61.

Lillard, A. S. (1993). Pretend play skills and the child's theory of mind. *Child Development, 64,* 348–371.

Lillard, A. S. (1997). Other folks' theories of mind and behavior. *Psychological Science, 8,* 268–274.

Lillard, A. S. (1998). Playing with a theory of mind. In O. N. Saracho & B. Spodek (Eds.), *Multiple perspectives on play in early childhood education.* Albany: State University of New York Press.

Lin, C. C., & Fu, V. R. (1990). A comparison of child-rearing practices among Chinese, immigrant Chinese, and Caucasian-American parents. *Child Development, 61,* 429–433.

Linn, M. C., Clement, C., Pulos, S., & Sullivan, P. (1989). Scientific reasoning during adolescence: The influence of instruction in science knowledge and reasoning strategies. *Journal of Research in Science Teaching, 26,* 171–187.

Linn, M. C., & Hyde, J. S. (1989). Gender, mathematics, and science. *Educational Researcher, 18*(8), 17–19, 22–27.

Linn, M. C., Songer, N. B., & Eylon, B. (1996). Shifts and convergences in science learning and instruction. In D. C. Berliner & R. C. Calfee (Eds.), *Handbook of educational psychology*. New York: Macmillan.

Linscheid, T. R., & Fleming, C. H. (1995). Anorexia nervosa, bulimia nervosa, and obesity. In M. C. Roberts (Ed.), *Handbook of pediatric psychology* (pp. 676–700). New York: Guilford Press.

Lipson, M. Y. (1983). The influence of religious affiliation on children's memory for text information. *Reading Research Quarterly, 18,* 448–457.

Liss, M. B. (Ed.). (1983). *Social and cognitive skills: Sex roles and children's play*. San Diego, CA: Academic Press.

Little, L. (2000a). *Differences in stress and coping for parents of children with Asperger-spectrum disorders*. Manuscript submitted for publication.

Little, L. (2000b, June). *Maternal discipline of children with Asperger-spectrum disorders*. Paper presented at the Youth and Victimization International Research Conference, Durham, NH.

Little, L. (2000c, June). *Peer victimization of children with Asperger-spectrum disorders*. Paper presented at the Youth and Victimization International Research Conference, Durham, NH.

Little, T. D., Oettingen, G., Stetsenko, A., & Baltes, P. B. (1995). Children's action-control beliefs about school performance: How do American children compare with German and Russian children? *Journal of Personality and Social Psychology, 69,* 686–700.

Littlewood, W. T. (1984). *Foreign and second language learning: Language-acquisition research and its implications for the classroom*. Cambridge, England: Cambridge University Press.

Livesley, W. J., & Bromley, D. B. (1973). *Person perception in childhood and adolescence*. New York: Wiley.

Livson, N., & Peshkin, H. (1980). Perspectives on adolescence from longitudinal research. In J. Adelson (Ed.), *Handbook of adolescent psychology* (pp. 47–98). New York: Wiley.

Lloyd, D. N. (1978). Prediction of school failure from third-grade data. *Educational and Psychological Measurement, 38,* 1193–1200.

Lobel, A. (1979). *Frog and Toad are friends*. New York: HarperCollins.

Lochman, J. E., & Dodge, K. A. (1994). Social–cognitive processes of severely violent, moderately aggressive, and nonaggressive boys. *Journal of Consulting and Clinical Psychology, 62,* 366–374.

Lochman, J. E., & Dodge, K. A. (1998). Distorted perceptions in dyadic interactions of aggressive and nonaggressive boys: Effects of prior expectations, context, and boys' age. *Development and Psychopathology, 10*(3), 495–512.

Lochman, J. E., Wayland, K. K., & White, K. J. (1993). Social goals: Relationship to adolescent adjustment and to social problem solving. *Journal of Abnormal Child Psychology, 21,* 1993.

Locke, E. A., & Latham, G. P. (1990). *A theory of goal setting and task performance*. Upper Saddle River, NJ: Prentice Hall.

Locke, J. L. (1993). *The child's path to spoken language*. Cambridge, MA: Harvard University Press.

Loeb, R. C., Horst, L., & Horton, P. J. (1980). Family interaction patterns associated with self-esteem in preadolescent girls and boys. *Merrill-Palmer Quarterly, 26,* 205–217.

Loeber, R. (1982). The stability of antisocial child behavior. *Annals of Child Development, 2,* 77–116.

Loeber, R., & Hay, D. F. (1993). Developmental approaches to aggression and conduct problems. In M. Rutter & D. F. Hay (Eds.), *Development through life: A handbook for clinicians* (pp. 488–516). Oxford, England: Blackwell.

Loeber, R., Lahey, B. B., & Thomas, C. (1991). Diagnostic conundrum of oppositional defiant disorder. *Journal of Abnormal Psychology, 100,* 379–390.

Loeber, R., & Schmaling, K. B. (1985). Empirical evidence for overt and covert patterns of antisocial conduct problems: A meta-analysis. *Journal of Abnormal Child Psychology, 13,* 227–252.

Loeber, R., & Stouthamer-Loeber, M. (1998). Development of juvenile aggression and violence. *American Psychologist, 53,* 242–259.

Logan, K. R., Alberto, P. A., Kana, T. G., & Waylor-Bowen, T. (1994). Curriculum development and instructional design for students with profound disabilities. In L. Sternberg (Ed.), *Individuals with profound disabilities: Instructional and assistive strategies* (3rd ed.). Austin, TX: Pro-Ed.

Logsdon, B. J., Alleman, L. M., Straits, S. A., Belka, D. E., Clark, D. (1997). *Physical education unit plans for grades 5–6* (2nd ed.). Champaign, IL: Human Kinetics.

Lomawaima, K. T. (1995). Educating Native Americans. In J. A. Banks & C. A. M. Banks (Eds.), *Handbook of research on multicultural education*. New York: Macmillan.

Lombroso, P. J., & Sapolsky, R. (1998). Development of the cerebral cortex: XII. Stress and brain development: I. *Journal of the American Academy of Child and Adolescent Psychiatry, 37,* 1337–1339.

London, P. (1970). The rescuers: Motivational hypotheses about Christians who saved Jews from the Nazis. In J. Macaulay & L. Berkowitz (Eds.), *Altruism and helping behavior* (pp. 241–250). New York: Academic Press.

Long, M. (1995). The role of the linguistic environment in second language acquisition. In W. C. Ritchie & T. K. Bhatia (Eds.), *Handbook of language acquisition: Vol. 2. Second language acquisition*. San Diego, CA: Academic Press.

Long, T. J., & Long, L. (1982). Latchkey children: The child's view of self care. Washington, DC: Catholic University. (ERIC Document Reproduction Service No. ED 211 229).

Lonigan, C. J., Burgess, S. R., Anthony, J. L., & Barker, T. A. (1998). Development of phonological sensitivity in 2- to 5-year-old children. *Journal of Educational Psychology, 90,* 294–311.

Lopez, E. C. (1997). The cognitive assessment of limited English proficient and bilingual children. In D. P. Flanagan, J. L. Genshaft, & P. L. Harrison (Eds.), *Contemporary intellectual assessment: Theories, tests, and issues* (pp. 503–516). New York: Guilford Press.

López del Bosque, R. (2000). Sticks and stones: What words are to self-esteem. *Intercultural Development Research Association Newsletter, 27*(5), 4–7, 16.

Lorch, E. P., Diener, M. B., Sanchez, R. P., Milich, R., Welsh, R., & van den Broek, P. (1999). The effects of story structure on the recall of stories in children with attention deficit hyperactivity disorder. *Journal of Educational Psychology, 91,* 251–260.

Lorenz, K. (1966). *On aggression*. New York: Harcourt.

Lorenz, K. Z. (1981). *The foundations of ethology* (K. Z. Lorenz & R. W. Kickert, Trans.). New York: Springer-Verlag.

Lortie, D. (1975). *Schoolteacher: A sociological study*. Chicago: University of Chicago Press.

Losey, K. M. (1995). Mexican American students and classroom interaction: An overview and critique. *Review of Educational Research, 65,* 283–318.

Lou, Y., Abrami, P. C., Spence, J. C., Poulsen, C., Chambers, B., & dApollonia, S. (1996). Within-class grouping: A meta-analysis. *Review of Educational Research, 66,* 423–458.

Lounsbury, J. H. (Ed.) (1984). *Perspectives: Middle school education 1964–1984*. Columbus, OH: National Middle School Association.

Lovell, K. (1979). Intellectual growth and the school curriculum. In F. B. Murray (Ed.), *The impact of Piagetian theory: On education, philosophy, psychiatry, and psychology*. Baltimore: University Park Press.

Lovett, M. W., Lacerenza, L., Borden, S. L., Frijters, J. C., Steinbach, K. A., & De Palma, M. (2000). Components of effective remediation for developmental reading disabilities: Combining phonological and strategy-based instruction to improve outcomes. *Journal of Educational Psychology, 92,* 263–283.

Lovett, S. B., & Flavell, J. H. (1990). Understanding and remembering: Children's knowledge about the differential effects of strategy and task variables on comprehension and memorization. *Child Development, 61,* 1842–1858.

Lowry, R., Sleet, D., Duncan, C., Powell, K., & Kolbe, L. (1995). Adolescents at risk for violence. *Educational Psychology Review, 7,* 7–39.

Lozoff, B. (1989). Nutrition and behavior. *American Psychologist, 44,* 231–236.

Luckasson, R., Coulter, D. L., Polloway, E. A., Reiss, S., Schalock, R. L., Snell, M. E., Spitalnik, D. M., & Stark, J. A. (1992). *Mental retardation: Definition, classification, and systems of supports*. Washington, DC: American Association on Mental Retardation.

Lueptow, L. B. (1984). *Adolescent sex roles and social change*. New York: Columbia University Press.

Lupart, J. L. (1995). Exceptional learners and teaching for transfer. In A. McKeough, J. Lupart, & A. Marini (Eds.), *Teaching for transfer: Fostering generalization in learning*. Mahwah, NJ: Erlbaum.

Luster, L. (1992). *Schooling, survival, and struggle: Black women and the GED*. Unpublished doctoral dissertation, Stanford University, School of Education, Stanford, CA.

Lutke, J. (1997). Spider web walking: Hope for children with FAS through understanding. In A. Streissguth & J. Kanter (Eds.), *The challenge of fetal alcohol syndrome: Overcoming secondary disabilities* (pp. 181–188). Seattle: University of Washington Press.

Lykken, D. T. (1997). The American crime factory. *Psychological Inquiry, 8,* 261–270.

Lynd, R. S., & Lynd, H. M. (1929). *Middletown*. New York: Harcourt, Brace.

Lyon, T. D., & Flavell, J. H. (1994). Young children's understanding of "remember" and "forget." *Child Development, 65,* 1357–1371.

Lytton, H., & Romney, D. M. (1991). Parents' differential socialization of boys and girls: A meta-analysis. *Psychological Bulletin, 109,* 267–296.

Lyytinen, P. (1991). Developmental trends in children's pretend play. *Child: Care, Health, and Development, 17,* 9–25.

Ma, X., & Kishor, N. (1997). Attitude toward self, social factors, and achievement in mathematics: A meta-analytic review. *Educational Psychology Review, 9,* 89–120.

MacArthur, C., & Ferretti, R. P. (1997, March). *The effects of elaborated goals on the argumentative writing of students with learning disabilities and their normally achieving peers.* Paper presented at the annual meeting of the American Educational Research Association, Chicago.

MacArthur, C., & Graham, S. (1987). Learning disabled students' composing with three methods: Handwriting, dictation, and word processing. *Journal of Special Education, 21,* 22–42.

Maccoby, E. E. (1980). *Social development: Psychological growth and the parent-child relationship.* New York: Harcourt Brace Jovanovich.

Maccoby, E. E. (1984). Middle childhood in the context of the family. In W. A. Collins (Ed.), *Development during middle childhood* (pp. 184–239). Washington, DC: National Academy Press.

Maccoby, E. E. (1990). Gender and relationships: A developmental account. *American Psychologist, 45,* 513–520.

Maccoby, E. E., & Hagen, J. W. (1965). Effects of distraction upon central versus incidental recall: Developmental trends. *Journal of Experimental Child Psychology, 2,* 280–289.

Maccoby, E. E., & Jacklin, C. N. (1974). *The psychology of sex differences.* Stanford, CA: Stanford University Press.

Maccoby, E., & Martin, J. (1983). Socialization in the context of the family: Parent-child interaction. In P. H. Mussen (Series Ed.) & E. M. Hetherington (Vol. Ed.), *Handbook of child psychology: Vol. 4. Socialization, personality and social development* (4th ed., pp. 1–102). New York: Wiley.

Mace, F. C., & Kratochwill, T. R. (1988). Self-monitoring. In J. C. Witt, S. N. Elliott, & F. M. Gresham (Eds.), *Handbook of behavior therapy in education.* New York: Plenum Press.

Macfarlane, J. W. (1971). From infancy to adulthood. In M. C. Jones, N. Bayley, J. W. Macfarlane, & M. P. Honzik (Eds.), *The course of human development* (pp. 406–410). Waltham, MA: Xerox College Publishing.

Mackintosh, N. J. (1998). *IQ and human intelligence.* London: Oxford University Press.

Madden, N. A., & Slavin, R. E. (1983). Mainstreaming students with mild handicaps: Academic and social outcomes. *Review of Educational Research, 53,* 519–569.

Madhubuti, H., & Madhubuti, S. (1994). *African-centered education.* Chicago: Third World Press.

Magnusson, S. J., Boyle, R. A., & Templin, M. (1994, April). *Conceptual development: Re-examining knowledge construction in science.* Paper presented at the annual meeting of the American Educational Research Association, New Orleans, LA.

Mahoney, G., O'Sullivan, P., & Robinson, C. (1992). The family environments of children with disabilities: Diverse but not so different. *Topics in Early Childhood Special Education, 12,* 386–402.

Main, M., & Solomon, J. (1986). Discovery of an insecure-disorganized/disoriented attachment pattern. In T. B. Brazelton & M. W. Yogman (Eds.), *Affective development in infancy* (pp. 95–124). Norwood, NJ: Ablex.

Main, M., & Solomon, J. (1990). Procedures for identifying infants as disorganized/disoriented during the Ainsworth Strange Situation. In M. T. Greenberg, D. Cicchetti, & E. M. Cummings (Eds.), *Attachment in the preschool years* (pp. 121–160). Chicago: University of Chicago Press.

Main, M., & Weston, D. (1981). The quality of the toddler's relationship to mother and father: Related to conflict behavior and readiness to establish new social relationships. *Child Development, 52,* 932–940.

Major, B., & Schmader, T. (1998). Coping with stigma through psychological disengagement. In J. K. Swim & C. Stangor (Eds.), *Prejudice: The target's perspective* (pp. 220–241). San Diego, CA: Academic Press.

Maker, C. J. (1993). Creativity, intelligence, and problem solving: A definition and design for cross-cultural research and measurement related to giftedness. *Gifted Education International, 9*(2), 68–77.

Maker, C. J., & Schiever, S. W. (Eds.). (1989). *Critical issues in gifted education: Vol. 2. Defensible programs for cultural and ethnic minorities.* Austin, TX: Pro-Ed.

Malatesta, C. Z., & Haviland, J. M. (1982). Learning display rules: The socialization of emotion expression in infancy. *Child Development, 53,* 991–1003.

Malinsky, K. P. (1997). Learning to be invisible: Female sexual minority students in America's public high schools. In M. B. Harris (Ed.), *School experiences of gay and lesbian youth: The invisible minority* (pp. 35–50). Binghamton, NY: The Harrington Park Press.

Maller, S. J. (2000). Item invariance of four subtests of the Universal Nonverbal Intelligence Test across groups of deaf and hearing children. *Journal of Psychoeducational Assessment, 18,* 240–254.

Malone, D. M., Stoneham, Z., & Langone, J. (1995). Contextual variation of correspondences among measures of play and developmental level of preschool children. *Journal of Early Intervention, 18,* 199–215.

Maloney, M. J., McGuire, J. B., & Daniels, S. R. (1988). Reliability testing of a children's version of the Eating Attitude Test. *Journal of the American Academy of Child and Adolescent Psychiatry, 27,* 541–543.

Manderson, L., Tye, L. C., & Rajanayagam, K. (1997). Condom use in heterosexual sex: A review of research, 1985–1994. In J. Catalan, L. Sherr, et al. (Eds.), *The impact of AIDS: Psychological and social aspects of HIV infection* (pp. 1–26). Singapore: Harwood Academic Publishers.

Manis, F. R. (1996). Current trends in dyslexia research. In B. J. Cratty & R. L. Goldman (Eds.), *Learning disabilities: Contemporary viewpoints.* Amsterdam: Harwood Academic.

Mansavage, N. M. (1999). *A study of hostility, hopelessness, and humor with incarcerated and nonincarcerated male adolescents.* Unpublished doctoral dissertation, University of Wisconsin, Madison.

Marcia, J. E. (1980). Identity in adolescence. In J. Adelson (Ed.), *Handbook of adolescent psychology.* New York: Wiley.

Marcia, J. E. (1988). Common processes underlying ego identity, cognitive/moral development, and individuation. In D. K. Lapsley & F. C. Power (Eds.), *Self, ego, and identity: Integrative approaches* (pp. 211–225). New York: Springer-Verlag.

Marcus, G. F. (1996). Why do children say "breaked"? *Current Directions in Psychological Science, 5,* 81–85.

Marcus, R. F. (1980). Empathy and popularity of preschool children. *Child Study Journal, 10,* 133–145.

Markman, E. M. (1977). Realizing that you don't understand: A preliminary investigation. *Child Development, 48,* 986–992.

Markman, E. M. (1979). Realizing that you don't understand: Elementary school children's awareness of inconsistencies. *Child Development, 50,* 643–655.

Marks, J. (1995). *Human biodiversity: Genes, race, and history.* New York: Aldine de Gruyter.

Markus, H. R., & Kitayama, S. (1991). Culture and the self: Implications for cognition, emotion, and motivation. *Psychological Review, 98,* 224–253.

Marsh, D. D., & Codding, J. B. (Eds.). (1999). *The new American high school.* Thousand Oaks, CA: Corwin Press/Sage.

Marsh, H. W. (1990a). Causal ordering of academic self-concept and academic achievement: A multi-wave, longitudinal panel analysis. *Journal of Educational Psychology, 82,* 646–656.

Marsh, H. W. (1990b). A multidimensional, hierarchical model of self-concept: Theoretical and empirical justification. *Educational Psychology Review, 2,* 77–172.

Marsh, H. W., & Craven, R. (1997). Academic self-concept: Beyond the dustbowl. In G. D. Phye (Ed.), *Handbook of classroom assessment: Learning, achievement, and adjustment.* San Diego, CA: Academic Press.

Marsh, H. W., & Yeung, A. S. (1997). Coursework selection: Relations to academic self-concept and achievement. *American Educational Research Journal, 34,* 691–720.

Marsh, H. W., & Yeung, A. S. (1998). Longitudinal structural equation models of academic self-concept and achievement: Gender differences in the development of math and English constructs. *American Educational Research Journal, 35,* 705–738.

Marshall, N. L., White, A. M., Keefe, N. E., & Marx, F. (1999, April). *When are children in self- or sibling care? Predicting entry into unsupervised care.* Paper presented at the biennial meeting of the Society for Research in Child Development, Albuquerque, New Mexico.

Martin, C., & Halverson, C. F. (1987). The roles of cognition in sex role acquisition. In D. B. Carter (Ed.), *Current conceptions of sex roles and sex typing: Theory and research.* New York: Praeger.

Martin, C. L. (1989). Children's use of gender-related information in making social judgments. *Developmental Psychology, 25,* 80–88.

Martin, C. L. (1991). The role of cognition in understanding gender effects. *Advances in Child Development and Behavior, 23,* 113–149.

Martin, C. L., & Halverson, C. F. (1981). A schematic processing model of sex typing and stereotyping in children. *Child Development, 52,* 1119–1134.

Martin, S. S., Brady, M. P., & Williams, R. E. (1991). Effects of toys on the social behavior of preschool children in integrated and nonintegrated groups: Investigation of a setting event. *Journal of Early Intervention, 15,* 153–161.

Mason, C. Y., & Jaskulski, T. (1994). HIV/AIDS prevention and education. In M. Agran, N. E. Marchand-Martella, & R. C. Martella (Eds.), *Promoting health and safety: Skills for independent living* (pp. 161–191). Baltimore: Brookes.

Massey, D. S., & Denton, N. A. (1993). *American apartheid: Segregation and the making of the underclass.* Cambridge, MA: Cambridge University Press.

Masten, A. S., & Coatsworth, J. D. (1998). The development of competence in favorable and unfavorable environments. *American Psychologist, 53,* 205–220.

Masten, A. S., Neemann, J., & Andenas, S. (1994). Life events and adjustment in adolescents: The significance of event independence, desirability, and chronicity. *Journal of Research on Adolescence, 4,* 71–97.

Mastropieri, M. A., & Scruggs, T. E. (1992). Science for students with disabilities. *Review of Educational Research, 62,* 377–411.

Masur, E. F., McIntyre, C. W., & Flavell, J. H. (1973). Developmental changes in apportionment of study time among items in a multitrial free recall task. *Journal of Experimental Child Psychology, 15,* 237–246.

Matheny, A. P. (1989). Children's behavioral inhibition over age and across situations: Genetic similarity for a trait during change. *Journal of Personality, 57,* 215–226.

Matthews, K. A., Batson, C. D., Horn, J., & Rosenman, R. H. (1981). Principles in his nature which interest him in the fortune of others: The heritability of empathic concern for others. *Journal of Personality, 49,* 237–247.

Mattison, R. E. (1992). Anxiety disorders. In S. R. Hooper, G. W. Hynd, & R. E. Mattison (Eds.), *Child psychopathology: Diagnostic criteria and clinical assessment* (pp. 179–202). Hillsdale, NJ: Erlbaum.

Mayall, B., Bendelow, G., Barker, S., Storey, P., & Veltman, M. (1996). *Children's health in primary schools.* London: Falmer Press.

Mayer, R. E. (1992). *Thinking, problem solving, cognition* (2nd ed.). New York: Freeman.

Mayer, R. E. (1996). Learning strategies for making sense out of expository text: The SOI model for guiding three cognitive processes in knowledge construction. *Educational Psychology Review, 8,* 357–371.

Mayer, R. E. (1998). Does the brain have a place in educational psychology? *Educational Psychology Review, 10,* 389–396.

Mayer, R. E. (1999). *The promise of educational psychology: Learning in the content areas.* Upper Saddle River, NJ: Merrill/Prentice Hall.

Mayes, L. C., & Bornstein, M. H. (1997). The development of children exposed to cocaine. In S. S. Luthar, J. A. Burack, D. Cicchetti, & J. R. Weisz (Eds.), *Developmental psychopathology: Perspectives on adjustment, risk, and disorder* (pp. 166–188). Cambridge, England: Cambridge University Press.

Mazza, J. J., & Overstreet, S. (2000). Children and adolescents exposed to community violence: A mental health perspective for school psychologists. *School Psychology Review, 29,* 86–101.

McAdoo, H. P. (1985). Racial attitude and self-concept of young Black children over time. In H. P. McAdoo & J. L. McAdoo (Eds.), *Black children: Social, educational, and parental environments.* Newbury Park, CA: Sage.

McAdoo, H. P. (1990). The ethics of research and intervention with ethnic minority parents and their children. In I. Sigel (Series Ed.), C. Fisher, & W. Tryon (Vol. Eds.), *Advances in applied developmental psychology: Vol. 4. Ethics in applied developmental psychology: Emerging issues in an emerging field* (pp. 273–283). Norwood, NJ: Ablex.

McAlpine, L. (1992). Language, literacy and education: Case studies of Cree, Inuit and Mohawk communities. *Canadian Children, 17*(1), 17–30.

McAlpine, L., & Taylor, D. M. (1993). Instructional preferences of Cree, Inuit, and Mohawk teachers. *Journal of American Indian Education, 33*(1), 1–20.

McCall, R. B. (1993). Developmental functions for general mental performance. In D. K. Detterman (Ed.), *Current topics in human intelligence* (Vol. 3). Norwood, NJ: Ablex.

McCall, R. B. (1994). Academic underachievers. *Current Directions in Psychological Science, 3,* 15–19.

McCallum, R. S. (1999). A "baker's dozen" criteria for evaluating fairness in nonverbal testing. *The School Psychologist, 53*(2), 41–60.

McCallum, R. S., & Bracken, B. A. (1993). Interpersonal relations between school children and their peers, parents, and teachers. *Educational Psychology Review, 5,* 155–176.

McCallum, R. S., & Bracken, B. A. (1997). The Universal Nonverbal Intelligence Test. In D. P. Flanagan, J. L. Genshaft, & P. L. Harrison (Eds.), *Contemporary intellectual assessment: Theories, tests, and issues* (pp. 268–280). New York: Guilford Press.

McCann, T. M. (1989). Student argumentative writing knowledge and ability at three grade levels. *Research in the Teaching of English, 23,* 62–72.

McCarty, T. L., & Watahomigie, L. J. (1998). Language and literacy in American Indian and Alaska Native communities. In B. Pérez (Ed.), *Sociocultural contexts of language and literacy.* Mahwah, NJ: Erlbaum.

McCaslin, M., & Good, T. L. (1996). The informal curriculum. In D. C. Berliner & R. C. Calfee (Eds.), *Handbook of educational psychology.* New York: Macmillan.

McClelland, D. C., Atkinson, J. W., Clark, R. A., & Lowell, E. L. (1953). *The achievement motive.* New York: Appleton-Century-Crofts.

McCormick, C. B., Busching, B. A., & Potter, E. F. (1992). Children's knowledge about writing: The development and use of evaluative criteria. In M. Pressley, K. R. Harris, & J. T. Guthrie (Eds.), *Promoting academic competence and literacy in school.* San Diego, CA: Academic Press.

McCourt, F. (1996). *Angela's ashes: A memoir.* New York: Scribner.

McCoy, K. (1994). *Understanding your teenager's depression.* New York: Perigee.

McCreary, M. L., Slavin, L. A., & Berry, E. J. (1996). Predicting problem behavior and self-esteem among African-American adolescents. *Journal of Adolescent Research, 11,* 216–234.

McCutchen, D. (1987). Children's discourse skill: Form and modality requirements of schooled writing. *Discourse Processes, 10,* 267–286.

McCutchen, D. (1996). A capacity theory of writing: Working memory in composition. *Educational Psychology Review, 8,* 299–325.

McDevitt, M., & Chaffee, S. H. (1998). Second chance political socialization: "Trickle-up" effects of children on parents. In T. J. Johnson, C. E. Hays, & S. P. Hays (Eds.), *Engaging the public: How government and the media can reinvigorate American democracy.* Lanhan, MD: Rowman & Littlefield.

McDevitt, T. M. (1990). Encouraging young children's listening skills. *Academic Therapy, 25,* 569–577.

McDevitt, T. M., & Ford, M. E. (1987). Processes in young children's communicative functioning and development. In M. E. Ford & D. H. Ford (Eds.), *Humans as self-constructing systems: Putting the framework to work.* (pp. 145–175). Hillsdale, NJ: Erlbaum.

McDevitt, T. M., Spivey, N., Sheehan, E. P., Lennon, R., & Story, R. (1990). Children's beliefs about listening: Is it enough to be still and quiet? *Child Development, 61,* 713–721.

McDonnell, L. M., & Hill, P. T. (1993). *Newcomers in American schools: Meeting the educational needs of immigrant youth.* Santa Monica, CA: RAND.

McGinn, P. V., Viernstein, M. C., & Hogan, R. (1980). Fostering the intellectual development of verbally gifted adolescents. *Journal of Educational Psychology, 72,* 494–498.

McGowan, R. J., & Johnson, D. L. (1984). The mother-child relationship and other antecedents of childhood intelligence: A causal analysis. *Child Development, 55,* 810–820.

McGrew, K. S., Flanagan, D. P., Zeith, T. Z., & Vanderwood, M. (1997). Beyond *g:* The impact of *Gf-Gc* specific cognitive abilities research on the future use and interpretation of intelligence tests in the schools. *School Psychology Review, 26,* 189–210.

McGue, M., Bouchard, T. J., Jr., Iacono, W. G., & Lykken, D. T. (1993). Behavioral genetics of cognitive ability: A life-span perspective. In R. Plomin & G. E. McClearn (Eds.), *Nature, nurture, and psychology.* Washington, DC: American Psychological Association.

McHale, J. P., & Rasmussen, J. L. (1998). Coparental and family group-level dynamics during infancy: Early family precursors of child and family functioning during preschool. *Development and Psychopathology, 10,* 39–59.

McHale, S. M., Bartko, W. T., Crouter, A. C., & Perry-Jenkins, M. (1990). Children's housework and psychosocial functioning: The mediating effects of parents' sex-role behaviors and attitudes. *Child Development, 61,* 1413–1426.

McKay, A. (1993). Research supports broadly-based sex education. *The Canadian Journal of Human Sexuality, 2*(2), 89–98.

McKenzie, J. K. (1993). Adoption of children with special needs. *The Future of Children, 3*(1), 26–42.

McKeough, A. (1995). Teaching narrative knowledge for transfer in the early school years. In A. McKeough, J. Lupart, & A. Marini (Eds.), *Teaching for transfer: Fostering generalization in learning.* Mahwah, NJ: Erlbaum.

McKeown, M. G., & Beck, I. L. (1994). Making sense of accounts of history: Why young students don't and how they might. In G. Leinhardt, I. L. Beck, & C. Stainton (Eds.), *Teaching and learning in history.* Hillsdale, NJ: Erlbaum.

McKey, R., Condelli, L., Ganson, H., Barrett, B., McConkey, C., & Plantz, M. (1985). *The impact of Head Start on children, families, and communities* (DHHS Publication No. OHDS 90-31193). Washington, DC: U.S. Government Printing Office.

McLane, J. B., & McNamee, G. D. (1990). *Early literacy.* Cambridge, MA: Harvard University Press.

McLoyd, V. C. (1990). The impact of economic hardship on black families and children: Psychological distress, parenting, and socioemotional development. *Child Development, 61,* 311–346.

McLoyd, V. C. (1998a). Children in poverty: Development, public policy, and practice. In W. Damon (Editor-in-Chief), I. E. Sigel, & K. A. Renninger (Vol. Eds.), *Handbook of child psychology: Vol. 4. Child psychology in practice* (5th ed., pp. 135–208). New York: Wiley.

McLoyd, V. C. (1998b). Socioeconomic disadvantage and child development. *American Psychologist, 53,* 185–204.

McMahon, S. (1992). Book club: A case study of a group of fifth graders as they participate in a literature-based reading program. *Reading Research Quarterly, 27*(4), 292–294.

McMillan, J. H., & Reed, D. F. (1994). At-risk students and resiliency: Factors contributing to academic success. *Clearing House, 67*(3), 137–140.

McMillan, J. H., Singh, J., & Simonetta, L. G. (1994). The tyranny of self-oriented self-esteem. *Educational Horizons, 72,* 141–145.

McNeill, D. (1966). Developmental psycholinguistics. In F. Smith & G. A. Miller (Eds.), *The genesis of language*. Cambridge, MA: MIT Press.

McNeill, D. (1970). *The acquisition of language: The study of developmental psycholinguistics*. New York: Harper & Row.

Mead, M. (1930). *Growing up in New Guinea*. New York: Mentor.

Mead, M. (1935). *Sex and temperament in three primitive societies*. New York: American Library.

Medrich, E. A., Roizen, J. A., Rubin, V., & Buckley, S. (1982). *The serious business of growing up: A study of children's lives outside school*. Berkeley, CA: University of California Press.

Medrich, E., & Marzke, C. (1991). *Young adolescents and discretionary time use: The nature of life outside school*. Washington, DC: Carnegie Council on Adolescent Development.

Meece, D., Colwell, M. J., & Pettit, G. (1999, April). *Infant-care, self-care, and early adolescent peer contact: A longitudinal study of developmental risk and continuity in nonparental care*. Paper presented at the biennial meeting of the Society for Research in Child Development, Albuquerque, NM.

Meece, J. L. (1994). The role of motivation in self-regulated learning. In D. H. Schunk & B. J. Zimmerman (Eds.), *Self-regulation of learning and performance: Issues and educational applications*. Hillsdale, NJ: Erlbaum.

Mehan, H. (1979). *Social organization in the classroom*. Cambridge, MA: Harvard University Press.

Meichenbaum, D. (1977). *Cognitive-behavior modification: An integrative approach*. New York: Plenum Press.

Meichenbaum, D. (1985). Teaching thinking: A cognitive-behavioral perspective. In S. F. Chipman, J. W. Segal, & R. Glaser (Eds.), *Thinking and learning skills: Vol. 2. Research and open questions*. Hillsdale, NJ: Erlbaum.

Meichenbaum, D., & Goodman, J. (1971). Training impulsive children to talk to themselves: A means of developing self-control. *Journal of Abnormal Psychology, 77*, 115–126.

Meindl, R. S. (1992). Human populations before agriculture. In S. Jones, R. Martin, D. Pilbeam, & S. Bunney (Eds.), *Cambridge encyclopedia of human evolution* (pp. 406–410). Cambridge, England: Cambridge University Press.

Meltzoff, A. N. (1988). Infant imitation after a 1-week delay: Long-term memory for novel acts and multiple stimuli. *Developmental Psychology, 24*, 470–476.

Menec, V. H., & Schonwetter, D. J. (1994, April). *Action control, motivation, and academic achievement*. Paper presented at the annual meeting of the American Educational Research Association, New Orleans, LA.

Menyuk, P., & Menyuk, D. (1988). Communicative competence: A historical and cultural perspective. In J. S. Wurzel (Ed.), *Toward multiculturalism: A reader in multicultural education*. Yarmouth, ME: Intercultural Press.

Mercer, C. D. (1997). *Students with learning disabilities* (5th ed.). Upper Saddle River, NJ: Merrill/Prentice Hall.

Mercer, C. D., Jordan, L., Allsopp, D. H., & Mercer, A. R. (1996). Learning disabilities definitions and criteria used by state education departments. *Learning Disabilities Quarterly, 19*, 217–231.

Merrill, M. D., & Tennyson, R. D. (1977). *Concept teaching: An instructional design guide*. Englewood Cliffs, NJ: Educational Technology.

Mervis, C. B. (1987). Child-basic object categories and early lexical development. In U. Neisser (Ed.), *Concepts and conceptual development: Ecological and intellectual factors in categorization*. Cambridge, England: Cambridge University Press.

Messick, S. (1983). Assessment of children. In W. Kessen (Ed.), *Handbook of child psychology* (Vol. 1). New York: Wiley.

Metz, K. E. (1995). Reassessment of developmental constraints on children's science instruction. *Review of Educational Research, 65*, 93–127.

Metz, K. E. (1997). On the complex relation between cognitive developmental research and children's science curricula. *Review of Educational Research, 67*, 151–163.

Meyer, D. K., Turner, J. C., & Spencer, C. A. (1994, April). *Academic risk taking and motivation in an elementary mathematics classroom*. Paper presented at the annual meeting of the American Educational Research Association, New Orleans, LA.

Meyer, D. K., Turner, J. C., & Spencer, C. A. (1997). Challenge in a mathematics classroom: Students' motivation and strategies in project-based learning. *Elementary School Journal, 97*, 501–521.

Meyer, M. S. (2000). The ability-achievement discrepancy: Does it contribute to an understanding of learning disabilities? *Educational Psychology Review, 12*, 315–337.

Meyers, D. T. (1987). The socialized individual and individual autonomy: An intersection between philosophy and psychology. In E. F. Kittay and D. T. Meyers (Eds.), *Women and moral theory*. Totowa, NJ: Rowman & Littlefield.

Micheli, L. J., & Melhonian, N. (1987). The child is sport. In *Proceedings of the Pan American Sports Medicine Congress XII*. Bloomington: Indiana University.

Middleton, M. J. (1999, April). *Classroom effects on the gender gap in middle school students' math self-efficacy*. Paper presented at the annual meeting of the American Educational Research Association, Montreal, Canada.

Middleton, M. R., & Cartledge, G. (1995). The effects of social skills instruction and parental involvement on the aggressive behaviors of African-American males. *Behavior Modification, 19*, 192–210.

Midgley, C., Feldlaufer, H., & Eccles, J. S. (1989). Change in teacher efficacy and student self- and task-related beliefs in mathematics during the transition to junior high school. *Journal of Educational Psychology, 81*, 247–258.

Milch-Reich, S., Campbell, S. B., Pelham, W. E., Jr., Connelly, L. M., & Geva, D. (1999). Developmental and individual differences in children's on-line representations of dynamic social events. *Child Development, 70*, 413–431.

Miller, B. C., & Benson, B. (1999). Romantic and sexual relationship development during adolescence. In W. Furman, B. B. Brown, & C. Feiring (Eds.), *The development of romantic relationships in adolescence* (pp. 99–121). Cambridge, England: Cambridge University Press.

Miller, C. T., & Myers, A. M. (1998). Compensating for prejudice: How heavyweight people (and others) control outcomes despite prejudice. In J. K. Swim & C. Stangor (Eds.), *Prejudice: The target's perspective* (pp. 191–218). San Diego, CA: Academic Press.

Miller, D. (1994). Suicidal behavior of adolescents with behavior disorders and their peers without disabilities. *Behavioral Disorders, 20*(1), 61–68.

Miller, G. A., & Gildea, P. M. (1987). How children learn words. *Scientific American, 257*, 94–99.

Miller, J. G. (1997). A cultural-psychology perspective on intelligence. In R. J. Sternberg & E. L. Grigorenko (Eds.), *Intelligence, heredity, and environment* (pp. 269–302). Cambridge, England: Cambridge University Press.

Miller, J. G., & Bersoff, D. M. (1995). Development in the context of everyday family relationships: Culture, interpersonal morality, and adaptation. In M. Killen & D. Hart (Eds.), *Morality in everyday life: Developmental perspectives* (pp. 259–282). Cambridge, England: Cambridge University Press.

Miller, L. S. (1995). *An American imperative: Accelerating minority educational advancement*. New Haven, CT: Yale University Press.

Miller, N., & Maruyama, G. (1976). Ordinal position and peer popularity. *Journal of Personality and Social Psychology, 33*, 123–131.

Miller, P. A., Eisenberg, N., Fabes, R. A., & Shell, R. (1996). Relations of moral reasoning and vicarious emotion to young children's prosocial behavior toward peers and adults. *Developmental Psychology, 32*, 210–219.

Miller, P. J. (1982). *Amy, Wendy, and Beth: Learning language in South Baltimore*. Austin: University of Texas Press.

Miller, P. J., & Goodnow, J. J. (1995). Cultural practices: Toward an integration of culture and development. In J. J. Goodnow & P. J. Miller (Eds.), *Cultural practices as contexts for development* (New Directions for Child Development, No. 67; pp. 5–16). San Francisco, CA: Jossey-Bass.

Miller, P. M., Danaher, D. L., & Forbes, D. (1986). Sex-related strategies of coping with interpersonal conflict in children aged five to seven. *Developmental Psychology, 22*, 543–548.

Mills, G. E. (2000). *Action research: A guide for the teacher researcher*. Upper Saddle River, NJ: Merrill/Prentice Hall.

Mills, K. (1998). *Something better for my children: The history and people of Head Start*. New York: Penguin/Dutton Books.

Mills, R. S. L., & Grusec, J. E. (1989). Cognitive, affective, and behavioral consequences of praising altruism. *Merrill-Palmer Quarterly, 35*, 299–326.

Milroy, L. (1994). Sociolinguistics and second language learning: Understanding speakers from different speech communities. In G. Brown, K. Malmkjær, A. Pollitt, & J. Williams (Eds.), *Language and understanding*. Oxford, England: Oxford University Press.

Minami, M., & Ovando, C. J. (1995). Language issues in multicultural contexts. In J. A. Banks & C. A. M. Banks (Eds.), *Handbook of research on multicultural education*. New York: Macmillan.

Minkler, M., & Roe, K. M. (1993). *Grandmothers as caregivers*. Newbury, CA: Sage.

Mintzes, J. J., Trowbridge, J. E., Arnaudin, M. W., & Wandersee, J. H. (1991). Children's biology: Studies on conceptual development in the life sciences. In S. M. Glynn, R. H. Yeany, & B. K. Britton (Eds.), *The psychology of learning science*. Hillsdale, NJ: Erlbaum.

Mischel, W. (1974). Processes in delay of gratification. In L. Berkowitz (Ed.), *Advances in experimental social psychology* (Vol. 7, pp. 249–292). New York: Academic Press.

Mischel, W., & Ebbesen, E. (1970). Attention in delay of gratification. *Journal of Personality and Social Psychology, 16*, 329–337.

Mischel, W., Shoda, Y., & Rodriguez, M. L. (1989). Delay of gratification in children. *Science, 244*, 933–938.

Mitchell, A. (1998). African American teachers: Unique roles and universal lessons. *Education and Urban Society, 31*(1), 104–122.

Miyake, K., Campos, J., Kagan, J., & Bradshaw, D. (1986). Issues in socioemotional development in Japan. In H. Azuma, K. Hakuta, & H. Stevenson (Eds.), *Kodomo: Child development and education in Japan* (pp. 238–261). San Francisco: Freeman.

Miyake, K., Chen, S.-J., & Campos, J. J. (1985). Infant temperament, mother's mode of interaction, and attachment in Japan: An interim report. In I. Bretherton & E. Waters (Eds.), Growing points of attachment theory and research. *Monographs of the Society for Research in Child Development, 50*(1–2, Serial No. 209), 276–297.

Mize, J., Pettit, G. S., & Brown, E. G. (1995). Mothers' supervision of their children's peer play: Relations with beliefs, perceptions, and knowledge. *Developmental Psychology, 31*, 311–321.

Moen, P., & Erickson, M. A. (1995). Linked lives: A transgenerational approach to resilience. In P. Moen, G. H. Elder, Jr., & K. Luscher (Eds.), *Examining lives in context: Perspectives on the ecology of human development* (pp. 169–207). Washington, DC: American Psychological Association.

Mohatt, G., & Erickson, F. (1981). Cultural differences in teaching styles in an Odawa school: A sociolinguistic approach. In H. T. Trueba, G. P. Guthrie, & K. H. Au (Eds.), *Culture and the bilingual classroom: Studies in classroom ethnography*. Rowley, MA: Newbury House.

Money, J. (1987). Sin, sickness, or status? Homosexual gender identification and psychoneuroendocrinology. *American Psychologist, 42*, 384–399.

Money, J. (1988). *Gay, straight, and in-between: The sexology of erotic orientation*. New York: Oxford University Press.

Montagu, A. (1999a). Introduction. In A. Montagu (Ed.), *Race and IQ* (expanded ed.; pp. 1–18). New York: Oxford University Press.

Montagu, A. (Ed.). (1999b). *Race and IQ* (expanded ed.). New York: Oxford University Press.

Montemayor, R. (1982). The relationship between parent-adolescent conflict and the amount of time adolescents spend with parents, peers, and alone. *Child Development, 53*, 1512–1519.

Montemayor, R. (1983). Parents and adolescents in conflict. *Journal of Early Adolescence, 3*, 83–103.

Montgomery, D. (1989). Identification of giftedness among American Indian people. In C. J. Maker & S. W. Schiever (Eds.), *Critical issues in gifted education: Vol. 2. Defensible programs for cultural and ethnic minorities*. Austin, TX: Pro-Ed.

Moon, S. M., Feldhusen, J. F., & Dillon, D. R. (1994). Long term effects of an enrichment program based on the Purdue three-stage model. *Gifted Child Quarterly, 38*, 38–47.

Moore, S. M., & Rosenthal, D. A. (1991). Condoms and coitus: Adolescents' attitudes to AIDS and safe sex behavior. *Journal of Adolescence, 14*, 211–227.

Moorehouse, M. J. (1991). Linking maternal employment patterns to mother-child activities and children's school competence. *Developmental Psychology, 27*, 295–303.

Moran, C. E., & Hakuta, K. (1995). Bilingual education: Broadening research perspectives. In J. A. Banks & C. A. M. Banks (Eds.), *Handbook of research on multicultural education*. New York: Macmillan.

Moran, S. (1991). Creative reading: Young adults and paperback books. *Horn Book Magazine, 67*, 437–441.

Morgan, B., & Gibson, K. R. (1991). Nutritional and environmental interactions in brain development. In K. R. Gibson & A. C. Petersen (Eds.), *Brain maturation and cognitive development: Comparative and cross-cultural perspectives*. New York: Aldine de Gruyter.

Morgan, J. L., & Demuth, K. (Eds.). (1996). *Signal to syntax: Bootstrapping from speech to grammar in early acquisition*. Mahwah, NJ: Erlbaum.

Morgan, M. (1985). Self-monitoring of attained subgoals in private study. *Journal of Educational Psychology, 77*, 623–630.

Morris, R. D., Stuebing, K. K., Fletcher, J. M., Shaywitz, S. E., Lyon, G. R., Shankweiler, D. P., Katz, L., Francis, D. J., & Shaywitz, B. A. (1998). Subtypes of reading disability: Variability around a phonological core. *Journal of Educational Psychology, 90*, 347–373.

Morrison, G., Furlong, M., & Smith, G. (1994). Factors associated with the experience of school violence among general education, leadership class, opportunity class, and special day class pupils. *Education and Treatment of Children, 17*, 356–369.

Morrow, S. L. (1997). Career development of lesbian and gay youth: Effects of sexual orientation, coming out, and homophobia. In M. B. Harris (Ed.), *School experiences of gay and lesbian youth: The invisible minority* (pp. 1–15). Binghamton, NY: Harrington Park Press.

Mortimer, J. T., Finch, M., Seongryeol, R., Shanahan, M. J., & McCall, K. T. (1993). *The effects of work intensity on adolescent mental health, achievement and behavioral adjustment: New evidence from a prospective study*. Paper presented at the biennial meeting of the Society for Research in Child Development, New Orleans, LA.

Mortimer, J. T., Shanahan, M., & Ryu, S. (1994). The effects of adolescent employment on school-related orientation and behavior. In R. K. Silbereisen & E. Todt (Eds.), *Adolescence in context: The interplay of family, school, peers and work in adjustment*. New York: Springer-Verlag.

Mueller, E. (1972). The maintenance of verbal exchanges between young children. *Child Development, 43*, 930–938.

Mueller, E., & Brenner, J. (1977). The origins of social skills and interaction among playgroup toddlers. *Child Development, 48*, 854–861.

Mueller, E., & Silverman, N. (1989). Peer relations in maltreated children. In D. Cicchetti & V. Carlson (Eds.), *Child maltreatment: Theory and research on the causes and consequences of child abuse and neglect* (pp. 529–579). New York: Cambridge University Press.

Mühlnickel, W., Elbert, T., Taub, E., & Flor, H. (1998). Reorganization of auditory cortex in tinnitus. *Proceedings of the National Academy of Sciences, USA, 95*, 10340–10343.

Mundy-Castle, A. C. (1974). Social and technological intelligence in western and non-western cultures. *Universitas, 4*, 46–52.

Munroe, R. L., & Munroe, P. J. (1992). Fathers in children's environments: A four culture study. In B. S. Hewlett (Ed.), *Father-child relations: Cultural and biosocial contexts* (pp. 213–230). New York: Aldine de Gruyter.

Murdock, T. B. (1999). The social context of risk: Status and motivational predictors of alienation in middle school. *Journal of Educational Psychology, 91*, 62–75.

Murray, B. A. (1998). Gaining alphabetic insight: Is phoneme manipulation skill or identity knowledge causal? *Journal of Educational Psychology, 90*, 461–475.

Murray, F. B. (1978). Teaching strategies and conservation training. In A. M. Lesgold, J. W. Pellegrino, S. D. Fokkema, & R. Glaser (Eds.), *Cognitive psychology and instruction*. New York: Plenum Press.

Muter, V. (1998). Phonological awareness: Its nature and its influence over early literacy development. In C. Hulme & R. M. Joshi (Eds.), *Reading and spelling: Development and disorders*. Mahwah, NJ: Erlbaum.

Nagy, L. (1912). *Psychologie des kindlichen Interesses*. Leipzig, Germany: Nemnich.

Nagy, W. E., Herman, P. A., & Anderson, R. C. (1985). Learning words from context. *Reading Research Quarterly, 20*, 233–253.

Narvaez, D. (1998). The influence of moral schemas on the reconstruction of moral narratives in eighth graders and college students. *Journal of Educational Psychology, 90*, 13–24.

Narvaez, D., Getz, I., Rest, J. R., & Thoma, S. J. (1999). Individual moral judgment and cultural ideologies. *Developmental Psychology, 35*, 477–488.

Narvaez, D., & Rest, J. (1995). The four components of acting morally. In W. M. Kurtines & J. L. Gewirtz (Eds.), *Moral development: An introduction*. Boston: Allyn & Bacon.

Nation, K., & Hulme, C. (1998). The role of analogy in early spelling development. In C. Hulme & R. M. Joshi (Eds.), *Reading and spelling: Development and disorders*. Mahwah, NJ: Erlbaum.

National Assessment of Educational Progress. (1985). *The reading report card: Progress toward excellence in our schools; trends in reading over four national assessments, 1971–1984*. Princeton, NJ: Author.

National Association of Secondary School Principals (NASSP). (1996). *Breaking ranks: Changing an American institution*. Reston, VA: Author.

National Center for Education Statistics. (1997). *Issue brief: Schools serving family needs: Extended-day programs in public and private schools*. Washington, DC: U.S. Department of Education.

National Center for Education Statistics. (1999a). *Digest of Education Statistics 1998* (NCES Publication No. 1999-036). Washington, DC: U.S. Department of Education.

National Center for Education Statistics. (1999b, August). *Snapshots of public schools in the United States: Results from the Schools and Staffing Survey*. Washington, DC: Author.

National Children and Youth Fitness Study II. (1987). *Journal of Physical Education, Recreation and Dance, 58*(9), 49–96.

National Council for Accreditation of Teacher Education. (2000). *Program Standards for Elementary Teacher Preparation*. Retrieved from the World Wide Web: http://www.ncate.org/elemstds.pdf.

National Joint Committee on Learning Disabilities (1994). Learning disabilities: Issues on definition, a position paper of the National Joint Committee on Learning Disabilities. In *Collective perspectives on issues affecting learning disabilities: Position papers and statements*. Austin, TX: Pro-Ed.

National Middle School Association (NMSA). (1995). *This we believe: Developmentally responsive middle-level schools*. Columbus, OH: Author.

National Research Council. (1993a). *Losing generations: Adolescents in high risk settings*. Washington, DC: National Academy of Sciences.

National Research Council. (1993b). *Understanding child abuse and neglect*. Washington, DC: National Academy Press.

Navarro, R. A. (1985). The problems of language, education, and society: Who decides. In E. E.

Garcia & R. V. Padilla (Eds.), *Advances in bilingual education research.* Tucson: University of Arizona Press.

NCSS Task Force on Ethnic Studies Curriculum Guidelines. (1992). Curriculum guidelines for multicultural education. *Social Education, 56,* 274–294.

Neapolitan, D. M., & Huston, A. C. (1994). *Educational content of children's programs on public and commercial television.* Lawrence, KS: Center for Research on the Influences of Television on Children, University of Kansas.

Neel, R. S., Jenkins, Z. N., & Meadows, N. (1990). Social problem-solving behaviors and aggression in young children: A descriptive observational study. *Behavioral Disorders, 16*(1), 39–51.

Neff, J. A., Hoppe, S. K., & Perea, P. (1987). Acculturation and alcohol use: Drinking patterns and problems among Anglo- and Mexican-American male drinkers. *Hispanic Journal of Behavioral Sciences, 9,* 151–181.

Neisser, U., Boodoo, G., Bouchard, T. J., Boykin, A. W., Brody, N., Ceci, S. J., Halpern, D. F., Loehlen, J. C., Perloff, R., Sternberg, R. J., & Urbina, S. (1996). Intelligence: Knowns and unknowns. *American Psychologist, 51,* 77–101.

Nel, J. (1993). Preservice teachers' perceptions of the goals of multicultural education: Implications for the empowerment of minority students, *Educational Horizons, 71,* 120–125.

Nelson, C. A. (1999). Neural plasticity and human development. *Current Directions in Psychological Science, 8,* 42–45.

Nelson, K. E. (Ed.). (1986). *Event knowledge: Structure and function in development.* Hillsdale, NJ: Erlbaum.

Neubauer, G., Mansel, J., Avrahami, A., & Nathan, M. (1994). Family and peer support of Israeli and German adolescents. In F. Nestemann & K. Hurrelmann (Eds.), *Social networks and social support in childhood and adolescence.* Berlin, Germany: Aldine de Gruyter.

Neuman, S. B. (1991). *Literacy in the television age: The myth of the TV effect.* Norwood, NJ: Ablex.

Newcomb, A. F., & Bagwell, C. L. (1995). Children's friendship relations: A meta-analysis review. *Psychological Bulletin, 117,* 306–347.

Newcomb, A. F., & Brady, J. E. (1982). Mutuality in boys' friendship relations. *Child Development, 53,* 392–395.

Newcomb, A. F., & Bukowski, W. M. (1984). A longitudinal study of the utility of social preference and social impact sociometric classification schemes. *Child Development, 55,* 1434–1447.

Newcomb, A. F., Bukowski, W. M., & Pattee, L. (1993). Children's peer relations: A meta-analytic review of popular, rejected, controversial, and average sociometric status. *Psychological Bulletin, 113,* 99–128.

Newcombe, N., & Huttenlocher, J. (1992). Children's early ability to solve perspective-taking problems. *Developmental Psychology, 28,* 635–643.

Newman, L. S. (1991). Why are traits inferred spontaneously? A developmental approach. *Social Cognition, 9,* 221–253.

Newman, R. S., & Schwager, M. T. (1992). Student perceptions and academic help seeking. In D. Schunk & J. Meece (Eds.), *Student perceptions in the classroom.* Hillsdale, NJ: Erlbaum.

Newport, E. L. (1990). Maturational constraints on language learning. *Cognitive Science, 14,* 11–28.

Newport, E. L. (1993). Maturational constraints on language learning. In P. Bloom (Ed.), *Language acquisition: Core readings.* Cambridge, MA: MIT Press.

Newson, J., & Newson, E. (1975). Intersubjectivity and the transmission of culture: On the origins of symbolic functioning. *Bulletin of the British Psychological Society, 28,* 437–446.

NICHD Early Child Care Research Network (1997). The effects of infant child care on infant-mother attachment security: Results of the NICHD study of early child care. *Child Development, 68,* 860–879.

Nicholls, J. (1990). What is ability and why are we mindful of it? A developmental perspective. In R. J. Sternberg & J. Kolligian (Eds.), *Competence considered.* New Haven, CT: Yale University Press.

Nicholls, J. G. (1979). Development of perception of own attainment and causal attributions for success and failure in reading. *Journal of Educational Psychology, 71,* 94–99.

Nicholls, J. G. (1984). Conceptions of ability and achievement motivation. In R. Ames & C. Ames (Eds.), *Research on motivation in education: Vol. 1. Student motivation.* San Diego, CA: Academic Press.

Nicholls, J. G., Cobb, P., Yackel, E., Wood, T., & Wheatley, G. (1990). Students' theories of mathematics and their mathematical knowledge: Multiple dimensions of assessment. In G. Kulm (Ed.), *Assessing higher order thinking in mathematics.* Washington, DC: American Association for the Advancement of Science.

Nichols, J. D., Ludwin, W. G., & Iadicola, P. (1999). A darker shade of gray: A year-end analysis of discipline and suspension data. *Equity and Excellence in Education, 32*(1), 43–55.

Nichols, M. L., & Ganschow, L. (1992). Has there been a paradigm shift in gifted education? In N. Coangelo, S. G. Assouline, & D. L. Ambroson (Eds.), *Talent development: Proceedings from the 1991 Henry B. and Jocelyn Wallace National Research Symposium on Talent Development.* New York: Trillium.

Nichols, P. D., & Mittelholtz, D. J. (1997). Constructing the concept of aptitude: Implications for the assessment of analogical reasoning. In G. D. Phye (Ed.), *Handbook of academic learning: Construction of knowledge.* San Diego, CA: Academic Press.

Nicklas, T. A., Webber, L. S., Johnson, C. C., Srinivasan, S. R., & Berenson, G. S. (1995). Foundations for health promotion with youth: A review of observations from the Bogalusa Heart Study. *Journal of Health Education, 26*(Suppl. 2), 18–26.

Niemi, R. G., & Junn, J. (1998). *Civic education: What makes students learn.* New Haven: Yale University Press.

Nieto, S. (1995). *Affirming diversity* (2nd ed.). White Plains, NY: Longman.

Nieto, S. (1995). A history of the education of Puerto Rican students in U.S. mainland schools: "Losers," "outsiders," or "leaders"? In J. A. Banks & C. A. M. Banks (Eds.), *Handbook of research on multicultural education.* New York: Macmillan.

Nippold, M. A. (1988). The literate lexicon. In M. A. Nippold (Ed.), *Later language development: Ages nine through nineteen.* Boston: Little, Brown.

Nix, R. L., Pinderhughes, E. E., Dodge, K. A., Bates, J. E., Pettit, G. S., & McFadyen-Ketchum, S. A. (1999). The relation between mothers' hostile attribution tendencies and children's externalizing behavior problems: The mediating role of mothers' harsh discipline practices. *Child Development, 70,* 896–909.

Noffke, S. (1997). Professional, personal, and political dimensions of action research. *Review of Research in Education, 22,* 305–343.

Nolen, S. B. (1996). Why study? How reasons for learning influence strategy selection. *Educational Psychology Review, 8,* 335–355.

Nolen-Hoeksema, S. (1987). Sex differences in unipolar depression: Evidence and theory. *Journal of Personality and Social Psychology, 101,* 259–282.

Norton, A. J., & Moorman, J. E. (1987). Current trends in marriage and divorce among American women. *Journal of Marriage and the Family, 49,* 3–14.

Nottelmann, E. D. (1987). Competence and self-esteem during transition from childhood to adolescence. *Developmental Psychology, 23,* 441–450.

Nsamenang, A. B., & Lamb, M. E. (1994). Socialization of the Nso children in the Bamenda Grassfields of northwest Cameroon. In P. M. Greenfield & R. R. Cocking (Eds.), *Cross-cultural roots of minority child development* (pp. 133–146). Hillsdale, NJ: Erlbaum.

Nucci, L. P., & Nucci, M. S. (1982a). Children's responses to moral and social conventional transgressions in free-play settings. *Child Development, 53,* 1337–1342.

Nucci, L. P., & Nucci, M. S. (1982b). Children's social interactions in the context of moral and conventional transgressions. *Child Development, 53,* 403–412.

Nucci, L. P., & Turiel, E. (1978). Social interactions and the development of social concepts in preschool children. *Child Development, 49,* 400–407.

Nucci, L. P., & Weber, E. K. (1991). The domain approach to values education: From theory to practice. In W. M. Kurtines & J. L. Gewirtz (Eds.), *Handbook of moral behavior and development: Vol. 3. Application* (pp. 251–266). Hillsdale, NJ: Erlbaum.

Nucci, L. P., & Weber, E. K. (1995). Social interactions in the home and the development of young children's conceptions of the personal. *Child Development, 66,* 1438–1452.

Nunner-Winkler, G. (1984). Two moralities? A critical discussion of an ethic of care and responsibility versus an ethic of rights and justice. In W. M. Kurtines & J. L. Gewirtz (Eds.), *Morality, moral behavior, and moral development.* New York: Wiley.

Nuthall, G. (1996). Commentary: Of learning and language and understanding the complexity of the classroom. *Educational Psychologist, 31,* 207–214.

Oakhill, J., Cain, K., & Yuill, N. (1998). Individual differences in children's comprehension skill: Toward an integrated model. In C. Hulme & R. M. Joshi (Eds.), *Reading and spelling: Development and disorders.* Mahwah, NJ: Erlbaum.

Oatley, K., & Nundy, S. (1996). Rethinking the role of emotions in education. In D. R. Olson & N. Torrance (Eds.), *The handbook of education and human development: New models of learning, teaching, and schooling.* Cambridge, MA: Blackwell.

O'Boyle, M. W., & Gill, H. S. (1998). On the relevance of research findings in cognitive neuroscience to educational practice. *Educational Psychology Review, 10,* 397–409.

O'Brien, S. F., & Bierman, K. L. (1987). Conceptions and perceived influence of peer groups: Interviews with preadolescents and adolescents. *Child Development, 59,* 1360–1365.

Ochs, E. (1982). Talking to children in western Samoa. *Language and Society, 11,* 77–104.

Ochs, E. (1988). *Culture and language development: Language acquisition and language socialization in a*

Samoan village. New York: Cambridge University Press.

O'Connor, M. J., Sigman, N., & Kasari, C. (1993). Attachment behavior of infants exposed prenatally to alcohol: Mediating effects of infant affect and mother-infant interaction. *Development and Psychopathology, 4,* 243–256.

Ogbu, J. U. (1992). Understanding cultural diversity and learning. *Educational Researcher, 21*(8), 5–14, 24.

Ogbu, J. U. (1994). From cultural differences to differences in cultural frames of reference. In P. M. Greenfield & R. R. Cocking (Eds.), *Cross-cultural roots of minority child development* (pp. 365–391). Hillsdale, NJ: Erlbaum.

Ogden, E. H., & Germinario, V. (1988). *The at-risk student: Answers for educators.* Lancaster, PA: Technomic.

O'Grady, W. (1997). *Syntactic development.* Chicago: University of Chicago Press.

Okagaki, L., & Frensch, P. A. (1998). Parenting and children's achievement: A multiethnic perspective. *American Educational Research Journal, 35,* 123–144.

Okagaki, L., & Sternberg, R. J. (1993). Parental beliefs and children's school performance. *Child Development, 64,* 36–56.

Oldfather, P., & West, J. (1999). *Learning through children's eyes: Social constructivism and the desire to learn.* Washington, DC: American Psychological Association.

O'Leary, K. D., & O'Leary, S. G. (Eds.). (1972). *Classroom management: The successful use of behavior modification.* New York: Pergamon Press.

Oliner, S. P., & Oliner, P. M. (1988). *The altruistic personality: Rescuers of Jews in Nazi Europe.* New York: Free Press.

Oliver, J. M., Cole, N. H., & Hollingsworth, H. (1991). Learning disabilities as functions of familial learning problems and developmental problems. *Exceptional Children, 57,* 427–440.

Olneck, M. R. (1995). Immigrants and education. In J. A. Banks & C. A. M. Banks (Eds.), *Handbook of research on multicultural education.* New York: Macmillan.

Olson, D. R. (1994). *The world on paper: The conceptual and cognitive implications of writing and reading.* New York: Cambridge University Press.

Olson, D. R., & Bruner, J. S. (1996). Folk psychology and folk pedagogy. In D. R. Olson & N. Torrance (Eds.), *The handbook of education and human development: New models of learning, teaching and schooling* (pp. 9–27). Cambridge, MA: Blackwell.

Olweus, D. (1993a). *Bullying at school: What we know and what we can do.* Oxford, England: Blackwell.

Olweus, D. (1993b). Victimization by peers: Antecedents and long-term outcomes. In K. H. Rubin & J. B. Asendorpf (Eds.), *Social withdrawal, inhibition and shyness in childhood* (pp. 315–341). Hillsdale, NJ: Erlbaum.

Olweus, D., Mattson, A., Schalling, D., & Low, H. (1988). Circulating testosterone levels and aggression in adult males: A causal analysis. *Psychosomatic Medicine, 42,* 253–269.

O'Malley, P. M., & Bachman, J. G. (1983). Self-esteem: Change and stability between ages 13 and 23. *Developmental Psychology, 19,* 257–268.

Oppenheimer, L. (1986). Development of recursive thinking: Procedural variations. *International Journal of Behavioral Development, 9,* 401–411.

Oppenheimer, L., & de Groot, W. (1981). Development of concepts about people in interpersonal situations. *European Journal of Social Psychology, 11,* 209–225.

O'Reilly, A. W. (1995). Using representations: Comprehension and production of actions with imagined objects. *Child Development, 66,* 999–1010.

Ormrod, J. E., & Jenkins, L. (1989). Study strategies in spelling: Correlations with achievement and developmental changes. *Perceptual and Motor Skills, 68,* 643–650.

Ormrod, J. E., & Wagner, E. D. (1987, October). *Spelling conscience in undergraduate students: Ratings of spelling accuracy and dictionary use.* Paper presented at the annual meeting of the Northern Rocky Mountain Educational Research Association, Park City, UT.

Ortony, A., Turner, T. J., & Larson-Shapiro, N. (1985). Cultural and instructional influences on figurative comprehension by inner city children. *Research in the Teaching of English, 19*(1), 25–36.

Osofsky, J. D. (1995). The effects of exposure to violence on young children. *American Psychologist, 50,* 782–788.

Owens, C. R., & Ascione, F. R. (1991). Effects of the model's age, perceived similarity, and familiarity on children's donating. *Journal of Genetic Psychology, 152,* 341–357.

Owens, R. E., Jr. (1996). *Language development* (4th ed.). Boston: Allyn & Bacon.

Owens, S. A., Steen, F., Hargrave, J., Flores, N., & Hall, P. (2000). Chase play: The neglected structure of a type of physical activity play. Manuscript submitted for publication.

Packard, V. (1983). *Our endangered children: Growing up in a changing world.* Boston: Little, Brown.

Paget, K. F., Kritt, D., & Bergemann, L. (1984). Understanding strategic interactions in television commercials: A developmental study. *Journal of Applied Developmental Psychology, 5,* 145–161.

Page-Voth, V., & Graham, S. (1999). Effects of goal setting and strategy use on the writing performance and self-efficacy of students with writing and learning problems. *Journal of Educational Psychology, 91,* 230–240.

Paik, H., & Comstock, G. (1994). The effects of television violence on antisocial behavior: A meta-analysis. *Communication Research, 21,* 516–546.

Paikoff, R. L., & Brooks-Gunn, J. (1991). Do parent-child relationships change during puberty? *Psychological Bulletin, 110,* 47–66.

Pajares, F. (1996). Self-efficacy beliefs in academic settings. *Review of Educational Research, 66,* 543–578.

Pajares, F., & Valiante, G. (1999). *Writing self-efficacy of middle school students: Relation to motivation constructs, achievement, gender, and gender orientation.* Paper presented at the annual meeting of the American Educational Research Association, Montreal, Canada.

Pajares, M. F. (1992). Teachers' beliefs and educational research: Cleaning up a messy construct. *Review of Educational Research, 62,* 307–332.

Palermo, D. S. (1974). Still more about the comprehension of "less." *Developmental Psychology, 10,* 827–829.

Paley, V. G. (1984). *Boys and girls: Superheroes in the doll corner.* Chicago: University of Chicago Press.

Palincsar, A. S., & Brown, A. L. (1984). Reciprocal teaching of comprehension-fostering and comprehension-monitoring activities. *Cognition and Instruction, 1,* 117–175.

Palincsar, A. S., & Brown, A. L. (1989). Classroom dialogues to promote self-regulated comprehension. In J. Brophy (Ed.), *Advances in research on teaching* (Vol. 1). Greenwich, CT: JAI Press.

Panel on Child Care Policy of the National Research Council. (1991). *Caring for America's children.* Washington, DC: National Academy Press.

Pang, V. O. (1995). Asian Pacific American students: A diverse and complex population. In J. A. Banks & C. A. M. Banks (Eds.), *Handbook of research on multicultural education.* New York: Macmillan.

Panksepp, J. (1998). Attention deficit hyperactivity disorders, psychostimulants, and intolerance of childhood playfulness: A tragedy in the making? *Current Directions in Psychological Science, 7,* 91–98.

Panofsky, C. P. (1994). Developing the representational functions of language: The role of parent-child book-reading activity. In V. John-Steiner, C. P. Panofsky, & L. W. Smith (Eds.), *Sociocultural approaches to language and literacy: An interactionist perspective.* Cambridge, England: Cambridge University Press.

Papernow, P. (1988). Stepparent role development: From outsider to intimate. In W. R. Beer (Ed.), *Relative strangers* (pp. 54–82). Totowa, NJ: Rowman & Littlefield.

Paris, S. G., & Ayres, L. R. (1994). *Becoming reflective students and teachers with portfolios and authentic assessment.* Washington, DC: American Psychological Association.

Paris, S. G., & Cunningham, A. E. (1996). Children becoming students. In D. C. Berliner & R. C. Calfee (Eds.), *Handbook of educational psychology.* New York: Macmillan.

Paris, S. G., & Jacobs, J. E. (1984). The benefits of informed instruction for children's reading awareness and comprehension skills, *Child Development, 55,* 2083–2093.

Paris, S. G., & Turner, J. C. (1994). Situated motivation. In P. R. Pintrich, D. R. Brown, & C. E. Weinstein (Eds.), *Student motivation, cognition, and learning: Essays in honor of Wilbert J. McKeachie.* Hillsdale, NJ: Erlbaum.

Paris, S. G., & Upton, L. R. (1976). Children's memory for inferential relationships in prose. *Child Development, 47,* 660–668.

Parish, P. (1985). *Amelia Bedelia goes camping.* New York: William Morrow.

Parke, R. D., & Bhavnagri, N. P. (1989). Parents as managers of children's peer relationships. In D. Belle (Ed.), *Children's social networks and social supports.* New York: Wiley.

Parke, R. D., & Buriel, R. (1998). Socialization in the family: Ethnic and ecological perspectives. In W. Damon (Editor-in-Chief) & N. Eisenberg (Vol. Ed.), *Handbook of child psychology: Vol. 3. Social, emotional, and personality development* (5th ed., pp. 463–552). New York: Wiley.

Parke, R. D., Ornstein, P. A., Rieser, J. J., & Zahn-Waxler, C. (1994). The past as prologue: An overview of a century of developmental psychology. In R. D. Parke, P. A. Ornstein, J. J. Rieser, & C. Zahn-Waxler (Eds.), *A century of developmental psychology* (pp. 1–70). Washington, DC: American Psychological Association.

Parke, R. D., & Tinsley, B. R. (1981). The father's role in infancy: Determinants of involvement in caregiving and play. In M. E. Lamb (Ed.), *The role of the father in child development* (pp. 429–458). New York: Wiley.

Parke, R. D., & Tinsley, B. R. (1987). Family interaction in infancy. In J. D. Osofsky (Ed.), *Handbook of infant development* (pp. 429–458). New York: Wiley.

Parke, R. D., & Walters, R. M. (1967). Some factors influencing the efficacy of punishment training for inducing response inhibition. *Monographs of the Society for Research in Child Development, 32*(1).

Parker, J. G. (1986). Becoming friends: Conversational skills for friendship formation in young children. In J. M. Gottman & J. G. Parker (Eds.), *Conversations of friends: Speculations on affective development* (pp. 103–138). Cambridge, England: Cambridge University Press.

Parker, J. G., & Gottman, J. M. (1989). Social and emotional development in a relational context: Friendship interaction from early childhood to adolescence. In T. J. Berndt & G. W. Ladd (Eds.), *Peer relations in child development* (pp. 95–131). New York: Wiley.

Parker, W. D. (1997). An empirical typology of perfectionism in academically talented children. *American Educational Research Journal, 34,* 545–562.

Parkhurst, J., & Gottman, J. M. (1986). How young children get what they want. In J. M. Gottman & J. G. Parker (Eds.), *Conversations of friends: Speculations on affective development* (pp. 315–345). Cambridge, England: Cambridge University Press.

Parkhurst, J. T., & Hopmeyer, A. (1998). Sociometric popularity and peer-perceived popularity: Two distinct dimensions of peer status. *Journal of Early Adolescence, 18,* 125–144.

Parks, C. P. (1995). Gang behavior in the schools: Reality or myth? *Educational Psychology Review, 7,* 41–68.

Parsons, J. E., Adler, T. F., & Kaczala, C. M. (1982). Socialization of achievement attitudes and beliefs: Parental influences. *Child Development, 53,* 310–321.

Parsons, J. E., Kaczala, C. M., & Meece, J. L. (1982). Socialization of achievement attitudes and beliefs: Classroom influences. *Child Development, 53,* 322–339.

Parten, M. B. (1932). Social participation among preschool children. *Journal of Abnormal and Social Psychology, 27,* 243–269.

Pascarella, E. T., & Terenzini, P. T. (1991). *How college affects students: Findings and insights from twenty years of research.* San Francisco: Jossey-Bass.

Passler, M., Isaac, W., & Hynd, G. W. (1985). Neuropsychological development of behavior attributed to frontal lobe functioning in children. *Developmental Neuropsychology, 1,* 349–370.

Pate, R. R., Long, B. J., & Heath, G. (1994). Descriptive epidemiology of physical activity in adolescents. *Pediatric Exercise Science, 6,* 434–447.

Patrick, H. (1997). Social self-regulation: Exploring the relations between children's social relationships, academic self-regulation, and school performance. *Educational Psychologist, 32,* 209–220.

Patterson, C. J. (1992). Children of lesbian and gay parents. *Child Development, 63,* 1025–1042.

Patterson, C. J. (1995). Sexual orientation and human development: An overview. *Developmental Psychology, 31,* 3–11.

Patterson, G. R., DeBaryshe, B. D., & Ramsey, E. (1989). A developmental perspective on antisocial behavior. *American Psychologist, 44,* 329–335.

Patterson, G. R., Littman, R., & Bricker, W. (1967). Assertive behavior in children: A step toward a theory of aggression. *Monographs of the Society for Research in Child Development, 32*(Serial No. 113).

Patterson, G. R., & Reid, J. B. (1970). Reciprocity and coercion: Two facets of social systems. In C. Neuringer & J. Michael (Eds.), *Behavior modification in clinical psychology.* New York: Appleton-Century-Crofts.

Patton, J. R., Blackbourn, J. M., & Fad, K. (1996). *Exceptional individuals in focus* (6th ed.). Upper Saddle River, NJ: Merrill/Prentice Hall.

Paul, R. (1990). Comprehension strategies: Interactions between world knowledge and the development of sentence comprehension. *Topics in Language Disorders, 10*(3), 63–75.

Pawlas, G. E. (1994). Homeless students at the school door. *Educational Leadership, 51*(8), 79–82.

Pea, R. D. (1993). Practices of distributed intelligence and designs for education. In G. Salomon (Ed.), *Distributed cognitions: Psychological and educational considerations.* Cambridge, England: Cambridge University Press.

Peak, L. (1993). Academic effort in international perspective. In T. M. Tomlinson (Ed.), *Motivating students to learn: Overcoming barriers to high achievement.* Berkeley, CA: McCutchan.

Pearson, P. D., Hansen, J., & Gordon, C. (1979). The effect of background knowledge on young children's comprehension of explicit and implicit information. *Journal of Reading Behavior, 11,* 201–209.

Pederson, D. R., Rook-Green, A., & Elder, J. L. (1981). The role of action in the development of pretend play in young children. *Developmental Psychology, 17,* 756–759.

Peláez-Nogueras, M., & Gewirtz, J. L. (1995). The learning of moral behavior: A behavior-analytic approach. In W. M. Kurtines & J. L. Gewirtz (Eds.), *Moral development: An introduction.* Boston: Allyn & Bacon.

Pellegrini, A. D. (1998). Play and the assessment of young children. In O. N. Saracho & B. Spodek (Eds.), *Multiple perspectives on play in early childhood education.* Albany: State University of New York Press.

Pellegrini, A. D., & Bartini, M. (2000). A longitudinal study of bullying, victimization, and peer affiliation during the transition from primary school to middle school. *American Educational Research Journal, 37,* 699–725.

Pellegrini, A. D., Bartini, M., & Brooks, F. (1999). School bullies, victims, and aggressive victims: Factors relating to group affiliation and victimization in early adolescence. *Journal of Educational Psychology, 91,* 216–224.

Pellegrini, A. D., & Bjorklund, D. F. (1997). The role of recess in children's cognitive performance. *Educational Psychologist, 32,* 35–40.

Pellegrini, A. D., & Horvat, M. (1995). A developmental contextualist critique of attention deficit hyperactivity disorder. *Educational Researcher, 24*(1), 13–19.

Pellegrini, A. D., & Smith, P. K. (1998). Physical activity play: Consensus and debate. *Child Development, 69,* 609–610.

Pennington, B. F., & Bennetto, L. (1993). Main effects of transactions in the neuropsychology of conduct disorder. Commentary on "The neuropsychology of conduct disorder." *Development and Psychopathology, 5,* 153–164.

Pérez, B. (Ed.). (1998). *Sociocultural contexts of language and literacy.* Mahwah, NJ: Erlbaum.

Perez-Granados, D. R., & Callanan, M. A. (1997). Parents and siblings as early resources for young children's learning in Mexican-descent families. *Hispanic Journal of Behavioral Sciences, 19,* 3–33.

Perfetti, C. A. (1985). Reading ability. In R. J. Sternberg (Ed.), *Human abilities: An information-processing approach.* New York: Freeman.

Perfetti, C. A. (1992). The representation problem in reading acquisition. In P. B. Gough, L. C. Ehri, & R. Treiman (Eds.), *Reading acquisition.* Hillsdale, NJ: Erlbaum.

Perfetti, C. A., & McCutchen, D. (1987). Schooled language competence: Linguistic abilities in reading and writing. In S. Rosenberg (Ed.), *Advances in applied psycholinguistics.* Cambridge, England: Cambridge University Press.

Perkins, D. (1992). *Smart schools: From training memories to educating minds.* New York: Free Press/Macmillan.

Perkins, D., Tishman, S., Ritchhart, R., Donis, K., & Andrade, A. (2000). Intelligence in the wild: A dispositional view of intellectual traits. *Educational Psychology Review, 12,* 269–293.

Perkins, D. N. (1995). *Outsmarting IQ: The emerging science of learnable intelligence.* New York: Free Press.

Perkins, D. N., & Grotzer, T. A. (1997). Teaching intelligence. *American Psychologist, 52,* 1125–1133.

Perner, J. (1991). *Understanding the representational mind.* Cambridge, MA: MIT Press.

Perner, J., Ruffman, T., & Leekam, S. R. (1994). Theory of mind is contagious: You catch it from your sibs. *Child Development, 65,* 1228–1238.

Perner, J., & Wimmer, H. (1985). "John *thinks that* Mary *thinks that.* . ." Attribution of second-order beliefs by 5- to 10-year-old children. *Journal of Experimental Child Psychology, 39,* 437–471.

Perry, C. L., Luepker, R. V., Murray, D. M., Hearn, M. D., Halper, A., Dudvitz, B., Mailie, M. C., & Smyth, M. (1989). Parent involvement with children's health promotion: A one-year follow-up of the Minnesota Home Team. *Health Education Quarterly, 16,* 71–180.

Perry, N. E. (1998). Young children's self-regulated learning and contexts that support it. *Journal of Educational Psychology, 90,* 715–729.

Perry, W. G., Jr. (1968). *Forms of intellectual and ethical development in the college years.* Cambridge, MA: President and Fellows of Harvard College.

Peters, A. M. (1983). *The units of language acquisition.* New York: Cambridge University Press.

Peterson, A. C., & Taylor, B. (1980). The biological approach to adolescence: Biological change and psychological adaptation. In J. Adelson (Ed.), *Handbook of adolescent psychology* (pp. 117–155). New York: Wiley.

Peterson, C. (1990). Explanatory style in the classroom and on the playing field. In S. Graham & V. S. Folkes (Eds.), *Attribution theory: Applications to achievement, mental health, and interpersonal conflict.* Hillsdale, NJ: Erlbaum.

Peterson, C., Maier, S. F., & Seligman, M. E. P. (1993). *Learned helplessness: A theory for the age of personal control.* New York: Oxford University Press.

Peterson, L. (1980). Developmental changes in verbal and behavioral sensitivity to cues of social norms of altruism. *Child Development, 51,* 830–838.

Peterson, M. E., & Haines, L. P. (1992). Orthographic analogy training with kindergarten children: Effects of analogy use, phonemic segmentation, and letter-sound knowledge. *Journal of Reading Behavior, 24,* 109–127.

Peterson, P. L. (1992). Revising their thinking: Keisha Coleman and her third-grade mathematics class. In H. H. Marshall (Ed.), *Redefining student learning: Roots of educational change.* Norwood, NJ: Ablex.

Petrill, S. A., & Wilkerson, B. (2000). Intelligence and achievement: A behavioral genetic perspective. *Educational Psychology Review, 12,* 185–199.

Pettit, G. S., Bates, J. E., Dodge, K. A., & Meece, D. W. (1999). The impact of after-school peer contact on early adolescent externalizing problems is moderated by parental monitoring, perceived neighborhood safety, and prior adjustment. *Child Development, 70,* 768–778.

Pettit, G. S., Brown, E. G., Mize, J., & Lindsey, E. (1998). Mothers and fathers socializing behaviors in three contexts: Links with children's peer competence. *Merrill-Palmer Quarterly, 44*(2), 173–193.

Pettit, G. S., Laird, R. D., Bates, J. E., & Dodge, K. A. (1997). Patterns of after-school care in middle childhood: Risk factors and developmental outcomes. *Merrill-Palmer Quarterly, 43*(3), 515–538.

Pettito, A. L. (1985). Division of labor: Procedural learning in teacher-led small groups. *Cognition and Instruction, 2,* 233–270.

Pettito, L. A. (1997). In the beginning: On the genetic and environmental factors that make early language acquisition possible. In M. Gopnik (Ed.), *The inheritance and innateness of grammars.* New York: Oxford University Press.

Phelan, P., Yu, H. C., & Davidson, A. L. (1994). Navigating the psychosocial pressures of adolescence: The voices and experiences of high school youth. *American Educational Research Journal, 31,* 415–447.

Phillips, M. (1997). What makes schools effective? A comparison of the relationships of communitarian climate and academic climate to mathematics achievement and attendance during middle school. *American Educational Research Journal, 34,* 633–662.

Phinney, J. S. (1989). Stages of ethnic identity development in minority group adolescents. *Journal of Early Adolescence, 9,* 34–49.

Phinney, J. S. (1990). Ethnic identity in adolescents and adults: Review of research. *Psychological Bulletin, 108,* 499–514.

Phinney, J. S., & Tarver, S. (1988). Ethnic identity search and commitment in Black and White eighth graders. *Journal of Early Adolescence, 8,* 265–277.

Piaget, J. (1926). *The language and thought of the child.* New York: Harcourt, Brace.

Piaget, J. (1928). *Judgment and reasoning in the child* (M. Warden, Trans.). New York: Harcourt, Brace.

Piaget, J. (1929). *The child's conception of the world.* New York: Harcourt, Brace.

Piaget, J. (1952a). *The child's conception of number* (C. Gattegno & F. M. Hodgson, Trans.). London: Routledge & Kegan Paul.

Piaget, J. (1952b). *The origins of intelligence in children.* New York: International Universities Press.

Piaget, J. (1959). *The language and thought of the child* (3rd ed.; M. Gabain, Trans.). London: Routledge & Kegan Paul.

Piaget, J. (1960). *The moral judgment of the child* (M. Gabain, Trans.). Glencoe, IL: Free Press. (First published in 1932)

Piaget, J. (1970). Piaget's theory. In P. H. Mussen (Ed.), *Carmichael's manual of psychology.* New York: Wiley.

Piaget, J. (1985). *The equilibration of cognitive structures: The central problem of intellectual development.* Chicago: University of Chicago Press.

Piaget, J., & Inhelder, B. (1969). *The psychology of the child* (H. Weaver, Trans.). New York: Basic Books.

Pianko, S. (1979). A description of the composing processes of college freshmen writers. *Research in the Teaching of English, 13,* 5–22.

Piche, C., & Plante, C. (1991). Perceived masculinity, femininity, and androgyny among primary school boys: Relationships with the adaptation level of these students and the attitudes of the teachers towards them. *European Journal of Psychology of Education, 6,* 423–435.

Pick, A. D., & Frankel, G. W. (1974). A developmental study of strategies of visual selectivity. *Child Development, 45,* 1162–1165.

Piirto, J. (1999). *Talented children and adults: Their development and education* (2nd ed.). Upper Saddle River, NJ: Merrill/Prentice Hall.

Pinker, S. (1982). A theory of the acquisition of lexical interpretive grammars. In J. Bresnan (Ed.), *The mental representation of grammatical notions.* Cambridge, MA: MIT Press.

Pinker, S. (1984). *Language learnability and language development.* Cambridge, MA: Harvard University Press.

Pinker, S. (1987). The bootstrapping problem in language acquisition. In B. MacWhinney (Ed.), *Mechanisms of language acquisition.* Hillsdale, NJ: Erlbaum.

Pinker, S. (1993). Rules of language. In P. Bloom (Ed.), *Language acquisition: Core readings.* Cambridge, MA: MIT Press.

Pinnegar, S. E. (1988, April). *Learning the language of practice from practicing teachers: An exploration of the term "with me."* Paper presented at the annual meeting of the American Educational Research Association, New Orleans.

Pintrich, P. R., & Garcia, T. (1994). Regulating motivation and cognition in the classroom: The role of self-schemas and self-regulatory strategies. In D. Schunk & B. Zimmerman (Eds.), *Self-regulation of learning and performance: Issues and educational applications.* Hillsdale, NJ: Erlbaum.

Pintrich, P. R., Marx, R. W., & Boyle, R. A. (1993). Beyond cold conceptual change: The role of motivational beliefs and classroom contextual factors in the process of conceptual change. *Review of Educational Research, 63,* 167–199.

Pintrich, P. R., & Schrauben, B. (1992). Students' motivational beliefs and their cognitive engagement in academic tasks. In D. Schunk & J. Meece (Eds.), *Students' perceptions in the classroom: Causes and consequences.* Hillsdale, NJ: Erlbaum.

Pintrich, P. R., & Schunk, D. H. (1996). *Motivation in education: Theory, research, and applications.* Upper Saddle River, NJ: Merrill/Prentice Hall.

Pipher, M. (1994). *Reviving Ophelia: Saving the selves of adolescent girls.* New York: Putnam.

Plomin, R. (1989). Environment and genes: Determinants of behavior. *American Psychologist, 44,* 105–111.

Plomin, R. (1994). *Genetics and experience: The interplay between nature and nurture.* Thousand Oaks, CA: Sage.

Plomin, R., & DeFries, J. C. (1985). *Origins of individual differences in infancy.* New York: Academic Press.

Plomin, R., Emde, R. N., Braungart, J. M., Campos, J., Kagan, J., Reznick, J. S., Robinson, J., Zahn-Waxler, C., & DeFries, J. C. (1993). Genetic change and continuity from fourteen to twenty months: The MacArthur Longitudinal Twin Study. *Child Development, 64,* 1354–1376.

Plomin, R., Fulker, D. W., Corley, R., & DeFries, J. C. (1997). Nature, nurture, and cognitive development from 1 to 16 years: A parent-offspring adoption study. *Psychological Science, 8,* 442–447.

Plomin, R., Owen, M. J., & McGuffin, P. (1994). The genetic basis of complex human behaviors. *Science, 24,* 1733–1739.

Plomin, R., & Petrill, S. A. (1997). Genetics and intelligence: What's new? *Intelligence, 24,* 53–77.

Plumert, J. M. (1994). Flexibility in children's use of spatial and categorical organizational strategies in recall. *Developmental Psychology, 30,* 738–747.

Pogrow, S., & Londer, G. (1994). The effects of an intensive general thinking program on the motivation and cognitive development of at-risk students: Findings from the HOTS program. In H. F. O'Neil, Jr., & M. Drillings (Eds.), *Motivation: Theory and research.* Hillsdale, NJ: Erlbaum.

Pollack, W. (1998). *Real boys: Rescuing our sons from the myths of boyhood.* New York: Henry Holt.

Pollard, S. R., Kurtines, W. M., Carlo, G., Dancs, M., & Mayock, E. (1991). Moral education from the perspective of psychosocial theory. In W. M. Kurtines & J. L. Gewirtz (Eds.), *Moral behavior and development: Vol. 3. Application.* Hillsdale, NJ: Erlbaum.

Poresky, R. H., Daniels, A. M., Mukerjee, J., & Gunnell, K. (1999, April). *Community and family influences on adolescents' use of alcohol and other drugs: An exploratory ecological analysis.* Paper presented at the Biennial Meeting of the Society for Research in Child Development, Albuquerque, NM.

Portes, P. R. (1996). Ethnicity and culture in educational psychology. In D. C. Berliner & R. C. Calfee (Eds.), *Handbook of educational psychology.* New York: Macmillan.

Posner, G. J., Strike, K. A., Hewson, P. W., & Gertzog, W. A. (1982). Accommodation of a scientific conception: Toward a theory of conceptual change. *Science Education, 66,* 211–227.

Posner, J. (1982). The development of mathematical knowledge in two West African societies. *Child Development, 53,* 260–266.

Pospisil, L. (1958). Kapauku Papuans and their law. *Yale University Publications in Anthropology, No. 54.* New Haven, CT: Yale University Press.

Pospisil, L. (1959). *The Kapauku Papuans and their kinship organization.* Unpublished manuscript in the Human Relations Areas Files, Yale University, New Haven, CT.

Poulin, F., & Boivin, M. (1999). Proactive and reactive aggression and boys' friendship quality in mainstream classrooms. *Journal of Emotional and Behavioral Disorders, 7,* 168–177.

Powell, G. J. (1983). *The psychosocial development of minority children.* New York: Brunner/Mazel.

Power, F. C., Higgins, A., & Kohlberg, L. (1989). *Lawrence Kohlberg's approach to moral education.* New York: Columbia University Press.

Powers, L. E., Sowers, J. A., & Stevens, T. (1995). An exploratory, randomized study of the impact of mentoring on the self-efficacy and community-based knowledge of adolescents with severe physical challenges. *Journal of Rehabilitation, 61*(1), 33–41.

Powers, S. I., Hauser, S. T., & Kilner, L. A. (1989). Adolescent mental health. *American Psychologist, 44,* 200–208.

Powlishta, K. K. (1995). Intergroup processes in childhood: Social categorization and sex role development. *Developmental Psychology, 31,* 781–788.

Powlishta, K. K., Serbin, L. A., Doyle, A.-B., & White, D. R. (1994). Gender, ethnic, and body type biases: The generality of prejudice in childhood. *Developmental Psychology, 30,* 526–536.

Pramling, I. (1996). Understanding and empowering the child as learner. In D. R. Olson & N. Torrance (Eds.), *The handbook of education and human development: New models of learning, teaching, and schooling.* Cambridge, MA: Blackwell.

Prawat, R. S. (1989). Promoting access to knowledge, strategy, and disposition in students: A research synthesis. *Review of Educational Research, 59,* 1–41.

Pressley, M. (1982). Elaboration and memory development. *Child Development, 53,* 296–309.

Pressley, M. (1994). State-of-the-science primary-grades reading instruction or whole language? *Educational Psychologist, 29,* 211–215.

Pressley, M., Almasi, J., Schuder, T., Bergman, J., Hite, S., El-Dinary, P. B., & Brown, R. (1994). Transactional instruction of comprehension strategies: The Montgomery County Maryland SAIL program. *Reading and Writing Quarterly, 10,* 5–19.

Pressley, M., Borkowski, J. G., & Schneider, W. (1987). Cognitive strategies: Good strategy users coordinate metacognition and knowledge. In R. Vasta (Ed.), *Annals of child development* (Vol. 4). Greenwich, CT: JAI Press.

Pressley, M., El-Dinary, P. B., Marks, M. B., Brown, R., & Stein, S. (1992). Good strategy instruction is motivating and interesting. In K. A. Renninger, S. Hidi, & A. Krapp (Eds.), *The role of interest in learning and development.* Hillsdale, NJ: Erlbaum.

Pressley, M., Goodchild, F., Fleet, J., Zajchowski, R., & Evans, E. D. (1989). The challenges of classroom strategy instruction. *Elementary School Journal, 89,* 301–342.

Pressley, M., Levin, J. R., & Ghatala, E. S. (1984). Memory strategy monitoring in adults and children. *Journal of Verbal Learning and Verbal Behavior, 23,* 270–288.

Pressley, M., & McCormick, C. B. (1995). *Advanced educational psychology for educators, researchers, and policymakers.* New York: HarperCollins.

Pressley, M., Ross, K. A., Levin, J. R., & Ghatala, E. S. (1984). The role of strategy utility knowledge in children's strategy decision making. *Journal of Experimental Child Psychology, 38,* 491–504.

Price, L. N., & Clarke-McLean, J. G. (1997, April). *Beyond stereotypes: Configurations and competence among African American inner city youth.* Poster presented at the biennial meeting of the Society for Research in Child Development, Washington, DC.

Price-Williams, D. R., Gordon, W., & Ramirez, M. (1969). Skill and conservation. *Developmental Psychology, 1,* 769.

Pritchard, R. (1990). The effects of cultural schemata on reading processing strategies. *Reading Research Quarterly, 25,* 273–295.

Proctor, R. W., & Dutta, A. (1995). *Skill acquisition and human performance.* Thousand Oaks, CA: Sage.

Pulkkinen, L. (1982). Self-control and continuity from childhood to adolescence. In P. B. Baltes & O. G. Brim (Eds.), *Life-span development and behavior* (Vol. 4). Orlando, FL: Academic Press.

Pulos, S., & Linn, M. C. (1981). Generality of the controlling variables scheme in early adolescence. *Journal of Early Adolescence, 1,* 26–37.

Purcell-Gates, V. (1995). *Other people's words: The cycle of low literacy.* Cambridge, MA: Harvard University Press.

Purcell-Gates, V., McIntyre, E., & Freppon, P. A. (1995). Learning written storybook language in school: A comparison of low-SES children in skills-based and whole language classrooms. *American Educational Research Journal, 32,* 659–685.

Purdie, N., & Hattie, J. (1996). Cultural differences in the use of strategies for self-regulated learning. *American Educational Research Journal, 33,* 845–871.

Purdie, N., Hattie, J., & Douglas, G. (1996). Student conceptions of learning and their use of self-regulated learning strategies: A cross-cultural comparison. *Journal of Educational Psychology, 88,* 87–100.

Putallaz, M., & Gottman, J. M. (1981). Social skills and group acceptance. In S. R. Asher & J. M. Gottman (Eds.), *The development of children's friendships* (pp. 116–149). New York: Cambridge University Press.

Putallaz, M., & Heflin, A. H. (1986). Toward a model of peer acceptance. In J. M. Gottman & J. G. Parker (Eds.), *Conversations of friends: Speculations on affective development* (pp. 292–314). Cambridge, England: Cambridge University Press.

Rabain-Jamin, J. (1994). Language and socialization in young African-American children. In P. M. Greenfield & R. R. Cocking (Eds.), *Cross-cultural roots of minority child development* (pp. 147–166). Hillsdale, NJ: Erlbaum.

Rabinowitz, M., & Glaser, R. (1985). Cognitive structure and process in highly competent performance. In F. D. Horowitz & M. O'Brien (Eds.), *The gifted and the talented: Developmental perspectives.* Washington, DC: American Psychological Association.

Radziszewska, B., & Rogoff, B. (1991). Children's guided participation in planning imaginary errands with skilled adult or peer partners. *Developmental Psychology, 27,* 381–389.

Raikes, H. (1993). Relationship duration in infant care: Time with high-ability teacher and infant-teacher attachment. *Early Childhood Research Quarterly, 8*(3), 309–325.

Raine, A., & Scerbo, A. (1991). Biological theories of violence. In J. S. Milner (Ed.), *Neuropsychology of aggression* (pp. 1–25). Boston: Kluwer Academic Press.

Rallison, M. L. (1986). *Growth disorders in infants, children, and adolescents.* New York: Churchill Livingstone.

Ramachandran, V. S., Rogers-Ramachandran, D., & Stewart, M. (1992). Perceptual correlates of massive cortical reorganization. *Science, 258,* 1159–1160.

Ramey, C. T. (1992). High-risk children and IQ: Altering intergenerational patterns. *Intelligence, 16,* 239–256.

Ramey, C. T., & Ramey, S. L. (1998). Early intervention and early experience. *American Psychologist, 53,* 109–120.

Ramsey, P. G. (1987). *Teaching and learning in a diverse world: Multicultural education for young children.* New York: Teachers College Press.

Ramsey, P. G. (1995). Growing up with the contradictions of race and class. *Young Children, 50,* 18–22.

Raudenbush, S. W. (1984). Magnitude of teacher expectancy effects on pupil IQ as a function of credibility induction: A synthesis of findings from 18 experiments. *Journal of Educational Psychology, 76,* 85–97.

Rayport, S. G. (1992). Cellular and molecular biology of the neuron. In S. C. Yudofsky & R. E. Hales (Eds.), *The American Psychiatric Press textbook of neuropsychiatry* (2nd ed., pp. 3–28). Washington, DC: American Psychiatric Press.

Reese, D. F., & Thorkildsen, T. A. (1999, April). *Perceptions of exclusion among eighth graders from low-income families.* Paper presented at the annual meeting of the American Educational Research Association, Montreal.

Reeve, J., Bolt, E., & Cai, Y. (1999). Autonomy-supportive teachers: How they teach and motivate students. *Journal of Educational Psychology, 91,* 537–548.

Reich, P. A. (1986). *Language development.* Englewood Cliffs, NJ: Prentice Hall.

Reid, N. (1989). Contemporary Polynesian conceptions of giftedness. *Gifted Education International, 6*(1), 30–38.

Reifman, A., Barnes, G. M., & Hoffman, J. H. (1999, April). *Physical maturation and problem behaviors in male adolescents: A test of peer and parent relations as mediators.* Paper presented at the Biennial Meeting of the Society for Research in Child Development, Albuquerque, NM.

Reimer, J., Paolitto, D. P., & Hersh, R. H. (1983). *Promoting moral growth: From Piaget to Kohlberg* (2nd ed.). White Plains, NY: Longman.

Reis, S. M. (1989). Reflections on policy affecting the education of gifted and talented students: Past and future perspectives. *American Psychologist, 44,* 399–408.

Reiss, I. R. (1980). *Family systems in America* (3rd ed.). New York: Holt, Rinehart & Winston.

Renninger, K. A., Hidi, S., & Krapp, A. (Eds.). (1992). *The role of interest in learning and development.* Hillsdale, NJ: Erlbaum.

Renzulli, J. S. (1978). What makes giftedness? Reexamining a definition. *Phi Delta Kappan, 60,* 180–184.

Renzulli, J. S., & Reis, S. M. (1986). The enrichment triad/revolving door model: A school wide plan for the development of creative productivity. In J. Renzulli (Ed.), *Systems and models for developing programs for the gifted and talented.* Mansfield Center, CT: Creative Learning Press.

Reschly, D. J. (1997). Diagnostic and treatment utility of intelligence tests. In D. P. Flanagan, J. L. Genshaft, & P. L. Harrison (Eds.), *Contemporary intellectual assessment: Theories, tests, and issues* (pp. 437–456). New York: Guilford Press.

Resnick, L. B. (1989). Developing mathematical knowledge. *American Psychologist, 44,* 162–169.

Resnick, L. B. (1995). From aptitude to effort: A new foundation for our schools. *Daedalus, 124*(4), 55–62.

Resnicow, K., Cross, D., & Wynder, E. (1991). The role of comprehensive school-based interventions. *Annals of the New York Academy of Sciences, 623,* 285–298.

Reutzel, D. R., & Cooter, R. B., Jr. (1999). *Balanced reading strategies and practices.* Upper Saddle River, NJ: Merrill/Prentice Hall.

Reyna, V. F. (1996, May 2). Fuzzy-trace theory, reasoning, and decision-making. Presentation at the University of Northern Colorado, Greeley.

Reynolds, A. (1994). Effects of a preschool plus follow-on intervention for children at risk. *Developmental Psychology, 30,* 787–804.

Reynolds, A. J., Mavrogenes, N. A., Bezruczko, N., & Hagemann, M. (1996). Cognitive and family-support mediators of preschool effectiveness: A confirmatory analysis. *Child Development, 67,* 1119–1140.

Reynolds, D. R. (1999). *There goes the neighborhood: Rural school consolidation at the grass roots in early twentieth century Iowa.* Iowa City: University of Iowa Press.

Reynolds, R. E., Taylor, M. A., Steffensen, M. S., Shirey, L. L., & Anderson, R. C. (1982). Cultural schemata and reading comprehension. *Reading Research Quarterly, 17,* 353–366.

Ricciuti, H. N. (1993). Nutrition and mental development. *Current Directions in Psychological Science, 2,* 43–46.

Rice, M., Hadley, P. A., & Alexander, A. L. (1993). Social biases toward children with speech and language impairments: A correlative causal model of language limitations. *Applied Psycholinguistics, 14,* 445–471.

Rice, M. L., Huston, A. C., Truglio, R., & Wright, J. (1990). Words from "Sesame Street": Learning vocabulary while viewing. *Developmental Psychology, 26,* 421–428.

Richman, A. L., Miller, P. M., & Solomon, M. J. (1988). The socialization of infants in suburban Boston. In R. A. LeVine, P. M. Miller, & M. M. West (Eds.), *Parental behavior in diverse societies* (pp. 65–74). San Francisco, CA: Jossey-Bass.

Richman, N., Stevenson, J., & Graham, P. J. (1982). *Preschool to school: A behavioural study.* London: Academic Press.

Rimm, D. C., & Masters, J. C. (1974). *Behavior therapy: Techniques and empirical findings.* San Diego, CA: Academic Press.

Rinehart, S. D., Stahl, S. A., & Erickson, L. G. (1986). Some effects of summarization training on reading and studying. *Reading Research Quarterly, 21,* 422–438.

Ripple, C. H., Gilliam, W. S., Chanana, N., & Zigler, E. (1999). Will fifty cooks spoil the broth? The debate over entrusting Head Start to the states. *American Psychologist, 54,* 327–343.

Ritchie, D., Price, V., & Roberts, D. F. (1987). Television, reading, and reading achievement: A reappraisal. *Communication Research, 14,* 292–315.

Rittle-Johnson, B., & Siegler, R. S. (1999). Learning to spell: Variability, choice, and change in children's strategy use. *Child Development, 70,* 332–348.

Ritts, V., Patterson, M. L., & Tubbs, M. E. (1992). Expectations, impressions, and judgments of physically attractive students: A review. *Review of Educational Research, 62,* 413–426.

RMC Research Corporation. (1989). *The impact of Reading Rainbow on libraries.* Hampton, NH: RMC Corporation.

Roberge, J. J. (1970). A study of children's abilities to reason with basic principles of deductive reasoning. *American Educational Research Journal, 7,* 583–596.

Roberts, D. F., Christenson, P., Gibson, W. A., Mooser, L., & Goldberg, M. E. (1980). Developing discriminating consumers. *Journal of Communication, 30,* 94–105.

Robinson, T. N., & Killen, J. D. (1995). Ethnic and gender differences in the relationship between television viewing and obesity, physical activity, and dietary fat intake. *Journal of Health Education, 26*(Suppl. 2), S91–S98.

Robinson, T. R., Smith, S. W., Miller, M. D., & Brownell, M. T. (1999). Cognitive behavior modification of hyperactivity-impulsivity and aggression: A meta-analysis of school-based studies. *Journal of Educational Psychology, 91,* 195–203.

Roderick, M., & Camburn, E. (1999). Risk and recovery from course failure in the early years of high school. *American Educational Research Journal, 36,* 303–343.

Roffwarg, H. P., Muzio, J. N., & Dement, W. C. (1966). Ontogenetic development of the human sleep-dream cycle. *Science, 152,* 604–619.

Rogoff, B. (1990). *Apprenticeship in thinking: Cognitive development in social context.* New York: Oxford University Press.

Rogoff, B. (1991). Social interaction as apprenticeship in thinking: Guidance and participation in spatial planning. In L. B. Resnick, J. M. Levine, & S. D. Teasley (Eds.), *Perspectives on socially shared cognition.* Washington, DC: American Psychological Association.

Rogoff, B. (1994, April). *Developing understanding of the idea of communities of learners.* Paper presented at the annual meeting of the American Educational Research Association, New Orleans, LA.

Rogoff, B., Matusov, E., & White, C. (1996). Models of teaching and learning: Participation in a community of learners. In D. R. Olson & N.

Torrance (Eds.), *The handbook of education and human development: New models of learning, teaching, and schooling.* Cambridge, MA: Blackwell.

Rogoff, B., Mistry, J., Gönsü, A., & Mosier, C. (1993). Guided participation in cultural activity by toddlers and caregivers. *Monographs of the Society for Research in Child Development, 58* (8, Serial No. 236).

Rogoff, B., & Morelli, G. (1989). Perspectives on children's development from cultural psychology. *American Psychologist, 44,* 343–348.

Rohner, R. P. (1998). Father love and child development: History and current evidence. *Current Directions in Psychological Science, 7,* 157–161.

Rohner, R. P., & Rohner, E. C. (1981). Parental acceptance-rejection and parental control: Cross-cultural codes. *Ethnology, 20,* 245–260.

Rondal, J. A. (1985). *Adult-child interaction and the process of language acquisition.* New York: Praeger.

Roopnarine, J. L., Lasker, J., Sacks, M., & Stores, M. (1998). The cultural contexts of children's play. In O. N. Saracho & B. Spodek (Eds.), *Multiple perspectives on play in early childhood education.* Albany: State University of New York Press.

Rose, A. J., & Asher, S. R. (1999). Children's goals and strategies in response to conflicts within a friendship. *Developmental Psychology, 35,* 69–79.

Rose, S. C., & Thornburg, K. R. (1984). Mastery motivation and need for approval in young children: Effects of age, sex, and reinforcement condition. *Educational Research Quarterly, 9*(1), 34–42.

Rosenberg, M. (1986). Self-concept from middle childhood through adolescence. In S. Suls & A. Greenwald (Eds.), *Psychological perspectives on the self* (Vol. 3, pp. 107–135). Hillsdale, NJ: Erlbaum.

Rosenberg, M. L., O'Carroll, P., & Powell, K. (1992). Let's be clear: Violence is a public health problem. *Journal of the American Medical Association, 267,* 3071–3072.

Rosenhan, D. L. (1970). The natural socialization of altruistic autonomy. In J. Macaulay & L. Berkowitz (Eds.), *Altruism and helping behavior* (pp. 251–268). New York: Academic Press.

Rosenshine, B., & Meister, C. (1992). The use of scaffolds for teaching higher-level cognitive strategies. *Educational Leadership, 49*(7), 26–33.

Rosenshine, B., & Meister, C. (1994). Reciprocal teaching: A review of the research. *Review of Educational Research, 64,* 479–530.

Rosenshine, B., Meister, C., & Chapman, S. (1996). Teaching students to generate questions: A review of the intervention studies. *Review of Educational Research, 66,* 181–221.

Rosenstein, D., & Oster, H. (1988). Differential facial responses to four basic tastes in newborns. *Child Development, 59,* 1555–1568.

Rosenthal, R. (1994). Interpersonal expectancy effects: A 30-year perspective. *Current Directions in Psychological Science, 3,* 176–179.

Rosenthal, T. L., & Bandura, A. (1978). Psychological modeling: Theory and practice. In S. L. Garfield & A. E. Begia (Eds.), *Handbook of psychotherapy and behavior change: An empirical analysis* (2nd ed.). New York: Wiley.

Ross, J. A. (1988). Controlling variables: A meta-analysis of training studies. *Review of Educational Research, 58,* 405–437.

Ross, S. M., Smith, L. J., Casey, J., & Slavin, R. E. (1995). Increasing the academic success of disadvantaged children: An examination of alternative early intervention programs. *American Educational Research Journal, 32,* 773–800.

Rosser, R. (1994). *Cognitive development: Psychological and biological perspectives.* Boston: Allyn & Bacon.

Rossi, A. S., & Rossi, P. H. (1990). *Of human bonding: Parent-child relations across the life course.* New York: Aldine de Gruyter.

Rossman, B. R. (1992). School-age children's perceptions of coping with distress: Strategies for emotion regulation and the moderation of adjustment. *Journal of Child Psychology and Psychiatry, 33,* 1373–1397.

Rotenberg, K. J., & Mayer, E. V. (1990). Delay of gratification in Native and White children: A cross-cultural comparison. *International Journal of Behavioral Development, 13,* 23–30.

Rotenberg, K. K., Simourd, L., & Moore, D. (1989). Children's use of verbal-nonverbal consistency principle to infer truth and lying. *Child Development, 60,* 309–322.

Roth, K. J. (1990). Developing meaningful conceptual understanding in science. In B. F. Jones & L. Idol (Eds.), *Dimensions of thinking and cognitive instruction.* Hillsdale, NJ: Erlbaum.

Roth, K. J., & Anderson, C. (1988). Promoting conceptual change learning from science textbooks. In P. Ramsden (Ed.), *Improving learning: New perspectives.* London: Kogan Page.

Roth, W., & Bowen, G. M. (1995). Knowing and interacting: A study of culture, practices, and resources in a grade 8 open-inquiry science classroom guided by a cognitive apprenticeship metaphor. *Cognition and Instruction, 13,* 73–128.

Rothbart, M. K., & Ahadi, S. A. (1994). Temperament and the development of personality. *Journal of Abnormal Psychology, 103,* 55–66.

Rothbart, M. K., & Bates, J. E. (1998). Temperament. In W. Damon (Editor-in-Chief) & N. Eisenberg (Vol. Ed.), *Handbook of child psychology: Vol. 3. Social, emotional, and personality development* (5th ed., pp. 105–176). New York: Wiley.

Rothbart, M. K., Hanley, D., & Albert, M. (1986). Gender differences in moral reasoning. *Sex Roles, 15,* 645–653.

Rothbaum, F., Weisz, J., Pott, M., Miyake, K., & Morelli, G. (2000). Attachment and culture: Security in the United States and Japan. *American Psychologist, 55,* 1093–1104.

Rowe, D. C., Almeida, D. M., & Jacobson, K. C. (1999). School context and genetic influences on aggression in adolescence. *Psychological Science, 10,* 277–280.

Rowe, D. C., Jacobson, K. C., & Van den Oord, E. J. C. G. (1999). Genetic and environmental influences on Vocabulary IQ: Parental education level as moderator. *Child Development, 70,* 1151–1162.

Rowe, D. W., & Harste, J. C. (1986). Metalinguistic awareness in writing and reading: The young child as curricular informant. In D. B. Yaden, Jr., & S. Templeton (Eds.), *Metalinguistic awareness and beginning literacy: Conceptualizing what it means to read and write.* Portsmouth, NH: Heinemann.

Rowe, E. (1999, April). *Gender differences in math self-concept development: The role of classroom interaction.* Paper presented at the annual meeting of the American Educational Research Association, Montreal, Canada.

Rowe, M. B. (1974). Wait-time and rewards as instructional variables, their influence on language, logic, and fate control: Part one—wait time. *Journal of Research in Science Teaching, 11,* 81–94.

Rowe, M. B. (1987). Wait-time: Slowing down may be a way of speeding up. *American Educator, 11,* 38–43, 47.

Rowland, T. W. (1990). *Exercise and children's health.* Champaign, IL: Human Kinetics.

Royce, J. M., Darlington, R. B., & Murray, H. W. (1983). Pooled analyses: Findings across studies. In Consortium for Longitudinal Studies (Ed.), *As the twig is bent: Lasting effects of preschool programs.* Hillsdale, NJ: Erlbaum.

Rubin, K., Fein, G., & Vandenberg, B. (1983). Play. In E. M. Hetherington (Ed.), *Handbook of child psychology: Vol. 4. Socialization, personality, and social development* (pp. 693–774). New York: Wiley.

Rubin, K. H., Bukowski, W., & Parker, J. G. (1998). Peer interactions, relationships, and groups. In W. Damon (Editor in Chief) & N. Eisenberg (Vol. Ed.), *Handbook of child psychology: Vol. 3. Social, emotional, and personality development* (pp. 619–700). New York: Wiley.

Rubin, K. H., Coplan, R. J., Fox, N. A., & Calkins, S. (1995). Emotionality, emotion regulation, and preschoolers' social adaptation. *Development and Psychopathology, 7,* 49–62.

Rubin, K. H., & Krasnor, L. R. (1986). Social-cognitive and social behavioral perspectives on problem solving. In M. Perlmutter (Ed.), *Minnesota symposia on child psychology: Vol. 19. Cognitive perspectives on children's social and behavioral development.* Hillsdale, NJ: Erlbaum.

Rubin, K. H., Lynch, D., Coplan, R., Rose-Krasnor, L., & Booth, C. L. (1994). "Birds of a feather": Behavioral concordances and preferential personal attraction in children. *Child Development, 65,* 1778–1785.

Rubin, K. H., & Pepler, D. J. (1995). The relationship of child's play to social-cognitive growth and development. In H. C. Foot, A. J. Chapman, & J. R. Smith (Eds.), *Friendship and social relations in children* (pp. 209–233). New Brunswick, NJ: Transaction.

Ruble, D. N., & Martin, C. L. (1998). Gender development. In W. Damon (Editor-in-Chief) & N. Eisenberg (Vol. Ed.), *Handbook of child psychology: Vol. 3. Social, emotional, and personality development* (5th ed., pp. 933–1016). New York: Wiley.

Rudlin, C. R. (1993). Growth and sexual development: What is normal, and what is not? *Journal of the American Academy of Physician Assistants, 6,* 25–35.

Rueda, R., & Moll, L. C. (1994). A sociocultural perspective on motivation. In H. F. O'Neil, Jr., & M. Drillings (Eds.), *Motivation: Theory and research.* Hillsdale, NJ: Erlbaum.

Ruff, H. A., & Lawson, K. R. (1990). Development of sustained, focused attention in young children during free play. *Developmental Psychology, 26,* 85–93.

Ruffman, T., Perner, J., Naito, M., Parkin, L., & Clements, W. A. (1998). Older (but not younger) siblings facilitate false belief understanding. *Developmental Psychology, 34*(1), 161–174.

Ruffman, T., Perner, J., Olson, D. R., & Doherty, M. (1993). Reflecting on scientific thinking: Children's understanding of the hypothesis-evidence relation. *Child Development, 64,* 1617–1636.

Rumberger, R. W. (1995). Dropping out of middle school: A multilevel analysis of students and schools. *American Educational Research Journal, 32,* 583–625.

Rushton, J. P. (1980). *Altruism, socialization, and society.* Upper Saddle River, NJ: Prentice Hall.

Rushton, J. P., Fulkner, D. W., Neal, M. C., Nias, D. K. B., & Eysenck, H. J. (1986). Altruism and aggression: The heritability of individual differences. *Journal of Personality and Social Psychology, 50,* 1192–1198.

Rushton, J. P., & Teachman, G. (1978). The effects of positive reinforcement, attributions, and punishment on model induced altruism in children. *Personality and Social Psychology Bulletin, 4,* 322–325.

Russell, A., & Russell, G. (1994). Coparenting early school-age children: An examination of mother-father independence within families. *Developmental Psychology, 30,* 757–770.

Rutter, M. (1989). Pathways from childhood to adult life. *Journal of Child Psychology and Psychiatry, 31,* 5–37.

Rutter, M., Champion, L., Quinton, D., Maughan, B., & Pickles, A. (1995). Understanding individual differences in environmental-risk exposure. In P. Moen, G. H. Elder, Jr., & K. Lüscher (Eds.), *Examining lives in context: Perspectives on the ecology of human development* (pp. 61–93). Washington, DC: American Psychological Association.

Rutter, M., & Garmezy, N. (1983). Developmental psychopathology. In P. H. Mussen (Series Ed.) & E. M. Hetherington (Vol. Ed.), *Handbook of child psychology: Vol. 4. Socialization, personality, and social development* (4th ed., pp. 775–911). New York: Wiley.

Rutter, M. L. (1997). Nature-nurture integration: The example of antisocial behavior. *American Psychologist, 52,* 390–398.

Ryan, A. M. (2000). Peer groups as a context for the socialization of adolescents' motivation, engagement, and achievement in school. *Educational Psychologist, 35,* 101–111.

Ryan, E. B., Ledger, G. W., & Weed, K. A. (1987). Acquisition and transfer of an integrative imagery strategy by young children. *Child Development, 58,* 443–452.

Ryan, R. M., Connell, J. P., & Grolnick, W. S. (1992). When achievement is *not* intrinsically motivated: A theory of internalization and self-regulation in school. In A. K. Boggiano & T. S. Pittman (Eds.), *Achievement and motivation: A social-developmental perspective.* Cambridge, England: Cambridge University Press.

Ryan, R. M., & Kuczkowski, R. (1994). The imaginary audience, self-consciousness, and public individuation in adolescence. *Journal of Personality, 62,* 219–237.

Ryan, R. M., & Lynch, J. H. (1989). Emotional autonomy versus detachment: Revisiting the vicissitudes of adolescence and young adulthood. *Child Development, 60,* 340–356.

Ryan, R. M., Mims, V., & Koestner, R. (1983). Relation of reward contingency and interpersonal context to intrinsic motivation: A review and test using cognitive evaluation theory. *Journal of Personality and Social Psychology, 45,* 736–750.

Ryan, R. M., Stiller, J. D., & Lynch, J. H. (1994). Representations of relationships to teachers, parents, and friends as predictors of academic motivation and self-esteem. *Journal of Early Adolescence, 14,* 226–249.

Saarni, C., Mumme, D. L., & Campos, J. J. (1998). Emotional development: Action, communication, and understanding. In W. Damon (Editor-in-Chief) & N. Eisenberg (Vol. Ed.), *Handbook of child psychology: Vol. 3. Social, emotional, and personality development* (5th ed., pp. 237–309). New York: Wiley.

Sacks, C. H., & Mergendoller, J. R. (1997). The relationship between teachers' theoretical orientation toward reading and student outcomes in kindergarten children with different initial reading abilities. *American Educational Research Journal, 34,* 721–739.

Sadker, M., & Sadker, A. (1988). *Sex equity handbook for schools* (2nd ed.). New York: Longman.

Sadker, M. P., & Sadker, D. (1994). *Failing at fairness: How our schools cheat girls.* New York: Touchstone.

Saffran, J. R., Aslin, R. N., & Newport, E. L. (1996). Statistical learning by 8-month-old infants. *Science, 274,* 1926–1928.

Sagi, A., & Lewkowicz, K. S. (1987). A cross-cultural evaluation of attachment research. In L. W. C. Tavecchio & M. H. van Ijzendoorn (Eds.), *Attachment in social networks* (pp. 427–459). Amsterdam, The Netherlands: Elsevier.

Salend, S. J., & Taylor, L. (1993). Working with families: A cross-cultural perspective. *Remedial and Special Education, 14*(5), 25–32, 39.

Salisbury, C. L., Evans, I. M., & Palombaro, M. M. (1997). Collaborative problem solving to promote the inclusion of young children with significant disabilities in primary grades. *Exceptional Children, 63,* 195–210.

Sallis, J. F. (1993). Epidemiology of physical activity and fitness in children and adolescents. *Critical Reviews in Food Science and Nutrition, 33*(4–5), 403–408.

Saltz, E. (1971). *The cognitive bases of human learning.* Homewood, IL: Dorsey.

Sameroff, A., Seifer, R., Barocas, R., Zax, M., & Greenspan, S. (1987). Intelligent quotient scores of 4-year-old children: Social environmental risk factors. *Pediatrics, 79*(3), 343–360.

Sameroff, A. J., Seifer, R., Baldwin, A., & Baldwin, C. (1993). Stability of intelligence from preschool to adolescence: The influence of social and family risk factors. *Child Development, 64,* 80–97.

Sampson, R. J., & Groves, W. B. (1989). Community structure and crime: Testing social disorganization theory. *American Journal of Sociology, 94,* 774–802.

Sanborn, M. P. (1979). Counseling and guidance needs of the gifted and talented. In A. H. Passow (Ed.), *The gifted and the talented: Their education and development. The seventy-eighth yearbook of the National Society for the Study of Education.* Chicago: University of Chicago Press.

Sanchez, F., & Anderson, M. L. (1990). Gang mediation: A process that works. *Principal, 69*(4), 54–56.

Sanders, C. E. (1997). Assessment during the preschool years. In G. D. Phye (Ed.), *Handbook of classroom assessment: Learning, achievement, and adjustment.* San Diego, CA: Academic Press.

Sanders, M. G. (1996). Action teams in action: Interviews and observations in three schools in the Baltimore School-Family-Community Partnership Program. *Journal of Education for Students Placed at Risk, 1,* 249–262.

Sands, D. J., & Wehmeyer, M. L. (Eds.). (1996). *Self-determination across the life span: Independence and choice for people with disabilities.* Baltimore: Brookes.

Sasso, G. M., Melloy, K. J., & Kavale, K. A. (1990). Generalization, maintenance, and behavior covariation associated with social skills training through structured learning. *Behavioral Disorders, 16*(1), 9–22.

Savin-Williams, R. C. (1989). Gay and lesbian adolescents. *Marriage and Family Review, 14*(3/4), 197–216.

Savin-Williams, R. C. (1995). Lesbian, gay male, and bisexual adolescents. In R. D'Augelli & C. J. Patterson (Eds.), Lesbian, gay, and bisexual identities over the lifespan: Psychological perspectives (pp. 165–189). New York: Oxford University Press.

Savin-Williams, R. C., & Demo, D. H. (1984). Developmental change and stability in adolescent self-concept. *Developmental Psychology, 20,* 1100–1110.

Savin-Williams, R. C., & Diamond, L. M. (1997). Sexual orientation as a developmental context for lesbians, gays, and bisexuals: Biological perspectives. In N. L. Segal, G. E. Weisfeld, & C. C. Weisfeld (Eds.), *Uniting psychology and biology: Integrative perspectives on human development* (pp. 217–238). Washington, DC: American Psychological Association.

Sawyer, R. J., Graham, S., & Harris, K. R. (1992). Direct teaching, strategy instruction, and strategy instruction with explicit self-regulation: Effects on the composition skills and self-efficacy of students with learning disabilities. *Journal of Educational Psychology, 84,* 340–352.

Saxe, G. B., & Posner, J. (1983). The development of numerical cognition: Cross-cultural perspectives. In H. P. Ginsburg (Ed.), *The development of mathematical thinking* (pp. 291–317). New York: Academic Press.

Scardamalia, M., & Bereiter, C. (1985). Fostering the development of self-regulation in children's knowledge processing. In S. F. Chipman, J. W. Segal, & R. Glaser (Eds.), *Thinking and learning skills: Vol. 2. Research and open questions.* Hillsdale, NJ: Erlbaum.

Scardamalia, M., & Bereiter, C. (1986). Research on written composition. In M. C. Wittrock (Ed.), *Handbook of research on teaching* (3rd ed.). New York: Macmillan.

Scardamalia, M., Bereiter, C., & Goelman, H. (1982). The role of production factors in writing ability. In M. Nystrand (Ed.), *What writers know: The language, process, and structure of written discourse.* New York: Academic Press.

Scarr, S. (1992). Developmental theories for the 1990s: Development and individual differences. *Child Development, 63,* 1–19.

Scarr, S. (1993). Biological and cultural diversity: The legacy of Darwin for development. *Child Development, 64,* 1333–1353.

Scarr, S. (1997). Behavior-genetic and socialization theories of intelligence: Truce and reconciliation. In R. J. Sternberg & E. L. Grigorenko (Eds.), *Intelligence, heredity, and environment* (pp. 3–41). Cambridge, England: Cambridge University Press.

Scarr, S. (1998). American child care today. *American Psychologist, 53,* 95–108.

Scarr, S., & McCartney, K. (1983). How people make their own environments: A theory of genotype environment effects. *Child Development, 54,* 424–435.

Scarr, S., & Weinberg, R. A. (1976). IQ test performance of black children adopted by white families. *American Psychologist, 31,* 726–739.

Schiefele, U. (1996). Topic interest, text representation, and quality of experience. *Contemporary Educational Psychology, 21,* 3–18.

Schiefele, U., Krapp, A., & Winteler, A. (1992). Interest as a predictor of academic achievement: A meta-analysis of research. In K. A. Renninger, S. Hidi, & A. Krapp (Eds.), *The role of interest in learning and development.* Hillsdale, NJ: Erlbaum.

Schimmoeller, M. A. (1998, April). *Influence of private speech on the writing behaviors of young children: Four case studies.* Paper presented at the annual meeting of the American Educational Research Association, San Diego, CA.

Schinke, S. P., Moncher, M. S., & Singer, B. R. (1994). Native American youths and cancer risk prevention. *Journal of Adolescent Health, 15,* 105–110.

Schlaefli, A., Rest, J. R., & Thoma, S. J. (1985). Does moral education improve moral judgment? A meta-analysis of intervention studies using the defining issues test. *Review of Educational Research, 55,* 319–352.

Schliemann, A. D., & Carraher, D. W. (1993). Proportional reasoning in and out of school. In P. Light and G. Butterworth (Eds.), *Context and cognition: Ways of learning and knowing.* Hillsdale, NJ: Erlbaum.

Schloss, P. J., & Smith, M. A. (1994). *Applied behavior analysis in the classroom.* Needham Heights, MA: Allyn & Bacon.

Schneider, J. J. (1998, April). *Developing multiple perspectives and audience awareness in elementary writers.* Paper presented at the annual meeting of the American Educational Research Association, San Diego, CA.

Schneider, W., & Pressley, M. (1989). *Memory development between 2 and 20.* New York: Springer-Verlag.

Schneider, W., Roth, E., & Ennemoser, M. (2000). Training phonological skills and letter knowledge in children at risk for dyslexia: A comparison of three kindergarten intervention programs. *Journal of Educational Psychology, 92,* 284–295.

Schneider, W., & Shiffrin, R. M. (1977). Controlled and automatic human information processing: I. Detection, search, and attention. *Psychological Review, 84,* 1–66.

Schnur, E., Brooks-Gunn, J., & Shipman, V. C. (1992). Who attends programs serving poor children? The case of Head Start attendees and nonattendees. *Journal of Applied Developmental Psychology, 13,* 405–421.

Schofield, J. W. (1995). Improving intergroup relations among students. In J. A. Banks & C. A. M. Banks (Eds.), *Handbook of research on multicultural education.* New York: Macmillan.

Schommer, M. (1994a). An emerging conceptualization of epistemological beliefs and their role in learning. In R. Garner & P. A. Alexander (Eds.), *Beliefs about text and instruction with text.* Hillsdale, NJ: Erlbaum.

Schommer, M. (1994b). Synthesizing epistemological belief research: Tentative understandings and provocative confusions. *Educational Psychology Review, 6,* 293–319.

Schommer, M. (1997). The development of epistemological beliefs among secondary students: A longitudinal study. *Journal of Educational Psychology, 89,* 37–40.

Schonert-Reichl, K. A. (1993). Empathy and social relationships in adolescents with behavioral disorders. *Behavioral Disorders, 18,* 189–204.

Schore, A. N. (1994). *Affect regulation and the origin of the self: The neurobiology of emotional development.* Hillsdale, NJ: Erlbaum.

Schratz, M. (1978). A developmental investigation of sex differences in spatial (visual-analytic) and mathematical skills in three ethnic groups. *Developmental Psychology, 14,* 263–267.

Schraw, G., Potenza, M. T., & Nebelsick-Gullet, L. (1993). Constraints on the calibration of performance. *Contemporary Educational Psychology, 18,* 455–463.

Schreibman, L. (1988). *Autism.* Newbury Park, CA: Sage.

Schroth, M. L. (1992). The effects of delay of feedback on a delayed concept formation transfer task. *Contemporary Educational Psychology, 17,* 78–82.

Schultz, G. F., & Switzky, H. N. (1990). The development of intrinsic motivation in students with learning problems: Suggestions for more effective instructional practice. *Preventing School Failure, 34*(2), 14–20.

Schumpf, F., Crawford, D., & Usadel, H. C. (1991). *Peer mediation: Conflict resolution in schools.* Champaign, IL: Research Press.

Schunk, D. H. (1989). Self-efficacy and cognitive skill learning. In C. Ames & R. Ames (Eds.), *Research on motivation in education: Vol. 3. Goals and cognitions.* San Diego, CA: Academic Press.

Schunk, D. H. (1990, April). *Socialization and the development of self-regulated learning: The role of attributions.* Paper presented at the annual meeting of the American Educational Research Association, Boston.

Schunk, D. H. (2000). *Learning theories: An educational perspective* (3rd ed.). Upper Saddle River, NJ: Merrill/Prentice Hall.

Schunk, D. H., & Hanson, A. R. (1985). Peer models: Influence on children's self-efficacy and achievement. *Journal of Educational Psychology, 77,* 313–322.

Schunk, D. H., Hanson, A. R., & Cox, P. D. (1987). Peer-model attributes and children's achievement behaviors. *Journal of Educational Psychology, 79,* 54–61.

Schunk, D. H., & Swartz, C. W. (1993). Goals and progress feedback: Effects on self-efficacy and writing achievement. *Contemporary Educational Psychology, 18,* 337–354.

Schunk, D. H., & Zimmerman, B. J. (1997). Social origins of self-regulatory competence. *Educational Psychologist, 32,* 195–208.

Schutz, P. A. (1994). Goals as the transactive point between motivation and cognition. In P. R. Pintrich, D. R. Brown, & C. E. Weinstein (Eds.), *Student motivation, cognition, and learning: Essays in honor of Wilbert J. McKeachie.* Hillsdale, NJ: Erlbaum.

Schwartz, D., Dodge, K. A., Coie, J. D., Hubbard, J. A., Cillessen, A. H., Lemerise, E. A., & Bateman, H. (1998). Social-cognitive and behavioral correlates of aggression and victimization in boys' play groups. *Journal of Abnormal Child Psychology, 26*(6), 431–440.

Schwartz, D., Dodge, K. A., Pettit, G. S., & Bates, J. E. (1997). The early socialization of aggressive victims of bullying. *Child Development, 68,* 665–675.

Schwartz, D., McFadyen-Ketchum, S., Dodge, K. A., Pettit, G. S., & Bates, J. E. (1999). Early behavior problems as a predictor of later peer victimization: Moderators and mediators in the pathways of social risk. *Journal of Abnormal Child Psychology, 27,* 191–201.

Schwartz, G. M., Izard, C. E., & Ansul, S. E. (1985). The 5-month-old's ability to discriminate facial expressions of emotion. *Infant Behavior and Development, 8,* 65–67.

Schweinhart, L. J., Barnes, H. V., & Weikart, D. P. (1993). *Significant benefits: The High/Scope Perry Preschool Study through age 27.* Ypsilanti, MI: High/Scope.

Schweinhart, L. J., & Weikart, D. (1983). The effects of the Perry Preschool Program on youths through age 15: A summary. In Consortium for Longitudinal Studies (Eds.), *As the twig is bent: Lasting effects of preschool programs* (pp. 71–101). Hillsdale, NJ: Erlbaum.

Scott-Jones, D. (1984). Family influences on cognitive development and school achievement. In E. W. Gordon (Ed.), *Review of research in education* (Vol. 11). Washington, DC: American Educational Research Association.

Scott-Jones, D. (1991). Black families and literacy. In S. B. Silvern (Eds.), *Advances in reading/ language research: Literacy through family,* community, and school interaction (pp. 173–200). Greenwich, CT: JAI Press.

Scott-Little, M., & Holloway, S. (1992). Child care providers' reasoning about misbehaviors: Relation to classroom control strategies and professional training. *Early Childhood Research Quarterly, 7,* 595–606.

Seaton, E., Rodriguez, A., Jacobson, L., Taylor, R., Caintic, R., & Dale, P. (1999, April). *Influence of economic resources on family organization and achievement in economically disadvantaged African-American families.* Paper presented at the annual meeting of the American Educational Research Association, Montreal.

Sebald, H. (1986). Adolescents' shifting orientation toward parents and peers: A curvilinear trend over recent decades. *Journal of Marriage and the Family, 48,* 5–13.

Seefeldt, C., Denton, K., Galper, A., & Younoszai, T. (1999). The relation between Head Start parents' participation in a transition demonstration, education, efficacy, and their children's academic abilities. *Early Childhood Research Quarterly, 14*(1), 99–109.

Seeley, K. (1989). Facilitators for the gifted. In J. Feldhusen, J. VanTassel-Baska, & K. Seeley, *Excellence in educating the gifted.* Denver, CO: Love.

Segal, B. M., & Stewart, J. C. (1996). Substance use and abuse in adolescence: An overview. *Child Psychiatry and Human Development, 26,* 193–210.

Segal, N. L. (2000). Virtual twins: New findings on within-family environmental influences on intelligence. *Journal of Educational Psychology, 92,* 442–448.

Seitz, V., Rosenbaum, L. K., & Apfel, N. H. (1985). Effects of family support intervention: A ten-year follow-up. *Child Development, 56,* 376–391.

Seligman, M. E. P. (1975). *Helplessness: On depression, development, and death.* San Francisco: Freeman.

Seligman, M. E. P. (1991). *Learned optimism.* New York: Knopf.

Selman, R. L. (1980). *The growth of interpersonal understanding.* San Diego, CA: Academic Press.

Selman, R. L., & Byrne, D. F. (1974). A structural-developmental analysis of levels of role taking in middle childhood. *Child Development, 45,* 803–806.

Selman, R. L., & Schultz, L. J. (1990). *Making a friend in youth: Developmental theory and pair therapy.* Chicago: University of Chicago Press.

Seltzer, V. C. (1982). *Adolescent social development: Dynamic functional interaction.* Lexington, MA: Heath.

Semrud-Clikeman, M., & Hynd, G. W. (1991). Specific nonverbal and social skills deficits in children with learning disabilities. In J. E. Obrzut & G. W. Hynd (Eds.), *Neuropsychological foundations of learning disabilities: A handbook of issues, methods, and practice* (pp. 603–630). San Diego, CA: Academic Press.

Sénéchal, M., Thomas, E., & Monker, J. (1995). Individual differences in 4-year-old children's acquisition of vocabulary during storybook reading. *Journal of Educational Psychology, 87,* 218–229.

Seuss, Dr. (1960). *One fish two fish red fish blue fish.* New York: Beginner Books.

Sewald, H. (1986). Adolescents' shifting orientation toward parents and peers: A curvilinear trend over recent decades. *Journal of Marriage and the Family, 48,* 5–13.

Shaffer, D. R. (1988). *Social and personality development* (2nd ed.). Pacific Grove, CA: Brooks/Cole.

Shanahan, T., & Tierney, R. J. (1990). Reading-writing connections: The relations among three perspectives. In J. Zutell & S. McCormick (Eds.), *Literacy theory and research: Analyses from multiple paradigms. Thirty-ninth yearbook of the National Reading Conference.* Chicago: National Reading Conference.

Share, D. L., & Gur, T. (1999). How reading begins: A study of preschoolers' print identification strategies. *Cognition and Instruction, 17,* 177–213.

Shatz, M., & Gelman, R. (1973). The development of communication skills: Modifications in the speech of young children as a function of the listener. *Monographs of the Society for Research in Child Development, 38*(5, Serial No. 152).

Shaw, C. C. (1993). Multicultural teacher education: A call for conceptual change. *Multicultural Education, 1*(2), 22–26.

Shaw, D. S., Vondra, J. I., Hommerding, K. D., Keenan, K., & Dunn, M. (1994). Chronic family adversity and early child behavior problems: A longitudinal study of low income families. *Journal of Child Psychology and Psychiatry, 35,* 1109–1122.

Shaywitz, S. E., Escobar, M. D., Shaywitz, B. A., Fletcher, J. M., & Makuch, R. (1992). Evidence that dyslexia may represent the lower tail of a normal distribution of reading ability. *The New England Journal of Medicine, 326,* 145–150.

Sheckley, B. G., & Keeton, M. T. (1997). Service learning: A theoretical model. In J. Schine (Ed.), *Service learning.* Chicago: The National Society for the Study of Education.

Sheehan, E. P., & Smith, H. V. (1986). Cerebral lateralization and handedness and their effects on verbal and spatial reasoning. *Neuropsychologia, 24,* 531–540.

Sheingold, K. (1973). Developmental differences in intake and storage of visual information. *Journal of Experimental Child Psychology, 16,* 1–11.

Sheldon, A. (1974). The role of parallel function in the acquisition of relative clauses in English. *Journal of Verbal Learning and Verbal Behavior, 13,* 272–281.

Shephard, L., & Smith, M. L. (1987, October). Effects of kindergarten retention at the end of the first grade. *Psychology in the Schools, 24,* 346–357.

Shephard, L., & Smith, M. L. (Eds.). (1989). *Flunking grades: Research and policy on retention.* Philadelphia: Falmer Press.

Shephard, L. A., & Smith, M. L. (1988). Escalating academic demand in kindergarten: Counterproductive policies. *The Elementary School Journal, 89,* 135–144.

Sheridan, M. D. (1975). *Children's developmental progress from birth to five years: The Stycar Sequences.* Windsor, England: NFER.

Sherif, M., Harvey, O. J., White, B. J., Hood, W. R., & Sherif, C. (1961). *Inter-group conflict and cooperation: The Robbers Cave experiment.* Norman: University of Oklahoma Press.

Sherrill, D., Horowitz, B., Friedman, S. T., & Salisbury, J. L. (1970). Seating aggregation as an index of contagion. *Educational and Psychological Measurement, 30,* 663–668.

Sheveland, D. E. (1994, April). *Motivational factors in the development of independent readers.* Paper presented at the annual meeting of the American Educational Research Association, New Orleans, LA.

Shoda, Y., Mischel, W., & Peake, P. K. (1990). Predicting adolescent cognitive and self-regulatory competencies from preschool delay of gratification: Identifying diagnostic conditions. *Developmental Psychology, 26,* 978–986.

Short, E. J., & Ryan, E. B. (1984). Metacognitive differences between skilled and less skilled read-

ers: Remediating deficits through story grammar and attribution training. *Journal of Educational Psychology, 76,* 225–235.

Short, E. J., Schatschneider, C. W., & Friebert, S. E. (1993). Relationship between memory and metamemory performance: A comparison of specific and general strategy knowledge. *Journal of Educational Psychology, 85,* 412–423.

Shrum, W., & Cheek, N. H. (1987). Social structure during the school years: Onset of the degrouping process. *American Sociological Review, 52,* 218–223.

Shuell, T. J. (1996). Teaching and learning in a classroom context. In D. C. Berliner & R. C. Calfee (Eds.), *Handbook of educational psychology.* New York: Macmillan.

Shulman, S., Elicker, J., & Sroufe, L. A. (1994). Stages of friendship growth in preadolescence as related to attachment history. *Journal of Social and Personal Relationships, 11,* 341–361.

Shultz, T. R. (1974). Development of the appreciation of riddles. *Child Development, 45,* 100–105.

Shultz, T. R., & Horibe, F. (1974). Development of the appreciation of verbal jokes. *Developmental Psychology, 10,* 13–20.

Shure, M. B., & Spivack, G. (1980). Interpersonal problem-solving as a mediator of behavioral adjustment in preschool and kindergarten children. *Journal of Applied Developmental Psychology, 1,* 29–44.

Shweder, R. A., Goodnow, J., Hatano, G., LeVine, R. A., Markus, H., & Miller, P. (1998). The cultural psychology of development: One mind, many mentalities. In W. Damon (Editor-in-Chief) & R. M. Lerner (Vol. Ed.), *Handbook of child psychology: Vol. 1. Theoretical models of human development* (5th ed., pp. 865–937). New York: Wiley.

Shweder, R. A., Mahapatra, M., & Miller, J. G. (1987). Culture and moral development. In J. Kagan & S. Lamb (Eds.), *The emergence of morality in young children* (pp. 1–83). Chicago: University of Chicago Press.

Shweder, R. A., & Miller, J. G. (1985). The social construction of the person: How is it possible? In K. J. Gergen & K. Davis (Eds.), *The social construction of the person* (pp. 41–69). New York: Springer-Verlag.

Shweder, R. A., Much, N. C., Mahapatra, M., & Park, L. (1997). The "big three" of morality (autonomy, community, and divinity) and the "big three" explanations of suffering. In A. Brandt & P. Rozin (Eds.), *Morality and health* (pp. 119–169). Stanford, CA: Stanford University Press.

Sickmund, M., Snyder, H. N., & Poe-Yamagata, E. (1997). *Juvenile offenders and victims: 1997 Update on violence.* Washington, DC: Office of Juvenile Justice and Delinquency Prevention.

Sidel, R. (1996). *Keeping women and children last: America's war on the poor.* New York: Penguin Books.

Siegler, R. S. (1976). Three aspects of cognitive development. *Cognitive Psychology, 8,* 481–520.

Siegler, R. S. (1978). The origins of scientific reasoning. In R. S. Siegler (Ed.), *Children's thinking: What develops?* Hillsdale, NJ: Erlbaum.

Siegler, R. S. (1981). Developmental sequences within and between concepts. *Monographs of the Society for Research in Child Development, 46*(2, Serial No. 189).

Siegler, R. S. (1989). Mechanisms of cognitive growth. *Annual Review of Psychology, 40,* 353–379.

Siegler, R. S. (1991). *Children's thinking* (2nd ed.). Upper Saddle River, NJ: Prentice Hall.

Siegler, R. S. (1994). Cognitive variability: A key to understanding cognitive development. *Current Directions in Psychological Science, 3,* 1–5.

Siegler, R. S. (1996a). A grand theory of development. In R. Case & Y. Okamoto, in collaboration with S. Griffin, A. McKeough, C. Bleiker, B. Henderson, & K. M. Stephenson (1996). The role of central conceptual structures in the development of children's thought. *Monographs of the Society for Research in Child Development, 61*(1, Serial No. 246).

Siegler, R. S. (1996b). *Emerging minds: The process of change in children's thinking.* New York: Oxford University Press.

Siegler, R. S., & Ellis, S. (1996). Piaget on childhood. *Psychological Science, 7,* 211–215.

Siegler, R. S., & Jenkins, E. (1989). *How children discover new strategies.* Hillsdale, NJ: Erlbaum.

Siegler, R. S., & Richards, D. D. (1982). The development of intelligence. In R. J. Sternberg (Ed.), *Handbook of human intelligence.* Cambridge, England: Cambridge University Press.

Siever, L., & Davis, K. (1985). Overview: Toward a dysregulation hypothesis of depression. *American Journal of Psychiatry, 142,* 1017–1031.

Sigman, M. (1995). Nutrition and child development: Food for thought. *Current Directions in Psychological Science, 4,* 52–55.

Sigman, M. D., Kasari, C., Kwon, J. H., & Yirmiya, N. (1992). Responses to the negative emotions of others by autistic, mentally retarded, and normal children. *Child Development, 63,* 786–807.

Signorielli, N., & Lears, M. (1992). Children, television, and conceptions about chores: Attitudes and behaviors. *Sex Roles, 27,* 157–170.

Silver, E. A., & Kenney, P. A. (1995). Sources of assessment information for instructional guidance in mathematics. In T. Romberg (Ed.), *Reform in school mathematics and authentic assessment.* Albany: State University of New York Press.

Silverman, I. W., & Ragusa, D. M. (1990). Child and maternal correlates of impulse control in 24-month-old children. *Genetic, Social, and General Psychology Monographs, 116,* 435–473.

Silverman-Watkins, T., & Sprafkin, J. N. (1983). Adolescents' comprehension of televised sexual innuendoes. *Journal of Applied Developmental Psychology, 4,* 359–369.

Silverstein, L. B., & Auerbach, C. F. (1999). Deconstructing the essential father. *American Psychologist, 54,* 397–407.

Simmons, R. G., & Blyth, D. A. (1987). *Moving into adolescence: The impact of pubertal change in school context.* New York: Aldine de Gruyter.

Simner, M. L. (1971). Newborn's response to the cry of another infant. *Developmental Psychology, 5,* 136–150.

Simons, R. L., Lorenz, F. O., Wu, C. I., & Conger, R. D. (1993). Social network and marital support as mediators and moderators of the impact of stress and depression on parental behavior. *Developmental Psychology, 29,* 368–381.

Simons, R. L., Robertson, J. F., & Downs, W. R. (1989). The nature of the association between parental rejection and delinquent behavior. *Journal of Youth and Adolescence, 18,* 297–310.

Simons, R. L., Whitbeck, L. B., Conger, R. D., & Conger, K. J. (1991). Parenting factors, social skills, and value commitments as precursors to school failure, involvement with deviant peers, and delinquent behavior. *Journal of Youth and Adolescence, 20,* 645–664.

Simons-Morton, B. G., Baranowski, T., Parcel, G. S., O'Hara, N. M., & Matteson, R. C. (1990). Children's frequency of consumption of foods high in fat and sodium. *American Journal of Preventive Medicine, 6,* 218–227.

Simons-Morton, B. G., Taylor, W. C., Snider, S. A., & Huang, I. W. (1993). The physical activity of fifth-grade students during physical education classes. *American Journal of Public Health, 83,* 262–264.

Simons-Morton, B. G., Taylor, W. C., Snider, S. A., Huang, I. W., & Fulton, J. E. (1994). Observed levels of elementary and middle school children's physical activity during physical education classes. *Preventive Medicine, 23,* 437–441.

Sims, M. (1993). How my question keeps evolving. In Cochran-Smith, M., & Lytle, S. L. (Eds.), *Inside/outside: Teacher research and knowledge* (pp. 283–289). New York: Teachers College Press.

Sims, M., Hutchins, T., & Taylor, M. (1997). Classroom "culture" and children's conflict behaviours. *Early Child Development and Care, 134,* 43–59.

Singer, D. G., & Singer, J. L. (1994). *Barney & Friends as education and entertainment: Phase 3. A national study: Can preschoolers learn through exposure to Barney & Friends?* New Haven, CT: Yale University Family Television Research and Consultation Center.

Singer, J. L., & Singer, D. G. (1994). *Barney & Friends as education and entertainment: Phase 2. Can children learn through preschool exposure to Barney & Friends?* New Haven, CT: Yale University Family Television Research and Consultation Center.

Sisk, D. A. (1989). Identifying and nurturing talent among American Indians. In C. J. Maker & S. W. Schiever (Eds.), *Critical issues in gifted education: Vol. 2. Defensible programs for cultural and ethnic minorities.* Austin, TX: Pro-Ed.

Sissel, P. A. (2000). *Staff, parents, and politics in Head Start: A case study in unequal power, knowledge, and material resources.* New York: Falmer Press.

Sjostrom, L., & Stein, N. (1996). *Bully proof: A teacher's guide on teasing and bullying for use with fourth and fifth grade students.* Wellesley, MA: Wellesley College Center for Women.

Skinner, B. F. (1953). *Science and human behavior.* New York: Macmillan.

Skinner, B. F. (1957). *Verbal behavior.* New York: Appleton-Century-Croft.

Skinner, B. F. (1968). *The technology of teaching.* New York: Appleton-Century-Crofts.

Skinner, B. F. (1971). *Beyond freedom and dignity.* New York: Knopf.

Slaby, R. G., & Frey, K. S. (1975). Development of gender constancy and selective attention to same-sex models. *Child Development, 52,* 849–856.

Slater, A. M., Mattock, A., & Brown, E. (1990). Size constancy at birth: Newborn infants' responses to retinal and real size. *Journal of Experimental Child Psychology, 49,* 314–322.

Slater, A. M., & Morison, V. (1985). Shape constancy and slant perception at birth. *Perception, 14,* 337–344.

Slavin, R. E. (1989). Students at risk of school failure: The problem and its dimensions. In R. E. Slavin, N. L. Karweit, & N. A. Madden (Eds.), *Effective programs for students at risk.* Needham Heights, MA: Allyn & Bacon.

Slavin, R. E. (1990). *Cooperative learning: Theory, research, and practice.* Upper Saddle River, NJ: Prentice Hall.

Sleeter, C. E., & Grant, C. A. (1991). Race, class, gender, and disability in current textbooks. In M. W. Apple & L. K. Christian-Smith (Eds.), *The politics of the textbook* (pp. 78–110). New York: Routledge.

Sleeter, C. E., & Grant, C. A. (1999). *Making choices for multicultural education: Five approaches to race, class, and gender* (3rd ed.). Upper Saddle River, NJ: Merrill/Prentice Hall.

Slonim, M. B. (1991). *Children, culture, ethnicity: Evaluating and understanding the impact.* New York: Garland.

Slusher, M. P., & Anderson, C. A. (1996). Using causal persuasive arguments to change beliefs and teach new information: The mediating role of explanation availability and evaluation bias in the acceptance of knowledge. *Journal of Educational Psychology, 88,* 110–122.

Smetana, J. G. (1981). Preschool children's conceptions of moral and social rules. *Child Development, 52,* 1333–1336.

Smetana, J. G. (1989). Toddlers' social interactions in the context of moral and conventional transgressions in the home. *Developmental Psychology, 25,* 499–508.

Smetana, J. G., & Asquith, P. (1994). Adolescents' and parents' conceptions of parental authority and adolescent autonomy. *Child Development, 65,* 1147–1162.

Smetana, J. G., & Braeges, J. L. (1990). The development of toddlers' moral and conventional judgments. *Merrill-Palmer Quarterly, 36,* 329–346.

Smetana, J. G., Killen, M., & Turiel, E. (1991). Children's reasoning about interpersonal and moral conflicts. *Child Development, 62,* 629–644.

Smith, C., Maclin, D., Grosslight, L., & Davis, H. (1997). Teaching for understanding: A study of students' preinstruction theories of matter and a comparison of the effectiveness of two approaches to teaching about matter and density. *Cognition and Instruction, 15,* 317–393.

Smith, H. L. (1998). Literacy and instruction in African American communities: Shall we overcome? In B. Pérez (Ed.), *Sociocultural contexts of language and literacy.* Mahwah, NJ: Erlbaum.

Smith, J., & Russell, G. (1984). Why do males and females differ? Children's beliefs about sex differences. *Sex Roles, 11,* 1111–1120.

Smith, L. (1994, February 16). Bad habits: Testament to the downward spiral of drugs and teen angst. *Los Angeles Times,* p. 1.

Smith, M. A., & Schloss, P. (1998). *Applied behavior analysis in the classroom* (2nd ed.). Needham Heights, MA: Allyn & Bacon.

Smith, M. C. (1978). Cognizing the behavior stream: The recognition of intentional action. *Child Development, 49,* 736–743.

Smith, N. R., Cicchetti, L., Clark, M. C., Fucigna, C., Gordon-O'Connor, B., Halley, B. A., & Kennedy, M. (1998). *Observation drawing with children: A framework for teachers.* New York: Teachers College Press.

Smith, P. B., & Bond, M. H. (1994). *Social psychology across cultures: Analysis and perspectives.* Needham Heights, MA: Allyn & Bacon.

Smith, R. E., & Smoll, F. L. (1997). Coaching the coaches: Youth sports as a scientific and applied behavioral setting. *Current Directions in Psychological Science, 6*(1), 16–21.

Smitherman, G. (1994). "The blacker the berry the sweeter the juice": African American student writers. In A. H. Dyson & C. Genishi (Eds.), *The need for story: Cultural diversity in classroom and community.* Urbana, IL: National Council of Teachers of English.

Snarey, J. (1995). In a communitarian voice: The sociological expansion of Kohlbergian theory, research, and practice. In W. M. Kurtines & J. L. Gewirtz (Eds.), *Moral development: An introduction.* Boston: Allyn & Bacon.

Snell, M. E., & Janney, R. (2000). *Social relationships and peer support.* Baltimore: Brookes.

Snow, C., & Ninio, A. (1986). The contracts of literacy: What children learn from learning to read books. In W. Teale & E. Sulzby (Eds.), *Emergent literacy: Writing and reading*. Norwood, NJ: Ablex.

Snow, C. E. (1990). Rationales for native language instruction: Evidence from research. In A. M. Padilla, H. H. Fairchild, & C. M. Valadez (Eds.), *Bilingual education: Issues and strategies*. Newbury Park, CA: Sage.

Snow, C. E., & Hoefnagel-Höhle, M. (1978). The critical period for language acquisition: Evidence from second language learning. *Child Development, 49,* 1114–1128.

Snow, R. E., Corno, L., & Jackson, D., III. (1996). Individual differences in affective and conative functions. In D. C. Berliner & R. C. Calfee (Eds.), *Handbook of educational psychology*. New York: Macmillan.

Snyder, H., Finnegan, T., Nimick, E., Sickmund, D., & Tierney, N. (1987). *Juvenile Court Statistics, 1984*. Pittsburgh: National Center for Juvenile Justice.

Solomon, D., Watson, M., Battistich, E., Schaps, E., & Delucchi, K. (1992). Creating a caring community: Educational practices that promote children's prosocial development. In F. K. Oser, A. Dick, & J. L. Patry (Eds.), *Effective and responsible teaching: The new synthesis*. San Francisco: Jossey-Bass.

Sonnenschein, S. (1988). The development of referential communication: Speaking to different listeners. *Child Development, 59,* 694–702.

Sorce, J. F., Emde, R. N., Campos, J., & Klinnert, M. D. (1985). Maternal emotional signaling: Its effects on the visual cliff behavior of 1-year-olds. *Developmental Psychology, 21,* 195–200.

Sorensen, R. (1983). *Adolescent sexuality in contemporary society*. New York: World Books.

Sosniak, L. A., & Stodolsky, S. S. (1994). Making connections: Social studies education in an urban fourth-grade classroom. In J. Brophy (Ed.), *Advances in research on teaching: Vol. 4. Case studies of teaching and learning in social studies*. Greenwich, CT: JAI Press.

South, D. (2000). What motivates unmotivated students? In G. Mills, *Action research: A guide for the teacher researcher* (pp. 2–3). Upper Saddle River, NJ: Merrill/Prentice Hall.

Sowell, E. R., & Jernigan, T. L. (1998). Further MRI evidence of late brain maturation: Limbic volume increases and changing asymmetries during childhood and adolescence. *Developmental Neuropsychology, 14,* 599–617.

Sowell, E. R., Thompson, P. M., Holmes, C. J., Jernigan, T. L., & Toga, A. W. (1999). In vivo evidence for post-adolescent brain maturation in frontal and striatal regions. *Nature Neuroscience, 2,* 859–861.

Spaulding, C. L. (1992). *Motivation in the classroom*. New York: McGraw-Hill.

Spearman, C. (1904). General intelligence, objectively determined and measured. *American Journal of Psychology, 15,* 201–293.

Spearman, C. (1927). *The abilities of man: Their nature and measurement*. New York: Macmillan.

Spelke, E. S. (1994). Initial knowledge: Six suggestions. *Cognition, 50,* 431–445.

Spencer, M. B., & Markstrom-Adams, C. (1990). Identity processes among racial and ethnic minority children in America. *Child Development, 61,* 290–310.

Sperling, M. (1996). Revisiting the writing-speaking connection: Challenges for research on writing and writing instruction. *Review of Educational Research, 66,* 53–86.

Spicker, H. H. (1992). Identifying and enriching: Rural gifted children. *Educational Horizons, 70*(2), 60–65.

Spivey, N. N. (1997). *The constructivist metaphor: Reading, writing, and the making of meaning*. San Diego, CA: Academic Press.

Sprafkin, C., Serbin, L. A., Denier, C., & Connor, J. M. (1983). Sex-differentiated play: Cognitive consequences and early interventions. In M. B. Liss (Ed.), *Social and cognitive skills: Sex roles and children's play*. San Diego, CA: Academic Press.

Squires, D. A., Howley, J. P., & Gahr, R. K. (1999). The developmental pathways study group. In J. P. Comer, M. Ben-Avie, N. M. Haynes, & E. T. Joyner (Eds.), *Child by child: The Comer process in education* (pp. 193–207). New York: Teachers College Press.

Sroufe, L. A. (1983). Infant-caregiver attachment and patterns of adaptation in preschool: The roots of maladaptation and competence. In M. Perlmutter (Ed.), Development and policy concerning children with special needs. *Minnesota Symposium on Child Psychology, 16,* 41–83. Hillsdale, NJ: Erlbaum.

Sroufe, L. A., Carlson, E., & Shulman, S. (1993). Individuals in relationships: Development from infancy through adolescence. In D. C. Funder, R. D. Parke, C. Tomlinson-Keasey, & K. Widaman (Eds.), *Studying lives through time: Personality and development* (pp. 315–342). Washington, DC: American Psychological Association.

Sroufe, L. A., & Fleeson, J. (1986). Attachment and the construction of relationships. In W. W. Hartup & Z. Rubin (Eds.), *Relationships and development* (pp. 51–71). New York: Cambridge University Press.

Stack, C. B., & Burton, L. M. (1993). Kinscripts. *Journal of Comparative Family Studies, 24,* 157–170.

Stahl, S. A., & Miller, P. D. (1989). Whole language and language experience approaches for beginning reading: A quantitative research synthesis. *Review of Educational Research, 59,* 87–116.

Stanley, J. C. (1980). On educating the gifted. *Educational Researcher, 9*(3), 8–12.

Stanovich, K. E. (2000). *Progress in understanding reading: Scientific foundations and new frontiers*. New York: Guilford Press.

Stanovich, K. E., West, R. F., & Harrison, M. R. (1995). Knowledge growth and maintenance across the life span: The role of print exposure. *Developmental Psychology, 31,* 811–826.

Statistical Abstract of the United States (111th ed.). (1991). Washington, DC: Department of Commerce, Bureau of the Census.

Stattin, H., & Magnusson, D. (1989). The role of early aggressive behavior in the frequency, seriousness, and types of later crime. *Journal of Consulting and Clinical Psychology, 57,* 710–718.

Stattin, H., & Magnusson, D. (1990). *Pubertal maturation in female development*. Hillsdale, NJ: Erlbaum.

Status of the American school teacher 1990–1991 (1992). Washington, DC: National Education Association, Research Division.

Staub, D. (1998). *Delicate threads: Friendships between children with and without special needs in inclusive settings*. Bethesda, MD: Woodbine House.

Staub, E. (1995). The roots of prosocial and antisocial behavior in persons and groups: Environmental influence, personality, culture, and socialization. In W. M. Kurtines & J. L. Gewirtz (Eds.), *Moral development: An introduction*. Boston: Allyn & Bacon.

Steen, F., & Owens, S. A. (2000, March). *Implicit pedagogy: From chase play to collaborative worldmaking*. Paper presented at the Evolution and Social Mind Speaker Series, University of California at Santa Barbara.

Stein, D. M., & Reichert, P. (1990). Extreme dieting behaviors in early adolescence. *Journal of Early Adolescence, 10,* 108–121.

Stein, N. L. (1982). What's in a story: Interpreting the interpretations of story grammars. *Discourse Processes, 5,* 319–335.

Stein, N. L., & Glenn, C. G. (1979). An analysis of story comprehension in elementary school children. In R. O. Freedle (Eds.), *New directions in discourse processing* (Vol. 2). Norwood, NJ: Ablex.

Stein, R. (1996). Physical self-concept. In B. A. Bracken (Ed.), *Handbook of self-concept: Developmental, social, and clinical considerations* (pp. 374–394). New York: Wiley.

Steinberg, L. (1986). Latchkey children and susceptibility to peer pressure: An ecological analysis. *Developmental Psychology, 22,* 433–439.

Steinberg, L. (1993). *Adolescence* (3rd ed.). New York: McGraw-Hill.

Steinberg, L., Blinde, P. L., & Chan, K. S. (1984). Dropping out among language minority youth. *Review of Educational Research, 54,* 113–132.

Steinberg, L., Brown, B. B., Cider, M., Kaczmarek, N., & Lazzaro, C. (1988). *Noninstructional influences on high school student achievement: The contributions of parents, peers, extracurricular activities, and part-time work*. Madison, WI: National Center on Effective Secondary Schools. (ERIC Document Reproduction Service No. ED 307 509)

Steinberg, L., Elmen, J., & Mounts, N. (1989). Authoritative parenting, psychosocial maturity, and academic success among adolescents. *Child Development, 60,* 1424–1436.

Steiner, J. E. (1979). Human facial expression in response to taste and smell stimulation. In H. W. Reese & L. P. Lipsitt (Eds.), *Advances in child development and behavior* (Vol. 13). New York: Academic Press.

Stenberg, C., & Campos, J. (1990). The development of anger expressions in infancy. In N. Stein, B. Leventhal, & T. Trabasso (Eds.), *Psychological and biological approaches to emotion* (pp. 247–282). Hillsdale, NJ: Erlbaum.

Stenberg, C., Campos, J., & Emde, R. (1983). The facial expression of anger in 7-month-old infants. *Child Development, 54,* 178–184.

Stern, B. M., & Finn-Stevenson, M. (1999). Preregistered for success: The Comer/Zigler initiative. In J. P. Comer, M. Ben-Avie, N. M. Haynes, & E. T. Joyner (Eds.), *Child by child: The Comer process for change in education* (pp. 63–77). New York: Teachers College Press.

Stern, W. (1912). *Die psychologischen Methoden der Intelligenzprufung*. Leipzig, Germany: Barth.

Sternberg, R. J. (1984). Toward a triarchic theory of human intelligence. *Behavioral and Brain Sciences, 7,* 269–287.

Sternberg, R. J. (1985). *Beyond IQ: A triarchic theory of human intelligence*. Cambridge, England: Cambridge University Press.

Sternberg, R. J. (1996). Myths, countermyths, and truths about intelligence. *Educational Researcher, 25*(2), 11–16.

Sternberg, R. J. (1997). The concept of intelligence and its role in lifelong learning and success. *American Psychologist, 52,* 1030–1037.

Sternberg, R. J. (1998). Abilities are forms of developing expertise. *Educational Researcher, 27*(3), 11–20.

Sternberg, R. J., & Detterman, D. K. (Eds.). (1986). *What is intelligence? Contemporary views on its nature and definition*. Norwood, NJ: Ablex.

Sternberg, R. J., & Wagner, R. K. (Eds.). (1994). *Mind in context: Interactionist perspectives on hu-*

man intelligence. Cambridge, England: Cambridge University Press.

Sternberg, R. J., & Zhang, L. (1995). What do we mean by giftedness? A pentagonal implicit theory. *Gifted Child Quarterly, 39,* 88–94.

Stevens, R. J., & Slavin, R. E. (1995). The cooperative elementary school: Effects of students' achievement, attitudes, and social relations. *American Educational Research Journal, 32,* 321–351.

Stevenson, H. W., Chen, C., & Uttal, D. H. (1990). Beliefs and achievement: A study of black, white, and Hispanic children. *Child Development, 61,* 508–523.

Stewart, R. B. (1983). Sibling interaction: The role of the older child as teacher for the younger. *Merrill-Palmer Quarterly, 29,* 47–68.

Sticht, T. G., Armstrong, W. B., Hickey, D. T., & Caylor, J. S. (1987). *Cast-off youth: Policy and training methods from the military experience.* New York: Praeger.

Stipek, D. J. (1981). Children's perceptions of their own and their classmates' ability. *Journal of Educational Psychology, 73,* 404–410.

Stipek, D. J. (1984). Sex differences in children's attributions for success and failure on math and spelling tests. *Sex Roles, 11,* 969–981.

Stipek, D. J. (1993). *Motivation to learn: From theory to practice* (2nd ed.). Needham Heights, MA: Allyn & Bacon.

Stipek, D. J. (1996). Motivation and instruction. In D. C. Berliner & R. C. Calfee (Eds.), *Handbook of educational psychology.* New York: Macmillan.

Stipek, D. J., & Kowalski, P. S. (1989). Learned helplessness in task-orienting versus performance-orienting testing conditions. *Journal of Educational Psychology, 81,* 384–391.

Stipek, D. J., Recchia, S., & McClintic, S. M. (1992). Self-evaluation in young children. *Monographs of the Society for Research in Child Development, 57*(2, Serial No. 226).

Stodolsky, S. S. (1974). How children find something to do in preschools. *Genetic Psychology Monographs, 90,* 245–303.

Stolley, K. S. (1993). Statistics on adoption in the United States. *The Future of Children, 3*(1), 26–42.

Storfer, M. D. (1995). Problems in left-right discrimination in a high-IQ population. *Perceptual & Motor Skills, 81*(2), 491–497.

Strage, A., & Brandt, T. S. (1999). Authoritative parenting and college students' academic adjustment and success. *Journal of Educational Psychology, 91,* 146–156.

Straus, M. A. (2000). The benefits of never spanking: New and more definitive evidence. In M. A. Straus, *Beating the devil out of them: Corporal punishment by American families and its effects on children.* New Brunswick, NJ: Transaction Publications.

Strauss, S., & Shilony, T. (1994). Teachers' models of children's mind and learning. In L. A. Hirschfeld & S. A. Gelman (Eds.), *Mapping the mind: Domain specificity in cognition and culture* (pp. 455–473). New York: Cambridge University Press.

Strayer, F. F. (1991). The development of agonistic and affiliative structures in preschool play groups. In J. Silverberg & P. Gray (Eds.), *To fight or not to fight: Violence and peacefulness in humans and other primates.* Oxford: Oxford University Press.

Strayer, F. F., & Trudel, M. (1984). Developmental changes in the nature and function of social dominance among young children. *Ethology and Sociobiology, 5,* 279–295.

Streigel-Moore, R., Silberstein, L. R., & Rodin, J. (1986). Toward an understanding of bulimia. *American Psychologist, 41,* 246–263.

Strike, K. A., & Posner, G. J. (1992). A revisionist theory of conceptual change. In R. A. Duschl & R. J. Hamilton (Eds.), *Philosophy of science, cognitive psychology, and educational theory and practice.* Albany: State University of New York Press.

Strozer, J. R. (1994). *Language acquisition after puberty.* Washington, DC: Georgetown University Press.

Strutt, G. F., Anderson, D. R., & Well, A. D. (1975). A developmental study of the effects of irrelevant information on speeded classification. *Journal of Experimental Child Psychology, 20,* 127–135.

Stukas, A. A., Jr., Clary, E. G., & Snyder, M. (1999). Service learning: Who benefits and why. *Social Policy Report, Society for Research in Child Development, 13*(4), 1–19.

Subar, A. F., Heimendinger, J., Krebs-Smith, S. M., Patterson, B. H., Kessler, R., & Pivonka, E. (1992). *Five a day for better health: A baseline study of American's fruit and vegetable consumptions.* Rockville, MD: National Cancer Institute.

Sue, S., & Chin, R. (1983). The mental health of Chinese-American children: Stressors and resources. In G. J. Powell (Ed.), *The psychosocial development of minority children.* New York: Brunner/Mazel.

Sugar, W. A., & Bonk, C. J. (1998). Student role play in the World Forum: Analyses of an Arctic learning apprenticeship. In C. J. Bonk & K. S. King (Eds.), *Electronic collaborators: Learner-centered technologies for literacy, apprenticeship, and discourse.* Mahwah, NJ: Erlbaum.

Suina, J. H., & Smolkin, L. B. (1994). From natal culture to school culture to dominant society culture: Supporting transitions for Pueblo Indian students. In P. M. Greenfield & R. R. Cocking (Eds.), *Cross-cultural roots of minority child development* (pp. 115–130). Hillsdale, NJ: Erlbaum.

Sullivan, L. W. (1987). The risks of the sickle-cell trait: Caution and common sense. *New England Journal of Medicine, 317,* 830–831.

Sullivan, P., & Knutson, J. F. (1998). The association between child maltreatment and disabilities in a hospital based epidemiological study. *Child Abuse and Neglect, 22,* 271–288.

Sullivan, R. C. (1994). Autism: Definitions past and present. *Journal of Vocational Rehabilitation, 4,* 4–9.

Sullivan-DeCarlo, C., DeFalco, K., & Roberts, V. (1998). Helping students avoid risky behavior. *Educational Leadership, 56*(1), 80–82.

Sulzby, E. (1985). Children's emergent reading of favorite storybooks: A developmental study. *Reading Research Quarterly, 20,* 458–481.

Sulzby, E. (1986). Children's elicitation and use of metalinguistic knowledge about *word* during literacy interactions. In D. B. Yaden, Jr., & S. Templeton (Eds.), *Metalinguistic awareness and beginning literacy: Conceptualizing what it means to read and write.* Portsmouth, NH: Heinemann.

Sulzby, E., & Teale, W. (1991). Emergent literacy. In R. Barr, M. L. Kamil, P. B. Mosenthal, & P. D. Pearson (Eds.), *Handbook of reading research* (Vol. II). New York: Longman.

Sund, R. B. (1976). *Piaget for educators.* Columbus, OH: Charles E. Merrill.

Super, C. M. (1981). Behavioral development in infancy. In R. H. Munroe, R. L. Munroe, & B. B. Whiting (Eds.), *Handbook of cross-cultural human development* (pp. 181–270). New York: Garland STPM Press.

Suskind, R. (1998). *A hope in the unseen: An American odyssey from the inner city to the Ivy League.* New York: Broadway Books.

Susman, E. J., Inoff-Germain, G., Nottelmann, E. D., Loriaux, D. L., Cutler, J., Gordon, B., & Chrousos, G. P. (1987). Hormones, emotional dispositions, and aggressive attributes in young adolescents. *Child Development, 58,* 1114–1134.

Susman, E. J., Nottelmann, E. D., Inhoff-Germain, G. E., Dorn, L. D., Cutler, G. B. Jr., Loriaux, D. L., & Chrousos, G. P. (1985). The relation of development and social-emotional behavior in young adolescents. *Journal of Youth and Adolescence, 14,* 245–264.

Susman, E. J., Nottelmann, E. D., Inhoff-Germain, G., Dorn, L. D., & Chrousos, G. P. (1987). Hormonal influences on aspects of psychological development during adolescence. *Journal of Adolescent Health Care, 8,* 492–504.

Suttles, G. D. (1970). Friendship as a social institution. In G. J. McCall, M. McCall, N. K. Denzin, G. D. Scuttles, & S. Kurth (Eds.), *Social relationships* (pp. 95–135). Chicago: Aldine de Gruyter.

Sutton-Smith, B. (1986). The development of fictional narrative performances. *Topics in Language Disorders, 7*(1), 1–10.

Sutton-Smith, B. (Ed.). (1979). *Play and learning.* New York: Gardner Press.

Swann, W. B., Jr. (1997). The trouble with change: Self-verification and allegiance to the self. *Psychological Science, 8,* 177–180.

Swanson, H. L. (1993). An information processing analysis of learning disabled children's problem solving. *American Educational Research Journal, 30,* 861–893.

Swanson, H. L., & Cooney, J. B. (1991). Learning disabilities and memory. In B. Y. L. Wong (Ed.), *Learning about learning disabilities.* San Diego, CA: Academic Press.

Swanson, H. L., Mink, J., & Bocian, K. M. (1999). Cognitive processing deficits in poor readers with symptoms of reading disabilities and ADHD: More alike than different? *Journal of Educational Psychology, 91,* 321–333.

Swim, J. K., Cohen, L. L., & Hyers, L. L. (1998). Experiencing everyday prejudice and discrimination. In J. K. Swim & C. Stangor (Eds.), *Prejudice: The target's perspective* (pp. 38–60). San Diego, CA: Academic Press.

Swope, G. W. (1980). Kids and cults: Who joins and why? *Media and Methods, 16,* 18–21.

Sylvester, R. (1995). *A celebration of neurosis: An educator's guide to the human brain.* Alexandria, VA: Association for Supervision and Curriculum Development.

Szynal-Brown, C., & Morgan, R. R. (1983). The effects of reward on tutor's behaviors in a cross-age tutoring context. *Journal of Experimental Child Psychology, 36,* 196–208.

Tager-Flusberg, H. (1993). Putting words together: Morphology and syntax in the preschool years. In J. Berko-Gleason (Ed.), *The development of language* (3rd ed.). Upper Saddle River, NJ: Merrill/Prentice Hall.

Takahashi, K. (1990). Are the key assumptions of the "Strange Situation" procedure universal? A view from Japanese research. *Human Development, 33,* 23–30.

Tallman, I., Gray, L. N., Kullberg, V., & Henderson, D. (1999). The intergenerational transmission of marital conflict: Testing a process model. *Social Psychology Quarterly, 62*(3), 219–239.

Tamburrini, J. (1982). Some educational implications of Piaget's theory. In S. Modgil and C. Modgil (Eds.), *Jean Piaget: Consensus and controversy.* New York: Praeger.

Tamis-LeMonda, C. S., & Cabrera, N. (1999). Perspectives on father involvement: Research and policy. *Society for Research in Child Development Social Policy Report, 13*(2), 1–25.

Tannen, D. (1990). *You just don't understand: Talk between the sexes*. New York: Ballantine.

Tanner, J. M. (1990). *Foetus into man: Physical growth from conception to maturity* (Rev. ed.). Cambridge, MA: Harvard University Press.

Taylor, J. M. (1994). *MDMA frequently asked questions list*. Retrieved from the World Wide Web: http://ibbserver.ibb.uu.nl/jboschma/ecstasy/xtc01.

Taylor, M., Esbensen, B. M., & Bennett, R. T. (1994). Children's understanding of knowledge acquisition: The tendency for children to report that they have always known what they have just learned. *Child Development, 65,* 1581–1604.

Taylor, R. D., & Roberts, D. (1995). Kinship support and maternal and adolescent well-being in economically disadvantaged African-American families. *Child Development, 66,* 1585–1597.

Taylor, R. D., Casten, R., Flickinger, S. M., Roberts, D., & Fulmore, C. D. (1994). Explaining the school performance of African American adolescents. *Journal of Research on Adolescence, 4,* 21–44.

Taylor, S. M. (1994, April). *Staying in school against the odds: Voices of minority adolescent girls*. Paper presented at the annual meeting of the American Educational Research Association, New Orleans.

Taylor, W. C., Beech, B. M., & Cummings, S. S. (1998). Increasing physical activity levels among youth: A public health challenge. In D. K. Wilson, J. R. Rodrigue, & W. C. Taylor (Eds.), *Health-promoting and health-compromising behaviors among minority adolescents* (pp. 107–128). Washington, DC: American Psychological Association.

Teale, W. H. (1978). Positive environments for learning to read: What studies of early readers tell us. *Language Arts, 55,* 922–932.

Teale, W. H. (1986). Home background and young children's literacy development. In W. H. Teale & E. Sulzby (Eds.), *Emergent literacy: Writing and reading*. Norwood, NJ: Ablex.

Teasley, S. D., & Parker, J. G. (1995, March). *The effects of gender, friendship, and popularity on the targets and topics of preadolescents' gossip*. Paper presented at the biennial meeting of the Society for Research in Child Development, Indianapolis, IN.

Teeter, P. A., & Semrud-Clikeman, M. (1997). *Child neuropsychology: Assessment and interventions for neurodevelopmental disorders*. Boston: Allyn & Bacon.

Tellegren, A., Lykken, D. T., Bouchard, T. J., & Wilcox, K. J. (1988). Personality similarity in twins reared apart and together. *Journal of Personality and Social Psychology, 54,* 1031–1039.

Tennyson, R. D., & Cocchiarella, M. J. (1986). An empirically based instructional design theory for teaching concepts. *Review of Educational Research, 56,* 40–71.

Terman, L. M. (1916). *The measurement of intelligence*. Boston: Houghton Mifflin.

Terman, L. M., & Merrill, M. A. (1972). *Stanford-Binet Intelligence Scale* (3rd ed.). Boston: Houghton Mifflin.

Terrell, S. L., & Terrell, F. (1993). African-American cultures. In D. E. Battles (Ed.), *Communication disorders in multicultural populations*. Stoneham, MA: Butterworth-Heinemann.

Thaler, R. H. (2000). Mental accounting matters. In D. Kahneman & A. Tversky (Eds.), *Choices, values, and frames* (pp. 241–287). New York: Russell Sage Foundation.

Tharp, R. G. (1989). Psychocultural variables and constants: Effects on teaching and learning in schools. *American Psychologist, 44,* 349–359.

Tharp, R. G. (1994). Intergroup differences among Native Americans in socialization and child cognition: An ethnogenetic analysis. In P. M. Greenfield & R. R. Cocking (Eds.), *Cross-cultural roots of minority child development* (pp. 87–105). Hillsdale, NJ: Erlbaum.

Tharp, R. G., & Gallimore, R. (1988). *Rousing minds to life: Teaching, learning, and schooling in social context*. Cambridge, England: Cambridge University Press.

Thomas, A., Chess, S., & Birch, H. (1968). *Temperament and behavior disorders in children*. New York: New York University Press.

Thomas, J. R., & French, K. E. (1985). Gender differences across age in motor performance: A meta-analysis. *Psychological Bulletin, 98,* 260–282.

Thomas, J. W. (1993). Promoting independent learning in the middle grades: The role of instructional support practices. *Elementary School Journal, 93,* 575–591.

Thomas, S., & Oldfather, P. (1997). Intrinsic motivations, literacy, and assessment practices: "That's my grade. That's me." *Educational Psychologist, 32,* 107–123.

Thomas, S. P., Groër, M., & Droppleman, P. (1993). Physical health of today's school children. *Educational Psychology Review, 5,* 5–33.

Thomas, W. P., Collier, V. P., & Abbott, M. (1993). Academic achievement through Japanese, Spanish, or French: The first two years of partial immersion. *Modern Language Journal, 77,* 170–179.

Thompson, H., & Carr, M. (1995, April). *Brief metacognitive intervention and interest as predictors of memory for text*. Paper presented at the annual meeting of the American Educational Research Association, San Francisco.

Thompson, L. A., Fagan, J. F., & Fulker, D. W. (1991). Longitudinal prediction of specific cognitive abilities from infant novelty preference. *Child Development, 62,* 530–538.

Thompson, R. A. (1994). The role of the father after divorce. *The Future of Children: Children and Divorce, 4*(1), 210–235.

Thompson, R. A. (1998). Early sociopersonality development. In W. Damon (Editor-in-Chief) & N. Eisenberg (Vol. Ed.), *Handbook of child psychology: Vol. 3. Social, emotional, and personality development* (5th ed., pp. 25–104). New York: Wiley.

Thompson, R. A., & Wyatt, J. M. (1999). Current research on child maltreatment: Implications for educators. *Educational Psychology Review, 11,* 173–201.

Thompson, R. F. (1975). *Introduction to physiological psychology*. New York: Harper & Row.

Thorkildsen, T. A. (1995). Conceptions of social justice. In W. M. Kurtines & J. L. Gewirtz (Eds.), *Moral development: An introduction*. Boston: Allyn & Bacon.

Thorndike, R., Hagen, E., & Sattler, J. (1986). *Stanford-Binet Intelligence Scale* (4th ed.). Chicago: Riverside.

Thornton, M. C., Chatters, L. M., Taylor, R. J., & Allen, W. (1990). Sociodemographic and environmental correlates of racial socialization by Black parents. *Child Development, 61,* 401–409.

Timmer, S. G., Eccles, J., & O'Brien, K. (1985). How children use time. In F. T. Juster & F. P. Stafford (Eds.), *Time, goods, and well-being* (pp. 353–383). Ann Arbor, MI: Survey Research Center, Institute for Social Research.

Tincoff, R., & Jusczyk, P. W. (1999). Some beginnings of word comprehension in 6-month-olds. *Psychological Science, 10,* 172–175.

Tisak, M. (1993). Preschool children's judgments of moral and personal events involving physical harm and property damage. *Merrill-Palmer Quarterly, 39,* 375–390.

Tobias, S. (1977). A model for research on the effect of anxiety on instruction. In J. E. Sieber, H. F. O'Neil, Jr., & S. Tobias (Eds.), *Anxiety, learning, and instruction*. Hillsdale, NJ: Erlbaum.

Tomblin, J. B. (1997). Epidemiology of specific language impairment. In M. Gopnik (Ed.), *The inheritance and innateness of grammars*. New York: Oxford University Press.

Tompkins, G. E., & McGee, L. M. (1986). Visually impaired and sighted children's emerging concepts about written language. In D. B. Yaden, Jr., & S. Templeton (Eds.), *Metalinguistic awareness and beginning literacy: Conceptualizing what it means to read and write*. Portsmouth, NH: Heinemann.

Torney-Purta, J. (1990). Youth in relation to social institutions. In S. S. Feldman & G. R. Elliott (Eds.), *At the threshold: The developing adolescent* (pp. 457–477). Cambridge, MA: Harvard University Press.

Torrance, E. P. (1989). A reaction to "Gifted black students: Curriculum and teaching strategies." In C. J. Maker & S. W. Schiever (Eds.), *Critical issues in gifted education: Vol. 2. Defensible programs for cultural and ethnic minorities*. Austin, TX: Pro-Ed.

Torrance, E. P. (1995). Insights about creativity: Questioned, rejected, ridiculed, ignored. *Educational Psychology Review, 7,* 313–322.

Torres-Guzmán, M. E. (1998). Language, culture, and literacy in Puerto Rican communities. In B. Pérez (Ed.), *Sociocultural contexts of language and literacy*. Mahwah, NJ: Erlbaum.

Tourniaire, F., & Pulos, S. (1985). Proportional reasoning: A review of the literature. *Educational Studies in Mathematics, 16,* 181–204.

Trainor, L. J., Austin, C. M., & Desjardins, R. N. (2000). Is infant-directed speech prosody a result of the vocal expression of emotion? *Psychological Science, 11,* 188–195.

Trawick-Smith, J. (1997). *Early childhood development: A multicultural perspective*. Upper Saddle River, NJ: Merrill/Prentice Hall.

Trawick-Smith, J. (2000). *Early childhood development: A multicultural perspective* (2nd ed.). Upper Saddle River, NJ: Merrill/Prentice Hall.

Treffert, D. A. (1989). *Extraordinary people: Understanding Savant syndrome*. New York: Harper & Row.

Treiman, R. (1993). *Beginning to spell: A study of first-grade children*. New York: Oxford University Press.

Treiman, R. (1998). Beginning to spell in English. In C. Hulme & R. M. Joshi (Eds.), *Reading and spelling: Development and disorders*. Mahwah, NJ: Erlbaum.

Tremblay, L. (1999, April). *Acceleration hypothesis: A meta-analysis of environmental stressors impact on puberty onset*. Paper presented at the Biennial Meeting of the Society for Research in Child Development, Albuquerque, NM.

Trevarthen, C. (1979). Communication and cooperation in early infancy: A description of primary intersubjectivity. In M. Bullowa (Ed.), *Before speech: The beginning of interpersonal communication* (pp. 321–347). Cambridge, England: Cambridge University Press.

Triandis, H. C. (1995). *Individualism and collectivism*. Boulder, CO: Westview Press.

Troiano, R. P., Flegal, K. M., Kuczmarski, R. J., Campbell, S. M., & Johnson, C. L. (1995).

Overweight prevalence and trends for children and adolescents. *Archives of Pediatric and Adolescent Medicine, 149,* 1085–1091.

Tronick, E. Z., Als, H., & Adamson, L. (1979). Structure of early face-to-face communication intent. In M. Bullowa (Ed.), *Before speech: The beginnings of human communication.* Cambridge, England: Cambridge University Press.

Trueba, H. T. (1988). Peer socialization among minority students: A high school dropout prevention program. In H. T. Trueba & C. Delgado-Gaitan (Eds.), *School and society: Learning content through culture.* New York: Praeger.

Tunmer, W. E., & Bowey, J. A. (1984). Metalinguistic awareness and reading acquisition. In W. E. Tunmer, C. Pratt, & M. L. Herriman (Eds.), *Metalinguistic awareness in children: Theory, research, and implications.* Berlin, Germany: Springer-Verlag.

Tunmer, W. E., Pratt, C., & Herriman, M. L. (Eds.), (1984). *Metalinguistic awareness in children: Theory, research, and implications.* Berlin, Germany: Springer-Verlag.

Turiel, E. (1983). *The development of social knowledge: Morality and convention.* Cambridge, England: Cambridge University Press.

Turiel, E. (1998). The development of morality. In W. Damon (Editor-in-Chief) & N. Eisenberg (Vol. Ed.), *Handbook of child psychology: Vol. 3. Social, emotional, and personality development* (pp. 863–932). New York: Wiley.

Turiel, E., Killen, M., & Helwig, C. C. (1987). Morality: Its structure, function, and vagaries. In J. Kagan & S. Lamb (Eds.), *The emergence of morality in young children* (pp. 155–243). Chicago: University of Chicago Press.

Turiel, E., Smetana, J. G., & Killen, M. (1991). Social contexts in social cognitive development. In W. M. Kurtines & J. L. Gewirtz (Eds.), *Moral behavior and development: Vol. 2. Research.* Hillsdale, NJ: Erlbaum.

Turnbull, A. P. (1974). Teaching retarded persons to rehearse through cumulative overt labeling. *American Journal of Mental Deficiency, 79,* 331–337.

Turnbull, A. P., Pereira, L., & Blue-Banning, M. (2000). Teachers as friendship facilitators: Respeto and personalismo. *Teaching Exceptional Children, 32*(5), 66–70.

Turnbull, A., Turnbull, R., Shank, M., & Leal, D. (1999). *Exceptional lives: Special education in today's schools* (2nd ed.). Upper Saddle River, NJ: Merrill/Prentice Hall.

Turner, J. C. (1995). The influence of classroom contexts on young children's motivation for literacy. *Reading Research Quarterly, 30,* 410–441.

Tversky, A., & Kahneman, D. (1990). Judgment under uncertainty: Heuristics and biases. In P. K. Moser (Ed.), *Rationality in action: Contemporary approaches* (pp. 171–188). New York: Cambridge University Press.

Uba, A., & Huang, K. (1999). *Psychology.* New York: Longman.

Udall, A. J. (1989). Curriculum for gifted Hispanic students. In C. J. Maker & S. W. Schiever (Eds.), *Critical issues in gifted education: Vol. 2. Defensible programs for cultural and ethnic minorities.* Austin, TX: Pro-Ed.

Udry, J. R. (1988). Biological predispositions and social control in adolescent sexual behavior. *American Sociological Review, 53*(5), 709–722.

Ulichny, P. (1994, April). *Cultures in conflict.* Paper presented at the annual meeting of the American Educational Research Association, New Orleans, LA.

Underwood, B., & Moore, B. (1982). Perspective-taking and altruism. *Psychological Bulletin, 91,* 143–173.

Upchurch, D. M., & McCarthy, J. (1990). The timing of first birth and high school completion. *American Sociological Review, 55,* 224–234.

Urban, J., Carlson, E., Egeland, B., & Sroufe, L. A. (1991). Patterns of individual adaptation across childhood. *Development and Psychopathology, 3,* 445–460.

Urdan, T. (1997). Achievement goal theory: Past results, future directions. In M. L. Maehr & P. R. Pintrich (Eds.), *Advances in motivation and achievement* (Vol. 10). Greenwich, CT: JAI Press.

Urdan, T. C., & Maehr, M. L. (1995). Beyond a two-goal theory of motivation and achievement: A case for social goals. *Review of Educational Research, 65,* 213–243.

U.S. Bureau of the Census. (1995). *Statistical Abstracts of the United States, 1995.* Washington, DC: U.S. Government Printing Office.

U.S. Bureau of the Census. (1996). *Statistical Abstracts of the United States, 1996.* Washington, DC: U.S. Government Printing Office.

U.S. Department of Education. (1992). *To assure the free appropriate public education of all children with disabilities: Fourteenth annual report to Congress on the implementation of the Individuals with Disabilities Education Act.* Washington, DC: Author.

U.S. Department of Education. (1993). *National excellence: A case for developing America's talent.* Washington, DC: Office of Educational Research and Improvement.

U.S. Department of Education. (1996). *To assure the free appropriate public education of all children with disabilities: Eighteenth annual report to Congress on the implementation of the Individuals with Disabilities Education Act.* Washington, DC: Author.

U.S. Department of Education. (1997). *To assure the free appropriate public education of all children with disabilities: Nineteenth annual report to Congress on the implementation of the Individuals with Disabilities Education Act.* Washington, DC: Author.

U.S. Department of Education, Office of Civil Rights. (1993). *Annual report to Congress.* Washington, DC: Author.

U.S. Department of Health and Human Services. (1994, April/May). *Reducing teenage pregnancy increases life options for youth* (U.S. Public Health Service Prevention Report, pp. 1–4). Washington, DC: Author.

U.S. Department of Health and Human Services. (1997). *Youth risk behavior surveillance—United States* (CDC MMWR Surveillance Summaries Vol. 45, No. SS-4). Washington, DC: Author.

U.S. Department of Health and Human Services. (1998). Youth risk behavior surveillance—United States, 1997. *Morbidity and Mortality Weekly Report, 47*(No. SS-3).

Uttal, D. H., Marzolf, D. P., Pierroutsakos, S. L., Smith, C. M., Troseth, G. L., Scudder, K. V., & DeLoache, J. S. (1998). Seeing through symbols: The development of children's understanding of symbolic relations. In O. N. Saracho & B. Spodek (Eds.), *Multiple perspectives on play in early childhood education.* Albany: State University of New York Press.

van Andel, J. (1990). Places children like, dislike, and fear. *Children's Environment Quarterly, 7*(4), 24–31.

Vandell, D. L., & Pierce, K. M. (1999, April). *Can after-school programs benefit children who live in high-crime neighborhoods?* Paper presented at the biennial meeting of the Society for Research in Child Development, Albuquerque, NM.

Vandell, D. L., & Posner, J. (1999). Conceptualization and measurement of children's after-school environments. In S. L. Friedman & T. D. Wachs (Eds.), *Assessment of the environment across the lifespan* (pp. 167–197). Washington, DC: American Psychological Association Press.

Vandell, D. L., & Shumow, L. (1999, Fall). After-school child care programs. *The Future of Children: When School Is Out, 9,* 64–80.

Vandenberg, B. (1978). Play and development from an ethological perspective. *American Psychologist, 33,* 724–738.

Van der Voort, T. H. A, & Valkenburg, P. M. (1994). Television's impact on fantasy play: A review of research. *Developmental Review, 14*(1), 227–251.

van Laar, C. (2000). The paradox of low academic achievement but high self-esteem in African American students: An attributional account. *Educational Psychology Review, 12,* 33–61.

Vasquez, J. A. (1990). Teaching to the distinctive traits of minority students. *Clearing House, 63,* 299–304.

Vaughn, B. E., Egeland, B., Sroufe, L. A., & Waters, E. (1979). Individual differences in infant-mother attachment at twelve and eighteen months: Stability and change in families under stress. *Child Development, 50,* 971–975.

Vaughn, B. E., Kopp, C. B., & Krakow, J. B. (1984). The emergence and consolidation of self-control from eighteen to thirty months of age: Normative trends and individual differences. *Child Development, 55,* 990–1004.

Vaughn, S. (1991). Social skills enhancement in students with learning disabilities. In B. Y. L. Wong (Ed.), *Learning about learning disabilities.* San Diego, CA: Academic Press.

Vega, W. A., Gil, A. G., Warheit, G. J., Zimmerman, R. S., & Apospori, E. (1993). Acculturation and delinquent behavior among Cuban American adolescents: Toward an empirical model. *American Journal of Community Psychology, 21,* 113–125.

Ventura, S. J., & Tappel, S. M. (1985). Child bearing characteristics of U.S. and foreign born Hispanic mothers. *Public Health Reports, 100,* 647–652.

Vermeer, H. J., Boekaerts, M., & Seegers, G. (2000). Motivational and gender differences: Sixth-grade students' mathematical problem-solving behavior. *Journal of Educational Psychology, 92,* 308–315.

Vernon, P. A. (1993). Intelligence and neural efficiency. In D. K. Detterman (Ed.), *Current topics in human intelligence* (Vol. 3). Norwood, NJ: Ablex.

Veroff, J., McClelland, L., & Ruhland, D. (1975). Varieties of achievement motivation. In M. T. S. Mednick, S. S. Tangri, & L. W. Hoffman (Eds.), *Women and achievement: Social and motivational analyses.* New York: Halsted.

Vignau, J., Bailly, D., Duhamel, A., Vervaecke, P., Beuscart, R., & Collinet, C. (1997). Epidemiologic study of sleep quality and troubles in French secondary school adolescents. *Journal of Adolescent Health, 21*(5), 343–350.

Vitaro, F., Gendreau, P. L., Tremblay, R. E., & Oligny, P. (1998). Reactive and proactive aggression differentially predict later conduct problems. *Journal of Child Psychology and Psychiatry and Allied Disciplines, 39,* 377–385.

Voelkl, K. E., & Frone, M. R. (2000). Predictors of substance use at school among high school students. *Journal of Educational Psychology, 92,* 583–592.

Vorrath, H. (1985). *Positive peer culture.* New York: Aldine de Gruyter.

Vosniadou, S. (1991). Conceptual development in astronomy. In S. M. Glynn, R. H. Yeany, & B. K.

Britton (Eds.), *The psychology of learning science.* Hillsdale, NJ: Erlbaum.

Vosniadou, S. (1994). Universal and culture-specific properties of children's mental models of the earth. In L. A. Hirschfeld & S. A. Gelman (Eds.), *Mapping the mind: Domain specificity in cognition and culture.* Cambridge, England: Cambridge University Press.

Vosniadou, S., & Brewer, W. F. (1987). Theories of knowledge restructuring in development. *Review of Educational Research, 57,* 51–67.

Voss, J. F., & Schauble, L. (1992). Is interest educationally interesting? An interest-related model of learning. In K. A. Renninger, S. Hidi, & A. Krapp (Eds.), *The role of interest in learning and development.* Hillsdale, NJ: Erlbaum.

Vygotsky, L. S. (1962). *Thought and language* (E. Haufmann & G. Vakar, Eds. and Trans.). Cambridge, MA: MIT Press.

Vygotsky, L. S. (1978). *Mind in society: The development of higher psychological processes.* Cambridge, MA: Harvard University Press.

Vygotsky, L. S. (1987). *The collected works of L. S. Vygotsky* (R. W. Rieber & A. S. Carton, Eds.). New York: Plenum Press.

Vygotsky, L. S. (1997). *Educational psychology.* Boca Raton, FL: St. Lucie Press.

Waddington, C. H. (1957). *The strategy of the genes.* London: Allyn & Bacon.

Wagner, M. M. (1995a). *The contributions of poverty and ethnic background to the participation of secondary school students in special education.* Washington, DC: U.S. Department of Education.

Wagner, M. M. (1995b). Outcomes for youths with serious emotional disturbance in secondary school and early childhood. *Critical Issues for Children and Youths, 5*(2), 90–112.

Wagner, R. K., Torgesen, J. K., & Rashotte, C. A. (1994). Development of reading-related phonological processing abilities: New evidence of bidirectional causality from a latent variable longitudinal study. *Developmental Psychology, 30,* 73–87.

Wahlsten, D., & Gottlieb, G. (1997). The invalid separation of effects of nature and nurture: Lessons from animal experimentation. In R. J. Sternberg & E. L. Grigorenko (Eds.), *Intelligence, heredity, and environment* (pp. 163–192). Cambridge, England: Cambridge University Press.

Walberg, H. J., & Paik, S. J. (1997). Home environments for learning. In H. J. Walberg & G. D. Haertel (Eds.), *Psychology and educational practice* (pp. 356–368). Berkeley, CA: McCrutchan.

Waldman, I. D., Weinberg, R. A., & Scarr, S. (1994). Racial-group differences in IQ in the Minnesota Transracial Adoption Study: A reply to Levin and Lynn. *Intelligence, 19,* 29–44.

Walker, J. E., & Shea, T. M. (1999). *Behavior management: A practical approach for educators* (7th ed.). Upper Saddle River, NJ: Merrill/Prentice Hall.

Walker, L. J. (1991). Sex differences in moral reasoning. In W. M. Kurtines & J. L. Gewirtz (Eds.), *Handbook of moral behavior and development: Vol. 2. Research* (pp. 333–364). Hillsdale, NJ: Erlbaum.

Walker, L. J. (1995). Sexism in Kohlberg's moral psychology? In W. M. Kurtines & J. L. Gewirtz (Eds.), *Moral development: An introduction.* Boston: Allyn & Bacon.

Walker, L. J., & Taylor, J. H. (1991). Family interactions and the development of moral reasoning. *Child Development, 62,* 264–283.

Wallerstein, J. S. (1984). Children of divorce: The psychological tasks of the child. *Annual Progress in Child Psychiatry & Child Development,* 263–280.

Wallerstein, J. S., & Kelly, J. B. (1980). *Surviving the break-up: How children and parents cope with divorce.* New York: Basic Books.

Walters, G. C., & Grusec, J. E. (1977). *Punishment.* San Francisco: Freeman.

Wang, P. P., & Baron, M. A. (1997). Language and communication: Development and disorders. In M. L. Batshaw (Ed.), *Children with disabilities* (4th ed.). Baltimore: Brookes.

Ward, R. A., & Spitze, G. (1998). Sandwiched marriages: The implications of child and parent relations for marital quality in midlife. *Social Forces, 77*(2), 647–666.

Warren, A. R., & McCloskey, L. A. (1993). Pragmatics: Language in social contexts. In J. Berko-Gleason (Ed.), *The development of language* (3rd ed.). New York: Macmillan.

Warren-Leubecker, A., & Bohannon, J. N. (1989). Pragmatics: Language in social contexts. In J. Berko-Gleason (Ed.), *The development of language* (2nd ed.). Upper Saddle River, NJ: Merrill/Prentice Hall.

Wartella, E. (1995). The commercialization of youth: Channel One in context. *Phi Delta Kappan, 76,* 448–451.

Warton, P. M., & Goodnow, J. J. (1991). The nature of responsibility: Children's understanding of "Your Job." *Child Development, 62,* 156–165.

Washington, V., & Bailey, U. J. O. (1995). *Project Head Start: Models and strategies for the twenty-first century.* New York: Garland.

Wasik, B., Karweit, N., Burns, L., & Brodsky, E. (1998, April). *Once upon a time: The role of rereading and retelling in storybook reading.* Paper presented at the annual meeting of the American Educational Research Association, San Diego, CA.

Waters, E., Merrick, S., Treboux, D., Crowell, J., Albersheim, L. (2000). Attachment security in infancy and early adulthood: A twenty-year longitudinal study. *Child Development, 71,* 684–689.

Waters, H. S. (1982). Memory development in adolescence: Relationships between metamemory, strategy use, and performance. *Journal of Experimental Child Psychology, 33,* 183–195.

Watson, J. (1928). *The psychological care of the infant and child.* New York: Norton.

Watson, R. (1996). Rethinking readiness for learning. In D. R. Olson & N. Torrance (Eds.), *The handbook of education and human development: New models of learning, teaching and schooling* (pp. 148–172). Cambridge, MA: Blackwell.

Waxman, S. R. (1990). Linguistic biases and the establishment of conceptual hierarchies: Evidence from preschool children. *Cognitive Development, 5,* 123–150.

Way, N. (1998). *Everyday courage: The lives and stories of urban teenagers.* New York: New York University Press.

Weaver, C. (1990). *Understanding whole language: From principles to practice.* Portsmouth, NH: Heinemann.

Weaver, C. A., III, & Kintsch, W. (1991). Expository text. In R. Barr, M. L. Kamil, P. B. Mosenthal, & P. D. Pearson (Eds.), *Handbook of reading research* (Vol. II). New York: Longman.

Webb, J. T., Meckstroth, E. A., & Tolan, S. S. (1982). *Guiding the gifted child: A practical source for parents and teachers.* Dayton: Ohio Psychology Press.

Webb, N. M., & Farivar, S. (1994). Promoting helping behavior in cooperative small groups in middle school mathematics. *American Educational Research Journal, 31,* 369–395.

Webb, N. M., & Palincsar, A. S. (1996). Group processes in the classroom. In D. C. Berliner & R. C. Calfee (Eds.), *Handbook of educational psychology.* New York: Macmillan.

Webber, J., Scheuermann, B., McCall, C., & Coleman, M. (1993). Research on self-monitoring as a behavior management technique in special education classrooms: A descriptive review. *Remedial and Special Education, 14*(2), 38–56.

Webster-Stratton, C., & Hammond, M. (1999). Marital conflict management skills, parenting style, and early-onset conduct problems: Processes and pathways. *Journal of Child Psychology & Psychiatry & Allied Disciplines, 40,* 917–927.

Wechsler, D. (1991). *Wechsler Intelligence Scale for Children* (3rd ed.). San Antonio, TX: Psychological Corporation.

Weinberg, R. A. (1989). Intelligence and IQ: Landmark issues and great debates. *American Psychologist, 44,* 98–104.

Weiner, B. (1984). Principles for a theory of student motivation and their application within an attributional framework. In R. Ames & C. Ames (Eds.), *Research on motivation in education: Vol. 1. Student motivation.* San Diego, CA: Academic Press.

Weiner, B. (1986). *An attributional theory of motivation and emotion.* New York: Springer-Verlag.

Weiner, L. (1999). *Urban teaching: The essentials.* New York: Teachers College Press.

Weinfeld, N. S., Sroufe, L. A., & Egeland, B. (2000). Attachment from infancy to early adulthood in a high-risk sample: Continuity, discontinuity, and their correlates. *Child Development, 71,* 695–702.

Weinstein, C. S. (1988). Preservice teachers' expectations about their first year of teaching. *Teaching and Teacher Education, 40*(2), 53–60.

Weinstein, R. S., Madison, S. M., & Kuklinski, M. R. (1995). Raising expectations in schooling: Obstacles and opportunities for change. *American Educational Research Journal, 32,* 121–159.

Weisner, T. S., & Gallimore, R. (1977). My brother's keeper: Child and sibling caregiving. *Current Anthropology, 18,* 169–190.

Weisner, T. S., Gallimore, R., & Jordan, C. (1988). Unpackaging cultural effects on classroom learning: Hawaiian peer assistance and child-generated activity. *Anthropology and Education Quarterly, 19,* 327–352.

Weiss, L. H., & Schwarz, J. C. (1996). The relationship between parenting types and older adolescents' personality, academic achievement, adjustment, and substance use. *Child Development, 67,* 2101–2114.

Weiss, M. J., & Hagen, R. (1988). A key to literacy: Kindergartners' awareness of the functions of print. *The Reading Teacher, 41,* 574–578.

Weissglass, J. (1998). *Ripples of hope: Building relationships for educational change.* Santa Barbara, CA: Center for Educational Change in Mathematics and Science, University of California.

Wellman, H., Harris, P. L., Banerjee, M., & Sinclair, A. (1995). Early understanding of emotion: Evidence from natural language. *Cognition and Emotion, 9,* 117–149.

Wellman, H. M. (1985). The child's theory of mind: The development of conceptions of cognition. In S. R. Yussen (Ed.), *The growth of reflection in children.* San Diego, CA: Academic Press.

Wellman, H. M. (1988). The early development of memory strategies. In F. Weinert & M.

Perlmutter (Eds.), *Memory development: Universal changes and individual differences.* Hillsdale, NJ: Erlbaum.

Wellman, H. M. (1990). *The child's theory of mind.* Cambridge, MA: MIT Press.

Wellman, H. M., & Estes, D. (1986). Early understanding of mental entities: A reexamination of childhood realism. *Child Development, 57,* 910–923.

Wellman, H. M., & Gelman, S. A. (1992). Cognitive development: Foundational theories of core domains. In M. R. Rosenzweig & L. W. Porter (Eds.), *Annual review of psychology* (Vol. 43). Palo Alto, CA: Annual Reviews, Inc.

Wellman, H. M., & Hickling, A. K. (1994). The mind's "I": Children's conception of the mind as an active agent. *Child Development, 65,* 1564–1580.

Wellman, H. M., Phillips, A. T., & Rodriguez, T. (2000). Young children's understanding of perception, desire, and emotion. *Child Development, 71,* 895–912.

Wellman, H. M., & Woolley, J. D. (1990). From simple desires to ordinary beliefs: The early development of everyday psychology. *Cognition, 35,* 245–275.

Wenar, C. (1972). Executive competence and spontaneous social behavior in 1–year-olds. *Child Development, 43,* 256–260.

Wentzel, K. R. (1999). Social-motivational processes and interpersonal relationships: Implications for understanding motivation at school. *Journal of Educational Psychology, 91,* 76–97.

Wentzel, K. R., & Asher, S. R. (1995). The academic lives of neglected, rejected, popular, and controversial children. *Child Development, 66,* 754–763.

Wentzel, K. R., & Wigfield, A. (1998). Academic and social motivational influences on students' academic performance. *Educational Psychology Review, 10,* 155–175.

Werker, J. F., & Lalonde, C. E. (1988). Cross-language speech perception: Initial capabilities and developmental change. *Developmental Psychology, 24,* 672–683.

Werner, E. (1989). High-risk children in adulthood: A longitudinal study from birth to 32 years. *American Journal of Orthopsychiatry, 59*(1), 72–81.

Werner, E. (1993). Risk, resilience, and recovery: Perspectives from the Kauai longitudinal study. *Development and Psychopathology, 5,* 505–515.

Werner, E. E. (1995). Resilience in development. *Current Directions in Psychological Science, 4,* 81–85.

Werner, E. E., & Smith, R. S. (1982). *Vulnerable but invincible: A longitudinal study of resilient children.* New York: McGraw-Hill. Reprinted 1989, 1998. New York: Adams, Bannister, Cox.

Wertsch, J. V. (1984). The zone of proximal development: Some conceptual issues. *Children's learning in the zone of proximal development: New directions for child development* (No. 23). San Francisco: Jossey-Bass.

Wertsch, J. V., & Tulviste, P. (1994). Lev Semyonovich Vygotsky and contemporary developmental psychology. In R. D. Parke, P. A. Ornstein, J. J. Rieser, & C. Zahn-Waxler (Eds.), *A century of developmental psychology* (pp. 333–355). Washington, DC: American Psychological Association.

West, M. J., & Rheingold, H. L. (1978). Infant stimulation of maternal instruction. *Infant Behavior and Development, 1,* 205–215.

White, R. (1959). Motivation reconsidered: The concept of competence. *Psychological Review, 66,* 297–333.

White, R., & Cunningham, A. M. (1991). *Ryan White: My own story.* New York: Signet.

White, S. H. (1992). G. Stanley Hall: From philosophy to developmental psychology. *Developmental Psychology, 28,* 25–34.

Whitehurst, G. J., Arnold, D. S., Epstein, J. N., Angell, A. L., Smith, M., & Fischel, J. E. (1994). A picture book reading intervention in day care and home for children from low-income families. *Developmental Psychology, 30,* 679–689.

Whiting, B. B., & Edwards, C. P. (1988). *Children of different worlds.* Cambridge, MA: Harvard University Press.

Whiting, B. B., & Whiting, J. W. M. (1975). *Children of six cultures: A psycho-cultural analysis.* Cambridge, MA: Harvard University Press.

Whiting, J. (1981). Environmental constraint on infant care practices. In R. H. Munroe, R. L. Munroe, & B. Whiting (Eds.), *Handbook of cross-cultural development.* New York: Garland STPM Press.

Wiesel, T. N., & Hubel, D. H. (1965). Extent of recovery from the effects of visual deprivation in kittens. *Journal of Neurophysiology, 28,* 1060–1072.

Wigfield, A. (1994). Expectancy-value theory of achievement motivation: A developmental perspective. *Educational Psychology Review, 6,* 49–78.

Wigfield, A. (1997). Reading motivation: A domain-specific approach to motivation. *Educational Psychologist, 32,* 59–68.

Wigfield, A., & Eccles, J. (1992). The development of achievement task values: A theoretical analysis. *Developmental Review, 12,* 265–310.

Wigfield, A., & Eccles, J. S. (1994). Children's competence beliefs, achievement values, and general self-esteem: Change across elementary and middle school. *Journal of Early Adolescence, 14,* 107–138.

Wigfield, A., Eccles, J., Mac Iver, D., Reuman, D., & Midgley, C. (1991). Transitions at early adolescence: Changes in children's domain-specific self-perceptions and general self-esteem across the transition to junior high school. *Developmental Psychology, 27,* 552–565.

Wigfield, A., Eccles, J. S., & Pintrich, P. R. (1996). Development between the ages of 11 and 25. In D. C. Berliner & R. C. Calfee (Eds.), *Handbook of educational psychology.* New York: Macmillan.

Wigfield, A., & Karpathian, M. (1991). Who am I and what can I do? Children's self-concepts and motivation in achievement situations. *Educational Psychologist, 26,* 233–262.

Wiig, E. H., Gilbert, M. F., & Christian, S. H. (1978). Developmental sequences in perception and interpretation of ambiguous sentences. *Perceptual and Motor Skills, 46,* 959–969.

Wilcox, S. (1994). Struggling for a voice: An interactionist view of language and literacy in Deaf education. In V. John-Steiner, C. P. Panofsky, & L. W. Smith (Eds.), *Sociocultural approaches to language and literacy: An interactionist perspective.* Cambridge, England: Cambridge University Press.

Wilder, D. A., & Shapiro, P. N. (1989). Role of competition-induced anxiety in limiting the beneficial impact of positive behavior by an out-group member. *Journal of Personality and Social Psychology, 56,* 60–69.

Williams, D. (1996). *Autism: An inside-outside approach.* London: Kingsley.

Williams, D. E., & D'Alessandro, J. D. (1994). A comparison of three measures of androgyny and their relationship to psychological adjustment. *Journal of Social Behavior and Personality, 9,* 469–480.

Williams, E., & Radin, N. (1993). Parental involvement, maternal employment, and adolescents' academic achievement: An 11-year follow-up. *American Journal of Orthopsychiatry, 63,* 306–312.

Williams, J., & Williamson, K. (1992). "I wouldn't want to shoot nobody": The out-of-school curriculum as described by urban students. *Action in Teacher Education, 14*(2), 9–15.

Willig, A. C. (1985). A meta-analysis of selected studies on the effectiveness of bilingual education. *Review of Educational Research, 55,* 269–317.

Willis, W. (1992). Families with African American roots. In E. W. Lynch & M. J. Hanson (Eds.), *Developing cross-cultural competence: A guide for working with young children and their families* (pp. 121–150). Baltimore: Brookes.

Wills, T. A., McNamara, G., Vaccaro, D., & Hirky, A. E. (1996). Escalated substance use: A longitudinal grouping analysis from early to middle adolescence. *Journal of Abnormal Psychology, 105,* 166–180.

Wilson, C. C., Piazza, C. C., & Nagle, R. (1990). Investigation of the effect of consistent and inconsistent behavioral example upon children's donation behavior. *Journal of Genetic Psychology, 151,* 361–376.

Wilson, D. K., Nicholson, S. C., & Krishnamoorthy, J. S. (1998). The role of diet in minority adolescent health promotion. In D. K. Wilson, J. R. Rodrigue, & W. C. Taylor (Eds.), *Health-promoting and health-compromising behaviors among minority adolescents* (pp. 129–151). Washington, DC: American Psychological Association.

Wilson, J. D., & Foster, D. W. (1985). *Williams textbook of endocrinology* (7th ed.). Philadelphia: Saunders.

Wilson, M. (1989). Child development in the context of the black extended family. *American Psychologist, 44,* 380–383.

Wilson, S. M., Shulman, L. S., & Richert, A. E. (1987). "150 different ways" of knowing: Representations of knowledge in teaching. In J. Calderhead (Ed.), *Exploring teachers' thinking* (pp. 104–124). London: Cassell Educational Limited.

Wimmer, H., Landerl, K., & Frith, U. (1999). Learning to read German: Normal and impaired acquisition. In M. Harris & G. Hatano (Eds.), *Learning to read and write: A cross-linguistic perspective.* Cambridge, England: Cambridge University Press.

Wimmer, H., & Perner, J. (1983). Beliefs about beliefs: Representation and constraining function of wrong beliefs in young children's understanding of deception. *Cognition, 13,* 103–128.

Winer, G. A., Craig, R. K., & Weinbaum, E. (1992). Adults' failure on misleading weight-conservation tests: A developmental analysis. *Developmental Psychology, 28,* 109–120.

Winne, P. H. (1995a). Inherent details in self-regulated learning. *Educational Psychologist, 30,* 173–187.

Winne, P. H. (1995b). Self-regulation is ubiquitous but its forms vary with knowledge. *Educational Psychologist, 30,* 223–228.

Winne, P. H., & Marx, R. W. (1989). A cognitive-processing analysis of motivation with classroom tasks. In C. Ames & R. Ames (Eds.), *Research on motivation in education* (Vol. 3). San Diego, CA: Academic Press.

Winner, E. (1988). *The point of words.* Cambridge, MA: Harvard University Press.

Winner, E. (1997). Exceptionally high intelligence and schooling. *American Psychologist, 52,* 1070–1081.

Winnick, J. P. (1995). An introduction to adapted physical education and sport. In J. P. Winnick (Ed.), *Adapted physical education and sport* (2nd ed., pp. 3–16). Champaign, IL: Human Kinetics.

Winsler, A., Díaz, R. M., Espinosa, L., & Rodriguez, J. L. (1999). When learning a second language does not mean losing the first: Bilingual language development in low-income, Spanish-speaking children attending bilingual preschool. *Child Development, 70,* 349–362.

Winston, P. (1973). Learning to identify toy block structures. In R. L. Solso (Ed.), *Contemporary issues in cognitive psychology: The Loyola Symposium.* Washington, DC: V. H. Winston.

Wise, F., & Miller, N. B. (1983). The mental health of the American Indian child. In G. J. Powell (Ed.), *The psychosocial development of minority children.* New York: Brunner/Mazel.

Witelson, S. F. (1985). The brain connection: The corpus callosum is larger in left-handers. *Science, 229*(4714), 665–668.

Wittmer, D. S., & Honig, A. S. (1994). Encouraging positive social development in young children. *Young Children, 49*(5), 4–12.

Wlodkowski, R. J., & Ginsberg, M. B. (1995). *Diversity and motivation: Culturally responsive teaching.* San Francisco: Jossey-Bass.

Wodtke, K. H., Harper, F., & Schommer, M. (1989). How standardized is school testing? An exploratory observational study of standardized group testing in kindergarten. *Educational Evaluation and Policy Analysis, 11,* 223–235.

Wolf, M., & Bowers, P. G. (1999). The double-deficit hypothesis for the developmental dyslexias. *Journal of Educational Psychology, 91,* 415–438.

Wolfe, D. A., & Wekerle, C. (1997). Pathways to violence in teen dating relationships. In D. Cicchetti & S. L. Toth (Eds.), *Developmental perspectives on trauma: Theory, research, and intervention. Rochester symposium on developmental psychology, 8,* 315–341. Rochester, NH: University of Rochester Press.

Wong, B. Y. L. (Ed.). (1991). *Learning about learning disabilities.* San Diego, CA: Academic Press.

Wong Fillmore, L. (1993). Educating citizens for a multicultural 21st century. *Multicultural Education, 1,* 10–12, 37.

Wood, D., Bruner, J. S., & Ross, G. (1976). The role of tutoring in problem-solving. *Journal of Child Psychology and Psychiatry, 17,* 89–100.

Wood, E., Motz, M., & Willoughby, T. (1997, April). *Examining students' retrospective memories of strategy development.* Paper presented at the annual meeting of the American Educational Research Association, Chicago.

Wood, E., Willoughby, T., McDermott, C., Motz, M., Kaspar, V., & Ducharme, M. J. (1999). Developmental differences in study behavior. *Journal of Educational Psychology, 91,* 527–536.

Wood, E., Willoughby, T., Reilley, S., Elliott, S., & DuCharme, M. (1994, April). *Evaluating students' acquisition of factual material when studying independently or with a partner.* Paper presented at the annual meeting of the American Educational Research Association, New Orleans, LA.

Wood, J. W. (1989). *Mainstreaming: A practical approach for teachers.* Upper Saddle River, NJ: Merrill/Prentice Hall.

Wood, J. W., & Rosbe, M. (1985). Adapting the classroom lectures for the mainstreamed student in the secondary schools. *The Clearing House, 58,* 354–358.

Wood, W., Wong, F. Y., & Chachere, J. G. (1991). Effects of media violence on viewers' aggression in unconstrained social interaction. *Psychological Bulletin, 109,* 371–383.

Woodward, A. L., & Sommerville, J. A. (2000). Twelve-month-old infants interpret action in context. *Psychological Science, 11,* 73–77.

Woody-Ramsey, J., & Miller, P. H. (1988). The facilitation of selective attention in preschoolers. *Child Development, 59,* 1497–1503.

Wright, J. C., & Huston, A. C. (1995, June). *Effects of educational TV viewing of lower income preschoolers on academic skills, school readiness, and school adjustment one to three years later* (report to Children's Television Workshop). Lawrence, KS: Center for Research on the Influences of Television on Children, University of Kansas.

Wright, R. (1994). *The moral animal: The new science of evolutionary psychology.* New York: Pantheon Books.

Wright, S., & Taylor, D. (1995). Identity and the language of the classroom: Investigating the impact of heritage versus second-language instruction on personal and collective self-esteem. *Journal of Educational Psychology, 87,* 241–252.

Wright, S. C., Taylor, D. M., & Macarthur, J. (2000). Subtractive bilingualism and the survival of the Inuit language: Heritage- versus second-language education. *Journal of Educational Psychology, 92,* 63–84.

Wu, Z. (1995). The stability of cohabitation relationships: The role of children. *Journal of Marriage and the Family, 57*(1), 231–236.

Yaden, D. B., Jr., & Templeton, S. (Eds.). (1986). *Metalinguistic awareness and beginning literacy: Conceptualizing what it means to read and write.* Portsmouth, NH: Heinemann.

Yarrow, M. R., Scott, P. M., & Waxler, C. Z. (1973). Learning concern for others. *Developmental Psychology, 8,* 240–260.

Yates, M., & Youniss, J. (1996). A developmental perspective on community service in adolescence. *Social Development, 5,* 85–111.

Yeager, E. A., Foster, S. J., Maley, S. D., Anderson, T., Morris, J. W., III, & Davis, O. L., Jr. (1997, March). *The role of empathy in the development of historical understanding.* Paper presented at the annual meeting of the American Educational Research Association, Chicago.

Yee, A. H. (1992). Asians as stereotypes and students: Misperceptions that persist. *Educational Psychology Review, 4,* 95–132.

Yee, A. H. (1995). Evolution of the nature-nurture controversy: Response to J. Philippe Rushton. *Educational Psychology Review, 7,* 381–390.

Yee, D. K., & Eccles, J. S. (1988). Parent perceptions and attributions for children's math achievement. *Sex Roles, 19,* 317–333.

Yell, M. L. (2001). Cognitive behavior therapy. In T. J. Zirpoli & K. J. Melloy, *Behavior management: Applications for teachers* (3rd ed.). Upper Saddle River, NJ: Merrill/Prentice Hall.

Young, E. L., & Assing, R. (2000). Review of *The Universal Nonverbal Intelligence Test. Journal of Psychoeducational Assessment, 18,* 280–288.

Youniss, J. (1980). *Parents and peers in social development.* Chicago: University of Chicago Press.

Youniss, J. (1983). Social construction of adolescence by adolescents and their parents. In H. D. Grotevant & C. R. Cooper (Eds.), *Adolescent development in the family: New directions for child development* (No. 22). San Francisco: Jossey-Bass.

Youniss, J., & Smollar, J. (1985). *Adolescent relations with mothers, fathers, and friends.* Chicago: University of Chicago Press.

Youniss, J., & Yates, M. (1999). Youth service and moral-civic identity: A case of everyday morality. *Educational Psychology Review, 11*(4), 361–376.

Ysseldyke, J. E., & Algozzine, B. (1984). *Introduction to special education.* Boston: Houghton Mifflin.

Yu, S. L., Elder, A. D., & Urdan, T. C. (1995, April). *Motivation and cognitive strategies in students with a "good student" or "poor student" self-schema.* Paper presented at the annual meeting of the American Educational Research Association, San Francisco.

Yude, C., Goodman, R., & McConachie, H. (1998). Peer problems of children with hemiplegia in mainstream primary schools. *Journal of Child Psychology and Psychiatry, 39,* 533–541.

Zahn-Waxler, C., Mayfield, A., Radke-Yarrow, M., McKnew, D. H., Cytryn, L., & Davenport, Y. B. (1988). A follow-up investigation of offspring of parents with bipolar disorder. *American Journal of Psychiatry, 145,* 506–509.

Zahn-Waxler, C., & Radke-Yarrow, M. (1982). The development of altruism: Alternative research strategies. In N. Eisenberg-Berg (Ed.), *The development of prosocial behavior.* Lincoln: University of Nebraska Press.

Zahn-Waxler, C., Radke-Yarrow, M., Wagner, E., & Chapman, M. (1992). Development of concern for others. *Developmental Psychology, 28,* 126–136.

Zahn-Waxler, C., Robinson, J., & Emde, R. N. (1992). The development of empathy in twins. *Developmental Psychology, 28,* 1038–1047.

Zahn-Waxler, C., & Smith, K. D. (1992). The development of prosocial behavior. In V. B. Van Hasselt & M. Hersen (Eds.), *Handbook of social development: A lifespan perspective* (Perspectives in Developmental Psychology, pp. 229–256). New York: Plenum Press.

Zajonc, R. B., & Mullally, P. R. (1997). Birth order: Reconciling conflicting effects. *American Psychologist, 52,* 685–699.

Zarbatany, L., Hartmann, D. P., & Rankin, D. B. (1990). The psychological function of preadolescent peer activities. *Child Development, 61,* 1067–1080.

Zelli, A., Dodge, K. A., Lochman, J. E., & Laird, R. D. (1999). The distinction between beliefs legitimizing aggression and deviant processing of social cues: Testing measurement validity and the hypothesis that biased processing mediates the effects of beliefs on aggression. *Journal of Personality and Social Psychology, 77,* 150–166.

Zervigon-Hakes, A. (1984). Materials mastery and symbolic development in construction play: Stages of development. *Early Child Development and Care, 17,* 37–47.

Zigler, E., & Berman, W. (1983). Discerning the future of early childhood intervention. *American Psychologist, 33,* 894–906.

Zigler, E., & Muenchow, S. (1992). *Head Start: The inside story of America's most successful educational experiment.* New York: Basic Books.

Zigler, E. F., & Finn-Stevenson, M. (1987). *Children: Development and social issues.* Lexington, MA: Heath.

Zigler, E. F., & Finn-Stevenson, M. (1992). Applied developmental psychology. In M. H. Bornstein & M. E. Lamb (Eds.), *Developmental psychology: An advanced textbook.* Hillsdale, NJ: Erlbaum.

Zill, N. (1983). *American children: Happy, healthy and insecure.* New York: Doubleday/Anchor Press.

Zill, N. (1985, April). *Behavior and learning problems among adopted children: Findings from a national survey of child health.* Paper presented at the meeting of the Society for Research in Child Development, Toronto.

Zill, N., Nord, C., & Loomis, L. (1995, September). *Adolescent time use, risky behavior, and outcomes:*

An analysis of national data. Rockville, MD: Westat.

Zimmerman, B. J., & Bandura, A. (1994). Impact of self-regulatory influences on writing course attainment. *American Educational Research Journal, 31,* 845–862.

Zimmerman, B. J., & Kitsantas, A. (1999). Acquiring writing revision skill: Shifting from process to outcome self-regulatory goals. *Journal of Educational Psychology, 91,* 241–250.

Zimmerman, B. J., & Risemberg, R. (1997). Self-regulatory dimensions of academic learning and motivation. In G. D. Phye (Ed.), *Handbook of academic learning: Construction of knowledge.* San Diego, CA: Academic Press.

Zirpoli, T. J., & Melloy, K. J. (1993). *Behavior management: Applications for teachers and parents.* Upper Saddle River, NJ: Merrill/Prentice Hall.

Zuckerman, G. A. (1994). A pilot study of a ten-day course in cooperative learning for beginning Russian first graders. *Elementary School Journal, 94,* 405–420.

Zwaan, R. A., Langston, M. C., & Graesser, A. C. (1995). The construction of situation models in narrative comprehension: An event-indexing model. *Psychological Science, 6,* 292–297.

Name Index

Newson, J., 137
Newson, M., 237
Nias, D. K. B., 497
Nicholls, J., 413
Nicholls, J. G., 342, 415, 416, 418, 421, 424, 440
Nichols, J. D., 559
Nichols, M. L., 227
Nichols, P. D., 223
Nicholson, S. C., 90
Nicklas, T. A., 90
Niemi, R. G., 371
Nieto, S., 266, 438
Nigg, J. T., 466
Nimick, E., 504
Ningiuruvik, L., 260
Ninio, A., 280
Nippold, M. A., 244, 245, 252
Nisbett, R. E., 124, 498
Nishina, A., 506
Nix, R. L., 496
Noffke, S., 60
Nolen, S. B., 414
Nolen-Hoeksema, S., 336
Nolin, M., 371
Nord, C., 461, 573
Norton, A. J., 458
Nottelman, E. D., 87
Nottelmann, E. D., 344
Novak, J. D., 245
Nowell, A., 219, 292, 306, 308
Nsamenang, A. B., 543
Nucci, L. P., 381, 384, 392, 393, 399
Nucci, M. S., 384
Nundy, S., 333
Nunner-Winkler, G., 394
Nuthall, G., 278
Nye, B., 573

Oakhill, J., 288, 291, 292
Oatley, K., 333
O'Boyle, M .W., 79
O'Brien, K., 576
O'Brien, S. F., 535
O'Carroll, P., 499
Ochs, E., 33, 258
O'Connor, M. J., 80
Oettingen, G., 341, 351, 353
Ogbu, J. U., 220, 261, 524, 547, 551
Ogden, E. H., 562
O'Grady, W., 237, 238, 242, 243, 248, 249
Ohana, J., 373
O'Hara, N. M., 90
Oishi, S., 458
Okagaki, L., 222, 456
Okamoto, Y., 84, 183, 184–187, 482, 560
Oldfather, P., 85, 416, 424
O'Leary, K. D., 405, 421
O'Leary, S. G., 405, 421
Oligny, P., 502
Oliner, P. M., 498
Oliner, S. P., 498
Olivárez, A., 228
Olneck, M. R., 350, 416, 438, 526
O'Loughlin, M., 124
Olson, D. R., 7, 32, 123
Olson, H. C., 80
Olweus, D., 86, 535
O'Malley, P. M., 96, 97, 343
Oppenheimer, L., 363, 368, 392
Orcutt, H. K., 530
O'Reilly, A. W., 138
Orlans, M., 325
Ormrod, J. E., 95, 159, 170, 171, 227, 232
Ormrod, R., 499, 502
Ornstein, P. A., 10, 158, 165, 168, 181
Ortony, A., 252, 256, 263

Osofsky, J. D., 499
Oster, H., 155
Osterman, K., 513
O'Sullivan, P., 476
Ovando, C. J., 267, 487
Overstreet, S., 499
Owen, M. J., 69
Owens, C. R., 497
Owens, R. E., Jr., 132, 236, 244, 245, 249, 252, 253, 254, 255, 256, 258, 263, 270, 285, 287, 290, 292, 302
Owens, S. A., 81
Owens, S. S., 573
Ozmun, J. C., 73, 74, 83, 92, 94, 95, 513

Packard, V., 344
Paget, K., 364
Page-Voth, V., 304
Paik, H., 578
Paik, S. J., 559
Paikoff, R. L., 86, 490, 530
Painter, K. M., 138
Pajares, F., 308, 341, 421
Pajares, M. F., 32, 33
Palermiti, A. L., 87
Palermo, D. S., 244
Paley, V. G., 297, 513
Palincsar, A. S., 52, 53, 130, 140, 145, 279, 293, 294, 295, 305, 307, 516, 540
Palombaro, M. M., 104
Pang, V. O., 350, 377, 424, 552, 553
Panksepp, J., 193
Panofsky, C. P., 279, 280, 281
Paolitto, D. P., 386
Papernow, P., 460
Paquette, A., 80
Parcel, G. S., 90
Paris, S. G., 52, 176, 278, 282, 288, 344, 351, 353, 410, 418, 419, 421
Parish, P., 264
Park, K., 511
Park, L., 396
Park, Y., 157
Parke, R. D., 10, 11, 381, 456, 457, 470, 509
Parker, D. A., 531
Parker, J. G., 507, 517, 518, 521, 522, 523
Parker, W. D., 228
Parkhurst, J., 509, 519
Parkin, L., 471
Parks, C. P., 525, 527
Parl, S., 569
Parsons, J. E., 341, 353, 481
Parten, Mildred, 506–7
Pascarella, E. T., 124
Pascual, L., 138
Passel, J. S., 22, 543
Passler, M., 78
Pasternack, J. F., 501
Pastorelli, C., 519
Pate, R. R., 92, 93
Patrick, H., 427, 514, 519
Pattee, L., 520
Patterson, C. J., 462, 531, 535
Patterson, G. R., 335, 506, 523
Patterson, M. L., 438
Patton, J. R., 231, 270, 432
Paul, R., 251
Pawlas, G. E., 560
Pea, R. D, 205, 226
Peak, L., 418, 421
Peake, P. K., 406
Pearson, D. A., 156
Pearson, P. D., 163, 266, 269, 287, 288
Pederson, D. R., 138
Peduzzi, J. D., 155
Peláez-Nogueras, M., 380

Pelham, W. E., Jr., 192, 376
Pellegrini, A. D., 83, 92, 93, 193, 216, 307, 505, 506, 518, 519
Pellegrino, J. W., 219
Pelletier, J., 32, 172, 173, 179, 180
Pellicer, L. O., 562, 563
Pence, A., 26
Pennington, B. F., 191, 502
Pepler, D. J., 367
Perea, P., 544
Pereira. L., 527
Pérez, B., 267, 280, 282, 283, 308, 309, 526, 547
Perez-Granados, D. R., 470
Perfetti, C. A., 177, 279, 285, 287, 302
Perkins, D., 136, 205, 222, 226, 231
Perner, J., 123, 179, 180, 368, 392, 471
Perret-Clermont, A., 130
Perry, C. L., 91
Perry, D., 506
Perry, D. G., 505
Perry, L. C., 505
Perry, N. E., 176
Perry, S., 569
Perry, W. G., Jr., 172
Perry-Jenkins, M., 455
Peshkin, H., 88
Pessar, L. F., 336
Peters, A. M., 236
Petersen, A., 90
Petersen, A. C., 348
Peterson, A. C., 88, 524
Peterson, C., 419, 421
Peterson, J. L., 461
Peterson, L., 502
Peterson, M. E., 287
Peterson, P. L., 137
Peterson, R. F., 516
Petrie, S., 512
Petrill, S. A., 7, 212, 213, 215
Pettit, G. S., 458, 496, 505, 506, 509, 519, 574
Pettito, A. L., 133
Pettito, L. A., 238, 266, 271
Phelan, P., 261, 416, 526
Phelps, L., 124, 211
Phillips, A. T., 367
Phillips, D., 569
Phillips, M., 219, 439
Phinney, J. S., 350, 375, 546
Piaget, Jean, 8, 9, 10, 13, 39–40, 52, 110–131, 158, 180–182, 345, 367, 373, 380–381, 410, 450, 510–511, 557
Pianko, S., 303, 304
Piazza, C. C., 497
Piche, C., 348
Pick, A. D., 156
Pickles, A., 50
Pierce, K. M., 572
Pierce, S. H., 174
Pietrucha, C. A., 505
Piirto, J., 228, 310
Pillard, R. C., 531
Pine, C. J., 350
Pinker, S., 237, 238, 239, 240
Pinnegar, S. E., 56
Pintrich, P. R., 83, 172, 173, 177, 341, 342, 345, 353, 410, 419
Pipher, Mary, 87, 91, 100, 105, 349, 490, 512, 557
Plante, C., 348
Plomin, R., 7, 8, 67, 69, 212, 215, 332, 497
Plowman, T. S., 427, 563
Plumert, J. M., 165
Poe-Yamagata, E., 574
Pogrow, S., 178, 427
Poling, D., 557
Polit, D., 471

Pollack, William, 65, 93, 331–332
Pollard, S. R., 396
Polloway, E. A., 192
Pomeroy, W. B., 530
Poresky, R. H., 97
Portes, P. R., 218, 308, 421, 488, 546, 547, 560
Posner, G. J., 173, 183
Posner, J., 545, 574
Pospisil, L., 50
Potenza, M. T., 176
Pott, M., 322
Poulin, R., 502
Powell, G. J., 356
Powell, K., 344, 499
Power, F. C., 393, 397
Power, T. G., 456
Powers, L. E., 424
Powers, S. I., 344
Powlishta, K. K., 374
Pramling, I., 58
Pratt, C., 263
Prawat, R. S., 183
Pressley, M., 35, 52, 166, 171, 172, 174, 177, 289, 292, 293, 418
Price, L. N., 566
Price-Spratlen, T., 370
Price-Williams, D. R., 125
Pritchard, R., 161
Proctor, R. W., 94
Pulkkinen, L., 465
Pulos, S., 124, 128, 228
Purcell-Gates, V., 250, 269, 292, 293
Purdie, N., 166, 172, 174
Putallaz, M., 496, 519, 520

Qualey, L. L., 505
Quay, H. C., 504
Quilitch, H. R., 516
Quintana, S., 345
Quinton, D., 50

Rabain-Jamin, J., 542
Rabinowitz, M., 35, 161
Radin, N., 469
Radke-Yarrow, M., 369, 392, 474, 499, 500, 513
Radziszewska, B., 145
Ragusa, D. M., 432
Raikes, H., 569
Raine, A., 502
Rajanayagam, K., 100
Rallison, M. L., 90
Ramachandran, V. S., 78
Ramey, C., 231, 571
Ramey, C. T., 40, 214, 219, 270, 427, 570, 571, 572
Ramey, S. L., 427, 570, 571, 572
Ramirez, M., 125
Ramsey, E., 335
Ramsey, P. G., 377, 553
Rankin, D. B., 509
Raphael, T. E., 278, 291, 297, 303
Rapson, R. L., 328
Rashotte, C. A., 285
Rasmussen, J. L., 458, 474
Raudenbush, S. W., 439
Raviv, A., 500
Rayport, S. G., 77
Recchia, S., 431
Reder, L. M., 135
Redfield, J., 498
Redler, E., 500, 516
Reed, D. F., 21, 561, 563
Reese, D. F., 518
Reese, H. W., 9
Reeve, J., 431
Reich, P. A., 248, 265
Reichert, P., 90

Subject Index